nutrition
& you

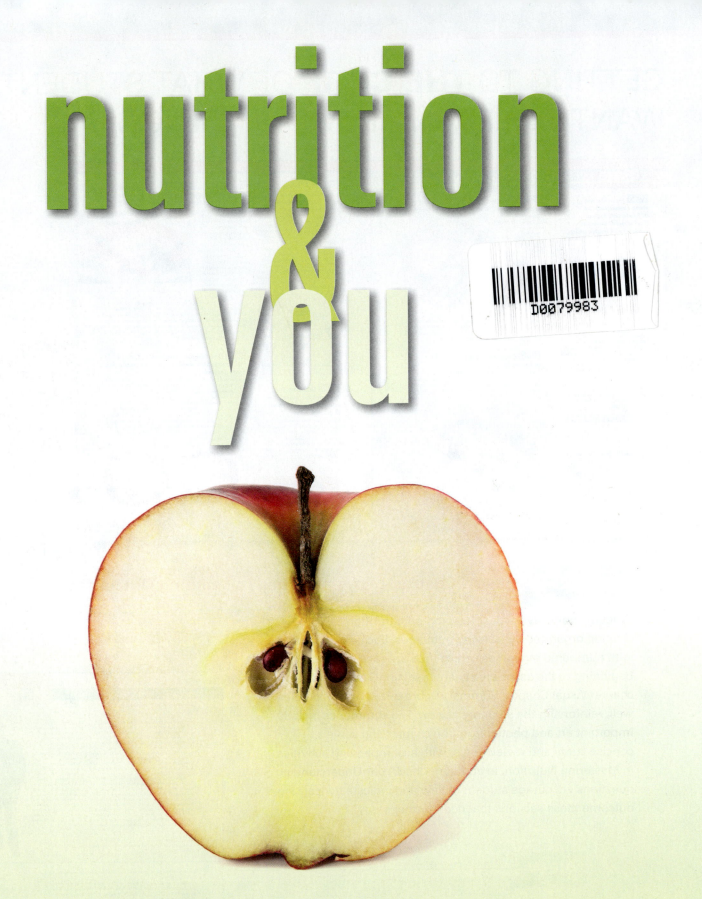

GUIDE STUDENTS TO A
DEEPER UNDERSTANDING OF NUTRITION

GETTING TO **THE CORE** OF WHAT STUDENTS WANT TO LEARN ABOUT NUTRITION

UPDATED **Visual Chapter Summaries tied to Learning Outcomes**

Students now have a clear learning path through each chapter, organized by learning outcomes. Each chapter starts with numbered outcomes, which then are repeated at the beginning of the associated chapter section. The end-of-chapter Visual Chapter Summary is organized by outcome as well, reinforcing the student's review. The summaries include important art and photos from the chapter and serve as concise study and review tools, with accompanying activities in Mastering Nutrition. In addition, Check Your Understanding questions encourage student review and indicate by learning outcome those sections that need further study.

NEW

Health Connection: A Case Study

The connections between nutrition and health are explored in new case studies written for every chapter. Students are introduced to a person experiencing a health problem and explore the interplay between nutrition and health, with follow-up critical thinking questions.

FOCUS

Figure 4.4 **Carbohydrate Digestion and Absorption**

FOCUS FIGURE WALKTHROUGH

Scan this QR code with your mobile device for a video tour of this figure by Joan Salge Blake.

Carbohydrate digestion begins in the mouth and ends with the absorption of the monosaccharides glucose, fructose, and galactose in the small intestine.

ORGANS OF THE GI TRACT

MOUTH
Mastication mixes food with saliva. Salivary amylase breaks down amylose and amylopectin into smaller chains of carbohydrates.

Amylose → Smaller chains

Amylopectin → Smaller chains

STOMACH
The acidity of the stomach inactivates the salivary amylase; thus, very little digestion of carbohydrates occurs in the stomach.

SMALL INTESTINE
Pancreatic amylase breaks down the amylose, amylopectin, and smaller chains of carbohydrates into maltose, a disaccharide.

Smaller amylose chains → Maltose

Smaller amylopectin chains → Maltose

Brush border enzymes break down all disaccharides to the monosaccharides glucose, fructose, and galactose, which are then absorbed into the bloodstream.

Sucrose → Glucose Fructose

Maltose → Glucose

Lactose → Glucose Galactose

Monosaccharides

Bloodstream

LARGE INTESTINE
All starches and simple sugars are broken down and absorbed in the small intestine; only fiber passes into the large intestine. Bacteria in the colon metabolize some of the fiber. The majority of fiber is eliminated in the stool.

ACCESSORY ORGANS

SALIVARY GLANDS
Produce salivary amylase.

PANCREAS
Produces pancreatic amylase that is released into the small intestine via the pancreatic duct.

LIVER
Glucose is taken up by the liver from the blood. Most glucose is returned to the blood to be picked up and used by body cells, or the body can use glucose for energy, convert it to glycogen, or store it as fat.

What Happens to the Carbohydrates You Eat? **105**

NEW

Focus Figure Walkthroughs

Author Joan Salge Blake narrates a video tour of full-page Focus Figures. These colorful figures, designed to teach key concepts in nutrition through bold, clear and detailed visual presentations, are now enhanced with dynamic media. When students scan the QR code, they see the figure come to life, accompanied by the author's detailed walkthrough of each part of the figure, as if she were breaking it down for a student in person. Already designed to guide students through complex processes using text and stepped-out art, these figures now make tough topics even clearer and easier to understand.

CONTINUOUS LEARNING
BEFORE, DURING, and AFTER CLASS with
MasteringNutrition™ with MyDietAnalysis

Mastering is the most effective and widely used online homework, tutorial, and assessment system for the sciences. MasteringNutrition with MyDietAnalysis includes content specific to introductory nutrition courses, delivering self-paced tutorials that focus on your course objectives, provides individualized coaching, and responds to each student's progress.

MyDietAnalysis is now available as single sign on to MasteringNutrition. For smartphone users, a new mobile website version of MyDietAnalysis is available. Students can track their diet and activity intake accurately, anytime and anywhere, from their mobile devices.

BEFORE CLASS

Dynamic Study Modules provide students with a preview of what's to come

Dynamic Study Modules enable students to study effectively on their own in an adaptive format. Students receive an initial set of questions with a unique answer format asking them to indicate their confidence.

Once completed, Dynamic Study Modules include explanations using material taken directly from the text.

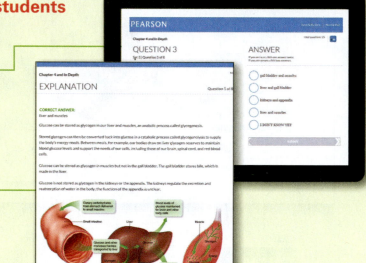

DURING CLASS

Learning Catalytics engage students during lecture

Learning Catalytics, a "bring your own device" student engagement, assessment, and classroom intelligence system, allows students to use their smartphone, tablet, or laptop to respond to questions in class.

Nutrition Animations explain tough topics during class

34 Nutrition Animations explain big picture concepts that help students learn the hardest topics in nutrition. These animations are provided as embedded media within your PowerPoint deck for easy play and review during class.

The updated animations are also mobile-ready and available with assessment within MasteringNutrition. These animations address tough topics and common misconceptions and feature a more contemporary look to appeal to today's students.

Topics include:

- DRI Determination
- Reading Labels
- Carbohydrate Digestion
- Lipid Digestion
- Basic Absorption Mechanisms
- Carbohydrate Absorption
- Protein Absorption
- Vitamin A and the Visual Cycle and much more

Additional Engaging In-Class Media

Instructors can also incorporate dynamic media from the Teaching Toolkit DVD into lecture and build class discussions and activities around Nutrition Animations, *ABC News* Lecture Launchers, and more. For more information, please see the last page of this walkthrough.

MasteringNutrition™

AFTER CLASS

Easy-to-Assign, Customize, and Automatically Graded Assignments

The breadth and depth of content available to you to assign in Mastering is unparalleled, allowing you to quickly and easily assign homework to reinforce key concepts.

NEW

Visual Chapter Summary Coaching Activities

These MasteringNutrition activities complement each Visual Chapter Summary with hints and feedback that help students with their understanding. Each covers one or more learning outcome and references each learning outcome within the activity.

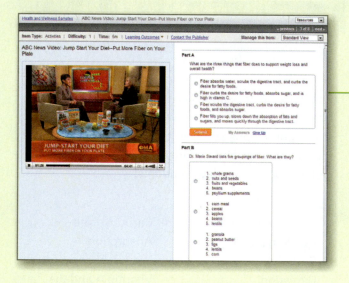

NEW

ABC News Lecture Launcher videos

Current videos cover up-to-date hot topics in the nutrition field, bringing nutrition to life and sparking discussion. These are accompanied by multiple-choice questions with wrong-answer feedback.

UPDATED

18 NutriTools Build-A-Meal Activities

Dynamic coaching activities allow students to apply nutrition concepts to improve their health through interactive mini-lessons that provide hints and feedback. The Build a Meal, Build a Pizza, Build A Salad, and Build A Sandwich tools have been carefully rethought to improve the user experience, making them easier to use. They are now HTML5 compatible.

YOUR COMPLETE INTERACTIVE eTEXT

Enhanced Interactive eText 2.0

This enhanced, interactive eText is complete with embedded videos, animations, author-narrated Focus Figure Video Walkthroughs, multiple choice questions, and drag and drop activities designed for students to interact with the material, not just read it. eText 2.0 is mobile friendly and ADA accessible.

- Now available on smartphones and tablets.
- Seamlessly integrated videos and other rich media.
- Accessible (screen-reader ready).
- Configurable reading settings, including resizable type and night reading mode.
- Instructor and student note-taking, highlighting, bookmarking, and search.

EVERYTHING YOU NEED
TO TEACH IN ONE PLACE

Teaching Toolkit DVD for *Nutrition & You*

The *Teaching Toolkit* DVD provides everything that you need to prep for your course and deliver a dynamic lecture, in one convenient place. These valuable resources are included on three disks:

DISK 1
Robust Media Assets for Each Chapter

- *ABC News* Lecture Launcher videos
- Practical Nutrition Tips videos
- Nutrition Animations
- PowerPoint Lecture Outlines
- Media-Only PowerPoint® slides for easy importing of videos and animations
- PowerPoint clicker questions and Jeopardy-style quiz show questions
- Files for all illustrations and tables and selected photos from the text

DISK 2
Comprehensive Test Bank

- Test Bank in Microsoft Word, PDF, and RTF formats
- Computerized Test Bank, which includes all the questions from the printed test bank in a format that allows you to easily and intuitively build exams and quizzes

DISK 3
Additional Innovative Supplements for Instructors and Students

For Instructors
- Instructor Resource and Support Manual in Microsoft Word and PDF formats
- Step-by-step MasteringNutrition tutorials
- Video introduction to Learning Catalytics™
- *Great Ideas in Teaching Nutrition*

For Students
- *Eat Right! Healthy Eating in College and Beyond*
- Food Composition Table

User's Quick Guide for Nutrition & You

This easy-to-use printed supplement accompanies the Teaching Toolkit and offers easy instructions for both experienced and new faculty members to get started with the rich Toolkit content and MasteringNutrition.

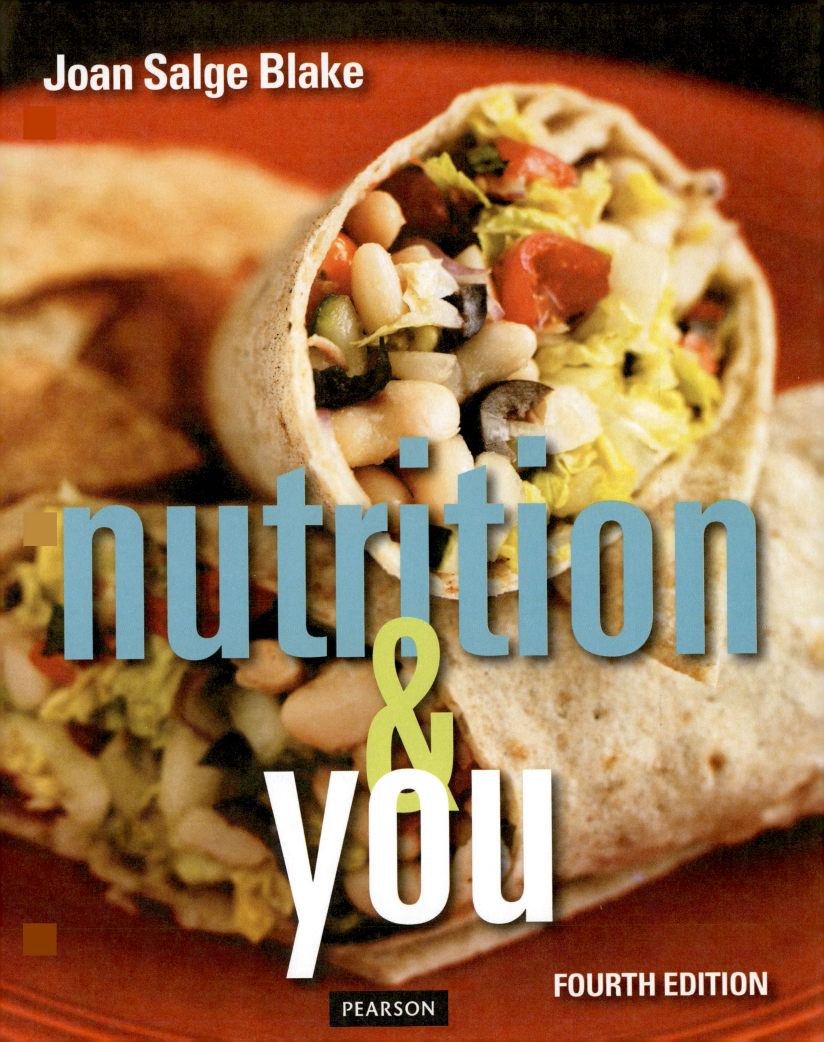

Joan Salge Blake

nutrition & you

FOURTH EDITION

PEARSON

Senior Acquisitions Editor: *Michelle Cadden*
Project Manager: *Caroline Ayres*
Program Manager: *Susan Malloy*
Editorial Assistant: *Heidi Arndt*
Director of Development: *Barbara Yien*
Development Manager: *Cathy Murphy*
Developmental Editors: *Suzanne Olivier, Alice Fugate, Kari Hopperstead*
Project Management Team Lead: *Nancy Tabor*
Program Management Team Lead: *Michael Early*
Director of Digital Product Development: *Lauren Fogel*
Executive Content Producer: *Laura Tommasi*
Senior Content Producer: *Aimee Pavy*
Copyeditor: *Anna Reynolds Trabucco*
Production Manager and Compositor: *Cenveo Publisher Services*

Design Manager; Cover Designer: *Side by Side Studios*
Text Designer: *Emily Friel, Integra Software Services*
Cover Designer: *Side by Side Studios*
Illustrator: *Lachina*
Rights and Permissions Project Manager: *William Opaluch*
Rights and Permissions Management: *Cordes Hoffman, PreMediaGlobal*
Senior Procurement Specialist: *Stacey Weinberger*
Executive Product Marketing Manager: *Neena Bali*
Field Marketing Manager: *Mary Salzman*
Text Printer: *LSC Communications*
Cover Printer: *LSC Communications*
Cover Photo Credit: *Heath Robbins/The Food Passionates/Corbis*

Library of Congress Cataloging-in-Publication Data
Names: Blake, Joan Salge.
Title: Nutrition & you / Joan Salge Blake.
Other titles: Nutrition and you
Description: Fourth edition. | Hoboken, New Jersey : Pearson, 2016. |
   Includes bibliographical references and index.
Identifiers: LCCN 2015038008 | ISBN 9780134167541
Subjects: LCSH: Nutrition--Textbooks.
Classification: LCC RA784 .B552 2016 | DDC 613.2--dc23 LC record available
at http://lccn.loc.gov/2015038008

ISBN 10: 0-13-416754-6; ISBN 13: 978-0-13-416754-1 (Student edition)
ISBN 10: 0-13-420930-3; ISBN 13: 978-0-13-420930-2 (Instructor Review Copy)
ISBN 10: 0-13-432484-6; ISBN 13: 978-0-13-432484-5 (Books A La Carte edition)

7   17

www.pearsonhighered.com

Brief Contents

1 What Is Nutrition?   2

2 Tools for Healthy Eating   30

3 The Basics of Digestion   68

4 Carbohydrates: Sugars, Starches, and Fiber   98

5 Fats, Oils, and Other Lipids   144

6 Proteins and Amino Acids   186

7 Vitamins   226

8 Minerals and Water   282

9 Alcohol   340

10 Weight Management and Energy Balance   368

11 Nutrition and Fitness   416

12 Consumerism and Sustainability: Food from Farm to Table   456

13 Food Safety and Technology   492

14 Life Cycle Nutrition: Pregnancy through Infancy   526

15 Life Cycle Nutrition: Toddlers through the Later Years   566

16 Hunger at Home and Abroad   600

A Calculations and Conversions   A-2

B Organizations and Resources   B-1

Glossary   G-1

References   R-1

Index   I-1

Credits   CR-1

Contents

Preface: Why I Wrote *Nutrition & You*   xvi

1

What Is Nutrition?   2

What Drives Our Food Choices?   4
We Need to Eat and Drink to Live   4
We Choose Foods for Many Other Reasons   5

What Is Nutrition and Why Is Good Nutrition So Important?   8

What Are the Essential Nutrients and Why Do You Need Them?   9
Carbohydrates, Fats, and Proteins Provide Energy   9
You Can Calculate the Amount of Energy a Food Provides   10
Vitamins and Minerals Are Essential for Metabolism   10
Water Is Vital for Many Processes in Your Body   11

How Should You Get These Important Nutrients?   11
The Best Way to Meet Your Nutrient Needs Is with a Well-Balanced Diet   11
You Can Meet Some Nutrient Needs with a Supplement   12

How Does the Average American Diet Stack Up?   12
The Quality of the American Diet   13
Rates of Overweight and Obesity in Americans   13
Improving Americans' Diets Is One Goal of *Healthy People 2020*   14

What's the Real Deal When It Comes to Nutrition Research and Advice?   15
Sound Nutrition Research Begins with the Scientific Method   17
Research Studies and Experiments Confirm Hypotheses   18
You Can Trust the Advice of Nutrition Experts   20
    Health Connection: Fast Food City   21
You Can Obtain Accurate Nutrition Information on the Internet   22
Visual Chapter Summary   26

2

Tools for Healthy Eating   30

What Is Healthy Eating and What Tools Can Help?   32

What Are the Dietary Reference Intakes?   34
DRIs Tell You How Much of Each Nutrient You Need   34
DRIs Encompass Several Reference Values   34
    Focus Figure 2.2 Dietary Reference Intakes   35
How to Use the DRIs   37

What Are the *Dietary Guidelines for Americans*?   37

What Are MyPlate and ChooseMyPlate.gov?   39
MyPlate and ChooseMyPlate.gov Emphasize Changes in Diet, Eating Behaviors, and Physical Activity   40
How to Use MyPlate and ChooseMyPlate.gov   42

What Is a Food Label and Why Is It Important?   48
The Food Label Tells You What's in the Package   49
The Food Label Can Help You Make Healthy Food Choices   51
    Focus Figure 2.12 Understanding the Nutrition Facts Panel   52

Functional Foods: What Role Do They Play in Your Diet?   60
Are There Concerns Associated with Consuming Functional Foods?   60
How to Use Functional Foods   61
    Health Connection: Functional Foods and Cholesterol   62
Visual Chapter Summary   64

3

The Basics of Digestion   68

What Is Digestion and Why Is It Important?   70
Digestion Occurs in the GI Tract   70
Digestion Is Mechanical and Chemical   70

What Are the Organs of the GI Tract and Why Are They Important?   73
Digestion Begins in the Mouth   73
   Focus Figure 3.3 The Digestive System   74
The Stomach Stores, Mixes, and Prepares Food for Digestion   75
Most Digestion and Absorption Occurs in the Small Intestine   76
   Focus Figure 3.6 Anatomy of the Small Intestine   77
The Large Intestine Eliminates Waste and Absorbs Water and Some Nutrients   78
The Liver, Gallbladder, and Pancreas Are Accessory Organs   79

How Do Hormones, Enzymes, and Bile Aid Digestion?   79
Hormones Regulate Digestion   79
Enzymes Drive the Process of Digestion   80
Bile Helps Digest Fat   80

How Are Digested Nutrients Absorbed?   81
Digested Nutrients Are Absorbed by Three Methods   82

What Happens to Nutrients after They Are Absorbed?   83
The Circulatory System Distributes Nutrients through Your Blood   83
The Lymphatic System Distributes Some Nutrients through Your Lymph Vessels   84
Your Body Can Store Some Surplus Nutrients   84
The Excretory System Passes Waste out of the Body   84

What Other Body Systems Affect Your Use of Nutrients?   84
The Nervous System Stimulates Your Appetite   85
The Endocrine System Releases Hormones That Help Regulate the Use of Absorbed Nutrients   85

What Are Some Common Digestive Disorders?   85
Disorders of the Mouth and Throat   85
Esophageal Problems   86
Disorders of the Stomach   87
Gallbladder Disease   87
Disorders of the Intestines   88
   Health Connection: Tired of Gluten   89
More Serious Intestinal Disorders   90
Visual Chapter Summary   94

4

Carbohydrates: Sugars, Starches, and Fiber   98

What Are Carbohydrates and Why Do You Need Them?   100
Simple Carbohydrates Contain One or Two Sugar Units   100
Polysaccharides Are Complex Carbohydrates   102
Starch Is the Storage Form in Plants   102
Fiber Is Nondigestible but Important   102
Glycogen Is the Storage Form in Animals   103

What Happens to the Carbohydrates You Eat?   104
You Digest Carbohydrates in Your Mouth and Intestines   104
What Is Lactose Maldigestion and Lactose Intolerance?   104
   Focus Figure 4.4 Carbohydrate Digestion and Absorption   105

How Does Your Body Use Carbohydrates?   106
Insulin Regulates Glucose in Your Blood   107
Carbohydrates Fuel Your Body between Meals and Help Spare Protein for Other Uses   107
   Focus Figure 4.6 Hormones Regulate Blood Glucose   108
Carbohydrates Fuel Your Body during Fasting and Prevent Ketosis   109

How Much Carbohydrate Do You Need and What Are the Best Food Sources?   110
You Need a Minimum Amount of Carbohydrates Daily   110
The Best Carbohydrates Are Found in These Foods   111
Whole Grains Can Help Meet Starch and Fiber Needs   112
Fruits and Vegetables Provide Simple Sugars, Starch, and Fiber   113
Legumes, Nuts, and Seeds Are Excellent Sources of Carbohydrates and Fiber   114
Low-Fat and Fat-Free Dairy Products Provide Some Simple Sugars   115
Packaged Foods Can Also Provide Carbohydrates   115

What's the Difference between Natural and Added Sugars?   115
Foods with Natural Sugars Usually Contain More Nutrients for Fewer Calories   116
Processed Foods and Sweets Often Contain Added Sugars   117
Are Added Sugars Bad for You?   117
Finding the Added Sugars in Your Foods   117
How Much Added Sugar Is Too Much?   121

Why Is Diabetes a Growing Epidemic?   121
What Are the Forms of Diabetes?   123
   Focus Figure 4.12 Diabetes   124
What Effects Does Diabetes Have on Your Body?   125
   Health Connection: Destined for Diabetes?   127
How Is Diabetes Treated and Controlled?   128
Why Is Diabetes Called an Epidemic?   129
Can Type 2 Diabetes Be Prevented?   129

What Are Sugar Substitutes and What Forms Can They Take?   130
Polyols Are Sugar Alcohols   130

Saccharin Is the Oldest Sugar Substitute   132
Aspartame Is Derived from Amino Acids   132
Neotame Is Also Made from Amino Acids   133
Acesulfame-K Contains Potassium   133
Sucralose Is Made from Sucrose   133
Rebaudioside A Is Derived from the Stevia Plant   133
Monk Fruit Is Another Sugar Substitute   134
Advantame Is the Newest Sugar Substitute   134

Why Is Fiber So Important?   134
Fiber Helps Prevent Constipation and Diverticulosis   134
Fiber Helps Prevent Obesity   135
Fiber Helps Prevent Heart Disease, Diabetes, and Cancer   136
Too Much Fiber Can Cause Health Problems   137
Visual Chapter Summary   140

5

Fats, Oils, and Other Lipids   144

What Are Fats and Why Do You Need Them?   146
Fats Serve Multiple Functions in Foods and in Your Body   146
Fatty Acids Are Found in Triglycerides and Phospholipids   146
Triglycerides Contain Three Fatty Acid Chains   149
Sterols Have a Unique Ring Structure   150

What Happens to the Fat You Eat?   151
You Digest Most Fat in Your Stomach and Small Intestine   151
Focus Figure 5.10 Fat Digestion and Absorption   152
Lipoproteins Transport Fat through the Lymph and Blood   153

How Does Your Body Use Fat and Cholesterol?   154
Fat Provides Energy   154
Fat Helps You Absorb Certain Compounds and Insulates the Body   154
Focus Figure 5.13 The Roles of Lipoproteins   155
Essential Fatty Acids Help Keep Cells Healthy   156
Cholesterol Has Many Important Roles   157

How Much Fat Do You Need Each Day?   157
You Need to Consume a Specific Percentage of Your Daily Calories from Fat   157
You Need to Consume a Specific Amount of Essential Fatty Acids Daily   158
Minimize Saturated and *Trans* Fats in Your Diet   158
The Impact of Cholesterol in Your Diet   160

What Are the Best Food Sources of Fats?   161

What Are Fat Substitutes and How Can They Be Part of a Healthy Diet?   164
Fat Substitutes Can Be Carbohydrate, Protein, or Fat Based   164
Reduced-Fat Products Aren't Calorie Free   165

What Is Heart Disease and What Increases Your Risk?   166
Heart Disease Begins with Buildup in the Arteries   167

What Are the Risk Factors for Heart Disease?   167
Focus Figure 5.20 Development of Atherosclerosis   168

What Can You Do to Maintain Healthy Blood Cholesterol Levels to Reduce Your Risk of Heart Disease?   170
Minimize Saturated Fats, *Trans* Fats, and Cholesterol in Your Diet   171
Include Fish in Your Weekly Choices   173
Health Connection: All Fats Are Not Created Equal   175
Eat Plenty of Plant Foods   175
Routinely Select Foods Rich in Antioxidants and Phytochemicals   177
Strive for Plenty of Exercise and Manage Your Weight   178
A Word about the Protective Effects of Red Wine   178
The Whole Is Greater Than the Sum of Its Parts   178
Visual Chapter Summary   182

6

Proteins and Amino Acids   186

What Are Proteins and Why Are They Important?   188
The Building Blocks of Proteins Are Amino Acids   188
Denaturation of Proteins Changes Their Shape   191

What Happens to the Protein You Eat?   192
You Digest and Absorb Dietary Proteins in Your Stomach and Small Intestine   192
Your Body Degrades and Synthesizes Proteins   192
Focus Figure 6.4 Protein Digestion and Absorption   193
DNA Directs the Synthesis of New Proteins   194
Focus Figure 6.6 Protein Synthesis   195

How Does Your Body Use Proteins?   196
Proteins Provide Structural and Mechanical Support and Help Maintain Body Tissues   196
Proteins Build Most Enzymes and Many Hormones   197
Proteins Help Maintain Fluid Balance   197
Proteins Help Maintain Acid-Base Balance   198
Proteins Transport Substances throughout the Body   198
Proteins Contribute to a Healthy Immune System   199
Proteins Can Provide Energy   199
Protein Improves Satiety and Appetite Control   199

How Much Protein Do You Need?   200
Healthy Adults Should Be in Nitrogen Balance   200
Not All Protein Is Created Equal   202
You Can Determine Your Personal Protein Needs   203

What Are the Best Food Sources of Protein?   204

What Happens If You Eat Too Much or Too Little Protein?   209
Eating Too Much Protein Can Be Unhealthy   209
Eating Too Little Protein Can Lead to Poor Health and Malnutrition   210

How Do Vegetarians Meet Their Protein Needs? 212
    Health Connection: Running on Empty 213
    The Potential Benefits and Risks of a Vegetarian Diet 216
    How You Can Be a Healthy Vegetarian 216
    Athletes Can Follow a Vegetarian Diet 219
Visual Chapter Summary 222

7

Vitamins 226

What Are Vitamins? 228
    Vitamins Are Either Fat-Soluble or Water-Soluble 229
    Some Vitamins Function as Antioxidants 229
    Vitamins Differ in Bioavailability 231
    Vitamins Can Be Destroyed by Air, Water, or Heat 232
    Overconsumption of Some Vitamins Can Be Toxic 233
    Provitamins Can Be Converted to Vitamins by the Body 233

The Storage of Fat-Soluble Vitamins 234

    Exploring Vitamin A 235
        What Is Vitamin A? 235
        Functions of Vitamin A 235
        Focus Figure 7.6 Retinal and Its Role in Vision 236
        Daily Needs 237
        Food Sources 238
        Too Much or Too Little 238

    Exploring Vitamin E 240
        What Is Vitamin E? 240
        Functions of Vitamin E 240
        Daily Needs 240
        Food Sources 240
        Too Much or Too Little 240

    Exploring Vitamin K 242
        What Is Vitamin K? 242
        Functions of Vitamin K 242
        Daily Needs 242
        Food Sources 242
        Too Much or Too Little 243

    Exploring Vitamin D 244
        What Is Vitamin D? 244
        Functions of Vitamin D 244
        Daily Needs 244
        Food Sources 245
        Too Much or Too Little 245

The Roles of the Water-Soluble B Vitamins and Vitamin C 247

    Exploring Thiamin (B$_1$) 248
        What Is Thiamin? 248
        Functions of Thiamin 248
        Daily Needs 248
        Food Sources 248
        Too Much or Too Little 248

    Exploring Riboflavin (B$_2$) 250
        What Is Riboflavin? 250
        Functions of Riboflavin 250
        Daily Needs 250
        Food Sources 250
        Too Much or Too Little 250

    Exploring Niacin (B$_3$) 252
        What Is Niacin? 252
        Functions of Niacin 252
        Daily Needs 252
        Food Sources 252
        Too Much or Too Little 252

    Exploring Vitamin B$_6$ 254
        What Is Vitamin B$_6$? 254
        Functions of Vitamin B$_6$ 254
        Daily Needs 254
        Food Sources 254
        Too Much or Too Little 254

    Exploring Folate 255
        What Is Folate? 255
        Functions of Folate 255
        Daily Needs 256
        Food Sources 256
        Too Much or Too Little 256

    Exploring Vitamin B$_{12}$ 258
        What Is Vitamin B$_{12}$? 258
        Functions of Vitamin B$_{12}$ 258
        Daily Needs 258
        Food Sources 258
        Too Much or Too Little 259

    Exploring Vitamin C 260
        What Is Vitamin C? 260
        Functions of Vitamin C 260
        Daily Needs 260
        Food Sources 260
        Too Much or Too Little 260

    Exploring Pantothenic Acid and Biotin 262
        What Are Pantothenic Acid and Biotin? 262
        Functions of Pantothenic Acid and Biotin 262
        Daily Needs 262
        Food Sources 262
        Too Much or Too Little 262

Are There Other Important Vitamin-Like Nutrients? 263
    Choline Is an Essential Nutrient 263
    Carnitine, Lipoic Acid, and Inositol Are Vitamin-Like Substances 263

How Should You Get Your Vitamins? 266
    Foods Are Still the Best Way to Meet Your Vitamin Needs 266
    Fortified Foods Can Provide Additional Nutrients, but at a Price 267
    Vitamin Supplements Are Not a Substitute for Healthy Eating 269
Visual Chapter Summary 275

8

Minerals and Water 282

Why Is Water So Important? 284
Water Is the Universal Solvent 284
Water Is a Transport Medium 285
Water Helps Maintain Body Temperature 285
Water Is a Lubricant and a Protective Cushion 286

What Is Water Balance and How Do You Maintain It? 286
You Take in Water through Beverages and Food 286
You Lose Water through Your Kidneys, Large Intestine, Lungs, and Skin 287
Losing Too Much Water Can Cause Dehydration 287
Consuming Too Much Water Can Cause Hyponatremia 289
Focus Figure 8.7 Fluid Balance during Exercise 290

How Much Water Do You Need and What Are the Best Sources? 291

What Are Minerals and Why Do You Need Them? 295
Bioavailability Affects Mineral Absorption 296
You Need Major Minerals in Larger Amounts 296
The Trace Minerals Are Needed in Small Amounts 296
Overconsumption of Minerals Can Be Toxic 298
Other Minerals: Arsenic, Boron, Nickel, Silicon, and Vanadium 298

Exploring Sodium 301
What Is Sodium? 301
Daily Needs 301
Food Sources 301
Too Much or Too Little 302
Health Connection: A High-Pressure Situation 303

Exploring Potassium 305
What Is Potassium? 305
Daily Needs 305
Food Sources 305
Too Much or Too Little 305

Exploring Calcium 307
What Is Calcium? 307
Daily Needs 307
Food Sources 307
Too Much or Too Little 308

Exploring Phosphorus 311
What Is Phosphorus? 311
Daily Needs 311
Food Sources 311
Too Much or Too Little 311

Exploring Magnesium 313
What Is Magnesium? 313
Daily Needs 313
Food Sources 313
Too Much or Too Little 313

Exploring Chloride 315
What Is Chloride? 315
Daily Needs 315
Food Sources 315
Too Much or Too Little 315

Exploring Sulfur 315
What Is Sulfur? 315
Food Sources 315
Daily Needs and Too Much or Too Little 315

Exploring Iron 316
What Is Iron? 316
Daily Needs 316
Food Sources 317
Too Much or Too Little 318

Exploring Copper 319
What Is Copper? 319
Daily Needs 319
Food Sources 319
Too Much or Too Little 319

Exploring Zinc 320
What Is Zinc? 320
Daily Needs 320
Food Sources 320
Too Much or Too Little 321

Exploring Selenium 322
What Is Selenium? 322
Daily Needs 322
Food Sources 322
Too Much or Too Little 323

Exploring Fluoride 324
What Is Fluoride? 324
Daily Needs 324
Food Sources 324
Too Much or Too Little 325

Exploring Chromium 326
What Is Chromium? 326
Daily Needs 326
Food Sources 326
Too Much or Too Little 327

Exploring Iodine 327
What Is Iodine? 327
Daily Needs 327
Food Sources 327
Too Much or Too Little 328

Exploring Manganese 329
What Is Manganese? 329
Daily Needs 329
Food Sources 329
Too Much or Too Little 329

Exploring Molybdenum 330
What Is Molybdenum? 330
Daily Needs 330
Food Sources 330
Too Much or Too Little 330

Visual Chapter Summary 333

9

Alcohol 340

What Is Alcohol and How Is It Made? 342

Why Do People Drink Alcohol? 342
People Drink to Relax, Celebrate, and Socialize 343
Moderate Alcohol Consumption May Have Health
 Benefits 343

What Happens to Alcohol in the Body? 344
You Absorb Alcohol in Your Stomach and Small
 Intestine 345
You Metabolize Alcohol Primarily in Your Liver 346
Alcohol Circulates in Your Blood 346
The Effects of Alcohol on Your Brain 346

How Can Alcohol Be Harmful? 349
Alcohol Can Disrupt Sleep and Cause Hangovers 349
Alcohol Can Interact with Hormones 351
Alcohol May Lead to Overnutrition and Malnutrition 351
Alcohol Can Harm Your Digestive Organs, Heart,
 and Liver 353
Alcohol Can Put a Healthy Pregnancy at Risk 355

What Is Alcohol Use Disorder? 356
Binge Drinking, Drinking and Driving, and Underage Drinking
 is Harmful 357
**Health Connection: Smashed:
 Story of a Drunken Girlhood 358**
How to Get Help for AUD 361
Some People Should Avoid
 Consuming Alcohol 361
Visual Chapter Summary 364

What Factors Are Likely to Affect Body Weight? 380
Hunger and Appetite Affect What You Eat 381
Physiological Mechanisms Help Regulate Hunger 381
Focus Figure 10.7 Your Brain Controls Hunger and Satiation 382
Genetics Partially Determine Body Weight 383
Environmental Factors Can Increase Appetite and Decrease
 Physical Activity 384

How Can You Lose Weight Healthfully? 387
Eat Smart, Because Calories Count 387
Move to Lose 393
Break Bad Habits 394
Dealing with Extreme
 Obesity 395
**Health Connection: Extreme
 Measures 398**
The Bottom Line 398

How Can You Maintain Weight Loss? 399

How Can You Gain Weight Healthfully? 399

What Is Disordered Eating and What Are the Warning Signs? 401
No Single Factor Causes Eating Disorders 401
Anorexia Nervosa Results from Severe Calorie Restriction 403
Bulimia Nervosa Involves Cycles of Binge Eating
 and Purging 405
Binge Eating Disorder Involves Compulsive Overeating 405
Other Disordered Eating Behaviors Can Be Harmful 406
There Are Some Common Signs of Disordered Eating 406
What Can You Do If You Suspect a Friend Has an
 Eating Disorder? 407
Eating Disorders Can Be Treated 407
Visual Chapter Summary 411

10

Weight Management and Energy Balance 368

What Is a Healthy Weight and Why Is Maintaining It Important? 370

How Do You Know If You're at a Healthy Weight? 372
BMI Measurements Can Provide a General Guideline 372
Measure Your Body Fat and Its Location 374

What Is Energy Balance and What Determines Energy Needs? 376
Energy Balance Is Calories In versus Calories Out 376
Focus Figure 10.5 Energy Balance and Imbalances 377
Energy Needs Are Different for Everyone 378
Calculating Your Energy Needs 379
Energy Imbalances over Time Can Lead to Changes
 in Body Weight 380

11

Nutrition and Fitness 416

What Is Physical Fitness and Why Is It Important? 418
Physical Fitness Has Five Basic
 Components 418
Physical Fitness Provides Numerous Benefits 419

What Does a Physical Fitness Program Look Like? 420
Cardiorespiratory Exercise Can Improve Cardiorespiratory
 Endurance and Body Composition 420
Strength Training Can Improve Muscle Strength, Muscle
 Endurance, and Body Composition 421
Stretching Can Improve Flexibility 422
The FITT Principle Can Help You Design a Fitness Program 422
The Progressive Overload Principle Can Help Improve Fitness
 over Time 424

How Are Carbohydrate, Fat, and Protein Used during Exercise? 425

Carbohydrate Is the Primary Energy Source during High-Intensity Exercise 426

Focus Figure 11.3 What Fuels Our Activities? 427

Fat Is the Primary Energy Source during Low-Intensity Exercise 429

Protein Is Primarily Needed to Build and Repair Muscle 433

Total Calorie Needs Depend on the Type and Schedule of Exercise 433

Health Connection: What Is the Female Athlete Triad? 434

Components of the Female Athlete Triad 434

Signs and Treatment 434

How Does the Timing of Meals Affect Fitness and Athletic Performance? 435

Optimal Foods before Exercise 435

Optimal Foods during Exercise 436

Optimal Foods after Exercise 436

What Vitamins and Minerals Are Important for Fitness? 437

Antioxidants Can Help Protect Cells from Damage Caused by Exercise 437

Some Minerals Can Be of Concern in Highly Active People 438

Vitamin and Mineral Supplements Are Generally Not Necessary 439

How Does Fluid Intake Affect Fitness? 439

Fluid and Electrolyte Balance and Body Temperature Are Affected by Exercise 440

You Need Fluids before, during, and after Exercise 441

Some Beverages Are Better than Others 441

Consuming Too Little or Too Much Fluid Can Be Harmful 442

Can Dietary Supplements Contribute to Fitness? 444

Dietary Supplements and Ergogenic Aids May Improve Performance, but Can Have Side Effects 444

Sports Bars, Shakes, and Meal Replacers May Provide Benefits 447

Visual Chapter Summary 452

12

Consumerism and Sustainability: Food from Farm to Table 456

How Do Advertising and Marketing Influence Your Food Choices? 458

Where Does Your Food Come From? 459

Food Comes from Farms, Not Stores 459

Food Production Outside the United States 465

What Is a Sustainable Food System? 466

Sustainable Food Systems Are Environmentally Friendly, Economically Viable, and Socially Equitable 467

The Most Sustainable Foods Are Locally Grown and Plant Based 469

How Do We Balance the World Population's Demand for Food with Sustainability? 473

Costs and Benefits of Using Hormones in Our Food Supply 473

Costs and Benefits of Using Antibiotics in Our Food Supply 474

Costs and Benefits of Using Pesticides in Our Food Supply 474

What Are the Risks and Benefits of Using Biotechnology in Agriculture? 477

Genetic Engineering 478

Concerns and Regulations Associated with GE Foods 479

How Does Food Policy Affect the Foods Available to You to Buy and Consume? 481

Food Policy Can Help Encourage Food Producers to Create Healthier Products 481

Food Policy Can Lead to Relabeling and Reformulating without Providing a Healthier Food Product 482

What Are the Politics of the Food Industry? 483

How Do You Know How Foods Were Produced? 484

Label Terms Provide Information about How Foods Were Produced 484

Understand the Meaning of the Term *Organic* 485

Visual Chapter Summary 488

13

Food Safety and Technology 492

What Causes Foodborne Illness? 494

Foodborne Illnesses Are Often Caused by Pathogens 494

Chemical Agents and Toxins Can Also Cause Illness 500

Some People Are at Higher Risk for Foodborne Illness 500

What Can You Do to Prevent Foodborne Illness? 501

Clean Your Hands and Produce 502

Combat Cross-Contamination 503

Cook Foods Thoroughly 504

Chill Foods at a Low Enough Temperature 505

Health Connection: Getting the Lowdown on *Listeria* 507

Who Protects Your Food and How Do They Do It? 510

Several Government Agencies Police the Food Supply 510

Food Manufacturers Use Preservation Techniques to Destroy Contaminants   512

Irradiation   513

Product Dating Can Help You Determine Peak Quality   514

What Are Food Additives and How Are They Used?   515

Preservatives Prevent Spoilage and Increase Shelf Life   515

Some Additives Enhance Texture and Consistency   516

Some Additives Improve Nutrient Content   516

Color and Flavor Enhancers Improve the Appeal of Foods   516

Food Additives Are Closely Regulated by the FDA   517

Some Food Additives Are Unintentional   518

What Are Toxins and Chemical Agents?   518

Toxins Occur Naturally   518

Contamination Is Sometimes Due to Pollution   520

What Is Bioterrorism and How Can You Protect Yourself?   521

Visual Chapter Summary   523

14

Life Cycle Nutrition: Pregnancy through Infancy   526

What Nutrients and Behaviors Are Important before Attempting a Healthy Pregnancy?   528

A Man's Diet and Lifestyle Affect the Health of His Sperm   528

Women Need to Adopt a Healthy Lifestyle before Conception   528

Health Connection: The Stress of Infertility   531

What Nutrients and Behaviors Are Important in the First Trimester?   532

During the First Trimester, the Fertilized Egg Develops into a Fetus   532

"Morning Sickness" and Cravings Are Common   533

Adequate Weight Gain Supports the Baby's Growth   534

The Need for Certain Nutrients Increases   534

Pregnancy Increases the Risk for Foodborne Illness   537

Pregnant Women Should Avoid Many Other Substances   537

The Importance of Critical Periods   538

What Nutrients and Behaviors Are Important in the Second Trimester?   539

Pregnant Women Need to Consume Adequate Calories, Carbohydrate, and Protein to Support Growth   539

Exercise Is Important for Pregnant Women   539

Potential Complications: Gestational Diabetes and Hypertension   540

What Nutrients and Behaviors Are Important in the Third Trimester?   542

What Special Concerns Might Younger or Older Mothers-to-Be Face?   542

What Is Breast-Feeding and Why Is It Beneficial?   543

Breast-Feeding Provides Physical, Emotional, and Financial Benefits for Mothers   544

Breast-Feeding Provides Nutritional and Health Benefits for Infants   545

What Are the Best Dietary and Lifestyle Habits for a Breast-Feeding Mother?   547

When Is Infant Formula a Healthy Alternative to Breast Milk?   548

Some Women May Not Be Able to Breast-Feed   549

Formula Can Be a Healthy Alternative to Breast-Feeding   549

What Are the Nutrient Needs of an Infant and Why Are They So High?   550

Infants Grow at an Accelerated Rate   551

Monitoring Infant Growth   551

Infants Have Higher Nutrient Needs   552

When Are Solid Foods Safe to Feed a Baby?   553

Solid Foods May Be Introduced Once Certain Milestones Are Met   553

Solid Foods Should Be Introduced Gradually   554

Some Foods Are Dangerous and Should Be Avoided   555

Putting It All Together   558

Visual Chapter Summary   561

15

Life Cycle Nutrition: Toddlers through the Later Years   566

What Are the Issues Associated with Feeding Young Children?   568

Young Children Need to Eat Frequent, Small Meals with Nutrient-Rich Foods   568

Young Children Have Special Nutrient Needs   570

Picky Eating and Food Jags Are Common in Small Children   571

Raising a Vegetarian Child   572

What Are the Nutritional Needs and Issues of School-Aged Children?   572

High Obesity Rates in School-Aged Children   574

Daily Food Plans For Kids Help Guide Food Choices   575

The Importance of Breakfast   576

School Meals Contribute to a Child's Nutritional Status   578

What Are the Nutritional Needs and Issues of Adolescents?   579

Peer Pressure and Other Factors Influence Teen
Eating Behaviors   579
Adolescents Need Calcium and Vitamin D for
Bone Growth   580
Teenage Girls Need More Iron   580
Adolescents: At Risk for Disordered Eating   581

**What Are the Nutritional Needs of Older
Adults?**   **581**
Older Adults Need Fewer Calories, Not Less Nutrition   582
Older Adults Need Adequate Fiber and Fluid   582
Older Adults Should Monitor Their Micronutrients   583

**What Additional Challenges Do Older
Adults Face?**   **585**
Eating Right for Health and to Prevent and Manage Chronic
Disease   585
Economic and Emotional Conditions Can Affect Nutritional
Health   591
Health Connection: A Wake-Up Call   593
Staying Physically Active   595
Visual Chapter Summary   597

16
Hunger at Home and Abroad   600

**What Are Food Insecurity, Food Security,
and Hunger?**   **602**
Many People Experience Food Insecurity in the United
States and Worldwide   602

**What Causes Food Insecurity in the United
States?**   **604**
In the United States, Food Insecurity Is Often Caused
by Poverty   604

Health Connection: Overweight and Undernourished   606
Health Problems Contribute to Food Insecurity among
Americans   606

**What Causes Food Insecurity and Poverty Around
the Globe?**   **607**
Discrimination and Inequality Promote Poverty   608
Political Sanctions and Armed Conflicts   608
Crop Failure, Natural Disasters, and Wasteful Agricultural
Practices   608
Population Overgrowth   610

Who Is at Increased Risk for Undernutrition?   **610**

What Are the Effects of Chronic Malnutrition?   **611**
Children Suffer Impaired Growth and Development   611
Impaired Immunity Can Result in Disease   612
Infant and Child Mortality Rates Increase   613

What Can Be Done to Reduce Food Insecurity?   **614**
Better Land Management and Proper Sanitation   614
Fortification of Foods   616
Education Is Key   616
You Can Help Reduce Food Insecurity   616
Visual Chapter Summary   619

Appendices

Appendix A
Calculations and Conversions   **A-2**

Appendix B
Organizations and Resources   **B-1**

Glossary   **G-1**

References   **R-1**

Index   **I-1**

Credits   **CR-1**

Special Features

FOCUS

Figure 2.2 Dietary Reference Intakes 35
Figure 2.12 Understanding the Nutrition Facts Panel 52
Figure 3.3 The Digestive System 74
Figure 3.6 Anatomy of the Small Intestine 77
Figure 4.4 Carbohydrate Digestion and Absorption 105
Figure 4.6 Hormones Regulate Blood Glucose 108
Figure 4.12 Diabetes 124
Figure 5.10 Fat Digestion and Absorption 152
Figure 5.13 The Roles of Lipoproteins 155
Figure 5.20 Development of Atherosclerosis 168
Figure 6.4 Protein Digestion and Absorption 193
Figure 6.6 Protein Synthesis 195
Figure 7.6 Retinal and Its Role in Vision 236
Figure 8.7 Fluid Balance during Exercise 290
Figure 10.5 Energy Balances and Imbalances 377
Figure 10.7 Your Brain Controls Hunger and Satiation 382
Figure 11.3 What Fuels Our Activities? 427

A CASE STUDY health CONNECTION

Fast-Food City 21
Functional Foods and Cholesterol 62
Tired of Gluten 89
Destined for Diabetes? 127
All Fats Are Not Created Equal 175
Running on Empty 213
A High-Pressure Situation 303
Smashed: Story of a Drunken Girlhood 358
Extreme Measures 398
What Is the Female Athlete Triad? 434
Getting the Lowdown on *Listeria* 507
The Stress of Infertility 531
A Wake-Up Call 593
Overweight and Undernourished 606

EXAMINING THE EVIDENCE

How Can I Evaluate Nutrition News? 16
Does the Time of Day You Eat Impact Your Health? 48
Do Sugar-Sweetened Beverages Cause Obesity? 122

The Mediterranean Diet: What Do People Living Near the Mediterranean Do Differently? 172
Protein Supplements: Are They Necessary? 206
Gesundheit! Myths and Facts about the Common Cold 266
Alcohol and Advertising 350
Evaluating Popular Diets 388
The Truth about the Fat-Burning Zone 432
Nutrition and Developmental Disabilities 573

nutrition IN THE Real World

Poor, Obese, and Malnourished: A Troubling Paradox 14
Don't Be Scammed! 23
The *Dietary Guidelines for Americans* at a Glance 38
When a Portion *Isn't* a Portion 46
Tinkering with Your Body's Digestive Process 72
Grains, Glorious Whole Grains 112
Avoiding a Trip to the Dentist 118
Mercury and Fish 176
The Joy of Soy 214
Tap Water or Bottled Water: Is Bottled Better? 292
A Closer Look at Body Image 404
Carbohydrate Loading 430
You as a Sustainable Farmer: Growing Vegetables in a Container 472
Sushi: A Cautionary Tale 501
Breast-Feeding at Work Can Work 547
Feeding the Baby 555
Drug, Food, and Drug-Herb Interactions 588
Natural Disasters and Food Insecurity: A Dire Combination 609
Food Insecurity among Us—and How You Can Help! 617

self-ASSESSMENT

Do Outside Factors Influence Your Food Choices? 7
What Does the Health of Your Family Tree Look Like? 8
Does Your Diet Have Proportionality? 41
Are You at Risk for Type 2 Diabetes? 126
How Much Fat Is in Your Diet? 161
Do You Have a Protein-Friendly Diet? 208
Are You Getting Enough Fat-Soluble Vitamins in Your Diet? 234

Are You Getting Enough Water-Soluble Vitamins in Your Diet?   247
Do You Consume Enough Water?   291
Are You at Risk for Osteoporosis?   310
Red Flags for Misusing Alcohol   359
What's Your Estimated Energy Requirement (EER)   379
Does Your Environment Affect Your Energy Balance?   384
Are You at Risk for an Eating Disorder?   408
Calculating Your Fluid Needs for Endurance Exercise   443
Are You Meeting Your Fitness Recommendations and Eating for Exercise?   445
How Sustainable Is Your Food Shopping?   471
How Do Your Food-Safety Habits Stack Up?   510
Are You Ready for a Healthy Pregnancy?   529
Are You at Nutritional Risk?   594
Which Is Cheaper: Fast Food or a Homemade Lunch?   605
Are You at Risk for Food Insecurity?   607

Table TIPS

Tip-Top Nutrition Tips   37
Digest It Right!   85
Eat Gluten Free   90
Ways to Enjoy Whole Grains   113
High Five! Five Ways to Increase Fiber Daily   115
Lowering Your Added Sugars   117
Easy Ways to Add Fish to Your Diet   176
Nuts about Nuts?   178
Eating for a Healthy Heart   179
Protein Power   199
Preserve Your Vitamins!   233
Score an A   239
Enjoying Your Es   241
Getting Your Ks   243
Dynamite Ways to Get Vitamin D   245
Thrive on Thiamin   249
Rally Your Riboflavin   251
Nail Your Niacin   253
Beam with B_6 255
Fulfill Your Folate Needs   257
Boost Your B_{12} 259
Juicy Ways to Get Vitamin C   261
Bottoms Up   295
Shake Your Salt Habit   302
Potassium Power!   306
Calcium Counts!   307
Fabulous Phosphorus   312
Magnificent Magnesium   314
Ironing Out Your Iron Needs   318
Counting Your Copper   319
Zapping Your Zinc Needs!   321
Seeking Out Selenium   323
Fabulous Ways to Get Fluoride   325
Cram in the Chromium   327
Iodine Impact   328
Managing Your Manganese   329
Keeping Your Drinking to a Moderate Amount   361
Eat More to Weight Less   393

Get UP and MOVE   394
Adopt Some Healthy Habits   395
Healthy Snacks for Healthy Weight Gain   400
Get Moving!   425
Don't Let Bad Bugs Ruin Your Trip   500
Scrub Away Pathogens   503
Ways to Avoid Toxins and Chemical Agents in Your Seafood   520
Avoid Foods that May Have Been Tampered With   521
Alleviating Morning Sickness   533
Exercising while Pregnant   540
Tasty Treats for Toddlers   569
Kid-Friendly, Iron-Rich Foods   570
Breakfast on the Go   577
Tips for Packing School Lunches   578
Teen Table Tips   581

MADE over MADE better

Try this to boost your fiber intake!   138
Try this to control your fat intake!   180
Try these healthier proteins!   220
Try these vitamin-rich foods!   273
Try these mineral-rich alternatives!   331
Try this mocktail!   362
Try these on-the-go options!   409
Try this to fuel your exercise!   450

POINTS OF VIEW

Should Food Advertising to Children Be Regulated by the Government?   25
Will Posting Nutritional Content in Restaurants Have a Positive Impact on the Obesity Epidemic?   63
Probiotics: Do You Need Them?   93
Should Food Labels Distinguish between Naturally Occurring and Added Sugars?   139
Is Wild Salmon a Better Choice Than Farmed Salmon?   181
Is the Paleo Diet a Good Choice for You?   221
Should Vegetarians Take Vitamin B_{12} Supplements?   274
Does Designer Water Have Nutritional Benefits?   332
Do the Health Benefits of Drinking Alcohol Outweigh the Risks?   363
Is Gastric Bypass Surgery a Healthy Weight-Loss Measure for Obese Adolescents   410
Should Energy Drinks Have Caffeine Limits Similar to Those for Soda?   451
Should the U.S. Federal Government Continue to Subsidize the Production of Corn and Wheat?   487
Is It Safe to Get Your Meals from a Food Truck?   522
Should Parents Make Their Own Baby Food?   560
Should School Meals Align with the *Dietary Guidelines for Americans?*   596
Food vs Cash: Which Is More Effective for Alleviating Hunger?   618

About the Author

Joan Salge Blake is a clinical associate professor and dietetics internship director at Boston University's Sargent College of Health and Rehabilitation Sciences. She teaches both graduate and undergraduate nutrition courses and has been a guest lecturer at both the Boston University Goldman School of Dental Medicine and the Boston University School of Medicine. She received the Whitney Powers Excellence in Teaching Award from Boston University. Joan completed her MS at Boston University and is currently working toward her doctorate.

Joan is a member of the Academy of Nutrition and Dietetics (AND) and the Massachusetts Dietetic Association (MDA). She has been a presenter and presiding officer at both the AND Annual Meeting and the MDA Annual Convention, and she was previously named the MDA's "Young Dietitian of the Year," Outstanding Dietitian (2009), and Outstanding Dietetic Educator (2007). Joan has served on the MDA board for more than a decade in many roles, including past MDA Director of Education and Nominating Committee Chairperson.

In addition to teaching and writing, Joan is also a national media spokesperson and is often asked to translate complex nutritional issues in understandable terms. She has conducted more than 1,000 media interviews. Joan is also a nutrition blogger for the *U.S. News & World Report*'s Eat + Run website.

Why I Wrote Nutrition & You

I wrote *Nutrition & You* for you. It is all about you. For more than a decade, I have taught an Introduction to Nutrition course to a packed classroom of almost 200 students, at the unseemly hour of 8 a.m. The students keep coming year after year because I not only deliver accurate nutrition science and information in an easy-to-understand, entertaining format, but more importantly, I personalize the information for them so that they can immediately apply it to their own lifestyles.

As a college student, you are exposed to a steady stream of nutrition and health information from the media, your family and friends, and the Internet. While you may think Google has the answer to your nutrition questions, I have seen students frequently fall victim to misinformation found via a quick Web search and a few glitzy websites. So I designed *Nutrition & You* to be as user friendly as possible, packed exclusively with sound nutrition information. The text goes beyond basic nutrition science and provides realistic advice and strategies to help you easily incorporate what you learn into your busy life. The text is written to meet *your* nutritional concerns and answer *your* questions.

As you read *Nutrition & You*, I want you to feel as though you are sitting in my class being entertained and informed. For this reason, I wrote the text in a conversational tone, and we designed it to visually communicate complex nutrition science and topics in an easy-to-understand way.

The information in this textbook is arranged in a deliberate **"What," Why,"** and **"How"** format. Each chapter will tell you:

➤ **"What"** the nutrition concept is;
➤ **"Why"** it is important and the role it plays in your body; and then, most importantly,
➤ **"How"** to easily adjust your lifestyle based on what you just learned.

Remember, nutrition matters to *you!* What you eat today and tomorrow will affect you and your body for years to come. Just as important, what you learn about nutrition today will enable you to make a positive effect on the lives of others from now on.

Joan Salge Blake

New to This Edition

Both nutrition research and personalized applications are continually expanding this dynamic science. To keep pace, we have reorganized the content, visually improved the figures and tables, and added new features to each chapter in the fourth edition of *Nutrition & You*. In addition, we have made these significant additions to the book and its digital accompaniments (for specific chapter-by-chapter updates, see the next section):

➤ **Interactive eText 2.0,** complete with embedded videos, animations, author-narrated Focus Figure Video Walkthroughs, multiple-choice questions, and drag-and-drop activities, is designed for students to interact with the material, not just read it. eText 2.0 is mobile friendly and ADA accessible.
- Now available on smart phones and tablets
- Seamlessly integrated videos and other rich media
- Accessible (screen-reader ready)
- Configurable reading settings, including resizable type and night reading mode
- Instructor and student note-taking, highlighting, bookmarking, and search

➤ **Focus Figure video walkthroughs** feature a narration for students to listen to as they watch a video walkthrough of each Focus Figure, where narrator Joan Salge Blake guides students through each section of the figure, highlighting important concepts and making connections. Access these by scanning the QR code on each Focus Figure.

➤ The new **Health Connection: A Case Study** feature box in each chapter examines the links between nutrition and disease. This new presentation is intended to:
- Take a more **case-study approach** to really engage students
- Add **key concepts** back into the **main narrative**
- Include new **Health Connection Case Study questions** in MasteringNutrition, making the feature assignable

Chapter-by-Chapter Updates

Chapter 1

➤ Updated information on added sugars and dietary fat, food and eating trends, leading causes of death among Americans, overweight and obesity rates among Americans, and key questions to ask when evaluating a nutrition- and health-related website
➤ Updated figure on nutrients and their functions in the body and added new obesity map
➤ Added a new Health Connection: A Case Study on weight gain called "Fast Food City"

Chapter 2

➤ Added new information about the Scientific Report of the 2015 *Dietary Guidelines for Americans* committee, the proposed new Nutrition Facts panel on the food label, functional foods, Health Claims, and circadian rhythms
➤ Added a new Health Connection: A Case Study on functional foods and cholesterol called "A Functionally Natural Approach"
➤ Updated Two Points of View feature box

Chapter 3

➤ Updated information regarding heartburn, foods that can contribute to acid reflux, celiac disease, and Alli
➤ Provided latest information regarding esophageal cancer, peptic ulcers, and irritable bowel syndrome
➤ Added a new Health Connection: A Case Study on celiac disease called "Tired of Gluten"

Chapter 4

➤ Updated lactose intolerance section, rates of per capita consumption of added sugars, per capita availability of grains among Americans, the glycemic index and diabetes, and the Examining the Evidence feature box about sugar-sweetened beverages
➤ Added new information regarding added sugars on the food label, advantame as a sugar substitute, and the dietary importance of whole grains among Americans
➤ Added a new Health Connection: A Case Study on prediabetes called "Destined for Diabetes?"

Chapter 5

➤ Updated the percentage of calories from fat consumed by Americans, information on the current consumption of dietary cholesterol by Americans and levels of cholesterol in foods, information about fat-free cookies, and research on nuts
➤ Added new information about *trans* fat labeling and the shopping habits of consumers
➤ Revised information on fish and pregnant women
➤ Incorporated information regarding heart disease into the text
➤ Added a new Health Connection: A Case Study on high cholesterol called "All Fats Are Not Created Equal"

Chapter 6

➤ Updated information about protein digestibility, soy and health, synthesis of new skin, and statistics about protein energy malnutrition
➤ Updated section on protein supplements and Bar Hopping chart
➤ Added new information about intake of fish
➤ Added a new Health Connection: A Case Study on vegetarian marathon runners called "Running on Empty"

Chapter 7

➤ Updated information on age-related macular degeneration and cataracts, vitamin losses in cooking, statistics on vitamin supplement usage, vitamin A and cell differentiation, daily intake of vitamin E by Americans, daily vitamin D needs, rickets and vitamin D deficiency, vitamin B_{12}, and vitamin C, echinacea, and zinc and the common cold
➤ Added new Figure 7.21 on food patterns and daily vitamin needs
➤ Changed Two Points of View feature box to address the new topic "Should vegetarians take vitamin B_{12} supplements?"

Chapter 8

➤ Updated information about bottled water, sodium recommendations in the *Dietary Guidelines for Americans* committee report, current intake of dairy foods among Americans, osteoporosis, current intake levels of all the minerals, and zinc and the common cold

➤ Updated figure showing fluoride map of the United States

➤ Added information regarding sustainability

➤ Changed Two Points of View feature box to address the new topic "Is there any nutritional benefit to consuming designer waters?"

➤ Added a new Health Connection: A Case Study on hypertension called "A High-Pressure Situation"

Chapter 9

➤ Updated statistics on the occurrence of cirrhosis in the U.S., drunk driving fatalities, and underage drinking

➤ Updated information on fetal alcohol spectrum disorders, and binge drinking

➤ Introduced new term, "heavy drinking"

➤ Updated criteria for alcoholism

Chapter 10

➤ Added Paleo Diet to coverage of popular diets and moved discussion of extreme measures to treat obesity to main text

➤ Updated trendy fad diet substances and statistics on weight loss and bariatric surgery

➤ Added new Focus Figure 10.7: Your Brain Controls Hunger and Satiation

➤ Added photo of realistic Lammily doll

➤ Added Health Connection: A Case Study on obesity called "Extreme Measures"

Chapter 11

➤ Updated calcium and creatine sections based on updated reference

➤ Updated Figure 11.3: What Fuels Our Activities?

➤ Developed a new Health Connection: A Case Study on the female athlete triad called "Sacrificing for Her Art"

➤ Changed Two Points of View feature box to address the new topic "Should energy drinks have caffeine limits similar to those for sodas?"

Chapter 12

➤ Modified chapter title, added new Learning Outcome, and created new text section to represent additional focus on sustainability

➤ Updated information in text and tables in section Where Does Your Food Come From? to reflect new agricultural census

➤ Added new figure showing a label of rBGH-free milk and updated Figure 12.3 map showing number of farms in America

➤ Updated text to reflect the focus on cost vs. benefits of using hormones, antibiotics, and pesticides

➤ Updated section on biotechnology, including information about the new USDA process of certification for GMO-free products

Chapter 13

➤ Added a new Health Connection: A Case Study about reducing risk of listeriosis in a pregnant woman called "Getting the Lowdown on *Listeria*"
➤ Added content in the food additives section discussing the risk/benefit ratio of using irradiation within the food supply
➤ Changed Two Points of View feature box to address the new topic "Is it safe to get your meal from a food truck?"

Chapter 14

➤ Updated content relating to fertility in men and women and regarding the benefits of breast-feeding
➤ Moved information on food allergies into the main text and added information about increased frequency of food allergies
➤ Added a new Health Connection: A Case Study called "The Stress of Infertility"

Chapter 15

➤ Updated calcium recommendations, statistics on eating frequency, physical activity, sedentary hours, obesity among children, and prevalence data for type 2 diabetes, and information on picky eating
➤ Added information about the School Breakfast Program and updated information on the National School Lunch Program to include policies from the Healthy Hunger-Free Kids Act
➤ Added a new Health Connection: A Case Study on breast cancer called "A Wake-Up Call"
➤ Changed Two Points of View feature box to address the new topic "Should school meals align with the *Dietary Guidelines for Americans*?"

Chapter 16

➤ Updated Figures 16.1 and 16.3 on food insecurity and updated information on U.S. and world food insecurity, illiteracy of women, AIDS orphans, worldwide childhood deaths resulting from malnutrition and diarrheal illnesses, and people served by Meals on Wheels
➤ Revised Health Connection: A Case Study called "Overweight and Undernourished"
➤ Added a new Self-Assessment, "Which Is Cheaper: Fast Food or a Homemade Lunch?"
➤ Updated Two Points of View feature box on "Food vs. Cash: Which Is More Effective for Alleviating Hunger?"

Other Key Features

➤ **Visual Chapter Summaries** are structured to mirror the organization of the chapter content and numbered to correspond with the chapter objectives. They contain important art and photos from the main chapter text and serve as concise study and review tools.
➤ **The learning outcomes, chapter headings, and summary sections** are linked together to provide a strong pedagogical structure that promotes comprehension and facilitates study and review.

- ➤ **Examining the Evidence** features look at the latest research on controversial or confusing "hot" topics in nutrition today and include critical-thinking questions. These features guide you to making better, informed choices in your personal nutrition, and becoming a critical media consumer of nutrition information.
- ➤ **MyDietAnalysis mobile website** is now available, so you can track your diet and activity accurately, anytime and anywhere, from your mobile device.
- ➤ **Exploring Micronutrients** within Chapters 7 and 8 are self-contained sections that incorporate photos, illustrations, and text to present each vitamin and mineral. Each micronutrient is discussed using the same categories (forms, functions, daily needs, food sources, toxicity and deficiency symptoms) for a consistent and easy-to-study format. These enable you to identify at a glance the key aspects of each nutrient.
- ➤ **Two Points of View** at the end of each chapter contains a summary of opposing viewpoints on a timely topic. This feature will encourage you to think critically about pro and con arguments on a given issue and decide for yourself which side you agree with. You will be applying the critical-thinking skills that you learned in the chapter as you think through each point of view presented.
- ➤ **True or False?** pretests open each chapter with 10 true/false statements that help you realize that the things you think you know about nutrition aren't always accurate. Answers are given at the end of the chapter, and a true/false icon emphasizes locations of answers within the chapter.
- ➤ **Nutrition in the Real World** features take a closer look at some of the ways nutritional information and issues affect daily life.
- ➤ **Practical Nutrition videos** show the dynamic and ever-interesting Joan Salge Blake walking you through making better eating choices in familiar environments, based on a choice related to the chapter topic. Examples include a pizza parlor, deli, coffee shop, breakfast choices on the go, fitness smoothies, and much more. QR codes appear throughout the text for direct links to the videos.
- ➤ **Table Tips** give practical ideas for incorporating adequate amounts of each nutrient into your diet using widely available foods.
- ➤ **Self-Assessments** throughout the book ask you to think about your own diet and behaviors and how well you are meeting your various nutrient needs.
- ➤ **Made Over, Made Better** food comparisons at the end of Chapters 4 through 11 can help you visually see how to make more nutritious decisions.
- ➤ **eLearn activities** within the chapters direct you to a website to complete an animated activity, assessment, or worksheet.

Digital Learning Products

MasteringNutrition™
www.masteringhealthandnutrition.com

MasteringNutrition is an online homework, tutorial, and assessment product designed to improve results by helping students quickly master concepts. Students benefit from self-paced tutorials that feature immediate wrong-answer feedback and hints that emulate the office-hour experience to help keep students on track. With a wide range of interactive, engaging, and assignable activities, students are encouraged to actively learn and retain tough course concepts.

Specific features include:

➤ **Interactive eText 2.0,** complete with embedded videos, animations, author-narrated Focus Figure Video Walkthroughs, multiple-choice questions, and drag-and-drop activities designed for students to interact with the material, not just read it. eText 2.0 is mobile friendly and ADA accessible.

➤ **Focus Figure video walkthroughs** feature Joan Salge Blake narrating a video walkthrough of each Focus Figure, guiding students through each section of the figure, highlighting important concepts and making connections.

➤ **Visual Chapter Summary coaching activities** complement each Visual Chapter Summary with hints and feedback that helps students with their understanding of one or more learning outcomes and reference each learning outcome within the activity.

➤ **Focus Figure coaching activities** guide students through key nutrition concepts with interactive mini-lessons that provide hints and feedback.

➤ **18 NutriTools Build-A-Meal coaching activities** allow students to apply nutrition concepts to improve their health through interactive mini-lessons that provide hints and feedback. The Build a Meal, Build a Pizza, Build a Salad, and Build a Sandwich tools have been carefully rethought to improve the user experience, making them easier to use. They are now HTML5 compatible.

➤ **Pre-lecture reading questions** ensure that students come prepared for lecture by answering multiple-choice questions related to the content in the text.

➤ *ABC News* **videos** cover up-to-date hot topics that occur in the nutrition field that bring nutrition to life and spark discussion. These are accompanied by multiple-choice questions with wrong-answer feedback.

➤ **34 nutrition animation activities** explain big-picture concepts that help students learn the hardest topics in nutrition. These animations include questions with wrong-answer feedback that address students' common misconceptions and have been refreshed and made compatible for MasteringNutrition and mobile devices.

➤ **Math activities** provide hands-on practice of important calculations with helpful wrong-answer feedback.

➤ **Scientific reporting lab activities** allow students to apply the principles of the scientific process to their own diet analysis project and determine if they are at risk for cardiovascular disease, diabetes, and more. These activities include short answer/essay questions.

➤ **Single sign-on for MyDietAnalysis,** a software system that allows students to complete a diet assignment. Students keep track of their food intake and exercise and enter the information to create a variety of reports (e.g., the balance between fats, carbohydrates, and proteins in their diet; how many calories they're eating vs. expending; whether they're meeting the RDAs for vitamins and minerals, etc.). A **MyDietAnalysis activity** has been added within MasteringNutrition for each text chapter that incorporates the use of MDA. A mobile version gives students 24/7 access via their smart phones to easily track food, drink, and activity on the go.

➤ **Chapter Summary MP3s** relate to chapter content and come with multiple-choice questions that provide wrong-answer feedback.

➤ **Get Ready for Nutrition** gives students extra help with math and chemistry skills.

➤ **Dynamic Study Modules** help students study effectively on their own by continuously assessing their activity and performance in real time. Here's how it works: Students complete a set of questions with a unique answer format that also asks them to indicate their confidence level. Questions repeat until the student can answer them all correctly and confidently. Once completed,

Dynamic Study Modules explain the concept using materials from the text. These are available as graded assignments prior to class, and accessible on smart phones, tablets, and computers.

➤ **Learning Catalytics™** is an interactive, student response tool that uses students' smart phones, tablets, or laptops to engage them in more sophisticated tasks and thinking. Now included with MyLab & Mastering with eText, Learning Catalytics enables you to generate classroom discussion, guide your lecture, and promote peer-to-peer learning with real-time analytics. Instructors, you can:

- Pose a variety of openended questions that help your students develop critical thinking skills
- Monitor responses to find out where students are struggling
- Use real-time data to adjust your instructional strategy and try other ways of engaging your students during class
- Manage student interactions by automatically grouping students for discussion, teamwork, and peer-to-peer learning

➤ **The Study Area** is broken down into learning areas and includes videos, animations, MP3s, and much more for student self-study.

 www.mydietanalysis.com

MyDietAnalysis was developed by the nutrition database experts at ESHA Research, Inc. and is tailored for use in college nutrition courses. This software system allows students to complete a diet assignment by keeping a diary of food intake and exercise and then creating a variety of reports (for example, the balance between fats, carbohydrates, and proteins in the diet; how many calories eaten vs. expended; whether the student is meeting the RDAs for vitamins and minerals, and so on). It has been updated to include a **mobile version** so students can access it from their smart phones to easily track food, drink, and activity on the go, 24/7.

Teaching Toolkit DVD for *Nutrition & You* (for instructors)

The Electronic Teaching Toolkit DVD provides everything an instructor needs to prep for the course, and deliver a dynamic lecture, in one convenient place. Resources include:

➤ NEW! *ABC News* Lecture Launcher videos covering the most up-to-date nutrition topics
➤ Updated 34 Nutrition Animations
➤ Practical Nutrition Tips videos
➤ Clicker questions
➤ Quiz Show questions
➤ PowerPoint® Lecture Outlines (including Media-only PowerPoints)
➤ PowerPoint step-edit Image Presentations
➤ Files for all illustrations and tables and selected photos from the text
➤ Microsoft® Word and PDF files for the Instructor Resource and Support Manual
➤ Microsoft® Word, RTF, and PDF files for the Test Bank
➤ Computerized Test Bank, which includes all the questions from the test bank in a format that allows instructors to easily and intuitively build exams and quizzes

➤ Printed *User's Quick Guide* with easy instructions for both experienced and new faculty members to get started with the rich toolkit content

Additional digital instructor and student resources include PDFs of:

➤ *Step-by-step MasteringNutrition tutorials*
➤ *Great Ideas in Teaching Nutrition*
➤ *Eat Right! Healthy Eating in College and Beyond*
➤ *Food Composition Table*

Acknowledgments

It takes a village, and then some, when it comes to writing a dynamic textbook. *Nutrition & You* is no exception. I personally want to thank all of those who passionately shared their expertise and support to make *Nutrition & You* better than I could have envisioned.

Beginning with the dynamic staff at Pearson, I would like to thank Michelle Cadden, who helped make my vision for this textbook a reality. Revising a text of this nature takes a lot of coordination, and Project Manager Caroline Ayres managed to keep us on track while still applying her eagle eye to every aspect of the revision. Diligent Developmental Editors Suzanne Olivier, Alice Fugate, and Kari Hopperstead brought their careful attention to each chapter. Program Manager Susan Malloy was invaluable in lending an extra set of eyes and an additional pair of hands when needed. Crackerjack Content Producer Aimee Pavy, Project Manager Caroline Ayres, and Project Manager Kyle Doctor worked diligently to create the best supplements for *Nutrition & You.*

A very special thanks to Mary Tindle, Senior Project Manager at Cenveo Publisher Services, for all of her hard work shepherding this book through production. My humble appreciation also goes to William Opaluch and Cordes McMahan Hoffman for obtaining the most vivid and unique photos available, as well as to Designer Emily Friel and Design Manager Mark Ong, whose design made the text, art, and photos all come alive and whom I must thank for the book's gorgeous cover.

Marketing takes energy, and that's exactly what Executive Product Marketing Manager Neena Bali and her team seem to generate nonstop. The many instructors who reviewed this book and supporting media, and who provided good insights and suggestions, are listed on the following pages; I am grateful to all of them for helping to inform the development of the fourth edition of *Nutrition & You.*

The village also included loyal contributors who lent their expertise to specific chapters. Courtney Robinson at East Carolina University revised the nutrition and fitness chapter as well as the disordered eating section of the weight-management chapter; E. Whitney Evans at Brown University revised the two "life cycle" chapters; Heidi Wengreen at Utah State University revised the food consumerism and sustainability chapter; Kellene A. Isom at Brigham and Women's Hospital revised the food safety and technology chapter; and Claire Alexander updated the hunger chapter as well as the Two Points of View features. Many thanks also to my accuracy reviewers, Keith Erikson of University of North Carolina at Greensboro and Ryan Paruch of Tulsa Community College.

Lastly, an endless thanks to my family, **A**dam, **B**rendan, and **C**raig, for their love and support when I was working more than I should have been.

Joan Salge Blake

Reviewers

Norman Temple
Athabasca University

Gabrielle Turner-McGrievy
University of Alabama

Simin Vaghefi
University of North Florida

Amy Vaughan
Radford University

John Warber
Morehead State University

Dana Wassmer
Cosumnes River College

Diana Watson-Maile
East Central University

Beverly Webber
University of Utah

Annie Wetter
University of Wisconsin, Stevens Point

Fred Wolfe
University of Arizona

Maureen Zimmerman
Mesa Community College

Donna Zoss
Purdue University

Second Edition

Barbara Bernardi
Lincoln Land Community College

Tracey Brigman
University of Georgia

Linda Brothers
Indiana University—Purdue University, Indianapolis

Lisa Duich-Perry
Chaminade University of Honolulu

Jerald C. Foote
University of Arkansas

Boyd Foster
Gonzaga University

Carol Friesen
Ball State University

Krista Jordheim
Normandale Community College

Lorri Kanauss
Western Illinois University

Kathleen M. Laquale
Bridgewater State College

Linda Johnston Lolkus
Indiana University—Purdue University, Indianapolis

Raymond McCormick
University of South Florida

Owen Murphy
University of Colorado, Boulder

Cheryl Neudauer
Minneapolis Community and Technical College

Patricia Plavcan
Cooking and Hospitality Institute of Chicago

Ramona Rice
Georgia Military College

Lisa Sasson
New York University

Tiffany Shurtz
University of Central Oklahoma

Priya Venkatesan
Pasadena City College

Third Edition

Lisa Aberle
Heartland Community College

Andrea Altice
Florida State College at Jacksonville

Joanne DeMarchi
Saddleback College

Linda Fleming
Middlesex Community College

Carol Friesen
Ball State University

Alvin Furiya
Purdue University, Indianapolis

Vijay Ganji
Georgia State University

Scott Johnson
Wake Technical Community College

Kathleen Laquale
Bridgewater State University

Esther Okeiyi
North Carolina Central University

Ryan Paruch
Tulsa Community College

Teresa Peeples
The College of Coastal Georgia

Janet Yarrow
Housatonic Community College

Fourth Edition

Keith Erikson
University of North Carolina at Greensboro

Carol Friesen
Ball State University

Alvin Furiya
Purdue University, Indianapolis

Kathleen Laquale
Bridgewater State University

Alison Miner
Prince George's Community College

Esther Okeiyi
North Carolina Central University

Ryan Paruch
Tulsa Community College

Teresa Peeples
The College of Coastal Georgia

Janet Yarrow
Housatonic Community College

MasteringNutrition™ Faculty Advisory Board

Brian Barthel
Utah Valley College

Melissa Chabot
University at Buffalo—The State University of New York

Julia Erbacher
Salt Lake Community College

Carol Friesen
Ball State University

Urbi Ghosh
Oakton Community College

Judy Kaufman
Monroe Community College

Michelle Konstantarakis
University of Nevada, Las Vegas

Milli Owens
College of the Sequoias

Janet Sass
Northern Virginia Community College

Dana Sherman
Ozarks Technical Community College

Priya Venkatesan
Pasadena City College

I am nothing without my ABCs.

Thanks.

1 What Is Nutrition?

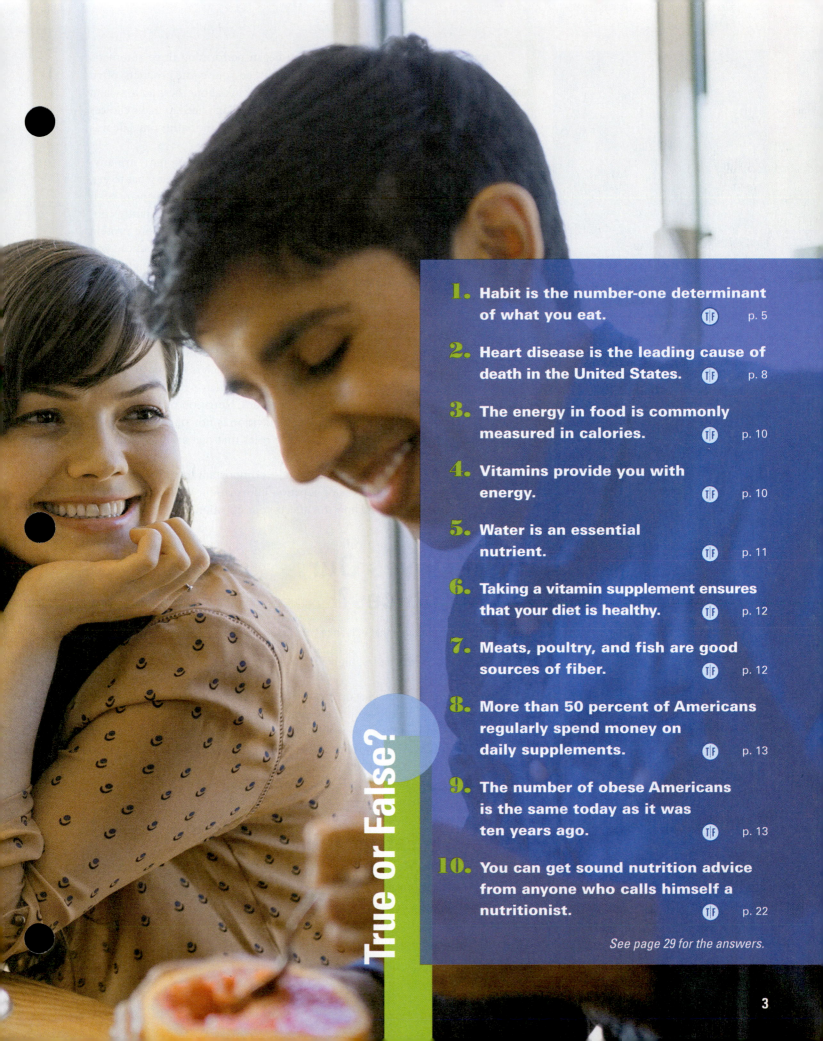

True or False?

1. Habit is the number-one determinant of what you eat. T|F   p. 5

2. Heart disease is the leading cause of death in the United States. T|F   p. 8

3. The energy in food is commonly measured in calories. T|F   p. 10

4. Vitamins provide you with energy. T|F   p. 10

5. Water is an essential nutrient. T|F   p. 11

6. Taking a vitamin supplement ensures that your diet is healthy. T|F   p. 12

7. Meats, poultry, and fish are good sources of fiber. T|F   p. 12

8. More than 50 percent of Americans regularly spend money on daily supplements. T|F   p. 13

9. The number of obese Americans is the same today as it was ten years ago. T|F   p. 13

10. You can get sound nutrition advice from anyone who calls himself a nutritionist. T|F   p. 22

See page 29 for the answers.

Learning Outcomes

After reading this chapter, you will be able to:

LO 1.1 Discuss the factors that influence your food choices.

LO 1.2 Define the term *nutrition*.

LO 1.3 Differentiate between the six categories of essential nutrients found in food and in the body.

LO 1.4 Understand the importance of a well-balanced diet in meeting your daily nutrient needs.

LO 1.5 Discuss the current nutritional state of the American diet.

LO 1.6 Understand the scientific method that is involved in nutrition research and identify reliable sources of nutrition information.

From the minute you were born, you began performing three automatic behaviors: You slept, you ate, and you expelled your waste products, often while you were sleeping. You didn't need to think about these actions, and you didn't have to decide to do them. You also didn't need to make choices about where to sleep, what to eat, or when to go to the bathroom. Life was so easy back then.

Now that you're older, these actions, particularly the eating part, are anything but automatic. You make numerous decisions every day about what to eat, and you make these decisions for reasons that you may not even be aware of. If your dietary advice comes from media sound bites, you may get constantly conflicting information. Yesterday's news flash announced that eating more protein would help you fight a bulging waist. Last week's headline boldly announced you should minimize added sugars in your diet to avoid becoming overweight. This morning, the TV news lead was a health report advising you to eat more whole grains to live longer, but to hold the line on sodium, otherwise your blood pressure may go up.

You may find it frustrating that dietary advice seems to change with the daily news (though it actually doesn't), but this bombardment of nutrition news is a positive thing. You are lucky to live in an era when so much is known and being discovered about what you eat and how it affects you. Today's research validates what nutrition professionals have known for decades: Nutrition plays an invaluable role in your health. As with any science, nutrition is not stagnant. Exciting discoveries will continue to be made about the roles that diet and foods play in keeping you healthy.

Let's find out more about nutrition, why it's so important to your health, and how you can identify sound sources of nutrition information. We'll start with the basic concept of why you eat and how this affects your nutrition.

What Drives Our Food Choices?

LO 1.1 Discuss the factors that influence your food choices.

What did you have for dinner last night? Where did you eat it? Who were you with? How did you feel?

Do you ever think about what drives your food choices? Or are you on autopilot as you stand in line at the sub shop and squint at yet another menu board? Do you adore some foods and eat them often, while avoiding others with a vengeance? Perhaps you have a grandparent who encourages you to eat more (and more!) of her traditional home cooking. You obviously need food to survive, but beyond your basic instinct to eat, there are many other factors that affect what goes into your stomach. Let's discuss some of these now.

We Need to Eat and Drink to Live

All creatures need fuel in order to function, and humans are no exception. We get our fuel from food in the form of chemical compounds that are collectively known as **nutrients**. These nutrients work together to provide energy, growth, and maintenance, and to regulate numerous body processes. Three of the six classes of nutrients—carbohydrates, fats (part of the larger class of lipids), and protein—provide energy in the form of **kilocalories**. Vitamins, minerals, and water help regulate many body processes, including **metabolism**. In fact, water is found in all foods and beverages and is so vital to life that you couldn't live more than a few days without it.

Foods also provide nonnutrient compounds that help maintain your body in order to keep it healthy. We will explore each of these nutrients in more depth later in this chapter, and in much more depth throughout the book.

Beyond the basic need to replenish our bodies with daily fuel are other factors that drive our food choices.

Nutrition knowledge

Trends

Habits

Taste

Emotions

Nutrients

Time

Food Choices

Cost

Convenience

Culture

Advertising

Social reasons

Figure 1.1 Many Factors Influence Your Food Choices

We Choose Foods for Many Other Reasons

Your favorite foods taste delicious—that's why they're your favorites. You also choose certain other foods because they're staples of your culture, or they've become an important aspect of your social life. Some of your food selections are determined by trends, influenced by media messages, or reflect the amount of time or money you have available (**Figure 1.1**). Sometimes, you choose a food just because it's there. Let's explore each of these factors more closely.

Taste and Culture

Research confirms that when it comes to making food choices, taste is the most important consideration.[1] This shouldn't be too much of a surprise, considering that there are at least 10,000 taste buds in your mouth, mainly on your tongue. Your taste buds tell you that chocolate cheesecake is sweet, fresh lemon juice is sour, and a pretzel is salty.

What you choose to put on your plate is often influenced by your culture. If you were a student in Mexico, you may be feasting on a dinner with corn tortillas and tamales, as maize (corn) is a staple of Mexican cuisine. In India, meals commonly include lentils and other legumes with rice and vegetables, whereas Native Americans often enjoy stews of mutton (sheep), corn, and other vegetables. In China, rice, a staple, would be front and center on your plate.

A culture's cuisine is greatly influenced by the environment. This includes not only the climate and soil conditions but also the native plants and animals, as well as the distance people live from rivers, lakes, or the sea. People tend to consume foods that are accessible and often have little experience eating foods that are scarce. For example, native Alaskans feast on fish because it is plentiful, but eat less fresh produce, which is difficult to grow locally. For most Americans, this is less of an issue today than in the past, due to global food distribution networks. However, it still rings true for some food items. People living in landlocked states may have less access to fresh fish, for example, while those outside the south may not see collard greens or beignets on local store shelves as often as their Gulf State counterparts do.

nutrients Compounds in foods that sustain your body processes. There are six classes of nutrients: carbohydrates, fats (lipids), proteins, vitamins, minerals, and water.

kilocalories The measurement of energy in foods. Commonly referred to as *calories*.

metabolism The numerous reactions that occur within the cell. The calories in foods are converted to energy in the cells of the body.

One in four Americans is of Hispanic, Native American, Asian, or African descent. Cultural food preferences often influence food choices.

Food, friends, and football . . . a way of life.

Social Reasons and Trends

Eating is an important way to bond with others. Every year, on the fourth Thursday in November, Americans gather with family and friends to consume close to 46 million turkeys as they celebrate Thanksgiving.[2] A person is likely to eat more on Thanksgiving than on any other Thursday, and this is partly because of all the other people eating with them. Eating dinner with others has been shown to increase the size of the meal by over 40 percent, and the more people present, the more you'll eat.[3]

For many people, activities like watching a football game with fellow fans or going to a movie with friends often involve particular foods. According to the National Restaurant Association, 48 million Americans will order take-out or delivery on Super Bowl Sunday, with chicken wings and pizza as their top foods to eat while watching the game.[4]

Your food choices are also affected by popular trends. For instance, home cooks in the 1950s bought bags of newfangled frozen vegetables in order to provide healthy meals in less time. A few decades later, vegetables went upscale and consumers bought them as part of ready-to-heat stir-fry mixes. Today, shoppers pay a premium price for bags of fresh veggies, like carrots, that have been prewashed and peeled, sliced, or diced. Similarly, decades ago, the only way to enjoy iced tea was to brew it and chill it yourself. Now most markets provide dozens of choices in flavored and enhanced bottled teas, a popular beverage for many college students. As food manufacturers pour more money into research and development, who knows what tomorrow's trendy food item will be?

Another trend is the number of men who are cooking meals for themselves and/or others. The proportion of men who are cooking has increased from 29 percent in the 1960s to 42 percent currently.[5]

Cost, Time, and Convenience

According to the United States Department of Agriculture, almost 15 percent of American households did not have access to enough healthy foods to satisfy their basic, daily food needs, often because of limited financial resources.[6] It's not surprising, then, that many people may be forced to base their food choices on cost. The large, store-brand bag of potato chips, on sale, may appear to be an economical way for a struggling family on a tight budget to fill a dinner plate, rather than with more nutritious fresh or frozen vegetables, which are assumed to be more expensive. The good news is that research has shown that many fruits and vegetables can actually be cheaper per serving than unhealthy junk foods that are high in fat, sugar, and sodium. Buying produce in season and using frozen varieties can actually be very economical ways to consume fruits and vegetables.[7]

For those with adequate food budgets, time is often at a premium. Because of this, the types of foods that many people choose have changed. Research shows that Americans, especially working women with families, want to spend less than 15 minutes preparing a meal.[8] Consequently, supermarkets have changed the types of foods they sell as well as how the food is presented.

If chicken is on the menu tonight, you can go to the poultry section in the store and buy it uncooked. Or you can go to the take-out section of the store and buy it hot off the rotisserie, precooked and stuffed with bread crumbs, or grilled with teriyaki sauce. You can also probably get the cooked vegetables and rice side dishes to take home and reheat with the chicken.

Convenience also influences food choices. Foods that are easily accessible to you are more likely to be eaten. Let's say you have a long walk back to your dorm

Do Outside Factors Influence Your Food Choices?

Rate yourself to see!

1. Whenever I meet friends, we get something to eat or drink, no matter the time of day.
   Yes ☐ No ☐

2. I sometimes find myself walking past a coffee shop, fast-food restaurant, or convenience store and am compelled to buy something to eat.
   Yes ☐ No ☐

3. When I am bored, stressed, or sad, I snack.
   Yes ☐ No ☐

4. I always eat or drink something when I am studying, even if I am not hungry.
   Yes ☐ No ☐

5. I always eat when I go out to a movie in a movie theater.
   Yes ☐ No ☐

Answers

If you answered "yes" to most of these questions, then you are not alone. Many of our food choices are driven by influences that surround us every day!

building after your last class of the day. On the way, you pass a food stand selling slices of delicious-looking pizza. The wonderful smell reminds you that you are hungry, so you buy a slice, or two. Or consider coffee. Decades ago, the most convenient way to get a hot cup of coffee was to brew it yourself. Americans today are more likely to get their java from one of the 20,000 coffee shops across the United States.[9] Pizza and coffee are just two examples of a broad trend of Americans spending more of their household food budget on eating out.

Habits and Emotions

Many people start their day with a bowl of cereal and a glass of orange juice. In fact, ready-to-eat cereals are the number-one breakfast food choice among Americans, and citrus juice is the top juice choice for most people in the morning.[10] Why? For many, the only answer is habit.

Your daily routine and habits can dictate not only what you eat but also *when* you eat. When you get home from work or school, do you head straight for the refrigerator, whether or not you're hungry? Do you always snack when you watch television at night? Or when you're studying?

Emotions also influence your food choices. When the going gets tough, the tough often eat. For many, food is used as an emotional crutch during times of stress, sadness, or joy. Happiness can also trigger eating. Many people celebrate their end-of-term good grades or a promotion at work with a celebratory meal with friends or family. On vacation, you likely reward yourself with fun, relaxation, and, of course, good food. No matter your mood, food is often part of how you express your emotions.

LO 1.1 **The Take-Home Message** Food provides the nutrients that your body needs to function, and the foods that you choose are influenced by many factors. Taste is the primary reason why certain foods have become your favorites. The availability of certain foods has made them a part of your culture and a habitual part of your day. Food trends, cost, limits on your time, convenience, and your emotions all can influence your food choices.

While brown rice is a healthy whole-grain addition to any meal, it can take close to an hour to cook. For time-strapped consumers, food manufacturers have developed instant brown rice that cooks in 10 minutes, and a precooked, microwavable variety that reheats in under 2 minutes.

What Does the Health of Your Family Tree Look Like?

Is there a history of heart disease, diabetes, or obesity in your family? What about other chronic diseases or conditions? Before you read this textbook and learn about the role that good nutrition plays in preventing chronic diseases and maintaining overall good health, ask your parents and grandparents about your family's health history. If there are certain diseases or conditions that run in your family, you'll want to pay particular attention to these as you read about them in this book.

An easy way to manage information about your family's health history is by visiting My Family Health Portrait at http://familyhistory.hhs.gov. When you input your family medical history, it provides a family tree report. Save a copy of this family health history for future reference.

Table 1.1

Leading Causes of Death in the United States

Disease/Cause of Death
Heart Disease (T/F)
Cancer
Respiratory Diseases
Accidents
Stroke
Alzheimer's Disease
Diabetes
Influenza/Pneumonia
Kidney Disease
Intentional Self-Harm

This isn't exactly what's meant by the phrase "You are what you eat," but it's close.

What Is Nutrition and Why Is Good Nutrition So Important?

LO 1.2 Define the term *nutrition*.

Whereas food is the source of nutrients that your body needs, **nutrition** is about more than just food. Nutrition is the science that studies how the nutrients and compounds in foods nourish you, help you function, and affect your health. In contrast, food science relates to the physical and chemical makeup of foods, and the culinary arts refers to the art of preparation of food for consumption.

Your body needs all the nutrients to function properly. An acute deficiency of even one nutrient will negatively affect your body's ability to function in the short term. Chronic deficiencies, excesses, and imbalances of many nutrients can also affect your long-term health.

Good nutrition plays a role in reducing the risk of four of the top ten leading causes of death in the United States—heart disease, cancer, stroke, and diabetes (listed in bold in **Table 1.1**).[11] Nutrition also plays an important role in preventing other diseases and conditions that can impede your lifestyle. A healthy diet can help keep your bones strong and reduce your risk of osteoporosis. Eating right will help you better manage your body weight, which in turn will reduce your risk of developing obesity, diabetes mellitus, and high blood pressure.

You are a product of what you eat, what you *don't* eat, or what you may eat *too much* of. You want to eat the best combination of a variety of foods to meet your nutritional needs and to be healthy. To do that, you need to understand the roles of the essential nutrients in your body and which foods to eat to get them.

LO 1.2 **The Take-Home Message** Nutrition is the scientific study of how the nutrients and compounds in foods nourish your body. Good nutrition plays a role in reducing the risk of many chronic diseases and conditions. Long-term imbalances of many nutrients will affect your health.

What Are the Essential Nutrients and Why Do You Need Them?

LO 1.3 Differentiate between the six categories of essential nutrients found in food and in the body.

The classes of nutrients that we introduced earlier are all *essential* because you must have them in order to function. (Alcohol, in contrast, is not an essential nutrient; even though it provides energy in the form of kilocalories, your body does not need it to function.) Your body is, in fact, made up of the same essential nutrients that are found in foods (see **Figure 1.2**).

Carbohydrates, lipids (fats), and proteins are called **macronutrients**, because you need higher amounts of them in your diet. Vitamins and minerals, though equally important to your health, are considered **micronutrients** because you need them in lesser amounts. You need to consume the final nutrient, water, in copious amounts daily so that you are well hydrated.

Kilocalories from the macronutrients are used as energy during the process of metabolism, and many vitamins, minerals, and water are essential to this process. Vitamins and minerals are also needed for growth and reproduction and to help repair and maintain your body (**Figure 1.3**).

Although each nutrient is unique, they are all equally important, as they work together in numerous ways to keep you healthy. An imbalance of just one will affect your health. Let's take a closer look at the macro- and micronutrients, and water.

Carbohydrates, Fats, and Proteins Provide Energy

Carbohydrates, fats (lipids), and proteins are the energy-providing nutrients, because they contain calories. When we talk about energy, we mean that your body breaks down these nutrients and "burns" them to fuel your activities and internal functioning. One kilocalorie equals the amount of energy needed to raise the temperature of 1 kilogram of water 1 degree Celsius. (Note that *kilocalories* are commonly referred to as *calories*, which is the term we will use from here on.) Carbohydrates and protein provide 4 calories per gram, and fats provide 9 calories per gram. The number of

Human body

Chicken breast

Broccoli (raw)

Figure 1.2 Nutrients in Foods and in the Body
The nutrients found in the foods that you eat are the same ones that provide structure for your body and allow your normal body processes to occur.

nutrition The science that studies how the nutrients and compounds in foods that you eat nourish and affect your body functions and health.

macronutrients The energy-containing essential nutrients that you need in higher amounts: carbohydrates, lipids (fats), and proteins.

micronutrients Essential nutrients that you need in smaller amounts: vitamins and minerals.

Figure 1.3 Nutrients and Their Functions
Nutrients work closely together to provide energy, structure, and support, and to regulate body processes.

Do you know how many calories are in your chips-and-soda "study snack"?

calories in a given food can be determined by measuring the weight, in grams, of each of the three nutrients in one serving of the food.

The amount of calories that you need daily to maintain your weight is estimated based on your age, gender, and activity level. However, you need these nutrients for many reasons beyond providing energy. You must consume a healthy combination of carbohydrates, fats, and protein so that excesses, deficiencies, and imbalances don't occur that may increase your risk of chronic diseases.

Carbohydrates supply the simple sugar, called glucose, that your cells use as the major energy source to fuel your body. Most of your daily calories should come from carbohydrates. Fats are another major fuel source. They also help cushion your organs to prevent damage and act as insulation under your skin to help maintain your body temperature. Proteins can be used as energy, but are better used to build and maintain your tissues, muscles, and organs. You also need protein to make most enzymes and some hormones, to help transport other nutrients, and for a healthy immune system. A healthy diet should provide adequate amounts of carbohydrates and fats for energy, and enough protein to maintain and repair your body.

Carbohydrates, fats, and proteins are all **organic** because they contain the element carbon (as opposed to **inorganic** substances, which don't contain carbon). They also contain two other elements, hydrogen and oxygen. Proteins also contain nitrogen, while carbohydrates and fats do not.

You Can Calculate the Amount of Energy a Food Provides

The number of calories in one serving of a given food can be determined based on the amount (weight in grams) of carbohydrates, protein, and fat in the food. For example, suppose you ate a half bag (4 ounces) of potato chips and drank a 20-ounce cola for a snack. Together these two items contain 125 grams of carbohydrate (in the cola and chips), 7 grams of protein (from the chips), and 38 grams of fat (also in the chips). How many calories did you consume?

To find this out, you need to multiply the total grams of each energy-yielding nutrient times the number of calories per gram of that nutrient. Remember, a gram of carbohydrates and protein each contain 4 calories and a gram of fat contains 9 calories. Let's do some simple math to find out the total calories in the snack:

$$125 \text{ grams carbohydrates} \times 4 \text{ calories} = 500$$
$$7 \text{ grams protein} \times 4 \text{ calories} = 28$$
$$38 \text{ grams fat} \times 9 \text{ calories} = 342$$
$$\textbf{Total calories} = \textbf{870}$$

Based on the amount of carbohydrates, protein, and fat that you consumed, it appears that your snack was rather hefty.

Vitamins and Minerals Are Essential for Metabolism

Even though vitamins and minerals do not provide calories, you need them to use the carbohydrates, fats, and proteins you consume and to sustain numerous chemical reactions in your body. A deficiency of vitamins and minerals can cause ill effects ranging from fatigue to stunted growth, weak bones, and organ damage.

Many vitamins and minerals aid **enzymes**, which are substances that speed up reactions in your body. For example, many of the B vitamins function as coenzymes in the metabolism of carbohydrates and fats. Many minerals, such as calcium and phosphorus,

organic Containing carbon.

inorganic Not containing carbon. Inorganic compounds include minerals, water, and salts.

enzymes Substances that speed up chemical reactions in your body.

work with protein-containing hormones and enzymes to maintain and strengthen your teeth and bones. The fate of carbohydrates, protein, and fats in your body is very much dependent upon your consuming enough vitamins and minerals in your daily diet.

Vitamins are organic compounds that usually have to be obtained from your foods. Your body is able to make some vitamins, such as vitamin D, but sometimes cannot make enough of it to maintain good health. In these situations, your diet has to supplement your body's efforts.

Minerals are inorganic substances that play a role in body processes and are key to the structure of some tissues, such as bone. A deficiency of any of the minerals can cause disease symptoms. Anyone who has ever suffered from iron-deficiency anemia can tell you that falling short of your daily iron needs, for example, can cause fatigue and interfere with your ability to function.

Water Is Vital for Many Processes in Your Body

Although plain water does not provide energy or calories, it is vital to many key body functions, and staying hydrated is therefore an important part of staying healthy. As part of the fluid medium inside your cells, water helps chemical reactions, such as those involved in the production of energy, take place. Water also bathes the outside of your cells, playing a key role in transporting vital nutrients and oxygen to, and removing waste products from, your cells. Water helps maintain your body temperature and acts as a lubricant for your joints, eyes, mouth, and intestinal tract. It surrounds your organs and cushions them from injury.

LO 1.3 **The Take-Home Message** Your body needs carbohydrates, fats (lipids), protein, vitamins, minerals, and water to survive. These six classes of nutrients have specific roles in your body, and you need them in specific amounts for good health. While carbohydrates, fats, and protein provide energy, vitamins, minerals, and water are needed to use the energy-containing nutrients and to maintain good health. The amount of calories you consume can be calculated based on the grams of carbohydrates, protein, and fat in the foods and beverages that you eat. Water is part of the medium inside and outside your cells that carries nutrients to, and waste products from, your cells. Water also helps maintain your body temperature and acts as a lubricant and protective cushion.

How Should You Get These Important Nutrients?

LO 1.4 Understand the importance of a well-balanced diet in meeting your daily nutrient needs.

There is no question that you need all six classes of nutrients to function properly. But is there an advantage to consuming them through food rather than taking them as supplements? Is there more to a healthy diet than just meeting your basic nutrient needs? Let's look at these questions in more detail.

The Best Way to Meet Your Nutrient Needs Is with a Well-Balanced Diet

Many foods provide a variety of nutrients. For example, low-fat milk is high in both carbohydrates and protein and provides a small amount of fat. Milk is also a good source of the vitamins A, D, and riboflavin, as well as the minerals potassium and

Low-fat milk provides a whole host of nutrients.

Carotenoids, the phytochemicals that give cantaloupe its orange color, may have cancer-fighting properties.

calcium, and is approximately 90 percent water by weight. Whereas milk contains a substantial variety of all six classes of nutrients, a single food item doesn't have to provide all nutrients in order to be good for you. Rather, a well-balanced diet composed of a variety of foods can provide you with all of these important nutrients.

A well-balanced diet will also provide other dietary compounds, such as **phytochemicals** (nonnutritive compounds in many foods) and **fiber**, which have been shown to help fight many diseases. At least 900 different phytochemicals have been identified in foods and more are likely to be discovered. However, don't assume that these compounds can be extracted from foods, put in a pill, and still produce the same positive effect on your health. The disease-fighting properties of phytochemicals likely go beyond the compounds themselves, and work with fiber, nutrients, or unknown substances in foods to provide a synergistic, positive effect on your health.

Fiber is the portion of plant foods that isn't completely digested in the stomach and small intestine. Some foods such as whole grains, fruits, and vegetables that are high in fiber are also phytochemical powerhouses. Studies have shown that diets rich in these plant-based foods fight many diseases. Fiber is not found in meat, poultry, or fish.

Also, let's not forget some of the obvious benefits of getting your nutrients from food. The delicious texture and aroma of foods, coupled with the social interaction of meals, are lost when you pop a pill to meet your nutrient needs. That said, some individuals *should* take a supplement if food alone can't meet their needs.

You Can Meet Some Nutrient Needs with a Supplement

Although many people can get all their nutrients through their diet, others have diet restrictions or higher nutrient needs such that they would benefit from taking a supplement in addition to consuming a healthy diet. For example, someone who is lactose intolerant (meaning they have difficulty digesting milk products) may have to meet his or her calcium needs from other sources. A calcium supplement could be an option for these individuals. Pregnant women should take an iron supplement because their increased need for this mineral is unlikely to be met through the diet alone. As you can see, a well-balanced diet and dietary supplements aren't mutually exclusive. In some situations, they should be partnered as the best nutritional strategy for good health.

A well-balanced, healthy diet can help reduce the risk of heart disease, cancer, stroke, and diabetes, which are leading causes of death among Americans.

LO 1.4 **The Take-Home Message** A well-balanced diet will likely meet all of your nutrient needs and also provide a variety of compounds that may help prevent chronic diseases. People who cannot meet their nutrient needs through food alone may benefit from taking a supplement.

How Does the Average American Diet Stack Up?

LO 1.5 Discuss the current nutritional state of the American diet.

The food supply in the United States provides an array of nutritious choices to meet the dietary needs of most Americans. Fresh fruits and vegetables, whole grains, and lean meats, fish, and poultry are usually easily accessible and affordable through

phytochemicals Nonnutritive compounds in plant foods that may play a role in fighting chronic diseases.

fiber The portion of plant foods that isn't digested in the small intestine.

grocery stores and farmers' markets. Yet, with such an abundance of healthy foods to choose from, are Americans adopting healthy diets?

The Quality of the American Diet

In general, Americans eat too much added sugar, sodium, and saturated fat, and too little fiber and some vitamins and minerals. Our low fiber intake is partly due to our inadequate consumption of fruits and vegetables and our overconsumption of refined rather than whole grains.[12] At the same time, while dietary fiber intakes are below recommended levels, Americans consume about 25 teaspoons of sugars daily. This is largely due to Americans' love of soft drinks and other sugary beverages, as well as sweets and treats. For most of us, our fat intake is at the higher end of the recommended range, at about 34 percent. We eat too much saturated fat, and many of us exceed the recommended sodium intake.[13]

With regard to the micronutrients, American men meet their recommendations for most vitamins and minerals but women often fall short of many—including iron, for example. Americans, in general, eat too much sodium, but not enough vitamin D, potassium, calcium, and fiber.[14] In an attempt to balance our lack of healthy food choices, more than 50 percent of Americans take at least one dietary supplement per day.[15]

The lack of a healthy diet may also be due to *where* we eat. Americans spend over 40 percent of their food budget consuming food outside the home.[16] As mentioned earlier, many of us buy prepared foods from the supermarket or take-out meals from restaurants. If you don't prepare a meal yourself, it can be more difficult to keep track of how much sugar, sodium, or saturated fat you're consuming. Research shows that prepared foods purchased outside the home tend to be less nutritious than those foods prepared in the home.[17, 18] Eating fast-food meals more frequently than once a week can increase the risk of weight gain, overweight, and obesity.[19]

Skipping breakfast may also hinder control of your waistline. Research suggests that children and adolescents who do not eat breakfast are at a higher risk for overweight and obesity.[20]

Rates of Overweight and Obesity in Americans

Americans have been battling the bathroom scale for decades, and the scale is winning. The prevalence of both **overweight** and **obesity** has become epidemic in the United States (see **Figure 1.4**). As people take in more calories than they burn, usually due to more sedentary lifestyles, they create a recipe for poor health. Over 65 percent of American adults are overweight and of those, approximately 35 percent are considered obese.[21] Whereas the latest statistics indicate that the epidemic of obesity may be slowing, the rate is still too high, and reducing it is a top health care priority.

Unfortunately, the rate of excessive weight gain is increasing for younger Americans. Currently, 15 percent of children and adolescents aged 2 to 19 years are overweight and 17 percent are considered obese.[22] Along with the weight gain have come higher rates of type 2 diabetes, particularly among children, and increased rates of heart disease, cancer, and stroke.

Ironically, being overweight doesn't necessarily mean being well fed. In fact, many of the poorest Americans are obese and malnourished. The Nutrition in the Real World feature "Poor, Obese, and Malnourished: A Troubling Paradox" looks at this growing problem among Americans.

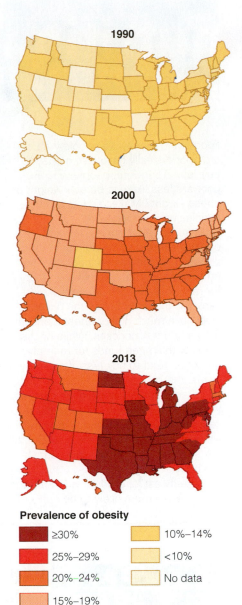

Prevalence of obesity

≥30%	10%–14%
25%–29%	<10%
20%–24%	No data
15%–19%	

Figure 1.4 **Obesity Trends among U.S. Adults**
Over the last two decades, rates of overweight and obesity have risen significantly in the United States.

overweight Carrying extra weight on your body in relation to your height. Clinically defined as having a body mass index (BMI) of 25 to 29.9.

obesity Carrying an excessive amount of body fat above the level of being overweight. Clinically defined as having a body mass index (BMI) of 30 or higher.

nutrition
IN THE Real World

Poor, Obese, and Malnourished: A Troubling Paradox

Food costs money, so people who are poor typically have less money to buy food. Therefore, people who are poor are less likely to be overweight or obese—right? Makes sense, but the conclusion is wrong.

In survey after survey, rates of obesity turn out to be highest among people with the lowest incomes. The numbers are greater for women than for men, but for both genders, Americans living near or below the poverty level have much higher rates of obesity than affluent Americans. While households with limited funds for monthly groceries tend to buy *less* of a variety of foods, the *quality* of the foods tends to be low in nutrients and high in calories.[1] When food insecurity, or the inability to satisfy the basic food needs of individuals, exists in the home, the goal is to fill the stomach, not necessarily nourish the body.

Obesity aside, children who are food insecure are more likely to be deficient in iron, have colds and headaches, and even have delayed cognitive development. These children are at risk for behavioral problems such as irritability, performing poorly academically, and being disruptive in class compared with their well-nourished peers.[2]

In addition to the lack of funds to buy adequate food, researchers have uncovered other factors that can lead to obesity for those who are food insecure, including:[3]

- **Inconsistent Meal Patterns.** Homes with food insecurity often experience "feast or famine" episodes in the kitchen. In other words, there may be times during the month when the kitchen shelves are full of food, only to have other days, and even weeks, where the pantry is bare. When food is plentiful, children often feast heartily, knowing that famine is just around the corner. Researchers speculate that these wide swings in the consumption of calories may wreak havoc with a person's metabolism as well as promote the storage of fat in the body.

- **Household Stress.** In addition to food insecurity, financial constraints also threaten a stable home and access to adequate health care, both of which can contribute to a stressful environment. Stress, anxiety, and depression can cause unhealthy eating, which can perpetuate obesity.

Individuals living in low-income neighborhoods also tend to have limited access to supermarkets to purchase healthy foods at a reasonable cost. In addition, poorer neighborhoods tend to be surrounded by convenience stores and fast-food restaurants, so high-fat, high-calorie foods may be plentiful but nutritious foods scarce. When money is scarce, the stage is set for the paradox of being poor, obese, and malnourished.

Practical Nutrition **VIDEO**

Shop Smart

Is it possible to eat healthfully on a tight budget? Take a trip to the supermarket with Joan to find out! Scan this QR code with your mobile device to access the video. You can also access the video in MasteringNutrition™.

Healthy People 2020 A set of disease prevention and health promotion objectives for Americans to meet during the second decade of the new millennium.

Improving Americans' Diets Is One Goal of *Healthy People 2020*

The U.S. Surgeon General has issued calls for a nationwide health improvement program since 1979. The latest edition of this report, *Healthy People 2020*, contains a set of health goals and objectives for the nation to achieve over the second decade of the twenty-first century.[23]

Healthy People 2020 focuses on several overarching goals:

- Attain high-quality, longer lives free of preventable disease, disability, injury, and premature death.
- Achieve health equity, eliminate disparities, and improve the health of all groups.
- Create social and physical environments that promote good health for all.
- Promote quality of life, healthy development, and healthy behaviors across every stage of life.

There are more than 35 topic areas in *Healthy People 2020*, ranging from ensuring that Americans have adequate access to health services to improvements in their diets and physical activity. Objectives are developed within each topic area.

For example, current research indicates that Americans' body weights are increasing rather than decreasing. Thus, "Nutrition and Weight Status" is one topic area. Its goal is to promote health and reduce chronic diseases associated with diet and weight. There are numerous objectives developed within this topic area that, if

Table 1.2

Healthy People 2020 Nutrition and Weight Status Objectives

Objectives	Target for Americans (%)	Status of Americans (%)
Increase the proportion of adults who are at a healthy weight	33.9	30.8
Reduce the proportion of adults who are obese	30.5	33.9
Reduce the proportion of children and adolescents who are considered obese	14.5	16.1
Increase the contribution of fruits to diets of the population aged 2 years and older	0.9 cups/1,000 calories	0.5 cups/1,000 calories
Increase the variety and contribution of vegetables to the diets of the population aged 2 years and older	1.1 cups/1,000 calories	0.8 cups/1,000 calories

fulfilled, will help Americans improve their diet and reduce their weight. See **Table 1.2** for the list of a few objectives in this area of focus.

As you can see from the table, consuming adequate amounts of fruits and vegetables is beneficial to managing one's weight. Americans should increase their intake of both of these food sources to help them improve their nutrition and weight status.

LO 1.5 **The Take-Home Message** Incidences of overweight and obesity among Americans are prevalent, yet many people are falling short of some nutrient needs. *Healthy People 2020* is a set of health objectives for the nation to achieve over the second decade of the twenty-first century.

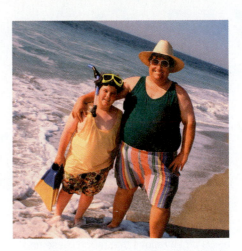

The incidence of overweight and obesity among adults and children is becoming more prevalent in the United States.

What's the Real Deal When It Comes to Nutrition Research and Advice?

LO 1.6 Understand the scientific method that is involved in nutrition research and identify reliable sources of nutrition information.

If you "Google" the word *nutrition*, you will get a list of about 408,000,000 entries instantly. Obviously, the world is full of nutrition information.

Just ask anyone who is trying to lose weight and that person will probably tell you how hard it is to keep up with the latest diet advice—because it seems to keep changing. In the 1970s, waist watchers were told that carbohydrates were the bane of their existence and that a protein-rich, low-carbohydrate diet was the name of the game when it came to shrinking their waistlines. A decade later, avoiding fat was the key to winning the battle of the bulge. By 2000, carbohydrates were being ousted yet again, and protein-rich diets were back in vogue. But now protein-heavy diets seem to be fading out of the limelight and higher carbohydrate diets—with plenty of fiber, fruits, and vegetables—are becoming the way to fight weight gain. So . . . are you frustrated yet?

Even though popular wisdom and trends seem to change with the wind, scientific knowledge about nutrition doesn't change this frequently. While the media publicize results from studies deemed newsworthy, in reality it takes many, many affirming research studies before a **consensus** is reached about nutrition advice. News of the results of one study is just that: news. In contrast, advice from an authoritative health organization or committee, such as the American Heart Association or the *Dietary Guidelines for Americans*, which is based on a consensus of research information, is sound information that can be trusted for the long term.

consensus The opinion of a group of experts based on a collection of information.

How Can I Evaluate Nutrition News?

Chocolate May Lower the Risk of Stroke in Men

Loren Grush, *FoxNews.com*

Based on this headline, you may be tempted to run out immediately and get yourself a couple of chocolate bars. However, you would be doing a disservice to your health if you didn't read below this tantalizing headline, to assimilate and analyze the evidence on which the headline is based.

The media are routinely bombarded by press releases sent from medical journals, food companies, organizations, and universities about research being conducted and/or conferences being sponsored by these institutions. These releases are sent for one reason: to gain publicity. Reputable news organizations that report these findings will seek out independent experts in the field to weigh in on the research and, just as importantly, explain how these findings relate to the public. If you don't read beyond the headlines, you are probably missing important details of the story. Even worse, if you begin making dietary and lifestyle changes based on each news flash, you become a scientific guinea pig.

When a headline piques your interest, read the article with a critical eye, and ask yourself the following questions.

1. Was the Research Finding Published in a Peer-Reviewed Journal?

You can be confident that studies published in a peer-reviewed journal have been thoroughly reviewed by experts in this area of research. If the research isn't published in a peer-reviewed journal, you have no way of knowing if the study was conducted in an appropriate manner and whether the findings are accurate. A study about the possible virtues of chocolate in fighting heart disease that is published in the *New England Journal of Medicine* has more credibility than a similar article published in a baking magazine.

2. Was the Study Done Using Animals or Humans?

Animals are animals and humans are humans. Experiments with animals are often used to study how a particular substance affects a health outcome. But if the study is conducted in rats, it doesn't necessarily mean that the substance will have the same effect if consumed by humans. This doesn't mean that animal studies are frivolous. They are important stepping-stones to designing and conducting similar experiments involving humans.

3. Do the Study Participants Resemble Me?

When you read or hear about studies involving humans, you should always seek more information about the individuals who took part in the research. For example, were the people in the chocolate studies college-aged subjects or older individuals with heart disease and high blood pressure? If older adults were studied, then would these findings be of any benefit to young adults who don't have high blood pressure or heart disease?

4. Is This the First Time I've Heard about This?

A single study in a specific area of research is a lonely entity in the scientific world. Is this the first study regarding the health benefits of chocolate? If the media article doesn't confirm that other studies have also supported these findings, this one study may be the *only* study of its kind. Wait until you hear that these research findings have been confirmed by a reputable health organization, such as the American Heart Association, before considering making any changes in your diet. Reputable organizations will only change their advice based on a consensus of research findings.

In your lifetime, you are going to read thousands of newspaper and website headlines, as well as watch and listen to who-knows-how-many similar television and radio reports. Your critical-thinking skills in evaluating the sources and information presented will be your best friend when it comes to deciding which blurbs to believe. These skills may also save you considerable money by helping you avoid nutrition gimmicks. When it comes to assessing nutrition information in the media, it's worth your time and effort to find out where it came from and why (or if) you should care.

WHAT DO YOU THINK?

1. Have you ever changed your food purchasing or consuming habits as the result of a story in the media?
2. What criteria did you use to evaluate that nutrition news?
3. What ethical obligations do news organizations have to protect the public from unreliable nutrition information?

Headlines in newspapers, lead articles on websites, and the sound bites on television often report the results of a single, recent research study. The Examining the Evidence feature "How Can I Evaluate Nutrition News?" discusses how to scrutinize information about current research findings and not get caught up in the media hype.

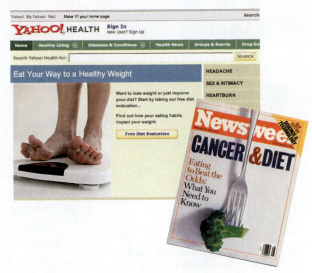

Nutrition-related research findings are often lead stories in newspapers, magazines, and on websites.

Sound Nutrition Research Begins with the Scientific Method

Research studies that generate enough information are based on a process called the **scientific method**. Scientists are like detectives. They observe something in the natural world, ask questions, come up with an idea (or **hypothesis**) based on their observations, test their hypothesis, and then see if their idea is correct. There are many steps in the scientific method and many adjustments made along the way before a scientist has gained enough information to support his or her hypothesis. In fact, the entire process can take years to complete.

Let's walk through a nutrition-related study in which scientists used the scientific method to study rickets. Rickets is a potentially severe and even fatal disease in children, whereby the bones throughout the body weaken. For instance, the spine and rib cage can become so distorted that breathing is impaired. The leg bones can become so weakened that they are unable to hold up the child's body weight, and they curve outward ("bow legs"). In the nineteenth century, parents often relied on folk remedies to treat diseases; in the case of rickets, they used cod-liver oil because it seemed to prevent the disorder as well as cure it, although no one knew how.

The first steps of the scientific method are to make an observation and ask questions (**Figure 1.5**). Originally, scientists were piqued by the cod-liver oil curing

scientific method A stepwise process used by scientists to generate sound research findings.

hypothesis An idea generated by scientists based on their observations.

Observe and ask a question
Why does cod-liver oil cure rickets?

Formulate a hypothesis
The vitamin A in cod-liver oil is the curative factor.

Conduct an experiment
Feed rats with rickets cod-liver oil that contains no vitamin A.

Hypothesis supported
Rats were not cured.

Hypothesis not supported
Rats were cured.

Revise or formulate a new hypothesis

Figure 1.5 Steps of the Scientific Method
The scientific method is used to conduct credible research in nutrition and other scientific fields.

What's the Real Deal When It Comes to Nutrition Research and Advice?   **17**

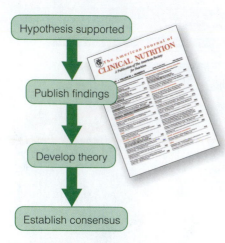

Figure 1.6 A Hypothesis Can Lead to a Scientific Consensus
When a hypothesis is supported by research, the results are published in peer-reviewed journals. Once a theory has been developed and supported by subsequent experiments, a consensus is reached in the scientific community.

phenomenon. They asked themselves why cod-liver oil cured rickets. In the second step of the scientific method, a hypothesis is formulated. Because cod-liver oil is very rich in vitamin A, scientists initially thought that this vitamin must be the curative factor. To confirm this, scientists proceeded to the next step in the scientific method, which was to conduct an experiment.

The scientists altered the cod-liver oil to destroy all of its vitamin A. The altered oil was given to rats that had been fed a diet that caused rickets. Surprisingly, the rats were still cured of rickets. This disproved the scientists' original hypothesis that vitamin A was the curative factor. They then needed to modify their hypothesis, as it was obvious that there was something else in the cod-liver oil that cured rickets. They next hypothesized that it was the vitamin D that cured the rats, and conducted another experiment to confirm this hypothesis, which it did.

The next step in the scientific method involves sharing these findings with the scientific community. What good would it be to make this fabulous discovery if other scientists couldn't find out about it? To do this, scientists summarize and submit their research findings to a **peer-reviewed journal** (**Figure 1.6**). Other scientists (peers) then look at the researchers' findings to make sure that they are sound. If so, the research study is published in the journal. (If this relationship between vitamin D and rickets were discovered today, it would probably be the lead story on CNN.)

As more and more studies were done that confirmed that vitamin D can cure and prevent rickets, a theory developed. We now know with great certainty that vitamin D can prevent rickets and that a deficiency of vitamin D will cause this type of deformed bones in children. Because of this, there is a consensus among health professionals as to the importance of vitamin D in the diets of children.

Research Studies and Experiments Confirm Hypotheses

Scientists can use different types of experiments to test hypotheses. The rickets experiment just described is called a **laboratory experiment**, as it was done in the confines of a lab. In the fields of nutrition and health, laboratory experiments are often conducted using animals, such as rats. Research conducted with humans is usually observational or experimental.

Observational Research
Observational research involves looking at factors in two or more groups of subjects to see if there is a relationship to a certain disease or another health outcome. For example, researchers might study rates of breast-feeding in infants with and without rickets, to see if breast-feeding influences the incidence of the disease.

One type of observational research is **epidemiological research**, which looks at populations of people. For example, scientists may look at people who live in Norway and notice that there is a higher incidence of rickets among children there than in Australia. Through their observation, they may find a relationship between the lack of sun exposure in Norway and the high incidence of rickets there compared with sunny Australia. However, the scientists can't rule out the possibility that the difference in the incidence of rickets in these two populations may also be due to other factors in the subjects' diet or lifestyle.

Experimental Research
Experimental research involves at least two groups of subjects. One group, the **experimental group**, is given a specific treatment, and another group, the **control group**, isn't. For instance, after hypothesizing that vitamin D cures rickets, scientists would have randomly assigned children with rickets to two groups. They would

peer-reviewed journal A research journal in which fellow scientists (peers) review studies to assess if they are accurate and sound before they are published.

laboratory experiment A scientific experiment conducted in a laboratory. Some laboratory experiments involve animals.

observational research Research that involves looking at factors in two or more groups of subjects to see if there is a relationship to certain outcomes.

epidemiological research Research that looks at populations of people; it is often observational.

experimental research Research involving at least two groups of subjects.

experimental group The group given a specific treatment.

control group The group given a placebo.

have given a vitamin D supplement to the children in the experimental group but would have given the children in the control group a substance, called a **placebo**, that looked just like the vitamin D supplement but contained only sugar or some other nonactive ingredient. If neither of the two groups of subjects knew which substance they received, then they were "blind" to the treatment. If the scientists who were giving the placebo and the vitamin D supplement also couldn't distinguish between the two treatments and didn't know which group received which, this would be called a **double-blind, placebo-controlled study**.

The scientists would also have to make sure that all other significant factors were the same for both groups during the experiment. For example, because the scientists knew that sun exposure has a therapeutic effect on rickets, they couldn't let the children in the control group go outside in the sunshine while keeping the children in the experimental group inside. The exposure to sunshine would change the outcome of the experiment. Similarly, they'd have to ensure that the children were eating exactly the same diet for the duration of the study.

A double-blind, placebo-controlled study is considered the "gold standard" of research, because all of the factors that might influence the study results are kept the same for the groups of subjects, and neither the subjects nor the researchers are biased, as they don't know which group has received which treatment (**Figure 1.7**).

placebo A sugar pill that has no impact on the individual's health when ingested.

double-blind, placebo-controlled study When the scientists and subjects in a research experiment can't distinguish between the treatments given to the subjects and don't know which group of subjects received which treatment.

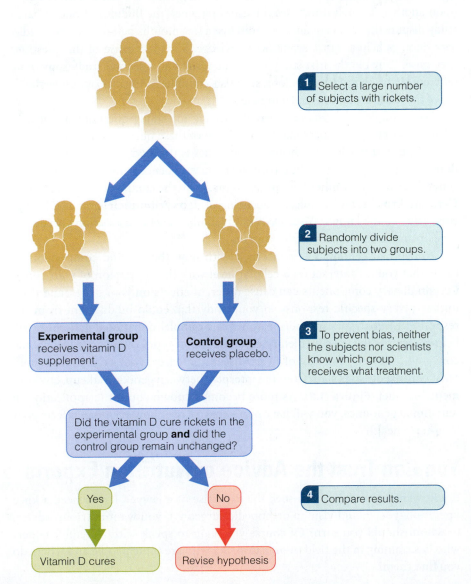

1 Select a large number of subjects with rickets.

2 Randomly divide subjects into two groups.

Experimental group receives vitamin D supplement.

Control group receives placebo.

3 To prevent bias, neither the subjects nor scientists know which group receives what treatment.

Did the vitamin D cure rickets in the experimental group **and** did the control group remain unchanged?

Yes

No

4 Compare results.

Vitamin D cures

Revise hypothesis

Figure 1.7 Controlled Scientific Experiments
Scientists use experimental research to test hypotheses.

Figure 1.8 Nutritional Genomics
Diet and lifestyle combine with your genetic makeup to influence your susceptibility to chronic disease.

Although the results of many experiments fail to support the initial hypotheses, a great many discoveries are made. With continuing research, one discovery builds upon another. Though it may seem frustrating when the findings of one research study dispute the results of another from just a few months before, even contradictory findings help advance scientific knowledge, in part because of the questions they raise. Why did the first study show one result and a second study something different? In tackling such questions, scientists continue to advance our understanding of the world around us, and within us.

For example, scientists are currently asking intriguing questions about how what we eat affects our personal health. Some of these questions lead to research in the field of **nutritional genomics**. Genomics is the study of genes, their functions in your body, and how the environment may influence **gene expression**. Your genes determine your inherited, specific traits. With the completion of the **Human Genome Project**, the complete sequencing of **deoxyribonucleic acid (DNA)** in your cells is now known. Your DNA contains the genetic instructions needed to develop and direct the activities of your body.

Nutritional genomics is concerned with how the specific components in foods that you eat interact on a cellular level with the expression of your genes. Certain dietary components can cause different effects on your genes, and thus, initiate a very specific response in your body that could be different from the response it initiates in another person. For example, nutritional genomics will help determine the specific dietary combination of types of fats that you should consume to lower your risk of heart disease based on your genetic makeup.[24] Most chronic diseases stem from the interplay between genetic makeup, environment, and diet (**Figure 1.8**). As more becomes known about the application of nutritional genomics, you will have more control over how your diet affects your long-term health.

You Can Trust the Advice of Nutrition Experts

If you want legal advice, you seek the expertise of a lawyer. If you need a knee operation, you should visit an orthopedic surgeon. If you want nutrition advice, to whom should you turn? Of course you want to speak with a credible expert who has training in the field of nutrition. So, who are these people and where do you find them?

nutritional genomics A field of study that researches the relationship between nutrition and genomics (the study of genes and gene expression).

gene expression The processing of genetic information to create a specific protein.

Human Genome Project A project sponsored by the United States government to determine the complete set and sequencing of DNA in human cells and identify all human genes.

deoxyribonucleic acid (DNA) Genetic material within cells that directs the synthesis of proteins in the body.

Brendan is a 23-year-old recent college graduate who majored in business and is working in New York City, miles away from his home in Boston. His workdays are long. He arrives at the office by 7:30 a.m. daily and most days doesn't leave his cubicle until 9 p.m. He skips breakfast and gets a fast-food meal for lunch. The office manager orders pizzas for dinner for those working past 7 p.m. While he has a gym in his apartment building, he rarely has time to use it during the week.

Within a year of living in the big city, he has gained 15 pounds. His girlfriend has noticed that he is unhappy about his weight and suggested that he make an appointment with her registered dietitian nutritionist (RDN) to help him figure out what the reasons may be for his recent weight gain.

Brendan mentions that both his grandfather and father were very overweight and have developed diabetes. His father's grandmother also is overweight. The RDN warns Brendan that because of his family history of obesity, he is genetically at a higher risk of developing weight issues. The RDN suggests that he make some changes in his lifestyle that would not only help him lose the recent 15-pound weight gain but also help him maintain a healthy weight as an adult.

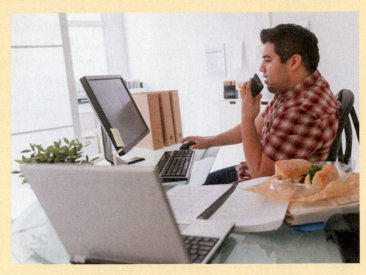

Chronic disease is caused by a mixture of genetic and environmental influences.

Think About It

Can you identify three changes that Brendan can make in his diet and lifestyle that may help him lower his risk of developing obesity?

One option is to seek the expertise of a **registered dietitian nutritionist (RDN)**. The RDN has completed at least a bachelor's degree at an accredited university or college in the United States that has incorporated specific coursework and supervised practice that have been approved by the accrediting body of the Academy of Nutrition and Dietetics (AND). RDNs have also passed a national exam administered by the credentialing body of AND. They have an understanding of **medical nutrition therapy**, which is an integration of nutrition counseling and dietary changes based on an individual's medical history and current health needs to improve that person's health.

RDNs work with their patients to make dietary changes that can help prevent diseases such as heart disease, diabetes, stroke, and obesity. Many physicians, based on the diagnoses of their patients, refer them to RDNs for nutrition advice and guidance. RDNs must participate in continuing professional education in order to remain current in the fast-changing world of nutrition, medicine, and health and maintain their registration. RDNs work in hospitals and other health care facilities, private practice, universities, medical schools, professional athletic teams, food companies, and other nutrition-related businesses. For the story of one person's visit with an RDN, see Health Connection: A Case Study, titled "Fast-Food City."

registered dietitian nutritionist (RDN) A health professional who has completed at least a bachelor's degree in nutrition from an accredited university or college in the United States, completed a supervised practice, and passed an exam administered by the Commission on Dietetic Registration, the credentialing agency for the Academy of Nutrition and Dietetics (AND).

medical nutrition therapy The integration of nutrition counseling and dietary changes based on an individual's medical and health needs to treat a patient's medical condition.

Individuals with advanced degrees, such as a PhD in nutrition, can also provide credible nutrition information. Sometimes physicians may have taken a nutrition course in medical school and gone on to get a master of science in public health (MPH), which involves some nutrition courses, or a master's degree in nutrition at an accredited university or college.

Some **public health nutritionists** may have an undergraduate degree in nutrition but didn't complete a supervised practice, so are not eligible to take the RDN exam. These credible individuals can work in the government organizing community outreach nutrition programs, such as programs for the elderly.

In order to protect the health of the public receiving nutrition information, more than 35 states in the United States currently license nutrition professionals who must meet specified educational and experience criteria to be considered experts in the field of nutrition. A person who meets these qualifications is a **licensed dietitian nutritionist (LDN)** and so will have the letters "LDN" after his or her name. Because RDNs have completed the rigorous standards set forth by the AND, they automatically meet the criteria for LDN and often will have both "RDN" and "LDN" after their names.

Be careful when taking nutrition advice from a trainer at the gym or the person who works at the local health food store. Whereas some of these people may be credible, many are not, and thus, less likely to give you valid information that's based on solid scientific evidence. Anyone who calls himself or herself a **nutritionist** may have taken few or no accredited courses in nutrition. As a consumer of nutrition information, you need to make sure that the person providing the information is credible. (T|F)

You also need to beware of individuals who specialize in health quackery or fraud. Such scammers will try to persuade you with false nutrition claims and anecdotal stories that aren't backed up by sound science and research. Americans spend billions of dollars annually on fraudulent health products, an injustice that the Food and Drug Administration (FDA) has been trying to fight for decades. The FDA's health fraud scams website helps consumers identify quackery and health fraud and make educated decisions about health-related information and products. Common deceptive statements made by health quacks are included in the Nutrition in the Real World feature, "Don't Be Scammed!"

Identifying quackery and fraud is important not only when you are seeking out an expert for advice, but also when you read about nutrition on the Internet. The Web is overflowing with nutrition information and *mis*information.

You Can Obtain Accurate Nutrition Information on the Internet

Mark Twain once said, "Be careful about reading health books. You could die of a misprint." If he were alive today, he probably would have included websites that dole out health advice. Approximately 60 percent of American adult Internet users have surfed millions of websites looking for health information.[25]

Don't assume that a slick website is a sound website. Although many websites, such as Let's Move! (www.letsmove.gov) and *Web*MD (www.webmd.com), provide credible, reliable, up-to-date nutrition information, a great many others do not. Remember, anyone with computer skills can put up a website. The National Institutes of Health (NIH) has developed several key questions that you should consider when viewing a nutrition- or health-related website.[26]

Who Runs and Pays for the Site?

Credible websites are willing to show their credentials. For example, the National Center for Complementary and Integrative Health (www.nccih.nih.gov) provides information about its association with the NIH and its extensive ongoing research

public health nutritionist An individual who may have an undergraduate degree in nutrition but isn't an RDN.

licensed dietitian nutritionist (LDN) An individual who has met specified educational and experience criteria deemed necessary by a state licensing board to be considered an expert in the field of nutrition. An RDN would meet all the qualifications to be an LDN.

nutritionist A generic term with no recognized legal or professional meaning. Some people may call themselves nutritionists without having any credible training in nutrition.

nutrition in the Real World

Don't Be Scammed!

Consumers beware. The snake-oil salespeople of yesteryear never left the building. They just left the oil behind and moved on to selling nutrition supplements and other products that are not based on science. These skilled salespeople introduce health fears into your mind and then try to sell services and products to allay these newly created fears. They make unrealistic promises and guarantees.

To avoid falling for one of their shady schemes, there are certain "red flags" that should alert and warn you to be leery of infomercials, magazine ads, mail-order catalogs, and websites that try to convince you that:

- There is a quick fix for what ails you.
- Their product causes miraculous cures.
- One product does it all.

- You can lose a lot of weight in a short amount of time without dieting or exercising.
- Other folks are claiming that the product worked for them.
- Conspiracies exist, such as the pharmaceutical industry and the government are working together to hide information about the product.

For more information, go to www.consumer.ftc.gov/scam-alerts. For practice detecting scams, look at www.wemarket4u.net. This site, which was created by the Federal Trade Commission, shows several examples of scams, both nutrition related and not.

Don't be a victim of health fraud scams. Be smart, be aware, and be careful. To report a problem, contact the FDA at www.fda.gov/Safety/Report-aProblem or call 1-888-463-6332.

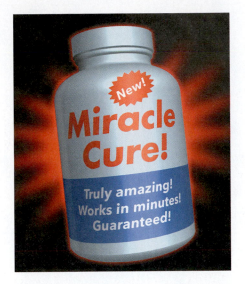

and educational programs. If you have to spend more than a minute trying to find out who runs the website, you should click to another site.

Also, running a website is expensive, and finding out who's paying for a particular site will tell you something about the reliability of its content. Websites sponsored by the government (with URLs ending in .gov) or an academic institution (.edu) are more reliable than many commercial websites (.com or .net). Some commercial websites, such as *Web*MD, carry articles that can be reliable if they are written by credible health professionals, but other websites may be promoting information to suit a company's own purposes.

For example, if the funding source for the website is a vitamin and mineral supplement company, are all the articles geared toward supporting the use of supplements? Does the website have advertisers, and do their products also influence the content on the website? You need to investigate whether the website content may be biased based on the funding source.

What Is the Purpose of the Site?

After you answer the first two questions, look for the "About This Site" link. This will help you understand the website's purpose. For example, at Nutrition.gov, the purpose is to "provide easy access to the best food and nutrition information across the federal government." This website doesn't exist to sell you anything, but to help you find reliable information.

What Is the Source of Information?

You should always know who wrote what you are reading. Is the author a qualified nutrition expert, or did she or he interview qualified individuals? If the site obtained information from another source, was that source cited?

When surfing the Internet for nutrition information, look for a credible, reliable site with up-to-date information.

What Is the Basis of the Information?

Is the article's information based on medical facts and figures that have references? For example, any medical news items released on the American Heart Association website (www.heart.org) will include the medical journal from which the information came. In fact, the website will often include the opinion of experts regarding the news items.

Is the Information Reviewed?

A physician who was a well-known medical expert for a major television network once commented that he spends most of his time not delivering medical advice, but trying to stop the networks from publicizing health news that isn't credible. Always look to see if the website has an editorial board of medical and health experts and if qualified individuals review or write the content before it is released.

How Current Is the Information?

Once a website is on the Internet, it will stay there until someone removes it. Consequently, the health information that you read may not be the most up to date. Always check to see when the content was written, and if it is over a year old, whether it has been updated.

What Is the Site's Policy about Linking to Other Sites?

Some medical sites don't like to link to other sites, as they don't have control over other sites' credibility and content. Others do link, if they are confident that these sites meet their criteria. Some sites receive financial reimbursement from the links that they post. Don't always assume that the link is credible.

How Does the Site Handle Personal Information?

Websites track the pages that you click on in order to analyze their more popular topics. Sometimes, they elicit personal information such as your gender, age, and health concerns. After collecting data on your viewing selections and your personal information, they can sell this information to interested companies. These companies can create promotional materials about their goods and services targeted to your needs. Credible sites should tell you about their privacy policy and if they will or will not give this information to other sources. A website's privacy policy is often found in a link at the bottom of its screen.

How Does the Site Manage Interactions with Visitors?

You should always be able to easily find the contact information of the website's owners should you have any concerns or questions that you want answered. If the site is associated with social media sites such as Twitter or Facebook, you should know how it is moderated. Read the postings before you jump in.

LO 1.6 **The Take-Home Message** Sound nutrition advice is based on years of research using the scientific method. You should only take nutrition advice from a credible source, such as a registered dietitian nutritionist (RDN) or other valid nutrition expert. When obtaining nutrition information from the Internet, you need to carefully peruse the site to make sure that it is credible, it contains up-to-date information, and its content isn't influenced by those that fund and support the website.

Should Food Advertising to Children Be Regulated by the Government? In 2012, the Better Business Bureau, working with several food industry companies, agreed to adhere to the Children's Food and Beverage Advertising Initiative, a voluntary program that was designed to "shift the mix of foods advertised to children under 12 to encourage healthier dietary choices and healthy lifestyles."[1] Still, children's advocacy groups argue that this isn't enough; they say we need laws that govern food advertising to children. Should the government regulate food advertising to children? Read the arguments, then consider the critical-thinking questions and decide for yourself.

yes

- Strong scientific evidence shows that the marketing of unhealthy foods to children is a significant risk factor contributing to childhood obesity.[2]

- Studies have shown that even at 10 years of age, children may not understand the persuasive intent of advertisements.[3]

- Cognitive research shows that young children don't understand that ads are trying to persuade them, nor can they evaluate commercials critically. Given that earlier legal cases set the precedent that it is OK for the government to restrict inherently misleading speech, it should be allowed to restrict advertising to children.[4]

- Dietary patterns that begin in childhood give shape to the health profiles of Americans at all ages. Dietary patterns reflect the influence of our culture, and our social and economic environments. Ensuring that these environments support good health is a fundamental responsibility, requiring leadership and action from all of us—not just parents.[5]

no

- Currently, advertisements to children are protected speech, under the First Amendment.[6]

- Parents can monitor how much TV their child is actually watching so that they are not overexposed to ads, and there are resources to help them sort out how to do this.[7]

- In 2011, McDonald's defended its right to advertise freely, insisting that it is a company's right to advertise so it can stay in business, and the consumer's right to make responsible personal choices.[8]

- Studies have shown that even though Sweden and Quebec have banned TV food advertising to children for over a decade, obesity rates are still comparable to those in the rest of Europe and Canada.[9]

what do you think?

1. Do you support the idea of regulating food advertising to children? **2.** Does food advertising really impact what children eat, given that parents are doing the shopping? **3.** How much impact should advertisers be allowed to have on children, whose minds can't discriminate the way adults' can?

VISUAL Chapter Summary

LO 1.1 Multiple Factors Influence Food Choices

Food choices are influenced by personal taste, culture, social life, accessibility, cost, and time constraints. You eat out of habit, in response to your emotions, and, of course, because food is delicious. However, taste is the most important consideration influencing what you eat.

Nutrition knowledge · Trends · Habits · Taste · Emotions · Nutrients · Time · **Food Choices** · Cost · Convenience · Culture · Advertising · Social reasons

LO 1.2 Nutrition Is the Science of Food

Nutrition is the science that studies how the nutrients and compounds in foods nourish you, help you function, and affect your health. Good nutrition plays an important role in preventing many of the leading causes of death in the United States, including heart disease, cancer, stroke, and diabetes.

LO 1.3 There Are Six Categories of Nutrients

Nutrients are classified as carbohydrates, lipids (fats), proteins, vitamins, minerals, and water. Carbohydrates, fats, and proteins provide the energy (calories) that your body needs. Carbohydrates are the body's preferred source of energy. Fats insulate the body and cushion internal organs. The primary role of dietary protein is to build and maintain body tissues. Protein also acts as enzymes that catalyze chemical reactions. Vitamins, minerals, and water do not provide energy, but are important for metabolism and to properly utilize carbohydrates, fats, and protein. Many vitamins aid enzymes in your body. Water is also vital for many functions. It bathes the inside and outside of your cells, helps maintain your body temperature, and acts as a lubricant and protective cushion.

Vitamins · Minerals · Carbohydrates · Protein · Water · 59% · 17% · 20% · Fat · **Human body**

LO 1.4 A Well-Balanced Diet Will Provide the Nutrients Your Body Needs

Your body needs a mixture of the six categories of nutrients in specific amounts to stay healthy. Eating a well-balanced diet is the best way to meet your nutrient and health needs. Vitamin and mineral supplements can help complete a healthy diet but should not replace foods.

LO 1.5 The American Diet Doesn't Stack Up

Most Americans are not meeting all their nutrient needs without exceeding their calorie requirements. The average American diet is high in protein, sugar, sodium, saturated fat, and calories, but low in vitamin E, calcium, and fiber. In addition, the rates of overweight and obesity among Americans are too high. Nutrition plays an important role in preventing many of the leading causes of death in the United States, including heart disease, cancer, stroke, and type 2 diabetes.

2013

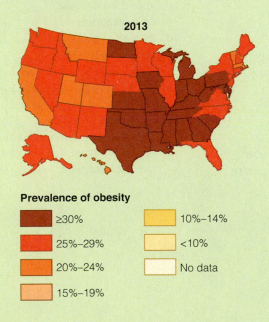

Prevalence of obesity

≥30%		10%–14%	
25%–29%		<10%	
20%–24%		No data	
15%–19%			

LO 1.6 Nutrition Is a Science and New Discoveries Are Continually Being Made

Sound nutrition information is the result of numerous scientific studies that are based on the scientific method. These research findings should be reviewed by and shared with the medical and scientific community. You should never change your diet or lifestyle based upon the findings of just one or a few studies. The science of nutritional genomics studies how diet may modify the way genes work and how genetic makeup affects nutrient requirements. Nutritional advice should come from credible sources. Individuals who call themselves nutritionists may or may not have a credible nutrition education.

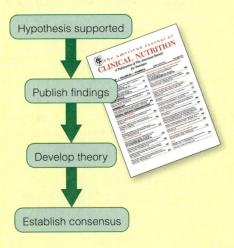

Hypothesis supported

↓

Publish findings

↓

Develop theory

↓

Establish consensus

VISUAL Chapter Summary

Check Your Understanding

LO 1.1 1. Megan picks up a sandwich at the campus food truck after class every afternoon before dashing off to her part-time job. Which of the following most likely influences Megan's food choices in this situation?

a. her ethnic background
b. her busy schedule
c. her emotions
d. her limited budget

LO 1.1 2. Nutrition is

a. the study of genes and their function in the body.
b. the study of how the body functions.
c. the scientific study of how compounds in foods affect body functions.
d. the study of hormones and how they function in the body.

LO 1.2 3. The energy in foods is measured in carbohydrates.

a. true
b. false

LO 1.2 4. A cookie with 13 grams of carbohydrates, 4 grams of fat, and 1 gram of protein contains

a. 54 calories.
b. 65 calories.
c. 70 calories.
d. 92 calories.

LO 1.3 5. The majority of your daily calories should come from

a. fats.
b. minerals.
c. vitamins.
d. carbohydrates.

LO 1.3 6. Which nutrients may help enzymes function in your body?

a. carbohydrates
b. vitamins
c. fat
d. protein

LO 1.4 7. Everyone needs to take vitamin and mineral supplements to be healthy.

a. true
b. false

LO 1.5 8. Over _____ percent of American adults are overweight.

a. 35
b. 45
c. 55
d. 65

LO 1.6 9. The first step in the scientific method is to

a. make observations and ask questions.
b. form a hypothesis.
c. do an experiment.
d. develop a theory.

LO 1.6 10. Which of the following individuals would be the best to approach for nutritional counseling?

a. a health food store employee
b. your personal trainer at the gym
c. a licensed dietitian nutritionist
d. your roommate, who runs for the campus track team

Answers

1. (b) While ethnic background, emotions, and costs all can influence food choices, in Megan's case her very busy schedule influences her food choices for a quick dinner.
2. (c) Nutrition is about how nutrients affect your body and health. The study of genes is genetics. Physiology is the study of how the body functions. The study of hormones is endocrinology.
3. (b) False. Carbohydrates are a source of energy in your foods. The energy in your foods is measured in units called calories (more specifically, kilocalories).
4. (d) Because both carbohydrates and protein have 4 calories per gram and fat has 9 calories per grams, the cookie contains 92 calories.
5. (d) The majority of your daily calories should come from carbohydrates. Vitamins and minerals don't provide calories. Fats do contain calories, but they shouldn't be the main source of energy in your diet.
6. (b) Vitamins can aid enzymes in your body. Carbohydrates, fat, and protein need enzymes to be properly metabolized.
7. (b) False. Many people can meet their vitamin and mineral needs with a well-balanced diet. Those who can't should take a supplement in addition to eating a healthy diet.
8. (d) Unfortunately, over 65 percent of American adults are overweight.
9. (a) The scientific method begins with scientists observing and asking questions. They then form a hypothesis and test it using an experiment. After many experiments confirm their hypothesis, a theory will be developed.
10. (c) Unless the salesperson, personal trainer, and your roommate are all licensed dietitian nutritionists, they are not qualified to provide nutrition counseling.

Web Resources

- Academy of Nutrition and Dietetics: www.eatright.org
- Agricultural Research Service: www.ars.usda.gov
- Center for Science in the Public Interest: www.cspinet.org
- Centers for Disease Control: www.cdc.gov
- Food and Drug Administration: www.fda.gov
- U.S. Department of Agriculture Food and Nutrition Center: www.fns.usda.gov
- National Institutes of Health: www.nih.gov
- Tufts University Health & Nutrition Newsletter: www.tuftshealthletter.com
- WebMD: www.webmd.com

Answers to True or False?

1. **False.** There are many outside factors that stimulate and motivate you to eat, but taste, not habits, is the most important consideration. To find out what the other factors are, turn to page 5.

2. **True.** Heart disease is the leading cause of death among Americans. The good news is that your diet can play an important role in preventing it. For more information, turn to page 8.

3. **True.** The energy in foods is measured in calories. To find out more, turn to page 10.

4. **False.** Vitamins do not provide calories so don't provide energy in the diet. Turn to page 10 to learn more.

5. **True.** Although water is often overlooked as an essential nutrient, it shouldn't be. To learn about the important roles water plays in your body, turn to page 11.

6. **False.** A supplement can augment a healthy diet, but it can't replace it. To find out why, turn to page 12.

7. **False.** Although lean meats, poultry, and fish are excellent sources of protein, they don't contain fiber. To find out how to get your fill of fiber, turn to page 12.

8. **True.** Shocked? Americans spend an enormous amount of money shopping for supplements. Turn to page 13.

9. **False.** Currently, obesity is at epidemic proportions in the United States, and it isn't just affecting adults. Turn to page 13 for more information.

10. **False.** Anyone can call himself or herself a nutritionist. To find out whose advice you can trust, turn to page 22.

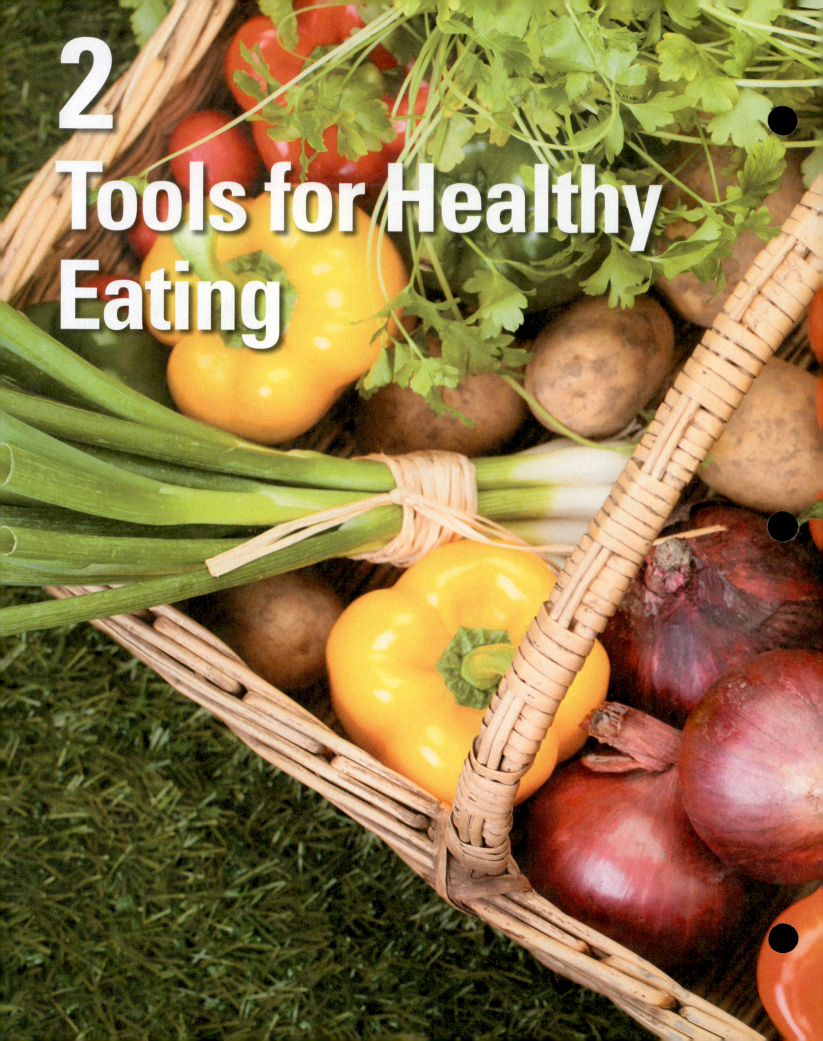

2 Tools for Healthy Eating

True or False?

1. There isn't any risk to overconsuming the essential nutrients in your diet. **T/F** p. 36

2. About 40 percent of your daily calories should come from protein-rich foods. **T/F** p. 36

3. The *Dietary Guidelines for Americans* were designed for almost all Americans to follow. **T/F** p. 38

4. Solid fats should be increased in your diet. **T/F** p. 41

5. Healthy oils are an important food group on MyPlate. **T/F** p. 42

6. To ensure that your diet is healthy, you should follow MyPlate exactly every day. **T/F** p. 45

7. All packaged foods must contain a food label. **T/F** p. 49

8. A nutrient claim on a food label tells you how healthy that nutrient is in the food. **T/F** p. 54

9. A health claim must state the beneficial component that the food contains and the disease or condition that it can improve. **T/F** p. 56

10. Adding functional foods to your diet will ensure that your diet is healthy. **T/F** p. 60

See page 67 for the answers.

Learning Outcomes

After reading this chapter, you will be able to:

LO 2.1 Describe the three key principles of a healthy diet and the tools you can use to help guide you.

LO 2.2 Explain what the DRIs are and the differences between the EAR, AI, RDA, UL, and AMDR.

LO 2.3 Describe the principles in the *Dietary Guidelines for Americans*.

LO 2.4 Explain the concept of MyPlate and name the five food groups and the typical foods represented in each group.

LO 2.5 Identify the required components of a food label and how to use it.

LO 2.6 Explain the role of functional foods in the diet.

Many Americans believe that to eat a healthful diet means giving up their favorite foods. Nothing could be farther from the truth! With a little planning, you can still occasionally eat almost any food even if it contains added sugars and fat and is high in calories. All it takes are the right tools to balance those higher calorie foods with more nutritious choices each day.

In this chapter, we'll discuss the various guidelines that exist to help you construct a healthy diet, as well as the tools, including food guidance systems and food labels, you can use to make the best food choices. At first, deciphering the information on the food label might seem confusing. But once you've cracked the code, you'll be able to confidently decide which foods to buy and which to leave on the store shelf.

What Is Healthy Eating and What Tools Can Help?

LO 2.1 Describe the three key principles of a healthy diet and the tools you can use to help guide you.

Healthy eating involves the key principles of balance, variety, and moderation. As a student, you are probably familiar with these principles from other areas of your life. Think about how you balance your time between work, school, and your family and friends. You engage in a variety of activities to avoid being bored, and you enjoy each in moderation, since spending too much time on one activity (such as working) would reduce the amount of time you could spend on others (such as studying, socializing, or sleeping). An unbalanced life soon becomes unhealthy and unhappy.

Likewise, your diet must be balanced, varied, and moderate in order to be healthy.

- A balanced diet includes healthy proportions of all nutrients. For instance, a student subsisting largely on bread, bagels, muffins, crackers, chips, and cookies might be eating too much carbohydrate and fat but too little protein, vitamins, and minerals.
- A varied diet includes many different foods. A student who habitually chooses the same foods for breakfast, lunch, and dinner is not likely to be consuming the wide range of phytochemicals, fiber, and other benefits that a more varied diet could provide.
- A moderate diet provides adequate amounts of nutrients and energy. Both crash diets and overconsumption are immoderate.

In short, you need to consume a variety of foods, some more moderately than others, and balance your food choices to meet your nutrient and health needs.

A diet that lacks variety and is unbalanced can cause **undernutrition**, a state in which you are not meeting your nutrient needs. If you were to consume only grains like white bread and pasta, and avoid other foods such as milk products, fruits, vegetables, and meats, your body wouldn't get enough fiber, calcium, protein, and other important nutrients. You would eventually become **malnourished**.

In contrast, **overnutrition** occurs when a diet provides too much of a nutrient such as iron, which can be toxic in high amounts, or too many calories, which

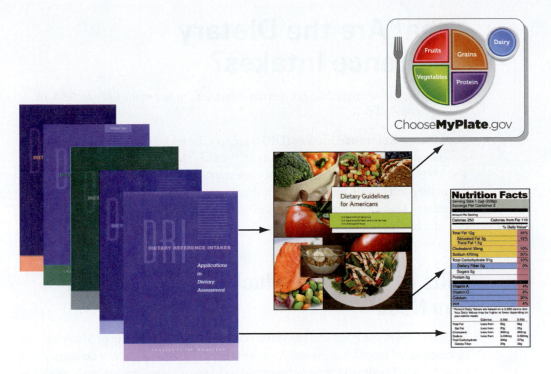

Figure 2.1 Dietary Recommendations and Implementation Tools
The science-based DRIs serve as the basis for information found in the *Dietary Guidelines*, MyPlate, and the Nutrition Facts panel.

can lead to obesity. A person who is overnourished can also be malnourished. For example, as you read in the previous chapter, a person can be overweight on a diet laden with less nutritious snack foods and sweets—foods that should be eaten in moderation—because he or she is taking in more calories than needed. These foods often displace more nutrient-rich choices, leaving the person malnourished.

Fortunately, the U.S. government provides several tools that can help you avoid both under- and overnutrition, including:

- The *Dietary Reference Intakes (DRIs)*, which provide recommendations regarding your nutrient needs
- The *Dietary Guidelines for Americans*, which provide broad dietary and lifestyle advice
- *MyPlate*, part of the ChooseMyPlate.gov Web-based initiative, which is designed to help you eat healthfully and implement the recommendations in the DRIs and the advice in the *Dietary Guidelines*
- The *Nutrition Facts panel* on food labels, which contains the Daily Values, and which can help you decide which foods to buy.

Together, these tools help you plan a balanced, moderate, and varied diet that meets your nutrient and health needs (**Figure 2.1**).

Let's look at each of these tools, beginning with the DRIs.

LO 2.1 **The Take-Home Message** A healthy diet is balanced, moderate, and varied. The U.S. government provides several tools to assist you in planning a healthy diet. These include the Dietary Reference Intakes, the *Dietary Guidelines for Americans*, the Nutrition Facts panel on food labels, and ChooseMyPlate.gov, the focal point for a multilevel, Web-based initiative that includes the MyPlate food guidance system.

Healthy eating is a way of life.

undernutrition A state of inadequate nutrition whereby a person's nutrient and/or calorie needs aren't met through the diet.

malnourished The long-term outcome of consuming a diet that doesn't meet nutrient needs.

overnutrition A state of excess nutrients and calories in the diet.

What Are the Dietary Reference Intakes?

Explain what the DRIs are and the differences between the EAR, AI, RDA, UL, and AMDR.

The **Dietary Reference Intakes (DRIs)** are specific reference values for each nutrient issued by the Institute of Medicine of the U.S. National Academy of Sciences. The DRIs are the specific amounts of each nutrient that one needs to consume to maintain good health, prevent chronic diseases, and avoid unhealthy excesses.[1] The Institute of Medicine periodically organizes committees of U.S. and Canadian scientists and health experts to update these recommendations based on the latest scientific research.

DRIs Tell You How Much of Each Nutrient You Need

Since the 1940s, the Food and Nutrition Board, part of the Institute of Medicine, has recommended amounts of essential nutrients needed daily to prevent a deficiency and promote good health. Because nutrient needs change with age, and because needs are different for men and women, different sets of recommendations were developed for each nutrient based on an individual's age and gender. In other words, a teenager may need more of a specific nutrient than a 55-year-old (and vice versa) and women need more of certain nutrients during pregnancy and lactation, so they all have different DRIs. Since the 1940s the DRIs have been updated more than ten times.

In the 1990s, nutrition researchers identified expanded roles for many nutrients. Though nutrient deficiencies were still an important issue, research suggested that higher amounts of some nutrients could play a role in disease prevention. Also, as consumers began using more dietary supplements and fortified foods, committee members grew concerned that excessive consumption of some nutrients might be as unhealthy as, or even more dangerous than, not consuming enough. Hence, the Food and Nutrition Board convened a variety of committees between 1997 and 2010 to take on the enormous task of reviewing the research on vitamins, minerals, carbohydrates, fats, protein, water, and other substances such as fiber, and developing the current DRI reference values for all the nutrients. As research evolves, changes are made in the DRIs.

DRIs Encompass Several Reference Values

The DRIs comprise five reference values: Estimated Average Requirement (EAR), Recommended Dietary Allowance (RDA), Adequate Intake (AI), the Tolerable Upper Intake Level (UL), and the Acceptable Macronutrient Distribution Ranges (AMDR) (**Figure 2.2**). Each of these values is unique, and serves a different need in planning a healthy diet. It may seem like a lot to remember, but you will use only the RDA or AI (not both), the AMDR, and the UL to assess whether your diet is meeting your nutrient needs. The EAR is the starting point in the process of determining the other values. Let's look at how the values are determined.

The DRI committee members begin by reviewing a variety of research studies to determine the **Estimated Average Requirement (EAR)** for the nutrient. They may look at studies that investigate the consequences of eating a diet too low in the nutrient and the associated side effects or physical changes that develop, as well as how much of the nutrient should be consumed to correct the deficiency. They may also review studies that measure the amount a healthy individual absorbs, stores,

Dietary Reference Intakes (DRIs) Reference values for the essential nutrients needed to maintain good health, to prevent chronic diseases, and to avoid unhealthy excesses.

Estimated Average Requirement (EAR) The average amount of a nutrient that is known to meet the needs of 50 percent of the individuals in a similar age and gender group.

Dietary Reference Intakes (DRIs) are specific reference values for each nutrient issued by the United States National Academy of Sciences, Institute of Medicine. They identify the amounts of each nutrient that one needs to consume to maintain good health.

FOCUS FIGURE WALKTHROUGH

Scan this QR code with your mobile device for a video tour of this figure by Joan Salge Blake.

DRIs FOR MOST NUTRIENTS

EAR The Estimated Average Requirement (EAR) is the average daily intake level estimated to meet the needs of half the people in a certain group. Scientists use it to calculate the RDA.

RDA The Recommended Dietary Allowance (RDA) is the average daily intake level estimated to meet the needs of nearly all people in a certain group. Aim for this amount!

AI The Adequate Intake (AI) is the average daily intake level assumed to be adequate. It is used when an EAR cannot be determined. Aim for this amount if there is no RDA!

UL The Tolerable Upper Intake Level (UL) is the highest average daily intake level likely to pose no health risks. Do not exceed this amount on a daily basis!

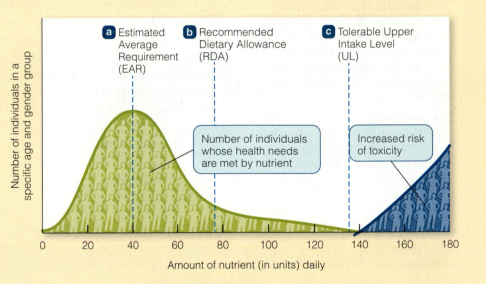

and maintains daily. Additionally, they look at research studies that address the role the nutrient plays in reducing the risk of associated chronic diseases, such as heart disease. After a thorough review process, the EAR for the nutrient is determined.

The EAR is the average amount of a nutrient that is known to meet the needs of 50 percent of the individuals in a similar age and gender group. The EAR is a starting point to determine the amount of a nutrient an individual should consume daily for good health. As you can see from Figure 2.2, if a nutrient's requirements were set using the EAR, 50 percent of the individuals would need more than this amount to meet their needs. This is where the **Recommended Dietary Allowance (RDA)** comes in. The RDA is based on the EAR, but it is set higher. It represents the average amount of a nutrient that meets the needs of nearly all (97 to 98 percent) of the individuals in a similar group.

If there is insufficient scientific information to determine the EAR for a nutrient, the RDA can't be developed. When this happens, an **Adequate Intake (AI)** is

Recommended Dietary Allowance (RDA) The average amount of a nutrient that meets the needs of 97 to 98 percent of individuals in a similar age and gender group. The RDA is higher than the EAR.

Adequate Intake (AI) The *approximate* amount of a nutrient that groups of similar individuals are consuming to maintain good health.

determined instead. The AI is the next best scientific estimate of the amount of a nutrient that groups of similar individuals should consume to maintain good health.

Because consuming too much of some nutrients can be harmful, the committees developed the **Tolerable Upper Intake Level (UL)**. The UL refers to the highest amount of a nutrient that is unlikely to cause harm if the amount is consumed daily. The higher the consumption above the UL, the higher the risk of **toxicity**. You should not try to consume the UL of a nutrient. There isn't any known benefit from consuming a higher amount, and it may cause health problems. ⓉⒻ

The DRI committee also developed ranges of intakes for the energy-containing nutrients, carbohydrates, proteins, and fats. These ranges are called the **Acceptable Macronutrient Distribution Ranges (AMDR)** and are as follows:

Carbohydrates should comprise 45 to 65 percent of your daily calories. ⓉⒻ
Fat should comprise 20 to 35 percent of your daily calories.
Proteins should comprise 10 to 35 percent of your daily calories.

Consuming these nutrient types in these ranges will ensure that you meet your calorie and nutrient needs, and reduce your risk of developing chronic diseases such as heart disease and obesity.

Although dietary recommendations have been established for carbohydrate, fat, protein, vitamins, and minerals that meet the optimal intake of nutrients, no DRI has been established for your energy (calorie) intake. The method used to determine the amount of energy you need, or your **Estimated Energy Requirement (EER)**, uses a different approach than the RDAs or AIs. In addition to taking into account your age and gender, the EER is calculated based on your height, weight, and activity level, and indicates the amount of energy *you* need daily to maintain energy balance. Individuals who consume more energy than they need will gain weight. Equations have been designed for men and women to provide a general estimate of energy needs. You can find the approximate amount of energy you require daily in **Table 2.1**. We will cover this in greater detail in Chapter 10.

Tolerable Upper Intake Level (UL) The highest amount of a nutrient that can be consumed daily without harm in a similar age and gender group of individuals.

toxicity The level at which exposure to a substance becomes harmful.

Acceptable Macronutrient Distribution Ranges (AMDR) A healthy range of intakes for the energy-containing nutrients—carbohydrates, proteins, and fats—in your diet, designed to meet your nutrient needs and help reduce the risk of chronic diseases.

Estimated Energy Requirement (EER) The amount of daily energy needed to maintain a healthy body weight and meet energy (calorie) needs based on age, gender, height, weight, and activity level.

Table 2.1

How Many Calories Do You Need Daily?

The amount of calories you need daily is based upon your age, gender, and activity level.*

	Males				Females		
Age	Sedentary	Moderately Active	Active	Age	Sedentary	Moderately Active	Active
16–18	2,400	2,800	3,200	16–18	1,800	2,000	2,400
19–20	2,600	2,800	3,000	19–20	2,000	2,200	2,400
21–25	2,400	2,800	3,000	21–25	2,000	2,200	2,400
26–30	2,400	2,600	3,000	26–30	1,800	2,000	2,400
31–35	2,400	2,600	3,000	31–35	1,800	2,000	2,200
36–40	2,400	2,600	2,800	36–40	1,800	2,000	2,200
41–45	2,200	2,600	2,800	41–45	1,800	2,000	2,200
46–50	2,200	2,400	2,800	46–50	1,800	2,000	2,200

*Note: These calorie levels are based on the Institute of Medicine's Estimated Energy Requirements from the *Dietary Reference Intakes: Macronutrients Report*, 2002.

Sedentary: Partaking in less than 30 minutes a day of moderate physical activity in addition to daily activities.

Moderately Active: Partaking in at least 30 minutes and up to 60 minutes a day of moderate physical activity in addition to daily activities.

Active: Partaking in 60 or more minutes a day of moderate physical activity in addition to daily activities.

Table 2.2
The Do's and Don'ts of the DRIs

The Reference Values and Their Meaning	When Planning Your Diet
Estimated Average Requirement (EAR)	**Don't** use this amount.
Recommended Dietary Allowance (RDA)	**Do** aim for this amount!
Adequate Intake (AI)	**Do** aim for this amount if an RDA isn't available.
Tolerable Upper Intake Level (UL)	**Don't** exceed this amount on a daily basis.
Acceptable Macronutrient Distribution Ranges (AMDR)	**Do** follow these guidelines regarding the percentage of carbohydrates, protein, and fat in your diet.

How to Use the DRIs

You can use the DRIs to make healthy food choices and plan a quality diet. To meet your needs, your goal should be to meet the RDA or the AI of all nutrients, but not exceed the UL. **Table 2.2** summarizes the DRIs for you. On the inside cover of your textbook, you will find the DRIs for all the nutrients that you need daily. For some ideas on how to use these in your daily life, see Table Tips: "Tip-Top Nutrition Tips."

Each chapter in this textbook will further explain what each nutrient is; why it is important; how much, based on the DRIs, you need to consume; and how to get enough, without consuming too much, in your diet.

Whereas the DRIs were released to prevent undernutrition, the *Dietary Guidelines for Americans* were developed out of concern over the incidence of overnutrition among Americans. Let's now look at the second tool that can help you attain a healthy diet and lifestyle, the *Dietary Guidelines for Americans*.

LO 2.2 **The Take-Home Message** The Dietary Reference Intakes (DRIs) are specific reference values that help you determine your daily nutrient needs to maintain good health, prevent chronic diseases, and avoid unhealthy excesses. The reference values include the EAR, RDA, AI, UL, and AMDR. Try to meet your RDA or AI and consume below the UL for each nutrient daily. The EER is calculated according to your height, weight, and activity level, in addition to your age and gender.

What Are the *Dietary Guidelines for Americans*?

LO 2.3 Describe the principles in the *Dietary Guidelines for Americans*.

By the 1970s, research had shown that Americans' overconsumption of foods rich in fat, saturated fat, cholesterol, and sodium was increasing their risk for chronic diseases, such as heart disease and stroke.[2] In 1977, the U.S. government released the *Dietary Goals for Americans,* which were designed to improve the nutritional quality of Americans' diets and to try to reduce the incidence of overnutrition and its associated health problems.[3]

Amid controversy over the scientific validity of the goals, the government asked scientists to lend credence to the goals and provide dietary guidance. Their work

Table TIPS

Tip-Top Nutrition Tips

Use traffic light colors to help you vary your lunchtime veggie choices. Add tomato slices (red) to your sandwich and carrots (yellow/orange) to your tossed salad (green).

Pop a snack-pack size of light microwave popcorn for a portion-controlled whole-grain snack.

Say "so long" to the elevator and hoof it up the stairs to work some extra physical activity into your day.

To keep your sweets to a discretionary amount, read the nutrition label and stick to a single serving that is no more than about 100 calories. Note that many big bars and bags contain more than double this amount.

Plan your dinner using at least one food from each of the food groups. Add tomato-pepper salsa (vegetables) and a can of rinsed black beans (protein) to your macaroni (grains) and cheese (dairy), and include an orange (fruits) for dessert to create a complete Mexican-influenced meal.

nutrition IN THE Real World

The Dietary Guidelines for Americans at a Glance

Currently, about half of all American adults have one or more preventable chronic diseases that are associated with diet and lifestyle choices. The science-based 2015 *Dietary Guidelines for Americans* are intended for people 2 years of age and older, including both those who are healthy and those at risk for chronic diseases. The following is a short overview of the recommendations. The complete guidelines are available at http://health.gov/dietaryguidelines/2015.

The five overarching guidelines are:

1. **Follow a healthy eating pattern across the lifespan.**
All food and beverage choices matter. Choose a healthy eating pattern at an appropriate calorie level to help achieve and maintain a healthy body weight, support nutrient adequacy, and reduce the risk of chronic disease.

2. **Focus on variety, nutrient density, and amount.**
To meet nutrient needs within calorie limits, choose a variety of nutrient-dense foods across and within all food groups in recommended amounts.

3. **Limit calories from added sugars and saturated fats and reduce sodium intake.**
Consume an eating pattern low in added sugars, saturated fats, and sodium. Cut back on foods and beverages higher in these components to amounts that fit within healthy eating patterns.

4. **Shift to healthier food and beverage choices.**
Choose nutrient-dense foods and beverages across and within all food groups in place of less-healthy choices. Consider cultural and personal preferences to make these shifts easier to accomplish and maintain.

5. **Support healthy eating patterns for all.**
Everyone has a role in helping to create and support healthy eating patterns in multiple settings nationwide, from home to school to work to communities.

What is an Eating Pattern?
The 2015 *Dietary Guidelines* define an *eating pattern* as "the combination of food and beverages that constitute an individual's complete dietary intake

over time." An eating pattern may also be described as a "dietary pattern." It refers to a person's customary way of eating or to a combination of foods and beverages that are recommended for consumption.

What to Eat?
An underlying premise of the guidelines is that nutritional needs should be met primarily from foods, without a heavy reliance on dietary supplements. All

Healthy Eating on a Budget

Healthy eating is not only better for your body, it's better for your wallet. According to the USDA, an individual between the ages of 20 and 50 can eat a healthy diet for as little as about $35 to $40 a week. If you want to learn how to eat healthfully and shop smart on a budget, visit http://people.bu.edu/salge/learning_budget.html.

culminated in the 1980 *Dietary Guidelines for Americans,* which emphasized eating a variety of foods to obtain a nutritionally well-balanced daily diet. Since 1990, the U.S. Department of Agriculture (USDA) and the Department of Health and Human Services (DHHS) have been mandated by law to update the guidelines every five years. The guidelines serve as one governmental voice to shape all federally funded nutrition programs in areas such as research and labeling, and to educate and guide consumers about healthy diet and lifestyle choices.[4]

The **Dietary Guidelines for Americans** reflect the most current nutrition and physical activity recommendations based on science for good health. They are designed to help individuals aged 2 and older improve the quality of their diet and lifestyle to lower their risk of chronic diseases and conditions, such as high blood pressure, high blood cholesterol levels, diabetes mellitus, heart disease, and certain cancers. The Nutrition in the Real World feature "The *Dietary Guidelines for Americans* at a Glance" provides an overview of the 2015 guidelines.

forms of foods, including fresh, frozen, canned, and dried, can be included in healthy eating patterns that emphasize nutrient-dense food choices. Nutrient-dense foods contain essential macro-nutrients, vitamins, minerals, and other naturally occurring substances (such as fiber) that our bodies need to maintain healthy function. For some people, forti-fied foods and/or dietary supplements may be useful in cases of specific nutri-ent deficiencies or to provide nutrients that are not easily obtained in the diet.

A healthy eating plan includes:

- A variety of vegetables from all sub-groups: dark green, red and orange, legumes (beans and peas), starchy, and other
- Fruits, especially whole fruits
- Grains, at least half of which are whole grains
- Fat-free or low-fat dairy (if tolerated), including milk, yogurt, cheese, and/or fortified soy beverages
- A variety of protein foods, including seafood, lean meats and poultry, eggs, legumes (beans and peas), and nuts, seeds, and soy products
- Oils

A healthy eating plan limits:

- Saturated fats and *trans* fats, added sugars, sodium, and alcohol. Specific recommendations include:
  - Consume less than 10 percent of calories daily from saturated fats.
  - Consume less than 10 percent of calories daily from added sugars.
  - Consume less than 2,300 mg of sodium daily.
  - If alcohol is consumed, recom-mended amounts are up to one drink per day for women and up to two drinks per day for men. (Note that there are many circumstances in which individuals should not consume any alcohol, such as during pregnancy, with certain medi-cal conditions, or when taking certain medications.)

Examples of Healthy Eating Patterns

The 2015 guidelines include several specific examples of healthy eating pat-terns: U.S.-Style, Mediterranean-Style, Vegetarian-Style, and the DASH dietary pattern. These examples demonstrate

how a variety of food and cultural prefer-ences can be integrated into a healthy eating plan.

While the information contained in the *Dietary Guidelines* may seem a bit intimidating at first, the good news is that the chapters in this textbook have been written to help you meet these guidelines, *one bite at a time*.

LO 2.3 **The Take-Home Message** The *Dietary Guidelines for Americans* provide dietary and lifestyle advice to individuals aged 2 and older. The goal of the guide-lines is to help individuals maintain good health and prevent chronic diseases.

What Are MyPlate and ChooseMyPlate.gov?

LO 2.4 Explain the concept of MyPlate and name the five food groups and the typical foods represented in each group.

With so many nutrient and dietary recommendations in the DRIs and the *Dietary Guidelines*, you may be wondering how to keep them straight and plan a balanced diet

Dietary Guidelines for Americans
Guidelines published every five years that provide dietary and lifestyle advice to individuals aged 2 and older to maintain good health and prevent chronic diseases.

Figure 2.3 Healthy Eating around the World
Many countries have developed their own food guidance systems, and they have a lot in common. For example, in Sweden, the Food Circle shown here is similar to MyPlate, as it emphasizes a plant-based diet with plenty of grains, fruits, and vegetables, and moderate amounts of milk products, meat, poultry, and fish.

Figure 2.4 MyPlate
The MyPlate icon reinforces important concepts of meal planning, healthful choices, proportionality, and moderation to be used in planning a healthful diet.

food guidance systems Visual diagrams that provide a variety of food recommendations to help create a well-balanced diet.

MyPlate A tool that depicts five food groups using the familiar mealtime visual of a place setting. It is part of a USDA Web-based initiative to provide consumer information with a food guidance system to help you build a healthy diet based on the current *Dietary Guidelines for Americans.*

proportionality The relationship of one entity to another. Vegetables and fruits should be consumed in a higher proportion than dairy and protein foods in the diet.

nutrient density The amount of nutrients per calorie in a given food. Nutrient-dense foods provide more nutrients per calorie than do less-nutrient-dense foods.

energy density A measurement of the calories in a food compared with the weight (grams) or volume of the food.

that meets all of your nutritional needs. Luckily, there are several carefully designed **food guidance systems** to help you select the best foods for your diet. These illustrated systems picture healthy food choices from a variety of food groups from which you can select, and show you how to proportion your food choices. Many countries have developed food guidance systems based on their food supply, cultural food preferences, and the nutritional needs of their population (**Figure 2.3**).

Some researchers have also developed food guidance systems to help individuals reduce their risk of certain diseases. For example, the DASH (Dietary Approaches to Stop Hypertension) diet is based on an eating style that has been shown to significantly lower a person's blood pressure. High blood pressure is a risk factor for heart disease and stroke.[6] (The DASH diet is discussed in more detail in Chapter 8.) The Mediterranean-style eating pattern is another food guidance system that emphasizes a plant-based diet rich in vegetables and fruits, nuts, olive oil, grains, and smaller amounts of meats and dairy. A Mediterranean-style eating pattern (discussed in Chapter 5) has been associated with a lower risk of heart disease.

In 2011, the USDA released the website www.ChooseMyPlate.gov and the tool MyPlate. **MyPlate** serves as an icon to remind consumers to eat healthfully. It depicts the five food groups using a familiar mealtime visual, a place setting (see **Figure 2.4**). MyPlate is the focal point for a larger, Web-based communication and education initiative at ChooseMyPlate.gov that provides information, tips, and tools to help you build a healthier diet based on the *Dietary Guidelines for Americans.* Also available at ChooseMyPlate.gov is an interactive food guidance system that is based on the USDA Food Patterns, which will provide you with a personalized food plan based on the latest nutrition and health recommendations. Consuming a calorie-appropriate, balanced diet that includes a variety of foods in moderation will also allow you to meet the DRIs for your nutrient needs and better manage your health and weight.

MyPlate and ChooseMyPlate.gov Emphasize Changes in Diet, Eating Behaviors, and Physical Activity

In addition to showing a variety of food groups that can make up a healthy diet, the tool MyPlate and the supporting information at ChooseMyPlate.gov promote proportionality, moderation, variety, and personalization.

As you can see from Figure 2.4, MyPlate shows a place setting split into sections, with each colored section representing one of five food groups: fruits, vegetables, grains, protein foods, and dairy. While oils are an important part of a healthy diet, they are not represented on the plate, as they are not considered a food group.

You can now easily see **proportionality** in how these food groups should dominate your diet. Half of your plate should be devoted to waist- and heart-friendly vegetables and fruits, with a smaller portion for grains (preferably whole grains) and lean protein foods such as fish, skinless poultry, lean meats, and dried beans and peas. The blue circle next to the plate is a visual reminder to make sure that fat-free and low-fat dairy foods such as milk should not be forgotten at mealtimes. With the majority of Americans overweight, this shift of food proportionality on your plate can have a dramatic effect on your calorie intake. Devoting more than half of the surface of the plate to low-calorie fruits and vegetables should crowd out higher calorie grains and protein food choices. Take the Self-Assessment to see how well-proportioned your diet is.

You should also choose mostly nutrient-dense foods from each food group. **Nutrient density** refers to the amount of nutrients a food contains in relationship

Does Your Diet Have Proportionality?

Answer yes or no to the following questions.

1. Are grains the main food choice at all your meals?
   Yes ☐ **No** ☐
2. Do you often forget to eat vegetables?
   Yes ☐ **No** ☐
3. Do you typically eat fewer than three pieces of fruit daily?
   Yes ☐ **No** ☐
4. Do you often have fewer than three cups of milk daily?
   Yes ☐ **No** ☐
5. Is the portion of meat, chicken, or fish the largest item on your dinner plate?
   Yes ☐ **No** ☐

Answers

If you answered yes to three or more of these questions, it is very likely that your diet lacks proportionality.

---

to the number of calories it contains. More nutrient-dense foods provide more nutrients per calorie (and in each bite) than less nutrient-dense foods, and so are better choices for meeting your DRIs without exceeding your daily calorie needs.

The foundation of your diet should be nutrient-dense foods with little solid fats and added sugars. Solid fats are solid at room temperature and contain a high percentage of heart-unhealthy saturated and/or *trans* fatty acids. Solid fats include butter, beef fat, chicken fat, pork fat (lard), stick margarine, and shortening. The fat in milk is also considered a solid fat, as it is solid at room temperature. Because of the homogenization process involved in processing milk, the solid fat is evenly dispersed and suspended in fluid milk, which masks its solid density. Saturated fat–laden coconut, palm, and palm kernel oils, as well as partially hydrogenated oils, which contain *trans* fatty acids, are also considered solid fats. Added sugars include sources such as brown sugar, corn syrup, molasses, and table sugar (you will learn about other sources in Chapter 4). Foods within each food group that contain solid fats and added sugars should be eaten in moderation because they add calories that are less nutrient dense to your diet.

Let's compare the nutrient density of two versions of the same food: a medium baked potato and an ounce of potato chips (**Figure 2.5**). Both have about the same number of calories, but the baked potato provides much more folate, potassium, and vitamin C, and is therefore much more nutrient dense, than the deep-fried chips. If you routinely choose foods with a lot of added sugar and solid fats, you will have to reduce your food intake elsewhere to compensate for the extra calories. This could cause you to displace healthier foods in your diet. If you don't adjust for these extra calories, but eat them in addition to your normal diet, you will soon experience weight gain.

In contrast to nutrient density, **energy density** refers to foods that are high in energy but low in weight or volume, such as that potato chip. A serving of deep-fried chips weighs much less than a plain baked potato, but is considerably higher in solid fats and calories. Therefore, the chip contains more calories per gram. A big, leafy green salad, on the other hand, is large in volume but low in energy density, due to its high water content. Most higher-fat foods and sweets and treats, such as fried foods and candy, are considered energy dense.

Individuals who choose low-energy-dense and high-nutrient-dense foods will generally have diets that are lower in solid fats and added sugars and higher in nutrient content. **Figure 2.6** helps you compare some nutrient-dense food choices with less-healthy food choices in each food group.

Eating a variety of foods among and within the food groups highlighted in MyPlate will increase your chances of consuming all 40 of the nutrients your

Figure 2.5 Which Is the Healthier Way to Enjoy Your Potatoes?
While one ounce of potato chips and one medium baked potato have similar amounts of calories, their nutrient content is worlds apart. A baked potato is more nutrient dense than potato chips.

*Note: Based on the percentage of the DRI for 19–50-year-old males. All these percentages apply to females in the same age range except for vitamin C. Females have lower vitamin C needs than males, so a baked potato provides more than 20 percent of the DRI for this vitamin for women.

	Vegetables	Fruits	Grains	Protein	Dairy	Oils
Foods with high amounts of added sugars and heart-unhealthy solid fats. These are less nutrient dense.	French fries, potato chips	Fruit canned in syrup, fruit drinks, sweetened dried fruit	Buttered popcorn, cake, cookies, doughnuts, pastries	Fatty cuts of meat and luncheon meats, fried chicken or fish, poultry with skin	Full-fat cheeses, fried mozzarella sticks, high-fat ice cream	Butter, hydrogenated oils
Foods that are more nutrient dense.	Fresh, frozen and canned vegetables, dried beans and peas	Dried fruit, whole fruit, 100% fruit juice	Brown rice, bulgur, couscous, oats, pasta, popcorn, rice, whole-grain cereals, bread, crackers	Dried beans and peas, eggs, fish, lean meat, nuts, skinless poultry, seeds	Low-fat or nonfat cheese, milk, or yogurt, low-fat ice cream or frozen yogurt	Vegetable oils

Eat **less** of these

Eat **more** of these

Figure 2.6 Nutrient-Dense Food Choices
Nutrient-dense foods provide more nutrition per calorie and fewer solid fats and added sugars.

body needs. Because no single food or food group provides all the nutrients, a varied diet of nutrient-dense foods is the savviest strategy. **Figure 2.7** provides tips on how to choose a variety of foods from each food group. The interactive website ChooseMyPlate.gov is designed to help you plan a personalized food plan based on your dietary and lifestyle needs. We will discuss this in more detail later in the chapter.

Lastly, physical activity is an important component in the *Dietary Guidelines*. Being physically active helps you stay fit and reduce your risk of chronic diseases such as heart disease and cancer. Advice regarding physical activity can also be found at ChooseMyPlate.gov.

Remember, "Rome wasn't built in a day." Adopting a healthier diet and lifestyle, and changing long-term eating habits, takes time. Taking small steps of improvement every day can be less overwhelming and will ultimately be beneficial to your health.

Let's next look at the foods of each food group, and why each group is uniquely important to you.

How to Use MyPlate and ChooseMyPlate.gov

You now know to eat a variety of nutrient-dense foods to be healthy, and that My-Plate reminds you to eat a diverse group of foods, but you may be wondering how much from each food group *you,* personally, should be eating. The ChooseMyPlate .gov interactive website will give you the exact numbers of servings to eat from each food group based on your daily calorie needs.

Recall that your calorie needs (your EER) are based upon your age and gender (two factors beyond your control) and your activity level (a factor you can control). As you just read, the more active you are, the more calories you burn to fuel your activities, and the more calories you can (and need to) consume in foods.

At the website, you will enter your age, gender, and activity level. Based on this information, your daily calorie needs will be determined and your personalized eating plan, specifying the exact number of servings from each of the five food groups, will be provided. (Oils are not considered a food group but should be added to your diet for good health.) With this information, you can plan your meals and snacks for the day. If you cannot go to the website, you can obtain similar information by using Tables 2.1 and 2.3 in this chapter. Let's use the tables to obtain your recommendations.

Practical Nutrition **VIDEO**

Portion Sizes

Who says you shouldn't eat with your hands? Let Joan show you how your hands can help you keep portions under control. Scan this QR code with your mobile device to access the video. You can also access the video in MasteringNutrition™.

The first step in creating your personalized daily food plan is to figure out how many calories you should be eating daily. To do this, you need to find out how active you are. If you participate in activities such as water aerobics, play doubles tennis, enjoy ballroom dancing, garden at home, or walk briskly, you are likely moderately active. You could consider yourself vigorously active if, for example, you race-walk, jog, run, swim laps, play singles tennis, or bicycle 10 miles per hour or faster. Based on these examples, are you moderately or vigorously active? Refer back to Table 2.1 on page 36 for the number of calories you need based on your activity level, age, and gender. When you know the number of calories you need daily, **Table 2.3** will tell you how many servings from each food group you should consume to healthfully obtain those calories. This is the equivalent of *your* personalized daily food plan.

Let's say that you are a moderately active female who needs 2,000 calories daily. To healthfully meet this level, you should consume each day:

- 6 servings from the grains group
- 2½ cups of dark green, orange, starchy, and other vegetables, and some legumes
- 2 cups of fruits
- 3 cups of fat-free or low-fat milk and yogurt
- 5½ ounces of lean meat, poultry, and fish or the equivalent in meat alternatives such as beans
- You should also add 6 teaspoons (2 tablespoons) of vegetable oils to your diet over the course of the day.

If you are having difficulty figuring out what 1 cup of vegetables, 3 ounces of meat, or 1 tablespoon of salad dressing looks like, use **Figure 2.8**. It provides an easy way to eyeball your serving sizes. Keep in mind that if you consistently eat oversized portions that are larger than those suggested in your daily food plan, you will consume too many calories and may gain weight. The Nutrition in the Real World feature "When a Portion *Isn't* a Portion" on pages 46–47 takes a look at how portion sizes have changed over the years, and how portion distortion can adversely affect our health.

If all of your food selections are low in solid fat and added sugars, the above menu will provide a total of about 1,740 calories. This means that, after meeting your nutrient requirements, you have a maximum of about 260 of your 2,000 calories left (see **Figure 2.9**). You can "spend" these calories on extra servings of foods such as grains, fruits, and/or vegetables, or on occasion, on a food such as a sweet or dessert that has added solid fats or added sugars. The calorie levels and distribution of food groups in daily food plans are calculated using the leanest food choices with no added sugars. So if you pour whole milk (high in solid fats) over your sweetened cereal (added sugars) instead of using skim milk (fat free and low in solid fats) to drench your shredded wheat (no added sugars), you will have added a fair amount of calories from solid fats and added sugars. As you can see from **Table 2.4**, your food choices could quickly provide less healthy calories from solid fats and added sugars and cause your diet to be less nutrient rich per bite.

Focus on fruits. Eat a variety of fruits—whether fresh, frozen, canned, or dried—rather than fruit juice for most of your fruit choices. For a 2,000-calorie diet, you will need 2 cups of fruit each day (for example, 1 small banana, 1 large orange, and ¼ cup of dried apricots or peaches).

Vary your veggies. Eat more dark green veggies, such as broccoli, kale, and other dark leafy greens; orange veggies, such as carrots, sweet potatoes, pumpkin, and winter squash; and beans and peas, such as pinto beans, kidney beans, black beans, garbanzo beans, split peas, and lentils.

Get your calcium-rich foods. Get 3 cups of low-fat or fat-free milk—or an equivalent amount of low-fat yogurt and/or low-fat cheese (1½ ounces of cheese equals 1 cup of milk)—every day. For kids aged 2 to 8, it's 2 cups of milk. If you don't or can't consume milk, choose lactose-free milk products and/or calcium-fortified foods and beverages.

Make half your grains whole. Eat at least 3 ounces of whole-grain cereals, breads, crackers, rice, or pasta every day. One ounce is about 1 slice of bread, 1 cup of breakfast cereal, or ½ cup of cooked rice or pasta. Look to see that grains such as wheat, rice, oats, or corn are referred to as "whole" in the list of ingredients.

Go lean with protein. Choose lean meats and poultry. Bake it, broil it, or grill it. And vary your protein choices—with more fish, beans, peas, nuts, and seeds.

Know the limits on fats, salt, and sugars. Read the Nutrition Facts label on foods. Look for foods low in saturated fats and *trans* fats. Choose and prepare foods and beverages with little salt (sodium) and/or added sugars (caloric sweeteners).

Figure 2.7 Mix Up Your Choices within Each Food Group

A woman's palm is the size of approximately 3 ounces of cooked meat, chicken, or fish

a

A woman's fist is the size of about 1 cup of pasta or vegetables (a man's fist is the size of about 2 cups)

b

The "O" made by a woman's thumb and forefinger is the size of about 1 tablespoon of vegetable oil

c

Figure 2.8 What's a Serving? Eat with Your Hands!
Your hands can guide you in estimating portion sizes.

260 calories (added fats and sugars)

1,740 calories (lean foods without added sugars)

2,000 total daily calories

Figure 2.9 How Solid Fats and Added Sugars Fit into a Healthy Diet
If you select mostly nutrient-dense, lean foods that contain few solid fats and added sugars, you may have leftover calories to "spend" on extra helpings or a small sweet dessert.

Table 2.3

How Much Should You Eat from Each Food Group?

The following are suggested amounts to consume daily from each of the basic five food groups and healthy oils based on your daily calorie needs. Remember that most of your choices should contain little solid fats and added sugar.

Calorie Level	Vegetables (cups)	Fruits (cups)	Grains (oz eq)	Protein (oz eq)	Dairy (cups)	Oil* (tsp)
1,600	2	1.5	5	5	3	5
1,800	2.5	1.5	6	5	3	5
2,000	2.5	2	6	5.5	3	6
2,200	3	2	7	6	3	6
2,400	3	2	8	6.5	3	7
2,600	3.5	2	9	6.5	3	8
2,800	3.5	2.5	10	7	3	8
3,000	4	2.5	10	7	3	10
3,200	4	2.5	10	7	3	11

Vegetables: Includes all fresh, frozen, canned, and dried vegetables, and vegetable juices. In general, 1 cup of raw or cooked vegetables or vegetable juice, or 2 cups of raw leafy greens, is considered 1 cup from the vegetable group.

Fruits: Includes all fresh, frozen, canned, and dried fruits, and fruit juices. In general, 1 cup of fruit or 100% fruit juice, or ½ cup of dried fruit, is considered 1 cup from the fruit group.

Grains: Includes all foods made with wheat, rice, oats, cornmeal, or barley, such as bread, pasta, oatmeal, breakfast cereals, tortillas, and grits. In general, 1 slice of bread, 1 cup of ready-to-eat cereal, or ½ cup of cooked rice, pasta, or cooked cereal is considered 1 ounce equivalent (oz eq) from the grains group. *At least half of all grains consumed should be whole grains such as whole-wheat bread, oats, or brown rice.*

Protein: In general, 1 ounce of lean meat, poultry, or fish, 1 egg, 1 tablespoon peanut butter, ¼ cup cooked dry beans, or ½ ounce of nuts or seeds is considered 1 ounce equivalent (oz eq) from the protein foods group.

Dairy: Includes all fat-free and low-fat milk, yogurt, and cheese. In general, 1 cup of milk or yogurt, 1½ ounces of natural cheese, or 2 ounces of processed cheese is considered 1 cup from the dairy group.

Oil: Includes vegetable oils such as canola, corn, olive, soybean, and sunflower oil, fatty fish, nuts, avocados, mayonnaise, salad dressings made with oils, and soft margarine.

*Oils are not considered a food group but should be added to your diet for good health.

Table 2.4

Choose Right!

As you can see, your daily food plan could provide a fair amount of solid fats and added sugars, depending on your food selections.

Choosing ...	Over ...	Will Cost You
Whole milk (1 cup)	Fat-free milk (1 cup)	65 calories of solid fats
Roasted chicken thigh with skin (3 oz)	Roasted chicken breast, skinless (3 oz)	70 calories of solid fats
Glazed doughnut, yeast type (3¾" diameter)	English muffin (1 muffin)	165 calories of solid fats and added sugars
French fries (1 medium order)	Baked potato (1 medium)	299 calories of solid fats
Regular soda (1 can, 12 fl oz)	Diet soda (1 can, 12 fl oz)	150 calories of added sugars

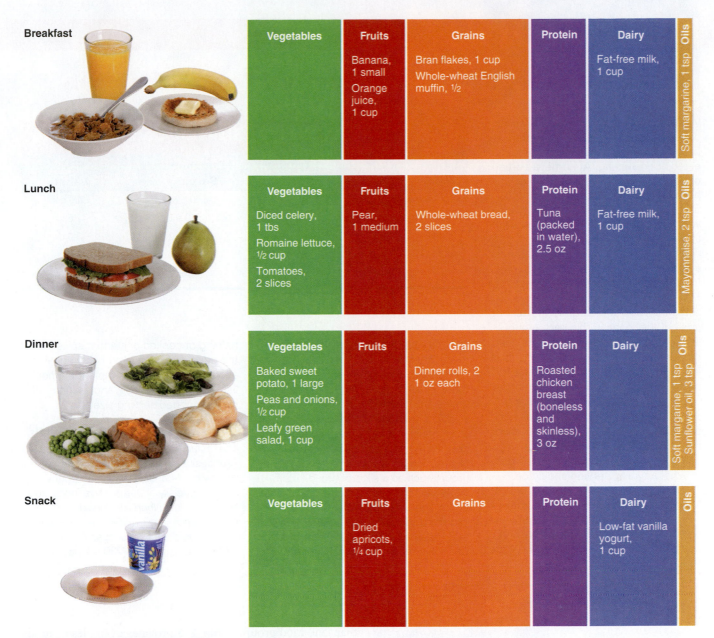

	Vegetables	Fruits	Grains	Protein	Dairy	Oils
Breakfast		Banana, 1 small Orange juice, 1 cup	Bran flakes, 1 cup Whole-wheat English muffin, ½		Fat-free milk, 1 cup	Soft margarine, 1 tsp
Lunch	Diced celery, 1 tbs Romaine lettuce, ½ cup Tomatoes, 2 slices	Pear, 1 medium	Whole-wheat bread, 2 slices	Tuna (packed in water), 2.5 oz	Fat-free milk, 1 cup	Mayonnaise, 2 tsp
Dinner	Baked sweet potato, 1 large Peas and onions, ½ cup Leafy green salad, 1 cup		Dinner rolls, 2 1 oz each	Roasted chicken breast (boneless and skinless), 3 oz		Soft margarine, 1 tsp Sunflower oil, 3 tsp
Snack		Dried apricots, ¼ cup			Low-fat vanilla yogurt, 1 cup	

Figure 2.10 A Healthy Daily Food Plan
A variety of foods from each group creates a well-balanced diet.

Let's now use these recommended amounts of servings from each food group and plan a 2,000-calorie menu. **Figure 2.10** shows how servings from the various food groups can create well-balanced meals and snacks throughout the day.

Although this particular menu is balanced and the foods are nutrient dense, it is unlikely that every day will be this ideal. The good news is that your nutrient needs are averaged over several days, or a week, of eating. If one day you eat insufficient servings of one food group or a specific nutrient, you can make up for it the next day. For example, let's say that you don't eat enough fruit one day but do eat an extra serving of grains. The next day you can adjust your diet by cutting back on your grain servings and adding an extra serving of fruit. Should you worry about *when* you eat? Read more about the time of day you should eat in the Examining the Evidence feature "Does the Time of Day You Eat Impact Your Health?" on pages 48–49.

If the foods at your meals are sometimes mixed dishes that contain a combination of ingredients, such as pizza, then they probably contribute servings to more

When a Portion *Isn't* a Portion

What is a portion of pasta? The answer depends on who is serving you the pasta. A *portion* is the amount of food eaten at one sitting. At home, a portion of pasta would be the amount that you heap on your plate. In a restaurant, it's the amount brought out on your plate, which can vary enormously among eating establishments.

On the other hand, the FDA defines a *serving size* as a standard amount of food that is customarily consumed. The FDA groups foods together into similar categories and standardizes the serving sizes of the foods within each group. These reference serving sizes are used on the Nutrition Facts panel of the food label. For example, the serving size for pasta is one cup, no matter what brand of pasta you purchase. Standardizing serving sizes among similar foods not only allows for consistency when choosing foods in the supermarket, but also helps the consumer get a ballpark idea of what a typical serving should be.

However, when following the online MyPlate recommendations, the portion size for pasta is only half a cup. Why the difference between the food label and this tool for healthy eating? The MyPlate

Comparison of Portion Sizes of Common Foods

Food	Typical Portion	Recommended Serving Size	FDA Label
Cooked pasta	2.9 cups	0.5 cup	1.0 cup
French fries	5.3 oz	10 fries	2.5 oz
Bagel	4.4 oz	1.0 oz	2.0 oz
Muffin	6.5 oz	1.5 oz	2.0 oz
Cookie, chocolate chip	4.0 oz	0.5 oz	1.1 oz

materials set portion sizes based on many different factors, one of which is the nutrient and calorie content of the foods in each group. All the foods in the grains group, which contains foods such as pasta, bread, and rice, provide similar amounts of nutrients and calories. The calories in half a cup of pasta are similar to the calories of the other foods in the group, such as a slice of bread.[1]

As you can see from the table, most times, the portions of the foods that you eat don't coincide with the standard serving size on the food label or the portion sizes recommended. A generous

helping of cooked pasta that spills over the edge of a plate is probably equal to about 3 cups, which is triple the amount listed on the food label and six times the recommended serving size.

How Have Portion Sizes Changed?

The restaurant industry has appealed to your desire to get the most food for your money by expanding restaurant portion sizes, especially of inexpensive foods, such as fast foods.[2] When McDonald's first introduced french fries in 1954, the standard serving weighed 2.4 ounces.[3] Although a small 2.6-ounce size (230 calories) is

Mixed dishes such as hamburgers and pizza are a major source of solid fats in the diets of Americans.

than one food group. **Table 2.5** provides examples of foods that contribute servings from multiple groups.

Now that you know what constitutes a healthy diet, the next step is to go food shopping. As you shop, you'll want to make sure you know the nutrient and calorie contents of the foods you buy. The food label will give you this information, and more.

LO 2.4 **The Take-Home Message** MyPlate depicts the five food groups using the familiar mealtime visual of a place setting. It is part of the USDA Web-based initiative at ChooseMyPlate.gov, providing information, a food guidance system, and a personalized daily food plan to help you build a healthy diet based on the *Dietary Guidelines for Americans*. The concepts of nutrient density and energy density refer to the amount of nutrients per bite of food and the number of calories per gram of food. You want to consume nutrient-dense foods such as fruits, vegetables, whole grains, and lean dairy and protein foods, but limit energy-dense foods, which provide calories from solid fats and added sugars but little nutrition. Daily physical activity is encouraged to better manage your weight and health.

available on the menu today, you can also choose the medium french fries weighing 3.9 ounces (340 calories) or the large at 5.9 ounces (510 calories). The difference in costs to the restaurants for the larger sizes is minuscule compared with the perceived "value" of the larger portion to the consumers.[4] Customers will frequent a restaurant more often if they think they are getting a bargain for their buck.

Unfortunately, from a health standpoint, research shows that even slight changes in the portion sizes of foods can lead to increased calorie intake and weight gain.[5] As you have read, being overweight increases the risk of developing heart disease, diabetes, joint problems, and even some types of cancers.[6] Downsizing your portions could down-size your health risks.

Here are some tips to help you control your portion sizes:

Controlling Portion Size

When You Are:	Do This:
At Home	Measure your food until you develop an "eye" for correct portion sizes.
	Use smaller plates so portions appear larger.
	Plate your food at the counter before sitting down at the table or in front of the television.
	Store leftover foods in portion-controlled containers.
	Don't eat snacks directly from the box or bag; measure a portion first, then eat only that amount.
	Cook smaller quantities of food so you don't pick at the leftovers.
Eating Out	Ask for half orders when available.
	Order an appetizer as your main entrée.
	Don't be compelled to "clean your plate"; stop eating when you're full and take the rest home.
Food Shopping	Divide a package of snacks into individual portion sizes and consume only one portion at any one sitting.
	Be aware of the number of servings in a package; read the labels.
	Buy foods in preportioned servings such as a 1-ounce sliced cheese or snack and 100-calorie microwave popcorn.

Table 2.5

A Combination of Good Food

Many of the foods you eat are probably mixed dishes that contain servings from multiple food groups. The following list should help you estimate the servings from each food group for some popular food items. Because the preparation process can vary greatly among recipes, these are only estimates.

Food and Sample Portion	Vegetables Group (cups)	Fruits Group (cups)	Grains Group (oz eq)	Protein Group (oz eq)	Dairy Group (cups)	Estimated Total Calories
Cheese pizza, with extra vegetables thick crust	1/2	0	3	0	3/4	380
Macaroni and cheese (1 cup, made from packaged mix)	0	0	2	0	1/4	335
Burrito with beans, cheese, onions, & salsa, meatless (1 small)	1/4	0	2	2	1¼	340
Chicken fried rice (1 cup)	1/4	0	1½	1	0	330
Double cheeseburger, with catsup, pickles, & onions on bun	1/4	0	2½	2	1/8	450
Tuna salad sandwich	1/4	0	2	2	0	290
Peanut butter and jelly sandwich (1)	0	0	2	1½	0	335
Apple pie (1 slice)	0	1/4	2	0	0	335–355

Does the Time of Day You Eat Impact Your Health?

We are all creatures of habit. Some of these habits, such as the time of day we eat, can either enhance or detract from overall health. Do you typically eat breakfast? Do you often snack after dinner or late at night? Do you overload on high-fat or fried foods when you go out on the weekends? The choice to skip breakfast, eat later in the day, or overeat on the weekend can impact your nutrient intake, appetite, and body weight.

Eating Breakfast Means More Energy and Fewer Calories throughout the Day

You probably know that grabbing a latte on the way to your morning class is not a healthy breakfast, but do you understand how such a habit impacts your overall nutrient intake? For one thing, skipping breakfast may affect the total number of calories you consume the rest of the day. Dr. John de Castro evaluated the timing of food intake in 867 people over a seven-day period and found that people who ate a larger proportion of food earlier in the day had a significantly lower intake of total calories.[7] In other words, if you eat breakfast, you are more likely to eat less by the end of the day than if you skip this important meal.

The reduction in total calories when you eat breakfast may be due to the size of the meal and how satisfied you feel. Most of us eat smaller meals at breakfast and more food at lunch and dinner. We also appear to spend less time eating breakfast than other meals. In Dr. de Castro's study, both of these factors affected satiety. Satiety ratios, or the time between meals based on the

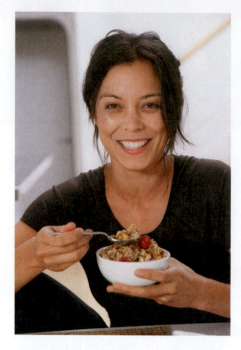

size of the previous meal, decreased over the day from breakfast through late-evening snacks.[8] Thus, a more substantial breakfast is more satiating than the evening meal.

One reason breakfast may be more satiating involves the types of foods consumed. Holt and colleagues investigated the effects of a high-fat breakfast versus a high-carbohydrate meal on the amount of snacking reported later in the day (see the figure).[9] If the breakfast included higher fiber foods, such as cereal, and a good protein source, the subjects ate less later in the day. Breakfast foods including potatoes, eggs, and high-fiber cereals ranked higher than doughnuts or white bread for satiety.

What if you skip breakfast? Not only will you eat more during the day, chances are you will choose less-nutrient-dense foods. Those who eat breakfast, lunch, and dinner tend to have higher calcium and iron intakes than individuals who skip breakfast.[10, 11]

Eating breakfast may also be a good strategy for weight control. Several studies have reported higher BMIs and body weight in subjects who don't consistently eat breakfast compared with their breakfast-eating counterparts.[12] In addition, eating breakfast helps maintain weight loss.[13]

Eating More during Evenings and Weekends Can Lead to Overconsumption of Calories

Do you eat after 7:00 p.m.? Most young adults do, especially during the weekend.[14] For most students, eating schedules are influenced by hunger, pressures from work and school, convenience, and social habits. Recent studies suggest that the craving for late-night carbohydrate snacks is related to your circadian rhythms.[15] Regardless of why you eat at various times, the timing of your meals can affect body weight, the level of hormones in the blood, body temperature, and blood pressure. Because eating later is less satisfying, you are likely to eat more food, and hence consume more calories, particularly from carbohydrates and fats, in the evening hours.

Though there is no current evidence that eating later in the day increases BMI or the risk of obesity,[16] timing of meals may impact changes in body composition during a weight-loss

What Is a Food Label and Why Is It Important?

LO 2.5 Identify the required components of a food label and how to use it.

Imagine walking down the supermarket aisle and finding that all the foods on the shelves are packaged in plain cardboard boxes and unmarked aluminum cans. How would you know if a brown box contained one pound of pasta or of crackers? Do the blank cans hold chicken noodle soup or crushed pineapple?

Food labels don't just make food shopping easier, they also serve important functions that make them helpful tools for anyone who wants to eat a healthy diet. First and foremost, they tell you what's inside the package. Second, they contain a program. In a controlled metabolic ward study, overweight women who ate the bulk of their calories in the morning hours had a slightly greater weight loss than when the bulk of the calories was consumed later in the day. However, when they ate more of their calories later in the day, they retained more lean muscle mass.[17] More research is needed before any strong conclusions can be drawn from these results.

Weekend eating patterns can also influence overall dietary intake. Haines reports that people in that study ate an average of 82 calories more per day on Friday, Saturday, and Sunday compared with weekdays.[18] These increases in calories were mostly due to an increase in fat (approximately 0.7 percent) and alcohol (1.4 percent); carbohydrates decreased by 1.6 percent. Over time, this increase in calorie intake may lead to weight gain.

Recommendations

Based on the current research on eating and time of day, it is recommended that you:

- Start your day with a nutrient-dense breakfast as part of a healthy eating pattern. Many breakfast foods, such as dry whole-grain cereals, fresh fruit, or whole-grain toast or bagels with low-fat cream cheese, can be eaten on the go. You'll have more energy and will most likely eat fewer total calories by the end of the day.
- Choose breakfast foods that are more satisfying to improve your appetite control throughout the day.

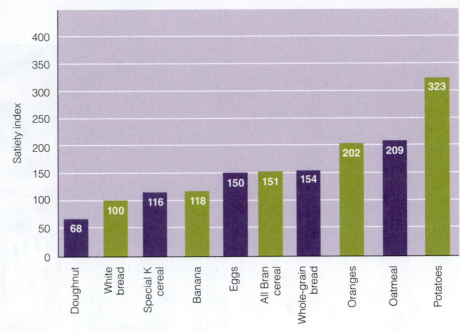

Satiety Index of Different Foods
Subjects were asked to rate their feelings of hunger every 15 minutes for 2 hours after eating 240-calorie portions of specific foods. All foods were compared with white bread, which scored a satiety index of 100.

Enjoy foods such as whole-grain cereals and whole fruits, which are higher in fiber, protein, and water, and lower in fat and sugar.

- Control calorie intake on nights and weekends. Monitor your weekend eating habits to maintain a consistent balance of carbohydrates, fats, and proteins and to reduce alcohol consumption.

WHAT DO YOU THINK?

1. What makes certain foods more satiating than others?
2. Have you ever significantly changed the timing or content of your meals?
3. What effects did you notice in your levels of hunger, satisfaction, and energy as a result of this change?

Nutrition Facts panel, which identifies the calories and nutrients in a serving of the food. Third, they list Daily Values (DVs), which help you determine how those calories and nutrients will fit into your overall diet.

The Food Label Tells You What's in the Package

To help consumers make informed food choices, the Food and Drug Administration (FDA) regulates the labeling of all packaged foods in the United States.[7] Currently, the FDA has mandated that every packaged food be labeled with:[8]

- The name of the food
- The net weight of the food (the weight of the food in the package, excluding the weight of the package or packing material)

The **Nutrition Facts panel** lists standardized serving sizes, specific nutrients, and shows how a serving of the food fits into a healthy diet by stating its contribution to the percentage of the Daily Value for each nutrient. The old cereal box doesn't contain this information.

The **name** of the product must be displayed on the front label.

The **ingredients** must be listed in descending order by weight. This format is missing in the old box. Whole-grain wheat is the predominant ingredient in the current cereal box.

The **net weight** of the food in the box must now be located at the bottom of the package.

Figure 2.11 The Food Label Provides Valuable Consumer Information
Manufacturers must adhere to strict labeling requirements mandated by the FDA.

- The name and address of the manufacturer or distributor
- A list of ingredients in descending order by weight, with the heaviest item listed first
- A Nutrition Facts panel that includes total calories, calories from fat, total fat, saturated fat, *trans* fats, cholesterol, sodium, total carbohydrate, dietary fiber, sugars, vitamin A, vitamin C, calcium, and iron (**Figure 2.11**)

The label must also contain:

- Serving sizes that are uniform among similar products, which allows for easier comparison shopping by the consumer
- An indication of how a serving of the food fits into an overall daily diet
- Uniform definitions for descriptive label terms such as "light" and "fat-free"
- Health claims that are accurate and science based, if made about the food or one of its nutrients
- The presence of any of eight common allergens that might be present in the food, including milk, eggs, fish, shellfish, tree nuts (cashews, walnuts, almonds, etc.), peanuts, wheat, and soybeans

Very few foods are exempt from carrying a Nutrition Facts panel on the label. Such foods include plain coffee and tea; some spices, flavorings, and other foods that don't provide a significant amount of nutrients; bakery foods, and other ready-to-eat foods that are prepared and sold in retail establishments; and foods produced by small businesses (for example, companies that have total annual sales of less than $500,000).[9]

Whereas raw fruits and vegetables and fresh fish typically don't have a label, these foods fall under the FDA's voluntary, point-of-purchase nutrition information program. Under the guidelines of this program, grocery stores must post the nutrition information of the most commonly eaten fruits, vegetables, and fish near where the foods are sold.[10] Nutrition labeling is mandatory for meat and poultry, which is regulated by the USDA. Meat and poultry items that are prepared and sold at the supermarket, such as take-out cooked chicken, do not have a nutrition label.[11]

The Food Label Can Help You Make Healthy Food Choices

Suppose you're in the dairy aisle of a supermarket trying to select a carton of milk. You want to watch your fat intake, so you have narrowed your choices to reduced-fat 2% milk or nonfat milk. How do they compare in terms of calories, fat, and other nutrients per serving? How do you decide which is more healthful? The answer is simple: Look at the labels. All the information that you need to make a smart choice is provided on one area of the label, the **Nutrition Facts panel**.

The Nutrient Fact Panel on the food label can help consumers make smart nutrition choices when shopping.

On the Label: The Nutrition Facts Panel

The Nutrition Facts panel provides a nutritional snapshot of the food inside a package. By law, the panel must list the following per serving of the food:

- Calories and calories from fat
- Total fat, saturated fat, and *trans* fat
- Cholesterol
- Sodium
- Total carbohydrate, dietary fiber, and sugars
- Protein
- Vitamin A, vitamin C, calcium, and iron

If an additional nutrient, such as vitamin E or vitamin B_{12}, has been added, or if the product makes a claim about a nutrient, then that nutrient must also be listed. Other nutrients, such as additional vitamins and minerals, can be listed by the manufacturer on a voluntary basis. The majority of the packaged foods you purchase will contain this nutrition information.

The content of the panel is regulated by the FDA, which is considering changes to the panel as this book goes to press. When the new panel is finalized, manufacturers will have two years to phase in the new format, so you are likely to see a mix of the existing and the new panel on foods for some time to come. Let's learn how to decipher the current Nutrition Facts panel (**Figure 2.12a**). At the top of the panel is the serving size. By law, the serving size must be listed both by weight in grams (less useful to you) and in common household measures, such as cups and ounces (more useful to you). Because serving sizes are standardized among similar food products, you can compare one brand of granola with a different brand to assess which one better meets your needs.

The rest of the information on the panel is based on the listed serving size (in this case, 2/3 cup) of the food. For example, if you ate two servings (1-1/3 cups) of this granola, you would double the nutrient information on the label to calculate the calories as well as the fat and other nutrients. The servings-per-container information is particularly useful for portion control.

Below the serving size is listed the calories per serving. The calories from fat give you an idea of what proportion of the food's calories comes from fat. In this box of granola, 72 out of a total of 230 calories per serving are from fat.

Nutrition Facts panel The area on the food label that provides a uniform listing of specific nutrients obtained in one serving of the food.

The U.S. Food and Drug Administration (FDA) is proposing new changes to the 20-year-old nutrition labels on packaged foods. The changes to the nutrition label provide information to help compare products and make healthy food choices.

FOCUS FIGURE WALKTHROUGH

Scan this QR code with your mobile device for a video tour of this figure by Joan Salge Blake.

ⓐ Current Label

GRANOLA

Nutrition Facts
Serving Size 2/3 cup (55g)
Servings Per Container About 8

Amount Per Serving

Calories 230	Calories from Fat 72

	% Daily Value*
Total Fat 8g	**12%**
Saturated Fat 1g	**5%**
Trans Fat 0g	
Cholesterol 0mg	**0%**
Sodium 160mg	**7%**
Total Carbohydrates 37g	**12%**
Dietary Fiber 4g	**16%**
Sugars 1g	
Protein 3g	

Vitamin A	10%
Vitamin C	8%
Calcium	20%
Iron	45%

* Percent Daily Values are based on a 2,000 calorie diet. Your daily value may be higher or lower depending on your calorie needs.

	Calories:	2,000	2,500
Total Fat	Less than	65g	80g
Sat Fat	Less than	20g	25g
Cholesterol	Less than	300mg	300mg
Sodium	Less than	2,400mg	2,400mg
Total Carbohydrate		300g	375g
Dietary Fiber		25g	30g

SERVINGS
• Serving sizes are standardized, making comparison shopping easier.

NEW
• Servings and serving sizes are larger and bolder.
• "Amount per serving" will be changed to "Amount per (serving size)" such as "Amount per cup."

CALORIES
• Calories per serving and the number of servings in the package are listed.

NEW
• Calories are larger to stand out more.
• "Calories from fat" is removed.

DAILY VALUES
• Daily Values are general reference values based on a 2,000 calorie diet.
• The %DV can tell you if a food is high or low in a nutrient or dietary substance.

NEW
• Daily Values are listed first.
• The meaning of the Daily Values will be explained in a new detailed footnote.

ADDED SUGARS
NEW
• Added sugars are listed.

VITAMINS & MINERALS
• Vitamin A, vitamin C, calcium, and iron are required.
• Other vitamins and minerals are voluntary.

NEW
• Vitamin D and potassium are required, in addition to calcium and iron.
• Vitamins A and C are voluntary.
• Actual amounts of each nutrient are listed as well as the %DV.

ⓑ Proposed New Label

GRANOLA

Nutrition Facts
8 servings per container
Serving size   2/3 cup (55g)

Amount per 2/3 cup

Calories   230

% DV*		
12%	**Total Fat** 8g	
5%	**Saturated Fat** 1g	
	Trans Fat 0g	
0%	**Cholesterol** 0mg	
7%	**Sodium** 160mg	
12%	**Total Carbs** 37g	
14%	Dietary Fiber 4g	
	Sugars 1g	
	Added Sugars 0g	
	Protein 3g	
10%	**Vitamin D** 2mcg	
20%	**Calcium** 260mg	
45%	**Iron** 8mg	
5%	**Potassium** 235mg	

* Footnote on Daily Values (DV) and calories reference to be inserted here.

Next are the nutrients that you should limit or add to your diet. Americans typically eat too much fat, including saturated fat, *trans* fat, and cholesterol, and too much sodium. In contrast, they tend to fall short in dietary fiber, vitamins A and C, calcium, and iron. These are on the label to remind you to make sure to eat foods rich in these substances. A food manufacturer voluntarily may list other nutrients that it is important to consume in sufficient amounts, such as potassium and vitamin D. The Nutrition Facts panel can be your best shopping guide when identifying and choosing foods that are low in the nutrients you want to limit (like saturated fat) and high in the nutrients that you need to eat in higher amounts (like fiber).

Are you wondering what determines if a food contains a "high" or "low" amount of a specific nutrient? That's where the Daily Values come into play.

On the Label: The Daily Values

Unlike the DRIs, which are precise recommended amounts of each nutrient that you should eat, the **Daily Values (DVs)** listed on the Nutrition Facts panel are general reference levels for the nutrients listed on the food label. The DVs give you a ballpark idea of how the nutrients in the foods you buy fit into your overall diet.

For example, if calcium is listed at 20 percent, a serving of that food provides 20 percent of most adults' daily requirement for calcium. However, if you are under 19 years of age or older than 70, your calcium needs are higher than the reference number used on the DV. Because the DVs on the food label are based on a 2,000-calorie diet, if you need more or fewer than 2,000 calories daily, some of your DV numbers may be higher or lower than those listed on the Nutrition Facts panel.

The DVs are based on older reference levels and are not as current as the DRIs. For example, whereas the DRIs recommend an upper level of dietary sodium of no more than 2,300 milligrams (daily), the DVs use less than 2,400 milligrams as the reference level.

There are no DVs listed on the label for *trans* fat, sugars, and protein. This is because there isn't enough information available to set reference values for *trans* fat and sugars. Although there are reference values for protein, consuming adequate amounts of protein isn't a health concern for most Americans over age 4, so listing the percent of the DV for this nutrient isn't warranted on the label. The DV for protein will only be listed if the product, such as a jar of baby food, is being marketed for children under the age of 4, or if a claim is made about the food, such as that it is "high in protein."[12]

If a serving provides 20 percent or more of the DV, it is considered high in that nutrient. For example, a serving of this granola is high in calcium (a healthy attribute). If you eat this cereal for breakfast, the good news is that a serving of this breakfast cereal provides 20 percent of the DV for calcium.

If a nutrient provides 5 percent or less of the DV, it is considered low in that nutrient. A serving of granola doesn't provide much saturated fat (another healthy attribute).

Lastly, depending on the size of the food package, there may be a footnote at the bottom of the label. This provides a summary of the DVs for a 2,000-calorie diet as well as a 2,500-calorie diet. This area of the panel provides you with a little "cheat sheet" to help you when you are shopping so that you don't have to memorize the values. As you can see from the footnote, you should try to keep your sodium intake to less than 2,400 milligrams daily. Because you know that this granola is low in

Virtual Food Label Fun

Take this virtual shopping trip challenge to see how food label–savvy you really are. Visit www.accessdata.fda.gov/videos/CFSAN/HWM/hwmintro.cfm for some comparison-shopping fun!

Daily Values (DVs) Established reference levels of nutrients, based on a 2,000-calorie diet, that are used on food labels.

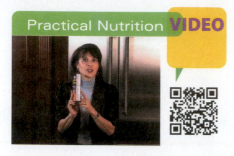

Reading a Food Label

The Nutrition Facts panel is easy to read—once you know what to look for. Scan this QR code with your mobile device to access the video. You can also access the video in MasteringNutrition™

Cereal-box readers will read the information on the box as many as 12 times before they consume the last spoonful!

sodium, providing 7 percent of the DV, or 160 milligrams, of sodium, you should try to keep the sodium in your remaining food choices during the day to less than 2,240 milligrams.

A new Nutrition Facts panel has been proposed by the FDA (see **Figure 2.12b**). The serving sizes are larger to reflect the amount of food and beverages people are actually consuming. The format on the label will be changed with key consumer information, such as calories, servings per container, and the percent daily value, more prominently displayed. Added sugars will be listed as well as vitamin D and potassium, two nutrients many Americans are falling short of in their diet. Listing the amounts of vitamin A and C in a food item will no longer be mandatory. The box between the old and new Nutrition Facts panels summarizes all the proposed changes.

While the Nutrition Facts panel on the side or back of the package can help you make healthier food choices, some foods carry claims on their front labels that may also influence your decision to buy. Let's look at these next.

On the Label: Label Claims

In the 1980s, the savvy Kellogg Company ran an ad campaign for its fiber-rich All Bran cereal reminding the public of the National Cancer Institute's recommendation to eat low-fat, high-fiber foods, fresh fruits, and vegetables to maintain a healthy weight. According to the FDA, sales of high-fiber cereals increased over 35 percent within a year.[13] Manufacturers realized that putting nutrition and health claims on labels was effective in influencing consumer purchases. Supermarket shelves were soon crowded with products boasting various claims.

So, can you feel confident that the jar of light mayonnaise is really lighter in calories and fat than regular mayonnaise? Yes, you can. The FDA mandates that all claims on labels follow strict guidelines.

Currently, the FDA allows the use of three types of claims on food products:

1. Nutrient content claims
2. Health claims
3. Structure/function claims

All foods displaying these claims on the label must meet specified criteria. Let's look at each of these claims closely.

Nutrient Content Claims

A food product can make a **nutrient content claim** about the amount of a nutrient it contains (or doesn't contain) by using descriptive terms such as *free* (fat-free yogurt), *high* (high-fiber crackers), *low* (low saturated fat granola), *reduced* (reduced-sodium soup), and *extra lean* (extra lean ground beef) as long as it meets the strict criteria designated by the FDA. These terms can help you identify at a glance the food items that best meet your needs.

Look at the labels of the canned soups in **Figure 2.13**. If you want a chicken soup with the least amount of sodium based on the three choices, look for the "low sodium" label on the can, as this nutrient claim means that the soup cannot contain more than 140 milligrams of sodium per serving. A next best choice would be the soup with the term "less sodium" on the label, which means that it must contain at least 25 percent less sodium than the regular variety. The classic can of chicken soup contains almost 900 milligrams for a serving, which is likely the same or even more

nutrient content claim Claim on the label that describes the level or amount of a nutrient in a food product.

a Because this can of chicken noodle soup displays the "low sodium" nutrient claim, it can't provide more than 140 milligrams of sodium in a serving.

b This can of soup has more than 25 percent less sodium than the classic version, so the term "less" can be displayed on its label.

c The classic variety of chicken noodle soup has the most sodium per serving.

Figure 2.13 Soup's On!
Nutrient claims on the food label must meet strict FDA criteria.

sodium you may consume at a meal. **Table 2.6** on page 56 provides some of the most common nutrient claims on food labels, the specific criteria that each claim must meet as mandated by the FDA, and examples of food products that carry these nutrient claims.

Health Claims

Suppose you are sitting at your kitchen table eating a bowl of Cheerios in skim milk, and staring at the front of the cereal box. You notice a claim on the front of the box that states: "The soluble fiber in Cheerios, as part of a heart healthy diet, can help you lower your cholesterol." Do you recognize this as a health claim that links Cheerios with better heart health?

Table 2.6

What Does That Labeling Term Mean?

Nutrient	Free	Low	Reduced/Less	Light
Calories	< 5 calories (cal) per serving	≤ 40 cal per serving	At least 25 percent fewer calories per serving	If the food contains 50 percent or more of its calories from fat, then the fat must be reduced
Fat	< 0.5 grams (g) per serving	≤ 3 g per serving	At least 25 percent less fat per serving	Same as above
Saturated Fat	< 0.5 g per serving	≤ 1 g per serving	At least 25 percent less saturated fat per serving	N/A
Cholesterol	< 2 milligrams (mg) per serving	≤ 20 mg per serving	At least 25 percent less cholesterol per serving	N/A
Sodium	< 5 mg per serving	<140 mg per serving	At least 25 percent less sodium per serving	If the sodium is reduced by at least 50 percent per serving
Sugars	< 0.5 g	N/A	At least 25 percent less sugar per serving	N/A

Other Labeling Terms

Term	Definition
"High," "Rich in," or "Excellent source of"	The food contains 20 percent or more of the DV of the nutrient in a serving. Can be used to describe protein, vitamins, minerals, fiber, or potassium.
"Good source of"	A serving of the food provides 10–19 percent of the DV. Can be used to describe meals or main dishes.
"More," "Added," "Extra," or "Plus"	A serving of the food provides 10 percent of the DV. Can only be used to describe vitamins, minerals, protein, fiber, and potassium.
"Lean"	Can be used on seafood and meat that contains less than 10 g of fat, 4.5 g or less of saturated fat, and less than 95 mg of cholesterol per serving.
"Extra lean"	Can be used on seafood and meat that contains less than 5 g of fat, less than 2 g of saturated fat, and less than 95 mg of cholesterol per serving.

Note: N/A = not applicable

> In one consumer survey, more than 40 percent of respondents said that they had purchased foods that claimed to reduce the risk of heart disease. Health claims do influence food decisions.

health claim Claim on the label that describes a relationship between a food or dietary compound and a disease or health-related condition.

A **health claim** must contain two important components:

1. A food or a dietary compound, such as fiber
2. A corresponding disease or health-related condition that is associated with the claim[14]

In the Cheerios example, the soluble fiber (the dietary compound) that naturally occurs in oats has been shown to lower blood cholesterol levels (the corresponding health-related condition), which can help reduce the risk of heart disease.

There are three types of health claims: (1) authorized health claims, (2) health claims based on authoritative statements, and (3) qualified health claims. The differences between them lie in the amount of supporting research and agreement among scientists about the strength of the relationship between the food or dietary ingredient and the disease or condition. See **Table 2.7** for a definition of these claims and examples of each.

Table 2.7

Sorting Out the Label Claims

Type of Claim	Definition	Examples (Claims of links between ...)
Authorized health claims (well-established)	Claims based on a well-established relationship between the food or compound and the health benefit. Food manufacturers must petition the FDA and provide the scientific research that backs up the claim. If there is significant agreement among the supporting research and a consensus among numerous scientists and experts in the field that there is a relationship between the food or dietary ingredient and the disease or health condition, the FDA will allow an authorized health claim. Specified wording must be used. The FDA has approved 12 authorized health claims.	• Calcium and osteoporosis • Sodium and hypertension • Dietary fat and cancer • Dietary saturated fat and cholesterol and risk of coronary heart disease • Fiber-containing grain products, fruits, and vegetables, and cancer • Fruits, vegetables, and grain products that contain fiber, particularly soluble fiber, and the risk of coronary heart disease • Fruits and vegetables and cancer • Folate and neural tube defects • Dietary noncarcinogenic carbohydrate sweeteners and dental caries • Soluble fiber from certain foods and risk of coronary heart disease • Soy protein and risk of coronary heart disease • Plant sterol/stanol esters and risk of coronary heart disease
Health claims based on authoritative statements (well-established)	Claims based on statements made by a U.S. government agency, such as the Centers for Disease Control and Prevention (CDC) and the National Institutes of Health (NIH). If the FDA approves the claim submitted by the manufacturer, the wording of these claims must include "may," as in "whole grains may help reduce the risk of heart disease," to illustrate that other factors in addition to the food or dietary ingredient may play a role in the disease or condition. This type of health claim can only be used on food and cannot be used on dietary supplements.	• Whole-grain foods and risk of heart disease and certain cancers • Potassium and risk of high blood pressure • Fluoridated water and risk of dental caries • Saturated fat, cholesterol, and *trans* fat and risk of heart disease • Substitution of saturated fat in the diet with unsaturated fatty acids and reduced risk of heart disease
Qualified health claims (less well-established)	Claims based on evidence that is still emerging. However, the current evidence to support the claim is greater than the evidence suggesting that the claim isn't valid. These are allowed in order to expedite the communication of potentially beneficial health information to the public. They must be accompanied by the statement "the evidence to support the claim is limited or not conclusive" or "some scientific evidence suggests. . . ." Qualified health claims can be used on dietary supplements if approved by the FDA.	• Selenium and cancer • Antioxidant vitamins and cancer • Nuts and heart disease • Omega-3 fatty acids and coronary heart disease • B vitamins and vascular disease • Monounsaturated fatty acids from olive oil and coronary heart disease • Unsaturated fatty acids from canola oil and risk of coronary heart disease • 0.8 mg folic acid and neural tube birth defects • Green tea and cancer • Chromium picolinate and diabetes • Calcium and colon/rectal cancer and calcium and recurrent colon/rectal polyps • Calcium and hypertension, pregnancy-induced hypertension, and preeclampsia • Tomatoes and/or tomato sauce and prostate, ovarian, gastric, and pancreatic cancers • Corn oil and corn oil–containing products and risk of heart disease • Walnuts and heart disease • Psyllium husk and diabetes

Antioxidants

With Antioxidants A*, C and E, including beta carotene to help support a healthy immune system.

Figure 2.14 A Structure/Function Label Claim
The structure/function claim is that the antioxidants added to this cereal support the immune system. The manufacturer cannot claim that the food lowers a consumer's risk of a chronic disease or health condition.

structure/function claim Claim on the label that describes how a nutrient or dietary compound affects the structure or function of the human body.

functional foods Foods that have a positive effect on health beyond providing basic nutrients.

Structure/Function Claims

The last type of label claim is the **structure/function claim**, which describes how a nutrient or dietary compound affects the structure or function of the human body.[15] The claims "calcium (nutrient) builds strong bones (body structure)" and "fiber (dietary compound) maintains bowel regularity (body function)" are examples of structure/function claims. Structure/function claims cannot state that the nutrient or dietary compound can be used to treat a disease or a condition (see **Figure 2.14**).[16] These claims can be made on both foods and dietary supplements. Unlike the other health claims, structure/function claims don't have to be preapproved by the FDA. They do have to be truthful and not misleading, but the manufacturer is responsible for making sure that the claim is accurate. These claims can be a source of confusion. Shoppers can easily fall into the trap of assuming that one brand of a product with a structure/function claim on its label is superior to another product without the claim. For instance, a yogurt that says "calcium builds strong bones" on its label may be identical to another yogurt without the flashy label claim. The consumer has to recognize the difference between claims that are supported by a significant amount of solid research and approved by the FDA, and structure/function claims that don't require prior approval for use.

If a dietary supplement such as a multivitamin is to contain a structure/function claim, its manufacturer must notify the FDA no later than 30 days after the product has been on the market. Dietary supplements that use structure/function claims must display a disclaimer on the label that the FDA did not evaluate the claim and that the dietary supplement is not intended to "diagnose, treat, cure, or prevent any disease." Manufacturers of foods bearing structure/function claims do not have to display this disclaimer on the label.

All foods that boast a health claim and/or a structure/function claim can also be marketed as **functional foods**. Although keeping the types of health and structure/function claims straight can be challenging, here's one way to remember them:

- Authorized health claims and health claims based on authoritative statements are the strongest, as they are based on years of accumulated research or an authoritative statement.
- Qualified health claims are less convincing. They are made on potentially healthful foods or dietary ingredients, but, because the evidence is still emerging, the claim has to be "qualified" as such.
- Structure/function claims are the weakest claims, as they are just statements or facts about the role the nutrient or dietary ingredient plays in your body. They can't claim that the food or dietary ingredient lowers your risk of developing a chronic disease such as heart disease or cancer. As you read the claims on the labels, you will quickly see that those with less established scientific evidence behind them have the weakest wording.

Table 2.8

A Summary of Tools for Healthy Eating

	DRIs	Dietary Guidelines for Americans	MyPlate	Nutrition Facts Panel	Label Claims
What Are They?	Specific reference values, for each nutrient by age and gender	Reflect the most current nutrition and physical activity recommendations for good health	A representational icon that depicts five food groups using the familiar mealtime visual of a place setting	Contains important nutrition information to be used to compare food products	There are three types of claims: 1. Nutrient content claims 2. Health claims 3. Structure/function claims
How Do They Guide You in Healthy Eating?	DRIs provide recommendations to prevent malnutrition and chronic diseases for each nutrient. The upper level is designed to prevent overnutrition or toxicity.	The *Dietary Guidelines* emphasize healthy food choices, maintaining healthy weight, and physical activity. Examples of healthy eating patterns and guidance on food safety and how to shift dietary choices to more nutrient-dense foods are included.	MyPlate is the focal point for the Web-based ChooseMyPlate.gov initiative, which provides information to build a healthy diet based on the *Dietary Guidelines for Americans.*	You can use the Nutrition Facts panel to compare the nutrient density of foods.	You can use these label terms to help you choose foods that may contain a specific amount of a nutrient or compound to improve your diet.
What Are They Made Up Of?	EARs, RDAs, AIs, ULs, and AMDRs	The key guidelines are: 1. Follow a healthy eating plan across the lifespan. 2. Focus on variety, nutrient density, and amount. 3. Limit calories from added sugars and saturated fats and reduce sodium intake. 4. Shift to healthier food and beverage choices. 5. Support healthy eating patterns for all.	Recommendations are made for physical activity as well as five food groups, plus oils: 1. Vegetables 2. Fruits 3. Grains 4. Protein 5. Dairy 6. Oils	Information is presented about: 1. Serving size 2. Servings per package 3. Total calories and calories from fat 4. Macronutrients 5. Vitamins and minerals 6. % Daily Values	1. Nutrient content claims describe the level or amount of a nutrient in a food product. 2. Health claims describe a relationship between a food or dietary compound and a disease or health-related condition. 3. Structure/function claims describe how a nutrient or dietary compound affects the structure or function of the body.

Table 2.8 summarizes the various areas of information you can use to help you achieve a healthful diet.

LO 2.5 The Take-Home Message The FDA regulates the labeling on all packaged foods. The Nutrition Facts panel and the Daily Values are found on all food labels. Every food label must include the name of the food, its net weight, the name and address of the manufacturer or distributor, a list of ingredients, and standardized nutrition information. The FDA allows and regulates the use of nutrient content claims, health claims, and structure/function claims on food labels. Any foods or dietary supplements displaying these claims on the label must meet specified criteria and be truthful.

Practical Nutrition VIDEO

Understanding Food Claims

Not all label claims are created equal! Let Joan show you how to recognize the different types. Scan this QR code with your mobile device to access the video. You can also access the video in MasteringNutrition™.

Functional Foods: What Role Do They Play in Your Diet?

LO 2.6 Explain the role of functional foods in the diet.

Have you ever eaten broccoli? Odds are that you have, but you may not have known that you were eating a functional food. In fact, some people have even called broccoli a superfood. Although there isn't a legal definition for either of these terms, the Academy of Nutrition and Dietetics defines *functional foods* as whole foods that, along with fortified, enriched, or enhanced foods, have a potentially beneficial effect on health when regularly consumed in enough quantity as part of a varied diet on a regular basis at effective levels based on significant standards of evidence. Broccoli is a functional food because it is rich in beta-carotene, which, in addition to being a key source of vitamin A, helps protect your cells from damaging substances that can increase your risk of some chronic diseases, such as heart disease. In other words, the beta-carotene's function goes beyond its basic nutritional role as a source of vitamin A, because it may also help fight heart disease. Broccoli is also a cruciferous vegetable, which, along with cauliflower and Brussels sprouts, is part of the cabbage family. These vegetables contain compounds such as isothiocyanates, which may also help fight cancer. Oats are also a functional food and are sometimes also referred to as a superfood, because they contain the soluble fiber beta-glucan, which has been shown to lower blood cholesterol levels. This can play a positive role in lowering the risk for heart disease.[17]

If the beneficial compound in the food is derived from plants, such as in the case of beta-carotene, isothiocyanates, and beta-glucan, it is called a **phytochemical** (*phyto* = plant). If it is derived from animals it is called a **zoochemical** (*zoo* = animal). Heart-healthy omega-3 fatty acids, found in fatty fish such as salmon and sardines, are considered zoochemicals. **Table 2.9** provides a list of currently known compounds in foods that have been shown to provide positive health benefits. Manufacturers are promoting foods containing naturally occurring phytochemicals and zoochemicals and have also begun fortifying other food products with these compounds. You can buy margarine with added plant sterols and a cereal with the soluble fiber, psyllium, which both help to lower blood cholesterol levels, as well as pasta and eggs that have had omega-3 fatty acids added.

Are There Concerns Associated with Consuming Functional Foods?

With so many labeling claims now adorning products on supermarket shelves, consumers have an array of enhanced functional foods from which to choose. Having so many options can be confusing. Consumers often cannot tell if a pricey box of cereal with added "antioxidants to help support the immune system" is really better than an inexpensive breakfast of oatmeal and naturally antioxidant-rich orange juice. There is also a concern that after eating a bowl of this antioxidant-enhanced cereal, consumers may think they are "off the hook" about eating healthfully the rest of the day. Often, more than one serving of a functional food is needed to reap

phytochemical Plant chemical that has been shown to reduce the risk of certain diseases such as cancer and heart disease. Beta-carotene is a phytochemical.

zoochemical Compound in animal food products that is beneficial to human health. Omega-3 fatty acids are an example of zoochemicals.

Table 2.9

Your Guide to Functional Foods

This Compound	Found in This/These Functional Food(s)	May Have This Health Benefit
Beta-carotene	Carrots, pumpkin, cantaloupe, broccoli	Functions as an antioxidant in the body
Lycopene	Tomatoes, tomato sauce	May lower risk of prostate cancer
Soy protein	Tofu, soy milk	Lowers risk of heart disease
Beta-glucan	Oatmeal, oats, oat bran	Lowers blood cholesterol
Plant sterol and stanol esters	Fortified margarines, like Benecol spreads	Lowers blood cholesterol
Omega-3 fatty acids	Salmon, sardines, tuna	May reduce the risk of heart disease
Whole grains	Whole-wheat bread, brown rice, popcorn	May reduce the risk of some cancers and heart disease
Flavanols	Dark chocolate, green apples	May contribute to heart health
Anthocyanins	Berries, red grapes, cherries	Act as antioxidants, may contribute to brain function
Probiotics	Active cultures in fermented dairy products such as yogurt	Support intestinal health

the beneficial effect of the food compound, but the consumer hasn't been educated appropriately about how much of such a food to consume.

Also, though functional foods do convey health benefits, they are not magic elixirs that can negate a poor diet. The best way to use functional foods is as part of a healthy diet that can help *prevent* adverse health conditions from occurring in the first place.

As with most dietary substances, problems may arise if too much is consumed (see Health Connection: A Case Study: Functional Foods and Cholesterol). For example, whereas consuming some omega-3 fatty acids can help reduce the risk of heart disease, consuming too much can be problematic for people on certain medications or for those at risk for a specific type of stroke.[18] A person can unknowingly overconsume a dietary compound if his or her diet contains many different functional foods enhanced with the same compound. Also, functional beverages, such as herbal beverages or vitamin-enhanced water, can have more calories and added sugar than soft drinks.

How to Use Functional Foods

Functional foods can be part of a healthy, well-balanced diet. Keep in mind that whole grains, fruits, vegetables, healthy vegetable oils, lean meat and dairy products, fish, and poultry all contain varying amounts of naturally occurring phytochemicals and zoochemicals and are the quintessential functional foods. If you consume other, packaged functional foods, take care not to overconsume any one compound. Seek out an RDN for sound nutrition advice on whether you would benefit from added functional foods, and, if so, how to balance them in your diet.

LO 2.6 **The Take-Home Message** Functional foods can be part of, but are not substitutes, for a well-balanced healthy diet.

Functional Foods and Cholesterol

Andy is a 45-year-old computer programmer who has just been told by his doctor that he has a high blood cholesterol level, which puts him at risk for heart disease. His diet of skipping breakfast, and having a cheeseburger for lunch and pizza for dinner has finally caught up with him.

To make matters worse, an elevated blood cholesterol is a family trait. Both his grandfather and father are taking doctor-prescribed medication to lower their blood cholesterol levels. Whereas his doctor wants him to take the same medication on a regular basis, Andy wants to break from this family tradition and look to his diet to help lower his cholesterol level in a natural way. He read about functional foods on the Internet and wants to try to lower his blood cholesterol level by adding these foods to his diet in lieu of taking medication.

Andy is not alone in his desire to turn to functional foods to help him improve his health. In one survey of 1,000-plus American adults, almost 90 percent of those surveyed believe that certain foods have health benefits beyond just providing basic nutrients.[19] Globally, it is estimated that the functional food and drink market will reach $130 billion by 2015.[20] Rising health care costs, the increasing age of the population, and the obesity epidemic are some of the factors driving this increased interest in functional foods.[21]

Functional foods are being used by some health care professionals to thwart patients' chronic diseases, and in some situations, as an economical way to treat a disease. Table 2.9 provides some examples of how functional foods could help individuals improve their health.

Think About It

Name three dietary changes that Andy could make that may help him lower his high blood cholesterol levels.

Will Posting Nutritional Content in Restaurants Have a Positive Impact on the Obesity Epidemic?

The Patient Protection and Affordable Care Act of 2010, also known as "Obamacare," has a provision that forces restaurants with more than 20 locations to disclose calories on the menu board and in written form by the end of 2013.[1] The idea behind this provision is that if people know what is in a food, they will make healthier choices. Is this true? Will posting this information make a dent in the obesity epidemic? Take a close look at the arguments for both sides and see what you think.

yes

- In 2009, a Healthy Eating Research review found that menu labeling reduces intentions to order high-calorie items.[2]

- Several studies reveal that people generally underestimate the calories and fat content in restaurant menu items.[3] If the nutrition information is provided, they will be able to adjust their choices accordingly.

- The Act requires a short statement about daily caloric intake, similar to that on the Nutrition Facts label, that helps consumers understand the calorie information within the context of a total daily diet.[4] Based on that information, they will be able choose a selection with an appropriate amount of calories.

- Having to post nutrition information may encourage restaurant owners to provide and promote healthier fare, as they seek to attract customers.[5]

- Some early studies show that posting caloric content and daily recommended intake does impact the amount of calories purchased.[6] A 2011 study from Stanford found that consumers purchased 6 percent fewer calories per transaction with menu labeling.[7]

no

- Most of the people who read and follow nutrition labels already do so as part of a healthy lifestyle.

- Posting nutritional content has had mixed results with Nutrition Facts labels in supermarkets. One analysis by the USDA's Economic Research Service found that Nutrition Facts label use was associated with higher fiber and iron intake, but not with reduced intake of calories, saturated fat, or cholesterol.[8]

- Surveys conducted about restaurant food choices show mixed results when people are given nutritional information. Some people make the healthier choice, and some don't depending on other factors, such as interest in losing weight.[9]

- A small study from Drexel University points out that while some restaurants add healthy choices to their menus, they also add unhealthy choices, which negates the positive change.[10]

- The groups of people impacted by menu labeling are already lean, already use nutrition labels to make healthy choices, and are, as a result, not part of the obesity epidemic.

what do you think?

1. Do you think that posting nutritional information will solve our obesity epidemic? **2.** Does reading nutritional information override the compulsion to order something unhealthy? **3.** How do you decide what to order in a restaurant?

LO 2.1 Healthful Eating Is Based on Key Principles

A healthy diet includes the key principles of balance, variety, and moderation of nutrient-dense foods. The Dietary Reference Intakes (DRIs), *Dietary Guidelines for Americans*, MyPlate, and the Nutrition Facts panel on food labels are all tools that can help you plan a healthy diet.

LO 2.2 The Dietary Reference Intakes Are Reference Values for Each Nutrient

The DRIs are specific reference values, based on your age and gender, for the essential nutrients you need daily. The DRIs are designed to prevent nutrient deficiencies, maintain good health, prevent chronic diseases, and avoid unhealthy excesses. The DRIs consist of the Estimated Average Requirement, Recommended Dietary Allowance, Adequate Intake, Tolerable Upper Intake Level, and the Acceptable Macronutrient Distribution Ranges.

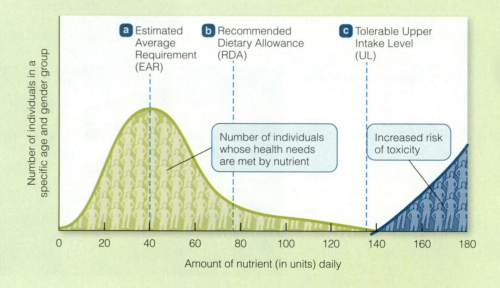

LO 2.3 The *Dietary Guidelines for Americans* Are Recommendations to Lower Risk of Disease

The *Dietary Guidelines for Americans* are the current nutrition and physical activity recommendations for Americans aged 2 and older. These guidelines are designed to help individuals improve their diet to lower their risk of chronic diseases and conditions such as diabetes mellitus, heart disease, certain cancers, high blood pressure, high blood cholesterol levels, and, most importantly, obesity.

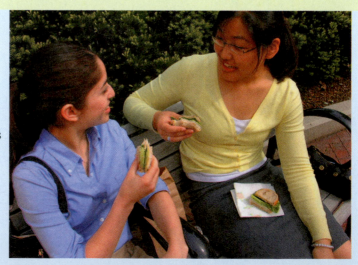

LO 2.4 MyPlate Is a Food Guidance System

MyPlate is the USDA's latest tool that visually represents the five food groups and many of the recommendations in the *Dietary Guidelines for Americans*. Together MyPlate and ChooseMyPlate.gov help you meet your daily DRIs and the recommendations for the number of servings that you should eat every day from each food group based on your calorie needs. The new recommendations emphasize daily physical activity, proportionality among the food groups, and variety within the food groups, as well as moderation when consuming foods with unhealthy solid fats and added sugars. ChooseMyPlate.gov provides a personalized eating plan based on your needs and encourages improvements in your diet and lifestyle choices to improve your health.

LO 2.6 Functional Foods Have Additional Health Benefits

Functional foods have been shown to have a positive effect on health beyond providing basic nutrients. Some foods are deliberately enhanced with compounds and marketed as functional foods. Functional foods can be used as part of a healthy, well-balanced diet, not in place of one.

LO 2.5 Food Labels Provide Nutrient Content Information

The FDA regulates all packaged foods to ensure that they are accurately labeled. The Nutrition Facts panel on the food label must list the serving size of the food. It must also show the corresponding amount of calories, fat, saturated fat, *trans* fat, cholesterol, sodium, sugars, protein, vitamins A and C, calcium, and iron that are contained in a serving of the food. Other nutrients can be listed by the manufacturer voluntarily. If a food product makes a claim about a nutrient, that nutrient must be listed in the Nutrition Facts panel. The food label helps you make healthy food choices.

GRANOLA

Nutrition Facts
8 servings per container

Serving size	2/3 cup (55g)

Amount per 2/3 cup

Calories 230

% DV*	
12%	**Total Fat** 8g
5%	**Saturated Fat** 1g
	Trans **Fat** 0g
0%	**Cholesterol** 0mg
7%	**Sodium** 160mg
12%	**Total Carbs** 37g
14%	Dietary Fiber 4g
	Sugars 1g
	Added Sugars 0g
	Protein 3g
10%	**Vitamin D** 2mcg
20%	**Calcium** 260mg
45%	**Iron** 8mg
5%	**Potassium** 235mg

* Footnote on Daily Values (DV) and calories reference to be inserted here.

VISUAL Chapter Summary

Check Your Understanding

LO 2.1 1. Healthy eating involves the following three principles:
- a. balance, portion control, and variety.
- b. variety, moderation, and portion control.
- c. balance, moderation, and variety.
- d. better nutrition, portion control, and moderation.

LO 2.2 2. The Dietary Reference Intakes (DRIs) are reference values for nutrients and are designed to
- a. only prevent nutritional deficiency.
- b. provide a ballpark range of your nutrient needs.
- c. prevent nutritional deficiencies by meeting your nutrient needs as well as prevent the consumption of excessive and dangerous amounts of nutrients.
- d. outline the health benefits of specific nutrients.

LO 2.2 3. The Estimated Average Requirement (EAR) is
- a. the estimated amount of a nutrient that you should consume daily to be healthy.
- b. the amount of a nutrient that meets the average needs of 50 percent of individuals in a specific age and gender group.

- c. the amount of a nutrient that meets the average needs of 100 percent of individuals in a specific age and gender group.
- d. the maximum safe amount of a nutrient that you should consume daily.

LO 2.3 4. The *Dietary Guidelines for Americans* recommend that you
- a. maintain calorie balance over time and sustain a healthy weight.
- b. stop smoking and walk daily.
- c. sleep eight hours a night and jog every other day.
- d. consume adequate nutrients within your calorie needs and stop smoking.

LO 2.3 5. The *Dietary Guidelines for Americans* is updated every
- a. 2 years.
- b. 3 years.
- c. 4 years.
- d. 5 years.

LO 2.4 6. A three-ounce serving of cooked chicken is approximately the size of
- a. a 5-year-old's palm.
- b. your adult brother's palm.
- c. your adult sister's palm.
- d. your great-uncle's palm.

LO 2.4 7. Which of the following foods is most nutrient dense?
- a. an orange ice pop
- b. an orange
- c. orange-flavored punch
- d. orange sherbet

LO 2.5 8. By law, which of the following MUST be listed on the food label?
- a. calories, fat, and magnesium
- b. fat, saturated fat, and vitamin E
- c. calories, fat, and saturated fat
- d. calories, sodium, and vitamin B_{12}

LO 2.5 9. The yogurt that you enjoy as a morning snack has a label stating that a serving provides 30 percent of the Daily Value for calcium. A serving of this yogurt is considered
- a. low in calcium.
- b. high in calcium.
- c. an insignificant source of calcium.
- d. a good source of both calcium and vitamin D.

LO 2.6 10. Oatmeal is a functional food. It contains a soluble fiber that can help lower your
- a. blood pressure.
- b. red blood cells.
- c. pulse.
- d. blood cholesterol.

Answers

1. (c) A healthy, nutritious diet encompasses three key principles: balance, moderation, and variety. Portion control is important, as it helps keep portions moderate so that a diet can have variety and balance.
2. (c) The DRIs tell you the amount of nutrients you need to prevent deficiencies, maintain good health, and avoid toxicity.
3. (b) The EAR is the amount of a nutrient that would meet the needs of half of the individuals in a specific age and gender group. The EAR is used to obtain the Recommended Dietary Allowance, which is the amount of a nutrient that you should be consuming daily to maintain good health. The Tolerable Upper Intake Level is the maximum amount of a nutrient that you can consume on a regular basis that is unlikely to cause harm.
4. (a) The *Dietary Guidelines for Americans* recommend that you maintain calorie balance over time and sustain a healthy weight. Though the *Dietary Guidelines* do not specifically address stopping smoking, this is a habit worth kicking. Walking or jogging daily are wonderful ways to be physically active. Sleeping eight hours a night isn't mentioned in the *Dietary Guidelines* but is another terrific lifestyle habit.
5. (d) The *Dietary Guidelines for Americans* are updated every 5 years.
6. (c) A three-ounce serving of cooked chicken (or meat and fish, for that matter) is approximately the size of an adult woman's palm.
7. (b) While an orange ice pop and orange sherbet may be refreshing treats on a hot day, the orange is by far the most nutrient-dense food among the choices because it provides the most nutrients for the fewest calories. The orange-flavored punch is a sugary drink with orange flavoring.
8. (c) The Nutrition Facts panel on the package must contain the calories, fat, and saturated fat per serving. Vitamins E and B_{12}, and magnesium do not have to be listed unless they have been added to the food and/or the product makes a claim about them on the label.
9. (b) If you consume 20 percent or more of the Daily Value for a nutrient, it is considered "high" in that nutrient. If a nutrient provides 5 percent or less of the Daily Value, it is considered "low" in that nutrient. This label doesn't make any reference to the vitamin D content of the serving of yogurt.
10. (d) Functional foods go beyond providing basic nutrients and also provide other health benefits. Oats contain the soluble fiber beta-glucan, which has been shown to help reduce blood cholesterol levels. Because of this, oatmeal is considered a functional food.

Web Resources

- For more tips and resources for MyPlate, visit www.ChooseMyPlate.gov
- For more on dietary guidelines, nutrition needs across the life span, and other nutrition topics, visit USDA's Food and Nutrition Information Center at http://fnic.nal.usda.gov
- For more on food labels, visit www.fda.gov

1. **False.** Because consuming too much of some essential nutrients can be harmful, the Tolerable Upper Intake Level (UL) of the DRIs was established for many nutrients. To learn more, turn to page 36.
2. **False.** Proteins should comprise only 10 to 25 percent of your daily calories. To find out why, turn to page 36.
3. **True.** The *Dietary Guidelines* are intended for those who are 2 years of age and older. To learn more, turn to page 38.
4. **False.** Solid fats are less nutrient dense, so should be reduced in your diet. Turn to page 41 to find out the sources of solid fats that you may be consuming.
5. **False.** Oils are not considered a food group, but you should add some daily for good health. Turn to page 42 to find out more.
6. **False.** The good news is that your nutrient needs are averaged over several days or a week of eating, so your plate doesn't have to perfectly match MyPlate daily. Turn to page 45 to learn how to do this.
7. **True.** The FDA requires a food label on all packaged food items, and specific information must be included. To find out exactly what must be disclosed on the food label, turn to page 49.
8. **False.** A nutrient claim uses descriptive terms to make a claim about the amount of a nutrient a serving of food contains (or doesn't contain). To find out what those terms are, turn to page 54.
9. **True.** However, more than one type of health claim is allowed on a label. Turn to page 56 to learn about the types of claims that food manufacturers may use.
10. **False.** Eating functional foods can have numerous health benefits, but they are not a magic potion. Find out which foods are functional foods, and why they are beneficial, on page 60.

3
The Basics of Digestion

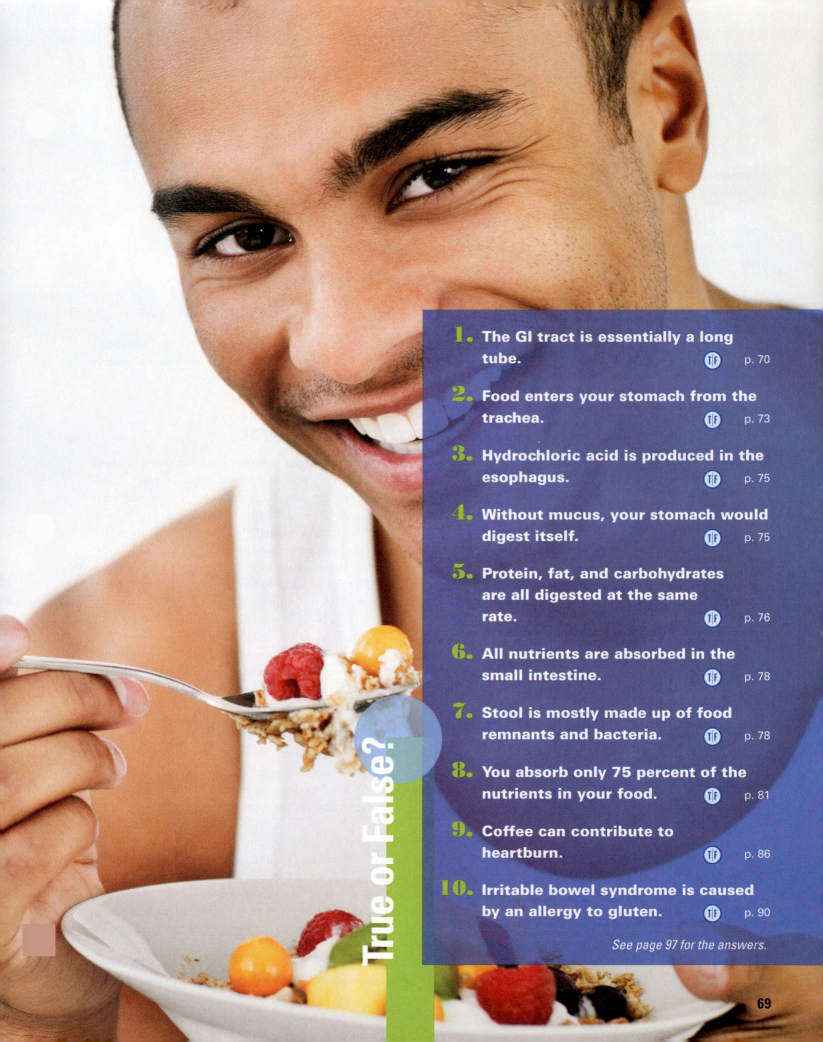

True or False?

1. The GI tract is essentially a long tube.   T|F   p. 70

2. Food enters your stomach from the trachea.   T|F   p. 73

3. Hydrochloric acid is produced in the esophagus.   T|F   p. 75

4. Without mucus, your stomach would digest itself.   T|F   p. 75

5. Protein, fat, and carbohydrates are all digested at the same rate.   T|F   p. 76

6. All nutrients are absorbed in the small intestine.   T|F   p. 78

7. Stool is mostly made up of food remnants and bacteria.   T|F   p. 78

8. You absorb only 75 percent of the nutrients in your food.   T|F   p. 81

9. Coffee can contribute to heartburn.   T|F   p. 86

10. Irritable bowel syndrome is caused by an allergy to gluten.   T|F   p. 90

See page 97 for the answers.

After reading this chapter, you will be able to:

LO 3.1 Define digestion and the processes involved in preparing food for absorption.

LO 3.2 Describe the organs involved in digestion and their primary functions.

LO 3.3 Explain the function of enzymes, hormones, and bile in digestion, including their primary action and their source of origin.

LO 3.4 Describe the process of absorption.

LO 3.5 Explain how the circulatory and lymphatic systems transport absorbed nutrients throughout the body.

LO 3.6 Describe the role of the nervous system and the endocrine system in keeping your body nourished.

LO 3.7 Describe the symptoms and causes of the most common digestive disorders.

Even before you take your first bite of food, the process of digestion begins. Just the smell of warm bread fresh out of the oven or the sight of home-made apple pie stimulates saliva to be released in the mouth. The secretion of saliva and other digestive juices sets in motion a cascade of events that prepares the body to digest your favorite foods. In this chapter you will explore the processes included in digestion and absorption, the organs involved, and the other biological mechanisms that regulate how you process the foods you enjoy. We'll also discuss the causes and treatments of some common gastrointestinal conditions and disorders.

What Is Digestion and Why Is It Important?

LO 3.1 Define digestion and the processes involved in preparing food for absorption.

The simple definition of digestion is the breaking down of foods into absorbable components in the **gastrointestinal (GI) tract**. Through a multistep **digestive process**, food is softened with moisture and heat, and then broken down into smaller particles by chewing and exposure to enzymes.

Digestion Occurs in the GI Tract

The GI tract consists of the mouth, esophagus, stomach, small intestine, and large intestine. Outside the GI tract are *accessory organs*—the pancreas, liver, and gallbladder—that aid in digestion by secreting digestive juices through ducts into the small intestine. The main roles of the organs of the GI tract are to (1) break food down into its smallest components; (2) absorb the nutrients; and (3) prevent microorganisms or other harmful compounds consumed with food from entering the tissues of the body.[1]

The GI tract is a muscular tube that coils and twists, beginning with the mouth and ending with the anus. The GI tract is nearly 30 feet long in a cadaver; it is significantly shorter in a living person because of muscle tone.[2] Stretched vertically, the GI tract would be about as high as a two-story building. The many circular folds, grooves, and projections in the stomach and intestines provide an extensive surface area over which absorption can occur. The cells lining your GI tract have a very brief life span. They function for three to five days and then they are shed into the **lumen** (interior of the intestinal tract) and are replaced with new, healthy cells.

Digestion Is Mechanical and Chemical

There are two forms of digestion: mechanical and chemical. **Mechanical digestion** involves chewing, grinding, and breaking food apart and then moving it through, the GI tract. **Chemical digestion** involves digestive juices and enzymes breaking down food into absorbable nutrients that are small enough to enter the cells of the GI tract, blood, or lymph tissue.

Both mechanical and chemical digestion occur in various organs throughout the GI tract. After food has been chewed and ground up in the mouth, mechanical digestion continues with wavelike actions of the muscles throughout the GI tract, called peristalsis, segmentation, and pendular movement. The muscular activity and rhythmic contractions, or **peristalsis** (**Figure 3.1**), occurs throughout the GI tract and helps mix food with digestive secretions and propel the mixture from the esophagus through the large intestine.

Segmentation is a "sloshing" motion that thoroughly mixes food with chemical secretions in the small intestine. Segmentation is different from peristalsis in that food is shifted back and forth along the small intestine to increase the time food comes into contact with the intestinal walls. **Pendular movement** is a constrictive wave that involves both forward and reverse movements and enhances nutrient absorption in the small intestine. Together, these three actions move chyme at a rate of 1 centimeter per minute.[3] Depending on the amount of food and the type of food consumed, the contact time in the small intestine is about 3 to 6 hours.[4]

The process of chemical breakdown can be interrupted. For example, the weight-loss drug orlistat, sold over the counter as Alli, interferes with the chemical digestion of fat (see the Nutrition in the Real World feature "Tinkering with Your Body's Digestive Process" on page 72).

Before we examine the individual roles of the organs, take a look at **Figure 3.2** and refresh your memory of how organs are built from cells and tissues and how they work together in various body systems. Understanding how cells build tissues will help you understand how digestion and absorption happen in the body.

LO 3.1 **The Take-Home Message** Digestion is a multistep process that takes place in the GI tract. Digestion is comprised of mechanical and chemical processes that break food into smaller units until it can be absorbed for use by the body. Food is propelled along the GI tract by peristalsis. Segmentation and pendular movement move chyme back and forth to allow mixing with the secretions of the small intestine.

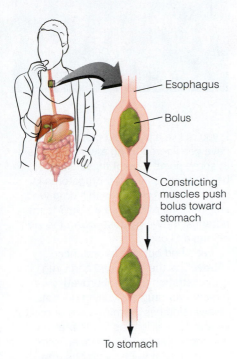

Figure 3.1 **Peristalsis**
Muscles around the organs of the GI tract constrict in a wavelike manner to help move food along.

a. Cells are the basic building blocks of life. All vital processes take place within cells.

Cells

b. Cells of similar structure and function combine to form tissues.

Tissue

c. Tissues combine to form organs, which perform specialized functions.

Organ

d. Organs work together in organ systems, such as the digestive system.

Organ system

Figure 3.2 **From Cells to Organs and Organ Systems**

gastrointestinal (GI) tract Body area containing the organs of the digestive tract. It extends from the mouth to the anus.

digestive process The breakdown of foods into absorbable components using mechanical and chemical means.

lumen The interior of the digestive tract, through which food passes.

mechanical digestion Breaking food down through chewing and grinding, or moving it through the GI tract with peristalsis.

chemical digestion Breaking down food with enzymes or digestive juices.

peristalsis The forward, rhythmic motion that moves food through the digestive system. Peristalsis is a form of mechanical digestion because it influences motion, but it does not add chemical secretions.

segmentation A "sloshing" motion that thoroughly mixes chyme with the chemical secretions of the intestine.

pendular movement A constrictive wave that involves both forward and reverse movements of chyme and enhances nutrient absorption.

nutrition
IN THE Real World

Tinkering with Your Body's Digestive Process

If you're like a lot of people, you may have considered using a weight-loss aid at some point. One of those aids, Alli, has popped up in many drugstores in recent years. How does this drug work, and will it help you lose weight? Is the potential for weight loss worth the side effects and costs?

Let's find out. Alli (pronounced "AL-eye") is the first Food and Drug Administration (FDA)–approved, over-the-counter drug containing orlistat. This version has 60 milligrams of orlistat versus 120 milligrams in the prescription form, Xenical. When taken with a meal, orlistat helps prevent some dietary fat from being absorbed into your body. Orlistat works its magic by preventing lipase, the enzyme secreted from the pancreas, from breaking down

Alli, the nonprescription version of the drug orlistat, was approved by the FDA for sale over the counter in 2007.

The drug orlistat prevents some of the fat in foods from being absorbed. This isn't a free ticket to eat a lot of fat-laden foods like pizza, however. Any fat that is consumed but not absorbed will be passed out of the body, potentially causing some unpleasant side effects.

dietary fat in the small intestines. If the fat isn't broken down, your body can't absorb it, and it will pass through the GI tract and be eliminated in stool. Alli blocks the absorption of about 25 percent of the fat at a meal. If you are taking Alli and eat a slice of pepperoni pizza containing 189 calories from fat for lunch, you will only absorb about 140 of them. Because fat—a hefty source of calories—isn't absorbed by your body, your body can end up with significantly fewer calories to potentially store as body fat.

Unfortunately, because this unabsorbed fat has to be eliminated from your body, there may be some not-so-pleasant side effects, including oily spotting, gas with discharge, the

feeling of having to go to the bathroom immediately, fatty/oily stools, and frequent bowel movements. Interestingly, because these side effects are so unpleasant, they may actually help an individual adhere to a well-balanced, low-fat diet (approximately 30 percent of calories from fat) when taking the drug. Orlistat taken with a very high-fat meal will make these side effects more pronounced.

Orlistat also reduces the absorption of some fat-soluble vitamins as well as beta-carotene. Consequently, individuals taking the drug are advised to take a supplement that contains the fat-soluble vitamins A, D, E, and K and the antioxidant beta-carotene.

According to the FDA, Alli is indicated for obese individuals or for people who are overweight and have other risk factors such as diabetes, high cholesterol, and elevated blood pressure. However, taking the drug won't let you off the hook when it comes to managing your weight. If you replace the unabsorbed fat calories with excess nonfat calories, such as from sweets, pretzels, and soda, or with hefty snacks between meals, you'll end up getting nowhere fast. There is also a cost factor. A month's supply of Alli costs approximately $70.

There isn't any quick fix when it comes to weight loss. Although Alli has been approved to help those who are obese, in the long term, eating healthfully, changing eating habits and behaviors, and exercising regularly are still, and always will be, the cornerstones and the *least expensive* methods of long-term weight management—for everyone.

What Are the Organs of the GI Tract and Why Are They Important?

LO 3.2 Describe the organs involved in digestion and their primary functions.

Figure 3.3 on page 74 illustrates the organs of the GI tract and the unique and crucial role each organ plays in digestion. Let's begin with your first bite and follow the process of digestion through the entire GI tract.

Digestion Begins in the Mouth

Both mechanical and chemical digestion begins in the mouth. Glands in your mouth release **saliva**, a watery fluid that will help soften the food you are about to eat. Once you take a bite and begin to chew, your teeth, powered by your jaw muscles, cut and grind the food into smaller pieces and with your tongue mix it with saliva. Saliva helps dissolve small food particles and allows you to comfortably swallow dry food. In addition to water, saliva contains electrolytes, a few enzymes (including amylase, which begins to break down carbohydrate), and **mucus**. The mucus helps lubricate the food, helps it stick together, and protects the inside of the mouth. Once food has been adequately chewed, it's pushed to the back of the mouth and through the **pharynx** by the tongue.

> You produce 1 to 1.5 liters of saliva every day.

Swallowing seems simple because we do it hundreds of times a day, but it is actually a complicated process. Pushing chewed food to the pharynx is a voluntary act—that is, you control it. Once the food mass (now called a **bolus**) enters the pharynx, the swallowing reflex kicks in, and you no longer control the action.

You have probably experienced an episode of "swallowing gone wrong" in which you've accidentally propelled food down the wrong pipe. When this happens (and you find yourself in a coughing fit trying to expel the item), it is because the

The smell, sight, and taste of food, such as freshly baked bread, triggers the release of saliva and other digestive juices.

Digestion converts whole foods into individual nutrients that can be used by the body's cells.

saliva Watery fluid secreted by the salivary glands in the mouth. Saliva moistens food and makes it easier to swallow.

mucus Viscous, slippery secretions found in saliva and other digestive juices.

pharynx The throat. Passageway for the respiratory (air) and digestive (food and beverages) tracts.

bolus Chewed mass of food.

The human digestive system consists of the organs of the gastrointestinal (GI) tract and associated accessory organs. The processing of food in the GI tract involves ingestion, mechanical digestion, chemical digestion, propulsion, absorption, and elimination.

FOCUS FIGURE WALKTHROUGH

 Scan this QR code with your mobile device for a video tour of this figure by Joan Salge Blake.

ORGANS OF THE GI TRACT

MOUTH

Ingestion Food enters the GI tract via the mouth.

Mechanical digestion Chewing tears and shreds food, and mixes it with saliva, forming a bolus.

Chemical digestion Carbohydrate enzymes secreted by the salivary glands begin carbohydrate breakdown.

PHARYNX AND ESOPHAGUS

Propulsion Swallowing and peristalsis move the bolus from mouth to stomach.

STOMACH

Mechanical digestion Movements mix and churn the bolus with acid, enzymes, and gastric fluid into a liquid called chyme.

Chemical digestion Stomach enzymes begin the digestion of proteins.

Absorption A few fat-soluble substances are absorbed through the stomach wall.

SMALL INTESTINE

Mechanical digestion and **Propulsion** Segmentation mixes chyme with digestive juices; peristaltic waves move it along tract.

Chemical digestion Digestive enzymes from pancreas and small intestine digest most classes of food.

Absorption Nutrients are absorbed into blood and lymph through the intestinal cells.

LARGE INTESTINE

Chemical digestion Some remaining food residues are digested by bacteria.

Absorption Reabsorbs salts, water, and some vitamins.

Propulsion Compacts waste into feces.

RECTUM

Elimination Temporarily stores stool before voluntary release through the anus.

ACCESSORY ORGANS

Salivary glands

LIVER
Produces bile to digest fats.

GALLBLADDER
Stores bile before release into the small intestine through the bile duct.

PANCREAS
Produces digestive enzymes and bicarbonate ions that are released into the small intestine via the pancreatic duct.

normal mechanism that protects your trachea (or windpipe) didn't engage properly. Usually, a small flap called the **epiglottis** closes off your trachea during swallowing (**Figure 3.4**). The epiglottis ensures that food and drink go down the correct pipe—the **esophagus**—rather than down the trachea. When the epiglottis doesn't work properly, food can get lodged in the trachea, which can potentially result in choking.

Once swallowed, a bolus of food is pushed down your esophagus by *peristalsis* (refer again to Figure 3.1). When the bolus of food reaches the stomach, the lower part of the esophagus relaxes, allowing the bolus to enter the stomach. Solid or partially chewed food passes through the esophagus in about 8 seconds. Soft food and liquids pass through in about 1 to 2 seconds.[5]

The esophagus narrows at the bottom (just above the stomach) and ends at a sphincter, or ring of muscle, called the **gastroesophageal sphincter**. Under normal conditions, when we swallow food, this sphincter relaxes and allows food to pass into the stomach. The stomach also relaxes to comfortably receive the food.[6] After food enters the stomach, the sphincter should close. If it doesn't, contents may flow back into the esophagus and irritate its lining. This is called *heartburn* because it may cause a burning sensation in the middle of the chest.

Chronic heartburn and the reflux of stomach acids are symptoms of gastroesophageal reflux disease (GERD). The condition, GERD, and the treatment for it will be discussed later in this chapter.

The Stomach Stores, Mixes, and Prepares Food for Digestion

[T|F] The **stomach** is a muscular organ that continues mechanical digestion by churning and contracting to mix food with digestive juices (**Figure 3.5**). The food is continuously mixed for several hours. The stomach also has a role in chemical digestion in that it produces powerful digestive secretions. These secretions include **hydrochloric acid (HCl)**, various enzymes, mucus, intrinsic factor (needed for vitamin B_{12} absorption), and the stomach hormone, **gastrin**. The swallowed bolus of food soon becomes **chyme**, a semiliquid substance that contains digestive secretions plus the original food. The stomach can expand to hold 2 to 4 liters of chyme.

[T|F] Hydrochloric acid has important digestive functions. You might think that such a strong chemical would digest the stomach itself, but mucus produced in the stomach acts as a barrier between the HCl and the stomach lining, protecting the

Bolus
Tongue
Epiglottis (up)
Trachea (open)
Esophagus

Bolus
Tongue
Epiglottis (down)
Trachea (closed)
Esophagus

Figure 3.4 The Epiglottis
The epiglottis prevents food from entering the trachea when you swallow.

epiglottis Flap of tissue that protects the trachea while swallowing.

esophagus Tube that extends from the throat to the stomach.

gastroesophageal sphincter A circular band of muscle between the esophagus and the stomach that opens and closes to allow food to enter the stomach.

stomach Digestive organ that holds food after it's moved down the esophagus and before it is propelled into the small intestine.

hydrochloric acid (HCl) A powerful acid made in the stomach that has digestive functions. It also helps to kill microorganisms and lowers the pH in the stomach.

gastrin A digestive hormone produced in the stomach that stimulates digestive activities and increases motility and emptying.

chyme The semiliquid, partially digested food mass that leaves the stomach and enters the small intestine.

Stomach
Esophagus
Lower esophageal sphincter
Small intestine
Inner stomach walls

Figure 3.5 Anatomy of the Stomach

lining from irritation or damage. Hydrochloric acid activates enzymes, including the protein-digesting enzyme **pepsin**, enhances the absorption of minerals, breaks down the connective tissue in meat, and destroys some ingested microorganisms.[7]

Have you ever noticed that some foods keep you feeling full longer than others? (T)(F) Foods high in refined carbohydrates exit the stomach faster, and therefore make you feel less full, than foods high in protein, fat, or fiber. Most liquids, carbohydrates, and low-fiber foods require minimal digestive activity, are easier to absorb, and have less surface area due to low fiber content.

Similarly, low-calorie foods exit the stomach faster than concentrated, high-calorie foods. This is because low-calorie foods frequently require minimal digestion. For example, a lightly sweetened cup of tea, a lower calorie beverage, requires less digestion than a higher-calorie, nutrient-dense milkshake. Digesting the tea involves only the breakdown of the sugar. In contrast, digesting the milkshake involves breaking down fat, protein, and carbohydrates.

As digestion continues, peristaltic contractions push the chyme toward the lower part of the stomach. As the chyme accumulates near the **pyloric sphincter**, the muscular sphincter relaxes and the chyme gradually enters the small intestine. Approximately 1 to 5 milliliters (1 teaspoon) of chyme are released into the small intestine every 30 seconds during digestion.[8] The pyloric sphincter prevents chyme from exiting the stomach too soon, and it prevents intestinal contents from returning to the stomach.

Most Digestion and Absorption Occurs in the Small Intestine

The **small intestine** is a long, narrow, coiled chamber in the abdominal cavity. The "small" in "small intestine" refers to its diameter, not its length, which accounts for about 20 feet of the GI tract. It consists of three segments—duodenum, jejunum, and ileum—and extends from the pyloric sphincter to the beginning of the large intestine. The first segment, the duodenum, is the shortest portion of the small intestine, followed by the jejunum, and finally the longest segment, called the ileum. While digestion continues along the small intestine, the duodenum is the primary site for food digestion within the human body.

> There are more microorganisms than human cells in your body, and many of them are located in your intestines.

The remarkable surface area (enough to cover a tennis court) of the folds and crevices of the small intestine lining allows for a continuous, efficient absorption of virtually all digested nutrients (**Figure 3.6**). The small intestine has tremendous surface area compared with the stomach, and its digestive secretions do most of the work when it comes to breaking down food into absorbable nutrients. The jejunum and ileum segments of the small intestine are where most of the absorption of digested nutrients takes place.

The interior of the small intestine is covered with thousands of small projections called **villi**. The villi increase the surface area of the small intestine's lining and mix the partially digested chyme with the intestinal secretions. Each individual villus is adjacent to a cluster of blood capillaries, lymph vessels, and nerve fibers.

The villi are covered by even smaller projections called **microvilli**, which provide additional surface area through which nutrients are absorbed into the blood capillaries and lymph vessels. The lining of the small intestine is also arranged in unique, circular folds, which further increase the absorptive surface area. The circular folds cause the chyme to spiral forward through the small intestine, rather than merely move in a straight line.

pepsin A digestive enzyme produced in the stomach that breaks down protein.

pyloric sphincter Sphincter in the bottom of the stomach that separates the pylorus from the duodenum of the small intestine.

small intestine Comprised of the duodenum, jejunum, and ileum, the small intestine is the longest part of the GI tract. Most of the digestion and absorption of food occurs in the small intestine.

villi Projections on the walls of the small intestine that increase the surface area over which nutrients can be absorbed.

microvilli Tiny projections on the villi in the small intestine that increase the surface area even more.

FOCUS FIGURE WALKTHROUGH

Scan this QR code with your mobile device for a video tour of this figure by Joan Salge Blake.

The small intestine is highly adapted for absorbing nutrients. Its length—about 20 feet—provides a huge surface area, and its wall has three structural features—circular folds, villi, and microvilli—that increase its surface area by a factor of more than 600.

CIRCULAR FOLDS

The lining of the small intestine is heavily folded, resulting in increased surface area for the absorption of nutrients.

Small Intestine

VILLI

The folds are covered with villi, thousands of fingerlike projections that increase the surface area even further. Each villus contains blood and lymph vessels that transport nutrients throughout the body.

Villi

Lymph vessel

Intestinal cell

Blood capillaries

MICROVILLI

The cells on the surface of the villi end in hairlike projections called microvilli that further increase the surface area of the small intestine.

Microvilli

Intestinal cell

The Large Intestine Eliminates Waste and Absorbs Water and Some Nutrients

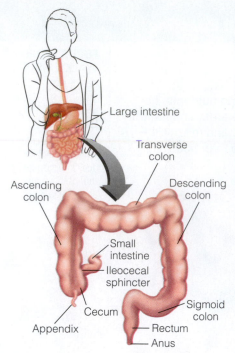

Figure 3.7 Anatomy of the Large Intestine By the time chyme reaches the large intestine, most of its nutrients have been absorbed. However, water and some electrolytes are absorbed in the colon. The final waste products of digestion pass out of the body as stool through the anus.

ileocecal sphincter Gateway between the end of the small intestine and the beginning of the large intestine. The sphincter prevents backflow of fecal contents from the large intestine into the small intestine.

large intestine Final organ of the GI tract. It consists of the cecum, appendix, colon, and rectum.

stool (feces) Waste products that are stored in the large intestine and then excreted from the body. Consists mostly of bacteria, sloughed-off gastrointestinal cells, inorganic matter, water, unabsorbed nutrients, food residue, undigested fibers, fatty acids, mucus, and remnants of digestive fluids.

rectum The lowest part of the large intestine, continuous with the sigmoid colon and the anus.

anus The opening at the end of the rectum where waste is eliminated from the body.

Once the chyme has passed through the small intestine, it comes to the **ileocecal sphincter**, which serves as the gateway to its next digestive destination, the **large intestine**. The primary purpose of the ileocecal sphincter is to prevent backflow of fecal contents from the large intestine into the ileum. In general, this sphincter is quite strong and resists reverse pressure. By the time food enters the large intestine, it has been digested and the majority of the nutrients have been absorbed. But the large intestine serves some important functions, including the absorption of water, production of a few vitamins, absorption of important electrolytes, and the formation and storage of fecal material.[9]

At approximately 5 feet long, the large intestine is one quarter the length of the small intestine, but it has twice the diameter. The structure of the large intestine borders the small intestine on three sides and unlike the small intestine, is not tightly coiled, nor does it secrete or use digestive enzymes. Rather, the chemical digestion that takes place in the large intestine is due to the efforts of bacteria. The large intestine produces mucus that protects the cells and acts as a lubricant for fecal matter. The cells of the large intestine absorb water and electrolytes much more efficiently than do the cells of the small intestine.

There are three segments of the large intestine: the cecum, colon, and rectum (**Figure 3.7**). The cecum is a small, pouchlike area that has the appendix hanging from one end. The middle section, or colon, is the largest portion of the large intestine. (Note that though the terms "colon" and "large intestine" are often used interchangeably, they're not technically the same thing.) The colon includes the ascending, transverse, descending, and sigmoid regions. These regions are relatively long and straight. Most of the vitamin production and absorption of water and electrolytes occur within the first half of the colon. The last half of the colon stores fecal matter.

The colon receives about l liter (about 1 quart) of fluid material each day from the cecum, consisting of water, undigested or unabsorbed food particles, indigestible residue, and bacteria. It slowly and gently mixes these intestinal contents and absorbs the majority of the fluid. The colon gradually produces a semisolid material of fecal matter (**stool,** or **feces**). The intestinal matter passes through the colon within 12 to 24 hours.[10]

Bacteria in the colon play a role in producing some vitamins, including the B vitamin biotin and vitamin K.[11] Bacteria also ferment some of the undigested and unabsorbed dietary carbohydrates into simpler compounds, including methane gas, carbon dioxide, and hydrogen. Similarly, some of the colon's bacteria break down undigested fiber and produce various compounds, including hydrogen and sulfide.

As in the small intestine, the colon moves contents via peristalsis. Peristalsis occurs within the ascending colon, but the waves of contraction are quite slow, which allows the fluids to be absorbed.[12]

The stool is propelled forward until it reaches the **rectum**, the final eight-inch portion of the large intestine, where it is stored. When stool distends the rectum, the action stimulates stretch receptors, which in turn stimulate the defecation reflex. This causes nerve impulses of the rectum to communicate with the rectum's muscles. The end result is relaxation of the internal sphincter of the anus.

The **anus** is connected to the rectum and controlled by two sphincters: an internal and an external sphincter. Under normal conditions, the anal sphincters are closed. Periodically, the anal sphincters will relax, stool will enter the anal canal, and defecation will occur. The final stage of defecation is under our voluntary control and influenced by age, diet, prescription medicines, health, and abdominal muscle tone.

The Liver, Gallbladder, and Pancreas Are Accessory Organs

Although food doesn't pass through the liver, gallbladder, or pancreas during digestion, these three accessory organs are still essential to the process (**Figure 3.8**).

Weighing about three pounds, the **liver** is the largest organ in the body. It is so important that you couldn't survive without it. The liver produces about 500 to 1,000 milliliters (about 2 pints) of bile each day[13] and helps regulate the metabolism of carbohydrates, fats, and protein. The liver also stores several nutrients, including vitamins A, D, and E; the minerals iron and copper; and glycogen, the storage form of glucose. The liver is essential for processing and detoxifying alcohol. You'll learn about each of these functions in more depth in later chapters of this book.

Once bile is formed in the liver, it is collected, drained, and released into the gallbladder to be stored. The **gallbladder** is attached to the liver and stores approximately 30 to 50 milliliters (1 to 2 ounces) of concentrated bile at a time.

The **pancreas** is an organ about the size of your hand that produces hormones, including the two blood glucose–regulating hormones, insulin and glucagon. It also produces digestive enzymes and bicarbonate that are delivered into the small intestine through the pancreatic duct. Bicarbonate neutralizes the acid found in the chyme (raises the pH), creating a neutral environment. This protects certain enzymes that would otherwise become inactivated in an acidic environment.

Figure 3.8 The Accessory Organs
The liver, gallbladder, and pancreas produce digestive secretions that flow into the small intestine through various ducts.

Liver
Gallbladder
Pancreas

LO 3.2 **The Take-Home Message** In the mouth, saliva mixes with food during chewing, moistening it and making it easier to swallow. Swallowed food that has mixed with digestive juices in the stomach becomes chyme. Maximum digestion and the absorption of digested nutrients occur in the small intestine. Undigested residue next enters the large intestine, where additional absorption of water and electrolytes occurs. Eventually, the remnants of digestion reach the anus and exit the body in stool. The liver, gallbladder, and pancreas are important accessory organs. The liver produces bile, which the gallbladder concentrates and stores. The pancreas produces enzymes and hormones.

How Do Hormones, Enzymes, and Bile Aid Digestion?

LO 3.3 Explain the function of enzymes, hormones, and bile in digestion, including their primary action and their source of origin.

The complete digestion of chyme requires chemical secretions, including hormones, enzymes, and bile. Supportive digestive organs such as the pancreas, liver, and gallbladder contribute or concentrate many of these fluids. The stomach and small intestine also produce digestive enzymes. **Table 3.1** summarizes the organs, secretions, and functions that take part in digestion as it proceeds from beginning to end.

Hormones Regulate Digestion

Hormones, released from endocrine glands scattered throughout the lining of the stomach and the small intestine, don't digest food, but regulate the activity of other cells. Eating or not eating stimulates the release of hormones from these glands. For example, when food reaches your stomach, *gastrin* is released to signal the rest of the GI tract to prepare for digestion. Gastrin stimulates the stomach to release HCl,

liver The largest gland of the body. It aids in digestive activity and is responsible for metabolism of nutrients, detoxification of alcohol, and some nutrient storage.

gallbladder A pear-shaped organ located behind the liver. The gallbladder stores bile produced by the liver and secretes the bile through the bile duct into the small intestine.

pancreas Accessory organ of digestion that produces hormones and enzymes. It's connected to the duodenum via the pancreatic duct.

hormones Chemical substances that regulate, initiate, or direct cellular activity.

Table 3.1

Functions of Digestive Secretions

Secretion	Secreted from	Function
Saliva	Glands in the mouth	Moistens food, eases swallowing, contains the enzyme salivary amylase
Mucus	Stomach, small and large intestines	Lubrication and coating of the internal mucosa to protect it from chemical or mechanical damage
Hydrochloric acid (HCl)	Stomach	Activation of enzymes that begin protein digestion
Bile	Liver (stored in the gallbladder)	Emulsifies fat in the small intestine
Bicarbonate	Pancreas	Raises pH and neutralizes stomach acid
Enzymes (amylases, proteases, and lipases)	Stomach, small intestine, pancreas	Chemicals that break down food into nutrient components that can be absorbed
Hormones (gastrin, secretin, cholecystokinin, and ghrelin)	Stomach, small intestine	Chemicals that regulate digestive activity, increase or decrease peristalsis, and stimulate various digestive secretions

increases gastric motility and emptying, and increases the tone of the LES.[14] Gastrin also causes the release of gastric secretions that contain the enzyme gastric lipase. When you haven't eaten, the hormone *ghrelin* is released to stimulate hunger.

The small intestine secretes the hormone *secretin* when acidic chyme enters the duodenum. Secretin in turn stimulates the pancreas to release *bicarbonate ions* to neutralize the HCl present in the chyme. When partially digested protein and fat enter the small intestine, the intestinal cells secrete the hormone *cholecystokinin*. This powerful hormone also stimulates the pancreas to secrete digestive enzymes, controls the pace of digestion, and contributes to meal satisfaction.

Enzymes Drive the Process of Digestion

The process of digestion is driven by a group of proteins called **enzymes**. Digestive enzymes speed up the chemical reactions that break apart food particles into smaller, unbound nutrients that can be easily absorbed. All macronutrients—carbohydrates, fats, and proteins—are broken down by their own specific enzymes without changing or consuming the enzymes in the process. For example, the enzyme *amylase*, secreted in saliva, starts digesting starch, whereas in the stomach, a *protease* or protein-digesting enzyme called *pepsin* and a fat-digesting enzyme called *gastric lipase* begin breaking down protein and a few fats. The pancreas produces the majority of digestive enzymes. These enzymes include *amylase*, which digests carbohydrate; *lipase*, which digests fat; and the precursors to the enzymes *trypsin*, *chymotrypsin*, and *carboxypeptidase*, which digest protein. The enzymes from the pancreas are responsible for the digestion of almost all (90 percent) of ingested fat, about half (50 percent) of all ingested protein, and half (50 percent) of all carbohydrates.[15]

Bile Helps Digest Fat

Bile, the yellowish-green substance made in the liver and stored in the gallbladder, helps digest fat. This dilute liquid consists of water, bile acids (and/or salts), various fats including cholesterol, and pigments. Bile is released from the gallbladder into the small intestine through the bile duct.

Bile breaks down large fat globules into smaller fat droplets much like dishwashing detergent breaks up the grease in a frying pan. This allows the fat-digesting enzymes to make contact with the fat and break it down to be absorbed.

enzymes Substances that produce chemical changes or catalyze chemical reactions.

bile A yellowish-green fluid made in the liver and concentrated and stored in the gallbladder. It helps emulsify fat and prepare it for digestion.

Table 3.2

Organs of Digestion and Their Functions

Organ or Tissue	Function	How They Work Together to Digest a Peanut Butter Sandwich
Mouth	Begins breaking down food into components through chewing	Saliva moistens the sandwich as your teeth grind the food. Amylase begins to break down the carbohydrate in the bread.
Esophagus	Transfers food from the mouth to the stomach	Bolus of sandwich moves through the esophagus to the stomach.
Stomach	Mixes food with digestive juices; breaks down some nutrients into smaller components	The HCl activates pepsin to begin digesting the protein in the sandwich. Gastric lipase starts breaking down the triglycerides in the peanut butter.
Small intestine	Completes digestion of food and absorbs nutrients through its walls	The carbohydrates, proteins, and fat are broken down further with the help of bile and enzymes so they can be absorbed.
Large intestine	Absorbs water and some nutrients; passes waste products out of the body	The fiber in the bread leaves the body in the stool.
Accessory organs	Release enzymes, bile, and bicarbonate ions	
liver		The liver produces the bile and regulates the metabolism of the absorbed nutrients.
gallbladder		The gallbladder releases stored bile into the small intestine to emulsify the fat in the peanut butter sandwich.
pancreas		The pancreas produces bicarbonate ions to neutralize the chyme, and the enzymes amylase, lipase, and protease to digest the sandwich.

Unlike other digestive juices, bile can be reused. From the large intestine, bile is recycled back to the liver through *enterohepatic* (*entero* = intestine, *hepatic* = liver) *circulation*. This recycling allows bile to be reused up to 20 times.

Table 3.2 not only summarizes the organs of the GI tract and their functions but also shows you how these organs work together to digest a peanut butter sandwich. The next several chapters will further illustrate how the specific nutrients in foods that you eat, such as pasta and pizza, travel through your GI tract and are digested, absorbed, and or/eliminated from your body.

LO 3.3 **The Take-Home Message** Hormones regulate digestion by stimulating secretions from the stomach, small intestine, pancreas, and gallbladder. They also control the pace of digestion. Specific digestive enzymes speed up the process that breaks apart food particles without being changed or consumed in the process. Bile breaks large fat globules into smaller fat droplets.

eLearn

Take a Ride through the GI Tract

Want to learn even more about the organs of the GI tract? Visit MasteringNutrition™ and slide through the organs and their functions.

How Are Digested Nutrients Absorbed?

LO 3.4 Describe the process of absorption.

Digestion is the forerunner to **absorption**. Once the nutrients have been completely broken down, they are ready to be used by the cells of the body. In order to reach the cells, however, they have to leave the GI tract and move to the other parts of the body. To accomplish this, nutrients are absorbed through the walls of the intestines and into the body's two transport systems: the circulatory and lymphatic systems. They

absorption The process by which digested nutrients move into the tissues where they can be transported and used by the body's cells.

are then taken to the liver for processing before moving on to their destination. The body is remarkably efficient when it comes to absorbing nutrients. Under normal conditions, you digest and absorb 92 to 97 percent of the nutrients from your food.[16]

Digested Nutrients Are Absorbed by Three Methods

Once digested nutrients reach the small intestine, they are absorbed by three methods: **simple diffusion**, **facilitated diffusion**, or **active transport** (**Figure 3.9**). Another method of absorption, called *endocytosis*, occurs when whole proteins, such as immunoglobulin from breast milk, are absorbed intact.

Simple diffusion is a process in which nutrients are absorbed due to a concentration gradient. When the concentration is greater in the GI tract than inside the intestinal cell, the nutrient is forced across the cell membrane. This simple process doesn't require energy or a special protein carrier to help the nutrient to cross inside the intestinal cell.

Facilitated diffusion is similar to simple diffusion in that nutrients are absorbed from a high to a low concentration and the process does not require energy. But facilitated diffusion does require a specialized protein to carry the nutrients across the cell membrane.

Active transport is different from both simple and facilitated diffusion. In this form of absorption, digested nutrients are absorbed from a low to a high concentration. This process requires both a carrier and energy to shuttle nutrients across the cell membrane.

simple diffusion The process of absorbing nutrients across the intestinal cell membrane from a high concentration to a low concentration.

facilitated diffusion The process of absorbing nutrients across the intestinal cell membrane with the help of a carrier molecule.

active transport The process of absorbing nutrients across the intestinal cell membrane with the help of a carrier molecule and energy.

LO 3.4 **The Take-Home Message** Absorption is the process by which the digested nutrients move into your tissues. You absorb more than 90 percent of the nutrients that you take in from eating food. Absorption occurs by simple diffusion, facilitated diffusion, or active transport.

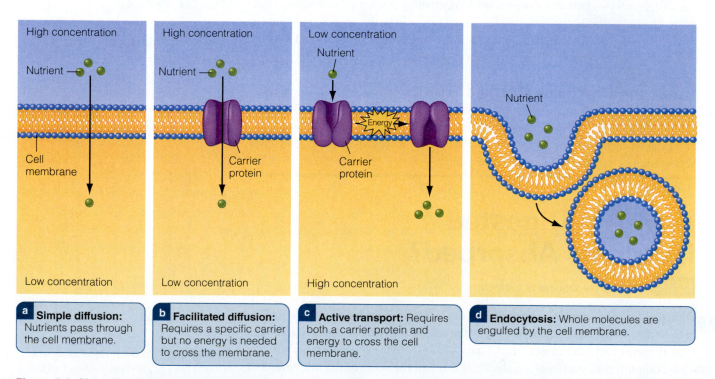

| a **Simple diffusion:** Nutrients pass through the cell membrane. | b **Facilitated diffusion:** Requires a specific carrier but no energy is needed to cross the membrane. | c **Active transport:** Requires both a carrier protein and energy to cross the cell membrane. | d **Endocytosis:** Whole molecules are engulfed by the cell membrane. |

Figure 3.9 Absorption Methods in the Small Intestine

What Happens to Nutrients after They Are Absorbed?

LO 3.5 Explain how the circulatory and lymphatic systems transport absorbed nutrients throughout the body.

Now that you know how the body digests and absorbs the nutrients from foods, you might be wondering what happens to the nutrients once they are absorbed. Once the nutrients are absorbed, they must be transported to the cells before they can be used by the body. Nutrients are transported either through the veins and arteries of the circulatory system or through the lymphatic vessels.

The Circulatory System Distributes Nutrients through Your Blood

Water-soluble nutrients are picked up through the capillary walls in the intestinal villi and are transported to the bloodstream. These nutrients circulate through the bloodstream to the liver. The liver regulates the use of the nutrients depending on your needs. Some of the nutrients may be stored in the liver, while others are released into the circulation and delivered to the cells of your body. The blood is the body's primary transport system, shuttling oxygen, nutrients, hormones, and waste products throughout the body (**Figure 3.10**). Without the circulatory system, nutrients that you eat would not reach your cells. Equally important, the blood removes excess water and waste products from the cells and brings these substances to the kidneys for excretion.

Fat-soluble nutrients transported in the lymph move through the thoracic duct into the blood through the left subclavian vein

Heart

Liver

Hepatic portal vein

Blood

Lymph

Intestinal villus

Water-soluble nutrients

Fat-soluble nutrients

Blood capillaries

Lymph vessel

Figure 3.10 The Circulatory and Lymphatic Systems
Blood and lymph are fluids that circulate throughout the body. They both distribute nutrients to cells and blood also picks up waste products for excretion.

The Lymphatic System Distributes Some Nutrients through Your Lymph Vessels

The lymphatic system is a complex network of capillaries, small vessels, valves, nodes, and ducts that helps maintain the internal fluid environment. Some absorbed nutrients, such as the products of fat digestion, must pass through the lymphatic system before they enter the bloodstream because they are too large to enter the bloodstream directly. Lymph also transports absorbed fat-soluble vitamins from the intestinal tract to your blood. The lymph eventually connects with the blood near the heart.

Your Body Can Store Some Surplus Nutrients

Whereas some nutrients are used immediately for energy and other functions, your body can store other, surplus nutrients to be used when you need them. For example, some excess carbohydrate is stored in your liver and muscles in a form called *glycogen*, to be available when you don't eat, such as between meals. Other excess energy (calories) is stored in fat cells. Some vitamins and minerals can also be stored. For example, storing calcium in your bones will help keep them strong. However, storing excessive amounts of fat-soluble vitamins, such as vitamin A, and some minerals, such as iron, can be toxic.

The Excretory System Passes Waste out of the Body

The excretory system eliminates wastes from the circulatory system. After the cells have gleaned the nutrients and other useful metabolic components they need, waste products accumulate. For example, the breakdown of proteins creates nitrogen-containing waste, such as urea, that must be eliminated. The kidneys allow these waste products to be concentrated in urine and excreted out of your body (**Figure 3.11**). Excess water-soluble vitamins are also excreted in urine. Finally, the kidneys play an important role in helping the body maintain water balance.

LO 3.5 **The Take-Home Message** Absorbed nutrients are transported throughout the bloodstream and lymph systems to be delivered to the cells. Some excess nutrients are stored, while the excretory system helps filter and eliminate waste products from the blood through the urine.

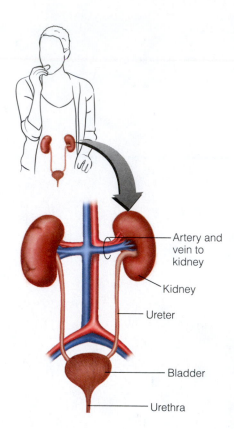

Figure 3.11 The Excretory System
Water and waste products from cells are filtered from your blood in the kidneys and expelled from your body in urine.

Artery and vein to kidney

Kidney

Ureter

Bladder

Urethra

What Other Body Systems Affect Your Use of Nutrients?

LO 3.6 Describe the role of the nervous system and the endocrine system in keeping your body nourished.

The human body is a well-coordinated organism. Each of us eats, drinks, sleeps, and lives a normal existence without too much thought about what we are consuming. We don't have to constantly worry about keeping ourselves nourished, or distributing nutrients to our cells, because numerous body systems are doing this work for us. In addition to the nutrient-related activities of the digestive, circulatory, lymphatic, and excretory systems, the nervous system reminds us to eat, and the endocrine system regulates what happens to the nutrients you absorb.

The Nervous System Stimulates Your Appetite

The main role of the nervous system in keeping you nourished is to let you know when you need to eat and drink and when to stop. Your brain, with the help of hormones, plays a central role in communicating and interpreting the message of hunger and encouraging you to seek food. For example, when your stomach is empty, the hormone ghrelin signals to your brain that you are hungry. If you ignore the signals of hunger or thirst sent by your nervous system, you may experience a headache, dizziness, or weakness. The nervous system helps each of us make daily decisions regarding what to eat, when to eat, where to eat, and, perhaps most important, when to stop eating.

The Endocrine System Releases Hormones That Help Regulate the Use of Absorbed Nutrients

The endocrine system consists of a series of glands, including the pancreas, the pituitary, the thyroid, and the adrenal glands, that release hormones into the bloodstream. The hormones regulate growth, reproduction, metabolism, and the cells' use of absorbed nutrients. For example, the hormones insulin and glucagon help regulate blood levels of glucose. When blood glucose levels get too high, the pancreas releases insulin, which directs the glucose out of the blood and into cells. On the flip side, if blood glucose levels dip too low, the pancreas releases glucagon, which directs the release of the body's stored glucose to increase the levels in blood. We will learn more about the important roles of hormones in future chapters.

LO 3.6 The Take-Home Message In addition to the digestive system, other body systems help us use the nutrients we take in from foods. The nervous system lets us know when we need to eat or drink, the blood and lymph systems deliver absorbed nutrients to cells, and the endocrine system releases hormones that regulate nutrient use in cells.

What Are Some Common Digestive Disorders?

LO 3.7 Describe the symptoms and causes of the most common digestive disorders.

Generally, the digestive tract works just fine. As a matter of fact, it doesn't usually require tinkering or medications to be healthy. But sometimes the digestive tract gets "off track" and the resulting symptoms can quickly catch your attention. Some of the problems are minor, like occasional heartburn or indigestion. Other problems such as ulcers or colon cancer are very serious.

Disorders of the Mouth and Throat

Oral health involves healthy teeth, gums, and supporting tissue. Maintaining a healthy oral environment is important because these tissues are used to bite, chew, taste, speak, smile, swallow, and communicate through facial expressions. Properly nourishing yourself can be difficult if you have chronic oral disease or extensive dental problems. There are many oral diseases, but we will only review some of the most common ones in this section.

Gingivitis causes redness and swelling of the gums and can lead to more serious gum disease and tooth loss.

Gingivitis and Periodontal Disease

In addition to tooth decay, which we'll discuss in depth in Chapter 4, common oral health problems include gingivitis and periodontal disease. Gingivitis is an early form of periodontal disease that involves gum swelling, bleeding, and oral pain. Periodontal disease is an inflammation of the gums that leads to multiple dental diseases. It is caused by infections or by plaque that adheres to the surface of the teeth.[17] Periodontitis results in a gradual loss of teeth as they loosen or partially separate from the gums and jawbone. Even though these conditions are serious, they are treatable with various dental procedures, optimal food choices, and excellent oral hygiene. Other oral health problems include dry mouth, inflamed oral tissue, cold sores, soft tissue ulceration, oral cancers, fungal infections, or various abnormalities of the tongue.

Swallowing Problems

Under some circumstances the ability to swallow is compromised. Difficult swallowing, or **dysphagia**, can have mechanical causes such as tumors, scar tissue, obstruction, cancer, trauma, or other barriers in the throat. Dysphagia can also result from nerve damage or a stroke.

Swallowing problems can lead to malnutrition, respiratory problems, tooth decay, nasal regurgitation, and compromised health. Various health care professionals are trained to help a person overcome swallowing difficulties.

Esophageal Problems

Several esophageal problems can lead to annoying symptoms such as belching, hiccups, burning sensations, or uncomfortable feelings of fullness. Some serious esophageal problems include cancer, obstruction from tumors, faulty nerve impulses, severe inflammation, and abnormal sphincter function.

One of the most common problems involving the esophagus is **heartburn**, or acid indigestion. Heartburn is caused by hydrochloric acid flowing from the stomach back into the esophagus or even the throat. The acid causes a lingering, unpleasant, sour taste in the mouth. Other symptoms include nausea, bloating, belching, a vague burning sensation in the midchest, or an uncomfortable feeling of fullness.[18] Chronic heartburn can be a symptom of **gastroesophageal reflux disease**, or **GERD**, when the acidic stomach contents reflux into the esophagus.

A weak lower esophageal sphincter is often the culprit in acid reflux, because it sometimes permits this backflow of stomach fluids into the esophagus. Certain foods, including chocolate, fried or fatty foods, spicy foods, coffee, tomato products, and alcoholic beverages can contribute to heartburn.[19] Lifestyle factors also play a role. For example, smoking cigarettes, drinking alcohol, wearing tight-fitting clothes, being overweight or obese, eating large evening meals, and reclining after eating tend to cause or worsen the condition. If dietary changes and behavior modification are insufficient to relieve the heartburn, over-the-counter antacids or prescription drugs may help. In rare circumstances, surgical intervention is required to treat severe, unrelenting heartburn.

Esophageal cancer is another medical condition that has serious consequences. According to the American Cancer Society, esophageal cancer makes up about one percent of the cancers in the United States. This type of cancer is three to four times

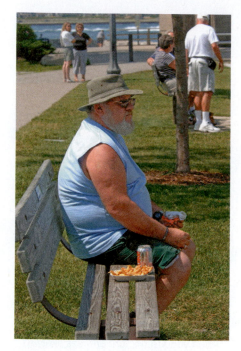
Certain foods and lifestyle factors contribute to heartburn.

dysphagia Difficult swallowing.

heartburn A burning sensation originating in the esophagus. Heartburn is usually caused by the reflux of gastric contents from the stomach into the esophagus. Chronic heartburn can lead to gastroesophageal reflux disease (GERD).

gastroesophageal reflux disease (GERD) The backward flow of stomach contents past the lower esophageal sphincter into the esophagus.

more likely to occur in men than in women. In addition, smoking, heavy drinking, and being overweight all increase the risk of this cancer.[20] Treatments include surgery, radiation, and chemotherapy.

Disorders of the Stomach

Does your stomach ever growl? A rumbling stomach, or *borborygmus,* isn't really a disorder (though if it's accompanied by pain or vomiting, it can be a sign of a larger problem, such as a mechanical obstruction).[21] Rather, the gurgling is due to the gas and air pockets that form as chyme is pushed through the stomach and small intestine. The best way to quiet the noise is to eat or drink something, or to apply mild pressure to the abdomen. Other stomach problems can range from the trivial, like an occasional stomachache, to life-threatening complications such as bleeding ulcers or stomach cancer.

At some point in time, everyone has had a stomachache. Common causes include overeating, gastric bloating, or eating too fast. Other possible causes include eating foods that are high in fat or fiber, eating spicy foods, lactose intolerance, or swallowing air while eating. More serious causes of a stomachache include the flu or consuming food or water that is contaminated with bacteria. Stomach flu or **gastroenteritis** is an inflammation of the stomach or intestines caused by a virus or bacteria. Flu symptoms include nausea, vomiting, diarrhea, and abdominal cramping. Sometimes the problem requires medical intervention, but usually rest, oral rehydration therapy, and a soft-food diet will help with the symptoms of this type of flu. (*Note:* The stomach flu is not the same as influenza (flu), which is a respiratory illness caused by the influenza virus.)

An ulcer is created when the mucosal lining of the GI tract erodes or breaks.

Peptic ulcers can occur in the lower region of the stomach and in the duodenum.[22] A peptic ulcer is a sore, or erosion, in the stomach or intestinal lining caused most often by the *Helicobacter pylori* bacterium. The main symptom of an ulcer is abdominal pain, but this condition may also involve weight loss, bloating, nausea, and vomiting. Smoking and drinking alcohol can exacerbate peptic ulcers. Medical treatments may consist of prescription drugs and avoiding foods that can cause discomfort.

Gallbladder Disease

One common problem of an unhealthy gallbladder is the presence of **gallstones**. Most people with gallstones have abnormally thick bile, and the bile is high in cholesterol and low in bile acids. Over an extended period of time, the high-cholesterol bile forms crystals, then sludge, and finally gallstones. Some individuals with gallstones experience no pain or mild pain. Others have severe pain accompanied by fever, nausea, vomiting, cramps, and obstruction of the bile duct.

Gallstones result from the crystallization of salts and other compounds in bile.

Medical treatment for gallstones may involve surgery to remove the gallbladder, prescription medicine to dissolve the stones, shock-wave therapy (a type of ultrasound treatment) to break them up, or a combination of therapies. If surgery is required to remove the gallbladder, patients typically recover quickly. After gallbladder removal surgery, the anatomy of the biliary tract adapts. The liver continues to produce the bile and secrete it directly into the duodenum. Interestingly, the remaining bile duct dilates, forming a simulated pouch that works in a manner very similar to the original gallbladder.

gastroenteritis Formal term for "stomach flu." Caused by a virus or bacteria and results in inflammation of the stomach and/or intestines.

peptic ulcers Sores, erosions, or breaks in the mucosal lining of the stomach.

gallstones Small, hard, crystalline structures formed in the gallbladder or bile duct due to abnormally thick bile.

Products like Beano contain enzymes that help reduce the production of gas in the large intestine.

Disorders of the Intestines

Disorders of the intestines can occur anywhere along the length of the small and large intestines. Common, temporary problems can include gassiness, diarrhea, constipation, and hemorrhoids; more serious disorders include celiac disease and Crohn's disease.

Flatulence

Flatulence is the release of intestinal gas from the rectum. It can be uncomfortable and sometimes embarrassing (but normal). Intestinal gas is produced for a variety of reasons, and most adults release it 10 to 20 times a day! Eating too fast, or drinking beverages with added air, such as beer and carbonated beverages, can result in the intake of air that makes its way through the GI tract. Legumes such as beans and lentils can lead to gas production because they contain indigestible carbohydrates that are fermented by intestinal bacteria. The bacteria produce the gas as a by-product. The gas is a mixture of carbon dioxide, hydrogen, nitrogen, oxygen, and methane. The offending odor comes from the gases that contain sulfur. Using products such as Beano, eating smaller meals, adding fiber gradually in your diet, and increasing your fluid intake can all help reduce the amount of gas.

Constipation and Diarrhea

Constipation is caused by excessively slow movements of the undigested residue through the colon, and is often due to insufficient fiber or water intake. Consuming an adequate amount of dietary fiber daily can help prevent constipation. Stress, inactivity, or various illnesses can also lead to constipation. It is usually treated with increasing the fiber and fluids in the diet. Daily exercise, establishing eating and resting routines, and using over-the-counter stool softeners are usually recommended to treat this condition.

    Diarrhea is the passage of frequent, watery, loose stools. It is considered more serious than constipation because of the loss of fluids and electrolytes. If the diarrhea continues for an extended period of time, you may malabsorb additional nutrients, which can lead to malnutrition. There are many causes of diarrhea, including contaminated water, various microorganisms, stress, or excessive fiber intake. Diarrhea is generally treated with fluid and electrolyte replacement. Most physicians identify the cause(s) of the diarrhea in addition to treating the symptoms.

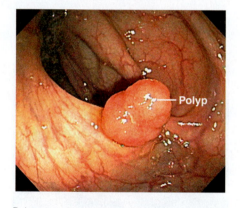

Polyps, or abnormal growths, on the lining of the large intestine may indicate early stages of colon cancer.

Hemorrhoids

Hemorrhoids are a condition in which pressure in the veins in the rectum and anus causes swelling and inflammation. The walls of the veins dilate, become thin, and bleed. As the pressure builds, the vessels protrude. Straining to pass dry stools, pregnancy, chronic constipation or diarrhea, and aging are all factors that can contribute to hemorrhoids. You may never know that you have hemorrhoids unless they begin to bleed (following a bowel movement), itch, or become painful. As with constipation, increasing both your fiber and fluid intake can treat hemorrhoids. Sometimes surgery may be necessary to remove hemorrhoids.

flatulence Production of excessive gas in the stomach or the intestines.

constipation Difficulty in passing stools.

diarrhea Frequent, loose, watery stools.

hemorrhoids Swelling in the veins of the rectum and anus.

Tired of Gluten

Elizabeth, a married 35-year-old woman, always thought that she followed a sensible diet. She ate a variety of whole grains, fruits, and vegetables, and consumed only lean meat and low-fat dairy products. Recently, however, she was continually feeling exhausted. At first, she thought it was the typical fatigue that accompanies a busy schedule of raising three active children and juggling her own life. Eventually, however, her daily fatigue became so prominent that it caused her to minimize the number of times that she climbed the stairs to the second floor of her home, as she found that the mere 14 steps left her feeling breathless. One afternoon, she dozed off at 4 p.m. while folding the wash, only to be awakened by her son at 6 p.m. asking about dinner. At this point, she nervously knew that something was very wrong. Thinking the worst, she made an appointment with her physician. After a number of tests, her doctor diagnosed her as having *celiac disease*, an autoimmune disorder.

Elizabeth isn't alone in having this disorder. According to the National Institutes of Health (NIH), more than 2 million people in this country have the disease, which amounts to about 1 in 141 Americans. Individuals with celiac disease can't tolerate specific proteins—collectively called "gluten"—that are found in the grains wheat, barley, and rye. Individuals with celiac disease can experience symptoms such as stomachaches, diarrhea, bloating, skin rashes, joint pain, and tiredness if gluten is consumed.

On the advice of her doctor, Elizabeth cut out gluten from her diet. She had to eliminate all breads, pasta, cereals, and other foods made with wheat, barley, or rye. It was difficult at first, having to remember to read food labels carefully and ask about the ingredients in menu items at restaurants. However, she found that there are many gluten-free foods to choose from, such as meat, milk, eggs, nuts, fruit, and vegetables.

She could also eat rice, potatoes, corn, and beans, as well as grains such as quinoa, amaranth, and millet.

Luckily for Elizabeth, the recently increased awareness of celiac disease has led to an exploding demand for gluten-free products. These products are so popular that the Food and Drug Administration (FDA) has created specific requirements for products that are listed as gluten free so that consumers can be sure that they are appropriate to eat. There are now smart phone apps to locate gluten-free–friendly restaurants, even while traveling to another country. Elizabeth found that the most problematic feature of the diet for her was avoiding the multiple foods that contain "latent," or hidden, sources of gluten. But soon after going gluten free she noticed that she was getting some of her energy back, so it motivated her to maintain the diet.

Think About It

List three days' worth of nutritious and gluten-free meals, including at least one meal at a restaurant.

More Serious Intestinal Disorders

The more serious small intestine and large intestine problems, such as irritable bowel syndrome, celiac disease, Crohn's disease, and colon cancer, tend to involve nutrient malabsorption, which can cause severe health consequences. The symptoms of these diseases vary, but they include abdominal pain, nausea, vomiting, bloating, loss of appetite, diarrhea, anxiety, weight loss, and fatigue. The medical problems that have to be addressed include various anemias, gastrointestinal blockages, inflammation, malnutrition, growth failure, vitamin and mineral deficiencies, and other medically complicated challenges.

Irritable Bowel Syndrome (IBS)

Globally, up to an estimated 15 percent of individuals have symptoms of **irritable bowel syndrome (IBS)**. IBS is a functional disorder that involves changes in colon rhythm—people with IBS have colons that overrespond to normal stimuli. This results in alternating patterns of diarrhea, constipation, and abdominal pain. The exact cause of IBS is unknown, but it is currently thought to be due to a combination of physical issues such as certain food sensitivities (to spicy or fatty foods, for example) and mental health problems such as anxiety and stress. Medical management includes dietary modification, including the addition of psyllium fiber, as well as stress management, and the use of prescription drugs, if necessary.[23]

Celiac Disease

Celiac disease is an autoimmune malabsorption disorder that causes a person's own immune system to damage the small intestine when gluten, a protein in wheat, rye, and barley, is consumed. A healthy small intestine contains numerous villi and microvilli that efficiently absorb nutrients from food. In people with celiac disease, the lining of the small intestine flattens due to an autoimmune reaction to gluten. This reduces the intestine's ability to absorb nutrients.

The exact cause of celiac disease is unknown, but it is believed to be genetic, and the disease is more common among people of European descent. Celiac disease is sometimes detected or triggered by surgery, pregnancy, a viral infection, or severe emotional stress.

The classic celiac symptoms include recurring abdominal bloating, cramping, diarrhea, gas, fatty and foul-smelling stools, weight loss, anemia, fatigue, bone or joint pain, and even a painful skin rash. Some people develop the symptoms of celiac disease in infancy or childhood. Others develop the disease later in life, after being misdiagnosed with irritable bowel syndrome or various food intolerances. Diagnosing celiac disease is sometimes difficult because it resembles other very similar malabsorption diseases.

Depending on the length of time between symptom development and diagnosis, the complications from celiac disease can be serious. They include increased

TableTIPS

Eat Gluten Free

Be a label reader to avoid products that contain all forms of wheat, barley, rye, triticale, or their hybrids.

Substitute whole-wheat bread with breads made from gluten-free whole grains, such as quinoa, buckwheat, amaranth, sorghum, and millet.

If you like a hot cereal for breakfast, try teff, a nutritious cereal grain from Ethiopia with a nutty, chewy texture.

Avoid packaged foods that contain modified food starch, dextrin, malt, or malt syrup, as these ingredients may be sourced from gluten-containing grains.

Enjoy coffee, tea, sodas, fruit juices, and even fermented or distilled beverages, such as wine, sake, and distilled spirits, on a gluten-free diet. But avoid coffee flavorings or creamers.

Maintain a high fiber intake by incorporating gluten-free fresh fruits, vegetables, beans, peas, and lentils into your diet.

Consume calcium-rich dairy or calcium-fortified gluten-free products, such as orange juice, soy products, or non-milk beverages made from rice or nuts.

Snack on gluten-free nuts, fruits, popcorn, raisins, rice cakes, and fruit smoothies.

Enjoy homemade meals to control gluten intake and eat a variety of nutrient-dense foods.

incidence of osteoporosis from poor calcium absorption, diminished growth because of nutrient malabsorption, and even seizures due to inadequate folate absorption.

There is no cure for celiac disease, and the only treatment is the consumption of a gluten-free diet. The Academy of Nutrition and Dietetics maintains a comprehensive list of foods allowed on a gluten-free diet on its website, www.eatright.org. This diet should stop the symptoms from progressing, allow the intestines to heal, and prevent further damage. The symptoms often improve within a few days after beginning the gluten-free diet. In children, the intestines can heal within three to six months. In adults, it may take two to three years of strict adherence to the diet for recovery to occur. Depending on the age at diagnosis and the severity of the disease, there may be some permanent health problems such as delayed or stunted growth.

Celiac disease is a manageable condition, and individuals with celiac disease can live normal lives. It's important that they learn about their condition by talking to health care professionals. Researchers are currently working to better diagnose the disease, to determine the exact component in gluten that causes celiac disease, and to develop enzymes that would detoxify the gluten before it enters the small intestine.

Crohn's Disease

Crohn's disease, or inflammatory bowel disease, is the general name for diseases that cause swelling in the intestines. Crohn's disease can affect any area of the GI tract, from the mouth to the anus, but it typically affects the ileum. The swelling can cause pain and diarrhea. Bleeding from the rectum, weight loss, and anemia are just some of the symptoms that can occur. Though there isn't a cure for Crohn's disease, medication, nutritional and dietary supplements, and/or surgery are currently used to manage the disease.[24]

Colon Cancer

Colon cancer is one of the leading forms of cancer and the second leading cause of cancer deaths. Fortunately, colon cancer is one of the most curable forms of cancer, if it is detected in the early stages.

Colon cancer often begins with polyps on the lining of the colon. They vary in size from that of a small pea to that of a mushroom or plum. The good news is that polyps can be removed surgically, and they are often small and benign. If the polyps are not removed or change to cancerous tumors, colon cancer can be more difficult to cure.

Individuals diagnosed with colon cancer may require radiation therapy, chemotherapy, and surgery to remove part of the colon or the entire colon. After surgery, patients are given dietary advice regarding the foods that would be the most comfortable to eat. Survival rates vary depending on the individual's age, health, treatment response, and stage of cancer diagnosis.

Table 3.3 on page 92 summarizes common digestive disorders.

Rice noodles are a good gluten-free substitute for pasta.

Practical Nutrition VIDEO

Probiotics: Do You Need Them?

Many products on the shelves today claim to provide probiotics that aid digestion. But what are they? Joan takes a look. Scan this QR code with your mobile device to access the video. You can also access the video in MasteringNutrition™.

irritable bowel syndrome (IBS) A functional disorder that involves changes in colon rhythm.

celiac disease An autoimmune disease of the small intestine that involves the inability to digest the protein gluten.

Crohn's disease An inflammatory bowel disease involving inflammation and swelling of the intestines.

Table 3.3

Common Digestive Disorders

Site	Disorder	Symptoms	Causes	Treatment
Esophagus and stomach	Gastrointestinal reflux disease (GERD)	Sore throat, burning sensation in the chest (heartburn)	Poor eating habits; overeating; other lifestyle choices	Eat smaller meals; eat more slowly; decrease fat and/or alcohol intake; quit smoking
Stomach or small intestine	Gastric and duodenal ulcers	Bleeding, pain, vomiting, fatigue, weakness	Multiple causes	Prescription drugs and an as-tolerated diet
Gallbladder	Gallstones	Cramps, bloating, intense abdominal pain, diarrhea	The concentration of high-cholesterol-containing bile that crystallizes and forms stones in the duct	Gallbladder removal, medication, or shock-wave therapy
Small intestine	Celiac disease	Malabsorption	Error of gluten metabolism	Gluten-free diet
Small intestine	Crohn's disease	Pain, diarrhea, rectal bleeding, weight loss, anemia	Swelling of the intestines	Medication, nutritional or dietary supplements, surgery
Large intestine	Constipation	Cramping, bloated uncomfortable feeling in abdomen	Too little water or too little fiber; inactivity	More water, fiber, and exercise
Large intestine	Diarrhea	Too-frequent, loose bowel movements	Multiple causes	Water and electrolyte replacement
Large intestine	Irritable bowel syndrome (IBS)	Diarrhea and constipation in alternating sequence; pain	Unknown cause(s); stress worsens the condition	Self-management with fiber therapy, stress relief, and good sleep habits
Large intestine	Colon cancer	Symptoms are often silent; may include weight loss, internal bleeding, iron-deficiency anemia, fatigue	Multiple causes (genetics, various colon diseases, smoking, exposure to dietary carcinogens)	Radiation therapy, chemotherapy, surgery

LO 3.7 **The Take-Home Message** Gastrointestinal diseases and digestive disorders include less serious conditions, like heartburn, GERD, indigestion, stomach flu, flatulence, constipation, diarrhea, and hemorrhoids, and more serious conditions, such as esophageal cancer, gastric ulcers, irritable bowel syndrome, celiac disease, Crohn's disease, and colon cancer. Disorders of the small intestine may result in malnutrition.

Probiotics: Do You Need Them? Probiotics are live microorganisms, usually bacteria, mainly found in cultured dairy foods.[1] Some research indicates that probiotics can have health benefits for the immune and digestive systems. However, the research is not conclusive, and some experts feel that adding probiotics to the diet is ineffective at best and possibly harmful at worst. Should you seek out fortified yogurt or probiotic supplements, or can you get along fine without them? Read the arguments below, then consider the critical-thinking questions and decide for yourself.

yes

- Research suggests that regular consumption of certain probiotics helps maintain the normal functioning of the digestive system. Studies indicate that probiotics can help in the prevention or treatment of antibiotic-associated disorders, in the treatment (and to a lesser extent prevention) of gastroenteritis (stomach inflammation) and diarrhea, and in the alleviation of lactose intolerance.[2]

- Some specific strains of probiotics have been shown to increase regularity in some people who have occasional constipation. Other strains have been studied for their role in decreasing the frequency of irritable bowel syndrome and some inflammatory bowel conditions.[3]

- Probiotics are generally considered safe. Their safety is somewhat evident by the fact that they have a long history of use in dairy foods like yogurt, cheese, and milk.[4]

- Though the burden lies with the manufacturer to make sure that the correct probiotic is added to the product and in adequate amounts, there is some regulation of probiotic labeling.[5] The FDA requires that the food label of these products contain accurate and relevant information.[6]

no

- We do not have sufficient information to say that probiotics are always beneficial and never harmful. Research is promising in several areas of digestive health but more research is needed to confirm their effectiveness, safety, and optimal dosage and duration.[7]

- Some products have been evaluated in well-controlled human studies, while others have no or not enough research to support their efficacy.

- Some consumers could experience gas or bloating when consuming probiotic products. The microorganisms may also have the potential to cause more serious side effects, especially in people with underlying health conditions.[8]

- People who have short bowel syndrome, a weakened immune system, a damaged intestinal lining, or are recovering from surgery are at a higher risk for side effects. These individuals should take probiotics only under the advice of a health care provider.

- Due to lack of strict FDA regulation, various probiotic products may not consistently contain the correct type of probiotics or enough of the probiotic to have an effect. Further, probiotics are not always delivered in an effective vehicle (foods versus supplements) and may be of variable quality.[9]

what do you think?

1. Do you think you should add probiotics to your diet? Why or why not? **2.** Which is the most compelling argument for taking probiotics? Which is the most compelling reason not to take them? Explain your rationale. **3.** Do you think we know enough about probiotics to recommend them to the public?

VISUAL Chapter Summary

LO 3.1 Digestion Breaks Down Foods for Absorption

Digestion is the process of breaking down whole food into absorbable nutrients. There are both mechanical and chemical aspects of digestion. Mechanical digestion includes chewing, peristalsis, segmentation, and pendular movement. Chemical digestion involves mixing consumed food with enzymes and gastric juices to break it down.

Esophagus

Bolus

Constricting muscles push bolus toward stomach

To stomach

LO 3.2 The Organs of the GI Tract and Their Accessory Organs Are Involved in Digestion

Digestion takes place in the organs of the GI tract—particularly the stomach and small intestine. Digestion begins in the mouth as chewing breaks down food and mixes it with saliva. Swallowing is a coordinated process that involves the mouth, throat, and esophagus. The stomach mixes food with enzymes and stores it before propelling it into the small intestine, where most of the digestion takes place. The large intestine absorbs water and some nutrients, before pushing waste through the colon and out of the body via the anus. Several sphincters control the entry and exit of food and chyme through the organs of the GI tract.

The accessory organs include the liver, gallbladder, and pancreas. The liver produces bile and stores it in the gallbladder. The pancreas produces both hormones and enzymes that play roles in digestion.

Salivary glands
Pharynx
Liver
Stomach
Pancreas
Gallbladder
Large intestine
Small intestine
Rectum
Anus

LO 3.3 Hormones Regulate Digestion, Enzymes Chemically Digest Food, and Bile Aids in Fat Digestion

Hormones, enzymes, and bile are necessary for efficient digestion. Hormones are chemical messengers that direct enzymes that do the actual work of breaking down food into smaller pieces for efficient absorption. Bile breaks large fat globules into smaller fat droplets to allow fat-digesting enzymes to come into contact with the fat.

Liver produces bile

Gallbladder stores bile

Pancreas produces hormones and secretes enzymes

LO 3.4 Nutrients Are Absorbed through the Small Intestine

The walls of the small intestine are covered with villi, which greatly increase its surface area and facilitate absorption. Digested nutrients pass through the small intestinal wall either by simple diffusion, facilitated diffusion, or active transport. Endocytosis is the process in which whole proteins, such as immunoglobulins, are absorbed intact.

Simple diffusion
High concentration
Nutrient
Cell membrane
Low concentration

Facilitated diffusion
High concentration
Nutrient
Carrier protein
Low concentration

Active transport
Low concentration
Nutrient
Energy
Carrier protein
High concentration

Endocytosis
Nutrient

LO 3.5 Nutrients Are Transported through the Circulatory and Lymphatic Systems

Water-soluble nutrients absorbed through the villi of the small intestine are transported through the circulatory system to the liver. Fat-soluble nutrients are transported through the lymphatic system before they enter the bloodstream.

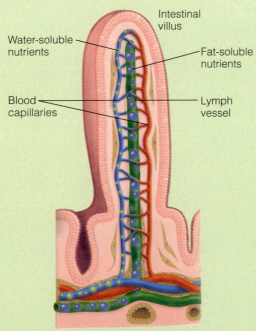

Water-soluble nutrients
Intestinal villus
Fat-soluble nutrients
Blood capillaries
Lymph vessel

LO 3.6 Other Body Systems Help You Use Digested Nutrients

Body systems other than the digestive system help you use the nutrients you eat. Your nervous system lets you know when you are hungry or thirsty. The endocrine system releases hormones that regulate the cells' use of nutrients.

VISUAL Chapter Summary

LO 3.7 There Are Many Digestive Disorders

Heartburn, constipation, diarrhea, and hemorrhoids are common digestive disorders. The more serious disorders such as ulcers, colon cancer, and even diarrhea can be potentially life-threatening. Colon cancer begins with polyps but is treatable if caught early. The causes of IBS and Crohn's disease are unknown but can lead to malabsorption and malnutrition. The autoimmune disorder celiac disease results in damage to the villi of the small intestine due to gluten, and can result in malabsorption.

Polyp.

Terms to Know

- gastrointestinal (GI) tract
- lumen
- mechanical digestion
- chemical digestion
- peristalsis
- segmentation
- pendular movement
- saliva
- mucus
- pharynx
- bolus
- epiglottis
- esophagus
- gastroesophageal sphincter
- stomach
- hydrochloric acid (HCl)
- gastrin
- chyme
- pepsin
- pyloric sphincter
- small intestine
- villi
- ileocecal sphincter
- large intestine
- stool (feces)
- rectum
- anus
- liver
- gallbladder
- pancreas
- hormones
- enzymes
- bile
- absorption
- simple diffusion
- facilitated diffusion
- active transport
- dysphagia
- gastroesophageal reflux disease (GERD)
- gastroenteritis
- peptic ulcers
- gallstones
- flatulence
- constipation
- diarrhea
- hemorrhoids
- irritable bowel syndrome (IBS)
- celiac disease
- Crohn's disease

MasteringNutrition™

Build your knowledge—and confidence—in the Study Area of MasteringNutrition with a variety of study tools.

 MyDiet Analysis

Access MyDietAnalysis through MasteringNutrition™ and track your diet and daily activities. In addition, a dietary analysis activity is available for every chapter in your book.

Check Your Understanding

LO 3.1 1. Food is moved through the GI tract by muscular waves called
- a. segmentation.
- b. peristalsis.
- c. bowel movement.
- d. pendular movement.

LO 3.2 2. _____ is the process that breaks down food into absorbable units.
- a. Circulation
- b. Digestion
- c. Absorption
- d. Excretion

LO 3.2 3. Chemical digestion begins in the
- a. liver.
- b. stomach.
- c. mouth.
- d. colon.

LO 3.2 4. The name of the protective tissue that covers the trachea when you swallow is the
- a. esophagus.
- b. tongue.
- c. pharynx.
- d. epiglottis.

LO 3.2 5. What causes heartburn?
- a. improper relaxation of the gastroesophageal sphincter
- b. improper contraction of the gastroesophageal sphincter
- c. improper and rapid swallowing
- d. improper breathing and chest congestion

LO 3.2 6. The name of the secretion produced in the stomach that helps break down protein and activates pepsin is
- a. hydrochloric acid (HCl).
- b. amylase.
- c. bile.
- d. gastrin.

LO 3.2 7. The sphincter that separates the stomach from the duodenum is the
- a. gastroesophageal sphincter.
- b. ileocecal sphincter.
- c. pyloric sphincter.
- d. colon sphincter.

LO 3.3 8. The compounds that directly help break down foods during digestion are
- a. enzymes.
- b. hormones.
- c. proteins.
- d. bicarbonate ions.

LO 3.7 9. A peptic ulcer is a sore, or erosion, in the stomach or intestinal lining caused most often by
- a. a diet too high in fiber.
- b. the *Helicobacter pylori* bacterium.
- c. acid reflux.
- d. hydrochloric acid.

LO 3.7 10. Celiac disease is an autoimmune malabsorption disorder that causes a person's own immune system to damage the small intestine when _____, a protein in wheat, rye, and barley, is consumed.
- a. glucose
- b. fiber
- c. gluten
- d. sodium

Answers

1. (b) Peristalsis is the process that moves food through the entire GI tract. Segmentation and pendular movements move food back and forth along the small intestine. A bowel movement involves peristalsis moving the feces through the large intestine.

2. (b) Digestion. Circulation is the process of distributing blood or lymph throughout the body. Absorption is the process of nutrients passing from the GI tract into the body. Excretion is the passing of waste products out of the body.

3. (c) Chemical digestion begins in the mouth, when the enzyme amylase secreted in the saliva begins to chemically break down carbohydrates. The liver is an accessory organ to digestion. The stomach and colon (part of the large intestine) are organs in the GI tract.

4. (d) Epiglottis. The esophagus is a tube that connects your mouth with your stomach. The tongue is a muscle that pushes food to the back of the mouth into the pharynx. The pharynx is a chamber that food passes through just before being swallowed.

5. (a) Heartburn occurs when the lower esophageal sphincter allows acid from the stomach back into the esophagus.

6. (a) Hydrochloric acid (HCl) is part of the gastric juices produced in the stomach; it activates pepsin, breaks down connective tissue in meat, and destroys some ingested microorganisms. Amylase is an enzyme in the mouth that begins breaking down carbohydrates. Bile is made by the liver and emulsifies fat. Gastrin is a hormone in the stomach that stimulates digestive activity.

7. (c) The pyloric sphincter allows chyme to pass from the bottom of the stomach to the beginning of the duodenum, the first part of the small intestine. The lower esophageal sphincter is between the mouth and the stomach. The ileocecal sphincter separates the ileum from the colon. The colon sphincter is also called the anal sphincter and it is the last part of the GI tract.

8. (a) Enzymes such as amylase and lipase break down the individual nutrients during digestion. Hormones are chemical messengers that regulate activities such as metabolism and the cells' use of nutrients. Protein is a macronutrient, and bicarbonate ions are released from the pancreas into the duodenum of the small intestine to neutralize the acids found in chyme.

9. (b) Peptic ulcers can occur in the lower region of the stomach and in the duodenum. They are sores, or erosions, in the stomach or intestinal lining caused most often by the *Helicobacter pylori* bacterium.

10. (c) Individuals with celiac disease must eliminate the protein gluten, which is found naturally in wheat, rye, and barley, from their diet.

Web Resources

- To find out more about celiac disease, visit www.celiac.org
- To learn about numerous types of cancer, cancer treatments, and preparation for treatment, visit www.cancer.gov
- To learn more about GI concerns, diseases, conditions, medicines, procedures, and treatments, go to www.medicinenet.com
- The National Library of Medicine is an abundant Internet resource for health care professionals, the public, researchers, and librarians; visit it at www.nlm.nih.gov
- To learn more about various digestive diseases, go to http://digestive.niddk.nih.gov

Answers to True or False?

1. **True.** The gastrointestinal, or GI, tract runs through the body and connects the mouth to the anus. Turn to page 70 to find out more about the organs that make up the GI tract.

2. **False.** The trachea is the windpipe. To find out what happens if food mistakenly enters it, turn to page 73.

3. **False.** Hydrochloric acid is only produced in the stomach. For more about digestive juices, turn to page 75.

4. **True.** The stomach secretes a powerful acid, HCl, which is strong enough to damage the stomach wall. A thick layer of mucus protects it. Turn to page 75 to find out more.

5. **False.** Fats and protein take longer to digest than carbohydrates. Turn to page 76 to find out why.

6. **False.** Though most absorption does take place in the small intestine, some nutrients, particularly water, are absorbed in the large intestine. Turn to page 78 to learn more.

7. **True.** Stool (or feces) contains leftover food residue, nondigestible fibers, bacteria, gases, and sloughed-off intestinal cells. Turn to page 78 to find out more about the waste products of digestion.

8. **False.** Your body is very efficient and absorbs more than 90 percent of the nutrients in food. To find out how this happens, turn to page 81.

9. **True.** Approximately 20 percent of adults experience heartburn every day. Turn to page 86 to learn what else can cause it.

10. **False.** The exact cause of irritable bowel syndrome is unknown. To find out more, turn to page 90.

4
Carbohydrates: Sugars, Starches, and Fiber

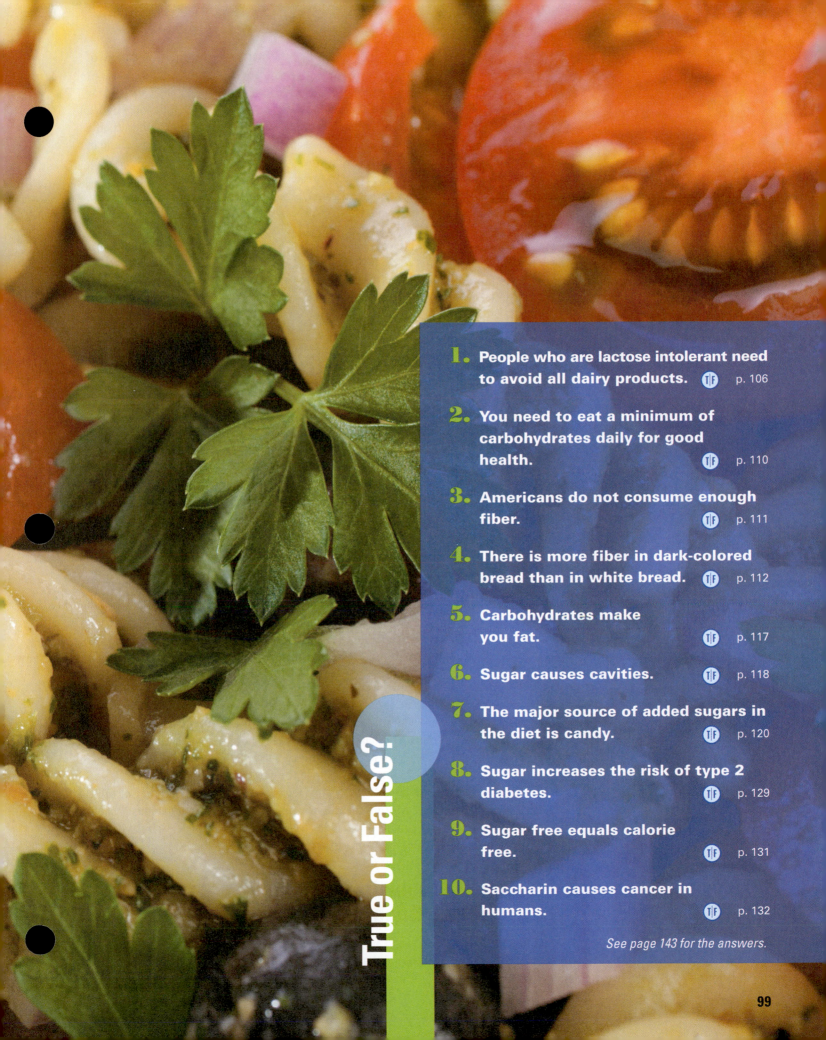

True or False?

1. People who are lactose intolerant need to avoid all dairy products. **T/F** p. 106

2. You need to eat a minimum of carbohydrates daily for good health. **T/F** p. 110

3. Americans do not consume enough fiber. **T/F** p. 111

4. There is more fiber in dark-colored bread than in white bread. **T/F** p. 112

5. Carbohydrates make you fat. **T/F** p. 117

6. Sugar causes cavities. **T/F** p. 118

7. The major source of added sugars in the diet is candy. **T/F** p. 120

8. Sugar increases the risk of type 2 diabetes. **T/F** p. 129

9. Sugar free equals calorie free. **T/F** p. 131

10. Saccharin causes cancer in humans. **T/F** p. 132

See page 143 for the answers.

Learning Outcomes

After reading this chapter, you will be able to:

LO 4.1 Describe what carbohydrates are and why you need them.

LO 4.2 Explain the process of digesting dietary carbohydrates.

LO 4.3 Explain how the body uses carbohydrates and regulates the blood glucose level.

LO 4.4 Describe the guidelines for carbohydrate intake, including the AMDR for carbohydrates, the DRI for fiber, and the recommendation for consuming added sugars.

LO 4.5 Describe the difference between natural and added sugars in the diet.

LO 4.6 Define type 1 and type 2 diabetes and describe how the types differ.

LO 4.7 List alternative sweeteners used as sugar substitutes.

LO 4.8 Describe the importance of fiber in the body and diet.

Carbohydrates are essential nutrients that make up the foundation of diets the world over. They are predominant in plant-based foods such as grains (rice and pasta), fruits, vegetables, nuts, and legumes (dry beans and peas), but are also found in dairy products such as milk and yogurt. These foods are staples in cuisines from Asia to Latin America, the United States to the Mediterranean. In Asia, rice is a dietary staple, and in Latin America, carbohydrate-laden bananas and nuts adorn most dinner plates. In the Mediterranean, grain-based pastas, breads, and couscous are plentiful, and here in the United States, many people consume bread on a regular basis.[1] In this chapter, you will learn about different types of carbohydrates and the functions they perform in the body. We will also discuss how we digest carbohydrates, how the body metabolizes glucose, and what happens when metabolic control fails, as in the disease diabetes mellitus. You will learn the role that certain types of carbohydrates can play in fighting obesity, heart disease, cancer, and diabetes. Finally, we will explore how to incorporate a rich balance of carbohydrates into your daily diet.

What Are Carbohydrates and Why Do You Need Them?

LO 4.1 Describe what carbohydrates are and why you need them.

Carbohydrates are the most desirable source of energy for your body. Providing four calories of energy per gram, their main role is to supply fuel, primarily in the form of **glucose**, the predominant sugar in high-carbohydrate foods, to your cells. Your brain in particular relies on glucose to function, as do your red blood cells.

The carbohydrates you eat come mostly from plant foods. Plants make carbohydrates to store energy and to build their root and stem structures. Animals, including humans, also store energy as carbohydrates, but in limited amounts. The storage form of carbohydrates in animals breaks down when the animal dies, so eating meat and poultry will not supply carbohydrates to our diets. Plants form the basic carbohydrate, glucose, in a process called **photosynthesis** (**Figure 4.1**). During photosynthesis, plants use the **chlorophyll** in their leaves to absorb the energy in sunlight. The absorbed energy splits water in the plant into its component parts: hydrogen and oxygen. Glucose is formed when the hydrogen joins with carbon dioxide that the plant has taken in from the air. The oxygen is released as a waste product.

Glucose is the most abundant carbohydrate in nature, and plants use it as energy, or combine it with minerals from the soil to make other compounds, such as protein and vitamins. They also link glucose units together and store them in the form of starch. Plants synthesize an estimated 145 billion tons of carbohydrates a year. This equals about 23 tons per person in the world.[2]

Carbohydrates are divided into two categories based on the number of units that are joined together. **Simple carbohydrates** include **monosaccharides** (*mono* = one, *saccharide* = sugar) and **disaccharides** (*di* = two), and **complex carbohydrates** include **polysaccharides** (*poly* = many).

Simple Carbohydrates Contain One or Two Sugar Units

Monosaccharides are found in foods. In addition to glucose, which we just discussed, there are **fructose** and **galactose** (**Figure 4.2** on page 102). Fructose is the

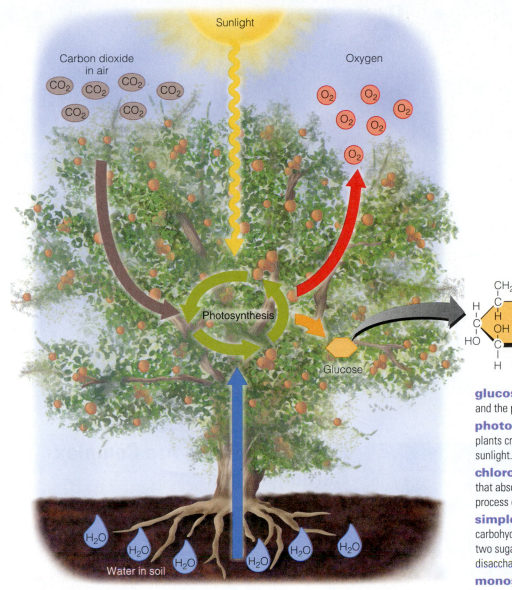

Figure 4.1 Photosynthesis: How Glucose Is Made
During photosynthesis, the leaves of green plants absorb the energy from sunlight. This energy splits six molecules of water (H_2O) into hydrogen and oxygen. The hydrogen joins with carbon dioxide in the plant to create glucose. In this process, six molecules of oxygen are released into the air. Glucose is the most abundant sugar in nature and the optimal fuel for your body.

glucose The most abundant sugar in foods and the primary energy source for your body.

photosynthesis A process by which green plants create carbohydrates using the energy from sunlight.

chlorophyll The green pigment in plants that absorbs energy from sunlight to begin the process of photosynthesis.

simple carbohydrates A category of carbohydrates that contain a single sugar unit or two sugar units combined. Monosaccharides and disaccharides are simple carbohydrates.

monosaccharide One sugar unit. There are three monosaccharides: glucose, fructose, and galactose.

disaccharide Two sugar units combined. There are three disaccharides: sucrose, lactose, and maltose.

complex carbohydrates A category of carbohydrates that contain many sugar units combined. A polysaccharide is a complex carbohydrate.

polysaccharide Many sugar units combined. Starch, glycogen, and fiber are all polysaccharides.

fructose The sweetest of the monosaccharides; also known as fruit sugar.

galactose A monosaccharide that links with glucose to create the sugar found in dairy foods.

sucrose A disaccharide composed of glucose and fructose; also known as table sugar.

maltose A disaccharide composed of two glucose units joined together.

lactose A disaccharide composed of glucose and galactose; also known as milk sugar.

sweetest of the simple sugars and is found abundantly in fruit. For this reason, it is often referred to as fruit sugar. Galactose is found in dairy foods. From these three sugars, the disaccharides can be created:

- When glucose and fructose join together, the disaccharide **sucrose**, or table sugar, is formed.
- When two glucose units join together, the disaccharide **maltose** is created. Maltose is the sugar found in grains, such as barley. It is used in the process of brewing beer.
- When glucose and galactose join together, the disaccharide **lactose** is created. Lactose is often called *milk sugar*, as it is found in dairy foods.

What Are Carbohydrates and Why Do You Need Them? **101**

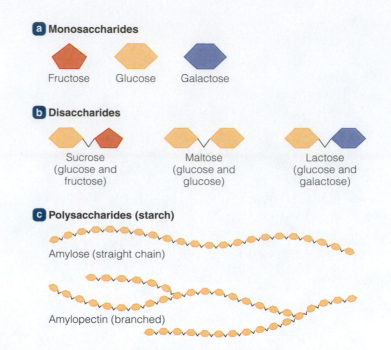

Figure 4.2 Creating Monosaccharides, Disaccharides, and Polysaccharides
(a) Fructose, glucose, and galactose are the three monosaccharides that are found in nature.
(b) The disaccharides sucrose, maltose, and lactose are created from the monosaccharides.
(c) The polysaccharide, starch, is composed of many glucose units joined together.

Polysaccharides Are Complex Carbohydrates

Polysaccharides consist of long chains of monosaccharides linked together. As you can see in Figure 4.2c, these chains contain many combined glucose units, which is why they are called complex carbohydrates. **Starch**, **fiber**, and **glycogen** are the three groups of polysaccharides.

Unripe fruit tastes more starchy than sweet. As fruit ripens, its complex carbohydrates are broken down into simple sugars, including fructose. The more it ripens, the more fructose it has.

Starch Is the Storage Form in Plants

Plants can store thousands of straight or branched glucose units strung together as starch. The straight chains of glucose units in starch are called amylose, whereas branched chains are called amylopectin. The many branches in amylopectin enable the body to break it down quickly and easily compared with amylose because there are so many sites where the enzymes can attach (Figure 4.2c). Starchy foods with highly branched amylopectin, such as potatoes, rice, bread, pasta, and cereals, are digested more rapidly than foods rich in amylose, such as legumes (dried peas, beans, and lentils).

Fiber Is Nondigestible but Important

Humans lack the digestive enzyme needed to break down fiber, so for the most part, fiber is the part of the plant that we eat but cannot digest. Plant components like cellulose, hemicellulose, lignins, gums, and pectin are all types of fibers. **Dietary fiber** is found naturally in foods and **functional fiber** is added to food for

starch The storage form of glucose in plants.

fiber A nondigestible polysaccharide.

glycogen The storage form of glucose in humans and animals.

dietary fiber Nondigestible polysaccharides found naturally in foods.

functional fiber The nondigestible polysaccharides that are added to foods because of a specific desired effect on health.

a specific, beneficial effect. For example, psyllium is a functional fiber derived from wheat husks. It can be added to breakfast cereals to help promote regular bowel movements. Together, dietary and functional fibers account for the *total fiber* that you eat.

Many compounds can be classified as both dietary fiber and functional fiber, depending on how they are used. Pectin occurs naturally in foods such as apples and citrus fruits and would be considered a source of dietary fiber. However, pectin can also be isolated and added to foods, such as nonfat yogurt, to add texture. In this situation, pectin is considered a functional fiber.

Fiber is sometimes also classified by its properties when combined with water. **Soluble fiber** dissolves in water, whereas **insoluble fiber** does not. Soluble fiber can be viscous (though not all soluble fibers are viscous); that is, it can have gummy or thickening properties. For example, the viscous soluble fiber in oats and beans thickens cooked oatmeal and bean chili. When you eat such foods, their soluble fiber is fermented (or digested) by bacteria in your large intestine. In contrast, insoluble fiber, found in foods such as bran flakes, is not viscous and is fermented less readily by bacteria.

A fiber's solubility affects how quickly it moves through the digestive tract. This classification system isn't exact, as most plant foods typically contain both types of fiber (**Figure 4.3**), and some fibers can have multiple effects in your body. In general, insoluble fibers include cellulose, hemicellulose, and lignins and are found in the bran portion of whole grains, cereal fiber, seeds, and in many fruits and vegetables. They typically move more quickly through your intestinal tract, so can have a laxative effect. Soluble fiber—like pectin in fruits and vegetables, beta-glucan in oats and barley, gums in legumes, and psyllium—is more viscous and moves slowly through your digestive system. Meat and dairy products do not contain fiber. Even though fiber is mostly nondigestible, it can have powerful health effects. We will discuss some of its effects in depth later in the chapter.

Glycogen Is the Storage Form in Animals

Glycogen is the storage form of glucose in humans and animals and is found in the liver and in muscle cells. Glycogen is branched glucose similar to amylopectin. Humans store only limited amounts of glycogen in their bodies, but it can be an important source of glucose for the blood. People can't access the carbohydrates stored in meats and poultry because the glycogen stored in animals breaks down when the animals die.

LO 4.1 **The Take-Home Message** Carbohydrates are found abundantly in plant-based foods. Your body cells use them for energy. Carbohydrates are divided into two categories: simple and complex. Simple carbohydrates include the monosaccharides and disaccharides; complex carbohydrates include polysaccharides. Glucose, fructose, and galactose are the three monosaccharides. Sucrose, lactose, and maltose are the three disaccharides. Starch, fiber, and glycogen are all polysaccharides. Dietary fiber occurs naturally in plant-based foods. Functional fiber has been added to foods because it has been shown to have a specific, functional effect. The total fiber in your diet is a combination of dietary and functional fiber. Viscous, soluble fiber has thickening properties and can be fermented by intestinal bacteria, and moves slowly through your intestinal tract. Insoluble fiber typically moves more quickly through your digestive system, so it can have a laxative effect.

Potatoes are a good source of complex carbohydrates.

Cellulose: insoluble fiber

Pectin: soluble fiber

Figure 4.3 Most Plant Foods Contain Both Soluble and Insoluble Fibers
The skin of an apple is high in cellulose, an insoluble fiber, while the pulp is high in pectin, a soluble fiber.

soluble fiber A type of fiber that dissolves in water and is fermented by intestinal bacteria. Many soluble fibers are viscous and have gummy or thickening properties.

insoluble fiber A type of fiber that doesn't dissolve in water and is not fermented by intestinal bacteria.

What Happens to the Carbohydrates You Eat?

LO 4.2 Explain the process of digesting dietary carbohydrates.

When you eat plant foods, your body breaks down the carbohydrates for energy. Let's look at how your body digests a sandwich.

You Digest Carbohydrates in Your Mouth and Intestines

The digestion of carbohydrates starts in your mouth (**Figure 4.4**). The act of chewing mixes the saliva in your mouth with the food. Your saliva delivers a powerful enzyme called amylase (*ase* = enzyme), which starts breaking down the starch in the fiber-rich whole-wheat bread in the sandwich, specifically the amylose and amylopectin, into smaller starch units. Some of the starch is broken down to the disaccharide, maltose.

This mixture of starch and amylase, along with the maltose and the fiber, travels down to your stomach. The amylase continues to break down the starch until your stomach acids deactivate this enzyme. Once the food leaves your stomach, it moves through your small intestine. The arrival of the food in the small intestine signals the pancreas to release another enzyme, pancreatic amylase. The pancreatic amylase breaks down the remaining starch units into maltose.

All the disaccharides—maltose, lactose, and sucrose—are absorbed in your small intestine. The disaccharides brush up against the lining of your digestive tract. A variety of enzymes such as maltase, lactase, and sucrase, called brush border enzymes, are housed in the microvilli in your small intestine. These enzymes break down the disaccharides into monosaccharides, specifically glucose, fructose, and galactose.

Once the dissacharides are broken down into monosaccharides, they are absorbed into the blood and travel to the liver. There the fructose and galactose are converted to glucose. The glucose is either stored in the liver or shipped back out into the blood for delivery to your cells.

The fiber continues down to the large intestine, where some of it is metabolized by bacteria in your colon. However, the majority of the fiber is eliminated from your body in stool.

What Is Lactose Maldigestion and Lactose Intolerance?

Lactose, or milk sugar, is the principal carbohydrate found in dairy products such as milk, yogurt, and cheese. People with a deficiency of the brush border enzyme lactase cannot properly digest lactose.

Lactose maldigestion is a natural part of the aging process and affects diverse populations in the United States, including people of Asian, African, Hispanic, and Native American backgrounds.[3] In fact, as soon as a child stops nursing, his body makes less lactase.

Though the term lactose maldigestion may sound serious, it doesn't mean that dairy foods have to be eliminated from the diet. In fact, the latest consensus is that people with lactose maldigestion can enjoy a serving of milk, yogurt, or cheese,

lactose maldigestion The inability to digest lactose in foods due to low levels of the enzyme lactase.

FOCUS

Figure 4.4 **Carbohydrate Digestion and Absorption**

Carbohydrate digestion begins in the mouth and ends with the absorption of the monosaccharides glucose, fructose, and galactose in the small intestine.

FOCUS FIGURE WALKTHROUGH

Scan this QR code with your mobile device for a video tour of this figure by Joan Salge Blake.

ORGANS OF THE GI TRACT

ACCESSORY ORGANS

MOUTH

Mastication mixes food with saliva. Salivary amylase breaks down amylose and amylopectin into smaller chains of carbohydrates.

Amylose   Smaller chains

Amylopectin   Smaller chains

STOMACH

The acidity of the stomach inactivates the salivary amylase; thus, very little digestion of carbohydrates occurs in the stomach.

SMALL INTESTINE

Pancreatic amylase breaks down the amylose, amylopectin, and smaller chains of carbohydrates into maltose, a disaccharide.

Smaller amylose chains   Maltose

Smaller amylopectin chains   Maltose

Brush border enzymes break down all disaccharides to the monosaccharides glucose, fructose, and galactose, which are then absorbed into the bloodstream.

Sucrose   Glucose   Fructose

Maltose   Glucose

Lactose   Glucose   Galactose

Monosaccharides

Bloodstream

LARGE INTESTINE

All starches and simple sugars are broken down and absorbed in the small intestine; only fiber passes into the large intestine. Bacteria in the colon metabolize some of the fiber. The majority of fiber is eliminated in the stool.

SALIVARY GLANDS
Produce salivary amylase.

PANCREAS
Produces pancreatic amylase that is released into the small intestine via the pancreatic duct.

LIVER
Glucose is taken up by the liver from the blood. Most glucose is returned to the blood to be picked up and used by body cells, or the body can use glucose for energy, convert it to glycogen, or store it as fat.

What Happens to the Carbohydrates You Eat?   **105**

Many products are available to help those who are lactose intolerant enjoy dairy foods.

especially with a meal or snack, without any problems or with only minor side effects.[4] This is good news, as dairy products can be an important source of calcium and vitamin D in the diet.

However, in some individuals the amount of lactase in the digestive tract decreases so much that they start to experience distressing symptoms. The undigested lactose draws water into the digestive tract, causing diarrhea. To make matters worse, once the lactose reaches the colon, the bacteria that normally live in the colon ferment this sugar and produce various gases. For some lactose-sensitive individuals, bloating, flatulence (gassiness), and cramps can sometimes be an unpleasant reminder that they ate lactose-containing foods. When these symptoms occur within two hours after eating or drinking foods that contain lactose, these people may be **lactose intolerant**.

You should never self-diagnose lactose intolerance, or any other medical condition. This could not only cause you to inflict unnecessary dietary restrictions on yourself, it could delay you from receiving an accurate diagnosis of a potentially more serious medical condition. It is best to leave medical diagnosis to your physician.

People with lactose maldigestion have varying thresholds for tolerating lactose-containing foods and beverages. Research suggests that these individuals can ingest at least 12 grams of lactose, the amount found in a cup of milk, with few or no symptoms.[5] Consuming smaller amounts of dairy foods throughout the day can be better tolerated than having a large amount at one time. Eating these foods with a meal or snack, rather than by themselves, can also influence how much can be tolerated. People tend to respond differently to various dairy foods. Whole milk tends to be better tolerated than skim milk. Cheeses (especially hard, aged cheeses, such as Swiss and Cheddar) typically have less lactose than milk, and so are better tolerated. Yogurts that contain active cultures are better tolerated than skim or low-fat milk.

For those who want to enjoy dairy foods without worrying about developing the unpleasant side effects, lactose-reduced dairy products such as milk, cottage cheese, ice cream, and other items are available in many supermarkets. Lactase pills are available that can be consumed with meals containing lactose.

LO 4.2 **The Take-Home Message** The digestion of carbohydrates begins in your mouth and continues in your stomach and small intestine. Enzymes help break down the carbohydrates into disaccharides and then monosaccharides so that they can be absorbed. All the monosaccharides are converted to glucose in your liver to be used as energy by your cells or stored as glycogen or fat. Fiber travels to your colon and then most of it is eliminated from your body. People with a deficiency of the brush border enzyme lactase cannot properly digest lactose, and so may experience lactose maldigestion and lactose intolerance.

How Does Your Body Use Carbohydrates?

LO 4.3 Explain how the body uses carbohydrates and regulates the blood glucose level.

Your body uses carbohydrates—specifically glucose—for energy (**Figure 4.5**). Chemical messengers called **hormones** regulate the amount of glucose in your blood. Hormones are like traffic cops, directing specific actions in your body. Let's take a closer look at how this works.

lactose intolerant When maldigestion of lactose results in symptoms such as nausea, cramps, bloating, flatulence, and diarrhea.

hormones Protein- or lipid-based chemical substances that act as "messengers" in the body to initiate or direct actions or processes. Insulin, glucagon, and estrogen are examples of hormones.

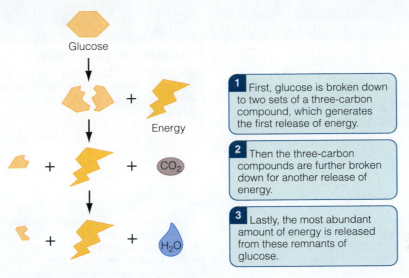

1 First, glucose is broken down to two sets of a three-carbon compound, which generates the first release of energy.

2 Then the three-carbon compounds are further broken down for another release of energy.

3 Lastly, the most abundant amount of energy is released from these remnants of glucose.

Glucose

Energy

CO_2

H_2O

Figure 4.5 Generating Energy from Glucose
When your body needs to break down glucose for energy, it begins a three-step process in your cells.

Insulin Regulates Glucose in Your Blood

After you eat a carbohydrate-heavy meal, your blood is flooded with glucose. To lower your blood glucose level, your pancreas releases the hormone **insulin** into the blood. Insulin helps direct the uptake of glucose by cells and also determines whether it will be used immediately as energy or stored for later use (**Figure 4.6**). When your cells need fuel, insulin stimulates the conversion of glucose to energy. If the amount of glucose in your blood exceeds your body's immediate energy needs, insulin directs it to be stored as glycogen and/or as fat if glycogen stores are maximized.

As mentioned, the surplus of glucose is stored in long, branched chains called glycogen. (Recall that plants store glucose as starch. Animals and humans store glucose as glycogen.) This process of generating glycogen for later use is called **glycogenesis** (*glyco* = sugar/sweet, *genesis* = origin). Glycogenesis occurs only in your liver and muscle cells. Whereas plants have an unlimited capacity to store glucose as starch, you can't squirrel away unlimited extra energy in the form of glycogen.

However, your body can store energy in another form: fat. Insulin can direct the conversion of the excess glucose to fat. In fact, most of the energy stored in your body is in the form of fat. Very little of it is in the form of glycogen. (Fat is covered in detail in Chapter 5.)

Carbohydrates Fuel Your Body between Meals and Help Spare Protein for Other Uses

Both glycogen and fat are important sources of stored fuel that meet your body's energy needs. These storage forms come in handy between meals when you aren't eating but your body continues to need fuel. Remember, your red blood cells and your brain, as well as the rest of your nervous system, rely on a steady supply of glucose to function properly. When your blood glucose level dips too low, such as if it has been longer than four hours since your last meal, your body calls upon its glycogen reserves to supply glucose to your blood. The glycogen in your liver is used to maintain your blood glucose level, and your muscle glycogen is used exclusively by the muscles for fuel. During this time, your body will also break down your fat stores to provide the energy for your tissues, such as your muscles. For example,

insulin The hormone, produced in and released from the pancreas, that facilitates the movement of glucose from the blood into cells.

glycogenesis The process of converting excess glucose into glycogen in your liver and muscle.

FOCUS

Figure 4.6 **Hormones Regulate Blood Glucose**

Our bodies regulate blood glucose levels within a fairly narrow range to provide adequate glucose to the brain and other cells. Insulin and glucagon are two hormones that play a key role in regulating blood glucose levels.

FOCUS FIGURE WALKTHROUGH

Scan this QR code with your mobile device for a video tour of this figure by Joan Salge Blake.

HIGH BLOOD GLUCOSE

1 **Insulin secretion:** When blood glucose levels increase after a meal, the pancreas secretes the hormone insulin into the bloodstream.

2 **Cellular uptake:** Insulin travels to the tissues where it alters the cell membranes to allow the transport of glucose into the cells by increasing the number of glucose transporters on the cell membrane.

3 **Glucose storage:** Insulin also stimulates the storage of glucose in body tissues. Glucose is stored as glycogen in the liver and muscles (glycogenesis), and is stored as triglycerides in fat tissue (lipogenesis).

LOW BLOOD GLUCOSE

1 **Glucagon secretion:** When blood glucose levels are low, the pancreas secretes the hormone glucagon into the bloodstream.

2 **Glycogenolysis:** Glucagon stimulates glycogenolysis in the liver to break down stored glycogen to glucose, which is released into the blood and transported to the cells for energy.

3 **Gluconeogenesis:** Glucagon also activates gluconeogenesis in the liver, stimulating the conversion of amino acids to glucose.

Oatmeal and other whole grain cereals are good sources of carbohydrates to start your morning off right.

let's say that your nutrition class is at 8 a.m. and that you overslept and didn't eat breakfast. The last time you ate was at dinner last night—more than 12 hours ago. As your blood glucose level begins to drop, your pancreas releases another hormone, **glucagon**, which directs the release of glucose from the stored glycogen in your liver to help raise your blood glucose level. This breakdown of glycogen is called **glycogenolysis** (*lysis* = loosening) (see Figure 4.6).

In addition to directing the breakdown of glycogen, glucagon signals the liver to start **gluconeogenesis** (*gluco* = sugar/sweet, *neo* = new, *genesis* = origin). This is the creation of glucose from noncarbohydrate sources, mostly from protein. Gluconeogenesis can only occur in your liver and kidneys, as these are the only organs that have all the enzymes needed. Most of the time, this glucose-generating process occurs in your liver. Gluconeogenesis kicks in from the kidney only after long periods of fasting. In times of deprivation, your body dismantles protein, using specific remnants (amino acids, which we will discuss in Chapter 6) to generate the glucose that it needs. If you don't feed your blood with glucose, your body will attempt to feed itself. Thus, consuming adequate amounts of carbohydrates is important to *spare* protein from being broken down to make glucose. You will learn in Chapter 6 that protein has so many other important functions in your body that you want to preserve it, rather than use it to make glucose. Once your blood glucose returns to normal, glucagon will no longer be released.

In addition to glucagon, other hormones can increase your blood glucose level. Epinephrine and norepinephrine, also known as adrenaline, act on the liver and muscle cells to stimulate glycogenolysis to quickly flood your blood with glucose. Emotional and physical forms of stress, such as fear, excitement, and bleeding, will increase your body's output of adrenaline. For example, if an aggressive dog was chasing you down the street, your body would be pumping out adrenaline to help provide the fuel you need to run. For this reason, epinephrine and norepinephrine are also referred to as the "fight-or-flight" hormones.

A low blood glucose level can also trigger the release of epinephrine. In fact, some of the symptoms that you may experience when your blood glucose level dips too low, such as anxiety, rapid heart beat, turning pale, and shakiness, are caused by the release of epinephrine.

Carbohydrates Fuel Your Body during Fasting and Prevent Ketosis

Skipping breakfast is one thing; fasting, or not eating for long periods of time, is quite another. After about 18 hours of fasting, your liver's glycogen stores are depleted, so your body must rely solely on fat and protein for fuel.

To burn fat thoroughly, you need adequate amounts of glucose. Without it, excessive amounts of **ketone bodies**, by-products of the incomplete breakdown of fat, are created and spill out into your blood. Because most ketone bodies are acids, excessive amounts can cause your blood to become slightly acidic. After about two days of fasting, the number of ketone bodies in your blood is at least doubled, and you are in a state of **ketosis**. Individuals who fast or follow strict low-carbohydrate diets are often in ketosis because they consume inadequate amounts of carbohydrates. Although the term *ketosis* sounds scary, the condition is not necessarily harmful as long as you are otherwise healthy.

During extended fasting, while your body continues to break down fat for fuel, it also breaks down the protein from your muscles and organs to generate glucose. If you continue to fast, your body's protein reserves will reach a dangerously low level and death will occur.

glucagon The hormone that directs glycogenolysis and gluconeogenesis to increase glucose in the blood. Glucagon is produced in and released from the pancreas.

glycogenolysis The breakdown of glycogen to release glucose.

gluconeogenesis The creation of glucose from noncarbohydrate sources, predominantly protein.

ketone bodies The by-products of the incomplete breakdown of fat.

ketosis The condition of increased ketone bodies in the blood.

LO 4.3 **LO 4.3** **The Take-Home Message** After a meal, when your blood glucose level begins to rise, the hormone insulin is released from the pancreas, directing glucose into your cells to be used for energy. Excess glucose is stored as glycogen or as fat. When your blood glucose drops too low, the hormone glucagon directs the release of glucose from glycogen in your liver to increase the glucose in your blood. Glucagon will also signal the start of gluconeogenesis in the liver, which is the creation of glucose from non-carbohydrate sources, such as protein. Epinephrine also plays a role in increasing your blood glucose level. When you fast, stored fat and ketone bodies become the primary source of energy to fuel your body. This spares your protein-rich tissues by reducing the amount of protein that needs to be broken down to generate glucose. If the fasting continues, death is inevitable.

How Much Carbohydrate Do You Need and What Are the Best Food Sources?

LO 4.4 Describe the guidelines for carbohydrate intake, including the AMDR for carbohydrates, the DRI for fiber, and the recommendation for consuming added sugars.

Although your body has mechanisms in place to provide the energy it needs on demand, you have to feed it the proper fuel to keep it running efficiently. Consequently, the question of how much carbohydrate you should consume daily has two answers. The first refers to the minimum amount of carbohydrates that you should eat to provide adequate fuel for your body, specifically your brain, to function efficiently. The longer, and more challenging, answer relates to the best type and source of carbohydrates that you should eat daily for long-term health. First, let's look at the amount of carbohydrates that you should eat daily.

You Need a Minimum Amount of Carbohydrates Daily

The latest Dietary Reference Intakes (DRIs) for carbohydrates recommend that adults and children consume a minimum of 130 grams daily. This is based on the estimated minimum amount of glucose your brain needs to function efficiently. This may sound like a lot, but 130 grams is less than the amount you would consume by eating the minimum recommended daily servings for each food group in MyPlate, that is, 6 servings from the grain group, 3 servings each from the vegetable and dairy groups, and 2 servings from the fruit group (**Figure 4.7**).

If your diet is well balanced, feeding your brain should be a no-brainer. In the United States, adult males consume, on average, just under 300 grams of carbohydrates daily, whereas adult females eat slightly over 200 grams daily, well over the minimum DRI.[6]

Recall from Chapter 2 that the AMDR for carbohydrates is 45 to 65 percent of your total daily calories. Adults in the United States consume about half of their calories from carbohydrate-rich foods, so they are easily meeting this optimal range.

For fiber, the current DRIs recommend that you consume 14 grams for every 1,000 calories you eat, to promote heart health. For example, individuals who need

Grams (g) of **Carbohydrates**

225 to 325*

| Vegetables | Fruits | Grains | Protein | Dairy | Daily Needs |

Lettuce, 2 cups — 2
Baby carrots, 1 cup — 10
Broccoli, cooked, 1 cup — 11
Peas, cooked, 1 cup — 25
Corn, cooked, 1 cup — 31
Cantaloupe, 1 cup — 13
Apple, 1 small (2.5" diameter) — 14
Orange, 1 large (3" diameter) — 22
Grapes, 1 cup — 28
Raisins, 1/2 cup — 58
Whole-wheat bread, 1 slice — 12
Crackers, whole-wheat, 5 — 16
Bagel, 1 oz — 18
Popcorn, 3 cups — 19
Pasta, cooked, 1/2 cup — 22
Walnuts, 7 halves — 2
Peanut butter, 1 tbs — 3
Sunflower seeds, 1/2 oz — 3
Kidney beans, cooked, 1/4 cup — 10
Mozzarella cheese (part skim) 1 1/2 oz — 1
Low-fat milk, 1 cup — 12
Low-fat yogurt (plain), 1 cup — 17
45 to 65% of calories

*Based on a 2,000 calorie diet

Figure 4.7 Food Sources of Carbohydrates
You need to eat at least 130 grams of carbohydrates daily. *Eating the minimum recommended servings from the grains, vegetables, fruits, and dairy groups will meet this need.
*Based on a 2,000-calorie diet.

2,000 calories daily to maintain their weight should consume 28 grams of fiber daily. Because few people know the exact number of calories they consume daily, the recommendations for fiber are categorized by both age and gender so that your estimated needs can be determined (**Table 4.1**). Unfortunately, most Americans fall short of this goal and consume approximately 15 to 18 grams of fiber a day, on average.[7]

The Best Carbohydrates Are Found in These Foods

Now let's turn to the second part of our answer and look at the best type and source of carbohydrates to choose for long-term health. As with other nutrients, not all carbohydrate-laden foods are created equal. For example, eating high-sugar foods containing lots of calories and saturated fat, but few other nutrients, can lead to weight gain and promote heart disease. It's best to choose carbohydrates from a variety of nutrient-dense, low-saturated-fat foods whenever possible. In general, the best strategy for long-term health is to eat a diet with fewer (low to moderate amounts of) simple carbohydrates and more complex carbohydrates.

Table 4.1
What Are Your Fiber Needs?

	Grams of Fiber Daily*	
	Males	**Females**
14 through 18 years old	38	26
19 through 50 years old	38	25
51 through 70+ years old	30	21
Pregnancy		28
Lactation		29

*Based on an Adequate Intake (AI) for fiber.

Grains are not only an important staple in the diet but also a wonderful source of nutrition. Americans' consumption of wheat, corn, oats, barley, and rice products has increased by over 40 percent since the 1970s. The availability of grain products for consumption is estimated to be approximately 122 pounds per person each year, or the equivalent of about 7 MyPlate servings daily.[1]

There are three edible parts in a kernel of grain: the bran, the endosperm, and the germ (see the figure). The **bran**, or outer shell of the wheat kernel, is rich in fiber, B vitamins, phytochemicals, and trace minerals such as chromium and zinc. The **germ**, or seed of the kernel, is a nutritional powerhouse providing vitamin E, heart-healthy fats, phytochemicals, and plenty of B vitamins. The **endosperm**, or starchy component of the grain, contains protein, B vitamins, and some fiber, although not as much as the bran.

bran The indigestible outer shell of the grain kernel.

germ In grains, the seed of the grain kernel.

endosperm The starchy part of the grain kernel.

refined grains Grain foods that are made with only the endosperm of the kernel. The bran and germ are not included.

whole grains Grain foods that are made with the entire edible grain kernel: the bran, the endosperm, and the germ.

enriched grains Refined grain foods that have folic acid, thiamin, niacin, riboflavin, and iron added.

Depending upon which parts of the kernel are used, grain products can be divided into two main categories: **refined grains** and **whole grains**. In refined grains, such as wheat or white bread and white rice, the grain kernel goes through a milling process that strips out the bran and germ, leaving only the endosperm of the kernel in the end product. As a result, some, though not all, of the B vitamins, iron, phytochemicals, and dietary fiber are removed. Though refined grains can still be a good source of complex carbohydrates, you can think of *refined* as having left some of the nutrition *behind*. From a health standpoint, what was left behind may end up being the most important part of the kernel.

To restore some of the nutrition lost from refined grains, **enriched grains** have folic acid, thiamin, niacin, riboflavin, and iron added to them. This improves their nutritional quality somewhat, but the fiber and the phytochemicals are lost.

Whole-grain foods, such as whole-wheat bread, white whole-wheat bread, brown rice, and oatmeal, contain all three parts of the kernel. (Note: White whole-wheat bread *is* a whole-grain product. It is made from a lighter variety of wheat, so although the bread is lighter in color, it has the same whole-grain nutrition as darker whole-wheat bread.) Whole grains are potential disease-fighting allies in the diet.[2] Research has shown that consuming whole grains protects against heart disease and may help individuals better manage their weight.[3] Several research studies have also shown that the fiber

in whole grains may help reduce the risk of diabetes.[4] Because whole grains are abundant in vitamins, minerals, fiber, and phytochemicals, it is uncertain which of these substances are the disease-fighting heroes, or if some or all of them work in a complementary fashion to provide the protection.[5]

The consumption of whole grains appears to have become an important dietary goal among Americans. A recent survey showed that eating both fiber and whole grains were Americans' top dietary priority.[6] The good news is that it's easy to incorporate more grains into your diet. When it comes to whole grain, you have a lot of choices:

- Brown rice
- Bulgur (cracked wheat)
- Graham flour
- Oatmeal
- Popcorn
- Pearl barley
- Whole-grain cornmeal
- Whole oats
- Whole rye
- Whole wheat

Dark bread is not necessarily whole-grain bread. Bread made with refined wheat flour can have caramel coloring added to give it a darker brown appearance.

Whole Grains Can Help Meet Starch and Fiber Needs

Starch is the primary complex carbohydrate found in refined grains, while fiber is found in whole grains. Select whole-grain breads and cereals that have at least 2 to 3 grams of total fiber per serving, such as quinoa, whole-wheat bread, bulgur, brown rice, and whole-wheat pasta. See the Nutrition in the Real World feature "Grains, Glorious Whole Grains" for more on what constitutes a whole grain.

A kernel of wheat

a

Bran
• High fiber
• B vitamins
• Phytochemicals
• Minerals

Germ
• Vitamin E
• Healthy unsaturated fats
• Antioxidants
• Phytochemicals
• Minerals
• B vitamins

Endosperm
• Starch
• Protein
• B vitamins

b Whole kernel used

c Only endosperm used

d Only endosperm used

Whole-Wheat Flour

Enriched Wheat Flour

Folic acid, thiamin, niacin, riboflavin, and iron added

Wheat Flour (not enriched)

Missing ingredients:
• Enriched folic acid

Missing ingredients:
• Bran (fiber)
• Phytochemicals
• Calcium
• Vitamin E
• Heart-healthy fats
• Antioxidants

Missing ingredients:
• Bran (fiber)
• Phytochemicals
• Calcium
• Vitamin E
• Heart-healthy fats
• Antioxidants
• Folic acid
• Thiamin
• Niacin
• Riboflavin
• Iron

The Table Tips box on Ways to Enjoy Whole Grains has some more useful ideas if you'd like to add more whole grains to your diet.

TableTIPS

Ways to Enjoy Whole Grains

Choose whole-grain cereal such as shredded wheat, bran flakes, raisin bran, and oatmeal in the morning.

Combine a 100% whole-wheat English muffin and low-fat Cheddar cheese for a hearty breakfast cheese melt.

Enjoy your lunchtime sandwich made with a whole-wheat pita or 100% whole-grain bread.

Try instant brown rice for a quick whole grain at dinner.

Snack on popcorn or 100% whole-wheat crackers for a high-fiber filler in the afternoon.

From Wheat Kernel to Flour
(a) The wheat grain kernel has three parts: the bran, germ, and endosperm. **(b)** Whole-wheat flour is made using the entire grain kernel. It is not enriched. **(c)** Enriched wheat flour doesn't contain the bran and germ, so it is missing nutrients and phytochemicals. Some nutrients, including folic acid, thiamin, niacin, riboflavin, and iron, are added back to the flour during an enrichment process. **(d)** Wheat flour that is not enriched lacks not only the bran and germ, but also many nutrients and phytochemicals.

Fruits and Vegetables Provide Simple Sugars, Starch, and Fiber

Whole fruits, 100 percent fruit juices, and vegetables are naturally good sources of simple carbohydrates. The flesh of fruit, for example, is rich in simple sugars, including fructose and glucose. Though you can also get simple sugars from processed foods and sweets, the higher calorie and lower nutrient levels in these foods make them a less healthy option (you'll learn more about the pros and cons

How Much Carbohydrate Do You Need and What Are the Best Food Sources?   **113**

An orange has four times the fiber of six ounces of orange juice.

of natural and added sugars in the next section). The skins of many fruits contain cellulose (a type of insoluble fiber), so eat unpeeled (but cleaned and scrubbed) fruit more often. Another type of fiber, pectin (a type of soluble fiber), is found in the flesh of fruit, and makes up about 15 percent to 30 percent of the fiber in fruit. Fruit overall contains about 2 grams of dietary fiber per serving (**Figure 4.8**). When selecting fruit, choose fresh or frozen versions over canned, but if canned is your only option, choose fruit packed in fruit juice rather than heavy syrup, to cut down on added sugar.

Vegetables contain abundant amounts of complex carbohydrates, including starch and fiber. A serving of vegetables contains approximately 2 grams of fiber. In general, starchy vegetables, such as corn and potatoes, contain more carbohydrate per serving than nonstarchy vegetables like green beans or carrots.

Legumes, Nuts, and Seeds Are Excellent Sources of Carbohydrates and Fiber

Legumes, such as kidney beans and chickpeas, are rich sources of both carbohydrates and fiber. Nuts and seeds are also good sources of fiber, providing over 1 gram in a ½ ounce or small handful. A ½ ounce of nuts is about 15 peanuts, 7 walnut halves, or 24 shelled pistachios. See the High Five! Table Tips for some ways to add legumes and other fiber-rich foods to your diet.

Figure 4.8 Food Sources of Fiber
Adults need to consume about 21 to 38 grams of fiber daily. Foods are a combination of soluble and insoluble fiber.

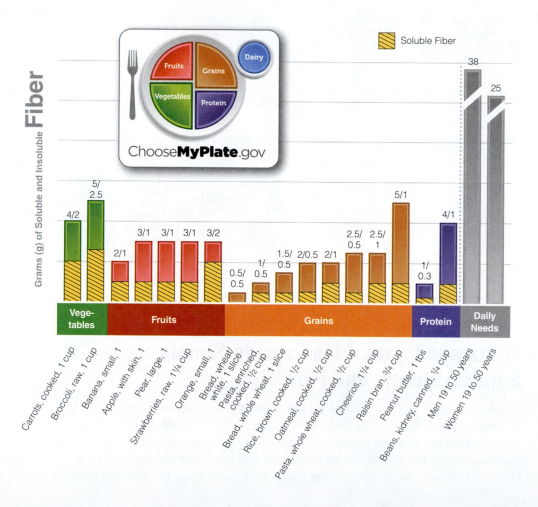

Low-Fat and Fat-Free Dairy Products Provide Some Simple Sugars

Milk and milk products, including cheese and yogurt, contain approximately 1 to 12 grams of lactose per serving. Choose low-fat or fat-free dairy products whenever possible, for the sake of your heart health. The lactose content is the same regardless of the fat content.

Packaged Foods Can Also Provide Carbohydrates

Packaged and processed foods, such as ready-to-eat cereals, crackers, and savory snacks, can be good sources of carbohydrate, but can also contain fair amounts of added sugar, salt, and fat. When selecting these packaged foods, choose products that contain at least 2 grams of dietary fiber per serving and be aware of the amounts of added sugar, salt, fat, and total calories. Choose whole-grain cereals with lower amounts of added sugar, whole-grain crackers, and baked rather than fried snacks. The Nutrition Facts panel and ingredients listings on the product can help you to choose healthier packaged foods.

LO 4.4 The Take-Home Message You need to consume a minimum of 130 grams of carbohydrates daily to provide adequate glucose for your brain. It is recommended that 45 to 65 percent of your daily calories come from carbohydrates. You should consume 14 grams of fiber for every 1,000 calories you eat. Whole grains, whole fruits and vegetables, legumes, and lean dairy products are the best food sources of simple carbohydrates and starch. Whole grains, fruits, vegetables, legumes, nuts, and seeds are excellent sources of fiber. Packaged foods can be good sources of carbohydrate, but the added sugars, fat, and total calories in such foods should be monitored.

What's the Difference between Natural and Added Sugars?

LO 4.5 Describe the difference between natural and added sugars in the diet.

Finding the taste of sweet foods pleasurable is an innate response. A child being fed puréed applesauce for the first time will probably show his pleasure with a big smile. You're not likely to see the same smile when Junior is eating plain oatmeal.

You don't have to fight this taste for sweetness. A modest amount of sweet foods can easily be part of a well-balanced diet. However, some sources of sugar provide more nutrition than others.

Your taste buds can't distinguish between **naturally occurring sugars**, which are found in foods such as fruit and dairy products, and **added sugars**, which are added by manufacturers to foods such as soda or candy. From a nutritional standpoint, however, there is a big difference between these sugar sources. Foods that contain naturally occurring sugar tend to be nutrient dense and thus provide more nutrition per bite. In contrast, foods that contain a lot of added sugar tend to give little else. The calories in foods with added sugars are often called **empty calories** because they provide so little nutrition.

naturally occurring sugars Sugars such as fructose and lactose that are found naturally in fruit and dairy foods.

added sugars Sugars that are added to processed foods and sweets.

empty calories Calories that come with little nutrition. Jelly beans are an example of a food that provides lots of calories from sugar but few nutrients.

Foods with Natural Sugars Usually Contain More Nutrients for Fewer Calories

Just one bite into a ripe peach, a crisp apple, or some chilled grapes will confirm that fruit can taste sweet, and not surprisingly, can contain more than 15 percent sugar by weight. There are many nutritional advantages of satisfying your sweet tooth with fruit rather than sweets with added sugar. Let's compare slices from a fresh navel orange with candy orange slices (**Figure 4.9**).

Six slices of a navel orange provides about 65 calories, more than 100 percent of the daily value for vitamin C, and 3.5 grams of fiber, which is more than 10 percent of the amount of fiber that many adults should consume daily. These juicy slices also provide fluid. In fact, more than 85 percent of the weight of the orange is water. The hefty amounts of fiber and water make whole fruits such as oranges a hearty, sweet snack that provides bulk. This bulk can increase eating satisfaction, or satiation. When you eat fruit, you not only satisfy your urge for a sweet, but you will also feel full before you overeat.

In contrast, six candy orange slices provide 300 calories of added sugar and little else. The candy is quite energy dense. It provides more than four times as many calories as the fresh orange. However, as it provides no fiber and only negligible amounts of water, it contains a concentrated amount of calories in relationship to the volume of food in the serving. You wouldn't likely feel satiated after consuming six candy orange slices. To consume close to the 300 calories found in the six pieces of candy, you would have to eat more than four oranges. It would be easier to overeat candy orange slices than fresh oranges.

Fiber-abundant whole fruits (and vegetables, for that matter) are not only very nutritious, but they are also kind to your waist, as their bulk tends to fill you up before they fill you out. In other words, it is more difficult to overconsume calories from fruits and vegetables because you will feel full and stop eating before you take in too many calories. In fact, eating adequate amounts of fruits and vegetables as

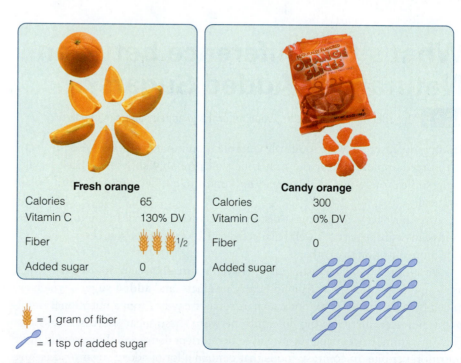

Fresh orange

Calories	65
Vitamin C	130% DV
Fiber	🌾🌾🌾1/2
Added sugar	0

Candy orange

Calories	300
Vitamin C	0% DV
Fiber	0
Added sugar	

🌾 = 1 gram of fiber

🥄 = 1 tsp of added sugar

Figure 4.9 Slices of an Orange versus Orange Slices
A fresh orange provides more nutrition for fewer calories and without any added sugars compared with candy orange slices.

part of a well-balanced diet is recommended to better manage your weight.[8] Substituting lower-calorie fruit for higher-calorie cake or other sweets on the dessert plate is a sweet way to cut calories.

Processed Foods and Sweets Often Contain Added Sugars

Americans have a sweet tooth. Unfortunately, the per capita availability of added sugars in our food supply is higher than it was in 1970.[9] Sugars are added to foods for many reasons. In baked goods, they can hold onto water, which helps keep the product moist and soft. They help provide a golden brown color to the finished product. Sugars function as preservatives and thickeners in foods such as sauces. Fermenting sugars in dough produce the carbon dioxide that makes yeast breads rise. And of course, sugars make foods taste sweet.

Are Added Sugars Bad for You?

Sugar has been blamed for everything from hyperactive children to diabetes, but are these claims myths or facts? Let's look at the most common claims:

- "Sugar causes hyperactivity in kids." Adults often point to sugary foods as the culprit behind the overly excited behavior of children at parties and holidays. However, research does not support the theory that sugar makes kids hyperactive.[10] The excitable behavior in the kids is more likely due to the festivities of the day rather than the sweets being consumed.
- "Too much sugar can contribute to dental caries." This is certainly true, but so can other sources of carbohydrates. See the Nutrition in the Real World feature, "Avoiding a Trip to the Dentist" on page 118 for information on how to prevent tooth decay.

Though these claims don't hold up, a high-sugar diet has been associated with some real health risks:

- Too much sugar in the diet can increase your blood level of triglycerides, the primary form of fat in your body. At the same time, it can lower the level of your "good" HDL cholesterol. Together, these changes may increase your risk for heart disease.[11] (This is discussed in Chapter 5.) Luckily, a reduction in dietary sugar coupled with an increase in dietary fiber can typically alleviate this problem.
- Consuming too much sugar can make weight management challenging. Eating sugar won't cause you to gain weight as long as you do not exceed the number of total calories that you need daily. However, it is easy to overeat high-calorie, sugary foods and quickly add excess calories to your diet. Added sugars are considered "empty calories" because they add calories to food but add few or no nutrients.
- Eating too much sugar may increase the risk of getting diabetes. Research shows that consuming a high intake of added sugars, especially from sugar-sweetened beverages, may play a role in type 2 diabetes. We will discuss diabetes in depth in the next section.

Finding the Added Sugars in Your Foods

While sucrose and fructose are the most common added sugars in our foods, sugars can appear on the food label under numerous different names. **Figure 4.10** includes some of the most common added sugars in foods.

Table TIPS

Lowering Your Added Sugars

Mix chocolate milk with an equal amount of regular low-fat milk.

Mix equal amounts of sweetened cereal with an unsweetened variety for a breakfast cereal with half the added sugar.

Drink water rather than soda or sweetened beverages throughout the day.

Buy sweets such as candy and cookies in individual serving sizes rather than large packages. The less you buy, the less you'll eat.

Choose canned fruit packed in juice rather than syrup.

Practical Nutrition VIDEO

Satisfy a Sweet Tooth

Hungry for something sweet? Look to nature for some of the sweetest treats around! Scan this QR code with your mobile device to access the video. You can also access the video in MasteringNutrition™.

Avoiding a Trip to the Dentist

Carbohydrates play a role in the formation of dental caries. Over the past few decades, the incidence of **dental caries** (tooth decay) in the United States has decreased as the use of fluoride has increased.[7] (The mineral fluoride is covered in more detail in Chapter 8.) Though things are improving in the world of dental health, an estimated 42 percent of children age 2 to 11 still have dental caries, and by the time these children reach age 19, almost 59 percent will have experienced a cavity, the later stage of dental caries. By age 64, over 90 percent of adults will have had dental caries in their permanent teeth.[8] To avoid dental caries, you need to understand the role your diet plays in tooth decay.

Feeding into Dental Caries

If you constantly eat carbohydrate-heavy foods, such as cookies, candy, crackers, and soft drinks, you are providing a continual buffet of easily fermentable sugars and starches to the bacteria that bathe your teeth. In addition, soft drinks can contain phosphoric acid and citric acid, which can erode teeth if consumed over a prolonged time.[9] Soft drinks are not the only beverage that may damage your teeth. Sports drinks, including energy drinks and vitamin waters, if consumed often, have been shown to be even more damaging to your teeth than soft drinks.[10]

Eating three balanced meals daily is best for minimizing tooth decay. Snacks should be kept to a minimum, and you should choose fruit or vegetables over candies or pastries. Whole fruits and raw vegetables tend not to cause tooth decay, so snack on these to your teeth's content.

Sticky foods like dried fruits, such as raisins and figs, can adhere to your teeth, so their fermentable sugars hang onto

dental caries The decay or erosion of teeth.

early childhood tooth decay The decay of baby teeth in children due to continual exposure to fermentable sugary liquids.

remineralization The repairing of teeth by adding back the minerals lost during tooth decay. Saliva can help remineralize teeth.

Sticky foods such as dried fruits can adhere to teeth and promote decay.

the tooth for longer periods. The longer the carbohydrate is in contact with your tooth, the more opportunity there is for the acids to do damage. Eating sticky foods in combination with other foods will discourage their adherence to your teeth. Drinking water after you eat will help by rinsing your teeth.

Fruit juice, even unsweetened juices, may be a problem for teeth, especially in small children. A child who routinely falls asleep with a bottle in his mouth that contains carbohydrate-containing beverages is at risk for developing **early childhood tooth decay** (also called baby bottle tooth decay) because the baby's teeth are continually exposed to fermentable sugars, especially during sleep.[11] Children need adequate amounts of fluids, such as water, but they should not be given a continual supply of sweetened beverages.

Foods That Fight Dental Caries

There are actually some foods that may help reduce the risk of acid attacks on your teeth. The texture of cheese stimulates the release of cleansing saliva. Cheese is also rich in protein, calcium, and phosphorus, all of which can help buffer the acids in your mouth following a meal or snack. The calcium can also assist in **remineralization** of your teeth. Eating as little as half an ounce of cheese after a snack, or eating cheese with a meal, has been shown to protect your teeth.[12] Chewing sugarless gum

can also be a healthy ending to a meal or snack if you can't brush your teeth. It encourages the production of saliva and provides a postmeal bath for your teeth. Xylitol, a sugar substitute often found in sugarless chewing gum, has also been shown to help protect the teeth against cavity-producing bacteria and acids in the mouth.[13]

With regular visits to your dentist, good dental hygiene, and a healthy diet, you can reduce the risk of dental caries. Follow these Do's and Don'ts to keep your teeth healthy:

DO eat three solid meals daily but keep snacks to a minimum.
DON'T graze all day long!
DO snack, if necessary, on whole fruit, raw vegetables, and low-fat cheese, which tend to be friendlier to your teeth.
DON'T munch on sugary foods such as candy, cookies, and other sweets.
DO drink plenty of water.
DON'T drink a lot of sugar-sweetened beverages.
DO chew sugarless gum or eat a piece of low-fat cheese after meals and snacks when you can't brush your teeth.
DON'T think that sugarless gum and cheese can replace a routine of brushing and flossing.
DO brush your teeth at least twice a day and floss daily.
DON'T forget this!

a Sugar can be called a number of different names on ingredient lists and labels.

Corn sweetener   Corn syrup

Dextrose   Sucrose   Brown sugar

Fructose   Lactose   Honey   Syrup

High-fructose corn syrup

Fruit juice concentrate

Invert sugar   Raw sugar

Malt syrup   Maltose

Molasses

b You can also look on the Nutrition Facts panel to see the total grams of sugar.

Nutrition Facts

Serving Size 1 Bar (24g)
Servings Per Container 10

Amount Per Serving	
Calories 90	Calories from Fat 20

	% Daily Value*
Total Fat 2g	3%
Saturated Fat 0.5g	3%
Trans Fat 0g	
Sodium 80 mg	3%
Total Carbohydrate 19g	6%
Dietary Fiber 1g	3%
Sugars 7g	
Protein 1g	

Calcium	8%	• Iron	4%

Not a significant source of Cholesterol, Vitamin A, Vitamin C

* Percent Daily Values are based on a 2,000 calorie diet. Your Daily Values may be higher or lower depending on your calorie needs:

	Calories:	2,000	2,500
Total Fat	Less than	65g	80g
Sat Fat	Less than	20g	25g
Cholesterol	Less than	300mg	300mg
Sodium	Less than	2,400mg	2,400mg
Total Carbohydrate		300g	375g
Dietary Fiber		25g	30g

Ingredients: Granola (whole grain rolled oats, sugar, rice flour, whole grain rolled wheat, partially hydrogenated soybean and cottonseed oils* with TBHQ and citric acid added to preserve freshness and/or sunflower oil with natural tocopherol added to preserve freshness, whole wheat flour, molasses, sodium bicarbonate, soy lecithin, caramel color, barley malt, salt, nonfat dry milk), corn syrup, crisp rice (rice, sugar, salt, barley malt), semisweet chocolate chunks (sugar, chocolate liquor, cocoa butter, soy lecithin, vanillin [an artificial flavor]), sugar, corn syrup solids, glycerin, high-fructose corn syrup, partially hydrogenated soybean and/or cottonseed oil*, sorbitol, fructose, calcium carbonate, natural and artificial flavors, salt, soy lecithin, molasses, water, BHT (a preservative), citric acid.

* Adds a dietarily insignificant amount of *trans* fat.

Figure 4.10 Finding Added Sugars on the Label
A food is likely to contain a large amount of sugar if added sugars appear first or second on the ingredients list and/or if many varieties of added sugars are listed.

Over the years, honey has been publicized in the popular press as being more nutritious than table sugar. This is an exaggeration. Honey provides a negligible amount of potassium, and it actually has more calories than table sugar. A teaspoon of honey contains 21 calories. The same amount of sugar provides only 16 calories. High-fructose corn syrup (HFCS), a sweetener produced from modified corn and composed of glucose and fructose, has also made media headlines because it has been blamed as a culprit in obesity. HFCS is less expensive than sucrose, and thus has replaced sucrose in some processed foods such as pastries, sweets, and soft drinks. Based on current research, the Academy of Nutrition and Dietetics states that it is unlikely that HFCS contributes more to obesity than any other sweetener in the diet.[12]

To find the amount and type of added sugars in the foods that you eat, read the ingredients on the food label. If added sugars appear first or second on the list or if the product contains many varieties of added sugars, it is likely to be high in sugar.

The Nutrition Facts panel that is currently used on food labels doesn't distinguish between naturally occurring and added sugars. For example, the nutrition

Honey should never be given to children younger than one year of age, as it may contain spores of the bacterium *Clostridium botulinum*. These spores can germinate in the immature digestive tracts of babies and cause deadly botulism. Adults do not face this risk.

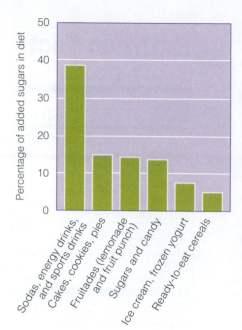

Figure 4.11 Where Are All These Added Sugars Coming From?
Sodas, energy drinks, and sports drinks are the number-one source of added sugars in American diets. Desserts, candy, fruit drinks, and some grains are also sources of added sugars.

labels on ready-to-eat cereals such as raisin bran and dairy products such as milk list 21 grams of sugars for raisin bran and 12 grams for low-fat milk. This can be misleading, as the grams of sugars listed for the raisin bran cereal include both the amount of naturally occurring sugars from the raisins and the sugars added to sweeten the cereal. For the milk, the sugar listed on the Nutrition Facts panel is just the naturally occurring sugar, lactose. With the growing concern about the rising levels of added sugars in the diets of Americans, various health professionals and organizations have pressured the FDA to require that all *added* sugars be disclosed on the food label. The proposed new Nutrition Facts panel includes added sugars (see Chapter 2 for an illustration). As you know, added sugars come from many sources and are found in many products. In fact, most Americans don't eat the majority of the added sugars in their diets—they drink them. The major sources of added sugars in the United States are sweetened sodas, fruit drinks, sweetened coffees and teas, and energy and sports drinks (**Figure 4.11**). To delve into how these facts relate to obesity, see the Examining the Evidence feature "Are Sugar-Sweetened Drinks Causing the Obesity Epidemic?" In addition to beverages, added sugars are hidden in many other foods (**Table 4.2**).

Table 4.2	
Sugar Smacked!	
Food Groups	**Teaspoons of Added Sugar**
Bread, Cereal, Rice, Pasta	
Bread, 1 slice	0
Cookies, 2 medium	🥄
Doughnut, 1 medium	🥄
Cereal, sweetened flakes	🥄🥄🥄🥄
Cake, frosted, 1/16 average	🥄🥄🥄🥄
Pie, fruit, 2 crust, 1/6, 8" pie	🥄🥄🥄🥄🥄🥄
Fruit	
Fruit, canned in juice, ½ cup	0
Fruit, canned in heavy syrup, ½ cup	🥄🥄🥄🥄
Milk, Yogurt, and Cheese	
Milk, 1% fat, 1 cup	0
Chocolate milk, 2% fat, 1 cup	🥄🥄🥄
Yogurt, low fat, plain, 8 oz	0
Yogurt, fruit, sweetened, 8 oz	🥄🥄🥄🥄🥄🥄🥄
Chocolate shake, 10 fl oz	🥄🥄🥄🥄🥄🥄🥄🥄
Other	
Energy drink, 8 oz	🥄🥄🥄🥄🥄🥄
Chocolate bar, 2 oz	🥄🥄🥄🥄🥄
Fruit drink, 12 fl oz	🥄🥄🥄🥄🥄🥄🥄🥄🥄🥄🥄

🥄 = 1 teaspoon of sugar

How Much Added Sugar Is Too Much?

The latest conclusion from the report of the 2015 *Dietary Guidelines for Americans* advisory committee is that a maximum of 10 percent of your total daily calories should come from added sugars.[13] Many Americans, especially women, sedentary individuals, and older adults who have lower daily calorie needs, would benefit from reducing the amount of added sugars in their diet. These individuals need to make sure that they are getting a substantial amount of nutrition from each bite of food. Eating excess amounts of foods with added sugars such as soda can displace more-nutritious food choices, such as vitamin D– and calcium-rich skim milk, in the diet, causing them to fall short of these important nutrients.[14] If you'd like to reduce the amount of added sugars in your diet, see Lowering Your Added Sugars Table Tips.

Concerned with the prevalence of obesity in Americans, the American Heart Association has recommended that women consume no more than 100 calories (6 teaspoons) of added sugar daily and that men consume no more than 150 calories (9 teaspoons) of added sugar daily.[15] American adults consume 99 grams of added sugars daily, which is the equivalent of approximately 25 teaspoons of added sugars daily.[16] Eating this much added sugar can have a major impact on daily nutrition and is one of the many reasons Americans are overweight.

LO 4.5 **The Take-Home Message** Your taste buds can't distinguish between naturally occurring and added sugars. Foods with naturally occurring sugars, such as whole fruit, tend to provide more nutrition and satiation than empty-calorie sweets such as candy. Sugar can contribute to dental caries, an elevated level of fat in your blood, and a lowering of the "good" HDL cholesterol. Foods with added sugars may displace more nutritious foods and quickly add excess calories to your diet. The current recommendation is to lower consumption of added sugars in the diet, as they are considered empty calories.

Why Is Diabetes a Growing Epidemic?

LO 4.6 Define type 1 and type 2 diabetes and describe how the types differ.

Diabetes mellitus, or *diabetes*, is becoming so common that it would be rare if you *didn't* know someone who has it. An estimated 25.8 million American adults—more than 8.3 percent of the population—have diabetes.[17]

Recall that the hormone insulin directs glucose into the cells to be used as immediate energy or stored in another form for later use. Individuals develop diabetes because they aren't producing enough insulin and/or they have developed **insulin resistance**, such that their cells do not respond to the insulin.[18] In essence, insulin is available in the blood, but the cells' decreased sensitivity interferes with its ability to work properly. Hence, the bloodstream is flooded with glucose that can't get into the cells. In this situation, the body thinks that it must be fasting and shifts into fasting mode. The liver begins the process of breaking down its glycogen stores (glycogenolysis) and making glucose from noncarbohydrate sources (gluconeogenesis) in an attempt to provide the glucose for its cells. This floods the blood with even more glucose. Eventually, the level of glucose accumulates in the blood and some of it spills into the urine and leaves the body.

diabetes mellitus A medical condition whereby an individual either doesn't have enough insulin or is resistant to the insulin available, causing the blood glucose level to rise.

insulin resistance The inability of cells to respond to insulin.

Do Sugar-Sweetened Beverages Cause Obesity?

The evidence is overwhelming: the United States is becoming an obese nation. Recent estimates suggest that more than 79 million adult Americans and over 12.5 million American children are obese.[14] Although there are many factors that contribute to this, some researchers note that this rise in obesity coincides with an increase in consumption of sugar-sweetened beverages, especially among children.[15] This observation has prompted some policy makers to propose new limits on soda purchases. To reverse this obesity epidemic, should the focus be placed squarely on sugar-sweetened beverages as the culprit?

Consumption of Sugar-Sweetened Beverages in the United States

A classic 8-ounce bottle of cola provides approximately 6 teaspoons of added sugars. In today's vending machine, you are more likely to find a 12-ounce can or

Table 1
Consumption Patterns of Sugar-Sweetened Beverages

Gender	Age	Teaspoons*	Calories**	% of Total Calories per Day
Males	12–19	18.4	294	11.6
	20–39	18.1	289	10.3
	40–59	12.6	202	7.7
	> 60	5.9	94	4.6
Females	12–19	12.1	194	10.5
	20–39	10.8	173	9.3
	40–59	7.7	123	6.9
	> 60	3.8	60	4.0

*Teaspoons of sugar consumed per day from sugar-sweetened beverages
**Total calories consumed per day from sugar-sweetened beverages
Adapted from P. E. Miller, et al., "Sugar-Sweetened Beverage Consumption in the U.S.: Novel Assessment Methodology," *American Journal of Preventive Medicine* 45, no. 4 (2013): 416–421.

Figure 1 The Many Sizes of Soft Drinks
A bottle or can of soda can provide from 6 to 17 teaspoons of added sugars, depending on the size of the container.

a 20-ounce bottle. People typically consume the entire can or bottle, regardless of its size, so they consume more sugar (**Figure 1**).

Currently, every day 50 percent of Americans consume some form of sugary drinks equivalent to about one 12-ounce soda.[16] Soda, fruit drinks, sweetened coffee and teas, and energy and sports drinks are the major sources of sweetened beverages in the diets of Americans.[17] The consumption patterns shown in **Table 1** suggest that males consume more of their total calories per day from sugar-sweetened beverages than do females, and both genders reduce consumption of sugary beverages as they age.

The good news is that the overall consumption of sugar-sweetened soda is declining.[18] Unfortunately, while Americans are drinking fewer sodas, they have almost tripled their consumption of sugar-sweetened sports and energy drinks.[19] Do these beverages contribute to our expanded waistlines?

Theories about the Relationship between Sugar-Sweetened Drink Consumption and Weight Gain

A couple of theories have been proposed to explain the possible connection between weight gain and our consumption of sugar-sweetened beverages. One theory suggests that the additional calories consumed in the sweetened beverages leads to excess overall calorie intake, and thus, weight gain. The second theory is that sugar in liquid form increases our appetite, leading to an increased consumption of calories from other foods. Research exploring both of these theories has yielded some interesting results.

Sugar-Sweetened and Artificially Sweetened Drinks, Water, and Weight Gain

According to the 2015 *Dietary Guidelines for Americans* advisory report, there is evidence that suggests that adding calories to your daily intake by

---

At the same time, the body has called on its energy reserve, fat, to be used as fuel. The body needs glucose in order to thoroughly burn fat; otherwise, it makes ketone bodies. In poorly managed diabetes, when glucose is unable to get into the cells, acidic ketone bodies build up in the blood to dangerous levels, causing diabetic **ketoacidosis**. Diabetic ketoacidosis can cause nausea and confusion, and in some cases, if left untreated, could result in coma or death.

ketoacidosis The buildup of ketone bodies to dangerous levels, which can result in coma or death.

drinking sugar-sweetened beverages adds body weight.[20] For example, normal-weight adults who drank one additional 12-ounce sugar-sweetened beverage each day gained an average of one extra pound every four years compared with people who did not add an extra beverage.[21] In another study, 641 children were given either an 8-ounce sugar-sweetened beverage containing 104 calories or an 8-ounce artificially sweetened beverage with 0 calories each day in school. After 18 months, the students who drank the sugar-sweetened beverage gained more weight and accumulated more body fat than did those who drank the artificially sweetened beverages.[22]

This research suggests that simply ingesting additional calories through sugar-sweetened beverages is enough to contribute to weight gain. But what if we replaced sugar-sweetened drinks with artificially sweetened beverages without calories?

In children at least, the research is promising. Results from the Double-blind, Randomized Intervention Study in Kids (DRINK) suggest that when the sugar in beverages was replaced with sucralose, healthy children lost weight, mostly due to loss of body fat.[23] Other studies contradict these results, however, and report that artificially sweetened beverages such as diet soda result in weight gain, not weight loss. Data from a 10-year longitudinal study indicated that adults who drank two or more diet sodas a day increased their waist size by six times more than those who did not drink diet sodas.[24] Another study found no effect on weight gain in individuals using sweetened cocoa versus sugar-free cocoa.[25] Thus the relationship of sugar-sweetened beverages versus artificially sweetened beverages on weight gain is still unclear.

If the increase in calories from sugary beverage consumption indeed causes weight gain, perhaps the best alternative is to switch from sugary drinks to calorie-free water. It appears that adults may gain less weight over time when they switch from sugar-sweetened beverages to water.[26] However, to add to the confusion, some published reviews suggest that switching to plain water had no effect overall on body weight.[27]

Sugar-Sweetened Beverages May Impact Satiation

Perhaps the answer lies in the second theory, that consuming sugar-sweetened beverages increases appetite or results in feeling less satisfied. Many beverages are sweetened with high-fructose corn syrup or sucrose. Sucrose and high-fructose corn syrup are both sweeteners that contain fructose. Some researchers have suggested that the fructose component of these sweeteners may change our appetite-control mechanisms, resulting in less satiation, or feeling of fullness, and thus a greater intake of calories from other foods during the day.[28] This theory is based on earlier studies conducted with individuals consuming pure fructose, which reported that this fructose ingestion resulted in a decrease in the hormones insulin and leptin, which suppress your appetite.[29] The flaw in this theory is that we rarely consume pure fructose in our diet.

The Bottom Line: Do Sugar-Sweetened Beverages Cause Obesity?

Obesity is the result of a combination of factors, including calories consumed from all food and beverage sources and physical activity. Currently, whereas there are some well-designed double-blind studies involving sugar-sweetened beverages and body weight, most of the studies involved are observational and of short duration. Because of this, there is no conclusive evidence that sugar-sweetened drinks *alone* contribute more to obesity than do other calorie sources.

While sugar-sweetened beverages may or may not be the main culprit in the dramatic rise in obesity, they do play a significant role in Americans' overall increased caloric intake, and so should be reduced in the diet. A recent study reported that over a four-year period, weight gain in adults was mostly associated with the intake of potato chips, potatoes, sugar-sweetened beverages, red meat, and processed meats, in that order.[30] Weight gain was inversely related to the ingestion of vegetables, whole grains, fruits, nuts, and yogurt. Thus it may be not just the sugary beverages but also other foods in the diet that cumulatively add up to a surfeit of calories being consumed. Sugar-sweetened beverages, including soda, fruit drinks, sweetened coffees and teas, and sports and energy drinks, add unnecessary calories to the diet and can contribute to weight gain.[31]

It is unlikely that one single dietary factor is the sole cause of obesity. Rather, it is more likely a combination of consuming too many calories from all foods and beverages and inadequate amounts of physical activity.

The conclusion from the 2015 Report of the *Dietary Guidelines* advisory committee is to reduce all sources of added sugars in the diet, whether from beverages or foods.[32] The "eat less and exercise more" approach may be the best strategy for reversing the obesity epidemic in the United States, including drinking fewer sugar-sweetened beverages.

> A super-large soda at the movie theater can be as large as 64 ounces! This giant beverage contains more than 800 calories and 50-plus teaspoons of added sugars.

What Are the Forms of Diabetes?

All forms of diabetes involve insulin and unregulated blood glucose levels. Some are due to insulin resistance, as just described, and others are due to a lack of insulin production. Still another form occurs only during pregnancy. The most prevalent types of diabetes are type 1 and type 2 (**Figure 4.12**).

FOCUS Figure 4.12 **Diabetes**

Diabetes is a chronic disease in which the body can no longer regulate glucose within normal limits, and blood glucose becomes dangerously high.

FOCUS FIGURE WALKTHROUGH

 Scan this QR code with your mobile device for a video tour of this figure by Joan Salge Blake.

NORMAL

1 Liver releases glucose into bloodstream.

2 The cells of the pancreas release insulin into bloodstream.

3 Insulin stimulates uptake of glucose into cells.

4 As glucose is taken into interior of cells, less glucose remains in the bloodstream.

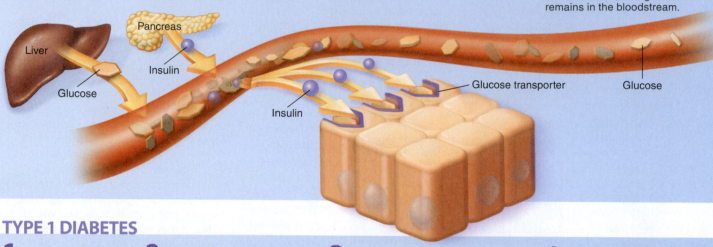

TYPE 1 DIABETES

1 Liver releases glucose into bloodstream.

2 The cells of the pancreas are damaged or destroyed. Little or no insulin is released into bloodstream.

3 In the absence of insulin, glucose is not taken up by cells.

4 High levels of glucose remain in the bloodstream.

TYPE 2 DIABETES

1 Liver releases glucose into bloodstream.

2 The cells of the pancreas release insulin into bloodstream.

3 Insulin is present, but cells fail to respond adequately. Progressively higher amounts of insulin must be produced to stimulate cells to uptake glucose.

4 High levels of glucose remain in the bloodstream.

Type 1 Diabetes Is an Autoimmune Disease

Type 1 diabetes is considered an *autoimmune* disease and is the rarer of the two forms. It usually begins in childhood and the early adult years and is found in about 5 to 10 percent of the individuals with diabetes in the United States.[19] The immune system of type 1 diabetics actually destroys the insulin-producing cells in the pancreas. Symptoms such as increased thirst, frequent urination, constant blurred vision, hunger, weight loss, and fatigue are common, as the glucose can't get into the cells of the body. If not treated with insulin, the person is susceptible to the dangers of ketoacidosis. Individuals with type 1 diabetes must take insulin every day in order to live a normal life.

Type 2 Diabetes Is More Common

Type 2 diabetes is the more common form of diabetes and is seen in people who have become insulin resistant. It accounts for 90 to 95 percent of diagnoses of the disease. Being overweight increases the risk of type 2 diabetes.[20] People with type 2 diabetes typically produce insulin but have become insulin resistant. After several years of exhausting their insulin-producing cells in the pancreas, their production of insulin decreases to the point where they have to take medication and/or insulin to manage their blood glucose level.

One of the major problems with type 2 diabetes is that this condition can go undiagnosed for some time. Whereas some people may have symptoms such as increased thirst, others may not. Consequently, diabetes can silently damage a person's vital organs without his or her being aware of it. Because of this, it is recommended that everyone 45 years of age and older undergo testing for diabetes. However, if a person is at a higher risk for developing diabetes, he or she shouldn't wait until age 45 to be tested. Take the Self-Assessment to see if you are at risk. Sometimes the medical testing will indicate that a person has higher than normal blood sugar but not yet high enough to be diabetic, a condition called prediabetes. See Health Connection: A Case Study for the story of one person with this condition.

Because the hormone insulin is a protein, it can't be taken orally, as it would be broken down in the same manner that other protein-containing foods are digested. Therefore, most individuals who need to take insulin have to inject themselves with a syringe. Researchers are continually testing alternative ways for those with diabetes to self-administer insulin. New methods include insulin pens, insulin jet injectors, and insulin pumps. Researchers hope that someday those with diabetes will no longer have to use needles to obtain the insulin they critically need.

What Effects Does Diabetes Have on Your Body?

Constant exposure to high blood glucose levels can damage vital organs over time. Diabetes, especially if it is poorly managed, increases the likelihood of a multitude of dire effects, such as nerve damage, leg and foot amputations, eye diseases, including blindness, tooth loss, gum problems, kidney disease, and heart disease.[21]

The longer the person has diabetes, the greater the risk for nerve damage. Numbness in the toes, feet, legs, and hands, as well as changes in bowel, bladder, and sexual function, are all signs of damage to nerves. This nerve damage can affect the ability to feel a change in temperature or pain in the legs and feet. A cut or sore on the foot could go unnoticed until it becomes infected. The poor blood circulation common in those with diabetes can also make it harder for sores or infections to heal. The infection could infiltrate the bone, causing the need for an amputation.

Diabetes can also damage the tiny blood vessels in the retina of the eye, which can cause bleeding and cloudy vision, and eventually destroy the retina and cause blindness. A high blood glucose level can cause tooth and gum problems, including the loss of teeth, and damage to the kidneys. If the kidneys are damaged, protein can

type 1 diabetes Autoimmune form of diabetes in which the pancreas does not produce insulin.

type 2 diabetes Form of diabetes characterized by insulin resistance.

Are You at Risk for Type 2 Diabetes?

Take the following quiz to assess if you are at a higher risk for developing type 2 diabetes. Whereas this list contains the presently known risk factors for type 2 diabetes, there may be others. If you have questions or doubts, check with your doctor.

Write Your Score

HOW DO YOU SCORE?

1 How old are you?
Less than 40 years (0 points)
40–49 years (1 point)
50–59 years (2 points)
60 years or older (3 points)

2 Are you female or male?
Female (0 points)   Male (1 point)

3 If you are a woman, have you ever been diagnosed with gestational diabetes?
Yes (1 point)   No (0 points)

4 Do you have a mother, father, sister, or brother with diabetes?
Yes (1 point)   No (0 points)

5 Have been diagnosed with high blood pressure?
Yes (1 point)   No (0 points)

6 Are you physically active?
Yes (0 points)   No (1 point)

7 What is your weight status?
(see chart below)

If your scored 5 or higher:
You are at increased risk for having type 2 diabetes. However only your doctor can tell for sure if you do have type 2 diabetes or prediabetes (a condition that precedes type 2 diabetes in which blood glucose levels are higher than normal). Talk to your doctor to see if additional testing is needed.

Type 2 diabetes is more common in African Americans, HIspanics/ Latinos, American Indians, and Asian Americans and Pacific Islanders.

TOTAL

Height	Weight (lbs.)		
4′ 10″	119–142	143–190	191+
4′ 11″	124–147	148–197	198+
5′ 0″	128–152	153–203	204+
5′ 1″	132–157	158–210	211+
5′ 2″	136–163	164–217	218+
5′ 3″	141–168	169–224	225+
5′ 4″	145–173	174–231	232+
5′ 5	150–179	180–239	240+
5′ 6″	155–185	186–246	247+
5′ 7″	159–190	191–254	255+
5′ 8″	164–196	197–261	262+
5′ 9″	169–202	203–269	270+
5′ 10″	174–208	209–277	278+
5′ 11″	179–214	215–285	286+
6′ 0″	184–220	221–293	294+
6′ 1″	189–226	227–301	302+
6′ 2″	194–232	233–310	311+
6′ 3″	200–239	240–318	319+
6′ 4″	205–245	246–327	328+
	(1 point)	(2 points)	(3 points)

Destined for Diabetes?

Joaquin is a 54-year-old math professor who weighs 50 pounds more than he did when he graduated from college. His annual physical at the campus health center uncovered that his blood glucose level classified him as having prediabetes: His level is higher than ideal but not high enough for a diagnosis of full-fledged diabetes. His father and grandfather both developed diabetes later in their lives. Joaquin's physical activity consists of walking less than one block from the faculty parking lot to his office. Because he doesn't like to cook, he eats breakfast at the donut shop and lunch at the hamburger fast-food joint on campus, and picks up takeout for dinner.

There are about 80 million individuals who, like Joaquin, have prediabetes and are at higher risk of developing not only diabetes, but also other health issues. A chronically higher level of glucose in the blood can cause damage to the heart, kidneys, eyes, and nerves. Factors that increase the risk of developing prediabetes include being 45 years of age and older; being overweight or obese; having a family history of diabetes; being of African-American, Hispanic/Latino, Native American, Asian-American, or Pacific Islander racial or ethnic background; having developed diabetes during a pregnancy (known as gestational diabetes) or having given birth to a baby weighing nine pounds or more; and being physically active less than three times a week.

Joaquin has one factor in his favor, which is that he now knows he is prediabetic; unfortunately, the majority of people with prediabetes don't even know that they have it. If people with this condition don't make any changes in their diet and lifestyle to improve their health, it is estimated that up to 30 percent of them will develop full-fledged type 2 diabetes within 5 years.[33] Joaquin now has the opportunity to try to reverse his prediabetic condition and so possibly avoid developing diabetes.

Think About It

What are three of Joaquin's risk factors for prediabetes? Which ones can he change and which ones can't he?

leak out into the urine, and at the same time, cause a backup of wastes in the blood. Kidney failure could result.

Diabetes is a risk factor for heart disease. The excess amount of fat often seen in the blood in poorly managed diabetes is most probably an important factor in the increased risk of heart disease in those with diabetes. Fortunately, good nutrition habits play a key role in both the prevention and management of diabetes.

Whereas a high level of glucose in your blood on a regular basis isn't healthy, a blood glucose level that is too low, or **hypoglycemia**, can be unpleasant for many of us and downright dangerous for some with diabetes. Individuals who experience hypoglycemia may feel hungry, nervous, dizzy, light-headed, confused, weak, or shaky, and even begin to sweat. Eating or drinking carbohydrate-rich foods, such as hard candies, juice, or soda, can relieve these symptoms quickly and raise the blood glucose level to a normal range.

Those with diabetes who need to use insulin and/or blood glucose–lowering medications daily are at risk of hypoglycemia if they skip meals and snacks or if they don't eat enough to cover the effects of the medication. If these individuals ignore their symptoms, their blood glucose level can drop so low that they could faint, or slip into a coma.[22] Those with diabetes need to eat regularly to maintain blood glucose levels that coincide with their medication. A change in their activities or exercise level can also lower the blood glucose level. Diabetics need to check their blood glucose level before they exercise to determine if a snack is needed.

hypoglycemia A blood glucose level that drops to lower than 70 mg/dl. Hunger, shakiness, dizziness, perspiration, and light-headedness are some signs of hypoglycemia.

Though not common, people without diabetes may also experience bouts of hypoglycemia after meals, better known as reactive hypoglycemia, which may be hormone related. Another type of hypoglycemia, called fasting hypoglycemia, can occur in individuals without diabetes in the morning, after fasting throughout the night. It can also occur during long stretches between meals or after exercise.

How Is Diabetes Treated and Controlled?

For years, people with diabetes have been advised to keep their blood glucose level under control. In the early 1990s, the research community gathered the evidence to back up that advice. The groundbreaking Diabetes Control and Complications Trial (DCCT), conducted from 1983 to 1993, involved more than 1,400 people with type 1 diabetes. It showed that controlling the level of blood glucose with an intense regimen of diet, insulin, and exercise, along with monitoring blood sugar levels and routinely visiting health care professionals, slowed the onset of some of the complications of diabetes. This study showed that reducing high blood glucose helped lower the risk of eye disease by 76 percent and the risk of kidney and nerve disease by at least 50 percent. However, the study did not cover this type of intensive therapy in young children or patients with multiple medical complications, those with a history of frequent hypoglycemia, or those who were terminally ill.[23]

The nutrition and lifestyle goals for individuals with type 1 or type 2 diabetes are the same: to minimize the complications of diabetes by adopting a healthy, well-balanced diet and participating in regular physical activity that maintains a blood glucose level in a normal or close to normal range. The ADA recommends that individuals with diabetes meet with a registered dietitian for individualized instruction regarding weight management, diet, and lifestyle changes.[24]

Whereas monitoring the overall amount of carbohydrate within a healthy diet along with weight management are key factors in managing diabetes, substituting low–glycemic load foods for higher–glycemic load foods may also modestly help those with diabetes better manage their blood glucose level, according to the ADA.[25]

The glycemic index (GI) and glucose load (GL) can be used to classify the effects of carbohydrate-containing foods on blood glucose. The GI refers to the measured upward rise, peak, and eventual fall of blood glucose following the consumption of a carbohydrate-intense food. Some foods cause a sharp spike and rapid fall in blood glucose levels compared with others that cause less of a spike and a more gradual decline.[26] The index ranks high-carbohydrate foods according to their effect on blood glucose levels compared with that of an equal amount of white bread or pure glucose.

If a carbohydrate-rich food causes your blood glucose level to produce a curve with a larger area than the standard curve of white bread, the food is considered a high-GI food. A carbohydrate-containing food that produces a smaller blood glucose level curve than that of white bread would be considered a low-GI food. For example, 50 grams of white bread has a glycemic index of 100. A 50-gram portion of kidney beans has a GI of 42, whereas the same amount of puffed wheat cereal has a GI of 105. Consequently, the kidney beans are considered a low-GI food compared with the white bread, while puffed wheat is considered a high-GI food (**Figure 4.13**). The problem with use of the GI is that 50 grams of puffed wheat would be more than 4 cups of cereal, an amount that is unlikely to be eaten in one sitting. The glycemic load (GL) adjusts the GI to take into account the amount of carbohydrate consumed in a typical serving of a food, and in the case of puffed wheat cereal would lower its effect on blood glucose dramatically.

Other factors can also affect the GI of a food. Overripe fruits have more easily digested sugar and a higher GI than underripe ones. Both cooking and food processing change the structure of foods and make them more easily digested, increasing the GI compared with raw, unprocessed equivalents. Larger chunks or bigger particle sizes of food contribute to slower digestion and lower GI than the same foods

There are many ways for an individual to monitor his or her blood glucose level.

chopped into smaller pieces. Foods with viscous, soluble fiber tend to be absorbed more slowly, so will have a lower GI than refined carbohydrates. In general, whole grains, vegetables, whole fruit, and legumes tend to have a low GI.[27] Lastly, eating carbohydrate-heavy foods with protein and/or fat can also lower the GI.[28]

(T/F) Though sugar was once thought of as a "diabetic no-no," it can now be part of a diabetic's diet. Research has found that eating sucrose doesn't cause a rise in a person's blood glucose level to any greater extent than does eating starch, so avoidance of sugar isn't necessary. Nor does eating a lot of sugar cause diabetes. However, being overweight is a risk factor for developing type 2 diabetes. And weight management is often a concern for diabetics, so there isn't room for a lot of sweets and treats in a diabetic diet (or *anyone's* diet, for that matter).

Why Is Diabetes Called an Epidemic?

The incidence of adults being diagnosed with diabetes in the United States has more than tripled since the early 1980s.[29] Our aging population is one of the reasons for this increase, as the occurrence of diabetes is about seven times as high for those 65 years of age or older as it is for younger adults aged 20 to 44 years.[30] Diabetes is the seventh leading cause of death in the United States. Diabetes is not only a deadly disease but also an extremely costly one. Disability insurance payments, time lost from employment, and the medical costs associated with diabetes cost the United States $245 billion annually.[31]

The number of people who have diabetes is not only strikingly high, but it's rising, particularly among children. Type 1 diabetes was formerly the only type of diabetes prevalent in children. Over the years, type 2 diabetes has been steadily increasing among children and adolescents in the United States.[32] Developing diabetes at a younger age means longer exposure to the disease and its medical complications.

Can Type 2 Diabetes Be Prevented?

Recent research has suggested that shedding some excess weight, exercising regularly, and eating a balanced, high-fiber, healthy diet that is lower in added sugars may be the best strategy to lower the risk of developing diabetes. The conclusion from the report of the 2015 *Dietary Guidelines* advisory committee, based on the latest research, is that a higher intake of added sugars, especially if they are consumed from sweetened beverages such as soda, fruits drinks, and sports and energy drinks, increases the risk of developing type 2 diabetes among adults.[33] According to the report, even when the excess body weight of the research subjects was taken into account, there was still a positive association between consuming too many sweetened beverages and the increased incidences of type 2 diabetes.

A landmark study by the Diabetes Prevention Program of more than 3,000 individuals with prediabetes showed that those who made changes in their lifestyle, such as losing weight, exercising 2.5 hours a week, eating a plant-based, heart-healthy diet, and meeting with a health professional for ongoing support and education, were 58 percent less likely to develop type 2 diabetes than those who did not partake in such intervention.[34] When it comes to winning the battle against diabetes, a healthful diet and lifestyle is the best game plan.

LO 4.6 The Take-Home Message Diabetes is a medical condition in which an individual either doesn't have enough insulin or their cells are resistant to the insulin available in their body. This causes their blood glucose level to rise to an unhealthy level. Type 2 diabetes is the most common form. Constant exposure to elevated blood glucose levels can damage your vital organs over time. Shedding some excess weight, exercising regularly, and eating a balanced, high-fiber, healthy diet that is lower in added sugars may be the best strategy to lower the risk of developing diabetes.

The Glycemic Index of Foods

Foods	GI*
Rice, low amylose	126
Potato, baked	121
Cornflakes	119
Jelly beans	114
Green peas	107
Cheerios	106
Puffed wheat	105
Bagel, plain	103
White bread	100
Angel food cake	95
Ice cream	87
Bran muffin	85
Rice, long grain**	80
Brown rice	79
Oatmeal	79
Popcorn	79
Corn	78
Banana, overripe	74
Chocolate	70
Baked beans	69
Sponge cake	66
Pear, canned in juice	63
Custard	61
Spaghetti	59
Rice, long grain***	58
Apple	52
Pear	47
Banana, underripe	43
Kidney beans	42
Whole milk	39
Peanuts	21

*GI = Glycemic Index
**Boiled for 25 minutes.
***Boiled for 5 minutes.

Figure 4.13 The Glycemic Index of Commonly Eaten Foods
The glycemic index of a variety of foods compared to white bread.

A variety of sugar substitutes is available to the consumer.

What Are Sugar Substitutes and What Forms Can They Take?

LO 4.7 List alternative sweeteners used as sugar substitutes.

Because eating too much sugar can be unhealthy, what's a person with a sweet tooth to do? Americans have looked to sugar-free beverages and foods over the years to limit their sugar intake while satisfying their yen for sugar (**Figure 4.14**). Such items contain **sugar substitutes** that are as sweet as—or sweeter than—sugar but contain fewer calories.

All sugar substitutes must be approved by the FDA and deemed safe for consumption before they are allowed in food products sold in the United States.[35] Several sugar substitutes are presently available to consumers, such as polyols, tagalose, saccharin, aspartame, acesulfame-K, sucralose, rebaudioside A, neotame, stevia, monk fruit, and advantame. Polyols don't promote dental caries and cause a slower rise in blood glucose than sugar does. Saccharin, aspartame, acesulfame-K, sucralose, rebaudioside A, tagalose, neotame, stevia, monk fruit, and advantame also won't promote dental caries and have the added advantage of not affecting blood glucose levels. All these sugar substitutes are either reduced in calories or are calorie free. See **Table 4.3** for a comparison of available sweeteners.

Polyols Are Sugar Alcohols

Polyols are often called sugar alcohols because they have the chemical structure of sugar with an alcohol component added. Whereas polyols such as sorbitol, mannitol, and xylitol are found naturally in plants, they are also produced synthetically and are used as sweeteners in foods such as chewing gum and candies. They can be used tablespoon for tablespoon to substitute for sucrose. Sorbitol and mannitol are also less likely to promote dental caries because the bacteria on your teeth

Figure 4.14 Growing Interest in Sugar-Free Foods and Beverages
The use of sugar-free products has more than doubled since 1986.

sugar substitutes Alternatives to table sugar that sweeten foods for fewer calories.

Table 4.3

Oh So Sweet!

	Calories/Gram	Trade Names	Sweetening Power	The Facts
Sweetener				
Sucrose	4	Table Sugar	—	Sweetens food, enhances flavor, tenderizes, and contributes browning properties to baked goods
Reduced-Calorie Sweeteners				
Sorbitol	2.6	Sorbitol	50–70% as sweet as sucrose	Found in foods such as sugarless chewing gum, jams, baked goods, and candy. May cause diarrhea when 50 grams (about 15 sugar-free candies) are consumed.
Mannitol	1.6	Mannitol	50–70% as sweet as sucrose	Found in foods such as chewing gum, jams, and as a bulking agent in powdered foods. Excessive amounts may cause diarrhea.
Xylitol	2.4	Xylitol	Equally sweet as sucrose	Found in foods such as chewing gum, candies; also in pharmaceuticals and hygiene products
Hydrogenated starch hydrolysates (HSH)	3.0	HSH	50–70% as sweet as sucrose	Found in confections and can be used as a bulking agent
Tagalose	1.5	Naturlose	92% as sweet as sucrose	Texture and taste similar to sucrose
Calorie-Free Sweeteners				
Saccharin	0	Sweet'N Low	200–700% the sweetness of sucrose	Retains its sweetening power at high temperatures such as baking
Aspartame	4*	Nutrasweet, Equal	Approximately 200% the sweetness of sucrose	Sweetening power is reduced at high temperatures such as baking. Can be added at end stages of recipes such as cooked puddings if removed from heat source. Individuals with PKU need to monitor all dietary sources of phenylalanine, including aspartame.
Neotame	0	Neotame	7,000–13,000% the sweetness of sucrose	Retains its sweetening power at high temperatures
Acesulfame-K	0	Sunette	200% the sweetness of sucrose	Retains its sweetening power at high temperatures
Sucralose	0	Splenda	600% the sweetness of sucrose	Retains its sweetening power at high temperatures
Rebaudioside A	0	Truvia, PureVia	200% the sweetness of sucrose	Retains its sweetening power at high temperatures
Monk fruit	0	Nectresse	150–300% the sweetness of sucrose	May have an aftertaste
Advantame	0	Not available	20,000 times the sweetness of sucrose	Retains its sweetening power at high temperatures

*Because so little aspartame is needed to sweeten foods, it provides negligible calories.

metabolize them so slowly. (Humans lack the enzyme needed to ferment xylitol.) Their slower absorption means that they do not produce a spike in blood glucose, which is a benefit for those with diabetes.

Chewing gums and candies that contain sugar alcohols can be labeled "sugar free" and boast that they don't promote tooth decay. Keep in mind, though, that even though these products are sugar free, they are not necessarily calorie free. Even more importantly, because polyols are incompletely absorbed in your digestive tract, they can cause diarrhea. For this reason, they should be used in moderation.

Another type of polyol is hydrogenated starch hydrolysates (HSH), which are made by partially breaking down corn, wheat, or potato starch into smaller pieces and then adding hydrogen to these pieces. The end product is a wide range of polyols, including those that can be strung together and used commercially. HSH adds sweetness, texture, and bulk to many sugarless products such as baked goods and candies.[36]

Tagalose is about 90 percent as sweet as sucrose and contains fewer calories per gram (see Table 4.3). It is derived from lactose that can be found naturally in some dairy products.

Saccharin Is the Oldest Sugar Substitute

Saccharin was first discovered in 1879, and during the two World Wars, when sugar was being rationed, it was used as a sugar substitute in the United States and Europe. Today, you probably know saccharin as those little pink packets often found on coffee shop counters or diner tables. It has been used in foods, beverages, vitamins, and pharmaceuticals. Because saccharin is not metabolized in your body, it doesn't provide any calories.

In 1977, the FDA banned saccharin due to reports from the research community that it could cause bladder cancer in rats. Congress immediately implemented an 18-month moratorium on this ban through the Saccharin Study and Labeling Act. This allowed the continued commercial use of saccharin, but required that any saccharin-containing products bear a warning label stating that saccharin was potentially hazardous to your health, as it caused cancer in laboratory animals.

In 2000, the National Toxicology Program (NTP) removed saccharin from the list of substances that could potentially cause cancer. After extensive review, the NTP determined that the observed bladder tumors in rats were actually from a mechanism that wasn't relevant to humans.[37] The lesson learned from this is that though you can safely consume saccharin in moderation, you shouldn't feed it to your pet rat. Saccharin is used in more than 100 countries in the world today.

> Substituting sweeteners for sugar isn't shaving off the pounds. Although the consumption of low-calorie sweeteners has tripled since 1980, the prevalence of overweight and obese Americans has increased by 60 percent.

Aspartame Is Derived from Amino Acids

In 1965, a scientist named James Schlatter was conducting research on amino acids in his quest to find a treatment for ulcers. To pick up a piece of paper in his laboratory, he licked his finger and stumbled upon a sweet-tasting compound.[38] It was the "lick" that was soon to be "tasted" around the world. Schlatter had just discovered aspartame, a substance that would change the world of sugar substitutes.

Aspartame is composed of two amino acids: a modified aspartic acid and phenylalanine. Enzymes in your digestive tract break down aspartame into its components, and the amino acids are absorbed, providing 4 calories per gram. Consequently, aspartame has the potential to provide calories to foods as an added sweetener. However, as aspartame is 200 times sweeter than sucrose, only a small amount is needed to sweeten a food.

In 1981, the FDA approved aspartame for use in tabletop sweeteners such as Equal and Nutrasweet, and for various other uses, such as to sweeten breakfast cereals, chewing gums, and carbonated beverages. The majority of the aspartame that is consumed in the United States is in soft drinks. In 1996, the FDA gave the food industry carte blanche to use aspartame in all types of foods and beverages. It is

Foods and beverages that contain aspartame must carry a warning label that says phenylalanine is present.

currently used as a sweetener in more than 100 countries, and can now be found in more than 6,000 foods, as well as pharmaceuticals and personal care products, sold in the United States.

Aspartame has undergone continual, vigorous reviews to ensure that it is safe for human consumption. The FDA considers it one of the most thoroughly studied and tested food additives approved by the agency. It is not associated with any adverse effects in the general population, including children.[39]

Individuals with a rare, inherited disorder known as phenylketonuria (PKU) are unable to metabolize one of the amino acids in aspartame, phenylalanine, and must adhere to a special diet.[40] PKU affects about 1 out of every 10,000 to 15,000 infants in the United States. While PKU can happen to anyone, it is more common in those who are Native American and Northern European.[41] It is the result of a deficiency of phenylalanine hydroxylase, an enzyme needed to properly metabolize phenylalanine.[42]

People with PKU need to control all dietary sources of this amino acid, including aspartame as well as protein-rich foods such as meat, milk, eggs, and nuts. These individuals do not necessarily have to avoid aspartame, but they need to monitor it as an additional source of phenylalanine in their diet. Because of the seriousness of this disorder, the FDA mandates that all food products that contain phenylalanine carry a label declaring its content.

Neotame Is Also Made from Amino Acids

Neotame, which the FDA approved in 2002, comprises the same two amino acids—aspartic acid and phenylalanine—as aspartame, but they are joined together in such a way that the body cannot break them apart. So, individuals with PKU can use neotame without concern. Neotame is completely eliminated in either the urine or stool. It has been approved as a sweetener and for a variety of uses, such as chewing gum, frostings, frozen desserts, puddings, fruit juices, and syrups.[43]

Acesulfame-K Contains Potassium

While less than sweet sounding, acesulfame-K (the K refers to the potassium component) is about twice as sweet as sucrose. It is available as a tabletop sweetener, called Sunette, and is currently used in chewing gum, candy, desserts, yogurt, and alcoholic beverages. Your body does not metabolize acesulfame-K.

Sucralose Is Made from Sucrose

Sucralose was developed in 1976 by changing the structure of the sucrose molecule. Unlike sucrose, sucralose isn't absorbed by your body—it is excreted in your urine. In 1998, sucralose was approved as a tabletop sweetener, and it's available commercially as Splenda.

Rebaudioside A Is Derived from the Stevia Plant

Rebaudioside A is a combination of a sugar alcohol with an extract from the stevia plant. Extracts from the stevia plant, which is native to Brazil and Paraguay, are currently used in Brazil and Japan as tabletop sweeteners and in some products, such as teas and yogurt. This zero-calorie sweetener is approximately twice as sweet as sugar and is available under trade names such as Truvia, Sun Crystals, and PureVia. It doesn't affect blood glucose levels, so those with diabetes can use it.

Monk Fruit Is Another Sugar Substitute

A new addition to the world of sugar substitutes is the extract of the luo han guo fruit, commonly called monk fruit. The name came from the Buddhist monks who discovered the fruit centuries ago. It has up to 150 to 300 percent the sweetness of sucrose but can have a lingering aftertaste when consumed in large amounts. It can be found in both foods and beverages.

Advantame Is the Newest Sugar Substitute

Advantame is chemically related to aspartame in that it is made from aspartame with the addition of vanillin, an ingredient of vanilla. It is about 20,000 times sweeter than sugar and 100 times sweeter than aspartame. It has been approved by the FDA to be used in baked goods, soft drinks, gum confections and frostings, frozen desserts, gelatins, jams, processed fruit juices, toppings, and syrups. Even though it contains phenylalanine as part of aspartame, advantame is such a high-intensity sweetener that only a very small amount is needed to sweeten a food or beverage. Thus, the amount of phenylalanine consumed with advantame will be so small that products containing it will not have to bear the warning label regarding phenylalanine that must accompany products containing aspartame.

LO 4.7 **The Take-Home Message** Millions of Americans consume reduced-calorie or calorie-free sugar substitutes. The FDA has approved polyols, tagalose, saccharin, aspartame, acesulfame-K, sucralose, neotame, rebaudioside A, monk fruit, and advantame to be used in a variety of foods. These sugar substitutes do not promote dental caries and can benefit those with diabetes who are trying to manage their blood glucose.

Why Is Fiber So Important?

LO 4.8 Describe the importance of fiber in the body and diet.

Even though fiber is a nondigestible substance that is resistant to being broken down in your small intestine, it can have many powerful health effects in your body. Fiber has been shown to help lower your risk of developing constipation, diverticulosis, obesity, heart disease, cancer, and diabetes mellitus (**Table 4.4**). Let's look closely at how this works.

Fiber Helps Prevent Constipation and Diverticulosis

More than 40 million Americans complain about being constipated, with women, especially pregnant women and adults 65 years of age and older, experiencing it more often than others. The uncomfortable, bloated, and sluggish feelings of constipation compel Americans to look to laxative products for relief.[44] Because a diet lacking sufficient high-fiber whole grains, fruits, and vegetables and abounding in cheese, eggs, and meats is a recipe for constipation, many people would be better off spending time in the produce and whole-grain aisles of the supermarket rather than shopping for laxatives.

As remnants of food move through your colon, water is absorbed, which causes the formation of solid waste products (stool). The contractions of the muscles in your colon push the stool toward your rectum to be eliminated. If these muscle contractions are sluggish, the stool may linger too long in your colon, which can cause too much water to be reabsorbed. This can create hard, dry stools that are more

Table 4.4

Type-Casting Fiber

Type	Found in	Can Help Reduce the Risk of
Insoluble Fiber		
Cellulose Hemicellulos Lignins	Whole grains, whole-grain cereals, bran, oats, fruit, and vegetables	Constipation Diverticulosis Certain cancers Heart disease Obesity
Soluble, Viscous Fibers		
Pectin Beta-glucan Gums Psyllium	Citrus fruits, prunes, legumes, oats, barley, brussels sprouts, carrots	Constipation Heart disease Diabetes mellitus Obesity

difficult and painful to expel. A diet adequate in insoluble fibers such as bran, whole grains, and many fruits and vegetables will help keep things moving along in your digestive tract and decrease your likelihood of becoming constipated. (Note: Some soluble fibers, such as psyllium, can also be an aid in relieving constipation, as its water-attracting capability allows the stool to increase in bulk and form a gel-like, soft texture, which makes it easier to pass.)

Constipation can become more frequent during different stages of your life. During pregnancy, hormonal changes as well as the pressure of the growing baby on the intestine can make regular bowel movements more difficult. As you age, your metabolism slows, which results in a slower-moving digestive tract as well as loss of intestinal muscle tone. Unfortunately, abusing laxatives can damage the nerve cells in the colon and disrupt the colon's natural movements. This can cause you to depend on laxatives in order to bring on a normal bowel movement.[45]

Long-term constipation may play a role in a disorder called **diverticulosis** (*osis* = condition). Constipation is the main cause of increased pressure in the colon and may cause the weak spots along your colon wall to bulge out, forming **diverticula** (**Figure 4.15**).

Infection of the diverticula, a condition known as **diverticulitis** (*itis* = inflammation), can lead to stomach pain, fever, nausea, vomiting, cramping, and chills. Though not proven, it is believed that the stool or bacteria in the colon may get stuck in the diverticula and cause the inflammation. Also, a decrease in healthy bacteria and a simultaneous increase in unhealthy bacteria may also cause inflammation.[46] The disorder is more common in developed countries, such as the United States and England, and is rarely found in areas where high-fiber diets are more commonplace, such as Asia and Africa. Consuming a diet with adequate fiber may reduce the symptoms associated with diverticulosis.

Fiber Helps Prevent Obesity

A fiber-rich diet can also be kind to your waistline. As mentioned earlier, high-fiber foods, such as whole grains, fruits, and vegetables, can add to satiation so that you need to eat fewer calories to feel full. Research studies suggest that this can aid in weight management.[47] Whereas some weight-loss diets restrict carbohydrates, these plans would work better if they *increased* high-fiber carbohydrates.

diverticulosis The existence of diverticula in the lining of the intestine.

diverticula Small bulges at weak spots in the colon wall.

diverticulitis Infection of the diverticula.

Fiber Helps Prevent Heart Disease, Diabetes, and Cancer

Viscous, soluble fibers have been shown to help lower elevated blood cholesterol levels. A high blood cholesterol level can increase the risk of heart disease. It is believed that viscous fiber interferes with the reabsorption of bile acids in the intestines. Bile acids are high in cholesterol and are released into your intestine by your gallbladder to help with the digestion of fat. The bile acids are likely "grabbed" by the fiber before they can be reabsorbed by the body. They then end up being excreted along with the fiber in your waste products. Your body replaces these lost bile acids by removing cholesterol from the blood to generate new bile acids in the liver. Blood cholesterol levels are lowered as a result.

Slow-moving, viscous, soluble fibers may reduce the rate at which fat and carbohydrates are absorbed from your meals. Delayed absorption can lower the surge of fat in your blood after a meal, and may help improve sensitivity to the hormone insulin. Both high levels of fat in the blood and a decreased sensitivity to insulin are considered risk factors for heart disease.

Viscous, soluble fiber may not be the only type of fiber that can promote heart health. Several research studies have shown that cereal and grains, which contain insoluble fiber, may help to lower the risk of heart disease.[48] Fiber from cereal has been associated with a reduction in blood pressure.[49] High blood pressure is a risk factor for both heart disease and stroke.

Viscous, soluble fibers have also been shown to help individuals with diabetes mellitus. They slow the release of food from your stomach, and thus slow down the digestion and absorption of glucose. This could help avoid a large spike in blood glucose after eating and help those with diabetes improve the long-term control of their blood glucose level.[50] Fiber may also play a role in preventing diabetes. Research suggests that diets that provide 30 to 50 grams of fiber from food sources daily can help lower blood glucose levels, reducing the risk of diabetes.[51]

Fiber is thought to have many positive and protective effects in the fight against certain cancers. Fiber from cereals has been shown to help lower the risk of breast cancer.[52] Research also suggests that as fiber consumption increases, the incidence of colorectal cancer is reduced.

Four mechanisms may account for fiber's role in fighting cancer:

- Fiber increases the bulk of stool, which can dilute cancer-promoting substances in the colon.
- Fiber helps keep things moving through the digestive tract so that potential cancer-promoting substances spend less time in contact with the intestinal lining.
- Fiber encourages the growth of friendly bacteria in the colon and their fermentation by-products, both of which may have cancer-fighting potential.
- Fiber binds with acids in bile, a substance produced by the liver and important in fat breakdown. This causes the acids to be expelled from the body in the stool, rather than being reabsorbed. Because an increased amount of bile acids in the colon is thought to be associated with colon and rectal cancer, fiber's ability to reduce the concentration of these acids is viewed as a cancer deterrent.[53]

Figure 4.15 Diverticula
Diverticula are small pouches that can occur along your colon. When stool gets trapped in them, they can become inflamed, and this can lead to diverticulitis.

Whole fruits and vegetables, whole grains, and legumes are the best food sources of fiber.

Whereas over the years some studies have challenged fiber's protective role against colorectal cancer, current research supports the cancer-fighting potential of fiber.[54] A large research study involving over 500,000 individuals recruited from 10 European countries showed that individuals who consumed the most fiber (35 grams of fiber daily, on average), compared with those eating the least amount of fiber daily (15 grams, on average), reduced their risk of colorectal cancer by about 40 percent.[55] The dietary sources of fiber were varied among the countries and included fiber from cereal, vegetables, fruits, and legumes. Because this large study was done with high-fiber foods and not fiber supplements, it is difficult to tease out if the potential cancer-fighting substance in these foods is only the fiber, or the other nutrients and phytochemicals in these plant-based foods operating in concert with the fiber.

Once again, the best advice is to eat a varied, balanced, plant-based diet rich in whole grains, fruits, vegetables, and legumes. This type of diet is also good for weight management. Obesity increases the risk of colorectal cancer.[56]

Too Much Fiber Can Cause Health Problems

A word of caution: Initially, a high-fiber diet can have negative side effects (flatulence and bloating). Consuming too much fiber can reduce the absorption of some vitamins and minerals and may cause diarrhea in some individuals.[57] Gradually increasing the fiber in your diet, rather than suddenly adding large amounts, will allow your body to adjust to the increased amount of fiber and minimize the side effects. A small, steady increase of fiber will be easier on your colon and on those around you. As you add more fiber to your diet, you should also drink more fluids.

LO 4.8 **The Take-Home Message** Fiber is a nondigestible substance that can help reduce the risk of constipation, diverticulosis, heart disease, obesity, diabetes mellitus, and certain cancers. Increasing fiber intake too quickly can cause diarrhea, constipation, and gassiness, so consumption should be increased gradually and be accompanied by plenty of fluids.

MADE over MADE better

Americans, on average, are consuming only about half of the amount of fiber recommended daily. Making some easy food substitutions can quickly bump up your daily fiber intake. Here are some typical foods made over and made nutritionally better!

If you like this. . .   **Try this to boost your fiber intake!**

Special K cereal
Serving size: 1 cup
Total Fiber: 1 gram

Wheaties cereal
Serving size: 1 cup
Total Fiber: 4 grams

Cheez-It
Serving size: 27 crackers
Total Fiber: 1 gram

Triscuit
Serving size: 6 crackers
Total Fiber: 3 grams

White bread
Serving size: 2 slices
Total Fiber: 1.2 grams

100% Whole-wheat bread
Serving size: 2 slices
Total Fiber: 8 grams

Pretzels
Serving size: 10 pretzels
Total Fiber: 0.9 grams

Popcorn
Serving size: 100-calorie microwave popcorn bag
Total Fiber: 4 grams

POINTS OF VIEW

Should Food Labels Distinguish between Naturally Occurring and Added Sugars?

The Food and Drug Administration (FDA) is considering a revision to the Nutrition Facts panel on food labels that would disclose the amount of added sugars per serving in foods and beverages. Currently, 16 percent of the calories in the American diet, on average, comes from added sugars.[1] Many experts recommend consuming fewer foods with a lot of added sugars. These sugary foods often displace more nutrient-rich foods, and at the same time, increase the overall calorie intake in the diet.[2, 3] However, some food industry representatives oppose the new rules, saying the mandates are unnecessary and harmful. One company even declared that separating out added sugars on the food label would confuse consumers.[4] Should added sugars appear on food labels? Take a close look at the arguments for both sides and see what you think.

yes

- In order to pursue a healthy diet, consumers need transparent information so they can make informed choices.[5]

- Labels with details about added sugars will increase consumer awareness about overall sugar consumption.[6]

- Consumers often overlook the fact that canned fruit in syrup has more sugar than canned fruit in juice.[7]

- With all the different names for sugar, it is necessary to clearly label products with added sugars.[8]

- Added sugars are a contributor to the obesity epidemic.[9] Most adults in the U.S. consume more sugar than is healthy.[10]

no

- Sugar is sugar, whether it is added or natural, and the label already lists the amount of sugar.[11]

- Putting "added sugars" on the label will unfairly hurt sales because it sounds unhealthy, even for products like cranberry juice, which needs added sugars in order to be palatable.[12]

- Consumers have information overload.[13] All this effort on the food label may be better spent on education on nutrition as a whole.

- Requiring companies to distinguish between sugars may drive them to disguise added sugars by adding sweetened juices, such as grape juice concentrate, to the product.[14]

- Singling out added sugars on the food label sets a precedent for targeting future ingredients.[15]

what do you think?

1. Do you think that including separate information about added sugars will help to solve our obesity epidemic? **2.** Does reading negative nutritional information override the impulse to consume something unhealthy? **3.** What effect do nutrition labels have on your decisions about what to buy at the supermarket?

LO 4.1 Carbohydrates Are Energy-Containing Nutrients

Carbohydrates are essential nutrients that are predominant in plant-based foods, and they make up the foundation of many diets around the world. You need carbohydrates on a daily basis because they are the most desirable source of energy for your body. Carbohydrates are divided into two categories or classifications based on the number of sugar units that are joined together. Simple carbohydrates, or sugars, include monosaccharides and disaccharides, and complex carbohydrates include polysaccharides.

Three monosaccharides are found in foods: glucose, fructose, and galactose. When two glucose units join together, the disaccharide maltose is created. When glucose and fructose pair up, the disaccharide sucrose, or table sugar, is formed. Galactose is joined with glucose to create lactose.

Starch, glycogen, and fiber are all polysaccharides. Starch is the storage form of glucose in plants, and glycogen is the storage form in your body. Fiber is nondigestible but important.

Monosaccharides

Fructose   Glucose   Galactose

Disaccharides

Sucrose (glucose and fructose)   Maltose (glucose and glucose)   Lactose (glucose and galactose)

Polysaccharides (starch)

Amylose (straight chain)

Amylopectin (branched)

LO 4.2 Carbohydrates Are Digested in Your Mouth and Intestines

Although the digestion of carbohydrates starts in your mouth with the help of the enzyme amylase, which is in your saliva, most carbohydrate digestion occurs in the small intestine, facilitated by pancreatic amylase. Sucrose, maltose, and lactose are digested by small intestine enzymes into glucose, fructose, and galactose. Fiber continues down to the large intestine, where the majority of it is eliminated from your body in your stool.

Glucose, fructose, galactose (monosaccharides)

Bloodstream

LO 4.3 Hormones Help the Body Regulate Glucose

Your body uses carbohydrates, specifically glucose, for energy. To lower your blood glucose level, your pancreas releases the hormone insulin into the blood. Insulin helps direct the uptake of glucose by cells and also determines whether it will be used immediately as energy or stored for later use. Surplus glucose is stored in long chains of glycogen in a process called glycogenesis, which occurs only in your liver and muscle cells. Once glycogen stores are full, excess glucose is stored as fat. Your pancreas releases another hormone, glucagon, when the body needs to direct the release of glucose from the stored glycogen in your liver to help raise your blood glucose level. This breakdown of glycogen is called glycogenolysis.

Pancreas

Insulin   Glucose

Blood vessel

Tissue cells

LO 4.4 You Need to Consume Carbohydrates Daily

The latest Dietary Reference Intakes (DRIs) for carbohydrates recommend that adults and children consume a minimum of 130 grams daily. This is based on the estimated minimum amount of glucose your brain needs to function efficiently. A quick look at MyPlate

shows that 130 grams is less than the amount you would consume by eating the minimum recommended daily servings from the grain group (6 servings), vegetable group (3 servings), fruit group (2 servings), and dairy group (3 servings). The latest DRIs indicate that 45 to 65 percent of your total daily calories should come from carbohydrates. Adults should consume 21 to 38 grams of fiber daily and minimize their intake of added sugars.

LO 4.5 There Is a Difference between Natural and Added Sugars

Your taste buds can't distinguish between naturally occurring sugars, which are found in foods such as fruit and dairy products, and added sugars, which are added by manufacturers to foods such as soft drinks. Foods that contain naturally occurring sugar tend to be nutrient dense and thus provide more nutrition per bite. In contrast, foods that contain a lot of added sugars tend to give little else. These sugar-laden foods are called empty calories.

LO 4.6 Diabetes Is Considered an Epidemic

Individuals develop diabetes because they aren't producing enough insulin (type 1 diabetes) and/or they have developed insulin resistance, such that their cells do not respond to the insulin when it arrives (type 2 diabetes). Type 1 diabetes is an autoimmune disease and is the rarer of the two forms. Type 2 is the more common form and is seen in people who have become insulin resistant. Type 2 diabetes accounts for 90 to 95 percent of diagnoses of the disease.

Diabetes, especially if it is poorly managed, increases the likelihood of a multitude of dire effects such as nerve damage, leg and foot amputations, tooth loss, gum problems, kidney disease, and heart disease. Diabetes can also damage the tiny blood vessels in the retina of the eye, which can cause bleeding and cloudy vision, and eventually destroy the retina and cause blindness. Good nutrition and lifestyle habits play a key role in both the prevention and management of diabetes.

LO 4.7 There Are Many Forms of Sugar Substitutes

Polyols, saccharin, aspartame, acesulfame-K, sucralose, rebaudioside A, tagalose, neotame, monk fruit, and advantame are all sugar substitutes currently deemed safe by the FDA. Americans are expressing a growing interest in sugar-free foods and beverages.

VISUAL Chapter Summary

LO 4.8 Fiber Has Many Health Benefits

Fiber has been shown to help lower your risk of developing constipation, obesity, heart disease, cancer, and diabetes mellitus. Meals high in fiber are typically digested more slowly, which allows the absorption of the nutrients to be extended over a longer period of time. Foods high in fiber, such as whole grains, fruits, and vegetables, can add to satiation so that you need to eat fewer calories to feel full. Viscous, soluble fibers have been shown to help lower elevated blood cholesterol levels. A high blood cholesterol level can increase the risk of heart disease.

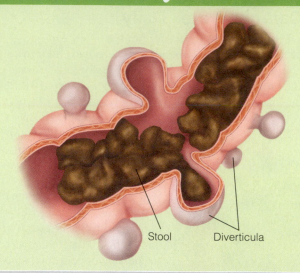
Stool Diverticula

Terms to Know

- glucose
- photosynthesis
- simple carbohydrates
- monosaccharides
- disaccharides
- complex carbohydrates
- polysaccharides
- fructose
- galactose
- sucrose
- maltose
- starch
- fiber
- glycogen
- hormones
- insulin
- glycogenesis
- glucagon
- glycogenolysis
- diabetes mellitus
- insulin resistance

MasteringNutrition™

Build your knowledge—and confidence—in the Study Area of MasteringNutrition with a variety of study tools.

Access MyDietAnalysis through MasteringNutrition™ and track your diet and daily activities. In addition, a dietary analysis activity is available for every chapter in your book.

Check Your Understanding

LO 4.1 1. _____ is the storage form of glucose in your body.
- a. Glucagon
- b. Glycogen
- c. Gluconeogenesis
- d. Glucose

LO 4.1 2. Sucrose is a
- a. monosaccharide.
- b. disaccharide.
- c. polysaccharide.
- d. starch.

LO 4.2 3. Which of the following can help someone who's lactose intolerant to enjoy dairy products?
- a. drinking Lactaid milk
- b. drinking milk on an empty stomach
- c. eating a large bowl of ice cream before going to bed
- d. having a milkshake for an afternoon snack

LO 4.3 4. The hormone that directs the breakdown of glycogen is
- a. galactose.
- b. glucagon.
- c. insulin.
- d. epinephrine.

LO 4.4 5. The minimum amount of carbohydrates needed daily is
- a. 75 grams.
- b. 100 grams.
- c. 120 grams.
- d. 130 grams.

LO 4.4 6. Which of the following nutrients are added to enriched grains?
- a. folic acid, thiamin, B_{12}, niacin, and calcium
- b. folic acid, thiamin, riboflavin, B_{12}, and iron
- c. fiber, thiamin, riboflavin, niacin, and iron
- d. folic acid, thiamin, riboflavin, niacin, and iron

LO 4.5 7. Reducing consumption of which item would have the biggest impact on decreasing the amount of added sugars that Americans consume?
- a. watermelon
- b. candy
- c. sugar-sweetened beverages
- d. desserts

LO 4.6 8. Which of the following can help reduce your risk of type 2 diabetes?
- a. playing computer games
- b. eating a high-fiber, plant-based diet lower in added sugars
- c. watching TV
- d. eating a high-calorie, high-fat diet

LO 4.7 9. Which sugar substitute is made of two amino acids?
- a. saccharin
- b. monk fruit
- c. aspartame
- d. sucralose

LO 4.8 **10.** Your blood cholesterol level is too high, so you would like to eat additional viscous, soluble high-fiber foods to help lower it. A good choice would be
  a. low-fat milk.
  b. chocolate chip cookies.
  c. orange juice.
  d. oatmeal.

Answers

1. (b) glycogen. Glycogen is stored in your liver and muscles and provides a ready-to-use form of glucose for your body. Glucagon is the hormone that directs the release of glucose from the stored glycogen. Gluconeogenesis is the creation of glucose from noncarbohydrate sources.
2. (b) Sucrose contains the two monosaccharides glucose and fructose, and is therefore a disaccharide. Starch contains many units of glucose linked together and is therefore a polysaccharide.
3. (a) Lactaid milk is pretreated to facilitate the breakdown of the lactose in the milk. Drinking milk on an empty stomach, eating a large bowl of ice cream before going to bed, and having a milkshake for an afternoon snack are all ways to consume a fair amount of lactose at one time and increase the symptoms of lactose intolerance.
4. (b) When your blood glucose level drops too low, glucagon is released from your pancreas to direct the breakdown of glycogen in your liver to raise your blood level of glucose. Insulin is a hormone that directs the uptake of glucose by your cells. Galactose is a monosaccharide found in dairy foods.
5. (d) You should consume at least 130 grams of carbohydrates daily to supply your body, particularly your brain, with the glucose needed to function effectively.
6. (d) These nutrients are added to enriched grains.
7. (c) Sugar-sweetened beverages are the number-one source of added sugars in the American diet, so reducing the intake of these sugary beverages would go a long way in reducing the amount of added sugars that Americans consume. Reducing the amount of candy and desserts that Americans consume would also help reduce the added sugars in the diet but not as much as cutting back on sugar-sweetened beverages.
8. (b) Unfortunately, if you want to try to prevent diabetes, playing sedentary computer games, watching TV, and eating a high-calorie, high-fat diet aren't healthy approaches. However, eating a high-fiber, plant-based diet lower in added sugars, getting regular exercise, and maintaining a healthy weight are all part of the best approach, at present, to help reduce your risk of developing type 2 diabetes.
9. (c) Aspartame is comprised of the amino acids aspartic acid and phenylalanine.
10. (d) Oatmeal is rich in beta-glucan, a viscous fiber that can help lower your cholesterol when eaten as part of a heart-healthy diet. Though nutrient dense, the orange juice and milk do not contain fiber. Cookies won't help lower your cholesterol.

Web Resources

- For more on fiber, visit the American Heart Association at www.heart.org
- For more on diabetes, visit the National Diabetes Education Program (NDEP) at www.ndep.nih.gov
- For more on lactose intolerance, visit the National Institute of Diabetes and Digestive and Kidney Disease (NIDDK) at http://digestive.niddk.nih.gov

Answers to True or False?

1. **False.** Many people who are lactose intolerant may still be able to enjoy some dairy products, especially if they are eaten with meals. In fact, dairy foods may be just what the doctor ordered. Turn to page 106 to learn why.
2. **True.** You need a *minimum* amount of carbohydrates daily to fuel your brain. See page 110 to find out how much you need to eat.
3. **True.** The average American consumes about half the amount of fiber that's recommended daily. Turn to page 111 to learn more about the potential problems associated with this shortfall.
4. **False.** Dark bread doesn't necessarily have more fiber than white bread. Learn why on page 112.
5. **False.** Calories, not carbs, are what you need to monitor to avoid weight gain. Turn to page 117 to find out why.
6. **True.** The more sugar you eat, the more likely you are to have tooth decay. Turn to page 118 to find out why this is the case.
7. **False.** The major source of added sugars in the diet is from sweetened beverages. Turn to page 120 to learn more.
8. **True.** Eating excess added sugars may increase the risk of developing diabetes. Turn to page 129 to learn more.
9. **False.** Foods that contain sugar alcohols, such as sorbitol or other sugar substitutes can be labeled "sugar free," but they still provide calories. Turn to page 131 to learn more.
10. **False.** Though saccharin once bore the stigma of being a cancer causer, it's no longer thought to cause cancer in humans. Turn to page 132 to learn more about this turnaround.

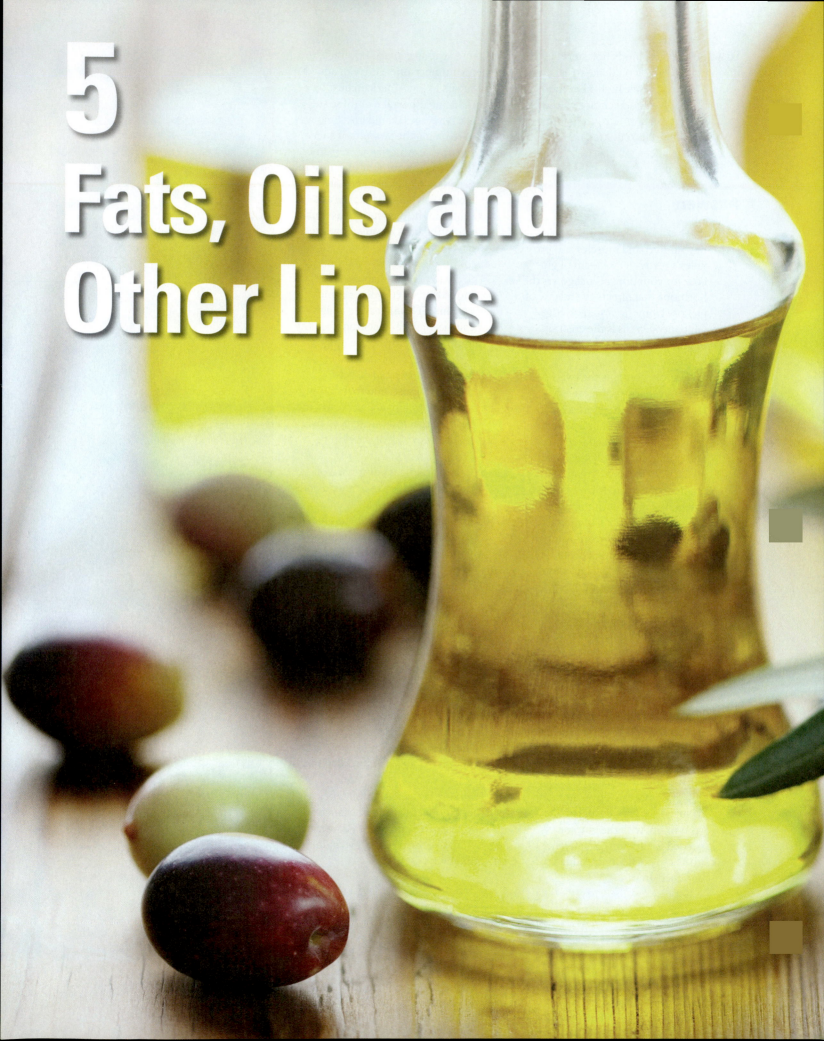

5
Fats, Oils, and Other Lipids

True or False?

1. You need to eat a small amount of cholesterol daily to meet your needs. **T/F** p. 150

2. Americans are eating too high a percentage of calories from fat daily. **T/F** p. 157

3. A healthy diet is very low in fat. **T/F** p. 157

4. The main source of saturated fat in the American diet is red meat. **T/F** p. 158

5. Fat-free cookies tend to have half the calories of full-fat varieties. **T/F** p. 165

6. A high amount of HDL cholesterol in your blood is bad for you. **T/F** p. 169

7. All-natural butter is better for you than margarine. **T/F** p. 171

8. Peanut butter is high in cholesterol. **T/F** p. 172

9. If you don't eat fish, you should take a fish-oil supplement. **T/F** p. 174

10. Oatmeal can help lower your cholesterol. **T/F** p. 176

See page 185 for the answers.

After reading this chapter, you will be able to:

LO 5.1 Describe the three classifications of lipids and explain the differences in the structure of triglycerides, phospholipids, and cholesterol.

LO 5.2 Describe how fat is digested, absorbed, and transported in the body.

LO 5.3 Describe the functions of fat in the body.

LO 5.4 Define the dietary recommendations for total fat, the essential fatty acids, saturated fat, cholesterol, and *trans* fat.

LO 5.5 Identify the major food sources of the different types of fats, including the essential fatty acids, saturated fats, and *trans* fats.

LO 5.6 Compare the different fat substitutes currently used in food products.

LO 5.7 Describe the development of atherosclerosis, including its role in the risk of heart disease.

LO 5.8 Explain the dietary changes you can make to maintain healthy blood cholesterol levels and reduce your risk of heart disease.

When you go shopping, what is on your grocery list? If you're like many Americans, you probably have the best intentions of filling your grocery cart with low-fat, nonfat, or cholesterol-free items to eat a more healthful diet. Even just saying the words *fat* or *cholesterol* brings up negative images of foods that we should avoid. The truth is, a small amount of dietary fat is essential to the body.

In this chapter, we will discuss the structure and functions of the different types of lipids, how they are handled in the body, and the amounts of each that should be consumed in a healthy diet. We will also explore the role of high-fat foods in the development of cardiovascular disease and other health conditions.

What Are Fats and Why Do You Need Them?

LO 5.1 Describe the three classifications of lipids and explain the differences in the structure of triglycerides, phospholipids, and cholesterol.

When you see the word *fat*, you may think of butter, mayonnaise, the cholesterol in meats and eggs, and even the fatty tissues in your own body. But technically speaking, these aren't all fats. Instead, they're examples of a broader category of substances known as **lipids**—compounds that contain carbon, oxygen, and hydrogen and which are **hydrophobic** (*hydro* = water, *phobic* = fearing), meaning they don't dissolve in water. If you were to drop lipids, such as butter or olive oil, into a glass of water, you would see them rise to the top and sit on the water's surface. This repelling of water enables lipids to play a unique role in foods and in your body.

To answer our original question, *fat* is the common name for just one type of lipid, known as a triglyceride. Because this is the type of lipid found most abundantly in foods, food labels and nutrition sources refer generally to this category as dietary *fat*—not dietary *lipid*—so fat is the term we'll use in this chapter.

Fats Serve Multiple Functions in Foods and in Your Body

Fats perform a variety of functions in cooking. They give a flaky texture to pie crusts and other baked goods, and they make meat tender and soups and puddings creamy. The flavor and aroma that fats provide can make your mouth water as you eye crispy fried chicken or smell baking cookies. Foods that are higher in fats contribute to satiety, that feeling of fullness you experience after eating.

In your body, fats are essential for energy storage and insulation. Two other types of lipids are also important as components of the membranes surrounding your cells and play a key role in transporting compounds in your blood.

The three types of lipids found in foods and in your body are triglycerides (*fats*), phospholipids, and sterols. Two of the three, triglycerides and phospholipids, are built from a basic unit called a fatty acid. So let's start our discussion of the structure of lipids with the fatty acids.

Fatty Acids Are Found in Triglycerides and Phospholipids

All **fatty acids** (**Figure 5.1**) consist of a chain of carbon and hydrogen atoms, with an acid group (COOH) at one end. There are more than 20 different fatty acids. They can vary by (1) the length of the chain, (2) whether the carbons have a single or a double bond between them (C—C or C==C), and (3) the total number of double bonds. The way and where carbon bonds occur in different types of fatty acids is what makes some fatty acids healthier than others.

There are three main types of fatty acids:

- *Saturated fatty acids.* When each carbon in a fatty acid chain is bonded with two atoms of hydrogen, as we saw in Figure 5.1, the chain is considered *saturated* with hydrogen. It cannot hold any more. We therefore call such a fatty acid a **saturated fatty acid**. For example, stearic acid is a saturated fatty acid (**Figure 5.2a**). It has 18 carbons, all of which are bound, or saturated, with hydrogen. Long fatty acids, such as stearic acid, are strongly

Acid group   Chain of carbon and hydrogen atoms

Figure 5.1 Structure of a Fatty Acid
Fatty acids are the building blocks of some lipids.

a Stearic acid, a saturated fatty acid

b Oleic acid, a monounsaturated fatty acid

Double bond in carbon chain creates a bend

c Linoleic acid, a polyunsaturated, omega-6 fatty acid

2 double bonds create 2 bends

d Alpha-linolenic acid, a polyunsaturated, omega-3 fatty acid

3 double bonds create 3 bends

Figure 5.2 Saturated and Unsaturated Fatty Acids
Fatty acids differ by the length of the fatty acid chain, whether or not there are double bonds between the carbons, and (if there are double bonds) how many double bonds they contain.

lipids A category of carbon, hydrogen, and oxygen compounds that are insoluble in water.

hydrophobic Having an aversion to water.

fatty acid The basic unit of triglycerides and phospholipids.

saturated fatty acid A fatty acid that has all of its carbons bound with hydrogen.

Figure 5.3 **Saturated and Unsaturated Fatty Acids Help Shape Foods**

Saturated fatty acids are able to pack tightly together and are solid at room temperature. The double bonds in unsaturated fatty acids cause kinks in their shape and prevent them from packing tightly together, so they tend to be liquid at room temperature.

a Saturated fatty acids

b Unsaturated fatty acids

Cocoa butter melts at body temperature. This is why solid milk chocolate melts in your mouth.

saturated fats Fats that contain mostly saturated fatty acids.

monounsaturated fatty acid (MUFA) A fatty acid that has one double bond.

unsaturated fatty acid A fatty acid that has one or more double bonds between carbons.

unsaturated fats Fats that contain mostly unsaturated fatty acids.

polyunsaturated fatty acid (PUFA) A fatty acid with two or more double bonds.

essential fatty acids The two polyunsaturated fatty acids that the body cannot make and therefore must be eaten in foods: linoleic acid and alpha-linolenic acid.

linoleic acid A polyunsaturated essential fatty acid; part of the omega-6 fatty acid family.

alpha-linolenic acid A polyunsaturated essential fatty acid; part of the omega-3 fatty acid family.

attracted to one another, and are relatively straight, so they are able to pack tightly together in food, and thus become solid fats at room temperature. Stearic acid can be found in cocoa butter (in chocolate) and in the fatty part of meat. Shorter saturated fatty acids (with fewer than 12 carbons) have a weaker attraction to one another, and so do not pack tightly together. Because of this, foods that contain them are liquid at room temperature. Whole milk contains short-chain saturated fatty acids. Fats made of mostly saturated fatty acids are called **saturated fats**. As you will learn later on in the chapter, saturated fats and other solid fats should be minimized in the diet, as they are not healthy for your heart.

● *Monounsaturated fatty acids (MUFAs)*. Take a look at the fatty acid shown in Figure 5.2b. Do you notice that, at one place in the chain, two carbons are each bound to only one atom of hydrogen, and are joined twice to each other? This double carbon bond means that the carbons are not "saturated" with hydrogen atoms at that point in the chain. This makes the chain unsaturated. When a double bond occurs at just one point in the chain, the molecule is called a **monounsaturated fatty acid** (recall that *mono-* means one). The example shown in Figure 5.2b is oleic acid. Like stearic acid, oleic acid contains 18 carbons, but two of them are paired with each other rather than with hydrogen, so it has one double bond. This one double bond makes oleic acid a monounsaturated fatty acid. It also makes it crooked. That is, double bonds cause a kink in the chain of the fatty acid. This kink keeps **unsaturated fatty acids** from packing together tightly. Thus, unsaturated fatty acids are liquid at room temperature. For instance, oleic acid is found in olive oil. You can see the effect of straight versus kinked fatty acid chains on foods in **Figure 5.3**. Fats made of mostly unsaturated fatty acids are called **unsaturated fats**. Whereas saturated fats are unhealthy, unsaturated fats are considered important to your health.

● *Polyunsaturated fatty acids (PUFAs)*. A **polyunsaturated fatty acid** (*poly* = many) contains more than one double bond and is even less saturated with hydrogen than a monounsaturated fatty acid. For instance, linoleic acid contains two double bonds and is polyunsaturated (Figure 5.2c). It is found in soybean oil. Like monounsaturated fats, polyunsaturated fats are considered healthy. Incidentally, your body can make most of the fatty acids it needs, but there are two that it cannot make, and both are polyunsaturated. Because you must consume them in your diet, they're known as **essential fatty acids**. They are **linoleic acid**, shown in Figure 5.2c, and **alpha-linolenic acid**, shown in Figure 5.2d. We'll discuss these essential fatty acids in more detail later.

Figure 5.4 Structure of a Triglyceride
A triglyceride consists of three fatty acids attached to a glycerol backbone. Note that a single triglyceride can contain different fatty acids.

Triglycerides Contain Three Fatty Acid Chains

Triglycerides are the most common lipids found in foods and in your body. Each **triglyceride** compound consists of three fatty acid chains (*tri* = three) connected to a **glycerol** "backbone." Glycerol is a compound containing carbon, hydrogen, and a type of alcohol. The three fatty acids join to the glycerol backbone to form the triglyceride (**Figure 5.4**). Any triglyceride can contain a variety of different fatty acids.

The more common name for triglycerides is **fat**, and this is the term we'll use throughout this chapter and the rest of the book. Most of the lipids that you eat and that are in your body are in the form of fat. Many fatty foods, such as butter, lard, and the fat in meats, are solid at room temperature so are often referred to as solid fats. **Oils** are fats that are liquid at room temperature.

Phospholipids Contain Phosphate

Like fats, **phospholipids** contain a glycerol backbone, but instead of three fatty acids, they contain two fatty acids and a phosphate group (a compound containing the mineral phosphorus) (**Figure 5.5**). The portion where the phosphate is attached to the glycerol is referred to as the head, which is *hydrophilic* (*philic* = loving), so it is able to attract water. In contrast, phospholipids' fatty acid tails are hydrophobic.

Phospholipids make up the phospholipid bilayer in cell membranes. Their water-loving heads face outward to the watery areas both outside and inside your cells, and their fat-loving tails line up with each other in the center, creating a phospholipid membrane that surrounds the cell and acts as a barrier (**Figure 5.6**). The cell membrane allows certain substances, such as water, to enter the cell but keeps others, like protein, from leaking out. You can visualize this phospholipid layer as being like a picket fence, acting as a barrier surrounding each cell.

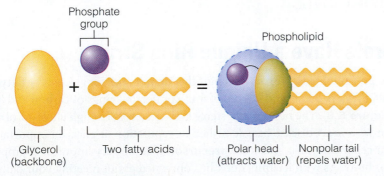

Figure 5.5 Structure of a Phospholipid
Phospholipids are similar to triglycerides but they have only two fatty acids and a phosphate group connected to the glycerol backbone. This configuration allows phospholipids, such as lecithin, to be attracted to both water and fat.

triglyceride Three fatty acids that are attached to a glycerol backbone.

glycerol The three-carbon backbone of a triglyceride.

fat The common name for triglycerides.

oils Fats that are liquid at room temperature.

phospholipids Lipids made of two fatty acids and a phosphate group attached to a glycerol backbone.

Figure 5.6 Phospholipids' Role in Your Cell Membranes

1 Because the phosphorus-containing head is polar, it attracts charged particles, such as water located both outside and inside your cells.

2 Its fatty acid–containing tail is nonpolar, so it mingles and lines up with other nonpolar molecules such as the fatty acid–containing ends of other phospholipids.

3 This creates a two-layer membrane that surrounds the cell and acts as a barrier, allowing certain substances to enter the cell but keeping others from leaving.

Cell

Outside of cell (watery extracellular fluid)

Cell membrane

Protein

Inside of cell (watery cytoplasm)

Phospholipid head

Phospholipid tails

Phospholipid tails

Phospholipid head

Cholesterol

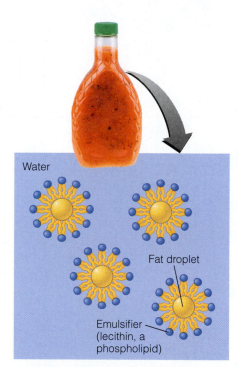

Water

Fat droplet

Emulsifier (lecithin, a phospholipid)

Figure 5.7 **Keeping a Salad Dressing Blended**
To prevent the fat from separating out in a salad dressing, an emulsifier is added. The emulsifier's fat-attracting tails surround the droplets of fat, whereas the water-attracting heads remain oriented toward the watery portion of the solution or dressing. This allows the fat droplet to stay suspended and blended in the dressing.

The major phospholipid in your cell membranes is lecithin. Even though lecithin plays an important role in your body, you don't have to worry about eating large amounts of lecithin in foods. As with all phospholipids, your body is able to make all the lecithin it needs. Because of its unique water- and fat-loving attributes, lecithin is used in many foods as an **emulsifier**, which helps keep incompatible substances, such as water and oil, mixed together. For example, an emulsifier is sometimes added to commercially made salad dressings to prevent the fat from separating and rising to the top of the dressing (**Figure 5.7**). The emulsifier's nonpolar, fat-attracting tail surrounds the droplets of fat, which orients the polar, water-attracting head of the emulsifier toward the watery solution of the dressing. This keeps the fat droplet suspended in the dressing and allows these two incompatible substances to stay blended together. We'll see the process of emulsification again when we discuss how the body uses fat.

Sterols Have a Unique Ring Structure

Unlike phospholipids, **sterols** are lipids that do not contain glycerol or fatty acids. Instead, they are composed mainly of four connecting rings of carbon and hydrogen (**Figure 5.8**). The best known sterol is cholesterol. Though cholesterol's association with heart disease has blemished its reputation, it plays an important role in your cell membranes and is the **precursor** of some very important compounds in your body. As with lecithin, don't be concerned about meeting your daily need for this important substance through your diet, since your body manufactures all the cholesterol you need. **Figure 5.9** summarizes the structures of the three types of lipids.

Figure 5.8 Structure of a Sterol
Rather than being made from fatty acids attached to a glycerol backbone, sterols have a carbon ring configuration with hydrogens and an oxygen attached. Cholesterol is the best-known sterol.

Lipid	Structure	Examples
Triglycerides	Glycerol — / Fatty acids	Saturated fat / Unsaturated fat / *Trans* fat
Phospholipids	Phosphate head / Fatty acids	Lecithin
Sterols	HO	Cholesterol

Figure 5.9 Three Types of Lipids
The three types of lipids vary in structure. Triglycerides and phospholipids are built from fatty acids, whereas sterols are composed of carbon rings.

LO 5.1 The Take-Home Message Lipids are hydrophobic compounds made of carbon, hydrogen, and oxygen. The three types of lipids are triglycerides, phospholipids, and sterols. Fatty acids, which consist of a carbon and hydrogen chain and an acid group, are the basic structural units of triglycerides and phospholipids. Triglycerides are formed from three fatty acids connected to a glycerol backbone and are the most prevalent lipids in your food and body. Phospholipids are made of two fatty acids and a phosphate-containing group attached to a glycerol backbone. Phospholipids are an important part of the structure of cell membranes. Cholesterol is an important sterol in your cell membranes and is the precursor to other essential compounds.

What Happens to the Fat You Eat?

LO 5.2 Describe how fat is digested, absorbed, and transported in the body.

As with all nutrients, the digestion of fat begins in your mouth (see **Figure 5.10** on page 152). Chewing mechanically breaks down the food—in this case, a slice of pizza. The enzyme lingual lipase in the mouth plays a minor role in breaking down some fat. Once food is swallowed, the stomach begins to breaks down fat further. Let's follow the fat in the cheese pizza through the rest of the GI tract.

You Digest Most Fat in Your Stomach and Small Intestine

In the stomach, fat mixes with gastric lipase, an enzyme that breaks down some of it into a fatty acid and a **diglyceride** (the remnant of fat digestion when only two fatty acids are left joined to the glycerol backbone). The majority of fat digestion occurs in your small intestine, where an enzyme released from your pancreas, pancreatic lipase, continues to break down the fat into two fatty acids and a **monoglyceride** (the remnant of fat digestion when only one fatty acid is left joined to the glycerol backbone).

Just as oil and water don't mix, fat can't mix with the watery fluids in your digestive tract. The fat globules tend to cluster together rather than disperse throughout the fluids. Mixing fats with watery fluids requires the addition of **bile**, which is made in your liver and stored in your gallbladder. When the fat from the pizza arrives

emulsifier A compound that keeps two incompatible substances, such as oil and water, mixed together.

sterol A lipid that contains four connecting rings of carbon and hydrogen.

precursor A substance that is converted into or leads to the formation of another substance.

diglyceride A glycerol with only two attached fatty acids.

monoglyceride A glycerol with only one attached fatty acid.

bile A substance produced by the liver, stored in the gallbladder, and secreted into the small intestine that emulsifies fat into smaller globules, allowing enzymes to break the fat down.

FOCUS FIGURE WALKTHROUGH

 Scan this QR code with your mobile device for a video tour of this figure by Joan Salge Blake.

Most fat digestion occurs in the small intestine with the aid of bile and lipase enzymes. The absorbed digestive by-products are transported via chylomicrons into the lymphatic system.

ORGANS OF THE GI TRACT

MOUTH

Chewing begins the mechanical digestion of food. Solid fat melts with the warmth of the body. Lingual lipase in the saliva begins the chemical digestion of fats.

STOMACH

Peristalsis mixes and churns the fat-containing food with gastric juices. Gastric lipase breaks down some fats, creating diglycerides and free fatty acids.

 →

SMALL INTESTINE

Bile secreted from the gallbladder through the common bile duct into the small intestine emulsifies fat into smaller globules.

Pancreatic lipase breaks down fats into monoglycerides, glycerol, and free fatty acids.

 →

The by-products of fat digestion are packaged into micelles for transport through the cells of the intestinal wall.

As they are absorbed, the micelles separate into their component parts. Short-chain fatty acids enter the bloodstream directly. Long-chain fatty acids, cholesterol, phospholipids, and other remnants are repackaged into chylomicrons for transport into the lymphatic system.

ACCESSORY ORGANS

LIVER

Produces bile, which is stored in the gallbladder.

GALLBLADDER

Releases bile into the small intestine through the common bile duct.

PANCREAS

Produces pancreatic lipase, which is secreted into the small intestine via the pancreatic duct.

Micelles

Chylomicron

Short fatty acid

Lymph

Blood

in your intestines, your gallbladder releases bile. Bile contains bile acids that help to emulsify the fat into smaller globules within the watery digestive solution. This keeps the smaller fat globules dispersed throughout the fluids, and provides more surface area so that the pancreatic lipase can more easily break down the fat.

Monoglycerides and fatty acids are next packaged with lecithin, which is in the bile, and other substances to create **micelles** (small carriers). Once close to the mucosa of your small intestine, micelles travel into your intestinal cells.

The length of the fatty acid chain determines what happens next. Short-chain fatty acids will enter your bloodstream and go directly to your liver. The long-chain fatty acids can't enter your bloodstream directly. They enter your **lymph** and need carriers.

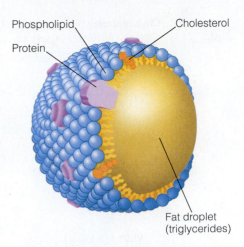

Lipoproteins Transport Fat through the Lymph and Blood

Long-chain fatty acids are reformulated into a fat within the cells of your intestinal wall as they are absorbed. These reformulated fats (as well as other lipids, such as cholesterol) are not soluble in your watery blood. They need to be packaged inside protein-containing carriers called **lipoproteins**. These capsule-shaped fat carriers have an outer shell high in protein and phospholipids and an inner compartment that carries the insoluble fat, as well as cholesterol, through your lymph and bloodstream. One example of a lipoprotein carrier that transports these lipids is a **chylomicron (Figure 5.11)**.

Chylomicrons are too large to be absorbed directly into your bloodstream, so they travel through your lymph system first and then enter your blood. Once in the blood, the fat is broken down into fatty acids and glycerol with the help of the enzyme lipoprotein lipase, which is located in the walls of the capillaries. After the fat is removed from the chylomicrons, the remnants of these lipoproteins go to your liver to be dismantled.

The liver produces other lipoproteins with different roles in your body:

- **Very-low-density lipoprotein (VLDL)**
- **Low-density lipoprotein (LDL)**
- **High-density lipoprotein (HDL)**

Although all lipoproteins contain fat, phospholipids, cholesterol, and protein, the proportion of the protein in these substances differs in the various types. Protein is denser than fat, so the proportion of protein in the lipoproteins determines their overall density (see **Figure 5.12** on page 154).

For example, VLDLs are composed mostly of triglycerides and have very little protein, so they are considered to be of very low density. The LDLs, which are approximately 50 percent cholesterol, have more protein than the VLDLs but less than HDLs, which have the highest density. The protein in lipoproteins helps them to perform their functions in your body. For example, the high protein content in HDLs not only helps remove cholesterol from your cells, but also enables the carrier to expand and contract, depending on the amount of fat and cholesterol it is carrying.

Why is the proportion of protein in a lipoprotein carrier important? Each lipoprotein has a different role. The main role of the VLDLs is to deliver fat that is made in the liver to your tissues. Once the fat is delivered, the VLDL remnants are converted into LDLs. The LDLs deliver cholesterol to your cells and are often referred to as the "bad" cholesterol carriers because they deposit cholesterol in the walls of your arteries, which can lead to heart disease. To help you remember this, you may want to think of the "**L**" in **L**DL as being of "**L**ittle" health benefit.

micelles Small carriers in the intestine that enable fatty acids and other compounds to be absorbed.

lymph Watery fluid that circulates through the body in lymph vessels and eventually enters the blood.

lipoproteins Capsule-shaped carriers that enable fat and cholesterol to travel through the lymph and blood.

chylomicron A type of lipoprotein that carries digested fat and other lipids through the lymph system into the blood.

very-low-density lipoprotein (VLDL) A lipoprotein that delivers fat made in the liver to the tissues. VLDL remnants are converted into LDLs.

low-density lipoprotein (LDL) A lipoprotein that deposits cholesterol in the walls of the arteries. Because this can lead to heart disease, LDL is referred to as the *bad* cholesterol carrier.

high-density lipoprotein (HDL) A lipoprotein that removes cholesterol from the tissues and delivers it to the liver to be used as part of bile and/or to be excreted from the body. Because of this, it is known as the *good* cholesterol carrier.

Figure 5.11 Chylomicron
Chylomicrons are one type of lipoprotein.

Chylomicron

Protein 2%

Phospholipids 3%

Cholesterol

5%

Triglycerides
90%

VLDL

Phospholipids

Protein
10%

18%

Triglycerides
60%

Cholesterol
12%

LDL

Triglycerides

10%

Protein
25%

Phospholipids
15%

Cholesterol
50%

HDL

Triglycerides

5%

Cholesterol
20%

Protein
50%

Phospholipids
25%

Figure 5.12 Lipoproteins
The various types of lipoproteins and their composition.

The HDLs are about 50 percent protein. They remove cholesterol from your cells and deliver it to your liver to be used to make bile or to be excreted from your body. For this reason, the HDLs are often referred to as the "good" cholesterol carriers, as they help remove cholesterol from your arteries. An easy way to remember this is to think of the "**H**" in HDL as referring to "**H**ealthy" (**Figure 5.13**).

LO 5.2 **The Take-Home Message** The digestion of fat begins in your mouth, and with the help of enzymes and emulsifying bile acids, most of it is digested and then absorbed in your small intestine. Fat is generally packaged as part of a chylomicron lipoprotein carrier, and travels in the lymph before entering your bloodstream. The other lipoproteins are VLDLs, LDLs, and HDLs. The VLDLs are converted to the "bad" LDL cholesterol carriers, which can deposit cholesterol in the walls of your arteries. The "good" HDL cholesterol carriers remove cholesterol from your arteries and deliver it to your liver to be excreted from your body.

How Does Your Body Use Fat and Cholesterol?

LO 5.3 Describe the functions of fat in the body.

Some people try to avoid fat in their diets, as they think it is unhealthy. This can actually be counterproductive, because fat plays many key roles in your body. Fat is an important source of energy and helps the absorption of some compounds. Fat also insulates your body and cushions your major organs. Some fats are essential for your good health. There are differences among the types of fat that you eat. Different fats can have different effects on your health, specifically your heart. Let's look at the roles that fats play in your body.

Fat Provides Energy

At 9 calories per gram, compared with 4 calories per gram for both carbohydrates and protein, fat is a major fuel source for your body. Your body has an *unlimited* ability to store excess energy (calories) as fat. In fact, your fat reserves have the capacity to enlarge as much as 1,000 times their original size, as more fat is added. If your cells fill to capacity, your body can add more fat cells.

Remember from Chapter 4 that your body only has a limited ability to store glucose, which is needed for the brain and red blood cells to function. When your blood glucose level begins to decline, the hormone glucagon promotes the release of glucose from the liver in order to supply the blood with glucose. Glucagon simultaneously promotes the release of fat from fat cells to provide additional energy for your body. Your heart, liver, and resting muscles prefer fat as their fuel source, which spares glucose to be used for your nervous system and red blood cells. In fact, fat is your main source of energy throughout the day. This fat stored in your fat cells provides a backup source of energy between meals. In a famine situation, some individuals could last months without eating, depending upon the extent of their fat stores and the availability of adequate fluids.

Fat Helps You Absorb Certain Compounds and Insulates the Body

Fat allows you to absorb the fat-soluble vitamins A, D, E, and K, as well as carotenoids, compounds that can have antioxidant properties in your body.[1] Consuming

FOCUS
Figure 5.13 The Roles of Lipoproteins

Fat and cholesterol are transported in the body via several different lipoprotein compounds, such as chylomicrons, VLDLs, LDLs, and HDLs.

FOCUS FIGURE WALKTHROUGH

Scan this QR code with your mobile device for a video tour of this figure by Joan Salge Blake.

CHYLOMICRONS

Chylomicrons transport fat and cholesterol from a meal via the lymphatic system to your cells. Once in the blood, lipoprotein lipase helps break down fat. The remaining chylomicron remnant is dismantled in the liver.

VLDLs

VLDLs (very-low-density lipoproteins), produced mainly in the liver, transport fat to the cells. Lipoprotein lipase helps with the uptake of fatty acids into the cells, primarily those in muscle and fat tissue, transforming VLDLs to LDLs (low-density lipoproteins).

LDLs

Low-density lipoproteins release cholesterol into body cells. LDLs not taken up by cells degrade over time, releasing cholesterol that may then adhere to blood vessel walls.

HDLs

HDLs (high-density lipoproteins) produced by the liver circulate in the blood, picking up cholesterol from cells. The cholesterol is returned to the liver and excreted through the bile, removing it from the bloodstream.

Small intestine cells — Fatty acids — Muscle cells — To blood vessel via lymphatic system — Chylomicron — Chylomicron remnant — Fat cells — Fatty acids — VLDL — Muscle cells — LDL — Fat cells — Cholesterol — Body cells — LDL — HDL — Back to liver to be recycled or eliminated — HDL — Cholesterol

How Does Your Body Use Fat and Cholesterol?   **155**

Fatty fish, such as salmon, are an excellent source of omega-3 fatty acids.

inadequate amounts of fat may impede your absorption of these fat-soluble vitamins and compounds. The fat that is located just under your skin helps to insulate your body and maintain your body temperature. Fat also acts as a protective cushion for your bones, organs, and nerves.

Essential Fatty Acids Help Keep Cells Healthy

Two polyunsaturated fatty acids, *linoleic acid* and *alpha-linolenic acid*, are essential, which means that your body can't make them; thus, you need to obtain them from your diet. Linoleic acid is also referred to as an *omega-6 fatty acid*, and alpha-linolenic acid is commonly called an *omega-3 fatty acid*. If this sounds like Greek to you, it should. The letters of the Greek alphabet help identify the placement of the carbons in fatty acids. Omega is the last letter of the Greek alphabet. Thus, the omega carbon is the *last* carbon of the fatty acid. In alpha-linolenic acid, the first double bond occurs at the third carbon from the omega end. Hence, it is referred to as an omega-3 fatty acid (refer again to Figure 5.2d).

The essential fatty acids help maintain healthy skin cells, nerves, and cell membranes. For example, a deficiency of linoleic acid can interfere with normal growth and result in inflammation of the skin. A deficiency in alpha-linolenic acid can affect the functioning of the brain and nervous system. Essential fatty acids are also necessary to make other substances your body needs. Linoleic acid is used to make another polyunsaturated fatty acid, called arachidonic acid (**Figure 5.14**). This fatty acid is important for your cells and for making **eicosanoids**, which are hormonelike substances. Among other roles, eicosanoids help with blood pressure, inflammation, and blood clotting.

A limited amount of alpha-linolenic acid can be converted to two other important omega-3 fatty acids: **eicosapentaenoic acid (EPA)** and **docosahexaenoic acid (DHA)**. EPA and DHA have been shown to reduce the risk of heart disease.[2] All fish contain EPA and DHA, although fatty fish such as salmon, herring, and sardines are especially rich sources. Cod-liver oil is abundant in EPA and DHA, but also in the fat-soluble vitamins A and D, which can both be toxic if consumed in high amounts. Eating fish is a safer way to obtain EPA and DHA, and it can also be very healthy for your heart, as discussed later in the chapter.

Some research suggests that a diet containing too much of the omega-6 fatty acids in comparison with omega-3 fatty acids may be unhealthy. Consensus on this matter hasn't yet been reached.[3]

A deficiency of linoleic acid can interfere with normal growth and result in inflammation of the skin. Scaly skin can be a sign of inadequate amounts of alpha-linolenic acid.

eicosanoids Hormonelike substances in the body. Prostaglandins, thromboxanes, and leukotrienes are all eicosanoids.

eicosapentaenoic acid (EPA) and docosahexaenoic acid (DHA) Two omega-3 fatty acids that are heart healthy.

Figure 5.14 Essential Fatty Acids
Both linoleic acid (an omega-6 fatty acid) and alpha-linolenic acid (an omega-3 fatty acid) are essential fatty acids that you have to obtain from your diet. Other fatty acids can be made from these fatty acids.

Cholesterol Has Many Important Roles

Your body needs cholesterol both as a part of your cell membranes and as the precursor for vitamin D and bile acids. Cholesterol is also the precursor for the sex hormones such as estrogen and testosterone, which help to determine sexual characteristics.

The confusion over cholesterol persists. Though dietary cholesterol has been proclaimed as unhealthy, the cholesterol in your blood can be either "good" or "bad" cholesterol. How can one substance be both Dr. Jekyll and Mr. Hyde? Later in this chapter, we will look at the health effects of cholesterol, and try to clear up this confusion. During the discussion, keep in mind that the cholesterol in your diet isn't the only factor that determines the levels of cholesterol in your blood.

LO 5.3 **The Take-Home Message** Fat contains 9 calories per gram and is an energy-dense source of fuel for your body. Fat cushions and protects your bones, organs, and nerves and insulates you to help maintain your body temperature. Fat also provides essential fatty acids and is needed for the absorption of fat-soluble vitamins and carotenoids. The essential fatty acids, linoleic acid (an omega-6 fatty acid) and alpha-linolenic acid (an omega-3 fatty acid), are necessary to keep cells healthy. Linoleic acid is necessary to make arachidonic acid and eicosanoids. A limited amount of alpha-linolenic acid can be converted to two other omega-3 fatty acids, EPA and DHA, which are also found in fish. Cholesterol is part of your cell membranes and is needed to make vitamin D, bile acids, and sex hormones.

How Much Fat Do You Need Each Day?

LO 5.4 Define the dietary recommendations for total fat, the essential fatty acids, saturated fat, cholesterol, and *trans* fat.

At first glance, it looks as though Americans' fat consumption has gone up and down over the last century. In the 1930s, Americans were consuming about 34 percent of their calories from fat; this number climbed to 42 percent in the mid-1960s. By 1984, fat consumption had declined to 36 percent of total calories, and current consumption is about 34 percent of calories.[4] However, while today's consumption levels are in line with the current recommendations, we can't break out the hot fudge sundaes just yet. Measuring fat consumption only as a percentage of total calories, and not including the type of fat, can be misleading. You will soon read that the amount of heart-unhealthy saturated fat that we are eating daily could use some adjusting.

But dietary fat is still essential for health. So, how much should you eat?

You Need to Consume a Specific Percentage of Your Daily Calories from Fat

The current AMDR (Acceptable Macronutrient Distribution Range) recommendation is that 20 to 35 percent of your daily calories should come from fat. For some individuals, especially sedentary, overweight folks, a very low-fat diet (providing less than 20 percent of daily calories from fat) that is consequently high in carbohydrates may cause an increase in fat in the blood and a lowering of the good HDL cholesterol—not exactly a healthy combination for the heart. For others, consuming more than 35 percent of their total daily calories from fat could perpetuate obesity, which is a risk factor for heart disease.[5]

Vegetable oils are good sources of essential fatty acids.

Although consuming fat won't increase your weight unless you consistently consume more calories than you need, remember that dietary fat has more than twice the calories per gram of carbohydrates or protein. Therefore, eating too many fatty foods could perpetuate a weight-management problem. Numerous research studies have shown that reducing dietary fat can also reduce dietary calories, which can result in weight loss.[6] Consequently, controlling one's fat in-take may help control one's weight.

According to the AMDR recommendation, if you need 2,000 calories daily to maintain your weight, you can consume between 44 and 78 grams of fat daily (**Table 5.1**). For your heart health, you should consume less than 10 percent (and ideally less than 7 percent) of your calories, or 16 to 22 grams, from saturated fats.

You Need to Consume a Specific Amount of Essential Fatty Acids Daily

To ensure that you consume enough linoleic acid and alpha-linolenic acid, a recommended amount has been set for each of these important nutrients. A minimum of 5 percent and up to 10 percent of the total calories in your diet should come from linoleic acid, and alpha-linolenic acid should make up 0.6 percent to 1.2 percent of your total calories.[7] These recommended amounts are based on the estimated daily caloric needs according to your gender and age. For example, men aged 19 to 50 need 17 grams of linoleic acid daily, and women aged 19 to 50 who aren't pregnant or lactating need 12 grams daily. For alpha-linolenic acid, men aged 14 to 70 need 1.6 grams daily, whereas women of the same age need 1.1 grams daily.

Minimize Saturated and *Trans* Fats in Your Diet

While your diet should include essential fatty acids, some types of fats should be avoided. Solid fats—like butter, chicken fat, cream, coconut oil, palm kernel and palm oils, and partially hydrogenated oils—are major sources of heart-unhealthy saturated fat and hydrogenated oils are significant sources of *trans* fat in the diet (as mentioned in Chapter 2). These solid fats are often found in mixed dishes, which include hamburger sandwiches, meat, poultry, seafood dishes, pizza, rice, pasta, and grain dishes, as well as snacks and sweets, and dairy foods.[8] Consuming too much saturated fat can lead to higher levels of the "bad" LDL cholesterol carrier (you'll learn more about how these lipoproteins affect heart disease risk later in the chapter).

Some of the *trans* fats in foods are created by food manufacturers through the process of **hydrogenation**. Hydrogenation involves heating an oil and exposing it to hydrogen gas, which causes some of the double bonds in the unsaturated fatty acid to become saturated with hydrogen. Typically, the hydrogens of a double bond are lined up in a *cis* (*cis* = same) configuration, that is, they are all on the same side of the carbon chain in the fatty acid. During hydrogenation, some hydrogens cross to the opposite side of the carbon chain, resulting in a *trans* (*trans* = cross) configuration (**Figure 5.15**). The newly configured fatty acid is now a synthetic **trans fatty acid**. These **trans fats** are actually worse for heart health than saturated fat because they not only raise the LDL cholesterol levels, but they also lower HDL cholesterol in the body.

Trans fats were initially used in many processed foods because they provide a richer texture, better resistance to rancidity and a longer shelf life than unsaturated fats. After saturated fat lost of favor in the 1980s, because of research that confirmed its association with heart disease, *trans* fats came into widespread commercial use.

cis Hydrogens are on the same side of the double bond

trans Hydrogens are on opposite sides of the double bond

Figure 5.15 Creating *Trans* Fatty Acids Hydrogenating, or adding hydrogen to, an unsaturated fatty acid will create a more saturated fatty acid. This process will also cause some of the double bonds to twist from a *cis* position to a *trans* position. This creates a *trans* fatty acid.

hydrogenation Adding hydrogen to an unsaturated fatty acid to make it more saturated and solid at room temperature.

***trans* fatty acids** Substances that result from the hydrogenating of an unsaturated fatty acid, causing a reconfiguring of some of its double bonds. A small amount of *trans* fatty acids occur naturally in animal foods.

***trans* fat** Substance that contains mostly *trans* fatty acids.

rancidity The decomposition, or spoiling, of fats through oxidation.

Table 5.1

Capping Your Fat Intake

If You Need This Many Calories to Maintain Your Weight	You Should Eat No More Than This Much	
	Fat (grams) (20% to 35% of total calories)	Saturated Fat (grams) (<7% to 10% of total calories)
1,600	36–62	12–18
1,700	38–66	13–19
1,800	40–70	14–20
1,900	42–74	15–21
2,000	44–78	16–22
2,100	47–82	16–23
2,200	49–86	17–24
2,300	51–89	18–26
2,400	53–93	19–27
2,500	56–97	19–28
2,600	58–101	20–29
2,700	60–105	21–30
2,800	62–109	22–31

Sedentary women should consume approximately 1,600 calories daily. Teenage girls, active women, and many sedentary men need approximately 2,200 calories daily. Teenage boys, many active men, and some very active women need about 2,800 calories daily. To determine the number of calories you should be eating daily, turn to Table 2.1 in Chapter 2.

The percentage of calories from fat and the corresponding grams of fat can be calculated by multiplying your number of daily calories by 20 percent and 35 percent and then dividing those numbers by 9. (Fat provides 9 calories per gram.)

For example, if you consume 2,000 calories daily:

$$2{,}000 \times 0.20 \text{ (20 percent)} = \underline{400} \text{ calories} \div 9 = \underline{44} \text{ grams}$$
$$2{,}000 \times 0.35 \text{ (35 percent)} = \underline{700} \text{ calories} \div 9 = \underline{78} \text{ grams}$$

Your range of fat intake should be 44 to 78 grams daily.
To find the maximum grams of saturated fat that you should be consuming daily, repeat the process:

$$2{,}000 \times 0.07 \text{ (7 percent)} = \underline{140} \text{ calories} \div 9 = \underline{16} \text{ grams}$$
$$2{,}000 \times 0.10 \text{ (10 percent)} = \underline{200} \text{ calories} \div 9 = \underline{22} \text{ grams}$$

The total amount of saturated fat intake should be no more than 22 grams daily.

Everything from cookies, cakes, and crackers to fried chips and doughnuts used *trans* fats to maintain their texture and shelf life. *Trans* fats were also frequently used for frying at fast-food restaurants.

To make consumers more aware of *trans* fat, the FDA mandated in 2006 that most foods, and even some dietary supplements such as energy bars, list the grams of *trans* fats per serving on the Nutrition Facts panel on the food label. The label allows you to quickly add up the saturated and *trans* fats listed and makes it easier for you to monitor the amount of these fats that you consume. Because of this labeling requirement, many food manufacturers reformulated their products to remove or reduce the amount of *trans* fats made with hydrogenation. The FDA has proposed a ban on partially hydrogenated oils in foods to reduce American consumption of *trans* fat. Reducing the amount of solid fats in your diet will help you reduce your consumption of both saturated fats and *trans* fats (see **Figure 5.16**).[9]

Commercially made peanut butter doesn't have any detectable levels of *trans* fatty acids. Even though partially hydrogenated oil is used as a stabilizer in many peanut butter brands, the amount is so small that it is insignificant.

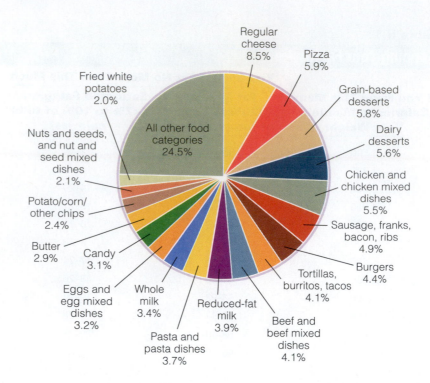

Figure 5.16 Major Food Sources of Saturated and *Trans* Fats for Americans Reducing the amount of food sources containing solid fats, such as cheese, pizza, grain-based desserts, and meat-containing dishes, will help you reduce saturated and *trans* fats in your diet.

Regular cheese 8.5%

Pizza 5.9%

Grain-based desserts 5.8%

Dairy desserts 5.6%

Chicken and chicken mixed dishes 5.5%

Sausage, franks, bacon, ribs 4.9%

Burgers 4.4%

Tortillas, burritos, tacos 4.1%

Beef and beef mixed dishes 4.1%

Reduced-fat milk 3.9%

Pasta and pasta dishes 3.7%

Whole milk 3.4%

Eggs and egg mixed dishes 3.2%

Candy 3.1%

Butter 2.9%

Potato/corn/other chips 2.4%

Nuts and seeds, and nut and seed mixed dishes 2.1%

Fried white potatoes 2.0%

All other food categories 24.5%

The Impact of Cholesterol in Your Diet

As mentioned earlier, your body can make all the cholesterol it needs. Therefore, you do not need to consume it in your diet. Adult males in the United States currently consume about 338 milligrams (mg) daily, whereas adult females eat 229 milligrams of cholesterol daily, on average, which is consistent with previous recommendations to limit dietary cholesterol to no more than 300 milligrams (mg) daily. The latest research suggests that dietary cholesterol has less impact on blood cholesterol levels than saturated fat and that the current intake of 229 to 338 mg of dietary cholesterol among healthy Americans has little effect on blood cholesterol levels.[10] However, very high intakes of dietary cholesterol can increase blood cholesterol levels.

Keeping the types of lipids straight, and remembering how much of each to consume or avoid, can be a challenge. The following summary should help you remember what you have learned thus far:

- **DO** be sure to get enough of the two heart-healthy essential fatty acids, linoleic acid and alpha-linolenic acid, in your diet by consuming adequate amounts of polyunsaturated fats in your daily meals.
- **DO** choose mono- and polyunsaturated fats over saturated fats when possible, as these unsaturated fats are better for you. Saturated fats should be kept to less than 10 percent of your total calories, because they aren't good for your heart or your blood cholesterol levels.
  - **DON'T** add *trans* fats to your diet. These are unhealthy for your heart and blood cholesterol levels and should be consumed as little as possible.
    - **DON'T** worry about eating enough cholesterol, because your body makes all it needs.

When it comes to keeping track of your fat intake, counting grams of fat in your foods is the best strategy. Table 5.1 provided you with a healthy range of recommended fat intake based on your daily caloric needs. (To figure out your approximate daily caloric needs, see Chapter 2.) Use the Self-Assessment to estimate how much fat and saturated fat you consume daily.

Vegetables are a low-saturated-fat topping for pizza.

How Much Fat Is in Your Diet?

Is your diet too overloaded with fat, and/or saturated fat? Are there surprising sources of fat in your diet? Use the diet analysis program, the Food Composition Table, and/or food labels to track your fat consumption for a day. How does your actual intake compare to the amount recommended for you in Table 5.1?

Food Log

	Food/Drink	Amount	Fat (g)	Saturated Fat (g)
Breakfast				
Snack				
Lunch				
Snack				
Dinner				
Snack				
Total				

LO 5.4 **The Take-Home Message** You need to consume some fat in your diet, particularly the essential fatty acids, but you should limit other fats, like saturated fats and *trans* fats. Your fat intake should range from 20 to 35 percent of your total calories. To meet your essential fatty acid needs, 5 to 10 percent of your calories should come from linoleic acid and 0.6 to 1.2 percent of your daily calories should come from alpha-linolenic acid. No more than 10 percent of your fat intake should come from saturated fat, and *trans* fats should be limited in your diet. You do not need to eat cholesterol in foods, as your body makes all the cholesterol it needs.

What Are the Best Food Sources of Fats?

LO 5.5 Identify the major food sources of the different types of fats, including the essential fatty acids, saturated fats, and *trans* fats.

Foods that contain unsaturated fats (both monounsaturated and polyunsaturated fats) are better for your health than foods high in saturated fat, cholesterol, and/or *trans* fat. So, where can you find the healthier fats in foods? Unsaturated fats are abundant in vegetable oils, such as soybean, corn, and canola oils, as well as soybeans, walnuts, peanut butter, flaxseeds, and wheat germ. Vegetable oils, nuts, and flaxseeds are also good sources of the essential fatty acids. In fact, all the foods listed in **Figure 5.17** are excellent sources of both unsaturated fats and essential fatty acids.

Figure 5.17 Food Sources of the Essential Fatty Acids
Many oils and nuts contain high amounts of the two essential fatty acids that you need to obtain in your diet.

The cheddar cheese on the top of a cheeseburger has more fat and saturated fat per ounce than the burger.

Most saturated fat in the diet comes from animal foods, such as whole-milk dairy products like cheese, butter, and ice cream, fatty cuts of meat, and the skin on poultry. Choosing lean meats and dairy foods, skinless poultry, and oil-based spreads will help you minimize the saturated fat in your diet. Certain vegetable oils, such as coconut, palm, and palm kernel oils, are very high in saturated fat. Although food manufacturers now use these highly saturated tropical oils less often, they may still be found in foods such as candies, commercially made baked goods, and gourmet ice cream. Checking the ingredient label on food packages is the best way to find out if these oils are in the foods that you eat (**Figure 5.18**).

Figure 5.18 Where's the Saturated Fat in Your Foods?
Saturated fat is found in animal products, tropical oils, and hydrogenated foods. Choosing less-saturated-fat versions of some of your favorite foods at meals and snacks can dramatically lower the amount of "sat" fat you consume in your diet.

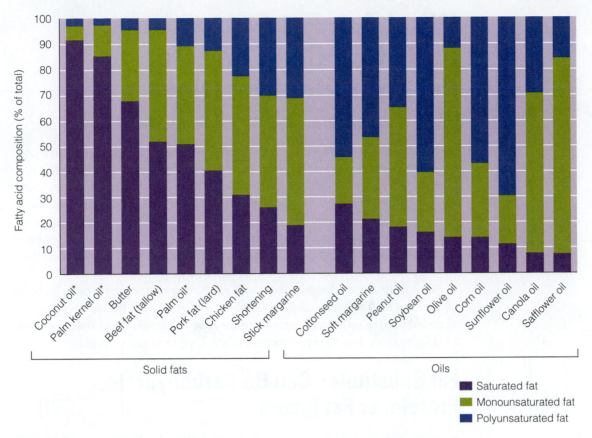

Figure 5.19
Composition of Various Fats
Foods vary in their composition of fat.

*Coconut oil, palm kernel oil, and palm oil are called oils because they come from plants. However, they are semi-solid at room temperature due to their high content of short-chain saturated fatty acids. They are considered solid fats for nutritional purposes.

Because all fats and oils are a combination of fatty acids, however, it's not only impossible to eliminate saturated fat entirely from your diet, it is unhealthy for you to do so (see **Figure 5.19**). Extreme trimming of fats and oils could lead to the unnecessary elimination of certain foods, such as soybean and canola oils, lean meats, fish, poultry, and low-fat dairy foods, which could cause you to fall short of important nutrients such as essential fatty acids, protein, and calcium. Just remember to keep your dietary intake of saturated fat to less than 10 percent of your daily total calories.

Americans on average consume 11 percent of their daily calories from saturated fat, so it's likely that you need to reduce your intake.[11] You can use Figure 5.18 to make low-saturated-fat food choices at some of your meals and snacks.

LO 5.5 **The Take-Home Message** Eating lean meats, skinless poultry, lean dairy products, and vegetable oils while limiting commercially prepared baked goods and snack items is a good strategy for overall good health. These foods will provide you with enough healthy unsaturated fats, with plenty of essential fatty acids, while limiting your intake of unhealthy, saturated fats.

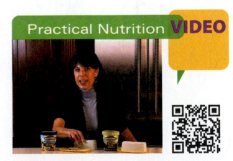

Practical Nutrition VIDEO

Making Low-Fat Choices

Do you know how much fat is in your ice cream? You may be surprised! Scan this QR code with your mobile device to access the video. You can also access the video in **Mastering**Nutrition™.

What Are Fat Substitutes and How Can They Be Part of a Healthy Diet?

LO 5.6 Compare the different fat substitutes currently used in food products.

If you adore the taste and texture of creamy foods but don't adore the extra fat in your diet, you're not alone. According to a recent survey, over 60 percent of consumers are trying to reduce the solid fats, saturated fat, and *trans* fat in their diet.[12] Because of this, 65 percent of shoppers say that they use the Nutrition Facts label to assess the total fat and solid fats in the products that they choose when shopping.[13] Today, with few exceptions, you will probably find a lower-fat alternative for almost any high-fat food on the grocery store shelves. The keys to these products' containing less fat than their counterparts are **fat substitutes**.

Fat substitutes are designed to provide all the creamy properties of fat for fewer calories and total fat grams. Because fat has more than double the calories per gram of carbohydrates or protein, fat substitutes have the potential to reduce calories from fat by more than 50 percent without sacrificing taste and texture.

Fat Substitutes Can Be Carbohydrate, Protein, or Fat Based

No single substitute works in all foods and with all cooking preparations, so there are several types of fat substitutes. They fall into three categories, depending on their primary ingredient:

- Carbohydrate-based substitutes
- Protein-based substitutes
- Fat-based substitutes[14]

Table 5.2 lists all three types of fat substitutes and their uses in foods.

Many fat substitutes in foods are carbohydrate based and use plant polysaccharides such as fiber, starches, gums, and cellulose to help retain moisture and provide a fatlike texture.[15] For example, low-fat muffins might have fiber added to them to help retain the moisture that is lost when fat is reduced. Carbohydrate-based fat substitutes have been used for years and work well under heat preparations other than frying.

Protein-based fat substitutes are created from the protein in eggs and milk. The protein is heated and broken down into microscopic balls that tumble over each other when you eat them, providing a creamy mouthfeel that's similar to that of fat. Because these are protein based, they break down under high temperatures and lose their creamy properties. Therefore, they are not suitable for frying and baking.[16]

Fat-based substitutes are fats that have been modified either to provide the physical attributes of fat for fewer calories or to interfere with the absorption of fat.[17] Mono- and diglycerides are used as emulsifiers in products such as baked goods and icings to provide moistness and mouth-feel. Though these remnants of fat have the same number of calories per gram as fat, fewer of them are needed to create the same effect, so the total levels of calories and fat are reduced in the food product.[18] One fat substitute is olestra, also known as Olean. Unlike fat, which contains three fatty acids connected to a glycerol backbone, olestra contains six to eight fatty acids connected to sucrose. The enzymes that normally break apart fatty acids from their glycerol backbones during digestion cannot disconnect the fatty acids in

fat substitutes Substances that replace added fat in foods by providing the creamy properties of fat for fewer calories and fewer total fat grams.

Table 5.2

The Lighter Side of Fat: Fat Substitutes

Name (trade names)	Calories per Gram	Properties	How It's Used
Carbohydrate Based			
Fibers from Grains (Beta-Trim)	1–4	Gelling, thickener	Baked goods, meats, spreads
Fibers, Cellulose (Avicel cellulose gel)	0	Water retention, texture, mouthfeel	Sauces, dairy products, frozen desserts, salad dressings
Gums (Slendid)	0	Thickener, texture, mouthfeel, water retention	Salad dressings, processed meats
Polydextrose (Litesse)	1	Water retention, adds bulk	Baked goods, dairy products, salad dressings, cookies, gum
Modified Food Starch (STA-SLIM)	1–4	Thickener, gelling, texture	Processed meats, salad dressings, frostings, fillings, frozen desserts
Protein Based			
Microparticulated Protein (Simplesse)	1–4	Mouthfeel	Dairy products, salad dressings, spreads
Fat Based			
Mono- or Diglycerides (Dur-Lo)	9*	Mouthfeel, moisture retention	Baked goods
Short-Chain Fatty Acids (Salatrim)	5	Mouthfeel	Confections, baked goods
Olestra (Olean)	0	Mouthfeel	Savory snacks

*Less of this fat substitute is needed to create the same effect as fat, so the calories are reduced in foods using this product.

olestra. Instead, olestra moves through your gastrointestinal tract intact and unabsorbed. Thus, it doesn't provide calories. Olestra is very heat stable, so it can be used in baked and fried foods.

In 1996, the FDA approved olestra for use in salty snacks such as potato and corn chips. An ounce of potato chips made with olestra can trim half the calories and all the fat from regular chips. Because of its inability to be absorbed, there was concern about olestra's interference with the absorption of fat-soluble vitamins and carotenoids.[19] (Absorption of water-soluble vitamins is not affected by olestra.) Consequently, the FDA has mandated that fat-soluble vitamins be added to foods containing olestra to offset these losses.[20] Because olestra travels through your digestive tract untouched, there was also a concern that it may cause stomach cramps and loose stools. Though there have been anecdotal studies of individuals experiencing bouts of diarrhea and cramps after consuming olestra-containing products, controlled research studies don't seem to support this phenomenon.[21]

Reduced-Fat Products Aren't Calorie Free

The use of fat substitutes doesn't seem to be helping Americans curb their calories or weight, and one reason for this may be people's overeating of low-fat and fat-free foods. Another reason may be that many reduced-fat products have close to the same number of calories as their regular counterparts. Also, research indicates that snacking on fat-reduced products may reduce overall fat intake, but not the overall intake of calories in a day.[22] As with sugar substitutes, consumers need to recognize that using reduced-fat or fat-free products is not a blank check for eating unlimited amounts of those foods. The foods still contain calories, and overconsuming calories leads to weight gain.

Foods made with fat substitutes aren't calorie free.

Table 5.3

Fat Free Doesn't Equal Calorie Free

	Serving Size	Calories	Fat (g)	Carbohydrates (g)	Calories Saved
Fig Newtons (Nabisco)	2 (31 g)	110	2	22	
Fat-Free Fig Newtons (Nabisco)	2 (29 g)	100	0	23	20

Also, some fat-free foods, especially baked goods, may have a reduced fat content but added carbohydrates, which will add back some calories. As you can see from **Table 5.3**, the calorie saving in these cookies is miniscule. In fact, the calorie difference between the two cookies is largely because the fat-free cookies are smaller. Do not assume that fat-free foods are healthy, because they often aren't. Jelly beans are fat free, but they don't provide the vitamins and minerals found in, for example, naturally fat-free green beans. Similarly, while choosing 4 ounces of fat-free chips will spare you half of the 600 calories found in the same amount of regular chips, those fat-free chips are also displacing 300 calories of more nutritious foods, such as fruits, vegetables, and whole grains, elsewhere in your diet. If you want chips, enjoy a handful rather than a large bag full, alongside your whole-grain sandwich and large salad at lunch.

Fats affect more than your weight and waistline. They also affect the health of your heart. In the next sections, we will take a closer look at how the lipids in your body and your lifestyle can affect your risk for heart disease.

LO 5.6 **The Take-Home Message** Fat substitutes are used in foods to provide the properties of fat for fewer calories and grams of fat. Fat substitutes can be carbohydrate based, protein based, or fat based. Though some fat substitutes provide fewer calories and fat grams than regular fat, others, such as olestra, aren't absorbed, so they are fat and calorie free. Reduced-fat or fat-free foods may help reduce the calories and fat in some foods, but shouldn't displace naturally low-fat and healthy foods such as fruits and vegetables.

What Is Heart Disease and What Increases Your Risk?

LO 5.7 Describe the development of atherosclerosis, including its role in the risk of heart disease.

Cardiovascular disease (CVD) encompasses several disorders affecting the heart and blood vessels, including problems with heart valves, heart beat irregularities, infections, and other problems. But the most common type of CVD is *coronary heart disease*, which affects the blood vessels that serve the heart muscle, and can lead to a heart attack. That's the type we focus on in this chapter.

Heart disease has been the number one killer of adults in the United States since 1918. Currently, it causes one of every six deaths among Americans.[23] Let's look at how heart disease develops, and the types of lipids that can accelerate it.

Heart Disease Begins with Buildup in the Arteries

Heart disease develops when the walls of coronary arteries, the large blood vessels that supply oxygen and other nutrients to the heart, accumulate a buildup of substances such as fat and cholesterol. As an artery gets narrower, blood flow is impeded and less oxygen and nutrients are delivered to the heart. If the heart doesn't receive enough oxygen, chest pains can result. A narrowed artery also increases the likelihood that a blood clot can block the vessel, leading to a **heart attack**. If the artery leads to the brain, a **stroke** can occur. Approximately every 34 seconds, an adult suffers a heart attack in the United States.[24]

The exact cause of the narrowed arteries, also known as **atherosclerosis** (*athero* = paste, *sclera* = hardness, *sis* = condition), is unknown, but researchers think it begins with an injury to the interior lining of an artery and subsequent inflammation in the injured area (see **Figure 5.20**). High blood levels of cholesterol and fat, high blood pressure, diabetes, and smoking likely contribute to this injury.

Over time, LDLs and other substances are deposited on an injured artery wall. The LDLs seep beneath the vessel lining, become oxidized, and attract macrophages (immune cells), which become enlarged with cholesterol-laden LDL and develop into foam cells. The foam cells build up in the wall of the artery, along with platelets (fragments of cells in the blood), calcium protein fibers, and other substances, to form **plaque**. The plaque narrows the passageway of the artery.

What Are the Risk Factors for Heart Disease?

While the primary risk factor for heart disease is an elevated LDL cholesterol level, other risk factors also exist. Some of these you can control; others you cannot (see **Table 5.4**).

Risk Factors You Can't Control

As your blood cholesterol increases, so does your risk of heart disease and heart attack. Your blood cholesterol level tends to rise with age until it stabilizes around the age of 65. Your gender also plays a role. Up until menopause, which is around the age of 50, women tend to have a lower blood cholesterol level than men and a reduced risk of heart disease. After menopause, a woman's blood cholesterol level tends to catch up and even surpass that of a man of the same age.[25] About one in eight American women between 45 and 64 years of age has heart disease, but this jumps to one out of every

> One in every 30 American women dies each year of breast cancer, but one in every four female adult deaths is from heart disease.[26]

Table 5.4	
Risk Factors for Heart Disease	
Factors You Cannot Control	**Factors You Can Control**
Your age and gender	Type 2 diabetes mellitus
Your family history of heart disease	High blood pressure
Type 1 diabetes mellitus	Smoking
	Physical inactivity
	Excess weight
	A low HDL "good" cholesterol level
	A high LDL "bad" cholesterol level

heart attack Permanent damage to the heart muscle that results from a sudden lack of oxygen-rich blood.

stroke A condition caused by a lack of oxygen to the brain that could result in paralysis and possibly death.

atherosclerosis Narrowing of the coronary arteries due to buildup of debris along the artery walls.

plaque The hardened buildup of cholesterol-laden foam cells, platelets, cellular waste products, and calcium in the arteries that results in atherosclerosis.

Figure 5.20 **Development of Atherosclerosis**

FOCUS FIGURE WALKTHROUGH

Scan this QR code with your mobile device for a video tour of this figure by Joan Salge Blake.

Plaque accumulation within coronary arteries narrows their interior and impedes the flow of oxygen-rich blood to the heart.

Red blood cell

Lipid

Micrograph of healthy artery cross-section

Injury

Immune cell (white blood cell)

Foam cell

Micrograph of artery with plaque cross-section.

HEALTHY ARTERY

Blood flows unobstructed through normal, healthy artery.

ARTERIAL INJURY

The artery's lining is injured, attracting immune cells, and prompting inflammation.

LIPIDS ACCUMULATE IN WALL

Lipids, particularly cholesterol-containing LDLs, seep beneath the wall lining. The LDLs become oxidized. Immune cells, attracted to the site, engulf the oxidized LDLs and are transformed into foam cells.

FATTY STREAK

The foam cells accumulate to form a fatty streak, which releases more toxic and inflammatory chemicals.

PLAQUE FORMATION

The foam cells, along with platelets, calcium, protein fibers, and other substances, form thick deposits of plaque, stiffening and narrowing the artery. Blood flow through the artery is reduced or obstructed.

four women over the age of 65. The decrease in the level of the hormone estrogen in postmenopausal women plays a part in this increased risk.[27]

Because high blood cholesterol levels can be partly determined by your genes, such levels can sometimes run in families.[28] If your father or brother had early signs of heart disease before age 55, or your mother or sister had them before age 65, then you are at a greater risk. Having diabetes also increases the risk. Though the less common form of diabetes, type 1, is not preventable, the more prevalent form, type 2 diabetes, can be controlled.

Risk Factors You Can Control

Controlling diabetes can help dramatically lower the risk of heart disease for those with this condition. Type 2 diabetes can be managed and, as you read in the last chapter, possibly even prevented, through diet, lifestyle changes, and medications. Adults with diabetes are two to four times more likely to die of heart disease than adults without diabetes.[29]

Blood pressure is another factor you can control. Blood pressure is the force of your blood against the walls of your arteries. A blood pressure reading consists of two numbers. The top number, called the *systolic pressure*, is the pressure within your arteries when your heart contracts. The bottom number, called the *diastolic pressure*, is the pressure in your arteries a moment later, when your heart is relaxed. A **normal blood pressure** is considered less than 120 millimeters of mercury (Hg) for the systolic pressure and less than 80 millimeters Hg for the diastolic pressure. You might hear this referred to as "120 over 80." A blood pressure reading of 140/90 or higher is considered **hypertension**, or high blood pressure. People with hypertension constantly have a higher-than-normal force pushing against the walls of their arteries. This is thought to damage the artery lining, prompt inflammation, and accelerate the buildup of plaque. Chronic high blood pressure also causes the heart to work harder than normal and can lead to an enlarged heart. (Chapter 8 contains a detailed discussion of hypertension and how a healthy diet can help lower high blood pressure.)

Smoking damages the walls of the arteries and accelerates atherosclerosis and heart disease. In fact, even light or occasional smoking can cause this damage.[30]

Because regular exercise can help lower your LDL cholesterol and raise your good HDL cholesterol, being inactive is a risk factor for heart disease. Whereas a high HDL cholesterol level can help protect you from heart disease, having an HDL level of less than 40 milligrams per deciliter (mg/dl) increases your risk of heart disease, as you don't have enough of this "good" cholesterol carrier in your body. In contrast, a high level of HDL cholesterol, 60 mg/dl or higher, is considered a "negative" risk factor. In other words, there is so much of this "good" cholesterol in your body helping to protect against heart disease that it allows you to "erase" a risk factor from your list.

In addition to exercising regularly, losing excess weight and quitting smoking can help increase your HDL cholesterol. Exercise can also help you manage your weight. Being overweight can raise your LDL cholesterol and increase your risk of heart disease. Whereas drinking modest amounts of alcohol has also been shown to raise HDL cholesterol, other problems can outweigh this benefit. In fact, for some individuals, drinking alcohol is not advised.[31]

Other Potential Risk Factors

Some individuals don't have elevated LDL cholesterol, yet still experience heart disease, which points to other factors that must be affecting their heart health. These other potential risk factors are referred to as *emerging risk factors*.

normal blood pressure Less than 120 mm Hg (systolic—the top number) and less than 80 mm Hg (diastolic—the bottom number). Referred to as 120/80.

hypertension High blood pressure.

Researchers are continually searching for clues or "markers" in the blood, other than cholesterol levels, that are signs of the presence of heart disease. Here are some:

- A high level of the amino acid homocysteine may injure arteries and promote the development of atherosclerosis.
- A high level of a protein called C-reactive protein can indicate that there is inflammation in the walls of the arteries, which can lead to plaque formation.[32]
- A lipid–protein compound called Lp(a) is being investigated for its role in promoting heart disease.
- Apolipoprotein B (ApoB) is a measure of the amount of "bad" LDL cholesterol in the blood. A high ApoB level indicates a higher risk for heart disease.

Though the name sounds mysterious, *syndrome X*, also called **metabolic syndrome**, refers to a cluster of many factors that increase the risk for heart disease. These include abdominal obesity (too much weight around the middle), insulin resistance, high blood pressure, elevated blood levels of triglycerides and the slower clearance of this fat from the blood, a low level of HDL cholesterol, smaller and more dense LDL cholesterol particles, the higher likelihood of forming and maintaining blood clots, too much insulin, and, possibly, too much glucose in the blood. Exercise and weight reduction can help reduce all of the risk factors associated with this syndrome.[33]

In the next section, we will look at what changes you can make in your diet and lifestyle to reduce your risk of heart disease.

LO 5.7 **The Take-Home Message** Heart disease begins with a buildup of substances, including fat and cholesterol, in the arteries. The narrowing of the arteries due to this plaque buildup is known as atherosclerosis. Your age, gender, and family history can affect your risk for heart disease. Having diabetes, high blood pressure, low HDL cholesterol, high LDL cholesterol, smoking, and being physically inactive and overweight can all increase your risk of heart disease.

What Can You Do to Maintain Healthy Blood Cholesterol Levels to Reduce Your Risk of Heart Disease?

LO 5.8 Explain the dietary changes you can make to maintain healthy blood cholesterol levels and reduce your risk of heart disease.

metabolic syndrome Refers to a cluster of many factors such as abdominal obesity, insulin resistance, high blood pressure, elevated blood levels of triglycerides and slower clearance of this fat from the blood, a low HDL level, smaller and more dense LDL cholesterol particles, higher likelihood of blood clots, too much insulin, and, possibly, too much blood glucose.

Numerous research studies have shown that reducing the amount of LDL cholesterol in your blood will reduce your risk for heart disease.[34] Starting at age 20, you should have your blood tested at least once every five years to obtain your "lipoprotein profile." This profile shows the total cholesterol, LDL cholesterol, and HDL cholesterol levels in your blood. **Table 5.5** provides the recommended goals for total cholesterol, LDL cholesterol, and HDL cholesterol. The good news is that there are several diet and lifestyle changes you can make to help lower your LDL cholesterol level. The Examining the Evidence feature "The Mediterranean Diet: What Do People Living in the Mediterranean Do Differently?" on page 172 addresses one diet approach to heart-healthy eating.

Table 5.5

What Your Cholesterol Level* Can Tell You

If Your Total Cholesterol Level Is	That Is Considered
<200	Fabulous! Keep up the good work!
200–239	Borderline high
≥240	High
If Your LDL Cholesterol Level Is	**That Is Considered**
<100	Fabulous! Congratulations!
100–129	Near or above optimal
130–159	Borderline high
160–189	High
190	Much too high!
If Your HDL Cholesterol Is	**That Is Considered**
≥60	Fabulous!
40–60	Good
<40	Too low

*All lipoprotein levels are measured in milligrams of cholesterol per deciliter of blood (mg/dl).

Practical Nutrition **VIDEO**

Pizza Parlor Strategies

Even pizza can be a heart-healthy choice if you follow Joan's suggestions on how to top it. Scan this QR code with your mobile device to access the video. You can also access the video in MasteringNutrition™.

Minimize Saturated Fats, *Trans* Fats, and Cholesterol in Your Diet

In general, saturated fats raise your LDL cholesterol level, while unsaturated fats, when they replace saturated fats in your diet, will have a cholesterol-lowering effect. (Note that saturated fats in your diet will raise your blood cholesterol level more than cholesterol in your diet will.) Typically, the higher your consumption of saturated fats, the higher the LDL cholesterol levels in your blood.[35]

Americans consume more saturated fat than *trans* fat. A food that is low in *trans* fats can still be heart unhealthy if it is high in saturated fat. For example, years ago, some consumers switched from using stick margarine, which is high in *trans* fat, to butter, thinking that butter was better for their blood cholesterol. As shown in **Figure 5.21**, although butter has less *trans* fat than stick margarine, if you combine both the saturated fat and *trans* fat in each spread, margarine would still be better for your blood cholesterol. For your heart's sake, cholesterol-raising saturated fat should contribute less than 10 percent of your daily calories (ideally, less than 7 percent) and *trans* fats should be as low as possible.[36] See the Health Connection: A Case Study called "All Fats Are Not Created Equal" on page 175 for one person's struggle with lowering their cholesterol levels.

The jury is still out on whether the consumption of dietary cholesterol, at Americans' current intake levels, has a major effect on LDL cholesterol.[37] Dietary cholesterol is found in foods from animal sources, with eggs being a significant source.[38] The cholesterol in an egg is contained entirely in the yolk—the egg white is cholesterol free. Research now suggests that consuming up to an egg daily may not be associated with an increased risk of heart disease in healthy individuals.[39]

Some shellfish, such as shrimp, are also high in cholesterol; however, these are very low in saturated fat and contain some heart-healthy omega-3 fatty acids.

Eggs are an excellent source of protein, but egg yolks are high in cholesterol.

The Mediterranean Diet: What Do People Living Near the Mediterranean Do Differently?

The Mediterranean diet doesn't refer to the diet of a specific country but to the dietary patterns found in the Mediterranean region, specifically Greece, Crete (a Greek island), and southern Italy. Compared with the diets of affluent Americans, the Mediterranean diet is dramatically lower in foods from animal sources, such as meat, eggs, and dairy products, and higher in fat (mostly from olive oil and olives) and grains, fruits, and vegetables.

Numerous studies associate this traditional Mediterranean diet with health benefits and greater longevity.[1] Adopting a Mediterranean-style diet has been shown to also help individuals who have experienced a heart attack reduce their risk of recurrent heart disease by 50 to 70 percent compared with those following a more classic low-saturated-fat, low-cholesterol diet.[2]

The Mediterranean Diet Pyramid shown here was designed to reflect these dietary patterns and lifestyle habits (see figure). Let's look a little closer at this pyramid, the dietary and lifestyle changes that augment it, and some potential changes that you can make in your diet and lifestyle to reap similar benefits.

The Mediterranean Lifestyle

First, notice that there are no portion recommendations in the Mediterranean Diet Pyramid. This purposeful omission portrays the relative importance and frequency of each grouping of foods as it contributes to the whole diet, rather than to a strict diet plan. It was designed to provide an overview of healthy food choices rather than dictate rigid amounts from each food group.[3]

The Healthy Mediterranean Diet Pyramid
A plant-based diet with minimal amounts of high-saturated-fat, high-sugar foods, coupled with daily physical activity, reflects the healthy habits of the Mediterranean lifestyle.

Next, note that physical activity is front and center, at the base of this pyramid, reflecting the foundation for the Mediterranean way of life. This is an important concept, as the Mediterranean residents are very active and, not surprisingly, much leaner than Americans. In addition to exercise,

Lobster has more than 40 percent less cholesterol than shrimp and is also very low in total fat. Unfortunately, the high price of shrimp and lobster limits their consumption for many people.

Because cholesterol is not found in foods from plant sources, you won't find it in vegetables, fruits, pasta, nuts, peanut butter, or vegetable oils. The best way to minimize both saturated fat and dietary cholesterol intake is to keep your portions of lean meat, skinless poultry, and fish to about 6 ounces daily; use only low-fat or nonfat dairy foods; use vegetable oils more often than butter; keep the consumption

Nonfat milk and yogurt, and low- or reduced-fat cheeses can be enjoyed on a daily basis when eating a Mediterranean-style diet. A small amount of grated Parmesan cheese sprinkled over vegetables and a grain-based meal can provide a distinct Mediterranean flavor.

Occasional Poultry, Eggs, and Meat

Foods from animal sources are limited in the Cretan diet. Local people consume less than 2 ounces of meat and poultry daily and no more than four eggs weekly, including those used in cooking and baking.[6] Following this trend, the Mediterranean Diet Pyramid suggests eating limited amounts of poultry and eggs weekly, but relegates red meat consumption to only occasionally.

Sweets, Water, and Wine

This pyramid recommends that consumption of honey- or sugar-based sweets remain modest. Water is recommended daily. The Cretans drink it all day long and with their meals. They also drink low to moderate amounts of wine, typically only with meals. Though the pyramid depicts wine consumption on a daily basis, it is actually considered optional and based on personal preferences, family and medical history, and social situations.

How Does the Mediterranean Diet Pyramid Compare with MyPlate?

There are many similarities between the Mediterranean Diet Pyramid and MyPlate. Both emphasize the importance of regular physical activity, and both encourage a plant-based diet rich in whole grains, fruits, and vegetables, and daily consumption of dairy products. Mediterranean-style eating encourages the use of olive oil, fish, and seafood. Vegetable oils are also encouraged on MyPlate, but more modestly. Whereas poultry, eggs, and meat are recommended more modestly in the Mediterranean Diet Pyramid than in MyPlate, both advise minimizing intake of sweets. Both tools can be used as a foundation for a healthy diet. The key is to stick to the recommendations.

WHAT DO YOU THINK?

1. What aspects of the Mediterranean diet do you think contribute to heart health?
2. How are the lifestyle habits commonly associated with the Mediterranean diet likely to impact heart health?
3. How does the Mediterranean diet compare to your own current diet?

eLearn

Dining Out with Your Heart In Mind

Having a yen for Mexican, Italian, Indian, or Chinese food, but not sure what to order? Visit the Healthy Dining Finder interactive website to help you choose a restaurant with menu options than will please your palate and be healthy for your heart. Dinner is a click away at www.healthydiningfinder.com.

Mediterranean citizens enjoy other lifestyle habits that have been known to promote good mental and physical health: a supportive community of family and friends, long relaxing family meals, and afternoon siestas (naps).[4] Exercising daily, resting, and relaxing with family and friends is good health advice for all, no matter what you eat.

A Diet of Well-Seasoned Plant Foods, Olive Oil, Fish, and Dairy

Plant-based foods such as whole grains, fruits, vegetables, legumes, and nuts are the focus of the Mediterranean diet. In fact, more than 60 percent of the calories of the Cretans' diet come from these high-fiber, nutritionally dense plant foods, and olives and olive oil supply more than 75 percent of the fat.[5] As previously discussed, vegetable oils are low in saturated fat, and olive oil in particular is high in monounsaturated fat.

of baked goods to a minimum; and fill up on cholesterol-free fruits, vegetables, and whole grains.

Include Fish in Your Weekly Choices

Decades ago, researchers suggested that the Greenland Eskimos' regular consumption of fatty fish (approximately 14 ounces a day), which is rich in EPA and DHA, played a key role in their low incidence of death from heart disease.[40] Ongoing

a Butter is a rich source of saturated fatty acids and cholesterol. One tablespoon of butter contains 8 grams of saturated fat.

b Margarine doesn't contain cholesterol but it may contain *trans* fat formed during hydrogenation of vegetable oils.

c Use liquid fats over solid fats on your food and in cooking. The more liquid a fat is at room temperature, the less saturated fat and *trans* fat it contains.

Figure 5.21 Read Food Labels to Lower Saturated and *Trans* Fat Intake

While fish-oil supplements contain omega-3 fatty acids, excessive amounts can be unhealthy for some individuals.

research continues to support the protective roles EPA and DHA may play in reducing the risk of heart disease and stroke.[41] These omega-3 fatty acids may prevent irregular heart beats, reduce atherosclerosis, mildly lower blood pressure, decrease the clustering or clumping of platelets, and lower the level of fat in the blood, to name a few protective actions.[42]

It is recommended that you consume at least two servings of fish (especially fatty fish such as salmon, sardines, or herring) per week, which is approximately 0.45 to 0.50 grams daily, to obtain these omega-3 fatty acids.[43] However, don't try to meet this quota at the fast-food drive-through. Fried fish that is commercially prepared tends to have few of these fatty acids and is often fried in unhealthy fat. Note some cautions regarding fish consumption in the Nutrition in the Real World feature "Mercury and Fish" on page 176.

Though consuming some omega-3 fatty acids is good, more may not be better. Because EPA and DHA interfere with blood clotting, consuming more than 3 grams, which typically only happens by taking supplements, can cause gastrointestinal discomfort, nausea, and the risk of excessive bleeding.[44] (Consuming large amounts

All Fats Are Not Created Equal

Adam, a 20-year-old junior in fine arts, took nutrition to fulfill his college's science requirement. In the class he found out that he might be at risk for having high LDL cholesterol, because his father had high cholesterol. Adam wasn't fond of physical activity, so the only exercise he had gotten recently was running from class to class. Because he was often in a rush, he had pastries and a latte for breakfast, and he often grabbed pizza for lunch and had a hamburger and French fries for dinner. On Sundays he usually had brunch with some friends, and ate scrambled eggs with sausage and hash browns.

Adam went to the campus clinic for a cholesterol test, and sure enough, he found out his blood LDL cholesterol level was high, and his HDL cholesterol was low. He decided to try to reduce his high cholesterol by cutting down on the cholesterol and *trans* fat in his diet. He found out that the pastries he had been eating had lots of *trans* fat, so he made time to have a breakfast at home of cereal with whole milk and orange juice. He also switched to pan-cakes for brunch, as

he now knew eggs have lots of cholesterol. But when he was away from his apartment, he mostly went back to his normal diet, although he did sometimes replace his French fries with a salad. He figured that cutting down would be enough, as he was young.

When Adam returned home from college for spring break, he went to the doctor for his annual physical to see if his efforts had paid off. Everything looked good at the doctor's, but when his laboratory reports came back, they showed that his LDL numbers were still high. The doctor told him that decreasing the *trans* fats in his diet at the expense of increasing the saturated fat wasn't healthy for his heart. Switching from eggs to pancakes might actually be worse for his cholesterol level, as pancakes can have a lot of saturated and *trans* fats. When it comes to lowering his LDL cholesterol level, he needed to limit both types of fats in his diet.[7] In other words, he needed to cut down on those pancakes, pizza slices, and hamburgers.

Think About It

Explain the relationships between dietary cholesterol, saturated fats, and *trans* fats and the blood LDL cholesterol level, and how it might have been easy for Adam to confuse them.

---

of fish-oil supplements can also leave a less-than-appealing fishy aftertaste in your mouth.) Because of these potential adverse side effects, omega-3 fatty acid supplements (fish-oil supplements) should only be consumed with the advice and guidance of a doctor.[45]

Americans are currently consuming only about 0.10 gram (as compared with the 0.50 grams recommended) of EPA and DHA daily.[46] **Figure 5.22** lists the omega-3 fatty acid content of some popular fish and seafood, and the Table Tips provide a few quick ways to add fish to your diet. Think of fish as food for your heart.

Eat Plenty of Plant Foods

In addition to fish, the American Heart Association also recommends that you consume plant-based foods such as walnuts and flaxseeds, as well as soybean and canola oils, which are all high in alpha-linolenic acid.[47] As mentioned, some alpha-linolenic acid is converted in the body to these heart-healthy omega-3 fatty acids.

Spreads and soft-gel tablets containing plant sterols and stanols can be used as part of a heart-healthy diet to lower LDL cholesterol.

Although the health benefits of eating fish are well established, not everyone should be eating unlimited amounts of *all* types of fish. In fact, pregnant and nursing women, women of childbearing age who may become pregnant, and young children should avoid certain types of seafood that may contain high amounts of methylmercury. This form of mercury can be harmful to the nervous systems of unborn children, especially during the first trimester of pregnancy, a time when women may not even realize that they are pregnant.[8]

Though mercury occurs naturally in nature, it is also a by-product of industrial processes and pollution. The airborne form of mercury accumulates on the surface of streams and oceans and is transformed in the water into the toxic form of methylmercury.[9] The fish absorb the methylmercury from the water, or get it by eating the organisms that live in the water. Because the ingested methylmercury accumulates over time, larger fish, such as swordfish, shark, king mackerel, and tilefish (golden bass or golden snapper), will have the highest concentration of methylmercury,

as they have a longer life span and feed on other, smaller fish. Women of childbearing age and young children should avoid eating these four types of fish.

However, eating fish, in particular the omega-3 fats from seafood, has been shown to *help* in the development of a fetus's nervous system. Thus, pregnant women and women of childbearing age should consume 8 to 12 ounces weekly of other types of cooked fish, including shellfish, and should choose from a variety of fish to get these omega-3 fats in their diet.[10] Luckily, the ten most popular types of seafood (canned *light* tuna, shrimp, pollock, salmon, cod, catfish, clams, flatfish, crabs, and scallops) contain only low amounts of methylmercury. Canned albacore (white) tuna has more mercury than the light variety, so should be limited to no more than 6 ounces weekly.[11] While the FDA regulates all commercial fish, the Environmental Protection Agency (EPA) oversees all freshwater fish caught recreationally, such as by family members and friends. This agency recommends that all women who are or may become pregnant, nursing mothers, and young

Large fish such as swordfish, shark, king mackerel, and tilefish are likely to contain high levels of methylmercury.

children should limit their consumption of freshwater fish to six ounces of cooked fish weekly for adults.[12] If you eat noncommercial fish from local waters, you should always check with your state or local health department for specific advice, as there could be additional fish consumption advisories based on your local waters. The EPA recommends that if you want to eat coastal and ocean fish that is caught recreationally, you should check with your local or state health department and follow the FDA advice referenced earlier.[13]

Eating more plant foods high in viscous, soluble fiber may be one of the easiest ways to decrease your LDL cholesterol level. In reviewing more than 65 studies, researchers found that each gram of viscous, soluble fiber consumed, in the range of 2 to 10 grams daily, from oatmeal, oat bran, legumes such as dried beans, psyllium, and/or pectin, lowered LDL cholesterol levels by more than 2.0 mg/dl on average.[48] Although the DRI for fiber ranges from consuming 20 to 38 grams daily, consuming about half of this amount, or 10 to 25 grams of viscous, soluble fiber, can help decrease high LDL cholesterol levels.[49] Increasing the soy in your diet may also help reduce the risk of heart disease.

Although all plant foods are cholesterol free, they do contain **phytosterols**, which are plant sterols similar to cholesterol that are found in the plant's cell membranes. Plant sterols can help lower LDL cholesterol levels by competing with cholesterol for absorption in the intestinal tract.[50] With less cholesterol being absorbed, there will be less in the blood. Plant sterols occur naturally in soybean oil, many fruits, vegetables, legumes, sesame seeds, nuts, cereals, and other plant foods.[51]

Research shows that consuming about 2 grams of plant stanols or sterols can lower LDL cholesterol by about 5 to 15 percent.[52] Products such as margarines, juices, snack items, and soft-gel tablets that contain plant sterols are now available.

Routinely Select Foods Rich in Antioxidants and Phytochemicals

You might think that a substance that starts with the prefix "anti" couldn't be good for you. However, antioxidants may help LDL cholesterol become more resistant to oxidants, products of cell processes that may play a role in the progression of heart disease.[53] Antioxidants appear to protect LDL cholesterol from being oxidized by inhibiting the formation of oxidants, intercepting them once they are created, or helping to repair any injury to cells due to these substances. However, when there are more oxidants than antioxidant defense mechanisms occurring in the body, an imbalance occurs. This can cause adverse effects, such as heart disease.

Antioxidant-rich plant foods such as fruits and vegetables contain many other vitamins and minerals, which are not only healthy for your heart in their own right, but may also work with antioxidants. These foods are naturally low in saturated fat and *trans* fat and are cholesterol free, so they can displace heart-unhealthy foods in your diet. Plant foods are also full of fiber, particularly soluble fiber. For all of these reasons, your heart will benefit if you eat plant foods high in antioxidants at each meal.

Nuts are one type of food that is rich in antioxidants and fiber, and they can have a positive effect on LDL cholesterol levels for other reasons. Research collecting data from 25 studies showed that daily nut consumption reduced LDL cholesterol slightly over 7 percent.[54] The FDA now allows the food label on certain nuts and nut products to claim that the product potentially helps fight heart disease.[55]

The only downside to nuts is that they're high in calories. A mere ounce of nuts (about 24 almonds or 28 peanuts) can contribute a hefty 160 to 200 calories to your diet. Routinely sitting down with a jar of peanuts to eat while studying can quickly have you overconsuming calories. The Table Tips called "Nuts about Nuts?" provides ideas on how to enjoy a modest amount of nuts in your diet.

There are other substances that may provide an extra boost to your heart health. Some research suggests that dark chocolate, due to its **flavonoid** content, may offer some antioxidant protection as well as potentially inhibiting platelet aggregation, which can perpetuate a blood clot.[56] However, keep in mind that the phytochemical, flavonoid, can vary among brands and that chocolate is a sweet that can contribute a hefty amount of calories if consumed in excess, which can lead to obesity, a risk factor for heart disease. When consumed in small amounts, as part of a healthy diet, flavonoid-rich chocolate will likely provide some heart-health benefits.[57]

Tea may also reduce your risk of heart disease. Research shows that consumption of tea is associated with a lower incidence of dying from heart disease.[58] Green tea in particular is not only high in catechins, which are antioxidants, but a review of 20 studies also showed that these substances may help reduce total and LDL cholesterol.[59] Drinking tea is good for your heart.

Grams (g) of Omega-3s (EPA and DHA)

Figure data (bar chart):
- Cod, 3 oz: 0.2
- Tuna, light, canned in water, 3 oz: 0.2
- Crab, 3 oz: 0.4
- Shrimp, 3 oz: 0.5
- Sardines, canned in oil, 3 oz: 0.8
- Salmon, 3 oz: 1.0
- Herring, 3 oz: 1.7
- Mackerel, 3 oz: 2.0
- Daily Needs / Adults 19 to 50 years: 0.25

Protein | Daily Needs

Figure 5.22 Food Sources of Omega-3 Fatty Acids Several types of fish, particularly fatty fish, are high in the heart-healthy omega-3 fatty acids.

Grind whole flaxseeds before eating them to best reap their nutritional benefits. Whole flaxseeds can pass through your gastrointestinal tract intact, keeping their essential fatty acids and vitamin E enclosed in the shell.

phytosterols Naturally occurring sterols found in plants. Phytosterols lower LDL cholesterol levels by competing with cholesterol for absorption in the intestinal tract.

flavonoids Phytochemicals found in fruits, vegetables, tea, nuts, and seeds.

Strive for Plenty of Exercise and Manage Your Weight

Routine exercise can help reduce LDL cholesterol levels, high blood pressure, insulin resistance, and excess weight, and improve HDL cholesterol levels.[60] To gain these health benefits, the current 2008 *Physical Activity Guidelines for Americans* recommend that adults should partake in 150 minutes (2 hours and 30 minutes) weekly of moderate-intensity activities such as walking briskly or 75 minutes (1 hour and 15 minutes) weekly of vigorous-intensity aerobic physical activity such as jogging, or a combination of the two.[61] Additional health benefits can be gained by increasing your physical activity above this level.[62]

Regular physical activity can also help accelerate weight loss. Losing excess weight can help not only to lower LDL cholesterol levels, high blood pressure, and the risk of developing type 2 diabetes, but also to raise HDL cholesterol levels. Hence, sedentary individuals should "move" and sedentary, overweight individuals should "move and lose" to lower their risk of heart disease. **Table 5.6** summarizes the diet and lifestyle changes you can make to reduce your LDL cholesterol and risk for heart disease.

A Word about the Protective Effects of Red Wine

Drinking alcohol in moderate amounts can reduce the risk of heart disease.[63] Alcohol can increase the level of the heart-protective HDL cholesterol. In fact, approximately 50 percent of alcohol's heart-protective effect is probably due to this positive effect on HDL cholesterol. Studies have also suggested that alcohol may decrease blood clotting by affecting the coagulation of platelets or by helping the blood to break up clots.[64]

Other studies have suggested that the antioxidants in wine as well as dark beer also contribute to the heart-protective aspects of alcohol.[65] Though some alcohol may be good, more is definitely not better. Drinking too much alcohol can increase the level of fat in your blood and lead to high blood pressure. Binge drinking, a common practice among young adults, is associated with an increased risk for heart disease and stroke.[66] We will talk more about alcohol consumption in Chapter 9.

The Whole Is Greater Than the Sum of Its Parts

When it comes to reducing the risk of heart disease, the whole diet may be greater than the sum of its parts. A study of more than 45 adults with elevated total and

Table 5.6	
To Decrease Excess LDL Cholesterol	
Dietary Changes	**Lifestyle Changes**
Consume less saturated fat	Lose excess weight
Consume less *trans* fats	Exercise more
Consume less dietary cholesterol	
Consume more soluble fiber–rich foods	
Consume a more plant-based diet	

LDL cholesterol levels illustrated that a diet "portfolio" consisting of a diet low in saturated fat and cholesterol that was also high in soluble fiber, soy protein, plant sterols, and nuts lowered LDL cholesterol levels by almost 30 percent.[67] This impressive reduction was similar to that observed in the group that was given a cholesterol-lowering drug and limited *only* the saturated fat and cholesterol in their diet. The latter group's diet did not include the other items in the portfolio diet. Hence, a dietary portfolio approach to eating may be a viable way for individuals to lower high cholesterol levels and avoid taking medication that could have potential side effects.[68] The Table Tips on Eating for a Healthy Heart provide eating tips for a heart-healthy diet.

LO 5.8 **The Take-Home Message** Limiting saturated fat, cholesterol, and *trans* fat, and increasing fish consumption, as well as consumption of antioxidant-rich fruits, vegetables, whole grains, and nuts, are associated with a reduction in the risk of heart disease. Regular exercise and weight loss can also help lower LDL cholesterol levels and raise HDL cholesterol levels. Drinking a moderate amount of alcohol may help reduce the risk of heart disease. Some individuals should avoid alcoholic beverages.

Table TIPS

Eating for a Healthy Heart

Choose only lean meats (round, sirloin, and tenderloin cuts) and skinless poultry and keep your portions of meat to about 6 ounces daily. Eat fish at least twice a week.

Use two egg whites in place of one whole egg when baking.

Use reduced-fat or nonfat dairy products, such as low-fat or skim milk, reduced-fat cheese, and low-fat or nonfat ice cream. Sprinkle cheese on top of your food rather than mixing it in so you use less. Be sure to keep ice cream servings small.

Substitute cooked beans for half the meat in chili, soups, and casseroles.

Use canola, olive, soybean, or corn oil, and *trans* fat–free margarine instead of butter or shortening.

MADE over MADE better

Many Americans' diets are too high in fat and heart-unhealthy saturated fat. A few tweaks in your diet selections can help you keep your fat intake within a healthy range of 20 to 35 percent of your daily calories and your saturated fat intake to no more than 7 to 10 percent of your calories every day. Here are some typical fat-rich foods made over and made nutritionally better!

If you like this. . .　　　　**Try this to control your fat intake!**

Mocha, 2% Milk, Whipped Cream
Serving size: 16 oz
Total Fat: 15 grams
Saturated Fat: 8 grams

Coffee, Brewed
Serving size: 16 oz
Total Fat: 0 grams
Saturated Fat: 0 grams

Butter
Serving size: 1 pat
Total Fat: 3.8 grams
Saturated Fat: 2.4 grams

Jelly
Serving size: 1 tbs
Total Fat: 0 grams
Saturated Fat: 0 grams

Cheddar Cheese
Serving size: 1.5 ounces
Total Fat: 14.1 grams
Saturated Fat: 9 grams

Reduced-fat Cheddar Cheese
Serving size: 2 ounces
Total Fat: 9 grams
Saturated Fat: 6 grams

Chocolate Ice Cream
Serving size: 1/2 cup
Total Fat: 14 grams
Saturated Fat: 9 grams

Low-fat Frozen Yogurt
Serving size: 1/2 cup
Total Fat: 1.5 grams
Saturated Fat: 1 gram

POINTS OF VIEW

Is Wild Salmon a Better Choice Than Farmed Salmon? Salmon is well known as an excellent source of omega-3 fatty acids. Both farmed and wild-caught salmon contain this essential nutrient; however, farmed salmon may also contain toxins such as methylmercury and polychlorinated biphenyls (PCBs).

Is the nutritional benefit of consuming high amounts of omega-3 fatty acids worth the risk of ingesting toxins? Should you avoid farmed salmon and eat only wild-caught salmon? After you've read the arguments for and against, answer the critical-thinking questions and decide for yourself.

yes

- Farmed salmon have much higher levels of toxic chemicals such as PCBs, dioxins, and certain pesticides than their wild-caught counterparts.[1] A review paper has found a possible link between PCBs and the development of type 2 diabetes mellitus.[2] The contamination source in farmed fish is fish oil and fishmeal in their feed. However, PCB levels vary greatly from farm to farm.

- There are some environmental concerns associated with farm-raised salmon. For instance, most salmon are farmed in open pens and cages in coastal waters. Waste from these farms is released directly into the ocean and can harm wild fish populations.[3]

- Salmon farms can be incubators of disease. One study found that reoccurring sea lice outbreaks killed up to 80 percent of young wild pink salmon whose migration paths crossed salmon farms.[4]

- Farmed salmon feed can contain high amounts of antibiotics and other chemicals, some of which are outlawed in the United States for threats to human and marine health.[5]

- It takes about 3 pounds of wild fish to grow 1 pound of farmed salmon. As global production increases, so does the environmental impact of farming salmon.[6]

no

- Farmed and wild salmon are both low in saturated fat and calories. Both are high in protein, and both are excellent sources of omega-3 fatty acids.[7]

- A study in 2004 found that farmed salmon had PCB levels 10 times as high as wild salmon,[8] but those levels were still very low[9] —well below those the Food and Drug Administration says are safe. And since then, PCB levels in farmed salmon have come down quite a bit.

- Researchers from the Harvard School of Public Health found that the benefits of eating oily fish outweighed the risk, even for the most sensitive parts of the population.[10]

- Most farm-raised salmon are Atlantic salmon and are readily available year-round. Wild populations of Atlantic salmon are generally at very low levels and their commercial harvest is limited.[11]

- Wild-caught salmon is often higher priced than farmed salmon.[12]

what do you think?

1. What is the most compelling argument for consuming wild rather than farm-raised salmon? Is this argument strong enough to influence your food choice? **2.** Do the benefits of eating farmed salmon outweigh the risks? **3.** How can consumers make the best choices when it comes to eating fish?

LO 5.1 Describe the three classifications of lipids and explain the differences in the structure of triglycerides, phospholipids, and cholesterol.

Lipids refer to a category of carbon, oxygen, and hydrogen compounds that do not dissolve in water. There are three types of lipids: triglycerides, phospholipids, and sterols. A triglyceride, also known as a fat, contains three fatty acids joined to a glycerol backbone and is the most abundant type of lipid in your body and in foods. A fatty acid without any double bonds is called a saturated fatty acid. If one or more double bonds is present, it is called an unsaturated fatty acid. A saturated fat contains mostly saturated fatty acids and tends to be solid at room temperature. An unsaturated fat has mostly unsaturated fatty acids, is liquid at room temperature, and is also known as an oil.

Phospholipids contain two fatty acids at their tail end and have a phosphate-containing head. Their polar heads and nonpolar tails cause them to be attracted to both water and fat. Lecithin is the major phospholipid in your cell membranes. Lecithin is often used as an emulsifier in foods. Cholesterol is the major sterol in your body and in foods. Cholesterol is the precursor of vitamin D, bile acids, and sex hormones. Your body makes all the cholesterol it needs.

Lipid	Structure
Triglycerides	Glycerol — [fatty acid structure] / Fatty acids
Phospholipids	Phosphate head [structure] / Fatty acids
Sterols	[cholesterol structure] HO

LO 5.2 Describe how fat is digested, absorbed, and transported in the body.

The majority of fat in your diet is digested and absorbed in your small intestine with the help of bile acids and pancreatic lipase. The digested fat is predominantly packaged in protein- and phosphorus-containing lipoproteins called chylomicrons, which travel in your lymph to your bloodstream.

Other lipoproteins include the "bad" LDL cholesterol carrier and the "good" HDL cholesterol carrier. LDL deposits cholesterol along your artery walls and contributes to atherosclerosis. HDL removes cholesterol from arteries and brings it to the liver to be used or excreted from your body.

LO 5.3 Describe the functions of fat in the body.

In your body, fat is used as a protective cushion for your bones, organs, and nerves, in your cell membranes, and as insulation to maintain your body temperature. In food, fat provides texture and flavor, and contributes to satiety. Fat in food also aids in the absorption of fat-soluble vitamins.

LO 5.4 Define the dietary recommendations for total fat, the essential fatty acids, saturated fat, cholesterol, and *trans* fat.

Your diet should contain 20 to 35 percent of calories coming from fat, with no more than 10 percent from saturated fat, and minimal amounts of *trans* fats. Because fat provides the essential fatty acids, linoleic acid and alpha-linolenic acid, a minimum of 5 percent and up to 10 percent of your total calories should be from linoleic acid, and 0.6 percent to 1.2 percent of total calories should be from alpha-linolenic acid.

LO 5.6 Compare the different fat substitutes currently used in food products.

Fat substitutes are designed to provide all the creamy properties of fat for fewer calories and total fat grams. Because fat has more than double the calories per gram of carbohydrates or protein, fat substitutes have the potential to reduce calories from fat.

LO 5.5 Identify the major food sources of the different types of fats, including the essential fatty acids, saturated fats, and *trans* fats.

Plant-based unsaturated fats are the best sources of fat and are abundant in vegetable oils, such as soybean, corn, and canola oils, as well as in soybeans, walnuts, peanut butter, and flaxseeds. Vegetables oils, nuts, and flaxseeds are good sources of essential fatty acids. A limited amount of alpha-linolenic acid can be converted to the omega-3 fatty acids, eicosapentaenoic acid (EPA) and docosahexaenoic acid (DHA), which have been shown to reduce the risk of heart disease and stroke. Because fish, especially fatty fish, are good sources of EPA and DHA, you should consume at least two servings of fish weekly. Most saturated fat in the diet comes from animal foods, including whole-milk dairy products such as cheese, butter, and ice cream, fatty cuts of meat, and the skin on poultry. The majority of *trans* fats in foods are created by food manufacturers through the process of hydrogenation. Reading food labels can help you lower your intake of both saturated and *trans* fats.

LO 5.7 Describe the development of atherosclerosis, including its role in the risk of heart disease.

Heart disease develops when the coronary arteries, the large blood vessels that supply oxygen and other nutrients to the heart, accumulate a buildup of LDLs and other substances along their walls. As the artery gets narrower, blood flow is impeded and less oxygen and nutrients are delivered to the heart; a blood clot could also block the narrowed artery, leading to a heart attack or stroke.

Heart disease is the leading cause of death in the United States. Risk factors that you can't control are your age, gender, family history of heart disease, and type 1 diabetes. Risk factors that you can control include preventing and controlling type 2 diabetes, high blood pressure, smoking, physical inactivity, excess weight, a low HDL cholesterol level, and an elevated LDL cholesterol level.

VISUAL Chapter Summary

Explain the dietary changes you can make to maintain healthy blood cholesterol levels and reduce your risk of heart disease.

Eating a well-balanced plant-based diet that contains moderate amounts of heart-healthy unsaturated fat and less heart-unhealthy saturated fat is the best strategy to lower your LDL blood cholesterol level and your risk of heart disease. Commercially prepared baked goods, snack items, and fried foods should be limited so as to decrease *trans* fats. Your diet should contain no more than 300 milligrams of cholesterol daily, on average. Soluble fiber–containing foods such as oats, and plant sterols can also help lower your LDL cholesterol level. Exercising and losing excess weight can help lower your LDL cholesterol level and increase your HDL cholesterol level. The Mediterranean Diet Pyramid is a heart-healthy diet that can help you maintain healthy blood cholesterol levels.

Terms to Know

- lipids
- hydrophobic
- fatty acids

- saturated fatty acid
- unsaturated fatty acid
- monounsaturated fatty acid
- polyunsaturated fatty acid

- essential fatty acids
- linoleic acid
- alpha-linolenic acid
- triglyceride
- glycerol

- fat
- phospholipids
- sterols
- bile
- micelles
- lipoprotein

- chylomicron
- very-low-density lipoprotein (VLDL)
- low-density lipoprotein (LDL)
- high-density lipoprotein (HDL)

- hydrogenation
- *trans* fatty acids
- atherosclerosis
- plaque
- hypertension

MasteringNutrition™

Build your knowledge—and confidence—in the Study Area of MasteringNutrition with a variety of study tools.

MyDiet Analysis

Access MyDietAnalysis through MasteringNutrition™ and track your diet and daily activities. In addition, a dietary analysis activity is available for every chapter in your book.

Check Your Understanding

LO 5.1 1. The primary lipid in your body is
a. cholesterol.
b. lecithin.
c. triglycerides.
d. chylomicrons.

LO 5.2 2. _____ help(s) to emulsify fat in your gastrointestinal tract.
a. Micelles
b. Lingual lipase
c. Gastric lipase
d. Bile

LO 5.3 3. Fat in foods is a source of
a. flavor.
b. carbohydrates.
c. minerals.
d. fiber.

LO 5.3 4. The type of lipoprotein that carries absorbed fat and other lipids through your lymph system is called
a. VLDL.
b. LDL.
c. bile acid.
d. a chylomicron.

LO 5.4 5. You should keep your dietary fat intake between
a. 8 and 10 percent of your daily calories.
b. 20 and 35 percent of your daily calories.
c. 35 and 40 percent of your daily calories.
d. 300 milligrams and 500 milligrams daily.

LO 5.5 6. Donald has heart disease. To obtain heart-healthy omega-3 fatty acids, he should eat
  a. a tuna fish sandwich at lunch and a Burger King fish sandwich for dinner.
  b. shrimp for lunch and salmon for dinner.
  c. fish and chips for lunch and flounder at dinner.
  d. fried fish sticks at lunch and steamed lobster for dinner.

LO 5.6 7. Fat substitutes are fats that have been modified either to provide the physical attributes of fat for fewer calories or to
  a. interfere with the absorption of fat.
  b. help the body burn more fat.
  c. increase the body's absorption of fat.
  d. affect the taste of dietary fat.

LO 5.7 8. The major dietary component that raises your LDL cholesterol is
  a. viscous, soluble fiber.
  b. green tea
  c. saturated fat.
  d. plant sterols.

LO 5.8 9. Which of the following are good sources of the essential fatty acids linoleic acid and alpha-linolenic acid?
  a. bananas
  b. walnuts
  c. oatmeal
  d. chocolate

LO 5.8 10. *Trans* fats are unhealthy for your heart because they
  a. lower LDL cholesterol levels.
  b. raise HDL and LDL cholesterol levels.
  c. raise LDL cholesterol and lower HDL cholesterol levels.
  d. have no effect on LDL cholesterol.

Answers

1. (c) The major lipid in your body is triglycerides, also known as fat. Cholesterol is another type of lipid but is not as abundant as fat. Lecithin is a phospholipid found in your cell membranes and is used as an emulsifier in some foods. Chylomicrons are lipoproteins that transport fat and other lipids to your liver.

2. (d) Bile helps to emulsify fat in your gastrointestinal tract. Micelles transport fatty acids through the cells of the intestinal wall. The enzyme lingual lipase in the mouth plays a minor role in fat digestion. Gastric lipase breaks down some fats in the stomach into diglycerides and free fatty acids.

3. (a) Fat provides flavor. It does not provide carbohydrates, minerals, or fiber.

4. (d) Chylomicrons enable insoluble fat as well as cholesterol and phospholipids to travel through the lymph system. Bile acids help emulsify fat in your GI tract. VLDLs and LDLs transport fat and other lipids through your blood.

5. (b) Your daily fat intake should be between 20 and 35 percent of your daily calories.

6. (b) Though tuna is a wonderful way to enjoy fish at lunch, the commercially prepared fried fish sandwich, fish and chips, and fish sticks have little of the omega-3 fatty acids that would help Donald's heart. Shrimp and salmon are much better choices.

7. (a) Fat substitutes are fats that have been modified either to provide the physical attributes of fat for fewer calories or to interfere with the absorption of fat.

8. (c) Saturated fat is the bigger culprit behind an elevated LDL cholesterol in the blood. Viscous, soluble fiber, green tea, and plant sterols can all help lower LDL cholesterol.

9. (b) Walnuts are a good source of essential fatty acids.

10. (c) *Trans* fats provide a double whammy for your heart because they raise the "bad" LDL cholesterol and lower the "good" HDL cholesterol in your body.

Web Resources

- National Heart, Lung, and Blood Institute at www.nhlbi.nih.gov
- American Heart Association at www.heart.org
- Centers for Disease Control and Prevention, at www.cdc.gov

1. **False.** Your body *does* need cholesterol for important functions. However, your body can manufacture it in sufficient amounts, so you don't need to eat any to meet your needs. See page 150.

2. **False.** However, don't start celebrating. We are still consuming too much fat from heart-unhealthy saturated fat in the diet. See page 157.

3. **False.** Whereas too much dietary fat may cause you to gain weight, eating too little isn't healthy either. A diet low in fat but high in added sugars may increase the level of fat in your blood. See page 157.

4. **False.** Red meat is not the major source of saturated fat in the diet. Turn to page 158 to find out what is.

5. **False.** Fat-free foods often have added carbohydrates, which add back calories. The savings in fat calories is usually not much of a savings in total calories. See page 165.

6. **False.** The HDL cholesterol in your body is healthy for you, and may protect against heart disease. Turn to page 169 to learn more.

7. **False.** Although stick margarines can contain heart-unhealthy *trans* fats, butter has more total cholesterol-raising fats than margarine, and so is ultimately less healthy. See page 171.

8. **False.** Because peanut butter doesn't come from an animal, it does not contain cholesterol. See page 172.

9. **False.** Consuming too much fish oil in supplement form can be unhealthy. See page 174.

10. **True.** The viscous, soluble fiber found in oatmeal and other foods can lower your blood cholesterol. See page 176.

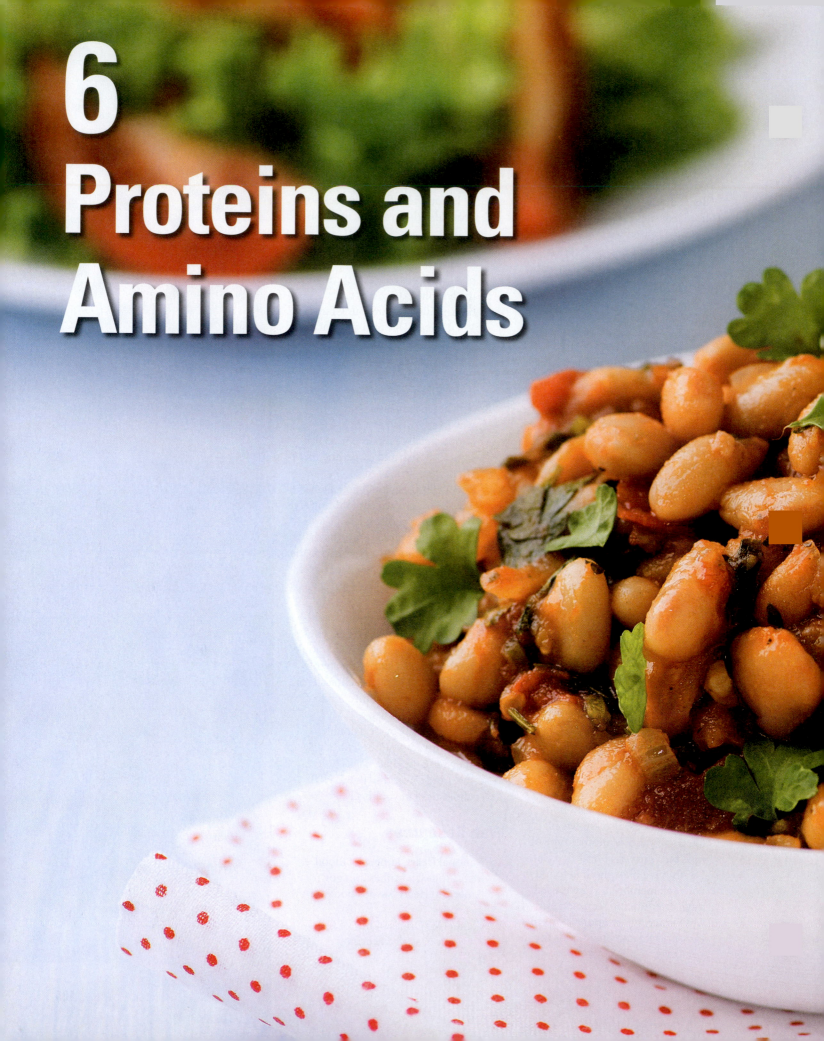

6
Proteins and Amino Acids

True or False?

1. Your body can use protein as an energy source. T|F p. 199

2. Proteins increase satiety after a meal. T|F p. 199

3. You can digest the protein in pasta as easily as the protein in a chicken breast. T|F p. 202

4. Soy is not as good a source of dietary protein as fish. T|F p. 202

5. Approximately one-half of your daily calories should come from protein. T|F p. 203

6. Most Americans are falling short of their protein needs. T|F p. 203

7. Americans are eating more red meat than they were in the 1970s. T|F p. 204

8. Protein bars are needed if you are very active. T|F p. 206

9. Eating too much protein-rich food may increase your blood risk of heart disease. T|F p. 209

10. Vegetarian athletes are at a competitive disadvantage compared with non-vegetarian competitors. T|F p. 219

See page 225 for the answers.

After reading this chapter, you will be able to:

Learning Outcomes

LO 6.1 Explain what proteins are and why they are important.

LO 6.2 Describe how your body digests and absorbs proteins.

LO 6.3 Describe the functions of protein in the body.

LO 6.4 Determine your daily protein needs.

LO 6.5 Identify healthy sources of protein in the diet.

LO 6.6 Explain the health consequences of consuming too little or too much protein.

LO 6.7 Describe the benefits and risks of a vegetarian diet.

Y ou have thousands of unique proteins in your body. Your protein-rich muscles enable you to swim, walk, stand, and hold your head up so you can read this information. Without adequate protein, your immune system wouldn't be able to fight off infections, your hair wouldn't grow, your fingernails would be mere stubs, and you wouldn't be able to digest your food.

In this chapter we discuss the structure and roles of proteins and how they are digested, absorbed, and used by the body. We will also cover the health risks associated with consuming too much or too little protein and the pros and cons of different eating patterns, including vegetarian diets.

What Are Proteins and Why Are They Important?

LO 6.1 Explain what proteins are and why they are important.

Proteins are the predominant structural and functional materials in every cell, and you have thousands of unique proteins in your body. These diverse molecules play a role in virtually every cellular activity, from building, repairing, and maintaining cells to storage, transport, and utilization of the nutrients you eat. Many hormones and enzymes, which control essential metabolic processes, are also made of proteins. In fact, proteins are involved in most of your body's functions and life processes; without them, you wouldn't survive.[1]

We'll begin our discussion of proteins with a look at how they're structured. Specifically, we'll start by looking at the amino acids.

The Building Blocks of Proteins Are Amino Acids

All proteins consist of a chain of some combination of 20 unique **amino acids**, and they are classified according to the number of amino acids in the chain. If the chain contains fewer than 50 amino acids linked together, it is called a peptide. Two joined amino acids form a *dipeptide*; three joined amino acids form a *tripeptide*; and a *polypeptide* is more than 10 amino acids joined together. A chain with more than 50 amino acids is called a protein. Proteins typically contain between 100 and 10,000 amino acids in a sequence. For instance, the protein that forms the hemoglobin in red blood cells consists of close to 300 amino acids, as compared with collagen, which contains approximately 1,000 amino acids.

Amino acids are like numeric digits, in that their specific sequence will determine a specific function. Consider that telephone numbers, Social Security numbers, and bank PIN numbers are all made up of the same digits (0 to 9) arranged in different sequences of varying lengths. Each of these number combinations has a specific purpose. Similarly, amino acids can be linked together to make unique sequences of varying lengths, each with a specific function.

Anatomy of an Amino Acid

As illustrated in **Figure 6.1a**, each amino acid contains a central carbon (C) surrounded by four parts: an **acid group** (COOH) (which is why it is called an amino "acid"), an **amine group** (NH_2) that contains nitrogen, a hydrogen atom, and a unique **side chain**. Whereas all 20 nutritionally important amino acids contain the same four parts, it is the side chain that makes each amino acid different.

The side chain can be as simple as a single hydrogen atom, as in the amino acid glycine; or it can be a combination of atoms, as in aspartic acid and phenylalanine (see **Figure 6.1b**). (Do these last two amino acids sound familiar? Recall that they are the major components of the sugar substitute aspartame, which we discussed in Chapter 4.)

Now let's look at how amino acids are linked together to build proteins.

Peptide Bonds and Side Chains Determine a Protein's Shape and Function

Amino acids are joined to each other by **peptide bonds** to build proteins. A peptide bond is created when the acid group (COOH) of one amino acid is joined with the amine group (NH₂) of another amino acid (**Figure 6.2**). The unique nature of each amino acid side chain prevents a protein from remaining in an orderly straight line. Rather, each polypeptide folds into a precise three-dimensional shape, such as a coil,

a **Amino acid structure.** All amino acids contain carbon, hydrogen, and oxygen, similar to carbohydrates and fat. They also contain a nitrogen-containing amine group and an acid group.

b **Different amino acids showing their unique side chains.** A unique side chain (shown in yellow) distinguishes the various amino acids.

Figure 6.1 The Structure of an Amino Acid

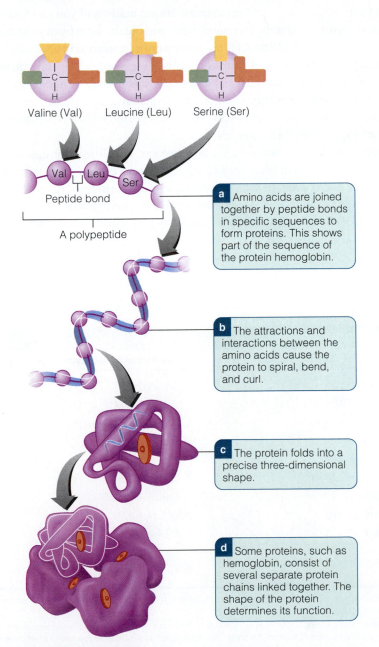

a Amino acids are joined together by peptide bonds in specific sequences to form proteins. This shows part of the sequence of the protein hemoglobin.

b The attractions and interactions between the amino acids cause the protein to spiral, bend, and curl.

c The protein folds into a precise three-dimensional shape.

d Some proteins, such as hemoglobin, consist of several separate protein chains linked together. The shape of the protein determines its function.

Figure 6.2 The Making of a Protein

proteins Compounds in your body that consist of numerous amino acids and are found in all living cells.

amino acids The building blocks of protein. Amino acids contain carbon, hydrogen, oxygen, and nitrogen. All amino acids are composed of an acid group, an amine group, and a unique side chain.

acid group The COOH group that is part of every amino acid; also called the *carboxyl group*.

amine group The nitrogen-containing part (NH₂) of an amino acid.

side chain The side group of an amino acid that provides it with its unique qualities; also referred to as the R group.

peptide bonds The bonds that connect amino acids, created when the acid group of one amino acid is joined with the nitrogen-containing amine group of another amino acid.

based on the interactions of its amino acid side chains with each other and the environment. Some side chains are attracted to other side chains; some are neutral; and some repel each other.

Additionally, side chains can be *hydrophilic* ("water-loving") or *hydrophobic* ("water-fearing"), and this affects how they react with their environment. The hydrophobic side chains tend to cluster together in the interior of the protein, causing the protein to be globular in shape. The hydrophilic side chains assemble on the outside surface of the protein, closer to the watery environments of blood and other body fluids. The shape of a protein determines its function in your body. Therefore, anything that alters the bonds between the side chains will alter its shape and thus its function.

Essential, Nonessential, and Conditionally-Essential Amino Acids

There are nine amino acids that your body cannot make and that you must therefore obtain from foods. These are the **essential amino acids**, and you can find them in foods such as meat and milk. It is *essential* that you obtain them from your diet.

The remaining 11 amino acids are **nonessential amino acids** because they can be synthesized, or created, in your body. It is *not essential* to consume them in the diet. Your body creates nonessential amino acids as needed by adding nitrogen to a carbon-containing structure. Some nonessential amino acids can also be made from other amino acids. This process occurs primarily in the liver. **Table 6.1** lists the 20 amino acids by their classification.

Some nonessential amino acids may become **conditionally essential** if the body cannot make them because of illness, or because the body lacks the necessary **precursors** or enzymes. In such situations, they are considered essential and must be consumed through food. An example of this is when premature infants are not able to make enough of the enzymes needed to create arginine, so they need to get this amino acid in their diet.[2]

essential amino acids The nine amino acids that the body cannot synthesize; they must be obtained through dietary sources.

nonessential amino acids The 11 amino acids that the body can synthesize.

conditionally essential amino acids Nonessential amino acids that become essential if the body cannot make them, such as during bouts of illness.

precursor A substance that is converted to another substance in the body.

Table 6.1

The Mighty Twenty

Essential Amino Acids	Nonessential Amino Acids
Histidine (His)[a]	Alanine (Ala)
Isoleucine (Ile)	Arginine (Arg)[b]
Leucine (Leu)	Aspartic acid (Asp)
Lysine (Lys)	Asparagine (Asn)
Methionine (Met)	Cysteine (Cys)[b]
Phenylalanine (Phe)	Glutamic acid (Glu)
Threonine (Thr)	Glutamine (Gln)[b]
Tryptophan (Trp)	Glycine (Gly)[b]
Valine (Val)	Proline (Pro)[b]
	Serine (Ser)
	Tyrosine (Tyr)[b]

[a]Histidine was once thought to be essential only for infants. It is now known that small amounts are also needed for adults.

[b]These amino acids can be "conditionally essential" if there are either inadequate precursors or inadequate enzymes available to create them in the body. This can happen in certain illnesses and in premature infants.

Heat →

Normal protein   Denatured protein

Figure 6.3 Denaturing a Protein
A protein can be denatured, or unfolded, by exposure to heat, mechanical agitation, acids, bases, or salts. Any change in a protein's shape will alter its function.

Denaturation of Proteins Changes Their Shape

Proteins can be unfolded or *denatured* (**Figure 6.3**) by heat, acids, bases, salts, or mechanical agitation. **Denaturation** doesn't alter the primary structure of the protein (amino acids will still be in the same sequence), but it does change the shape. As mentioned earlier, changing the protein's shape will alter its function, sometimes permanently.

The protein found in eggs can be used to illustrate denaturation. When you apply heat to a raw egg, such as by frying it, the heat denatures the protein in both the yolk and the egg white. Heat disrupts the bonds between the amino acid side chains, causing the protein in the egg to uncoil. New bonds then form between the side chains, changing the shape and structure of the protein and the texture of the egg. As the egg cooks, it solidifies, illustrating the permanent change in the protein's shape and structure.

Similarly, mechanical agitation, such as beating egg whites when you prepare a meringue, can denature protein. Beating an egg white uncoils the protein, allowing the hydrophilic side chains to react with the water in the egg white, while the hydrophobic portions of the side chains form new bonds, trapping the air from the whipping. The stiffer the peaks of egg white, the more denatured the protein.[3]

Salts and acids can also denature proteins. For example, when you marinate a chicken breast or a steak before cooking, you might use salt (such as in soy sauce) or acid (such as wine or vinegar) to denature its protein. The end result is juicier, more tender meat.[4] During digestion, acidic stomach juices help denature and untangle proteins to reveal the peptide bonds. This allows digestive enzymes to break them apart.

Cooking denatures protein and will often improve the quality, structure, and texture of the protein-rich foods you eat. Raw eggs, meat, and poultry are basically inedible, but cooking these foods greatly increases their palatability.

LO 6.1 **The Take-Home Message** An amino acid is made up of carbon, oxygen, hydrogen, a nitrogen-containing amine group, and a unique side chain. There are 20 side chains and so 20 unique amino acids. Whereas all 20 amino acids are needed to make proteins, 11 of these can be synthesized in your body and are thus nonessential. The remaining nine amino acids are the essential amino acids that your body cannot synthesize. Essential amino acids must be obtained in your diet. Amino acids are joined together by peptide bonds to create proteins. The attractions and interactions between the side chains cause the protein to fold into a precise three-dimensional shape. The protein's shape determines its function. Heat, mechanical agitation, acids, bases, and salts can break, or denature, a protein and alter its shape and function.

denaturation The alteration of a protein's shape, which changes the structure and function of the protein.

What Happens to the Protein You Eat?

LO 6.2 Describe how your body digests and absorbs proteins.

When you enjoy a tasty peanut butter sandwich, what happens to the protein from the peanut butter once it's in your body? How is the protein in the peanuts broken down so that the valuable amino acids can be efficiently digested, absorbed, and used to synthesize other proteins?

You Digest and Absorb Dietary Proteins in Your Stomach and Small Intestine

Protein digestion begins after chewed food enters your stomach (**Figure 6.4**). Stomach acids denature the protein strands, breaking their bonds. This allows the digestive enzyme pepsin, which is produced in your stomach lining and activated by its acidic environment, to begin breaking the proteins down and preparing them for absorption. Pepsin splits the protein into shorter polypeptide strands, and these strands are propelled into the small intestine.

In the small intestine, other enzymes further break down the strands into tripeptides and dipeptides, as well as some amino acids. The protein remnants are then absorbed into the cells of the small intestine lining, where the remaining tripeptides and dipeptides are broken down into single amino acids, which enter the blood and travel to the liver.

How the liver uses these amino acids depends on the needs of your body. For example, they might be used to make new proteins or, if necessary, as an energy source. They can also be converted to glucose if you are not getting enough carbohydrate in your diet. Some of these amino acids also travel back out to the blood to be picked up and used by your cells.

Your Body Degrades and Synthesizes Proteins

Your diet provides essential and nonessential amino acids. Your body stockpiles a limited amount of all these in **amino acid pools** in your blood and inside your cells. Because your body can't make the essential amino acids, the pools need to be constantly restocked.

Your body is also constantly degrading its proteins, that is, breaking them down into their component parts, to synthesize other needed proteins. Hence, amino acids are continually being removed from your amino acid pools to create proteins on demand. This process of continually degrading and synthesizing protein is called **protein turnover** (see **Figure 6.5** on page 194). In fact, more than 200 grams of protein are turned over daily. The proteins in your intestines and liver—two active areas in your body—account for as much as 50 percent of this turnover.[5] The cells that make up the lining of your intestines are continually being sloughed off and replaced. The proteins in these sloughed-off cells are degraded, and most of the resulting amino acids are absorbed and recycled in your body, although some are lost in your stool and urine. Proteins and amino acids are also lost daily through sloughed-off skin, hair, and nails. Replacements for these proteins must be synthesized, and the amino acid pools provide the building materials to do this. Some of the amino acids in the pools are used to synthesize nonprotein substances, including thyroid hormones and melanin, the pigment that gives color to dark skin and hair.

amino acid pools A limited supply of amino acids stored in your blood and cells and used to build new proteins.

protein turnover The continual process of degrading and synthesizing protein. When the daily amount of degraded protein is equivalent to the amount that is synthesized, you are in protein balance.

192 Chapter 6 | Proteins and Amino Acids

FOCUS

Figure 6.4 **Protein Digestion and Absorption**

FOCUS FIGURE WALKTHROUGH

Scan this QR code with your mobile device for a video tour of this figure by Joan Salge Blake.

Protein digestion begins in the stomach with the aid of hydrochloric acid (HCl) and the enzyme pepsin. Other enzymes continue the digestion in the small intestine, breaking the protein down to single amino acids that are absorbed into the bloodstream.

ORGANS OF THE GI TRACT

ACCESSORY ORGANS

MOUTH

Mechanical digestion of protein begins with chewing, tearing, and mixing food with salivary juices to form a bolus.

STOMACH

Hydrochloric acid denatures protein and activates pepsinogen to form pepsin.

Pepsin breaks the polypeptide chain into smaller polypeptides.

PANCREAS

Produces enzymes that are released into the small intestine via the pancreatic duct.

LIVER

Uses some amino acids to make new proteins or converts them to glucose. Most amino acids pass through the liver and return to the blood to be picked up and used by body cells.

SMALL INTESTINE

Enzymes continue to cleave peptide bonds, resulting in dipeptides, tripeptides, and single amino acids.

Enzymes in the lining of the small intestine finish the digestion to yield single amino acids, which can then be absorbed into the bloodstream and travel through the portal vein to the liver.

Amino acids

Intestinal cells

Blood

a The foods that you eat contain both essential and nonessential amino acids.

b A limited supply of all the amino acids exists in amino acid pools in your blood and inside your cells; this supply is used to create proteins.

c Some amino acids in the pools are used to make nonprotein products, such as some hormones.

d Protein turnover involves the degradation (breaking down) of protein and synthesis of its amino acids into new proteins.

e Amino acids are degraded and their nitrogen-containing amine groups are removed. The nitrogen generates ammonia (NH_3), which is converted to urea and excreted in urine. The carbon-containing remains are either used to make glucose or energy, or are stored as fat.

Figure 6.5 The Fate of Amino Acids in Your Body

Amino acids are also broken down into their component parts for other uses or stored in another form. To begin the breakdown process, the amino acids lose their amine groups. The nitrogen in the amine groups forms ammonia (NH_2), which can be toxic to your cells in high amounts. Your liver converts the ammonia to **urea**, a waste product that is excreted in your urine via the kidneys.

The carbon-containing remnants of the amino acids are then converted to glucose, used as energy, or stored as fat, depending on the needs of your body. When your diet is too low in carbohydrates, the amino acids will be used to make glucose. When calories are inadequate, the amino acids can be sacrificed for energy. Surplus amino acids (beyond what is needed in the amino acid pools) from excess dietary protein can't be stored as protein in your body and so must be stored predominantly as fat. Hence, as you know from the last two chapters, *all* excess calories—whether from carbohydrates, proteins, or fats—will be stored as fat in your body.

Proteins don't have minds of their own. How does your body know when to create or synthesize more proteins? Let's look at how proteins are synthesized in your body.

DNA Directs the Synthesis of New Proteins

Protein synthesis is directed by a molecule in the nucleus of your cells called **DNA** (**d**eoxyribo**n**ucleic **a**cid). DNA is the blueprint for every cell in your body.

Each DNA molecule carries the code to synthesize every protein that you need. A **gene** is a DNA segment that codes for a specific protein. However, your cells' protein-producing capabilities are specialized. For example, only cells in the pancreas make the hormone insulin, because no other cell in the body expresses the gene to make insulin. Several compounds prompt DNA to synthesize proteins as needed.

As with any blueprint, DNA doesn't do the actual building or synthesizing; it only provides the instructions. DNA can't leave the nucleus of the cell, so it directs another important molecule within the cell, called **RNA** (**ribon**ucleic **a**cid), to carry out its instructions for building a protein. There are two specialized RNAs, called **messenger RNA (mRNA)** and **transfer RNA (tRNA)** that perform very specific roles during protein synthesis. See **Figure 6.6** to view how protein synthesis takes place in a cell.

urea A nitrogen-containing waste product that is excreted in urine.

DNA The blueprint in cells that stores all genetic information. DNA remains in the nucleus of the cell and directs the synthesis of proteins.

gene A DNA segment that codes for a specific protein.

RNA A molecule that carries out the orders of DNA.

messenger RNA (mRNA) A type of RNA that copies the genetic information encoded in DNA and carries it out of the nucleus of the cell to synthesize the protein.

transfer RNA (tRNA) A type of RNA that collects the amino acids within the cell that are needed to make a specific protein.

FOCUS

Figure 6.6 **Protein Synthesis**

FOCUS FIGURE WALKTHROUGH

 Scan this QR code with your mobile device for a video tour of this figure by Joan Salge Blake.

Protein synthesis is the process by which the DNA code within a cell's nucleus directs the cell's production of specific proteins.

1 Each strand of DNA holds the the code to create specific proteins. Because the DNA can't leave the nucleus of the cell, a copy of the code, called messenger RNA (mRNA) is made.

2 The mRNA takes this information outside the nucleus and brings it to the ribosome.

3 The ribosome moves along the mRNA, reading the code.

4 Another type of RNA, called transfer RNA (tRNA), collects the specific amino acids that are needed to make the protein. There are 20 different tRNAs, one for each amino acid.

5 The tRNA brings the amino acid to the ribosome.

6 The ribosome then builds a chain of amino acids (the protein) in the proper sequence, based on the code in the mRNA.

7 The ribosome continues to move down the mRNA strand until all the appropriate amino acids are added and the protein is complete.

Cell

Nucleus

DNA

Inside the nucleus

Inside the cell

1 DNA

2 mRNA

3

4

Amino acids

tRNA

mRNA

Ribosome

5

6

Protein

7

When abnormalities occur during protein synthesis, serious medical conditions may result. One such condition is **sickle-cell anemia**. The most common inherited blood disorder in the United States, sickle-cell anemia is caused by the abnormal formation of the protein hemoglobin. According to the National Institutes of Health (NIH), approximately one in 12 African-Americans and one in 100 Hispanics have the mutated gene that causes the disease.[6]

The mutation in the gene causes a change in the amino acid sequence in the hemoglobin molecule. In sickle-cell anemia, there is a displacement of just *one* amino acid, glutamine, with another amino acid, valine, in the polypeptide chains of hemoglobin. This causes the chains to stick to one another and form crescent-shaped

sickle-cell anemia A blood disorder caused by a genetic defect in the development of hemoglobin. Sickle-cell anemia causes the red blood cells to distort into a sickle shape and can damage organs and tissues.

structures rather than the normal globular ones. Whereas red blood cells with normal hemoglobin are smooth and round, those with this mutation are stiff and form a sickle or crescent-moon shape under certain conditions, such as after vigorous exercise, when oxygen levels in the blood are low. These abnormal sickle cells are easily destroyed, which can lead to anemia, and they can build up in blood vessels, causing painful blockages and damage to tissues and organs.

Another rare genetic disorder, phenylketonuria (PKU), is caused by the body's inability to properly degrade phenylalanine, causing a buildup of this amino acid in the blood. If not identified and treated early in life, PKU can cause mental retardation. To prevent this, infants are screened for PKU at birth.

Red blood cells with normal hemoglobin, like the three similar ones, are smooth and round. A person with sickle-cell anemia has red blood cells like the one on the right; these cells are stiff and form a sickle (crescent-moon) shape when blood oxygen levels are low.

LO 6.2 The Take-Home Message With the help of gastric juices and enzymes in your stomach and small intestine, proteins are broken down into amino acids and absorbed into your blood to be used by your cells. A limited supply of amino acids exists in pools in your body, which act as a reservoir for the synthesis of proteins as needed. Surplus amino acids are broken down, and the carbon-containing remains can be used for glucose or energy, or are stored as fat, depending on your body's needs. The nitrogen in the amine groups is eventually converted to the waste product urea and excreted in your urine. Amino acids can be used to create nonprotein substances, including certain hormones. The synthesis of proteins is directed in the cell nucleus by DNA, which carries the code for the amino acid sequences necessary to build the proteins that you need.

How Does Your Body Use Proteins?

LO 6.3 Describe the functions of protein in the body.

Proteins play many important roles in the body, from providing structural and mechanical support and maintaining your body's tissues to creating enzymes and hormones and helping maintain acid-base and fluid balance. They also transport nutrients, assist your immune system, and, when necessary, become a source of energy.

Proteins Provide Structural and Mechanical Support and Help Maintain Body Tissues

Proteins provide much of the structural and mechanical support that keeps you upright, moving, and flexible. Just as wood, nails, and plaster are the behind-the-scenes materials holding up the room around you, several fibrous proteins in your bones, muscles, and other tissues help hold up your body.

Collagen, the most abundant protein in your body, is found in all of your **connective tissues**, including the bones, tendons, and ligaments, that support and connect your joints and other body parts. This fibrous protein is also responsible for the elasticity in your skin and helps form scar tissue to repair injuries such as wounds. Two other proteins, actin and myosin, provide mechanical support by helping your muscles contract so you can run, walk, sit, and lie down.

The daily wear and tear on your body causes the breakdown of hundreds of grams of proteins each day. For example, the protein-rich cells of your skin are constantly sloughing off, and proteins help create a new layer of outer skin every

Proteins play an important role in keeping your skin healthy and your nails strong.

collagen A ropelike, fibrous protein that is the most abundant protein in your body.

connective tissue The most abundant tissue type in the body. Made up primarily of collagen, it supports and connects body parts as well as providing protection and insulation.

40 to 56 days.[7] Because your red blood cells have a short life span—only about 120 days—new red blood cells must continually be regenerated. The cells that line the inner surfaces of your organs, such as your lungs and intestines, are also constantly sloughed off, excreted, and replaced.

In addition to regular maintenance, extra protein is sometimes needed for emergency repairs. Protein is essential in healing, and a person with extensive wounds, such as severe burns, may have dietary protein needs that are more than triple his or her normal needs.

Proteins Build Most Enzymes and Many Hormones

When your body needs a reaction to take place promptly, such as breaking down carbohydrates after a meal, it calls upon **enzymes**, biological **catalysts** that speed up reactions. Without enzymes, reactions would occur so slowly that you couldn't survive. Most enzymes are proteins, although some may also have a **coenzyme**, such as a vitamin, that aids in initiating a reaction.

Each of the thousands of enzymes in your body catalyzes specific reactions. Some enzymes, such as digestive enzymes, break compounds apart. (Recall from Chapter 4 that the enzyme lactase is needed to break down the milk sugar lactose.) Other enzymes, such as those used to synthesize proteins, help compounds combine. Enzymes aren't changed, damaged, or used up in the process of speeding up a particular reaction. **Figure 6.7** shows how an enzyme breaks apart two compounds, yet isn't changed in the process. Thus, the enzyme is available to catalyze additional reactions.

While enzymes expedite reactions, hormones direct them. Many **hormones** are proteins that direct or signal an activity, often by turning on or shutting off enzymes. (Recall from Chapter 5 that some hormones can also be lipids.) Hormones are released from tissues and organs and travel to target cells in another part of your body to direct an activity. There are more than 75 trillion cells in your body, and all of these cells interact with at least one of more than 50 known hormones.[8]

Let's consider an example of one hormone in action. When your blood glucose level rises after a meal or snack, your pancreas (an organ) releases insulin (a hormone) into your blood, which in turn directs the uptake of glucose in your cells (the activity). If your blood glucose level drops too low, such as between meals, your pancreas (an organ) releases glucagon (a hormone), which promotes the release of glucose (the activity) from the glycogen stored in your liver, which in turn raises your blood glucose level.

Proteins Help Maintain Fluid Balance

Your body is made up predominantly of water, which is distributed throughout various body compartments. Proteins help ensure that all this water is dispersed evenly, keeping you in a state of **fluid balance**.

Normally, your blood pressure forces the nutrient- and oxygen-rich fluids out of your capillaries and into the spaces between your cells. Whereas fluids can flow easily in these spaces, proteins can't, because they are too big to cross the cell membranes. Proteins attract water, so the proteins remaining in the capillaries eventually draw the fluids back into the capillaries. Hence, protein plays an important role in the movement of fluids and in keeping the fluids balanced among these compartments. (Note: The mineral sodium also plays a major role in fluid balance.)

When fewer proteins are available to draw the fluid from between the cells back into the bloodstream, as during severe malnutrition, a fluid imbalance results. The

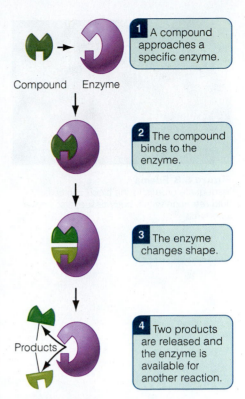

1 A compound approaches a specific enzyme.

Compound   Enzyme

2 The compound binds to the enzyme.

3 The enzyme changes shape.

4 Two products are released and the enzyme is available for another reaction.

Products

Figure 6.7 An Enzyme in Action
Enzymes speed up reactions in your body, yet they aren't changed, damaged, or used up in the process.

enzymes Substances that act as catalysts and speed up reactions.

catalysts Substances that aid and speed up reactions without being changed, damaged, or used up in the process.

coenzyme Substances, often vitamins, that are needed by enzymes to perform many chemical reactions in your body.

hormones Protein- or lipid-based chemical messengers that initiate or direct a specific physiological response. Insulin, glucagon, and estrogen are examples of hormones.

fluid balance The equal distribution of water throughout your body and within and between cells.

Figure 6.8 Edema
Inadequate protein in the blood can cause fluid retention within body tissue, also known as edema.

spaces between the cells become bloated and the body tissue swells, a condition known as **edema** (**Figure 6.8**).

Proteins Help Maintain Acid-Base Balance

Proteins can alter the pH (the concentration of hydrogen ions) of your body fluids. Normally, your blood has a pH of about 7.4, and the fluid in your cells has a pH of about 7.0. Even a small change in the pH of your blood in either direction can be harmful or even fatal. With a blood pH below 7.35, a condition called acidosis sets in, which can result in a coma. A blood pH above 7.45, known as alkalosis, can result in convulsions.

Proteins act as **buffers** and minimize the changes in acid-base levels by picking up or donating hydrogen ions in the blood. Should your blood become too acidic, some of the amino acid side chains in the proteins will pick up excess hydrogen ions. Other side chains can donate hydrogen ions to your blood if it becomes too basic.

Proteins Transport Substances throughout the Body

Transport proteins shuttle oxygen, waste products, lipids, some vitamins, and sodium and potassium through your blood and into and out of cells through cell membranes. Hemoglobin acts as a transport protein that carries oxygen to cells from the lungs. Hemoglobin also picks up carbon dioxide from cells for transport to your lungs to be exhaled from your body. Once in your blood, vitamin A travels to your liver and is bound to yet another protein to be transported to your cells.

Transport proteins in cell membranes form a doorway that allows substances such as sodium and potassium to pass in and out of cells (**Figure 6.9**). Substances

edema The accumulation of excess fluid in the spaces surrounding your cells, which causes swelling of the body tissue.

buffers Substances that help maintain the proper pH in a solution by attracting or donating hydrogen ions.

transport proteins Proteins that carry lipids (fat and cholesterol), oxygen, waste products, and vitamins through the blood to various organs and tissues, or that serve as channels to allow substances to pass through cell membranes.

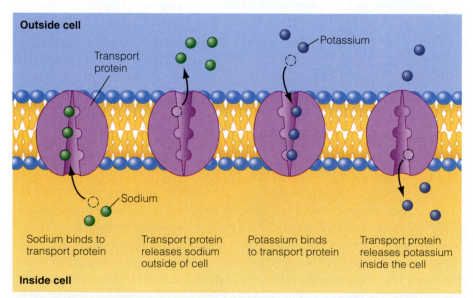

Figure 6.9 Proteins as Transport Channels
Transport proteins in cell membranes form a channel, or doorway, through which substances such as sodium and potassium can move from one side of the cell membrane to the other.

that are not lipid soluble or that are simply too big to pass through the lipid-rich membrane have to enter the cell through a protein channel.

Proteins Contribute to a Healthy Immune System

Your immune system works like an army to protect your body from foreign invaders, such as disease-causing bacteria and viruses. Specialized protein "soldiers" called **antibodies** that inactivate these potentially harmful substances.

Once your body knows how to create antibodies against a specific invader, such as a virus, it stores that information, and you have **immunity** to that pathogen. The next time the invader enters your body, you can respond very quickly (producing up to 2,000 precise antibodies per second!) to fight it. When this rapid immune response works efficiently, it prevents the virus or other invader from multiplying to levels high enough to make you sick.

Sometimes, your body incorrectly perceives a nonthreatening substance as an invader and attacks it. This perceived invader is called an *allergen*. All food allergens contain proteins.[9] Individuals who react to these allergens are diagnosed with food allergies. You will learn more about food allergies in Chapter 15.

Proteins Can Provide Energy

Since proteins provide 4 calories per gram, they can be used as an energy source. However, the last thing you want to do is use this valuable nutrient, which plays so many important roles in your body, as a regular source of fuel, especially because carbohydrates and fats are far better suited for providing energy. When your diet contains adequate amounts of calories from carbohydrates and fat, proteins are used for their other important roles.

When your diet doesn't provide adequate amounts of calories—for example, in times of starvation—your body begins to break down its protein, mainly from muscles, into its amino acid components. The carbon skeletons of the amino acids are used for energy and for gluconeogenesis, the creation of glucose from non-carbohydrate sources. (Remember that your brain and nervous system need a minimum amount of glucose to function properly.) However, when proteins are used for energy, they create waste products that must be eliminated from your body, which is particularly burdensome for your liver and kidneys.

Protein Improves Satiety and Appetite Control

In addition to the structural and functional roles protein plays in the body, protein also helps increase satiety, the feeling of fullness, after a meal more than do either carbohydrate or fat.[10] Eating a meal that contains a good source of protein will leave you more satisfied than a meal containing the same amount of calories but with the majority of them coming from carbohydrate. Although the mechanism behind protein's effect on your appetite is not yet known, some research studies suggest that it may be due to several factors, such as changes in appetite-suppressing hormones in the body, how the body metabolizes protein, and the levels of the amino acids in the blood.[11] Including protein in each meal can help control your appetite, which in turn can help you maintain a healthy weight.

Table 6.2 summarizes the many roles that proteins play in your body.

antibodies Proteins made by your body to bind to and neutralize foreign invaders, such as harmful bacteria, fungi, and viruses, as part of the body's immune response.

immunity The state of having built up antibodies to a particular foreign substance so that when particles of the substance enter the body, they are destroyed by the antibodies.

Table 6.2

The Many Roles of Proteins

Role of Proteins	How They Work
1. Provide structural and mechanical support and maintenance	Proteins are your body's building materials, providing strength and flexibility to your tissues, tendons, ligaments, muscles, organs, bones, nails, hair, and skin. Proteins are needed for the ongoing maintenance of your body.
2. Build enzymes and hormones	Proteins are needed to make most enzymes that speed up reactions in your body and many hormones that direct specific activities, such as regulating your blood glucose level.
3. Maintain fluid balance	Proteins play a major role in ensuring that your body fluids are evenly dispersed in your blood and inside and outside your cells.
4. Maintain acid-base balance	Proteins act as buffers to help keep the pH of your body fluids balanced within a tight range. A drop in pH will cause your body fluids to become too acidic, whereas a rise in pH can make them too basic.
5. Transport substances	Proteins shuttle substances such as oxygen, waste products, and nutrients through your blood and into and out of your cells.
6. Provide antibodies for the immune response	Proteins create specialized antibodies that attack pathogens in your body that can make you sick.
7. Provide energy	Because proteins provide 4 calories per gram, they can be used as fuel or energy in your body.
8. Improve satiety	Proteins increase satiety, which can help control your appetite and weight.

LO 6.3 **The Take-Home Message** Proteins play many important roles in the body, including: (1) structural and mechanical support, (2) building enzymes and some hormones, (3) maintaining fluid balance, (4) maintaining acid-base balance, (5) transporting substances throughout the body, (6) providing antibodies for a strong immune system, (7) providing energy, and (8) improving satiety.

How Much Protein Do You Need?

LO 6.4 Determine your daily protein needs.

Healthy adults should consume enough dietary protein to replace the amount they use each day. Pregnant women, people recovering from surgery or an injury, and growing children need more protein to supply the necessary amino acids and nitrogen to build new tissue. **Nitrogen balance** studies have been used to determine how much protein individuals need to replace or build new tissue.

Healthy Adults Should Be in Nitrogen Balance

nitrogen balance The state in which an individual is consuming the same amount of nitrogen (from protein) in the diet as he or she is excreting in the urine.

A person's daily protein requirement can be estimated by using what we know about the structure of an amino acid. We know that 16 percent of every dietary protein molecule is nitrogen, and we also know that this nitrogen is retained by the body during protein synthesis. With this information, we can assess a person's protein status by measuring the amount of nitrogen consumed and subtracting the amount of nitrogen excreted. The goal is to achieve nitrogen balance.

If the nitrogen intake from dietary protein is equivalent to the amount of nitrogen excreted (mostly as urea) in the urine, then a person is in nitrogen balance. Such an individual is consuming a balanced diet with adequate amounts of protein and excreting an equally balanced amount of nitrogen. Healthy, nonpregnant adults are typically in nitrogen balance or equilibrium.

A body that retains more nitrogen than it excretes is in positive nitrogen balance. Rapidly growing babies, children, or teenagers are all in positive nitrogen balance because their bodies use nitrogen to build new tissues that aid growth, build muscles, and expand the supply of red blood cells. They therefore excrete less nitrogen in their urine. When your mother was pregnant with you, she was in positive nitrogen balance because she was building a robust baby.

Negative nitrogen balance occurs when the body excretes more nitrogen than is consumed due to some physical impairment, such as a serious injury, infection, malnutrition, or other trauma, where the body cannot synthesize protein as quickly as it's broken down. These situations all increase the body's need for both calories and protein. If the calories and protein in the diet are inadequate to cover the increased demands, then proteins from tissues are broken down to meet the body's needs. **Figure 6.10** lists some of the situations that lead to nitrogen balance or imbalance in the body.

While it is important to eat a sufficient quantity of protein to meet your needs, the quality of protein also matters.

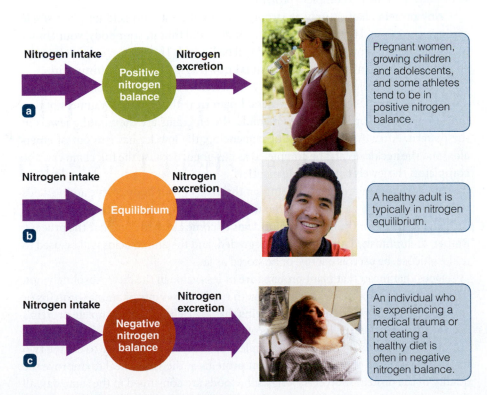

Figure 6.10 Nitrogen Balance and Imbalance

Not All Protein Is Created Equal

A high-quality protein is digestible, contains all the essential amino acids, and provides sufficient protein to be used to synthesize the nonessential amino acids. **Protein quality** is determined by two factors: your body's ability to digest the protein (the protein's **digestibility**) and the types and amounts of amino acids (essential, nonessential, or both) that the protein contains.

Digestibility

The digestibility of proteins varies, depending on their source. In general, animal proteins are more digestible than plant proteins. Some of the plant proteins, especially when consumed raw, are protected by the plant's cell walls and cannot be broken down by the enzymes in your intestinal tract. Whereas about 99 percent of the proteins from animal sources (cheese and other dairy foods) are digestible, only 87 percent of plant proteins, such as peas, are typically digestible.[12]

Amino Acid Profile

The second factor that affects protein quality concerns the types and amounts of amino acids that the protein contains, or its **amino acid profile**. A protein that provides all nine of the essential amino acids, along with some of the 11 nonessential amino acids, is considered a **complete protein**. A protein that is low or deficient in one or more of the essential amino acids is considered an **incomplete protein**. A complete protein is considered of higher quality than an incomplete protein. Protein from animal sources, such as meat, fish, and poultry is typically complete protein, whereas protein from plant foods tends to be incomplete.

The exceptions to this generalization are gelatin and soy. Gelatin, an animal protein, is not a complete protein because it is missing the amino acid tryptophan. Soy, a plant protein, has an amino acid profile that resembles the protein needs in your body, making it a complete protein.

Any protein chain is only as strong as its weakest amino acid link. If a single essential amino acid is in low supply in your diet, and thus in your body, your ability to synthesize the proteins that you need will be limited. The amino acid that is in the shortest supply in an incomplete protein is known as the **limiting amino acid**.

Imagine a jeweler trying to create a necklace. If the jeweler attempts to make a necklace using a diamond-ruby-emerald pattern with unlimited numbers of diamonds and rubies but only three emeralds, the emeralds are the limiting jewels in the pattern. After the third round of sequencing, the jeweler has run out of emeralds, and the necklace can't be completed as designed. Because the full chain can't be completed, the jewels have to be dismantled.

Similarly, when proteins are being synthesized in your body, all the amino acids have to be available at the same time to complete the protein. A half-synthesized protein can't wait for the needed amino acids to come along to complete the process. Rather, the unfinished protein will be degraded, and the amino acids will be used to make glucose, be used as energy, or be stored as fat.

Does that mean that plant proteins are of less value in the diet? Absolutely not. When incomplete proteins are coupled with modest amounts of animal proteins or soy, or combined with other plant proteins that are rich in the incomplete protein's limiting amino acids, the incomplete protein is **complemented**. In other words, its amino acid profile is upgraded to a complete protein. You don't have to eat the two food sources of the complementing plant proteins at the same meal to improve the quality of the protein source. As long as the foods are consumed in the same day, all the essential amino acids will be provided to meet your daily needs.

protein quality The measure of a protein's digestibility and how its amino acid pattern compares with your body's needs. Proteins that are more easily digested and have a complete set of amino acids are of higher quality.

digestibility A food's capacity to be broken down so that it can be absorbed.

amino acid profile The types and amounts of amino acids in a protein.

complete protein A protein that provides all the essential amino acids that your body needs, along with some nonessential amino acids. Soy protein and protein from animal sources, in general, are complete.

incomplete protein A protein that is low in one or more of the essential amino acids. Protein from plant sources tends to be incomplete.

limiting amino acid The amino acid that is in the shortest supply in an incomplete protein.

complemented proteins Incomplete proteins that are combined with modest amounts of animal or soy proteins or with other plant proteins that are rich in the limiting amino acids to create a complete protein.

Once the digestibility and the amino acid profile of a protein are known, the quality of a protein can be determined.

Protein Scoring

The **protein digestibility corrected amino acid score (PDCAAS)**, which is measured as a percentage, takes into account both the amino acid profile and digestibility of a protein to give a good indication of its quality. Milk protein, which is easily digested and meets essential amino acid requirements, has a PDCAAS of 100 percent. In comparison, chickpeas garner a PDCAAS of 87 percent, and wheat has a score of only 44 percent. If your only dietary source of protein is wheat, you are not meeting your essential amino acid needs.

The Food and Drug Administration (FDA) uses the PDCAAS to assess the quality of dietary proteins. On a food label, when protein is listed as a percentage of the daily value, this percentage is determined based on its PDCAAS.

You Can Determine Your Personal Protein Needs

There are two ways to determine protein intake in the diet. It can be measured as a percentage of total calories or as grams of protein eaten per day. The latest dietary recommendation, based on data from numerous nitrogen balance studies, is to consume from 10 to 35 percent of your total daily calories from protein. Currently, adults in the United States consume about 15 percent of their daily calories from protein, which falls within this range.[13]

The current recommendation for the grams of protein that you need daily is based on your age and your weight (**Table 6.3**). Adults age 19 and older should consume 0.8 gram (g) of protein for each kilogram (kg) of body weight. For example, a person who weighs 176 pounds (lb) would weigh 80 kg (176 lb ÷ 2.2 = 80 kg) and should consume 80 kg × 0.8 g, or 64 g of protein a day. A person who weighs 130 lb should consume approximately 47 g of protein daily (130 lb ÷ 2.2 = 59 kg × 0.8 g = 47 g). In the United States, men age 20 and older consume, on average, 99 grams of protein daily, while women of the same age consume, on average, 68 grams every day.[14] As you can see, Americans are typically meeting, and even exceeding, their dietary protein needs.

Even though most Americans consume more protein than they need, their percentage of daily calories contributed by protein (approximately 15 percent) falls

Table 6.3
Calculating Your Daily Protein Needs

If You Are	You Need
14–18 years old	0.85 g/kg
≥19 years old	0.80 g/kg

To calculate your needs, first convert your body weight from pounds (lb) to kilograms (kg) by dividing by 2.2, like this:

Your weight in pounds:_____ lb ÷ 2.2 = _____ kg

Then, multiply your weight in kilograms by 0.8 or 0.85:

Your weight in kilograms: _____ kg × 0.8 g = _____ g/day

protein digestibility corrected amino acid score (PDCAAS) A score measured as a percentage that takes into account both digestibility and amino acid profile and gives a good indication of the quality of a protein.

Practical Nutrition VIDEO

Healthy Snacks to Fuel Your Day

Snacks can be a great way to keep you going *and* help you meet your daily protein needs. Scan this QR code with your mobile device to access the video. You can also access the video in MasteringNutrition™.

within the recommended range. This is because they consume an abundant amount of calories from carbohydrates and fats, which lowers the percentage of their total calories coming from protein.

An overweight individual's protein needs are not much greater than those of a healthy-weight person of similar height. This is because the Recommended Dietary Allowance (RDA) for dietary protein is based on a person's need to maintain protein-dependent tissues like lean muscle and organs and to perform protein-dependent body functions. Because most overweight people carry their extra body weight predominantly as fat, not muscle, they do not need to consume significantly more protein than normal-weight people.

The American College of Sports Medicine, the Academy of Nutrition and Dietetics, and other experts have advocated an increase of 50 to 100 percent more protein for competitive athletes participating in endurance exercise (marathon runners) or resistance exercise (weight lifters) to meet their needs.[15] However, because of their active lifestyles, athletes typically have a higher intake of food and thus already consume higher amounts of both calories and protein. Protein supplements are not needed. Now let's look at how you can meet your daily protein needs through a well-balanced diet.

LO 6.4 **The Take-Home Message** Protein quality is determined by the protein's digestibility and by the types and amounts of amino acids (essential versus nonessential) it contains. Protein from animal foods is more easily digested than protein from plant foods. A complete protein, which is typically found in animal foods and soy, provides a complete set of the essential amino acids along with some nonessential amino acids. Plant proteins are typically incomplete, as they are missing one or more of the essential amino acids. Plant proteins can be complemented with protein from other plant sources or animal food sources to improve their protein quality. Adults should consume 0.8 gram of protein for each kilogram of body weight. In the United States, men, on average, consume nearly 100 grams of protein daily, while women, on average, are consuming 68 grams—in both cases, more than is needed.

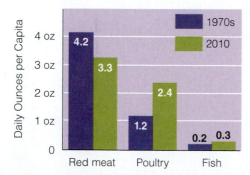

Figure 6.11 What Types of Proteins Are Americans Eating? Americans' consumption of red meat has been declining, and they are eating more poultry and fish.

What Are the Best Food Sources of Protein?

LO 6.5 Identify healthy sources of protein in the diet.

Although some amount of protein is found in many foods, it is particularly abundant in meat, fish, poultry, and meat alternatives such as dried beans, peanut butter, nuts, and soy. Americans, on average, not only consume more than the recommended servings of the protein-rich foods in the meat and beans group, but also eat approximately 4 percent more than they did in the 1970s.[16] A 3-ounce serving of cooked meat, poultry, or fish, which is about the size of a woman's palm or a deck of cards, provides approximately 21 to 25 grams of protein, or about 7 grams per ounce, and is plenty of protein for one meal.

While red meat is still the most popular food in the protein group, Americans' love of meat has declined over the last four decades. In contrast, Americans currently eat more than double the amount of poultry, and about 40 percent more fish, than they did in 1970 (see **Figure 6.11**).[17] Dried beans such as kidney beans, pinto beans, and black beans not only provide an excellent source of protein, but are also a potent source of fiber (as you saw in Chapter 4). Dairy foods and eggs are also an excellent source of protein, and though grains and vegetables are less robust protein sources, as part of a varied, balanced diet they can aid significantly in meeting your daily needs.

Eating a wide variety of foods is the best approach to meeting your protein needs (**Figure 6.12**). A diet that consists of the recommended servings from the five food groups based on 1,600 calories, which is far less than most adults consume daily, will supply the protein needs for adult women and most adult men (see **Table 6.4** on page 208). In fact, many people have already met their daily protein needs before they even sit down to dinner! The Examining the Evidence further evaluates if protein supplements are needed in your diet.

How does your diet stack up when it comes to protein? Take the Self-Assessment on page 208 to find out.

More than half of the protein in an egg is in the white. In fact, two large egg whites provide 7 grams of protein, compared with only 6 grams in a large whole egg.

LO 6.5 **The Take-Home Message** A well-balanced diet can easily meet your daily protein needs. Meat, fish, poultry, and meat alternatives such as dried beans, peanut butter, nuts, and soy are particularly abundant in protein. Dairy products and some vegetables can also be good sources.

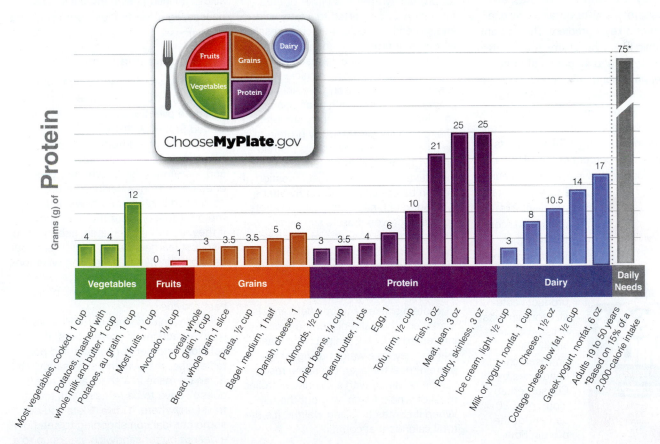

Figure 6.12 **Food Sources of Protein**
Food choices from the meat, poultry, fish, meat alternative, and milk groups are the most abundant sources of dietary protein. Grains and vegetables provide less protein per serving but as part of a varied, balanced diet can add significantly to meeting your daily needs.

USDA National Nutrient Database for Standard Reference (www.nal.usda.gov).

Protein Supplements: Are They Necessary?

The sale of protein supplements has skyrocketed over the last decade, generating almost two billion dollars in the United States annually.[1] However, with very few exceptions, these products are, at best, a waste of money, and at worst, potentially harmful.

Protein supplement manufacturers use phrases such as "scientifically proven," "nutritious and time-saving snack or meal replacement," and "look years younger" as a promise to consumers. Unfortunately, dietary supplements do not go through rigorous testing for quality or efficacy. So how do you know if these supplements contain what they say they contain and do what they say they do? Is more protein always better?

Protein Shakes and Powders

Most protein shakes and powders use whey (concentrates, isolates, and hydrolysates), soy, or occasionally rice protein as a key ingredient. The amount of protein their label claims they contain ranges from 10 to 40 grams of protein per serving, along with added vitamins and minerals. Muscle Milk® lists 25 grams of protein per serving and suggests three servings per day for a total of 75 grams of protein. This amounts to almost 100 percent of the RDA for protein for a male weighting 176 pounds (RDA = 80 grams per day). This does not account for the other foods consumed during the day.

Do these products actually contain what is listed on the label? Based on research conducted by ConsumerLab .com, over 30 percent of the protein powders and drinks tested revealed problems with quality, including containing 16 grams of protein less per serving, being contaminated with 12.7 milligrams of lead per serving, and having more cholesterol per serving than was listed on the label.[2] Other labs reported arsenic, cadmium, lead, and mercury in 15 tested samples.[3] Chronic ingestion of these toxic metals can cause severe health consequences, including kidney and pulmonary damage, anemia, and osteoporosis. Exposure is avoidable because most consumers more than meet their daily protein requirements by choosing whole foods.

Protein intake does enhance muscle synthesis.[4] But athletes consume enough protein for muscle growth and repair in an average mixed diet. Whey protein used in protein supplements is abundant in milk and dairy products.[5] The additional protein consumed through powders and shakes not used for protein synthesis is either burned for energy or converted to a fatty acid and stored in fat cells. In fact, excessive amounts of protein can be unhealthy and produce undesirable results.

The key to increasing muscle weight is a well-designed strength-training program combined with additional calories from all three macronutrients. These calories allow dietary protein to be used for muscle synthesis instead of energy. Another important key is timing. Research suggests that ingestion of protein before and immediately after a workout combined with a carbohydrate source improves muscle synthesis.[6] Choose a glass of nonfat milk, rather than a protein supplement, before and after a workout. Milk provides both key amino acids and the carbohydrate to stimulate muscle growth.

Protein shakes and powders are also marketed as meal replacers to those interested in losing weight. Whereas dieters may lose weight using a high-protein meal replacer, the same results can be obtained with a calorie-controlled meal of whole foods, without the risk. When it comes to losing weight, it's the total calories that count.

Amino Acid Supplements

Amino acid supplements, including those containing individual amino acids

such as tryptophan and lysine, are marketed as remedies for a range of health issues, including pain, depression, insomnia, and certain infections. These supplements contain single amino acids often in amounts or combinations not found naturally in foods. Consuming single amino acids in unnatural doses can compete with other amino acids for absorption, possibly resulting in a deficiency of other amino acids. Further, overconsuming specific amino acids can lead to side effects such as nausea, light-headedness, vomiting, and drowsiness.

Protein Bars and Energy Bars

The sale of snack and nutrition bars is a growing industry that is expected to generate over $6 billion annually in the United States by 2018.[7]

As you learned from the previous two chapters, all foods provide calories and therefore energy. Whether your calories come from a balanced meal or a "balanced bar," your body will either use them for fuel or store them as body fat if they are not immediately needed. You also just learned that you can meet your daily protein needs by making wise food choices. Given this knowledge, what advantage, if any, do you think protein bars provide?

If convenience and portability are the main attractions of protein bars, then consider another convenient and portable food, the peanut butter sandwich. It can be made in a snap, and since it doesn't have to be refrigerated, it can travel anywhere. **Table 1** lets you do some comparison shopping to see how a peanut butter sandwich stacks up to a protein bar.

From a price standpoint, a peanut butter sandwich is a bargain compared with bars that can cost ten times more.

While the calories and protein content of the sandwich are similar to that in many bars, the saturated fat and sugar contents are not. Some bars provide 4 or more grams of saturated fat, which is about 18 percent of the upper limit recommended for many adults daily. In contrast, the sandwich contains less saturated fat than most of the bars listed. These bars can contain up to 7.5 teaspoons of sugar, so much of the "energy" in an energy bar is simply sugar. Because the peanut butter sandwich has less sugar and more fiber than almost all of the bars, it's actually healthier.

WHAT DO YOU THINK?

1. Do you think most people would benefit from consuming protein bars or shakes? Why or why not?
2. Are there any benefits of protein supplements that cannot be achieved by consuming protein-rich foods? If yes, what are they?
3. What role does marketing play in promoting protein shakes and supplements?

Table 1
Bar Hopping

Product	Price ($)	Calories	Protein (g)	Total Carb (g)	Total Fat (g)	Sat. Fat (g)	Sugar	Fiber (g)
Peanut butter (1 tbs) on 2 slices whole-wheat bread	0.59	215	8.5	27	9	1.75	5% (1 tsp)	5
Balance, Chocolate Craze	$1.29	200	14	21	7	4	14% ½ (3.5 tsp)	2
Zone Perfect, Chocolate Peanut Butter	$1.19	210	14	24	7	4	12% (3 tsp)	3
PowerBar Protein Plus, Chocolate Brownie	$2.99	330	30	40	9	4.5	22% ½ (5.5 tsp)	5
Clif Luna, Nutz over Chocolate	$1.39	180	9	25	6	2.5	8% (2 tsp)	4
Slim-fast Meal Options, Chocolate Fudge Brownie	$1.29	200	10	30	4	2.5	10% ½ (2.5 tsp)	9
Clif Bar, Chocolate Brownie	$1.49	240	9	44	4.5	1.5	18% ½ (4.5 tsp)	5
Larabar, Chocolate Chip Brownie	$1.59	200	4	31	9	2	23% ¾ (5.75 tsp)	4
Health Warrior Chia Bars, Coconut	$1.29	110	3	13	6	2.5	5% (1 tsp)	4

Key: = 1 tsp sugar; = 1 g fiber

self-ASSESSMENT

Do You Have a Protein-Friendly Diet?

Take this brief self-assessment to see if you have adequate amounts of protein-rich foods in your diet.

1. Do you eat at least 5 to 7 ounces of meat, fish, and/or poultry on most days of the week?
   Yes ☐ No ☐

2. Do you have at least 2 to 3 cups of milk, yogurt, soy milk, and/or soy yogurt daily?
   Yes ☐ No ☐

3. Do you enjoy at least 6 ounces of grains every day? (An ounce is considered 1 slice of bread, 1 cup of ready-to-eat cereal, or ½ cup of pasta or rice.)
   Yes ☐ No ☐

4. Do you eat at least 1 ounce of cheese or soy cheese daily?
   Yes ☐ No ☐

5. Do you eat at least 1 tablespoon of peanuts daily?
   Yes ☐ No ☐

6. Do you eat at least ½ cup of dried beans or peas, such as kidney beans or chickpeas, every day?
   Yes ☐ No ☐

7. Do you eat soy-based foods such as soy burgers and tofu daily?
   Yes ☐ No ☐

Answers

If you answered yes to at least the first three questions and are also meeting your calorie needs on a daily basis, you have a *very* protein-friendly diet! If you answered no to question 1 but yes to most of the other questions, you are also likely meeting your protein needs if your daily calories are adequate. If you have more no than yes answers, your diet may be in need of a protein makeover. Read on in the chapter to learn how you can easily add healthy sources of protein to your diet.

Table 6.4

It's Easy to Meet Your Daily Protein Needs

Food	Amount	Calories	Protein (g)	Vegetable Group (servings)	Fruit Group (servings)	Grain Group (servings)	Protein Group (oz)	Dairy Group (servings)	Oil Group (tsp)
Breakfast									
Bran flakes	2 cups	256	7.5			2			
Milk, nonfat	1 cup	83	8					1	
Orange juice	8 oz	117	2		1				
Lunch									
Turkey and cheese sandwich:									
Turkey breast	2 oz	69	11				2		
Cheese, low fat	2 oz	98	14					1	
Whole-wheat bread	2 slices	138	7			2			
Tossed salad	3 cups	66	15	1.5					
Italian dressing	1 tbs	35	0						3
Snack									
Yogurt, vanilla	8 oz	160	8					1	
Banana	1	105	1		1				
Dinner									
Chicken breast, skinless	3 oz	144	27				3		
Brown rice	1 cup	218	5			2			
Broccoli, cooked	1 cup	27	2	1					
Margarine	2 tsp	67	0						2
Totals		1,583	97	2.5	2	6	5	3	5

Note: A 140-pound adult needs 51 g of protein daily. A 180-pound adult needs 65 g of protein daily.

What Happens If You Eat Too Much or Too Little Protein?

LO 6.6 Explain the health consequences of consuming too little or too much protein.

While protein is essential to health and normal body function, eating too much or too little can be unhealthy. Let's look at what happens to the human body when it gets too much or too little protein.

Eating Too Much Protein Can Be Unhealthy

Although consuming protein is a key to good health, eating more is clearly not necessarily eating better. In fact, a diet that is too high in protein is associated with the following risks:

- *Heart disease.* A high-protein diet may increase your risk for heart disease and dying prematurely from heart disease. Many foods rich in protein are also rich in heart-unhealthy saturated fats. Although lean meats and skinless poultry contain less saturated fat than some other cuts of meat, they are not completely free of saturated fat. Hence, a high protein intake can make a low saturated fat intake challenging (see **Figure 6.13**). Lowering the saturated fat in your diet is important in lowering your risk for heart disease.

Figure 6.13 Where Are the Protein and Saturated Fat in Your Foods?
While many foods, in particular dairy foods and meats, can provide a hefty amount of protein, they can also provide a large amount of saturated fat. Choose nonfat and low-fat dairy foods and lean sources of meats and skinless poultry to enjoy your protein without consuming too much saturated fat.

- *Kidney stones.* A high-protein diet may also increase your risk for kidney stones, which commonly contain calcium. Kidney stones are one of the most common disorders of the urinary tract, sending more than 300,000 Americans to emergency rooms annually.[18]
- *Osteoporosis.* A high-protein diet may also increase your risk of osteoporosis (poor bone density). Although still a controversial issue, numerous research studies have shown that bones lose calcium when a person's diet is too high in protein. The loss seems to occur because calcium is taken from bone to act as a buffer, offsetting the acid generated when specific amino acids are broken down.[19] Other research has attempted to determine if calcium loss leads to osteoporosis when there is an adequate amount of calcium in a high-protein diet. If a higher dietary protein intake is coming from foods such as low-fat milk, yogurt, and cheese, it can add calcium to the diet.[20] Unfortunately, many American adults are falling short of their recommended calcium intake. If their diets are also high in protein, this isn't a healthy combination for their bones.
- *Cancer.* A high-protein diet may increase your risk for cancer; however, this relationship is also less than clear. While large amounts of meat, especially red and processed meats, may increase the risk for colon cancer, research doesn't necessarily support a connection between high amounts of total protein and increased colon cancer risk.[21]

One final health concern surrounding a high-protein diet is the displacement of other foods. If your diet is overloaded with protein-rich foods, such as meat, fish, and poultry, they will likely crowd out other nutrient- and fiber-rich foods. As you know, a diet that contains high fiber and a wide variety of nutrient-dense foods can help you reduce your risk for several chronic diseases, such as cancer, heart disease, diabetes, and stroke. If you fill up on meat and milk at meals, you might be short-changing yourself on foods, such as whole grains, fruits, and vegetables, that contain disease-fighting compounds.

While many individuals have the luxury of worrying about consuming too much protein, others are desperately trying to meet their daily needs. Let's look at the serious health implications of chronically eating too little dietary protein.

Eating Too Little Protein Can Lead to Poor Health and Malnutrition

Almonds and other nuts are also good sources of protein. An ounce of almonds provides 6 grams of protein.

Eating too little protein can lead to many health problems, especially in older adults. A diet that is chronically inadequate in protein can lead to the reduction of lean body mass. In older individuals, this can contribute to the increased risk of becoming frail, impairing wound healing, and decreasing immune function.[22] Consuming adequate protein throughout the day is important to preserving lean body mass as you age.

Protein-Energy Malnutrition

protein-energy malnutrition (PEM) A lack of sufficient dietary protein and/or calories.

Every day, nearly 845 million people, or one in eight, around the world don't have access to enough food.[23] Their diets are inadequate in either protein or calories or both, a condition known as **protein-energy malnutrition (PEM)**. When calories and protein are inadequate, dietary protein is used for energy rather than reserved for its numerous other roles in the body. Other important nutrients, such as vitamins and minerals, also tend to be in short supply, which further compounds PEM.

Many factors can lead to PEM, including poverty, poor food quality, insufficient food intake, unsanitary living conditions, ignorance regarding the proper feeding of children, and stopping lactation (nursing) too early. PEM can cause children to become stunted (too short for their age) and have a low body weight.[24] Because they are growing, infants and children have higher nutritional needs for their size than adults. They are also dependent on others to provide them with food. For these reasons, PEM is more frequently seen in infants and children than in adults.

Because protein is needed for so many functions in the body, it isn't surprising that a chronic protein deficiency can lead to many health problems. For example, without adequate dietary protein, the cells in the lining of the gastrointestinal tract aren't adequately replaced when they are routinely sloughed off. The inability to regenerate these cells inhibits their function. Absorption of the little food that may be available is reduced, and bacteria that normally stay in the intestines can get into the blood and poison it, causing septicemia. Malnourished individuals frequently have a compromised immune system, which can make fighting even a minor infection impossible. Over 7.5 million children die annually due to malnutrition.[25]

While deficiencies of both calories and protein often occur simultaneously, sometimes one condition may be more prevalent than the other. A severe deficiency of protein is called **kwashiorkor**, whereas a severe deficiency of calories is called **marasmus**. A condition that is caused by a chronic deficiency of both calories and protein is called marasmic kwashiorkor.

Figure 6.14 Kwashiorkor
The edema in this child's belly is a classic sign of kwashiorkor.

Kwashiorkor

Kwashiorkor was first observed in the 1930s in tribes in West Africa: Often the first-born child became sick when a new sibling became part of the family. Typically, the newborn displaced the first child, usually around 18 months of age, from his or her lactating mother and her nutritionally balanced breast milk. The first child was then relegated to an inadequate and unbalanced diet high in carbohydrate-rich grains but severely deficient in protein. This sets the stage for serious medical complications.

A classic symptom of severe kwashiorkor is edema in the legs, feet, and stomach (see **Figure 6.14**). As we discussed earlier, protein plays an important role in maintaining fluid balance in the blood and around the cells. With protein deficiency, fluid accumulates in the spaces surrounding the cells, causing swelling. The body wastes away as the muscle proteins are broken down to generate the amino acids needed to synthesize other proteins. Consequently, muscle tone and strength diminish. Those with kwashiorkor often have dry, peeling skin and brittle hair.[26]

Marasmus and Marasmic Kwashiorkor

The bloating seen in kwashiorkor is the opposite of the frail, emaciated appearance of marasmus (**Figure 6.15**). Because they are not consuming enough calories, marasmic individuals are starving. They body fat can be as low as 5 percent and their protein mass can decrease as much as 30 percent. Marasmic children's bodies use all available calories to stay alive; thus, growth is interrupted. These children are weakened and apathetic.[27]

Individuals with marasmic kwashiorkor have the worst of both conditions. They often have edema in their legs and arms, yet have a "skin and bones" appearance in other parts of the body.

More than 59 percent of childhood deaths globally are due to undernutrition.[28] Appropriate medical treatment can dramatically reduce the mortality rate. The treatment for PEM involves a multiple-step approach that addresses life-threatening dehydration and nutrient imbalances, then restores the individual's depleted tissues by gradually providing nutritionally dense calories and high-quality protein.[29]

Figure 6.15 Marasmus
The emaciated appearance of this child is a sign (and symptom) of marasmus.

kwashiorkor A state of PEM where there is a severe deficiency of dietary protein.

marasmus A state of PEM where there is a severe deficiency of calories that perpetuates wasting; also called starvation.

The Take-Home Message A high-protein diet may play a role in increasing the risk of heart disease, kidney problems, and calcium loss from bone. Consuming too much protein from animal sources can increase the amount of heart-unhealthy saturated fat in your diet. Too many protein-rich foods in the diet can displace whole grains, fruits, and vegetables, which have been shown to help reduce many chronic diseases. A high-protein diet has also been shown to lead to loss of bone mass. PEM is caused by an inadequate amount of protein and/or calories in the diet. A severe deficiency of protein is called kwashiorkor; a deficiency of calories is called marasmus. These conditions can be improved with proper food and treatment.

How Do Vegetarians Meet Their Protein Needs?

LO 6.7 Describe the benefits and risks of a vegetarian diet.

What do spaghetti topped with marinara sauce, cheese pizza, and macaroni and cheese all have in common? These common, classic **vegetarian** meals all lack meat.

For many people, being a vegetarian is a lifestyle choice made for a particular reason. While some vegetarians avoid foods from animal sources for ethical, religious, or environmental reasons, others choose a vegetarian lifestyle because they believe it's better for their health.[30] An estimated 5 percent of Americans consider themselves vegetarians.[31]

Because vegetarians avoid meat, which is high in protein, they need to be sure to get adequate protein from other food sources. Vegetarians can meet their daily protein needs by consuming a varied plant-based diet that contains protein-rich meat alternatives such as soy, dried beans and other legumes, and nuts. Some vegetarians include protein-rich eggs, dairy foods, and fish as part of their diet. There are several types of vegetarians and associated ranges of acceptable foods. See **Table 6.5** for a description of vegetarian diets and the foods associated with each.

vegetarian A person who doesn't eat meat, fish, or poultry or (sometimes) foods made from these animal sources.

Table 6.5

The Many Types of Vegetarians

Type	Dietary Patterns	
	Does Eat	Doesn't Eat
Semivegetarian	Grains, vegetables, fruits, legumes, seeds, nuts, dairy foods, eggs	Meat, fish, and poultry, except on occasion
Pesco-vegetarian	Grains, vegetables, fruits, legumes, seeds, nuts, dairy foods, eggs, and fish	Meat and poultry
Lacto-ovo-vegetarian	Grains, vegetables, fruits, legumes, seeds, nuts, dairy foods, eggs	Meat, fish, and poultry
Lacto-vegetarian	Grains, vegetables, fruits, legumes, seeds, nuts, dairy foods	Meat, fish, poultry, and eggs
Ovo-vegetarian	Grains, vegetables, fruits, legumes, seeds, nuts, eggs	Meat, fish, poultry, and dairy foods
Vegan	Grains, vegetables, fruits, legumes, seeds, nuts	Any animal foods, meat, fish, poultry, dairy foods, and eggs

Running on Empty

Megan is a 19-year-old business major who also runs marathons on the weekends. She has been reading about the resources that it takes to produce meat, and has decided that she wants to become a vegetarian. Megan did this by cutting out all meat from her diet, including beef, pork, and poultry, as well as fish and shellfish. She then just ate the rest of her usual diet.

After a week or so on this diet, though, Megan started noticing problems with her athletic performance. When she did her weight training, she noticed she wasn't feeling as strong as she had before. After her training runs, her muscles seemed to take longer to recover. And she was just feeling tired in general. Something was definitely not working here. Megan thought about giving up the idea of going vegetarian, but decided to get more information first.

After doing some Internet research on vegetarian diets for athletes, she found out that sports dietitians agree that athletes consuming a vegetarian diet can keep their competitive edge—with careful planning. She decided to talk to a registered dietitian to plan a nutritionally complete diet.

A week later at her appointment, the dietitian, Sandy, told Megan that her symptoms meant that she probably wasn't getting enough protein to fuel her athletic activities. Sandy recommended that Megan add soy products, eggs, yogurt, cow's milk, cheese, or protein shakes to her daily diet to help get needed amounts of protein as well as vitamin B_{12}, calcium, and vitamin D. For athletes like Megan who don't consume fish, soy products, walnuts, flaxseeds, soybean oil, and canola oil provide omega-3 fatty acids. In addition, Sandy said that Megan also needed to pay some attention to the minerals in her diet, including iron, which is a critical nutrient for athletes because it carries oxygen to working muscles, and zinc, which is important to help tissues recover from the stress of training. Fortified foods can help increase the level of these minerals in a vegetarian diet, and a daily multivitamin/mineral supplement can provide added insurance. After this Megan felt like she finally had the information she needed to plan a vegetarian diet that can support her endurance running.

Think About It

Plan three days of vegetarian meals for Megan that will include enough protein for her activities.

In the United States, the vegetarian food market continues to grow as manufacturers accommodate increased consumer demand with an array of new vegetarian products each year.[32] Many sit-down restaurants offer vegetarian entrées on their menus, and even some fast-food restaurants now offer veggie burgers. University food services are increasingly making vegetarian options available to meet growing student demand. The Joy of Soy on pages 214–215 gives an overview of the abundance of soy products available on the market.

The Joy of Soy

Soy has been used as a dietary staple for centuries in Asia. In recent decades, soy consumption in the United States has increased to an all-time high and is rising at 5 percent annually.[8] Consumers not only perceive soy foods as being healthy, but also an abundance of new products is contributing to the increased consumption of soy foods.[9]

isoflavones Naturally occurring phytoestrogens, or weak plant estrogens, that function in a fashion similar to the hormone estrogen in the human body.

estrogen The hormone responsible for female sex characteristics.

Consumers choosing soy for its health benefits are doing so for its protein-rich, heart-healthy, and high-fiber properties.[10] Soy is a high-quality protein source that is low in saturated fat and that contains **isoflavones**, which are naturally occurring phytoestrogens (*phyto* = plant). These plant estrogens have a chemical structure similar to human **estrogen**. While they are considered weak estrogens (they have less than a thousandth of the potential activity of estrogen), they may interfere with or mimic some of estrogen's activities in certain cells in the body.[11] Although isoflavones can also be found in other plant foods, such as grains, vegetables,

and legumes, soybeans contain the largest amount found in food.

Eating soy protein as part of a heart-healthy diet may reduce the risk of heart disease by lowering cholesterol levels. Research suggests that soy protein can lower the "bad" LDL cholesterol by about 3 percent.[12] Soy protein may also help lower blood pressure.[13] High blood pressure is a risk factor for heart disease.

Some studies suggest that isoflavones may also reduce the risk of certain cancers. Interest in soy as a cancer fighter was sparked after researchers observed that Asian countries had lower rates of breast cancer than Western

What's on the Soy Menu?

Tofu

- Cooked, puréed soybeans that are processed into a silken, soft, or firm texture; has a neutral flavor, which allows it to blend well
- Use the silken version in dips, soups, and cream pies. Use the firm variety in stir-fries or on salads, or marinate it and then bake or grill it.

Soy Flour

- Made from ground, roasted soybeans
- Use it in baked goods such as pancakes, muffins, and cookies. It can also substitute for eggs in baked goods: Use 1 tbs soy flour combined with 1 tbs of water for each whole egg.

Edamame

- Tender young soybeans; can be purchased fresh, frozen, or canned
- Use them in salads, grain dishes, stir-fries, and casseroles.

Soy Milk

- A soy beverage made from a mixture of ground soybeans and water
- Use it in place of cow's milk. Combine soy milk with ice and fruit in a blender for a soy shake.

countries, including the United States. Numerous studies suggest that the isoflavones in soy may have anticancer functions in the body. One of these functions is that isoflavones compete with the hormone estrogen for its binding site on specific cells. The isoflavone latches onto the cell and blocks the binding of the hormone. Because estrogen may increase the risk of breast cancer, inhibiting or blocking the actions of estrogen may help reduce the risk. Other research suggests that isoflavones may latch on to a different cell receptor that potentially could suppress the production of a tumor.[14] This weak estrogen-like activity may also protect against other hormone-related cancers such as prostate, ovarian, and uterine cancer. Other compounds in soy may also have anticancer properties.[15]

Timing may be an important part of the preventive role that soy plays in breast cancer. A study of Chinese women found that those who ate the most soy during their adolescent years had a reduced risk of breast cancer in adulthood.[16]

There was some concern that once the isoflavones are bound to the estrogen receptors, they can initiate the production of cancer cells, which can *raise* the risk of breast cancer.[17] However, research supports the safety of soy isoflavones when consumed as soy and soy products.[18]

According to the American Cancer Society, current research suggests that eating a moderate amount of soy foods is not harmful for breast cancer survivors, although less is known about the consumption of soy supplements.[19] A moderate amount is considered 1 to 2 standard servings of whole soy foods, such as soy milk, tofu, edamame, and soy nuts. A serving provides about 7 grams of protein and 25 milligrams of isoflavones.[20] Soy can be an inexpensive, heart-healthy protein source that may also help modestly lower your blood cholesterol, high blood pressure, and risk of certain cancers.

Tempeh

- Made from cooked whole soybeans that are condensed into a solid block
- Can be seasoned and used as a meat substitute

Soy Meat Analogs

- Products such as hot dogs, sausages, burgers, cold cuts, yogurts, and cheese that are made using soy
- Use them as meat substitutes at meals and snacks.

Miso

- A flavorful paste of fermented soybeans used to season foods
- Use it in soups, stews, and sauces.

Textured Soy Protein

- Created from defatted soy flour that has been compressed and dehydrated
- Use it as a meat substitute in foods such as meatballs, meatloaf, chili, tacos, and spaghetti sauce.

The Potential Benefits and Risks of a Vegetarian Diet

A plant-based diet can be rich in high-fiber whole grains, vegetables, fruits, legumes, and nuts and thus naturally lower in saturated fat and cholesterol. This type of diet contains the fundamentals for reducing the risk of the following diseases:

- *Heart disease.* Vegetarian food staples, such as soy, nuts, and soluble fiber–rich foods, such as beans and oats, have been shown to reduce blood cholesterol levels. Numerous studies have shown that a vegetarian diet is associated with a lower risk of dying from heart disease.[33]

- *High blood pressure.* Vegetarians tend to have lower blood pressure than meat eaters. Vegetarians tend to have a lower BMI (body mass index) as well as consume higher amounts of fruits and vegetables compared with nonvegetarians, both of which can play a role in lowering blood pressure.[34] High blood pressure is a risk factor not only for heart disease but also for stroke.

- *Type 2 diabetes.* You know from Chapter 4 that a plant-based diet can help reduce the risk for type 2 diabetes, so it shouldn't surprise you that vegetarians tend to have a lower risk for diabetes. Diabetes is also a risk for heart disease. For people with diabetes, consuming foods rich in fiber and low in saturated fat and cholesterol makes eating a vegetarian diet an attractive strategy to better manage this disease.[35]

- *Certain types of cancer.* Vegetarians tend to have a lower cancer rate compared with the general population. The latest American Cancer Society guidelines recommend that Americans maintain a healthy weight, stay physically active, and consume a plant-based diet that is high in nutrients and dietary fiber yet low in calorie-dense foods (highly processed foods and beverages with a lot of added sugars), processed meat, and red meat to reduce the risk for cancer.[36]

- *Obesity.* A plant-based diet containing mostly fiber-rich whole grains and low-calorie, nutrient-rich vegetables and fruits tends to "fill you up before it fills you out," making you more likely to eat fewer calories overall. Hence, the plant-based foods of a vegetarian diet can be a healthy, satisfying strategy for those fighting the battle against obesity.

In addition to diet, other lifestyle habits such as not smoking, abstaining from alcohol and recreational drugs, and enjoying daily physical activity, which are all common among vegetarians, may also contribute to their lower risk of the above conditions.

The biggest risk of a vegetarian diet is in not consuming enough of the nutrients, such as protein and vitamin B_{12}, that are found in abundance in animal foods. Strictly avoiding meat, fish, poultry, and foods derived from animal sources can be *unhealthy* if you don't replace these foods with healthy, nutrient-dense, nonmeat alternatives. Also, vegetarian meals may not always be low in saturated fat if full-fat dairy products are heavily used. Planning is needed to be a healthy vegetarian.

How You Can Be a Healthy Vegetarian

To avoid nutrient deficiencies, vegetarians and vegans must consume adequate amounts of all nutrients by eating a wide variety of foods (see **Figure 6.16**). Some nutrients found in abundance in animal foods, including protein, iron, zinc, calcium, vitamin D, riboflavin (a B vitamin), vitamin B_{12}, vitamin A, and omega-3 fatty acids, are particularly important to monitor. The tips in **Table 6.6** can help you incorporate these nutrients in a vegetarian diet.

Figure 6.16 My Vegan Plate
Please see Table 6.7 for specific nutrients that could be missing in action in a vegetarian diet.

Table 6.6

Nutrients That Could Be MIA (Missing in Action) in a Vegetarian Diet

Vegetarians need to take care in planning a diet that meets all their nutritional needs. Here are the nutrients that a vegetarian diet could fall short of, some vegetarian food sources for these nutrients, and tips on how to enjoy these foods as part of a balanced diet.

Nutrient	Risks	Vegetarian Food Sources	Table Tips
Protein	A vegetarian's protein needs can be met by consuming a *variety* of plant foods. A combination of protein-rich soy foods, legumes, nuts, and/or seeds should be eaten daily.	Soybeans, soy burgers, tofu, tempeh, nuts, peanuts, peanut butter, legumes, sunflower seeds, milk, soy milk, yogurt, cheese	• Add nuts to your morning cereal. • Add beans to your salads, soups, and main entrées. • Have a soy burger for lunch. • Use tofu in stir-fries, rice and pasta dishes, and casseroles. • Snack on a soy milk and banana or berry shake.
Iron	The form of iron in plants is not as easily absorbed as the type in meat, milk, and poultry. Also, phytate in grains and rice and polyphenols in tea and coffee can inhibit iron absorption. The iron needs of vegetarians are about 1½ times higher than those of nonvegetarians. Vitamin C enhances the absorption of the iron in plant foods.	Iron-fortified cereals, enriched grains, pasta, bread, oatmeal, potatoes, wheat germ, cashews and other nuts, sunflower seeds, legumes, soybeans, tofu, bok choy, broccoli, mushrooms, dried fruits, raisins	• Make sure your morning cereal is iron fortified. • Add soybeans to your lunchtime salad. • Eat bread with your salad lunch or make a sandwich. • Pack a trail mix of dried fruits and nuts for a snack. • Add vitamin C–rich foods (broccoli, tomatoes, citrus fruits) to all your meals.

Table 6.6 (continued)

Nutrients That Could Be MIA (Missing in Action) in a Vegetarian Diet

Nutrient	Risks	Vegetarian Food Sources	Table Tips
Zinc	The absorption of zinc is enhanced by animal protein. Eating a vegetarian diet means that you lose out on this benefit and are more likely to develop a deficiency. Phytate in grains also binds zinc, making it unavailable to your body. A vegan's zinc needs may be as much as 50 percent higher than a nonvegetarian's.	Soybeans, soy milk, tofu, tempeh, fortified soy burgers, legumes, nuts, sunflower seeds, wheat germ, fortified ready-to-eat cereals, mushrooms, low-fat or nonfat milk, yogurt, and cheese	• Douse your morning cereal with low-fat milk. • Add low-fat cheese and soybeans to your lunchtime salad. • Snack on sunflower seeds. • Top an afternoon yogurt with wheat germ. • Add soybeans to your dinner rice.
Calcium	Calcium is abundant in lean dairy foods such as nonfat or low-fat milk, yogurt, and cheese, so obtaining adequate amounts shouldn't be difficult if you consume these foods. Calcium-fortified soy milk and orange juice, as well as tofu, can provide about the same amount of calcium per serving as is found in dairy foods. Green vegetables can also provide calcium in the diet.	Low-fat or nonfat milk, yogurt, and cheese, fortified soy milk, soy yogurt, and soy cheese, calcium-fortified orange juice, legumes, sesame tahini, tofu processed with calcium, bokchoy, broccoli, kale, collard greens, mustard greens, okra	• Add milk to your morning cereal and coffee. • Have at least one yogurt a day. • Have a glass of calcium-fortified orange juice with lunch. • Snack on low-fat cheese or yogurt in the afternoon. • Eat green vegetables often at dinner.
Vitamin D	Some vegetarians will need to consume vitamin D–fortified milk or soy products.	Low-fat or nonfat milk, egg yolk, fortified yogurt, soy milk, soy yogurt, ready-to-eat cereals; a vitamin supplement	• Have a glass of milk or soy milk at breakfast every day. • Make sure your morning cereal is vitamin D fortified. • Use fortified evaporated skim milk as a base for cream sauces. • Snack on fortified cereals. • Have a fortified yogurt each day.
Vitamin B$_{12}$	Animal foods are the only naturally occurring food source of B$_{12}$, so it is extremely important that vegetarians, especially strict vegans, look to fortified cereals and soy milk or a supplement to meet their daily needs.	Low-fat and nonfat milk, yogurt, or cheese, eggs, fortified soy milk, ready-to-eat cereals, soy burgers, egg substitutes; vitamin supplement	• Make sure your morning cereal is fortified with vitamin B$_{12}$. • Drink a cup of milk or fortified soy milk with your meals. • Top an afternoon yogurt snack with a fortified cereal. • Try an egg-substitute omelet for lunch. • Use fortified soy "meat" alternatives at dinner.
Vitamin A	Vitamin A is found only in animal foods. However, vegetarians can meet their needs by consuming the vitamin A precursor, beta-carotene.	Fortified low-fat or nonfat milk and soy milk, apricots, cantaloupe, mangoes, pumpkin, kale, spinach	• Enjoy a slice or bowl of cantaloupe in the morning. • Snack on dried apricots. • Add spinach to your lunchtime salad. • Drink a glass of fortified milk or soy milk with dinner. • Try mangoes for a sweet dessert.
Omega-3 fatty acids	If your vegetarian diet doesn't include fish, you may not be consuming enough of the essential omega-3 fatty acid called alpha-linolenic acid.	Fish, especially fatty fish such as salmon and sardines, walnuts, flaxseed and flaxseed oil, soybean and canola oil	• Add walnuts to baked breads and muffins. • Try canned salmon on top of your lunchtime salad. • Top your yogurt with ground flaxseed. • Have fish regularly for dinner. • Cook with canola and flaxseed oil.

Table 6.7

How Does a Vegetarian Meal Compare?

Similar to meat meals, vegetarian meals can provide a robust amount of protein and iron with less heart-unhealthy saturated fat and cholesterol. While a tofu stir-fry doesn't provide as much zinc or vitamin B_{12} as meat, it is a fabulous source of calcium, a mineral many adults are falling short of.

	Beef Stir-Fry (per Serving)	vs.	Tofu Stir-Fry (per Serving)
Protein	38 grams		26 grams
Saturated Fat	3.3 grams		1.8 grams
Dietary Cholesterol	105 milligrams		0
Iron	3.9 milligrams		5.1 milligrams
Calcium	34 milligrams		450 milligrams
Zinc	6.8 milligrams		2.9 milligrams
Vitamin B_{12}	2.5 micrograms		0

Table 6.7 compares the nutrient composition of a traditional meat-based meal and a similar meal made solely from plant foods. Comparing these nutrient profiles may surprise you! Finally, when following a vegetarian diet, a vitamin and mineral supplement may be necessary.

Athletes Can Follow a Vegetarian Diet

Sports dietitians agree that athletes consuming a vegetarian diet can keep their competitive edge—with careful planning. Soy products, eggs, yogurt, cow's milk, cheese, and protein shakes can help a vegetarian athlete get needed amounts of protein, vitamin B_{12}, calcium, and vitamin D. Iron is a critical nutrient for athletes, because it carries oxygen to working muscles. Zinc is important to help tissues recover from the stress of training. Fortified foods can help increase the level of these minerals in a vegetarian diet, and a daily multivitamin/mineral supplement can provide added insurance. For athletes who don't consume fish, soy products, walnuts, flaxseed, soybean oil, and canola oil provide omega-3 fatty acids. Vegetarian athletes should consult a registered dietitian to plan a nutritionally-complete diet.

LO 6.7 **The Take-Home Message** Vegetarian diets can be a healthy eating style that may help reduce the risk of some chronic diseases. Some vegetarians abstain from all animal foods, while others may eat animal foods (such as eggs and dairy products) in limited amounts. All vegetarians must take care in planning a varied diet that meets their nutrient needs, especially for protein, iron, zinc, calcium, vitamin D, riboflavin (a B vitamin), vitamin B_{12}, vitamin A, and omega-3 fatty acids.

Practical Nutrition VIDEO

Getting the Nutrients You Need within Limitations

You don't need to eat meat in order to eat healthfully. Join Joan at the salad bar as she puts together a protein-packed, meat-free meal. Scan this QR code with your mobile device to access the video. You can also access the video in MasteringNutrition™.

MADE over MADE better

Although protein is an important nutrient in your diet, you don't want to consume protein-rich sources at the expense of your heart. Your best bet is to choose leaner protein foods, as they contain less heart-unhealthy saturated fat.

Here are some typical protein-rich foods made over and made nutritionally better!

If you like this... | Try these healthier proteins!

Fried Chicken
3 oz = 246 calories
Protein: 19 grams
Fat: 15 grams
Saturated Fat: 4 grams

Roasted Chicken
3 oz = 147 calories
Protein: 26 grams
Total Fat: 4 grams
Saturated Fat: 1 gram

Hamburger
3 oz = 230 calories
Protein: 22 grams
Fat: 15 grams
Saturated Fat: 6 grams

Veggie Burger
3 oz = 119 calories
Protein: 12 grams
Fat: 4 grams
Saturated Fat: 1 gram

Bologna
3 oz = 261 calories
Protein: 12 grams
Fat: 24 grams
Saturated Fat: 10 grams

Turkey
3 oz = 72 calories
Protein: 13 grams
Fat: 1 gram
Saturated Fat: 0 grams

Fried Fish
3 oz = 195 calories
Protein: 15 grams
Fat: 11 grams
Saturated Fat: 3 grams

Grilled Fish
3 oz = 129 calories
Protein: 16 grams
Fat: 1 gram
Saturated Fat: 0 grams

Is the Paleo Diet a Good Choice for You?

Is the Paleo Diet a Good Choice for You? Named for the Paleolithic era, the Paleo Diet is supposed to imitate the diets of humans who lived before the advent of agriculture. Hence, it emphasizes foods that could be hunted and gathered: meats, fresh vegetables, and fruits. It frowns on cereal grains, refined sugars, dairy, and legumes, among other things. The diet has a large following of people who claim to have lost a lot of weight and improved their health by adhering to the diet.

Would the Paleo Diet be a good fit for you? After you've read the arguments for and against, answer the critical-thinking questions and decide for yourself.

yes

- The Paleo Diet consists of lots of plants, meat, and less grain.[1] The diet is a good fit for omnivores, and including lean meats and fresh vegetables is a good idea.[2]

- The diet avoids refined grains, which are bad for us—they cause a spike in blood sugar, are lower in fiber, and exclude some healthy nutrients.[3]

- The diet encourages consumption of nonstarchy fresh fruits and vegetables as the main carbohydrate source.[4]

- This diet is an improvement over the average American's diet, given that it does not include refined sugar, processed foods, and added salt.[5]

no

- The diet is restrictive, which could make it difficult to stick to.[6]

- The diet excludes dairy and whole grains. This creates a risk of nutrient deficiency; moreover, research supports a recommendation that diets include a broad variety of foods to prevent metabolic syndrome.[7]

- Some varieties of the diet call for raw milk consumption. Without pasteurization, raw milk may contain *Salmonella*, *E. coli*, and *Campylobacter*, which can cause foodborne illness.[8]

- Humans have evolved genes to digest things that early humans couldn't digest, so the idea that our guts are exactly like cavemen's is disingenuous.[9]

what do you think?

1. Which side do you think has the more compelling argument? Why? **2.** Do you think that the Paleo Diet is a healthful diet choice? **3.** Do you think you could stick to the Paleo Diet?

LO 6.1 Proteins Are Made of Amino Acids

Proteins are made of amino acids, which contain an acid group, an amine group, and a unique side chain. Each group is made of carbon, hydrogen, oxygen, and, in the case of the amine group, nitrogen. There are 20 unique side chains and therefore 20 unique amino acids. Amino acids are joined together by peptide bonds to form proteins.

The interactions between the amino acids cause individual proteins to fold into precise three-dimensional shapes. The shape of a protein determines its function. Heat, acids, bases, and salts denature these bonds and disrupt the shape and function of a protein.

Of the 20 amino acids, 9 are essential, so you need to obtain them through your diet. Your body can synthesize the remaining 11 amino acids, so they are nonessential.

LO 6.2 Your Body Digests, Absorbs, and Synthesizes Protein

With the help of stomach juices and intestinal enzymes, your body digests and breaks down proteins into amino acids to make them available for use. A limited amount of amino acids exists in pools in your body. The DNA in your cells directs the synthesis of proteins. Excess amino acids are also broken down and either stored in another form or used as energy, depending on your needs. The nitrogen is converted to the waste product urea and excreted in your urine.

LO 6.3 Protein Plays Many Roles in Your Body

Protein provides structural and mechanical support, supplies materials for ongoing maintenance, forms enzymes and hormones, maintains acid-base and fluid balance, transports nutrients, and aids your immune system. Protein can provide energy, be used to make glucose, and increase satiety at meals. Calories from excess protein will be stored as fat.

LO 6.4 Protein Needs Are Determined by Nitrogen Balance in Your Body

Healthy adults are usually in a state of nitrogen balance, which means they excrete as much nitrogen as they consume. Pregnant and lactating women and growing children are in a state of positive nitrogen balance because they use additional nitrogen to grow new tissues. People who are malnourished or experiencing medical trauma may be in negative nitrogen balance.

Adults should consume 0.8 gram of protein for each kilogram of body weight. Protein quality is determined by the protein digestibility corrected amino acid score (PDCAAS), which is based on the protein's digestibility and its amino acid profile. Protein from animal foods is more easily digested than protein from plant foods. Proteins from animal foods and soy are typically complete proteins and provide all of the essential amino acids along with some nonessential amino acids. Plant proteins are typically incomplete, as they are missing one or more essential amino acids.

LO 6.5 Protein Is Found in Many Foods

Protein is abundant in meat, fish, poultry, and meat alternatives such as dried beans, peanut butter, nuts, and soy. Dairy foods are also excellent sources of protein. Grains and vegetables are less robust protein sources. A varied, balanced diet can easily meet your daily protein needs.

LO 6.7 Vegetarian Diets Can Reduce the Risk of Certain Chronic Diseases and Conditions

A well-balanced, healthy vegetarian diet can help reduce the risk of heart disease, high blood pressure, type 2 diabetes, certain types of cancer, and obesity. Some vegetarians abstain from all animal foods, while others may eat a limited amount. All vegetarians must take care to eat a varied diet that meets all of their nutrient needs, especially for protein, iron, zinc, calcium, vitamin D, riboflavin, vitamin B_{12}, vitamin A, and omega-3 fatty acids.

LO 6.6 Too Much or Too Little Protein Is Linked to Health Problems

Consuming too much protein from animal sources can increase the amount of heart-unhealthy saturated fat in your diet. A high-protein diet has been associated with the loss of calcium from the body, the development of kidney stones, and certain cancers. An excess of protein-rich foods in the diet can displace whole grains, fruits, and vegetables, and can be associated with excess saturated fat consumption, which may contribute to overweight or obesity.

Protein-energy malnutrition (PEM) is caused by an inadequate amount of protein and/or calories in the diet. Kwashiorkor is a severe deficiency of protein; marasmus is a severe deficiency of calories. A deficiency of both calories and protein is known as marasmic kwashiorkor.

Terms to Know

- amino acid
- acid group
- amine group
- side chain
- peptide bonds
- essential amino acid
- nonessential amino acid
- conditionally essential amino acid
- denaturation
- amino acid pools
- protein turnover
- DNA
- gene
- RNA
- messenger RNA (mRNA)
- transfer RNA (tRNA)
- collagen
- enzymes
- catalysts
- hormones
- edema
- buffers
- transport proteins
- antibodies
- nitrogen balance
- protein quality
- digestibility
- amino acid profile
- complete protein
- incomplete protein
- limiting amino acid
- complemented protein
- protein digestibility corrected amino acid score (PDCAAS)
- protein-energy malnutrition (PEM)
- kwashiorkor
- marasmus
- vegetarian
- isoflavones

MasteringNutrition™   Build your knowledge—and confidence—in the Study Area of MasteringNutrition with a variety of study tools.

 MyDiet Analysis

Access MyDietAnalysis through MasteringNutrition™ and track your diet and daily activities. In addition, a dietary analysis activity is available for every chapter in your book.

Check Your Understanding

LO 6.1 1. A protein's shape, and therefore its function in your body, is determined by the interactions of _____ with each other and their environment.
- a. the amino acids in the protein
- b. the water molecules in the protein
- c. the carbons in protein
- d. the peptide bonds in the protein

LO 6.1 2. There are _____ essential amino acids that cannot be made by the body.
- a. 7
- b. 9
- c. 10
- d. 11

LO 6.1 3. Which of the following will NOT denature a protein?
- a. grilling a chicken breast
- b. frying an egg
- c. marinating a steak in red wine
- d. refrigerating milk

LO 6.2 4. Limited amounts of surplus amino acids are stored in your body in your
- a. muscles.
- b. fat stores.
- c. amino acid pools.
- d. stomach.

LO 6.3 5. Protein plays many important roles in your body. Which role does it NOT play in your body?
- a. helping you fight the flu
- b. allowing you to walk, run, sit, and lie down
- c. helping you absorb fat-soluble vitamins in the diet
- d. transporting fat and cholesterol through your blood

LO 6.4 6. Brendan is a 20-year-old male. How much protein does he need daily?
- a. 0.70 gram per kilogram body weight.
- b. 0.80 gram per kilogram body weight.
- c. 0.85 gram per kilogram body weight.
- d. 1.0 gram per kilogram body weight.

LO 6.5 7. Protein is found abundantly in the
- a. dairy group and the fat group.
- b. protein group and the fruit group.
- c. fruit group and the dairy group.
- d. dairy group and the protein group.

LO 6.5 8. Which of the following is a source of complete protein?
- a. kidney beans
- b. peanut butter
- c. soy milk
- d. pasta

LO 6.6 9. Kwashiorkor is a type of PEM that develops when
- a. there is a severe deficiency of protein in the diet but an adequate amount of calories.
- b. there are inadequate amounts of both protein and calories in the diet.
- c. there is an inadequate amount of animal protein in the diet.
- d. there are adequate amounts of both protein and calories in the diet.

LO 6.7 10. A lacto-ovo-vegetarian is coming to your house for dinner. You need to make a meal that she will enjoy. Which would NOT be an acceptable entrée?
- a. stir-fried tofu and vegetables over brown rice
- b. a cheese and broccoli omelet
- c. baked ziti with ricotta cheese, spinach, and tomato sauce
- d. an anchovy pizza

Answers

1. (a) The interactions of the amino acids with each other and with their environment determine the shape, and thus the function, of the proteins in your body.
2. (b) There are 9 essential amino acids that cannot be made in the body, so you must obtain these from foods.

3. (d) Heat and acids will denature proteins. Refrigeration does not alter the bonds between the amino acid side chains and so does not denature proteins.

4. (c) Limited amounts of all the amino acids exist in amino acid pools in your blood and inside your cells, not your stomach. Your muscles contain protein but don't store surplus amino acids. Your fat stores are the result of excess calories from carbohydrates, proteins, and/or fats.

5. (c) You need adequate amounts of protein to fight infections such as the flu, to provide structural and mechanical support when you're moving or lying down, and to transport substances such as fat and cholesterol through your blood. Protein does not help with the absorption of fat-soluble vitamins in your body.

6. (b) Individuals who are 19 years of age and older need 0.80 gram per kilogram body weight of protein daily.

7. (d) Both the dairy group and the protein foods group are full of protein-rich food sources. While there is some protein in vegetables, there is little in fruits. Fats do not contain protein.

8. (c) Soy foods such as soy milk provide all the essential amino acids that you need, along with some nonessential amino acids, and thus are a source of complete protein. Kidney beans, peanut butter, and pasta are missing adequate amounts of some essential amino acids.

9. (a) Kwashiorkor occurs when protein is deficient in the diet even though calories may be adequate. Marasmus occurs when calories are inadequate in a person's diet and thus he or she is starving. Protein from animal sources is not necessary because people can meet their protein needs from a combination of plant proteins, such as soy, legumes, grains, and vegetables, as part of a well-balanced diet.

10. (d) Because a lacto-ovo-vegetarian avoids meat, poultry, and fish, the anchovy (fish) pizza would not be an acceptable dinner option. However, because lacto-ovo-vegetarians eat a predominantly plant-based diet with dairy foods and eggs, the tofu stir-fry, cheese omelet, and baked ziti are all fine.

Web Resources

- For information on specific genetic disorders, including those that affect protein use in the body, visit the National Human Genome Research Institute at www.genome.gov
- For more information on vegetarian diets, visit the Vegetarian Research Group at www.vrg.org
- For more information on soy foods, visit the United Soy Board at www.unitedsoybean.org

Answers to True or False?

1. **True.** However, burning proteins, rather than carbohydrates or fat, for energy is an inefficient way to use this precious nutrient. To learn why, turn to page 199.

2. **True.** Protein increases satiety, the feeling of fullness, after a meal more than either carbohydrates or fat. Turn to page 199 to learn more.

3. **False.** Although both pasta and chicken can contribute to your daily protein needs, the protein in poultry is more easily digested than the protein found in grains. Turn to page 202 to learn why.

4. **False.** Soy foods contain complete proteins, as do fish, so they are both good sources of protein. Turn to page 202 and find out more.

5. **False.** Proteins do play a vital role in your body, but a little can go a long way. For most healthy adults, less than one-fifth of their daily calories should come from dietary protein. For more on how to meet your protein needs, see page 203.

6. **False.** On average, most Americans are not only meeting their daily protein needs but are also surpassing them. Turn to page 203 to learn how.

7. **False.** Contrary to media headlines, Americans are eating less red meat than they were decades ago. To find out what they are eating more of, turn to page 204.

8. **False.** Even an extremely active person can easily meet his or her protein needs through a well-balanced diet. To learn more about protein bars, turn to page 206.

9. **True.** A high-protein diet is usually associated with high levels of artery-clogging saturated fat and low amounts of whole grains, fruits, and vegetables. This type of diet is not heart friendly and may raise your blood cholesterol. To learn more, turn to page 209.

10. **False.** Vegetarian athletes can keep their competitive edge if they are consuming a well-balanced vegetarian diet. Turn to page 219 to find out what that is.

7
Vitamins

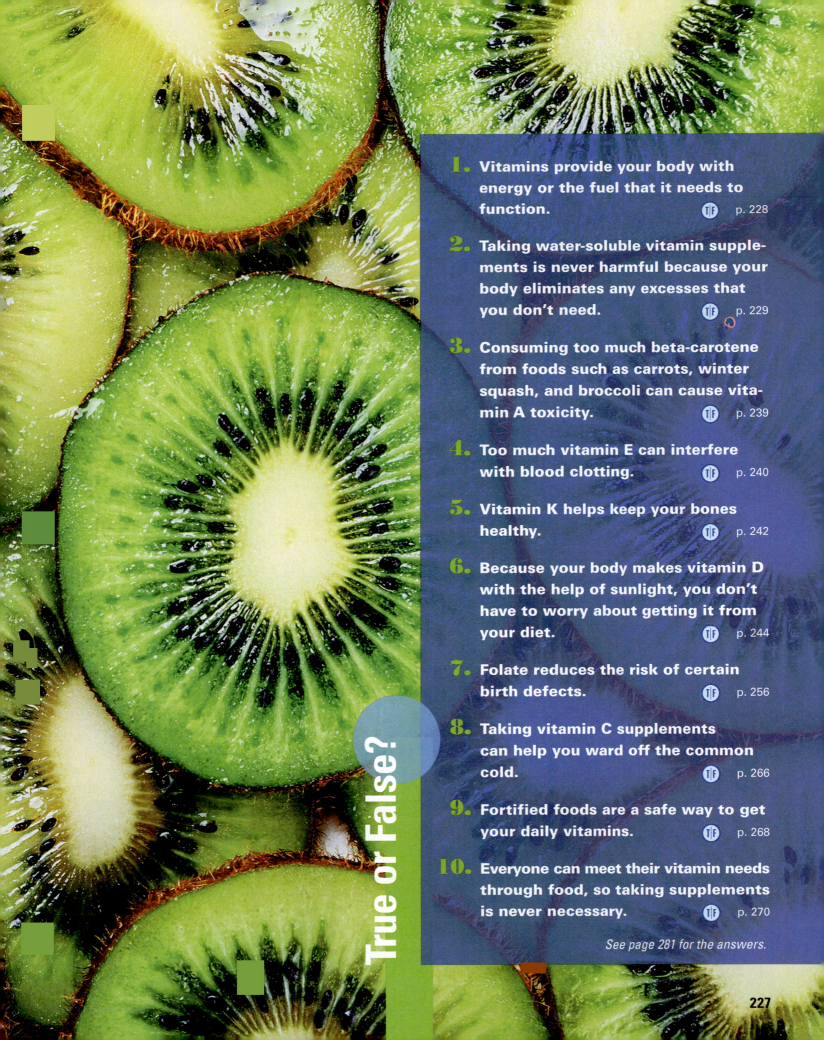

True or False?

1. Vitamins provide your body with energy or the fuel that it needs to function.   T/F   p. 228

2. Taking water-soluble vitamin supplements is never harmful because your body eliminates any excesses that you don't need.   T/F   p. 229

3. Consuming too much beta-carotene from foods such as carrots, winter squash, and broccoli can cause vitamin A toxicity.   T/F   p. 239

4. Too much vitamin E can interfere with blood clotting.   T/F   p. 240

5. Vitamin K helps keep your bones healthy.   T/F   p. 242

6. Because your body makes vitamin D with the help of sunlight, you don't have to worry about getting it from your diet.   T/F   p. 244

7. Folate reduces the risk of certain birth defects.   T/F   p. 256

8. Taking vitamin C supplements can help you ward off the common cold.   T/F   p. 266

9. Fortified foods are a safe way to get your daily vitamins.   T/F   p. 268

10. Everyone can meet their vitamin needs through food, so taking supplements is never necessary.   T/F   p. 270

See page 281 for the answers.

Learning Outcomes

After reading this chapter, you will be able to:

LO 7.1 Explain what vitamins are, their functions, and how to preserve them in food.

LO 7.2 Describe the storage of the fat-soluble vitamins.

LO 7.3 Name functions, food sources, and deficiency and toxicity symptoms for vitamin A.

LO 7.4 Name functions, food sources, and deficiency and toxicity symptoms for vitamin E.

LO 7.5 Name functions, food sources, and deficiency and toxicity symptoms for vitamin K.

LO 7.6 Name functions, food sources, and deficiency and toxicity symptoms for vitamin D.

LO 7.7 Describe the role water-soluble vitamins play as coenzymes.

LO 7.8 Name functions, food sources, and deficiency and toxicity symptoms for thiamin.

LO 7.9 Name functions, food sources, and deficiency and toxicity symptoms for riboflavin.

LO 7.10 Name functions, food sources, and deficiency and toxicity symptoms for niacin.

LO 7.11 Name functions, food sources, and deficiency and toxicity symptoms for vitamin B_6.

LO 7.12 Name functions, food sources, and deficiency and toxicity symptoms for folate.

LO 7.13 Name functions, food sources, and deficiency and toxicity symptoms for vitamin B_{12}.

LO 7.14 Name functions, food sources, and deficiency and toxicity symptoms for vitamin C.

LO 7.15 Name functions, food sources, and deficiency and toxicity symptoms for pantothenic acid and biotin.

LO 7.16 Name other vitamin-like substances the body needs.

LO 7.17 Explain the role of vitamin supplements and fortified foods in your diet.

While vitamins (*vita* = vital) have always been in foods, they remained nameless and undiscovered substances as recently as 100 years ago. If you were to flash back to the early part of the twentieth century, you would find scientists hard at work searching for substances to cure diseases such as beriberi, scurvy, and rickets.[1] These may sound like the names of rock bands to you, but they're actually the devastating diseases caused by deficiencies of thiamin (for beriberi), vitamin C (for scurvy), and vitamin D (for rickets). Throughout the twentieth century, scientists received Nobel Prizes for their discoveries of the vitamins that cured these and other diseases. By the 1940s, the U.S. government mandated that specific vitamins be added to grains and milk to improve the nation's health by improving people's diet.

Now flash forward to the latter part of the twentieth century, when an improved diet meant that vitamin deficiencies became less of an issue for most Americans. Scientists shifted their focus from using vitamins to cure disease to using them to prevent disease. Today, research is being done to find out how vitamins affect and prevent everything from birth defects to heart disease and cancer.

What Are Vitamins?

LO 7.1 Explain what vitamins are, their functions, and how to preserve them in food.

Vitamins are organic compounds that you need in small amounts for growth, reproduction, and overall good health. Although they don't provide energy (calories) for your body, they are essential nutrients for your well-being. A deficiency of any one will cause physiological symptoms. There are 13 vitamins, and you get most of them by eating a variety of foods from each of the food groups (see **Figure 7.1**), though the vitamins D, K, niacin, and biotin can also be synthesized in your body or by microorganisms in the intestinal tract.

A chronic deficiency of any of the essential vitamins can cause a cascade of symptoms, from scaly skin to blindness. However, consuming too much of some vitamins can also cause adverse effects that can be as damaging as consuming too little. Balance is always your best bet when it comes to meeting your vitamin needs.

Vegetables	Fruit	Grains	Protein	Dairy
Folate	Folate	Folic acid	Niacin	Riboflavin
Vitamin A	Vitamin C	Niacin	Thiamin	Vitamin A
Vitamin C	Vitamin A	Vitamin B_6	Vitamin B_6	Vitamin B_{12}
Vitamin E		Vitamin B_{12} (if fortified)	Vitamin B_{12}	Vitamin D
Vitamin K		Riboflavin		
		Thiamin		

Figure 7.1 Vitamins Found Widely in the Food Groups
Eating a wide variety of foods from all food groups will ensure that you meet your vitamin needs.

Vitamins Are Either Fat-Soluble or Water-Soluble

A vitamin is classified as either fat soluble or water soluble, depending on its chemical structure. Fat-soluble vitamins need dietary fat to be properly absorbed, whereas water-soluble vitamins are absorbed with water. Vitamins A, D, E, and K are fat soluble; the B vitamins and vitamin C are water soluble (**Figure 7.2**).

The fat-soluble vitamins are absorbed at the beginning of your small intestine (**Figure 7.3**). They are packaged with fatty acids and bile in micelles, small transport carriers that shuttle them close to the intestinal wall. Once there, the fat-soluble vitamins travel through the cells in the intestinal wall and are packaged with fat and other lipids in chylomicrons (one of the lipoprotein carriers discussed in Chapter 5). The vitamins then travel through your lymph system before they enter your bloodstream.

Water-soluble vitamins are absorbed with water and enter your bloodstream directly (see Figure 7.3). Most water-soluble vitamins are absorbed in the upper portion of your small intestine, although vitamin B_{12} is absorbed in the lower part of your small intestine. Water-soluble vitamins are typically not stored in your body for long periods of time (vitamin B_{12} is the exception), and excess amounts are excreted, so it's important to consume adequate amounts of them every day. **Table 7.1** provides a summary of the two categories of vitamins.

Some Vitamins Function as Antioxidants

Antioxidants (*anti* = against; *oxidants* = oxygen-containing substances) are a group of compounds that includes vitamins E and C, beta-carotene, the mineral selenium, and certain phytochemicals. Just as their name implies, antioxidants counteract

Fat-soluble vitamins **Water-soluble vitamins**

Figure 7.2 Categorizing the Vitamins: Fat Soluble and Water Soluble
Fat-soluble vitamins need dietary fat to be properly absorbed, whereas water-soluble vitamins are absorbed with water.

Figure 7.3 Absorbing Vitamins
Once in the small intestine, fat-soluble vitamins are packaged with fatty acids and bile in micelles that transport them into the intestinal wall. The fat-soluble vitamins travel through the cells in the intestinal wall and are packaged with fat and other lipids in chylomicrons. The chylomicrons travel through the lymph system and into the bloodstream. Water-soluble vitamins are absorbed directly into the bloodstream from the small intestine.

vitamins Non-energy-providing organic essential nutrients that your body needs in small amounts to grow, reproduce, and maintain good health.

antioxidants Substances that neutralize free radicals. Vitamins A, C, and E and beta-carotene are antioxidants.

Table 7.1

Fat-Soluble vs Water-Soluble Vitamins

	Fat Soluble: A, D, E, K	Water Soluble: Bs and C
Requirements	Needed in small amounts	Needed in small amounts
Absorption	Need fat to be absorbed	Absorbed with water
	Absorbed in upper part of small intestine	Most absorbed in upper part of the small intestine
		Vitamin B_{12} absorbed in the lower part of the small intestine
Transport through Body	Packed in micelles and chylomicrons in lymph	Enter bloodstream directly
Storage in Body	Stored in liver, fat, and muscle tissue	Not stored in body
		Excess amounts excreted in the urine
Toxicity	Can be toxic in high doses	Low risk of toxicity, *but* excesses can be harmful
Major Food Sources	Fortified milk, oils	Fortified grains, whole fruits, vegetables, and some animal food sources

oxidation, a harmful chemical reaction that takes place in your cells. During oxidation, oxygen-containing molecules called **free radicals** can damage cell structure, cell proteins, and even DNA.[2] Like prowling thieves, the unstable free radicals steal electrons from other molecules in order to stabilize themselves. The robbed molecule then itself becomes a free radical, and looks for another molecule to attack. This chain reaction, if not stopped, can significantly damage cells.

Free radicals are normal by-products of your body's metabolic reactions, which convert energy from food. They can also result from exposure to chemicals in the environment (such as cigarette smoke and air pollution) and from the damaging effects of the sun's ultraviolet rays on unprotected skin.

Antioxidants are part of your body's natural defense system to harness free radicals and stop them from damaging cells (**Figure 7.4**). If free radicals accumulate

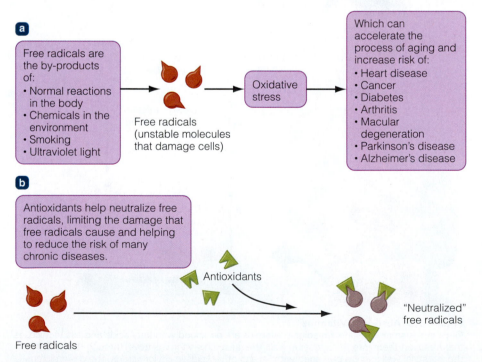

oxidation The process during which oxygen combines with other molecules.

free radicals Unstable oxygen-containing molecules that can damage the cells of the body and possibly contribute to the increased risk of chronic diseases.

a
Free radicals are the by-products of:
• Normal reactions in the body
• Chemicals in the environment
• Smoking
• Ultraviolet light

Free radicals (unstable molecules that damage cells)

Oxidative stress

Which can accelerate the process of aging and increase risk of:
• Heart disease
• Cancer
• Diabetes
• Arthritis
• Macular degeneration
• Parkinson's disease
• Alzheimer's disease

b
Antioxidants help neutralize free radicals, limiting the damage that free radicals cause and helping to reduce the risk of many chronic diseases.

Antioxidants

Free radicals

"Neutralized" free radicals

Figure 7.4 Free Radicals and Antioxidants

faster than your body can neutralize them (a condition known as *oxidative stress*), their effects can contribute to various health problems, including heart disease, cancer, arthritis, and Alzheimer's disease.[3]

Free radicals can also damage your eyes by contributing to age-related macular degeneration and cataracts. **Age-related macular degeneration (AMD)** results from damage to the macula, a tiny area of the retina that is needed for central vision (the ability to see things that are directly in front of you). AMD can make activities such as reading, driving, and watching television difficult (compare **Figure 7.5a** with **Figure 7.5b**). It is a common eye condition among those who are 50 years of age and older and a leading cause of vision loss among older individuals.[4] A study conducted by the National Eye Institute (NEI) discovered that supplements containing large amounts of antioxidants (vitamin C, vitamin E, beta-carotene, lutein, and zeaxanthin), with the minerals zinc and copper, are effective in reducing the risk for AMD, as well as the extent of vision loss.[5]

A **cataract** is a disorder in which the lens of the eye becomes cloudy, resulting in blurred vision (see **Figure 7.5c**). More than half of all Americans have experienced cataracts by the time they reach 80 years of age, and many undergo surgery to remove them.[6] The NIH recommends consuming antioxidant-rich fruits and vegetables, such as leafy dark green vegetables, and fish, for the health of your eyes.[7]

There is no question that diets high in antioxidant-rich fruits, vegetables, and whole grains are associated with a lower incidence of some diseases. However, these foods contain other compounds that may work with antioxidants to provide protection. For example, **phytochemicals** (*phyto* = plant), naturally occurring plant compounds that give fruits and vegetables their vibrant colors, have many beneficial functions in the body, such as acting as antioxidants, which can help protect against cancer.[8]

The big question that remains is if antioxidant *supplements* provide the same health protection as antioxidants consumed in foods. As you will soon read, too much of vitamins C and E, as well as beta-carotene supplements—all of which are antioxidants—can cause health problems. At this time, both the Academy of Nutrition and Dietetics and the *Dietary Guidelines for Americans* advocate that your nutrition needs should be met primarily through foods as part of a well-balanced diet.[9] Filling your plate with a colorful variety of antioxidant- and phytochemical-rich plant-based foods is currently one of the best-known strategies to fight chronic diseases. **Table 7.2** provides you with a list of disease-fighting phytochemicals and their food sources.

a Normal vision and the ability to clearly see the world around you is often taken for granted.

b People with age-related macular degeneration (AMD) have difficulty seeing things directly in front of them.

c Cataracts cause vision to become cloudy.

Figure 7.5 **Normal and Impaired Vision**

Vitamins Differ in Bioavailability

Not all of the vitamins consumed in foods are available to be used in the body. In other words, they are not 100 percent bioavailable. The **bioavailability** of individual vitamins varies according to several factors, including the amount of the vitamin in the food; whether the food is cooked, raw, or refined; how efficiently the food is digested and absorbed; the individual's nutritional status; and whether or not the vitamin is natural or synthetic. In general, if the body needs more vitamins, a greater percentage will be absorbed. For example, a young child or pregnant woman will absorb more ingested vitamins than will a nonpregnant adult.

The bioavailability of fat-soluble vitamins is usually less than that of water-soluble vitamins because fat-soluble vitamins require bile salts and the formation of a micelle to be absorbed. Vitamins in plant foods are typically less bioavailable than those in animal foods because plant fiber can trap vitamins.

age-related macular degeneration (AMD) A disease that affects the macula of the retina, causing blurry vision.

cataract A common eye disorder that occurs when the lens of the eye becomes cloudy.

phytochemicals Naturally occurring substances in fruits, vegetables, and whole grains that protect against certain chronic diseases.

bioavailability The degree to which a nutrient is absorbed from foods and used in the body.

Table 7.2

The Phytochemical Color Guide

The National Cancer Institute recommends eating a variety of colorful fruits and vegetables daily to provide your body with valuable vitamins, minerals, fiber, and disease-fighting phytochemicals. Whole grains also have phytochemicals and have been added to this list.

Color	Phytochemical	Found In
Red	Anthocyanins	Apples, beets, cabbage, cherries, cranberries, red cabbage, red onion, red beans, peppers
	Lycopene	Tomatoes, watermelon, pink grapefruit
Yellow/Orange	Beta-carotene	Apricots, butternut squash, cantaloupe, carrots, mangoes, peaches, pumpkin, sweet potatoes
	Flavonoids	Apricots, clementines, grapefruits, lemons, papaya, pears, pineapple, yellow raisins
White	Alliums/allicin	Chives, garlic, leeks, onions, scallions
Green	Lutein, zeaxanthin	Broccoli, collard greens, honeydew melon, kale, kiwi, lettuce, mustard greens, peas, spinach
	Indoles	Arugula, broccoli, bok choy, brussels sprouts, cabbage, cauliflower, kale, Swiss chard, turnips
Blue/Purple	Anthocyanins	Blackberries, black currants, elderberries, purple grapes
	Phenolics	Eggplant, plums, prunes, raisins
Brown	Beta-glucan, lignans, phenols, plant sterols, phytoestrogens, saponins, tocotrienols	Barley, brown rice, oats, oatmeal, whole grains, whole-grain cereals

Salad Bar Savvy

A trip to your local salad bar can be a wonderful way to add vitamin-rich vegetables to your diet. However, some of the food choices at a salad bar may also be high in heart-unhealthy saturated fat. To learn how to build a heart-friendly, vitamin-rich salad at the salad bar, try the Build-a-Salad NutriTool in MasteringNutrition™.

Vitamins were originally called *vitamines*. Casimir Funk, a chemist and early vitamin researcher, believed that vitamins were vital to life (he was correct) and were probably also a nitrogen-containing amine (he was incorrect). When later discoveries found that an amine wasn't present, the *e* was dropped from the word.

Vitamins Can Be Destroyed by Air, Water, or Heat

Water-soluble vitamins can be destroyed by exposure to air, water, or heat. In fact, vegetables and fruits begin to lose their vitamins almost immediately after being harvested, and some preparation and storage methods can accelerate vitamin loss. Although the fat-soluble vitamins tend to be more stable than water-soluble vitamins, some food preparation techniques can cause the loss of these vitamins as well.

Don't Expose Your Produce to Air

Air (oxygen) exposure can destroy the water-soluble vitamins and the fat-soluble vitamins A, E, and K. For this reason, fresh vegetables and fruits should be stored in airtight, covered containers and used soon after being purchased. Cutting vegetables and fruits increases the amount of surface exposed to air, so cut your produce close to the cooking and serving time to minimize vitamin loss.

A Little Water Is Enough

When you toss out the water that cooks your vegetables, you are also tossing out some water-soluble vitamins. Soaking foods will cause water-soluble vitamins to leach out of the food and into the liquid.[10] To reduce vitamin loss, cook vegetables in a minimal amount of liquid—just enough to prevent the pot from scorching and to keep your vegetables crisp. Steaming or microwaving vegetables, using minimal water, may help preserve some vitamins in vegetables.

Reduce Cooking Time

Heat, especially prolonged heat from cooking, will also destroy water-soluble vitamins, especially vitamin C. Because they are exposed to less heat, vegetables cooked by microwaving, steaming, or stir-frying can have approximately 1½ times more vitamin C after cooking than if they were boiled, which involves longer heat exposure.[11] The first three cooking methods are faster than boiling, reducing the length of time the food is in direct contact with the heat, and they all use less added water. (Stir-frying typically uses only oil.) Cooking vegetables until just tender is best, as it reduces the cooking time and heat exposure and preserves the vitamins. If you find yourself with a plate full of limp and soggy vegetables, this is a sure sign that vitamins have been lost.

Keep Your Food Cool

Whereas heat causes foods to lose vitamins, cooler temperatures help preserve them. For this reason, produce should be stored in your refrigerator rather than on a counter or in a pantry. A package of fresh spinach left at room temperature will lose more than half of its folate, a B vitamin, after four days. Keeping the spinach in the refrigerator delays that loss until eight days.[12] See the Table Tips for ways to preserve the vitamins in your foods.

Overconsumption of Some Vitamins Can Be Toxic

Vitamin **toxicity**, or *hypervitaminosis,* is very rare. This condition results from ingesting more of the vitamin than the body needs, to the point where tissues become saturated. The excess vitamin can damage cells, sometimes permanently. Vitamin toxicity does not occur by eating a normal balanced diet. It can result when individuals consume **megadose** levels of vitamin supplements, usually in the mistaken belief that more is better. Many individuals, for example, overload on vitamin C tablets to ward off a cold, despite the fact that there is no evidence showing that vitamin C prevents the common cold, and despite the fact that too much vitamin C in the body can lead to unpleasant side effects.

To prevent excessive intake, the Dietary Reference Intakes include a tolerable upper intake level for most vitamins. Even though some vitamins lack sufficient evidence to establish a UL, there still may be risks in taking them in megadose amounts.

Provitamins Can Be Converted to Vitamins by the Body

Provitamins are substances found in foods that are not in a form directly usable by the body, but that can be converted into an active form once they are absorbed. The best-known example of this is beta-carotene, which is split into two molecules of vitamin A in the small intestinal cell wall or in the liver cells. Vitamins found in foods that are already in the active form, called **preformed vitamins**, do not undergo conversion in the body.

Now that we've discussed the general characteristics of vitamins, let's review them individually.

Table TIPS

Preserve Your Vitamins!

Cook your vegetables in a small amount of water. If you have to boil vegetables, use the leftover cooking liquid as a soup or gravy base.

Don't rinse rice before cooking it or pasta after cooking it. You'll wash away water-soluble vitamins.

Steam, microwave, or stir-fry vegetables instead of boiling them to reduce the amount of time they are exposed to heat and therefore the amount of vitamins that are lost.

Store produce in a refrigerator and eat it soon after purchase.

Cut vegetables and fruits close to the time that they are going to be cooked and/or served.

toxicity The accumulation of a substance to the level of being poisonous.

megadose A very large dose or amount.

provitamins Substances found in foods that can be converted into an active vitamin form once they are absorbed.

preformed vitamins Vitamins that are found in active form in foods.

Are You Getting Enough Fat-Soluble Vitamins in Your Diet?

Take this brief self-assessment to see if your diet contains enough food sources of the four fat-soluble vitamins.

1. Do you eat at least 1 cup of deep yellow or orange vegetables, such as carrots and sweet potatoes, or dark green vegetables, such as spinach, every day?
   Yes ☐ **No** ☐

2. Do you consume at least 2 glasses (8 ounces each) of milk daily?
   Yes ☐ **No** ☐

3. Do you eat a tablespoon of vegetable oil, such as corn or olive oil, daily? (Tip: Salad dressings, unless they are fat free, count!)
   Yes ☐ **No** ☐

4. Do you eat at least 1 cup of leafy green vegetables in your salad and/or put lettuce in your sandwich every day?
   Yes ☐ **No** ☐

Answers

If you answered yes to all four questions, you are on your way to acing your fat-soluble vitamin needs! If you answered no to any one of the questions, your diet needs some fine-tuning. Deep orange and dark green vegetables are excellent sources of vitamin A, and milk is an excellent choice for vitamin D. Vegetable oils provide vitamin E, and if you put them on top of your vitamin K–rich leafy green salad, you'll hit the vitamin jackpot.

LO 7.1 **The Take-Home Message** Vitamins are essential nutrients needed in small amounts for growth, reproduction, and overall good health. All vitamins are either fat soluble or water soluble. The fat-soluble vitamins, A, D, E, and K, require fat for absorption. The water-soluble B and C vitamins are absorbed with water. Some vitamins, such as vitamins E and C, as well as the mineral selenium, and carotenoids, act as antioxidants because they help counteract the damaging effects of oxygen-containing molecules called free radicals. If free radicals accumulate faster than your body can neutralize them, their damaging effects can contribute to chronic diseases and conditions. Fruits, vegetables, and whole grains are robust sources of antioxidants. Many vitamins in foods can be destroyed or lost by exposure to air, water, and heat. The overconsumption of some vitamins can be toxic. Provitamins can be converted to vitamins in the body.

The Storage of Fat-Soluble Vitamins

LO 7.2 Describe the storage of the fat-soluble vitamins.

Because vitamin A is stored in the liver, chicken liver is a potent source of this vitamin.

Fat-soluble vitamins are stored in your body and used as needed when your dietary intake falls short. Your liver is the main storage depot for vitamin A and to a lesser extent vitamins K and E, whereas vitamin D is mainly stored in your fat and muscle tissues. Because they are stored in the body, large quantities of some of the fat-soluble vitamins, particularly A and D, can build up to the point of toxicity, causing harmful symptoms and conditions.

Before we begin our discussion of the fat-soluble vitamins, take the Self-Assessment to see if your diet is rich in foods containing these important nutrients.

LO 7.2 **The Take-Home Message** Fat-soluble vitamins are stored in your body. For this reason, chronic dietary excesses of some fat-soluble vitamins can be toxic.

Vitamin A

What Is Vitamin A?

LO 7.3 Name functions, food sources, and deficiency and toxicity symptoms for vitamin A.

Vitamin A is actually a family of substances called **retinoids** that includes retinol, retinal, and retinoic acid. These are called **preformed vitamin A** because they are in a form that your body readily uses. **Retinol** is the most usable of the three forms and can be converted to both retinal and retinoic acid in your body.[13]

Preformed vitamin A is found only in foods from animal sources, such as liver and eggs, and is added to all processed milk. Plant food sources do not contain preformed vitamin A, but some do contain **provitamin A carotenoids**, which can be converted to retinol in your body. Carotenoids are the yellow-red pigments that give carrots, butternut squash, and cantaloupe their vibrant, deep orange color.

There are more than 600 different carotenoids, but only 3—beta-carotene (β-carotene), beta-cryptoxanthin (β-cryptoxanthin), and alpha-carotene (α-carotene)—can be converted to vitamin A. These three provide approximately 25 to 35 percent of the dietary vitamin A consumed by adults in the United States, with the majority of it coming from beta-carotene.[14] Other nutritionally

The carotenoid lycopene, found in tomatoes and tomato products, functions as an antioxidant in the body.

significant carotenoids, including lycopene, lutein, and zeaxanthin, may function as antioxidants or provide health benefits, but cannot be converted to vitamin A.

Functions of Vitamin A

Vitamin A Is Essential for Vision

Rays of light are bouncing off this page. For you to read this sentence, your eyes receive this reflection of light and begin the process of translating the light into visible images. After light enters your eye through the cornea, it travels to the back of your eye to the retina and macula (which is located in the retina and allows you to see fine details and things that are straight in front of you).

Vitamin A is a component of two light-sensitive proteins that are essential for vision. The two proteins, **rhodopsin** and **iodopsin**, are in the light-absorbing cells in the retina called **rods** and **cones**, respectively.

As rhodopsin absorbs incoming light, the shape of vitamin A is altered, and it detaches from its protein (**Figure 7.6** on page 236). This causes a cascade of events that transmits visual messages through your optic nerve to your brain. This change in rhodopsin is called **bleaching**. Although the breakdown of iodopsin is similar, rhodopsin is more sensitive to dim light than iodopsin and is more likely to become bleached. After bleaching, the vitamin A returns to its original shape and becomes part of the protein again, regenerating the eye's light-absorbing capabilities. This regeneration process can take a few moments.

Have you ever been outside on a sunny day without sunglasses and then entered a dark building? Was it difficult for you initially to see the objects in the room? In this situation, your eyes needed an adjustment period because much of your rhodopsin had been bleached in the bright outdoor sun and your eyes needed to regenerate it once you were in the dark room. Luckily, there is a pool of vitamin A in your retina to help with this regeneration.

Vitamin A Is Involved in Cell Differentiation, Reproduction, Bone Health, and Immunity

Vitamin A plays an important role in cell division and **cell differentiation**, the processes that determine what a cell becomes in your body.[15]

Vitamin A affects cell division by prompting gene expression, a process that uses genetic information to make the proteins needed to begin the process of cell division. As cells divide and cluster together, changes occur that cause them to become different from their initiating cells. This differentiation determines what they become in your body. When immature skin cells differentiate into mature skin cells, for example, vitamin A acts as a signal to turn on the genes to create the proteins needed to make healthy skin.

This role of vitamin A is one reason dermatologists prescribe retinoid-containing medicines, such as Retin-A or Accutane, to treat acne (see photo on page 237). Retin-A is a topical medication that works by enhancing the turnover of skin cells and inhibiting the formation of acne.

retinoids The family or group of substances that include retinol, retinal, and retinoic acid.

preformed vitamin A The form of vitamin A that is readily used by the body.

retinol The most usable form of preformed vitamin A.

provitamin A carotenoids The family of compounds that includes beta-carotene that can be used to make vitamin A in the body.

rhodopsin A compound found in the rods of the eye that is needed for night vision.

iodopsin The compound found in the cones of the eye that is needed for color vision.

rods Light-absorbing cells responsible for black-and-white vision and night vision.

cones Light-absorbing cells responsible for color vision.

bleaching When light enters the eye and interacts with and changes rhodopsin.

cell differentiation The process that determines what a cell becomes in your body.

CONTINUED

FOCUS

Figure 7.6 Retinal and Its Role in Vision

FOCUS FIGURE WALKTHROUGH

Scan this QR code with your mobile device for a video tour of this figure by Joan Salge Blake.

Light

Vitamin A is a component of two light-sensitive proteins, rhodopsin and iodopsin, that are essential for vision. Here we examine rhodopsin's role in vision. Although the breakdown of iodopsin is similar, rhodopsin is more sensitive to light than iodopsin and is more likely to become bleached.

EYE STRUCTURE

Eye cross-section

Cornea

Light

Retina

Macula

Optic nerve

1 After light enters your eye through the cornea, it travels to the back of your eye to the macula, which is located in the retina. The macula allows you to see fine details and things that are straight in front of you.

Rod and cone cells in retina

Rhodopsin protein in rod cell membrane

Rhodopsin

Rod

Cone

Vitamin A

2 Inside the retina are two types of light-absorbing cells, rods and cones. Rods contain the protein rhodopsin, while cones contain the protein iodopsin.

EFFECT OF LIGHT ON RHODOPSIN

Vitamin A detaches from protein

Light

1 As rhodopsin absorbs incoming light, the shape of vitamin A is altered, and it detaches from the rhodopsin.

Some vitamin A is lost

2 This process, called bleaching, causes a cascade of events that transmits visual messages through your optic nerve to your brain. After bleaching, some vitamin A is lost.

Vitamin A from bloodstream

3 Vitamin A from the blood is brought in to replenish what is lost. The vitamin A returns to its original shape and becomes part of rhodopsin again, regenerating the eye's light-absorbing capabilities. This regeneration can take a few moments.

Microgrames (μg) RAE of **Vitamin A**

Value	Food
234	Red peppers, 1 cup
266	Green leaf lettuce, 2 cups
268	Squash, winter, cooked, ½ cup
281	Spinach, raw, 2 cups
690	Carrots, baby, raw, 10 medium
956	Kale, frozen, cooked, 1 cup
978	Collards, frozen, cooked, 1 cup
1,096	Sweet potato, baked, 1 medium
1,906	Pumpkin, canned, 1 cup
89	Mango, sliced, raw, 1 cup
117	Apricots, dried, ½ cup
270	Cantaloupe, cubed, 1 cup
6,582	Liver, pan-fried, 3 oz
149	Milk, low fat or skim, 8 oz
900	Men 19 to 50 years
700	Women 19 to 50 years

Categories: Vegetables | Fruits | Protein | Dairy | Daily Needs

Figure 7.7 **Vitamin A Content in Selected Foods**

Accutane is a medication taken orally that, among other things, affects cell differentiation by manipulating the gene expression of acne-producing cells to alter their development in the skin.[16]

During the early stages of pregnancy, vitamin A signals cells to differentiate into tissues that form the baby's body. Vitamin A plays a particularly important role in the development of the lungs, heart, kidneys, ears, and other organs.[17]

Vitamin A may help regulate the cells involved in bone growth through gene expression. Too much vitamin A, however, may negatively affect healthy bones.

Vitamin A is important for keeping your skin and the mucous membranes of your lungs, intestinal tract, and kidneys healthy and structurally sound. If these linings are weakened or damaged, bacteria and viruses can infiltrate your body and make you sick.

Vitamin A helps keep your skin, which acts as another barrier to infections, healthy to prevent harmful

bacteria from entering your body. Vitamin A also works with your immune system to create white blood cells that fight pathogens that enter your bloodstream.

Daily Needs

Vitamin A in foods and supplements can be measured in two ways: in micrograms (μg) of **retinol activity equivalents (RAE)** and in **international units (IU)**.

Because retinol is the most usable form of vitamin A and because

*Throughout this book, the amount of each nutrient that is needed daily is based on adults age 19 to 50. If you are younger than 19 or older than 50, your needs may be different. See the inside cover of this textbook for the specific amount of each nutrient you need daily based on your age and gender.

provitamin A carotenoids can be converted to retinol, the preferred way to measure vitamin A in foods is its conversion to RAE. However, some vitamin supplements and food labels use the older measure, IU, on their products. (One RAE in micrograms is the equivalent of 3.3 IU.)

Adult females need 700 micrograms RAE of vitamin A daily, whereas adult males need 900 micrograms RAE daily.* This is the average amount needed to maintain adequate stores in your body to keep it healthy.[18]

A daily recommendation for beta-carotene hasn't been established, but the Institute of Medicine suggests consuming 3 to 6 milligrams of beta-carotene every day from foods.[19] (Beta-carotene is measured in milligrams.) You can obtain this easily by eating five or more servings of fruits and vegetables. This amount will provide about 50 percent of the recommended vitamin A intake.

Vegetarians who eat no animal foods, including vitamin A–rich milk and eggs, need to be especially conscientious about eating carotenoids and beta-carotene-rich foods to meet their daily vitamin A needs.

Vitamin A can aid in the treatment of acne.

retinol activity equivalents (RAE) The unit of measure used to describe the total amount of all forms of preformed vitamin A and provitamin A carotenoids in food.

international units (IU) A system of measurement of a biologically active ingredient such as a vitamin.

CONTINUED

Vitamin A

The upper level for adults has been set at 3,000 micrograms of preformed vitamin A daily.

Overconsumption of preformed vitamin A is usually due to taking supplements and is less likely to occur from overeating vitamin A in foods. Consuming more than 15,000 micrograms of preformed vitamin A at one time or over a short period of time can lead to nausea, vomiting, headaches, dizziness, and blurred vision.[21]

Chronic daily consumption of more than 30,000 micrograms of vitamin A (more than 300 times the amount that adults need daily) can lead to **hypervitaminosis A** (hyper = over, osis = condition), an extremely serious condition in which the liver accumulates toxic levels of vitamin A. Hypervitaminosis A can lead to deterioration and scarring of the liver and even death.[22]

High intake of preformed vitamin A during pregnancy, particularly in the first trimester, can cause birth defects in the face and skull and lungs.[23] All women of childbearing age who are using retinoids for acne or other skin conditions should take the proper steps to avoid becoming pregnant.

Although vitamin A is needed for bone health, some research suggests that consuming too much may lead to **osteoporosis** (osteo = bone, porosis = porous), or thinning of the bone, which in turn increases the risk of fractures. Osteoporosis-related hip fractures

Food Sources

Organ meats (liver), milk, and eggs are the most popular sources of preformed vitamin A in the U.S. diet. Carrots, spinach, and sweet potatoes are American favorites for provitamin A carotenoids, including beta-carotene (**Figure 7.7**). Similar to vitamin A and other fat-soluble vitamins, carotenoids are absorbed more efficiently when fat is present in your intestinal tract. Adding a reduced-fat or full-fat salad dressing to a salad can significantly increase the amount of carotenoids absorbed compared with a salad topped with a nonfat dressing.[20] For more ideas on how to get vitamin A into your daily diet, see Table Tips "Score an A."

Too Much or Too Little

Because vitamin A is stored in your body, excessive amounts of preformed vitamin A can accumulate to toxic levels.

hypervitaminosis A The serious condition in which the liver accumulates toxic levels of vitamin A.

osteoporosis A condition in which bones become brittle and porous.

The hand on the right exhibits the orange-tinged skin characteristic of carotenodermia.

TableTIPS

Score an A

Dunk baby carrots in a tablespoon of low-fat ranch dressing for a healthy snack.

Keep dried apricots in your backpack for a sweet treat.

Add baby spinach to a lunchtime salad.

Bake sweet potatoes rather than white potatoes at dinner.

Buy frozen mango chunks for a ready-to-thaw beta-carotene-rich addition to cottage cheese or yogurt.

appear to be prevalent in Swedes and Norwegians, who tend to have high consumption of vitamin A–rich cod-liver oil and specialty dairy products that have been heavily fortified with vitamin A.[24] As little as 1,500 micrograms (3,000 IU) of retinol, which is slightly more than twice the RDA recommended for women, has been shown to be unhealthy for bones, although not all studies support this finding.[25]

The upper level applies *only* to preformed vitamin A from foods, fortified foods, and supplements. Provitamin A carotenoids in foods are not toxic and do not pose serious health problems. Your body has a built-in safeguard to prevent provitamin A carotenoids from contributing to vitamin A toxicity, birth defects, or bone damage. If you consume more carotenoids than you need to meet your vitamin A needs, your body will decrease their conversion to retinol. Extra amounts of carotenoids are stored in your liver and in the fat under your skin.[26]

Eating too many carotenoids can cause a nonthreatening condition called **carotenodermia** (*carotene* = carotene, *dermia* = skin) which results in orange-tinged skin, particularly on the palms of the hands and soles of the feet. Because these areas are cushioned with fat, they become more concentrated with the pigments and more visibly orange in color (right hand in photo). Cutting back on carotenoid-rich foods will reverse carotenodermia.

Though a diet abundant in carotenoid-rich foods is not dangerous, carotenoid supplements may be. In a study of adult male smokers, those who consumed beta-carotene supplements were shown to have significantly higher rates of lung cancer than those who didn't take the supplements.[27] There is no known benefit associated with taking beta-carotene supplements. Eating a variety of fruits and vegetables is the safest and most healthful way to meet your vitamin A needs.

A chronic vitamin A deficiency can lead to an inability to regenerate rhodopsin, causing **night blindness**. Individuals with night blindness have difficulty seeing at dusk, because they can't adjust from daylight to dark, and may not be able to drive a car during this time of the day. If diagnosed early, night blindness can be reversed by taking vitamin A.

A prolonged vitamin A deficiency can also lead to dryness and permanent damage to the cornea, a condition called **xerophthalmia** (*xero* = dry, *ophthalm* = eye). Vitamin A deficiency is the number-one cause of preventable blindness in children.[28]

A deficiency of vitamin A is also associated with stunting, or reduction in the growth, of bones.

carotenodermia The presence of excess carotene in the blood resulting in an orange skin color, due to excessive intake of carotene-rich vegetables.

night blindness The inability to see in dim light or at night due to a deficiency of vitamin A.

xerophthalmia Permanent damage to the cornea causing blindness, due to a prolonged vitamin A deficiency.

The Storage of Fat-Soluble Vitamins **239**

exploring
Vitamin E

What Is Vitamin E?

LO 7.4 Name functions, food sources, and deficiency and toxicity symptoms for vitamin E.

Vitamin E is sometimes referred to as a vitamin in need of a disease to cure. For almost 40 years after its discovery, scientists searched unsuccessfully for a curative role for vitamin E. They now have shifted their focus and begun valuing the vitamin's importance as an effective antioxidant.[29]

There are eight different forms of naturally occurring vitamin E, but one form, **alpha-tocopherol (α-tocopherol)**, is most active in your body. The synthetic form of vitamin E found in dietary supplements is only half as active as the natural form.[30]

Functions of Vitamin E
Vitamin E as an Antioxidant

Vitamin E's nutritional claim to fame is its role as a powerful antioxidant. This role is extremely important in protecting cell membranes and preventing oxidation of the "bad" LDL cholesterol carrier.

As you recall from Chapter 5, phospholipids (lipids that contain phosphorus and two fatty acids) are critical components of cell membranes. Many phospholipids contain unsaturated fatty acids, which are vulnerable to the damaging effects of free radicals. As an antioxidant, vitamin E neutralizes free radicals before they can harm cell membranes (see **Figure 7.8**).

When the bad LDL cholesterol carrier is oxidized, it contributes to the buildup of artery-clogging plaque. Antioxidants, including vitamin E, can help protect the LDL cholesterol carrier from being oxidized and reduce the buildup in the arteries, called atherosclerosis.[31]

Other Functions of Vitamin E

Vitamin E is an **anticoagulant** (*anti* = against, *coagulant* = causes clotting), which means that it inhibits platelets (fragments of cells used in blood clotting) from unnecessarily clumping together and creating a damaging clot in your bloodstream. Vitamin E also alters the stickiness of the cells that line your lymph and blood vessels. This decreases the ability of blood components to stick to these walls and clog these passageways.

However, research to date on the use of vitamin E to prevent heart disease is conflicting, and at this time, studies do not support the use of vitamin E supplements to protect against heart disease.[32]

Daily Needs

Adults need to consume 15 milligrams of vitamin E daily. Because alpha-tocopherol is the most active form of vitamin E in your body, your vitamin E needs are expressed in alpha-tocopherol equivalents.

Currently, American adults, on average, are consuming less than 10.5 milligrams of vitamin E daily, so are falling short of their dietary needs.[33]

Food Sources

Because vitamin E is fat soluble, vegetable oils, foods that contain these oils, nuts, and seeds are good sources (**Figure 7.9**). Some green leafy vegetables, avocado, and fortified cereals can also contribute to your daily needs. For more ideas on how to get vitamin E into your daily diet, see Table Tips "Enjoying Your Es."

Too Much or Too Little

There isn't any known risk of consuming too much vitamin E from natural food sources. However, overconsumption of the synthetic form that is found in supplements and/or fortified foods could pose risks.

Because vitamin E can act as an anticoagulant and interfere with blood

alpha-tocopherol (α-tocopherol) The most active form of vitamin E in the body.

anticoagulant A substance that interferes with blood coagulation.

hemorrhage Excessive loss of blood or bleeding.

Free radicals
Damaged phospholipids
Vitamin E (antioxidant)
Phospholipid membrane

Free radicals damage phospholipids, essential components of the cell membrane.

Vitamin E in cell membranes can neutralize free radicals, preventing them from damaging phospholipids.

Figure 7.8 Vitamin E as an Antioxidant

Figure 7.9 Vitamin E Content in Selected Foods

Vitamin E

Milligrams (mg) of Vitamin E

ChooseMyPlate.gov

	Vegetables			Fruits			Grains	Protein			Oils			Daily Needs

- Spinach, raw, 2 cups — 1.2
- Carrots, boiled, 1 cup — 1.6
- Broccoli, chopped, boiled, 1 cup — 2.4
- Kiwi, 1 fruit, sliced — 1.1
- Nectarine, 1 medium — 1.1
- Mango, pieces, 1 cup — 1.5
- Avocado, cubed, 1 cup — 3.1
- Wheat germ, 1/4 cup — 4.5
- Peanut butter, 1 tbs — 1.5
- Almonds, dry roasted, 1/2 oz — 3.4
- Sunflower seed kernels, dry roasted, 1/2 oz — 3.7
- Italian salad dressing, 1 tbs — 0.3
- Corn oil, 1 tbs — 1.9
- Olive oil, 1 tbs — 1.9
- Sunflower oil, 1 tbs — 5.6
- Adults 19 to 50 years — 15

of their vitamin E needs. Though rare, a chronic deficiency can cause nerve problems, muscle weakness, and uncontrolled movement of body parts. Because vitamin E is an antioxidant and is found in the membranes of red blood cells, a deficiency can also increase the susceptibility of cell membranes to damage by free radicals.

clotting, excess amounts in your body increase the risk of **hemorrhage**. Because of this, the upper level from supplements and/ or fortified foods is 1,000 milligrams for adults. This applies only to healthy individuals consuming adequate amounts of vitamin K. (Vitamin K also plays a role in blood clotting. A deficiency of vitamin K can exacerbate the anticoagulant effects of vitamin E.) Individuals taking anticoagulant medication and vitamin E supplements should be monitored by their physician to avoid the serious situation in which the blood can't clot quickly enough

to stop the bleeding from a wound.

Although the upper level of 1,000 milligrams was set to keep you safe, it may actually be too high. A study showed that those at risk of heart disease who took 400 IU (265 milligrams) or more of vitamin E daily for at least one year had an overall higher risk of dying during that time.[34] One theory is that too much vitamin E may disrupt the balance of other antioxidants in the body, causing more harm than good.

Individuals who can't absorb fat properly may fall short

The Storage of Fat-Soluble Vitamins   **241**

exploring
Vitamin K

What Is Vitamin K?

LO 7.5 Name functions, food sources, and deficiency and toxicity symptoms for vitamin K.

There are two forms of vitamin K: **menaquinone** and **phylloquinone**. Menaquinone is synthesized by the bacteria that exist naturally in your intestinal tract. Phylloquinone is found in green plants, and is the primary source of vitamin K in your diet.

Bacteria in your GI tract synthesize one form of vitamin K.

Functions of Vitamin K

Vitamin K Is Essential for Blood Clotting

An easy way to remember vitamin K's major function is to associate the letter *K* with "klotting."

Vitamin K plays a major role in blood **coagulation**, or clotting. Blood clotting is a complex chain of events involving substances in your blood, many of which are proteins, called clotting factors. Vitamin K plays a role in synthesizing four of these **clotting factors**. Without vitamin K, a simple cut on your finger would cause uncontrollable bleeding.

menaquinone The form of vitamin K produced by bacteria in the colon.

phylloquinone The form of vitamin K found in green plants.

coagulation The process of blood clotting.

clotting factors Substances involved in the process of blood clotting.

osteocalcin The protein in bone that binds with bone-strengthening calcium.

Vitamin K Is Important to Bone Health

Acting as a coenzyme, vitamin K aids an enzyme that alters the bone protein **osteocalcin**. Vitamin K enables osteocalcin to bind with the bone-strengthening mineral calcium.

Chronic inadequate amounts of dietary vitamin K may be a factor in osteoporosis. In a study of women over a ten-year period, researchers found that a low dietary intake of vitamin K was associated with an increased risk of hip fractures.[35] Research continues in the area of vitamin K and bone health.

Daily Needs

Currently, it is not known how much of the vitamin K made from bacteria in your intestinal tract truly contributes to meeting your daily needs. Because of this, it is hard to pinpoint the exact amount you need to consume daily in your foods. Therefore, the recommendation for dietary vitamin K is based on the current amount that is consumed, on average, by healthy Americans.[36]

Adult women need 90 micrograms of vitamin K per day, and men need 120 micrograms daily.

Food Sources

When it comes to meeting your vitamin K needs, think green. Vegetables like broccoli, spinach, salad greens, brussels sprouts, and cabbage are all rich in vitamin K (**Figure 7.10**). Vegetable oils and margarine are the second largest source of vitamin K in the diet. For more ideas on how to get vitamin K into your daily diet, see Table Tips "Getting Your Ks."

Figure 7.10 Vitamin K Content in Selected Foods

Vitamin K — Micrograms (µg) of Vitamin K

Vegetables:
- Romaine lettuce, raw, 2 cups: 96
- Green cabbage, raw, 2 cups: 135
- Brussels sprouts, raw, 1 cup: 156
- Coleslaw, 1 cup: 159
- Broccoli, cooked, 1 cup: 220
- Parsley, raw, 1/2 cup: 246
- Spinach, raw, 2 cups: 290
- Collards, raw, 2 cups: 368
- Swiss chard, raw, 2 cups: 598
- Kale, raw, 2 cups: 944

Oils:
- Olive oil, 1 tsp: 2.7
- Canola oil, 1 tsp: 3.2
- Margarine, regular, 80% fat, 1 tsp: 3.9
- Soybean oil, 1 tsp: 8.3

Daily Needs:
- Men 19 to 50 years: 120
- Women 19 to 50 years: 90

TableTIPS

Getting Your Ks

Have a green salad daily.

Cook with soybean oil.

Add shredded cabbage to your salad, or top it with a scoop of coleslaw.

Add a tad of margarine to your steamed spinach. Both will provide some vitamin K.

Dunk raw broccoli florets in salad dressing for two sources of vitamin K.

A green salad with oil and vinegar dressing at lunch and 3/4 cup broccoli at dinner will meet your vitamin K needs for the entire day.

Too Much or Too Little

There are no known adverse effects of consuming too much vitamin K from foods or supplements, so an upper intake level hasn't been set for healthy people.

Individuals taking anticoagulant (anticlotting) medications such as **warfarin** (also known as Coumadin) need to keep a consistent intake of vitamin K. This medication decreases the activity of vitamin K and prolongs the time it takes for blood to clot. If these individuals suddenly increase the vitamin K in their diets, the vitamin can override the effect of the drug, enabling the blood to clot too quickly. In contrast, a sudden decline in dietary vitamin K can enhance the effectiveness of the drug.[37]

A vitamin K deficiency severe enough to affect blood clotting is extremely rare in healthy individuals.[38] People with illnesses affecting absorption of fat in the intestinal tract, which is necessary to absorb fat-soluble vitamin K, may be at risk of not meeting their vitamin K needs.

warfarin An anticoagulant drug given to prevent blood from clotting.

exploring
Vitamin D

What Is Vitamin D?

LO 7.6 Name functions, food sources, and deficiency and toxicity symptoms for vitamin D.

Vitamin D is called the "sunshine vitamin" because it is made in your body with the help of **ultraviolet (UV) rays** from sunlight.[39] Many individuals do not obtain enough sun exposure, so they must meet their needs through their diets.

Whether from food or sunlight, vitamin D enters your body in an inactive form. The ultraviolet rays of the sun convert a cholesterol-containing compound in your skin to previtamin D, which is then converted to an inactive form of vitamin D in your blood. The vitamin D in your foods is also in this inactive form.

This inactive form travels in your blood to your liver, where it is changed into a circulating form of vitamin D and is released back into your blood. Once in your kidneys, it is converted to an active form of vitamin D.

Functions of Vitamin D
Vitamin D Helps Bone Health by Regulating Calcium and Phosphorus

Once in an active form, vitamin D acts as a hormone and regulates two important bone minerals, calcium and phosphorus. Vitamin D stimulates the absorption of calcium and phosphorus in the intestinal tract, helping to keep the levels of these minerals within a healthy range in your blood. Because of its role in regulating these minerals, vitamin D helps to build and maintain your bones.

Although phosphorus deficiency is very rare, dietary calcium deficiencies do occur, causing blood levels of calcium to drop. When this happens, vitamin D and **parathyroid hormone** cause calcium

ultraviolet (UV) rays The rays from sunlight that cause the production of vitamin D in the skin.

parathyroid hormone (PTH) The hormone secreted from the parathyroid glands that activates vitamin D formation in the kidney.

to leave your bones to maintain the necessary levels in your blood. Vitamin D then signals your kidneys to decrease the amount of calcium excreted in the urine. All of these actions help to regulate the amount of calcium in your blood.

Vitamin D May Prevent Some Cancers and Other Conditions

The role of vitamin D in preventing cancer has produced interesting but mixed research results. Some research studies suggest that vitamin D may help protect against breast, colon, and prostate cancers.[40] Unfortunately, other studies suggest that some individuals with excessive blood levels of vitamin D may be at higher risk for pancreatic cancer.[41]

Because of this discrepancy, further research is needed to determine whether vitamin D could play a protective role in certain cancers, how much would be protective, and most importantly, if excessive amounts may be detrimental.[42]

Exciting research is also emerging as to the role that vitamin D may play in preventing or treating diabetes, heart disease, high blood pressure, and auto-immunue disorders such as multiple sclerosis, as well as other conditions.[43] Until more is known to confirm the association of vitamin D and these numerous medical conditions, your daily needs are based on the amount needed for healthy bones.

Daily Needs

Most individuals can synthesize some of their needed vitamin D with adequate exposure to the sun. However, the seasons of the year and time of day can affect ultraviolet radiation and vitamin D synthesis in your body.

Also, individuals with darker skin, such as African-Americans, have a higher amount of the skin pigment melanin, which reduces vitamin D production from sunlight. These individuals need a longer period of sun exposure, compared with a person who has less melanin, to derive the same amount of vitamin D. The amounts of cloud cover, smog, and air pollution can all reduce the amount of vitamin D produced in the skin.

Figure 7.11 Vitamin D Content in Selected Foods

keep in mind that the Daily Value (DV) on the Nutrition Facts panel is set at 400 IU, less than the current amount recommended for adults.

Food Sources

One of the easiest ways to get your vitamin D from food is to drink fortified milk, which provides 100 IU, or 2.5 micrograms, of vitamin D per cup. Other than fatty fish (such as sardines and salmon), fortified milk, breakfast cereals, juice, and yogurt, very few foods provide ample amounts of vitamin D (**Figure 7.11**). With this scarcity of naturally occurring vitamin D–rich sources, it isn't surprising that many Americans are not meeting their daily dietary vitamin D needs.[46] For more ideas on how to get vitamin D into your daily diet, see Table Tips "Dynamite Ways to Get Vitamin D."

Too Much or Too Little

Consuming too much vitamin D can cause loss of appetite, weight loss, irregular heart beat, and increased urination.

TableTIPS

Dynamite Ways to Get Vitamin D

Use low-fat milk, not cream, in your hot or iced coffee.

Buy vitamin D–fortified yogurts and have one daily as a snack. Top it with a vitamin D–fortified cereal for another boost of D.

Start your morning with cereal, and douse it with plenty of low-fat or skim milk.

Flake canned salmon over your lunchtime salad.

Make instant hot cocoa with hot milk rather than water.

Although the use of sunscreen with a sun protective factor (SPF) of 8 or more can also block the body's ability to synthesize vitamin D, individuals typically do not apply enough of it, cover all of their skin, or reapply it during the day, so some synthesis likely occurs.[44]

Because of these variables involving sun exposure, your daily vitamin D needs are based on the amount you would need to eat in foods and are not based on the synthesis of vitamin D in your skin from sunlight.

Based on the important roles that vitamin D plays in your body, it is currently recommended that adults age 19 to 70 consume 15 micrograms, or 600 IU, of vitamin D daily. This is a significant increase from previously recommended daily amounts. Also, based on revised Dietary Reference Intakes, adults over the age of 70 should incorporate 20 micrograms, or 800 IU, into their daily consumption.[45]

When you are reading labels to assess the amount of vitamin D in your foods,

CONTINUED

The Storage of Fat-Soluble Vitamins **245**

Vitamin D

The upper level for vitamin D has been set at 4,000 IU (100 micrograms), which is five to six times higher than the daily recommendation.

As with the other fat-soluble vitamins, excess amounts of vitamin D are stored in the fat cells, and an accumulation can reach toxic levels, causing **hypervitaminosis D**. This condition causes overabsorption of calcium from the intestines as well as calcium loss from bones. When both of these symptoms occur, blood calcium levels can become dangerously high.

A chronically high amount of calcium in the blood, or **hypercalcemia** (*hyper* = over, *calc* = calcium, *emia* = blood), can cause damaging calcium deposits in the tissues of your kidneys, lungs, blood vessels, and heart.[47]

The good news is that it is highly unlikely that you will get hypervitaminosis D from foods, even fortified foods. The only exception is fish oils, specifically cod-liver oil, which provides 1,360 IU of vitamin D per tablespoon. Luckily, the less-than-pleasant taste of this oil is a safeguard against overconsumption. A more likely culprit behind hypervitaminosis D is the overuse of vitamin D supplements.

Sun worshippers don't have to worry about getting hypervitaminosis D from the sun (although they should be concerned about the risk of skin cancer). Overexposing the skin to UV rays will eventually destroy the inactive form of vitamin D in the skin, causing the body to shut down production of vitamin D.

Are Rickets a New Problem?

Rickets is a vitamin D deficiency disease that occurs in children. The bones of

hypervitaminosis D A condition resulting from excessive amounts of vitamin D in the body.

hypercalcemia A chronically high amount of calcium in the blood.

rickets A vitamin D deficiency in children, resulting in soft bones.

osteomalacia The adult equivalent of rickets, causing muscle and bone weakness, and pain.

A child with rickets.

children with rickets aren't adequately mineralized with calcium and phosphorus, and this causes them to weaken. Because of their "soft bones," these children develop bowed legs, as they are unable to hold up their own body weight when they are standing upright.[48]

Since milk became fortified with vitamin D in the 1930s, rickets has been considered a rare disease among children in the United States. Unfortunately, research now shows that milk consumption among adolescent girls has declined, and currently American children and adolescents, on average, are not consuming adequate amounts of dietary vitamin D to meet their daily needs.[49]

Changes in the lifestyles of children may also be part of the problem. In a study of over 4,000 children, those who watched more television, played less outside, and biked less to school were shown to have a deficiency of vitamin D in their blood compared with those who were more active outdoors.[50] The

increased concern over skin cancer may also be contributing to less vitamin D synthesis in the body. Skin cancer is the most common form of cancer in the United States, and childhood sun exposure appears to increase the risk of skin cancer in later years. Because of this, organizations such as the Centers for Disease Control and the American Cancer Society have run campaigns that recommend limiting exposure to ultraviolet light. People are encouraged to use sunscreen, wear protective clothing when outdoors, and minimize activities in the sun.[51, 52]

The American Association of Pediatricians also recommends that infants younger than 6 months not be exposed to direct sunlight and that children use sunscreen to avoid sunburns.[53]

Other Vitamin D Deficiency Disorders

Osteomalacia is the adult equivalent of rickets and can cause muscle and bone weakness and pain. The bones can't mineralize properly because there isn't enough calcium and phosphorus available in the blood.[54] Although there may be adequate amounts of these minerals in the diet, the deficiency of vitamin D hampers their absorption.

Vitamin D deficiency and its subsequent effect on decreased calcium absorption can lead to osteoporosis, a condition in which the bones can mineralize properly, but there isn't enough calcium in the diet to maximize the bone density, or mass.

The Roles of the Water-Soluble B Vitamins and Vitamin C

LO 7.7 Describe the role water-soluble vitamins play as coenzymes.

There are nine water-soluble vitamins, and eight of them belong to the vitamin B complex. When initially discovered in the early 1900s, the "water-soluble B" was thought to be one vitamin. After years of research, it became apparent that this was not a single substance but rather many vitamins—thiamin, riboflavin, niacin, vitamin B_6, folate, vitamin B_{12}, pantothenic acid, and biotin—known collectively as the B vitamins. The ninth water-soluble vitamin is vitamin C.

Water-soluble vitamins are different from fat-soluble vitamins in that they dissolve in water, are generally not stored in the body, and are often excreted in the urine. Consumers who take large amounts of water-soluble vitamins in an attempt to beef up their vitamin stores literally end up flushing their vitamins, and their money, down the toilet. Because excess amounts are not stored, most water-soluble vitamins are not toxic. However, routine intakes of excessive amounts can be harmful. Underconsuming the water-soluble vitamins can lead to deficiency symptoms, and because many B vitamins are found in similar food sources, an individual experiencing a deficiency of one B vitamin is likely also deficient in others.

Water-soluble vitamins serve numerous similar functions in the body. The B vitamins share a common role as **coenzymes** (see **Figure 7.12**), helping numerous enzymes produce reactions in your cells. Although vitamins don't provide calories and thus aren't sources of energy, you need many of the B vitamins to use the three energy-yielding nutrients (carbohydrates, proteins, and fat). Each vitamin has other important functions in your body. Vitamin C plays important roles in the immune system and in bone health, in addition to its other functions. Take the Self-Assessment to see if you are consuming foods that are rich in the B vitamins and vitamin C.

LO 7.7 **The Take-Home Message** There are nine water-soluble vitamins: eight B-complex vitamins and vitamin C. All water-soluble vitamins dissolve in water, are generally not stored in the body, and are excreted through the urine. The B-complex vitamins function as coenzymes in energy production and have roles in other important functions. Vitamin C acts as an antioxidant and is necessary for immune system health and bone health.

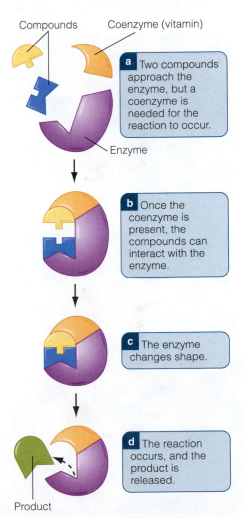

Compounds   Coenzyme (vitamin)

a Two compounds approach the enzyme, but a coenzyme is needed for the reaction to occur.

Enzyme

b Once the coenzyme is present, the compounds can interact with the enzyme.

c The enzyme changes shape.

d The reaction occurs, and the product is released.

Product

Figure 7.12 How B Vitamins Function as Coenzymes

coenzymes Substances needed by enzymes to perform many chemical reactions in your body. Many vitamins act as coenzymes.

exploring
Thiamin (B₁)

What Is Thiamin?

LO 7.8 Name functions, food sources, and deficiency and toxicity symptoms for thiamin.

Thiamin, or vitamin B_1, was the first B vitamin to be discovered. The path to its discovery began in the 1890s in East Asia. A Dutch doctor, Christiaan Eijkman, noticed that chickens and pigeons that ate polished rice (rice with the nutrient- and thiamin-rich outer layer and germ stripped away) developed **polyneuritis** (*poly* = many, *neur* = nerves, *itis* = inflammation). This debilitating nerve condition resulted in the birds not being

able to fly or stand up. Eijkman noted that polyneuritis was also a symptom of beriberi, a similar disease that had been observed in humans.

When Eijkman changed the birds' diet to unpolished rice, with the outer layer and germ intact, the birds were cured.[55] Though Eijkman realized that the unpolished rice eliminated the symptoms, he didn't know why. Finally, in 1911, Casimir Funk identified thiamin as the curative factor in the unpolished rice.

Functions of Thiamin

Thiamin plays a role in the transmission of nerve impulses and so helps keep nerves healthy and functioning properly.

You also need thiamin for the metabolism of carbohydrates and certain amino acids. Thiamin also plays a role in breaking down alcohol in the body.

Daily Needs

The RDA for thiamin for adults is 1.1 milligrams for women and 1.2 milligrams for men. Currently, adult American men consume close to 2 milligrams of thiamin daily, whereas women, on average, eat approximately 1.4 milligrams daily, so both groups are meeting their daily needs.[56]

Food Sources

Enriched and whole-grain foods, such as bread and bread products, ready-to-eat cereals, pasta, and rice, and combined foods, such as sandwiches, are the biggest contributors of thiamin in the American diet (**Figure 7.13**). A medium-sized bowl

of ready-to-eat cereal in the morning and a sandwich at lunch will just about meet your daily thiamin requirement.

Pork is the richest source of naturally occurring thiamin. For more ideas on how to get thiamin into your daily diet, see Table Tips "Thrive on Thiamin."

Too Much or Too Little

There are no known toxicity symptoms from consuming too much thiamin from food or supplements, so no upper level has been set.

The disease that occurs in humans who are deficient in thiamin is **beriberi**. There are two types of beriberi. Wet beriberi affects the cardiovascular system, so symptoms often include a rapid heart beat, shortness of breath, and edema (swelling) in a person's calves and feet. Dry beriberi affects the nervous system, so symptoms may include difficulty in walking, tingling and loss of feeling in the hands and feet, confusion, and problems with coordination.[57] The populations of poor countries with an inadequate food supply rely heavily on refined grains that are not enriched (recall that enriched grains have the B vitamins thiamin,

polyneuritis Inflammation of the peripheral nerves.

beriberi A thiamin deficiency that can affect the cardiovascular and nervous systems and results in weakness in the body.

Figure 7.13 **Thiamin Content in Selected Foods**

Thiamin — Milligrams (mg) of

Peas, boiled, 1 cup — 0.4
Oatmeal, cooked, ½ cup — 0.09
Rice, brown, cooked, ½ cup — 0.1
Wheat bread, 1 slice — 0.14
Pasta (spaghetti), enriched, cooked ½ cup — 0.19
Wheat crackers, 1 oz — 0.19
Pretzels, hard, 10 pretzels — 0.3
Bagel, medium, ½ — 0.32
Ready-to-eat cereal, whole wheat, ¾ cup — 0.38
Pistachios, dry roasted, ½ oz — 0.1
Lentils, boiled, 1 cup — 0.33
Beans, black, cooked, 1 cup — 0.42
Ham, extra lean, 2 oz — 0.43
Pork, center loin, lean, broiled, 3 oz — 0.53
Men 19 to 50 years — 1.2
Women 19 to 50 years — 1.1

Vegetables | Grains | Protein | Daily Needs

Table TIPS

Thrive on Thiamin

Sprinkle cereal on your yogurt.

Toss pasta with peas. Both foods will boost your thiamin.

Add cooked rice to soups.

Have a sandwich daily.

Enjoy oatmeal for breakfast.

Try a mushroom omelet with feta cheese and spinach to increase your thiamin.

Enjoy a snack of dry-roasted almonds.

riboflavin, niacin, and folic acid, as well as the mineral iron, added to them). These people are more susceptible to a thiamin deficiency and the side effects of beriberi.

In the United States, widespread use of enriched grains means that instances of beriberi are rare. Americans, however, are not completely immune to thiamin deficiencies. Those who chronically abuse alcohol tend to have a poor diet that is probably deficient in thiamin. Alcohol consumption also interferes with the absorption of the small amounts of thiamin that may be in the diet, accelerating its loss from the body. Alcoholics may find themselves battling a thiamin deficiency that can cause beriberi, and chronic alcohol abuse can lead to an advanced form of thiamin deficiency called **Wernicke-Korsakoff syndrome**. The syndrome is a progressively damaging brain disorder that can cause mental confusion and memory loss, loss of muscle coordination, leg tremors, abnormal eye movements, and hallucinations.

Edema is one of the symptoms of beriberi.

Although some of these symptoms can be reversed after the person is medically treated with thiamin, some of the memory loss may be permanent.[58]

Wernicke-Korsakoff syndrome
A progressively damaging brain disorder due to chronic thiamin deficiency.

The Roles of the Water-Soluble B Vitamins and Vitamin C   **249**

Riboflavin (B$_2$)

What Is Riboflavin?

LO 7.9 Name functions, food sources, and deficiency and toxicity symptoms for riboflavin.

Riboflavin, also known as vitamin B$_2$, is a light-sensitive B vitamin that is abundant in milk. One of the reasons that milk is packaged in opaque bottles or cardboard containers is to prevent its riboflavin content from being destroyed by light.

Not so long ago, milk made its way to a household not via the grocery store cooler, but by way of a daily visit from a milkman in the early hours of the morning. At each delivery, the milkman placed the clear glass milk bottles inside a covered "milk box" outside the home. The milk box helped protect the light-sensitive riboflavin in the milk from being destroyed by the morning sunlight. Sunlight destroys riboflavin quickly. In fact, just 30 minutes of midday summer sun will destroy more than 30 percent of the riboflavin in glass-bottled milk.[59]

Functions of Riboflavin

Your body needs riboflavin to turn the carbohydrates, proteins, and fats that you eat into energy, and to keep the cells in your body healthy. Riboflavin also enhances the functions of other B vitamins, such as niacin and B$_{12}$.

Daily Needs

You need to consume a little over 1 milligram of riboflavin daily to be healthy.

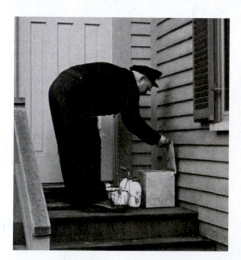

Adult males should consume 1.3 milligrams and females, 1.1 milligrams of riboflavin, every day. Americans, on average, typically exceed their daily needs.[60]

Food Sources

Milk and yogurt are the most popular sources of riboflavin in the diets of American adults, followed by enriched cereals and grains (**Figure 7.14**). A breakfast of cereal and milk and a lunchtime pita sandwich and yogurt will meet your riboflavin needs for the day. For more ideas on how to get riboflavin into your daily diet, see Table Tips "Rally Your Riboflavin."

Too Much or Too Little

Your body has a limited ability to absorb riboflavin, so excessive amounts are

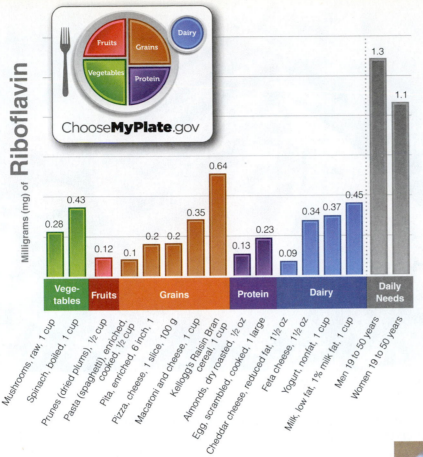

Riboflavin

Milligrams (mg) of

ChooseMyPlate.gov

| Vegetables | Fruits | Grains | Protein | Dairy | Daily Needs |

- Mushrooms, raw, 1 cup — 0.28
- Spinach, boiled, 1 cup — 0.43
- Prunes (dried plums), ½ cup — 0.12
- Pasta (spaghetti) enriched, cooked, ½ cup — 0.1
- Pita, enriched, 6 inch, 1 — 0.2
- Pizza, cheese, 1 slice, 100 g — 0.2
- Macaroni and cheese, 1 cup — 0.35
- Kellogg's Raisin Bran cereal, 1 cup — 0.64
- Almonds, dry roasted, ½ oz — 0.13
- Egg, scrambled, cooked, 1 large — 0.23
- Cheddar cheese, reduced fat, 1½ oz — 0.09
- Feta cheese, 1½ oz — 0.34
- Yogurt, nonfat, 1 cup — 0.37
- Milk, low fat, 1% milk fat, 1 cup — 0.45
- Men 19 to 50 years — 1.3
- Women 19 to 50 years — 1.1

Figure 7.14 Riboflavin Content in Selected Foods

Table TIPS

Rally Your Riboflavin

Have a glass of milk with your meals.

A yogurt snack is a riboflavin snack.

Add spinach to your salad for a riboflavin bonus.

Enriched pasta will enrich your meal with riboflavin.

Macaroni and cheese provides a double source of riboflavin from the pasta and the cheese.

excreted in urine. No upper level for riboflavin has been determined. However, because riboflavin is a bright yellow compound, consuming large amounts through supplements will turn urine as yellow as a school bus. While this isn't dangerous to your health, it isn't beneficial either, so you should skip the supplements and pour yourself a glass of milk instead.

If you don't consume enough of this B vitamin, the cells in the tissues that line your throat, mouth, tongue, and lips will be the first to signal a deficiency. Your throat would be sore, the inside of your mouth would swell, your tongue would be inflamed and look purplish red, and your lips would be dry, cracked, and scaly. Deficiencies are rarely seen in healthy individuals who eat a balanced diet.

An inflamed tongue (glossitis) is one symptom of a riboflavin deficiency.

exploring
Niacin (B₃)

What Is Niacin?

LO 7.10 Name functions, food sources, and deficiency and toxicity symptoms for niacin.

Niacin, or vitamin B₃, is the generic term for **nicotinic acid** and **nicotinamide**, which are the two active forms of niacin that are derived from foods.

Functions of Niacin

Niacin Is Needed to Use the Energy in Your Food

Niacin is another nutrient your body needs in order to use carbohydrates, proteins, and fats. Without niacin, you wouldn't be able to create energy from the foods that you eat. Niacin is also needed to synthesize fat and cholesterol.

Other Functions of Niacin

Niacin is needed to keep your skin cells healthy and your digestive system functioning properly.

Niacin has been shown to lower the total amount of cholesterol in the blood and the "bad" LDL cholesterol carrier. It can also lower high levels of fat (triglycerides) in the blood and simultaneously raise the level of the "good" HDL cholesterol carrier. The nicotinic acid form of niacin is sometimes prescribed by physicians for patients with high blood cholesterol levels. When niacin is used to treat high blood cholesterol, it is considered a drug. The amount prescribed by a physician is often more than 50 times the upper level for niacin.

nicotinic acid One of the two active forms of niacin that are derived from foods.

nicotinamide One of the two active forms of niacin that are derived from foods.

tryptophan An amino acid that can be converted to niacin in the body.

niacin equivalents (NE) A measurement that reflects the amount of niacin and tryptophan in foods that can be used to synthesize niacin.

flushing A reddish coloring of the face, arms, and chest.

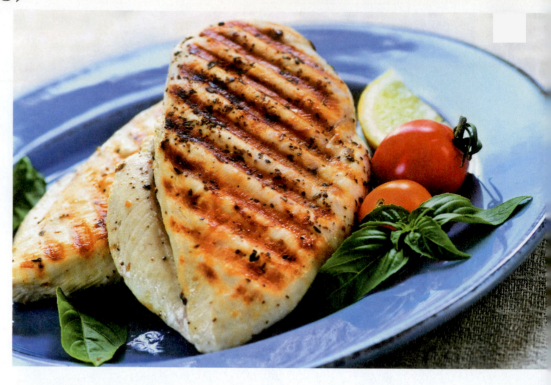

Note that you should *never* consume high amounts of niacin unless a physician is monitoring you.

Daily Needs

The recommended daily amount for adults is 14 milligrams for women and 16 milligrams for men, an amount set to prevent the deficiency disease pellagra. American adults, on average, far exceed their daily niacin needs.[61]

Niacin is found in many foods, but it can also be synthesized in the body from the amino acid **tryptophan**. For this reason, your daily niacin needs are measured in **niacin equivalents (NE)**. It is estimated that 60 milligrams of tryptophan can be converted to 1 milligram of niacin or 1 milligram NE.

Food Sources

Niacin is found in meat, fish, poultry, enriched whole-grain breads and bread products, and fortified cereals (**Figure 7.15**). Protein-rich foods, particularly animal foods such as meat, are good sources of tryptophan and thus of niacin. However, if you are falling short of both your dietary protein and niacin, tryptophan will first be used to make protein in your body, at the expense of your niacin needs.[62]

As with thiamin, your niacin needs are probably met after you eat your breakfast and lunch, especially since similar foods contain both vitamins. For more ideas on how to get niacin into your daily diet, see Table Tips "Nail Your Niacin."

Too Much or Too Little

As with most water-soluble vitamins, there isn't any known danger from consuming too much niacin from foods such as meat and enriched grains. However, overconsuming niacin by taking supplements or eating too many overly fortified foods can cause **flushing**, a reddish coloring of the face, arms, and chest. Too much niacin consumption can also cause nausea and vomiting, be toxic to your liver, and raise your blood glucose levels.

The upper level for niacin for adults is 35 milligrams to prevent flushing, the first side effect to be observed when too much niacin is consumed. This upper

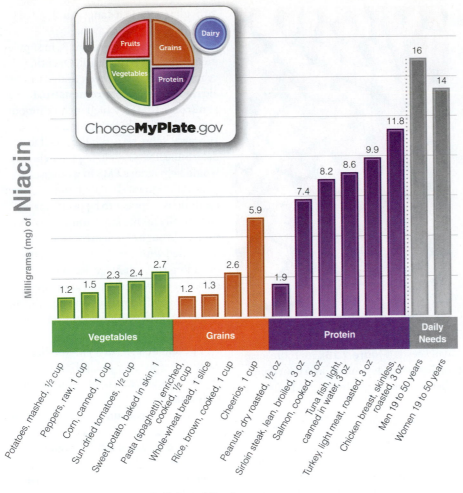

Figure 7.15 Niacin Content in Selected Foods

Chart: Milligrams (mg) of Niacin

ChooseMyPlate.gov

Vegetables
- Potatoes, mashed, 1/2 cup: 1.2
- Peppers, raw, 1 cup: 1.5
- Corn, canned, 1 cup: 2.3
- Sun-dried tomatoes, 1/2 cup: 2.4
- Sweet potato, baked in skin, 1: 2.7

Grains
- Pasta (spaghetti), enriched, cooked, 1/2 cup: 1.2
- Whole-wheat bread, 1 slice: 1.3
- Rice, brown, cooked, 1 cup: 2.6
- Cheerios, 1 cup: 5.9

Protein
- Peanuts, dry roasted, 1/2 oz: 1.9
- Sirloin steak, lean, broiled, 3 oz: 7.4
- Salmon, cooked, 3 oz: 8.2
- Tuna fish, light, canned in water, 3 oz: 8.6
- Turkey, light meat, roasted, 3 oz: 9.9
- Chicken breast, skinless, roasted, 3 oz: 11.8

Daily Needs
- Men 19 to 50 years: 16
- Women 19 to 50 years: 14

Inflamed skin (dermatitis) can result from pellagra.

pellagra The disease caused by a deficiency of niacin in the body.

dermatitis Inflammation or irritation of the skin.

dementia Loss of memory along with confusion and disorientation.

level applies only to healthy individuals. It may be too high for those with certain medical conditions, such as diabetes mellitus and liver disease.[63]

Too little niacin in the diet can result in the deficiency disease called **pellagra**.

In the early 1900s, pellagra was widespread among the poor living in the southern United States, where people relied on corn—a poor source of niacin—as a dietary staple. The symptoms of pellagra—**dermatitis** (inflammation or irritation of the skin), **dementia** (loss of memory along with confusion and disorientation), and **d**iarrhea—led to its being known as the disease of the three Ds. A fourth D, **d**eath, was often associated with the disease.

Once other cereal grains were available, pellagra disappeared as a widespread disease in the United States. The niacin in the grains was later identified as the curative factor for pellagra. Although no longer common in the United States, pellagra does occur among individuals who abuse alcohol and have a very poor diet.

exploring
Vitamin B₆

What Is Vitamin B₆?

LO 7.11 Name functions, food sources, and deficiency and toxicity symptoms for vitamin B₆.

Vitamin B₆ is a collective name for several related compounds, including **pyridoxine**, the major form found in plant foods and the form used in supplements and fortified foods.[64] Two other forms, pyridoxal and pyridoxamine, are found in animal food sources such as chicken and meat.

Functions of Vitamin B₆

Vitamin B₆ Is an Active Coenzyme

Vitamin B₆ acts as a coenzyme with more than 100 enzymes involved in the metabolism of proteins. It is needed to create non-essential amino acids and to convert the amino acid tryptophan to niacin.[65] Vitamin B₆ also helps your body metabolize fats and carbohydrates and break down glycogen, the storage form of glucose.

Other Functions of B₆

Vitamin B₆ is needed to make the oxygen-carrying hemoglobin in your red blood cells and to keep your immune and nervous systems healthy.[66]

Daily Needs

Adult women need 1.3 to 1.5 milligrams and men need 1.3 to 1.7 milligrams of vitamin B₆ daily, depending on their age.

Food Sources

Because vitamin B₆ is found in so many foods, including ready-to-eat cereals, meat, fish, poultry, many vegetables and fruits, nuts, peanut butter, and other legumes, Americans on average easily meet their

pyridoxine The major form of vitamin B₆ found in plants foods, supplements, and fortified foods.

premenstrual syndrome (PMS) A variety of symptoms such as moodiness, irritability, bloating, and anxiety that some women may experience during the menstrual cycle.

anemia A condition in which your blood has a lower than normal number of red blood cells than it should be to be healthy.

daily needs (**Figure 7.16**). For more ideas on how to get vitamin B₆ into your daily diet, see Table Tips "Beam with B₆."

Too Much or Too Little

To protect against potential nerve damage, the upper level for vitamin B₆ is set at 100 milligrams daily for adults over the age of 19. Luckily, it would be extremely difficult to take in a dangerous level of vitamin B₆ from food alone.

However, taking vitamin B₆ in supplement form can be harmful. Over the years, vitamin B₆ has been touted to aid the symptoms of **premenstrual syndrome (PMS)**, which include moodiness, irritability, bloating, and anxiety. However, more research is needed to determine if vitamin B₆ supplements would help reduce PMS in women.

While high intakes of vitamin B₆ from foods do not appear to be problematic, chronically taking large amounts of vitamin B₆ through supplements has been associated with a variety of ill effects, including nerve damage, losing control of bodily movements, and gastrointestinal issues such as nausea and heartburn. Typically these symptoms subside once supplement consumption stops.[67]

The telltale signs of a vitamin B₆ deficiency are a sore tongue, inflammation of the skin, depression, confusion, and possibly **anemia**.

Those who consume too much alcohol are more likely to fall short of their needs. Not only does alcohol cause your body to lose vitamin B₆, but those suffering from alcoholism are likely to have an unbalanced diet, with little variety.

Milligrams (mg) of Vitamin B₆

Category	Food	mg
Vegetables	Baked potato, with skin, 1 small	0.29
Vegetables	Broccoli, cooked, 1 cup	0.31
Vegetables	Winter squash, baked, 1 cup	0.33
Vegetables	Sweet red pepper, raw, 1 cup	0.43
Vegetables	Spinach, cooked, 1 cup	0.44
Fruits	Prunes (dried plums), 1/2 cup	0.27
Fruits	Banana, medium	0.43
Grains	Barley, cooked, 1/2 cup	0.1
Protein	Kidney beans, cooked, 1/4 cup	0.1
Protein	Pinto beans, cooked, 1/4 cup	0.1
Protein	Flounder, cooked, 3 oz	0.1
Protein	Peanut butter, 1 tlbs	0.1
Protein	Hamburger, lean, 3 oz	0.35
Protein	Chicken breast, skinless, roasted, 3 oz	0.52
Protein	Chickpeas, canned, 1 cup	1.1
Daily Needs	Adults 19 to 50 years	1.3

Figure 7.16 Vitamin B₆ Content in Selected Foods

TableTIPS

Beam with B₆

Have a stuffed baked potato with steamed broccoli and grilled chicken for lunch.

Grab a banana for a midmorning snack.

Add cooked barley to your soup.

Snack on prunes.

Add kidney beans to your chili.

Sprinkle garbanzo beans onto your salad for a Vitamin B₆ addition.

Try steamed spinach with your dinner.

Pack peanuts and dried fruits for a snack.

exploring
Folate

What Is Folate?

LO 7.12 Name functions, food sources, and deficiency and toxicity symptoms for folate.

There are two forms of the vitamin **folate**: the naturally occurring folate in foods and the synthetic form, **folic acid**, which is added to foods (such as ready-to-eat cereals and grains) and found in supplements. (A very small amount of folic acid can occur naturally in foods. But, for practical purposes here, *folic acid* refers to the synthetic variety.)

Functions of Folate

Folate Is Vital for DNA Synthesis

Folate is vital to making the DNA in your cells. If the synthesis of DNA is disrupted, your body's ability to create and maintain new cells is impaired.[68] For this reason, folate plays many important roles, from maintaining healthy blood cells and preventing birth defects to possibly fighting cancer. Folate also helps your body use amino acids and is needed to help red blood cells divide and increase in adequate numbers.

folate The naturally occurring vitamin found in foods.

folic acid The form of folate used in vitamin supplements and fortification of foods.

CONTINUED ▶

Folate

FOLATE

Folate Prevents Birth Defects

Folate plays an extremely important role during pregnancy, particularly in the first few weeks after conception, often before the mother knows she is pregnant. Folate is needed to create new cells so that the baby can grow and develop. A deficiency during pregnancy can result in birth defects called **neural tube defects**. The neural tube forms the baby's spine, brain, and skull and is formed during the first 12 weeks of gestation. If the neural tube doesn't develop properly, two common birth defects, **anencephaly** and **spina bifida**, can occur. In anencephaly, the brain doesn't completely form, so the baby can't move, hear, think, or function. An infant with anencephaly dies soon after birth. In spina bifida (see photo), the baby's spinal cord and backbone aren't properly developed, causing physical disabilities, such as the inability to walk.[69] Folic acid could possibly reduce the risk of these birth defects by 50 to 60 percent if consumed at least the month prior to conception and during the early part of pregnancy.[70]

Infant with spina bifida.

neural tube defects Any major birth defect of the central nervous system, including the brain, caused by failure of the neural tube to properly close during fetal development.

anencephaly A neural tube defect that results in the absence of major parts of the brain and spinal cord.

spina bifida A serious birth defect in which the spinal cord is malformed and lacks the protective membrane coat.

dietary folate equivalents (DFE) A measurement used to express the amount of folate in a food or supplement.

Folate Reduces Some Cancer Risks

Inadequate amounts of folate in the body can disrupt the cell's DNA, potentially triggering the development of cancer. While research has shown that an adequate intake of folate may help reduce the risk of certain cancers, specifically colon cancer, some studies suggest that folate supplements may actually increase the risk of prostate cancer.[71] This suggests that while some may be good, more (through supplements) may not be better.

Daily Needs

Your body absorbs the synthetic folic acid more easily than it absorbs naturally occurring folate. In fact, synthetic folic acid is absorbed 1.7 times more efficiently than most folate that is found naturally in foods.[72] Because of this, your folate needs are measured in **dietary folate equivalents (DFE)**. Most adults should consume 400 micrograms DFE of folate daily.

While the foods in your diet analysis program database list the micrograms of folate as DFE, the Nutrition Facts panel on the food label doesn't make this distinction. To convert the micrograms of folic acid found on the food labels of foods with folic acid added, such as enriched pasta, rice, cereals, and bread, to dietary folate equivalents, multiply the amount listed on the label by 1.7:

$$100\ \mu g \times 1.7 = 170\ \mu g\ DFE$$

Women who are planning to become pregnant should consume 400 micrograms of synthetic folic acid daily from fortified foods or supplements, along with a diet high in naturally occurring folate. Women with a family history of neural tube defects should, under the guidance of their physicians, take even larger amounts.[73] Because 50 percent of pregnancies in the United States are unplanned, any woman who may become pregnant is advised to follow these same recommendations.

Food Sources

Since 1998, the FDA has mandated that folic acid be added to all enriched grains and cereal products. This enrichment program has reduced the incidence of neural tube defects by 25 to 30 percent.[74] Enriched pasta, rice, breads and cereals, legumes (dried peas and beans), leafy green vegetables (spinach, lettuce, collards), broccoli, asparagus, and orange juice are all good sources of this vitamin (**Figure 7.17**). For more ideas on how to get folate into your daily diet, see Table Tips "Fulfill Your Folate Needs."

Too Much or Too Little

There isn't any danger in consuming excessive amounts of naturally occurring folate in foods. However, consuming too much folic acid, either through supplements or fortified foods, can be harmful for individuals who are deficient in vitamin B_{12}. A vitamin B_{12} deficiency can cause anemia and, more dangerous, crippling and irreversible nerve damage. Too much folate in the diet masks the symptoms of B_{12}-deficiency anemia and may even exacerbate the anemia. Though the folate can correct anemia, the nerve damage due to the vitamin B_{12} deficiency persists. This delays a proper diagnosis and corrective therapy with vitamin B_{12}. By the time the person is given the vitamin B_{12}, irreversible nerve damage may have

Figure 7.17 **Folate Content in Selected Foods**

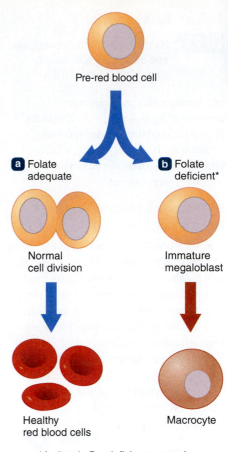

a Folate adequate

Normal cell division

Healthy red blood cells

b Folate deficient*

Immature megaloblast

Macrocyte

*A vitamin B₁₂ deficiency can also cause the formation of macrocytes.

Figure 7.18 **Altered Red Blood Cells with Folate Deficiency**

Table TIPS

Fulfill Your Folate Needs

Have a bowl of cereal in the morning.

Add chickpeas to your salad.

Enjoy a tossed salad with your lunch.

Add fresh spinach leaves to your sandwich.

Have a handful of crackers as a late afternoon snack.

occurred. While, as you read, low folate intake may be associated with increased cancer risk, studies suggest that folate consumption double the DRI or even higher may also increase the risk of cancer.[75]

A folate deficiency can also result in abnormally large and immature blood cells known as **megaloblasts** (*megalo = large*). These megaloblasts develop into abnormally large red blood cells, or **macrocytes**, that have a diminished oxygen-carrying capacity. Eventually, **macrocytic anemia** causes a person to feel tired, weak, and irritable and to experience shortness of breath. Because folate acts with vitamin B₁₂ to produce healthy red blood cells, a deficiency of either vitamin can lead to macrocytic anemia (**Figure 7.18**).

An upper level of 1,000 micrograms has been set for folic acid from enriched and fortified foods and supplements to safeguard those who may be unknowingly deficient in vitamin B₁₂.

megaloblasts Large, immature red blood cells.

macrocytes Abnormally large cells such as red blood cells.

macrocytic anemia A form of anemia characterized by large, immature red blood cells, due to a vitamin B₁₂ deficiency.

exploring
Vitamin B$_{12}$

What Is Vitamin B$_{12}$?

LO 7.13 Name functions, food sources, and deficiency and toxicity symptoms for vitamin B$_{12}$.

The family of compounds referred to as vitamin B$_{12}$ is also called cobalamin because it contains the metal cobalt.[76] Vitamin B$_{12}$ is the only water-soluble vitamin that can be stored in your body, primarily in your liver.

B$_{12}$ Needs Intrinsic Factor to Be Absorbed

A protein produced in your stomach called **intrinsic factor** is needed to promote vitamin B$_{12}$ absorption. Intrinsic factor binds with vitamin B$_{12}$ in your small intestine, where the vitamin is absorbed. Individuals who cannot produce intrinsic factor are unable to absorb vitamin B$_{12}$ and are diagnosed with **pernicious anemia** (*pernicious* = harmful). Individuals with this condition are given regular shots of vitamin B$_{12}$, which inject the vitamin directly into the blood, bypassing the intestine. Because your body stores plenty of vitamin B$_{12}$ in the liver, the symptoms of pernicious anemia can take years to develop.

intrinsic factor (IF) A protein secreted by the stomach that helps in the absorption of vitamin B$_{12}$.

pernicious anemia A form of anemia characterized by large, immature red blood cells, due to a lack of intrinsic factor.

Functions of Vitamin B$_{12}$
Vitamin B$_{12}$ Is Vital for Healthy Nerves and Red Blood Cells

Your body needs vitamin B$_{12}$ to use certain fatty acids and amino acids and to make the DNA in your cells. Vitamin B$_{12}$ is also needed for healthy nerves and tissues. Like folate, vitamin B$_{12}$ plays an important role in keeping your cells, particularly your red blood cells, healthy.[77]

Daily Needs

Adults need 2.4 micrograms of vitamin B$_{12}$ daily. American adults, on average, consume more than 4 micrograms daily.

The body's ability to absorb naturally occurring vitamin B$_{12}$ from foods diminishes with age. This decline appears to be due to a reduction in the acidic juices in the stomach, which are needed to break the bonds that bind the B$_{12}$ to the proteins in food. If the bonds aren't broken, the vitamin can't be released. Up to 30 percent of individuals over the age of 50 experience this decline in acidic juices in their stomachs. Not surprisingly, the

pernicious anemia associated with a vitamin B$_{12}$ deficiency occurs in about 1 to 2 percent of older adults.[78]

With less acid present, the bacteria normally found in the intestines aren't properly destroyed and so tend to overgrow. This abundance of bacteria feed on vitamin B$_{12}$, diminishing the amount of the vitamin that may be available. Luckily, the synthetic form of vitamin B$_{12}$ that is used in fortified foods and supplements isn't bound to a protein, so it doesn't depend on your stomach secretions to be absorbed. (Synthetic vitamin B$_{12}$ still needs intrinsic factor to be absorbed.)

Because the synthetic variety is a more reliable source, individuals over the age of 50 should meet their vitamin B$_{12}$ needs primarily from fortified foods or a supplement.[79]

Food Sources

Naturally occurring vitamin B$_{12}$ is found only in foods from animal sources, such as meat, fish, poultry, and dairy products. (See **Figure 7.19**.) A varied diet that includes the minimum recommended servings of these food groups will easily meet your daily needs.

Synthetic vitamin B$_{12}$ is found in fortified soy milk and some ready-to-eat cereals, which are ideal sources for older adults and strict vegetarians, who avoid all foods from animal sources. If you are relying solely on fortified foods to

Figure 7.19 **Vitamin B₁₂ Content in Selected Foods**

Microgram (µg) of **Vitamin B₁₂**

Food	µg
Total Raisin Bran Cereal, 1 cup	6.0
Turkey breast, 3 oz	0.08
Chicken, dark meat, without skin, cooked, 3 oz	0.3
Egg, hard cooked, 1 large	0.6
Soy milk, calcium fortified, 1 cup	2.0
Hamburger, 90% lean, broiled, 3 oz	2.1
Tuna, light, canned in water, 3 oz	2.5
Salmon, cooked, 3 oz	4.8
Mozzarella cheese, part skim, 1½ oz	0.4
Cottage cheese, low fat, 1% milk fat, ½ cup	0.7
Feta cheese, 1½ oz	0.7
Milk, low fat, 1% milk fat, 1 cup	1.2
Yogurt, nonfat, plain, 8 oz	1.4
Adults 19 to 50 years (Daily Needs)	2.4

Categories: Grains, Protein, Dairy, Daily Needs

meet your vitamin B₁₂ needs, continually check the labels on these products to make sure they haven't unexpectedly been reformulated to exclude the vitamin. For more ideas on how to get vitamin B₁₂ into your daily diet, see Table Tips "Boost Your B₁₂."

Too Much or Too Little

At present, there are no known risks of consuming too much vitamin B₁₂ from foods, fortified foods, or supplements, and no upper level has been set. There is also no known

benefit from taking B₁₂ supplements if your diet contains foods from animal sources and/or fortified foods.

A Vitamin B₁₂ Deficiency Can Cause Macrocytic Anemia

Because vitamin B₁₂ and folate work closely together to make healthy red blood cells, a vitamin B₁₂ deficiency can cause macrocytic anemia, the same type of anemia caused by a folate deficiency. In macrocytic anemia due to a vitamin B₁₂ deficiency, there is enough folate available for red blood cells to divide, but the folate

can't be utilized properly because there isn't enough vitamin B₁₂ available. In fact, the true cause of macrocytic anemia is more likely a B₁₂ deficiency than a folate deficiency.

Because pernicious anemia (caused by a lack of intrinsic factor) is a type of macrocytic anemia, its initial symptoms are the same as those seen in folate deficiency: fatigue and shortness of breath.

Vitamin B₁₂ is needed to protect nerve cells, including those in your brain and spine, so one long-term consequence of pernicious anemia is nerve damage marked by tingling and numbness in the arms and legs and the inability to maintain balance. If diagnosed early enough, these symptoms can be reversed with treatments of vitamin B₁₂.

Vitamin C

What Is Vitamin C?

LO 7.14 Name functions, food sources, and deficiency and toxicity symptoms for vitamin C.

You don't have to go out of your way to ensure that your dog's daily chow contains enough vitamin C. Dogs and many other animals possess an enzyme that can synthesize vitamin C from glucose. Humans, however, lack the necessary enzyme for this conversion and have to rely on food to meet their daily vitamin C needs.[80]

Functions of Vitamin C

Vitamin C Acts as a Coenzyme

Vitamin C, also known as **ascorbic acid**, acts as a coenzyme that is needed to synthesize and use certain amino acids. In particular, vitamin C is needed to make collagen, the most abundant protein in your body. Collagen is plentiful in your connective tissue, which supports and connects all your body parts, so this protein is needed for healthy bones, teeth, skin, and

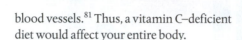

blood vessels.[81] Thus, a vitamin C–deficient diet would affect your entire body.

Vitamin C Acts as an Antioxidant

Like beta-carotene and vitamin E, vitamin C acts an antioxidant that may help reduce the risk of chronic diseases such as heart disease and cancer. It also helps you absorb the iron in plant foods such as grains and cereals and break down histamine, the component behind the inflammation seen in many allergic reactions.[82]

Vitamin C Boosts Your Immune System

Vitamin C helps keep your immune system healthy by enabling your body to make white blood cells, like the ones shown in the photo. These blood cells

fight infections, and this immune-boosting role has fostered the belief that high doses of vitamin C can cure the common cold. (The Examining the Evidence feature "Gesundheit! Myths and Facts about the Common Cold" on pages 266–267 takes a look at this theory.)

Daily Needs

Women need to consume 75 milligrams of vitamin C daily, and men need to consume 90 milligrams daily to meet their needs.

Smoking accelerates the breakdown and elimination of vitamin C from the body, so smokers need to consume an additional 35 milligrams of vitamin C every day to make up for these losses.[83]

Food Sources

Most Americans can meet their vitamin C needs by consuming fruits and vegetables. One serving of either orange or grapefruit juice will just about meet an adult's daily needs. Tomatoes, peppers, potatoes, broccoli, oranges, and cantaloupe are also excellent sources (**Figure 7.20**). For more ideas on how to get vitamin C into your daily diet, see Table Tips "Juicy Ways to Get Vitamin C."

Too Much or Too Little

Though excessive amounts of vitamin C aren't known to be toxic, consuming more than 3,000 milligrams daily through the use of supplements has been shown to cause nausea, stomach cramps, and diarrhea.

The upper level for vitamin C for adults is set at 2,000 milligrams to avoid the intestinal discomfort that excessive amounts of the vitamin can cause. Too much vitamin C can also lead to the

Vitamin C contributes to healthy, glowing skin by facilitating the production of collagen.

White blood cells.

ascorbic acid The active form of vitamin C.

Vitamin C

Milligrams (mg) of

ChooseMyPlate.gov

Fruits Grains Dairy
Vegetables Protein

Vegetables	Fruits	Daily Needs

209
120
102
72
52
35
19 19
17
8

98
79
70
64
58
17

90 75

Vegetables: Tomato, ½ medium · Baked potato, with skin, 1 small · Sweet potato, boiled, 1 · Tomato soup, 1 cup · Peas, frozen, low sodium, cooked, 1 cup · Cauliflower, raw, 1 cup · Vegetable juice, low sodium, 1 cup · Broccoli, boiled, 1 cup · Green pepper, raw, 1 cup · Red pepper, 1 raw

Fruits: Pineapple, chunks, canned, 1 cup · Cantaloupe, 1 cup · Kiwi, 1 · Orange, 1 medium · Grapefruit, sections, 1 · Strawberries, raw, 1 cup

Daily Needs: Men 19 to 50 years · Women 19 to 50 years

Figure 7.20 **Vitamin C Content in Selected Foods**

formation of kidney stones in individuals with a history of kidney disease.

Because vitamin C helps to absorb the form of iron found in plant foods, those with a rare disorder called **hemochromatosis** (*hemo* = blood, *chroma* = color, *osis* = condition), which causes the body to store too much iron, should avoid excessive amounts of vitamin C. Iron toxicity is extremely dangerous and can damage many organs in your body, including the liver and heart.

For centuries, **scurvy**, the disease of a vitamin C deficiency, was the affliction of sailors on long voyages. After many weeks at sea, sailors would run out of vitamin C–rich produce and then develop the telltale signs of scurvy: swollen and bleeding gums, a rough rash on the skin, coiled or curly arm hairs, and wounds that wouldn't heal. Because vitamin C is needed for healthy blood vessels, a deficiency also often causes purple-colored spots, a sign of skin hemorrhages, to appear on the skin and in mucous membranes of the body such as the lining of the mouth.

In 1753, a British naval surgeon discovered that orange and lemon juice prevented scurvy. Decades later, the British government added lemon or lime juice to their standard rations for sailors to thwart scurvy. In 1919, vitamin C was discovered as the curative factor in these juices.[84]

Vitamin C deficiency can cause skin hemorrhages.

Table TIPS

Juicy Ways to Get Vitamin C

Have at least one citrus fruit (such as an orange or grapefruit) daily.

Put sliced tomatoes on your sandwich.

Enjoy a fruit cup for dessert.

Drink low-sodium vegetable juice for an afternoon refresher.

Add strawberries to your low-fat frozen yogurt.

hemochromatosis A blood disorder characterized by the retention of an excessive amount of iron.

scurvy A disease caused by a deficiency of vitamin C and characterized by bleeding gums and a skin rash.

exploring
Pantothenic Acid and Biotin

LO 7.15 Name functions, food sources, and deficiency and toxicity symptoms for pantothenic acid and biotin.

What Are Pantothenic Acid and Biotin?

Pantothenic acid and biotin are B vitamins.

Functions of Pantothenic Acid and Biotin

Pantothenic acid and biotin aid in the metabolism of the nutrients that provide you with energy: carbohydrates, proteins, and fats.

Daily Needs

Adults need 5 milligrams of pantothenic acid and 30 micrograms of biotin daily.

Food Sources

Both pantothenic acid and biotin are widely available in foods, including whole grains and whole-grain cereals, nuts and legumes, broccoli, peanut butter, meat, milk, and eggs. Most Americans easily meet their needs.[85]

Biotin deficiency is so rare that an accurate list of the amount in foods is hard to find. In addition to its abundance in foods, biotin can be synthesized by the bacteria in your intestinal tract, providing yet another avenue to meet your needs.

Eating a healthy diet to meet all of your other B vitamin needs will ensure that you meet your needs for pantothenic acid and biotin.

Too Much or Too Little

Like many of the other B vitamins, there are no known adverse effects from consuming too much pantothenic acid or biotin. An upper level has not been determined for either of these vitamins.

Although a pantothenic acid deficiency is rare, if you do fall short of your needs, your symptoms might include fatigue, nausea, vomiting, numbness, muscle cramps, and difficulties walking.

During World War II, prisoners of war in Asia experienced a "burning feet" syndrome. The symptoms ranged from heat sensations and tingling on the soles of their feet to a painful burning intense enough to disrupt sleep. Their diet consisted predominantly of nutrient-poor polished rice. A doctor in India who was studying an identical phenomenon in his patients discovered that when he gave them supplements of pantothenic acid, the condition stopped.[86] In both cases, the syndrome was later attributed to a diet deficient in pantothenic acid.

Consuming inadequate amounts of biotin can cause hair loss, skin rash, and feelings of depression, fatigue, and nausea.[87] Though deficiencies are rare, they can occur if you eat a lot of raw egg whites. The protein avidin, found in egg whites, binds with biotin and blocks it from being absorbed in your intestine. Cooking the egg denatures and inactivates the protein, eliminating the problem.[88]

Are There Other Important Vitamin-Like Nutrients?

LO 7.16 Name other vitamin-like substances the body needs.

Choline Is an Essential Nutrient

Choline is an essential nutrient that your body needs for healthy cells and nerves and the transportation of lipids, but it is not classified as a vitamin. Although your body can synthesize it, it does not make enough to meet your daily needs.[89] To be safe, the current dietary recommendation of 425 milligrams for women and 550 milligrams for men is based on the amount needed to protect the liver.

Although choline is widely available in foods, especially milk, liver, eggs, wheat germ, and peanuts, Americans' diets appear to be falling short of this nutrient. Too much choline from supplements can cause sweating and vomiting as well as **hypotension** (*hypo* = low), or low blood pressure. Too much choline can also cause a person to emit an unpleasant fishy odor as the body tries to get rid of the excess. The upper level of 3,500 milligrams for choline has been set to prevent your blood pressure from dropping too low and to keep you from smelling like a fish.

Carnitine, Lipoic Acid, and Inositol Are Vitamin-Like Substances

Certain vitamin-like substances are needed for overall health and important body functions, but they are not considered essential nutrients because your body can synthesize them in adequate amounts without consuming them in foods, and deficiency symptoms are not known to occur in humans.

Carnitine (*carnus* = flesh) is needed to properly utilize fat. It is abundant in foods from animal sources, such as meat and dairy products. Although there is no research to support the claim, carnitine supplements are sometimes promoted to help athletes improve their performance.[90]

Similar to many B vitamins, **lipoic acid** helps your cells generate energy, and it was in fact initially thought to be a vitamin. Lipoic acid is also being studied for its potential role in obesity.[91]

Lastly, **inositol** is needed to keep cell membranes healthy. Inositol can be found in foods from plant sources. As with the other important vitamin-like substances, healthy individuals can synthesize enough inositol to meet their needs, so supplements are not necessary.

Table 7.3 on pages 264–265 provides you with a quick guide to your vitamin needs.

LO 7.16 **The Take-Home Message** Choline, carnitine, lipoic acid, and inositol are vitamin-like substances. Choline is an essential nutrient that is needed for healthy cells and nerves. Americans' diets may be falling short of choline. Carnitine, lipoic acid, and inositol are needed for important body functions and overall health, but are not essential nutrients. Your body can synthesize these substances in adequate amounts, and there are no known deficiency symptoms.

choline A vitamin-like substance needed for healthy cells and nerves.

hypotension Low blood pressure.

carnitine A vitamin-like substance needed to properly utilize fat.

lipoic acid A vitamin-like substance that your body needs for energy production; it may also act as an antioxidant.

inositol A vitamin-like substance synthesized in your body that helps to keep your cells and their membranes healthy.

Table 7.3

Vitamins at a Glance

	Major Functions	Adult DRI, Age 19 to 50 Years	Food Sources	Toxicity Symptoms/UL	Deficiency Symptoms/ Conditions
Fat-Soluble Vitamins					
Vitamin A	Vision, cell differentiation, reproduction, bone health, immune function	700–900 µg RAE/day	Beef liver, fortified dairy products	Compromised bone health, birth defects during pregnancy UL: 3,000 µg RAE/day of preformed vitamin A	Night blindness, xerophthalmia, stunting of bones
Beta-carotene	Provitamin A carotenoid, antioxidant		Sweet potatoes, carrots, winter squash, cantaloupe	Carotenodermia	
Vitamin D	Calcium balance, bone health, cell differentiation, immune system	15 µg (600 IU)/day	Fatty fish (salmon, tuna, sardines) Fortified foods (dairy products, orange juice, cereals)	Hypercalcemia UL: 100 µg (4,000 IU)/day	Rickets and osteomalacia
Vitamin E	Antioxidant, health of cell membranes, heart health	15 mg alpha-tocopherol/day	Vegetable and seed oils, nuts, seeds, fortified cereals, green leafy vegetables	Interference with blood clotting and increased risk of hemorrhage UL: 1,000 mg AT/day from supplements and/or fortified foods	Nerve problems, muscle weakness, and uncontrolled movement of body parts
Vitamin K	Blood clotting, bone health	90–120 µg/day	Green leafy vegetables, soybeans, canola and soybean oils, beef liver	None known	Excessive bleeding
Water-Soluble Vitamins					
Thiamin (B₁)	Coenzyme, needed for nerve function and energy metabolism	1.1–1.2 mg/day	Pork, enriched and fortified foods, whole grains	None known	Beriberi, Wernicke-Korsakoff syndrome
Riboflavin (B₂)	Coenzyme in energy metabolism, enhances function of other B vitamins	1.1–1.3 mg/day	Milk, enriched and fortified grains, whole grains	Can turn urine bright yellow	Sore throat, inflammation of the mouth, tongue, and lips
Niacin (B₃)	Coenzyme in energy metabolism, needed to synthesize fat and cholesterol	14–16 mg/day	Lean meats, fish, poultry, enriched and fortified grains and cereals, whole grains, corn, sweet potatoes	Flushing, nausea, vomiting, toxic to liver, may raise blood glucose levels UL: 35 mg/day	Pellagra, characterized by dermatitis, diarrhea, and dementia

Table 7.3

Vitamins at a Glance (continued)

	Major Functions	Adult DRI, Age 19 to 50 Years	Food Sources	Toxicity Symptoms/UL	Deficiency Symptoms/Conditions
Water-Soluble Vitamins					
Vitamin B$_6$	Coenzyme in energy metabolism, hemoglobin, healthy immune and nervous systems, homocysteine metabolism	1.3–1.7 mg/day	Fortified cereals, meat, fish, poultry, many vegetables and fruits, nuts, peanut butter, and other legumes	Nerve damage, tingling in hands and feet UL: 100 mg/day	Sore tongue, inflammation of skin, depression, possible anemia, confusion
Folate	DNA and red blood cell formation, prevention of specific birth defects, homocysteine metabolism	400 µg DFE/day	Dark green leafy vegetables, enriched pasta, rice, breads and cereals, legumes, orange juice, asparagus, spinach	Masks vitamin B$_{12}$ deficiency UL: 1,000 µg/day from supplements and/or fortified foods	Macrocytic anemia
Vitamin B$_{12}$	Synthesis of new cells, especially red blood cells, healthy nerves and tissues Activates folate	2.4 µg/day	Animal products, including lean meats, fish, poultry, eggs, cheese, fortified foods	None known	Pernicious anemia, macrocytic anemia, nerve damage as indicated by tingling and numbness in the hands and feet
Vitamin C	Collagen formation, antioxidant, enhanced iron absorption, healthy immune system	75–90 mg/day (an additional 35 mg if a smoker)	Citrus fruit, tomatoes, peppers, potatoes, broccoli, cantaloupe	Nausea, diarrhea, stomach cramps UL: 2,000 mg/day	Scurvy; characterized by bleeding gums, skin hemorrhages, coiled or curly arm hairs
Biotin and Pantothenic Acid	Aid in the metabolism of the energy nutrients	Pantothenic acid: 5 mg/day Biotin: 30 µg/day	Both are widespread in foods	No known adverse effects UL has not been set	For pantothenic acid: fatigue, nausea, vomiting, numbness, muscle cramps, and difficulty walking For biotin: hair loss, skin rash, depression, fatigue, nausea

Gesundheit! Myths and Facts about the Common Cold

You probably know the symptoms well. Your nose runs like a leaky faucet and turns beet red from constant wiping. Your head seems stuffed with cotton, and it feels like someone is playing bongo drums under your scalp.

Between coughing and sneezing, you can't get the rest you need to relieve what feels like constant fatigue. The diagnosis? At least one of the more than 200 varieties of cold virus has invaded your body, and you have a cold that could last as long as two weeks.

You're never alone if you have a case of the common cold—Americans will suffer a billion of them this year alone.[1] Colds are the main reason for children to miss school and for adults to miss work annually. Students miss more than 22 million school days every year battling the common cold.[2]

The Truth about Catching a Cold

Contrary to popular belief, you can't catch a cold from being outside on a cold day without a coat or hat. Rather, the only way to catch a cold is to come into contact with a cold virus. Contact can be direct, such as when you hug or shake hands with someone who is carrying the virus; or indirect, such as when you touch an object like a keyboard or telephone contaminated with a cold virus. The next time you touch your nose or rub your eyes, you transfer these germs from your hands into your body.

You can also catch a cold virus by inhaling virus-carrying droplets from a cough or sneeze of someone with the cold.

The increased frequency of colds during the fall and winter is likely due to people spending more time indoors in the close quarters of classrooms, dorm rooms, and the workplace, which makes the sharing of germs easier. The low humidity of the winter air can also cause the inside of your nose to be drier and more permeable to the invasion of these viruses.

Vitamin C and the Common Cold

In the 1970s, a scientist named Linus Pauling theorized that consuming at least 1,000 milligrams of vitamin C daily would prevent the common cold. The latest extensive review of almost 30 controlled studies involving over 11,000 individuals who consumed 200 milligrams or more of vitamin C daily suggests that the regular ingestion of a supplement doesn't prevent healthy individuals from getting a cold.[3] However, this research did show that individuals who are involved in short periods of heavy physical stress, such as marathon runners and skiers, may gain some

How Should You Get Your Vitamins?

LO 7.17 Explain the role of vitamin supplements and fortified foods in your diet.

Store vitamin B–rich whole-wheat flour in an airtight container in your refrigerator or freezer. Because whole-wheat flour contains the germ of the wheat kernel, which is rich in unsaturated fatty acids, it is more susceptible to becoming rancid than refined white flour.

Natural food sources, like fruits and vegetables, have long been advocated as an excellent way to get your vitamins. With advances in fortified foods and supplements, new options became available for meeting your nutrient needs. Let's look next at the pros and cons of each of these.

Foods Are Still the Best Way to Meet Your Vitamin Needs

Because foods provide more than just vitamins (many are also rich in disease-fighting phytochemicals, antioxidants, and fiber), they are the best way to meet your vitamin needs. The substances and nutrients in foods all work together to keep you healthy. For example, the fat in your salad dressing helps you absorb the carotenoids in the carrots in your salad. The vitamin protection against the common cold when routinely taking a supplement. Some research also suggests that regularly consuming vitamin C may reduce the severity of symptoms and decrease the duration of a cold should you catch it.[4] While it is very individualized, the reduction is only about a day *annually*, and it is still unknown what amount is needed to reap this very small benefit.

Other Cold Remedies: The Jury Is Still Out

Recently, other dietary substances, such as the herb *Echinacea* and the mineral

zinc, have emerged as popular treatment strategies for the common cold. *Echinacea* had been used centuries ago by some Native American populations to treat coughs and sore throats. A review of 24 studies did not show any significant difference in the use of *Echinacea* in preventing or reducing the duration of the cold.[5] Results are mixed as to whether the herb can reduce the duration or the severity of cold symptoms. A major issue with using *Echinacea* is that the available supplements on the market vary greatly between the nine different species of the herb as well as the various parts of the plant used in the product.

Zinc may be helpful. In a review of 14 studies, zinc lozenges or syrup were shown to help reduce the duration of colds in healthy people, when consumed within the first 24 hours of the first sign of a cold.[6] But there is a catch. Those taking zinc lozenges may experience nausea and a bad aftertaste in their mouth. More research is needed to determine the correct dosage and usage for the general population, especially those with chronic illnesses. You will learn more about zinc and its role in the immune system in Chapter 8.

What You Can Do

One of the best ways to reduce your chances of catching a cold is to wash your hands frequently with soap and water. This will lower the likelihood of germs being transmitted from your hands to your mouth, nose, or eyes. When soap and water aren't available, gel sanitizers or disposable alcohol-containing hand wipes can be an effective alternative. Covering your mouth and nose when you cough or sneeze and then immediately washing your hands will help you keep from contaminating the people around you.

WHAT DO YOU THINK?

1. Given your knowledge of the functions of vitamin C in the body, why do you think it has been theorized that vitamin C may combat colds?
2. Many people have anecdotal accounts of vitamin C or other supplements preventing or helping them recover from a cold. Why are these accounts not considered scientific evidence?
3. How do folk remedies like the use of vitamin C or *Echinacea* for colds come about, and why do you think so many people trust them?

C–rich tomatoes on your sandwich help you absorb the iron in the wheat bread. The whole is indeed greater than the sum of its parts when it comes to eating a balanced diet to meet your vitamin needs.

The *Dietary Guidelines for Americans* recommend eating a wide variety of foods from each food group with ample amounts of vitamin-rich fruits, vegetables, whole grains, and lean dairy foods. **Figure 7.21** on page 268 shows the estimated intake of each nutrient among all age and gender groups when following the USDA Food Patterns that are used in MyPlate.[92]

If you are falling short of some vitamins in your diet, fortified foods can help make up the difference.

Fortified Foods Can Provide Additional Nutrients, but at a Price

When you pour your morning glass of orange juice, you know that you are getting a significant splash of vitamin C. However, depending on the brand of orange juice, you may also be meeting your vitamin E and vitamin D needs—two nutrients that are not (and never have been) naturally found in oranges. Welcome to the world of fortified foods.

Practical Nutrition VIDEO

When Is a Fruit Smoothie Not a Healthy Smoothie?

Pre-made fruit smoothies may not be as healthy as you think! Scan this QR code with your mobile device to access the video. You can also access the video in MasteringNutrition™.

Percent of Daily Needs Met (Shown as Range)

(y-axis: Percentages — 0, 50, 100, 150, 200, 250, 300, 350, 400, 450)

(x-axis categories: Vitamin B₁₂, Selenium, Riboflavin, Protein, Manganese, Folate, Niacin, Vitamin K, Vitamin B₆, Thiamin, Copper, Zinc, Phosphorus, Vitamin C, Fiber, Vitamin A, Carbohydrate, Calcium, Iron, Magnesium, Choline, Vitamin E, Potassium, Vitamin D)

Figure 7.21 What We Eat in America
With the exception of a few nutrients, a person's daily needs can be met by following the USDA Food Patterns that are recommended in MyPlate. Bars set in green indicate that daily needs are met by following the USDA Food Patterns. Orange bars indicate needs that are not met by following the MyPlate Food Patterns and may need to be supplemented.

Fortified foods can give your diet a vitamin boost.

fortified foods Foods with added nutrients.

Fortified foods—that is, foods that have nutrients added to them—can be a valuable option for individuals whose diets fall short of some nutrients. For instance, someone who doesn't drink milk, such as a strict vegetarian or an individual who is lactose intolerant, may benefit from drinking vitamin D- and calcium-fortified soy milk. Older adults who are inactive, and thus have lower calorie needs, may choose fortified foods to add nutrients, such as vitamins B₁₂ and E, to their limited dietary selections. Women in their childbearing years may look to folic acid–fortified cereals to help them meet their daily needs of this B vitamin.

Fortified foods can do a disservice in the diet if they displace other vitamin- and mineral-rich foods. For example, a sugary orange drink that has vitamin C added to it should not replace vitamin C–rich orange juice. Although the vitamin C content of the two beverages may be the same, the orange-flavored drink doesn't compare well to the juice when it comes to providing other nutrients and phytochemicals. As you can see from **Figure 7.22**, the orange drink is basically orange-flavored water sweetened with 7 teaspoons of sugar and enriched with vitamin C.

A diet containing numerous fortified foods can put you at risk of overconsuming some nutrients. If a heavily fortified food, like some cereals, snack bars, and beverages, claims to contain "100% of the vitamins needed daily," then eating several servings of the food or a combination of several fortified foods is similar to taking several multivitamin supplements. You are more likely to overconsume vitamins from fortified foods than from whole foods.

Figure 7.22 What Are You Pouring in Your Glass?
Although both of these beverages are a good source of vitamin C, they are worlds apart in their nutrition.

Added sugar = 0

Added sugar =

a Pure orange juice is an excellent source of the mineral potassium and doesn't contain any added sugar.

b Orange drink is basically sugar water with vitamin C added to it. A glass will contain the equivalent of 7 teaspoons of added sugar.

= 1 tsp of added sugar

Vitamin Supplements Are Not a Substitute for Healthy Eating

Americans spend more than $13 million on vitamin- and mineral-containing supplements annually, including more than $5 billion on multivitamin/mineral supplements.[93] The aging of the population appears to be one of the forces driving this increase in the use of supplements—older people may use vitamins and minerals in an attempt to mitigate ongoing medical issues.[94]

Vitamin supplements are called supplements for a reason: A vitamin pill or a combined multivitamin and mineral pill may be used to *supplement* your diet. Supplements should never be used to replace a healthy diet. A consistent diet of nonnutritious foods followed by a daily supplement won't transform your less-than-desirable eating habits into a healthy diet. The disease-fighting phytochemicals, fiber, and other substances that your body needs are all missing from a bottle of supplements.

Practical Nutrition VIDEO

Do You Need a Supplement to Meet Your Vitamin C Needs?

For most people and most nutrients, consuming a healthy, varied diet trumps taking supplements. Let Joan show you how. Scan this QR code with your mobile device to access the video. You can also access the video in MasteringNutrition™.

Supplements are useful for people who cannot meet their nutrient needs through a regular, varied diet. Among those who may benefit from taking a dietary supplement are:[95]

- Women of childbearing age who may become pregnant, as they need to consume adequate amounts of folic acid to prevent certain birth defects
- Pregnant and lactating women who can't meet their nutrient needs with foods
- Older individuals, who need adequate amounts of vitamin D and synthetic vitamin B_{12}
- Individuals who do not drink enough milk and/or do not have adequate sun exposure to meet their vitamin D needs
- Individuals on low-calorie diets that limit the amount of vitamins and minerals they can consume through food
- Strict vegetarians, who have limited dietary options for vitamins B_{12} and D and other nutrients
- Individuals with food allergies or lactose intolerance that limit food choices
- Individuals who abuse alcohol, have a poor appetite, have medical conditions such as intestinal disorders, or are taking medications that may increase their need of certain vitamins
- Individuals who are food insecure and those who are eliminating food groups from their diet
- Infants who are breast-fed should receive 400 IU of vitamin D daily until they are consuming at least 1 quart of formula daily. Children age 1 and older should receive 400 IU of vitamin D daily if they consume less than one quart of milk per day. Adolescents who consume less than 400 IU of vitamin D daily from their diet would also benefit from a supplement.

Always talk to your health care professional or a registered dietitian nutritionist (RDN) before taking a vitamin or mineral supplement to make sure it is appropriate based on your medical history, especially if you are taking prescription medications. Supplements can interact or interfere with certain medications. If you regularly eat many fortified foods, the addition of a supplement could cause you to overconsume some nutrients. A meeting with an RDN for a diet checkup can help you decide if a supplement is needed.

See **Table 7.4** for a brief consideration of the pros and cons of relying on foods, supplements, and fortified foods to meet your vitamin needs.

Who's Minding the Vitamin Store?

Dietary supplements, a category that includes vitamins, minerals, and herbs, are regulated less stringently by the Food and Drug Administration (FDA) than are drugs. In 1994, Congress passed the Dietary Supplement Health and Education Act, which shifted the responsibility for determining the quality, effectiveness, and safety of dietary supplements from the FDA to the manufacturers. Unlike drugs, dietary supplements do not require FDA approval before they can be marketed to the public, unless they contain a new ingredient that hadn't been used prior to 1994. Recall from Chapter 2 that supplement manufacturers are legally permitted to make structure/function claims on the labels of dietary supplements. The FDA cannot remove a supplement from the marketplace unless it has been shown to be unsafe or harmful to the consumer.[96]

The FDA is trying to tighten its regulation of dietary supplements to better safeguard the public against harmful products and misleading claims. One way it plans to do this is to improve the criteria that it uses to make enforcement decisions about dietary supplements. The FDA has improved its process for evaluating potential

U.S. Pharmacopeia (USP) A nonprofit organization that sets purity and reliability standards for dietary supplements.

Table 7.4

Foods, Fortified Foods, and Supplements

There are a variety of ways to meet your vitamin needs. Consider the pros and cons to find out the best combination for you.

Foods

Pros: Sources of other nutrients and energy; can supply phytochemicals, antioxidants, and fiber; delicious and satisfying

Cons: Need to shop for and prepare meals; need to plan for in diet

Fortified Foods

Pros: Easy to obtain a specific nutrient; can be delicious and satisfying

Cons: Often more expensive than regular variety; risk of overconsumption of nutrients; can displace a more nutrient-dense food

Supplements

Pros: Easy to obtain; no planning or preparation involved

Cons: Can be expensive; risk of overconsumption of nutrients; lack of antioxidants, phytochemicals, and fiber found naturally in foods; not satisfying

safety concerns and adverse reports that may arise from a variety of sources, including consumers, media reports, consumer groups, and experts. An option exists to help consumers choose among dietary supplements. The **U.S. Pharmacopoeia (USP)** is a nonprofit organization that sets standards for dietary supplements.[97] Although it does *not* endorse or validate health claims that the supplement manufacturers make, it sets standards for the performance, strength, quality, consistency, and purity of dietary supplements. Supplement manufacturers can voluntarily submit their products to the USP's staff of scientists for review. USP verifies supplements through a comprehensive testing and evaluation process and awards its USP Verified Mark only after rigorous facility audits, product documentation reviews, and product testing have been completed and approved.

a The FDA allows the term "high potency" to be used as long as at least two-thirds of the nutrients contain at least 100 percent of the Daily Value.

b All supplements must clearly identify what is in the bottle.

c Always look for the USP seal of approval for quality and purity. Choose the cheapest supplement with the seal to save a few dollars.

d The FDA disclaimer is a reminder that this product doesn't have the FDA seal of approval for effectiveness.

e The net quantity of contents must be listed. The Supplement Facts panel lists the serving size, the vitamins in the supplement, and the amount of the vitamin in each capsule.

f The structure/ function claim explains that vitamin C is beneficial for your immune system.

g The amount of each supplement is also given as a percentage of the Daily Value. Remember, the Daily Value may be higher than you actually need.

h All the ingredients must be listed in descending order by weight.

i The name and address of the manufacturer or distributor must be provided.

Figure 7.23 Supplement Smarts
The FDA has strict guidelines for the information that must appear on any supplement label.

What's a Consumer to Do?

With hundreds of bottles of vitamin and mineral supplements available on the store shelves, you could get dizzy trying to find one that's right for you. The best place to start when picking a supplement is to carefully read the label. The FDA has strict guidelines for the information that must appear on any supplement label. For example, the term "high potency" can be used only if at least two-thirds of the nutrients in the supplement contain at least 100 percent of the daily value (**Figure 7.23**). The label must also clearly identify the contents of the bottle. While a supplement may have the USP seal of approval for quality and purity, it doesn't have the FDA's approval, even if it makes a claim. Supplements must contain a panel that lists the serving size, the number of units in the bottle, the amount of the vitamin in each unit, and the percentage of the Daily Value. All the ingredients must also be listed.

LO 7.17 The Take-Home Message A well-balanced diet that provides adequate calories can meet most individuals' daily vitamin needs. Fortified foods, as part of a healthy diet, can provide extra nutrients for those whose diets fall short. A vitamin supplement is another option for individuals unable to meet their daily vitamin needs. The consumer needs to take care when selecting a dietary supplement and should seek advice and guidance from a qualified health professional.

MADE *over* MADE *better*

Including vegetables in your diet is a good step in the right direction, but sometimes there are improvements that can be made to increase the vitamin content and/or improve the nutritional quality of your meals and snacks.

Here are some typical vitamin-rich foods made over and made nutritionally better!

If you like this. . .	Try this instead!

Creamed Spinach
1 cup: 180 calories
Vitamin A: 600 micrograms RAE

Steamed Spinach
1 cup: 54 calories
Vitamin A: 4,437 micrograms RAE

Fried, Breaded Onion Rings
10 rings: 244 calories
Vitamin C: 0.8 milligrams

Sautéed Onions
1 onion: 115 calories
Vitamin C: 1.6 milligrams

Cheese & Bacon Stuffed Baked Potato
1 loaded potato: 451 calories
Folate: 30 micrograms

Baked Potato
1 plain potato: 161 calories
Folate: 49 micrograms

Milk Chocolate Bar with Almonds
1.5 ounce bar: 216 calories
Vitamin E: 1.3 milligrams

Almonds, Raw
1 ounce: 169 calories
Vitamin E: 1.3 milligrams

POINTS OF VIEW 2

Should Vegetarians Take Vitamin B_{12} Supplements?

It seems that everywhere we turn we are encouraged to take a vitamin supplement. Despite consuming a generally healthy diet, vegetarians are often advised to make sure that they get the vitamins that they could fall short of by not eating meat from either a supplement or fortified foods. Vegans are particularly at risk for a B_{12} deficiency.[1] Can vegetarians, if they eat a balanced diet, get all the vitamins they need from food instead of taking a supplement or should they supplement their diets with a B_{12} pill? Take a close look at the arguments for both sides and see what you think.

yes

- It's difficult to get enough B_{12} especially on a vegan diet. Indeed, vegetarians are listed as an "at risk" group for vitamin B_{12} deficiency because they do not eat animal products.[2]

- Excess B_{12} is excreted in urine (B_{12} is water soluble), so there isn't a threat that a supplement will cause toxicity in the body.[3]

- Screening for B_{12} deficiency is not routine in the United States so there is a real possibility that many people, vegetarian or not, are undiagnosed.[4]

- Not getting enough B_{12} can result in anemia, nerve damage, and/or dementia.[5] The risk of damage to the nerves outweighs the risk of taking too much B_{12}, for most people, especially vegetarians.

no

- It is better to get vitamins from food to avoid excess vitamin intake and because foods work together. Foods provide phytochemicals and fiber that are missing in a supplement.[6, 7]

- Excessive levels of B_{12} can cause side effects in some people with underlying conditions, such as those with a history of cancer.[8]

- It can be possible to get enough B_{12} from a well-planned vegetarian diet that includes eggs, milk, yogurt, and fortified foods.[9]

- Excessive vitamin B_{12} can interfere with the action of some medicines.[10] It is critical to check with your doctor before starting to take vitamin supplements.

what do you think?

1. Do you or anyone you know currently take a B_{12} supplement? If so, is it to supplement a vegetarian diet? **2.** Compare the benefits of a vegetarian diet to the difficulties in achieving a balanced nutritonal intake without consuming meat. **3.** What are the most compelling reasons for and against taking a B_{12} supplement? Which reason do you think is the most convincing?

VISUAL Chapter Summary

LO 7.1 Vitamins Are Essential Nutrients Needed by Your Body to Grow, Reproduce, and Maintain Good Health

A vitamin is either fat-soluble or water-soluble, depending on how it is absorbed and handled in your body. The fat-soluble vitamins A, D, E, and K are stored in your body and require fat for absorption. They can accumulate to the point of toxicity if your intake is excessive. The water-soluble B vitamins and vitamin C are absorbed with water and typically aren't stored for extended periods. Excess amounts of water-soluble vitamins do not accumulate to toxic levels, but can be harmful if you routinely consume too much.

Antioxidants, such as vitamins E and C and beta-carotene, neutralize harmful oxygen-containing molecules called free radicals that can damage cells. Free radicals can contribute to chronic diseases such as cancer and heart disease and accelerate the aging process. They also contribute to age-related macular degeneration and cataracts, two common eye disorders. Diets abundant in antioxidant-rich fruits, vegetables, and whole grains are associated with a lower incidence of many diseases.

Vitamins are found naturally in foods, added to fortified foods, or are available in a pill form through dietary supplements. Food preparation techniques can cause the loss of vitamins, particularly from fruits and vegetables. To preserve the vitamins in your produce, limit its exposure to air, keep it cool, use less water in cooking it, and reduce cooking time.

Fat-soluble vitamins

Water-soluble vitamins

LO 7.2 Fat-Soluble Vitamins Are Stored in the Liver as Well as in Fat and Muscle Tissues

Vitamins A, K, and E are stored in the liver. Vitamin D is mainly stored in fat and muscle tissues. Because they are stored in the body, large quantities of some of the fat-soluble vitamins, particularly A and D, can build up to the point of toxicity, causing harmful symptoms and conditions.

LO 7.3 Vitamin A

Vitamin A refers to a family of retinoids, which are needed for strong vision, reproduction, and healthy fetal development. Carotenoids are yellow-reddish pigments that give some fruits and vegetables their vibrant yellow-red color. The carotenoid beta-carotene is a common provitamin that can be converted to vitamin A in your body. Two other carotenoids, lutein and zeaxanthin, are being investigated for their potential role in eye health. The carotenoid lycopene acts as an antioxidant in the body. Preformed vitamin A is found in milk, organ meats, and eggs, whereas carrots, spinach, and sweet potatoes are good sources for provitamin A carotenoids. Toxic amounts of preformed vitamin A can compromise bone health and cause birth defects during pregnancy. Deficiencies of vitamin A can result in vision problems.

LO 7.4 Vitamin E

Vitamin E is an antioxidant that protects your cells' membranes. Vitamin E plays an important role in helping prevent the "bad" LDL cholesterol carrier from being oxidized. High levels of artery-clogging, oxidized LDL cholesterol are a risk factor for heart disease. Vegetable oils, avocados, nuts, and seeds are good sources of vitamin E.

Green leafy vegetables and fortified cereals also contribute to your daily intake. The recommended intake for vitamin E is presented in alpha-tocopherol equivalents. Excessive amounts of vitamin E from supplements may cause hemorrhage. Too little vitamin E, although rare, may result in nerve problems, muscle weakness, and increased susceptibility to free radical damage.

Free radicals   Damaged phospholipids   Vitamin E (antioxidant)

Phospholipid membrane

Free radicals damage phospholipids, essential components of the cell membrane.

Vitamin E in cell membranes can neutralize free radicals, preventing them from damaging phospholipids.

LO 7.5 Vitamin K

Vitamin K helps your blood to clot and helps synthesize proteins that keep bones healthy. Dietary sources of vitamin K include leafy greens, vegetable oils, and margarine. While there are no known toxicity problems, a deficiency of vitamin K may result in hemorrhage and bone fractures. Individuals taking anticoagulant medications need to carefully monitor their vitamin K intake.

LO 7.6 Vitamin D

Vitamin D is necessary for absorption of calcium and phosphorus. Although vitamin D can be made in your body with the help of ultraviolet rays from the sun, some individuals are not exposed to enough sunlight to meet their needs. Milk and fortified yogurts are excellent sources of vitamin D. Consuming too much vitamin D can cause loss of appetite, nausea, vomiting, and constipation. A deficiency of vitamin D can cause rickets in children and osteomalacia in adults.

LO 7.7 Water-Soluble Vitamins Act as Coenzymes in Metabolic Processes

The B-complex vitamins thiamin, riboflavin, niacin, vitamin B_6, vitamin B_{12}, pantothenic acid, and biotin function as coenzymes in the conversion of carbohydrates, proteins, and fats to energy; in fatty acid, cholesterol, and protein synthesis; and in glycogenolysis and gluconeogenesis. Vitamins catalyze enzyme activity when they bind to the active site of an enzyme. Water-soluble vitamins also act as anti-oxidants (vitamin C) aid in nerve function (thiamin), DNA synthesis (folate), and red blood cell formation (vitamin B_{12}).

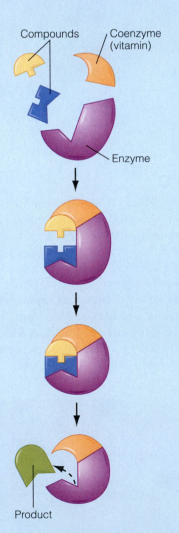

Compounds

Coenzyme (vitamin)

Enzyme

Product

LO 7.8 Thiamin

Thiamin is needed for nerve function and energy metabolism. The best sources of thiamin are lean pork, enriched and whole-grain foods, ready-to-eat cereals, pasta, rice, and nuts. There are no known toxicity problems for thiamin, but a deficiency can result in beriberi. Chronic alcohol abuse can lead to an advanced form of thiamin deficiency called Wernicke-Korsakoff syndrome.

LO 7.9 Riboflavin

Riboflavin is important for energy metabolism and healthy cells. Milk and yogurt are the most popular sources of riboflavin. Excess amounts are excreted in urine and there are no known toxicity symptoms. A deficiency in riboflavin results in symptoms such as a sore throat, a swelling in the inside of the mouth, an inflamed tongue, and dry and scaly lips.

LO 7.10 Niacin

Niacin is needed for the body to use the energy in your food. In larger doses, niacin has been shown to lower LDL blood cholesterol levels. When it is used to treat high blood cholesterol levels, it is considered a drug. Niacin is found in a variety of foods, including meat, fish, poultry, fortified cereals, and enriched breads. There is no danger of consuming too much niacin through foods, although overconsumption of niacin supplements can cause flushing. A deficiency of niacin results in pellagra.

VISUAL Chapter Summary

LO 7.11 Vitamin B₆

Vitamin B₆ also known as pyridoxine, acts as a coenzyme for over 100 enzymes. Vitamin B₆ is also a key player in red blood cell synthesis, and in keeping the immune and nervous systems healthy. Vitamin B₆ is found in meat, fish, poultry, legumes, bananas, and fortified cereals. Consuming excessive amounts from supplements may cause neurological damage. A deficiency of vitamin B₆ can result in anemia, depression, and inflammation of the skin. Drinking too much alcohol can deplete the body of vitamin B₆.

LO 7.12 Folate

Folate is vital for DNA synthesis and critical in cell division. Folate is naturally found in foods but is more easily absorbed as the synthetic form, folic acid. Folic acid is found mostly in fortified foods and supplements. Folate is found in leafy green vegetables, enriched pasta, rice, breads, and cereals. Consuming too much folate can obscure a vitamin B₁₂ deficiency. A deficiency of folate results in macrocytic anemia. Babies born to mothers who are deficient in folate have a higher risk of neural tube defects such as anencephaly and spina bifida.

LO 7.13 Vitamin B₁₂

Vitamin B₁₂ is a family of compounds also referred to as cobalamin. Vitamin B₁₂ is vital for healthy nerves and red blood cells. It requires the aid of intrinsic factor from the stomach to be properly absorbed. Vitamin B₁₂ is found naturally in animal foods, and the synthetic form is used in fortified soy milk and some cereals. There are no known toxicity risks of consuming too much vitamin B₁₂. A deficiency of vitamin B₁₂ causes macrocytic anemia and nerve damage.

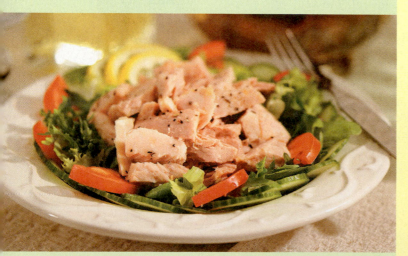

LO 7.14 Vitamin C

Vitamin C, also known as ascorbic acid, assists in the formation of collagen. Collagen, the most abundant protein in the body, is necessary for healthy bones, teeth, skin, and blood vessels. As an antioxidant, vitamin C reduces free radical damage and supports a healthy immune system. Vitamin C also improves the absorption of nonheme iron. Vitamin C is found in a wide variety of fruits and vegetables, including citrus fruits, tomatoes, potatoes, and broccoli. Excessive amounts can cause intestinal discomfort. A deficiency of vitamin C results in scurvy. The regular ingestion of a supplement doesn't prevent healthy individuals from getting a cold.

LO 7.15 Pantothenic Acid and Biotin

Pantothenic acid and biotin are both B vitamins that aid in metabolism. Pantothenic acid and biotin are found in a wide variety of foods, including whole-grain cereals, nuts and legumes, peanut butter, milk, meat, and eggs. There are no known adverse effects from consuming too much pantothenic acid and biotin from foods, and deficiencies are rare.

Deficiencies of biotin can occur when large amounts of raw eggs are consumed. Avidin in raw egg whites binds biotin in the intestinal tract and prevents it from being absorbed.

LO 7.16 Other Vitamin-Like Compounds Are Not Essential

Choline is a conditionally essential nutrient that the body needs for healthy cells and nerves. Carnitine, lipoic acid, and inositol are vitamin-like compounds that are used for important body functions and overall health. They are not considered essential because they can be synthesized in sufficient amounts in the body.

LO 7.17 Fortified Foods and Supplements Can Provide Vitamins

Fortified foods and vitamin supplements can help individuals with inadequate diets to meet their nutrient needs. However, supplements should never replace a healthy diet. The U.S. Pharmacopoeia (USP) seal on a supplement label indicates that the supplement has been tested and meets the USP's criteria for purity and accuracy.

VISUAL Chapter Summary

Terms to Know

- vitamins
- antioxidants
- oxidation
- free radicals
- age-related macular degeneration (AMD)
- cataract
- phytochemicals
- bioavailability
- toxicity
- megadose
- provitamins
- preformed vitamins
- retinoids
- preformed vitamin A
- retinol
- rhodopsin
- iodopsin
- rods
- cones
- bleaching
- cell differentiation
- retinol activity equivalents (RAE)
- international units (IU)
- hypervitaminosis A
- osteoporosis
- carotenodermia
- night blindness
- xerophthalmia
- alpha-tocopherol
- anticoagulant
- hemorrhage
- menaquinone
- phylloquinone
- coagulation
- clotting factors
- osteocalcin
- warfarin
- ultraviolet (UV) rays
- parathyroid hormone
- hypervitaminosis D
- hypercalcemia
- rickets
- osteomalacia
- coenzymes
- polyneuritis
- beriberi
- Wernicke-Korsakoff syndrome
- nicotinic acid
- nicotinamide
- tryptophan
- niacin equivalents (NE)
- flushing
- pellagra
- dermatitis
- dementia
- pyridoxine
- premenstrual syndrome (PMS)
- anemia
- folate
- folic acid
- neural tube defects
- anencephaly
- spina bifida
- dietary folate equivalents (DFE)
- megaloblasts
- macrocytes
- macrocytic anemia
- intrinsic factor
- pernicious anemia
- ascorbic acid
- hemochromatosis
- scurvy
- choline
- hypotension
- carnitine
- lipoic acid
- inositol
- fortified foods
- U.S. Pharmacopeia (USP)

MasteringNutrition™

Build your knowledge—and confidence—in the Study Area of MasteringNutrition with a variety of study tools.

 MyDietAnalysis

Access MyDietAnalysis through MasteringNutrition™ and track your diet and daily activities. In addition, a dietary analysis activity is available for every chapter in your book.

Check Your Understanding

LO 7.1 1. Which of the following is a water-soluble vitamin?
   a. vitamin A
   b. vitamin E
   c. niacin
   d. vitamin K

LO 7.3 2. The most usable form of vitamin A in your body is
   a. retinol.
   b. retinal.
   c. retinoic acid.
   d. retinoids.

LO 7.4 3. You are enjoying a salad bar lunch (good choice!). You want to top your greens with vitamin E–rich foods. You could choose
   a. olive oil.
   b. pickles.
   c. tomatoes.
   d. vinegar.

LO 7.5 4. Which of the following vitamins is needed in order for your blood to clot?
   a. vitamin D
   b. vitamin K
   c. beta-carotene
   d. vitamin A

LO 7.6 5. Vitamin D is
   a. a carbohydrate.
   b. made in your body with the help of sunscreen.
   c. found in fortified milk.
   d. water soluble.

LO 7.8 6. A deficiency of thiamin can cause
   a. rickets.
   b. beriberi.
   c. scurvy.
   d. osteomalacia.

LO 7.12 7. Folic acid can help reduce the risk of
   a. acne.
   b. neural tube defects.
   c. night blindness.
   d. pellagra.

LO 7.13 8. Adam Craig is 55 years old. Which of the following might his body have difficulty absorbing?
   a. the vitamin B_{12} in a piece of steak
   b. the vitamin B_6 in liver
   c. the folate in spinach
   d. the riboflavin in milk

LO 7.14 9. You are enjoying a breakfast of raisin bran cereal in skim milk accompanied by a glass of orange juice. The vitamin C in the orange juice will enhance the absorption of
   a. the calcium in the milk.
   b. the vitamin D in fortified milk.
   c. the iron in the cereal.
   d. the fiber in the cereal.

LO 7.17 10. Which of the following statements is NOT correct? The USP seal on the vitamin label means that the dietary supplement has been tested and shown to
   a. contain the amount of the substance that is stated on the label.
   b. be of good quality.
   c. be free of any contaminants.
   d. meet your daily needs of that vitamin.

Answers

1. (c) Niacin is water soluble, whereas vitamins A, E, and K are fat soluble.
2. (a) Retinol is the most usable form of vitamin A in your body. Retinoids include all three forms of preformed vitamin A: retinol, retinal, and retinoic acid.
3. (a) Go for the olive oil for a good source of fat-soluble vitamin E.
4. (b) Vitamin K is needed in order for your blood to clot.
5. (c) Vitamin D is a hormone that can be obtained by drinking fortified milk. It can be made in your body with the help of adequate exposure to the sun's ultraviolet rays.
6. (b) A chronic deficiency of thiamin can cause beriberi. A vitamin D deficiency can cause rickets in children and osteomalacia in adults. Scurvy is the result of a vitamin C deficiency.
7. (b) If consumed prior to and during the first several weeks of pregnancy, adequate amounts of folic acid can reduce the risk of neural tube defects, including spina bifida and anencephaly. Vitamin A–containing medication may be used to treat acne. Vitamin A can also help prevent night blindness. Consuming adequate amounts of niacin prevents pellagra.
8. (a) Approximately 10 to 30 percent of adults over the age of 50 have reduced secretions of acidic stomach juices, which affects the absorption of the vitamin B_{12} that is found naturally in food. The other B vitamins should be readily absorbed regardless of Adam's age.
9. (c) Vitamin C will help your body absorb the iron in grain products and cereals. Vitamin C does not affect the absorption of calcium, vitamin D, or fiber. However, the vitamin D in the milk will help you absorb the mineral calcium.
10. (d) Manufacturers of dietary supplements can voluntarily have their products tested for the strength, quality, and purity of the supplement. The USP seal does not confirm that the product will meet your daily need for the vitamin.

Web Resources

- To learn more about fulfilling your needs for fruits and vegetables, visit www.fruitsandveggiesmorematters.org
- For more information on the disease-fighting capabilities of fruits and vegetables, visit www.cdc.gov/nutrition/everyone/fruitsvegetables/nutrient-info.html
- To find out the latest recommendations for vitamins, see the dietary supplements fact sheets in the Health Information section at http://ods.od.nih.gov

1. **False.** Although vitamins perform numerous functions in your body, they don't provide energy, as do carbohydrates, proteins, and fats. To find out more, turn to page 228.
2. **False.** Routinely taking an excess of many vitamins, including many water-soluble vitamins, can be harmful. To find out more, turn to page 229.
3. **False.** Deep orange vegetables and some green vegetables are good sources of the vitamin A precursor beta-carotene, which is converted to vitamin A in your body. While an excess of beta-carotene will not cause vitamin A toxicity, it could make your skin change color. To find out more, turn to page 239.
4. **True.** Consuming excessive amounts of vitamin E supplements can interfere with blood clotting. To learn more, turn to page 240.
5. **True.** Vitamin K helps a protein in your bones bind with the bone-strengthening mineral calcium. To learn about other functions of vitamin K, turn to page 242.
6. **False.** Many people are unable to meet their vitamin D needs through sunlight exposure alone. To find out if you are at risk, turn to page 244.
7. **True.** Folate can lower the risk of some birth defects during pregnancy. However, timing is everything. To find out when a pregnant woman needs to be taking this B vitamin, turn to page 256.
8. **False.** There is no clear evidence that taking megadoses of vitamin C, such as from supplements, protects you from the common cold. To find out what role it does play in combating colds, turn to page 266.
9. **False.** Fortified foods are not always a safe way to meet your vitamin needs. To find out why, turn to page 268.
10. **False.** While foods are an excellent source of vitamins, some individuals may need extra vitamin support from a supplement. To find out who would benefit from a supplement, turn to page 270.

8 Minerals and Water

True or False?

1. Vitamin waters are healthier for you than plain water. T|F p. 293

2. Your morning mug of coffee counts toward fulfilling your daily water needs. T|F p. 294

3. Most of your dietary sodium comes from the salt that you shake on your foods. T|F p. 301

4. A serving of milk will provide about one-third of an adult's daily calcium needs. T|F p. 307

5. Magnesium can help lower your blood pressure. T|F p. 313

6. Meat is the major source of iron in the American diet. T|F p. 317

7. Zinc can prevent the common cold. T|F p. 320

8. Fluoride has been added to bottled waters. T|F p. 325

9. Chromium can help you build bigger muscles and stay lean when you are lifting weights. T|F p. 326

10. Kosher salt is a good source of iodine. T|F p. 328

See page 339 for the answers.

Learning Outcomes

After reading this chapter, you will be able to:

LO 8.1 Explain the importance and functions of water in the body.

LO 8.2 Describe water balance and how the body maintains it.

LO 8.3 Identify daily water needs and the best sources for it.

LO 8.4 Explain what minerals are and why you need them.

LO 8.5 Name functions, sources, and deficiency/toxicity of sodium.

LO 8.6 Name functions, sources, and deficiency/toxicity of potassium.

LO 8.7 Name functions, sources, and deficiency/toxicity of calcium.

LO 8.8 Name functions, sources, and deficiency/toxicity of phosphorus.

LO 8.9 Name functions, sources, and deficiency/toxicity of magnesium.

LO 8.10 Name functions, sources, and deficiency/toxicity of chloride.

LO 8.11 Name functions, sources, and deficiency/toxicity of sulfur.

LO 8.12 Name functions, sources, and deficiency/toxicity of iron.

LO 8.13 Name functions, sources, and deficiency/toxicity of copper.

LO 8.14 Name functions, sources, and deficiency/toxicity of zinc.

LO 8.15 Name functions, sources, and deficiency/toxicity of selenium.

LO 8.16 Name functions, sources, and deficiency/toxicity of fluoride.

LO 8.17 Name functions, sources, and deficiency/toxicity of chromium.

LO 8.18 Name functions, sources, and deficiency/toxicity of iodine.

LO 8.19 Name functions, sources, and deficiency/toxicity of manganese.

LO 8.20 Name functions, sources, and deficiency/toxicity of molybdenum.

You could survive for weeks without food, but only a few days without water. Water is needed for chemical reactions that take place in your cells, and essential for maintaining the fluid balance inside your body. Minerals also participate in fluid balance, along with performing many other structural and functional roles in the body. In this chapter we will explore these vital nutrients.

Why Is Water So Important?

LO 8.1 Explain the importance and functions of water in the body.

The average healthy adult is about 50 to 60 percent water, which makes water the most abundant substance in your body. However, individuals vary in the exact amount of water they carry, because factors such as age, gender, and the body's amount of fat and muscle tissue affect body water (**Figure 8.1**). Muscle tissue is approximately 75 percent water, whereas fat tissue is up to 20 percent water.[1] Generally, men have a higher percentage of muscle mass and a lower percentage of fat tissue than women of the same age, so they have more body water. For the same reason, muscular athletes have a higher percentage of body water than do sedentary individuals.

You learned in Chapter 6 that fluid balance refers to the equal distribution of fluid among several compartments in your body. The fluid inside your cells is in the **intracellular fluid compartment**, whereas the fluid in the space outside your cells is in the **extracellular fluid compartment**. The extracellular fluids are further broken down into (1) **interstitial fluids**, which are in the space immediately outside your cells, and (2) the fluids in your blood (see **Figure 8.2**). The interstitial fluids act as an area of exchange between your blood fluids and your cells.

Maintaining the equal distribution of all this body fluid is crucial to health, and water and dissolved minerals play key roles. The minerals important in fluid balance are called **electrolytes** (*electro* = electricity, *lytes* = soluble). They include sodium, potassium, phosphate, magnesium, calcium, and chloride. Water in your body is drawn into and out of your cells by the "pull" of electrolytes. When cells have more electrolytes than the fluid outside them, water flows in, and vice versa.

Water Is the Universal Solvent

Water is a wonderful **solvent**, a liquid in which substances dissolve. In fact, water is commonly known as the universal solvent. As a solvent, water is part of the medium in which molecules come in contact with each other. This contact

~5% minerals and other nutrients

~5% minerals and other nutrients

~14% protein

~17% protein

29% fat

20% fat

59% water

52% water

Female, 137 lbs.   Male, 168 lbs.

Figure 8.1 Your Body Is Mostly Water

between molecules allows chemical reactions to take place. For example, the combining of specific amino acids to synthesize a protein occurs in the watery medium inside your cells.

Water Is a Transport Medium

The water in blood and lymph helps transport substances throughout your body. Did you know that only about 45 percent of your blood is red blood cells? Most of the rest is water. As part of blood, water helps transport oxygen, nutrients, and other important substances to your cells. It also helps transport waste products away from cells to be excreted in urine and stool. Like the fluid in blood, lymph fluid is almost entirely water. Lymph transports proteins back to the bloodstream, and it is important in the absorption of fats. Lymph also transports wastes and microbes through "cleaning stations" called *lymph nodes,* where defensive cells consume these harmful substances before the lymph returns to the blood.

Water Helps Maintain Body Temperature

The water in your blood is like the coolant that runs through a car. They both absorb, carry, and ultimately release heat in order to keep a running machine from overheating. In a car, the coolant absorbs the heat from a running engine and carries it to the radiator for release. In your body, the water in your circulating blood absorbs the heat from your internal core—the center of your body, where your most important organs are located—and carries it to the skin for release (**Figure 8.3**). Water

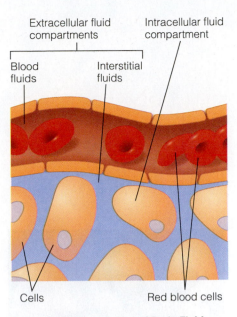

Figure 8.2 Water as Part of Body Fluids Water is a key component of the fluid compartments both inside and outside cells.

1. The water in blood carries heat to the capillaries at the skin surface.

2. The heat is released at the skin surface. Evaporation of sweat cools the skin.

3. Cooled blood returns to the body core.

Figure 8.3 Water Helps Regulate Your Body Temperature

intracellular fluid compartment The fluid located inside your cells.

extracellular fluid compartment The fluid located outside your cells. Interstitial fluids and fluids in the blood are extracellular fluids.

interstitial fluids Fluids located between cells.

electrolytes Charged ions that conduct an electrical current in a solvent such as water. Sodium, potassium, and chloride are examples of electrolytes in the body.

solvent A liquid that acts as a medium in which substances dissolve. Water is considered the universal solvent.

works so well as a coolant in both your car and your body because it has a unique ability to absorb and release a tremendous amount of heat. Like a car, your body sometimes gets overheated. For instance, if you were to go jogging on a hot summer day, the enormous amount of internal heat that would be generated would probably overwhelm the heat-absorbing capacity of your body's water. The increasing heat would break apart the molecules of water on your skin, transforming them from a liquid (sweat) to a vapor. The evaporation of sweat from your skin would release the heat and cool you down, enabling you to maintain a safe body temperature. When you are cold, less blood flows to your body surface, so that your core stays warm. That's why your hands, feet, and face can become so cool to the touch on a cold day.

Water Is a Lubricant and a Protective Cushion

Water, combined with other molecules, acts as a lubricant for your joints, helping to promote easy, reduced-friction movement. The water in tears lubricates your eyes and helps flush out dust and other debris. Water is also part of the saliva that moistens your mouth and foods and the mucus that lubricates your intestinal tract. Water is the main part of the fluid that surrounds certain organs, including your brain; thus, it acts as a cushion to protect them from injury during a fall or other trauma. During pregnancy, a developing fetus is surrounded by a sac of watery amniotic fluid, which helps protect it from physical harm.

LO 8.1 **The Take-Home Message** Your body is mostly water. Muscle tissue has more water than does fat tissue. The water inside your body cells is balanced by the water outside your cells. Electrolytes help maintain fluid balance. Water is a universal solvent that helps transport oxygen and nutrients throughout your body. It also absorbs and releases heat to regulate your body temperature, acts as a lubricant through saliva and mucus, and provides a protective cushion for your brain and other organs.

A developing fetus is cushioned in a sac of watery amniotic fluid to protect it from physical harm during pregnancy.

What Is Water Balance and How Do You Maintain It?

LO 8.2 Describe water balance and how the body maintains it.

When the amount of water you consume is equal to the amount you lose daily, you are in **water balance**. When you are not in water balance—that is, having too much or too little water in your system—health problems can occur. Thus, maintaining water balance is very important.

There are several ways in which water is lost from your body and several mechanisms that help you replenish those losses. Let's look at this next.

You Take in Water through Beverages and Food

The first aspect of being in water balance is consuming enough water. You get most of your daily water from beverages such as tap or bottled water, milk, juices, and soft drinks. You also get some water from the foods that you eat, although much less in comparison (**Figure 8.4**). Even the driest foods, like oatmeal and bread, provide some water. A small amount of water is also generated during metabolism.

water balance The state whereby an equal amount of water is lost and replenished daily in the body.

Figure 8.4 The Concept of Water Balance: Intake Equals Output
You get most of your water from foods and beverages, though a small amount is also generated through the process of metabolism. You lose water in your urine, stool, sweat, and exhaled breath. The amount of water that you take in is balanced with the amount that you excrete every day.

Labels in figure:
1 cup Metabolism
3 cups Food
6.5 cups Beverages
Water Intake
10.5 cups

0.5 cup — Intestines (stool)
1 cup — Sweat
3 cups Skin and Lungs
6 cups Kidneys (urine)
Water Output
10.5 cups

You Lose Water through Your Kidneys, Large Intestine, Lungs, and Skin

The other aspect of water balance is excreting excess water so that you don't have too much in your body. You normally lose water daily through these four routes:

- Via your kidneys in the form of urine
- Via intestinal fluids in your stool (unless you are experiencing diarrhea, the amount of water lost in stool is normally small)
- Via the water that evaporates when you exhale
- Via your skin when you release the heat produced in your body core

The water that evaporates when you exhale and the water lost through your skin when you release the heat generated during normal reactions is called **insensible water loss**, as it occurs without your noticing it. An individual loses about 3 cups of water daily due to insensible water loss.[2]

Insensible water loss doesn't include the water lost in sweat. Sweating is your body's way of releasing a higher than normal amount of heat. The amount of water lost during sweating varies greatly and depends upon many environmental factors, such as the temperature, the humidity, the wind, the sun's intensity, clothing worn, and the amount of physical activity you are doing.[3] For example, if you jump rope in the noontime sun on a summer day wearing a winter coat, you'll soon be losing a lot of water as sweat. In contrast, little or no sweat will leave your body if you sit under a shady tree on a dry, cool day wearing shorts and a light tee shirt.

Losing Too Much Water Can Cause Dehydration

Dehydration is a state in which you've lost too much, or aren't taking in enough, water. Dehydration can result from not drinking enough fluids and/or from conditions that result in too much water (and sodium) being lost from the body, such as diarrhea, vomiting, high fever, or the use of **diuretics**. If dehydration persists, a person can experience weight loss, fever, dizziness, and confusion, as well as impaired physical coordination, and, in extreme situations, death.[4]

insensible water loss The water that is lost from the body daily through exhalation from the lungs and evaporation off the skin.

dehydration The state whereby there is too little water in the body due to too much water being lost, too little being consumed, or a combination of both.

diuretics Substances such as alcohol and some medications that cause the body to lose water.

Water is vital for many body functions, but it isn't stored in the body, so it's important to take in enough water every day.

Your Thirst Mechanism Signals Dehydration

Have you ever been outside for a while on a hot day and noticed that your mouth was as dry as the Sahara Desert? The dry mouth is part of your **thirst mechanism**, and is your body's way of telling you to find a water source—you are on the road to dehydration. The thirst mechanism plays an important role in helping you avoid dehydration and restore the water balance in your body.

The dry mouth that makes you thirsty when you are dehydrated is due to the increased concentration of electrolytes in your blood. As the concentration of these minerals increases, less water is available to your salivary glands to make saliva.[5] Thus, your mouth feels very dry.

When you are dehydrated, the fluid volume in your blood decreases, resulting in a higher concentration of sodium in the blood. To restore balance, the fluid inside your cells will move through the membrane to the outside of the cell and into your blood to balance the concentration of sodium between these compartments. This movement of water across the cell membrane is called **osmosis** (see **Figure 8.5**).

Your brain detects the increased concentration of sodium in your blood and triggers your thirst mechanism, reminding you to drink fluids. Your brain will also trigger the secretion of **antidiuretic hormone (ADH)** from the pituitary gland. ADH causes your kidneys to decrease further loss of water and thus concentrate your urine.[6] These mechanisms work together to keep your body in water balance.

Other Ways to Tell If You Are Dehydrated

Just quenching your thirst will not typically provide enough fluids to remedy dehydration. This isn't a concern for moderately active individuals eating a balanced diet,

thirst mechanism Various bodily reactions caused by dehydration that signal you to drink fluids.

osmosis The movement of a solvent, such as water, from an area of lower concentration of solutes across a membrane to an area of higher concentration of solutes. It balances the concentration of solutes between the compartments.

antidiuretic hormone (ADH) A hormone that directs the kidneys to concentrate urine and reduce urine production in order to reduce water loss from the body.

1 A selectively permeable filter is placed in a glass of pure water.

2 Salt is added to the water on one side of the filter.

3 Drawn by the high concentration of electrolytes, pure water flows to the "salt water" side of the filter.

Figure 8.5 A Simple Demonstration of Osmosis

as fluids from beverages and food throughout the day can eventually restore water balance.[7] However, older adults, and individuals who are very physically active and/or who have physically vigorous jobs, such as firefighters, are at higher risk of dehydration because they don't take in enough fluid, or they lose body water copiously through sweating. These individuals need to take additional steps to ensure that they are properly hydrated.

One way to monitor hydration is the cornerstone method, which involves measuring body weight before and after long bouts of intense physical activity or labor and noting any changes. If a person weighs less after an activity than before, the weight change is due to loss of body water, and that water must be replenished. (Alternatively, if a weight gain is noted, overhydration is likely, and you need to drink less before your next activity.)

Urine color can also be used to assess hydration. When you are dehydrated, you produce less urine due to the release of ADH. The urine you do produce is more concentrated, as it contains a higher proportion of compounds to the smaller volume of water. This causes the urine to be darker in color.[8] The National Athletic Trainers Association has created a chart to help individuals assess if they are drinking enough fluids to offset the amount of water lost through sweating (see **Figure 8.6**).[9] If you are very physically active and the color of your urine darkens during the day, to the point where it resembles the shade of a "yield" sign or darker, you likely need to increase the amount of fluids in your diet. (Note: Other factors, such as consuming excessive amounts of the B vitamin, riboflavin, and certain medications can also affect the color of urine.)

Figure 8.06 **Urine Color Can Signal Dehydration**
If you collect your urine in a cup and it looks like the color of 1 through 3 on the chart, you are well hydrated. If it resembles color 7 or is darker, you are dehydrated and need to drink more fluids.

Consuming Too Much Water Can Cause Hyponatremia

For healthy individuals who consume a balanced diet, it's hard to consume too much water, because the body will just produce more urine to eliminate the excess. However, some individuals, particularly soldiers during military training and athletes who participate in endurance events such as marathons, have experienced water toxicity in certain circumstances.[10]

In April 2002, 28-year-old Cynthia Lucero was running the Boston Marathon. About five miles from the finish line, Lucero began to feel wobbly and mentioned to a friend that she felt dehydrated even though she had been consuming fluids throughout her run. She suddenly collapsed and was taken to a nearby hospital. She died the next day, not of dehydration, but of overhydration. In January 2007, 28-year-old Jennifer Strange collapsed after competing in a California radio contest to see who could drink the most water without using the restroom. She was found dead in her home a few hours after completing the contest.[11] The cause of death for both of these individuals was swelling of the brain brought on by **hyponatremia** (*hypo* = under, *natrium* = sodium, *emia* = blood), caused by overconsumption of fluids. In both cases, drinking too much fluid diluted the blood to the point where sodium levels were too low, which in turn resulted in the swelling of body tissues (see **Figure 8.7** on page 290). When swelling occurs in the brain, the person can experience symptoms similar to those of dehydration—confusion and disorientation.[12] Mistakenly treating these symptoms by consuming more fluids will only make matters worse.

Even though dehydration is more common and a bigger challenge to physically active individuals than overhydration, the seriousness of overhydration has prompted the USA Track & Field association to revise its hydration guidelines for long-distance and marathon runners to avoid hyponatremia. Chapter 11 will provide these guidelines and show you how to calculate how much fluid you need during exercise.

hyponatremia A condition of too little sodium in the blood.

FOCUS FIGURE WALKTHROUGH

 Scan this QR code with your mobile device for a video tour of this figure by Joan Salge Blake.

The health of our body's cells depends on maintaining the proper balance of fluids and electrolytes on both sides of the cell membrane, both at rest and during exercise. Let's examine how this balance can be altered under various conditions of exercise and fluid intake.

MODERATE EXERCISE

When you are appropriately hydrated, engaged in moderate exercise, and not too hot, the concentration of electrolytes is likely to be the same on both sides of cell membranes. You will be in fluid balance.

Concentration of electrolytes about equal inside and outside cell

STRENUOUS EXERCISE WITH RAPID AND HIGH WATER INTAKE

If a person drinks a great deal of water quickly during intense, prolonged exercise, the extracellular fluid becomes diluted. This results in the concentration of electrolytes being greater inside the cells, which causes water to enter the cells, making them swell. Drinking moderate amounts of water or sports drinks more slowly will replace lost fluids and restore fluid balance.

Lower concentration of electrolytes outside

H_2O

Higher concentration of electrolytes inside

STRENUOUS EXERCISE WITH INADEQUATE FLUID INTAKE

If a person does not consume adequate amounts of fluid during strenuous exercise of long duration, the concentration of electrolytes becomes greater outside the cells, drawing water away from the inside of the cells and making them shrink. Consuming sports drinks will replace lost fluids and electrolytes.

Higher concentration of electrolytes outside

H_2O

Lower concentration of electrolytes inside

Do You Consume Enough Water?

Do you think you are consuming enough fluids each day? Answer these questions to find out.

1. Do you drink a glass (8 ounces) of orange juice or other juices in the morning?
   Yes ☐ **No** ☐
2. Do you have at least two cups (16 ounces) of coffee or tea daily?
   Yes ☐ **No** ☐
3. Do you drink at least 2 cups (16 ounces) of water daily?
   Yes ☐ **No** ☐

4. Do you drink 1 to 3 cups (8 to 24 ounces) of milk daily?
   Yes ☐ **No** ☐
5. Do you consume at least 5 servings of fruits and vegetables daily?
   Yes ☐ **No** ☐

Answers

If you answered yes to at least four questions, it's likely that you are easily meeting your daily water needs.

LO 8.2 **The Take-Home Message** You lose water daily through your kidneys, intestinal tract, lungs, and skin. If you lose more water than you take in, you will become dehydrated. Your thirst mechanism reminds you to drink fluids and helps restore water balance. Although rare, overconsumption of fluids can lead to an electrolyte imbalance (hyponatremia) and can be fatal.

How Much Water Do You Need and What Are the Best Sources?

LO 8.3 Identify daily water needs and the best sources for it.

Your daily water requirements may be different from those of your grandparents, parents, siblings, and even the classmate sitting next to you. The amount of water a person needs depends on his or her physical activity, environmental factors such as air temperature, and diet. (Recall from Chapter 4 that increasing the fiber in your diet should be accompanied by an increase in water consumption.)

The current recommendation for the amount of water you should consume daily is based on the reported total water intake (from both beverages and food) of healthy Americans. Currently, healthy female adults consume about 12 cups, whereas men consume about 16 cups of water daily.[13] About 80 percent of this intake is from beverages. Therefore, adult women should ingest about 9 cups (~80 percent of 12 cups) and adult males approximately 13 cups (~80 percent of 16 cups) of beverages daily.[14] People who are very active will have higher water requirements because they lose more water by sweating. Complete the Self-Assessment to see if you are meeting your daily fluid needs.

If you think that sounds like a lot, keep in mind that a well-balanced, 2,200-calorie diet that includes beverages at all meals and snacks will provide about 12 cups of water.[15] Drinking water (either from the tap or from a bottle), milk, and juices throughout the day can help you meet your needs. The Nutrition in the Real World feature "Tap Water or Bottled Water: Is Bottled Better?" on pages 292–293 discusses the differences and similarities between tap water and bottled water.

Practical Nutrition **VIDEO**

Are Enhanced Waters Necessary?

Bottled water gets fancier all the time as new "enhanced waters" hit the shelves. You may buy these products for their added vitamins and minerals, but are they really a nutritional bargain? Scan this QR code with your mobile device to access the video. You can also access the video in Mastering Nutrition™.

nutrition
in the Real World

Tap Water or Bottled Water: Is Bottled Better?

What items do you *have* to have when you walk out the door in the morning? Your keys? Your student ID? Your wallet? What about a bottle of water? Would you never leave home without it? Are you one of the many individuals who drink *only* bottled water because you think it is superior to tap water? If you are, you're certainly not alone. But is bottled water really better or safer for you than tap water?

Although many individuals drink bottled water thinking that it is "pure," consuming 100 percent *pure* water is impossible. Whether you fill your reusable water bottle from the tap or purchase bottled water, the water will contain some impurities. However, this does not mean that the water is unsafe for most individuals to drink. (Note that individuals with a weakened immune system, such as those with HIV/AIDS, undergoing chemotherapy, and/or taking steroids, should speak with their health care provider prior to drinking any water. These individuals may need to take precautions such as boiling their water—no matter the source—before consuming it.[1])

The source of any water will vary from faucet to faucet and bottle to bottle, so it is virtually impossible to make a direct comparison. There are some basic points to understand about each type, though. Let's look at how tap

A Well of Sources for Bottled Water	
Mineral water	Water derived from an underground source that contains a specific amount of naturally occurring minerals and trace elements. The minerals and elements cannot be added to the water after bottling.
Spring water	Water that is obtained from underground water that flows naturally to the surface. The water is collected at the spring or at the site of the well purposefully drilled to obtain this water.
Sparkling water	Spring water that has carbon dioxide gas added to supply "bubbles" before bottling. Also sold as seltzer water or club soda. *Note:* This is technically considered a soft drink and does not have to adhere to FDA bottled water regulations.
Distilled water	Water that has been boiled and processed to remove most, but not all, contaminants.
Flavored water	Water that has a flavor such as lemon or lime added. It may also contain added sugars and calories.
Vitamin or enhanced waters	Water that has vitamins, protein, herbs, and/or caffeine added to it. Such water may also contain added sugars and calories.

Water can be classified according to its source or how it is treated prior to bottling.

and bottled water compare in terms of regulation, cost, and safety.

Turn on the Tap

Most Americans obtain their drinking water from a community water system. The source of this municipal water can be underground wells or springs, or rivers, lakes, or reservoirs. Regardless of the source, all municipal water is sent to a treatment plant where any dirt and debris are filtered out, bacteria are killed, and other contaminants are removed. The Environmental Protection Agency (EPA) oversees the safety of public drinking water with national standards that set limits for a wide variety of contaminants, either naturally occurring ones, such as bacteria, or man-made ones, such as chemicals, that may find their way into your drinking water. Hundreds of billions of dollars have been invested in these treatment systems to ensure that the public water is safe to drink.[2] Each year, the water supplier in your community must provide you

with an annual report about the quality and source of your tap water. In fact, many of these regional reports can be accessed online at www.epa.gov. Even with these precautions, some individuals, who may not like the taste of their tap water or have health concerns, use an in-home water treatment device to further filter their water. Filter devices can range from a less costly pitcher or device mounted on the kitchen faucet to a more costly, larger system that treats all the water that enters the home. Depending upon the device, it can filter out contaminants such as bacteria, viruses, lead, nitrates, and pesticides. Whatever the device used, it is important that it be maintained regularly to ensure that it is working effectively.

You may have heard the terms "hard" or "soft" water used to describe tap water. The "hardness" refers to the amount of metals—specifically, calcium and magnesium—in the water. The higher the amount, the harder the water.

There aren't any health concerns from drinking hard water. In fact, there may be a benefit, as hard water may contribute small amounts of these minerals to your daily diet. Whether your water is hard or soft is less important than meeting your daily need for enough water.

Another benefit of consuming tap water is that many municipalities add fluoride to their water. About 74 percent of Americans who drink from public systems have fluoride in their water (see the map on page 324).[3] Fluoridation of public water has had a positive impact on the nation's dental health, reducing the incidence of dental caries.

Lastly, tap water costs less than a penny a gallon, making it a very affordable way to stay hydrated.

Bottling Boom

Bottled water is second only to carbonated soft drinks in popularity among Americans. Bottled water that is sold through interstate commerce is regulated by the FDA. Thus, as with other food products, manufacturers must adhere to specific FDA regulations, such as standards of identity. In other words, if the label on the bottle states that it is "spring water," the manufacturer must derive the water from a very specific source (see the table on page 292). Interestingly, some bottled water may actually be from a municipal water source. The bottled water must also adhere to a standard of quality set forth by the FDA, which specifies the maximum amount of contaminants that can be in the water for it still to be considered safe for consumption. The FDA sets its standards for bottled water based on the EPA's standards for public drinking water.[4]

The price of bottled water can be hefty, ranging from $1 to $4 a gallon. If you pay $1.50 per bottle and buy two bottles daily, you will be shelling out more than $20 a week and $80 monthly buying bottled water. Over the course of a nine-month term at college, you would be spending more than $750 on a beverage that you can get free from the campus water fountain. Finally, not all bottled waters contain fluoride, so bottled water drinkers may be losing out on this important cavity fighter if this is their predominant source of drinking water.

Another costly bottled beverage option is the "designer" drinks such as vitamin waters and enhanced waters. Although bottled plain water has become increasingly popular in the past few decades, it seems to be losing ground to these new types of waters. These drinks often advertise health benefits beyond just keeping you hydrated. Sold under brand names such as Vitamin Water and SmartWater, they are often enhanced or fortified with additional compounds such as vitamins, sugar, and caffeine, as well as calories, though most Americans typically consume enough or even too much of these in their diet. These designer waters can cost more than $2.50 for a 20-ounce bottle—more than $10 a gallon!

Keep in mind that reusing the bottles from bottled water is not advised. The plastic containers cannot withstand repeated washing and the plastic can actually break down, causing chemicals to leach into the water. Sturdier water bottles that are designed for reuse must be thoroughly cleaned with hot soapy water after each use to kill germs.

Lastly, there is a sustainability issue. Bottled water requires fossil fuel to produce and distribute. It is estimated that only about 20 percent of plastic water bottles are recycled by the customer. This means that these bottles create garbage that end up in our landfills.[5]

The bottom line is that both tap water and bottled water can be safe to drink. Your choice is likely to come down to personal preference and costs. Consider your choice carefully using the table below.

Bottled vs. Tap Water: A Summary

Bottled Water	Tap Water
Cost to Consumers	
• About $1.00–$4.00 per gallon (plain water) • Designer waters can cost more than $10 per gallon and may contain added sugar and calories	• About $0.003 per gallon
Safety and Sustainability	
• Generally safe • Regulated by the FDA. • May not contain fluoride. • If not recycled, end up as garbage in landfills.	• Municipal water is regulated by EPA, state, and local regulations • EPA guidelines require that the public have access to water quality reports and be notified if water quality is outside established bounds
Benefits to Consumers	
• Packaging of bottled water may make it more convenient than tap water • May taste better than tap water	• Available at the faucet • Often contains fluoride, which helps to prevent tooth decay • Doesn't contain any added sugar or calories

Figure 8.8 Water Content of Foods
Approximately 20 percent of the water you consume comes from foods. Fruits, vegetables, and cooked grains all contain a high percentage of water by weight.

The remaining 20 percent of your water can come from foods. All foods contain some water. Cooked hot cereals and many fruits and vegetables are robust sources of water (see **Figure 8.8**).

Contrary to popular belief, beverages like caffeinated coffee, tea, and soft drinks will contribute to your daily water needs. Caffeine is a diuretic, so it causes water to be excreted, but the water loss it causes is short lived. In other words, the caffeine doesn't cause a significant loss of body water over the course of a day compared with noncaffeinated beverages. In fact, research suggests that individuals who routinely consume caffeinated beverages actually develop a tolerance to its diuretic effect and experience less water loss over time.[16]

Even though caffeinated beverages can count as a water source, this doesn't mean you should start guzzling caffeinated colas and other soft drinks. Their high calorie and sugar contents can quickly have you drinking your way into a very unbalanced, high-calorie diet. These soft drinks also contain acids that can contribute to erosion of tooth enamel. See **Figure 8.9** for a list of the healthiest fluids to drink and the Table Tips for more suggestions on ways to meet your daily water needs.

Figure 8.9 The Best Way to Meet Your Daily Water Needs

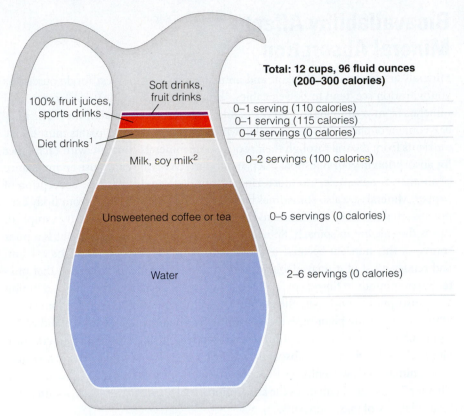

Total: 12 cups, 96 fluid ounces (200–300 calories)

Soft drinks, fruit drinks — 0–1 serving (110 calories)

100% fruit juices, sports drinks — 0–1 serving (115 calories)

Diet drinks[1] — 0–4 servings (0 calories)

Milk, soy milk[2] — 0–2 servings (100 calories)

Unsweetened coffee or tea — 0–5 servings (0 calories)

Water — 2–6 servings (0 calories)

[1] Includes diet soft drinks and tea or coffee with sugar substitutes.
[2] Includes fat-free or 1% milk and unsweetened fortified soy milk.

LO 8.3 **The Take-Home Message** Adult women should ingest about 9 cups of water daily, whereas adult men should drink about 13 cups daily. Those who are very active will need more water to avoid dehydration. Foods and beverages, even caffeinated beverages, contribute to your daily water needs.

What Are Minerals and Why Do You Need Them?

LO 8.4 Explain what minerals are and why you need them.

What do a cast-iron skillet, the salt on an icy road, and the copper plumbing pipes in some houses all have in common? They're made from some of the same **minerals** that play essential roles in your body. From iron to sodium to copper, these rocky substances occur as part of the earthen world around you and are necessary for your day-to-day functioning. You already read that electrolytes (minerals that are charged ions in your body fluids) help maintain fluid balance. Minerals can also be part of enzymes, work with your immune system, and play an invaluable role in structural growth. They help chemical reactions take place in your cells, help your muscles contract, and keep your heart beating. Your body needs these **inorganic** elements in relatively small amounts. Like vitamins, minerals don't provide calories, so they aren't a source of energy themselves, but they work with other nutrients to enable your body to function properly.

minerals Inorganic elements essential to the nutrition of humans.

inorganic Not containing carbon and not formed by living things.

Bioavailability Affects Mineral Absorption

Minerals are found in both plant and animal foods, but the best food sources, as you will soon see, tend to be vegetables, legumes, milk, and meats. Absorption of minerals from your foods can vary depending upon their **bioavailability**. The mineral content of plants reflects the soil in which they are grown, as plants must derive nutrients from the soil through their roots. Some minerals compete with each other for absorption in your intestinal tract, and too much of one can cause an imbalance of another. For example, too much zinc in your diet can decrease the absorption of copper. Minerals are also sometimes bound to other substances and your body cannot absorb them (they are eliminated from your body in your stool). An example of this is the calcium in spinach. Spinach is technically high in calcium, but is a poor source of this nutrient because it contains oxalates, which bind with the calcium and render most of it unavailable for absorption. Recall from Chapter 6 that phytates, compounds in fibrous plant foods, can bind to both iron and zinc and inhibit their absorption. This is why the DRI for both zinc and iron is increased for vegans, who consume only plant-based foods. Similarly, the polyphenols in tea and coffee can inhibit your body's absorption of iron, reducing its bioavailability. In contrast, vitamin C will enhance the absorption of iron that is found in plant foods. Protein from animal foods will enhance the absorption of zinc and iron, and (as you read in Chapter 7) vitamin D enhances the absorption of calcium. All these factors affect the bioavailability of these nutrients.

You Need Major Minerals in Larger Amounts

Minerals are categorized into two groups, depending on how much of them you need. The **major minerals**, known also as *macrominerals,* are needed in amounts greater than 100 milligrams per day, and the **trace minerals**, known also as *microminerals,* are needed in amounts less than 15 milligrams per day.[17] The major minerals are major because you need more of them in your body, and thus, you need more of them in your diet (**Figure 8.10**). Your daily needs for the major minerals range from hundreds of milligrams daily to more than a thousand. The major minerals include sodium, chloride, potassium, calcium, phosphorus, magnesium, and sulfur.

Many of these minerals work closely together to perform major body functions. For example, the sodium and chloride located mainly outside your cells, and the potassium, calcium, magnesium, and sulfur, which are mostly inside your cells, all play a key role in maintaining fluid balance. Calcium, phosphorus, and magnesium work together to strengthen your bones and teeth. **Table 8.1** provides a summary of the major minerals.

The Trace Minerals Are Needed in Small Amounts

The trace minerals—iron, zinc, selenium, fluoride, chromium, copper, iodine, manganese, and molybdenum—are needed in much smaller amounts, less than 15 milligrams daily, compared with the major minerals.[18] However, don't assume that this diminishes their importance. Trace minerals play essential roles that are as important as those of the major minerals. Some (chromium, iodine) help certain

bioavailability The degree to which a nutrient from foods is available for absorption by the body.

major minerals Minerals needed from your diet and in your body in amounts greater than 100 milligrams per day. These include sodium, chloride, potassium, calcium, phosphorus, magnesium, and sulfur. Also called *macrominerals*.

trace minerals Minerals needed from your diet and in your body in small amounts, less than 20 milligrams daily. These include iron, zinc, selenium, fluoride, chromium, copper, manganese, and molybdenum. Also called *microminerals*.

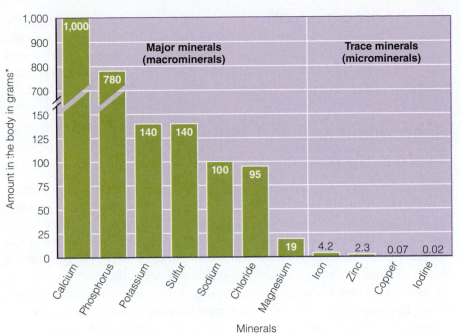

Figure 8.10 The Amounts of the Different Minerals in Your Body
The major minerals are present in larger amounts than the trace minerals. However, all are equally important to your health.

* Based on a 154-pound person

Table 8.1

Minerals at a Glance: Major Minerals

Major Minerals	Major Functions	Adult DRI, 19 to 50 years	Food Sources	Excessive/ Toxicity Symptoms/UL	Deficiency Symptoms/ Conditions
Sodium	Major electrolyte outside the cell; helps regulate body water and blood pressure	1,500 mg/day	Processed foods, table salt, meat, seafood, milk, cheese, eggs	Hypertension UL: 2,300 mg/day	Rare in individuals consuming a healthy diet
Potassium	Major mineral inside the cell, needed for muscle contraction and nerve impulses; regulates body water and blood pressure	4,700 mg/day	Potatoes, melons, citrus fruits, most fruits and vegetables, meat, milk, legumes	Hyperkalemia	Hypokalemia
Calcium	Formation of bones and teeth, muscle contraction and relaxation, blood clotting, heart and nerve function	1,000 mg/day	Milk and dairy products, leafy greens, broccoli, salmon, sardines, tofu	Hypercalcemia UL: 2,500 mg/day	Osteoporosis
Phosphorus	Formation of bones and teeth	700 mg/day	Meat, fish, poultry, eggs, dairy, cereals	Hyperphosphatemia UL: 4,000 mg/day	Muscle weakness, bone pain, rickets, confusion, and death
Magnesium	Participates in muscle contraction and nerve conduction	310 to 420 mg/day	Meat, seafood, nuts, legumes, dairy, whole grains	Large intakes from supplements can cause diarrhea, cramps, and nausea	Rare
Chloride	Helps maintain fluid and acid-base balance	2,300 mg/day	Found as sodium chloride in foods	UL: 3,600 mg/day	Rare
Sulfur	A part of other compounds in body; helps give some amino acids their three-dimensional shape	None	Meats, fish, poultry, eggs, dairy foods, fruits, vegetables	None	None

hormones, such as insulin and thyroid hormones, function. They are indispensable for maintaining healthy red blood cells (iron) and protecting your teeth (fluoride), and can be cofactors (iron, zinc, copper, manganese, and molybdenum) that work with enzymes to ensure that numerous critical reactions occur. **Table 8.2** provides a summary of the trace minerals.

Overconsumption of Minerals Can Be Toxic

As with many other nutrients, consuming large amounts of some minerals, particularly the trace minerals, including iron and copper, can have toxic effects. In fact, for some minerals such as magnesium, there isn't a huge difference between the amount that is recommended daily for good health and the excessive amount that can cause gastrointestinal problems such as diarrhea and cramps. The good news is that foods alone rarely provide excessive amounts of any of the minerals; toxicities are usually the result of the use of supplements. This is one more reason why you should try to eat a wide variety of foods to meet your daily needs. **Figure 8.11** gives examples of minerals that are often obtained by following the MyPlate plan. In the following pages, we will look at each of the major and trace minerals closely, considering their functions, recommended intake, food sources, and the possible health consequences of over- or underconsumption.

Other Minerals: Arsenic, Boron, Nickel, Silicon, and Vanadium

A few other minerals exist in your body, but their nutritional importance in humans has not yet been established. These minerals include arsenic, boron, nickel, silicon, and vanadium. Although limited research suggests that these may have a function in animals, there isn't enough data to confirm an essential role in humans.[19]

Figure 8.11 Minerals Are Found Widely in MyPlate
Eating a variety of foods from all food groups is the best strategy to meet your daily mineral needs.

ChooseMyPlate.gov

Vegetables	Fruits	Grains	Protein	Dairy
Potassium	Potassium	Sodium	Sodium	Potassium
Calcium	Calcium	Phosphorus	Phosphorus	Calcium
Magnesium	(fortified juice)	Magnesium	Magnesium	Phosphorus
Chromium	Manganese	Iron	Iron	
Manganese	Boron	Zinc	Copper	
		Selenium	Zinc	
		Chromium	Selenium	
		Manganese		

Table 8.2

Minerals at a Glance: Trace Minerals

Trace Minerals	Major Functions	Adult DRI, 19 to 50 years	Food Sources	Excessive/Toxicity Symptoms/UL	Deficiency Symptoms/Conditions
Iron	As a major component of hemoglobin and myoglobin, helps transport oxygen throughout the body; enhances brain function	8 to 18 mg/day	Meat, fish, poultry, enriched and fortified breads and cereals	Vomiting, nausea, diarrhea, constipation, organ damage including the kidney and liver UL: 45 mg/day	Fatigue, iron-deficiency anemia, growth retardation in infants
Copper	A component of several enzymes; involved in iron transport; needed for healthy connective tissue enzymes; role in blood clotting and a healthy immune system	900 µg/day	Organ meats, nuts, seeds, cocoa, whole grains, legumes, and shellfish	Vomiting, abdominal pain, nausea, diarrhea, liver damage UL: 10,000 µg/day	Impaired growth and development
Zinc	Cofactor for several enzymes; DNA and RNA synthesis; needed for a healthy immune system, wound healing, and taste acuity	8 to 11 mg/day	Meat, poultry, seafood, whole grains	Nausea, vomiting, cramps, diarrhea, impaired immune function UL: 40 mg/day	Skin rash and hair loss, diarrhea, loss of taste and smell
Selenium	A component of enzymes; antioxidant	55 µg/day	Meat, seafood, fish, eggs, whole grains	Selenosis, brittle hair and nails, skin rash, garlic breath odor, fatigue UL: 400 µg/day	Keshan disease
Fluoride	Makes teeth stronger	3.1 to 3.8 mg/day	Fluoridated water, tea	Fluorosis in teeth and skeletal fluorosis UL: 10 mg/day	Increased susceptibility to dental caries
Chromium	Improves insulin response	20 to 35 µg/day	Pork, egg yolks, whole grains, nuts	Unconfirmed toxicity effects	Potential increase of insulin resistance
Iodine	Component of a thyroid hormone	150 µg/day	Iodized salt, seafood, dairy products	Impaired functioning of thyroid UL: 1,100 µg/day	Goiter, cretinism
Manganese	Cofactor involved in metabolism	1.8 to 2.3 mg/day	Beans, oats, nuts, tea	Abnormal central nervous system effects UL: 11 mg/day	Deficiency rare; rash and scaly skin
Molybdenum	Cofactor for a variety of enzymes	45 µg/day	Legumes, nuts, leafy vegetables, dairy, cereals	Unknown in humans UL: 2 mg/day	Unknown in humans

Table 8.3

Additional Minerals

Mineral	Potential Role and Deficiency Symptoms	Food Sources	Potential Toxicity
Arsenic	May be needed in the metabolism of a specific amino acid in rats. A deficiency may impair growth and reproduction in animals.	Dairy products, meat, poultry, fish, grains, and cereal products	No known adverse effect in humans from the organic form of arsenic found in foods. The inorganic form is poisonous to humans.
Boron	A deficiency may be associated with reproductive abnormalities in certain fish and frogs, which suggests a possible role in normal development in animals.	Grape juice, legumes, potatoes, pecans, peanut butter, apples, and milk	No known adverse effect from boron in food. Some research suggests that high amounts of boron may cause reproductive and developmental problems in animals. Because of this, the upper limit for human adults has been set at 20 mg daily, which is more than 10 times the amount American adults consume daily, on average.
Nickel	May be needed by specific enzymes in the body. It is considered an essential mineral in animals.	Grains and grain products, vegetables, legumes, nuts, and chocolate	No known toxicity of nickel in humans when consuming a normal diet. In rats, high exposure to nickel salts can cause toxicity, with symptoms such as lethargy, irregular breathing, and lower than normal weight gain. Because of this, the upper limit for adults is set at 1 mg daily for nickel salts.
Silicon	May be needed for bone formation in animals.	Grains, grain products, and vegetables	No known risk of silicon toxicity in humans from food sources.
Vanadium	In animals, vanadium has insulin-like actions and a deficiency increases the risk of abortion.	Mushrooms, shellfish, parsley, and black pepper	No known risk of toxicity in humans from vanadium in foods. Too much has been shown to cause kidney damage in animals. Vanadium can be purchased as supplements. Because of the known toxicity in animals, the upper limit for adults is set at 1.8 mg daily.

Table 8.3 summarizes these minerals, their potential role in animal health, their food sources, and the levels of deficiency and toxicity, if known, in humans.

LO 8.4 **The Take-Home Message** Minerals are essential nutrients needed in relatively small amounts to enable your body to function properly. All minerals are inorganic elements. The body's absorption of minerals from foods varies, depending on their bioavailability. The seven major minerals are needed in amounts greater than 100 milligrams per day, and the nine trace minerals are needed in amounts less than 20 milligrams per day. Several minerals, particularly the trace minerals, can be toxic if consumed in high amounts.

exploring
Sodium

What Is Sodium?

LO 8.5 Name functions, sources, and deficiency/toxicity of sodium.

Sodium is an electrolyte in your body. Most sodium in your body is in your blood and in the fluid surrounding your cells. About 90 percent of the sodium you consume is in the form of sodium chloride, commonly known as table salt.

Functions of Sodium

Sodium's chief role is regulation of fluid balance. Sodium also plays an important role in transporting substances such as amino acids across cell membranes.

Salt is frequently added to foods to enhance flavor and as a preservative. It is also used to reduce the growth of bacteria and mold in many bread products and deli meats. Sodium phosphate, sodium carbonate, and sodium bicarbonate (baking soda) are food additives and preservatives that perform similar functions in foods. Monosodium glutamate (MSG) is a common additive in Asian cuisines that is used to intensify the flavor of foods.

Sodium Balance in Your Body

Physiological processes maintain the amount of sodium in your body at a certain level. When your body needs more sodium, your kidneys reduce the amount that is excreted in your urine. Likewise, when you take in too much sodium, you excrete the excess. For example, when you eat salty pretzels or potato chips, your kidneys will excrete the extra sodium you take in from these snacks.

Smaller amounts of sodium are lost in your stool and through daily perspiration. The amount of sodium lost through perspiration depends upon the rate at which you are sweating, the amount of sodium you have consumed (the more sodium in your diet, the higher the loss), and the intensity of heat in the environment. As you get acclimated to environmental heat, less sodium will be lost over time

in your sweat.[20] This built-in protective mechanism helps to prevent the loss of too much sodium from your body.

Daily Needs

The penny shown below is covered with about 180 milligrams of sodium. This is the bare minimum you need daily. It is based on the amount of sodium needed by individuals who live in temperate climates and those who have become acclimated to hotter environments.[21]

Planning a balanced diet with such a small amount of sodium is virtually impossible, so the recommended sodium intake for adults up to 51 years of age is set at 1,500 milligrams daily. This sodium recommendation allows you to eat a variety of foods from all the food groups so that you can meet your other nutrient needs. It also covers any sodium that is lost in sweat by moderately active individuals, or those who are not acclimated to the environmental temperature. Those who are very physically active and/or not acclimated to heat will likely need to consume a higher amount of sodium. This can easily be obtained in the diet.

Americans currently consume more than double the recommended amount, or more than 3,400 milligrams of sodium daily, on average (**Figure 8.12**).

Food Sources

Sodium is so widely available in foods that you don't have to go out of your way to meet your needs (**Figure 8.13**).

About 10 percent of Americans' consumption of sodium is from foods in which it occurs naturally, such as fruits, vegetables, milk, meat, fish, poultry, and legumes.[22] Another 5 to 10 percent gets added during cooking and to season foods at the table.

Processed foods contribute a hefty 75 percent of the sodium in the diet of Americans.[23] Comparing the amount of sodium in a fresh tomato (6 milligrams) with the amount found in a cup of canned tomatoes (355 milligrams) aptly illustrates just how much more sodium is found in processed foods.

Because the majority of your sodium comes from processed foods, and a fair amount comes from the salt that you add to your foods, cutting back on these two sources is the best way to lower your intake. When you buy processed foods, look for the terms "low sodium," "reduced sodium," or "sodium free" on the labels. Further, bypass the salt shaker at the table and season foods with black pepper, Tabasco sauce, lemon juice, or a no-salt seasoning blend. For more ideas on how avoid excess sodium in your daily diet, see Table Tips: "Shake Your Salt Habit."

Figure 8.12 Recommended Intake of Sodium

CONTINUED

Sodium

ChooseMyPlate.gov

Milligrams (mg) of

Figure 8.13 Sodium Content of Selected Natural and Processed Foods
While sodium is naturally occurring in many foods, processing adds a tremendous amount, as you can see by the pairing of items within each food group (e.g., compare 2 mg of sodium in 1 cup of cucumbers to 1,356 mg of sodium in 1 cup of pickles).

Too Much or Too Little

There is a direct relationship between sodium and blood pressure in many people. In general, as a person's intake of sodium increases, so does his or her blood pressure. Blood pressure that becomes too high, known as hypertension, increases the risk for heart disease, stroke, and kidney disease (see the Health Connection Case Study). Unfortunately, many Americans will develop hypertension sometime during their lives. Researchers estimate that if Americans reduced their sodium intake by 40 percent over the next ten years, over 275,000 deaths from cardiovascular disease could be prevented.[24] To help reduce the risk of high blood pressure, the upper level for adults for daily sodium intake is set at 2,300 milligrams. Many Americans exceed this upper limit daily.

Sodium deficiency is rare in healthy individuals consuming a balanced diet.

Controlling Hypertension

There are factors that increase the chances of developing hypertension, some of which you can control and others you cannot.

Your family history, the aging process, and your race all affect the likelihood that you will develop high blood pressure. These are the risk factors that you can't control. If your parents, siblings, and/or grandparents have or had hypertension, you are at a higher risk of developing it

Practical Nutrition VIDEO

Sodium: What You Need Compared to What You Consume

Even if you never pick up a salt shaker, you may be far exceeding your daily sodium needs. Scan this QR code with your mobile device to access the video. You can also access the video in MasteringNutrition™.

TableTIPS

Shake Your Salt Habit

When buying canned soups, look for the reduced-sodium or low-sodium versions.

Keep your portions of deli meats to no more than 3 ounces and build a "meaty" sandwich by adding naturally low-sodium vegetables. Remember to skip the high-sodium pickles!

Nibble on low-sodium dried fruits (apricots, raisins) and unsalted walnut pieces.

Skip the salty French fries and potato chips and enjoy the sodium-free baked potato at dinner.

Use olive oil and balsamic vinegar for a salad dressing with less sodium than is in bottled dressings. Or, dilute regular salad dressing with an equal portion of vinegar to cut the sodium.

yourself. Typically, the risk of hypertension increases with age. It is more likely to occur after the age of 35 for men, and women generally experience it after menopause. Hypertension is more prevalent in African-Americans, and tends to occur earlier and be more severe than in Caucasians.[25]

The good news is that there are more risk factors that you *can* control than those that you can't. You can change several dietary and lifestyle habits to help reduce your risk (see **Table 8.4**), such as your weight and your physical activity level. Individuals who are obese are twice as likely to have hypertension as those at a healthy weight. Even a modest weight loss can have an impact. Losing as little as 10 pounds can reduce a person's blood pressure, and may actually prevent

hypertension even if a healthy weight has not yet been reached. Additional weight loss can have an even more dramatic effect on blood pressure. Regular physical activity can lower blood pressure even if weight loss hasn't occurred.[26]

You can also control your alcohol consumption, which affects your risk of developing high blood pressure. Studies have shown that drinkers who consumed 3 to 6 drinks daily and then reduced their alcohol consumption by 67 percent, on average, were able to reduce their systolic pressure by more than 3 mm Hg and their diastolic pressure by 2 mm Hg.[27] Less drinking and more physical activity is the name of the game when it comes to keeping high blood pressure at bay.

Lastly, eating a balanced diet is a proven strategy to lower your blood pressure. A large research study, called the DASH (Dietary Approaches to Stop Hypertension) study, followed individuals on three different diets. One diet was a typical American diet: low in fruits, vegetables, and dairy products and high in fat, saturated fat, and cholesterol. A second

hypertension High blood pressure.

systolic pressure The force of your blood against the artery walls when your heart beats.

diastolic pressure The pressure of your blood against the artery walls when the heart is at rest between beats.

A CASE STUDY
A High-Pressure Situation

health CONNECTION

Kegan, a young African-American man, landed his dream job at a major financial institution soon after he graduated from college. Kegan works over 12 hours a day, has no free time to work out, and eats take-out foods for all of his three meals. Not surprisingly, he has gained over 25 pounds since graduation, which classifies him as obese. At a recent "Wellness Workplace" event, his blood pressure reading categorized him just shy of having **hypertension**, or high blood pressure.

While many folks his age think that they don't have to worry about high blood pressure until their later adult years, this couldn't be farther from the truth. In a recent study, researchers looked at the hospital records of over 2,200 young adults, aged 19 to 49, and uncovered that those individuals who were obese were more likely to have experienced a stroke than were leaner young adults.[28] These stroke victims were also more likely to be smokers, and have high blood pressure and/or diabetes. As a young adult, Kegan is setting the stage for a disease that was once experienced only by his older relatives.

Your blood pressure is a measure of the force your blood exerts against the walls of your arteries. With every beat, your heart pumps blood into your arteries, and thus to all the areas in your body. Blood pressure is highest at the moment of the heart beat. This is known as your **systolic pressure**. Pressure is lower when your heart is at rest between beats. This is called your **diastolic pressure**. Your blood pressure is expressed

using these two measurements: systolic pressure/diastolic pressure. Blood pressure of less than 120/80 mm Hg (millimeters of mercury) is considered normal. Your blood pressure rises naturally as you age, which is believed to be due in part to the increased stiffness of the arteries.[29] As blood pressure begins to rise above normal—that is, systolic is 120 or above and diastolic is 80 or above—it is classified as prehypertension. Many individuals with prehypertension will develop hypertension if they don't lower their blood pressure. A blood pressure of 140/90 mm Hg or above is classified as high blood pressure or hypertension.

Individuals with chronic high blood pressure have a higher than normal force pounding against the walls of their arteries, which makes the walls thicker and stiffer, and contributes to atherosclerosis. The heart becomes enlarged and weakened, as it has to work harder to pump enough oxygen- and nutrient-laden blood throughout the body. This can lead to fatigue, shortness of breath, and possibly heart attack. Hypertension can also damage the arteries leading to the brain and kidneys, which increases the risk of stroke and kidney disease.[30]

Think About It
Can you name two risk factors that increase Kegan's chances for a stroke at an early age?

Sodium

was rich in just fruits and vegetables, and a third, the DASH diet, was a balanced diet that was lower in fat, saturated fat, cholesterol, and sweets, and high in whole grains, fruits, vegetables, and low-fat dairy products (see **Figure 8.14**).

The individuals in the study who followed the DASH diet experienced a significant reduction in blood pressure compared with those who followed the other two diets. Because the sodium content of all three diets was the same, about 3,000 milligrams, which is the approximate amount that Americans consume daily, on average, the blood-pressure lowering effect was attributed to some other substance, or a combination of nutrients working together. For example, due to its abundance of fruits and vegetables, the DASH diet provides healthy doses of potassium and magnesium, and because of its numerous servings of dairy foods, it is also rich in calcium. Dietary potassium, magnesium, and calcium can all play a role in lowering blood pressure.[31]

A follow-up to the DASH study, called the DASH-Sodium study, investigated whether reducing the amount of dietary sodium in each of the three diets could also help lower blood pressure. Not surprisingly, it did. In general, as a person's sodium intake increases, so does the blood pressure. Although this study showed that reducing dietary sodium from about 3,300 milligrams to 2,400

Figure 8.14 The DASH diet, rich in whole grains, fruits, vegetables, and low-fat dairy foods, can help lower blood pressure.

milligrams daily lowered blood pressure, the biggest reduction occurred when sodium intake was limited to only 1,500 milligrams daily. Most importantly, the overall best diet combination for lowering blood pressure was the DASH diet plus consuming only 1,500 milligrams of sodium daily.[32] The latest scientific report of the *Dietary Guidelines for Americans* Advisory Committee concluded that Americans should consume no more than 2,400 milligrams daily and that a further reduction to 1,500 milligrams daily can have a greater effect on lowering blood pressure.[33]

eLearn

Calculating Your Risk for Hypertension

Would you like to find out *your* risk for developing high blood pressure and learn how lifestyle changes can affect your personal risk? Visit the American Heart Association website at www.heart.org and search for the "High Blood Pressure Health Risk Calculator."

Table 8.4

Take Charge of Your Blood Pressure!

If You	By	Your Systolic Blood Pressure* May Be Reduced by
Reduce your sodium intake	Keeping dietary sodium consumption to less than 2,400 mg daily	8–14 mm Hg
Lose excess weight	Modifying your diet and exercise to reach and maintain a normal, healthy body weight	5–20 mm Hg for every 22 lbs of weight loss
Stay physically active	Partaking in 30 minutes of aerobic activity (e.g., brisk walking) on most days of the week	4–9 mm Hg
Drink alcohol only in moderation	Limiting consumption to no more than 2 drinks daily for men and 1 drink daily for women	2–4 mm Hg
Follow the DASH diet	Consuming this diet, which is abundant in fruits and vegetables and low-fat dairy products	8–14 mm Hg

*Controlling the systolic pressure is more difficult than controlling the diastolic pressure, especially for individuals 50 years of age and older. Therefore, it is the primary focus for lowering blood pressure. Typically, as systolic pressure goes down with diet and lifestyle changes, the diastolic pressure will follow.

exploring
Potassium

What Is Potassium?

LO 8.6 Name functions, sources, and deficiency/toxicity of potassium.

Potassium is an important mineral with numerous functions in your body. Luckily, it is also found in numerous foods, so it's not difficult to meet your needs for it.

Functions of Potassium

Potassium Is Needed for Fluid Balance and as a Blood Buffer

More than 95 percent of the potassium in your body is inside your cells, with the remainder in the fluids outside your cells, including your blood. As with other electrolytes, potassium helps maintain fluid balance and keeps your blood pH and acid-base balance correct.

Potassium Is Needed for Muscle Contraction and Nerve Impulse Conduction

Potassium plays a role in the contraction of your muscles, including your heart, and the conduction of nerve impulses. Because of this, a dramatic increase of potassium in your body can lead to irregular heart beats or heart attack, whereas dangerously low levels could cause paralysis. Thus, potassium is tightly controlled and balanced in your body with the help of your kidneys.

Potassium Can Help Lower High Blood Pressure

A diet with plentiful potassium has been shown to help lower blood pressure, especially in salt-sensitive individuals who respond more intensely to sodium's blood pressure–raising capabilities. Potassium causes the kidneys to excrete excess sodium from the body, and keeping sodium levels low can help lower blood pressure. The DASH diet is abundant in foods with potassium.

Potassium Aids in Bone Health and Reduces Kidney Stones

Because potassium plays a buffering role in your blood, it helps keep the bone-strengthening minerals, calcium and phosphorus, from being lost from the bones and kidneys. Numerous studies suggest that having adequate amounts of potassium in your diet helps increase the density, and thus the strength, of your bones.[34]

Potassium also helps reduce the risk of **kidney stones** by causing the body to excrete citrate,[35] a compound that binds with calcium to form kidney stones, shown in **Figure 8.15**.

Daily Needs

Adults should consume 4,700 milligrams of potassium daily. This amount is recommended to help reduce the risk of high blood pressure. Potassium can also help lower the risk of developing kidney stones and preserve bone health.

Figure 8.15 Kidney Stone

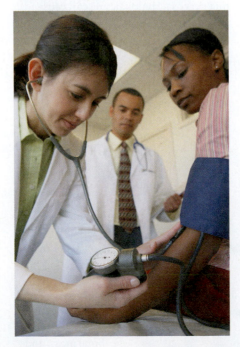

Because Americans fall short of their servings of fruits, vegetables, and lean dairy, they are also falling short of their daily potassium needs. Adult females are consuming only about 2,400 milligrams of potassium daily, and adult males are consuming only about 3,195 milligrams daily, on average.[36]

Food Sources

Consume an abundance of fruits and vegetables so as to meet your potassium needs. A diet that includes at least 4½ cups of fruits and vegetables, especially leafy greens, which is the *minimum* amount you should be consuming daily, can help you meet your potassium needs. Dairy foods, nuts, and legumes are also good sources (**Figure 8.16**). For more ideas on how to get potassium into your daily diet, see Table Tips: "Potassium Power."

Too Much or Too Little

There isn't any known danger from consuming too much potassium that occurs naturally in foods. These excesses will be excreted in your urine. However, consuming too much from supplements or salt substitutes (the sodium in some salt substitutes is replaced with potassium) can cause **hyperkalemia** (*hyper* = too much, *kalemia* = potassium in the blood) for some individuals. Hyperkalemia can cause irregular heart beats, damage the heart, and be life-threatening.[37]

kidney stone A solid mass formed in the kidneys from dietary minerals.

hyperkalemia Abnormally high levels of potassium in the blood.

hypokalemia Abnormally low levels of potassium in the blood.

CONTINUED ▸

Figure 8.16 Potassium Content in Selected Foods

Those at a higher risk for hyperkalemia include individuals with impaired kidneys, such as people with type 1 diabetes mellitus, those with kidney disease, and individuals taking medications for heart disease or diuretics that cause the kidneys to block the excretion of potassium. These individuals may also need to consume less than the recommended amount of potassium daily, as advised by their health care professional.

Although a deficiency of dietary potassium is rare, too little potassium can cause **hypokalemia** (*hypo* = too little, *kalemia* = potassium in the blood). This may occur during bouts of vomiting and/or diarrhea. It has been seen in individuals who have anorexia nervosa and/or bulimia nervosa. Hypokalemia can cause muscle weakness and spasms, fatigue, and, in severe situations, irregular heart beats and paralysis.[38]

Individuals who consume high-protein diets that contain few fruits and vegetables may be depriving themselves of the buffering actions of potassium.[39] The breakdown of excessive amounts of dietary protein causes the formation of acids that are balanced by the buffering action of potassium. A diet too low in fruits and vegetables is setting the stage for an imbalance of acids and bases in the blood and the increased risk of kidney stones, loss of bone mass, and high blood pressure.

TableTIPS

Potassium Power!

Slice a banana on your oatmeal at breakfast to begin the day with a potassium boost.

Add leafy greens to all your sandwiches. Spinach in particular is a potassium dynamo!

Add a spoonful of walnuts to your mid-morning yogurt for a one-two (nuts and dairy) potassium punch.

Have bean soup with your lunchtime sandwich for a warm way to enjoy your potassium.

Baked regular or sweet potatoes are potassium powerhouses on your dinner plate.

exploring
Calcium

What Is Calcium?

LO 8.7 Name functions, sources, and deficiency/toxicity of calcium.

Calcium is one of the most abundant minerals in nature and is found in everything from pearls to seashells to eggshells. Calcium is also the most abundant mineral in your body. More than 99 percent of your body's calcium is located in your bones and teeth.

Functions of Calcium

Calcium Helps Build Strong Bones and Teeth

Calcium couples with phosphorus to form *hydroxyapatite*, providing strength and structure in your bones and the enamel on your teeth. Adequate dietary calcium is needed to build and maintain bone mass. Calcium makes up almost 40 percent of the weight of your bones.[40]

Calcium Plays a Role in Your Muscles, Nerves, and Blood

The remaining 1 percent of calcium is in your blood, in the fluids that surround your cells, in your muscles, and in other tissues. Calcium is needed for muscle contraction, and to help your nervous system transmit messages. Calcium is also involved in the dilation and contraction of blood vessels, and it helps your blood clot. Finally, calcium is necessary

for the secretion of some hormones and enzymes. It must be maintained at a constant level for your body to function properly.[41]

Calcium May Help Lower High Blood Pressure

Studies have shown that a heart-healthy diet rich in calcium, potassium, magnesium, fruits, vegetables, and low-fat dairy products can help lower blood pressure.[42] One example of such a diet, the DASH diet, contains three servings of lean dairy foods daily, the minimum amount of servings recommended to obtain this protective effect[43] (see the Exploring Sodium section for more on the DASH diet).

Calcium May Help Prevent Colon Cancer

A diet with plenty of calcium has been shown to help reduce the risk of developing benign tumors in the colon that may eventually lead to cancer.[44] Calcium may protect the lining of the colon from damaging bile acids and cancer-promoting substances.

Calcium May Reduce the Risk of Kidney Stones

Approximately a million American adults visit their health care providers annually with kidney stones.[45] Most of these stones are composed mainly of calcium oxalate.[46] Although health professionals in the past often warned those who suffer with kidney stones to minimize their dietary calcium, this advice has since been reversed. Research has shown that a balanced diet, along with adequate amounts of *dietary* calcium, may actually reduce the risk of developing kidney stones.[47] Calcium binds with the oxalates in foods in the intestines and prevents their absorption. With fewer oxalates filtering through the kidneys, fewer stones are formed. Research involving calcium supplements has not indicated the same protective effect. In fact, high intake of calcium supplements, not food sources, has been shown to increase the risk of kidney stones[48] (see the section on Too Much or Too Little). The current upper levels set for calcium are based on research related to risk for increased kidney stones.[49]

Daily Needs

Adults age 19 to 50 need 1,000 milligrams of calcium daily. Women older than 50, and men age 70 and beyond, should increase their daily intake to 1,200 mg.[50] Most women and many older males do not meet their daily calcium needs.[51]

Food Sources

Milk, yogurt, and cheese are the major sources of calcium in the American diet (**Figure 8.17**). Each serving from the dairy group will provide approximately 300 milligrams of calcium. (Choose nonfat, low- or reduced-fat, or skim milk versions to reduce the amount of saturated fat in these foods.) Although three servings of dairy foods will just about meet many adults' daily needs, American adults consume less than 2 servings of dairy daily, on average.[52]

hypercalcemia Abnormally high levels of calcium in the blood.

CONTINUED ▸

exploring continued
Calcium

Broccoli, kale, canned salmon with bones (the calcium is in the bones), and tofu that is processed with calcium can also add calcium to the diet. Calcium-fortified foods, such as juices and cereals, are also excellent sources. Spinach, rhubarb, and okra also contain calcium, but these foods are also high in calcium-binding oxalates, so less than 10 percent of the mineral is absorbed in the body (**Figure 8.18**). For more ideas on how to get calcium into your daily diet, see Table Tips: "Calcium Counts."

Too Much or Too Little

The upper level for calcium has been set at 2,500 milligrams daily for adults age 19 to 50, and at 2,000 milligrams for those age 51 and beyond, to avoid kidney stones. Too much dietary calcium can also cause constipation and interfere with the absorption of other minerals, such as iron, zinc, magnesium, and phosphorus. **Hypercalcemia**, or having abnormally high blood levels of calcium, can potentially impair kidney function and lead to calcium deposits in the body.

If your diet is low in calcium, calcium leaves your bones in order to maintain a constant level in your blood. A chronic deficiency of dietary calcium can lead to less dense, weakened, and brittle bones and increased risk for osteoporosis and bone fractures (**Figure 8.19**). Read on to find out more about the importance of forming and maintaining healthy bone.

Osteoporosis: Not Just Your Grandmother's Problem

If you are fortunate enough to have elders, such as grandparents, in your life, you may have heard them comment that they are shrinking as they age. Of course, they aren't really shrinking, but they may be losing height as the tissues supporting their spine lose mass and elasticity and the joint capsules between the bones (or vertebrae) of the spine lose their cushion of fluid. This is normal. In many older adults, however, the vertebrae themselves lose mass and begin to collapse, so that it becomes more difficult for the spine to hold the weight of the head and upper body. This leads to a gradual curvature of the spine, which affects their posture (**Figure 8.20**). As older individuals begin to hunch over, they can lose as much as a foot in height.[53]

Figure 8.17 **Calcium Content in Selected Foods**

Figure 8.18 **Bioavailability of Calcium**

Figure 8.19 **Healthy Bone (left) vs Weakened Bone (right)**

Figure 8.20 **Weak bones cause the spine to collapse over time**

Bones are a dynamic, living tissue. Older layers of bones are constantly removed, and new bone is constantly added. In fact, your entire skeleton is replaced with new bone about every decade. During childhood and adolescence, more bone is added than is removed, as the bones grow in length and mass. Although growth of bone length typically ceases during the teenage years, bone mass will continue to accumulate into the early years of young adulthood (**Figure 8.21**). **Peak bone mass**, which is the genetically determined maximum amount of bone mass an individual can build up, typically occurs when a person reaches his or her 30s. After peak bone mass is reached, the loss of bone mass begins to slowly exceed the rate at which new bone is added.[54]

As bones lose mass, they become porous, and **osteoporosis** (*osteo* = bone, *porosis* = porous) can develop. The weakened, fragile bones are prone to fractures. A minor stumble while walking can result in a broken ankle, rib cage, or arm bone as the result of an ensuing fall. Shopping for groceries, showering, dressing, and even brushing one's teeth become challenges for many older people with osteoporosis.

Hip fractures can be devastating because they often render a person immobile, which quickly affects quality of life. Individuals with hip fractures are never able to regain the quality of life they had prior to the injury and have an increased risk of dying.[55] Osteoporosis causes 1.5 million fractures annually in the United States.[56]

Adults can have a bone test done by their doctors to assess how their **bone mineral density (BMD)** compares with that of a healthy 30-year-old. BMD refers to the amount of minerals, in particular calcium, per volume in an individual's bone. The denser the bones, the stronger the bones. A low test score indicates **osteopenia** (*penia* = poverty), which signals low bone mass. A very low test score indicates osteoporosis.

Ironically, though osteoporosis is often thought of as a condition of the elderly, it has its roots in childhood and must be prevented throughout adulthood. Saving up bone mass is like saving money for retirement. The more you save when you are young and preserve throughout your adulthood, the more you will have for your later years. Conversely, if you don't save enough early in life, you may end up with little to fall back on when you need it later.

It's never too late to try to reduce your risk of osteoporosis. To take a look at the risk factors involved, see the Self-Assessment.

After you have completed the Self-Assessment, look at the skeleton. If it has mostly shaded areas, you have fewer risk factors for osteoporosis; the less shaded the skeleton, the more risk factors you have, and the higher your risk of developing osteoporosis. Many of these risk factors can be reduced by a healthy diet and lifestyle.

Although you cannot control the first five risk factors (your gender, ethnicity, age, body type, and family history), you can control the remaining six risk factors. If your sex hormone levels are lower than they should be and/or if you are taking medications that may increase your risk of osteoporosis, talk to your doctor. Quitting smoking, exercising regularly, and limiting or avoiding alcohol will help reduce your risk. Lastly, make sure that you consume adequate amounts of vitamin D (Chapter 7) and calcium. If you can't meet your calcium needs through food, a supplement may be necessary.

Calcium Supplements

Some individuals are advised by their health care provider to take a calcium supplement. The calcium in supplements is part of a compound, typically either calcium carbonate or calcium citrate. Calcium carbonate tends to be the form of calcium most commonly purchased. It is most effective when consumed with a meal, as the acidic juices in your stomach help with its absorption.[57] Calcium citrate can be taken any time throughout the day, as it doesn't need the help of acidic juices to be absorbed.

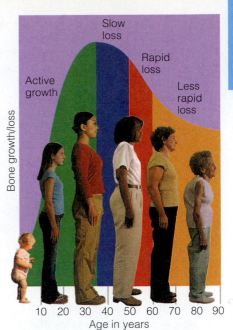

Figure 8.21 Change in Bone Mass over Time
In your early years, more bone mass is added than lost in your body. In their mid-30s, women begin to slowly lose bone mass until menopause, when the rate of loss is accelerated for several years. Bone loss continues after age 60 but at a slower rate. Bone loss also occurs in men as they age.

Regardless of the form, all calcium, whether from supplements or from fortified or naturally occurring foods, should be consumed in doses of 500 milligrams or less, as this is the maximum that your body can absorb efficiently at one time.[58]

Be cautious about adding a calcium supplement to your diet if you are already consuming plenty of dairy foods and/or calcium-fortified foods.

peak bone mass The genetically determined maximum amount of bone mass an individual can build up.

osteoporosis A condition in which the bones are less dense, increasing the risk of fractures.

bone mineral density (BMD) The amount of minerals, in particular calcium, per volume in an individual's bone.

osteopenia A condition in which bone mineral density is lower than normal but not low enough to be classified as osteoporosis.

CONTINUED ▶

self-ASSESSMENT

Are You at Risk for Osteoporosis?

Answer the following questions to determine how many risk factors you have for osteoporosis. Shade in each part of the skeleton based on your answers.

1. *Gender:* Are you female?
   Yes ☐ **No** ☐ (If you answered no, shade in the left arm of the skeleton.)
   Females are at higher risk for osteoporosis than males because they have smaller bones, and thus less bone mass. Also, bone mass is lost at a faster rate right after menopause due to the decline of estrogen in women's bodies. However, men can suffer from osteoporosis and can experience it at a fairly young age.[59]

2. *Ethnicity:* Are you a Caucasian or Asian-American female?
   Yes ☐ **No** ☐ (If no, shade in the right arm of the skeleton.)
   Caucasian and Asian women typically have lower bone mass than other women.

3. *Age:* Are you over 30 years of age?
   Yes ☐ **No** ☐ (If no, shade in the left hand of the skeleton.)
   You begin to lose bone mass after about age 30, which increases your risk of osteoporosis and fractures.

4. *Body Type:* Are you a small-boned or petite woman?
   Yes ☐ **No** ☐ (If no, shade in the right hand of the skeleton.)
   Thin women have lower bone mass and increased risk of fractures. A higher body weight puts more weight-bearing, mechanical stress on bones, helping them to stay healthy. A healthy body weight also means you'll have some padding should a fall occur. Also, since most of the estrogen produced in menopausal women's bodies is formed in fat tissue, thinner women have less bone-protecting estrogen.[60]

5. *Family History of Fractures:* Have your parents or grandparents ever experienced any bone fractures in their golden years?
   Yes ☐ **No** ☐ (If no, shade in the left leg of the skeleton.)
   A family history of bone fractures in your relatives' later years increases your risk of osteoporosis.

6. *Level of Sex Hormones:* Are you a premenopausal woman who has stopped menstruating, a menopausal woman, or a male with low testosterone levels?
   Yes ☐ **No** ☐ (If no, shade in the right leg of the skeleton.)
   Women with amenorrhea (the absence of menstrual periods) experience hormonal imbalances, especially if they are at a dangerously low body weight.[61] Menopausal women, or men with low levels of sex hormones, which are protective against bone loss, are also at a higher risk.

7. *Medications:* Are you taking certain medications such as glucocorticoids (prednisone), antiseizure medications (phenytoin), aluminum-containing antacids, and/or excessive amounts of thyroid replacement hormones?
   Yes ☐ **No** ☐ (If no, shade in the torso of the skeleton.)

The long-term use of glucocorticoids, antiseizure medicines, certain antacids, or too much thyroid hormone–replacing medication can lead to a loss of bone mass and increase the risk of fractures.[62] Certain cancer treatments can also cause bone loss. Though you shouldn't stop taking any prescribed medications, you should speak to your doctor regarding your bone health.

8. *Smoking:* Do you smoke?
   Yes ☐ **No** ☐ (If no, shade in the left foot of the skeleton.)
   Smokers absorb less calcium than do nonsmokers. Women smokers have lower levels of estrogen in their bodies and begin menopause earlier than do nonsmokers.

9. *Physical Activity:* Do you spend less than 30 minutes exercising daily?
   Yes ☐ **No** ☐ (If no, shade in the left hip of the skeleton.)
   Regular physical activity contributes to higher peak bone mass in a person's early years, and strength and weight-bearing activities such as walking, hiking, and tennis help maintain bone mass during adulthood. These activities cause you to work against gravity, which helps strengthen your bones. Regular exercise also helps you maintain healthy muscles and improves your coordination and balance, which can help prevent falls.[63]

10. *Alcohol:* Do you consume more than one alcoholic drink a day if you are a woman or consume more than two alcoholic drinks daily if you are a man?
    Yes ☐ **No** ☐ (If no, shade in the right hip of the skeleton.)
    Heavy consumption of alcohol can reduce bone mass by inhibiting the formation of new bone, preventing the activation of vitamin D, and increasing the loss of calcium. It can also increase the risk of stumbling and falling.[64]

11. *Inadequate Amounts of Calcium and Vitamin D:* Do you consume less than 3 cups daily of milk or yogurt that has been fortified with vitamin D?
    Yes ☐ **No** ☐ (If no, shade in the right foot of the skeleton.)
    Because calcium is needed to build and maintain bone mass, and vitamin D is needed for your body to absorb this mineral, having inadequate amounts of either or both of these nutrients increases your risk of low bone mass, bone loss, and bone fractures.

exploring
Phosphorus

What Is Phosphorus?

LO 8.8 Name functions, sources, and deficiency/toxicity of phosphorus.

Phosphorus is the second most abundant mineral in your body. The majority of phosphorus—about 85 percent—is in your bones. The remainder is in your cells and fluids outside your cells, including your blood.

Functions of Phosphorus

Phosphorus Is Needed for Bones and Teeth and Is an Important Component of Cells

As mentioned, phosphorus combines with calcium to form hydroxyapatite, the strengthening material found in bones and teeth.

Phosphorus is part of phospholipids, which give your cell membranes their structure (**Figure 8.22**). Phospholipids act as a barrier to keep specific substances out of the cells, while letting others in.

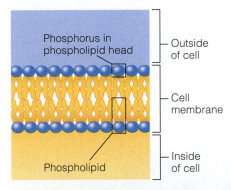

Figure 8.22 Phosphorus in Phospholipids Phosphorus makes up part of the phospholipids found in cell membranes.

Phosphorus Is Needed during Metabolism

Phosphorus helps your body store the energy generated from the metabolism of carbohydrates, protein, and fat for later use. Your body can draw upon these stores as needed.

Phosphorus Acts as a Buffer and Is Part of the DNA and RNA of Every Cell

If your blood becomes too acidic or too basic, phosphorus can act as a buffer to help return your blood pH to normal.

Your blood pH must stay within a very narrow range to prevent damage to your tissues.

Phosphorus is part of your DNA and RNA. The instructions for your genes are coded in your DNA and transcribed in your RNA to make the proteins needed in your body.

Daily Needs

Adults, both male and female, need 700 milligrams of phosphorus daily. Americans, on average, consume more than 1,000 milligrams of phosphorus daily.[65]

Food Sources

A balanced, varied diet will easily meet your phosphorus needs. Foods from animal sources such as meat, fish, poultry, and dairy products are excellent sources of phosphorus (**Figure 8.23**). Phosphorus is also part of many food additives. For more ideas on how to get phosphorus into your daily diet, see Table Tips: "Fabulous Phosphorus."

Too Much or Too Little

Typically, consuming too much dietary phosphorus and its subsequent effect, **hyperphosphatemia**, is an issue only for individuals with kidney problems who cannot excrete excess phosphorus.

Constantly high phosphorus intake and low calcium intake can cause the

hyperphosphatemia Abnormally high levels of phosphorus in the blood.

Phosphorus

Figure 8.23 Phosphorus Content of Selected Foods

Table TIPS

Fabulous Phosphorus

Layer sliced bananas, yogurt, and raisin bran cereal for a high-phosphorus breakfast that tastes like a dessert.

Blend together orange juice and slightly thawed frozen strawberries for a refreshing smoothie.

Skip the butter and sprinkle sliced almonds over your dinner vegetables for a crunchy topping.

Dunk raw broccoli florets in a spicy salsa for a snack with a kick.

Combine shredded wheat cereal, mixed nuts, and raisins for a sweet and crunchy snack mix.

loss of calcium from your bones and a subsequent decrease in bone mass. Loss of bone mass increases the risk of osteoporosis. Hyperphosphatemia can also lead to calcification of tissues in the body. To protect against this, the upper level for phosphorus has been set at 4,000 milligrams daily for adults age 19 to 50 and 3,000 milligrams for those 50 years of age and older.

Too little phosphorus in the diet can cause its level in your blood to drop dangerously low and result in muscle weakness, bone pain, rickets, confusion, and, at the extreme, death. Because phosphorus is so abundant in the diet, a deficiency is rare. In fact, a person would have to be in a state of near starvation before experiencing a phosphorus deficiency.[66]

Magnesium

What Is Magnesium?

LO 8.9 Name functions, sources, and deficiency/toxicity of magnesium.

Magnesium is another abundant mineral in your body. While about half of the magnesium is in your bones, most of the remaining magnesium is inside the cells. A mere 1 percent is found in your blood and, like calcium, this amount must be maintained at a constant level.

Functions of Magnesium

Magnesium Is Needed for Metabolism and to Maintain Healthy Muscles, Nerves, Bones, and Heart

Magnesium helps more than 300 enzymes produce reactions inside your cells. It is needed for the metabolism of carbohydrates, proteins, and fats. Magnesium is used during the synthesis of protein and to help your muscles and nerves function properly. It is also needed to help you maintain healthy bones and a regular heart beat.[67]

Magnesium May Help Lower High Blood Pressure

Studies have shown that magnesium supplements may help lower blood pressure slightly and that a plant-based diet abundant in fruits and vegetables, which are rich in magnesium as well as other minerals, can also lower blood pressure.[68]

The blood-pressure-lowering DASH diet, which has been clinically proven to lower blood pressure, is rich in magnesium as well as calcium and potassium (see the Exploring Sodium section for more on the DASH diet).[69]

Magnesium May Help Reduce the Risk of Diabetes Mellitus

Some studies suggest that a diet with higher amounts of magnesium may help decrease the risk of type 2 diabetes mellitus. Low blood levels of magnesium, which often occur in individuals with type 2 diabetes, may be involved in insulin resistance in the body. This may lead to elevated blood glucose levels in those with preexisting diabetes, and may contribute to higher than normal blood glucose levels in those at risk for type 2 diabetes.[70]

Daily Needs

Adult females age 19 to 30 need 310 milligrams of magnesium, whereas men of the same age need 400 milligrams daily. Females age 31 and over need 320 milligrams; men of this age need 420 milligrams of magnesium daily.

Currently, many adult Americans fall short of their magnesium needs. Women consume only about 85 percent of their needs, or about 274 milligrams daily, on average. Men consume approximately 350 milligrams daily, on average, which is only about 85 percent of the amount recommended daily.[71] Because older adults tend to consume fewer calories, and thus less dietary magnesium, elders are at an even higher risk of falling short of their needs.

Food Sources

The biggest contributors of magnesium to Americans' diets are vegetables, whole grains, nuts, and fruits (**Figure 8.24**). Milk, yogurt, meat, and eggs are also good sources. Because the majority of the magnesium is in the bran and germ of the grain kernel, products made with refined grains, such as white flour, are poor sources.

It's not difficult to meet your magnesium needs. A peanut butter sandwich on whole-wheat bread, chased with a glass of low-fat milk and a banana, will provide over 200 milligrams, or about half of an adult's daily needs. For more ideas on how to get magnesium into your daily diet, see Table Tips: "Magnificent Magnesium."

Too Much or Too Little

There isn't any known risk in consuming too much magnesium from food sources. However, consuming large amounts from supplements has been shown to cause intestinal problems such as diarrhea, cramps, and nausea. In fact, some laxatives purposefully contain magnesium because of its known purgative effect. Because of the potential for distress to the intestinal system, the upper level for magnesium from supplements, not foods, is set at 350 milligrams for adults. This level is to prevent diarrhea, the first symptom that typically

CONTINUED

Magnesium

MAGNESIUM

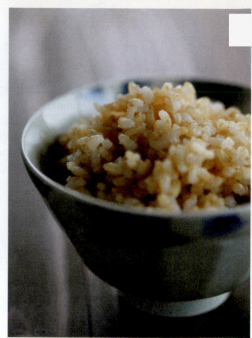

Milligrams (mg) of **Magnesium**

Food	mg
Romaine lettuce, 2 cups	12
Spinach, fresh, 2 cups	47
Pineapple, diced, 1 cup	20
Banana, 1 medium	32
Oatmeal, 1/2 cup	30
Wheat germ, 2 tbs (approx. 1/8 cup)	34
Brown rice, cooked, 1/2 cup	43
Kidney beans, cooked, 1/2 cup	19
Chickpeas, cooked, 1/2 cup	20
Edamame, 1/2 cup	49
Peanut butter, 2 tbs	49
Almonds, 1 oz	80
Milk, low fat, 1 cup	27
Yogurt, low fat, strawberry, 1 cup	30
Men 19 to 30 years	400
Men 31 to 50 years	420
Women 19 to 30 years	310
Women 31 to 50 years	320

Categories: Vegetables · Fruits · Grains · Protein · Dairy · Daily Needs

Figure 8.24 Magnesium Content of Selected Foods

arises when too much magnesium is consumed.[72] As mentioned earlier in this chapter, the difference between consuming enough and getting too much magnesium is rather narrow. Look to food to meet your magnesium needs rather than supplements, which can quickly cause you to consume too much.

Even though many Americans don't meet their magnesium needs, deficiencies are rare in healthy individuals because the kidneys compensate for low magnesium intake by excreting less of it. However, some medications may cause magnesium deficiency. Certain diuretics can cause the body to lose too much magnesium, and some antibiotics, such as tetracycline, can inhibit the absorption of magnesium, both of which can lead to a deficiency. Individuals with poorly controlled diabetes or who abuse alcohol can experience excessive losses of magnesium in the urine, which could also cause a deficiency. A severe magnesium deficiency can cause muscle weakness, seizures, fatigue, depression, and irregular heart beats.

Table TIPS

Magnificent Magnesium

Sprinkle chopped almonds over your morning whole-grain cereal for two crunchy sources of magnesium.

Add baby spinach to your salad.

Add rinsed, canned beans to salsa for a veggie dip with a magnesium punch.

Spread peanut butter on whole-wheat crackers for a satisfying afternoon snack.

Try precooked brown rice for an easy way to add whole grains to your dinner!

exploring
Chloride

What Is Chloride?

LO 8.10 Name functions, sources, and deficiency/toxicity of chloride.

Chloride is a form of chlorine, an element you've surely smelled in bleach. Chlorine is a powerful disinfectant that if inhaled or ingested can be poisonous.

Fortunately, most of the chlorine in your body is in the nontoxic form of chloride (Cl^-). Chloride is part of hydrochloric acid, a strong acid in your stomach that enhances protein digestion and kills harmful bacteria that may be consumed with your foods.

Functions of Chloride

Sodium and chloride are the major electrolytes outside your cells and in your blood. They help maintain fluid balance between these two compartments. Chloride also acts as a buffer to help keep your blood at a normal pH.

Daily Needs

Adults age 19 to 50 should consume 2,300 milligrams of chloride a day.

Food Sources

Sodium chloride, which is 60 percent chloride, is the main source of chloride in your diet, so the food sources for it are the same as those for sodium (**Figure 8.25**).

Because Americans consume plenty of salt, it is estimated that they are consuming, on average, 3,400 milligrams to just over 7,000 milligrams of dietary chloride daily.

Too Much or Too Little

Because sodium chloride is the major source of chloride in the diet, the upper level for adults for chloride is set at 3,600 milligrams to coincide with the upper level for sodium.[73]

Figure 8.25 Table Salt Is Composed of Sodium and Chloride

A chloride deficiency rarely occurs in healthy individuals. Individuals who experience significant bouts of vomiting and diarrhea may become deficient as chloride is lost from the body.

exploring
Sulfur

What Is Sulfur?

LO 8.11 Name functions, sources, and deficiency/toxicity of sulfur.

Sulfur is typically found in your body as part of other compounds. For example, sulfur is part of the vitamins thiamin, biotin, and pantothenic acid.

Functions of Sulfur

Sulfur Helps Shape Some Amino Acids

The amino acids methionine, cystine, and cysteine all contain sulfur. The sulfur part of these amino acids helps give some proteins their three-dimensional shape. This enables these proteins to perform effectively as enzymes and hormones.[74]

Sulfites Are Preservatives

Sulfur-based substances called *sulfites* are often used as a preservative by food

manufacturers. They help prevent food spoilage and discoloration. (We discuss sulfites further in Chapter 13.)

Food Sources

Foods that contain the amino acids mentioned above are the major dietary sources of sulfur. A varied diet that contains meat, poultry, fish, eggs, legumes,

dairy foods, fruits, and vegetables will provide sulfur.

Daily Needs and Too Much or Too Little

There isn't any recommendation for the amount of sulfur to be consumed daily, nor are there any known toxicity or deficiency symptoms. Most people get plenty of sulfur in their diet.

exploring
Iron

What Is Iron?

LO 8.12 Name functions, sources, and deficiency/toxicity of iron.

Iron is the most abundant mineral on Earth, and the most abundant trace mineral in your body. A 130-pound female has more than 2,300 milligrams of iron in her body—about the weight of a dime—whereas a 165-pound male will have 4,000 milligrams of iron in his body—slightly less than the weight of two dimes.

As a key component of blood, iron is highly valuable to the body and is treated accordingly. For the most part, iron is not excreted in the urine or stool, so once absorbed very little of it leaves the body. Approximately 95 percent of your iron is recycled and reused.[75] Whereas some iron is shed in hair, skin, and sloughed-off intestinal cells, most iron loss is due to bleeding.

Iron Occurs in Two Forms: Heme and Nonheme

Foods from animal sources, such as meat, poultry, and fish, provide heme iron in your diet. Heme iron (**Figure 8.26**) is part of the protein **hemoglobin** in your red blood cells and the protein **myoglobin** in your muscles. Heme iron is easily absorbed by your body.

Figure 8.26 Hemoglobin Contains Heme Iron

Heme

hemoglobin The oxygen-carrying, heme-containing protein found in red blood cells.

myoglobin The oxygen-carrying, heme-containing protein found in muscle cells.

Plant foods such as grains and vegetables are the main sources of nonheme iron in your diet. Nonheme iron is not as easily absorbed as heme iron. This is because other compounds in foods, such as phytates in legumes, rice, and grains, the polyphenols in tea, and the protein in soy products, all inhibit its absorption.

In general, your body absorbs only about 10 to 15 percent of the iron you eat. However, if your body stores are low, the amount you absorb from foods will increase. You can enhance your nonheme iron absorption by eating a food that's high in vitamin C along with iron-rich foods. Vitamin C and the acids in your stomach change the configuration of nonheme iron, which improves its absorption. As little as 25 milligrams of vitamin C—the amount in about one-quarter cup of orange juice—can double the amount of nonheme iron you absorb from your meal, and 50 milligrams of vitamin C can increase the amount absorbed about sixfold.[76] Keep this in mind when you make your next peanut butter-on-whole-wheat sandwich and have an orange for dessert.

Another way to enhance nonheme iron absorption from foods is to eat meat, fish, or poultry at the same meal as the nonheme iron–containing food. The peptides in these animal-derived foods are thought to be the enhancing factors. The meat in your next turkey sandwich will help enhance the absorption of the nonheme iron in the whole-wheat bread.

Functions of Iron

Hemoglobin and Myoglobin Transport Oxygen

Approximately two-thirds of the iron in your body is in hemoglobin, the oxygen-carrying transport protein in your red blood cells. The iron-containing heme group binds with oxygen from your lungs and is transported to your tissues for their use. Hemoglobin also picks up carbon dioxide waste products from your cells and brings them to your lungs to be exhaled from your body. Similarly, iron is part of the myoglobin that transports and stores oxygen in your muscles.

Iron Is Needed for Brain Function

Iron helps enzymes that are involved in the synthesis of neurotransmitters in your brain, which send messages to the rest of your body. A deficiency of iron in children can reduce their ability to learn and retain information. Studies have shown that children with iron-deficiency anemia in their early years can have persistent, decreased cognitive ability.[77]

Daily Needs

Adult females, age 19 to 50, need 18 milligrams daily to cover the iron lost during menstruation. During pregnancy, a

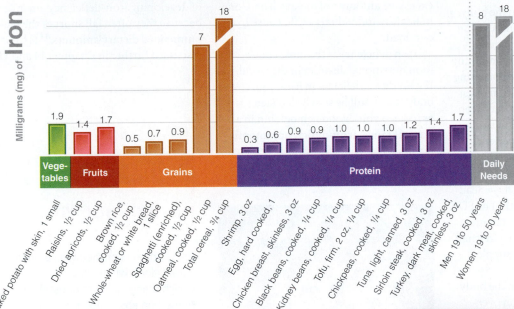

Milligrams (mg) of **Iron**

Vegetables	1.9
Fruits	1.4, 1.7
Grains	0.5, 0.7, 0.9, 7, 18
Protein	0.3, 0.6, 0.9, 0.9, 1.0, 1.0, 1.0, 1.2, 1.4, 1.7
Daily Needs	8, 18

Baked potato with skin, 1 small • Raisins, 1/2 cup • Dried apricots, 1/2 cup • Brown rice, cooked, 1/2 cup • Whole-wheat or white bread, 1 slice • Spaghetti (enriched), cooked, 1/2 cup • Oatmeal, cooked, 1/2 cup • Total cereal, 3/4 cup • Shrimp, 3 oz • Egg, hard cooked, 1 • Chicken breast, skinless, 3 oz • Black beans, cooked, 1/4 cup • Kidney beans, cooked, 1/4 cup • Tofu, firm, 2 oz, 1/4 cup • Chickpeas, cooked, 1/4 cup • Tuna, light, canned, 3 oz • Sirloin steak, cooked, 3 oz • Turkey, dark meat, cooked, skinless, 3 oz • Men 19 to 50 years • Women 19 to 50 years

Figure 8.27 Iron Content of Selected Foods

woman's iron needs increase to 27 milligrams per day to support her growing fetus. After a woman stops menstruating, usually around age 50, her daily iron needs drop to 8 milligrams because she is no longer losing blood monthly.

Adult males need 8 milligrams of dietary iron daily. These recommendations for women and men take into account a typical American diet, which includes both heme and nonheme iron sources.

Adult men consume more than twice their recommended iron needs—more than 17 milligrams, on average, daily.[78] Adult premenopausal women consume only about 70 percent of their daily need, or approximately 13 to 14 milligrams, on average.[79] Postmenopausal women consume approximately 13 milligrams of

iron daily, so, like men, they are meeting their needs.

The iron needs of vegetarians are 1.8 times higher than those of nonvegetarians due to components in plant foods that inhibit iron absorption.[80]

Food Sources

About half of Americans' dietary iron intake comes from iron-enriched bread and other grain foods such as cereals (**Figure 8.27**).[81] The richest sources of heme iron are meat, fish, and poultry. For more ideas on how to get iron into your daily diet, see Table Tips: "Ironing Out Your Iron Needs."

CONTINUED

Iron

IRON

Too Much or Too Little

Consuming too much iron from supplements can cause constipation, nausea, vomiting, and diarrhea. The upper level for iron for adults is set at 45 milligrams daily, as this level is slightly less than the amount known to cause these intestinal symptoms. This upper level doesn't apply to individuals with liver disease or other diseases, such as hemochromatosis, which can affect iron stores in the body. It is too high for these individuals.

In the United States, the accidental consumption of supplements containing iron has been known to cause poisoning deaths among children. Ingestion of as little as 200 milligrams of iron has been shown to be fatal. Children who swallow iron supplements can experience symptoms such as nausea, vomiting, and diarrhea within minutes. Intestinal bleeding can also occur, which can lead to shock, coma, and even death. The FDA has mandated that a warning statement about the risk of iron poisoning in small children be put on every iron supplement label.[82]

Excessive storing of iron in the body over several years is called iron overload and, if undetected, can damage a person's tissues and organs, including the heart, kidneys, liver, and nervous system. **Hemochromatosis**, a genetic disorder in which individuals absorb too much dietary iron, can cause iron overload. Though this condition is congenital, its symptoms often aren't manifested until adulthood. If not diagnosed and treated early enough, organ damage can occur. These individuals need to avoid iron supplements throughout their lives, as well as large amounts of vitamin C supplements, which enhance iron absorption.

hemochromatosis A genetic disorder that causes the body to store excessive amounts of iron.

iron-deficiency anemia An anemia caused by low hemoglobin levels due to insufficient dietary intake and absorption of iron.

Iron overload from consuming too much dietary iron has occurred in South Africans and Zimbabwean natives who consume large amounts of beer.[83] The iron content in the particular beer that they drink is high: 80 milligrams per liter. However, these individuals may also have a genetic disorder that contributes to excessive iron storage in the body. It is not known if excessive amounts of dietary iron alone in healthy individuals could cause iron overload.

Iron deficiency is the most common nutritional disorder in the world. If your diet is deficient in iron, your body stores will be slowly depleted so as to keep your blood hemoglobin in a normal range. **Iron-deficiency anemia** occurs when your stores are so depleted

a Normal red blood cells

b Red blood cells affected by anemia

Figure 8.28 Normal and Anemic Red Blood Cells
Red blood cells affected by anemia are small and pale in color compared with normal red blood cells due to lower heme concentration.

that your hemoglobin levels decrease (**Figure 8.28**). This will diminish the delivery of oxygen through the body, causing fatigue and weakness. Premenopausal females, menstruating women and teenage girls (especially those with heavy blood losses), pregnant women (because of their increased iron needs), preterm and low birth weight infants, and older infants and toddlers are at risk of developing iron-deficiency anemia because they often fall short of the recommended dietary amounts.[84] (This is discussed further in Chapters 14 and 15.)

Table TIPS

Ironing out Your Iron Needs

Enjoy an iron-enriched whole-grain cereal along with a glass of vitamin C–rich orange juice to boost the nonheme iron absorption from your bowl of cereal.

Add plenty of salsa (vitamin C) to your bean burritos to enhance the absorption of the nonheme iron in both the beans and the flour tortilla.

Stuff a cooked baked potato (nonheme iron, vitamin C) with shredded cooked chicken (heme iron) and broccoli (vitamin C) and top it with melted low-fat cheese for a delicious dinner.

Eat a small box of raisins (nonheme iron) and a clementine or tangerine (vitamin C) as a sweet, iron-rich afternoon snack.

Add chickpeas (nonheme iron) to your salad greens (vitamin C). Don't forget the tomato wedges for another source of iron-enhancing vitamin C.

exploring
Copper

What Is Copper?

LO 8.13 Name functions, sources, and deficiency/toxicity of copper.

Copper may bring to mind ancient tools, great sculptures, or American pennies (although pennies are no longer made of solid copper), but it is also associated with several key body functions.

Functions of Copper

Copper is part of many enzymes and proteins. It is important for iron absorption and transfer and the synthesis of hemoglobin and red blood cells. Copper helps generate energy in your cells, synthesize melanin (the dark pigment found in skin), and link the proteins collagen and elastin together in connective tissue. It works with enzymes to protect your cells from free radicals. Copper also plays an important role in blood clotting and in maintaining a healthy immune system.[85]

Daily Needs

Both adult women and men need 900 micrograms of copper daily. American women consume 1,200 micrograms, whereas men consume 1,600 micrograms daily, on average.

Figure 8.29 Copper Content of Selected Foods

Food Sources

Organ meats such as liver, seafood, nuts, and seeds are abundant in copper (**Figure 8.29**). Bran cereals, whole-grain products, and cocoa are also good sources. Whereas potatoes, milk, and chicken are low in copper, they are consumed in such abundant amounts that they contribute a fair amount of copper to Americans' diets. For more ideas on how to get copper into your daily diet, see Table Tips: "Counting Your Copper."

Too Much or Too Little

Too much copper can cause stomach pains and cramps, nausea, diarrhea, vomiting, and even liver damage. The upper level for copper for adults is set at 10,000 micrograms daily.

Copper deficiency is rare in the United States. It has occurred in premature babies fed milk formulas, malnourished infants fed cow's milk, and individuals given intravenous feedings that lacked adequate amounts of copper.

Table TIPS

Counting Your Copper

Make your hot cocoa with milk, rather than water, for two sources (cocoa and milk) of copper in your mug.

Mix raisins with your brown rice at dinner.

Top chocolate pudding with a sprinkling of crushed walnuts for a dessert that is both sweet and crunchy.

Choose sunflower seeds for an afternoon snack.

Ladle black beans and salsa into a whole-wheat pita. Top with reduced-fat Cheddar cheese. Zap it in the microwave for a Mexican lunch with a copper kick.

exploring
Zinc

What Is Zinc?

LO 8.14 Name functions, sources, and deficiency/toxicity of zinc.

Zinc is found in almost every cell of your body. It is involved in the function of more than 100 enzymes, including those used for protein synthesis. As important as it is, it was not considered an essential nutrient until 1974.

Functions of Zinc

Zinc Is Needed for DNA Synthesis and Growth and Development

Zinc plays a role in the structure of both RNA and DNA in your cells and in gene expression. Zinc is needed for adequate growth in developing infants and throughout the adolescent years.[86]

Zinc Helps Keep Your Immune System Healthy and Helps Wounds Heal

Zinc is needed for production of white blood cells, so it helps keep your immune system healthy. It helps reduce the inflammation that can accompany skin wounds. Zinc also helps in wound healing by being part of enzymes and proteins that repair and enhance the proliferation of skin cells.[87]

Zinc Brings Out the Best in Your Taste Buds

One lick of a chocolate ice cream cone or a forkful of cherry cheesecake will make you appreciate the role that zinc plays in taste acuity, which is the ability to savor the flavors of your foods. A deficiency of zinc has been shown to alter taste perceptions.[88]

Zinc and the Common Cold

A recent review of 14 studies of healthy individuals has shown promise that zinc can affect the common cold.[89] In these studies, those who consumed zinc lozenges or syrup within 24 hours of the onset of the first sniffle or sneeze appeared to somewhat benefit from a reduction in the duration and severity of a cold. These were healthy individuals so it is too early to say if these results would occur in people with chronic illnesses or a compromised immune system. Also, those who

took zinc lozenges were more likely to experience side effects such as nausea and a bad aftertaste in their mouth. More studies are needed to determine if zinc could be safely used in the general population to treat the common cold, and to determine a safe dose and appropriate duration without adverse effects.[90] (T|F)

Recent research suggests that zinc lozenges and nasal gels may help reduce the severity and duration of cold symptoms.

Zinc May Help Fight AMD

Research studies do support the assertion that zinc may play a role in reducing the risk of age-related macular degeneration (AMD), a condition that hampers central vision. Zinc may work with an enzyme in your eyes that's needed to properly utilize vitamin A for vision. Zinc may also help mobilize vitamin A from the liver to ensure adequate blood levels of this vitamin. Supplements that contain antioxidants along with zinc have been shown to delay the progression of AMD.[91] (See the section on antioxidants in Chapter 7.)

Daily Needs

Adult males need 11 milligrams of zinc, whereas women need 8 milligrams daily.

American adults, on average, are meeting their daily zinc needs. Men are consuming approximately 14 milligrams and women are consuming 10 milligrams of zinc daily, on average.

Vegetarians, especially strict vegetarians, can have as much as a 50 percent higher need for zinc. Phytates in grains and legumes, which are staples of vegan diets, can bind with zinc, reducing its absorption in the intestinal tract.

Food Sources

Red meat, some seafood, and whole grains are excellent sources of zinc (**Figure 8.30**). Because zinc is found in the germ and bran portion of the grain, refined grains stripped of these components have as much as 80 percent less

Figure 8.30 Zinc Content of Selected Foods

zinc than whole grains. For more ideas on how to get zinc into your daily diet, see Table Tips: "Zapping Your Zinc Needs."

Too Much or Too Little

The upper level for zinc in food and/or supplements for adults is set at 40 milligrams daily. Consuming too much zinc, as little as 50 milligrams, can cause stomach

Skin rash is one of the symptoms of zinc deficiency.

pains, nausea, vomiting, and diarrhea. Consuming large amounts of zinc daily has been shown to lower the level of copper in your body by competing with this mineral for absorption in the intestinal tract. This is an excellent example of how the overconsumption of one mineral can compromise the benefits of another.

Excessive amounts of zinc daily have also been shown to suppress the immune system and lower blood levels of HDL (good) cholesterol.[92]

A deficiency of zinc can cause hair loss, loss of appetite, impaired taste of foods, diarrhea, and delayed sexual maturation, as well as impotence and skin rashes.

Because zinc is needed during development, a deficiency can slow and impair growth. Classic studies of groups of people in the Middle East showed that people who consumed a diet mainly of unleavened bread, which is high in zinc-binding phytates, experienced impaired growth and dwarfism.[93]

TableTIPS

Zapping Your Zinc Needs!

Enjoy a tuna fish sandwich on whole-wheat bread at lunch for a double serving (fish and bread) of zinc.

Add kidney beans to your cup of soup. (These beans are often at cafeteria salad bars, so add a spoonful to your soup-and-salad lunch.)

Pack a small handful of mixed nuts and raisins in a zip-closed bag for a snack on the run.

Top your breakfast yogurt with cereal for two servings of zinc in one bowl!

Add cooked green peas to casseroles, stews, soups, and salads.

exploring
Selenium

What Is Selenium?

LO 8.15 Name functions, sources, and deficiency/toxicity of selenium.

The mineral selenium is often incorporated into a class of proteins called selenoproteins, many of which are enzymes. Selenoproteins have important functions in your body.

Functions of Selenium

Selenium Is Needed by Your Thyroid

Selenium-containing enzymes help regulate thyroid hormones in your body.

Selenium Plays an Antioxidant Role

Selenoproteins can also function as antioxidants that protect your cells from free radicals. (See the section on antioxidants in Chapter 7.) As you recall, free radicals are natural by-products of metabolism and can also result from exposure to chemicals in the environment. If free radicals accumulate faster than your body can neutralize them, their damaging effects can contribute to chronic diseases, such as heart disease.[94]

Selenium May Help Fight Cancer

Research studies have suggested that deaths from cancers, such as lung, colon, and prostate cancers, are lower in groups of people that consume more selenium. Selenium's antioxidant capabilities, and its ability to potentially slow the growth of tumors, are thought to be the mechanism behind its anticancer effects.

The FDA now allows a Qualified Health Claim on food labels and dietary supplements stating that "selenium may reduce the risk of certain cancers but the evidence is limited and not conclusive to date."[95]

Daily Needs

Both adult females and males need 55 micrograms of selenium daily. American adults are more than meeting their needs—they consume about 94 micrograms to 135 micrograms daily, on average.

Food Sources

Meat, seafood, pasta, grains, dairy foods, and fruits and vegetables can all contribute to dietary selenium (**Figure 8.31**). However, the amount of selenium in the foods you eat depends upon the soil where the plants were grown and the animals grazed. For example, wheat grown in selenium-rich soil can have more than ten times as much selenium as an identical wheat grown in selenium-poor soil. For more ideas on how to get selenium into your daily diet, see Table Tips: "Seeking Out Selenium."

Figure 8.31 Selenium Content of Selected Foods

Chart data (Micrograms (µg) of Selenium):

Vegetables
- Green beans, frozen, boiled, 1 cup: 1
- Baked potato, with skin, 1 medium: 1
- Broccoli, frozen, boiled, 1 cup: 2

Fruits
- Watermelon, raw, 1 cup: 1
- Banana, 1 medium: 1

Grains
- Wheat crackers, 5 crackers, 1 oz: 2
- Frozen waffle, 1: 8
- Brown rice, long grain, cooked, 1/2 cup: 10
- Whole-wheat bread, 1 slice: 11
- Spaghetti, cooked, 1/2 cup: 18

Protein
- Walnuts, 1/2 oz: 1
- Peanut butter, 1 tbs: 1
- Egg, hard-boiled, 1 large: 15
- Roast beef, 3 oz: 23
- Chicken breast, cooked, 3 oz: 24
- Cod, 3 oz: 32
- Shrimp, 3 oz: 42
- Salmon, cooked, 3 oz: 47
- Tuna, light, canned in water, 3 oz: 68
- Brazil nuts, 1/2 oz: 544

Dairy
- Cheddar cheese, reduced fat, 1 1/2 oz: 5
- Milk, skim, 1 cup: 8
- Cottage cheese, low fat, 2 cups: 22

Daily Needs
- Adults 19 to 50 years: 55

Too Much or Too Little

Too much selenium can cause toxicity and a condition called **selenosis**. A person with selenosis will have brittle nails and hair, both of which may fall out. Other symptoms include stomach and intestinal discomfort, a skin rash, garlicky breath, fatigue, and damage to the nervous system. The upper level for selenium for adults is set at 400 micrograms per day to prevent the loss and brittleness of nails and hair, which is the most common symptom of selenosis.

Though rare in the United States, a selenium deficiency is associated with **Keshan disease**, which damages the heart. However, some researchers speculate that selenium deficiency alone may not cause Keshan disease; the selenium-deficient individual may also be exposed to a virus, which, together with the selenium deficiency, leads to the damaged heart.[96]

selenosis The presence of toxic levels of selenium.

Keshan disease A disease related to a deficiency of selenium.

Table TIPS

Seeking Out Selenium

Top a toasted whole-wheat bagel with a slice of reduced-fat Cheddar cheese.

Spread peanut butter on whole-wheat crackers and top with a slice of banana.

Top your dinner pasta with broccoli for a selenium-smart meal.

Zap sliced apples, sprinkled with a little apple juice and cinnamon, in the microwave and top with vanilla yogurt.

Spoon a serving of low-fat cottage cheese into a bowl and top with canned sliced pears and walnuts.

exploring
Fluoride

What Is Fluoride?

LO 8.16 Name functions, sources, and deficiency/toxicity of fluoride.

Fluoride is the safe ion form of fluorine, a poisonous gas. Calcium fluoride is the form that is found in your bones and teeth.

Functions of Fluoride

Fluoride Protects against Dental Caries

The best known function of fluoride is its role in keeping teeth healthy. Your teeth have an outer layer called enamel (**Figure 8.32**), which can become eroded over time by acids and result in dental caries. The acids are produced by the bacteria in your mouth when they feast on the carbohydrates that you eat. Continual exposure of your teeth to these acids can cause erosion and create a cavity.

Fluoride from food, beverages, and dental products, such as toothpaste, helps protect your teeth in several ways. It helps to repair the enamel that has already started to erode, and it interferes with the ability of the bacteria to metabolize carbohydrates, thus reducing the amount of acid they produce. Finally, fluoride provides a protective barrier between your tooth and the destructive acids. As a component of saliva, it provides a continual fluoride bath to your teeth's surfaces.[97]

Consuming adequate amounts of fluoride is extremely important during infancy and childhood, when teeth are developing, and for maintenance of healthy teeth throughout your life.

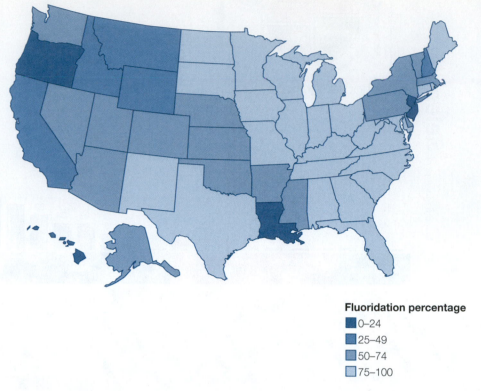

Fluoridation percentage
- 0–24
- 25–49
- 50–74
- 75–100

Figure 8.33 Percentage of Americans Living in Communities with a Fluoridated Water Supply, by State. 2012

Enamel
Gum
Bone

Figure 8.32 Structure of a Tooth

Fluoride in Drinking Water Has Improved the Nation's Dental Health

In the 1930s, scientists noticed lower rates of dental caries among individuals whose community water systems contained significant amounts of fluoride. Studies confirmed that the fluoride was the protective factor in the water that helped fight dental decay. Since 1945, most communities have fluoridated their water, and today, over 74 percent of Americans live in communities that have a fluoridated water supply (**Figure 8.33**).

The increase in access to fluoridated water is one of the major reasons why there has been a decline in dental caries in the United States, and fluoridation of water is considered one of the ten greatest public health advances of the twentieth century.[98]

To find out if your community water is fluoridated and how much fluoride is added, visit the Centers for Disease Control and Prevention's website, My Water's

Fluoride, at http://apps.nccd.cdc.gov/MWF/Index.asp.

Daily Needs

Adult men should consume 3.8 milligrams and women 3.1 milligrams of fluoride daily to meet their needs. If the tap water in your community is fluoridated at 0.7 milligram/liter, you would have to consume more than 15 cups of water daily, through either beverages or cooking, to meet your fluoride needs (1 liter = 4.2 cups). The toothpaste that you use to brush your teeth can also be a source of fluoride.

Food Sources

Foods in general are not a good source of fluoride. The best sources are fluoridated water and beverages and foods made with this water, such as coffee, tea, and soups. Another source of fluoride can be juices made from concentrate using fluoridated tap water. For more ideas on how to get fluoride into your daily diet, see Table Tips: "Fabulous Ways to Get Fluoride."

If you shy away from tap water and drink and cook predominantly with bottled water, you may be robbing yourself of some cavity protection. Most bottled waters sold in the United States have less than the optimal amount of fluoride. It is difficult to determine the fluoride content of many bottled waters because currently, the amount of fluoride in bottled water has to be listed on the label only if fluoride has been specifically added. Check the label to see if your bottled water contains added fluoride. For more information about the differences between bottled and tap water, and their advantages and disadvantages, see the Nutrition in the Real World feature "Tap Water or Bottled Water: Is Bottled Better?" on pages 292–293.

Teeth pitted by fluorosis

Too Much or Too Little

Because of fluoride's protective qualities, too little exposure to or consumption of fluoride increases the risk of dental caries.

Having some fluoride is important for healthy teeth, but too much can cause **fluorosis**, a condition whereby the teeth become pitted and develop white patches or stains on the surface, which can become brownish as the disease progresses. Fluorosis creates teeth that are extremely resistant to caries but cosmetically unappealing (see photo).

Fluorosis occurs when teeth are forming, so only infants and children up to 8 years of age are at risk. Once teeth break through the gums, fluorosis can't occur. Fluorosis results from overfluoridation of water, the misuse of dietary fluoride supplements, or excessive use of dental products that contain fluoride.[99]

Skeletal fluorosis can occur in bones when a person consumes at least 10 milligrams of fluoride daily for 10 or more years. This is a rare situation that occurs when water is mistakenly overfluoridated. This can cause bone concentrations of fluoride that are up to five times higher than normal and result in stiffness or pain in joints, osteoporosis, and calcification of the ligaments.[100]

TableTIPS

Fabulous Ways to Get Fluoride

Pour orange juice into ice cube trays and pop a couple of frozen cubes into a glass of tap water for a refreshing and flavorful beverage.

Use tap water when making coffee, tea, or juice from concentrate, and for food preparation.

Brew a mug of flavored decaffeinated tea, such as French vanilla or gingerbread, to keep you warm while you're hitting the books.

The upper level for adults has been set at 10 milligrams to reduce the risk of fluorosis in the bones. (Note, however, that the upper level for infants and children is much lower, to prevent fluorosis in teeth. See the inside cover of the textbook for this upper level.)

fluorosis A condition caused by excess amounts of fluoride, resulting in mottling of the teeth.

exploring
Chromium

What Is Chromium?

LO 8.17 Name functions, sources, and deficiency/toxicity of chromium.

The most recent mineral to be found necessary in humans, chromium, was identified as an essential mineral in 1977, although researchers have had an interest in chromium and its roles in the metabolism of glucose since the 1950s.

Functions of Chromium

Chromium Helps Insulin in Your Body

The main function of this mineral is to increase insulin's effectiveness in cells. The hormone insulin plays an important role in the metabolism and storage of carbohydrates, fats, and protein in your body. Individuals who were intravenously fed a chromium-free diet experienced high blood levels of glucose, weight loss, and nerve problems—all telltale signs of uncontrolled diabetes and poor blood glucose control. The problems were corrected when chromium was provided.[101]

Chromium May Reduce Prediabetes

Because it works with insulin, some researchers think that chromium may help individuals who have diabetes mellitus or prediabetes (glucose intolerance) improve their blood glucose control. There has yet to be a large research study in the United States that confirms this theory.

One small study suggests that a chromium supplement may reduce the risk of insulin resistance, and therefore, favorably affect the handling of glucose in the body.[102] Improving the body's sensitivity to insulin and maintaining a normal blood glucose level can possibly lower the incidence of type 2 diabetes in individuals at risk.

Based on this one study, the FDA has

Figure 8.34 Chromium Content of Selected Foods

allowed a Qualified Health Claim on chromium supplements. However, the supplement label must state that the evidence regarding the relationship between chromium supplements and either insulin resistance or type 2 diabetes is not certain at this time.[103]

Chromium Does Not Help Build Muscle Mass

Although advertisements have sometimes touted chromium supplements as an aid to losing weight and building lean muscle, the research doesn't support the claim. A review of more

than 20 research studies didn't find any benefits from taking up to 1,000 micrograms of chromium daily.[104] If you are trying to become lean and mean, taking chromium supplements isn't going to help.

Daily Needs

Adult men age 19 to 50 need 30 to 35 micrograms of chromium daily, whereas women of the same age need 20 to 25 micrograms daily, on average, depending upon their age. It is estimated that American men consume 39 to 54 micrograms of chromium from foods, and women consume 23 to 29 micrograms, on average, daily.[105]

Food Sources

Grains are good sources of chromium (**Figure 8.34**). Meat, eggs, and poultry and some fruits and vegetables can also provide chromium, whereas dairy foods are low in the mineral. For more ideas on how to get chromium into your daily diet, see Table Tips: "Cram in the Chromium."

Too Much or Too Little

As yet, there is no known risk from consuming excessive amounts of chromium from food or supplements, so no upper level has been set.

A chromium deficiency is very rare in the United States. The jury is still out on whether individuals with diabetes who did not have a chromium deficiency would benefit by taking a supplement. More research is needed in this area.[106]

exploring
Iodine

What Is Iodine?

LO 8.18 Name functions, sources, and deficiency/toxicity of iodine.

Like the fluoridation of community drinking water, the iodization of salt was a significant advance for public health in the United States. Prior to the 1920s, many Americans suffered from the iodine-deficiency disease, goiter. Once salt manufacturers began adding iodine to their product, incidence of the disease dropped. Today, rates of the disease are very low in the United States, though not in other parts of the world.

Functions of Iodine

Iodine is an essential mineral for your thyroid, a butterfly-shaped gland located in your neck (**Figure 8.35**). The thyroid needs iodine to make some essential

Figure 8.35 Location of Thyroid Gland

hormones. In fact, approximately 60 percent of your thyroid hormones are comprised of iodine.

Thyroid hormones affect the majority of your cells, regulate your metabolic rate, and help your heart, nerves, muscles, and intestines function properly. Children need thyroid hormones for normal bone growth and brain development.[107]

Daily Needs

Adult men and women need 150 micrograms of iodine daily to meet their needs. Americans currently consume 138 micrograms to 353 micrograms of iodine from foods daily, on average, depending upon their age and gender. This does not include the amount that they get from iodized salt that they may be adding to their foods.

Food Sources

The amount of iodine that occurs naturally in foods is typically low, approximately 3 to 75 micrograms in a serving, and is influenced by the amount of iodine in the soil, water, and fertilizers used to grow foods (**Figure 8.36**).

CONTINUED

Iodine

Fish can provide higher amounts of iodine, as they concentrate it from sea-water. Iodized salt provides 284 micro-grams of iodine per teaspoon. Note that not all salt has added iodine. Kosher salt, for example, has no additives, including iodine. Processed foods that use iodized salt or iodine-containing preservatives are also a source. For more ideas on how to get iodine into your daily diet, see Table Tips: "Iodine Impact."

Too Much or Too Little

Consuming too much iodine can challenge the thyroid, impairing its function and reducing the synthesis and release of thyroid hormones. Because of this, the upper level for adults for iodine is 1,100 micrograms.

An early sign of iodine deficiency is **goiter**, which is an enlarged thyroid gland. An iodine-deficient thyroid has to work harder to make the thyroid hormones, causing it to become enlarged.[108]

A deficiency of iodine during the early stages of fetal development can damage the brain of the developing baby, causing

goiter Enlargement of the thyroid gland, mostly due to iodine deficiency.

cretinism A condition caused by a deficiency of thyroid hormone during prenatal development, resulting in abnormal mental and physical development in children. It is also known as *congenital hypothyroidism*.

Figure 8.36 **Iodine Content of Selected Foods**

mental retardation. Inadequate iodine during this critical time can cause lower IQ scores. Depending upon the severity of the iodine deficiency, **cretinism**, also known as *congenital hypothyroidism*, can occur. Individuals with cretinism can experience abnormal sexual development, mental retardation, and dwarfism.

Early detection of an iodine deficiency and treatment in children is critical to avoiding irreversible damage.

Goiter is an enlarged thyroid gland caused by an iodine deficiency.

Cretinism can result in a child born to a mother who was iodine deficient during early pregnancy.

TableTIPS

Iodine Impact

Add a hard-cooked egg to your breakfast.

Add beans to your lunchtime soup.

Sprinkle tuna fish flakes on your dinner salad.

exploring
Manganese

ChooseMyPlate.gov

What Is Manganese?

LO 8.19 Name functions, sources, and deficiency/toxicity of manganese.

Manganese is either part of, or activates, many enzymes in your body.

Functions of Manganese

This mineral is involved in the metabolism of carbohydrates, fats, and amino acids. Manganese is needed for the formation of bone.

Daily Needs

Adult women need 1.8 milligrams, whereas men need 2.3 milligrams, of manganese daily. Americans are easily meeting their manganese needs. Adult women consume more than 2 milligrams of manganese daily, and adult men consume more than 2.8 milligrams daily, on average, from the foods in their diet.[109]

Food Sources

When it comes to meeting your manganese needs, look to whole grains, nuts, legumes, tea, vegetables, and fruits such as pineapples, strawberries, and bananas (**Figure 8.37**). A teaspoon of ground cinnamon provides just under 0.5 milligram of manganese. For more ideas on how to

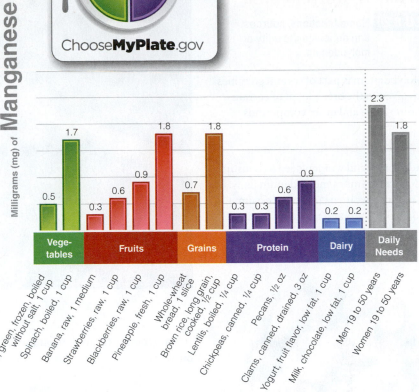

Figure 8.37 Manganese Content of Selected Foods

get manganese into your daily diet, see Table Tips: "Managing Your Manganese."

Too Much or Too Little

Manganese toxicity, which has occurred in miners who have inhaled manganese dust, can cause damage to the nervous system and symptoms that resemble Parkinson's disease.[110] A study of individuals who drank water with high levels of

manganese showed that they also experienced Parkinson's disease–like symptoms.

To protect against this toxicity, the upper level has been set at 11 milligrams daily.

A deficiency of manganese is rare in healthy individuals who have a balanced diet. Individuals fed a manganese-deficient diet developed a rash and scaly skin.

TableTIPS

Managing Your Manganese

Sprinkle your whole-wheat toast with a dusting of cinnamon to spice up your morning.

Combine cooked brown rice, canned and rinsed lentils, and chickpeas for a dinner in a snap.

Spoon vanilla yogurt over canned crushed pineapple and sliced bananas for a tropical treat.

exploring
Molybdenum

What Is Molybdenum?

LO 8.20 Name functions, sources, and deficiency/toxicity of molybdenum.

Molybdenum is part of several enzymes involved in the breakdown of certain amino acids and other compounds.

Daily Needs

Adult men and women need to consume 45 micrograms of molybdenum daily. American women currently consume 76 micrograms and men consume

109 micrograms of molybdenum daily, on average.

Food Sources

Legumes are excellent sources of molybdenum. Grains and nuts are also good sources.[111]

Too Much or Too Little

There is limited research on the adverse effects of too much dietary molybdenum in humans. In animal studies, too much can cause reproductive problems. Because of this finding in animals, the upper level for molybdenum in humans has been set at 2 milligrams for adults.

A deficiency of molybdenum has not been seen in healthy individuals. However, a deficiency was observed in an individual who was fed intravenously for years and developed symptoms that included rapid heart beats, headaches, and night blindness.

MADE over MADE better

Snacks can be a great way to give your diet a mineral boost. Bananas, for example, are packed with potassium, raisins are naturally high in iron, peanuts are rich in magnesium, and cheese is a ringer for calcium. However, depending upon how these foods are processed, they may be higher in calories, fat, and saturated fat than you bargained for.

Here are some typical mineral-rich snacks made over and made nutritionally better!

If you like this. . .

Try this healthy alternative!

Banana Chips
Serving size: ½ cup
Calories: 300
Fat: 14 grams
Saturated Fat: 12 grams

Banana
1 small
Calories: 90
Fat: < 0.5 grams
Saturated Fat: 0 grams

Yogurt-Covered Raisins
Serving size: ½ cup
Calories: 280
Fat: 12 grams
Saturated Fat: 9 grams

Raisins
Serving size: ½ cup
Calories: 123
Fat: 0 grams
Saturated Fat: 0 grams

Trail Mix
Serving size: ½ cup
Calories: 300
Fat: 20 grams
Saturated Fat: 4 grams

Peanuts in Shell
Serving size: ½ cup
Calories: 170
Fat: 13 grams
Saturated Fat: 2 grams

Cheddar Cheese
Serving size: 1 ounce
Calories: 120
Fat: 10 grams
Saturated Fat: 6 grams

String Cheese
Serving size: 1 ounce
Calories: 80
Fat: 6 grams
Saturated Fat: 3 grams

Does Designer Water Have Nutritional Benefits?

Supermarket shelves seem to be loaded with bottles touting the benefits of "smart" water. You can find water with vitamins, water with electrolytes, water for energy, and even water for a good night's sleep.[1] Sales of Glaceau Vitaminwater™ and SmartWater combined topped $1 billion in 2014.[2] Marketers are aiming designer water at everyone from athletes to people trying to recover from hangovers. Designer waters can have a variety of different ingredients, including added sugar, extra caffeine, extra sodium, and a wide range of vitamins. With zippy names and promises of health and hydration, they can be tempting. But are they good for you? Do designer waters have a place in a healthy diet? Take a close look at the arguments for both sides and see what you think.

yes

- If you cannot meet your vitamin needs from your diet, you may be able to get a percentage of them in these bottles.[3]

- If you exercise for long periods in the heat or if you live in a hot place, you need fluids, and possibly electrolytes to recover from your physical activity. Designer waters can provide electrolytes, and can encourage fluid intake.[4]

- If they have less sugar and no phosphates, designer waters can be healthier than soda.[5] People may be able to use designer waters to wean off of soda.

- Drinking plain old water can get boring, and dehydration can be a serious matter.[6] If it is a matter of staying hydrated or chronically being thirsty, it's better to drink a designer water.

no

- A recent study showed that many designer waters have an excess of the vitamins needed in a healthy diet.[7] Drinking too much of these products could lead to a vitamin overdose.

- Studies show that drinking water alone is perfectly adequate for recovery from most forms of exercise.[8] Designer water is more expensive than tap water and provides extra calories.

- The *Dietary Guidelines* for *Americans* recommend getting vitamins primarily from food.[9] Food also contains fiber and phytochemicals, among other things that promote good health.[10]

- You can make water more interesting by adding lemon, lime, or cucumber slices or by drinking sparkling water.[11]

what do you think?

1. If you drink designer waters, what is your rationale for doing so? **2.** What is the strongest argument for not drinking designer waters? **3.** Do you think it is realistic for people to use designer waters to wean off of soda? Why or why not?

LO 8.1 Water Is an Important Nutrient in the Diet

Water is the universal solvent that helps transport oxygen, nutrients, and other substances throughout your body and that carries waste products away from your cells. It helps regulate body temperature and cushion organs. Combined with other substances to form saliva and mucus, it acts as a lubricant in your mouth and intestines.

~5% minerals and other nutrients

~5% minerals and other nutrients

~14% protein

~17% protein

29% fat

20% fat

52% water

59% water

Female, 137 lbs.   Male, 168 lbs.

LO 8.2 Water Balance Is Maintained through the Food and Beverages You Consume and the Amount You Excrete

When the amount of water consumed in foods and beverages is equal to the amount excreted, the body is in water balance. You lose water through your kidneys, large intestines, lungs, and skin. Consuming too little will cause dehydration, whereas consuming excessive amounts could cause hyponatremia.

1 cup Metabolism

3 cups Food

6.5 cups Beverages

Water Intake

Water Output

0.5 cup | Intestines (stool)

1 cup | Sweat

3 cups Skin and Lungs

6 cups Kidneys (urine)

10.5 cups   10.5 cups

LO 8.3 You Need to Consume Water Daily to Meet Your Needs

Adult women should consume 9 cups of water, and adult men should drink approximately 13 cups of water, daily. Caffeinated beverages, juices, and milk can all count toward meeting your water needs. Many foods are also a good source of water.

LO 8.4 Minerals Are Essential Micronutrients That Play Many Roles in the Body

Many minerals are part of enzymes. Minerals help maintain fluid and acid-base balance; play a role in nerve transmission and muscle contractions; help strengthen bones, teeth, and the immune system; and are involved in growth. Minerals are found in both plant and animal foods, but often vary in bioavailability due to binding agents (oxalates, phytates) or competition with other minerals for absorption in the intestinal tract.

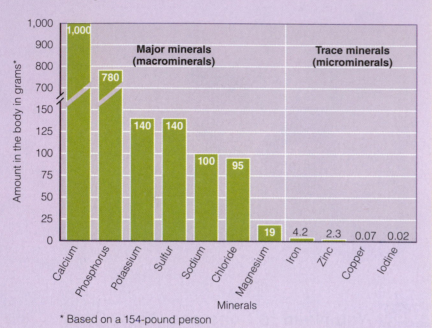

Amount in the body in grams*

Major minerals (macrominerals): Calcium 1,000; Phosphorus 780; Potassium 140; Sulfur 140; Sodium 100; Chloride 95; Magnesium 19

Trace minerals (microminerals): Iron 4.2; Zinc 2.3; Copper 0.07; Iodine 0.02

Minerals

* Based on a 154-pound person

LO 8.5 Sodium

Sodium plays an important role in balancing the fluid between your blood and cells. Americans currently consume more than double the sodium recommended daily, predominantly as sodium chloride (table salt). Processed foods are the major source of sodium chloride in the diet. Consuming too much sodium can contribute to hypertension. Reducing dietary sodium and following the DASH diet, which is abundant in foods rich in potassium, magnesium, and calcium, can help lower blood pressure. Losing excess weight, being physically active, and limiting alcohol can also lower blood pressure.

Milligrams of Sodium

American adult daily consumption (> 3,400 mg)

Adult upper level daily (2,300 mg)

Adult recommended daily (1,500 mg)

Adult needed daily (180 mg)

LO 8.6 Potassium

Potassium helps keep your heart, muscles, nerves, and bones healthy. It can help lower high blood pressure by causing the kidneys to excrete excess sodium, and it may help prevent kidney stones. It also is involved in the maintenance of fluid balance and acid-base balance in the blood. The current recommendations to increase the fruits and vegetables in your diet will help you meet your potassium needs. Too much potassium from supplements results in hyperkalemia, whereas too little causes hypokalemia.

LO 8.7 Calcium

Calcium, along with phosphorus, forms hydroxyapatite, which provides strength and structure for bones and teeth. Dairy foods are a good source of calcium. A diet adequate in protein, vitamin K, calcium, and vitamin D, along with regular physical activity, is needed to build and maintain healthy bones. Consuming too much calcium causes hypercalcemia and may cause kidney stones or constipation. Osteoporosis is a condition caused by frail bones. A chronic deficiency of dietary calcium and/or vitamin D, excess alcohol consumption, and smoking can all increase the risk of osteoporosis.

LO 8.8 Phosphorus

Phosphorus is a major component of bones, teeth, and cell membranes. It is needed during metabolism, acts as an acid-base buffer, and is part of your DNA and RNA. Meat, fish, poultry, and dairy products are good sources of phosphorus. Consuming too much can result in hyperphosphatemia. Too little phosphorus in the diet can result in muscle weakness, bone pain, and confusion.

LO 8.9 Magnesium

Magnesium is needed for metabolism and to maintain healthy muscles, nerves, bones, and heart. Magnesium is abundant in leafy green vegetables, almonds, and legumes. Too much magnesium from taking supplements can cause intestinal problems such as diarrhea, cramps, and nausea. Deficiencies are rare but the use of some medications can result in magnesium deficiency.

LO 8.10 Chloride

Chloride works with sodium to maintain fluid balance as well as acid-base balance in the body. Table salt accounts for almost all the chloride you consume. Chloride toxicity is rare but hyperchloremia can occur due to extreme dehydration. Deficiencies are also rare and are generally caused by extreme vomiting and diarrhea, resulting in hypochloremia.

LO 8.11 Sulfur

In the body, sulfur provides shape to amino acids. Sulfites are used as a preservative in processed foods. The best food sources of sulfur are meats, chicken, and fish. It can also be found in fruits and vegetables. There are no known toxicity or deficiency symptoms.

VISUAL Chapter Summary

LO 8.12 Iron

Iron is part of the oxygen-carrying transport proteins—hemoglobin in your red blood cells and myoglobin in your muscles. Heme iron is found in meat, poultry, and fish. Nonheme iron is found in plant foods, such as grains and vegetables. Nonheme iron is the predominant source of the iron in your diet but isn't absorbed as readily as heme iron. Too much iron from supplements can cause constipation, nausea, vomiting, and diarrhea. A deficiency of iron in children can reduce their ability to learn and retain information. Iron-deficiency anemia can cause fatigue and weakness.

Heme

LO 8.13 Copper

Copper is part of many enzymes and proteins that are involved in the absorption and transfer of iron and the synthesis of hemoglobin and red blood cells. Other enzymes containing copper are involved in energy production and protecting cells from free radicals. Copper is found in a variety of foods, especially seafood, nuts, and seeds. Too much copper can cause stomach pains, nausea, diarrhea, vomiting, and even liver damage. A copper deficiency is rare in the United States.

LO 8.14 Zinc

More than 100 enzymes in your cells need zinc to function properly. Zinc plays a role in the structure of both RNA and DNA, in your taste acuity, and in helping fight age-related macular degeneration (AMD). Meat, fish, and whole grains are good sources of zinc. Too much zinc can cause intestinal problems, nausea, and vomiting, and can lower the HDL cholesterol in the body. A deficiency can cause hair loss, loss of appetite, impaired taste of foods, diarrhea, skin rashes, and delayed sexual maturation.

LO 8.15 Selenium

Selenium acts as an antioxidant in your body and may help fight cancer. It is also a component of enzymes that help regulate thyroid hormones. All food groups contribute selenium, including nuts, meat, and seafood. Too much selenium can cause selenosis, the symptoms of which include brittle teeth and fingernails, garlic odor in the breath, gastrointestinal problems, and damage to the nervous system. A deficiency of selenium can lead to Keshan disease, which damages the heart.

336   Chapter 8 | Minerals and Water

LO 8.16 Fluoride

Fluoride helps maintain the structure of bones and teeth and helps prevent dental caries. The primary dietary source of fluoride is a fluoridated water supply and the consumption of foods and beverages prepared using fluoridated water. In children, consumption of too much fluoride during tooth development can result in fluorosis. In adults, too much fluoride can cause skeletal fluorosis, which results in joint stiffness or pain, osteoporosis, and calcification of the ligaments.

LO 8.17 Chromium

Chromium helps the hormone insulin function, but has not been proven to enhance weight loss or build muscle mass during exercise. It may reduce insulin resistance and help lower the risk of type 2 diabetes. Grains, meat, eggs, poultry, and some fruits and vegetables are good sources of chromium. A chromium deficiency is very rare in the United States.

LO 8.18 Iodine

Iodine is essential to make thyroid hormones, which affect the majority of the cells and help regulate metabolic rate. Children need iodine for normal growth and development. Iodine is found mostly in iodized salt, seafood, and foods processed using iodized salt or iodine-containing perservatives. A deficiency of iodine during pregnancy can cause mental retardation and cretinism in the child. A deficiency of iodine during adulthood causes goiter, which is an enlarged thyroid gland.

LO 8.19 Manganese

Manganese assists enzymes involved in metabolism, and functions in the formation of bone. Manganese is found in legumes, nuts, fruits, and whole grains. A deficiency of manganese causes a rash and scaly skin. Manganese is generally not toxic except due to environmental contamination, osteoporosis, and calcification of the ligaments.

LO 8.20 Molybdenum

Molybdenum also is a part of several enzymes involved in the breakdown of amino acids and other compounds. Molybdenum is found in legumes, whole grains, and nuts. A deficiency of molybdenum causes cardiovascular problems and headaches. Molybdenum does not appear to be toxic in humans, but in animal studies excess amounts of it can cause reproductive problems.

Terms to Know

- intracellular fluid compartment
- extracellular fluid compartment
- interstitial fluids
- electrolytes
- solvent
- water balance
- insensible water loss
- dehydration
- diuretics
- thirst mechanism
- osmosis
- antidiuretic hormone (ADH)
- hyponatremia
- minerals
- inorganic
- bioavailability
- major minerals
- trace minerals
- hypertension
- systolic pressure
- diastolic pressure
- kidney stones
- hyperkalemia
- hypokalemia
- hypercalcemia
- peak bone mass
- osteoporosis
- bone mineral density (BMD)
- osteopenia
- hyperphosphatemia
- hemoglobin
- myoglobin
- hemochromatosis
- iron-deficiency anemia
- selenosis
- Keshan disease
- fluorosis
- goiter
- cretinism

MasteringNutrition™

Build your knowledge—and confidence—in the Study Area of MasteringNutrition with a variety of study tools.

 MyDiet Analysis

Access MyDietAnalysis through MasteringNutrition™ and track your diet and daily activities. In addition, a dietary analysis activity is available for every chapter in your book.

Check Your Understanding

LO 8.1 1. The most abundant substance in your body is
   a. magnesium.
   b. iron.
   c. sodium.
   d. water.

LO 8.3 2. Bottled water is regulated by the FDA.
   a. true
   b. false

LO 8.4 3. In your body, minerals cannot
   a. help maintain fluid balance.
   b. be part of enzymes.
   c. work with your immune system.
   d. help absorb vitamin C.

LO 8.5 4. The daily recommendation for dietary sodium intake for adults up to age 51 is
   a. 3,400 milligrams.
   b. 2,300 milligrams.
   c. 1,500 milligrams.
   d. 180 milligrams.

LO 8.6 5. Which are NOT good sources of potassium?
   a. fruits and vegetables
   b. healthy unsaturated oils
   c. dairy and protein
   d. vegetables and grains

LO 8.7 6. One cup of skim milk, 8 ounces of low-fat yogurt, and 1½ ounces of reduced-fat Cheddar cheese *each* provide
   a. 100 milligrams of calcium.
   b. 200 milligrams of calcium.
   c. 300 milligrams of calcium.
   d. 400 milligrams of calcium.

LO 8.12 7. You are having pasta for dinner. You want to enhance your absorption of the nonheme iron in the pasta. To do that, you could top your spaghetti with
   a. butter.
   b. olive oil.
   c. tomato sauce.
   d. nothing; eat it plain.

LO 8.15 8. Which of the following is NOT a function of selenium?
   a. It helps regulate thyroid hormones in your body.
   b. It may help fight against certain cancers.
   c. It functions as an antioxidant.
   d. It is needed to prevent anemia.

LO 8.16 9. Fluoride will help strengthen and repair the enamel on your teeth. What other mineral strengthens your teeth?
   a. chloride
   b. phosphorus
   c. sulfur
   d. zinc

LO 8.17 10. Chromium increases the effectiveness of
   a. thyroid hormones.
   b. the hormone insulin.
   c. antidiuretic hormone (ADH).
   d. hemoglobin.

Answers

1. (d) Your body is about 60 percent water. Water bathes the trillions of cells in your body and is part of the fluid inside your cells where reactions take place. Iron, though part of hemoglobin, is a trace mineral, so you only have small amounts in your body. Both magnesium and sodium are major minerals used in your body but are not as abundant as water.

2. (a) True. The FDA regulates all bottled water sold in the United States.

3. (d) Although you need only small amounts of minerals in your diet, they play enormously important roles in your body, such as helping to maintain fluid balance, being part of enzymes, and working with your immune system to keep you healthy. Unfortunately, they can't help absorb vitamin C.

4. (c) The daily recommended amount of sodium for adults up to age 51 is 1,500 milligrams. The upper level for sodium daily is 2,300 milligrams, whereas the absolute minimum that should be consumed is 180 milligrams per day. Unfortunately, Americans far exceed these recommendations and consume more than 3,400 milligrams of sodium daily, on average.

5. (b) While oils are a heart healthy way to get some fat in your diet, they are not a good source of potassium. The good news is that fruits, vegetables, protein, and dairy products are good sources of this mineral.

6. (c) Each of these servings of dairy foods provides 300 milligrams of calcium. Consuming the recommended three servings of lean dairy products daily will just about meet the amount of calcium recommended daily (1,000 milligrams) for many adults.

7. (c) Ladle the tomato sauce on your pasta—the vitamin C in it can enhance nonheme iron absorption. Though the butter and olive oil will give your spaghetti flavor, they won't help you absorb iron.

8. (d) Selenium helps regulate thyroid hormones, may play a role in fighting certain cancers, and functions as an antioxidant, but it does not prevent anemia. Iron is the mineral most associated with preventing anemia.

9. (b) Phosphorus, along with calcium, forms hydroxyapatite, which is the strengthening material found in your teeth. Chloride is one of the electrolytes in your blood that helps maintain fluid and acid-base balance. Sulfur plays an important role as part of many compounds in your body, such as certain amino acids. Zinc helps with wound healing and maintaining a healthy immune system.

10. (b) Chromium increases insulin's effectiveness in your cells. Iodine is needed to make thyroid hormones, and ADH is the hormone that directs kidneys to minimize water loss and concentrate urine.

Web Resources

- To learn more about the safety of your local water supply, visit the EPA's website at www.epa.gov
- For more on the DASH diet, visit DASH for Health at www.dashforhealth.com
- For more on osteoporosis, visit the National Osteoporosis Foundation at www.nof.org
- For more on high blood pressure, visit www.nhlbi.nih.gov

Answers to True or False?

1. **False.** Vitamin waters contain additional calories that you may not need. To improve your fluid intake, plain water is just as healthy and much cheaper. Turn to page 293 to learn more about these waters.

2. **True.** Your mug of java does contribute to meeting your daily water needs, even though it may contain caffeine, a diuretic. Turn to page 294 to find out why.

3. **False.** Although seasoning your food with salt adds sodium, it is not the major culprit in sodium overload. Turn to page 301 to find out what is.

4. **True.** In fact, the recommended three servings of dairy foods, including milk, yogurt, and/or cheese, will almost nail your calcium needs for the day. Unfortunately, most Americans' diets fall short in regard to this food group. To find out how to meet your needs, turn to page 307.

5. **True.** Magnesium, along with calcium and potassium, is part of a diet that has been shown to substantially lower blood pressure. To find out more, turn to page 313.

6. **False.** Although meat, fish, and poultry are fabulous sources of iron, they are not the main sources in Americans' diets. Turn to page 317 to find out what contributes the most iron to our diets.

7. **False.** Taking a zinc lozenge doesn't prevent the common cold but it may help reduce the severity and duration of a cold. But there is a catch. Turn to page 320 to find out what the side effects can be.

8. **False.** Most bottled water sold in the United States does not contain fluoride. Turn to page 325 to find out why this could be bad news for your teeth.

9. **False.** Dream on. Turn to page 326 to learn the truth.

10. **False.** Kosher salt doesn't contain iodine. Turn to page 328 to find foods that are good sources of this mineral.

9
Alcohol

True or False?

1. **A shot of whiskey contains more alcohol than a can of beer.** T|F p. 343

2. **Red wine contains phytochemicals that are good for your heart.** T|F p. 344

3. **Women feel the effects of alcohol sooner than men.** T|F p. 348

4. **Drinking a Bloody Mary (tomato juice and vodka) will help with a hangover.** T|F p. 351

5. **Drinking alcohol will improve sexual function.** T|F p. 351

6. **Alcohol provides 7 calories per gram.** T|F p. 351

7. **Binge drinking is considered drinking 7 or more drinks in a very short time.** T|F p. 357

8. **If you passed out from heavy drinking, your blood alcohol level would stabilize and gradually return to normal.** T|F p. 359

9. **Some states in the United States have lowered the legal drinking age to 18.** T|F p. 360

10. **There is no cure for alcohol use disorder.** T|F p. 361

See page 367 for the answers.

341

Learning Outcomes

After reading this chapter, you will be able to:

LO 9.1 Explain what alcohol is and how it is made.

LO 9.2 Explain why people drink alcohol.

LO 9.3 Describe how alcohol is absorbed and metabolized in the body.

LO 9.4 List the harmful effects of alcohol in the body.

LO 9.5 Describe alcohol use disorder.

The nature of alcohol is discussed in this chapter, including its various forms, how it is digested and absorbed in the body, and its potential short-term and long-term health effects. We also explore alcohol use and abuse, and steps you can take if you suspect that you or someone close to you is abusing alcohol.

What Is Alcohol and How Is It Made?

LO 9.1 Explain what alcohol is and how it is made.

Your body doesn't need alcohol to survive. Therefore, alcohol is not an essential nutrient. You don't gain any nutrition from drinking it, other than calories. Ounce for ounce, it can cost 100 times more than bottled water. It's legally sold in the United States, but supposedly off limits to those who aren't adults, even though teenagers often feel under social pressure to consume it. Some medical reports say that in moderation, it can be good for you, while others tell you that drinking too much of it can kill you.

A bottle of beer, a glass of wine, or a rum and cola are all drinks that might come to mind when we consider the term **alcohol**. Technically, these beverages aren't alcohol by themselves, but they all contain a type of alcohol called **ethanol**.

Ethanol is one of three similar compounds in the chemical category of alcohol. The other two compounds, methanol (used in antifreeze) and isopropanol (used in rubbing alcohol), are both poisonous when ingested. Ethanol is considered safe for consumption, but it is not harmless. Consuming excessive amounts of ethanol can be toxic and damage your body. Too much can even kill you.

Ethanol is made through the **fermentation** of yeast and the natural sugars in grains (glucose and maltose) and fruits (fructose and glucose). The yeast breaks down the sugar into ethanol and carbon dioxide. The carbon dioxide evaporates, leaving an alcohol-containing beverage. Grapes provide the sugar for making wine, whereas the starch from grains provides the sugar when producing beer.

Liquors, such as rum, scotch, and whiskey, are made through a process called **distillation** and are more accurately called distilled spirits.[1] In this process, an alcoholic beverage is heated, causing the ethanol to vaporize. The vapor is collected, cooled, and condensed into a very concentrated liquid called liquor.

Although ethanol is the scientific name for the alcohol found in beverages, we will use the more common term *alcohol* throughout this chapter.

LO 9.1 **The Take-Home Message** Ethanol is the type of alcohol consumed in alcoholic beverages. Alcoholic beverages are made by the processes of fermentation or distillation. Alcohol is not an essential nutrient because your body does not need it to survive.

Why Do People Drink Alcohol?

LO 9.2 Explain why people drink alcohol.

People around the world drink alcohol in many different forms and for many different reasons. The sake (rice wine) of Japan is used during tea and Shinto ceremonies, while the dark beer of the Irish is consumed by many pub patrons celebrating their favorite sport. The vodka of Russia and the chardonnay of Napa Valley are consumed in the pursuit of relaxation and pleasure. Globally, wine is part of many religious traditions, including the Catholic Mass and the Jewish Sabbath, and in some cultures, it's the beverage of choice during the main meal of the day. For parts of human history, wine and beer were safer to drink than water, which was often polluted.

In the United States, more than half of adults consume at least one alcoholic beverage per month.[2] Americans drink alcohol for many of the same reasons people in other parts of the world do. We use it to relax, celebrate, and socialize. We have also found that it may provide health benefits. Let's explore these motives for drinking alcohol more closely.

People Drink to Relax, Celebrate, and Socialize

Alcohol is a drug that alters your conscious mind.[3] Within minutes of sipping an alcoholic beverage, a person will feel more relaxed. After a few more sips, a mild, pleasant euphoria sets in and inhibitions begin to loosen. By the end of the first or second drink, a person will often feel more outgoing, happy, and social. This anxiety-reducing, upbeat initial effect is why people seek out and continue to drink alcohol.

Having a drink with another person symbolizes social bonding. When it comes to mingling with others or celebrating a special occasion, whether it's with friends, coworkers, or even strangers, pubs and parties are common gathering spots, and alcoholic drinks are commonly served. This is considered **social drinking**, which is defined as drinking patterns that are considered acceptable by society.[4] Social drinking is not the same as moderate drinking (see the next section), as consuming too much alcohol, even in socially acceptable situations, can be harmful, even if it is only done on the weekends. Later in this chapter we discuss binge drinking, which often occurs in social settings.

Moderate Alcohol Consumption May Have Health Benefits

Some people drink alcohol because of its health benefits. That's right. Some studies have suggested that moderate alcohol consumption may reduce the risk of heart disease, and the risk of dying in general, for middle-aged and older adults.[5] **Moderate alcohol consumption** is defined as an average daily consumption of up to one drink per day for women and up to two drinks per day for men.

A standard drink is any one of the following:

- One 12-ounce serving of beer
- One 1.5-ounce shot of liquor
- One 5-ounce glass of wine

(T/F) Each of these contains about half an ounce of alcohol (**Figure 9.1**).

On November 17, 1991, the television news show *60 Minutes* aired a segment called "The French Paradox," touting the benefits of modest amounts of red wine to help reduce the risk of heart disease. The French Paradox is so called because the people of France have lower rates of heart disease even though their saturated fat intake mimics that of Americans. They also drink more red wine than Americans do, which is thought to be the differentiating factor. (However, the French also consume fewer *trans* fats and have a less stressful lifestyle and better developed social networks, which can also contribute to their impressively lower risk of heart disease.) In the four weeks after the segment was aired, sales of red wine increased by about 45 percent.[6] Suddenly,

Beer is made from the fermentation of yeast and the natural sugars from grains.

Figure 9.1 What Is a Standard Drink? One standard drink of beer (12 ounces), wine (5 ounces), or liquor (1½ ounces) contains the same amount of alcohol.

alcohol A chemical class of substances that include ethanol, methanol, and isopropanol.

ethanol The type of alcohol in alcoholic beverages such as wine, beer, and liquor.

fermentation The process by which yeast converts sugars in grains or fruits into ethanol and carbon dioxide.

distillation The evaporation and then collection of a liquid by condensation.

social drinking Drinking patterns that are considered acceptable by society.

moderate alcohol consumption An average consumption of up to one drink per day for women and up to two drinks per day for men, as well as no more than three drinks in any single day for women and no more than four drinks in a single day for men.

Understanding Alcohol Serving Sizes

Do you really know the number of drinks you've had? Be careful how much you pour! Scan this QR code with your mobile device to access the video. You can also access the video in MasteringNutrition™.

12 oz
(1 drink)

16 oz
(1⅓ drink)

5 oz
(1 drink)

8 oz
(1½ drink)

Figure 9.2 When a Drink Is More Than a Drink…
Depending on the size, one drink may actually be the equivalent of 1⅓ to 2 drinks or more.

instead of thinking that "an apple a day keeps the doctor away," people were hoping that "a drink a day keeps the cardiologist at bay." Were these people on the right track?

Red wine contains resveratrol, a flavonoid and type of phytochemical, which acts as an antioxidant. (Dark beer also contains flavonoids.) Antioxidants help prevent the "bad" LDL cholesterol from becoming oxidized, which leads to its accumulation in the artery wall and atherosclerosis. Flavonoids help inhibit the stickiness of platelets in the blood. Alcohol also helps inhibit the stickiness of platelets in the blood, just like flavonoids, but also increases the level of heart-protective "good" HDL cholesterol. Because of these potential heart-healthy attributes, alcohol and red wine have been in the media limelight since the 1990s.

There isn't enough evidence to support the theory that wine, whether red, white, or rosé, has any health superiority over beer and distilled spirits. In fact, some studies comparing various alcohol sources have found that the majority of heart-protective effects are attributable to the alcohol content regardless of the source.[7] In other words, a beer, a glass of cabernet, or a shot of scotch all appear to have similar heart-protective effects. When it comes to the health benefits of alcohol, the source is unlikely to make much of a difference.

Before you crack open a beer to celebrate though, be aware that the people who gain the health benefits from moderate alcohol consumption are women age 55 and older and men age 45 and older. Alcohol consumption by younger people has not been shown to provide many—if any—health benefits. In fact, drinking alcohol during your younger years increases the risk of injuries and violent, traumatic deaths, which offsets any possible health benefits from the alcohol.[8]

All individuals who choose to drink alcohol need to stick to moderate drinking, and even then they need to carefully monitor their intake. Moderate drinkers need to watch out for (1) the size of their drinks and (2) the frequency of their drinking. As mentioned earlier, a standard drink contains about 0.5 ounce of alcohol. If your 8-ounce wine glass gets filled to the brim, or you chug an oversized mug of beer, you could consume close to two standard drinks in one glass or mug (**Figure 9.2**). A 750-milliliter bottle of wine contains five, 5-ounce glasses of wine. If you split a bottle with a friend, you are consuming the equivalent of 2½ standard drinks. One rum and cola can provide the equivalent of more than 2½ alcoholic drinks. Another important point to remember is that abstaining from drinking through the week and then having seven drinks on a single Friday night does not count as moderate drinking. When it comes to alcohol, no "banking" is allowed.

LO 9.2 **The Take-Home Message** People drink alcohol to relax, celebrate, and socialize. Moderate alcohol consumption, which means 1 to 2 drinks per day for men and 1 drink per day for women, may provide health benefits in some older adults. While the flavonoids in red wine and dark beer are thought to be beneficial compounds, the alcohol itself may also provide protective benefits, such as increasing "good" HDL cholesterol levels. Individuals who choose to drink alcohol need to do so in moderation and monitor both the size of their drinks and the frequency of their drinking.

What Happens to Alcohol in the Body?

LO 9.3 Describe how alcohol is absorbed and metabolized in the body.

Your body treats alcohol differently from any other substance. Unlike the other energy-containing nutrients, such as carbohydrates and fats, your body cannot

Blood vessels

Alcohol

Alcohol dehydrogenase

Liver

1 Some alcohol is metabolized in the stomach by the enzyme alcohol dehydrogenase.

2 Some alcohol is absorbed through the stomach. Food in the stomach slows the absorption of alcohol.

3 Most alcohol is absorbed in the small intestine.

4 Most alcohol is metabolized in the liver.

5 Alcohol that is not metabolized will return to the blood and circulate throughout the body, including the brain.

Stomach

Small intestine

Figure 9.3 The Metabolism of Alcohol

store alcohol. Because alcohol is a toxin, the body quickly works to metabolize and eliminate it.

Many factors, including your gender, your body type, the amount of food in your stomach, and the amount of alcohol you drink, will affect how quickly you absorb and metabolize it.[9] Alcohol travels through the body in the blood, and is distributed throughout the watery tissues, including the brain. Let's follow a swallow of beer through your digestive system and see how it's handled along the way (**Figure 9.3**).

You Absorb Alcohol in Your Stomach and Small Intestine

Within seconds of the first sip of the beer, about 20 percent of the alcohol will be directly absorbed through the stomach and into your blood. Some alcohol is also metabolized in the stomach by an enzyme called **alcohol dehydrogenase** before it is absorbed. The majority of alcohol, about 80 percent, is absorbed in the small intestine.

The amount and type of food in the stomach determine how long alcohol lingers there before entering the small intestine. If your swallow of beer chases a bacon cheeseburger and fries, the alcohol will take longer to leave the stomach than if the beer was consumed without food after a period of fasting. One study showed that an alcoholic drink consumed after a meal was absorbed about three times more slowly than if it was consumed on an empty stomach.[10] This is why you should always try to avoid drinking alcohol on an empty stomach. Fat also slows down the departure

Light beer has about the same amount of alcohol as regular beer.

alcohol dehydrogenase One of the alcohol-metabolizing enzymes found in the stomach and the liver.

of food from the stomach, so a large amount of fat in the food, as in this burger meal, will help delay the arrival of the alcohol into the small intestine.

Keep in mind, however, that though a stomach full of high-fat food will delay the arrival of alcohol in the small intestine, the alcohol will still eventually arrive there. If a person drinks several glasses of beer with dinner, the alcohol will be absorbed once the stomach starts emptying. Intoxication could be an unexpected post-dinner surprise.

You Metabolize Alcohol Primarily in Your Liver

Once in your blood, alcohol travels to the liver, where the majority of it is metabolized. Enzymes in the liver, most importantly alcohol dehydrogenase, convert the alcohol to **acetaldehyde**, which is eventually metabolized to carbon dioxide and water.[11] A healthy liver can metabolize about one alcoholic drink in about 1½ to 2 hours. Regardless of the amount consumed, the metabolism of alcohol occurs at a steady rate in your body.

There is a second enzyme system in the liver that metabolizes alcohol: the **microsomal ethanol-oxidizing system (MEOS)**. Individuals who consume a lot of alcohol will have a somewhat more active MEOS because this system is revved up when chronically high levels of alcohol are present in the liver.

Alcohol Circulates in Your Blood

If your liver cannot handle the amount of alcohol all at once, the extra alcohol reenters the blood and is distributed in the watery tissues in your body. Your **blood alcohol concentration (BAC)** is the amount of alcohol in your blood, measured in grams of alcohol per deciliter of blood, usually expressed as a percentage.[12] **Table 9.1** gives you a ballpark idea of how your BAC is affected by the number of alcoholic beverages you consume. As you can see, the more you drink, the higher your BAC. Because alcohol infiltrates your brain, as your BAC increases so does your level of mental impairment and intoxication.

Though the liver will eventually metabolize most of the alcohol that is consumed, a small amount will leave your body intact through your breath and urine. Because the amount of alcohol in your breath correlates with the amount of alcohol in your blood, a Breathalyzer test can be used to measure your BAC. Police officers often use this device when they suspect that a person has consumed too much alcohol.

A Breathalyzer is used to measure a person's blood alcohol concentration (BAC).

acetaldehyde An intermediary by-product of the breakdown of ethanol in the liver.

microsomal ethanol-oxidizing system (MEOS) The other major enzyme system in the liver that metabolizes alcohol.

blood alcohol concentration (BAC) The measurement of the amount of alcohol in your blood. BAC is measured in grams of alcohol per deciliter of blood, usually expressed as a percentage.

The Effects of Alcohol on Your Brain

Alcohol is a *depressant*, a substance that slows the transmission of nerve impulses. Your brain is very sensitive to the depressant effect of alcohol. For instance, alcohol slows down your reaction time to stimuli (such as a car coming toward you on the road), confuses your thoughts, impairs your judgment, and induces sleepiness. The more you drink, the more areas of the brain are affected. **Table 9.2** and **Figure 9.4** on page 348 show how increasing BAC levels affect specific areas of the brain, and how body movements and behaviors are affected. (*Note:* A person's BAC can continue to rise even when unconscious.) If enough alcohol has been consumed, the activities of the brain stem, which controls breathing and heart rate, can be suppressed, and ultimately cause death. Excessive amounts

Table 9.1
Blood Alcohol Concentration Tables

For Women
Body Weight in Pounds

Drinks per Hour	100	120	140	160	180	200
1	0.05	0.04	0.03	0.03	0.03	0.02
2	0.09	0.08	0.07	0.06	0.05	0.05
3	0.14	0.11	0.10	0.09	0.08	0.07
4	0.18	0.15	0.13	0.11	0.10	0.09
5	0.23	0.19	0.16	0.14	0.13	0.11
6	0.27	0.23	0.19	0.17	0.15	0.14
7	0.32	0.27	0.23	0.20	0.18	0.16
8	0.36	0.30	0.26	0.23	0.20	0.18
9	0.41	0.34	0.29	0.26	0.23	0.20
10	0.45	0.38	0.32	0.28	0.25	0.23

For Men
Body Weight in Pounds

Drinks per Hour	100	120	140	160	180	200
1	0.04	0.03	0.03	0.02	0.02	0.02
2	0.08	0.06	0.05	0.05	0.04	0.04
3	0.11	0.09	0.08	0.07	0.06	0.06
4	0.15	0.12	0.11	0.09	0.08	0.08
5	0.19	0.16	0.13	0.12	0.11	0.09
6	0.23	0.19	0.16	0.14	0.13	0.11
7	0.26	0.22	0.19	0.16	0.15	0.13
8	0.30	0.25	0.21	0.19	0.17	0.15
9	0.34	0.28	0.24	0.21	0.19	0.17
10	0.38	0.31	0.27	0.23	0.21	0.19

Notes: The darkly shaded areas indicate legal intoxication.
Blood alcohol concentrations are expressed as percent, meaning grams of alcohol per 10 milliliters (per deciliter) of blood.

of alcohol can cause "brain shrinkage," which can impair memory and learning as well as coordination and balance. Heavy drinking also reduces blood flow to the brain, which can similarly impair balance and coordination, such as for walking.[13]

Because alcohol is a depressant, it can be very unhealthy, and even dangerous, to mix it with a stimulant, such as the high amounts of caffeine found in energy drinks. In a study of more than 4,000 college students, research found that those who consumed alcohol mixed with caffeinated energy drinks were twice as likely to be injured, require medical attention, ride with an intoxicated driver, and either take sexual advantage of someone or be the victim of sexual aggressiveness.[14] Because energy drinks can reduce the symptoms of alcohol intoxication, such as tiredness, individuals may continue drinking to the point where the BAC increases to dangerous levels, affecting both the body's mental and physical functions.[15]

Mixing alcohol with caffeinated energy drinks can have dangerous consequences.

Table 9.2
Progressive Effects of Alcohol

Blood Alcohol Concentration	Changes in Feelings and Personality	Brain Regions Affected	Impaired Functions (continuum)
0.01–0.05	Relaxation, sense of well-being, loss of inhibition	Cerebral cortex	Alertness; judgment
0.06–0.10	Pleasure, numbing of feelings, nausea, sleepiness, emotional arousal	Cerebral cortex and forebrain	Coordination (especially fine motor skills); visual tracking
0.11–0.20	Mood swings, anger, sadness, mania	Cerebral cortex, forebrain, and cerebellum	Reasoning and depth perception; appropriate social behavior
0.21–0.30	Aggression, reduced sensations, depression, stupor	Cerebral cortex, forebrain, cerebellum, and brain stem	Speech; balance; temperature regulation
0.31–0.40	Unconsciousness, coma, death possible	Entire brain	Bladder control; breathing
0.41 and greater	Death		Heart rate

Figure 9.4 The Brain and Alcohol
As you consume more alcohol, additional areas of your brain are affected. Your cerebral cortex is affected first, followed by your forebrain, cerebellum, and brain stem. The greater the alcohol intake, the greater the physical and behavioral changes in your body.

Labels: Cerebral cortex, Forebrain, Brain stem, Cerebellum

Women Are More Susceptible to the Effects of Alcohol Than Men

In essence, every alcoholic beverage that a male consumes is equivalent to about 1$\frac{1}{3}$ alcoholic beverages for a woman. Two factors contribute to women's greater susceptibility to alcohol:

- Women have about 20 to 30 percent less alcohol dehydrogenase in their stomachs than men, so more alcohol will enter the blood immediately through women's stomachs.[16]
- Women generally have less muscle mass, and thus less body water, than men. (Recall from Chapter 8 that muscle tissue has a higher percentage of water than fat.) Because alcohol is diluted in water, people with more muscle are able to distribute more of the alcohol throughout their body than people who have more fat.

Because of these factors, women will feel alcohol's effects sooner than men. Women take note: It's dangerous to try to keep up, drink for drink, with male companions. You will begin to feel the effects of alcohol long before a man will.

Finally, people of Asian descent also need to be aware of a potential lower tolerance to alcohol. About 50 percent of Asians (both men and women) experience "alcohol flush," a reddish skin reaction that occurs because of an enzyme deficiency. Symptoms include facial flushing, nausea, and rapid heart beat, and one study has shown that people who experience this condition, particularly East Asians, are at higher risk of esophageal cancer.[17]

LO 9.3 **The Take-Home Message** Alcohol is absorbed in the stomach and small intestine and is metabolized primarily in the liver. Your sex, body type, the amount of food in your stomach, and the quantity of alcohol consumed will affect the rate of absorption and metabolism in your body. The blood alcohol concentration (BAC) is the measurement of alcohol in your blood. Alcohol is a central nervous system depressant. Because your brain is sensitive to alcohol, alcohol affects your behavior. Because of having less alcohol dehydrogenase in the stomach and less body water, women will feel the effects of the same amount of alcohol before men will.

How Can Alcohol Be Harmful?

LO 9.4 List the harmful effects of alcohol in the body.

Although alcohol is often advertised in magazines, billboards, and television commercials as a trendy and sexy way to relax and socialize (see the Examining the Evidence feature "Alcohol and Advertising"), it can cause a number of problems for those who abuse it. Some of these problems merely cause temporary discomfort, but other long-term effects can be extremely damaging to health.

Alcohol Can Disrupt Sleep and Cause Hangovers

Many people wrongly think that a drink before bed will help them sleep better, but it will actually have the opposite effect. Whereas having a drink within an hour before bed may help you to fall asleep sooner, it will disrupt your sleep cycle, potentially causing you to awaken in the middle of the night, and making returning to sleep a challenge. As a result, you will likely feel tired the next morning, and you may find it harder to pay attention to what you are learning in class.[18] Even a moderate amount of alcohol consumed at dinner—or even late in the afternoon during happy hour—can disrupt that night's sleep.

If you have a bad night's sleep, it's a bad idea to drink alcohol the next day. Studies have shown that a night of sleep disruption followed by even small amounts of alcohol the next day reduces the reaction time and alertness in individuals performing a simulated driving test. Being tired and then drinking alcohol exacerbates alcohol's sedating effect.[19]

A **hangover** is your body's way of saying, "don't do that to me again." After a bout of heavy drinking, individuals can experience hangover symptoms ranging from a pounding headache, fatigue, nausea, and increased thirst to a rapid heart beat, tremors, sweating, dizziness, depression, anxiety, and irritability. A hangover begins within hours of your last drink, as your BAC begins to drop. The symptoms will appear in full force once all the alcohol is gone from your blood, and these symptoms can linger for up to an additional 24 hours.[20] In other words, a few hours of excessive alcohol consumption on a Saturday night can not only ruin your entire Sunday but even disrupt part of your Monday morning.

There are several ways that alcohol contributes to the symptoms of a hangover. Alcohol is a diuretic, so it can cause dehydration, and thus, electrolyte imbalances. It inhibits the release of antidiuretic hormone from your pituitary gland, which in turn causes your kidneys to excrete water, as well as electrolytes, in your urine. Vomiting and sweating during or after excessive drinking will further contribute to dehydration and electrolyte loss. Dehydration also increases your thirst and can make you

Practical Nutrition **VIDEO**

Step Up to the Bar

Joan has some flavorful "mocktail" ideas that will help you avoid dehydration and a hangover. Scan this QR code with your mobile device to access the video. You can also access the video in MasteringNutrition™.

hangover A collective term for the unpleasant symptoms, such as a headache and dizziness, that occur after drinking an excessive amount of alcohol.

Alcohol and Advertising

Advertising for alcoholic beverages is pervasive and persuasive. You need only drive down a major highway or turn on your television to see billboards and commercials for a beer or liquor brand. In some media, including popular magazines like *Rolling Stone* and *Sports Illustrated*, alcohol ads can outnumber non–alcohol ads by almost 3 to 1.[1]

Companies that make alcoholic beverages pay large sums of money to create and show these ads for one reason: They work. Studies have shown that advertisements for alcoholic beverages are associated with an increase in drinking among adolescents.[2] Many ads tend to emphasize sexual and social stereotypes. When targeted to underage drinkers, this type of message has been shown to increase adolescents' desire to emulate those portrayed in the advertisements.[3]

Alcohol ads should be viewed with caution, as the messages in them are often misleading and in some cases blatantly false. Let's take a look at the messages and realities in a typical alcohol advertisement that might appear in a magazine.

WHAT DO YOU THINK?

1. Do advertisements for alcoholic beverages in trendy magazines, television commercials, and on the Internet motivate adolescents to drink?
2. Should advertisements for alcoholic beverages be banned in media outlets that attract a younger audience?
3. Should advertisements for alcohol geared to underage drinkers also state the dangers of consuming it?

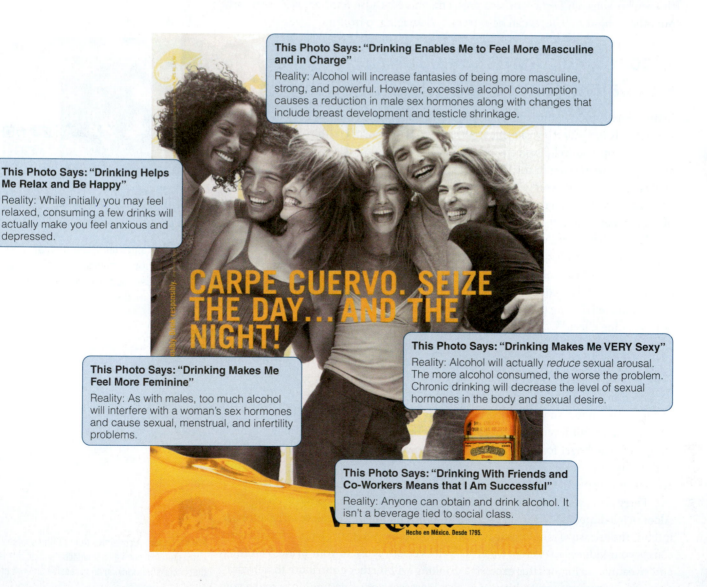

This Photo Says: "Drinking Enables Me to Feel More Masculine and in Charge"
Reality: Alcohol will increase fantasies of being more masculine, strong, and powerful. However, excessive alcohol consumption causes a reduction in male sex hormones along with changes that include breast development and testicle shrinkage.

This Photo Says: "Drinking Helps Me Relax and Be Happy"
Reality: While initially you may feel relaxed, consuming a few drinks will actually make you feel anxious and depressed.

This Photo Says: "Drinking Makes Me Feel More Feminine"
Reality: As with males, too much alcohol will interfere with a woman's sex hormones and cause sexual, menstrual, and infertility problems.

This Photo Says: "Drinking Makes Me VERY Sexy"
Reality: Alcohol will actually *reduce* sexual arousal. The more alcohol consumed, the worse the problem. Chronic drinking will decrease the level of sexual hormones in the body and sexual desire.

This Photo Says: "Drinking With Friends and Co-Workers Means that I Am Successful"
Reality: Anyone can obtain and drink alcohol. It isn't a beverage tied to social class.

CARPE CUERVO. SEIZE THE DAY... AND THE NIGHT!

Hecho en México. Desde 1795.

feel lightheaded, dizzy, and weak. Increased acid production in the stomach and secretions from the pancreas and intestines can cause stomach pain, nausea, and vomiting.

Lastly, alcoholic beverages often contain compounds called **congeners**, which enhance their taste and appearance but may contribute to hangover symptoms. Congeners can be produced during the fermentation process or be added during production of the alcoholic beverages. The large number of congeners in red wine can cause headaches in some people.[21]

Coffee will not sober you up. An intoxicated person who drinks coffee will end up being a stimulated drunk. It takes time to sober up because your liver has to metabolize all the alcohol that you consumed.

(T|F) Forget the old wives' tale of consuming an alcoholic beverage to cure a hangover. Drinking more alcohol, even if it is mixed with tomato or orange juice, during a hangover only prolongs the recovery time. In fact, time is the only true remedy for hangover symptoms. Whereas aspirin and other nonsteroidal anti-inflammatory medications, such as ibuprofen, can ease a headache, these medications can also contribute to stomachache and nausea. Taking acetaminophen (Tylenol) during and after alcohol consumption, when the alcohol is being metabolized, has been shown to intensify this pain reliever's toxicity to the liver and may cause liver damage in some cases.[22] The best strategy for dealing with a hangover is to avoid it by limiting the amount of alcohol consumed.

Alcohol Can Interact with Hormones

Many individuals who overindulge in alcohol tend not to eat enough while they are drinking, which causes their body's glucose stores to become depleted and their blood glucose levels to fall. Typically, the hormones insulin and glucagon would automatically be released to make glucose, but alcohol interferes with this process. Because the brain needs glucose to function properly, a low blood glucose level can contribute to the feelings of fatigue, weakness, mood changes, irritability, and anxiety often experienced during a hangover.

(T|F) In addition to the hormones that regulate your blood glucose level, alcohol can interfere with other hormones. Alcohol can also increase estrogen levels in women, which may increase the risk of breast cancer.[23] Drinking alcohol can affect reproductive hormones and is associated with both male and female sexual dysfunction, and alcohol abuse has been associated with infertility.[24]

Alcohol May Lead to Overnutrition and Malnutrition

(T|F) At 7 calories per gram, alcohol provides fewer calories than fat (9 calories per gram) but more than either carbohydrates or protein (4 calories per gram each). However, unless you are drinking a straight shot of liquor, your alcoholic beverages will contain additional calories (see **Table 9.3**). For example, a rum and cola contains the calories from both the rum and the cola, making the drink more than three times as high in calories as the rum itself. Depending on the mixers and ingredients added to your beverage, the calorie count in your drink can escalate to that of a meal. A mudslide, for example, made with vodka, Irish cream, coffee liqueur, ice cream, and cream, should be ordered from the dessert menu and served with a spoon.

If you consistently add extra calories from alcoholic beverages—or any food or beverage source—to a diet that is already meeting your daily calorie needs, you will gain weight. Excessive consumption of alcohol has also been shown to increase fat and weight around the stomach. Though this is usually referred to as a "beer" belly, extra calories from any type of alcoholic beverage can contribute to a paunch.

congeners Compounds in alcohol that enhance the taste but may contribute to hangover symptoms.

Table 9.3

Calories in Selected Alcoholic Drinks

Beer
Serving size: 12 oz
Alcohol serving: 1
Calories per drink: 150

Light Beer
Serving size: 12 oz
Alcohol serving: 1
Calories per drink: 110

Mudslide
Serving size: 12 oz
Alcohol servings: 4
Calories per drink: 820

Distilled Spirits (e.g., whiskey, vodka, gin, rum)
Serving size: 1.5 oz
Alcohol serving: 1
Calories per drink: 100

Bloody Mary
Serving size: 5.5 oz
Alcohol serving: 1
Calories per drink: 97

Wine (white or red)
Serving size: 5 oz
Alcohol serving: 1
Calories per drink: 100–105

Margarita
Serving size: 6.3 oz
Alcohol servings: 3
Calories per drink: 327

Cosmopolitan
Serving size: 2.5 oz
Alcohol servings: 1.7
Calories per drink: 131

Rum and Cola
Serving size: 12 oz
Alcohol servings: 2.7
Calories per drink: 361

Note: Alcohol servings are per beverage.

If high-calorie "bar foods" are consumed with the drinks, the calories can add up rapidly (**Figure 9.5**).

Compensating for calories in alcoholic beverages by cutting out more nutritious foods will cause you to fall short of your nutrient needs. If you drink a daily glass of beer instead of an equal amount of low-fat milk, your waist may not suffer, but your bones could. You will rob yourself of an excellent source of calcium and vitamin D that the milk, but not the beer, provides. A chronic substitution of excessive amounts of alcohol for nutritious foods in the diet can lead to malnutrition.

Dinner 1

5 12-oz beers

1,719 total calories

8 BBQ chicken wings

1 large serving nachos with cheese

1 handful goldfish crackers

Total fat (g)	**51**	
Saturated fat (g)	**16**	
Cholesterol (mg)	**154**	

Dinner 2

724 total calories

2 oz whole-wheat dinner roll
4 tsp soft margarine

1 cup fat-free milk

4 oz grilled chicken breast
3/4 cup mashed potatoes
1 1/2 cup steamed carrots

28	Total fat (g)
8	Saturated fat (g)
89	Cholesterol (mg)

Figure 9.5 Too Much Alcohol Costs You Good Nutrition
A dinner of several alcoholic beverages and bar foods not only adds calories, fat, and saturated fat to your diet, but also displaces healthier foods that would provide better nutrition.

Individuals who drink excessively often eat diets inadequate in nutrients, especially vitamins and minerals. Often, they drink too much and don't eat enough. Those who consume more than 30 percent of their daily calories from alcohol tend to consume less protein, fiber, vitamins A, C, D, riboflavin, and thiamin, and the minerals calcium and iron.[25] This isn't surprising once you consider that if a person consuming 2,000 calories daily devotes 600 (30 percent) of these calories to alcohol, there would only be 1,400 calories left to meet all of his or her nutrient needs. When you're routinely limited to a diet of 1,400 calories daily, you're bound to have nutrient deficiencies.

Excessive alcohol consumption can also affect how the body handles the essential nutrients it actually gets. Routinely drinking too much alcohol can interfere with the absorption and/or use of protein, zinc, magnesium, the B vitamins thiamin, folate, and B$_{12}$, and the fat-soluble vitamins A, D, E, and K. As you have read in previous chapters, a chronic deficiency of nutrients can cause a cascade of ill health conditions and diseases. In particular, a thiamin deficiency can affect brain function, including memory loss, and increase the risk of Wernicke-Korsakoff syndrome, which includes mental confusion and uncontrolled muscle movement (see Chapter 7).

Alcohol Can Harm Your Digestive Organs, Heart, and Liver

Chronically drinking too much alcohol can lead to an inflamed esophagus. Alcohol inhibits the ability of the esophagus to contract. This enables the acid juices in the stomach to flow back up into the esophagus, causing inflammation. Chronic inflammation can be a stepping-stone to esophageal cancer. If you smoke when you drink, your chances of developing esophageal cancer, as well as mouth and throat cancer, are even higher.[26] Individuals who are heavy drinkers also have increased incidences of **gastritis** (*gastr* = stomach, *itis* = inflammation) and stomach ulcers.[27]

gastritis Inflammation of the stomach.

| a Normal liver | b Fatty liver A fatty liver can occur after just a few days of overconsumption. | c Cirrhosis By the cirrhosis stage, permanent damage is done and scar tissue has developed. |

Figure 9.6 Alcoholic Liver Disease

Excessive amounts of alcohol can also affect the beating and rhythm of the heart, which likely plays a role in the sudden deaths of some individuals who abuse alcohol.[28] It can damage heart tissue and increase the risk of hypertension. Hypertension is a risk factor for both heart disease and stroke.

Alcohol can also damage your liver and cause **alcoholic liver disease** (**Figure 9.6**). The disease develops in three stages, although some stages can occur simultaneously. The first stage of the disease is **fatty liver**, which can result from just a weekend or a few days of excessive drinking. Because alcohol metabolism takes top priority in the liver, the metabolism of other nutrients, including fats, will take a back seat to alcohol. Thus, the liver isn't able to metabolize all the fat that arrives in the liver, causing a buildup in this organ. Simultaneously, the liver uses some of the by-products of alcohol metabolism to make even more fat. The net effect is a liver that has cells that are full of fat.[29] A fatty liver can reverse itself *if* the alcohol consumption is stopped.

If the drinking doesn't stop, the second stage of liver disease, **alcoholic hepatitis**, can develop. In alcoholic hepatitis, the liver basically becomes irritated by various by-products of alcohol metabolism. Some by-products, namely acetaldehyde, are toxic to the liver. Free radicals, another by-product of alcohol metabolism, react with the proteins, lipids, and DNA in your cells, causing damage. Nausea, vomiting, fever, jaundice, and loss of appetite are signs of alcoholic hepatitis. Chronic, excessive amounts of alcohol may also impair your immune system, which can contribute to liver damage and increase the susceptibility to pneumonia and other infectious diseases.

Heavy drinking can also cause the increased passage of destructive **endotoxin**, which is released from bacteria in your intestines into your blood. Once endotoxin arrives in your liver, it can cause the release of substances called *cytokines* that further damage healthy liver cells and perpetuate scarring.[30]

As bouts of heavy drinking continue, chronic inflammation further injures the liver cells and can cause scarring. **Cirrhosis** is the third and final stage of alcoholic

alcoholic liver disease A degenerative liver condition that occurs in three stages: (1) fatty liver, (2) alcoholic hepatitis, and (3) cirrhosis.

fatty liver Stage 1 of alcoholic liver disease.

alcoholic hepatitis Stage 2 of alcoholic liver disease; due to chronic inflammation.

endotoxin A damaging product produced by intestinal bacteria that travels in the blood to the liver and initiates the release of cytokines that damage liver cells, leading to scarring.

cirrhosis Stage 3 of alcoholic liver disease in which liver cells die, causing severe scarring.

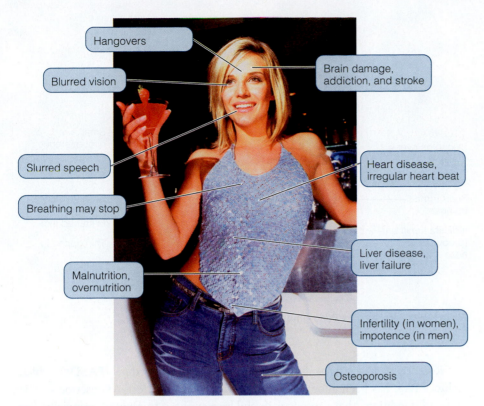

Figure 9.7 **Effects of Alcohol on the Body**

liver disease. In cirrhosis, the cells of the liver die and form scar tissue, which prevents this organ from performing critical metabolic roles, such as filtering toxins and waste products in the blood and out of the body. If these toxins and waste products build up, it can lead to mental confusion, nausea, tremors or shakiness, and even coma.

As many as 70 percent of individuals with alcoholic hepatitis end up developing cirrhosis.[31] Unfortunately, cirrhosis is among the 12 leading causes of death among Americans.[32] **Figure 9.7** summarizes the many harmful effects of excessive drinking.

Alcohol Can Put a Healthy Pregnancy at Risk

More than 30 years ago, Drs. David Smith and Kenneth Jones noticed an interesting trait among children in their clinic at the University of Washington School of Medicine. Some children looked alike even though they weren't related. Many had facial abnormalities such as eyes with very small openings and thin upper lips (**Figure 9.8** on the next page). These children also weren't physically growing as normally as other children their age, and they seemed to have some mental and behavioral difficulties, such as reduced attention span and memory, and learning disabilities. The scientists discovered that these children were all born to women who drank alcohol during their pregnancy. The doctors coined the term "fetal alcohol syndrome" (FAS) to describe these physical, mental, and behavioral abnormalities.[33]

When a pregnant woman drinks, she is never drinking alone—her fetus becomes her drinking partner. Because the baby is developing, the alcohol isn't broken down as quickly as in the mother's body. The baby's BAC can become higher and stay higher longer than the mother's, causing serious damage to its central nervous system, particularly the brain. Children exposed to alcohol during pregnancy may have problems in school and interacting socially with others, poor coordination, low IQ, and problems with everyday living.[34]

Skin folds over the eyes

Low nasal bridge

Short turned up nose

Indistinct philtrum (groove between nose and upper lip)

Small head circumference

Small eye opening

Small midface

Flattened face

Thin upper lip

Figure 9.8 **Fetal Alcohol Syndrome**
Children born with fetal alcohol syndrome often have facial abnormalities.

eLearn

What Are Those Drinks Costing You?

Did you ever consider how much you're spending on alcohol in a given year? Use the Alcohol Cost Calculator in the Calculators section of www.collegedrinkingprevention.gov to see how quickly a few drinks will add up.

Recently a newer term, **fetal alcohol spectrum disorders (FASDs)**, which includes FAS, has been adopted by major health organizations to describe a wide range of conditions that can occur in children exposed to alcohol prenatally. For example, not all children exposed to alcohol during pregnancy may experience *all* of the physical, mental, and behavioral abnormalities seen in FAS, which is the severe end of the FASDs. However, no matter the degree of abnormalities, FASDs are permanent. The only proven, safe amount of alcohol a pregnant woman can consume is *none*. Women should avoid alcohol if they think they are, or could become, pregnant.

LO 9.4 **The Take-Home Message** Excessive drinking can disrupt your sleep, cause hangovers, and add extra calories to your diet, which can lead to weight gain. Drinking too much alcohol can also cause hormone imbalances; lead to malnutrition; harm your digestive organs, heart, and liver; and cause irreversible damage to a developing fetus during pregnancy. Individuals with alcoholic liver disease can experience a fatty liver and deterioration of the liver that develops into alcohol-related hepatitis and cirrhosis.

What Is Alcohol Use Disorder?

LO 9.5 Describe alcohol use disorder.

When people choose not to drink alcohol responsibly, they often end up misusing it. **Alcohol use disorder (AUD)** is an illness that occurs when individuals exhibit impaired control over their drinking, they continually drink even though they know of the negative consequences of their excessive consumption, and they neglect the responsibilities in their life due to their drinking.[35] **Table 9.4** lists the 11 symptoms of AUD. Individuals experiencing two or more of these symptoms in a 12-month period are diagnosed with mild AUD. Those that experience 4 to 5 of these symptoms are classified as moderate AUD, and if a person manifests 6 or more symptoms, they are classified as having severe AUD. Individuals who have milder AUD are considered abusing alcohol whereas those with severe AUD have developed a dependence on alcohol.

fetal alcohol spectrum disorders (FASDs) A range of conditions that can occur in children who are exposed to alcohol in utero. Fetal alcohol syndrome (FAS) is the most severe of the FASDs; children with FAS will display physical, mental, and behavioral abnormalities.

alcohol use disorder (AUD) The continuation of alcohol consumption even though this behavior has created social, psychological, and/or physical health problems.

binge drinking The consumption of 5 or more alcoholic drinks by men, or 4 or more drinks by women, in a very short time.

blackouts Periods of time when an intoxicated person cannot recall part or all of an event.

Table 9.4

The Symptoms of Alcohol Use Disorder

1. Alcohol is often taken in larger amounts or over a longer period than was intended.
2. There is a persistent desire or unsuccessful efforts to cut down or control alcohol use.
3. A great deal of time is spent in activities necessary to obtain alcohol, use alcohol, or recover from its effects.
4. Craving or a strong desire or urge to use alcohol.
5. Recurrent alcohol use resulting in a failure to fulfill major role obligations at work, school, or home.
6. Continued alcohol use despite having persistent or recurrent social or interpersonal problems caused or exacerbated by the effects of alcohol.
7. Important social, occupational, or recreational activities are given up or reduced because of alcohol use.
8. Recurrent alcohol use in situations in which it is physically hazardous, such as driving an automobile or operating a machine, when impaired.
9. Alcohol use is continued despite knowledge of having a persistent or recurrent physical or psychological problem that is likely to have been caused or exacerbated by alcohol.
10. Tolerance, as designated by either of the following:
    a. A need for markedly increased amounts of alcohol to achieve intoxication or desired effect.
    b. A markedly diminished effect with continued use of the same amount of alcohol.
11. Withdrawal, as manifested by either of the following:
    a. The characteristic withdrawal syndrome for alcohol.
    b. Alcohol is taken to relieve or avoid withdrawal symptoms.

Binge Drinking, Drinking and Driving, and Underage Drinking Is Harmful

Binge drinking and drunk driving are situations in which alcohol is being abused. Because 21 is the legal drinking age in the United States, anyone under this age who consumes alcohol is abusing it. Let's take a closer look at each of these.

Binge Drinking

Binge drinking refers to a man consuming 5 or more drinks or a woman consuming 4 or more drinks in about two hours. It is estimated that one in six American adults binge drinks about four times a month.[36]

College students who binge drink are more likely to miss classes and experience unintentional injuries, such as falling and motor vehicle accidents, and may even die (**Figure 9.9**).[37] Binge drinking can increase the risk of engaging in unplanned sexual activity and failure to use safe-sex strategies. Sexual aggression and assaults on campus increase when drinking enters the picture.[38] Alcohol is involved in thousands of reported sexual assaults and rapes on college campuses. Victims are often too drunk to consent to or refuse the actions of the other person. Binge drinking is associated with many other health problems, such as hypertension, heart attack, sexually transmitted infections, unintended pregnancy, and sexual dysfunction.[39] Binge drinking can also cause **blackouts**, which are periods of time that a person cannot remember, even though he or she may have been conscious. A research study of more than 700 college students found that more than half of them had blacked out at least once in their lives, and many found out after the fact that they had taken part in activities such as vandalism, unprotected sex, and driving a motor vehicle during the blackout period.[40]

College students many times have exaggerated perceptions of the amount of alcohol their peers consume. Many college-aged binge drinkers think that everyone is drinking all the time, but this isn't always the case. Those who think binge drinking is just a normal part of the college experience often have a circle of like-minded buddies who reinforce their misperceptions.

Drinking in groups is also associated with an increased intake of alcohol. Joining a fraternity or sorority tends to increase alcohol consumption among college students and frequenting frat parties raises the bar as to what is the normal amount

Number of college students, 18–24, per year

1,825	97,000	599,000	696,000
Deaths	Sexual assaults	Injuries	Assaults

Figure 9.9 Consequences of College Binge Drinking
Alcohol use by college students results in numerous assaults, injuries, and deaths each year.

Smashed: Story of a Drunken Girlhood

health CONNECTION

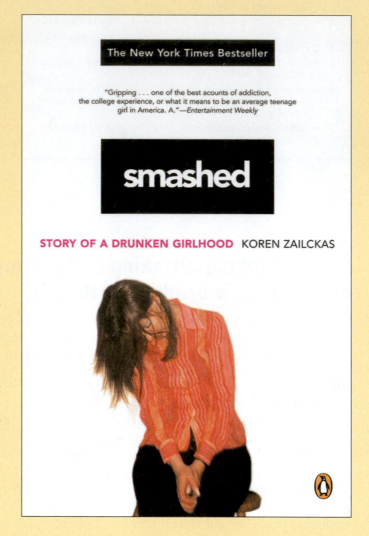

The New York Times Bestseller

"Gripping . . . one of the best acounts of addiction, the college experience, or what it means to be an average teenage girl in America. A."—*Entertainment Weekly*

smashed

STORY OF A DRUNKEN GIRLHOOD KOREN ZAILCKAS

Koren Zailckas was a shy, insecure girl raised in an upscale town in the Boston suburbs. She started drinking at the age of 14, and almost from her first sip, there was no turning back. During a socially awkward adolescence, Koren found it difficult to be at ease around other people, particularly girls her own age. When she drank, she became assertive and friendly. She bonded with other girls and met tons of guys. Throughout her high school and college years, alcohol was her crutch and best pal.

Koren didn't think of herself as an alcoholic, but she was a binge drinker. She drank herself into her first blackout with a thermos full of vodka at the age of 16. She woke up in her bedroom wearing a hospital Johnny and a pink plastic bracelet on her wrist. The bracelet was compliments of her local hospital emergency room. The Johnny had replaced her vomit-covered clothes from the night before. Her stomach had been pumped. Her parents had carried her from the back seat of the family car to her bedroom in the middle of the night. They were devastated.

As a freshman entering college, Koren used beer and liquor to make friends and be accepted. She pledged a sorority for the sisterhood and booze. She frequently drank herself into a state of numbness and allowed sorority sisters and male friends to make many of her decisions. She was often the last girl to leave the party because she was too drunk to know that she should have left an hour before.

After college graduation, Koren continued her drunken lifestyle in New York City. She worked hard during the day and drank hard at night. One morning she woke up in a strange bed, in a strange condo, next to a stranger from the cab ride the night before. For Koren, this was rock bottom. She realized that her chronic drinking was a magnet for like-minded people who similarly abused alcohol and were as damaged in life as she. But she wanted a good life. She wanted sound friendships and self-confidence, and she recognized that she wasn't going to achieve these goals with alcohol. At that moment, she decided to get help.

Through guidance from an addiction counselor and her own drive to quit drinking, Koren stopped her destructive behavior and began surrounding herself with a healthier circle of friends. Today, she is sober, and has a new lease on life.

You can read more about Koren's struggles and triumphs in her best-selling book, *Smashed* (Penguin, 2006).

Think About It

1. Can you identify the behaviors that may have encouraged Koren's binge drinking?
2. How do these behaviors make it more likely that a young adult will abuse alcohol?

and frequency of alcohol consumption during college life. College students are more likely to binge drink compared to their peers who are not in college.[41] The Health Connection feature "Smashed: Story of a Drunken Girlhood" describes the true story of Koren Zailckas and her struggles with abusing alcohol during college. The Self-Assessment will help you recognize some red flags of alcohol abuse.

Red Flags for Misusing Alcohol

Complete the following self-assessment to see if you may be at increased risk for alcohol abuse.

1. Do you fail to fulfill major work, school, or home responsibilities because of your consumption of alcohol?
   Yes ☐   No ☐
2. Do you drink in situations that are potentially dangerous, such as while driving a car or operating heavy machinery?
   Yes ☐   No ☐
3. Do you experience repeated alcohol-related legal problems, such as being arrested for driving while intoxicated?
   Yes ☐   No ☐
4. Do you have relationship problems that are caused or made worse by alcohol?
   Yes ☐   No ☐
5. Do you try to hide your alcohol consumption from family or friends because you know they will tell you to stop?
   Yes ☐   No ☐

Answers

If you answered yes to any of these questions, you should speak with your health care provider for insight and guidance.

Binge drinking can lead to **alcohol poisoning**, which can have devastating results. Bradley was a junior at Michigan State University. At midnight on the eve of Brad's twenty-first birthday, he and a group of friends went to a bar to celebrate his birthday. A birthday tradition around campus was to "drink your age" in shots of liquor. Brad not only drank 21 shots but gulped down another three for a grand total of 24 shots in less than two hours. On the way out of the bar, Brad passed out. His friend brought him home and put him in his bed to "sleep it off." Unfortunately, because he had drunk an enormous amount of alcohol, his BAC level continued to rise to a lethal level, even though he was unconscious and no longer taking in alcohol. Brad stopped breathing and died before the sun came up on his twenty-first birthday.[42]

Chronic drinking can lead to **alcohol tolerance**, which occurs over time as the body adjusts to long-term alcohol use. As the brain becomes less sensitive to alcohol, more is needed to get the same intoxicating effect.[43] People who've developed an alcohol tolerance should not think they can drink more without damaging the body. The harmful effects that you read about in the previous section still occur.

Drinking and Driving

If you have spent any time behind a steering wheel, you know that you can't *just* drive. You have to drive defensively. Driving involves multitasking. You need to keep the car within your lane, stay within the speed limit, make constant quick decisions, and, of course, maneuver the car based on these decisions. Alcohol intake impairs all of these skills. It is illegal to drive in the United States with a BAC of 0.08 (some states in the United States have set their legal limit even lower), but the level of alcohol in the blood doesn't have to get that high to impair your driving. As we saw in Table 9.1, even the lowest level of BAC, the level that occurs after one alcoholic beverage, will impair alertness, judgment, and coordination. In 2013, over 10,000 people died in alcohol-related, driving-impaired automobile accidents, accounting for 31 percent of total traffic fatalities that year.[44]

The latest data regarding the alcohol intake of Americans shows that adults admitted to driving while alcohol impaired over 110 million times and 1.4 million Americans were arrested for driving under the influence (DUI) of alcohol.[45] Legal penalties for DUI can be severe, ranging from stiff fines and loss of license to jail time in some states.

alcohol poisoning When the BAC rises to such an extreme level that a person's central nervous system is affected and his or her breathing and heart rate are interrupted.

alcohol tolerance When the body adjusts to long-term alcohol use by becoming less sensitive to the alcohol. You need to consume more alcohol in order to get the same effect.

The "It's Only Another Beer"
Black and Tan

8 oz. pilsner lager
8 oz. stout lager
1 frosty mug
1 icy road
1 pick-up truck
1 10-hour day
1 tired worker
A few rounds with the guys

Mix ingredients.
Add 1 totaled vehicle.

Never underestimate 'just a few.'
Buzzed driving is drunk driving.

Ad Council.org

U.S. Department of Transportation

"Buzzed driving is drunk driving" was a successful ad campaign that underscored the dangers of drinking and driving.

> As the price of alcohol goes up, the number of people involved in fatal traffic accidents goes down.[52]

Drinking and driving can be deadly.

heavy drinking The consumption of 5 or more drinks on the same occasion in each of 5 or more days in the past month.

People who ride with drunk drivers put themselves at high risk of being involved in an accident. To educate the public about the risks of drinking and driving, the Ad Council and the United States Department of Transportation launched a campaign in the early 1980s to promote the Designated Driver Program. The concept of the program was to designate a sober driver at social gatherings to ensure that people who choose to drink have a safe ride home. The "Friends Don't Let Friends Drive Drunk" tagline has been instrumental in reducing the annual number of alcohol-related automobile fatalities since its inception in 1983. Unfortunately, many people think they can still drive safely as long as they consume "only a few" drinks. But because even one alcoholic beverage can affect the skills needed when driving, the only sober driver is one who completely abstains from drinking alcohol.

Another campaign, entitled "Buzzed Driving Is Drunk Driving," has been launched to reinforce the concept that the designated driver shouldn't be the least drunk member of the group, but rather the one who hasn't consumed any alcohol.

Underage Drinking

By age 15, more than 30 percent of adolescents in the United States have consumed alcohol.[46] In fact, over 14 percent of surveyed individuals age 12 through 20 admitted to binge drinking.[47] Even more importantly, 3.7 percent of this age group reported engaging in **heavy drinking**, which means that they consume 5 or more drinks on the same occasion on each of 5 or more days in the past month.[48] Underage drinking not only increases the risk of violence, injuries, and other health risks, as discussed earlier, but alcohol consumption at this age can also interfere with brain development and lead to permanent cognitive and memory damage in teenagers.

Underage drinking, coupled with driving, is a disaster waiting to happen. Adolescent drivers are inexperienced behind the wheel to begin with, so it isn't surprising that automobile accidents are the number-one cause of death of young people between the ages of 15 and 20.[49] In 2012, 22 percent of young drivers, 15 to 20 years of age, involved in fatal crashes had drunk alcohol prior to getting behind the wheel of the car.[50] In fact, this is why the minimum legal drinking age in the United States is 21. Studies conducted between 1970 and 1975, when several states had lowered the legal drinking age to under 21, showed that the rate of motor vehicle crashes and fatalities increased among teenagers.[51] Since 1984, all states have adopted 21 as the minimum legal drinking age and prohibited the sale of alcohol to underage individuals.

There is another danger in consuming alcohol at a young age. The earlier in life a person starts drinking, the higher the chances that alcohol will become a problem later in life. A person who starts drinking at age 15 is five times more likely to develop alcohol dependency or abuse later in life than an individual who doesn't start drinking until after the age of 21.[53]

How to Get Help for AUD

(T|F) Those who have AUD should seek the guidance from their health care provider. Research has shown that support from such a provider can reduce alcohol consumptions among those with mild AUD.[54] Setting a goal for reduced drinking, alternating alcoholic drinks with nonalcoholic beverages, and spacing the time between drinks are some examples of strategies that can help reduce alcohol consumption.[55]

Those with more severe AUD may need to seek specialized counseling as well as medical support.

Some individuals have found success with ongoing support programs such as Alcoholics Anonymous (AA). AA was created in 1935 by Bill Wilson, a stockbroker, and Dr. Robert Smith, a surgeon, who together declared themselves hopeless drunks. They founded AA to help themselves and others stay sober. With more than 100,000 groups worldwide AA is a global fellowship of men and women with various backgrounds, lifestyles, and educational levels who meet, bond, and support each other, with the sole purpose of remaining sober. AA's 12 steps for recovery and supportive group meetings help individuals maintain sobriety.[56]

If you are interested in learning more about AA or finding a group in your area, look in your local telephone directory or online at www.alcoholics-anonymous.org. Everyone is welcomed at their meetings, including family members, friends, and coworkers.

Some People Should Avoid Consuming Alcohol

According to the *Dietary Guidelines for Americans*, the following people should also abstain from drinking alcohol:[57]

- Women of childbearing age who may become pregnant
- Pregnant women
- Children and adolescents
- Those taking medications that can interact with alcohol, which include prescription and over-the-counter medications
- Those with specific medical conditions, such as liver disease
- Those engaging in activities that require attention, skill, or coordination, such as driving or operating machinery
- Those who cannot restrict their alcohol intake

For these individuals, abstinence is the best option, as even modest amounts of alcohol can have detrimental health effects.

LO 9.5 **The Take-Home Message** Alcohol use disorder (AUD) is an illness that that occurs when individuals exhibit impaired control over their drinking, they continually drink even though they know of the negative consequences of their excessive consumption, and they neglect the responsibilities in their life due to their drinking. Individuals with AUD should seek support. Binge drinking, drinking and driving, and underage drinking all increase the risk of injuries, violence, and even death. Many individuals should avoid alcohol entirely. These include pregnant and lactating women; women who may become pregnant; anyone who is under the legal drinking age; those with specific medical conditions or taking certain medications; people who operate heavy machinery; those who plan to drive, operate machinery, or take part in activities (such as swimming or climbing a ladder) in which impaired judgment could provoke an injury; and those who cannot control their intake.

MADE over MADE better

Trendy "mocktails" are increasing in popularity. These nonalcoholic beverages can be a caloric bargain in comparison with traditional cocktails.

Here are some typical cocktails made over and made nutritionally better!

Instead of this cocktail...   **Try this mocktail!**

Pomegranate Cosmo
(vodka, triple sec, pomegranate juice, lime juice)
Calories: 124

Virgin Pomegranate Cosmo
(pomegranate juice, club soda, lime juice)
Calories 20

Grey Goose L'Orange
(Grey Goose L'Orange, Cointreau, cranberry juice, lime)
Calories: 110

Maui Punch
(pineapple juice, orange juice, soda water, grenadine)
Calories: 33

Vodka Tonic
(vodka, tonic, lime)
Calories: 114

Tonic with a Twist
(diet tonic, lime)
Calories: 2

Beer
Calories: 140

Nonalcoholic Beer
Calories: 67

POINTS OF VIEW

Do the Health Benefits of Drinking Alcohol Outweigh the Risks?

Many people have heard about the supposed health benefits of moderate alcohol consumption, but the potential negative health effects of drinking alcohol in excess—alcohol use disorder, cirrhosis, and behavioral issues—are still very big problems in the United States.

Should young adults drink alcohol for its health benefits? Or do the risks associated with alcohol consumption outweigh those benefits? After you've read the arguments for and against, answer the critical-thinking questions and decide for yourself.

yes

- There is evidence that moderate alcohol consumption reduces the risk of heart attack and stroke.[1]

- Moderate alcohol consumption may also lead to fewer gallstones, fewer kidney stones, and improved cognitive function in the elderly.[2]

- People who drink alcohol in moderation have been shown to have greater longevity than those who abstain or those who abuse alcohol.[3]

- One review of several studies concludes that moderate use of alcohol may reduce the risk of type 2 diabetes.[4]

- Beer and wine can provide some nutrients, including soluble fiber, vitamins, antioxidants, and minerals.[5]

no

- Alcohol consumption is disproportionately risky for college students, for whom binge drinking is often an issue.[6]

- It is estimated that each year, among college students aged 18–24, 1,825 die from alcohol-related unintentional injuries, including motor vehicle crashes, 599,000 are unintentionally injured under the influence of alcohol, more than 690,000 are assaulted by another student who has been drinking, 97,000 are victims of alcohol-related sexual assault or date rape, and 3,360,000 drive under the influence of alcohol.[7]

- Because the brain is not fully developed until the early twenties, underage consumption of alcohol can compromise the development of the brain.[8]

- People who start drinking at an early age are more likely to become addicted.[9]

what do you think?

1. Are the benefits of alcohol consumption worth the risks? **2.** How are those risks different for you and your peers as opposed to the general population? **3.** Why do you think overconsumption of alcohol is so prevalent among college students? **4.** Aside from abstaining from alcohol entirely, how can some of the potential risks associated with drinking be avoided?

VISUAL Chapter Summary

LO 9.1 Alcohol Is a Nonessential Nutrient That Is Made through Fermentation or Distillation

Ethanol is the type of alcohol found in alcoholic beverages. While it provides calories, you don't need to consume alcoholic beverages to maintain good health. Alcoholic beverages are made via the processes of fermentation (turning sugars into alcohol and carbon dioxide; examples include beer and wine) or distillation (causing alcohol to vaporize and then collecting and condensing the vapor; examples include distilled spirits).

LO 9.2 People Drink Alcohol for Many Reasons

Alcohol produces an initial euphoric, pleasurable state of mind. Drinking alcohol in moderation may help reduce the risk of heart disease in older adults. For adults who choose to drink, moderate alcohol consumption is considered up to one drink for women daily and up to two drinks a day for men. A standard drink is 12 ounces of beer, 5 ounces of wine, or 1.5 ounces of liquor.

LO 9.3 Your Body Works to Metabolize Alcohol As Soon As You Drink It

About 20 percent of the alcohol you drink is absorbed in the stomach. The rest is absorbed in the small intestine. Alcohol dehydrogenase begins to metabolize some of the alcohol in the stomach before it reaches your blood. Alcohol mixes with water and is distributed in the watery tissues of the body. Women have less body water and less alcohol dehydrogenase in their stomachs than men. Both of these factors cause women to feel the narcotic effects of alcohol sooner than men do.

The majority of the alcohol you consume is metabolized in your liver. Some alcohol is lost from your body in your breath and urine. Your liver can only metabolize about one standard drink in about 1½ to 2 hours. As you drink more alcohol, your BAC goes up, as does your level of impairment and intoxication.

Whereas alcohol is often thought of as a stimulant, it is actually a central nervous system depressant. Your brain is sensitive to the effects of alcohol, and depending on the amount you consume, alcohol can cause numerous mental, behavioral, and physical changes in your body. Your alertness, judgment, and coordination will initially be affected. As you drink more alcohol, your vision, speech, reasoning, and balance will be altered. An excessive amount of alcohol can interfere with your breathing and heart rate.

Blood vessels

Alcohol

Alcohol dehydrogenase

Liver

Stomach

Small intestine

LO 9.4 Alcohol Can Have Short-Term and Long-Term Effects on the Body and Brain

Alcohol can have short-term effects on your body such as disrupting your sleep, causing hangovers, interfering with hormones, adding excess calories, and displacing healthier food choices from your diet. Chronically consuming excessive amounts of alcohol can harm your digestive organs, heart, and liver. It can also do long-term damage to the brain. The three stages of alcoholic liver disease are fatty liver, alcoholic hepatitis, and cirrhosis. Liver disease is one of the 12 leading causes of death among Americans. Maternal alcohol consumption can put a fetus at risk for fetal alcohol spectrum disorders.

Hangovers

Blurred vision

Brain damage, addiction, and stroke

Slurred speech

Breathing may stop

Heart disease, irregular heart beat

Liver disease, liver failure

Malnutrition, overnutrition

Infertility (in women), impotence (in men)

Osteoporosis

LO 9.5 Alcohol Use Disorder Can Negatively Affect One's Life and Health

Misusing alcohol can negatively affect a person's life. Individuals with AUD should seek support. Individuals who binge drink, many of whom are also underage, are at risk for blackouts and alcohol poisoning. Individuals who chronically drink alcohol often develop alcohol tolerance, which occurs when the brain becomes less sensitive to alcohol. Because alcohol affects alertness and judgment, the only safe amount of alcohol to consume when driving is none.

Alcohol should be avoided by women of childbearing age who may become pregnant, or who are pregnant or lactating; anyone under the age of 21; those engaging in activities that require attention, skill, or coordination, such as driving or operating machinery; those taking certain medications or with specific medical conditions; and those who cannot restrict or limit their intake of alcohol.

VISUAL Chapter Summary

Terms to Know

- alcohol
- ethanol
- fermentation
- distillation
- social drinking
- moderate alcohol consumption
- alcohol dehydrogenase
- blood alcohol concentration (BAC)
- hangover
- congeners
- gastritis
- alcoholic liver disease
- fatty liver
- alcoholic hepatitis
- cirrhosis
- fetal alcohol spectrum disorders (FASDs)
- alcohol use disorder (AUD)
- binge drinking
- blackouts
- alcohol poisoning
- alcohol tolerance
- heavy drinking

MasteringNutrition™

Build your knowledge—and confidence—in the Study Area of MasteringNutrition with a variety of study tools.

MyDiet Analysis

Access MyDietAnalysis through MasteringNutrition™ and track your diet and daily activities. In addition, a dietary analysis activity is available for every chapter in your book.

Check Your Understanding

LO 9.1 1. Alcohol provides
  a. 9 calories per gram.
  b. 7 calories per gram.
  c. 4 calories per gram.
  d. 0 calories per gram.

LO 9.2 2. Which of the following is NOT considered a standard drink?
  a. a 12-ounce can of beer
  b. a 7-ounce glass of red wine
  c. a shot (1.5 ounces) of liquor
  d. a 5-ounce glass of white wine

LO 9.3 3. The major site of alcohol metabolism in your body is your
  a. kidneys.
  b. lungs.
  c. liver.
  d. stomach.

LO 9.3 4. Which of the following factors affect(s) your rate of absorption and the metabolism of alcohol?
  a. whether you're male or female
  b. the place where you are drinking
  c. the time of day you drink
  d. the individuals you are drinking with

LO 9.3 5. Blood alcohol concentration (BAC) is the
  a. minimum amount of alcohol needed in your blood daily.
  b. amount of alcohol in your blood, measured in grams of alcohol per deciliter of blood.
  c. number of drinks you consumed in an hour.
  d. grams of alcohol per liter of beverage.

LO 9.4 6. The *best* cure for a hangover is
  a. chicken soup.
  b. a light beer.
  c. time and abstinence.
  d. taking acetaminophen (Tylenol).

LO 9.4 7. The first stage in alcoholic liver disease is
  a. malnutrition.
  b. a fatty liver.
  c. cirrhosis.
  d. alcoholic hepatitis.

LO 9.5 8. AUD refers to
  a. addiction use disorder.
  b. alcohol use disorder.
  c. allowing unsupervised drinking.
  d. alcohol use deprivation.

LO 9.5 9. Drinking 4 to 5 alcoholic beverages on one occasion in a very short time is called
  a. alcohol tolerance.
  b. drunk driving.
  c. blackout.
  d. binge drinking.

LO 9.5 10. Of the following list, who shouldn't drink alcohol?
  a. your pregnant aunt
  b. your high school–aged brother
  c. your father while he is riding the lawn mower
  d. all of the above

Answers

1. (b) Alcohol serves up 7 calories per gram, which is less than fat at 9 calories per gram, and more than carbohydrates and protein, which each provide 4 calories per gram. Alcohol isn't an essential nutrient—your body doesn't need it to survive—and it's not calorie free.

2. (b) Five ounces of wine is considered a standard drink, so a 7-ounce glass of red wine is the equivalent of almost 1.5 drinks.

3. (c) Most alcohol in the body is metabolized in the liver. A small amount of alcohol is lost in your urine (kidneys) and in your breath (your lungs). Some alcohol is also metabolized in your stomach, though substantially less than in your liver.

4. (a) Your gender will affect the rate of absorption and the metabolism of alcohol. Women have less of the enzyme alcohol dehydrogenase in their stomachs, which means they metabolize less alcohol in the stomach and more alcohol will be absorbed into the blood. They also tend to have less body water, so the concentration of alcohol in their systems is higher. The time of day and the place where you drink do not have any effect on the absorption and metabolism of alcohol. Your drinking partners also won't alter the absorption and metabolism of alcohol. Of course, they could influence the *amount* of alcohol you consume.

5. (b) Your BAC is the concentration of alcohol in your blood. It is measured in grams of alcohol per deciliter of blood. Your body doesn't need a minimum intake of alcohol daily. The number of drinks that you consume in an hour will affect your BAC; the more you drink, the higher the concentration of alcohol in your blood. BAC has nothing to do with the concentration of alcohol in a drink.

6. (c) The best cure is to stop drinking and let your body have the time it needs to recover from consuming too much alcohol. Neither chicken soup nor coffee nor any other food or beverage will cure the fatigue and other ill effects of drinking too much alcohol. Taking acetaminophen is not recommended, as its toxicity to your liver is enhanced if it is consumed while alcohol is being metabolized. The worst thing you can do for a hangover is to have another alcoholic beverage.

7. (b) The first stage of alcoholic liver disease is a fatty liver. Alcoholic hepatitis is the second stage, followed by cirrhosis. Some people who have alcoholic liver disease are also malnourished.

8. (b) AUD is alcohol use disorder.

9. (d) Consuming that much alcohol in a very short time is considered binge drinking. Binge drinking can lead to alcoholism. Individuals who binge drink may experience blackouts or may drive while drunk.

10. (d) All pregnant women should avoid alcohol, as drinking during pregnancy will increase the risk of fetal alcohol spectrum disorders (FASDs). Unless your brother is 21 years old, he shouldn't be drinking alcohol. Your father should wait until he has finished mowing the lawn before having a drink, as this chore involves operating machinery that requires attention, skill, and coordination.

Web Resources

- For more information about drinking at college, visit www.collegedrinkingprevention.gov
- For more information about alcohol and your health, visit the National Institute on Alcohol Abuse and Alcoholism (NIAAA) at www.niaaa.nih.gov
- For more information about alcohol consumption and its consequences, visit the Centers for Disease Control and Prevention's Alcohol and Public Health section, at www.cdc.gov

Answers to True or False?

1. **False.** A straight shot of liquor may look and taste more potent than a can of beer, but it isn't. To learn more, turn to page 343.

2. **True.** Red wine does contain heart-healthy compounds. To find out more about them, turn to page 344.

3. **True.** Women respond more quickly to the narcotic effects of alcohol than do men. To find out why, turn to page 348.

4. **False.** Drinking more alcohol isn't going to take away the ill effects of a hangover. To find out what will, turn to page 351.

5. **False.** Alcohol can interfere with your sex hormones and may impair your sexual function. To find out more, turn to page 351.

6. **True.** However, not all alcoholic beverages contain equal amounts of calories. For an eye-opener as to the amount of calories in some common alcoholic drinks, turn to page 351.

7. **False.** Binge drinking is considered the consumption of 5 or more alcoholic drinks by men, or 4 or more drinks by women, in a very short time. To find out more, turn to page 357.

8. **False.** The alcohol in your stomach and small intestine would continue to be absorbed, your blood alcohol concentration would continue to rise, and you could die from alcohol poisoning. See page 359 for more.

9. **False.** Decades ago, some states lowered their legal drinking age, but today you have to be 21 to legally purchase and consume alcohol anywhere in the United States. Turn to page 360 to learn more.

10. **False.** Although counseling is an important component of alcoholism recovery, it will not cure it. Page 361 explains why.

10
Weight Management and Energy Balance

True or False?

1. **Overweight people often have less restful sleep compared with people who are at a healthy weight.** T/F   p. 371

2. **Being skinny is always healthy.** T/F   p. 371

3. **One of the best ways to tell if you are at a healthy weight is to compare yourself to celebrities.** T/F   p. 372

4. **Fat around the hips is as unhealthy as fat stored around the waist.** T/F   p. 374

5. **The number of calories you burn daily is affected by your body size.** T/F   p. 378

6. **Your body weight is affected by your genes and your environment.** T/F   p. 383

7. **Eating more vegetables and fruits can help you lose weight.** T/F   p. 390

8. **The nutrient that has the most effect on satiety is fat.** T/F   p. 392

9. **Disordered eating and eating disorders are the same thing.** T/F   p. 401

10. **Eating disorders can be fatal.** T/F   p. 405

See page 415 for the answers.

369

Learning Outcomes

After reading this chapter, you will be able to:

LO 10.1 Explain the concept of a healthy weight, and differentiate between the conditions of underweight, overweight, and obesity.

LO 10.2 Define healthy weight and identify how to determine if you are at a healthy weight.

LO 10.3 Explain what energy balance is, and what determines your daily energy needs; describe the effects of energy imbalance.

LO 10.4 Explain the factors that affect body weight.

LO 10.5 Explain how to lose weight healthfully.

LO 10.6 Identify two strategies that help foster healthy weight maintenance.

LO 10.7 Describe how to gain weight healthfully.

LO 10.8 Define disordered eating and discuss the warning signs and treatment options for eating disorders.

F lip through a magazine, watch a little television, or spend some time online, and before long you'll find someone talking about weight loss. You may be used to so much coverage of weight management, but it hasn't always been that way. In the early 1960s, fewer than 32 percent of Americans were overweight, so weight didn't receive much media attention. Today, the majority of Americans are overweight, so it's a much hotter topic.[1] In fact, obesity is one of the most frequently covered health stories in the media.[2]

Americans currently spend more than $60 billion on everything from over-the-counter diet pills to books, magazines, online support groups, and commercial dieting centers to help shed excess weight.[3] Unfortunately, these programs usually aren't successful, and the U.S. health care system bears more than $145 billion in costs of treating the medical complications associated with being overweight.[4] No matter what you personally weigh, some of your tax dollars are supporting these costs. Despite spending so much money on the battle of the bulge, we are not winning the war for weight control.

What is causing this trend, and how unhealthy is it? What does it mean to manage your weight, and what are the best strategies for doing so? Lastly, should we strive to be thin at all costs—or can this be equally unhealthy?

Let's try to figure this all out.

What Is a Healthy Weight and Why Is Maintaining It Important?

LO 10.1 Explain the concept of a healthy weight, and differentiate between the conditions of underweight, overweight, and obesity.

A **healthy weight** is considered a body weight that doesn't increase your risk of developing weight-related health problems or diseases. Rather than a single number, it's a range of weight that is appropriate for your gender, height, and muscle mass, a weight at which you feel energetic and fit. A healthy weight is also a *realistic* weight, one that you can maintain naturally through consuming a nourishing diet and engaging in regular physical activity. As the U.S. Centers for Disease Control and Prevention (CDC) puts it, a healthy weight is not a diet; it's a healthy lifestyle![5]

Weight management, then, means maintaining your weight within a healthy range. Either extreme—being very overweight or very underweight—can be unhealthy, a red flag for undernutrition of some nutrients, overnutrition of others, and impending health problems. Being **overweight**, or weighing 10 to 15 pounds more than your healthy weight, tends to be a stepping stone to **obesity**. A person with 25 to 40 or more pounds of weight above his or her healthy weight is considered obese. With more than 65 percent of Americans overweight and close to 35 percent of those obese, the American Medical Association now recognizes obesity as a disease.[6]

In addition to potentially leading to obesity, being overweight can increase your risk of numerous other health problems, including:

- Hypertension and stroke
- Heart disease
- Gallbladder disease
- Type 2 diabetes
- Osteoarthritis
- Some cancers
- Sleep apnea

T|F Generally, as a person's weight increases, so does his or her blood pressure. Overweight individuals can experience increased retention of sodium, which causes both increased blood volume and resistance in the blood vessels. This and additional demands on the heart all likely contribute to high blood pressure.[7] High blood pressure increases the risk of stroke and heart disease. Overweight people also tend to have high blood levels of both fat and the "bad" LDL cholesterol, and less of the "good" HDL cholesterol, which is an unhealthy combination for the heart. High blood cholesterol levels increase the risk for gallstones and gallbladder disease. They are also more likely to contribute to an enlarged gallbladder, impeding its function.

Being overweight increases the risk of developing type 2 diabetes. Excess weight causes the body's cells to become insulin resistant. Over time, this resistance causes the pancreas to work harder to produce more insulin and can eventually cause the pancreas to stop producing it altogether. Incidences of cancers of the colon, uterus, and breast (in postmenopausal women) are also higher. Excess weight means extra stress on joints, especially in the knees, hips, and lower back, and contributes to osteoarthritis. Sleep apnea, a condition in which breathing stops for brief periods during sleep, disrupts a person's ability to obtain a restful slumber. The fat stored around the neck, as well as fat-induced inflammation in that area, may contribute to a smaller airway and interfere with breathing.[8]

Although being overweight can lead to many unhealthy conditions and diseases, the good news is that losing as little as 5 to 10 percent of a person's body weight can produce health benefits such as lower blood pressure, cholesterol, and glucose levels in the body.[9]

T|F While overweight and obesity are currently far more prevalent among Americans, being **underweight** is also of concern, especially among teens and young adults, because of the potential negative health effects that are associated with it. Being underweight means that a person's weight is not sufficient for his or her height or to sustain health. For some, being very slender is their natural, healthy body shape, but for others, it's a sign of malnutrition. Excessive calorie restriction and/or physical activity, emotional stress, or an underlying medical condition such as cancer or an intestinal disorder can often cause someone to be underweight.[10] Young adults who are underweight often face health challenges, including nutrient deficiencies, electrolyte imbalance, low energy levels, and decreased concentration. Over time, more serious health effects can arise, such as heart complications that can be fatal. For older adults (those over age 65), being undernourished means an increased risk for low body protein and fat stores and a depressed immune system, which makes it more difficult to fight infections. Injuries, wounds, and illnesses that would normally abate in healthy individuals can cause serious medical complications, including death, for older undernourished individuals.[11]

LO 10.1 **The Take-Home Message** A healthy weight is a body weight that doesn't increase your risk of developing weight-related health problems or diseases. It's realistic for your build and can be attained with a nourishing diet and regular exercise. Weight management means maintaining a healthy weight to reduce your risk for specific health problems. Being overweight, obese, or underweight can be unhealthy.

Weight management is such a hot topic in the United States that it is frequently covered by the mainstream media.

American people aren't the only ones getting bigger—American pets are also putting on pounds. According to the National Academy of Sciences, there has been an epidemic of obesity among pet dogs and cats.

healthy weight A body weight in relationship to your height that doesn't increase the risk of developing any weight-related health problems or diseases.

weight management Maintaining your weight within a healthy range.

overweight Carrying extra weight on your body in relation to your height. Clinically defined as having a body mass index (BMI) of 25 to 29.9.

obesity Carrying an excessive amount of body fat above the level of being overweight. Clinically defined as having a body mass index (BMI) of 30 or higher.

underweight Weighing less than is healthy for your height. Clinically defined as having a body mass index (BMI) below 18.5.

How Do You Know If You're at a Healthy Weight?

LO 10.2 Define healthy weight and identify how to determine if you are at a healthy weight.

Over the years, varying body shapes have trended in and out of Ⓣ Ⓕ the media spotlight. In the 1980s, fashion models were 8 percent thinner than the average woman. Today, the typical cover girl is more than 20 percent thinner. The male physique is being held to a similarly unattainable standard. Witness the change from average to beefy in toy action figures over the years.[12] Although models, celebrities, and dolls may reflect the "in" look, they don't necessarily correlate with good health, nor should they be your reference for the body weight that *you* should strive to obtain. However, there are some signs that healthy body weight is being more represented and celebrated in our culture, such as the new realistic Lammily doll.

So, how can you determine if your body weight is within a healthy range? Following are a few methods that can be helpful.

BMI Measurements Can Provide a General Guideline

One of the most common and inexpensive ways to assess a healthy weight is to measure **body mass index (BMI)**. BMI is a calculation of weight in relationship to height using the following formula:

$$BMI = \frac{\text{weight (pounds)} \times 703}{\text{height squared (inches}^2)}$$

Here's how to interpret your BMI:

- *Underweight.* If your BMI falls in the first part of the graph (shaded orange in **Figure 10.1**), it is below 18.5

and you are considered underweight. Although people who are underweight are at reduced risk for the chronic diseases associated with obesity, they are at increased risk for infection, and their overall risk of mortality is higher than for people of healthy weight.

Over the past few years, the idealized model look has gone from curvy to stick thin to sporty and back to waiflike again. Today, superslender women are the norm in magazines and movies.

The male physique depicted in popular action figures in the 1970s, like Luke Skywalker and sHan Solo from *Star Wars*, was more realistic than the bulked-up versions of the late 1990s.

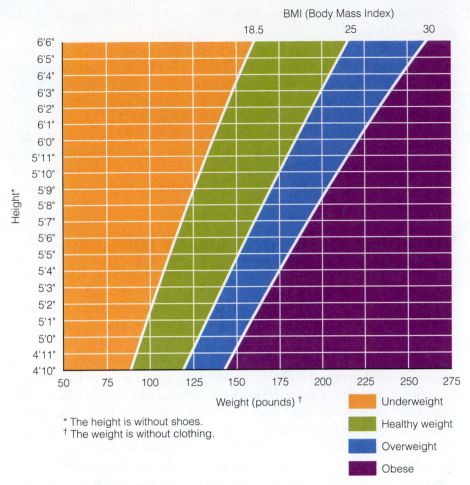

BMI (Body Mass Index)

* The height is without shoes.
† The weight is without clothing.

- Underweight
- Healthy weight
- Overweight
- Obese

Figure 10.1 What's Your BMI?
As your BMI increases, you are more likely to be overweight or obese. A BMI between 18.5 and 25 is considered healthy. A BMI of 25 and over is considered overweight, and a BMI of 30 and over is obese. A BMI under 18.5 is considered underweight, and can also be unhealthy.

- *Healthy weight.* If your BMI falls between 18.5 and 24.9 (the green part of the graph), it is considered healthy.
- *Overweight.* If your BMI falls between 25 and 29.9 (the blue area of the graph), you are considered overweight. As the amount you are overweight increases, so does your risk of dying from certain chronic diseases, although research shows that the risk is modest until a person reaches a BMI of closer to 30.
- *Obese.* If your BMI is 30 or over (the purple part of the graph), you are considered obese. Obese individuals have a 50 to 100 percent higher risk of dying prematurely, compared with those at a healthy weight.[13]

BMI is used as a screening tool to identify potential weight problems and should not be used as a diagnostic tool for specific medical conditions. Also, because BMI is not a direct measure of percentage body fat, it may not be accurate for everyone. This is particularly true for athletes. Many athletes have a BMI that should put them in the "unhealthy" category, but they aren't unhealthy because their body weight is predominantly muscle, not fat. For example, Peyton Manning, the quarterback for the Denver Broncos, has a BMI of 27. He is not "overfat" and unhealthy, and his muscular weight does not increase his health risk. Therefore, athletes and other people with a high percentage of muscle mass may have a BMI over 25 yet still be healthy, as they have a low percentage of body fat. Many young, athletic adults may also have BMI results similar to those of these professional athletes, but once again, they are

The Lammily doll is part of a current push to create dolls for children that represent a more realistic, healthy, and obtainable body weight.

body mass index (BMI) A calculation of your weight in relationship to your height. A BMI between 18.5 and 24.9 is considered healthy.

Determining Your BMI

Want to know your exact BMI based on your height and weight? Use the BMI calculator at www.nhlbi.nih.gov/health/educational/lose_wt/BMI/bmicalc.htm.

central obesity An excess storage of visceral fat in the abdominal area, which increases the risk of heart disease, diabetes, and hypertension.

visceral fat The fat stored in the abdominal area.

subcutaneous fat The fat located under the skin.

not considered "unhealthy" or at risk for other health conditions because of their muscular physique.

In contrast, a person may be in a healthy weight range, but may have been steadily losing weight due to an unbalanced diet or poor health. This chronic weight loss is a loss of muscle mass and the depletion of nutrient stores in the body, which increases health risks even though the BMI seems healthy. Lastly, because height is factored into the BMI, individuals who are very short—under 5 feet—may have a high BMI, but, similar to athletes, may not be unhealthy.[14] In general, BMI is best used to assess overweight and obesity for populations rather than individuals. If someone is classified as underweight, overweight, or obese according to BMI, further assessments by a health care provider will determine health risks or present medical conditions associated with weight.

Measure Your Body Fat and Its Location

There are several techniques you can use to measure total body fat, including skin-fold thickness measurements, bioelectrical impedance, dual-energy X-ray absorptiometry, underwater weighing, and air displacement. These tests must be conducted by trained technicians and some of them can be expensive. **Table 10.1** describes the ways to measure body fat.

How much fat you carry isn't the only determinant of health risk—where you carry it also matters. **Central obesity**, that is, carrying excess fat around the waist (sometimes referred to as an "apple" body shape) versus carrying it around the buttocks, hips, and thighs (a "pear" body shape), has been shown to increase the risk of heart disease, diabetes, and hypertension.[15] Central obesity is due to storing too much **visceral fat** (the fat that surrounds organs in your chest and stomach and above your hips) around your waist (see **Figure 10.2**). (Another type of fat, called **subcutaneous fat**, is the fat beneath your skin.) On average, men tend to be apple-shaped and women more pear-shaped, because of the hormone estrogen. This hormone is made by the ovaries and the presence of estrogen causes more fat to be stored in the lower body than the abdomen, resulting in women of childbearing

Figure 10.2 Visceral and Subcutaneous Fat Storage in the Body
Visceral fat stored around the waist is more likely to lead to health problems than subcutaneous fat stored elsewhere in the body.

Table 10.1

Ways to Measure Percentage of Body Fat

Skinfold Thickness Measurements

How It Is Done: Calipers are used to measure the thickness of fat that is located just under the skin in the arm, in the back, on the upper thigh, and in the waist area. From these measurements, percent body fat can be determined.
Cost: $

Bioelectrical Impedance

How It Is Done: An electric current flows through the body and its resistance is measured. Lean tissue is highly conductive and less resistant than fat mass. Based on the current flow, the volume of lean tissue can be estimated. From this information, the percentage of body fat can be determined.
Cost: $

Dual-Energy X-Ray Absorptiometry (DXA)

How It Is Done: An X-ray is used to measure bone, fat, and lean tissue. The type of tissue that the X-ray passes through will absorb different amounts of energy. The amount of energy lost will allow the percentage of body fat to be determined.
Cost: $$$

Underwater Weighing

How It Is Done: A person is weighed on land and also suspended in a water tank. This is done to determine the density of the body. Fat is less dense and weighs less than muscle mass and will be reflected as such when the person is weighed in the water. The difference of a person's weight in water and on land is then used to calculate the percentage of body fat.
Cost: $$

Air Displacement Using a BodPod

How It Is Done: A person's body volume is determined by measuring air displacement from a chamber. The person sits in a special chamber (called the BodPod) and the air displacement in the chamber is measured. From this measurement, the percentage of body fat can be estimated.
Cost: $$$

$ = very affordable
$$ = less affordable
$$$ = expensive

age being generally more likely to be pear-shaped. People of both genders can be of either shape and develop health risks associated with it.

Because visceral fat is located near the liver, it is believed that fatty acids released from the fat storage area travel to the liver and can lead to insulin resistance, high levels of fat, low levels of the good HDL cholesterol, and high levels of LDL cholesterol in the blood, which all increase the risk of heart disease and diabetes. Insulin resistance also increases the risk for hypertension.[16] Men, postmenopausal women, and obese people tend to have more visceral fat than young adults and lean individuals.

Measuring a person's waist circumference can quickly reveal whether he or she is at risk. (**Figure 10.3** shows how to make this measurement accurately.) A woman with a waist measurement of more than 35 inches or a man with a belly that's more than 40 inches around is at a higher health risk than people with slimmer middles.

Figure 10.3 Waist Measurement
Your waist circumference should be measured around your bare abdomen just above your hip bone.

Extremely High Risk
BMI 40+ and high waist circumference

Very High Risk
BMI 30–39.9 and high waist circumference

High Risk
BMI 25–29.9 and high waist circumference
or
BMI 30–34.9 and low waist circumference

Increased Risk
BMI 25–29.9 and low waist circumference

Low Risk
BMI under 25

Figure 10.4 How at Risk Are You?
Considering both your BMI and your waist circumference can give you a good idea of your level of risk for health problems.

energy balance The state at which energy (calorie) intake and energy (calorie) output in the body are equal.

energy excess Consuming more energy than is expended. Also called *positive energy balance.*

energy deficit Expending more energy than is consumed. Also called *negative energy balance.*

Carrying extra fat around your waist can increase health risks even if you are not overweight. In other words, a person who may be at a healthy weight according to BMI, but who has excess fat around the middle, is at a higher health risk. A person who has both a BMI 25 and a large waist circumference is considered at a higher risk for health problems than if he or she only had a high BMI (**Figure 10.4**).

LO 10.2 **The Take-Home Message** Body mass index (BMI) is a calculation of weight in relationship to height and can be used to assess if weight increases health risks. It is not a direct measure of body fat and may be inaccurate for people who are muscular or who are frail due to illness. Skinfold thickness measurements using calipers, bioelectrical impedance, dual-energy X-ray absorptiometry, underwater weighing, and air displacement are all techniques that can be used to measure the percentage of body fat. Individuals with central obesity, who carry excess fat around the middle, have an increased risk of several chronic diseases, regardless of BMI.

What Is Energy Balance and What Determines Energy Needs?

LO 10.3 Explain what energy balance is, and what determines your daily energy needs; describe the effects of energy imbalance.

To maintain your weight, you need to make sure that you don't consume more calories than you expend daily. Spending as many calories as you consume is the concept behind energy balance.

Energy Balance Is Calories In versus Calories Out

Energy balance is the state at which your energy intake and your energy expenditure, both measured in calories, are equal (**Figure 10.5**). When you consume more calories than you expend, you have **energy excess** and are in *positive energy balance*. Routinely eating more calories than you expend will cause the storage of fat and weight gain. When your calorie intake falls short of your needs, you have an **energy deficit** and are in *negative energy balance*. Imbalances that occur over a long time period, such as weeks and months, are what change body weight.

You can determine whether you are in positive or negative energy balance by comparing the number of calories you consume to the number of calories you expend on a given day. Determining how many calories you consume is fairly straightforward. You can use the food label or a diet analysis program (like the one available with this book) to find out how many calories are in the foods and beverages you eat and drink.

You can also use the grams of macronutrients in foods to calculate the number of total calories they contain. Recall from Chapter 1 that carbohydrates and protein each contain 4 calories/gram and fat contains 9 calories/gram. (Note that alcohol, at 7 calories/gram, can also contribute calories.) Multiplying the number of grams of carbohydrates, protein, or fat by the calories per gram and then adding these numbers reveals the total amount of calories in the food.

Calculating the number of calories you expend daily is a little more complicated.

Energy balance is the relationship between the food we eat and the energy we expend each day. Finding the proper balance between energy intake and energy expenditure allows us to maintain a healthy body weight.

FOCUS FIGURE WALKTHROUGH

Scan this QR code with your mobile device for a video tour of this figure by Joan Salge Blake.

ENERGY INTAKE = ENERGY EXPENDITURE = WEIGHT MAINTENANCE

ENERGY BALANCE

When the calories you consume meet your needs, you are in energy balance. Your weight will be stable.

Calories in   Calories out

ENERGY INTAKE < ENERGY EXPENDITURE = WEIGHT LOSS

ENERGY DEFICIT

When you consume fewer calories than you expend, your body will draw upon your stored energy to meet its needs. You will lose weight.

Calories in   Calories out

ENERGY INTAKE > ENERGY EXPENDITURE = WEIGHT GAIN

ENERGY EXCESS

When you take in more calories than you need, the surplus calories will be stored as fat. You will gain weight.

Calories in   Calories out

What Is Energy Balance and What Determines Energy Needs?   **377**

Table 10.2

Factors That Affect Your Basal Metabolic Rate

Factor	Explanation
Lean body mass	Lean body mass, which is mostly muscle mass, is more metabolically active than fat tissue, so more calories are needed to maintain it. Athletes who have a large percentage of lean body mass due to their increased muscle mass will have a higher BMR than individuals who aren't athletic.
Age	For adults, BMR declines about 1 to 2 percent per decade after the early adult years, but it increases by 15 percent during pregnancy. For children, BMR increases during times of rapid growth such as infancy and adolescence.
Gender	Women have less lean body mass, and typically have a higher percentage of body fat than men. This results in women having up to a 10 percent lower BMR. Women also tend to have a smaller body size.
Body size	Larger individuals will have a higher BMR due to increased surface area compared with smaller individuals. More surface area means more heat lost from the body, which causes the metabolism rate to increase to maintain the body's temperature.
Genes	Research suggests that genes may affect BMR, as individuals within families have similar metabolic rates.
Ethnicity	African-Americans have BMRs that are about 10 percent lower than that of Caucasians.
Stress	Hormones such as epinephrine, which are released during emotional stress, increase BMR. Physiological stress on the body caused by injury, fever, burns, and infections also causes the release of hormones that raise BMR. Heat lost from the body through wounds, as well as the response of the immune system during infection, increase BMR.
Hormones	An increase in thyroid hormone increases BMR, whereas too little of this hormone lowers BMR. Hormone fluctuations during a woman's menstrual cycle lower BMR during the phase before ovulation.
Starvation	Both starvation and fasting for more than about 48 hours lower BMR.
Environmental temperature	Being very cold or very hot can increase BMR, but the change is minimal if you make adjustments in your clothing or in the temperature of your surroundings.
Caffeine	Caffeine can raise BMR, but only slightly, when consumed regularly in moderate amounts.
Drugs	Nicotine may increase BMR.* Drugs such as amphetamines and ephedrine increase BMR.

*Note: Smoking is not a weight-management strategy. Some people may think that replacing snacks with cigarettes helps them stay slim, but the health risks associated with smoking, such as lung cancer, heart disease, and stroke, make it a foolish habit. Anyone concerned about weight gain when quitting smoking can minimize the chances of this with exercise (plus, you'll be able to run farther and faster with your cleaner lungs!).

Figure 10.6 The Three Components of Energy Needs
The "calories out" side of the energy balance equation includes your basal metabolic rate (BMR), the thermic effect of food (TEF), and the energy you use to fuel physical activity.

basal metabolism The amount of energy the body expends to meet its basic physiological needs. Also referred to as *basal metabolic rate (BMR)*.

Energy Needs Are Different for Everyone

Energy needs are unique to every individual, and your energy needs are different from those of your 80-year-old grandparents, your 50-year-old parents, and your marathon-running roommate. Your energy needs are comprised of your basal metabolism, the thermic effect of food (TEF), and the calories needed to fuel your physical activities. (See **Figure 10.6**.)

Your BMR Is the Minimum Amount of Energy You Need to Function

Even when you're not at the gym or sprinting to class, your body is using energy. Pumping your blood, expanding your lungs, and using your brain all require energy every moment of your life. **Basal metabolism** is the amount of energy expended to meet the basic physiological needs that enable your organs and cells to function. Also referred to as your *basal metabolic rate (BMR)*, it is the minimum energy needed to keep you alive.

Approximately 60 percent of your daily energy need is determined by your BMR. The factor that most affects your BMR, **lean body mass**, accounts for about 70 percent of your BMR. Age, gender, body size, genes, ethnicity, emotional and physical stress, thyroid hormone, nutritional state, and environmental temperature, as well as your caffeine and nicotine intake, affect your BMR. **Table 10.2** explains each of these factors.

What's Your Estimated Energy Requirement (EER)?

Calculating your EER is a two-step process.
1. First, complete the information below.
   a. My age is _____.
   b. My physical activity during the day based on the chart below is

Physical Activity	Male	Female
Sedentary (no exercise)	1.00	1.00
Low active (walks about 2 miles daily at 3–4 mph)	1.11	1.12
Active (walks about 7 miles daily at 3–4 mph)	1.25	1.27
Very active (walks about 17 miles daily at 3–4 mph)	1.48	1.45

   c. My weight in pounds is ____ divided by 2.2 = ____ kg.
   d. My height in inches is ____ divided by 39.4 = ____ meters.

2. Using your answers from each part of step 1, complete the following calculation based on your gender and age.

Males, 19+ years old, use this calculation:

$$662 - (9.53 \times \underset{a}{\underline{\quad}}) + \underset{b}{\underline{\quad}} \times [(15.91 \times \underset{c}{\underline{\quad}}) + (539.6 \times \underset{d}{\underline{\quad}})] = \underset{\text{EER}}{\underline{\quad}}$$

Females, 19+ years old, use this calculation:

$$354 - (6.91 \times \underset{a}{\underline{\quad}}) + \underset{b}{\underline{\quad}} \times [(9.36 \times \underset{c}{\underline{\quad}}) + (726 \times \underset{d}{\underline{\quad}})] = \underset{\text{EER}}{\underline{\quad}}$$

The Thermic Effect of Food Is the Energy Your Body Needs to Process Food

Your body uses energy to extract the calories from the foods that you consume. The **thermic effect of food (TEF)** is the amount of calories you expend to digest, absorb, metabolize, and store your food. Approximately 10 percent of calories in the food consumed is used for TEF. In other words, if you eat a 100-calorie cookie, about 10 calories will be used to metabolize the cookie. The TEF varies by the type of food you eat. Protein and carbohydrate have a higher TEF than dietary fat. This is because your body requires more energy to digest, absorb, and metabolize amino acids, starches, and sugar into stored body fat than to metabolize dietary fat into body fat.

Physical Activity Increases Your Energy Expenditure

If you are very physically active, you're going to need more energy than someone who is sedentary. For sedentary people, the amount of energy expended in physical activity is less than half of their BMR. For very physically active individuals, such as athletes, it can be as much as double their BMR. The more physical activity you routinely incorporate into your day, the more calories you will need to eat to meet your energy needs. The amount of energy expended during physical activity goes beyond the activity itself. Exercise causes a small increase in energy expenditure for some time after the activity has stopped.[17]

Calculating Your Energy Needs

Recall Table 2.1 from Chapter 2, which helped you estimate your energy needs. This table was derived from the DRIs' estimated energy requirement (EER). The **estimated energy requirement (EER)** is the average calorie intake that is estimated to maintain energy balance based on a person's gender, age, height, body weight, and level of physical activity. (Physical activity levels are separated into categories ranging from sedentary to very active.) While Table 2.1 used a reference height and weight for each age grouping, you can calculate your own EER using your specific height and weight with the Self-Assessment "What's Your Estimated Energy Requirement (EER)?"

eLearn

An Estimated Energy Requirement Online Tool

To calculate a more precise EER, you need to record all of your daily physical activity. Visit the interactive tracker tool at www.ChooseMyPlate.gov and enter your gender, height, weight, age, and all the activities you do in a 24-hour period. The Tracker will then calculate your EER.

lean body mass The body mass once the fat mass has been subtracted. It contains mostly muscle but also organs and fluids.

thermic effect of food (TEF) The amount of calories the body uses to digest, absorb, metabolize, and store food.

estimated energy requirement (EER) The amount of daily energy needed to maintain a healthy body weight and meet energy (calorie) needs based on age, gender, height, weight, and activity level.

Energy Imbalances over Time Can Lead to Changes in Body Weight

The handful of cheese curls that Pam eats every night while watching television is adding about 100 more calories than she needs daily. After three months, she's gained a little over two pounds. Bryan, in contrast, is so busy juggling studying with tennis practice that he consumes about 50 calories fewer daily than he expends. After four months, he has dropped about 1½ pounds from his already light frame. Over time, a chronic energy imbalance results in a change in body weight. Let's look at what is happening inside your body when an energy imbalance occurs.

Reducing Calories Can Lead to Weight Loss

Consuming fewer calories than you need daily will cause your body to draw upon its energy stores to overcome the deficit. In Chapter 4, you learned that when you don't eat for a period of time, glycogen and fat are used as fuel sources to meet your body's glucose and energy needs until your next meal or snack. Amino acids from the breakdown of body protein, particularly muscle, can also be used to make glucose.

In prolonged fasting, all of the glycogen in your liver is depleted. The breakdown of body fat contributes to your energy needs, while the breakdown of muscle pro-

> Your body contains about 35 billion fat cells, which can expand to accommodate a surplus of calories.

vides materials to meet your glucose needs. Ketone bodies are also generated through the incomplete breakdown of fat, and these are used as an energy source. People starting at a healthy weight can't live much beyond 60 days of fasting, as their fat stores, as well as about one-third of their lean tissue mass, will be depleted by this time.[18]

Excess Calories Can Lead to Weight Gain

Eating more calories than you need, regardless of the foods they come from, will result in your body storing the excess as fat. Recall from Chapters 4 and 6 that you have limited capacity to store glucose as glycogen and you can't store extra protein. However, you have unlimited capacity to store fat.

Although the relationship between eating too many calories and gaining weight appears straightforward, this isn't necessarily the case. The causes of overweight and obesity and the ability to prevent them can be complex, as there is more to eating than just nourishing the body. Let's look at this next.

LO 10.3 **The Take-Home Message** Energy balance is the relationship between your energy intake and your energy expenditure, which are both measured in calories. Your basal metabolism, the thermic effect of food (TEF), and your physical activities all determine your daily energy needs. When you don't eat enough calories to meet your needs, your glycogen and fat stores, as well as muscle mass, will be broken down for fuel. A chronic deficit of calories will produce weight loss. When you chronically consume more calories than you need, the excess will be stored as fat, and weight gain will occur.

What Factors Are Likely to Affect Body Weight?

LO 10.4 Explain the factors that affect body weight.

Numerous factors influence weight management, starting with what and how often you eat. Physiology, genetics, and your environment also play a role. Let's look at how each of these can affect your body weight.

Hunger and Appetite Affect What You Eat

Recall from Chapter 3 that there is a difference between your physiological need for food (or hunger) and the psychological factors that prompt you to eat (your appetite). Hunger is the physical need for nourishment that drives you to consume food. Once you start eating, hunger will subside as the feeling of **satiation** begins to set in. Satiation will determine how long and how much you eat. **Satiety** is the sensation that you feel when you have had enough to eat. Satiety determines the length of time between eating episodes.[19] An increase in satiety will delay the start of your next meal or snack.

Your appetite is affected by hunger, as well as environmental factors, like seeing or smelling something that you think will taste good, your social setting, your stress level, and so forth. Hunger, in turn, is affected by many physiological mechanisms, as well as genetics. Both hunger and appetite ultimately affect what you eat.

> Being sleep deprived can increase your appetite by lowering the levels of leptin and increasing the amount of ghrelin in your body.

Physiological Mechanisms Help Regulate Hunger

Various physiologic feedback mechanisms involving the mouth, stomach, intestines, and brain all work together to increase or decrease your hunger (**Figure 10.7**). For example, many hormones play a role. When your stomach is empty, the hormone **ghrelin**, which is produced mainly in the stomach, signals your brain that you need to consume food. Your body produces more ghrelin during fasting (such as between meals) in order to stimulate hunger, and it produces less after food is consumed. Another hormone, **leptin**, which is produced in fat cells, helps regulate your body fat by affecting hunger. As your fat stores increase, leptin signals the brain to decrease your level of hunger and food intake.

Once food enters your mouth, sensory signals are sent to the brain to tell you whether or not to continue eating. The feedback mechanism is very much affected by your prior experience of tasting that food.[20] For example, a spoonful of your favorite ice cream is a pleasant stimulus, and your brain would encourage you to keep eating it. However, if you took a sip of sour milk, this stimulus would be unacceptable to the brain, especially if the last time you drank sour milk it made you sick. Your brain will instruct you to spit out the sour milk so that you don't swallow it.

Once food is in your stomach, other factors, such as the size of the meal, come into play. After you eat a large meal, your stomach becomes distended. This signals the brain to decrease your hunger, and you will stop eating. A distended stomach also causes the release of **cholecystokinin**, a hormone that is associated with the feeling of satiation.[21]

When the food reaches your small intestine, the nutrients, protein, fatty acids, and monosaccharides all stimulate feedback to the brain to decrease your hunger. Once these nutrients are absorbed, the hormone insulin is released, which also causes the brain to decrease your hunger.[22]

Changes in your food intake can also cause changes in your hunger cues. If you suddenly decrease the size of your meals, you may feel an initial increase in hunger. If you continue eating smaller meals, your stomach adapts to the reduced quantity and the feelings of extreme hunger diminish over time. After a while, a larger meal can make you feel extremely full and uncomfortable because your stomach has gotten used to smaller meals.[23] People sometimes refer to this effect as the "shrinking" of the stomach, but the organ itself does not get smaller.

satiation The feeling during eating that determines how long and how much you eat.

satiety The sensation that you feel when you have had enough to eat. It determines how long you will go between meals and/or snacks.

ghrelin A hormone produced mainly in the stomach that increases hunger.

leptin A hormone produced in fat tissue that helps regulate body fat by signaling the reduction of food intake in the brain and interfering with the storage of fat in the cells.

cholecystokinin A hormone released when the stomach is distended. It is associated with the feeling of satiation.

F⊙CUS

Figure 10.7 **Your Brain Controls Hunger and Satiation**

FOCUS FIGURE WALKTHROUGH

Scan this QR code with your mobile device for a video tour of this figure by Joan Salge Blake.

Two regions of the brain—the ventromedial nucleus and the lateral hypothalamus—control eating behaviors in response to hormones released from the stomach, pancreas, small intestine, fat cells, and the hypothalamus. The ventromedial nucleus responds to hormones to stimulate satiety. Hunger is triggered by hormones that stimulate the lateral hypothalamus.

HORMONES THAT STIMULATE SATIETY

HORMONES THAT STIMULATE HUNGER

INSULIN
Insulin is released from the **pancreas** following carbohydrate ingestion.

LEPTIN
Leptin produced in the **fat cells** is released into the blood to stimulate satiety.

GHRELIN
Ghrelin is secreted from the **stomach** when the stomach is empty to stimulate hunger.

CHOLECYSTOKININ
Cholecystokinin (CCK) is released from the **small intestine** when chyme enters the duodenum.

In a perfect world, all these physiologic mechanisms, when recognized and responded to appropriately, would keep you in perfect energy balance. When you are hungry, you eat, and when you are satiated, you stop. The reality, however, is that many people override these mechanisms and end up in energy imbalance. Factors like genetics and the environment also affect how much energy you consume and expend.

Genetics Partially Determine Body Weight

Genetics also influence your body weight.[24] Studies on separated identical twins raised in different home environments confirm this, as both twins showed similar weight gain and body fat distribution.[25]

People who share genes will often have similar body weights.

Research suggests that genetic differences in the level or the functioning of some hormones can influence a person's body weight and appetite. For example, genetically high levels of ghrelin may cause some people to overeat and become obese.[26] Individuals who are genetically prone to being leptin deficient become massively obese, yet when they are given leptin, their appetite decreases and their weight falls to within a healthy range.[27] Ironically, many obese people have adequate amounts of leptin but the brain has developed a resistance to it, rendering its appetite control ineffective.[28] For these individuals, other mechanisms prevent leptin from functioning as a regulator of their appetite.

Genetics may also affect how calories are expended in the body by affecting **thermogenesis** (*thermo* = heat, *genesis* = origin), which is the production of heat in body cells. Genes may cause different rates of **nonexercise-associated thermogenesis (NEAT)**, which is the energy you expend during fidgeting, standing, chewing gum, texting on your smart phone, and other nonexercise movement throughout the day. When some individuals overeat, they are able to rev up their NEAT to expend some of the excess calories and are thus better able to manage their energy balance.[29] Many overweight individuals don't appear to have this compensatory mechanism.

Some researchers have described a genetic "set point" that determines body weight. This theory holds that the body fights to remain at a specific body weight and opposes attempts at weight loss. The body may even enable very easy weight gain in order to get back to this "set point" when weight is lost. In other words, a person's weight remains fairly constant because the body "has a mind of its own." Given that the weight of Americans has disproportionately increased over the last few decades relative to previous decades, this theory either isn't true or the set point can be overridden.[30]

Research also suggests that people with a genetic propensity to become overweight experience greater challenges to preventing obesity in an environment that is conducive to gaining weight. This relationship is referred to as a **gene–environment interaction**. To explain how these two entities interact with each other, researchers have used the analogy that genes load the gun but an obesity-promoting environment pulls the trigger.[31] For instance, if a person's lifestyle stays the same, his or her weight should remain fairly stable. However, if the environment shifts to make it easier to gain weight, the body will also shift, and then the person will gain weight. This means that an environment in which people can easily and cheaply obtain endless amounts of energy-dense food may be one of the biggest culprits in the current obesity epidemic. In one study, rats, which should genetically be able to maintain a healthy body weight, were shown to overeat and become fat when they had access to unlimited fatty foods and sweets.[32]

The same effect has been observed in human populations. For instance, Pima Indians of the southwestern United States have a high rate of obesity. Research comparing Pimas in Mexico with Pimas living in Arizona suggested that the environment promoted weight gain in the latter, weight-susceptible population. The traditional Mexican Pimas whom the researchers studied lived an active lifestyle and

thermogenesis The production of heat in body cells.

nonexercise-associated thermogenesis (NEAT) The energy expenditure that occurs during nonexercise movements, such as fidgeting, standing, and chewing gum.

gene–environment interaction The interaction of genetics and the environment that increases the risk of obesity in some people.

Does Your Environment Affect Your Energy Balance?

1. Do you eat out at least once a day?
   Yes ☐ No ☐

2. Do you often buy snacks at convenience stores, coffee shops, vending machines, sandwich shops, or other eateries?
   Yes ☐ No ☐

3. Do you buy the largest portions of fast foods or snacks because you think you're getting more for your money?
   Yes ☐ No ☐

4. When you order pizza, do you have it delivered?
   Yes ☐ No ☐

5. Do you drive around the parking lot to get the closest parking space to the entrance?
   Yes ☐ No ☐

6. Do you get off at the subway or bus stop that is nearest to your destination?
   Yes ☐ No ☐

7. Do you take the elevator when stairs are available in a building?
   Yes ☐ No ☐

8. Do you e-mail or call your friends and neighbors rather than walk next door to talk to them in person?
   Yes ☐ No ☐

Answers

All of the habits listed above contribute to an obesity-promoting environment. If you answered yes to more than half, you should think about how you can improve your lifestyle habits.

Practical Nutrition VIDEO

Coffee Shop Strategies

Is stopping at a coffee shop part of your daily morning routine? If so, a few small changes to what you order could make a big difference to your waistline! Scan this QR code with your mobile device to access the video. You can also access the video in MasteringNutrition™.

ate a diet rich in complex carbohydrates and lower in animal fats than that of the "Americanized" Pimas in Arizona, who had a more sedentary lifestyle and fatty diet. The overweight Mexican Pimas, on average, had a BMI of about 25, compared with the obese Arizona Pimas, who had, on average, a BMI of over 33.[33] The traditional Pimas had a better chance of avoiding obesity because they lived in a healthier environment. As this study suggests, even if you have a genetic predisposition to being overweight, it's not guaranteed. Genetics may increase your risk of obesity, but eating and exercising properly will allow you to maintain a healthy body weight.

Environmental Factors Can Increase Appetite and Decrease Physical Activity

How many times have you eaten a satisfying meal before going to the movies, but bought a bucket of popcorn at the theater anyway? You didn't buy the popcorn because you were hungry. You just couldn't resist the buttery smell and the allure of munching during the film. Environmental factors don't just affect people who are genetically prone to being overweight—anyone can fall prey to an environment that encourages eating! In fact, there are many stimuli in the environment that can drive your appetite. In addition to aromas and certain venues such as movie theaters, events such as holidays and sporting events, people such as your friends and family, and even the convenience of obtaining food can all encourage you to eat even when you're not hungry.

Over the past few decades, the environment around us has changed in ways that have made it easier for many of us to incur an energy imbalance and a propensity to gain weight. Take the Self-Assessment "Does Your Environment Affect Your Energy Balance?" to reflect upon how your environment may influence the lifestyle decisions that you make throughout your day.

Let's look at some environmental issues that are feeding Americans' energy imbalance.

We Work More and Cook Less

One reason Americans are getting larger is that they often don't eat at home. Research shows that adults today spend more time traveling to work and devote more of their daily hours to work than in previous decades.[34] This longer workday means there is less time to devote to everyday activities, such as food preparation. In fact, the amount of time devoted to food preparation has declined by over 40 percent since 1965.[35]

Today, 32 percent of Americans' daily calories come from ready-to-eat foods that are prepared outside the home, and this is having an effect on the quality of their diets.[36] Research shows that when compared with foods made at home, foods that are obtained away from home, from establishments such as sit-down restaurants and fast-food outlets, contain more total fat, saturated fat, sodium, and cholesterol but less calcium, fiber, and iron. Not surprisingly, the food choices at these establishments are less likely to contain whole grains, fruit, and lean dairy foods.[37] Cooking less in the home and obtaining ready-to-eat foods outside the home isn't a formula that is healthy for the diets of Americans.

Dining out frequently is also associated with a higher BMI. Research suggests that there is a strong association between the consumption of one or more fast-food meals a week and obesity. However, research suggests that when families share meals at home, not only does the quality of their diet improve, but they are better able to manage their weight.[38]

Research has shown that women who dine out five or more times weekly consume close to 300 calories smore on dining-out days than do women who eat at home.

We Eat More (and More)

In the United States, food is easy to get, there's a lot to choose from, and portion sizes are generous. All of these factors are associated with consuming too many calories.[39]

Years ago, people went to a bookstore for the sole purpose of buying a book. Now they go to a bookstore to sip a mocha latte and nibble on cookie while they ponder which book to buy. Americans can grab breakfast at a hamburger drive-through, lunch at a fast-food court, a sub sandwich at many gas stations, and a three-course meal of nachos, pizza, and ice cream at a movie theater. At any given moment of your day, you can probably easily find a bundle of calories to consume.

This access to a variety of foods is problematic for weight-conscious individuals. While the appeal of a food diminishes as it continues to be eaten (that is, the first bite will taste the best, but each subsequent bite loses some of that initial pleasure), having a variety of foods available allows the eater to move on to another food once boredom sets in.[40] The more good-tasting foods that are available, the more a person will eat. For example, during that three-course meal at the movie theater, once you're tired of the nachos, you can move on to the pizza, and when that loses its appeal, you can dig into the ice cream. If the pizza and ice cream weren't available, you would have stopped after the nachos and consumed fewer calories.

Portion size also plays a large role in overeating. Research shows that people tend to eat more of a food, and thus more calories, when larger portions are served.[41] Because the supersize portions often cost only slightly more than the regular size, they are perceived as bargains by the consumer and a license to overeat.

When serving yourself at home, the size of the serving bowl or package of food influences the amount of the food you put on your plate. Serving yourself from a large bowl or package has been shown to increase the serving size by more than 20 percent.[42] This means that you are more likely to scoop out (and eat) a bigger serving of ice cream from a half-gallon container than from a pint container. To make matters worse, most people don't compensate for these extra calories by reducing the portions at the next meal.[43]

Portion sizes of French fries have more than doubled from the past. Choose the smaller size to reduce your ingestion of calories.

The size of the average dinner plate has increased by more than 20 percent since 1960. The larger the plate, the more food it will hold, and the more food you will likely consume.

Increased amounts of "screen time" are contributing to decreased amounts of physical activity.

**Less in-home food preparation
More dining out**

**Larger portion sizes
More energy-dense foods**

Higher calorie intake

Lack of physical activity

**Weight gain
Higher BMI**

Figure 10.8 Environmental and Lifestyle Factors of Weight Gain
This flowchart shows how eating out more often leads to consuming larger portion sizes of energy-dense foods, which leads to intake of excess calories. Combine this with less physical activity and the result is weight gain and a higher BMI.

We Sit More and Move Less

Compared to past decades, Americans today have more food options and consume more calories daily—about 600 more since 1970. On average, we're also expending fewer calories per day at work and at leisure, which has contributed significantly to the obesity epidemic.[44]

When your great-grandparents went to work in the morning, they probably headed out to the fields or off to the factory. Your parents and older siblings, though, are more likely to go to an office and sit in front of a computer, and you probably sit at a desk for much of your day. This shift from jobs that required manual labor to jobs that are more sedentary has been shown to increase the risk of becoming overweight or obese.[45] One study found that men who sit for more than 6 hours during their workday are at higher risk of being overweight than those who sit for less than an hour daily.[46] Technology in the workplace now allows us to communicate with everyone without having to leave our desks. This means that people no longer have to get up and walk to see the colleague down the hall or the client across town. Researchers estimate that a 145-pound person expends 3.9 calories for each minute of walking, compared with 1.8 calories per minute sitting. Thus, walking 10 minutes during each workday to communicate in person with coworkers would expend 10,000 calories annually, yet only about 5,000 calories would be expended if the person spent those daily 10 minutes sitting in the office sending e-mails or calling colleagues on the phone.[47]

Labor-saving devices have also affected energy expenditure outside of work. Driving short distances is now the norm, while walking and biking have decreased over the years.[48] Dishes aren't washed by hand but are stacked in a dishwasher.[49] Labor-saving devices can reduce our daily energy expenditure by more than 100 calories.[50] As technology continues to advance and allows you to become more energy efficient in your work and lifestyle habits, you need to offset this conservation of energy with *planned* physical activity at another time of the day.

More than half of Americans do not accumulate the recommended minimum 150 minutes (2 hours and 30 minutes) weekly of moderate-intensity aerobic activity such as brisk walking.[51] In fact, more than 20 percent of Americans report no leisure-time physical activity daily.[52] Unfortunately, Americans are spending more than 41 hours weekly viewing their televisions, computers, and mobile phones.[53] Young adults in particular have increased their screen time, due in part to a growing trend for watching videos on handheld mobile devices.[54]

We are moving less during both work and play. With less energy being expended, weight gain is becoming easier and the need for weight loss even greater. Combine this with an environment that is conducive to eating and with the genetic makeup of many Americans, and it's not difficult to see why many people are becoming overweight or obese (**Figure 10.8**). Many Americans have to begin making conscious diet and lifestyle changes that will help them lose weight, or at the very least, prevent further weight gain.

Let's look at what is a realistic amount of weight to lose and how to do it healthfully.

LO 10.4 **The Take-Home Message** Your appetite is your desire to eat and is affected by hunger, satiation, and satiety. It is influenced by your physiology, your genes, and your environment. Physiological mechanisms, such as hormones, signal your brain to increase your hunger when you are hungry and decrease it after you have eaten. Genetics can make it more difficult for some individuals to manage their weight. The current environment—which provides easy access to a variety of excessive amounts of energy-dense foods and at the same time decreases energy expenditure—encourages obesity.

How Can You Lose Weight Healthfully?

LO 10.5 Explain how to lose weight healthfully.

According to the National Institutes of Health, overweight individuals should aim to lose about 10 percent of their body weight over a six-month period.[55] This means that the goal for an overweight 180-pound person should be to shed 18 pounds over six months, about 3 pounds a month, or ¾ pound weekly. Because a person must have an energy deficit of approximately 3,500 calories over time to lose a pound of fat, a deficit of 250 to 500 calories daily will result in a weight loss of about ½ to 1 pound weekly. This is a healthy rate of weight loss that you can sustain. Although fad diets promise dramatic weight loss "overnight," don't be fooled. These plans are not based on legitimate science, and some can endanger your health. We talk more about fad diets in the Examining the Evidence feature "Evaluating Popular Diets" on page 388.

Although there is no single diet approach that has been universally embraced, many health experts agree that a person needs to adjust three areas of life for successful, long-term weight loss (**Figure 10.9**):

- Diet
- Physical activity
- Behavior modification

Let's start with the diet.

Eat Smart, Because Calories Count

When it comes to losing weight, you need to remember two important words: *calories count*—no matter where they come from. Because an energy imbalance of too many calories in and not enough calories out causes weight gain, reversing the imbalance will cause the opposite. That is, taking in fewer calories and burning more will result in weight loss. However, cutting back too drastically on calories often results in a failed weight-loss attempt. If a person skips meals or isn't satiated at each meal because of skimpy portions, the person will experience hunger between meals and be more inclined to snack on energy-dense foods. Thus, a key strategy during the weight-loss process is for the person to eat a healthy, balanced diet that is

HEALTHY WEIGHT

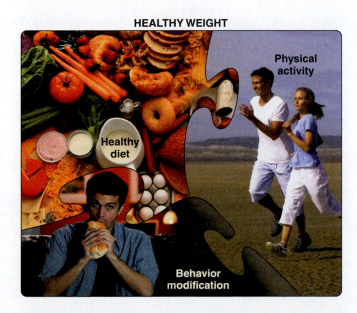

Figure 10.9 Three Pieces of the Long-Term Weight-Loss Puzzle
Diet, physical activity, and behavior modification are all necessary for long-term weight management.

Evaluating Popular Diets

Americans spend over $60 billion annually on weight-loss programs, products, and pills and are more than willing to keep reaching into their wallets for the next quick diet fix.[1] Though it may seem that there is a new fad diet around every corner, many of these diets have actually been around for years.

The low-carbohydrate, high-protein, and high-fat diets of the 1970s (Dr. Atkins' Diet Revolution) were replaced by the very high-carbohydrate and very low-fat diets of the 1980s (Pritikin diets), which continued into the early 1990s (Dr. Ornish's diet). These diets led the way to the more carbohydrate-restricted, moderate protein and fat diets of the late 1990s (the Zone diet), only to flip back to the low-carbohydrate, high-protein and high-fat diets in the early part of 2000s (Dr. Atkins' New Diet Revolution, South Beach). In the later part of the last decade, portion sizes and an emphasis on increasing whole grains, fruits, and vegetables in the diet became the talk of the diet scene. We are now back to lower carbohydrate and higher protein diets, such as the Paleo Diet and The New Atkins for a New You diet. The table on the next page summarizes the main types of popular diet plans and the differences among them.

After decades of clashing diet books and plans, does one emerge as the clear winner in the battle of the bulge? The answer is no. Research supports that it's the calories, not the composition of the diet, that count when it comes to losing weight.[2] In fact, a study comparing the Atkins, Ornish, Weight Watchers, and Zone diets showed that no matter what diet the individuals followed, they all lost about the same amount of weight, on average, by the end of one year.[3] Whereas each of these diets provides a different percentage of carbohydrates, protein, and fat, they all had one important thing in common: They all reduced calories.

A very interesting point emerged from this study: People who were most diligent about adhering to the diet—no matter which one—experienced the most weight loss.[4] However, more than 20 percent of the dieters quit just two months into the study, and more than 40 percent of them dropped out after one year. The highest dropout rates occurred among followers of the Atkins or Ornish diets. The researchers speculate that the rigidity of these extreme diets may have caused the higher dropout rates. Thus, the problem with many fad diets is that people give up on them long before they meet their weight-loss goals. A fad diet doesn't fix anything in the long term. If it did, there wouldn't be new (or recycled) fad diets continually appearing on the market. Some extreme diets may also be unhealthy in the long term. In fact, the high dropout rate for some fad diets has probably protected many individuals from serious ill health effects and long-term nutrient deficiencies.

Red Flags for Diet Hype

Marketers often make sensational claims about fad diets and weight-loss products. These red flags can often tell you if a diet is questionable.

🚩 It's the Carbs, Not the Calories, That Make You Fat!

Some fad diet ads claim that you can eat as much protein and fat as you want as long as you keep away from the carbs. These diets claim that your consumption of pasta, breads, rice, and many fruits and vegetables should be limited, but fatty meats such as ribs, salami, bologna, and poultry with skin, as well as butter, bacon, and cheeses should be on the menu often.

The Truth behind the Hype

Diets that severely limit carbohydrates (< 130 grams daily) eliminate so many foods, as well as sweets and treats, that it is impossible for a person not to consume at least 500 fewer calories daily.

This will theoretically produce about one pound of weight loss per week.[5] When you curtail the carbohydrates, you likely will also be cutting back on fat.[6] When you stop eating the bagel (carbs), you'll also eliminate the cream cheese (fat) you slather on each half. Also, the monotonous nature of these diets causes people to become bored with eating, so they stop. Because the bread, mashed potatoes, and corn are off limits at dinner, the dieter is limited to fatty steak and not much else. Most people can only eat so much of this before it loses its appeal, so they're likely to stop eating sooner. As always, putting down the fork will cut calorie consumption.

Buyer Beware

A diet high in saturated fat and low in fiber and phytochemicals because it is low in whole grains, fruits, and vegetables is a recipe for heart disease, cancer, constipation, elevated blood cholesterol levels, and deficiencies in many vitamins and minerals, such as vitamins A, E, and B_6, folate, calcium, iron, zinc, and potassium.[7] So each time you follow a diet low in whole grains, fruits, and vegetables and high in animal fats, you are robbing your body of the protection of plant foods and overfeeding it the wrong type of fat. The high protein content of these diets may also cause the loss of calcium, and thus increase the risk of osteoporosis, as well as kidney stones.

🚩 Lose Seven Pounds in One Week!

Many diets guarantee rapid weight loss. This may happen on a low-carbohydrate diet—but only during the first few days, and only temporarily.

The Truth behind the Hype

The 4- to 7-pound weight loss during the first week of low-carbohydrate dieting is due to loss of body water that results from two physiological processes. First, because the reduced amount of carbohydrates can't support the body's need for glucose, the stored glycogen in the liver and muscle will be broken down. Each gram of glycogen removed from storage causes the loss of 2 grams of water with it. Because you store about 500 grams of glycogen in your body, you can expect

Distinguishing Among Popular Diets

Dietary Approach	Weight-Loss Claim	What You Eat	Pros	Cons	Examples
Very low-calorie diet (VLCD)	Severely limiting calories burns fat and reduces body weight	400 to 800 calories per day; liquid meals containing vitamins, electrolytes, minerals, and essential fatty acids; high in protein (up to 125 g/day)	Quick weight loss of 15–20% in 12–16 weeks; improves glycemic control in type 2 diabetics, reduced hypertension and hyperlipidemia	Numerous side effects: fatigue, hypotension, headaches, dizziness, constipation, and gallstones in long-term use; loss of lean body tissue; regain 50% of weight lost in one year	• Medifast • Cabbage Soup • Cookie Diet
Balanced, reduced calorie	Moderate reduction of calories promotes weight loss at a healthy rate	1,200 to 1,800 calories per day; balanced 45–65% carbohydrate, 20–35% fat, and 10–35% protein; wide variety of foods; portions are controlled	Average weight loss of 1 to 2 pounds per week; approach balances reduced food intake by portion sizes and exercise, which helps maintain lean body mass; incorporates behavior modification	Low adherence rates; some programs require prepackaged foods	• Jenny Craig • Weight Watchers • Nutri-System • The Biggest Loser
Restricted carbohydrate, high protein	Insulin promotes fat storage; low glycemic foods are more satisfying, which limits total food intake	< 20% carbohydrate, 55–65% fat, 25–30% protein; less than 100 g carbohydrate per day; excludes most fruits, grains, starchy vegetables, and legumes; allows meat, limited dairy, and fats	Hunger is controlled, weight loss, improved glycemic control; may improve HDL and triglycerides	Reduced glycogen, loss of lean body tissue and electrolytes; side effects include fatigue, headaches, dizziness, and constipation; nutritional deficiencies	• Dr. Atkins • South Beach • Belly Fat Cure • Wheat Belly Diet • Paleo Diet
High carbohydrate, low fat	When fat is restricted, fewer calories are consumed	> 65% carbohydrate, < 20% fat, 10–20% protein; low-energy-dense plant foods: fruits, vegetables, whole grains; low or void of animal foods; limited nuts and seeds	Significant weight loss due to low calorie intake; allows you to eat more	Low adherence rates; limited food options; may have poor nutrient absorption due to low fat intake and high fiber	• Ornish • Pritikin • Pasta Diet

to lose approximately 2 pounds of water weight during the first week of a low-carbohydrate diet. Secondly, the ketone bodies generated by the breakdown of fat are lost from the body through the kidneys. This will also cause the body to lose sodium. As you know from Chapter 8, where sodium goes, water follows. Therefore, the ketone bodies that cause you to lose sodium will also cause you to lose water.[8]

Buyer Beware

Though water weight may be lost during the first week, the rate of weight loss after that will be determined by the energy imbalance in the body, as in any calorie-reducing diet. As soon as carbohydrates are added back to the diet, the body will retain water and some water weight will come back on. When it comes to shedding weight, quick loss usually means quick regain.

⚑ Celebrity-Endorsed Miracle Weight-Loss Products with a Money-Back Guarantee!

Just because a celebrity actor or model tries to sell you a product doesn't mean that the product is valid. It just means that the celebrity is being paid to do what he or she does best: act.

The Truth behind the Hype

No cream, shake, or potion will magically melt away body fat, and many marketers who claim that their products do this end up paying millions of dollars in fines to the Federal Trade Commission (FTC) for public deception.[9]

Buyer Beware

Forget about getting your money back. The FTC has received numerous complaints from dissatisfied customers who have unsuccessfully tried to get a refund. The more miraculous the claim, the more likely you are to lose (money, that is, not weight).

How Can You Lose Weight Healthfully? **389**

Naturally Occurring Plants, Herbs, and Other Substances Will Help You Lose Weight without Risk!

"Natural" substances, such as gluco-mannan, guar gum, acai berries, chito-san, green tea extracts, bitter orange, and hoodia are not necessarily safer or more effective for weight loss.

The Truth behind the Hype

Glucomannan is a compound found in the root of the starchy konjac plant, and guar gum is a type of dietary fiber found in a specific bean. Acai berries are reddish purple and are native to Central and South America. All of these substances are ineffective in weight loss. Hoodia is a cactus-like plant found in southern Africa, and there haven't been any studies published that back its claim as an aid in weight loss. Chitosan is produced from a substance found in shellfish. Though the claim is that these substances decrease the absorption of fat in the body, research doesn't back up the claim. While green tea extracts have been marketed to help with weight loss, there isn't research evidence to support the hype. In fact, there have been reports of liver problems in people taking concentrated green tea extracts.[10] Bitter orange is a plant that is touted as a substitute for ephedra (see the medications listed in the Health Connection feature "Extreme Measures" on page 398), yet the research is not definitive on its ability to stimulate weight loss.

Buyer Beware

Guar gum has been shown to cause diarrhea, flatulence, and gastrointestinal disturbances. Chitosan may cause nausea and flatulence.[11] There are some reports of individuals having adverse effects such as fainting and heart attack when taking bitter orange supplements alone or with caffeine.[12] Naturally occurring substances are not necessarily safe to consume, and there's no evidence that they help you lose weight.

WHAT DO YOU THINK?

1. How can you best evaluate new diet products, programs, and books?
2. What marketing ploys have you noticed in advertisements for diet products and programs?
3. Why do you think some of the popular diet plans seem to contradict each other?

Practical Nutrition VIDEO

What Does 100 Calories Look Like?

Every calorie counts! Let Joan show you how much more food you can get per calorie when you make high-volume, low-energy-density choices. Scan this QR code with your mobile device to access the video. You can also access the video in MasteringNutrition™.

not only lower in calories, but is also *satisfying*. One way you can add heft and satiation to your lower-calorie meals is by including higher-volume foods.

Eat More Vegetables, Fruit, and Fiber

People tend to eat the same amount of food regardless of its energy density—that is, the amount of calories in the meal.[56] In other words, you need a certain volume of food in order to feel full. As you learned in Chapter 4, it is very easy to overeat energy-dense, low-volume foods such as candy, which can easily fill you *out* before they fill you *up*. You'll overeat them before you become satiated. The reverse of this—eating high-volume, low-energy-density foods that fill you up before they fill you out—can help in weight management. High-volume foods include fruits and vegetables, which are bulked up because of their water content, and whole grains, which contain a lot of fiber. These foods are also low in fat (which contains 9 calories/gram) and high in carbohydrate (which contains only 4 calories/gram). Research shows that these foods are associated with increased satiety and reduced feelings of hunger and calorie intake.[57]

In fact, consuming a large, high-volume, low-energy-density salad before a meal can reduce the calories eaten at that meal by more than 10 percent.[58] Adding vegetables to sandwiches and soups will increase both the volume of food consumed and meal satisfaction and help displace higher-calorie items (**Figure 10.10**). If you are full after eating a sandwich loaded with vegetables, you'll eat less from the bag of energy-dense chips. This is important because you don't need to eliminate chips from your diet if you enjoy them. Any food—from chocolate to chips—can be modest in calories if you eat modest amounts. **Table 10.3** provides examples of low-, moderate-, and high-energy-density foods. See the Table Tips called "Eat More to Weigh Less" for ways to increase the volume of foods you consume, while decreasing your overall caloric intake.

Fiber also contributes to the bulk of vegetables and fruits and their ability to prolong satiety.[59] Overweight individuals have been shown to consume less dietary fiber and fruit than normal-weight people.[60] For these reasons, high-fiber foods, such as vegetables, fruit, and whole grains, are a key part of a weight-loss diet.

Change low-volume...

¾ cup chicken broth: **29** calories
½ cup chicken (white meat): **106** calories
1 cup noodles: **212** calories

347 total calories

2 slices whole-wheat bread: **138** calories
4 oz ham: **125** calories
2 oz American cheese: **213** calories

476 total calories

...to high volume

¾ cup chicken broth: **29** calories
½ cup chicken (white meat): **106** calories
½ cup noodles: **106** calories
½ cup mixed vegetables: **59** calories

300 total calories

2 slices whole-wheat bread: **138** calories
2 oz ham: **63** calories
1 oz American cheese: **106** calories
2 slices tomato: **7** calories
2 leaves Romaine lettuce: **10** calories

324 total calories

Figure 10.10 Adding Volume to Your Meals Aids Weight Loss
Adding high-volume foods like fruits and vegetables to your sandwiches, soups, and meals can add to satiety and displace higher-calorie foods, two factors that can help in weight management.

Table 10.3

The Energy Density of Foods

Low

These foods provide 0.7 to 1.5 calories per gram and are high in water and fiber. Examples include most vegetables and fruits—tomatoes, cantaloupe, strawberries, broccoli, cauliflower—as well as broth-based soups, fat-free yogurt, and cottage cheese.

Medium

These foods have 1.5 to 4 calories per gram and contain less water. They include bagels, hard-cooked eggs, dried fruits, lean sirloin steak, hummus, whole-wheat bread, and part-skim mozzarella cheese.

High

These foods provide 4 to 9 calories per gram, are low in moisture, and include chips, cookies, crackers, cakes, pastries, butter, oil, and bacon.

Low-volume, high-calorie

16 oz Dunkin Donuts Coffee Coolata®
with cream: **350** calories

460 total calories

Dunkin Donuts chocolate
chunk cookie: **110** calories

Pizza Hut Pepperoni Lover's® Pizza
2 slices, large pizza: **570** calories

890 total calories

Cheese breadstick
320 calories

High-volume, low-calorie

Pop Secret Snack popcorn,
94% fat free, butter:
110 calories

180 total calories

16 oz Dunkin Donuts Hot Latte Lite
made with skim milk: **70** calories

Pizza Hut Veggie Lover's® Pizza
3 slices, large pizza: **610** calories

676 total calories

1 cup Romaine lettuce: **8** calories
½ cup cherry tomatoes: **13** calories
½ cup sliced cucumbers: **7** calories
1 tbs light ranch dressing: **38** calories

Figure 10.11 The Volume of Food You Eat Affects Satiety
Low-volume, high-calorie foods can be much less satisfying than higher-volume, lower-calorie foods.

Include Some Protein and Fat in Your Meals

Of all the dietary substances that increase satiety, protein will have the most dramatic effect. Even though the mechanism is unknown, this is likely one of the reasons why high-protein diets tend to reduce hunger and can help in weight loss.[61] Because fat slows the movement of food from the stomach into the small intestine, it can also prolong satiety. Therefore, including some lean protein and fat in all meals and even with snacks can help increase satiety between meals.

However, you don't want to add high-saturated-fat foods such as whole milk and/or whole-milk cheese, fatty cuts of meat, and butter, because eating these foods to feel full will come at the expense of your heart. It would be better to add lean meat, skinless chicken, fish, nuts, and oils, which are kinder to a person's waist and heart. (Note: Unsaturated fat still contains 9 calories per gram, so excessive amounts of nuts and oils, even though these are heart healthy, can quickly add excess calories.)

Look at the difference between the foods shown in **Figure 10.11**. The snack and dinner on the left are low in volume, but high in calories. The foods on the right are high in volume but have almost 500 fewer calories combined! These higher-volume foods will be more satisfying for fewer calories.

Use MyPlate as a Weight-Loss Guide

Meals that contain a high volume of fruits and vegetables, whole grains, some lean protein, and modest amounts of fat are a smart combination for weight loss, so a diet that contains all the five food groups can be used to lose weight. Most importantly, this type of diet is well balanced and will meet your daily nutrient needs.

Reducing caloric intake a little at a time can result in healthy weight loss. A 180-pound, overweight person who consumes 2,800 calories daily can reduce his or her intake to 2,400 to 2,600 calories for a calorie deficit of 200–400 calories per day. He or she will then lose 5 to 10 pounds in about three months. Small changes, like switching from full-fat to nonfat dairy products or replacing the afternoon soda with a glass of water, will contribute to this calorie reduction. Use ChooseMyPlate .gov to eat a variety of foods, and replace higher-calorie foods with lower-calorie options within each food group for a satisfying diet.

If this person added some extra physical activity, he or she could further increase that daily calorie deficit. Let's now look at the other side of the energy equation: energy expenditure.

Move to Lose

Research shows that regular physical activity is associated with a healthier body weight. Some individuals may need to devote 45 minutes or more to participation in moderate-intensity activities daily to prevent overweight or to aid in weight loss for those who need to lose weight.[62] Moderately intense physical activity would be the equivalent of walking 3.5 miles per hour (**Table 10.4**). Regular physical activity can also displace sedentary activity such as watching television, which often leads to mindless snacking on energy-dense foods.[63] Going for a walk and expending calories rather than watching television while snacking on a bag of chips will provide caloric benefits beyond the exercise alone.

A way to assess if you are incorporating enough physical activity into your day is to count your steps (such as with a pedometer). Research suggests that accumulating 10,000 steps daily, which is the equivalent of walking 5 miles, can help reduce the risk of becoming overweight.[64] Americans, on average, accumulate only 900 to 3,000 steps daily.[65] To reach 10,000 steps, a conscious effort is needed by most people to keep moving. See the Table Tips called "Get UP and MOVE" for some ideas for fun ways to expend more energy during the day.

Table 10.4
Calories Used during Activities

Moderate Physical Activity	Approximate Calories/Hour for a 154-lb Person*	Vigorous Physical Activity	Approximate Calories/Hour for a 154-lb Person*
Hiking	370	Running/jogging (5 mph)	590
Light gardening/yard work	330	Bicycling (> 10 mph)	590
Dancing	330	Swimming (slow freestyle laps)	510
Golf (walking and carrying clubs)	330	Aerobics	480
Bicycling (< 10 mph)	290	Walking (4.5 mph)	460
Walking (3.5 mph)	280	Heavy yard work (chopping wood)	440
Weight lifting (general light workout)	220	Weight lifting (vigorous effort)	440
Stretching	180	Basketball (vigorous)	440

*Note: Calories burned per hour will be higher for persons who weigh more than 154 lbs (70 kg) and lower for persons who weigh less.

Wearing a pedometer, like the one shown here, can help you track your steps. Remember to aim for 10,000 steps per day.

behavior modification Changing behaviors to improve health. Identifying and altering eating patterns that contribute to weight gain or impede weight loss is behavior modification.

Break Bad Habits

Have you ever heard about the "freshman 15"? If you have, you may be relieved to find out that a 15-pound weight gain is not inevitable for college freshmen. In fact, research to support the "freshman 15" is rather slim. Some research has found that weight gain didn't occur at all or didn't occur in the majority of the students during the first semester (the length of the study) or the entire first year.[66] Other studies found that students gained less than 5 pounds, on average, and one of these studies showed that certain behaviors such as snacking in the evening, consumption of junk foods, and the number of meals eaten on weekends were associated with weight gain.[67]

However, if students get in the habit of skipping breakfast, hitting the vending machine for a midmorning snack, and mindlessly munching late at night, they may find weight management during their freshman year to be an uphill struggle and would benefit from some behavior modification.

Behavior modification focuses on changing the behaviors that contribute to weight gain or impede weight loss. Several behavior-modification techniques can be used to identify and change poor eating behaviors. These techniques include self-monitoring the behaviors by keeping a food log, controlling environmental cues that trigger eating when not hungry, and learning how to better manage stress.

Do you really know when, why, and what you eat? Understanding the habits and emotions that drive your eating patterns can help you change your less-than-healthy eating behaviors. In a 12-month study of over 120 overweight/obese women, journaling in a food log was found to be one of the key strategies that helped the women not only meet their weight-loss goal of losing 10 percent of their body weight by 6 months but also to maintain the weight loss at 12 months.[68] In fact, the women in the study who consistently kept food logs lost about 6 pounds more than those who didn't journal.

Keeping a food log is a great way to track the kinds of foods you eat during the day, when and where you eat them, your moods, and hunger ratings. You can use this information to minimize or eliminate the eating behaviors that interfere with weight management.

A typical day's log might be similar to the one in **Figure 10.12** and is a good way to uncover habits that are common to people who struggle with their weight. For example, a study of overweight women who typically skipped breakfast showed that once they started consuming cereal for breakfast, they indulged in less impulsive snacking.[69] Eating a bowl of high-fiber whole-grain cereal (approximately 200 calories) will likely appease a person's morning hunger and help bypass an 11 a.m. vending machine snack such as a package of 270-calorie cookies and a 210-calorie sports drink. This one behavior change would not only save 280 calories in the morning, but also reduce the calories from added sugars in the diet and add more nutrition to the day. Similarly, adding a less-energy-dense salad at lunch could help increase satiety and lessen the desire to eat a couple of the cookies.

Because studying for exams can be anxiety-inducing for students and cause them to munch even though they aren't hungry, they should think twice about studying in their dorm rooms or other areas where they are surrounded by snacks. Rather, studying at the campus library, an environment where eating is typically prohibited, would be a better bet. Exercising before or after studying would also be a healthier way for students to relieve stress rather than eating their way through a bag of snacks.

Changing behaviors that have become unhealthy habits is another important piece of improving weight management. Individuals who eat "out of habit" and in response to their emotions need to replace this unnecessary eating to better manage their weight. The Table Tips called "Adopt Some Healthy Habits" lists some healthy behaviors that can easily be incorporated into your life.

Food Log

For: Hannah

Date: Monday, September 6

Food and drink	Time eaten	What I ate/ Where I ate it	Hunger level*	Mood †
Breakfast		Skipped it	3	G
Snack	11 a.m.	Oreo cookies, PowerAde from vending machine during morning class.	5	E
Lunch	1:30 p.m.	Ham and cheese sandwich, 2 large M&M cookies in student union cafeteria.	4	B
Snack				
Dinner	6:30 p.m.	Hamburger, french fries, salad at kitchen table	4	F
Snack	7 p.m. to 10 p.m.	Large bag of tortilla chips and entire bag of Pepperidge Farm Milano cookies while studying at kitchen table	1	I

*Hunger levels (1–5): 1 = not hungry; 5 = super hungry

† **Moods:**
A = Happy; B = Content; C = Bored; D = Depressed; E = Rushed; F = Stressed; G = Tired; H = Lonely; I = Anxious; J = Angry

Figure 10.12 Food Log
Keeping track of when, where, and what you eat, as well as why you ate it, can yield some surprising information. Do you think you sometimes eat out of boredom or stress, rather than because you're hungry?

Dealing with Extreme Obesity

Very obese people are at a high risk for conditions such as heart disease and stroke, and even premature death. More aggressive treatments that go beyond just trying to eat less and exercise more, such as following a very low-calorie diet, medications, and/or surgery, are often recommended for these individuals. Let's look at each of these options.

A Very Low-Calorie Diet

On her television show in 1988, a very petite Oprah Winfrey beamed with joy after having lost 67 pounds using a **very low-calorie diet**. Oprah achieved her weight loss by consuming a liquid protein diet, or *protein-sparing modified fast*. Such protein-rich diets provide fewer than 800 calories daily, are very low in or devoid of carbohydrates, and have minimal amounts of fat. They are designed to help individuals at high risk of disease drop a substantial amount of weight in a short amount of time. However, they are not a long-term solution. After consuming the diet for 12 to 16 weeks, the dieter is switched over to a well-balanced, low-calorie diet.

Very low-calorie diets have to be supplemented with vitamins and minerals and must be supervised by a medical doctor, as they can cause dangerous electrolyte imbalances as well as gallstones, constipation, fatigue, hair loss, and other side effects. The National Institutes of Health doesn't recommend very low-calorie diets because well-balanced low-calorie diets are just as effective in producing a similar amount of weight loss after one year and are less dangerous.[70]

In the 1980s Oprah Winfrey reached her goal weight by consuming a very low-calorie, liquid-protein diet. She has since regained and lost the weight several times, and often publicly discusses the challenges of maintaining a stable, healthy weight.

very low-calorie diet A diet of fewer than 800 calories per day and high in protein.

The average weight gain between Thanksgiving and New Year's Day is about a pound. But many people don't lose this extra weight and add to it every year.

Medication

Some prescription medications can help a person lose weight. The drugs either suppress the appetite or inhibit the absorption of fat in the intestinal tract. For example, the drug sibutramine (trade name Meridia) reduces hunger and increases thermogenesis, which increases energy expenditure. The drug can also increase a person's heart rate and blood pressure. Therefore, it may not be appropriate for those who have hypertension, which tends to occur often in overweight individuals. In fact, because all drugs have side effects, their use must be monitored by a doctor.

Orlistat (trade name Xenical; recall that this drug is discussed in Chapter 3) inhibits an intestinal enzyme that is needed to break down fat. If it isn't broken down, the fat (and calories) will not be absorbed by the body. Up to about one-third of the dietary fat will be blocked and expelled in the stool. Orlistat has to be taken at each meal and should accompany a diet that provides no more than about 30 percent of its calories from fat. Because fat is lost in the stool, the drug can cause oily and more frequent stools, flatulence, and oily discharge.[71] Ironically, these side effects may help an individual adhere to a low-fat diet, as these effects are more pronounced if a high-fat meal is consumed. Today, a reduced-strength version of orlistat (trade name Alli) is approved for over-the-counter sale. It is intended to be used in conjunction with a low-fat, low-calorie diet and regular exercise to treat obesity, and can have the same unpleasant side effects as the full-strength version. Because of the recent reports of rare, but serious, cases of liver damage in individuals using Xenical and Alli, both of these drugs must now carry warnings on their labels.

Other weight-loss drugs that have been approved by the FDA include Belviq and Qsymia. Belviq works by affecting a part of the brain that regulates hunger. Qsymia is a combination of two drugs, phentermine, an appetite suppressant, and topiramate, used to treat epilepsy and migraines. Both drugs should be consumed in conjunction with a healthy diet and routine exercise program and have been shown in studies to help individuals lose from 3 to 9 percent of their body weight compared with those who were given a placebo.[72]

Sometimes the side effects of weight-loss medications can be so serious that the medication must be withdrawn from the market. For instance, the FDA has prohibited the sale of supplements that contain ephedra (also called ma huang), the plant source for ephedrine.[73] Ephedrine has been shown to cause an increased risk of hypertension, stroke, and heart problems. In 2003, baseball player Steve Bechler died at age 23 after taking a weight-loss supplement containing ephedrine during spring training. Ephedrine was determined to have contributed to his death.

Whereas individuals who take prescription medications to lose weight have been shown to lose as much as 20 pounds, these drugs should be coupled with, and can't replace, a lower-calorie diet, regular physical activity, and behavior modification for long-term weight loss.

Surgery

In 1998, approximately 13,000 obese patients went under the knife to reduce the size of their stomachs. Years later, in 2014, an estimated 193,000 people in the United Stated had **bariatric surgery**.[74] In one version of this surgery, **gastric bypass surgery**, the majority of the stomach is stapled shut (shown in **Figure 10.13a**). This reduces the size of the stomach so that it holds about ¼ cup of fluid. Food consumed leaves the small stomach pouch through a surgically added intestinal loop that bypasses the original stomach and attaches directly to the small intestine. After the surgery, these individuals need to consume small, frequent meals because the

bariatric surgery Surgical procedures that reduce the functional volume of the stomach so that less food is eaten. Such surgeries are sometimes used to treat extreme obesity.

gastric bypass surgery A type of bariatric surgery that reduces the functional volume of the stomach to minimize the amount of food eaten.

a In gastric bypass, the stomach is closed off and a small pouch is left that can hold about ¼ cup of food at a time.

Path of food

Staples

Bypassed stomach

Unused portion of small intestine

Small intestine

b In gastric banding, a silicone band is placed around the top of the stomach to greatly reduce its size.

Path of food

New, smaller stomach pouch

Band

Stomach

Figure 10.13 Surgeries for Extreme Obesity
Bariatric surgeries such as gastric bypass and gastric banding restrict food intake and promote malabsorption.

stomach pouch can only expand to a maximum of about 5 ounces, the size of a woman's fist. Individuals not only eat less because of their smaller stomachs, but have higher levels of satiety and lower levels of hunger after the surgery. This effect on their appetite may be associated with lower levels of the hormone ghrelin due to the loss of stomach area after the surgery.[75]

Because both the majority of the stomach and the upper part of the small intestine are bypassed after the surgery, individuals can experience deficiencies of vitamin B_{12}, iron, and calcium. (Vitamin B_{12} needs intrinsic factor from the stomach to be absorbed, which is missing after surgery. Iron and calcium are typically absorbed in the upper part of the small intestine, which is now bypassed.) Supplements must be given because of these deficiencies.

Another type of bariatric surgery is **gastric banding**, in which a silicone band is placed around the top of the stomach to create a small pouch with a very narrow opening at the bottom for the food to pass through (Figure 10.13b). This delays the emptying of the stomach contents so that a person will feel fuller longer. The doctor can adjust the opening of the pouch by inflating or deflating the band.

Although dramatic amounts of weight loss can occur and research has shown that incidences of hypertension, diabetes, high blood cholesterol levels, and sleep apnea have been reduced among people who've had the surgery, there are also risks involved. Less than 1 percent of those undergoing bariatric surgery experience complications such as gallstones and less than 0.1 percent die from the surgery.[76] After surgery, individuals need to be monitored long term by medical and nutrition professionals to ensure that they remain healthy and meet their nutritional needs.

Another type of surgery, **liposuction**, is less about health and more about physical appearance. During this procedure, a doctor removes subcutaneous fat from the abdomen, hips, or thighs (and sometimes other areas of the body) by suctioning it out with a penlike instrument. People often undergo liposuction to get rid of **cellulite**, which isn't a medical term, but refers to the fat cells that give the skin a dimpled appearance. Complications such as infections, scars, and swelling can arise after liposuction. Fat can also reappear at the site where it was removed, so the results of liposuction may not be permanent.

gastric banding A type of bariatric surgery that uses a silicone band to reduce the size of the stomach so that less food is needed to feel full.

liposuction The surgical removal of subcutaneous fat with a penlike instrument. Usually performed on the abdomen, hips, and thighs, and/or other areas of the body.

cellulite A nonmedical term that refers to fat cells under the skin that give it a ripplelike appearance. Contrary to popular belief, cellulite is no different from other fat in the body.

Extreme Measures

Desiree is 40 years old, 5 feet 4 inches tall, and weighs 235 pounds, which is 100 pounds more than she should in order to be healthy. She has spent the majority of her adult life trying to lose this excessive amount of weight, which she has been carrying around since her college graduation decades ago. She works as an accountant, and so sits at her desk all day crunching numbers for her company. Her days are long, and her job is stressful. She often gets home late and feels too tired to cook herself a healthy meal. Take-out dinners and frozen yogurt is her go-to daily dinner and sweet treat to release her stress. Frustrated with her weight, Desiree is always trying the latest diet trend, but any weight loss that she achieves is quickly followed with regaining all of it back once she stops the diet.

Because Desiree's BMI is over 40, she is considered to have **extreme obesity**. Her weight and other related factors have caused her blood pressure to skyrocket. Because her high blood pressure is increasing her risk for stroke, her doctor wants her to consider a more aggressive weight-loss treatment to help her lower her weight.

Desiree decided to get serious about losing weight and started to look into her options. Her doctor told her that she could go on a medically supervised very low-calorie diet and work with a registered dietitian nutritionist (RDN) to help her change her eating behaviors, take medication to help her lose some weight, or undergo bariatric surgery.

Think About It

Based on Desiree's lifestyle and behaviors, which weight-loss option do you think would be best for her?

The Bottom Line

Very low-calorie diets, medications, and surgery may be viable options for those with extreme obesity, but they are not without risks. For one woman's experience of deciding how to deal with her obesity, see the Health Connection: A Case Study, called "Extreme Measures." For those who are overweight, the safest route to a healthy weight is to make incremental diet and lifestyle changes to take in fewer calories and expend more calories. Of course, the best overall strategy for weight management is to avoid becoming overweight in the first place.

LO 10.5 **The Take-Home Message** For successful, long-term weight loss, people need to reduce their daily calorie intake, increase their physical activity, and change their behavior. Adding low-energy-dense, high-volume vegetables, fruit, and fiber along with some lean protein and healthy oils to the diet can help in satiety and reduce unplanned snacking. Incorporating physical activity daily can help with weight loss. Changing unhealthy habits by restructuring the environment to minimize or eliminate the eating behaviors that interfere with weight loss can also help shed extra pounds.

extreme obesity Having a BMI > 40.

How Can You Maintain Weight Loss?

LO 10.6 Describe a basic plan for healthy weight maintenance.

You, or someone you know, may be familiar with the typical fad diet experience: the triumphant rush associated with the dropping of 10 pounds, the disappointment that sets in when 15 pounds are regained, then a new round of hope when 10 of them are re-shed. This fluctuation is known as **weight cycling**, and some research suggests that it can lead to problems such as diabetes and gallbladder disease, not to mention depression and feelings of frustration.[77] However, other research suggests that it does not cause major health issues.[78]

Research suggests that weight cycling may not be as common as previously thought. Studies have shown that people who lose weight are able to keep it off for at least 5 years.[79] These people were successful because they maintained their physical activity habits and positive behavior changes after they reached their weight goal. They commonly limited the intake of fatty foods, monitored their calorie intake, consumed breakfast, and ate nearly five times a day, on average. (For many people, eating smaller meals allows them to avoid becoming ravenous and overeating at the next meal.) The majority of them routinely weighed themselves and maintained a high level of daily physical activity, expending the energy equivalent of walking four miles a day.[80] This suggests that weight loss can be maintained as long as the individual doesn't abandon the healthy habits that promoted the weight loss and revert to the unhealthy habits that caused the excess weight in the first place.

Physical activity can also help those who've lost weight close the "energy gap." After weight loss, a person will have lower overall energy needs, as there is less body weight to maintain. The **energy gap** is the difference in daily calories that are needed for weight maintenance before and after weight loss.[81] Researchers have estimated that the energy gap is about 8 calories per pound of lost weight.[82]

For example, someone who lost 30 pounds would need approximately 240 fewer calories a day to maintain the new, lower body weight. This person can eat 240 fewer calories, expend this amount of calories through added physical activity, or do a combination of both. Because the environment we live in seems to encourage eating more than discourage it, researchers feel that increasing daily physical activity is likely the easier way to close the energy gap and help maintain the weight loss.[83] *Adding* something (physical activity) to your lifestyle is often easier than *removing* something (calories). Regular physical activity may help prevent weight gain as you age.[84]

LO 10.6 **The Take-Home Message** People who lose weight are most likely to keep it off if they maintain the positive diet and lifestyle habits that helped them lose the weight. Eating less and/or exercising more will help close the energy gap after weight loss.

How Can You Gain Weight Healthfully?

LO 10.7 Describe how to gain weight healthfully.

For people who are underweight, weight gain can be as challenging and frustrating as losing weight is for an overweight individual. The major difference is that the thin

weight cycling The repeated gain and loss of body weight.

energy gap The difference between the numbers of calories needed to maintain weight before and after weight loss.

person rarely gets sympathy from others. Like overweight individuals, those who are underweight experience an energy imbalance. In their case, however, they consume fewer calories than they expend.

People who want to gain weight need to do the opposite of those who are trying to lose weight. Whereas waist watchers hunt for the lower-calorie foods, individuals seeking to gain weight should make each bite more energy dense. These individuals need to add at least 500 calories to their daily energy intake. This will enable them to add about a pound of extra body weight weekly.

Of course, someone who wants to gain weight should not just load up on high-fat, high-calorie foods. The quality of the extra calories is very important. Snacking on an extra 500 calories of jelly beans will add 500 calories of sugar and little nutrition. Rather, these individuals should make energy-dense, nutritious choices from a variety of foods within each food group. For example, instead of eating a slice of toast in the morning, they should choose a waffle. Adding coleslaw rather than cabbage will increase the calories in a salad-bar lunch more than tenfold. **Figure 10.14** contrasts more- and less-energy-dense foods within each food group. Eating snacks during the day will also add calories. The Table Tips on "Healthy Snacks for Healthy Weight Gain" provides easy and portable snack ideas.

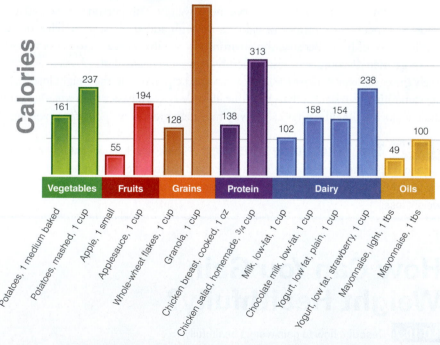

Figure 10.14 More- and Less-Energy-Dense Food Choices, by Food Group
Choosing more energy-dense, but still nutritious, foods can help those who are underweight gain weight.

Regular exercise and resistance training will stimulate muscle growth and help avoid excess fat storage. Remember that it takes time to gain weight and build sufficient muscle mass. Be patient and continue to choose healthy foods until you reach your goal weight.

LO 10.7 **The Take-Home Message** People who want to gain weight need to add energy-dense foods to their diet so that they take in more energy than they expend. Adding nutrient-dense snacks between meals is an easy way to increase the number of calories consumed daily.

What Is Disordered Eating and What Are the Warning Signs?

LO 10.8 Define disordered eating and discuss the warning signs and treatment options for eating disorders.

Attaining a healthy weight, whether it means gaining or losing a few pounds, is a worthwhile goal that can result in lowered risk of disease and a more productive life. However, it's important to reach and maintain a healthy weight in a positive way. Patterns of eating that involve severe calorie restriction, purging, or other abnormal behaviors can be severely damaging to health. Whereas disordered eating and eating disorders are diagnosed as psychological disorders rather than nutrition-related issues, it's important to be aware of them and recognize their symptoms.

The term **disordered eating** is used to describe a variety of eating patterns considered abnormal and potentially harmful. Refusing to eat, compulsive eating, binge eating, restrictive eating, vomiting after eating, and abusing diet pills, laxatives, or diuretics are all examples of disordered eating behaviors. **Eating disorders**, in contrast, are diagnosed by meeting specific criteria that include disordered eating behaviors as well as other factors (see **Table 10.5**). It is possible for someone to engage in disordered eating patterns without having a clinically diagnosed eating disorder.

There are three main types of eating disorders that someone could develop, including anorexia nervosa, bulimia nervosa, and binge eating disorder. In the United States, approximately 20 million women and 10 million men struggle with eating disorders at some time in their life.[85] Adolescent and young adult females in predominantly white upper-middle- and middle-class families are the population with highest prevalence. However, eating disorders and disordered eating among males, minorities, and other age groups are increasing.[86] In fact, about 10 percent of all cases of anorexia nervosa and bulimia nervosa occur in men. And this may be an underestimate, as many men, as well as women, feel ashamed or embarrassed and may hide their problem. The prevalence of eating disorders among both males and females is probably higher than reported. Anyone can develop one of these conditions regardless of gender, age, race, ethnicity, or social status.

Although the highest rates of disordered eating patterns occur among females, males are not simmune. Adolescents in particular can feel pressure to achieve a certain body image.

No Single Factor Causes Eating Disorders

Although there is typically no one cause of disordered eating and eating disorders, there are certain factors that may increase one's risk for developing these conditions. Current research suggests that eating disorders are prompted by a complex network of sociocultural, genetic, and preexisting psychological factors (**Figure 10.15**).

disordered eating Abnormal and potentially harmful eating behaviors that do not meet specific criteria for an eating disorder.

eating disorders The term used to describe psychological illnesses that involve specific abnormal eating behaviors, such as anorexia nervosa (self-starvation), bulimia nervosa (bingeing and purging), and binge eating disorder.

Table 10.5

Diagnostic Criteria for Eating Disorders

Eating Disorder	Diagnostic Criteria
Anorexia Nervosa	• Restriction of energy intake relative to requirements leading to a significantly low body weight in the context of age, sex, developmental trajectory, and physical health • Intense fear of gaining weight or becoming fat, even though underweight • Disturbance in the way one's body weight or shape is experienced, undue influence of body weight or shape on self-evaluation, or denial of the seriousness of the current low body weight

Bulimia Nervosa	• Recurrent episodes of binge eating, which is characterized by BOTH of the following:
	  ➤ Eating in a discrete amount of time (within a 2-hour period) large amounts of food
	  ➤ Sense of lack of control over eating during an episode
	• Recurrent inappropriate compensatory behavior in order to prevent weight gain (purging)
	• The binge eating and compensatory behaviors both occur, on average, at least once per week for three months.
	• Self-evaluation is unduly influenced by body shape and weight.
	• The disturbance does not occur exclusively during episodes of anorexia nervosa.

Binge Eating Disorder	• Recurrent episodes of binge eating. An episode of binge eating is characterized by both of the following:
	  ➤ Eating, in a discrete period of time, an amount of food that is definitely larger than most people would eat in a similar period of time under similar circumstances
	  ➤ A sense of lack of control over eating during the episode (for example, a feeling that one cannot stop eating or control what or how much one is eating)
	• The binge eating episodes are associated with three (or more) of the following:
	  ➤ Eating much more rapidly than normal
	  ➤ Eating until feeling uncomfortably full
	  ➤ Eating large amounts of food when not feeling physically hungry
	  ➤ Eating alone because of feeling embarrassed by how much one is eating
	  ➤ Feeling disgusted with oneself, depressed, or very guilty afterward
	• Marked distress regarding binge eating is present.
	• The binge eating occurs, on average, at least once a week for three months.
	• The binge eating is not associated with the recurrent use of inappropriate compensatory behavior (for example, purging) and does not occur exclusively during the course of anorexia nervosa, bulimia nervosa, or avoidant/restrictive food intake disorder.

Feeding or Eating Disorders Not Elsewhere Classified	• Disordered eating behaviors that do not meet the criteria for anorexia nervosa, bulimia nervosa, or binge eating disorder, including orthorexia and night eating syndrome.

Sociocultural Factors

Some researchers theorize that the higher prevalence of eating disorders in females is due in part to the greater societal pressure they experience to be thin and have a "perfect" figure.[87] Thinness is too often associated with beauty, success, and happiness in our society, as evidenced by images in magazines and on billboards of fashion models and celebrities with abnormally low body weights. Even the average BMI of Miss America winners has decreased from 22 to 16.9 in the past 80 years, while BMIs of girls and women has increased.[88] Many females don't realize that nearly all media images have been digitally enhanced and do not depict the people as they appear in real life. Instead, they come to believe that extreme thinness is both possible and desirable and that they cannot be beautiful, successful, or happy unless they achieve it. Some may feel such extreme body dissatisfaction that they try to lose weight at any cost, including engaging in disordered eating behaviors.

Men also experience societal pressure to have a specific look, often focusing on muscle mass and looking "cut." They, too, can be influenced by images of professional athletes, body builders, celebrities, and models in advertising, and some may strive to achieve the same look through extreme, unhealthy behaviors.

Genetic Factors

Researchers have not found a gene or genes that promote eating disorders; however, they theorize that a combination of genetic predisposition and environmental

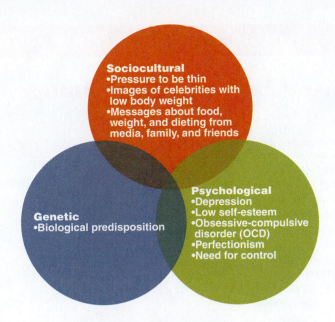

Figure 10.15 Factors That Contribute to Eating Disorders

Sociocultural
•Pressure to be thin
•Images of celebrities with low body weight
•Messages about food, weight, and dieting from media, family, and friends

Genetic
•Biological predisposition

Psychological
•Depression
•Low self-esteem
•Obsessive-compulsive disorder (OCD)
•Perfectionism
•Need for control

factors can increase an individual's risk. Certainly, eating disorders have been observed to "run in families." For example, an adolescent female has a greatly increased risk of developing an eating disorder if she has a sibling with an eating disorder, even if she does not live with that sibling.[89]

Psychological Factors

Depression and anxiety are common in people with an eating disorder,[90] as is obsessive-compulsive disorder (OCD),[91] a psychiatric illness characterized by intrusive thoughts that something bad will happen if a certain behavior is not repeated in a certain way. Not only women but men diagnosed with eating disorders have higher rates of other psychiatric illness, compared with men who do not have eating disorders.[92] Alcohol and other substance abuse disorders are four times more common in people with eating disorders than in the general population.[93]

A personality trait that can contribute to eating disorders is perfectionism, as an inability to reach unrealistic standards (such as in school or in athletic competition) can lead to a sense of failure and lowered self-worth. Many people who struggle with eating disorders are trying to gain some control in their lives. When external factors feel out of control, the person with an eating disorder gets a sense of security from being able to control food intake and body weight. Other common psychological factors include lack of self-esteem, high family expectations, and family dysfunction.

The most common eating disorders are anorexia nervosa, bulimia nervosa, and binge eating disorder. Let's take a look at each type of disorder and the characteristics that make each one unique.

Anorexia Nervosa Results from Severe Calorie Restriction

Anorexia nervosa is a serious, potentially life-threatening eating disorder that is characterized by self-starvation and excessive weight loss. People who suffer from anorexia nervosa have an intense fear of gaining weight or being fat. This fear causes them to control their food intake by restricting the amount they consume, resulting in significant weight loss.

People with anorexia nervosa have a distorted sense of body image and usually see themselves as fat even though they are underweight (you can read more about the concept of body image in the Nutrition in the Real World feature, "A Closer Look at Body Image" on page 404). This misperception of body size contributes to

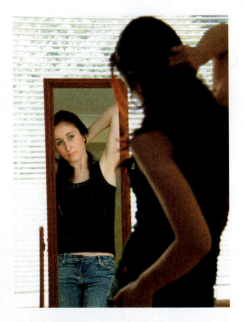

Societal pressure to be thin can cause people to feel fat when they look in the mirror regardless of their body weight. Dissatisfaction with one's body can lead to disordered eating behaviors.

nutrition in the Real World

A Closer Look at Body Image

What Is Body Image?

Body image refers to the way that you perceive and what you believe about your physical appearance, whether you are looking in the mirror or picturing yourself in your mind.[13] Most people think of body image as being about body weight and shape, but it actually refers to any physical attribute such as skin color, hair texture, or height.

Body image can be further defined as having positive or negative characteristics. People with a positive body image view themselves as they truly are (no distortion) and overall feel comfortable and confident in and about their body. They engage in healthy eating and exercise behaviors and don't spend a lot of time worrying about weight, dieting, or changing their looks using extreme measures. They accept their body and don't define their self-worth based on physical appearances.[14] In contrast, those with a negative body image often have distorted views of the way they look and may view their shape as larger than they actually are. This is especially true of people with anorexia nervosa. Additionally, they may feel ashamed, uncomfortable, or self-conscious about their physical appearance and spend a large amount of time focusing on their weight or aspects of their looks that they perceive as unattractive. They often believe that only others are attractive.[15] A negative body image can contribute to the development or continuation of unhealthy behaviors, like eating disorders, in many individuals.

What Is Body Dysmorphic Disorder?

Body dysmorphic disorder (BDD) is a mental illness in which a person's preoccupation with minor or imaginary physical flaws causes significant distress or impairment in work, school, or other areas of functioning. BDD is estimated to affect slightly more than 2 percent of the U.S. population and frequently occurs along with other psychiatric disorders, such as obsessive-compulsive disorder, anorexia nervosa, and clinical depression.[16]

Muscle dysmorphia, also referred to as "bigorexia" or "reverse anorexia," is a specific type of BDD that typically occurs in males who have a well-defined muscular build but view themselves as being small or weak.[17] Symptoms of muscle dysmorphia include extreme exercise (especially weight lifting) and attention to diet, anxiety when missing a workout, constant mirror checking, use of anabolic steroids to enhance muscle mass, and neglecting family, friends, or work in order to exercise. Media influence on men and their muscle mass and size is thought to be a major contributing factor in the increasing prevalence of muscle dysmorphia. Anyone with these symptoms should seek professional help and treatment, as they can get worse over time.

How Can You Attain a Positive Body Image?

Many factors can influence your body image, including family, friends, peers, media, and culture. We live in a society where certain images are labeled "ideal," yet are not achievable by most. Nonetheless, we strive to get the

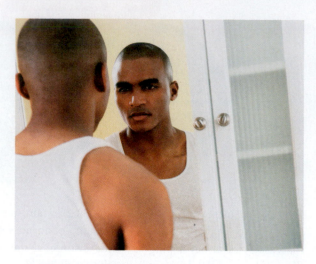

Both men and women can experience issues with body image.

"perfect" body through any means necessary. Comparing our bodies to those of friends, models, and celebrities that we view as more attractive only leads to lowered self-esteem and feeling "not good enough."

The following are strategies to help you attain a positive body image:[18]

- Know and accept what determines your physical characteristics (genetics, stage of life, nutritional intake, activity levels).
- Avoid dieting and eat normally by responding to hunger and fullness cues.
- Avoid comparing yourself to others, especially models and celebrities, based on weight, shape, or size.
- Recognize that you are a whole person and not just individual parts.
- Respect yourself and others based on the qualities of character and accomplishments, rather than appearance.

---

body dysmorphic disorder A mental illness in which a person is excessively concerned about and preoccupied by a perceived defect in his or her body.

the behavior of restricting food intake in order to lose (more) weight. For instance, someone with anorexia nervosa might eat only a piece of fruit and a small container of yogurt during an entire day. They may also have a fear of eating certain foods, such as those that contain fat and sugar. They believe that these foods (and possibly others) will make them fat, regardless of how much they eat. Some may also exercise excessively as a means of controlling their weight.

There are numerous health consequences that can occur with anorexia nervosa, and some can be fatal.[94] A recent study that reviewed nearly fifty years of research found that anorexia nervosa has the highest mortality rate of any psychiatric disorder.[95] One of the most serious health effects is an electrolyte imbalance, specifically low blood potassium, which can also occur if someone with anorexia nervosa engages in episodes of purging. An electrolyte imbalance can lead to an irregular heart rhythm and possibly heart failure, which can be fatal. Because someone with anorexia nervosa is not getting enough calories, the body begins to slow or shut down some processes in an effort to conserve energy for its most vital functions. The person may experience a decrease in heart rate and blood pressure, overall weakness and fatigue, and hair loss. The digestive process also slows down, which often results in constipation, bloating, and delayed gastric emptying.

Someone who's lost an extreme amount of body fat may experience a drop in body temperature and feel cold even when it is hot outside. In an effort to regulate body temperature, this person's body may begin to grow **lanugo** (downy hair), particularly on the face and arms. Dehydration, iron deficiency, menstrual disturbances, and osteoporosis are also negative health effects caused by anorexia nervosa.

Bulimia Nervosa Involves Cycles of Binge Eating and Purging

Bulimia nervosa is another type of eating disorder that can be life-threatening. During times of binge eating, the person lacks control over eating and consumes larger than normal amounts of food in a short period of time. Following the binge, the person counters the binge with some type of **purging**. Many people assume that bulimics purge only by vomiting, but self-induced vomiting is just one form. Purging can be described as any behavior that assists in "getting rid" of food to prevent weight gain or to promote weight loss. This can include excessive exercise; abuse of diet pills, laxatives, or diuretics; and strict dieting or fasting.

Most of the health consequences that occur with bulimia nervosa are associated with self-induced vomiting, such as tears in the esophagus, swollen parotid glands, tooth decay and gum disease (due to stomach acid in the mouth), and broken blood vessels in the eyes (due to pressure from vomiting). Electrolyte imbalance may occur with bulimia nervosa and can be fatal, just as with anorexia nervosa. People with bulimia nervosa may also experience dehydration and constipation due to frequent episodes of binge eating and purging.[96]

Laxative abuse can also cause serious medical complications depending on the type, amount, and length of time the person has used them. Laxatives used repeatedly can cause constipation, dehydration due to fluid loss in the intestines, electrolyte imbalances, fluid retention, bloody stools, and impaired bowel function.

People with binge eating disorder often eat in secret.

Binge Eating Disorder Involves Compulsive Overeating

Binge eating disorder is characterized by recurrent episodes of binge eating without purging. People who have binge eating disorder eat without regard to physiological cues. They may eat for emotional reasons, and feel out of control while eating. The overeating results in physical and psychological discomfort. Many people who struggle with this type of eating disorder will often eat in secret and feel ashamed about their behaviors.

The health effects of binge eating disorder are commonly those that are associated with obesity, because most people who struggle with binge eating disorder are of

lanugo Very fine, soft hair on the face and arms of people with anorexia nervosa.

purging Measures taken to prevent weight gain or to lose weight after consuming food; examples include self-induced vomiting, laxatives, diuretics (water pills), excessive exercise, and/ or fasting.

People with night eating syndrome may consume more than half their day's calories between 8 p.m. and 6 a.m.

normal or heavier-than-average weight. Health effects may include high blood pressure, high cholesterol levels, heart disease, type 2 diabetes, and gallbladder disease.[97]

Other Disordered Eating Behaviors Can Be Harmful

In addition to anorexia nervosa, bulimia nervosa, and binge eating disorder, there are other abnormal eating behaviors that can be harmful and require treatment. These include orthorexia, night eating syndrome, and pica.

Orthorexia is defined as an obsession with "healthy or righteous eating" and often begins with someone's simple desire to live a healthy lifestyle. Someone with orthorexia fixates on defining the "right" foods, and will spend just as much time and energy thinking about food as someone with anorexia nervosa or bulimia nervosa. While this person may not obsess about calories, they think about the overall health benefits and how the food was processed, prepared, etc. Various factors can contribute to this obsession for healthy foods, including hearing something negative about a food or food group, which then leads to completely eliminating the food or foods from their diet. Be aware that the restrictive nature of orthorexia has the potential to develop into anorexia nervosa.

Night eating syndrome is a unique combination of disordered eating, a sleep disorder, and a mood disorder.[98] Someone with this syndrome consumes the majority of daily calories after the evening meal, as well as wakes up during the night, possibly even several times, to eat. In addition, the person typically does not have an appetite during the morning hours and consumes very little throughout the day. One study found that people with night eating syndrome consume 56 percent of their 24-hour calorie intake between the hours of 8:00 p.m. and 6:00 a.m. This study also found that people with night eating syndrome generally do not binge eat with each awakening; rather, they eat smaller portions of food on several occasions throughout the night.[99]

Pica refers to a strong, persistent desire to eat, lick, or chew nonnutritive substances, such as clay, dirt, or chalk, for a period of at least 1 month. Consuming nonfood substances can cause serious medical complications such as intestinal obstruction, intestinal perforation, infections, or lead poisoning.

Because orthorexia, night eating syndrome, and pica do not meet the diagnostic criteria for anorexia nervosa, bulimia nervosa, or binge eating disorder, but still require treatment, they fall into the diagnostic category of "Feeding and Eating Disorders Not Elsewhere Classified." Other behaviors in this category include purging without binging, restrictive eating by people who are in a normal weight range despite having significant weight loss, binging and purging but not frequently enough to meet criteria for bulimia, and chewing and spitting out food instead of swallowing it.

There Are Some Common Signs of Disordered Eating

There are both physical and behavioral warning signs of eating disorders and disordered eating (**Table 10.6**). Hair loss is very common among people with anorexia nervosa and bulimia nervosa, as the body does not receive adequate nutrients for hair maintenance and growth. You may also notice significant weight changes, such as sudden weight loss in anorexia nervosa, and sudden weight gain in bulimia nervosa or binge eating disorder. *Russell's sign,* which is scar tissue on the knuckles of fingers used to induce vomiting, is one indicator of bulimia nervosa. This is caused by scraping the knuckles when removing the fingers from the mouth during purging.

Table 10.6

Warning Signs for Eating Disorders

Symptom	Explanation/Example
Weight is below 85% of ideal body weight	Refusal to accept and maintain body weight (even if it is within normal range)
Exercising excessively	Often exercise daily for long periods of time to burn calories and prevent weight gain. May skip work or class to exercise.
Preoccupation with food, weight, and diet	Constantly worry about amount and type of food eaten. May weigh themselves daily or several times per day.
Distorted body image	Do not see themselves as they truly are. May comment on being fat even if underweight.
Refusing to eat	Will avoid food in order to lose weight or prevent weight gain. May avoid only certain foods, such as those with fat and sugar.
Diet pill use or laxative use	Evidence of pill bottles, boxes, or packaging
Changes in mood	May become more withdrawn, depressed, or anxious, especially around food
Hair loss	Hair becomes thinner and falls out in large quantities.
Avoiding eating around others	Want to eat alone. Make excuses to avoid eating with others.

People with disordered eating often avoid social situations because they know food will be present and do not feel comfortable eating around others. Preoccupation with food and body weight is also present among people with eating disorders, such as weighing several times each day or obsessively counting calories. They may also deny unusual eating behaviors if confronted about them.

What Can You Do If You Suspect a Friend Has an Eating Disorder?

You may know someone with an eating disorder, but do not know how to help them, or you may be concerned about your own eating patterns (see the Self-Assessment "Are You at Risk for an Eating Disorder?"). Learning about eating disorders will help you understand why a friend or loved one can have destructive eating behaviors and be seemingly unaware of the damage, pain, or danger they can cause. Knowing the warning signs can also help you identify disordered eating behaviors that could progress into more serious eating disorders.

If you are concerned about someone, find a good time and place to gently express your concerns without criticism or judgment. Realize that you may be rejected or your friend may deny the problem. Be supportive and let them know that you are available if they want to talk to you at another time. Unfortunately, there are many things that you cannot do to help a loved one or friend get better. You cannot force an anorexic to eat, keep a bulimic from purging, or make a binge eater stop overeating. It is up to the individual to decide when he or she is ready to deal with the issues in life that led to the eating disorder.

The best thing you can do is learn to listen to your friend or loved one. Find out about resources in your area for treating eating disorders so that you can refer someone there when that person is ready to get help. Some Web-based resources are listed on page 415.

Eating Disorders Can Be Treated

The most effective treatment for eating disorders is a multidisciplinary team approach including psychological, medical, and nutrition professionals. All members of the team must be knowledgeable and experienced with eating disorders

Are You at Risk for an Eating Disorder?

Check the appropriate box in the following statements to help you find out.

1. I constantly think about eating, weight, and body size.
   Yes ☐ No ☐
2. I'm terrified of being overweight.
   Yes ☐ No ☐
3. I binge eat and can't stop until I feel sick.
   Yes ☐ No ☐
4. I weigh myself several times each day.
   Yes ☐ No ☐
5. I exercise too much or get very rigid about my exercise plan.
   Yes ☐ No ☐
6. I have taken laxatives or forced myself to vomit after eating.
   Yes ☐ No ☐
7. I believe food controls my life.
   Yes ☐ No ☐
8. I feel extremely guilty after eating.
   Yes ☐ No ☐
9. I eat when I am nervous, anxious, lonely, or depressed.
   Yes ☐ No ☐
10. I believe my weight controls what I do.
    Yes ☐ No ☐

Answers

These statements are designed to help you identify potentially problematic eating behavior. These statements do *not* tell you if you have an eating disorder. Look carefully at any statement you marked as yes and decide if this behavior prevents you from enjoying life or makes you unhealthy. Changing these behaviors should be done gradually, making small changes one at a time. Contact your student health services center or your health care provider if you suspect you need help.

---

because it is a complex area that some health care professionals do not feel comfortable treating. A psychologist can help the person deal with emotional and other psychological issues that may be contributing to the eating disorder. Anyone who struggles with an eating disorder should be closely monitored by a physician or other medical professional, as some eating disorders can be life-threatening. A registered dietitian nutritionist can help someone with an eating disorder establish normal eating behaviors.

Some nutritional approaches to eating disorders include identifying binge triggers, safe and unsafe foods, and hunger and fullness cues. Food journals are often helpful to identify eating patterns, food choices, moods, eating disorder triggers, eating cues, and timing of meals and snacks. Meal plans are also used in some instances to ensure intake of adequate calories and nutrients among those with anorexia nervosa, and to help avoid overeating among those with bulimia nervosa or binge eating disorder.

Many people recover from eating disorders and do not struggle with them for the rest of their lives. When treatment is sought in the early stages, there is a better chance that the person will recover fully and have a shorter recovery process than someone who begins treatment after many years.[100] Some people continue to have the desire to engage in disordered eating behaviors; however, they are able to refrain from actually doing these behaviors. Unfortunately, some individuals may never fully recover from an eating disorder. Caregivers must recognize that recovery is a process that often takes years; it is not a quick fix.

LO 10.8 **The Take-Home Message** Disordered eating is characterized by an abnormal eating pattern. Eating disorders include disordered eating behaviors and other specific criteria. Eating disorders are prompted by a complex network of factors, including sociocultural, genetic, and preexisting psychological factors. The most common eating disorders include anorexia nervosa, bulimia nervosa, and binge eating disorder. Eating disorders are most effectively treated with a multidisciplinary team of psychologists, physicians, and registered dietitians. A full recovery takes time but is possible, especially if the disorder is treated in the early stages.

MADE over MADE better

Eating on the run doesn't have to ruin your health. Many eateries are now offering a wide range of options for the health-conscious consumer—if you make the right selection. Try these options the next time you're eating on the fly!

If you like this. . .	Try this instead!
Double Chocolaty Chip Blended Beverage Calories: 410 **Fat: 20 grams** **Saturated Fat: 12 grams**	**Iced Coffee with Skim Milk** Calories: 110 **Fat: 0 grams** **Saturated Fat: 0 grams**
Dunkin' Donuts Coffee Cake Muffin Calories: 660 **Fat: 26 grams** **Saturated Fat: 7 grams**	**Dunkin' Donuts Multigrain Bagel** Calories: 390 **Fat: 8 grams** **Saturated Fat: 0.5 grams**
Taco Bell Grilled Stuffed Beef Burrito Calories: 700 **Fat: 30 grams** **Saturated Fat: 10 grams**	**Fresco Burrito Supreme®— Steak** Calories: 330 **Fat: 8 grams** **Saturated Fat: 3 grams**
Pizza Hut Meat Lovers Pan Pizza Calories: 480 (1 slice) **Fat: 28 grams** **Saturated Fat: 10 grams**	**Pizza Hut Veggie Lovers Thin Crust Pizza** Calories: 410 (1 slice) **Fat: 9 grams** **Saturated Fat: 4 grams**

Is Gastric Bypass Surgery a Healthy Weight-Loss Measure for Obese Adolescents?

Gastric bypass surgery is the most commonly performed bariatric surgery in the United States.[1] By changing the digestive system, it limits the amount of food a person can eat.[2] In recent years, this type of surgery has been increasingly performed on adults, and scientists expect the number of surgeries for adolescents to increase as well.[3]

Is this type of surgery a healthy weight-loss measure for young people? Or are the risks too great? Take a close look at the arguments for both sides and see what you think.

yes

- In the past 30 years, the rate of obesity among children has more than doubled, and the rate of obesity among adolescents has tripled, leaving children and teens at greater risk for a host of diseases, including cardiovascular disease and diabetes, at earlier ages.[4]

- Childhood obesity can also lead to depression and increased tendency toward risk-taking behaviors.[5]

- As with adults, gastric bypass surgery does have risks, and as a result is not for everyone. Only severely obese children and teens, with a BMI in the 95th percentile and with other medical complications as a result of obesity, should be considered, and then only after all other weight-loss measures have failed.[6]

- One study has shown that surgery could actually reverse the effects of type 2 diabetes in obese adolescents.[7]

- As gastric banding becomes more commonly used among adolescents, outcomes are even better. One study found that 24 of 25 adolescent patients who underwent gastric banding lost more than 50 percent of their excess weight.[8]

no

- Because of the drastically reduced amount of food their bodies are taking in, adolescents who have undergone gastric bypass surgery are at a heightened risk of nutritional deficiencies, especially iron, which is normally absorbed through the duodenum, a section of the digestive tract that is bypassed in the surgery.[9]

- Whereas young people tend to dramatically shed excess weight during the first year after surgery, as with adults, the weight loss tends to slow over time; their BMI tends to level off in the second year at a point that remains above normal.[10]

- Some researchers fear that as weight-loss surgery for teenagers becomes more popular, some doctors—because they are either tempted by a potentially lucrative market or motivated by a sincere desire to help—will operate on patients who should not have the surgery.[11]

- More research is needed on the long-term outcomes of bariatric surgery in adolescents. Some patients are likely to have later complications that are not yet apparent.[12]

- Adolescents are at risk for bone loss after bariatric surgery, according to a case review of 61 patients.[13]

what do you think?

1. Imagine you had an obese child whom doctors recommended for surgery. What factors would you consider in deciding whether or not your child should have it? **2.** Do you think rates of gastric surgery among adolescents are likely to increase or decrease in the future? Explain your answer.

LO 10.1 A Healthy Body Weight Is Healthy for You

A healthy body weight is considered a body weight that doesn't increase the risk of developing any weight-related health problems. Being very underweight increases the risk of nutritional deficiencies and related health problems. Being overweight increases the risk of chronic diseases such as heart disease, cancer, and type 2 diabetes.

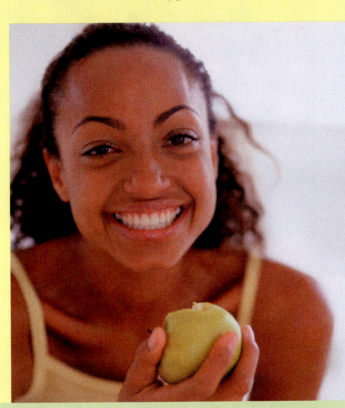

LO 10.2 Your BMI Can Help You Determine If You Are at a Healthy Weight

To assess if you are at a healthy weight, you can consider your BMI (body mass index), which is your weight in relationship to your height. A BMI of 18.5 to 24.9 is considered healthy. A BMI of 25 up to 29.9 is considered overweight. A BMI of 30 or higher is considered obese. As your BMI increases above 25, so does your risk of dying from many chronic diseases. However, some individuals, such as athletes, may have a high BMI but their weight doesn't put them at a health risk because they are not overfat. In contrast, some individuals who have unintentionally lost weight may have a healthy BMI but be at nutritional risk. In general, BMI is best used to assess overweight and obesity for populations rather than individuals. Excess weight around the middle, measured by your waist circumference, could put you at a higher health risk, regardless of your BMI.

Extremely High Risk
BMI 40+ and high waist circumference

Very High Risk
BMI 30–39.9 and high waist circumference

High Risk
BMI 25–29.9 and high waist circumference
or
BMI 30–34.9 and low waist circumference

Increased Risk
BMI 25–29.9 and low waist circumference

Low Risk
BMI under 25

LO 10.3 Energy Balance Is Achieved When Energy (Calories) In Equals Energy (Calories) Out

Body weight remains constant when energy (calorie) intake equals energy (calorie) expenditure. When you consume more energy (calories) than you expend, you have an energy excess, or positive energy balance, and weight gain occurs. When your calories fall short of your needs and/or you expend more energy, you have an energy deficit, or negative energy balance, and you will lose weight. Your basal metabolic rate (BMR), the thermic effect of food (TEF), and your physical activities all factor into your daily energy (calorie) needs. Your BMR is influenced mainly by your lean body mass, but also by your age, gender, body size, genes, ethnicity, emotional and physical stress, thyroid hormone, nutritional state, and environmental temperature. Your caffeine intake and use of nicotine can also affect your BMR.

VISUAL Chapter Summary

LO 10.4 Many Factors Affect Your Body Weight

Appetite is your psychological desire for food and is affected by hunger, satiety, and satiation, as well as your emotions and your environment. Hunger prompts you to eat, and it will subside as the feeling of satiation sets in after you start eating. Satiety is the feeling you experience when you have had enough to eat and determines the length of time between meals or snacks. Physiological mechanisms such as hormones, sensory signals, and a distended stomach, as well as the size of the meal and the nutrients in your foods, all influence your appetite. Genetics and your environment also play a role in your appetite and weight. If your parents were overweight, you are at a higher risk of developing obesity. An environment that enables easy access to a variety of large portions of foods, and encourages you to be sedentary, will also promote obesity.

LO 10.5 Losing Weight Healthfully Involves Diet, Physical Activity, and Behavior Modification

Losing 10 percent of your body weight over a six-month period is considered a reasonable rate of weight loss. Losing weight rapidly can cause a person to fall short of meeting nutrient needs. Many fad diets promise quick results but can be unhealthy for the long term.

Eating more low-energy-density, high-volume foods, such as vegetables and fruit, can help you lose weight because you will feel full for fewer calories. Fiber also promotes satiation. Because protein has the most dramatic effect on satiety, eating high-protein lean meats, chicken, and fish at meals can help reduce hunger between meals. Because fat slows the movement of food out of the stomach into the intestines, it can also prolong satiety.

Changing the eating behaviors that contribute to weight gain or impede weight loss is necessary for long-term weight-loss success. Self-monitoring of these behaviors by keeping a food record, controlling environmental cues that trigger eating when not hungry, and learning how to better manage stress are all behavior modification techniques that can be used by individuals who eat out of habit and in response to their environment. Routine physical activity can add to the daily energy deficit needed for weight loss.

HEALTHY WEIGHT

Healthy diet

Physical activity

Behavior modification

LO 10.6 Maintaining Weight Loss Involves a Lifetime of Healthy Habits

Weight cycling is the repeated gain and loss of body weight. Individuals who lose weight often experience an "energy gap" due to their lower overall energy needs because there is less body weight to maintain. In order to account for the energy gap and successfully maintain their new weight, individuals who have lost weight must continue to eat a healthy diet, follow healthy habits, and maintain a high level of physical activity.

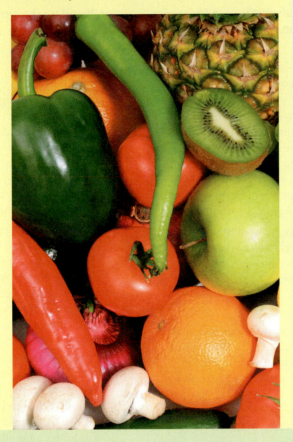

LO 10.7 Consuming a Healthy Diet Is Important When Trying to Gain Weight

Individuals who are trying to gain weight should consume a healthy diet that is calorie and nutrient rich and exercise to build muscle mass. Consuming larger portions at mealtimes and energy-dense snacks between meals can help with weight gain.

LO 10.8 Disordered Eating Describes a Variety of Abnormal Eating Patterns

Disordered eating includes restrictive eating, binge eating, vomiting after eating, and abusing laxatives or diet pills. Eating disorders are diagnosed by meeting specific criteria that include disordered eating behaviors.

Anorexia nervosa is characterized by self-starvation and excessive weight loss. Bulimia nervosa involves repeated cycles of binge eating and purging. Binge eating disorders are characterized by binge eating without purging. Orthorexia is an obsession with "healthy or righteous eating." Night eating syndrome is described as excessive calorie intake in the evening and waking up during the night to eat. Pica is a compulsion to eat nonnutritive substances.

Numerous health consequences can occur with eating disorders, such as hair loss, digestive problems, electrolyte imbalances, changes in heart rate and blood pressure, dehydration, and nutrient deficiencies. The most effective treatment for eating disorders involves a multidisciplinary team approach including psychological, nutrition, and medical professionals.

Terms to Know

- healthy weight
- overweight
- obesity
- underweight
- body mass index (BMI)
- energy balance
- energy excess
- energy deficit
- basal metabolism
- thermic effect of food (TEF)
- estimated energy requirement (EER)
- satiety
- behavior modification
- disordered eating
- eating disorders

MasteringNutrition™

Build your knowledge—and confidence—in the Study Area of MasteringNutrition with a variety of study tools.

 Access MyDietAnalysis through MasteringNutrition™ and track your diet and daily activities. In addition, a dietary analysis activity is available for every chapter in your book.

Check Your Understanding

LO 10.1 1. Which one of the following is NOT influenced by being overweight?
  a. heart disease
  b. osteoarthritis
  c. gallbladder disease
  d. hair loss

LO 10.2 2. Bryan has a BMI of 27. He is considered
  a. underweight.
  b. overweight.
  c. at a healthy weight.
  d. obese.

LO 10.2 3. Central obesity refers to
  a. the accumulation of excess fat in your hips and thighs.
  b. the accumulation of excess fat in your stomach area.
  c. the accumulation of excess fat in your arms and legs.
  d. the accumulation of excess fat in your ankles and feet.

LO 10.3 4. Your basal metabolic rate (BMR) refers to
  a. the amount of energy you expend during physical activity.
  b. the amount of energy you expend digesting your food.
  c. the amount of energy (calories) that you consume daily.
  d. the amount of energy expended to meet your basic physiological needs.

LO 10.4 5. You just ate a large plate of pasta and tomato sauce, so your stomach is full and distended. Which hormone is released because of the distention of your stomach?
  a. cholecystokinin
  b. insulin
  c. thyroid hormone
  d. leptin

LO 10.4 6. Which of the following can increase your risk of becoming overweight?
  a. having a parent who is obese
  b. consuming more meals at home than dining out
  c. reducing the amount of "screen time" during the day
  d. decreasing your portion sizes

LO 10.5 7. Which are examples of low-energy-density, high-volume foods that can aid in weight loss?
  a. raw vegetables and salsa
  b. jelly beans
  c. olive oil
  d. ice cream

LO 10.6 8. Research suggests that accumulating _____ daily, which is the equivalent of walking 5 miles, can help reduce the risk of becoming overweight.
  a. 1,000 steps
  b. 5,000 steps
  c. 7,500 steps
  d. 10,000 steps

LO 10.7 9. You are trying to gain weight in a healthy way, and so are looking for foods that add healthy calories. Which of the following foods is both nutrient dense and energy dense?
  a. mixed nuts
  b. candy
  c. black coffee
  d. soda

LO 10.8 10. Lanugo, or downy hair growth, is common in what type of eating disorder?
  a. anorexia nervosa
  b. bulimia nervosa
  c. binge eating disorder
  d. night eating syndrome

Answers

1. (d) Hair loss. Being overweight increases your risk of all these diseases and conditions, as well as type 2 diabetes, some cancers, and sleep apnea.

2. (b) Because Bryan's BMI falls between 25 and 29.9, he is considered overweight. If his BMI was under 18.5, he would be underweight, whereas a BMI of 18.5 to 24.9 would put him in the healthy weight category. A BMI of 30 and higher is considered obese.

3. (b) Central obesity refers to the accumulation of excess fat in the stomach area and can be determined by measuring a person's waist circumference. Central obesity increases the risk of heart disease, diabetes, and hypertension.

4. (d) Your BMR refers to the bare minimum amount of energy (calories) your body expends to keep your blood circulating and lungs breathing so that you can stay alive. The amount of energy or calories that you expend during physical activity is not factored into your BMR. The energy that you expend digesting, absorbing, and processing food is called the thermic effect of food (TEF) and is also not part of your BMR. The amount of energy or calories that you consume daily doesn't factor into your BMR.

5. (a) A distended stomach causes the release of cholecystokinin, which is associated with the feeling of satiation and the ending of eating. Insulin will be released once

this carbohydrate-heavy meal is digested and absorbed into the blood. Thyroid hormone affects your BMR and is not associated with your stomach being distended, and leptin is secreted from fat cells and decreases hunger.

6. (a) Having a parent who is obese can increase your risk of becoming overweight. Consuming more meals at home, reducing your "screen time," and decreasing your portion sizes can all help you reduce your risk of becoming overweight.

7. (a) Vegetables, including the salsa, are low-energy-density, high-volume foods. These foods will increase satiation, contain few calories per bite, and can displace more energy-dense foods in the diet, all of which can help promote weight loss. The jelly beans, olive oil, and ice cream are all very energy dense.

8. (d) Accumulating 10,000 steps daily can help reduce the risk of becoming overweight.

9. (a) Mixed nuts are a nutrient- and energy-rich snack that can add healthy calories to a person's diet.

10. (a) Lanugo grows typically on the face and arms of people with anorexia nervosa as a way of regulating body temperature.

Web Resources

- For more on overweight and obesity, visit the Centers for Disease Control and Prevention at www.cdc.gov
- For more information on weight control and physical activity, visit the Weight-control Information Network (WIN) at http://win.niddk .nih.gov
- For more weight-loss shopping tips, recipes, and meal plans, visit the USDA's MyPlate website at www .ChooseMyPlate.gov
- For more on eating disorders, visit the National Eating Disorders Association at www .nationaleatingdisorders.org

Answers to True or False?

1. **True.** Overweight people can suffer from a condition called sleep apnea. To find out what this is and why being overweight contributes to it, turn to page 371.

2. **False.** Being underweight due to a poor diet can have serious health risks. Turn to page 371 to find out why.

3. **False.** Celebrities and models in magazine photos may reflect social trends, but they often don't reflect a healthy body weight. Turn to page 372 to find out more.

4. **False.** Fat around the belly puts a person at a higher health risk than fat stored on the hips and thighs. To find out why, turn to page 374.

5. **True.** But this isn't the only factor. Turn to page 378 to find out the others.

6. **True.** To find out why and how these factors interact with each other, turn to page 383.

7. **True.** Surprising as it may be, eating *more* of certain foods can help you lose weight. To find out why, turn to page 390.

8. **False.** Whereas fat makes food stay in the stomach longer, which slows its digestion and absorption, it isn't the nutrient that provides the greatest level of satiety. You may be surprised to learn what is. Turn to page 392 to find out.

9. **False.** Technically, disordered eating describes abnormal eating behaviors, whereas eating disorders are clinically diagnosed illnesses. Turn to page 401 to learn more about these behaviors and illnesses.

10. **True.** Some eating disorders can be life-threatening. Turn to page 405 to learn about the health effects of eating disorders.

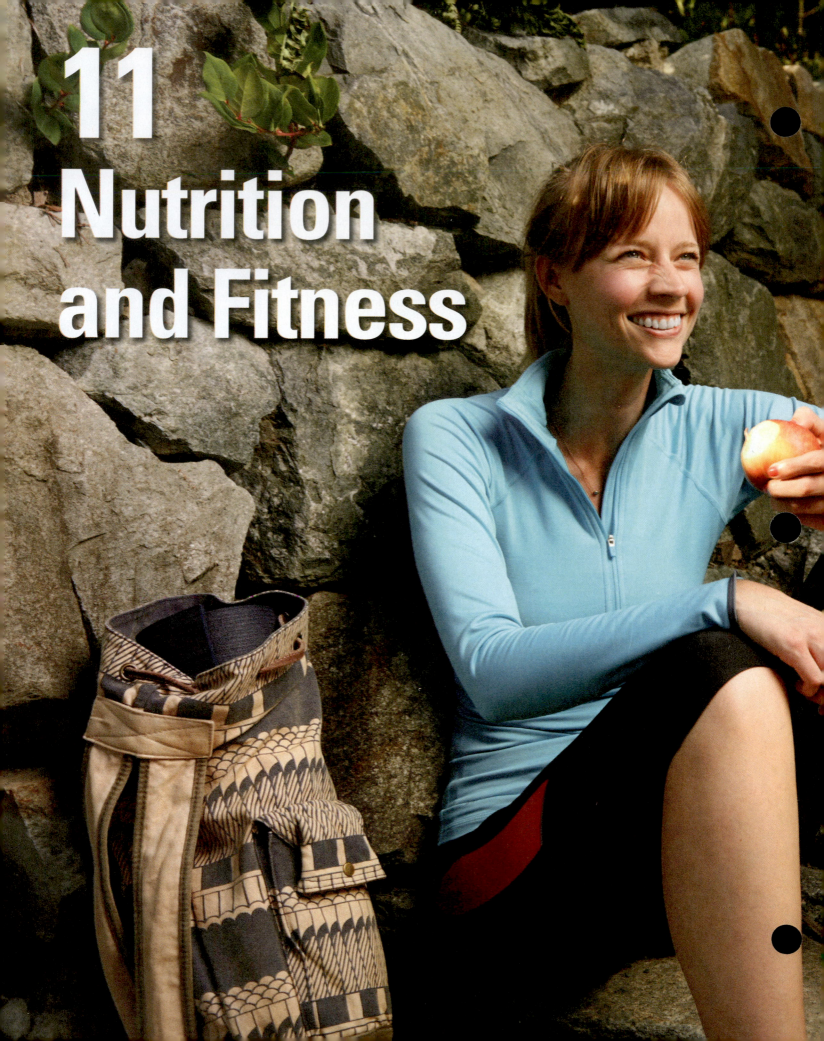

11 Nutrition and Fitness

True or False?

1. Physical activity and exercise are technically the same. **T|F** p. 418

2. As little as 60 minutes of physical activity per week is enough to provide health benefits. **T|F** p. 423

3. Energy for exercise is derived from both anaerobic and aerobic metabolic pathways. **T|F** p. 426

4. Eating a high-carbohydrate meal before an exercise session will always result in improved energy and performance. **T|F** p. 429

5. Athletes should eat immediately after training. **T|F** p. 436

6. Vitamins and minerals are not as important to exercise as are carbohydrate, protein, and fat. **T|F** p. 437

7. Many athletes are at risk for iron deficiency. **T|F** p. 438

8. Everyone who exercises should consume sports drinks. **T|F** p. 442

9. Thirst is the best indicator for monitoring fluid needs. **T|F** p. 442

10. The National Collegiate Athletic Association (NCAA) classifies caffeine as a banned substance when consumed in high amounts. **T|F** p. 446

See page 455 for the answers.

417

Learning Outcomes

After reading this chapter, you will be able to:

LO 11.1 List and describe the five basic components of fitness.

LO 11.2 Describe the FITT principle and how to use it to create a fitness program.

LO 11.3 Describe the roles of carbohydrate, fat, and protein during physical activity.

LO 11.4 List optimal food sources before, during, and after exercise.

LO 11.5 Describe the importance of vitamins and minerals for physical fitness.

LO 11.6 Explain the relationship between fluid intake and fitness.

LO 11.7 List and describe ergogenic aids that claim to improve athletic performance and physical fitness.

hether you are a competitive athlete or strive to stay "in shape," your eating habits are just as important to your fitness and performance as the exercise itself. Your body is like a car: It requires fuel to make it move and proper maintenance to keep it in good working condition. If you are driving a car in a race, you will make sure that you have enough gas to make it through the competition. Similar to gas in a car, nutrients from food provide the energy needed to move the body, especially during exercise. The more you move, the more energy is needed. Nutrients are necessary to help the body recover after exercise so that you receive the benefits of the activity and have energy to repeat the activity. Fueling your body with the proper balance of nutrients is essential to achieving optimal fitness levels and optimal athletic performance.

What Is Physical Fitness and Why Is It Important?

LO 11.1 List and describe the five basic components of fitness.

Physical fitness is simply defined as good health or physical condition, primarily as the result of exercise and proper nutrition. Some people think of exercise and physical activity as the same thing, but this isn't technically the case. **Physical activity** refers to body movement that results in expending calories. Activities such as gardening, walking the dog, and playing with children can all be regarded as physical activity. **Exercise** is defined as formalized training or structured activity, like step aerobics, running, or weight lifting. For the purpose of this chapter, though, the terms *exercise* and *physical activity* are used interchangeably.

Being physically active and consuming a healthy diet are the two most important components of overall health and fitness. You will not achieve optimal fitness if you ignore either of these areas.

Physical Fitness Has Five Basic Components

The five basic components of fitness include cardiorespiratory endurance, muscular strength, muscular endurance, flexibility, and body composition. Most strength training programs blend muscular strength and muscular endurance, which is generally referred to as *muscular fitness*. To be physically fit, one must consider all five variables.

Cardiorespiratory endurance is the ability to sustain cardiorespiratory exercise, such as running and biking, for an extended length of time. This requires that the body's cardiovascular and respiratory systems provide enough oxygen and energy to the working muscles without becoming overly fatigued or exhausted. Someone who can run a leisurely mile without being too out of breath to talk has good cardiorespiratory endurance. Someone who is out of breath after climbing one flight of stairs, in contrast, does not.

Muscle strength is the ability to produce force for a brief period of time, while **muscle endurance** is the ability to exert force over a long period of time without fatigue. Increasing muscle strength and muscle endurance is best achieved with **strength training**. You probably associate muscle strength with bodybuilders or weight lifters, and it's true that these people train to be particularly strong. However, other athletes, such as cheerleaders and ballet dancers, also work hard to strengthen their muscles. Consider the strength it takes to lift another person above your head. If you could hold the person up for several minutes, that would show exceptional muscle endurance.

Flexibility is the range of motion around a joint and is improved with stretching. Athletic performance and joint and muscular function are all enhanced with improved flexibility, which also reduces the likelihood of injury. A gymnast exhibits high flexibility when performing stunts and dance routines. In contrast, someone with low flexibility might not be able to bend over and touch his toes from a standing or sitting position.

Finally, **body composition** is the proportion of muscle, fat, water, and other tissues in the body. Together, these tissues make up your total body weight. Your body composition can change without your total body weight changing, due to the fact that muscle takes up less space (per pound) than does body fat. This is why you can lose inches on your body without losing pounds of weight when you increase your lean muscle mass and decrease body fat.

Running is a great way to improve cardiorespiratory endurance.

Physical Fitness Provides Numerous Benefits

We have long heard that eating a balanced diet and exercising regularly maintains good health. We also know that even modest amounts of exercise will provide health benefits, and the more you exercise, the more fit you'll be. However, despite knowing the benefits that exercise brings, more than half of the adults living in the United States do not meet the recommendations for regular physical activity.[1]

So, how does physical activity improve and maintain good health? One of the most obvious ways is that it helps you achieve or maintain a healthy body weight, which in turn helps reduce the risk of developing chronic diseases like type 2 diabetes mellitus and heart disease. In addition, being physically fit can improve overall health in other ways, like helping you get restful sleep and reducing stress. **Table 11.1** on the next page lists some of the numerous health benefits that result from being physically active on a regular basis. You have to be cautious, however, not to overexercise and increase your risk of injury.

To improve the health of American adults and children through regular physical activity, the U.S. Department of Health and Human Services developed the *2008 Physical Activity Guidelines for Americans*. This publication gives information and guidance on the types and amounts of physical activity that provide substantial health benefits for Americans age 6 and older. The recommendations are based on a review of scientific research on the benefits of physical activity, and conclude with the main idea that regular physical activity over time can produce long-term health benefits.[2]

LO 11.1 **The Take-Home Message** Physical fitness is the state of being in good physical condition through proper nutrition and regular physical activity. The five components of physical fitness are cardiorespiratory endurance, muscle strength, muscle endurance, flexibility, and body composition. To achieve optimal fitness, all five components must be considered. The numerous health benefits of physical activity include higher likelihood of a healthy body weight, as well as reduced risk of several chronic diseases, including type 2 diabetes, heart disease, and cancer; improved body composition, bone health, immune function, and mental well-being; more restful sleep; and reduced stress.

physical fitness The ability to perform physical activities requiring cardiorespiratory endurance, muscle endurance, and strength and/or flexibility; physical fitness is acquired through physical activity and adequate nutrition.

physical activity Voluntary movement that results in energy expenditure (burning calories).

exercise Any type of structured or planned physical activity.

cardiorespiratory endurance The body's ability to sustain prolonged exercise.

muscle strength The greatest amount of force exerted by a muscle at one time.

muscle endurance The ability of a muscle to produce prolonged effort.

strength training Exercising with weights or other resistance to build, strengthen, and tone muscle to improve or maintain overall fitness; also called *resistance training*.

flexibility A joint's ability to move freely through a full and normal range of motion.

body composition The relative proportion of muscle, fat, water, and other tissues in the body.

Table 11.1

The Benefits of Physical Fitness

Reduced Risk of Heart Disease

How It Works: Research has shown that moderate physical activity lowers blood pressure.[3] In addition, exercise is positively associated with high-density lipoprotein (HDL) cholesterol.[4]

Reduced Risk of Type 2 Diabetes

How It Works: Exercise helps control blood glucose levels by increasing insulin sensitivity.[6] This not only reduces risk for type 2 diabetes, but also improves blood glucose control for those who have been diagnosed with type 2 diabetes.

Improved Body Composition

How It Works: Exercise helps burn excess stored body fat and builds muscle, resulting in a leaner body mass. Individuals with moderate cardiorespiratory fitness have less total fat and abdominal fat compared with people with low cardiorespiratory fitness.[5]

Reduced Risk of Some Forms of Cancer

How It Works: Increased physical activity has been associated with a reduced risk of colon, breast, endometrial, and lung cancers. This reduced risk is likely the result of a reduction in overall body weight and other hormonal and metabolic mechanisms.[7]

What Does a Physical Fitness Program Look Like?

LO 11.2 Describe the FITT principle and how to use it to create a fitness program.

Physical fitness programs are generally based on the five components of fitness, and include aerobic exercise, resistance training, and stretching. A successful fitness program should be tailored to meet the needs of the individual and performed consistently so that any gains in physical fitness are not lost. It is also important to incorporate activities that are enjoyable so that they become a regular part of your lifestyle. If you dislike jogging, for example, you won't be likely to consistently work a daily run into your schedule.

Cardiorespiratory Exercise Can Improve Cardiorespiratory Endurance and Body Composition

Between birth and old age, you will walk about 70,000 miles. Walking is one of the best activities you can do to improve cardiovascular health and maintain a healthy weight. Plus, it can be done anywhere!

Cardiorespiratory exercise usually involves continuous activities that use large muscle groups, such as high-impact aerobics, stair climbing, and brisk walking. This type of exercise is predominantly aerobic because it uses oxygen. During cardiorespiratory exercise, your heart beats faster and more oxygen-carrying blood is delivered to your tissues. How does this work? As you begin to exercise, your body requires more oxygen to break down nutrients for energy, so it increases blood flow (volume) to the working muscles. It accomplishes

Improved Bone Health

How It Works: Bone density has been shown to improve with weight-bearing exercise and resistance training, thereby reducing the risk for osteoporosis.[8]

Improved Mental Well-Being

How It Works: Regular exercise protects against the onset of depression and anxiety disorders, reduces symptoms in people diagnosed with depression and anxiety, delays the incidence of dementia, and overall enhances mental well-being.[10]

Improved Immune System

How It Works: Regular moderate exercise can enhance the immune system by increasing immunoglobulins in the body. Immunoglobulins function like antibodies, protecting against colds and other infectious diseases.[9]

Improved Sleep

How It Works: People who engage in regular exercise often have better quality of sleep due to anxiety reduction, antidepressant effect, and changes in body temperature that promote sleep.[11]

---

this by increasing your heart rate and **stroke volume**. Your body also redistributes blood from your internal organs to maximize the volume of blood that is delivered to the muscles during exercise.

Your level of cardiorespiratory fitness can be measured by the maximum amount of oxygen your muscles can consume during exercise, or **VO₂max**. People who are more physically fit have a higher VO₂max and can exercise at a higher intensity without fatigue than someone who is not as fit.

Cardiorespiratory exercise provides the most benefits to your cardiovascular system (heart, blood, and blood vessels), which improves your cardiorespiratory endurance. In addition, it reduces stress and lowers your risk of heart disease by maintaining normal cholesterol levels, heart rate, and blood pressure. Cardiorespiratory exercise also helps you maintain a healthy weight and improve your body composition by burning excess calories, leading to a reduction of body fat.

Strength Training Can Improve Muscle Strength, Muscle Endurance, and Body Composition

Strength (or resistance) training has long been associated with gaining muscle mass, strength, and endurance. Maintaining adequate muscle mass and strength is important for everyone. Just because you engage in resistance training does not mean that you will develop large, bulky muscles. Many females, as well as males, use resistance training to tone and define their muscles to improve their physical appearance and body composition.

To increase muscle strength, you should perform a low number of repetitions using heavy weights or other resistance. If you want to increase muscle endurance, you should perform a high number of repetitions using lighter resistance. However,

Resistance training improves muscle strength and endurance.

stroke volume The amount of blood pumped by the heart with each heart beat.

VO₂max The maximum amount of oxygen (ml) a person uses in one minute per kilogram of body weight.

heavier resistance can also be used to improve muscle endurance by allowing short rest intervals between repetition sets.

Rest periods between sets of an exercise and between workouts are important so that you do not overwork your muscles and increase your risk of muscle strains or other injury. If you don't allow time for your muscles to rest, your muscles may break down and not recover, leading to a loss of muscle mass. The amount of rest depends on your fitness goals and level of **conditioning**. If increasing strength is your goal, you should allow long rest periods of 2 to 3 minutes between sets. If increasing muscle endurance is your goal, shorter rest periods of 30 seconds or less are recommended.

Between workouts, the general guideline to reduce the risk of injury is to allow 48 hours between sets that use the same muscle groups. However, strength training can be done daily as long as different muscles are used on consecutive days.

Stretching Can Improve Flexibility

When you think about your flexibility, you are likely considering how far you can stretch in a particular way without feeling pain or discomfort. Improving flexibility can improve balance, posture, and circulation of blood and nutrients throughout your body. The most common exercise used to improve flexibility is stretching.

There are several types of stretching. The most common form is *static stretching*, which consists of relaxing a muscle, then extending it to a point of mild discomfort for about 10 to 30 seconds, and then relaxing it again. You can use static stretching exercises to stretch one muscle at a time, or you can stretch more than one muscle or muscle group simultaneously.

A form of stretching used by many professional athletes as a pre-event warm-up is *dynamic stretching*, which stretches muscles while moving, for example, by performing arm swings, kicks, or lunges. A form of exercise called *yoga* incorporates aspects of both static and dynamic stretching, and individuals who perform yoga on a regular basis can significantly improve their flexibility. Note that when you perform these stretches for the first time, you'll need to consult a qualified trainer, coach, or physician on proper techniques to reduce your risk of injury.

Another form of stretching, called *ballistic stretching*, involves a repetitive, bouncing motion while you are stretching. Some believe that ballistic stretching increases your risk for pulling a muscle; therefore, it is less favored than static and dynamic stretching. Other, less common forms of stretching are types that involve a partner or machine to create the force needed to stretch the muscle, and controlled stretches that use momentum to create the force needed to extend the muscle.

Recommendations about stretching often conflict and the research to sort it out is limited. Some researchers have concluded that stretching before exercise does not prevent muscle soreness after exercise, nor does it prevent acute sports injuries.[12] However, stretching afterward has been shown to relax and reduce tension on muscles that were just exercised.[13]

Improving your flexibility can help you reduce muscle soreness and lower your risk of injury.

The FITT Principle Can Help You Design a Fitness Program

One easy way to design a successful physical fitness program is to follow the FITT principle. FITT is an acronym for frequency, intensity, time, and type. Let's take a closer look at each of these components:

- **F**requency is how often you do the activity, such as the number of times per week.
- **I**ntensity refers to the degree of difficulty at which you perform the activity. Common terms used to describe **intensity** are low, moderate, and vigorous

conditioning The process of improving physical fitness through repeated activity.

intensity The level of difficulty of an activity.

Table 11.2
Target Heart Rate

Age	Percent of Maximum Heart Rate*			
	55%	65%	85%	95%
20	106	126	164	184
25	105	124	162	181
30	103	121	159	177
35	101	119	156	174
40	99	117	153	171
45	97	115	150	168
50	95	113	147	165

*Maximum heart rate (HRmax) can be estimated using the following equation:
206.9 − (age in years × 0.67) = estimated HRmax.

(high). One measure of intensity for cardiorespiratory exercise is the **rating of perceived exertion (RPE)**, in which the person performing the activity self-assesses the level of intensity. The RPE is based on your current level of fitness and your perception of how hard you are working. The scale ranges from 1 (rest) to 10 (maximal exertion). A range of 5 to 7 on the RPE scale (somewhat hard to hard) is recommended for most adults to achieve fitness. A more precise method of measuring intensity is using your **target heart rate** (see **Table 11.2**). Your target heart rate is the range (given in percentages of maximum heart rate) that your heart rate should fall within to ensure that you are training aerobically. A target heart rate of 55 percent to 64 percent of maximum heart rate is considered low intensity, 65 percent to 84 percent of maximum heart rate is defined as moderate intensity, and 85 percent to 95 percent is considered high intensity. For strength training, intensity is referred to as **repetition maximum (RM)**. For example, 1 RM is the maximum amount of weight that can be lifted one time; 10 RM is the maximum amount of weight that can be lifted ten times.

- Time, or **duration**, is how long you performed the activity, such as a 30-minute run.
- Type means the specific activity that you are doing, such as step aerobics or cycling.

The frequency, intensity, time (duration), and type of exercise that are right for you depend partly on what goal you are trying to achieve. For some health benefits, the *2008 Physical Activity Guidelines* state that as little as 60 minutes a week of moderate-intensity activity, such as brisk walking or dancing, will help you achieve that goal. However, adults who wish to see substantial health benefits, including a reduced risk of many chronic diseases, need a total amount of 150 minutes (2 hours and 30 minutes) of moderate-intensity aerobic activity per week. Additionally, resistance training, such as by lifting weights, at a moderate or high intensity, should be performed two or more days per week. Anyone who wants to maintain body weight and prevent gradual weight gain should participate in approximately 60 minutes of moderate- to vigorous-intensity activity on most days of the week while not consuming excess calories. Those wishing to lose weight need to participate in at least 60 to 90 minutes of daily moderate-intensity physical activity and make calorie adjustments to their diet. You can use the Physical Activity Pyramid to help you become more physically active or improve your current level of fitness (**Figure 11.1** on the next page). People with diabetes, high blood pressure, and other types of heart disease should consult with a health care provider before participating in any exercise program, especially one to be performed at a vigorous intensity.

Small Steps for Big Gains

You have numerous opportunities every day to be physically active. Go to www .choosemyplate.gov/physical-activity to see how you can incorporate little changes into your daily routine to attain the health benefits of physical activity.

rating of perceived exertion (RPE) A subjective measure of the intensity level of an activity using a numerical scale.

target heart rate A heart rate in beats per minute (expressed as a percentage of maximum heart rate) achieved during exercise that indicates the intensity of the exercise.

repetition maximum (RM) The maximum amount of weight that can be lifted for a specified number of repetitions.

duration The length of time of performing an activity.

Helpful tips:

- Join a yoga or pilates class
- Use household objects as free weights (soup cans, gallon water jugs)
- Use resistance bands

- Increase treadmill speed
- Play team sports with friends

- Walk rather than drive for short trips
- Take stairs instead of elevator
- Ride bikes with children or walk dog

Minimize sedentary activities
Watching TV
Computer use
Examples

2–3 days/week
Flexibility and muscular fitness
Stretching
Yoga
Pilates
Weight lifting

3–5 days/week
Cardiorespiratory
Moderate–high intensity
Brisk walking
Basketball
Soccer
Jogging
Racquetball

Daily
Low–moderate intensity
Walking
Climbing stairs
Light bicycling
Playing with pets

Figure 11.1 Physical Activity Pyramid
Participating in a variety of activities, such as those shown in this Physical Activity Pyramid, will have you on your way to physical fitness.

Do you feel like you don't have a 30-minute block of time to exercise? The good news is that you don't have to do an activity for 30 consecutive minutes to get health benefits. You can break this time up into three 10-minute bouts of activity and still receive the same benefits as if you were to do it all at one time.[14]

The key to being physically active is to find activities that you enjoy so that you continue to do them on a regular basis. If you don't like jogging, you don't have to do it! Just find other activities that you like. Maybe you enjoy playing basketball, going for a walk, or hiking. It doesn't really matter what the activity is, as long as you take pleasure in what you are doing and do it regularly. See the Get Moving! Table Tips for more ideas on how to increase the amount of exercise you're getting.

You can use the FITT approach to meet the American College of Sports Medicine's guidelines for cardiorespiratory endurance, muscular fitness, and flexibility for healthy adults, which are summarized in **Table 11.3.** For example, for your FITT program, you may want to jog three days a week for 30 minutes on Tuesday, Thursday, and Friday to attain your cardiorespiratory fitness. On Monday and Wednesday, you may want to lift weights for muscular fitness and make sure that you incorporate stretching throughout the week to improve your flexibility.

The Progressive Overload Principle Can Help Improve Fitness over Time

During conditioning, the body gradually adapts to the activities that are being performed. Over time, if the activity is kept exactly the same, the body doesn't have to work as hard and fitness levels will plateau as a result. To continue to improve

Table 11.3
Using FITT to Improve Fitness

	Cardiorespiratory Fitness	Muscular Fitness	Flexibility
Frequency	3–5 days per week	2–3 days per week	2–3 days per week
Intensity	64–95% of maximum heart rate	60–80% of 1 RM	To the point of feeling tightness or slight discomfort
Time	20–60 minutes per day (150 minutes per week), continuous or intermittent (minimum of 10-minute bouts)	8–10 different exercises performed in 2–4 sets, 8–12 repetitions	2–4 repetitions for each muscle group; hold static stretch for 10–30 seconds
Type	Brisk walking, jogging, biking, step aerobics	Free weights, machines with stacked weights, resistance bands	Stretching, yoga

your fitness level, you must challenge your body by using the **progressive overload principle**. Modifying one or more of the FITT principles so that you gradually increase exercise demands on the body will improve fitness. For example, if you are trying to improve cardiorespiratory endurance, you might gradually increase the duration of a run. To increase muscle strength, you may gradually increase the amount of weight being lifted.

As your body responds to the work that it is being asked to do, physical fitness will be attained. Muscles will increase in size, endurance, and strength and you will notice increased cardiorespiratory endurance and improved flexibility. However, if conditioning is executed improperly or nutrient intake is inadequate for physical activity, muscles can lose mass, endurance, and strength, and cardiorespiratory fitness levels will suffer.

LO 11.2 **The Take-Home Message** Cardiorespiratory exercise improves cardiorespiratory endurance and body composition. Strength training can improve muscle strength and endurance as well as body composition. Flexibility can be enhanced by stretching. An effective training program can be designed using the FITT principle, which stands for frequency, intensity, time, and type of activity. Most people should aim for 60 minutes of moderate activity per week for some health benefits; greater amounts of exercise are needed for substantial health benefits, weight management, and physical fitness improvement. Applying the progressive overload principle to workouts will help you achieve optimal fitness levels.

How Are Carbohydrate, Fat, and Protein Used during Exercise?

LO 11.3 Describe the roles of carbohydrate, fat, and protein during physical activity.

In addition to regular physical activity, you need the right foods and fluids in order to be physically fit. When you eat and drink, you meet your nutrient needs for physical activity in two ways: (1) You supply the energy, particularly from carbohydrate and fat, that your body needs for the activity; and (2) you provide the nutrients, particularly carbohydrate and protein, that will help you recover properly so that you can repeat the activity.

TableTIPS

Get Moving!

Schedule physical activity into your day, just like you would schedule a meeting, class, or work.

Find activities that you enjoy. Make exercise something you look forward to, so that you're more likely to keep it up.

Ask a friend or coworker to exercise with you. Many people are more likely to exercise if they have a partner to motivate them.

Track your exercise in a log or journal so you see how much you are getting and note your improvements over time.

Be adventurous and try new activities. If you're used to jogging or going to the gym, try hiking or racquetball. Mixing up your routine will help prevent boredom.

progressive overload principle
A gradual increase in exercise demands resulting from modifications to the frequency, intensity, time, or type of activity.

Figure 11.2 Energy Metabolism
During anaerobic metabolism, energy is derived from the breakdown of ATP and creatine phosphate. (a) Energy is released when one phosphate group is removed from ATP, leaving ADP. (b) Creatine phosphate directly provides energy when the phosphate group is removed from creatine, as well as donates the phosphate group to ADP, regenerating ATP, thereby facilitating energy production as described in (a).

We mentioned earlier in the chapter that much energy production during cardiorespiratory exercise is **aerobic** because it uses oxygen. But during the first few seconds of exercise, energy production occurs under **anaerobic** conditions, or without oxygen. For the anaerobic production of energy, the body relies heavily on two high-energy molecules in muscle cells:

- **Adenosine triphosphate (ATP)** is a compound composed of a molecule called adenosine attached to a "tail" of three phosphates (*tri* = three). When one of these phosphates is removed from ATP, energy is released as a by-product (**Figure 11.2**). The remaining compound is called adenosine diphosphate (ADP), because it contains only two phosphates (*di* = two). The amount of ATP (energy) in cells is limited, so its breakdown can support only a few seconds of intense exercise.

- **Creatine phosphate** is a compound containing the molecule creatine attached to a single phosphate. Your body produces creatine with the help of the liver and kidneys and then stores it in skeletal muscle and other tissues. Your body also gets some creatine from foods, including meat and fish. Direct energy is produced when the phosphate is split off from the creatine, and indirect energy is produced when the phosphate is donated to ADP, thereby regenerating ATP. Because these processes work together, these molecules are sometimes referred to as ATP-CP. The amount of creatine that can be stored in the muscles is very limited and becomes depleted after about 10 seconds of high-intensity activity.

As you continue exercising, you will breathe more heavily and take in an increased amount of oxygen. At this point your body begins to rely more on aerobic energy production because the amount of ATP needed to support your activity cannot be generated fast enough by anaerobic energy production to meet the energy demands. To supply your body with the energy it needs, you begin to oxidize carbohydrate (glucose), fat (fatty acids), and, to a minimal extent, protein (amino acids) to produce energy in the form of ATP.

Your body relies on carbohydrate, fat, and protein for energy during exercise, but the type and amount of energy that is used depends highly on the intensity and duration of the exercise, your nutritional status, and your level of physical fitness. Carbohydrate and fat contribute most of the energy needed for activity (**Figure 11.3**), while protein is best used to promote muscle growth and recovery. The following section discusses the roles of carbohydrate, fat, and protein during exercise.

Carbohydrate Is the Primary Energy Source during High-Intensity Exercise

aerobic With oxygen.

anaerobic Without oxygen.

adenosine triphosphate (ATP) A compound that is broken down to produce energy for working muscles and other tissues.

creatine phosphate A compound stored in the muscles that is broken down to replenish ATP stores.

During exercise, you obtain energy from carbohydrate through blood glucose and stored glycogen in the muscles and the liver. In an average-sized man, about 525 grams of glycogen are stored in the muscle, 100 grams of glycogen are stored in the liver, and 25 grams of glucose are in the blood.

The total amount of energy stored as carbohydrate in the body is about 2,600 calories (650 grams multiplied by 4 calories per gram), of which 2,000 calories can be used. This is enough energy to perform about 2 hours of moderate exercise, and then glycogen stores are almost completely depleted.

FOCUS

Figure 11.3 **What Fuels Our Activities?**

FOCUS FIGURE WALKTHROUGH

Scan this QR code with your mobile device for a video tour of this figure by Joan Salge Blake.

Depending on the duration and intensity of the activity, our bodies may use ATP and creatine phosphate (CP), carbohydrate, or fat in various combinations to fuel muscular work. Keep in mind that the amounts and sources shown below can vary based on the person's fitness level and health, how well fed the person is before the activity, and environmental temperatures and conditions.

SPRINT START (0–3 seconds)
A short, intense burst of activity like sprinting is fueled by ATP and under anaerobic conditions.

— 100% ATP-CP

100-M DASH (10–12 seconds)
ATP and CP provide energy for about 10 seconds of quick, intense activity, after which energy is provided as ATP from the breakdown of carbohydrates.

— 50% ATP-CP

— 50% Carbohydrates

1500-M RACE (4–6 minutes)
Energy derived from ATP and CP is small and would be exhausted after about 10 seconds of the race. At this point, most of the energy is derived from aerobic metabolism of primarily carbohydrates.

— 6% ATP-CP

— 94% Carbohydrates

10-KM RACE (30–40 minutes)
During moderately intense activities such as a 10-kilometer race, ATP is provided by fat and carbohydrate metabolism. As the intensity increases, so does the utilization of carbohydrates for energy.

— 40% Fat

— 60% Carbohydrates

MARATHON (2.5–3 hours)
During endurance events such as marathons, ATP is primarily derived from carbohydrates, and to a lesser extent fat. A very small amount of energy is provided by the breakdown of amino acids to form glucose.

— 5% Other

— 20% Fat

— 75% Carbohydrates

DAY-LONG HIKE (5.5–7 hours)
The primary energy source for events lasting several hours at low intensity is fat (free fatty acids in the bloodstream which derive from triglycerides stored in fat cells). Carbohydrates contribute a lesser percentage of energy needs.

— 35% Carbohydrates

— 65% Fat

Glucose derived from stored muscle glycogen is the preferred carbohydrate source for energy during exercise. However, liver glycogen stores are just as important to your body during activity. Glycogen stored by the liver can be converted into glucose and delivered to the bloodstream in order to maintain normal blood glucose levels, both during times of activity and while you are at rest.

While muscle glycogen provides energy for the muscles during activity, blood glucose is the energy source for your brain. If you are not supplying your brain with the energy it needs, you may feel a lack of coordination or a lack of concentration—two things you especially *don't* want to experience during exercise or a sport competition.

Intensity Affects How Much Glucose and Glycogen You Use

Your muscles will use carbohydrates for energy no matter how intense the exercise. However, the *amount* of carbohydrate used is affected by intensity, as well as your level of fitness, initial muscle glycogen stores, and whether you're consuming carbohydrates during exercise. Research shows that as the intensity of exercise increases, so does the use of glucose and glycogen for energy.[15] At very high intensities (85 percent of VO$_2$max), most of the energy is supplied by carbohydrates in the form of muscle glycogen. During exercise of moderate intensity (65 percent of VO$_2$max), carbohydrate (in the form of blood glucose and muscle glycogen) contributes to approximately half to two-thirds of the energy needed, with the remainder coming from fat (more on this in a later section). Although carbohydrates are not the main energy source during exercise of low intensity (25 percent of VO$_2$max), they still provide some energy for the working muscles from glucose in the bloodstream. Additionally, if carbohydrates are consumed before or during exercise, the use of carbohydrates as an energy source would be greater, even at lower intensities.

When glucose is broken down at a very high rate and there is not enough oxygen, the muscles produce a by-product called **lactate**. Lactate is continuously produced and removed from the body at all times, even at rest. When produced at a low rate, the muscles can effectively clear lactate from the blood and use it directly as an energy source or convert it to glucose (which can also be used for energy). For example, during low-intensity exercise, the body is able to oxidize the lactate that is produced by the muscles for energy and therefore it does not accumulate in the working muscle tissue. This makes it an important fuel source for exercise. The body also shuttles excess lactate to other tissues, such as the brain, heart, and liver, to prevent excessive accumulation.

As exercise intensity increases, the body relies more heavily on breaking down glucose as an energy source, which occurs at a faster rate, and less oxygen becomes available. As a result, more lactate is formed and begins to accumulate in the muscles faster than it can be used for energy or shuttled elsewhere in the body. This can potentially negatively affect exercise performance due to a reduction in pH in the muscle cell. The good news is that the ability of the muscles to effectively use and shuttle lactate to other tissues improves with training.

Duration Affects How Much Glucose and Glycogen You Use

In addition to intensity, the duration of exercise also affects the source and amount of carbohydrate that you use to fuel physical activity. At the start of low- to moderate-intensity exercise, stored muscle glycogen is the main carbohydrate source of energy, although fat contributes most of the total energy at lower intensities. After about 20 minutes, as low- to moderate-intensity exercise continues, muscle glycogen stores diminish and your muscles rely more on fat for fuel (more on this in a later discussion). As your muscle glycogen stores diminish, the liver also contributes its glycogen to be converted to glucose for energy and to prevent hypoglycemia.

A pre-exercise meal must contain adequate amounts of carbohydrate.

lactate A by-product of rapid glucose metabolism.

Remember that your body will always use glycogen for energy during exercise, and if the intensity and duration of the exercise last long enough, muscle and liver glycogen stores become depleted and the activity that you are doing can no longer be sustained. Many endurance runners refer to this as "hitting the wall" or "bonking."

Conditioning Affects How Much Glucose and Glycogen You Use

Research has shown that the amount of glycogen that muscles can hold can be affected by training.[16] When your muscles are well trained, they have the ability to store 20 to 50 percent more glycogen than untrained muscles. More stored glycogen means more fuel for your working muscles, which means you can exercise for a longer period of time and increase your endurance. Just eating a high-carbohydrate meal before an exercise session or athletic competition will not increase your muscles' ability to store glycogen or optimize your performance. You need to train your muscles *and* eat a high-carbohydrate diet regularly to improve endurance.

How Much Carbohydrate Do I Need for Exercise?

Most adults should be getting 45 to 55 percent of their daily energy intake from carbohydrates. Glycogen stores are continuously being depleted and replenished. If you exercise often, eating carbohydrate-rich foods on a regular basis is important to provide your muscles with adequate glycogen. When glycogen stores are inadequate, the muscles have only a limited amount of energy available to support activity, which has been shown to reduce performance and promote fatigue.[17] Keep in mind that the glycogen storage capacity of both the muscles and the liver is limited. Once your muscles and liver have stored all of the glycogen possible, any excess glucose will be converted into fatty acids and stored in the form of body fat.

The best types of carbohydrates to eat during and/or immediately after exercise are simple carbohydrates such as sports drinks, bars, and gels, bananas, bagels, or corn flakes because they are quickly absorbed and enter the bloodstream, and therefore can be used immediately for energy (glucose) or to replenish glycogen stores. Complex carbohydrates like whole grains, rice, pasta, oatmeal, and corn are ideal a couple of hours before exercise because they take longer to digest than simple carbohydrates and enter the bloodstream much more slowly, thereby providing a sustained source of energy. Remember, however, that complex carbohydrates are generally high in fiber, and too much fiber can cause bloating, gas, and diarrhea.

You will learn more about timing your nutrient intake in a later section of this chapter. Carbohydrate recommendations for athletes range from 5 to 12 grams per kilogram of body weight per day. **Table 11.4** shows the amount of carbohydrate needed for different durations and intensities of physical activity.[18] **Carbohydrate loading** is one training strategy that athletes use to build up muscle glycogen stores before a competition (see the Nutrition in the Real World feature "Carbohydrate Loading" on the next page).

Table 11.4

Carbohydrate Needs for Activity and Recovery

Duration/ Intensity of Activity (per Day)	Grams Carbohydrate/ Kg Body Weight (per Day)
60 to 90 minutes moderate intensity	5–7
1 to 3 hours moderate to high intensity	7–12
4 to 6+ hours extreme endurance	10–13

Fat Is the Primary Energy Source during Low-Intensity Exercise

Fat supplies nearly all of the energy required during prolonged low-intensity activity. Even at rest, your body uses fat as its main energy source. Unlike glycogen, fat does not contain water, so the amount of energy stored in the form of body fat is far greater, and more concentrated, than the amount of energy that is stored as glycogen.

Fat is supplied as an energy source during exercise in two forms: fatty acids in the bloodstream (derived from food and triglycerides released from fat stores) and fatty acids in muscle tissue (also in the form of triglycerides). When the body uses stored

carbohydrate loading A diet and training strategy that maximizes glycogen stores in the body before an endurance event.

Carbohydrate Loading

The goal of carbohydrate loading before an endurance event is to maximize the storage capacity of muscle glycogen. Increasing the amount of stored muscle glycogen can improve an athlete's endurance performance by giving the energy to fuel activity at an optimal pace for a longer period of time.

Not all athletes or physically active people will have improved performance with carbohydrate loading. The people who are likely to benefit the most from this strategy are those who participate in endurance events or exercise that lasts more than 90 minutes. Examples of endurance events include marathons, triathlons, cross-country skiing, and long-distance cycling and swimming. If you exercise or train for less than 90 minutes, you should follow the standard recommendations for carbohydrate intake for athletes to ensure that you have adequate muscle glycogen stores. Research has also shown that women are less likely than men to have improved performance with carbohydrate loading because women oxidize significantly more fat and less carbohydrate and protein compared with men during endurance exercise.[1] Additionally, recall that when the muscles store more glycogen, they also hold more

water (3 grams per 1 gram of glycogen). This additional water causes an increase in weight and potential decrease in flexibility, therefore making this method less desirable for some athletes.

So how do athletes start carbohydrate loading? When this concept was first recognized by athletes, they began by training very hard for three

to four days in addition to eating a low-carbohydrate diet (less than 5 to 10 percent of total calories). This period was called the depletion phase and was thought to be necessary to increase glycogen stores during the next phase, called the loading phase. The loading phase involved three to four days of minimal or no training while eating a diet

- Taper exercise
- Eat 4–5 g carbohydrates per kg body weight each day

- Taper exercise
- Eat 10 g carbohydrates per kg body weight each day

- Eat 250–300 g carbohydrates 3–4 hours before event

Carbohydrate loading involves tapering exercise and gradually increasing carbohydrate intake the week before a competitive endurance event. On the day of the competition, a high-carb meal is eaten 3 to 4 hours before the event begins.

fat for energy, it is broken down into fatty acids and then supplied to the muscles via the bloodstream, where it is converted into energy (ATP). Muscle triglycerides are directly oxidized to provide energy to the working muscles in which they are stored.

Intensity, Duration, and Training Affect How Much Fat You Use

For low-intensity exercise, your body uses mostly fat for energy in the form of free fatty acids in the blood rather than fatty acids stored in muscles. Oxidation of fat from fat (adipose) tissue typically occurs after 15 to 20 minutes of aerobic exercise. When exercising at a low intensity for a period of up to 2 hours, fatty acids in the bloodstream that are used for energy are replaced by fatty acids from adipose tissue to sustain energy levels. During moderate exercise, approximately one-third to half of the energy needed is supplied by fat and the rest is supplied by carbohydrates. For moderate-intensity exercise lasting up to 3 hours, your body begins to use equal amounts of fatty acids derived from muscle triglycerides and fatty acids in the bloodstream (derived from adipose tissue). This, in turn, results in an increase in total fat oxidation compared with a lower intensity at which muscle triglycerides are not significantly used. At high levels of activity, fatty acids cannot be converted into high in carbohydrates. This resulted in higher muscle glycogen stores and better endurance performance.

Many people found the depletion phase hard to endure and would often experience irritability, hypoglycemia, and fatigue. In fact, today, many endurance athletes have modified this training strategy to exclude the depletion phase. Research has shown that depleting muscle glycogen stores is not necessary to increase the amount of stored muscle glycogen. However, there will be greater increases in muscle glycogen by initially depleting muscle glycogen stores.[2]

To begin a modified carbohydrate loading regimen, you should taper your exercise about seven days prior to the event by doing a little bit less activity each day. This is often the hardest recommendation to follow because many athletes feel that they will be out of shape if they stop training before competition. But tapering your exercise is necessary to increase muscle glycogen; otherwise, you will continue to burn glycogen for fuel rather than storing it to be used for energy during the upcoming event. One study showed that you can decrease your training by 70 percent of your normal training schedule about one week prior to an endurance event without negatively affecting your performance.[3]

In addition to tapering your exercise, you should eat a high-carbohydrate diet that provides about 4 to 5 grams of carbohydrate per kilogram of body weight for the first three to four days. During the last three days of tapering exercise, increase your intake of carbohydrates to 10 grams per kilogram of body weight. Lastly, a meal that is high in carbohydrate (providing about 250 to 300 grams of carbohydrate), moderate in protein, and low in fat should be consumed about 3 to 4 hours prior to the start of the event to further maximize glycogen stores.

Despite the emphasis on carbohydrates, you do not want to compromise your intake of protein and fat by eating too much carbohydrate. Remember to include at least 0.8 grams of protein per kilogram of body weight (some athletes may require more protein) in your training diet, as well as about 20 to 25 percent of calories coming from fat, preferably unsaturated fats. Below is a sample one-day menu that is high in carbohydrate, adequate in protein, and low in fat.

Table 1
Sample One-Day Menu

Breakfast	Lunch	Dinner	Snack
1 cup orange juice ½ cup Grape-Nuts 1 medium banana 1 cup 2% milk 1 English muffin 1 tbs jelly	2 slices oatmeal bread 3 oz turkey breast with lettuce, tomato 8 oz apple juice 1 cup frozen yogurt	3 cups spaghetti (6 ounces uncooked) 1 cup tomato sauce 2 oz ground turkey ¼ loaf multigrain bread (4 ounces)	1 cup vanilla yogurt 6 fig bars
750 calories	750 calories	1,300 calories	500 calories
85% carbohydrates	65% carbohydrates	70% carbohydrates	80% carbohydrates

Total: 3,300 calories: 75% carbohydrates (610 g), 15% protein (125 g), 10% fat (40 g)

energy fast enough to meet the demand; therefore, fat use decreases and carbohydrates become the preferred energy source. Also note that your body requires more oxygen to convert fat into energy compared with carbohydrate, which creates more stress for the cardiovascular system.

Your level of training can affect how much fat your body will use for energy. Muscles that are well trained will burn more fat than muscles that are not as well trained. This is thought to be caused by an increase in enzymes that are necessary to burn fat for energy. As a result, well-trained muscles use less glycogen for energy and more fat, thereby having the potential to increase endurance by "saving" your glycogen stores for later energy use. So, if you are trying to lose weight and body fat, should you reduce the intensity of your workout? The Examining the Evidence feature "The Truth about the Fat-Burning Zone" on the next page addresses this question.

How Much Fat Do I Need for Exercise?

Dietary recommendations for fat intake are generally the same for active people as for the average adult population, with 20 to 35 percent of calories coming from fat.[19] Recall from Chapter 5 that high intakes of saturated and *trans* fats have been linked to

The Truth about the Fat-Burning Zone

Many people recognize the importance of exercise, especially of the cardiovascular system, for weight loss. They head off to the gym and jump on an exercise machine to start their workout. Once on the machine, they hook up to a device that monitors their heart rate, which lets them know if they are in the "fat-burning" zone (65 to 73 percent of one's maximum heart rate) or the "cardio" zone (more than 73 percent of one's maximum heart rate). Because most people seek to lose body fat, they exercise in the fat-burning zone, believing that this is the most effective way to lose weight. After all, it is true that the body will burn more fat at lower intensities and will burn more carbohydrate as the intensity increases. So, is staying in the fat-burning zone the best advice to follow if you are trying to lose weight? The simple answer is no. Let's look at some calculations to better understand why.

If you are trying to lose weight, you need to burn more calories than you consume. Working out is an excellent way to do this, but you need to be aware of how many calories you are burning, and aim to work off as many as possible. In the fat-burning zone at 65 percent of maximum heart rate, a moderately fit person will burn an average of 220 calories during 30 minutes of exercise. Also at this same intensity, fat supplies about 50 percent of the total calories burned for energy. This means that the person is burning an average of 110 fat calories (50 percent of 220). As the intensity increases to

about 85 percent of maximum heart rate, this same person burns an average of 330 calories during 30 minutes of exercise, with fat supplying only about 33 percent of the total calories burned. Guess what? The person still burns the same number of fat calories (33 percent of 330, or 110), but is burning more total calories (330 calories) at a higher intensity, which will help meet the weight-loss goal sooner than exercising at a lower intensity (burning 220 calories). The bottom line is, you don't need to stay in the fat-burning zone to effectively lose body fat. You just need to burn calories so that there is an overall calorie deficit.

If you prefer not to exercise at a high intensity, there is an advantage to exercising at a lower intensity. If you have time for a long workout, you can probably exercise at a lower intensity for a longer period of time without getting tired. In other words, if you are jogging at 6 mph (high intensity) you may get tired after you cover 3 miles. However, if you are walking briskly at 4 mph (lower intensity), you may be able to cover 4 miles because you aren't as fatigued. Walking the extra 30 minutes and covering that extra mile will allow you to expend more overall calories during your workout (330 calories for 30 minutes of jogging versus 440 calories for 60 minutes of walking). But if you have a busy lifestyle and feel pressed for time to exercise, don't be afraid to go out of the fat-burning zone to get the most out of your workout and effectively lose weight!

Exercising in the "fat-burning" zone or the "cardio" zone are both effective methods to burn calories and reduce body weight.

WHAT DO YOU THINK?

1. What are some examples of exercises that would keep you in the fat-burning zone and in the cardio zone?
2. Have you or someone that you know stayed in the fat-burning zone to lose weight?
3. Knowing what you know now, would you still exercise in the fat-burning zone to lose weight?

high blood cholesterol levels and heart disease. Physically active people sometimes assume that because they're in shape, they don't have to worry about these diseases. While it is true that physical activity grants some protection against heart disease, athletes and other fit people can also have high cholesterol, heart attacks, and strokes. Everyone, regardless of activity level, should limit saturated fat to no more than 10 percent of total calories, while consuming 10 percent of total calories from monounsaturated fat and 10 percent of total calories from polyunsaturated fat.[20]

Some athletes, such as endurance runners and those in sports in which low body weight is important, like gymnasts and figure skaters, may feel they can benefit from a very low-fat diet (less than 20 percent). Though consuming too much dietary fat is a concern, you don't want to limit your fat intake too much. When you consume less than adequate amounts of fat, you are more likely at risk for consuming inadequate calories, essential fatty acids, and fat-soluble vitamins, which can negatively affect exercise performance.[21]

Protein Is Primarily Needed to Build and Repair Muscle

Amino acids obtained from protein are the main nutrients needed to promote muscle growth and recovery. Muscle damage is one of the most significant physiological effects of exercise, especially in weight or strength training. You need to supply your muscles with protein so that this muscle damage does not result in decreased muscle mass and strength. Not all muscle damage is bad, however. It can stimulate remodeling of the muscle cells, which increases muscle strength and mass.

The Body Can Use Protein for Energy

Your body prefers to use carbohydrate and fat as its main energy sources during exercise (refer again to Figure 11.3). Small amounts of protein are used for energy, but greater amounts are used when calorie intake and carbohydrate stores are insufficient. When needed, proteins can be broken down into amino acids and oxidized to provide energy directly to the working muscles in the form of ATP. Excess protein that is not used by your body for its normal functions is converted into glycogen or fatty acids, which can provide energy at a later time.

Muscle protein can also be an energy source by being broken down into amino acids that are then released into the bloodstream. These amino acids are carried to the liver, where they get converted into glucose, which supplies the working muscles with energy. If the body has to use a significant amount of protein for energy, including muscle protein, that protein is not available to build and repair tissues. If this occurs too often, muscle mass will likely be lost.

How Much Protein Do I Need for Exercise?

Many athletes and exercisers assume that they need substantially more protein than nonexercisers need. It is true that those who are fit and physically active need more protein than those who are sedentary, but those needs are not significantly higher. Recall from Chapter 6 that the RDA for protein for most healthy adults is 0.8 gram per kilogram of body weight per day, and most people, including athletes, far exceed this.

People who are recreational exercisers can meet their needs for protein with a balanced diet. The increased protein needs of competitive and elite athletes, as well as bodybuilders, can also be met with a balanced diet. Endurance athletes are advised to consume 1.2 to 1.4 grams of protein per kilogram of body weight per day. People who primarily participate in resistance and strength activities may need to consume as much as 1.2 to 1.7 grams of protein per kilogram of body weight per day.[22]

Total Calorie Needs Depend on the Type and Schedule of Exercise

Your daily calorie needs depend on the type of exercise (such as swimming, volleyball, or tennis) you choose and your training schedule. Playing an hour of Frisbee with your friends will use a little over 200 calories (based on a 150-pound person). Compare that with an hour of downhill skiing, which will burn over 500 calories. When eight-time Olympic gold medal champion swimmer Michael Phelps is training, he needs to thousands of calories daily to fuel his activities and maintain his weight. However, if the average jogger were to adopt this eating pattern, he would quickly gain a lot of body fat. The best way to determine if you are consuming enough calories is to monitor your weight. If your weight doesn't decrease, you are consuming enough calories. If your weight *increases*, and it's not due to an increase in muscle mass, you are consuming too many calories.

What Is the Female Athlete Triad?

Katie Sutton tried out for her school's dance program at a healthy weight of 130 pounds on her 5'5" frame. The instructors in the dance program suggested that Katie could improve her endurance if she was leaner. Over the next month, Katie added several hours a day of additional exercise to her current dance schedule, while following a very low-calorie diet. By the end of the semester, Katie's weight had dropped to 105 pounds. Katie's low-calorie diet and excessive exercise resulted in a stress fracture in her foot that prevented her from performing in the final dance performance of the semester.

The low-calorie diet that Katie followed is one part of the *female athlete triad*, a syndrome of interrelated conditions existing on a continuum of severity: low energy availability, menstrual dysfunction, and low bone mineral density. Female athletes are often pressured to reach or maintain an unrealistically low body weight and/or level of body fat. This pressure contributes to the development of disordered eating, which helps to initiate the triad. Of major concern with this disorder is that it not only reduces the performance of the athlete, but may have serious medical and psychological consequences later in life.

Components of the Female Athlete Triad

Let's look at the major components of the triad in a bit more detail.

Low Energy Availability/Disordered Eating

Athletes wishing to lose weight or maintain a low body weight may restrict their energy intake or develop abnormal eating behaviors. At the most extreme, an athlete with disordered eating may fulfill the diagnostic criteria for anorexia nervosa or bulimia nervosa. However, disordered eating occurs on a continuum and is not always so pronounced. Many athletes mistakenly believe that losing weight by any method enhances performance, and that disordered eating is harmless. Disordered eating is most common among athletes in sports where appearance is important, such as figure skating, gymnastics, and ballet, but can occur in athletes in all types of sports. It is also possible for athletes who do not exhibit disordered eating patterns to unintentionally take in fewer calories than they need, such as in Katie's case. They may appear to be eating a healthy diet—one that would be adequate for a sedentary individual—but their caloric needs are higher due to their level of physical activity.

Menstrual Dysfunction/Amenorrhea

The failure to consume enough energy to compensate for the "energy cost" of the exercise can lead to disruption of the menstrual cycle. At its most extreme and recognizable, this results in amenorrhea, the absence of three or more consecutive menstrual cycles. In Katie's case, she started to notice irregularities in her period as the semester progressed, but she didn't know

it could be a symptom of a larger problem. Unfortunately, many females welcome the convenience of not menstruating and do not report it.

Low Bone Mineral Density/Osteoporosis

Energy deficiency and decreased estrogen levels due to menstrual dysfunction contribute to bone loss and low bone mineral density. At its most extreme this causes premature osteoporosis, putting the athlete at risk for stress fractures, hip and vertebral fractures, and the loss of bone mass, which may be irreplaceable. Katie's low-calorie diet, excessive exercise, and menstrual disruption created the conditions that led to the stress fracture in her foot.

Female athletes for whom body size or appearance is an issue, such as dancers, gymnasts, and skaters, are often particularly vulnerable to the female athlete triad.

Signs and Treatment

All individuals, including friends, teachers, and coaches, involved with female athletes should be aware of the warning signs because the triad components are very often not recognized, not reported, or denied. Warning signs include menstrual changes, weight changes, disordered eating patterns, cardiac arrhythmia, depression, or stress fractures. Those working with athletes should provide a training environment in which athletes are not pressured to lose weight, and should be able to recommend appropriate nutritional, medical, and/or psychological resources if needed. Treatment of an athlete with this disorder is multidisciplinary, and needs to involve cooperation among the athlete's physician, dietitian, psychologist, coach or trainer, family, and friends.

In Katie's situation, the symptoms were caught too late and she missed out on the most important performance of the season. However, Katie's physician recognized the components of the female athlete triad and referred her to a registered dietitian. Katie was able to meet with the registered dietitian, who helped Katie create a more balanced diet to support her level of exercise and help her stress fracture heal. In the future, as Katie continues to eat adequate calories to fuel her body, her estrogen levels should return to normal and her menstrual cycle should regulate, decreasing her risk of any new stress fractures.[4, 5, 6]

Think About It

What are some strategies that could have been implemented in Katie's dance program to prevent a situation like this from happening?

Unfortunately, some female athletes in certain "lean-build" sports are under pressure to maintain a low weight that's not conducive to good health. This pressure can contribute to a complex condition known as the **female athlete triad**, as discussed in the Health Connection: A Case Study feature called "What Is the Female Athlete Triad?"

LO 11.3 **The Take-Home Message** Carbohydrate and fat are the primary sources of fuel during exercise. Carbohydrates provide energy in the form of blood glucose and muscle and liver glycogen, and are the main energy source during high-intensity exercise. Fat is the main energy source during low-intensity exercise. Carbohydrate and fat contribute equally as energy sources during moderate-intensity exercise. Protein provides amino acids that are necessary to promote muscle growth and repair muscle damage caused by exercise.

How Does the Timing of Meals Affect Fitness and Athletic Performance?

LO 11.4 List optimal food sources before, during, and after exercise.

Timing the foods that you eat around exercise has a significant impact on energy levels and recovery time. As you learned in Chapter 6, inadequate calorie intake leads to muscles being broken down for energy. This in turn can lead to loss of muscle mass and strength, and lack of energy, which can negatively affect exercise performance.

During exercise, especially weight training, muscles are under a great deal of stress, which can result in overstretching and tearing of proteins and potential inflammation. After exercise, the body is in a catabolic (breaking down) state: Muscle and liver glycogen stores are low or depleted, muscle protein is broken down, and the immune system is suppressed. Therefore, supplying the body with the nutrients needed to reverse this catabolic state into an anabolic (building up) state is crucial and necessary for optimal fitness.

Optimal Foods before Exercise

You need to eat before exercise or a competition so that you have enough energy for optimal performance. However, one of the most important considerations about eating before exercise is allowing sufficient time for the food to be digested so that it doesn't negatively affect your performance. In general, larger meals (making you feel quite full) may take 3 to 4 hours to digest, whereas smaller meals (making you feel satisfied but not overly full) may take only 2 to 3 hours to digest. If you are drinking a liquid supplement or having a small snack, you should allow about 30 minutes to 1 hour for digestion. These are general guidelines and may not apply to everyone, so be sure that you experiment with your own eating and exercise schedule well before a workout or competition so that you know how long you need to wait before starting your activity.

You just learned that carbohydrates are one of the main sources of energy during exercise. Thus, your pre-exercise meal should contain adequate amounts of carbohydrate so that you maximize muscle and liver glycogen stores and maintain normal blood glucose levels. In general, your pre-exercise meal should contain 1 to 4.5 grams of carbohydrate per kilogram of body weight and be consumed 1 to 4 hours prior to exercise.

Consuming carbohydrate immediately before exercise (about 15 to 30 minutes prior to the start) provides an advantage because it gives your muscles an immediate

Crackers can be consumed before and during endurance exercise to supply an easily digestible source of carbohydrate and help prevent early fatigue.

female athlete triad A syndrome of the three interrelated conditions occurring in some physically active females: low energy availability, menstrual dysfunction, and low bone density.

source of energy (glucose) and spares your glycogen stores so that you can exercise for a longer period or at a higher intensity without becoming tired as quickly.[23] Carbohydrate intake prior to the start of exercise can also help reduce muscle damage by causing the release of insulin, which promotes muscle protein synthesis.

Just as your body needs a continuous supply of carbohydrate, it also needs moderate amounts of protein throughout the day. Timing your protein intake around activity will have a significant impact on muscle preservation, growth, and recovery.

The consumption of foods with both protein *and* carbohydrate before exercise, such as fruit and yogurt, benefits the body by causing a greater increase in muscle glycogen synthesis than consuming carbohydrate alone. With more glycogen in your muscles, you can increase endurance. Another benefit of consuming both protein and carbohydrate before exercise is that it results in greater protein synthesis after the exercise is over compared with either protein or carbohydrate alone.[24] The making of new proteins, including muscles, is necessary for optimal fitness and muscle preservation, repair, and growth.

Foods with a higher fat content take longer to digest than foods that are higher in carbohydrate and protein. For this reason, high-fat foods should generally be avoided several hours before exercise. If you eat high-fat foods before exercise, you may feel sluggish or have stomach discomfort, which can impair your performance. Of course this is a general guideline, and not all active people have difficulty during exercise if they consume higher-fat foods before starting to exercise.

Optimal Foods during Exercise

For exercise lasting longer than 1 hour, carbohydrate intake should begin shortly after the start of exercise and continue at 15- to 20-minute intervals throughout. For long-lasting endurance activities, a total of 30 to 60 grams of carbohydrate should be consumed per hour to prevent early fatigue.[25] Sports drinks and gels are one way to take in carbohydrate immediately before and/or during activity, but foods such as crackers and sports bars are also commonly eaten.

The best types of carbohydrate to consume during exercise are glucose, sucrose, and maltodextrin because they are absorbed by the body more quickly than other carbohydrates. Fructose, the sugar found in fruit and fruit juice, should generally be avoided because it may cause gastrointestinal problems or stomach discomfort.

Many sports drinks and gels contain only carbohydrate and electrolytes; others also contain protein. For endurance athletes, consuming both carbohydrate and protein during exercise has been shown to improve net protein balance at rest as well as during exercise and postexercise recovery.[26] This will, in turn, have an effect on muscle maintenance and growth.

Optimal Foods after Exercise

What you eat after exercise will affect how fast you recover, which may affect how soon you're ready for your next workout or training session. This is especially important for competitive athletes who train more than once per day. Some people who load up on high-fat foods after a workout or competition experience fatigue that may result in less-than-optimal performance during the next workout.

The best postexercise meal is consumed quickly and contains both carbohydrate and protein. The muscles are most receptive to storing new glycogen within the first 30 to 45 minutes after you have finished exercising, so this is a crucial time period in which to provide the body with carbohydrate.[27] Research shows that consuming carbohydrate immediately after exercise also results in a more positive body protein balance.[28] In addition, protein intake immediately after exercise rather than several hours later results in greater muscle protein synthesis. Finally, the

Low-fat chocolate milk is a low-cost option for providing the whey protein and carbohydrate that help with muscle and glycogen synthesis after exercise.

consumption of protein with carbohydrate causes an even greater increase in glycogen synthesis than carbohydrate or protein alone.[29] In short, both nutrients should be consumed soon after exercise.

What is the best way to get these two nutrients? Studies have shown that consumption of carbohydrate and protein in a ratio of approximately 3:1 (in grams) is ideal to promote muscle glycogen synthesis, protein synthesis, and faster recovery time.[30] Whey protein (such as in milk) is the preferred protein source because it is rapidly absorbed and contains all of the essential amino acids that your body needs. You can use commercial shakes and drinks, but they can be expensive. A cheaper alternative is low-fat chocolate milk, which will provide you with adequate amounts of carbohydrate and protein to assist in recovery after exercise.[31] If you consume a liquid supplement or small snack after exercise, this should be followed by a high-carbohydrate, moderate-protein, low-fat meal within the next 2 hours. An old-fashioned peanut butter and jelly sandwich or a slice of cheese pizza are inexpensive and can help you recover after exercise too.

If you are a competitive athlete, always experiment with timing your nutrient intake and consuming new foods and beverages during practice, not on the day of competition. You don't want to be unpleasantly surprised to find that a particular food doesn't agree with you a few hours before an important race or other event.

In addition to consuming adequate protein and carbohydrate, drinking adequate fluids is important for exercise performance and recovery. You will learn more about hydration in a later section of this chapter.

LO 11.4 **The Take-Home Message** Consuming the right balance of nutrients at the right time can improve exercise performance and recovery time. Higher fat foods should generally be avoided before exercise, while carbohydrate and protein are important for energy and recovery before, during, and after exercise.

What Vitamins and Minerals Are Important for Fitness?

LO 11.5 Describe the importance of vitamins and minerals for physical fitness.

In addition to several other important functions, vitamins and minerals play a major role in the metabolism of carbohydrate, fat, and protein for energy during exercise. Some also act as antioxidants and help protect cells from the oxidative stress that can occur with exercise.

Antioxidants Can Help Protect Cells from Damage Caused by Exercise

Your muscles use more oxygen during exercise than while you are at rest. As a result, your body increases its production of free radicals that damage cells, especially during intense, prolonged exercise. Antioxidants, such as vitamins E and C, are known to protect cells from the damage of free radicals. Vitamin C also assists in the production of collagen, which provides most of the structure of connective tissues like bone, tendons, and ligaments. This, in turn, can affect your likelihood of developing strains, sprains, and fractures that may occur as a result of exercise.

Research has not proven that supplementation with vitamins E or C improves athletic performance, nor that it decreases oxidative stress in highly trained athletes.[32]

Therefore, you do not need to consume more than the RDA of these vitamins, but you do need to be sure to consume adequate amounts from foods like nuts, vegetable oils, broccoli, and citrus fruits to meet your needs.

Some Minerals Can Be of Concern in Highly Active People

You learned in Chapter 8 that minerals have important roles in normal body functions and health. Minerals are also essential to physical fitness and athletic performance. Though active people do not need more minerals than less active individuals, there are two minerals they must be careful to consume in adequate amounts.

Iron

Iron is important to exercise because it is necessary for energy metabolism and transporting oxygen throughout the body and within muscle cells. Iron is a structural component of hemoglobin and myoglobin, two proteins that carry and store oxygen in the blood and muscle, respectively. If iron levels are low, hemoglobin levels can also fall, diminishing the blood's ability to carry oxygen to the cells. If this occurs during exercise, you will experience early fatigue. (You can also feel tired if iron levels are low and you are not exercising.) Iron supplementation can improve aerobic performance for people with depleted iron stores.[33]

Many athletes and physically fit people are prone to iron-deficiency anemia. Although iron-deficiency anemia can occur in both females and males, female athletes are at a greater risk. Long-distance runners, as well as athletes in sports where they must "make weight," have also been noted to be at higher risk for iron-deficiency anemia. Athletes in other sports such as basketball, tennis, softball, and swimming also have been shown to have suboptimal iron status.[34]

Low iron levels can be a result of poor dietary intake or increased iron losses. Women can lose a lot of iron during menstruation, depending on their iron status and menstrual blood flow. Iron is also lost in sweat, but not in amounts significant enough to lead to iron deficiency.

Another effect of exercise on iron is intravascular hemolysis (*hemo* = blood, *lysis* = breaking down), which is the bursting of red blood cells. This happens when you are running and your feet repeatedly hit the ground (a hard surface), causing red blood cells to burst and release iron. This iron is recycled by the body and not lost, and therefore does not typically contribute to iron deficiency.

Some people experience decreased levels of hemoglobin because of training, especially when the training is quite strenuous. During exercise your blood volume increases, which in turn causes lower concentrations of hemoglobin in the blood. This is often referred to as sports anemia, or pseudoanemia, and is not the same as iron-deficiency anemia. Iron-deficiency anemia typically has to be treated with iron supplementation. Sports anemia can be corrected on its own because the body can adapt to training and produce more red blood cells, which restores normal hemoglobin levels.

Whether you exercise or not, you can maintain your iron status by consuming adequate amounts of iron-rich foods, and supplements if necessary. However, many female athletes do not consume enough iron to meet their needs, which often leads to low iron levels. Vegetarian athletes are especially susceptible to iron deficiency and need to plan their diets appropriately so they consume adequate amounts of foods plentiful in iron.

Calcium

Most people know about the importance of calcium to maintain bone health, but athletes are particularly susceptible to broken bones and fractures. Therefore, they need to consume enough calcium in their diets to reduce their risk of sustaining

Kidney beans, steak, and iron-fortified bread and cereal are good sources of iron. Female and vegetarian athletes are at higher risk of iron deficiency.

these types of injuries. Calcium affects both skeletal and heart muscle contraction, and hormone and neurotransmitter activity during exercise. It also assists in blood clotting when you have a cut or other minor hemorrhage, which may occur during exercise or competition.

Many people may not be aware that calcium is lost in sweat, and the more you sweat the more calcium you lose. One study concluded that exercise can increase bone mineral content (the mass of all minerals in bone) even when calcium intake is below the recommended amount. The exercise effects on bone mineral density were sufficient to compensate for the calcium lost through sweating.[35]

Calcium supplements are not recommended unless your intake from food and beverages is inadequate and you are not meeting your daily needs. Choosing foods that are high in calcium, including fortified foods, can ensure that athletes meet their needs for calcium.

Vitamin and Mineral Supplements Are Generally Not Necessary

Active people generally do not need more vitamins than sedentary people, because vitamins can be used repeatedly in metabolic reactions. Many athletes mistakenly believe that vitamins and minerals themselves supply energy, and often consume extra vitamins and minerals so that they can perform better. In fact, studies have shown that multivitamin and mineral supplements are the supplements most commonly used by college athletes.[36] As you know by now, vitamins and minerals themselves don't provide energy. But can taking these supplements improve athletic performance for other reasons? The answer is: not unless you are experiencing a deficiency. For people who consume enough vitamins and minerals in their diet, taking more than the RDA will not result in improved performance during exercise.[37]

Everyone, not just athletes, should obtain vitamins and minerals through nutrient-dense foods before considering the use of supplements. Eating a wide variety of foods that meets your calorie needs will likely provide your body with plenty of vitamins and minerals. Thus, it is probably a waste of money to use vitamin and mineral supplements.

Eating calcium-rich foods daily assists with bone health, muscle contraction, and blood clotting.

LO 11.5 **The Take-Home Message** Athletes need to pay special attention to their intakes of certain vitamins and minerals. Antioxidants such as vitamins E and C are not needed in excessive amounts, as they have not been proven to reduce oxidative damage to cells from exercise. Iron is important because of its role in transporting oxygen in blood and muscle, and deficiency is prevalent among athletes, especially females and vegetarians. Calcium intake is important for bone health and muscle contraction. Adequate amounts of all nutrients can be consumed in foods, so supplements are not usually necessary.

How Does Fluid Intake Affect Fitness?

LO 11.6 Explain the relationship between fluid intake and fitness.

As basic as it sounds, water is one of the most important nutrients during physical activity. When you drink too little fluid, or you lose too much fluid and electrolytes through sweating, this causes physiological changes that can negatively affect exercise performance and health. You may experience early fatigue or weakness when your body doesn't have sufficient amounts of water. Consuming adequate fluids on a

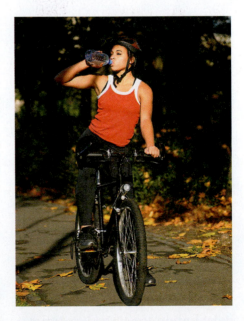

Staying hydrated during physical activity is important to maintain electrolyte balance and help regulate body temperature.

regular basis, as well as monitoring fluid losses during physical activity, are key to maintaining optimal performance and preventing **dehydration** and electrolyte imbalance.

Fluid and Electrolyte Balance and Body Temperature Are Affected by Exercise

You learned in Chapter 8 that water and some electrolytes are necessary to maintain the fluid balance in your body. When you are physically active, your body will lose more water via sweat and exhalation of water vapor than when you are less active, so you need to replace water lost during exercise to maintain normal fluid balance.

Sodium and chloride are the two primary electrolytes that are lost in sweat. Potassium is also lost in sweat, but to a lesser extent than sodium and chloride. An electrolyte imbalance can cause heat cramps, as well as nausea, lowered blood pressure, and edema in the hands and feet, all of which can hinder your performance. When electrolyte losses are within the range of normal daily dietary intake, they can easily be recovered by consuming a balanced meal within 24 hours after exercise. Electrolytes can also be replaced by beverages that contain them, such as sports drinks, if food is not available.

The sweat you produce during exercise releases heat and helps keep your body temperature normal. The amount of fluid lost through sweating depends on the type, intensity, and duration of exercise and varies from person to person. Some people sweat heavily, while others may sweat very little. Regardless of how much you sweat, it is important that you don't allow your body to lose too much fluid without replacing it with water or other beverages.

Exercising in hot, humid weather results in more fluid lost in breathing in addition to sweating, which will increase your body's need for fluids. However, if the air outside is very humid (that is, it contains a lot of water), sweat may not evaporate off the skin, and the body won't cool down. This can cause heat to build up in your body, placing you at risk for heat exhaustion or heat stroke. One significant warning sign of heat stroke is if you are *not* sweating when you should be. This happens when you are extremely dehydrated and cannot produce sweat, which prevents the release of heat and causes your body temperature to rise. Other warnings signs of heat exhaustion and heat stroke are shown in **Table 11.5**.

Table 11.5
Warning Signs of Heat Exhaustion and Heat Stroke

Heat Exhaustion	Heat Stroke
Profuse sweating	Extremely high body temperature (above 103°F [39.4°C], measured orally)
Fatigue	
Thirst	Red, hot, and dry skin (no sweating)
Muscle cramps	Rapid, strong pulse
Headache	Rapid, shallow breathing
Dizziness or light-headedness	Throbbing headache
Weakness	Dizziness
Nausea and vomiting	Nausea
Cool, moist skin	Extreme confusion
	Unconsciousness

dehydration Loss of water in the body as a result of inadequate fluid intake or excess fluid loss, such as through sweating.

You Need Fluids before, during, and after Exercise

Many active people are aware that it's important to stay hydrated during exercise, but your need for water doesn't begin with your first sit-up or lap around the track. Meeting your fluid needs before and after activity is also important to maintain fluid and electrolyte balance and optimize performance.

Consuming adequate fluid every day is important for everyone, from sedentary individuals to competitive athletes. Recall from Chapter 8 that most healthy adult women need approximately 9 cups of beverages daily, while most healthy adult men need about 13 cups. This is a general guideline to follow for adequate hydration. Another way to determine your estimated daily fluid needs is to divide your body weight by 2. This tells you the number of ounces of fluid you need (8 ounces = 1 cup) on a daily basis, not including the additional needs associated with exercising.

For active individuals, pre-exercise hydration is essential to replace sweat losses. As you learned in Chapter 8, you can determine your fluid needs during exercise by weighing yourself both before and after an activity. Because the amount of weight that is lost is mainly due to losses in body water, you should consume 16 to 24 fluid ounces (about 2 to 3 cups) of fluid for every pound of body weight lost.[39] The American College of Sports Medicine (ACSM) has specific recommendations for how much fluid to drink before and during exercise. See **Table 11.6** for these recommendations.

Some Beverages Are Better than Others

Beverages like tea, coffee, soft drinks, fruit juice, and, of course, water contribute to your daily fluid needs. But what is the best type of fluid for preventing dehydration prior to and during activity? What about for rehydrating your body after activity? For these purposes, not all beverages are equal.

Sports drinks are popular in the fitness world and are often marketed as tasty beverages to all groups of people, not just athletes. They typically contain 6 to 8 percent carbohydrate as well as sodium and potassium, two electrolytes that are critical in muscle contraction and maintaining fluid balance. One purpose of sports drinks is to replace fluid and electrolytes that are lost through sweating. These drinks have been shown to be superior to water for rehydration, mostly because their flavor causes people to drink more than they would of just plain water.[40]

Sports drinks can replace electrolytes and fluids lost during exercise.

Table 11.6	
ACSM Hydration Recommendations	
When?	**How Much Fluid?**
4 hours before exercise	16–20 fl oz (2–2½ cups)
10 to 15 minutes before exercise	8–12 fl oz (1–1½ cups)
At 15- to 20-minute intervals when exercising less than 60 minutes	3–8 fl oz (3/8–1 cup)
At 15- to 20-minute intervals when exercising more than 60 minutes	3–8 fl oz (3/8–1 cup) sports beverage (5–8 percent carbohydrate with electrolytes)
After exercise for every pound of body weight lost	20–24 fl oz (2½–3 cups)

For most people, water will provide adequate hydration before, during, and after exercise, and it's lower in both calories and cost than sports drinks.

Sports drinks also provide additional carbohydrate to prevent glycogen depletion. This is beneficial if you engage in long endurance events or exercise when glycogen stores may be running low. When you consume a sports drink during exercise, you provide your body with glucose to be used as an immediate energy source and prevent further decline in muscle glycogen stores.

However, not everyone actually needs sports drinks in order to stay adequately hydrated, and at about 60 calories per 8-ounce cup, they can be a source of unwanted extra calories. For exercise that lasts less than 60 minutes, water is sufficient to replace fluids lost through sweating and food consumption following exercise will adequately replace electrolytes. A sports drink is most appropriate when physical activity lasts longer than 60 minutes.[41]

Other beverages may be suboptimal for hydration during physical activity. Fruit juice and juice drinks contain a larger concentration of carbohydrate and do not hydrate the body as quickly as beverages with a lower concentration of carbohydrates (like sports drinks). Carbonated drinks contain a large amount of water; however, the air bubbles from the carbonation can cause stomach bloating and may limit the amount of fluid consumed.

Though alcohol may seem like an unlikely choice for rehydration, some people may drink alcoholic beverages, such as beer, in order to quench thirst. But because alcohol is a diuretic, it can actually contribute to dehydration. Alcohol during athletic performance can also impair your judgment and reasoning, which can lead to injuries not only for you, but for those around you.

Another diuretic, the caffeine found in coffee and some soft drinks, should only be consumed in moderate amounts, because excessive intake can cause increased heart rate, nausea, vomiting, excessive urination, restlessness, anxiety, and difficulty sleeping. Moderate caffeine intake is about 250 milligrams (the amount found in about three cups of coffee) per day.[42]

Consuming Too Little or Too Much Fluid Can Be Harmful

As your body loses fluid through sweating and exhalation during physical activity, it will let you know that you need to replace these fluids by sending a signal of thirst. However, by the time you're thirsty, you may already be dehydrated. **Figure 11.4** shows the effect of dehydration on exercise performance. As you can see from the figure, thirst is not a good indicator of fluid needs for most athletes and physically active people. Knowing the warning signs of dehydration so that you can respond by drinking adequate fluids will help prevent health consequences and impaired exercise performance.

If you become dehydrated over a short period of time, such as during a single exercise session or sport competition, **acute dehydration** may set in. Acute dehydration most commonly occurs if you are not adequately hydrated before beginning a hard exercise session, especially if you have been sick, if it is extremely hot and humid, or if the temperature is significantly different from what you are used to. To prevent acute dehydration, follow a regimented hydration schedule using water or sports drinks to hydrate before, during, and after exercise sessions and/or competition.

Chronic dehydration refers to when you are not adequately hydrated over an extended period of time, such as during several sport practices or games. The most common warning signs of chronic dehydration include fatigue, muscle soreness, poor recovery from a workout, headaches, and nausea. If your urine is very dark and you do not need to go to the bathroom every 3 or 4 hours, then you could be experiencing chronic dehydration. As with acute dehydration, following a regimented hydration schedule throughout the day will help prevent chronic dehydration.

When speaking of hydration and physical activity, we are usually concerned about consuming *enough* fluids so that we do not become dehydrated. As you recall

acute dehydration Dehydration starting after a short period of time.

chronic dehydration Dehydration over a long period of time.

Calculating Your Fluid Needs for Endurance Exercise

The next time you take a 1-hour training run, use the following process to determine your fluid needs.

1. Make sure that you are properly hydrated before the workout. Your urine should be clear.
2. Do a warm-up run to the point where you start to sweat, then stop. Urinate if necessary.
3. Weigh yourself on an accurate scale.
4. Run for one hour at an intensity similar to your targeted race.
5. Drink a measured amount of a beverage of your choice during the run to quench your thirst. Be sure to keep track of how much you drink.
6. Do not urinate during the run.
7. After you have finished the run, weigh yourself again on the same scale you used in Step 3.

8. Calculate your fluid needs using the following formula:
   a. Enter your body weight from Step 3 in pounds _____
   b. Enter your body weight from Step 7 in pounds – _____
   c. Subtract b from a = _____
      × 15.3
   d. Convert the pounds of weight in c to fluid ounces by multiplying by 15.3 _____
   e. Enter the amount of fluid you consumed during the run in ounces + _____
   f. Add e to d = _____

The final figure is the number of ounces of fluid that you must consume per hour to remain well hydrated.

from Chapter 8, consuming too much fluid can also be harmful. Taking in too much water without sufficient electrolytes can result in **hyponatremia**. Symptoms of severe hyponatremia may include rapid weight gain, bloated stomach, nausea, vomiting, swollen hands and feet, headache, dizziness, confusion, disorientation, and lack of coordination. Hyponatremia is more likely to occur in those who participate in endurance sports or prolonged exercise periods (greater than 4 hours), in which fluid and sodium loss is more likely.

Figure 11.4 Effects of Dehydration on Exercise Performance
Failing to stay hydrated during exercise or competition can result in fatigue and cramps and, in extreme cases, heat exhaustion. Because the thirst mechanism doesn't kick in until after dehydration has begun, replacing fluids throughout physical activity is important.

hyponatremia Dangerously low levels of sodium in the blood.

Drinking as much fluid as possible and "staying ahead of thirst" has been the recommendation for hydration among long-distance runners for quite some time. Due to the growing concern about overhydration and hyponatremia, USA Track & Field (USATF) provides guidelines on hydration in order to lower the risk of hyponatremia among long-distance runners. USATF recommends consuming 100 percent of fluids lost due to sweat while exercising, and to be sensitive to the onset of thirst as the signal to drink, rather than "staying ahead of thirst."[43]

If you are a distance runner, take the Self-Assessment called "Calculating Your Fluid Needs for Endurance Exercise" on the previous page to determine your fluid needs during long-distance races.[44] Keep in mind that you should perform this hydration test well before a competition or event, and perform the test again if your level of fitness improves or if the climate changes from when you initially determined your fluid needs. If you're not a runner, you can take the Self-Assessment called "Are You Meeting Your Fitness Recommendations and Eating for Exercise?" to determine if you are meeting exercise and dietary recommendations.

LO 11.6 **The Take-Home Message** Being adequately hydrated before, during, and after exercise is important to sustain fluid and electrolyte balance and a normal body temperature. Inadequate hydration can impair performance. Water is the preferred beverage for hydration, but sports drinks can be beneficial during moderate- or vigorous-intensity exercise that lasts longer than 60 minutes. Too little fluid intake can result in acute or chronic dehydration, while consuming too much water can lead to hyponatremia.

Can Dietary Supplements Contribute to Fitness?

LO 11.7 List and describe ergogenic aids that claim to improve athletic performance and physical fitness.

Competitive athletes are always looking for an edge, and many turn to supplements in the hope of improving their performance. The pill and powder manufacturers may claim that their products enhance immunity, boost metabolism, improve memory, or provide some other physical advancement. Because dietary supplements are not strictly regulated by the Food and Drug Administration, their manufacturers do not have to prove the purity, quality, safety, or efficacy of any of their products or claims. As a result, many athletes risk their health and, in some cases, eligibility for competition by taking supplements that can be ineffective, dangerous, or contain banned substances. Proper nutrition and exercise should be first and foremost in any training regimen. Once these requirements have been met, then supplementation can be considered to improve health and overall fitness. Meeting with a sports dietitian will help you determine if you need supplements and what risks you might be taking by consuming them.

Dietary Supplements and Ergogenic Aids May Improve Performance, but Can Have Side Effects

The term **ergogenic aid** describes any substance, including dietary supplements, used to improve athletic performance. Although the makers of dietary supplements do not have to prove their effectiveness, researchers have examined several supplements and their effects on athletic performance. Studies have indicated that

ergogenic aid A substance, such as a dietary supplement, used to enhance athletic performance.

some dietary supplements have a positive effect on performance, while others do not. Further, some ergogenic aids cause serious side effects. Let's take a closer look at some of the most popular dietary supplements and ergogenic aids in the fitness industry.

Creatine

Creatine is one of the best-known dietary supplements in the fitness industry today. In the early 1990s, research revealed that creatine supplementation increased creatine stores in the muscles (in the form of creatine phosphate), which increased the amount of ATP generated and improved performance during high-intensity, short-duration exercise.[45]

However, the data on whether creatine enhances performance is mixed. Studies have shown that creatine supplementation does improve athletic performance in high-intensity, short-duration activities such as weight training, when the body relies on anaerobic energy metabolism. Creatine supplementation has also been shown to increase muscle strength and muscle mass.[46] But research yields mixed results as to whether creatine supplementation improves sprint-running performance, with some studies showing improvement and others showing no benefit.[47]

To date, creatine has not been found to have negative effects on blood pressure, or kidney or liver function among healthy people, when taken within recommended usage guidelines.[48] Still, anyone considering taking creatine supplements should check with a health care provider first.

Athletes sometimes take supplements, such as creatine or caffeine, to enhance their athletic performance. Supplements are not strictly regulated by the FDA, so their quality and effectiveness can vary widely.

Caffeine

Caffeine used to be known mostly in the context of its negative effect on hydration (recall that caffeine is a diuretic). Today, caffeine has gained popularity as an ergogenic aid among athletes, trainers, and coaches. Caffeine may decrease perception of effort by stimulating the central nervous system, directly affect the breakdown of muscle glycogen, and increase the availability of fatty acids during exercise, therefore sparing glycogen stores. Studies on the effects of caffeine on exercise have shown that caffeine does enhance athletic performance, mostly during endurance events.[49] However, research has not proven that caffeine provides any benefit during short-duration activities, such as sprinting.[50] Caffeine is considered a banned substance by some athletic associations when consumed in high amounts. For example, the National Collegiate Athletic Association (NCAA) classifies caffeine as a banned substance when urine concentrations exceed 15 micrograms per milliliter. For most people, this would be the equivalent of drinking four or five cups of coffee within one hour.

Anabolic Steroids

Anabolic steroids are sometimes used by athletes seeking to bulk up. Because they are testosterone based, they can have undesirable effects on the body for both men and women.

Anabolic steroids (*anabolic* = to stimulate growth) are testosterone-based substances designed to mimic the bodybuilding traits of testosterone. There are two primary effects of anabolic steroids. The anabolic effect, which is the one users are seeking, results in the promotion of protein growth and muscle development, which leads to bigger muscles and greater strength. Most athletes want to be stronger and will often turn to anabolic steroids to build up muscle to a level that's not naturally possible.

The other, undesirable, effect of anabolic steroids is the androgenic effect (*andro* = testosterone promoting). Taking in testosterone causes the body to decrease its own production of the hormone, leading to a hormone imbalance. In men, this can cause shrinkage of the testicles, decreased sperm production, impotence, painful urination, severe acne (especially on the back), and changes in hair growth (an increase in facial hair and a decrease in hair on the head). Men may also experience psychiatric side effects such as extreme mood swings and aggressiveness, which can lead to violence.

Women who use anabolic steroids also experience androgenic effects. Just as with men using anabolic steroids, women experience severe acne, increased facial and body hair, and loss of hair on the head. Additionally, women may experience a lower voice, increased aggressiveness, amenorrhea, and increased sex drive.

Although anabolic steroids can increase muscle mass and strength, their use among collegiate and professional athletes is prohibited by most governing agencies. Abusing anabolic steroids, to improve performance or physical appearance, can lead to severe health consequences such as liver and kidney tumors, liver cancer, high blood pressure, trembling, and increases in LDL cholesterol.

Growth Hormone

Growth hormone has been promoted with claims that it will increase muscle mass and strength and decrease body fat, thereby improving performance. Some competitive athletes use growth hormone instead of anabolic steroids to build muscles because they believe it is less likely to be detected through current testing methods.

Growth hormone is naturally produced by the pituitary gland to stimulate growth in children. Synthetic, or man-made, growth hormone was originally created for children with growth hormone deficiency to enable them to grow to their full height. It targets numerous tissues, including bones, skeletal muscle, fat cells, immune cells, and liver cells. Growth hormone increases protein synthesis by increasing amino acid transport across cell membranes, causing an increase in muscle mass but not strength. This increased muscle mass but not strength could actually impair performance by reducing one's power, speed, and endurance.

Growth hormone also decreases glycogen synthesis and the use of glucose for energy, causing an increase in fat breakdown and the use of fatty acids for energy. This, in turn, can improve body composition by decreasing body fat. For these reasons, many people assume they can improve their performance with the use of growth hormone.

Little research exists on the effectiveness of growth hormone on improving fitness and athletic performance, and the results of studies that have been done are mixed. Growth hormone has been shown to reduce body fat and increase fat-free mass in well-trained adults.[51] However, other studies show that it does not improve muscle strength or lean body mass in healthy adult athletes or the elderly.[52] It also appears to have no positive effect on cardiovascular performance in adults with growth hormone deficiency.[53]

Abuse of growth hormone can have serious health effects, including the development of diabetes, atherosclerosis (hardening of the arteries), and hypertension. Excess growth hormone can also cause **acromegaly**, a condition in which tissues, bones, and internal organs grow abnormally large.

Erythropoietin and Blood Doping

Erythropoietin is a hormone produced by the kidneys when there is a decrease in blood oxygen levels. The hormone travels to the bone marrow and stimulates the formation of red blood cells, which carry oxygen to tissues. Synthetic versions of erythropoietin are used as ergogenic aids by athletes because increasing the number of red blood cells increases the oxygen-carrying capacity of the blood. This results in the athlete's being able to train at a higher intensity without becoming fatigued as quickly,[54] thereby having the potential to improve performance and overall physical fitness. Despite its popularity among competitive athletes, synthetic erythropoietin is a banned substance in most athletic organizations.

Before synthetic erythropoietin was discovered, the most common way to increase the oxygen-carrying capacity of the blood was blood doping. Blood doping, or red blood cell reinfusion, involves removing 250 to 500 milliliters (about 0.5 to 1 pint) of an athlete's own blood, extracting the red blood cells, and storing them for a few weeks prior to competition, during which time the athlete's body produces more red blood cells. The stored red blood cells are reinfused as the competition day approaches, so that the athlete has a higher than normal number of blood cells in his or her body. This results in an increase in the amount of oxygen in the blood, which can increase aerobic endurance.

Synthetic erythropoietin and blood doping can be dangerous because they increase blood viscosity (thickness). If the blood becomes too thick, it moves slowly and can clog capillaries. If this occurs in the brain, it can result in a stroke. If there is a blood clot in the heart, it can cause a heart attack. Both of these can be life-threatening. Erythropoietin may also cause sudden death during sleep, which is believed to have been a contributing factor in numerous deaths among professional European cyclists.

In 2012, U.S. cyclist Lance Armstrong shocked the sports world after he admitted to using performance-enhancing drugs including steroids, erythropoietin, and growth hormones. Consequently, he received a lifetime ban from sports from the U.S. Anti-Doping Agency and was stripped of all seven Tour de France titles, in addition to having a tarnished image and lack of respect from other athletes, sports organizations, and devoted fans.

Table 11.7 summarizes the supplements that are often used to enhance athletic performance.

Sports Bars, Shakes, and Meal Replacers May Provide Benefits

Sports bars and shakes are not considered dietary supplements because they are more like food and contain one or more macronutrients.

The main energy source in most sports bars and shakes is carbohydrate, with protein and fat contributing smaller amounts of energy. The ratio of the

The man on the right, who is more than eight feet tall, has acromegaly caused by a tumor on his pituitary gland. Growth hormone abuse can also cause acromegaly in specific tissues, bones, or organs of the body.

acromegaly A condition caused by excess growth hormone in which tissues, bones, and internal organs grow abnormally large.

Table 11.7

The Truth about Supplements and Ergogenic Aids

Supplement/Ergogenic Aid	Belief or Claim	Evidence/Potential Side Effects
Multivitamin/mineral (most common among college athletes)	Improves overall health and performance; provides energy	Will improve health and performance only when deficiencies exist. Avoid multivitamin/mineral supplements containing more than 100% RDA of contents. Vitamins and minerals do not directly supply energy, but assist with the breakdown of carbohydrate, fat, and protein to use for energy.
Creatine	Increases muscle mass and strength; makes athlete faster and stronger	Mixed results in clinical trials. Has been shown to increase muscle mass and strength and improve performance in high-intensity, short-duration exercise by increasing ATP. Mixed results in improving performance in exercise of longer duration. No negative effects seen in healthy individuals.
Caffeine	Improves endurance	Has been shown to improve endurance in some athletes, but no improvement shown in short-duration activities. NCAA lists caffeine as a banned substance when urine concentrations exceed 15 mcg/ml.
Anabolic steroids	Increase muscle mass, size, and strength	Have been shown to increase muscle mass, size, and strength, but also contribute many negative side effects such as hormone imbalance, changes in hair growth, shrinkage of testicles and decreased sperm count in men, and psychiatric effects like extreme mood swings and aggressiveness. Steroids are illegal in the United States unless prescribed by a physician.
Growth hormone	Increases muscle mass and strength, decreases body fat	Mixed results in clinical trials regarding improved athletic performance. May improve body composition in well-trained adults, but not others. Can have negative side effects such as acromegaly, and the development of diabetes, atherosclerosis, and hypertension. NCAA lists GH as a banned substance.
Erythropoietin	Improves cardiorespiratory fitness and endurance	Has been shown to improve cardiorespiratory fitness and endurance in athletes, but can be dangerous by increasing blood thickness and possibly forming blood clots. Has been linked to sudden death during sleep among European cyclists. NCAA lists erythropoietin as a banned substance.

Practical Nutrition VIDEO

Energy Bars: Are They Needed?

Energy bars can seem like the most simple choice for food on the go. But are they really the best option for fueling your active lifestyle? Scan this QR code with your mobile device to access the video. You can also access the video in MasteringNutrition™.

macronutrients in these foods varies depending on the purpose. Bars and shakes that are intended to provide energy for and recovery from exercise have a greater proportion of energy supplied by carbohydrates. Those that are promoted for muscle protein synthesis typically contain more protein than carbohydrate and fat. Bars and shakes that are high in protein are often used by vegetarians and some athletes who may think that they need additional sources of protein in their diet. Most bars and shakes also contain a variety of vitamins and minerals. Of course, these vitamins and minerals may not be necessary if you are consuming balanced meals regularly or taking a daily multivitamin. **Table 11.8** separates fact from fiction when it comes to using protein supplements to bulk up.

If you're a supremely busy person, these products may be a convenient alternative to meals or snacks prepared at home. However, keep in mind that these items are often expensive. An energy bar may be trendy and easy to stash in your book bag, but an old-fashioned peanut butter sandwich on whole-grain bread would cost less and be just as easy to carry. Alternatively, you could even make your own energy bars for much less than it costs to buy them (see **Figure 11.5**).

Table 11.8

Bulking Up on Protein to Bulk Up?

Probably one of the biggest dietary misconceptions related to fitness is that to bulk up your muscles, you need to bulk up the protein or amino acids in your diet. Although athletes need more dietary protein than less active folks, their diets are likely supplying more than enough to build muscle. Expensive protein supplements are not only unnecessary, but may actually provide undesirable results.

The following chart will help you separate fact from fiction:

Fact	Fiction
You need weight-resistance training to build muscle mass. The purpose of resistance training is to stress the muscle tissue so it increases its bulk. This is the only process that will result in increased muscle strength.	**Protein intake is more important than weight-resistance training to build muscle.** This is pure fiction, as regularly scheduled weight-resistance exercises are a key component to building muscle. No matter how much protein you consume, you won't build muscle without proper training.
Consuming adequate daily calories, especially from carbohydrates and fat, are vital to building muscle. A diet adequate in all three nutrients—carbohydrates, fat, and protein—is a muscle must! You need adequate carbohydrates and fats to fuel your workouts so that your dietary protein will be preserved to build and repair your muscles.	**There isn't any downside to eating a lot of protein.** Excessive amounts of protein, beyond your daily calorie needs, will be stored as body fat. Also, excessive protein burdens the kidneys to excrete the excess nitrogen as urea in urine.
The best recovery snack after your workout is one that will supply both carbohydrates and protein. Carbohydrates are needed for post-workout recovery to replenish your glycogen stores. Protein is also needed to aid in muscle repair and growth. Peanut butter on crackers with a glass of milk, yogurt and fruit, or chocolate milk all make excellent post-workout snacks.	**The protein and amino acids in supplements are more easily used by the body.** Your body doesn't distinguish between sources of protein and amino acids, but your wallet does. A supplement can cost more than $25 for 12 servings. Whole foods not only provide all three nutrients needed to build muscle, but they are also less expensive than overpriced supplements.
For best results, your recovery snack or meal should occur within 30 to 45 minutes of your workout. It's a fact!	**It doesn't matter when you eat after your workout.** Wrong again. Timing is everything, and waiting too long will diminish the body's ability to use the newly consumed carbohydrate and protein for glycogen replacement and muscle repair.

No Oven Needed Energy Bars

Ingredients:
5 Tablespoons natural peanut butter
6 scoops chocolate whey protein (~130 grams protein)
1 cup dry oats
1 cup non-fat dry milk
1 teaspoon vanilla
1/2 cup water

Directions:
Spray an 8x8 inch baking dish with non-stick cooking spray. Mix oats, whey protein, and non-fat dry milk in a bowl. Stir in peanut butter (mixture will look crumbly and dry). Add water and vanilla to mixture and stir until it forms a dough. Spray a clean spatula with non-stick cooking spray and use it to spread dough in baking dish. Refrigerate for a few hours, then cut into squares. Wrap bars individually in plastic wrap and keep in refrigerator until you are ready to eat them!

Figure 11.5 "No Oven Needed" **Energy Bars**
Try this recipe as an inexpensive alternative to commercial energy bars.

LO 11.7 The Take-Home Message Dietary supplements and ergogenic aids, such as creatine, caffeine, anabolic steroids, growth hormone, erythropoietin, and blood doping, may enhance performance, but can have serious health effects. Sports bars and shakes are convenient sources of energy, but are more expensive than whole foods and should only be included as a minor part of an overall healthy diet.

MADE over MADE better

Many athletes choose quick, convenient foods that are often processed, high in refined sugars, and low in protein. Making a few small changes in your diet can result in big gains in your physical fitness. Here are some typical foods consumed by athletes made over to provide more balanced nutrients and fuel the body for exercise.

If you like this. . .

Try this to fuel your exercise!

Pop Tarts
2 pastries = 360 calories
Fat: 2 grams
Carbohydrates: 76 grams
Protein: 4 grams

Whole-Wheat Bagel with Peanut Butter
1 bagel with 1 tbs peanut butter = 345 calories
Fat: 10 grams
Carbohydrates: 54 grams
Protein: 16 grams

Potato Chips
1 oz = 160 calories
Fat: 10 grams
Carbohydrates: 15 grams
Protein: 2 grams

Trail Mix (dried fruit and nuts)
1 oz = 140 calories
Fat: 10 grams
Carbohydrates: 10 grams
Protein: 5 grams

Ramen Noodles
1 package = 380 calories
Fat: 14 grams
Carbohydrates: 26 grams
Protein: 4 grams

Baked Potato Topped with Beans
1 large potato with 1/2 cup beans = 380 calories
Fat: 0.5 gram
Carbohydrates: 83 grams
Protein: 14 grams

Soda (cola)
12 oz = 140 calories
Fat: 0 grams
Carbohydrates: 65 grams
Protein: 0 grams

Low-Fat Chocolate Milk
12 oz = 270 calories
Fat: 4 grams
Carbohydrates: 44 grams
Protein: 17 grams

Should Energy Drinks Have Caffeine Limits Similar to Those for Soda?

In 2013, doctors at Johns Hopkins University School of Medicine and the University of Maryland School of Public Health called on the Food and Drug Administration (FDA) to limit caffeine in energy drinks.[1] Drinking more than the recommended maximum amount of caffeine—400 milligrams, or about 4 8 ounce cups of coffee a day—can result in side effects such as insomnia, irritability, fast heart beat, and even death in extreme cases.[2] Ingesting too much caffeine is a serious health concern, especially for children and adolescents.[3] Energy drinks, which have increased dramatically in popularity, may contain 200 mg or more of caffeine—half the recommended daily dose for an adult. A person using energy drinks to boost their workout or to stay awake during an evening outing could easily overdose on caffeine, and caffeine overdose is an increasing problem in the United States.[4] Should the FDA limit the amount of caffeine allowed in energy drinks? Take a close look at the arguments for both sides and see what you think.

yes

- Energy drinks are similar to soda, and like soda, they can be consumed quickly. This combined with the amount of caffeine in energy drinks makes it easy to overdose.[5]

- *Consumer Reports* reviewed the caffeine labeling on energy drinks and found that labels do not always list the correct amount of caffeine per serving.[6] A limit on the amount of caffeine might help to curb overdose.

- Energy drinks are used as mixers in alcoholic beverages, which has been shown to increase the number of drinks people consume.[7, 8] When a partygoer might normally call it a night, an energy drink could give them the wakefulness to keep drinking to excess.

- Younger people are advised to get less caffeine in their diets, and since the marketing for these drinks is aimed at younger people, it makes sense to limit the amount of caffeine in these drinks.[9]

no

- Energy drinks are not the same as soda; they are intended to give a boost of energy.[10] Part of the boost of energy comes from caffeine.

- What we need is not more limits but more education. Caffeine is added to many foods—from gum to syrup.[11] We should be teaching people about the need to limit caffeine.

- People can read labels and decide for themselves whether they are having too much caffeine. While the FDA doesn't require energy drinks to provide caffeine content on the label, there are websites that provide this information.[12, 13]

- Limiting the amount of caffeine in individual energy drinks won't stop people from having a second energy drink to get a larger dose of caffeine.

what do you think?

1. Are you aware of your total caffeine intake? Do you consider it too high, too low, or just right? **2.** Do you or your friends drink energy drinks? If yes, what effects are you trying to obtain by consuming them? **3.** Would limiting the amount of caffeine in energy drinks affect your consumption of them? If so, how? What would the impact on your health be?

VISUAL Chapter Summary

LO 11.1 Physical Fitness Includes Five Components for Health

Physical fitness is defined as good health or physical condition, especially as the result of exercise and proper nutrition. There are five basic components of physical fitness: cardiorespiratory endurance, muscle strength, muscle endurance, flexibility, and body composition.

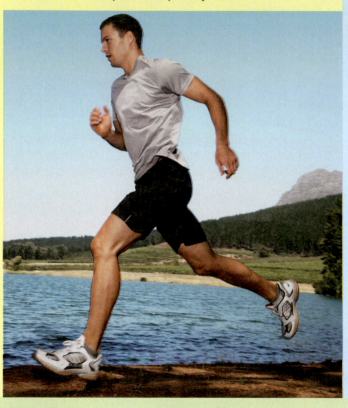

LO 11.2 A Successful Physical Fitness Program Uses FITT Principles

Fitness programs generally incorporate exercises that are based on the five components of fitness, and include aerobic activities, resistance training, and stretching. A successful fitness program should be tailored to meet the needs of the individual and performed consistently so that any gains in physical fitness are not lost. FITT is an acronym for frequency, intensity, time and type of activity.

Minimize sedentary activities

2–3 days/week
Flexibility and muscular fitness

3–5 days/week
Cardiorespiratory
Moderate–high intensity

Daily
Low–moderate intensity

LO 11.3 Carbohydrate, Fat, and Protein Fuel Exercise

Carbohydrate, fat, and protein are all used by the body during exercise. The source of energy needed to fuel exercise depends on the intensity and duration of the activity, and an individual's current level of fitness. The body relies heavily on anaerobic energy from ATP and creatine phosphate during the first few seconds of exercise. As exercise continues, the body relies on aerobic production of ATP mainly from carbohydrate and fat, obtained from blood glucose and stored glycogen, and fatty acids stored in muscle tissue and free fatty acids in the blood derived from fat tissue. Fat supplies nearly all of the energy required during rest and low- to moderate-intensity activity. Protein primarily functions to maintain, build, and repair tissues, including muscle tissue. As long as the diet is adequate in total calories, carbohydrate, and fat, only small amounts of protein are used for energy during exercise.

50% ATP-CP 50% Carbs
100-M DASH (brief, high-intensity)

35% Fat 65% Carbs
10-KM RACE (moderate intensity)

35% Carbs 65% Fat
DAY-LONG HIKE (low intensity)

LO 11.4 The Timing of Meals Affects Fitness Performance

The timing of meals before, during, and after exercise impacts energy levels and recovery time. Consuming both carbohydrate and protein 1 to 4 hours before exercise produces a greater increase in muscle glycogen synthesis, promotes greater endurance, and results in greater protein synthesis after exercise is over. Consuming carbohydrate 15 to 30 minutes prior to the start of exercise give muscles an immediate source of energy, spares glycogen stores, and protects muscles from damage. Within the first 30 to 45 minutes after exercise, carbohydrate helps replenish glycogen stores and stimulates muscle protein synthesis, with protein intake immediately following exercise resulting in greater protein synthesis.

LO 11.5 Vitamins and Minerals Assist in Energy Metabolism

Vitamins and minerals assist in energy metabolism and are necessary for fitness. Athletes do not have greater needs for vitamins and minerals than do nonathletes, and intakes of vitamins and minerals above the RDA do not improve athletic performance. Supplements containing vitamins and minerals are not necessary when adequate amounts are obtained through consuming a variety of foods. Female and vegetarian athletes are at greater risk of developing iron deficiency and should consume iron-rich foods regularly. Athletes also need to be sure their calcium intake is adequate to help reduce their risk of bone fractures during physical activity.

LO 11.6 Fluid Intake Affects Fitness and Performance

Being adequately hydrated before, during, and after exercise helps maintain fluid and electrolyte balance and normal body temperature. Water is the best fluid for hydration during exercise, though sports drinks can be beneficial for moderate- to vigorous-intensity exercise. Dehydration and overhydration should both be avoided because they can be harmful to health.

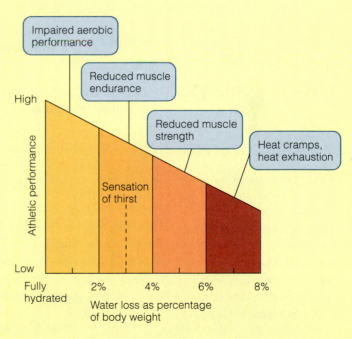

LO 11.7 Some Dietary Supplements Can Contribute to Fitness

Dietary supplements are not strictly regulated for their safety and efficacy; those who choose to use them may be placing their health at risk. Some dietary supplements, such as creatine and caffeine, are used as ergogenic aids to improve athletic performance. Creatine has been shown to increase both muscle strength and mass. Caffeine has been shown to improve endurance performance, but has not shown any benefit in activities of short duration. Anabolic steroids can increase muscle mass and strength, but will also cause undesirable androgenic side effects for both men and women. Growth hormone may increase muscle mass and decrease body fat, but also has serious health effects. Synthetic erythropoietin and blood doping can improve endurance, but can also thicken the blood, which may lead to a stroke, heart attack, or death.

Terms to Know

- physical fitness
- cardiorespiratory endurance
- muscle strength
- muscle endurance
- strength training
- flexibility
- body composition
- stroke volume
- VO₂max
- intensity
- rating of perceived exertion (RPE)
- repetition maximum (RM)
- duration
- progressive overload principle
- aerobic
- anaerobic
- adenosine triphosphate (ATP)
- creatine phosphate
- female athlete triad
- dehydration
- hyponatremia
- ergogenic aid

MasteringNutrition™ Build your knowledge—and confidence—in the Study Area of MasteringNutrition with a variety of study tools.

 MyDiet Analysis Access MyDietAnalysis through MasteringNutrition™ and track your diet and daily activities. In addition, a dietary analysis activity is available for every chapter in your book.

Check Your Understanding

LO 11.1 1. Which of the following is *not* a component of physical fitness?
- a. muscle strength
- b. cardiorespiratory endurance
- c. stress
- d. body composition

LO 11.1 2. If you are able to do 100 consecutive push-ups without taking a break, you are exhibiting great
- a. cardiorespiratory endurance.
- b. muscle endurance.
- c. flexibility.
- d. muscle strength.

LO 11.2 3. Which component of the FITT principle refers to the degree of difficulty at which you perform an activity?
- a. frequency
- b. intensity
- c. duration
- d. type

LO 11.3 4. During low-intensity activity, your body obtains most of its energy from
- a. muscle glycogen.
- b. liver glycogen.
- c. muscle protein.
- d. fatty acids.

LO 11.3 5. Under what conditions will the body use significant amounts of protein for energy during exercise?
- a. inadequate calorie and fluid intake
- b. inadequate carbohydrate and protein stores
- c. inadequate protein stores and fluid intake
- d. inadequate calorie intake and carbohydrate stores

LO 11.4 6. A pregame meal should be
- a. high in carbohydrate, low in fat.
- b. high in carbohydrate and high in fat.
- c. low in carbohydrate, high in fat.
- d. low in protein, high in fat.

LO 11.5 7. Which mineral is necessary for energy metabolism and for transporting oxygen throughout the body and within muscle cells?
   a. calcium
   b. iron
   c. vitamin E
   d. vitamin C

LO 11.6 8. A commercial sports drink might be beneficial after 60 minutes or more of exercise because it
   a. provides electrolytes and carbohydrates, and contributes to hydration.
   b. is marketed to everyone, not just athletes.
   c. typically contains 12 to 16 percent carbohydrate.
   d. tastes good so you will drink more.

LO 11.6 9. An appropriate exercise recovery beverage would be
   a. a soft drink.
   b. coffee.
   c. low-fat chocolate milk.
   d. orange juice.

LO 11.7 10. Acromegaly can be caused by abuse of which ergogenic aid?
   a. creatine
   b. growth hormone
   c. anabolic steroids
   d. erythropoietin

Answers

1. (c) Muscle strength, cardiorespiratory endurance, and body composition, along with muscle endurance and flexibility, are the five basic components of physical fitness. Stress is not a component of physical fitness.
2. (b) Performing 100 consecutive push-ups without resting shows great muscle endurance because you are able to exert the force needed to push yourself up over a long period of time without getting tired.
3. (b) Intensity refers to the degree of difficulty at which you perform an activity.
4. (d) Fatty acids are the main source of energy during low-intensity activity. As the intensity increases, the body will use fewer fatty acids and more glycogen for energy.

5. (d) The body will use larger amounts of protein for energy if overall calorie intake is inadequate and if carbohydrate stores are low.
6. (a) A meal before a game or workout should be high in carbohydrate to maximize glycogen stores and low in fat to prevent feelings of fatigue or discomfort.
7. (b) Iron is necessary for energy metabolism and for transporting oxygen throughout the body and within muscle cells.
8. (a) Sports drinks supply fluids to rehydrate the body during and after exercise, electrolytes to replace those lost during sweating, and carbohydrate, which acts as an immediate source of energy that can potentially improve performance.
9. (c) Low-fat chocolate milk is a good exercise recovery beverage because it contains an appropriate ratio of carbohydrate and protein that is necessary for optimal recovery. Soft drinks, coffee, and orange juice will provide your body with fluids, but lack other nutrients that are ideal for recovery after exercise.
10. (b) Abusing growth hormone causes acromegaly, a disease in which tissues, bones, and internal organs grow abnormally large in size.

Web Resources

- The President's Council on Physical Fitness and Sports, www.fitness.gov
- Let's Move, www.letsmove.gov
- American Council on Exercise, www.acefitness.org
- American College of Sports Medicine, www.acsm.org
- Academy of Nutrition and Dietetics, www.eatright.org
- Sports, Cardiovascular, and Wellness Nutritionists: A Dietetics Practice Group of the Academy of Nutrition and Dietetics, www.scandpg.org
- Gatorade Sports Science Institute, www.gssiweb.org
- For information on independent testing and product reviews about dietary supplements, visit www.ConsumerLab.com

Answers to True or False?

1. **False.** Physical activity refers to general body movement such as walking the dog, while exercise is defined as formalized training or structured activity like weight lifting. Refer to page 418 for more information.

2. **True.** You don't have to be an Olympian to enjoy the health benefits of exercise. With as little as 60 minutes per week, you can burn more calories and lower your risk of certain diseases. Turn to page 423 for more information.

3. **True.** Energy is produced anaerobically during the first few seconds of exercise, and aerobically as exercise continues beyond several seconds. Turn to page 426 to learn about energy sources during exercise.

4. **False.** It is necessary to eat a high-carbohydrate diet on a regular basis to improve athletic performance, not just before exercise or competition. Turn to page 429 to learn more.

5. **True.** Consumption of nutrients immediately after stopping exercise will improve recovery. Find out more on page 436.

6. **False.** Vitamins and minerals have important roles in exercise, including assisting in the metabolism of carbohydrate, fat, and protein for energy. Turn to page 437 to learn more about the roles of vitamins and minerals during exercise.

7. **True.** Female and vegetarian athletes are at higher risk for iron deficiency. Turn to page 438 to find out why this is the case.

8. **False.** Sports drinks are generally beneficial only when you exercise for longer than one hour. Find out more about fluid needs during exercise on page 442.

9. **False.** Once you feel the sensation of thirst, you are already experiencing dehydration. Turn to page 442 to learn more about proper hydration during exercise.

10. **True.** You may be surprised to learn that just a few cups of coffee can supply excessive amounts of caffeine. To learn more, turn to page 446.

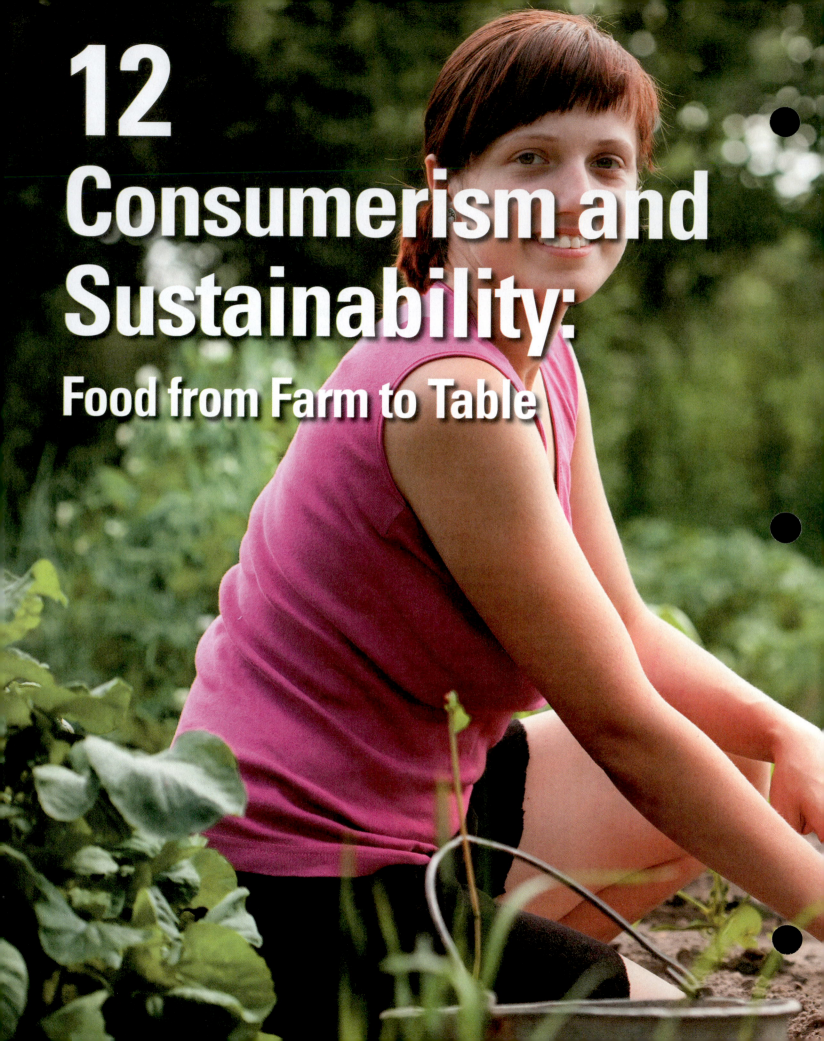

12
Consumerism and Sustainability:
Food from Farm to Table

True or False?

1. Food advertising has little effect on what foods most Americans buy and consume. **T|F** p. 458

2. Most farms in the United States are family farms. **T|F** p. 460

3. The U.S. government currently provides monetary incentives for farmers to grow a variety of fruits and vegetables. **T|F** p. 462

4. Most of the corn grown in the United States is used to feed animals, not humans. **T|F** p. 463

5. Plant-based diets are more sustainable than are diets high in animal-based foods. **T|F** p. 469

6. Energy costs, such as the cost of oil, influence the cost of food. **T|F** p. 470

7. The FDA requires special labels for products produced from the milk of cows treated with synthetic hormones. **T|F** p. 473

8. The majority of soybeans grown in the United States to produce soybean oil and other products are genetically modified. **T|F** p. 478

9. All organic foods certified by the USDA are 100 percent pesticide free. **T|F** p. 485

10. Organic foods are more nutritious than nonorganic foods. **T|F** p. 485

See page 491 for the answers.

The fact that we buy food, whether at the dining hall, mini mart, grocery store, or a restaurant, makes us all **food consumers**. As such, we command a great deal of influence on the **food industry**, which is a global, $4 *trillion*-a-year business.[1] We literally speak with our food dollars. The foods we choose to buy, where we choose to buy them, and how often we make these purchases are decisions that are tremendously important to the environment as well as the people who grow, process, distribute, advertise, and sell our food products. Although you may think that you are "in the driver's seat" when choosing the foods you eat, this isn't entirely the case. In fact, there are many outside factors that influence the foods that you have access to and end up purchasing. At least partially because of these factors, the dietary choices of most Americans don't match the dietary patterns that promote both health and sustainability.

How Do Advertising and Marketing Influence Your Food Choices?

LO 12.1 Describe how food advertising and marketing affect your food choices.

Every year, vast amounts of money are spent by food companies to persuade you to buy their products. Whether they are advertised on television, radio, magazines, or the Internet, or placed in movies, these products' manufacturers spend close to $10 billion annually to promote them. Much of the promotion is for highly processed and packaged foods. In fact, 20 percent of the total amount of money spent on advertising by food companies is focused on breakfast cereal, 19 percent on candy and gum, and 14 percent on carbonated soft drinks. In contrast, only 3 percent is spend on advertising fruits and vegetables.[2] You can probably think of an ad campaign you've seen recently for a particular brand of soda or fast-food chain. In comparison, when was the last time you saw an advertisement for broccoli? Have you *ever* seen an ad for broccoli?

A growing trend in food advertising is to market heavily to college-aged and young adults by targeting college campuses and social venues that are popular with this age group. For example, one marketing strategy for Red Bull, a caffeinated energy drink, was to give away free samples on college campuses, at sports events, and in trendy clubs and bars. And it worked like a charm. Within three years of rolling out this product in the United States, Red Bull sparked a booming trend in energy beverage consumption. In 2008, Red Bull enjoyed $1 billion in sales.[3] Why did this advertising and marketing strategy work? Red Bull astutely identified where the members of its target audience hang out, and then the beverage company hung out with them.

More recently, Red Bull has followed its target audience online to social media sites, including Facebook, MySpace, and Twitter.[4] Facebook users can "like" Red Bull, and those on Twitter

Red Bull uses strategies that help it target college-aged, young-adult consumers.

Figure 12.1 From Farm to Consumer
Many individuals make it easier for you to obtain the foods you consume and enjoy.

1 **Farm:** Trees, bushes, plants, and animals produce the raw materials that eventually end up on your plate.

2 **Food Processor:** Food processors clean and sort the raw food products. The food is then either ready for shipping (in the case of whole foods like fruits, vegetables, and grains), or processed with heat, salt, or sugar, or combined with other ingredients to convert it into a packaged food.

3 **Distributor:** Once processed, foods are transported via truck, ship, or train from the plant to a retail outlet, where consumers can buy them.

4 **Seller:** While people buy food from several sources, including family farms, restaurants, farmers' markets, and convenience stores, most food shopping takes place at the grocery store.

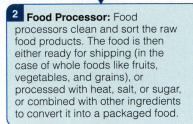

5 **Consumer:** You, the consumer, are the final step in the process.

can "follow" the company's tweets. While you may think you are immune to the influence of these techniques, companies like Red Bull put a lot of thought and effort into keeping you excited about their brand, and they do it because they think it works. Wherever you, and your wallet go, they will follow.

In contrast, advertising for fruits and vegetables is almost nonexistent, which is a shame because healthy foods can be successfully marketed. When the dairy industry noted a decline in milk consumption among Americans in the early 1990s, it launched the *Got Milk?* ad campaign, which featured celebrities wearing milk mustaches. This campaign strove to make drinking milk sexy, and it worked. Milk sales increased by nearly 1.5 billion pounds, the equivalent of about 45 million pounds of milk being sold for each ad dollar spent.[5]

LO 12.1 **The Take-Home Message** The food industry spends large amounts of money on marketing and advertising its products, often to target audiences. The most heavily advertised foods are often the least nutritious.

Where Does Your Food Come From?

LO 12.2 Recognize where your food comes from.

Most people don't think too much about where their food comes from before it appears on the supermarket shelf. Have you ever considered where the ingredients in your morning cereal and orange juice, for example, originate? Unless you're growing wheat and oranges and keeping a cow in your backyard, you're depending on the work of numerous individuals, from the farmer to the food distributor, to transform raw milk and stalks of wheat into the foods that you have available to you. No matter what you're eating, in some form or another, it started out on a farm (see **Figure 12.1**).[6]

Food Comes from Farms, Not Stores

In the United States, a **farm** is considered an establishment that produces and sells at least $1,000 of agricultural products annually. By this definition, there are just over 2 million farms in the United States, and they're largely concentrated in the Midwest,

food consumers Individuals who make decisions about which foods to buy.

food industry The collective efforts of various businesses that provide food to consumers.

farm An establishment that produces and sells at least $1,000 of agricultural products annually.

Figure 12.2 The Location and Number of Farms in the United States, 2012

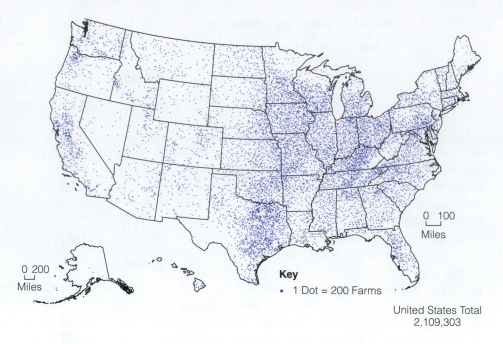

Key

• 1 Dot = 200 Farms

United States Total
2,109,303

Great Plains, and California (**Figure 12.2**). Although 2 million may sound like a lot of farms, it's actually many fewer than in the past. This decrease is surprising, considering that farmers are feeding more people now than ever before. In 1935, there were more than 6.5 million farms feeding approximately 127 million Americans.[7] Currently, fewer than 960,000 hard-working Americans—less than 1 percent of the population—are producing food to feed the country's 300+ million people. This lopsided scenario, with fewer farms but more people, has forced farmers to become more efficient in the ways they produce food. We will read more about this later in the chapter.

You probably think that to feed all these people, farms must be mammoth, but most American farms (more than 80 percent) are actually small farms (see **Table 12.1**). However, larger farms produce more food; in fact, approximately 10 percent of farms

Nearly all the food that you consume originates on a farm.

are responsible for more than 60 percent of all agricultural product sales. Further, more than 97 percent of U.S. farms, both large and small, are owned and operated by families. However, these families are not necessarily passing the business on to the next generation, and the age of the average farmer is increasing.[8]

Approximately 40 percent of farmers in the United States are 55 years old or older.

Challenges of Farming

While running a family farm may sound like a desirable career path—after all, you'd spend much of your time outside and, if you're working for your family, would probably enjoy a flexible schedule—the challenges farmers face are actually quite steep. High costs, a demand for low food prices, competition, and a dependence on the cooperation of Mother Nature can all derail a farmer's bottom line. In fact, less than one in four farms generates gross revenues (this is revenue before expenses) of more than $50,000 per year.[9] Because land, equipment, facilities, fuel, and fertilizer are all expensive (a combine used for harvest, for example, can cost upwards of $200,000), farmers must depend on a hearty yield to cover their costs and make a profit.[10]

Fortunately, technology and machinery allow today's farmers to produce food more efficiently. Whereas a farmer in the 1930s could expect to harvest about 100 bushels (1 bushel is equal to 32 quarts) of corn daily, current farmers can harvest as much as 900 bushels of corn every hour.[11] But again, the machines that allow them to do this are very expensive. Thus, farmers are caught in a cycle of having to continually invest in new machines and technology to ensure a hearty and bountiful crop in order to make enough money to pay for the expense of farming.

Some farmers use computers and the Internet to farm more efficiently. Known as **precision agriculture** or *satellite farming*, these farmers use a Global Positioning System (similar to the GPS in a car) along with other technologies to help collect and evaluate data on the soil, pests, and disease at specific field locations. The farmers then enter that information into a computer and, based on the findings, adjust their farming practices to optimize returns while preserving natural resources. For example, information gained by practicing precision agriculture may allow a farmer to use less water and/or less fertilizer in specific areas of a field.[12]

The consumer is also squeezing the farmer's bottom line, as there is a limit to what people are willing to spend for food. In the 1930s, Americans spent 25 percent of their disposable income on food. Today, Americans allocate less than 7 percent of their earnings to what they eat.[13] Once again, farmers are forced to produce large volumes in order to keep foods affordable for consumers, cover their expenses, and still make a profit.[14]

Table 12.1
Types of Farms in the United States

Farm Type	Number of Farms	Percent of Total Farms
Small Family Farms		
(annual sales less than $250,000)	1,925,799	87.3
Large Farms		
(annual sales greater than $250,000)	278,993	12.7
Non-family	91,177	4.1
Family	187,816	8.6
Total Farms in the United States	2,204,792	100

precision agriculture A cost-efficient, precise farming method that uses new technologies to collect data about variations in field soil to better manage the use of appropriate seeds, fertilizer, water, and pesticides for the growing of crops with less waste. Also known as *satellite farming*.

Modern machinery has helped farmers increase yields.

To try to offset their rising costs, many farmers take advantage of government-sponsored financial subsidies paid to farmers for growing select **commodity crops**, such as corn, wheat, and soybeans. The government subsidy program has helped to manage and ensure the supply of these crops over time. However, because not all crops are subsidized, farmers may opt to grow subsidized commodity crops over other specialty crops such as fruits and vegetables. To obtain these government-sponsored subsidies farmers must grow the approved crops in accordance with conservation plans that protect the environment.[15] Unfortunately, even with this support, there has been a trend toward larger farms, which are sometimes owned by giant corporations, producing large amounts of agricultural products in America. This can make it more difficult for small farms, especially those that specialize in non–commodity crops such as fruits and vegetables, to stay in business.[16]

The Role of Agribusiness

All farming, large and small, is part of a wider field known as **agribusiness**—the blending of agricultural and business entities that affect how food, as well as the clothes in your closet and the furnishings in your home, are developed, processed, distributed, and purchased in the United States. The food component of agribusiness includes not only food production, distribution, marketing, and retail sales, but also agrichemicals, finance, management, and other environmental and land use entities. In essence, it involves all of the major elements needed in the efficient meshing of agriculture and the food business.[17]

The agribusiness sector employs approximately 16 million Americans, or about 5 percent of the U.S. population.[18] *Food-processing companies*, which take raw fruits, vegetables, grains, meats, and dairy products and convert them into edible food, comprise a large segment of those employed in agriculture (**Figure 12.3**). While agribusiness is "big business" because it employs many individuals, this doesn't mean that it consists only of enormous conglomerates. In fact, two-thirds of the more than 20,000 processing operations in the United States have fewer than 20 employees.[19]

commodity crops Crop products such as corn and soybeans that can be used for commerce.

agribusiness The businesses collectively associated with the production, processing, and distribution of agricultural products, including food.

Corn Belt The parts of the United States where corn is grown in abundance. This includes Iowa, Indiana, most of Illinois, and parts of Kansas, Missouri, Nebraska, South Dakota, Minnesota, Ohio, and Wisconsin.

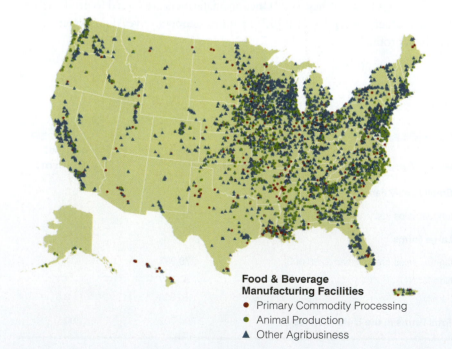

Figure 12.3 The Location and Number of Food- and Beverage-Processing Facilities, 2007 Food- and beverage-processing facilities employ many of the 16 million people who work in the American agriculture sector.

Food & Beverage Manufacturing Facilities
- ● Primary Commodity Processing
- ● Animal Production
- ▲ Other Agribusiness

Crops Grown for Food

T/F The top three agricultural food crops grown in the United States are corn, soybeans, and wheat (see **Table 12.2**). The United States is the largest producer of corn in the world, with 10 billion bushels harvested on more than 400,000 farms spread out over 84 million acres, primarily located in the **Corn Belt** (**Figure 12.4**). Most of that corn, however, isn't consumed as cornflakes, corn syrup, cornmeal, high-fructose corn syrup, or other human food products. Rather, about 80 percent ends up as feed for livestock, poultry, and fish.

Fifty percent of the world's soybean production occurs on just over 290,000 U.S. farms (see Figure 12.4). In addition to products like tofu, soy sauce, and edamame, soy is used to produce soybean oil, the number-one oil consumed by Americans. More than 30 million tons of soybean meal (the part of the soybean left after the oil is extracted) are used to feed livestock annually.[20]

The United States produces about 10 percent of the world's wheat, which is harvested from more than 160,000 farms clustered in the Great Plains from Texas to Montana (see Figure 12.4). More than 70 percent of this wheat is used for food products, such as bread and cereal; about 22 percent is used for animal feed; and the rest is left for seeds to replenish the crops.[21]

As you can tell from these statistics, most of the staple crops grown in the United States are used not to feed humans, but to feed animals that will themselves

Table 12.2

Major Agricultural Crops Produced in the United States, 2011

Crop	Harvested Area (millions of acres)
Corn for grain	87.4
Soybeans	76.1
Hay	55.8
Wheat	46.9
Cotton	9.4
Sorghum for grain	5.1
Vegetables	4.5

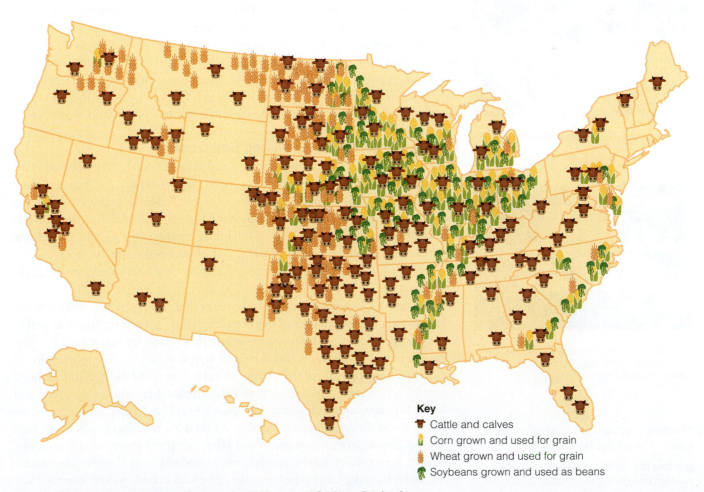

Key
- Cattle and calves
- Corn grown and used for grain
- Wheat grown and used for grain
- Soybeans grown and used as beans

Figure 12.4 Major U.S. Centers of Cattle, Corn, Wheat, and Soybean Production

This is a soybean. Soy is used to make numerous food products, including soybean oil, which is the number-one oil used by Americans.

Some pork by-products have medical applications: insulin for managing diabetes used to be extracted from pig pancreases, and pig heart valves have been used for heart surgery in humans.

Americans eat more poultry than either beef or pork.

Many countries do not produce enough food and need to import food from the United States to meet their needs.

feedlot A facility where cattle are fed grain and other foods before being slaughtered.

globesity A blend of the words *global* and *obesity*, coined by the World Health Organization, which refers to the worldwide obesity epidemic.

later enter our food supply. Does it surprise you to learn that livestock in the United States consume a substantial amount of the crops that are grown in the United States? Should we be growing crops to feed animals, or should we be eating fewer animal foods and eating more crops? Later on in the chapter we will look at this important question.

Animals Raised for Food

By far, the dominant food animals in the United States are cows, pigs, and chickens. Beef products such as steaks, roasts, and hamburger originate from animals raised on more than 700,000 beef farms, concentrated in Texas, Colorado, Nebraska, Kansas, Iowa, California, Missouri, and Oklahoma (see Figure 12.4). Calves (young cattle) typically graze on croplands after harvest or in open grass pasturelands until they reach a certain weight. They are then confined to **feedlots**, where they are fed predominantly roughage (hay and inedible plant parts such as cornstalks) and grains (such as corn, soybeans, and wheat), so that they will grow to 1,000 pounds or more before being slaughtered.[22]

There are about 60,200 U.S. pig farms, concentrated in the Corn Belt and in North Carolina, producing pork products such as bacon, pork chops, and ham. Unlike their ancestors, most of today's hogs are raised indoors to protect them from weather, predators, and the spread of disease. They're also leaner and meatier than ever, with a 250-pound animal producing 150 pounds of pork.[23] However, the reduced price that you are used to paying for pork has forced smaller pork farmers out of business. They can't compete with larger-scale farms to produce the volume of product necessary to make a profit.

If you enjoy eggs with your bacon, you can thank the more than 145,000 poultry farms located in the Corn Belt, North Carolina, and the southern United States that focus on poultry and egg production.[24] Americans eat more poultry products than either beef or pork.[25] As with pork, raising poultry indoors has increased production and reduced labor, and thus has resulted in lower poultry and egg prices.

Exporting Foods: The Good and Bad News

In addition to producing enough food to feed Americans, U.S. farmers help feed the world. An estimated 30 percent of the income from a U.S. farm is derived from trading with other countries.[26] Since the mid-1940s, the United States has exported more agricultural products than it has imported.[27] In 2013, agricultural exports were predicted to top $139.5 billion, an increase of $3.7 billion from the previous year.[28] Grains (corn, soybeans, and wheat) and oilseeds (seeds used to make oils such as corn oil and soybean oil) are the most popular exports from the United States.

We are also exporting many of our unhealthy eating habits, including the consumption of large amounts of high-calorie, high-fat, processed foods as well as animal foods, many of which are made primarily from or are being fed corn, soybeans, and wheat. According to the Economic Research Service, the globalization of the food industry has caused the "Americanization" of many food cultures around the world, which is less sustainable than the native food culture. As the income of individuals in countries such as Mexico, Poland, Brazil, and China has increased, so has their desire for an American-like diet. As these more-affluent individuals shift their food choices from native grains and other carbohydrate-rich staples to more expensive meats, dairy foods, confectionery products, soft drinks, convenience foods, and fast foods,[29] they experience the same shift in body weight as we are seeing in the United States. That is, they also experience a growing problem with obesity.

Globesity, or the rapidly growing incidence of obesity worldwide, is becoming a global threat. For example, in the late 1980s, less than 10 percent of Mexicans were overweight. Currently, approximately 70 percent of citizens in Mexico are overweight or obese, which, not coincidentally, is very similar to the prevalence of these problems here in the United States, where 69 percent of adult citizens are also overweight or obese.[30] It is now estimated that more than 115 million people worldwide suffer health problems related to being overweight and obese.[31]

Food Production Outside the United States

Other countries are "Americanizing" their local culture's diet with sugary and/or high-fat foods that add little nutrition to the diet.

So, if we are exporting so much food and we are producing plenty of food here at home, does that mean we don't import foods from other countries? In a word, no. The next time you are in a supermarket, look beyond the colorful fruits and vegetables in the produce aisle, and read the signs posted alongside these foods. It's not uncommon for those juicy green grapes to be from Chile, the vibrant red peppers from Mexico, the fresh shrimp from Canada, and the nuts from Costa Rica. You may feel as though you are traveling around the world rather than around the grocery aisles.

Americans' plates are filled with more imported foods than ever before. In fact, most fish and shellfish eaten in the United States is now imported from other countries, including China and Thailand, and about 39 percent of the fruit and nuts that we buy originate outside the United States (see **Figure 12.5**). The United States currently imports close to $2 billion worth of bananas annually from Guatemala, Ecuador, Costa Rica, Colombia, and Honduras.[32] Vegetable imports have doubled, and importation of fruits, juices, and nuts has increased by 20 percent from decades ago.[33] The majority of our coffee comes from Colombia and Brazil. All told, approximately 17 percent of your food comes from outside the United States, and this number has continued to climb over the past several years.[34]

Importing Foods: The Good and Bad News

Why do we get so much of our food from other countries? Two primary reasons are our demand for a diverse array of products year round, regardless of U.S. growing seasons, and our demand for cheap food.

Americans have lost their patience for waiting. Even with a foot of snow on the ground, Northerners in the United States still want to wake up to fresh cantaloupe for breakfast, so retailers have the fruit shipped in from Mexico. The novelty of waiting until the summer to enjoy melons is, well, a novelty.

Also, as already mentioned, farming in the United States is an expensive endeavor. This opens the door to the outsourcing of agricultural production to poorer, developing nations that have lower overhead costs, and hence, can provide cheaper food to the consumer.[35] Although this outsourcing can provide jobs and income for developing countries (good news), you will learn in the next section that there are environmental costs (bad news) of shipping these foods long distances to the United States and ultimately to your plate.

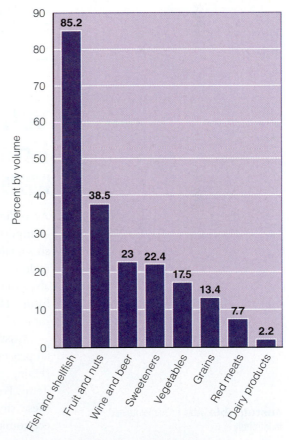

Figure 12.5 Percent of Selected Foods and Beverages Consumed in the United States That Are Imported, by Volume
America is importing foods such as seafood now more than ever before.

In addition to the environmental costs, the other downside to importing foods is the potential for contamination. There have been reports of imported foods containing excessive amounts of pesticides and foodborne pathogens compared with similar domestic products.[36] This increased risk of contamination places an increased burden on the FDA, the agency that polices the safety of the domestic food supply. Because of the tremendous volume of imports, the FDA only inspects less than 2 percent of all food products brought into the United States.[37] The FDA can't inspect everything, but it takes a targeted and risk-based approach. In the past, the FDA has had to block contaminated farm-raised fish imported from China because the fish contained additives that have been shown to cause cancer in animals.[38] The globalization of the food supply is going to require that uniform, global food-safety standards be developed and implemented to keep imported foods safe.[39] This will entail an enormous, unified effort among many countries.

Let's now look at how all of this modernization and globalization of the food supply affect the environment.

LO 12.2 **The Take-Home Message** The majority of the food that you consume originates on a farm. Most farms in the United States are small and family operated. Agribusiness is a blending of agriculture and business and affects how foods are developed, processed, distributed, and purchased. The major crops grown in the United States are corn, soybeans, and wheat, and the major animals raised for food are cows, pigs, and chickens. Many of the crops grown in the United States are used to feed the animals that are raised for food. Some of the foods you consume are grown in the United States but a good portion is likely imported from other countries. Many countries rely on the United States for part of their food supply. There are pros and cons to both the import and export of foods.

What Is a Sustainable Food System?

LO 12.3 Describe what factors contribute to a sustainable food system.

According to a recent survey, two-thirds (66 percent) of American consumers say it is important to them that the foods they purchase and consume are produced in a sustainable way.[40] The aspects of sustainability most important to those consumers include conserving natural resources, making sure that the food supply is affordable, and that there is enough food to feed the world's population now and in the future. However, only one-quarter of American consumers are willing to pay more for foods that they perceive as being more sustainable.

Sustainable means able to be maintained indefinitely. A food system includes all processes involved in feeding populations, including growing, harvesting, processing, packaging, transporting, marketing, and disposing of food and food-related items. Food systems involve the natural and human resources needed for each of these steps, and are influenced by external factors such as agricultural policy, economics, and social values. A **sustainable food system** is one that addresses concerns regarding the health of individuals, the community, and the environment in a way that intends to provide healthy food for the world's population for generations to come.

sustainable Able to be maintained indefinitely.

sustainable food system A food-providing system that conserves natural resources and can be maintained indefinitely.

Figure 12.6 Sustainable Food Systems Model

Environmental Stewardship
- Conserves, protects and renews natural resources (soil, water, air, energy, biodiversity)
- Supports vibrant ecosystems
- Promotes a low-carbon footprint
- Mitigates climate change

Economic Vitality
- Builds community wealth
- Is economically viable and sustainable

SUSTAINABLE, RESILIENT, AND HEALTHY FOOD AND WATER SYSTEMS

Nutrition and Health
- Assure dietary diversity
- Assures safety of food and water supplies
- Assures optimal access to food and water in order to meet nutritional requirements

Social, Cultural and Ethical Capital
- Promotes cultural diversity
- Empowers social responsibility and community engagement
- Advances ethical, humane, and fair treatment of individuals and animals

Sustainable Food Systems Are Environmentally Friendly, Economically Viable, and Socially Equitable

Sustainable food systems must address the three "E"s of sustainability: they must be environmentally friendly, economically viable, and socially equitable. The Academy of Nutrition and Dietetics developed a model that provides a useful way to think about the factors that contribute to a sustainable food system (see **Figure 12.6**).[41] In a sustainable food system the natural resources used to produce, transport, and distribute foods are conserved and protected instead of destroyed or depleted. Foods are produced, transported, and distributed using methods that support existing ecosystems and emit as few greenhouse gases as possible. Economic viability means that people can afford to buy food, and farmers and other workers can afford to provide food in a system that builds community wealth. In addition, a sustainable food system is one that provides all people with access to healthy as well as culturally and socially acceptable foods in a way that empowers social responsibility and community engagement in the system. In fact, because food systems are meant to nourish individuals, a sustainable food system should be one that assures access to diverse and safe foods and provides all of the nutrients needed to support health.

The prevailing industrial agriculture system has delivered enormous gains in the yield of product, but at what cost? America's industrialized agriculture system is using topsoil, fossil fuel, and water—all precious natural resources—at unsustainable rates. Many food systems are currently degrading the environment, reducing **biodiversity**, and polluting the air and water.[42] Striving for more sustainable

biodiversity Having a wide variety of plant and animal species within an environment.

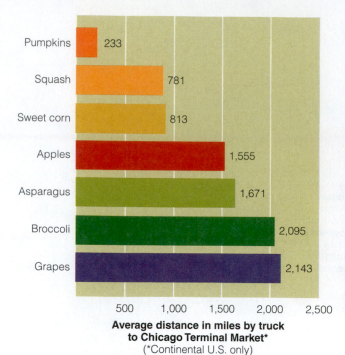

Figure 12.7 How Far Did Your Food Travel?
You might be surprised to learn just how far some of your food travels to get to your local supermarket.

methods of producing, transporting, and distributing food is our best shot at making sure future generations will have access to the food needed to sustain life and health.

Any factor that leads to the abuse or unnecessary waste of inputs, especially nonrenewable natural resources, may prevent sustainability. Many of the current practices involving the use of soil, energy, and water in industrial agriculture provide cause for concern.

Concerns about Energy Use

Research suggests that almost 16 percent of the total energy consumption in the United States is used in the production, processing, transport, and preparation of our food.[43] One obvious use of energy in food systems is the energy used to transport food. Depending on where you live and shop, the lettuce, orange, or cantaloupe that you buy could easily have traveled 1,500 or more miles to reach you. The Leopold Center for Agriculture compiled data from the USDA and found that the average mileage for produce to travel to a Chicago market was just over 1,500 miles, which is more than a 20 percent increase from that observed in the early 1980s (see **Figure 12.7**).[44] A study conducted in Iowa showed that produce imported into the United States from different countries used 4 to 17 times more fuel and released 5 to 17 times more carbon dioxide gas emissions than produce that was locally produced.[45]

The use of energy to transport food not only increases the cost of food, but is harmful to the environment because it contributes to a phenomenon known as global warming. Global warming is a term that describes the observed rise in the average temperature of the Earth due to the release of carbon dioxide (a greenhouse gas) from the burning of fossil fuels.[46] Global warming is worrisome because it contributes to rising sea levels and extreme weather patterns that make it difficult for farmers to provide food. Sustainable food systems use as little fossil fuel in the production and transport of food as possible.

A less obvious use of energy in food systems is the energy used to produce chemical fertilizers and pesticides for crops. The production of these products requires large amounts of fossil fuels, which also increases the cost of food and contributes to global warming.[47] Avoiding these chemicals and using natural fertilizers, such as animal manure, not only cuts the use of fossil fuel, but also can make soil more fertile.[48] Research also shows that crop rotation and other aspects of organic farming result in less soil erosion than nonorganic methods.[49]

Concerns about the Use of Soil

More than 99 percent of the food you eat is produced on land, compared to less than one percent that comes from the sea. All land crops are dependent upon the thin layer of topsoil that sits atop the Earth's crust.[50] Topsoil is regenerated from decaying plants, microorganisms, and animals, and provides the oxygen and nutrients needed to support the growth of hearty plants. Plants in turn contribute to the health of the topsoil by providing nutrients back to the soil and having roots that help prevent the erosion of topsoil by wind and water.

Problems arise when the topsoil cannot be regenerated and/or is less fertile. When this happens plants can't grow, and nourishment for all—the animals, microorganisms, and *you*—suffers.[51] Unfortunately, the natural process of regenerating *one inch* of nutrient-rich topsoil takes more than 500 years.[52] Improper agricultural practices, such as planting one crop year after year, facilitate soil erosion faster than it can be regenerated, depleting the soil and resulting in lower crop yields.[53] Overgrazing of land by animals leads to topsoil erosion. This is a growing problem in areas of the world like parts of Africa. In addition, planting one crop year after year promotes soil depletion and may increase the need for pesticides.[54]

Farmers' markets provide fresh, local produce to consumers.

Concerns about Water Use

According to the EPA, since the 1950s the population in America has nearly doubled, while our water consumption has more than tripled.[55] Americans, on average, use 100 gallons—about 1,600 full glasses—of water per person each day.[56]

Water shortages in many places are due to the use of ground and surface water for irrigation without consideration of the natural ecosystem. All plants and animals, including humans, need water to survive, so the potential for water shortage is not only a danger to the environment but also to your health. Conserving water now to ensure a healthy supply in the future makes sense. There are several steps you and/or your family can take to conserve water. Installing water-efficient appliances, including washing machines and dishwashers, helps cut down on water used for daily chores. If all households installed water-efficient appliances, the United States would save more than 3 trillion gallons annually.[57] Low-flow toilets and showerheads can also help save water, as can turning off the tap while washing dishes or brushing your teeth. When it comes to individual water conservation, think of saving water "one gallon at a time." If each American set a goal to incorporate three "greener" habits in his or her daily life over the next year, the reduction in the use of natural resources and thus improvement in sustainability would be dramatic.

The Most Sustainable Foods Are Locally Grown and Plant Based

Obviously it takes less fuel to transport locally grown food to local consumers than it does to transport a watermelon grown in Mexico to consumers in Denver, Colorado, but did you know that it also takes fewer natural resources to produce plant-based foods than it does to produce animal-based foods?

In a recent study using data from the annual use of land, irrigation water, and fertilizer from the USDA and the Department of Energy (2000–2010), livestock (cows, pigs, and chickens) required significantly more (two- to sixfold more) natural resources in the form of land and water, and produced more greenhouse gas emissions than did staple plant foods such as corn and wheat. Beef production required 6–11 times more natural resources than did other livestock.[58] Animal-based foods are high in protein and provide many essential nutrients, and do not need to be eliminated from our diets, but most Americans could benefit from consuming fewer animal-based foods and more plant-based foods. According to the Scientific Report of the Dietary Guidelines for Americans Advisory Committee, diets higher in plant-based foods

The Oxford American Dictionary declared the word *locavore* the 2007 Word of the Year!

Table 12.3
Food Miles in a Meal

Food Item	Local Source	Distance Traveled from Local Source	Conventional Source	Distance Traveled through Conventional Channels
Chuck roast	Local grass-fed beef farm	75 miles	Colorado	675 miles
Potatoes	Farmers' market	10–15 miles	Idaho	1,300 miles
Carrots	Backyard garden	40 feet	California	1,700 miles
Green beans	Backyard garden	40 feet	California	1,700 miles

are not only more sustainable, but also more health promoting.[59] Choosing to eat less meat than you usually do, or even eating meat from locally grown animals, can also help to support sustainable food systems.

The movement for "eating locally" has gained momentum for numerous reasons. Among these is that most people perceive locally grown foods as tasting better. A locally grown summer tomato, for example, is usually much more flavorful than one that has been shipped in a refrigerated truck for 1,500 miles. Similarly, a New England Macintosh apple tastes much better picked off a tree at the height of apple season than after sitting in a cold-storage room for three months. As previously discussed, eating locally also has environmental benefits, because the less your food travels, the less energy is being used to get it to you.

Small farms often provide foods to people living in their communities in different ways, including **community-supported agriculture (CSA)**, farmers' markets, and contracts through local grocery stores. Produce is often picked at the peak of ripeness, and sold without having to be processed or packaged. While fuel and environmental costs are lower for locally grown food compared with food that has to travel long distances from farm to consumers, these costs depend on the type of food and the type of transportation used. **Table 12.3** shows the distance traveled for the ingredients in a meal that was obtained locally or from conventional sources. For example, a meal consisting of foods obtained at a local supermarket can travel as much as 60 times the miles as the same meal made from locally grown foods.

Many large supermarkets now sell locally grown produce. This combining of locally grown foods with conventionally grown foods allows the consumer to do "one-stop shopping" rather than having to drive to the farmers' markets, farm stands, and CSA pick-ups in addition to the supermarket. Corporate America is also making it easier to eat locally. It is becoming more common for some large corporations and industrial complexes to host weekly farmers' markets on their premises and for restaurants to feature menu items from locally grown products.[60] USDA's "Know Your Farmer Know Your Food (KYF2)" initiative provides resources to support and strengthen local and regional food systems.[61] Local food is a billion dollar industry that continues to grow.

However, when making individual food choices, remember that buying food from small local farms doesn't guarantee that the foods were grown in a sustainable way, nor does being from a distant farm mean that those farmers didn't practice sustainable agriculture. Many factors impact the sustainability of individual food choices. The "How Sustainable Is Your Food Shopping?" Self-Assessment can help you determine if the foods that you purchase were provided in a sustainable way. Think about these questions as you plan, shop for, and prepare your next meal, and consider following some of the suggestions in the "Go Green" table (**Table 12.4**). If

community-supported agriculture (CSA) An arrangement whereby individuals pay a fee to support a local farm, and in exchange receive a weekly or biweekly box of fresh produce from the farm.

How Sustainable Is Your Food Shopping?

Use the following checklist to assess a food or beverage product before you purchase it. Check the box next to each statement that is true of the product you are considering. The more check marks, the greater contribution the food product makes to a sustainable food system.

☐ The producer or farmer who grew the food is known.

☐ The location where the food originated is known.

☐ The food traveled the least distance possible.

☐ The food is fresh, seasonal, and grown without harming soil, water, or air quality.

☐ The food was raised humanely without synthetic hormones or antibiotics.

☐ The process used to produce the food conserves genetic biodiversity and ecological integrity.

☐ The farm workers, processors, or food-service workers earned a fair wage, worked in safe conditions, and were not exploited in the making of this food.

☐ The nutritional value of the food is maintained and it is free of artificial ingredients.

☐ There were no or low environmental impacts as a result of processing and transporting the food.

☐ The food packaging is minimal, made from renewable resources, and is recyclable.

☐ The label on the food product directs you to find more information. Product labeling is transparent.

☐ The name and any claims of the food product are specific, meaningful, and logical.

☐ The food product has a legitimate and reputable third-party seal or certification.

☐ The local, national, and global implications of this food product are known.

Table 12.4

Go Green: Tips for Making More Sustainable Food Choices

Purchase locally grown, seasonal foods when possible	Visit the Natural Resources Defense Council for an interactive guide to the seasonal foods available in your area at www.nrdc.org.
Waste not, want not	Don't buy excessive amounts of food at one time. If you can't eat the food that you purchased before it goes bad, consider donating it to a food pantry and/or shelter. Your excess is someone else's dinner.
Eat more plant protein	Go meatless at least one meal a week. For delicious meatless ideas, visit www.meatlessmonday.com.
Plant your own garden	For the ultimate reduction in food miles, plant your produce in your backyard or in containers. To help you develop a green thumb, visit the National Gardening Association's Food Gardening Guide, the ultimate source for information on growing your favorite vegetables, fruits, and herbs, at www.garden.org.
Buy from local farm stands, farmers' markets, and community-supported agriculture (CSA) farms	Shop at local farmers' markets and roadside farm stands to find just-picked fruits and veggies (which will be at their peak nutritional value) for minimal food miles. You can also join a CSA to enjoy weekly or monthly boxes of farm-fresh produce delivered to your doorstep or a local pick-up site.
	Find local farmers' markets and community-supported farms in your area at http://ams.usda.gov and www.localharvest.org.

you want to try growing your food, which is as local as it gets, see Nutrition in the Real World, "You as a Sustainable Farmer: Growing Vegetables in a Container."

LO 12.3 **The Take-Home Message** Numerous natural resources are used when growing crops and raising animals for food. Natural resources are used internally to produce foods and externally to move these food products from the farm to the consumer. By-products that are produced during food production and processing can affect the environment. Locally grown foods use fewer external resources. Food systems involve all aspects of food production, transportation, and distribution. Sustainable food systems are environmentally friendly, economically sound, and socially equitable (the 3 Es). Individuals can eat more sustainably by choosing to eat more locally grown and plant-based foods.

You as a Sustainable Farmer: Growing Vegetables in a Container

You might think you need a yard, a hoe, and a shovel to have a garden, but this isn't necessarily the case. Edible plants can grow in all kinds of environments and containers, and for those living in dorms or apartments, a sunny window sill, a balcony, or your front step will provide enough space to create your own garden. All you need are a container, potting soil, water, a plant, and sun. In fact, there are even advantages to growing plants in containers rather than in the ground. There won't be any weeds to pull, and you'll have fewer pests to damage your plants. Your garden is also transportable so you can move it if you need to.

Here's what you need to get started:[1]

The Container
Almost any container, such as a ceramic pot, planter box, one- to five-gallon tubs, or even the plastic trash container under your desk, will do. The size of the container will depend on what you want to grow (see table). Drainage is key to growing a hearty plant. So, your container must have two important elements: (1) ¼-inch drilled holes, evenly spaced along the bottom of the container, and (2) an inch-thick layer of coarse gravel, pebbles, or broken pieces of a clay pot in the bottom of the container. This layer will allow excess water to drain from the plant.

The Potting Mixture
In place of soil, potting mixtures, which may be a combination of several compounds such as sawdust, peat moss, and vermiculite (a mineral that puffs up when exposed to heat such as from the sun), can be purchased at most garden centers, many hardware stores, and even on the Internet. The amount of potting mixture that you need will depend on the type of vegetables you want to grow and the size of your container.

The Plant
Many of the vegetables that grow in a backyard garden will also sprout quite nicely in a container garden. The table

provides a list of the easier-to-grow vegetables for first-time gardeners that are ideal for containers. Transplants (small plants that you transfer to the container) can be purchased at garden centers, farmers' markets, local farm stands, and even some supermarkets. When these transplants become available in your area, it is time to begin your vegetable garden.

Fertilizing
Because the rejuvenating, nutrient-rich soil of a backyard is missing in a container garden, you will need to routinely fertilize your plants. You can purchase a powdered fertilizer at your local supermarket, garden center, or hardware store and dilute it with water as directed on the package. Pour this diluted nourishment around the plant once a week or every other week.

Watering
Container plants tend to dry out more quickly than plants grown in outdoor gardens. Depending on the plant, you may need to water daily. Avoid waiting until the soil is completely dried out. Pour enough water so that some liquid will drain out the bottom of the container. (Put a foil pan under your plant if you are growing it inside your home to catch any excess water.) Avoid overwatering, which can be as damaging to a grown plant as underwatering. If your plant becomes waterlogged, the roots won't be able to "breathe" and receive the oxygen the

Growing plants in a container garden can provide healthy, nutritious vegetables for your dinner table.

plant needs to grow. You'll end up with root rot, and the plant may not survive.

Harvesting
The best part of gardening of any type is getting to harvest and eat what you grew. Plants like cabbage, cucumbers, green beans, and lettuce take about six weeks to mature before they are ready to harvest and eat. Tomatoes and peppers take about three months.

Vegetables: From Plant to Plate				
Vegetable	Minimum Container Size	Number of Plants	Amount of Sunlight	Approximate Number of Days to Harvest
Cabbage	1 gallon	1 plant	Partial shade	48–53
Cucumbers	1 gallon	2 plants	Full sun	46–66
Green beans	1 gallon	2–3 plants	Full sun	37–58
Lettuce	1 gallon	4–6 plants	Partial shade	41–56
Peppers	2 gallon	2 plants	Full sun	82–112
Tomatoes	3 gallon	1 plant	Full sun	84–124

How Do We Balance the World Population's Demand for Food with Sustainability?

LO 12.4 Describe the costs and benefits of using hormones, antibiotics, and pesticides in food production.

There are currently more than 7 billion people in the world, and that number is expected to reach between 8 and 11 billion people by 2050.[62] Providing food to the world's population is a challenge now, and will become more difficult in the future as population continues to grow. According to the United Nations, one in nine people in the world suffered from chronic hunger because they didn't have access to food in 2012–2014. Resources are limited, and questions remain about how farmers will be able to continue to feed the world given these limited resources. Many farmers are using different food technologies to enhance food products, but at what cost? For example, sometimes farmers use hormones, antibiotics, and pesticides to try to improve the yield of their crops and livestock. Even though these methods are beneficial because they allow farmers to produce food more efficiently, at least regarding the amount of land required, introducing these compounds into the food supply may be cause for some concern.

Costs and Benefits of Using Hormones in Our Food Supply

Scientists and dairy farmers have known for years that cows injected with a naturally occurring bovine **growth hormone**, also known as bovine somatotropin, produce more milk. Cows injected with a synthetic version of this hormone, **recombinant bovine somatotropin (rbST)**, also known as recombinant bovine growth hormone (rBGH), produce more milk than untreated cows. Recombinant bovine somatotropin has been used in the United States for more than 20 years.[63] The U.S. FDA and the Food and Agriculture Organization of the United Nations have reviewed the use of rbST in the United States and found no evidence that milk from cows treated with it is significantly different than milk from untreated cows, and have not found that it poses any long-term health threat to humans.[64] Other consumer groups, including Health Canada (the FDA equivalent in Canada) continue to question the long-term safety of the use of rbST in the food supply. There is some concern that milk from cows treated with rbST may contain higher amounts of other hormones as well, including insulin-like growth factor (IGF), and the consequences of humans consuming milk with these higher amounts of hormones are unknown.[65] Currently, the FDA does not require that manufacturers include information about whether or not cows that produced the milk in their products were treated with rbST, although this information is often voluntarily provided. If manufacturers make a statement about products being made from cows not treated with rBGH, they must also include a disclaimer statement that the FDA has said there is no significant difference between milk from cows treated with rBGH and those not treated (**Figure 12.8**).

Other hormones are sometimes used to increase the amount of weight that cattle gain and the amount of meat that they produce.[66] An additional concern is that the runoff from sewage sludge containing these hormones can reach surface waters and may interfere with the reproductive cycle of wildlife.[67] Hormones cannot be used in animals used to produce USDA organic–verified products.

growth hormone A protein-based hormone that stimulates cell growth and reproduction in humans and animals.

recombinant bovine somatotropin (rbST) A synthetically made hormone identical to a cow's natural growth hormone, somatotropin, that stimulates milk production. Also known as rbGH (recombinant bovine growth hormone).

Figure 12.8 Milk Label Containing Information about the Use of rBGH

Cows being raised for beef are often confined to feedlots, where they may be treated with antibiotics to prevent disease transmission, or hormones to facilitate greater weight gain.

Costs and Benefits of Using Antibiotics in Our Food Supply

Antibiotics, whether injected into food-producing animals or given via feed, are used for three purposes: (1) to treat animals that are sick; (2) to preventively treat animals that may be at risk of being sick (for example, if one animal becomes ill, the entire herd may be given antibiotics); and (3) to promote growth. When antibiotics are used for the first two purposes, they are used for a relatively short period of time. This isn't true when antibiotics are used for the third purpose. Low-dose antibiotics are sometimes put in animal feed, because animals that consume this feed gain more weight than animals fed antibiotic-free feed.

Pathogenic bacteria such as *Campylobacter, E. coli* O157:H7, and *Salmonella* are commonly found in the gastrointestinal tracts of animals without making them sick. However, when animals are given antibiotics chronically, **antibiotic-resistant bacteria** strains can sometimes grow in their intestinal tracts. If a human contracts a foodborne illness from this animal food source, treatment with the same antibiotic that was used in the feed, which killed the bacteria in the past, may no longer be effective. One example of this occurred as follows: In the late 1980s, the antibiotic fluoroquinolone was successfully used to treat *Campylobacter*, which is commonly found in chickens. In 1995, this antibiotic began to be used regularly in poultry. Shortly after, doctors began seeing patients with *Campylobacter*-induced foodborne illness whose infections were resistant to treatments with fluoroquinolone.[68] More recent outbreaks of antibiotic-resistant strains of *Salmonella* traced to ground beef and poultry demonstrate the need for ongoing concern.[69] The National Antimicrobial Resistance Monitoring System–Enteric Bacteria (NARMS) has been established, which is a joint effort between the Food and Drug Administration's Center for Veterinary Medicine (FDA CVM), the U.S. Department of Agriculture (USDA), and the Centers for Disease Control and Prevention (CDC), to monitor this important issue of preventing antibiotic-resistant bacteria strains in animals and humans.[70] The Center for Veterinary Medicine has developed guidelines for the judicious use of antibiotics in food-producing animals in order to minimize the development of antibiotic-resistant bacteria.[71] Antibiotics cannot be used to treat animals used to produce USDA organic–verified products.[72] The risk of finding antibiotic-resistant bacteria was found to be 33 percent higher in livestock grown with conventional methods than in organically grown livestock.[73]

Costs and Benefits of Using Pesticides in Our Food Supply

antibiotics Drugs that kill or slow the growth of bacteria.

antibiotic-resistant bacteria Bacteria that have developed a resistance to an antibiotic such that they are no longer affected by antibiotic medication.

pesticides Substances that kill or repel pests such as insects, weeds, microorganisms, rodents, or fungi.

You have probably been handling **pesticides** for years without even realizing it. If you use a disinfectant to control the mold in your shower, bug spray to ward off flesh biters on muggy summer nights, or a flea collar to keep your pet itch free, you're making use of chemicals that destroy or mitigate pests. These chemicals are collectively known as pesticides. Whereas pesticides can cause harm if consumed in high enough quantities, some more so than others, they are needed to control disease-causing organisms and pests that threaten or affect the food supply. By using pesticides on agricultural crops, food plants can flourish and produce a hearty bounty. This enables farmers to offer affordable crops to consumers.

Types of Pesticides

Several different types of pests can diminish or destroy crop yields, including insects, microorganisms (bacteria, viruses), fungi (mold), and rodents (rats and mice). Pesticides used to kill weeds are called **herbicides**, whereas those used on microorganisms are **antimicrobials**. **Fungicides** are used to destroy fungi.

Pesticides can be chemically or biologically based. Biologically based pesticides, such as **biopesticides** and sex pheromones, use materials from animals, plants, bacteria, and some minerals. Biopesticides are less toxic than chemically based pesticides, generally affect only the targeted pest, and often decompose relatively quickly, minimizing the potential for environmental pollution. For example, baking soda (sodium bicarbonate) can be diluted with water and sprayed onto plants to inhibit the growth of fungi without any known risk to humans or birds. The most commonly used biopesticides are strains of the bacterium *Bacillus thuringiensis*, or *Bt*, which kills developing insects.[74] Insect **sex pheromones** can be used to interfere with the mating of certain pests. Scented extracts from plants can also be used to lure and then trap insects. Biopesticides are typically safer than chemical pesticides; however, for biopesticides to be effective the user must understand exactly which pests are the problem.[75]

Chemically based **organophosphates** make up about half of all the insecticides used in the United States and are used on fruits, nuts, vegetables, corn, wheat, and other crops, as well as on commercial and residential lawns and plants.[76] These pesticides affect the nervous systems of the pests they destroy, but also affect other animals and even humans. The EPA (Environmental Protection Agency) banned residential use of most organophosphates, but some are still used in agriculture for the production of fruits and vegetables. Organophosphates degrade relatively quickly when exposed to light and oxygen, but small quantities can still be detected in the U.S. food supply. All pesticides, including organophosphates, are continually re-reviewed by the EPA to ensure their safety.

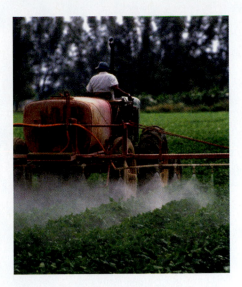

Farmers use pesticides on food crops to diminish the damage from pests.

Risks and Regulation of Pesticides

The problem with pesticides, especially chemically based pesticides, is that they can cause unintended harm to the environment, animals, and humans. Chemical pesticides require a large amount of fossil fuel to produce, have been shown to affect the fertility of soil, and may pollute the environment in unintended ways. The American bald eagle almost became extinct due to a now-banned pesticide that was ingested by the eagles.[77] Research has shown that some pesticides, depending upon their level of toxicity and how much is consumed, may cause serious health problems, such as cancer, birth defects, and nerve damage, in humans.[78] Infants and young children are especially susceptible to the ill effects of organophosphates as their internal organs are continuing to develop.[79]

To prevent potential harm to consumers, pesticide use is regulated in the United States. The Food Quality Protection Act of 1996 allowed the FDA to enforce stricter safety standards for the use of pesticides in the United States. Risk for pesticide contamination is 30 percent lower for organically grown produce compared with conventionally grown produce. However, there is little difference in the risk of going over the maximum allowed limits between organic and conventional methods.[80] The EPA evaluates all food pesticides with a four-part **risk assessment** to ensure that they can be used with "a reasonable certainty of no harm." The risk assessment process includes the following:

1. *Hazard identification.* Identify the potential hazards or ill effects that may develop after exposure to a specific pesticide in animals.

herbicides Substances that are used to kill and control weeds.

antimicrobials Substances or a combination of substances, such as disinfectants and sanitizers, that control the spread of bacteria and viruses on nonliving surfaces or objects.

fungicides Chemicals used to kill mold.

biopesticides Substances used to kill pests that are derived from natural materials such as animals, plants, bacteria, and certain minerals.

sex pheromones Naturally occurring chemicals secreted by one organism to attract another; used as a biopesticide to control pests by interfering with their mating.

organophosphates A group of synthetic pesticides that adversely affect the nervous systems of pests.

risk assessment The process of determining the potential human health risks posed by exposure to substances such as pesticides.

Wash: Thoroughly wash and scrub all fresh fruits and vegetables with a vegetable brush with sturdy surfaces under running water to dislodge bacteria and some of the pesticide residue. Running water is more effective for this purpose than soaking the fruit and vegetables.

Peel and trim: Peeling fruits and vegetables and tossing the outer leaves of leafy vegetables helps reduce pesticides. Trimming the visible fat from meat and the fatty skin from poultry and fish helps reduce some of the pesticide residue that remains in the fatty tissue of the animal.

Eat a variety of foods: Eating a variety of foods reduces your chances of being overexposed to any particular pesticide.

Figure 12.9 Reducing Pesticides in Food

2. *Dose-response assessment.* Determine the dose at which these ill effects occur in animals and then use this information to identify a potentially equal dose in humans.

3. *Exposure assessment.* Determine all the ways that a person could typically be exposed to that pesticide. Exposure could occur orally when you eat food or drink water, or by inhalation or absorption through your skin when you are using household disinfectants or gardening pesticides around your home.

4. *Risk characterization.* Use the information obtained in the first three steps to determine the overall risk of the pesticide.[81]

Because there are potential differences between the effects of a pesticide on animals and its effect on humans, as well as differences among humans, the EPA builds in a margin of safety when determining the health risk. An extra safety factor is added, up to a tenfold difference, to protect the most vulnerable groups, such as infants and children, who could be exposed to the pesticide. Before a pesticide can be registered by the EPA, the manufacturer must submit it to more than 100 health and environmental tests, at a cost of over $150 million, and it takes approximately nine years before being approved.[82] Thus, much effort goes into ensuring that the foods you eat are safe, yet affordable, in order for you to reap their health benefits and minimize any known risks. **Figure 12.9** shows what you can do to reduce the pesticides on the foods that you consume. Even crops labeled USDA organic may contain some pesticides.

The EPA also conducts environmental risk assessments to make sure that a pesticide doesn't pose any risk to wildlife and the environment. If it does, or is even thought to hurt the environment, acceptable levels are determined to prevent any known harm.[83]

Alternatives to Pesticides

Rather than use pesticides, some growers, including those certified as organic farmers, use an approach called **integrated pest management (IPM)** to manage pests in their crops. The goal of this approach is to use the most economical methods

integrated pest management (IPM) Alternative to pesticides that uses the most economical and the least harmful methods of pest control to minimize risk to consumers, crops, and the environment.

to control pests while causing the least risk of harm to the consumer, the crops, or the environment. The IPM method includes preventive measures, such as rotating crops and choosing pest-resistant strains of crops, to reduce the likelihood of attracting pests. When these measures aren't adequate to control pests, biologically based alternatives, such as biopesticides or the introduction of natural predators (specific insects that eat the unwanted pests), may be used to curtail an infestation. If all these methods don't control the spread of the pests, targeted spraying of chemically based pesticides is then considered.[84] Note that foods grown using IPM methods typically aren't labeled, so the consumer can't easily spot them in the supermarket, although organic food production applies many of the same concepts as IPM.

LO 12.4 **The Take-Home Message** Hormones, antibiotics, and pesticides are used to increase food production, but may impact the environment and human health. Cows treated with synthetic growth hormone produce more milk than untreated cows. The FDA says milk from cows treated with synthetic hormone is safe, but some question its long-term safety for humans. Animals treated chronically with antibiotics may grow to be larger than untreated animals, but may develop antibiotic-resistant strains of bacteria that may be passed on to humans through foodborne illness. Pesticides control the growth of disease-causing organisms and pests that threaten the food supply. The FDA, USDA, and EPA regulate the use of pesticides, but some pose risks to humans if consumed at high doses. The FDA does not require food manufacturers to include information about the use of hormones, antibiotics, or pesticides on food labels. Foods that carry the USDA organic seal are guaranteed to be produced without the use of hormones or antibiotics, but may contain some pesticides.

What Are the Risks and Benefits of Using Biotechnology in Agriculture?

LO 12.5 Describe the benefits and risks of using biotechnology, including genetic engineering, in agriculture.

Another strategy of the food industry to maximize food production is the use of **biotechnology**. Although this sounds like a high-tech term, humans have actually been manipulating the genes of food products for generations. In years past, they did this through selective breeding. In fact, the fresh apples that you eat today look nothing like their small, sour Asian ancestors. Because apples have been intentionally grown (or cultivated) by humans for thousands of years, apple farmers have had plenty of time to crossbreed different versions of the tree to produce more desirable offspring. For example, if one tree produced large, fleshy apples with thinner skins, and another produced smaller, sour apples with thicker skins, an ancient apple farmer might have bred the two in the hope of producing a tree with large, fleshy, hardy fruit. This process is a form of selective **plant breeding**.

Historically, farmers have crossbred plants by trial and error, hoping for the best results and using the best offspring to further breed more desirable plants. Farmers in the United States and around the world routinely use selectively bred plants to create bigger and better produce and disease-resistant crops, and to increase crop yields. In fact, you would be hard pressed to find many fruits and vegetables today that aren't a product of genetic modification through this type of selective plant

biotechnology The application of biological techniques to living cells, which alters their genetic makeup.

plant breeding A type of biotechnology in which two plants are crossbred to produce offspring with desired traits from both.

The apples of today are larger and sweeter than their ancestors, thanks to hundreds of years of selective breeding.

breeding. In the past two centuries, as scientists learned more about DNA and its workings, and how to manipulate it, the process of genetic modification has become faster and more controlled.

Genetic Engineering

Today's versions of bioengineered foods include new techniques, such as **genetic engineering (GE)**, to alter the genetic makeup of an organism. In this type of bioengineering, the exact gene or genes from the DNA of a plant cell are isolated and inserted into the DNA of another cell to create the genetically modified product (**Figure 12.10**). This cutting and splicing of genes into the DNA of another cell is called *recombinant DNA (rDNA)* technology. Organisms that have been genetically engineered to contain both original and foreign genes are called **genetically modified organisms (GMOs)**. These GMOs are used to grow GE plants that produce GE foods.

Genetically modified crops were first grown in the early 1990s, and by 2007, 140 million acres of bioengineered crops, including corn, cotton, canola, and soybeans, had been planted in the United States. In fact, by 2014 85 percent of the soybeans grown in the United States were genetically engineered.[85] Bioengineered crops are being cultivated in 23 countries worldwide.[86] While some individuals and groups have expressed concern about the use of genetically modified foods (sometimes calling them "frankenfoods"), proponents believe that GMOs can be good for

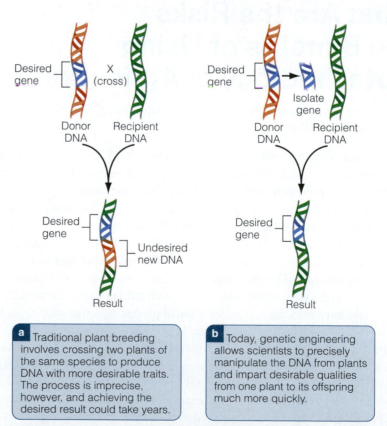

a Traditional plant breeding involves crossing two plants of the same species to produce DNA with more desirable traits. The process is imprecise, however, and achieving the desired result could take years.

b Today, genetic engineering allows scientists to precisely manipulate the DNA from plants and impart desirable qualities from one plant to its offspring much more quickly.

Figure 12.10 Plant Breeding versus Genetic Engineering

genetic engineering (GE) A biological technique that isolates and manipulates the genes of organisms to produce a targeted, modified product.

genetically modified organisms (GMOs) Organisms that have been genetically engineered to contain both original and foreign genes.

the environment, help feed countries that have an inadequate food supply, improve the quality and quantity of foods available all year round, and create new uses for plants in industries such as pharmaceuticals and manufacturing. In the words of former President Jimmy Carter, "Responsible biotechnology is not the enemy; starvation is."[87]

The original purpose of using biotechnology in plants was to reduce the amount of pesticides used on food crops. For example, the bacterium *Bacillus thuringiensis*, mentioned previously and found naturally in soil, produces a toxin that is poisonous to certain pests but not to humans or other animals. When the gene for this toxin is inserted into a crop plant, the plant becomes resistant to these pests. Some corn crops in the United States contain the *Bt* gene, which makes them resistant to some insect pests. The use of biotechnology to reduce the use of pesticides is working—the total amount of pesticides has declined by 2.5 million pounds by using bioengineered crops.[88]

Bt corn has been genetically engineered to produce a protein that is toxic to the larva of the European corn borer, the most damaging insect pest of corn in North America.

First-generation bioengineered products were also created to improve a crop's tolerance to herbicides. With an herbicide-resistant version of a desired crop, a farmer can spray herbicide over a field to kill a variety of weeds without harming the crop. Approximately 93 percent of soybeans grown in the United States in 2013 were varieties that had been genetically modified to be herbicide resistant.[89]

The second-generation bioengineered products were designed to provide consumers with added nutritional value as well as other attributes, such as increasing the crop's shelf life. For example, "golden" rice contains foreign gene segments that encode the rice grain to make beta-carotene and to stockpile extra iron. This "super" rice, if planted by farmers and accepted by consumers in southeast Asia, could help eliminate the epidemic of vitamin A and iron deficiency in children there.[90] Bioengineered, high-oleic-acid oil is less prone to becoming rancid, and thus is more stable when used for frying foods.[91]

Third-generation bioengineered products hold promise in the pharmaceutical, environmental, and industrial arenas. In fact, the first such bioengineered product created for commercial use was human insulin (needed by diabetics) produced by genetically engineered *E. coli*. Other examples are delivering vaccinations for the hepatitis B virus in tomatoes and lettuce.[92]

Concerns and Regulations Associated with GE Foods

While many professional organizations, such as the American Medical Association, the National Academy of Sciences, the World Health Organization, and the Society of Toxicology, have supported agricultural biotechnology, some opponents of bioengineered foods fear that biotechnology can cause the creation of "Frankenstein" foods.[93] Though bioengineering in agriculture is regulated by the federal government, there are many unanswered questions regarding the development of GMOs. For example, in many cases we are not aware of how GMOs may change or impact the natural environment or ecological balance of the ecosystems in which they are allowed to grow. Other concerns have arisen about the production of plant toxins, the introduction of new allergens into the human food chain, changes in the nutrient content and creation of new substances in foods, the production of unsafe animal feed, and horizontal transfer of genes to humans as they consume these products. **Table 12.5** lists some of the concerns and regulatory safeguards that are in place to address these issues. In addition, some people have ethical and religious concerns about introducing GMOs into the U.S. food supply.

Bioengineered foods in the United States are regulated by the same three government agencies that regulate pesticides: the FDA, USDA, and EPA. The FDA's role is to ensure that foods are safe to eat, and the USDA's role is to ensure that the plants are safe to grow. The EPA's role is to ensure that foods will not negatively affect the environment, for example, that the gene for any pesticide, such as that for *Bt* toxin, inserted into a plant is safe and won't hurt the environment. Though these agencies work together to ensure the safety of these foods, the FDA has the overall authority to remove any food that doesn't meet the same high safety standards that are set for its conventionally grown equivalent.[94] Currently, labeling of GMO foods is not mandated by the FDA because the FDA says that in most cases there is little scientific evidence that GE foods are different in nutritional content than conventional foods. This continues to be a current topic of controversy. The FDA does require labeling if the food is significantly different than the conventional food in the nutrients it provides, if it introduces an allergen that consumers may not expect, or if it contains a toxicant. Though not mandated to do so, some companies choose to include information about genetic engineering on their food labels. The USDA recently developed a new government certification and labeling for foods that are free of genetically modified ingredients. So far, the certification is voluntary, but foods that meet the guidelines could carry a label indicating that the food is "USDA Process Verified" and GMO free. Genetic engineering cannot be used to produce USDA organic–verified products. In addition, in 2015 the U.S. federal government released a memorandum outlining steps to review and revise current regulations for biotechnology including genetically engineered foods.

Table 12.5

Concerns and Regulations for GE Foods

Concern	FDA Regulation
Undesirable genetic modification	To avoid the creation of undesirable products, genes used must not have prior evidence of encoding any harmful substances. The genes must also be stably inserted into the plant in order to avoid any rearranging of genetic information that would produce an undesirable substance.
Introduction of allergens	GE foods must be monitored for food allergens. Protein encoded from common allergen food sources (such as milk, eggs, fish, tree nuts, and legumes) should be presumed to be allergens and should be labeled as such on the GE food.
Excessive level of toxins	GE foods should not contain natural toxins at levels that are higher than those found naturally in plants.
Changes in nutrients	All GE foods should be monitored to assess unintentional changes in the nutrient levels in the plants and their ability to be utilized in the human body as compared with their conventional counterparts.
Creation of new substances	If the genes that are introduced into plants encode substances that are different in structure and function than those normally found in foods, these substances would have to be approved by the FDA, as would any other food additive. However, if these substances are GRAS (generally recognized as safe) or "substantially equivalent" to substances that already exist in foods, they do not require premarket approval from the FDA.
Unsafe animal feeds	Because a single plant type may be the predominant food source in an animal feed, all GE animal feeds must meet the same strict safety standards that are in place for food that is grown for humans.

The public seems to be warming up to bioengineered foods because of their health benefits and improved quality. In a 2014 survey of 1,000 Americans, 50 percent agreed that biotechnology is one way to help ensure we have enough food for everyone as the world population continues to climb. Thirty-seven percent of Americans knew that bioengineered foods are currently available in the United States. More than 60 percent stated that they would likely purchase bioengineered foods if they provided health benefits such as being lower in saturated fat and *trans* fats or having lower levels of pesticides. Interestingly, Millennials (those born from 1980 to 2000) have more favorable views about food biotechnology than do older age groups.[95]

LO 12.5 **The Take-Home Message** Both plant breeding and genetic engineering are types of biotechnology that alter the genetic makeup of an organism's cells to create a new plant with more desirable traits. Genetically engineered corn and soybeans are more resistant to pests and have been grown in the United States since the early 1990s. The majority of corn and soybeans grown in the United States are genetically engineered. Genetic engineering of plants has also led to the development of rice that is a good source of beta-carotene and vegetables that deliver vaccinations. Some consumers worry that genetically modified organisms may alter the natural environment or ecological balance of the food system in unpredictable ways, but there is little scientific evidence to support these concerns.

How Does Food Policy Affect the Foods Available to You to Buy and Consume?

LO 12.6 Explain how food policy affects the foods that are available to you to buy and consume.

Farmers and food companies aren't the only ones responsible for keeping food safe, healthy, available, and sustainable. Several government agencies, including the USDA, FDA, EPA, and the Federal Trade Commission (FTC), regulate the food industry and set national food and nutrition policy (see **Table 12.6**). These policies have a dramatic effect on the foods available to you to purchase and consume. For example, some farmers in the United States receive a form of government financial aid known as subsidies to grow certain commodity crops such as corn and soybeans. It may surprise you to learn that many of these crops are used to either feed animals or make processed foods. Sometimes policy drives the production of healthier foods and sometimes it doesn't.

Food Policy Can Help Encourage Food Producers to Create Healthier Products

In 2005, the Department of Health and Human Services (DHHS) and USDA's *Dietary Guidelines for Americans* not only encouraged the public to eat more whole grains, but for the first time in history made a specific recommendation that at least half of daily grain servings should come from whole grains. This policy released a tidal wave of reaction in the food industry. Manufacturers quickly scrambled to increase the production of good-tasting whole-grain products to keep up with consumer demand. In 2006, soon after the release of the *Dietary Guidelines*, whole-grain bread sales increased more than 200 percent.[96] This increased demand caused a change in crop production

Table 12.6

Who Oversees the Food Supply?

Agency	Responsible for
United States Department of Agriculture (USDA)	Monitoring agriculture and food production and ensuring safe and accurately labeled meat, poultry, and eggs. The USDA enforces tolerances for pesticide residues in meat, poultry, and eggs set forth by the EPA.
Food and Drug Administration (FDA)	Overseeing domestic and imported foods except for meat and poultry products. Ensuring that these foods are safe, sanitary, nutritious, wholesome, and honestly and adequately labeled. Overseeing food-processing plants and approval and surveillance of food-animal drugs, feed additives, and all food additives. FDA enforces tolerances for pesticide residues that are set by the EPA.
Environmental Protection Agency (EPA)	Protecting you and the environment from harmful pesticides. EPA is responsible for the safe use of pesticides and fertilizers, as well as food-plant detergents and sanitizers on foods and in the environment. It establishes the safe tolerances for pesticide residues in or on food commodities and animal feed.
Animal and Plant Health Inspection Service (APHIS)	Protecting against plant and animal pests and disease
National Marine Fisheries Service (NMFS)	Overseeing a voluntary seafood inspection for quality and a grading program
Centers for Disease Control and Prevention (CDC)	Surveillance and investigation of human and animal diseases
Federal Trade Commission (FTC)	Regulating food advertising
Department of Health and Human Services (DHHS)	Protecting the health of and providing essential human services to Americans, including those who are less able

Food policy can drive the food industry. The recommendation for Americans to consume more whole grains caused food manufacturers to increase their production of whole-grain products.

at the farm level, as farmers switched from growing crops such as red winter wheat to a different variety that can be used in processed whole-grain food products.[97] In essence, the farmers had to catch up to the demands of consumers.

Interestingly, this industry shift of offering more whole-grain products to the consumer also had an impact on the American diet. The availability of a slew of newly reformulated whole-grain products enabled even the less motivated, less health-conscious consumers to more easily incorporate this recommendation into their lives. Americans increased their whole-grain consumption by 20 percent from 2005 to 2008, but most people still get far fewer whole grains than recommended.[98]

In fact, according to a report published by the Whole Grain Council, only 11 percent of the grains that Americans eat are whole grains.[99] Nevertheless, it appears that food consumers may have increased whole grains in their diet without even realizing it, as their favorite reformulated products continued to taste good.[100] This is an example of how food policy and food production can work together to make it easier for the food consumer to consume healthy foods.

Food Policy Can Lead to Relabeling and Reformulating without Providing a Healthier Food Product

Unfortunately, changes in nutrition and food policy can also sometimes result in less-than-healthy consequences. For example, the food labeling policy on *trans* fats caused some manufacturers to reformulate their products in ways that did not benefit the consumer. In 2003, based on the research documenting the heart-unhealthy attributes of *trans* fat, the FDA issued a policy for the mandatory labeling of *trans* fats on the Nutrition Facts panel of food labels. Major food manufacturers, such as Kraft, Campbell's, and Frito-Lay, reformulated some of their cookies, crackers, chips, and bakery items to remove *trans* fat. While some of these products were reformulated to replace the *trans* fats with healthy vegetable oils, others were reformulated using heart-unhealthy saturated fats, such as butter and palm oil.[101] As a result, the products ended up containing little or no *trans* fat, but often containing other varieties of unhealthy fats. Also, the removal of the *trans* fats from these products enabled manufacturers to boast "0 grams *trans* fats" on the food label (as long as the product contains <0.5 gram of *trans* fat per serving). This kind of labeling can lead to a "halo effect" on these foods, leaving consumers with the impression that these no-*trans*-fat foods are good for them because they contain no *trans* fats, and they need not worry about the consequences of eating them. In reality, these foods may or may not be foods that contribute to a healthy and balanced diet.[102] Let's face it, when you take the *trans* fats out of the doughnut, you are still left with a doughnut. The doughnut didn't magically morph into an apple. No matter what type of fat is in the bakery item, few Americans have room in their diets for a lot of doughnuts—or other sweets, for that matter—especially when they displace much-needed fruit or vegetables.

What Are the Politics of the Food Industry?

The intersection of food policy (set by various government agencies) and the interests of the food industry (made up of hundreds of companies that produce, distribute, and sell food) can often yield interesting results. The National School Lunch Program, which you will learn more about in Chapter 15, is one example. This program supplies American children with reduced-price, nutritionally regulated lunches via the standard school cafeteria. Who supplies the schools with the massive amounts of food needed for this nationwide program? The answer is the federal government, the nation's biggest food consumer.

Government Programs Are Food Consumers

The U.S. government provides more than $11 billion in money and free food commodities, including poultry, eggs, fruits, vegetables, peanut butter, and dairy products, to support federal school nutrition programs. Providing schools with commodities helps to keep the cost of the school lunch at an affordable rate. Where do these commodities come from? They are the surplus, unsold foods grown and raised on our U.S. farms. The government buys these foods from the farmers and gives them to schools.[103]

In addition to the National School Lunch Program, other U.S. programs, such as the Summer Food Service Program, the Emergency Food Assistance Program, and the Child and Adult Care Food Program, all have access to these commodities.[104] In 2008, the U.S. Congress passed a Farm Bill that, among other things, reauthorized the distribution of surplus commodities to these special nutrition projects. The advantage of this arrangement is twofold: The government provides a market for farmers' surplus foods while ensuring that American citizens get fed.

Food Lobbyists Exert Influence

Food companies and other members of the food industry often voice their preferences to government agencies and politicians via individuals known as *lobbyists*. A lobbyist is paid to meet with and persuade politicians to vote on pending legislation in a direction that would favor the interests of the party the lobbyist represents. All lobbyists must be registered, make the parties that they represent publicly known, and report how they are funded.[105]

Sometimes research can prompt food companies and businesses to spring food lobbyists into action. In 2009, a report published in the *New England Journal of Medicine* by a group of prominent researchers claimed that the consumption of sugar-sweetened beverages was linked to an increased risk of obesity, diabetes, and heart disease among Americans. The researchers' solution: to tax these beverages to dissuade consumption.[106] They also recommended that monies generated from the tax could be used to support childhood nutrition and obesity prevention programs, and fund health care in general. The makers of these sweetened beverages, supermarket companies, fast-food restaurants, and other organizations with a vested interest in maintaining high sales of sugary beverages such as the National Corn Growers Association (whose products create high-fructose corn syrup, the main sweetener found in soft drinks) spent more than $20 million on lobbying efforts to convince Congress to block this (for them) not-so-sweet proposal.[107] Will sweetened beverages be taxed? You can be sure that businesses that will be impacted by this tax aren't going to leave Washington, D.C. without a fight.

LO 12.6 **The Take-Home Message** Several government agencies, including the FDA, FTC, USDA, and EPA, regulate the food industry and set national food and nutrition policy. The U.S. government is also a food consumer, and it purchases large amounts of surplus commodities that are used in various national food and nutrition programs. Large food companies often hire lobbyists to persuade politicians about food policy.

How Do You Know How Foods Were Produced?

LO 12.7 Recognize how label terms can help you know how food was produced.

As you just read, many factors, including decisions made by farmers, food companies, grocery stores, and government agencies, will affect the foods that are available to you. At the end of the day, though, you get to choose which food products to buy and consume. Knowing and understanding the terms found on food labels or posted near foods can help you select the healthiest, most environmentally friendly options.

Label Terms Provide Information about How Foods Were Produced

Both the FDA and the USDA are the consumer watchdogs for food labeling, and labeling of animal food products is essential when it comes to determining how the animals were fed, raised, and treated. The label terms for meat and poultry are determined and defined by the USDA. The following list includes terms often found on prepackaged meat products:[108]

The term "natural," when used on the packaging of meat and poultry, indicates that no artificial ingredients were added and that the product is minimally processed.

- *Certified.* Indicates that the USDA has evaluated a meat product for class, grade, or other quality characteristics (for example, "Certified Angus Beef").
- *Fresh Poultry.* Poultry that has never had an internal temperature below 26°F.
- *Free Range.* Producers must demonstrate that the animal has been allowed access to the outdoors each day, but does not designate a specific time allotment.
- *Kosher.* Meat and poultry products that were prepared under the supervision of a rabbi, thus satisfying the requirements of Jewish law.
- *Natural.* The FDA has no definition for the use of the term "natural." However, it doesn't object to the use of this term if the food does not contain artificial ingredients or added color and is only minimally processed; that is, using processes that do not fundamentally alter the raw product. The label must explain the use of the term natural (such as "no added colorings or artificial ingredients").
- *No Hormones (pork or poultry).* Hormones are not allowed in raising hogs or poultry. Therefore, the claim "no hormones added" cannot be used on the labels of pork or poultry unless it is followed by the statement, "Federal regulations prohibit the use of hormones."

- *No Hormones (beef)*. The phrase "no hormones administered" may be approved for use on the label of bovine products, including milk, if no hormones were used in raising the animals.
- *No Antibiotics*. May be used on labels for meat or poultry products if the animals were raised without antibiotics.

In addition to these common terms, the use of the term "organic" is appearing on increasing numbers of products on supermarket shelves.

Understand the Meaning of the Term *Organic*

As more consumers become concerned about how their food is grown and raised, the popularity of **organic** foods has increased, with sales rising from $11 billion in 2004 to an estimated $27 billion in 2012, which is more than double the annual growth rate for all food sales.[109] In fact, a broader segment of the U.S. population is buying organic foods and organic food options are becoming more and more prevalent even in mainstream supermarkets and warehouse- or club-style stores. Organic foods are now available in three out of four conventional grocery stores. More than one-third of Americans buy organic products at least monthly.[110] Learn more about how to decide if it makes sense for you to buy organic products in the Practical Nutrition Video titled "Are Organic Foods Necessary? Or Just Expensive?"

This growing interest in organic foods prompted the USDA to develop National Organic Standards (NOS) in 2002. The NOS provide specific criteria that food producers must meet during production, handling, and processing to label their products organic. As a result of these standards, you can be confident that if the food is labeled as organic, it was produced and handled using specific guidelines and certified by a USDA-accredited inspector.[111]

Organic farming involves growing crops without the use of *some* synthetic pesticides, synthetic fertilizers, bioengineering, or irradiation. Contrary to popular belief, organic foods are not necessarily free of all pesticides. Organically grown crops may come into contact with chemicals due to drift from wind and rainwater. Also, though organic farmers use IPM, sometimes synthetic pesticides and biopesticides may still be needed. The National Organic Program has created the National List of Allowed and Prohibited Substances that identifies substances that can and cannot be used in organic crop production. According to the list, several synthetic pesticides, such as insecticidal soaps, are allowed, while some natural substances, such as ash from the burning of manure, cannot be used in organic farming.[112] For animal food products, only antibiotic-free or growth hormone–free animals can be used to produce organic meat, poultry, eggs, and dairy foods.[113]

You can identify organically produced foods in your supermarket by looking for the USDA Organic seal (**Figure 12.11**). Foods that display this seal or otherwise state that they are organic must contain at least 95 percent organic ingredients. However, organic food producers can choose whether or not to display this seal, so it may not be on all such products. There are other label claims and standards for foods that are 100 percent organic, or that use organic ingredients. **Table 12.7** on the next page describes the standards that organic label claims must meet.

There is little scientific evidence supporting the idea that organic foods are nutritionally superior to those grown in a conventional manner.[114] However, organically grown food is less likely to have detectable levels of pesticides or antibiotics (for animal food products) than conventionally grown food.[115] Studies have shown that organic farming can help the environment by reducing pesticide use, energy use, and greenhouse emissions, and by increasing biodiversity in fields.[116] Unfortunately, organic foods tend to cost more than those that are conventionally grown. For example, organic produce can cost anywhere from 5 to 70 percent more than conventional

Practical Nutrition VIDEO

Are Organic Foods Necessary? Or Just Expensive?

When organic foods cost more, it can be difficult to determine whether they are worth the expense. Join Joan in the produce aisle for advice that may help you decide. Scan this QR code with your mobile device to access the video. You can also access the video in MasteringNutrition™.

Figure 12.11 The USDA Organic Seal
Foods that are labeled or advertised with the USDA Organic seal must contain at least 95 percent organic ingredients.

organic Being free of chemical-based pesticides, synthetic fertilizers, irradiation, and bioengineering. A USDA-accredited certifying inspector must certify organic foods.

Table 12.7

Various Levels of Organic

If the label says "100% Organic"

Then: The food must be composed entirely of organic ingredients. *Note:* These foods cannot contain sulfites and must declare the certifying agent. The USDA Organic seal may be displayed.

If the label says "Made with Organic Ingredients"

Then: The food contains at least 70 percent organic ingredients.

If the label says "Organic" and/or displays the USDA Organic seal

Then: The food contains at least 95 percent organic ingredients.

If the label says nothing about organic claims

Then: The food contains less than 70 percent organic ingredients.

foods. The price isn't likely to decline any time soon, as the demand for organic food is currently higher than the supply. Another issue to consider when choosing organic foods is where they were grown. The USDA currently has trade arrangements with India, Israel, Japan, and New Zealand to allow organic foods from these countries to enter the U.S. market.[117] Keep in mind that if your organic food has to travel from New Zealand, the food miles that it travels may negate some of the environmental benefits described earlier.[118] Finally, organic foods are not always healthy foods. There are plenty of processed foods that contain high amounts of salt, sugar, and fat that are made with some organic ingredients, and therefore bear the organic label.

LO 12.7 **The Take-Home Message** Food labels provide information that help consumers know how their food was produced. Foods labeled as organic are grown without the use of some synthetic pesticides, synthetic fertilizers, bioengineering, or irradiation. Organically produced animal foods are produced without antibiotics or hormones. The National Organic Standards provide specific criteria and guidelines for the production, handling, processing, and labeling of organic foods, as well as mandatory certification by an accredited inspector. Organic foods usually cost more than conventionally grown foods, and there is little scientific evidence that they are more nutritious than conventionally grown foods, though they may have lower levels of pesticides and antibiotics than do conventionally grown foods.

Should the U.S. Federal Government Continue to Subsidize the Production of Corn and Wheat?

Farm subsidies are funds given to farmers by the U.S. government to encourage them to grow certain crops. Subsidies help to manage crop supply and thus influence the cost of these crops. Most farm subsidies in the United States go to farmers of grains such as corn and wheat. In times of plenty, when supply exceeds demand, the U.S. government purchases the excess and uses these crops in national food programs such as the National School Lunch Program.[1] Take a look at both sides of the issue and decide what you think.

yes

- Subsidizing crops that are in high demand, such as corn and wheat, helps provide farmers with a stable income even when weather and other conditions make it difficult to produce other crops. Without subsidies many farmers could go out of business, which would result in an increase in the demand for, and thus the price of, food.

- Subsidies help to control the price of food. Ensuring American farmers a decent return on their labor, even in tough times, helps to smooth out the constant fluctuations in the supply and demand of commodities.

- The United States is not the only country to subsidize farmers. Many farmers in Europe and Japan also receive government subsidies to raise certain crops. Governments see farm subsidies as a way to boost their local production of food and decrease the need for foreign foods or aid.

- It may be less expensive to pay farmers in your own country to produce the food needed than to import it from abroad. In the United States, subsidies help to ensure that U.S. farmers are growing enough food to meet demands. Subsidies help to ensure that low-cost food is available both in the United States and abroad.

no

- Subsidies are expensive and cost American taxpayers money. The United States spends more than $44 billion on subsidies and other farm support every year. Farmers continue to receive subsidies even when times are favorable.

- Subsidies have a negative impact on the global economy. Subsidies artificially maintain the price of a commodity crop, which does not reflect the true cost of its production.

- Subsidies are bad for the environment. Farm subsidies encourage large-scale production of single crops, which contributes to soil erosion and depletion. Growing one crop on the same land year after year often requires a large amount of fertilizer for success.

- Subsidies discourage farmers from growing crops not currently subsidized, which includes the variety of fruits and vegetables that people need to support optimal health. The majority of crops currently subsidized in the United States are used to feed animals and in the production of processed foods. It would make more health sense to subsidize the production of a variety of fruits and vegetables.

what do you think?

1. Who benefits from government farm subsidies besides the farmer? Does the consumer benefit? **2.** How might subsidies be harming the environment? **3.** Should the U.S. government continue to subsidize commodity crops such as corn and wheat? Why or why not? If yes, should other crops be added to the program?

LO 12.1 Food Advertising and Marketing Affects Your Food Choices

The food industry spends large amounts of money on marketing and advertising its products, often to target audiences. The most heavily advertised foods are often the least nutritious.

LO 12.2 Whole Foods and Ingredients Used to Make Processed Foods Come from Farms

Only 2 percent of the American public are farmers, yet more food is produced today than ever before in history. Farming is a type of agribusiness, a sector that encompasses how foods are developed, processed, distributed, and purchased. The major crops grown in the United States are corn, soybeans, and wheat, and the major animals raised for food are cows, pigs, and chickens. Many of the crops grown in the United States are used to feed the animals that are raised for food. The United States participates in both the import and export of foods.

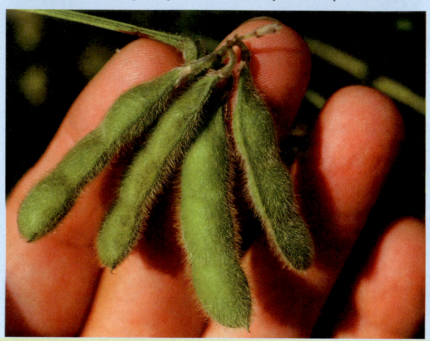

LO 12.3 Sustainable Food Systems Are Environmentally Friendly, Economically Sound, and Socially Equitable

Food systems involve all aspects of producing, transporting, and distributing foods. Sustainable food systems are those that can be maintained for the long term in a manner that (1) protects and preserves natural resources, (2) provides access to affordable healthy foods and builds community wealth, and (3) advances ethical and fair treatment of individuals and animals in a way that empowers social responsibility. Locally grown and plant-based foods use fewer external resources and are the most sustainable food choices.

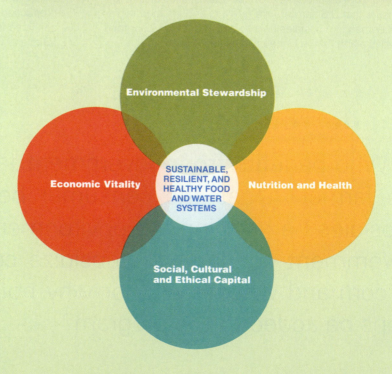

LO 12.4 Food Additives, Chemical Enhancers, and Pesticides Play a Role in Food Production and Safety

Hormones, antibiotics, and pesticides are used to increase the yield of animal foods and crops. The FDA, USDA, and EPA regulate the use of these products, but some people have concerns over the long-term safety for humans when products from animals and plants treated with these substances are consumed by humans. In addition, contamination of water supplies by these products may harm the environment.

LO 12.5 Biotechnology Is Used to Alter the Genetic Makeup of Plants

Genetically modified corn and soybeans, developed using a type of biotechnology known as bioengineering, have been grown in the United States for several years. Biotechnology may lead to the development of plants that have more desirable traits than the original, such as rice that is a good source of beta-carotene. Some consumers worry that genetically modified plants may alter the natural environment or ecological balance of the food system in unpredictable ways, but there is little scientific evidence to support these views.

LO 12.6 Food Policy Affects the Foods That Are Available to You to Buy and Consume

Several government agencies, including the FDA, FTC, USDA, and EPA, regulate the food industry and set national food and nutrition policy. The U.S. government is also a food consumer, and it purchases large amounts of surplus commodities that are used in various national food and nutrition programs. Large food companies often hire lobbyists to persuade politicians about food policy.

LO 12.7 Label Terms Can Help You Know How Food Was Produced

Foods labeled as organic certified are grown without the use of some synthetic pesticides, synthetic fertilizers, bioengineering, or irradiation. Organically produced animal foods are produced without antibiotics or hormones. Organic foods usually cost more than conventionally grown foods, and there is little scientific evidence that they are more nutritious than conventionally grown foods, though they may have lower levels of pesticides and antibiotics than do conventionally grown foods.

Terms to Know

- food consumers
- food industry
- farm
- agribusiness
- sustainable food system
- community-supported agriculture (CSA)
- growth hormone
- recombinant bovine somatotropin (rbST)
- antibiotics
- pesticides
- integrated pest management (IPM)
- biotechnology
- genetic engineering (GE)
- genetically modified organisms (GMOs)
- organic

MasteringNutrition™

Build your knowledge—and confidence—in the Study Area of MasteringNutrition with a variety of study tools.

 Access MyDietAnalysis through MasteringNutrition™ and track your diet and daily activities. In addition, a dietary analysis activity is available for every chapter in your book.

Check Your Understanding

LO 12.1 1. Food manufacturers spend the least amount of money on advertising which of the following foods?
   a. breakfast cereal
   b. candy and gum
   c. fruits and vegetables
   d. carbonated soft drinks

LO 12.2 2. The majority of farms in the United States are
   a. small family run farms.
   b. large farms run by the United States government.
   c. large farms run by private companies.
   d. large farms run by overseas companies.

LO 12.2 3. Most of the corn grown in the United States is
   a. used in the National School Lunch Program.
   b. used to feed animals.
   c. used to make high-fructose corn syrup.
   d. sold to local markets and eaten by Americans.

LO 12.3 4. Pound for pound, which of the following takes the greatest amount of natural resources to grow?
   a. poultry
   b. beef
   c. corn
   d. soy

LO 12.3 5. Which of the following represents the most sustainable food choice?
   a. purchasing watermelon in Alaska in December (the middle of winter)
   b. eating a diet high in animal protein purchased from large chain suppliers
   c. purchasing only organically grown fruits and vegetables
   d. eating a mostly plant-based diet of mostly locally grown foods

LO 12.4 6. Which of the following practices is a way to protect natural resources?
   a. growing as much of a single crop as possible year after year on a plot of land designated for the sole purpose of growing that specific crop
   b. chronically treating all livestock used in food production with antibiotics
   c. practicing integrated pest management
   d. growing livestock used in food production centrally in large feedlots, then transporting food produced from that livestock to consumers all over the country

LO 12.5 7. The process of isolating and inserting a gene from the DNA of one organism into the DNA of another organisms is called
   a. plant breeding.
   b. DNA insertion.
   c. bioterrorism.
   d. genetic engineering.

LO 12.6 8. U.S. farmers may receive subsidies from the U.S. government for growing which of the following products?
   a. corn
   b. carrots
   c. watermelon
   d. strawberries

LO 12.6 9. A food lobbyist works for
   a. the government.
   b. the interests of all food consumers.
   c. a food company or organization that has a vested interest in the outcome of food policy.
   d. only those in health care.

LO 12.7 10. You are in the supermarket shopping for cereal and find a package of raisin bran that bears the USDA Organic seal. You can be assured that in this cereal
   a. 100 percent of the ingredients are certified organic.
   b. only ingredients that were grown without the use of any pesticide, even if some of the ingredients are not organic certified, are used.
   c. at least 95 percent of the ingredients are certified organic.
   d. at least 50 percent of the ingredients are certified organic.

Answers

1. (c) Food manufacturers spend the least amount of money on advertising foods that are the healthiest for you, such as fruits and vegetables. Most advertising dollars are spent on foods that are processed, packaged, and high in added sugar and fat.

2. (a) The majority of farms in the United States are small family farms, though the total number of U.S. farms today is less than it has been in the past, in part because fewer family farmers are passing farms on to the next generation.

3. (b) Eighty percent of the corn grown in the United States is used to feed animals, not humans.

4. (b) It takes more natural resources to grow livestock than it does grain. Of the common types of livestock grown for food in the United States, it takes more natural resources to raise beef than it does poultry.

5. (d) A sustainable diet is a healthy diet for you and for future generations. Plant-based protein requires fewer natural resources to produce than does animal-based protein. Locally grown food requires fewer energy resources to produce than does food that has to be transported long distances from farm to consumer.

6. (c) Practicing integrated pest management relies as much as possible on biological measures instead of chemical pesticides to control pests. In this method chemical pesticides are used only as a last resort. Chemical pesticides require large amounts of fossil fuels to produce; deplete the soil of nutrients, making it less fertile; and may pollute the environment in unintended ways.

7. (d) Genetic engineering is the term used to describe the technique of inserting a segment of DNA from one organism into the DNA of another organism. The products of genetic engineering are genetically modified organisms (GMOs).

8. (a) U.S. farmers may be eligible to receive subsidies (a form of financial aid) from the government when they grow specific crops such as corn, wheat, and soybeans. Farmers who grow a variety of fruits and vegetables are typically not eligible for government subsidies.

9. (c) While it would be nice to think that a food lobbyist works for the interests of all food consumers, in reality the lobbyist works for a company or organization that has an interest in the outcome of food policy. A lobbyist's job is to persuade government officials to vote in a direction favorable to the companies or organizations the lobbyist represents.

10. (c) Only foods made with at least 95 percent organic ingredients can display the USDA Organic seal. If a product is made with at least 70 percent organic ingredients, an organic statement can be made, but the seal cannot be displayed. Some pesticides may be used to grow organic ingredients.

Web Resources

- Looking to help the environment? Pick five easy changes you can make that are environmentally friendly, by visiting "30 Ways to Protect the Environment" at www.epa.ohio.gov/pic/facts/30years/tips.aspx.
- For more on living green, visit "Learn the Issues" at www2.epa.gov/learn-issues
- To help you pick environmental products while shopping, visit "While Shopping" at www.epa.gov/epahome/shopping.htm
- For help in finding local farms, visit www.localharvest.org

1. **False.** Although you may think you are indifferent to food advertising, it likely has a significant impact on your food decisions. See page 458.

2. **True.** Small family farms comprise the majority of farms in the United States. Learn more on page 460.

3. **False.** The U.S. federal government provides monetary incentives for farmers producing commodity crops such as corn and soybeans, but not a variety of fruits and vegetables. Learn more on page 462.

4. **True.** Although corn is the number-one food crop grown by American farmers, the majority is used to feed animals and not humans. Find out more about factors that impact what plants and animals U.S. farmers grow on page 463.

5. **True.** It takes fewer natural resources to raise plants for food than it does to raise animals for food, so a plant-based diet is more sustainable than a diet high in foods derived from animals. Turn to page 469 to learn more.

6. **True.** Because much of our food in the United States travels long distances from farm to consumers, when the price of fuel such as oil increases, so must the cost of food. To find out more, turn to page 470.

7. **False.** The U.S. government currently does *not* require label information to indicate whether or not animals were treated with synthetic hormones. Turn to page 473 to learn more about this interesting point of controversy.

8. **True.** Genetically engineered forms of soybeans have been the mainstay in the United States since the 1990s. Find out more about bioengineering on page 478.

9. **False.** Organic foods are not necessarily pesticide free. To learn more, turn to page 485.

10. **False.** Although organic foods do have some advantages when it comes to preserving the environment and introducing fewer pesticides and antibiotics into the food supply, there is little scientific evidence that they are more nutritious than foods that were grown using traditional methods. Learn more on page 485.

13
Food Safety and Technology

True or False?

1. The most common type of virus that causes foodborne illness is *Salmonella*. T|F p. 495

2. Foods that smell bad will give you foodborne illness if you consume them. T|F p. 495

3. Washing your hands for 10 seconds under running water is necessary to reduce your chances of getting foodborne illness. T|F p. 502

4. Grilled chicken that is pink in the middle is never safe to eat. T|F p. 505

5. The temperature for your refrigerator should be set at 40°F or below. T|F p. 506

6. Freezing foods kills bacteria. T|F p. 506

7. Leftovers that have been stored in the fridge for a week will still be safe to eat. T|F p. 507

8. Food irradiation makes food radioactive. T|F p. 513

9. As long as the expiration date hasn't passed, packaged food is always safe to eat. T|F p. 514

10. *E. coli* is considered a bacterium that could be used for bioterrorism. T|F p. 521

See page 525 for the answers.

Learning Outcomes

After reading this chapter, you will be able to:

LO 13.1 Name the pathogens and other agents that cause foodborne illness.

LO 13.2 Identify the four Cs that can prevent foodborne illness.

LO 13.3 Discuss how the food supply is protected in the United States.

LO 13.4 Explain the role that food additives play in food production.

LO 13.5 Explain what are toxins and chemical agents in the food supply.

LO 13.6 Explain how food can play a role in bioterrorism.

Although the United States enjoys one of the safest food supplies in the world, millions of Americans still suffer annually from some type of **foodborne illness**. In fact, cases of foodborne illness cause millions of illnesses and thousands of deaths per year, and the medical costs and lost wages associated with just one type of illness, that due to the bacterium *Salmonella*, are estimated to top $1 billion per year.[1] These illnesses often result in distressing gastrointestinal symptoms such as cramps, diarrhea, and vomiting.

Efforts to prevent foodborne illnesses have led to the development of extensive **food safety** practices and guidelines. Several government agencies work together to ensure the safety of foods from the farm to the table. Food safety is also the practice of minimizing your risk of contaminating foods as you store and prepare them in your kitchen. There are several strategies consumers can use to make sure the foods they eat and serve are safe. We'll find out more about all of these in this chapter.

What Causes Foodborne Illness?

LO 13.1 Name the pathogens and other agents that cause foodborne illness.

Most people do not question the safety of the foods they eat until there is a national food-safety recall or they experience firsthand the effects of foodborne illness. A classic example of emerging public awareness occurred in 1906 with the publication of *The Jungle*, by Upton Sinclair. The descriptions of the unsanitary conditions in the Chicago meat-packing plants,[2] which among other atrocities included rodent droppings and body parts making their way into consumer-bound meat products, horrified the public. Meat sales plummeted as a result of consumer fear about eating contaminated foods. Due to the enormous public health risks associated with these unsanitary practices, President Theodore Roosevelt incited the United States Congress to pass the Meat Inspection Act.[3] The act demanded a continuous inspection of all meat-processing plants by the United States Department of Agriculture.[4] Other improvements in food safety, such as pasteurization of milk, safe canning, and disinfection of water supplies, conquered the common foodborne illnesses of the era. Before long, these food-safety precautions resulted in positive effects on the nation's health. By 1920, instances of one foodborne illness, typhoid fever, had declined by about two-thirds, and by the 1950s it had virtually disappeared in the United States.[5]

Today, advances in production and distribution, new food sources, and the growing volume of food imports continue to present challenges to maintaining a safe food supply. Prior to the advent of convenience foods like bagged lettuce, a contaminated head of lettuce might have affected only one family. Now, however, contaminated lettuce may be processed with thousands of other heads and placed into bags that end up in thousands of homes. This could lead to large outbreaks, making the source difficult to pinpoint.[6] Prevention of such outbreaks remains a public health priority for governmental agencies.

Even with stringent regulations in place, however, bouts of foodborne illness still happen. Let's take a look at the causes of foodborne illness.

Foodborne Illnesses Are Often Caused by Pathogens

To contract a foodborne illness, you must eat foods or beverages that contain one or more harmful agents. The agents can be disease-causing microbes, also known as

pathogens, such as viruses, bacteria, parasites, fungal agents, or prions. Pathogens can be found in the stool or droppings of infected humans and/or animals. Drinking water that has been contaminated with infected droppings, or putting anything in your mouth (such as food or your hands) that has been in contact with fecal matter, are common ways to become infected. This route of transmission is known as **fecal-to-oral transmission**, and this is why people should always wash their hands after using the bathroom and before preparing foods. Eating raw or undercooked meat, poultry, or fish from an infected animal can also expose you to pathogens.

Pathogenic viruses and bacteria are the most common causes of foodborne illness in the United States. Parasites, fungi, and prions are less common causes. Let's begin with the various viruses that can make you sick.

Viruses, such as the hepatitis B virus shown here, need a host to survive and multiply.

Viruses

The term **virus** denotes a microscopic infectious agent that contains chromosomes that carry genetic information (DNA or RNA) for its own replication. Viruses must have a living **host**, such as a plant or an animal, to survive. When an individual eats a contaminated plant or animal as food, the pathogen can invade the cells of the stomach and intestinal walls. The virus can then cause the cells' genetic material to start producing more viruses, ultimately leading to illness.[7]

The most common type of virus that causes foodborne illness is the **norovirus**. In fact, norovirus is the most common cause of foodborne illness in the United States (see **Table 13.1**).[8] Norovirus are named after the original strain of the virus, Norwalk virus, which was the cause of **gastroenteritis** (*gastro* = stomach, *entero* = intestines, *itis* = inflammation), or the "stomach flu," in a school in Norwalk, Ohio, in 1968.[9] (Note: The stomach flu is not the same as influenza (flu), which is a respiratory illness caused by the influenza virus.)

Another foodborne virus, hepatitis A, caused a multistate outbreak among young concertgoers in 2003.[10] The concerts were often multiday events at campgrounds that had less than optimal sanitary conditions. The unofficial food vendors were the attendees themselves. Many of the concert attendees traveled from concert to concert. This type of living environment, in which people are living, cooking, and eating in unsanitary conditions, practicing poor hand washing and hygiene, and traveling from state to state, can create a breeding ground for an outbreak. Approximately 300 attendees had to be vaccinated against hepatitis A.

Bacteria

If you were to swab your kitchen sink right now and look at the results under a microscope, you would find that there are about 16 million **bacteria** living on each square centimeter (less than half an inch) of your sink. Whereas viruses need a host to survive, bacteria can flourish on both living and nonliving surfaces. They live on your computer mouse, keyboard, body, clothing, and in every room of your house. In fact, there are hundreds of different types of bacteria on your skin alone.[11] The majority of bacteria around you are harmless, and some are even essential, such as the ones in your intestine that synthesize biotin and vitamin K. Bacteria are also used to make some of the foods we enjoy, like yogurt, cheese, and buttermilk.

A few bacteria are harmful, however, and can cause food spoilage or illness. The bacteria that cause food spoilage are not the same as those that cause foodborne illness. Food spoilage bacteria cause the deterioration of the quality of food. For example, a carton of sour milk and that forgotten Chinese takeout in the back of your refrigerator have gone "bad" because of food spoilage bacteria. Though most individuals will not become seriously ill after eating spoiled foods, these items can cause nausea and shouldn't be eaten. (Luckily, the less-than-pleasant odor of sour milk or spoiled food usually leads to it being thrown away.) In contrast to spoiled foods, contaminated foods that contain bacterial pathogens may look and smell

foodborne illness Sickness caused by consuming contaminated food or beverages. Also known as foodborne disease or food poisoning.

food safety Guidelines and procedures that help keep foods free from contaminants.

pathogens Collective term for disease-causing microorganisms (microbes). Includes viruses, bacteria, and parasites. The most common source of foodborne illness.

fecal-to-oral transmission The spread of pathogens by putting something in the mouth that has been in contact with infected stool. Poor hygiene, such as not washing hands after using the bathroom, can lead to this type of contamination.

virus A microscopic organism that carries genetic information for its own replication; can infect a host and cause illness.

host A living plant or animal (including a human) that a virus or parasite infects for the sake of reproducing.

norovirus The most common type of virus that causes foodborne illness. Noroviruses can cause gastroenteritis, or the "stomach flu." Also known as Norwalk-like viruses.

gastroenteritis Inflammation of the stomach and intestines.

bacteria Single-celled microorganisms without an organized nucleus. Some are benign or beneficial to humans, while others can cause disease.

Table 13.1

Pathogens That Cause Foodborne Illness

Microbe	Where You Find It	How You Can Get It	What You May Experience	Treatment
Viruses				
Norovirus	In the stool or vomit of infected individuals	Fecal-to-oral transmission; eating ready-to-eat foods or drinking liquids contaminated by an infected person; eating contaminated shellfish; touching contaminated objects and then putting hands in mouth	Watery diarrhea, nausea, vomiting, flulike symptoms; possible fever Can appear 12 to 48 hours after onset and last 12 to 60 hours Typically not serious	Symptoms usually abate without treatment; fluid replacement may be necessary to treat dehydration due to vomiting and/or diarrhea.
Hepatitis A (HAV)	In the stool of infected individuals	Fecal-to-oral transmission; eating raw produce irrigated with contaminated water; eating raw or undercooked foods that have not been properly reheated; drinking contaminated water	Diarrhea, vomiting, muscle aches, jaundice, inflammation of the liver that can appear 30 days after incubation Can last 2 weeks to 6 months	Treatment of symptoms only. Vaccination is the most effective means of preventing HAV transmission among persons at risk for infection.
Bacteria				
Campylobacter jejuni	Intestinal tracts of animals and birds, raw milk, untreated water, and sewage	Drinking contaminated water or raw milk; eating raw or undercooked meat, poultry, or shellfish	Fever, headache, and muscle pain followed by diarrhea (sometimes bloody), abdominal pain, and nausea Appears 2 to 5 days after eating; may last 2 to 10 days. Guillain-Barré syndrome may occur.	Almost all persons infected with *Campylobacter* recover without any specific treatment. Patients should drink extra fluids as long as the diarrhea lasts. In more severe cases, antibiotics such as erythromycin and quinolones can shorten the duration of symptoms if given early in the illness.
Clostridium botulinum	Widely distributed in nature in soil, water, on plants, and in the intestinal tracts of animals and fish Grows only in environments with little or no oxygen	Eating improperly canned foods, garlic in oil, vacuum-packaged and tightly wrapped food	Bacteria produce a toxin that causes illness by affecting the nervous system. Symptoms usually appear after 18 to 36 hours. May experience double vision, droopy eyelids, trouble speaking and swallowing, and difficulty breathing. Fatal if not treated immediately.	The respiratory failure and paralysis that occur with severe botulism may require a patient to be on a breathing machine (ventilator) for weeks, plus intensive medical and nursing care. After several weeks, the paralysis slowly improves. If diagnosed early, foodborne and wound botulism can be treated with a botulinum antitoxin.
Clostridium perfringens	Soil, dust, sewage, and intestinal tracts of animals and humans Grows only in environments with little or no oxygen.	Called "the cafeteria germ" because many outbreaks result from eating food left for long periods in steam tables at improper temperatures or at room temperature. Bacteria are destroyed by cooking, but some spores may survive.	Diarrhea and gas pains may appear 8 to 24 hours after eating; usually last about 1 day, but less severe symptoms may persist for 1 to 2 weeks.	Supportive care; avoid dehydration

Table 13.1 continued

Pathogens That Cause Foodborne Illness

Microbe	Where You Find It	How You Can Get It	What You May Experience	Treatment
Escherichia coli O157: H7	Intestinal tracts of some mammals, raw milk, unchlorinated water; one of several strains of *E. coli* that can cause human illness	Drinking contaminated water, unpasteurized apple juice or cider, or raw milk, or eating raw or rare ground beef or uncooked fruits and vegetables	Diarrhea or bloody diarrhea, abdominal cramps, nausea, and weakness. Can begin 2 to 5 days after food is eaten, lasting about 8 days. Small children and elderly adults may develop hemolytic uremic syndrome (HUS) that causes acute kidney failure. A similar illness, thrombotic thrombocytopenic purpura (TTP), may occur in adults.	Supportive care and avoidance of dehydration. Antibiotics should not be used to treat this infection. There is no evidence that treatment with antibiotics is helpful, and taking antibiotics may increase the risk of HUS.
Enterotoxigenic *Escherichia coli* (major cause of traveler's diarrhea)	Intestinal tracts of some mammals and unpasteurized dairy products. More common in developing countries	Fecal-to-oral transmission. Consuming stool-contaminated water and foods from unsanitary water supplies and food establishments	Diarrhea, nausea, vomiting, stomach cramping, bloating, fever, and weakness	Traveler's diarrhea often resolves without specific treatment; however, oral rehydration is often beneficial to replace lost fluids and electrolytes.
Listeria monocytogenes	Intestinal tracts of humans and animals, milk, soil, leafy vegetables; can grow slowly at refrigerator temperatures	Eating ready-to-eat foods such as hot dogs, luncheon meats, cold cuts, fermented or dry sausage, other deli-style meat and poultry, or soft cheeses; drinking unpasteurized milk	Fever, nausea, vomiting, headache, aches; may take hours to up to 3 months to become ill; may later develop more serious illness in high-risk individuals	When infection occurs during pregnancy, antibiotics given promptly to the pregnant woman can often prevent infection of the fetus or newborn. Babies with listeriosis receive the same antibiotics as adults. Even with prompt treatment, some infections result in infant death.
Salmonella (more than 2,500 types)	Intestinal tracts and feces of animals; *Salmonella enteritidis* in eggs	Eating raw or undercooked eggs, poultry, and meat, raw milk and dairy products, and seafood. Can also be spread by infected food handlers	Stomach pain, diarrhea, nausea, chills, fever, and headache usually appear 6 to 72 hours after eating; may last 4 to 7 days.	Supportive care and plenty of fluids. Antibiotics are not usually necessary unless the infection spreads from the intestines.
Shigella (more than 30 types)	Human intestinal tract; rarely found in other animals	Fecal-to-oral transmission by consuming contaminated food and water. Most outbreaks result from eating food, especially salads, prepared and handled by workers with poor personal hygiene.	Disease referred to as "shigellosis" or bacillary dysentery. Diarrhea containing blood and mucus, fever, abdominal cramps, chills, and vomiting begins 8 to 50 hours from ingestion of bacteria; typically resolves in 5 to 7 days.	Persons with mild infections usually recover quickly without antibiotic treatment. However, an appropriate antibiotic may be needed.

CONTINUED ▶

Table 13.1 continued

Pathogens That Cause Foodborne Illness

Microbe	Where You Find It	How You Can Get It	What You May Experience	Treatment
Staphylococcus aureus	On human skin and the mucous membranes of the mouth	Consuming foods that were contaminated by being improperly handled Bacteria multiply rapidly at room temperature.	Severe nausea, abdominal cramps, vomiting, and diarrhea occur 1 to 6 hours after eating; recovery within 1 to 2 days.	The best treatments are rest and plenty of fluids.
Parasites				
Cryptosporidium parvum	In the intestines of humans and animals	Fecal-to-oral transmission; drinking contaminated water, eating contaminated vegetables and fruits	Stomach pains, diarrhea, cramps, fever, and vomiting Usually goes away without medical intervention in 2 days to 2 weeks.	Adequate fluids are necessary to avoid dehydration For individuals with weakened immune systems, cryptosporidiosis can be serious, long-lasting, and sometimes fatal.
Cyclospora cayetanensis	Human stool	Fecal-to-oral transmission Drinking contaminated water, eating contaminated produce	Diarrhea, loss of appetite, bloating, cramps, fatigue	Can be treated with antibiotics
Giardia duodenalis	In the intestines of humans and animals	Fecal-to-oral transmission Drinking contaminated water, eating contaminated produce	Diarrhea, stomach pains, flatulence	Several prescription drugs are available to treat *Giardia* infection. Although *Giardia* can infect all people, young children and pregnant women might be more susceptible to dehydration resulting from diarrhea and should, therefore, drink plenty of fluids while ill.
Toxoplasma gondii	Develops in cats and passed on through their feces	Fecal-to-oral transmision Can also get it from eating raw or uncooked meat and seafood	In pregnant women, can cause miscarriages, and birth defects.	Can be treated with sulfa drugs
Trichinella spiralis	In undercooked or raw meats containing *Trichinella* worms	Eating raw or undercooked contaminated meat, usually pork or game meats	Nausea, vomiting, diarrhea, fever, aching joints and muscles	Safe and effective prescription drugs are available to treat trichinellosis.

perfectly fine. Pathogenic bacteria can cause illness in several ways: 1) by directly invading the intestinal wall and multiplying; 2) by producing an infection via a toxin that is absorbed into your blood; or 3) by invading deeper body tissues.[12]

The most common bacteria that cause foodborne illness are *Campylobacter*, *Escherichia coli (E. coli)* O157: H7, and *Salmonella* (see Table 13.1). Another bacterium, *Listeria monocytogenes*, a less prevalent cause of foodborne illness, is still of concern for individuals most likely to get foodborne illness, especially pregnant women and newborns.

Campylobacter is one of the most common causes of bacteria-related diarrhea in the United States.[13] It is estimated that 1.3 million people are infected annually in the United States.[14] It is found mostly in contaminated water, raw milk, and raw meat products, particularly poultry. Some individuals may develop a rare nerve disease called **Guillain-Barré syndrome** after contracting a *Campylobacter* infection, which causes a person's immune system to attack the body's own nerves and results in temporary paralysis.[15]

Guillain-Barré syndrome A condition that can result from a *Campylobacter* infection. It causes the immune system to attack the body's own nerves and can lead to temporary paralysis.

hemolytic uremic syndrome A rare condition caused by *E. coli* O157: H7 that results in the destruction of red blood cells and kidney failure.

Though most strains of *E. coli* are harmless, *E. coli* O157: H7 is estimated to cause more than 90,000 cases of foodborne illness[16] in the United States annually. Contaminated cattle have been the culprits behind most cases of foodborne illness caused by *E. coli* O157: H7. Because bacteria live in the gastrointestinal tract of healthy cattle, they can easily come into contact with the meat of the animal during the slaughtering process. Proper cooking can destroy these bacteria. In people at highest risk for foodborne illness (the very young, the elderly, and those with compromised immune systems), *E. coli* O157: H7 can cause **hemolytic uremic syndrome** (HUS; *hemo* = blood, *lyti* = destroyed, *uremic* = too much urea in blood), which results in the destruction of red blood cells and damage to and eventual failure of the kidneys.[17]

E. coli O157: H7 is the strain of *E. coli* bacteria that causes the most foodborne illness.

Another type of *E. coli*, called enterotoxigenic (*entero* = intestines, *toxi* = toxin, *genic* = forming) *E. coli*, is a common cause of **traveler's diarrhea**. Each year, up to 50 percent of international travelers have their trips interrupted by unpleasant intestinal side effects. Traveler's diarrhea is primarily caused by consuming contaminated food or water. People visiting countries where proper sanitation is in question, including some developing countries in Latin America, Africa, the Middle East, and Asia, are at a higher risk of contracting it.[18] See the Table Tips called "Don't Let Bad Bugs Ruin Your Trip" for suggestions on how to avoid traveler's diarrhea.

Reptiles (lizards, snakes, and turtles) often carry *Salmonella*. You should always wash your hands after touching a reptile, and keep reptiles away from small children.

There are several types of *Salmonella* bacteria. *Salmonella enteritidis* is one of the most common varieties found in the United States. An estimated 40,000 incidences of *Salmonella*-related foodborne illness occur annually, and about 400 individuals die yearly due to this bacterium.[19] *S. enteritidis* is most commonly found in raw eggs, so foods that contain raw eggs, such as the dressing on homemade Caesar salad, raw cookie dough, or cake batter, can potentially cause illness.

Parasites

Parasites are microscopic animals that take their nourishment from hosts. They can be found in food and water and are often transmitted through the fecal-to-oral route.[20] The most common parasitic illness outbreaks in the United States have been caused by just a few types: *Crytosporidium parvum*, *Cyclospora cayatenensis*, *Giardia duodenalis*, *Toxoplasma gondii*, and *Trichinella spiralis*.[21]

Crytosporidium parvum, *Cyclospora cayatenensis*, and *Giardia duodenalis* can be found in contaminated water or food sources, and individuals can also get infected by the fecal-to-oral route. *Toxoplasma gondii* is the third leading cause of death from foodborne illness. It develops in cats and is passed on through their feces. Cleaning a cat's litter box but not washing your hands could cause fecal-to-oral transmission. *Trichinella spiralis* is an intestinal worm whose larvae (hatched eggs) can travel from the digestive tract to the muscles of the body. *Trichinella spiralis* is typically transmitted by eating undercooked or raw pork or wild game. Refer to Table 13.1 for a summary of these parasites and the foodborne illnesses they cause. Consuming undercooked or raw fish can also cause foodborne illness; see the Nutrition in the Real World feature "Sushi: A Cautionary Tale" on page 501.

The parasitic roundworm *Trichinella spiralis*.

traveler's diarrhea A pathogen-induced intestinal disorder experienced by some travelers who visit areas with unsanitary conditions.

parasites Organisms that live on or in another organism, obtaining nourishment from it.

prions Misfolded proteins that can act as disease agents. An abnormal prion protein is the cause of mad cow disease.

bovine spongiform encephalopathy (BSE) A slow, degenerative, and deadly disease that attacks the central nervous system of cattle. Also known as *mad cow disease*.

Prions

Prions are an extremely rare but deadly infectious agent. **Bovine spongiform encephalopathy (BSE)** is a slow, degenerative, and deadly disease caused by an unusual protein called a prion that attacks the central nervous system of cattle. Cattle can become infected by consuming feed that is contaminated with BSE.[22] Individuals who are exposed to BSE by eating beef from infected cattle experience neurological symptoms and damage.

TableTIPS

Don't Let Bad Bugs Ruin Your Trip

If you are traveling abroad, look up the country you're visiting on the Travelers' Health website at www.cdc.gov/travel to find out about any *specific* health advisories for that area.

Do not eat raw or undercooked meat or seafood.

Do not consume raw fruits and vegetables unless you peel them. Thoroughly cooked fruits and vegetables should be safe to eat.

Do not consume foods or beverages from street vendors or restaurants that appear to be unsanitary.

Do not drink tap water or use ice made from tap water unless it has been boiled first or treated with iodine or chlorine.

Do not consume unpasteurized milk or other unpasteurized dairy foods.

Meat and bone meal given to young calves and cattle that was rendered from contaminated tissues, such as the brain or spinal cord of infected bovines, is the primary source of BSE.[23] In 1986, BSE was first observed in the United Kingdom, where the majority of cases have occurred worldwide.[24] Since then, the FDA has banned the use of contaminated meat and bone meal as feed for all animals, including cattle and sheep, as this type of feed has been identified as a major route of BSE transmission.[25] Also, meat and meat products from animals that were given animal feed that contains animal protein derived from countries that are at risk for BSE cannot be imported into the United States.[26] In addition, the United States Department of Agriculture has established an ongoing BSE Surveillance Program to monitor cattle in the United States.[27]

All of these measures have played a part in limiting the incidences of BSE in the United States to only four cases to date.[28] The contaminant that causes BSE in animals is thought to cause a similar disease, called *variant Creutzfeldt-Jakob Disease (vCJD)*, in humans. vCJD causes a degenerative, fatal brain disorder in humans. Luckily, no one has acquired vCJD from cattle in the United States.[29]

Chemical Agents and Toxins Can Also Cause Illness

Foodborne illnesses can also be caused by **toxins** and chemical agents that occur naturally in foods, such as those found in certain fungi (including poisonous mushrooms) and some fish. Chemical agents, such as antibiotics and pesticides that are intentionally added to foods, can also cause foodborne illness. We'll discuss specific toxins and chemicals later in the chapter.

Some People Are at Higher Risk for Foodborne Illness

Some individuals are at greater risk of developing foodborne illness than others. Older adults, young children, and those with a compromised immune system are more susceptible to the adverse effects of foodborne illness.

In older adults, the age-related deterioration of the immune system increases the risk for foodborne illness. Also, because less acidic gastric juice is produced in the stomach as you age, fewer foodborne pathogens are destroyed during digestion, resulting in greater risk of gastrointestinal infections and their complications. In fact, the elderly are at higher risk of dying of gastroenteritis, which is a severe complication of foodborne illness.[30]

Young children, because of their underdeveloped immune systems, are also more vulnerable to foodborne illness. Children are also smaller and weigh less than adults, and can become sickened by exposure to a smaller quantity of pathogens. Also, their reduced production of stomach acids impedes their ability to destroy harmful bacteria that may be in foods.[31]

Any condition that weakens a person's immune system can increase his or her risk of contracting foodborne illness. This applies to individuals with HIV, AIDS, cancer, and diabetes.[32] The hormonal shifts seen during pregnancy can affect a pregnant woman's immune system, making her more vulnerable to certain foodborne illnesses such as listeriosis. Often in cases of foodborne illness in pregnancy, the mother is mildly sick, but the risk to the fetus can be great and often can lead to death of the baby.

Individuals in institutional settings (such as nursing homes, hospitals, and schools); where groups of people eat foods from the same source, are also at higher risk of foodborne illness. Improper handling of foods and poor hygiene practices of

toxins Poisons produced by living organisms.

Sushi: A Cautionary Tale

Are you looking for a delicious meal that's typically low in calories, high in nutrients, and a good source of omega-3 fatty acids? Well, then, sushi may be for you! But before we declare sushi the next great superfood, we need a reality check. When improperly handled, some types of sushi can be a significant harbor for organisms that cause foodborne illness.

Sushi is a traditional Japanese food that contains vinegared rice, seaweed (*nori*), vegetables (such as cucumber, radish, or avocado), and seafood (for example, tuna, yellowtail, salmon, squid, octopus, shrimp, eel, or roe, among many others). Some types of sushi are made with vegetables and rice only, or use cooked fish or other seafood, and therefore create less risk of harm. However, sushi that specifically contains raw fish, including the type of sushi known as **sashimi**, carries a greater potential risk.

Raw-fish versions of sushi can sometimes carry illness-inducing parasites, including nematodes (roundworms),

tapeworms, and flukes, in the flesh or organs of the fish.[1] These parasites can be killed with heat (by cooking) or cold (by freezing). However, freezing will not kill other pathogens, such as bacteria, so using cooked seafood would more effectively reduce the risk of foodborne illness.[2]

If you make your own sushi at home, make sure that you buy high-quality seafood that is very fresh. Store it in your refrigerator at 40°F or less and eat it promptly. Always wash your hands thoroughly before and after handling it to avoid cross-contamination. Remember that even the rice that has come into contact with sushi or sashimi can make you sick if you don't keep it refrigerated. When dining out, frequent only restaurants that are reputable and have a chef who has been trained to safely prepare raw seafood.

Pregnant women, young children, and older adults are more susceptible to

foodborne illness and should avoid raw seafood—as should anyone with a compromised immune system.[3]

sushi A Japanese dish of cooked, vinegared rice served with fish or other seafood, vegetables, and/or seaweed.

sashimi A type of sushi that primarily consists of raw seafood, sliced into thin pieces and served with a dipping sauce (soy sauce with wasabi paste) or other condiments (such as fresh ginger).

food-service workers are often the cause of foodborne disease outbreaks in institutional settings. Luckily, there are many ways to reduce your risk of contracting such an illness.

LO 13.1 **The Take-Home Message** Foodborne illness is frequently caused by consuming pathogens in contaminated food or drinks. Viruses and bacteria are the most common causes in the United States, though parasites, prions, and fungal agents can cause some foodborne illness as well. Natural toxins and chemical agents can also cause illness. Certain populations, including the elderly, children, and those with compromised immune systems, are at higher risk of contracting foodborne illness.

What Can You Do to Prevent Foodborne Illness?

LO 13.2 Identify the four Cs that can prevent foodborne illness.

Because foods may harbor some contamination even when you bring them home from the store, the best way to fight foodborne illness is to take action in your kitchen to kill any disease-causing microbes and to prevent them from flourishing.

Figure 13.1 A Bulk Recipe for Bacteria

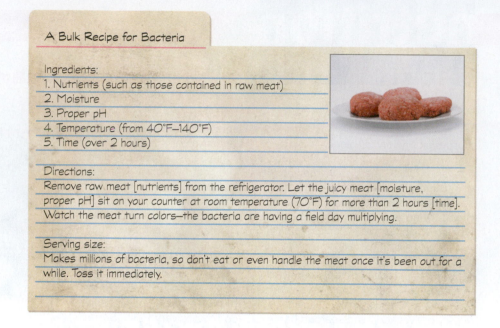

A Bulk Recipe for Bacteria

Ingredients:
1. Nutrients (such as those contained in raw meat)
2. Moisture
3. Proper pH
4. Temperature (from 40°F–140°F)
5. Time (over 2 hours)

Directions:
Remove raw meat [nutrients] from the refrigerator. Let the juicy meat [moisture, proper pH] sit on your counter at room temperature (70°F) for more than 2 hours [time]. Watch the meat turn colors—the bacteria are having a field day multiplying.

Serving size:
Makes millions of bacteria, so don't eat or even handle the meat once it's been out for a while. Toss it immediately.

Bacteria, for instance, thrive and multiply in an environment with the following characteristics (see **Figure 13.1**):

- *Adequate nutrients.* Protein- and nutrient-rich animal foods, such as raw and undercooked meat, poultry, seafood, eggs, and unpasteurized milk, are the most common havens for bacterial growth.
- *Moisture.* Bacteria thrive in moist environments, such as in raw chicken that is sitting in its own juices.[33]
- *A change in pH.* Over time, a food's pH may change and allow for the growth of bacteria.[34]
- *The correct temperature.* Bacteria multiply most abundantly between the temperatures of about 40°F and 140°F.
- *Time.*

Perishable food, such as raw meat, left at room temperature for an extended period can become a feast for bacterial growth.

You can reduce your risk for foodborne illness by practicing proper food-handling and -storage strategies. They're easy to remember as the "four Cs" of food safety: cleaning, combating cross-contamination, cooking, and chilling (**Figure 13.2**). Let's look at each of these four steps individually.

Figure 13.2 Fight BAC!
The Fight BAC! symbol sums up the four Cs of keeping food safe in your kitchen: clean, combat cross-contamination (separate raw meats from ready-to-eat foods), cook thoroughly, and chill to a cold enough temperature.

Clean Your Hands and Produce

You were probably taught as a child to wash your hands before eating, and guess what? Your parents were right. Hand washing is one of the most important strategies for preventing foodborne illness. In fact, research suggests that nearly 50 percent of all cases of food poisoning could be prevented if everyone correctly washed their hands.[35] However, washing your hands *correctly* is where many people fall short. In a recent study, researchers watched and collected data on over 3,700 individuals who used the bathroom in bars, restaurants, and other public establishments. Their results showed that about 15 percent of the men didn't wash their hands at all, compared with 7 percent of women.[36] When the men did wash their hands, only 50 percent of them used soap, compared with 79 percent of women. Washing your hands *correctly* means wetting them under clean running water, adding soap, rubbing your hands together to make lather, scrubbing, rinsing, and then air drying your hands or drying them with a *clean* towel. This whole procedure should take at least 20 seconds.

In addition to your hands, anything that touches your food, such as knives, utensils, and countertops, should be thoroughly cleaned between each use. Cutting boards should be placed in the dishwasher or scrubbed with hot soapy water and rinsed after each use. Nonporous cutting boards made of plastic, marble, and tempered glass are typically easier to keep clean than the more porous wood cutting boards or wooden surfaces. Cracks in a cutting board can become a hideaway for microbes, so try to keep only unbroken boards on hand. You can routinely sanitize your cutting board by flooding it in your sink in a solution of one teaspoon bleach in one quart of water. Let the board sit in the sanitizing liquid for a few minutes to kill the microbes, then rinse it thoroughly.

A moist sponge that contains food scraps and has been left at room temperature is an ideal environment for bacteria. Sponges and dishcloths should be washed often in the hot cycle of your washing machine, preferably with bleach in addition to the soap. Sponges can also be put in your dishwasher or microwave.

Fruits and vegetables should be thoroughly washed under cold running tap water before eating. This will help remove any dirt or microbes on their surfaces. Produce with a firm surface can be scrubbed with a vegetable brush. The Table Tips called "Scrub Away Pathogens" summarize the cleaning strategies you should apply when preparing food.

You should also keep your refrigerator clean. Research shows that many Americans, especially young adults, neglect to properly clean their refrigerators adequately and often enough.[37] Interestingly, research has shown that the vegetable drawer was found to harbor more bacteria than the meat drawer.[38] The interior of your refrigerator should be cleaned weekly with hot, soapy water and then thoroughly rinsed. Toss out leftovers and perishable foods that are no longer safe to eat.[39]

Combat Cross-Contamination

Produce, especially if it's going to be eaten raw, should never come in contact with raw meat, poultry, or fish during the food preparation process. If these items do come in contact, they could **cross-contaminate** each other, meaning that microbes from one could move to the other and vice versa. Microbe-containing raw meat, poultry, and fish should be kept separate from ready-to-eat foods during food preparation, and stored separately in your refrigerator. You should even keep these products apart on the trip home from the grocery store.

Marinades that are used to tenderize and flavor meats, poultry, or fish shouldn't be used as a serving sauce unless they have been boiled for several minutes to kill any pathogens; instead of reusing, set aside an amount for sauces before marinating.

The knife and cutting board used to cut and prepare raw meat, poultry, or fish shouldn't be used to slice vegetables or bread unless both have been thoroughly cleaned. Your best bet is to use separate cutting boards for meat and nonmeat foods to avoid cross-contamination. Keep one board for slicing raw meats, poultry, and fish, and use another one for cutting fresh produce, breads, rolls, and other ready-to-eat foods. All plates and bowls that have contained raw meats, poultry, and fish should be thoroughly washed before they are reused. For example, at a barbecue, the plate that held the raw hamburgers should *never* be used to serve the cooked burgers unless it has been thoroughly washed between each use. In addition, the tongs that you use to handle the raw meat should be either cleaned or exchanged for a clean pair as the meat cooks.

cross-contaminate Transfer pathogens from a food, utensil, cutting board, kitchen surface, and/or hands to another food.

Packaging materials like zip-close bags, egg cartons, and takeout containers should be thrown away after use. Even if you clean them, pathogens can cling to these items and contaminate other foods.

Soiled dish towels shouldn't be used to dry clean dishes or utensils. A towel that was used to wipe up raw meat juices from a counter or your hands can transfer any microbes from the juices to your clean dishes or utensils. You could easily coat those clean surfaces with a layer of germs. Dishes and utensils should air-dry for the least contamination. **Figure 13.3** illustrates more ways to combat cross-contamination when you prepare food.

Cook Foods Thoroughly

Though you may assume that brown meat is cooked meat, this is often not the case. Look at the two hamburger patties in **Figure 13.4**. Which one do you think looks safe to eat? The answer may surprise you. The patty on the bottom looks as though it is more thoroughly cooked than the patty on the top, but it's actually not. Color is not always a proper indication that meat is safe to eat; some lean varieties of beef can remain pink even though they have reached an internal temperature of 160°F, high enough to kill any potential pathogens.

The color of beef is largely determined by *myoglobin*, a protein that provides the purplish-red pigment in meat (and poultry). Whereas meat typically turns from pink to brown during cooking, if it starts out brown, this color change won't occur. Thus, the burger could look "done" when it may still be raw in places. Research has shown that hamburgers can look "well done" while having reached an internal temperature of only approximately 135°F.[40]

Do marinate raw meat in the refrigerator in sealed containers.

Do sanitize sponges and cutting boards with chlorine bleach solution.

Don't reuse the marinade unless it has been boiled.

Do wash utensils, countertops, and cutting boards thoroughly with hot soapy water after they touch raw meat, fish, or poultry.

Do separate raw meats from produce in the refrigerator.

Don't use dirty towels to dry clean dishes.

Do discard worn cutting boards with lots of cuts and scratches.

Figure 13.3 The Do's and Don'ts of Cross-Contamination

Table 13.2
Cook It Until It's Done!

If You Are Cooking This Food	The Food Thermometer Should Reach (°F)*
Ground Meat and Meat Mixtures	
Beef, pork, veal, lamb	160
Turkey, chicken	165
Fresh Beef, Veal, Lamb	145**
Poultry	
Chicken, turkey, whole or parts	165
Duck and goose	165
Fresh Pork	145**
Ham, raw	145**
Ham, precooked (to reheat)	140
Eggs and Egg Dishes	
Eggs	Cook until yolk and white are firm
Egg dishes	160
Leftovers and Casseroles	165

*The thermometer should be placed in the thickest part of the food item.

**Meat should rest for 3 minutes before consumption to ensure that pathogens are destroyed.

Figure 13.4 Color Is Not Always an Indicator of Whether Meat Is Thoroughly Cooked
A hamburger needs to reach an internal temperature of 160°F to ensure that all foodborne pathogens are killed. Can you tell which of these two hamburgers is safe to eat? (If you answered "a," you're right!)

Poultry can also remain pink after thorough cooking. Gases in your oven can cause a chemical reaction in the poultry that will give the meat a pink tinge. Because younger birds have thin skins, the gases can react with their flesh more easily and make the meat look pinker than that of older birds. Also, if nitrates and nitrites are added as a preservative, these can give poultry a pink tinge (see the discussion of food additives later in the chapter).[41]

With so many variables in fresh meat and poultry, color is not a reliable indicator that food is safe to eat. The only way to determine if your food has reached an appropriate internal temperature, high enough to kill pathogens, is to use a food thermometer. **Figure 13.5** shows several types of food thermometers you can use when cooking.

When it comes to foodborne pathogens, always remember that though eating raw meats, poultry, and fish can make you *ill*, cooking to the proper temperature will *kill* the pathogens. **Table 13.2** provides a list of the internal temperatures that your foods should reach to ensure that they are safe to eat.

Chill Foods at a Low Enough Temperature

Just as cooking foods to a high enough temperature to kill pathogens is essential, chilling foods at a low enough temperature to inhibit pathogenic growth is also important. Foodborne bacteria multiply most rapidly in temperatures between 40°F and 140°F (or 5°C to 60°C), a range known as the **danger zone**. To keep foods out of the danger zone, make sure that you keep hot foods *hot*, above 140°F, and cold foods *cold*, 40°F or below (**Figure 13.6**). In other words, the lasagna on a buffet table should be sitting on a hot plate or other heat source that keeps its temperature above 140°F, while the potato salad should be sitting on ice that will keep it chilled and at 40°F or below at all times.

danger zone The range of temperatures (between 40°F and 140°F) at which foodborne bacteria multiply most rapidly. Room temperature falls within the danger zone.

Temperature		
170°		Well-done meats
165°		Stuffing, poultry, reheated leftovers
160°	Safe zone (above 140°)	Medium-done meats, raw eggs, egg dishes, pork, ground meats
145°		Medium-rare beef steaks, roasts, veal, lamb
140°		Hold hot foods
	Danger zone	Do not keep foods between 40°F and 140°F for more than 2 hours or for more than 1 hour when the air temperature is greater than 90°F
68°		Room temperature
40°		Refrigerator temperatures
	Safe zone (below 40°F)	
0°		Freezer temperatures

Temperature (Fahrenheit)

Figure 13.6 The Danger Zone
Bacteria multiply rapidly in the "danger zone," between temperatures of 40°F and 140°F.

listeriosis A disease caused by infection of the bacterium, *Listeria monocyotogenes*, typically caused by eating food contaminated with *Listeria*.

Thermocouple digital food thermometer displays the temperature of the food within 6 seconds after placement.

Thermometer fork combination thermometers allow you to stab and check. A device that measures the temperature in the food is located in the tines of the fork.

Thermistor digital food thermometers take approximately 10 seconds to display the temperature of the food on the dial.

Oven-safe bimetallic-coil thermometers are most useful when cooking thick foods such as roasts and turkeys. They are unique, as they can stay in the food during cooking.

Figure 13.5 Food Thermometers
There are several types of food thermometers you can use to tell if your food is safe to eat. The thermometer should be inserted at least ½ inch deep into the food. It should be washed thoroughly after each use, before it is inserted back into food.

Cold temperatures will slow down microbes' ability to multiply to dangerous levels. Because of this, the temperature in your refrigerator should be set at or below 40°F. The only way to know if the temperature in your refrigerator or freezer is low enough is to use a thermometer.

The only exception to this guideline is *Listeria*. Because the bacterium *Listeria monocytogenes* can multiply at refrigerator temperatures, cross-contamination of foods carrying *Listeria* is more likely, so there is greater concern for foodborne illness in individuals most likely to get foodborne illness. *Listeria* causes a foodborne illness called **listeriosis** that affects approximately 1,600 Americans annually, with 14 percent of cases being in pregnant women.[42] Because a pregnant woman's immune system is altered during pregnancy, she is at higher risk for foodborne illnesses. *Listeria* can reach the fetus through the placenta, be transmitted to the newborn, and lead to severe problems in the fetus or newborn such as premature delivery, miscarriage, or stillbirth.[43] Listeriosis is the third leading cause of death from food poisoning in the United States.[44] See the Health Connection: A Case Study called "Getting the Lowdown on *Listeria*" for how one pregnant woman went about reducing her chances of contracting listeriosis.

The temperature for the freezer should be set at 0°F or below. Food will stay safe in the freezer indefinitely, though its quality may deteriorate. (For example, freezer burn may occur if frozen food is not tightly wrapped and gets exposed to air. Freezer burn causes food to dry out and taste less pleasant, but it isn't harmful.) Most microbes become dormant and are unable to multiply when they are frozen, but they aren't destroyed. In fact, once the frozen foods are defrosted, many microbes can "thaw out" and thrive if given the proper conditions.

Perishables such as raw meat and poultry shouldn't be left out at room temperature (a temperature within the danger zone) for more than two hours. If the air temperature is above 90°F, foods shouldn't be left out for more than one hour.[45]

Getting the Lowdown on *Listeria*

What Is *Listeria* and Listeriosis?

When Monica learned she was pregnant, she wanted to provide herself with good nutrition that would help her baby grow and develop. She met with her doctor and a registered dietitian who explained her overall nutrient needs for pregnancy. In addition, they advised her to avoid certain foods that could cause listeriosis, an infection caused by the bacterium *Listeria*.

The dietitian told Monica that animals can harbor *Listeria*, which can lead to contamination of meat and dairy foods. Contamination can occur after processing, and *Listeria* can also continue to multiply at refrigerated temperatures. Therefore, many outbreaks have been associated with foods such as hot dogs, luncheon meats, and salami. In dairy products, cooking and pasteurization will kill *Listeria*, but the lower cooking temperature used during the processing of soft cheeses isn't high enough to destroy this bacterium. Finally, produce such as cantaloupes, raw sprouts, and celery can be contaminated with *Listeria*.

In order to reduce her chances of getting this illness, Monica followed guidelines for avoiding foodborne illnesses, including *Listeria*.[4] During her pregnancy, Monica avoided soft cheeses, including her favorite, queso fresco. When eating out, she ordered baked or grilled meat instead of sandwiches made with deli cuts, and when preparing food at home, she reheated luncheon meats and hot dogs. She also used separate cutting boards in the kitchen for meat and produce, and she made sure to wash her hands after touching these foods. She didn't eat smoked seafood (which she didn't like anyway).

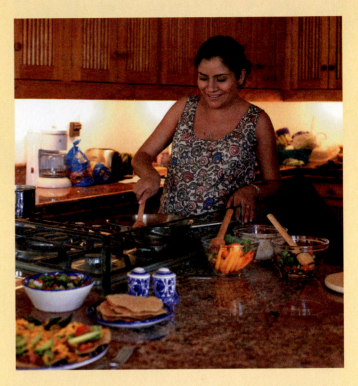

And finally, she avoided eating sprouts in her salads, temporarily gave up eating cantaloupe, and washed other produce thoroughly. She stayed healthy throughout her pregnancy, and delivered a healthy 7.5-lb. baby boy. She found she continued some of these practices, especially reducing cross-contamination, even after her son was born.

Think About It

What foods should a pregnant woman avoid to reduce the chance of listeriosis?

Leftovers should be refrigerated within two hours of being served. Large roasts and pots of soup or stews should be divided into smaller batches in order to cool down more quickly in the refrigerator. If these items have been left in the danger zone for too long or have been mishandled, bacteria can not only grow, but can also produce toxins that are heat resistant. These toxins won't be destroyed even if the food is cooked to a proper internal temperature, and could make you sick if consumed.[46]

Even stored at a proper temperature, foods shouldn't remain in the refrigerator for more than a few days. The rule of thumb is that leftovers can be in the refrigerator at 40°F or below for no more than four days. Here's an easy way to remember this: After *four* days in the refrigerator, leftovers are ready *for* disposal.

Raw eggs and other perishables should not be stored in your refrigerator door, as temperature swings there are more likely. Store perishables in the back of the refrigerator, for a colder and more constant temperature.

Raw meats and poultry can be kept for a maximum of two days in the refrigerator. **Table 13.3** provides a listing of the storage times for various foods. If you are unsure about the safety of a food, remember this: *When in doubt, throw it out.*

Now that you've read about how cleaning, cooking, chilling, and avoiding cross-contamination can help keep your foods safe, think about how many of these strategies you use in your own kitchen. The Self-Assessment will help you identify areas in which you may need to improve your food-safety habits.

Table 13.3
Keeping It Cool!

Follow these guidelines to keep your perishable foods safe.

Preparation	Type or Description	Refrigerate (40°F)	Freeze (0°F)*
Beef, Lamb, Pork, Veal			
Fresh beef, lamb, veal, and pork	Ground, hamburger, stew meat, variety meat (tongue, liver, heart, kidney, chitterlings)	1–2 days	3–4 months
	Chops, roasts, steaks	3–5 days	4–12 months
	Chops, prestuffed	1 day	Does not freeze well
Leftovers	Including casseroles	3–4 days	2–3 months
Corned beef	In pouch, with pickling juices	5–7 days	Drained, 1 month
Bacon	Bacon	7 days	1 month
Ham (Precooked)			
Fully cooked	Slices	3–4 days	1–2 months
	Half	3–5 days	1–2 months
	Whole	7 days	1–2 months
Canned, labeled "keep refrigerated"	Opened	3–5 days	1–2 months
	Unopened	6–9 months	Do not freeze
Vacuum sealed	Unopened, fully cooked, vacuum sealed, dated	"Use by" date	1–2 months
	Unopened, fully cooked, vacuum sealed, undated	2 weeks	1–2 months
Chicken, Turkey, Other Poultry			
Fresh	Chicken breast, prestuffed	1 day	Does not freeze well
	Ground, patties, giblets	1–2 days	3–4 months
	Pieces	1–2 days	9 months
	Whole	1–2 days	1 year
Leftovers	Casseroles	3–4 days	4–6 months
	Chicken nuggets, patties	1–2 days	1–3 months
	Pieces, plain or fried	3–4 days	4 months
	Pieces in broth or gravy	3–4 days	6 months
Eggs			
Fresh	In shell	3–5 weeks	Do not freeze
	Yolk, whites	2–4 days	1 year

Table 13.3 continued

Keeping It Cool!

Preparation	Type or Description	Refrigerate (40°F)	Freeze (0°F)*
Leftovers (egg dishes)	Casserole, quiche, omelet	3–4 days	2 months
	Hard-cooked	1 week	Does not freeze well
Opened	Liquid pasteurized eggs, egg substitutes	3 days	Does not freeze well
Unopened	Liquid pasteurized eggs, egg substitutes	10 days	1 year
Sausages, Lunch Meats			
Hard sausage	Jerky sticks, pepperoni	2–3 weeks	1–2 months
Raw sausage	Beef, chicken, pork, turkey	1–2 days	1–2 months
Smoked sausage	Breakfast links, patties	7 days	1–2 months
Lunch meat	Deli-sliced or store-prepared	3–5 days	1–2 months
Opened	Hot dogs	1 week	1–2 months
	Lunch meat—vacuum packed, sliced	3–5 days	1–2 months
	Summer sausage labeled "keep refrigerated"	3 weeks	1–2 months
Unopened	Hot dogs	2 weeks	1–2 months
	Lunch meat—vacuum packed, sliced	2 weeks	1–2 months
	Summer sausage labeled "keep refrigerated"	3 months	1–2 months
Seafood			
Fresh	Fish	1–2 days	3–8 months
	Shellfish	1–2 days	3–12 months
Leftovers	Fish and shellfish	3–4 days	3 months
Miscellaneous			
Frozen dinners and entrées	"Keep frozen"	Unsafe to thaw	3–4 months
Mayonnaise	Commercial, "refrigerate after opening"	2 months	Do not freeze
Other leftovers	Gravy and meat broth	3–4 days	2–3 months
	Pizza	3–4 days	1–2 months
	Soups and stews	3–4 days	2–3 months
	Stuffing	3–4 days	1 month
Salads	Egg, chicken, ham, macaroni, tuna (store-prepared, homemade)	3–5 days	Does not freeze well

*Because freezing at 0°F keeps food safe indefinitely, recommended storage times are for quality only.

LO 13.2 **The Take-Home Message** Proper food-handling and food-storage strategies, particularly cleaning, combating cross-contamination, cooking, and chilling, can help reduce your risk of foodborne illness. Anything that comes in contact with your foods, including your hands, should be thoroughly washed. You should always wash produce before eating it, and separate raw meats, poultry, and fish, plus any utensils that touch them, from ready-to-eat foods to prevent cross-contamination. A food thermometer is the only accurate way to tell if your cooked food is safe to eat. Perishables should be properly and promptly chilled to minimize the growth of bacteria.

Test Your Food-Safety Smarts in the Kitchen

Download this app, "Is My Food Safe?" to learn more about reducing your risk of food poisoning. www.homefood-safety.org/video/is-my-food-safe-app

How Do Your Food-Safety Habits Stack Up?

Take the following quiz to find out.

How Often Do You	Always	Sometimes	Never
Wash your hands before preparing food?			
Scrub your fruits and vegetables under cold, running water before eating them?			
Use an insulated pouch and an ice pack to transport your perishable lunches and snacks?			
Wash your hands after using the bathroom?			
Throw out refrigerated leftovers after four days?			
Chop raw vegetables on a clean chopping board rather than the one you just used for raw meat, fish, or poultry?			
Use a thermometer to determine if the meat or poultry is done cooking?			

Answers

If you answered "Always" to all of the above, you are a food-safety superstar. If you didn't, there's more you can do to reduce your chances of contracting a foodborne illness. This chapter will help!

Practical Nutrition VIDEO

Food Safety with Picnics

Now that you know how to practice food safety in the kitchen, let's take it on the road! Joan shows you how to pack a picnic without bringing along unwanted pathogens. Scan this QR code with your mobile device to access the video. You can also access the video in MasteringNutrition™.

Food Safety Initiative (FSI) The program that coordinates the research, surveillance, inspection, outbreak response, and educational activities of the various government agencies that work together to safeguard food.

Who Protects Your Food and How Do They Do It?

LO 13.3 Discuss how the food supply is protected in the United States.

Foods don't originate in the grocery store. Whether in a bag, box, or bin, nearly every food you buy starts life on a farm. Keeping food safe from the time it's harvested until you buy it is the responsibility of farmers, food manufacturers, and several government agencies. In this section, we'll look at the regulations, food preservation techniques, product dating, and irradiation that are done during various steps between the farm and the table. We'll start by looking at the government agencies that keep an eye on the food supply.

Several Government Agencies Police the Food Supply

Today, several federal agencies share responsibility for food safety in the United States.[47] **Table 13.4** lists these agencies and summarizes the roles they each play in safeguarding your foods. This shared responsibility has paid off. There has been a 24 percent decline in foodborne illness since 1996.[48] Much of this decline can be attributed to the **Food Safety Initiative (FSI)**, which was begun in 1997. The FSI coordinates the research, inspection, outbreak response, and educational activities of the various government agencies. The goal of the FSI is to make sure that government agencies work collaboratively.[49]

One FSI program is FoodNet, a combined effort among the Centers for Disease Control and Prevention (CDC), the United States Department of Agriculture (USDA), the Food and Drug Administration (FDA), and other health departments to conduct ongoing active monitoring of specific foodborne illnesses when they arise in the United States. Improved reporting and monitoring systems, as well as outbreak investigations, have helped to quickly identify and trace the causes of foodborne illness.

Table 13.4

Who's Policing the Food Supply?

Agency	Responsible for
USDA Food Safety and Inspection Service (FSIS)	Ensuring safe and accurately labeled meat, poultry, and eggs
Food and Drug Administration (FDA)	Ensuring the safety of all other foods besides meat, poultry, and eggs
Environmental Protection Agency (EPA)	Protecting you and the environment from harmful pesticides
Animal and Plant Health Inspection Service (APHIS)	Protecting against plant and animal pests and disease

PulseNet, another foodborne disease watchdog, is a network of government and public health laboratories that specializes in detecting foodborne diseases using **DNA fingerprinting**. Finding similar strains of a bacterium in both a person and a food suggests a common source and potential connection.[50] Once these patterns are determined, they are entered into an electronic database at a local or state health department, maintaining an ongoing collection of DNA fingerprints. These patterns are also sent to the CDC's central computer. If similar patterns emerge at the same time in different states, this could indicate a potential outbreak. Once a suspicious foodborne illness outbreak is reported, several government agencies work together to contain the disease.

The *E. coli* O157: H7 outbreak in spinach that occurred in the fall of 2006 provides one example of how these multiple agencies work together to identify and contain an outbreak. First, the CDC alerted the FDA of an outbreak of illness due to *E. coli* O157: H7 that spanned 26 states in the United States. PulseNet used DNA fingerprinting to determine that the strain of *E. coli* was the same in all those infected. The suspected food was bagged raw spinach grown in California. The CDC issued an official health alert about the outbreak, and the FDA advised consumers to stop eating raw spinach. Before it was over, more than 200 people were infected, and more than half of them were hospitalized. Three individuals died and 31 developed hemolytic uremic syndrome from the infection. However, the swift, coordinated action of these federal and state agencies helped curtail the outbreak and kept it from being much worse.[51] Investigators from the FDA, CDC, and USDA worked with the state of California to conclude that the infected spinach came from one grower and most likely occurred because of cross-contamination of infected water and animals with the produce in the field. The same strain of *E. coli* was found in a nearby stream and in the feces of cattle on a neighboring farm.

The FDA and USDA have also adopted a food-safety program called Hazard Analysis and Critical Control Points (HACCP; pronounced "hassip") that is used to identify and control foodborne hazards that may occur in all the stages of the food production process.[52] HACCP procedures are in place for food manufacturers and transporters to help safeguard food. Manufacturers also apply food preservation techniques to some foods to make them safer when you buy them. These techniques will be discussed in the next section.

Once the food arrives at retail and food-service establishments such as grocery stores and restaurants, these outlets use the Food Code, a reference document published by the FDA. The Food Code provides practical, science-based guidance, including HACCP guidelines, and provisions to help purveyors minimize foodborne illness.[53] The FDA updates the Food Code periodically to keep pace with emerging science, and states use the FDA Food Code to present their food codes and laws. The Partnership for Food Safety Education (PFSE) is a program designed to educate the public about safe food handling after purchase.

The FDA, CDC, and USDA worked together to combat an outbreak of *E. coli* O157: H7 in 2006 that was traced to bagged prewashed spinach.

DNA fingerprinting A technique in which DNA "gene patterns" (or "fingerprints") are detected and analyzed. Used in food safety to distinguish between different strains of a bacterium.

1 **Farm: Use good agricultural practices.** Farmers grow, harvest, sort, pack, and store their crops in ways that help reduce food safety hazards.

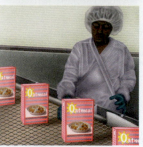

2 **Processing: Monitor at critical control points.** During processing, HACCP measures are implemented.

3 **Transportation: Use clean vehicles and maintain the proper temperature.** Food is kept at a proper temperature during transportation to reduce the growth of foodborne microbes.

4 **Retail: Follow the Food Code guidelines.** Retail outlets, including restaurants, grocery stores, and institutions (such as hospitals), use the Food Code guidelines to reduce the risk of foodborne illness.

5 **Consumer: Always follow the four Cs of food safety (clean, combat cross-contamination, cook, chill).** The consumer uses the four Cs to reduce the risk of foodborne illness.

Figure 13.7 The Farm-to-Table Continuum
Every step in the farm-to-table continuum plays an important role in reducing microbes and the spread of foodborne illness.

From the farmer to the consumer, everyone involved in the production and preparation of food plays a role in making sure the food we eat is safe. The **farm-to-table continuum** is a visual tool that shows how farmers, food manufacturers, transporters of food, retailers, and you, the consumer, can help ensure a safe food supply. **Figure 13.7** shows the steps in this continuum.

In addition to government efforts to help prevent foodborne illness, food manufacturers also work to safeguard food. Food processing, preservation techniques, and irradiation help destroy contaminants and/or maintain a food's color and freshness, and product dating can help you know when a food is past its prime and should be tossed.

Food Manufacturers Use Preservation Techniques to Destroy Contaminants

One way to control foodborne hazards is to use **food preservation** methods. Pickling (adding an acidic substance such as vinegar to the food), salting, drying, heating, freezing, and newer techniques such as irradiation and the use of food additives are all methods of food preservation. You use some of these yourself when you cook (apply heat to) or freeze (apply cold to) foods. Pickling, drying, and canning (a form of heating) have been in use for centuries, though today they're more often done by food manufacturers than home cooks.

Pasteurization is a technique that involves heating foods and liquids to a high enough temperature to kill pathogens. The process kills *E. coli* O157: H7 as well as other bacteria. In addition to dairy foods, most juices sold in supermarkets in the United State are pasteurized. Juices that aren't pasteurized must display a warning on the label.[54] Another method of pasteurization is ultra-high temperature (UHT) pasteurization, which is often used to aseptically package juice and some milk in "boxes." These are shelf stable until opened, which saves manufacturers (and you) a lot of money because the products don't have to be shipped and stored under expensive refrigeration. Once they are opened, they do have to be refrigerated.

Pasteurizing milk and dairy foods improves their quality and helps them stay fresh longer. Though raw (unpasteurized) milk and cheese are sometimes touted as being more healthful, this is an unfounded claim and can be dangerous, as raw milk can contain *Salmonella, E. coli* O157: H7, and *Listeria monocytogenes*.

Canning goes a step beyond pasteurization by packing food in airtight containers after heating it to a temperature high enough to kill most bacteria. Though this preserves the safety of most foods, botulism is one illness that can still result from improperly canned foods. The bacterium *Clostridium botulinum* can survive environments without air, such as sealed cans, and creates **spores** that are not destroyed at normal cooking temperatures; a temperature higher than boiling (212°F) is needed to kill these spores.[55] **Retort canning** has eliminated botulism from commercially canned foods. Because of the success of retort canning, the very rare cases of botulism typically result from products that have been home canned. This is a great reason to make sure you are using modern canning methods at home. If you have an old recipe from Grandma, you need to modify Grandma's instructions to make the product safe.

Many people were initially resistant to the processes of pasteurization and canning because they thought the techniques would promote the use of inferior ingredients. The federal government helped address such fears by putting formal food grading processes in place to reassure consumers that only quality foods would be used. Both of these preservation methods are now widely used and generally regarded as effective to thwart foodborne illness.

Two newer preservation methods used to keep foods fresh are MAP and HPP. **Modified atmosphere packaging (MAP)** is a process during which the manufacturer changes the composition of the air surrounding the food in a package. Usually, the amount of oxygen is reduced, which delays the decay of packaged fruits and vegetables. MAP is used in such foods to extend their shelf life and preserve their quality.[56] **High-pressure processing (HPP)** is a newer method in which foods are exposed to pulses of high pressure, which destroys microorganisms. If bacterial spores are present on the food, heat may also have to be applied along with the HPP. Foods such as jams, fruit juices, ham, rice cakes, guacamole, and pourable salad dressing can be treated with HPP.[57]

Irradiation

Another method of food preservation that manufacturers and growers use to keep food safe is **irradiation**. After foods have been packaged by a manufacturer, they may undergo irradiation, at either the manufacturing plant or another facility. During this process, foods are subjected to a radiant energy source. This level of energy damages the harmful organisms, either killing them all or greatly reducing their numbers, thus reducing the risk of foodborne disease.[58] Irritation also destroys the bacteria that cause food spoilage.[59] This will allow foods to have a longer shelf life.[60] Foods that have been irradiated are not radioactive and don't undergo any harmful or dangerous chemical changes.[61]

The temperature of the food isn't significantly raised during irradiation, which helps prevent nutrient losses.[62] Irradiation destroys bacteria such as *Campylobacter*, *E. coli* O157: H7, and *Salmonella* and helps control insects and parasites. It does not destroy viruses such as norovirus and hepatitis A, however, because the higher radiation levels needed to destroy the DNA of these smaller microbes have not yet been approved by the FDA.[63]

Food irradiation has been studied and tested for more than 50 years and remains the most researched food-related technology ever approved in the United States.[64] Irradiation has been used for years to sterilize surgical instruments and implants. Hospitals have used irradiation to destroy disease-promoting microbes in foods served to patients with cancer and others who have weakened immune systems.

Foods that are irradiated must bear the "radura" logo, along with the phrase "treated by irradiation" or "treated with radiation" on the package (**Figure 13.8**).[65] A label is not required if a minor ingredient, such as a spice, has been irradiated and used in the product. Foods that are currently approved for irradiation in the United States include:[66]

- Fruits and vegetables
- Herbs and spices

Figure 13.8 The International Radura Symbol
The radura symbol must appear on all irradiated foods.

farm-to-table continuum Illustrates the roles that farmers, food manufacturers, food transporters, retailers, and consumers play in ensuring that the food supply, from the farm to the plate, remains safe.

food preservation The treatment of foods to reduce deterioration and spoilage, and help prevent the multiplication of pathogens that can cause foodborne illness.

pasteurization The process of heating liquids or food at high temperatures to destroy foodborne pathogens.

canning The process of heating food to a temperature high enough to kill bacteria and then packing the food in airtight containers.

spores Hardy reproductive structures that are produced by certain bacteria. Some bacterial spores can survive boiling temperature (212°F).

retort canning The process of subjecting already-canned foods to an additional high-temperature heat source to destroy potential pathogens.

modified atmosphere packaging (MAP) A food preservation technique that changes the composition of the air surrounding the food in a package to extend the food's shelf life.

high-pressure processing (HPP) A method used to pasteurize foods by exposing the items to pulses of high pressure, which destroys the microorganisms that are present.

irradiation A process in which foods are placed in a shielded chamber, called an irradiator, and subjected to a radiant energy source. This kills specific pathogens in food by breaking up the cells' DNA.

Figure 13.9 Closed and Open Food Product Dating

- Fresh meat, pork, and poultry
- Wheat flour
- White potatoes
- Molluscan shellfish (oysters, clams, mussels, scallops)
- Alfalfa sprouts
- Shell eggs

Though irradiation has many advantages, it doesn't guarantee that a food is safe, and some foods should still not be eaten raw, even if they have been irradiated. Steak tartare (a dish that contains raw ground beef) isn't a safe menu option even if it is made with irradiated ground beef, because the beef could be recontaminated after irradiation. Proper food-handling, preparation, and cooking techniques must still be used for foods that have been irradiated.

Despite the advantages of irradiated food, there is some public concern about whether this process will cause the food to become radioactive. To assess the changes in foods caused by irradiation, the FDA formed the Bureau of Foods Irradiated Food Committee (BFIFC). Currently approved radiation sources are not of concern because their energy at the recommended doses is too low to induce radioactivity.[67]

Product Dating Can Help You Determine Peak Quality

Although food product dating isn't federally mandated, except for infant formula and some baby foods, more than 20 states in the United States require some form of food product dating. There are two types of food product dating: closed dating and open dating. **Closed** (or **"coded"**) **dating** refers to the packing numbers used by manufacturers that are often found on nonperishable, shelf-stable foods, such as cans of soup and fruit (see **Figure 13.9**). This type of dating is used by the manufacturer to keep track of product inventory, rotate stock, and identify products that may be involved in a recall.[68]

Open dating is typically found on perishable items such as meat, poultry, eggs, and dairy foods, and is more useful for the consumer. Open dating must contain a calendar date that includes at least a month and day. (If the product is shelf stable or frozen and a calendar date is used, the year must also be included in the date.) You can use open dating to help you decide when to buy and consume a product while it is at its peak quality. Note: This date does not refer to food safety, but to the *quality* of the food. For example, a carton of yogurt that has been mishandled and not refrigerated for several hours may be unsafe to eat even though the date on the container hasn't passed.

When open dating is used, there must be a phrase next to the date that tells you how to interpret it. If there is "Sell By" next to the date, you should purchase the product on or before that date. If there is "Best if Used By" or "Use By" next to it, this refers to the date by which you should consume the product in order to enjoy it at its

closed or "coded" dating Refers to the packing numbers that are decodable only by manufacturers and are often found on nonperishable, shelf-stable foods.

open dating Typically found on perishable items such as meat, poultry, eggs, and dairy foods; must contain a calendar date.

best.[69] If you don't plan to consume a product by its Use By date, you can freeze it; once frozen, the Use By date doesn't apply.

LO 13.3 **The Take-Home Message** Several government agencies share responsibility for food safety in the United States. HACCP is a food safety program used to identify and control hazards that may occur in any part of the food system. Manufacturers may use other techniques such as pasteurization, canning, and irradiation to preserve food and destroy contamination.

What Are Food Additives and How Are They Used?

LO 13.4 Explain the role that food additives play in food production.

Food manufacturers use **food additives** for numerous reasons: to increase the shelf life of products, enrich nutrient content, and improve the flavor and texture of foods. Commonly used additives include preservatives (such as antioxidants and sulfites), nutrients, and flavor enhancers (such as MSG).

Preservatives Prevent Spoilage and Increase Shelf Life

Most additives are *preservatives* that are added to foods to prevent spoilage (usually by destroying microbes) and increase shelf life. The most common antimicrobial preservatives are salt and sugar. Salt has been used for centuries, particularly in meat and fish, to create a dry environment in which bacteria cannot multiply. Sugar is used for the same preserving effect in products such as canned and frozen fruits and condiments.

Nitrites and **nitrates** are salts that are added to foods to prevent microbial growth and are used in cured meats such as hot dogs and ham to prevent the growth of *Clostridium botulinum*. They are also the chemicals that give these foods their pink color. The use of these salts has been controversial due to the fact that they form **carcinogenic** nitrosamines in the digestive tract of animals.

The addition of antioxidants to foods can prevent an off taste or off color in a product that's vulnerable to damage by oxidation. Currently two vitamins have been approved for use as food additives due to their actions as antioxidants: vitamin E and vitamin C. Vitamin E is added to oils and cereals to prevent the fats in them from becoming rancid, and vitamin C is often added to cut fruit to prevent premature browning. Butylated hydroxyanisole (BHA) and butylated hydroxytoluene (BHT) are two chemical antioxidants that are also used as preservatives.

Sulfites are a group of antioxidants that are used as preservatives to help prevent the oxidation and browning of some foods and to inhibit the growth of microbes.[70] Sulfites are often found in dried fruits and vegetables, packaged and prepared potatoes, wine, beer, bottled lemon and lime juice, and pickled foods.

For most people, sulfites pose no risk, but there are people who experience adverse reactions. Individuals who are sensitive to sulfites may experience symptoms ranging from chest tightness and difficulty breathing to hives.[71] People at highest risk for negative reactions include people who suffer from asthma and others who are sensitive to sulfites. Due to the risk of adverse reactions in people who are sulfite sensitive, the FDA has prohibited the use of sulfites on fruits and vegetables that are served raw, such as in a salad bar, or are advertised as "fresh." Foods that contain sulfite additives or

Dried fruits often have sulfur dioxide or other sulfites added to them to preserve color and flavor. People with sulfite sensitivity should avoid products containing these additives.

food additives Substances added to food that affect its quality, flavor, freshness, and/or safety.

nitrates (nitrites) Substances that can be added to foods to function as a preservative and to give meats such as hot dogs and luncheon meats a pink color.

carcinogenic Cancer causing.

sulfites Preservatives used to help prevent foods from turning brown and to inhibit the growth of microbes. Often used in wine and dried fruit products.

ingredients treated with sulfites must declare "added sulfites" in the ingredients listing on the label. Food sold in bulk, such as dried fruit treated with sulfites, must display the ingredients on a sign near the food. Because sulfites destroy the B vitamin thiamin, the FDA prohibits their use in foods that are good sources of the vitamin.[72]

Some Additives Enhance Texture and Consistency

Food additives can improve food quality in a number of ways. Gums and pectins are used to improve consistency and texture and are added to thicken yogurts and puddings. Emulsifiers improve the stability, consistency, and homogeneity of products like mayonnaise and ice cream. Lecithin is an example of an emulsifier that is added to some salad dressing. Leavening agents are added to breads to incorporate gases that cause them to rise. Anti-caking agents prevent products like powdered sugar that are crystalline in nature from absorbing moisture and lumping. Humectants such as propylene glycol are added to increase moisture in products so that they stay fresh.

Some Additives Improve Nutrient Content

Additives can be used to enhance a product's nutrition content, such as when refined grains are enriched with added B vitamins and iron. In some cases, such additions are mandated. This was the case in 1996 when the FDA published regulations requiring the addition of folic acid to enriched breads, cereal, and other grain products in order to help decrease the risk of neural tube defects in newborns.

Color and Flavor Enhancers Improve the Appeal of Foods

Additives can be used to enhance the color of foods. Two main categories make up the FDA's list of permitted colors. "Certifiable" color additives are man-made and are derived primarily from petroleum and coal sources. You can recognize these types of additives by the prefixes FD&C, D&C, or Ext. An example is FD&C Yellow, which is often found in cereals and baked goods. The second main category of color additives includes those obtained largely from plant, animal, or mineral sources. Examples include caramel color and grape color extract. Reactions to color additives are rare, though FD&C Yellow No. 5 may cause itching and hives in some people. This additive is found in beverages, desserts, and processed vegetables and is required to be listed on food labels. **Table 13.5** provides a list of commonly used additives and their functions in foods.

MSG Is a Common Flavor Enhancer

Monosodium glutamate (MSG) is often used as a flavor enhancer in Asian foods, canned vegetables and soups, and processed meats. Consumers can buy it in a form that is similar in texture to salt; although it doesn't have a strong taste of its own, it enhances sweet, salty, sour, and bitter tastes in other foods. Because of its long history of safe use, MSG is **generally recognized as safe (GRAS)**. However, the FDA has received numerous consumer complaints that it can cause symptoms such as headaches and nausea, along with concerns that it can contribute to Alzheimer's disease, brain tumors, and nerve cell damage.[73]

After an extensive review, the FDA confirmed that MSG is safe to consume in the amounts typically used in processed foods and cooking (a typical meal that

monosodium glutamate (MSG) A flavor enhancer.

generally recognized as safe (GRAS) Describes a substance that is believed to be safe to consume based on a long history of use by humans or a substantial amount of research that documents its safety.

Table 13.5

Commonly Used Food Additives

Additive(s)	Function(s)	Where You'll Find Them
Alginates, carrageenan, glyceride, guar gum, lecithin, mono- and diglycerides, methyl cellulose, pectin, sodium aluminosilicate	Impart/maintain desired consistency	Baked goods, cake mixes, coconut, ice cream, processed cheese, salad dressings, table salt
Ascorbic acid (vitamin C), calcium carbonate, folic acid, thiamine (B$_1$), iron, niacin, pyridoxine (B$_6$), riboflavin (B$_2$), vitamins A and D, zinc oxide	Improve/maintain nutritive value	Biscuits, bread, breakfast cereals, desserts, flour, gelatin, iodized margarine, milk, pasta, salt
Ascorbic acid, benzoates, butylated hydroxyanisole (BHA), butylated hydroxytoluene (BHT), citric acid, propionic acid and its salts, sodium nitrite	Maintain palatability and wholesomeness	Bread, cake mixes, cheese, crackers, frozen and dried fruit, lard, margarine, meat, potato chips
Citric acid, fumaric acid, lactic acid, phosphoric acid, sodium bicarbonate, tartrates, yeast	Produce light texture and control acidity/alkalinity	Butter, cakes, cookies, chocolates, crackers, quick breads, soft drinks
Annatto, aspartame, caramel, cloves, FD&C Red No. 40, FD&C Blue No. 1, fructose, ginger, limonene, MSG, saccharin, turmeric	Enhance flavor or provide desired color	Baked goods, cheeses, confections, gum, spice cake, gingerbread, jams, soft drinks, soup, yogurt

contains MSG has less than 0.5 gram). However, when consumed in large quantities such as 3 or more grams at a time, it may cause short-term reactions in people who are sensitive to it.[74] These reactions, which are called the **MSG symptom complex**, can include numbness, burning sensation, facial pressure or tightness, chest pain, rapid heartbeat, and drowsiness. In addition, people with asthma may have difficulty breathing after consuming MSG. For these reasons, the FDA requires that all foods containing MSG declare this ingredient on the food label.

Food Additives Are Closely Regulated by the FDA

Food additives are under strict regulation by the FDA, with consumer safety a top priority. The Federal Food, Drug and Cosmetic Act of 1938 gave the FDA authority to regulate food and food ingredients, including the use of food additives. The 1958 Food Additives Amendment further mandated that manufacturers document the safety of a food additive and obtain FDA approval before using it in a food.[75]

Two categories of food additives were exempted from this amendment. The first category includes substances that were known to be safe before 1958 and were given **prior-sanctioned** status. For example, because nitrates were used to preserve meats before 1958, they have prior-sanctioned status, but *only* for their use in meats. They cannot be used in other foods, such as vegetables, without FDA approval.[76] The second category includes substances that have a long history of being safe for consumption, such as salt, sugar, and spices, or have extensive research documenting that they are safe to consume, such as vitamins. These additives are exempt from FDA approval because they are "generally recognized as safe" (GRAS).[77]

MSG symptom complex A series of reactions such as numbness, burning sensation, facial pressure or tightness, chest pain, rapid heart beat, and drowsiness that can occur in some individuals after they consume MSG.

prior-sanctioned Having previous approval.

The FDA continually monitors both prior-sanctioned additives and those with GRAS status to ensure that current research continues to support their safety. To remain on the GRAS list, an additive must not have been found to be cancer causing in animals or humans. The 1958 Food Additives Amendment also included the *DeLaney Clause*, which was created to protect consumers from additives found to cause cancer. The clause states that no substances that have been shown to cause cancer in animals or humans at any dosage may be added to foods. However, with the present increases in technology and the ability to detect substances at very low levels, the clause is considered outdated. To address this issue, the FDA deems additives safe if lifetime use presents no more than a one-in-a-million risk of cancer in human beings. If an additive is suddenly called into question, the FDA can prohibit its use or require that the food manufacturer conduct additional studies to ensure its safety.[78] Even with these safeguards in place, some additives, such as MSG and sulfites, may cause adverse reactions in some people and should be avoided by those who are sensitive to them.

Some Food Additives Are Unintentional

The food additives already discussed are all *intentional food additives* used to improve the quality of food products. However, *unintentional food additives* may sometimes be added indirectly to a food. For example, very small amounts of substances used during packaging or processing may inadvertently end up in the food. The safety of packaging must therefore be determined by manufacturers to ensure that packing substances aren't harmful to the consumer. Unintentional additives may also include chemicals from processing, and *dioxins* used during the manufacture of bleached paper such as coffee filters. Dioxins can accumulate in the food chain and cause cancer in animals. The FDA monitors the level of dioxins in food that you consume and in the feed that animals consume.[79]

LO 13.4 **The Take-Home Message** Food additives are often used by manufacturers to preserve foods, enhance their color or flavor, or add to their nutrient content. Some additives, such as MSG and sulfites, may cause unpleasant symptoms in sensitive individuals, but all additives are strictly regulated by the FDA. All intentional food additives must be listed on food labels. Some additives may be added unintentionally during processing or cause adverse reactions in sensitive individuals.

What Are Toxins and Chemical Agents?

LO 13.5 Explain what are toxins and chemical agents in the food supply.

In addition to pathogens, naturally occurring toxins can contaminate foods, and chemicals can accumulate in foods. In this section we'll discuss some of these toxins.

Toxins Occur Naturally

Toxins frequently occur in nature to help a plant or animal fend off predators or capture its meals. In many cases, toxins in food animals exist in amounts too small to harm humans, but there are instances in which the toxins found in plant and animal foods can make a person ill, or worse.

marine toxins Chemicals that occur naturally and contaminate some fish.

scombrotoxic fish poisoning A condition caused by consuming spoiled fish that contain large amounts of histamines.

ciguatera poisoning A condition caused by marine toxins produced by *dinoflagellates* (microscopic sea organisms).

Marine Toxins

Although there are numerous reasons to include fish and seafood in your diet (recall their omega-3 fatty acid and low saturated fat content from Chapter 5), you should be aware of the risks involved. Some seafood, such as some of the raw fish used in sushi, can contain pathogens, and some can harbor naturally occurring **marine toxins**. Thorough cooking will kill many harmful bacteria and viruses found in seafood, but it won't destroy any of the marine toxins.

Spoiled finfish, such as tuna and mackerel, can cause **scombrotoxic fish poisoning**, in which the spoilage bacteria break down proteins in the fish and generate histamine. Other by-products are created that block the breakdown of histamine. Consuming fish that contain large amounts of histamine can cause symptoms such as diarrhea, flushing, sweating, and vomiting within 2 minutes to 2 hours.[80]

Eating large, predatory reef fish, such as barracuda and grouper, can sometimes result in **ciguatera poisoning**, which is caused by ciguatoxins. These toxins originate in microscopic sea organisms called *dinoflagellates*, which are then eaten by small tropical fish. As larger fish eat the smaller fish, the toxins **bioaccumulate** and become more concentrated in the larger fish.[81] **Figure 13.10** shows how these toxins can accumulate in the food chain. In addition to experiencing various gastrointestinal discomforts, individuals infected with ciguatera may have temperature sensation reversal in the mouth when they eat.[82] To them, ice cream feels hot and hot coffee feels cold.

Certain shellfish, such as mussels, clams, scallops, oysters, crabs, and lobsters, that typically live in the coastal waters of New England and the Pacific states can be contaminated with **neurotoxins** (*neuro* = nerve, *toxin* = toxic). Neurotoxins are also produced by dinoflagellates, and the particular reddish-brown-colored dinoflagellates that contain them can become so abundant that the ocean appears to have red streaks, also known as "red tides." Eating contaminated shellfish can lead to **paralytic shellfish poisoning**. Symptoms include mild numbness or tingling in the face, arms, and legs, as well as headaches and dizziness. Muscle paralysis, inability to breathe, and, in severe cases, death could result.[83] See Table Tips on "Ways to Avoid Toxins and Chemical Agents in Your Seafood" for a useful summary of these points.

Toxins in Other Foods

Many plant foods naturally contain toxins in small amounts, so though they're generally safe to eat, consuming them in very large amounts could be harmful.

Warning signs like this one are often posted when local waters have been found to contain high amounts of pollutants. Fish caught in such waters should never be eaten.

bioaccumulate When a substance or chemical builds up in an organism over time, so that the concentration of the chemical is higher than would be found naturally in the environment.

neurotoxins Toxins that affect the nerves and can cause symptoms including mild numbness or tingling in the face, arms, and legs, as well as headaches and dizziness. Severe cases could result in death.

paralytic shellfish poisoning A condition caused by consuming shellfish contaminated with neurotoxins.

Level 1 Dinoflagellates produce toxin and/or other microscopic organisms become contaminated with toxins.

Level 2 Small fish eat the dinoflagellates. Over time, the toxins accumulate and become more concentrated in their bodies.

Level 3 Large, predatory fish consume the smaller contaminated fish, which increases their toxin concentration.

Level 4 Fishermen catch the larger fish for human consumption.

Increasing accumulation of biotoxins

Figure 13.10 Bioaccumulation of Toxins

Keep fish, especially finfish, such as fresh tuna, mackerel, grouper, and mahi mahi, chilled in the refrigerator to prevent spoilage and the formation of histamine toxins.

Never consume finfish or shellfish that are sold as bait, as these do not meet food-safety regulations.

Observe all fish consumption advisories. To learn if an advisory is in place for the fish in your area, visit the EPA's Fish and Wildlife Consumption website at www.epa.gov.

If you fish recreationally, you should always check with the local or state health department for specific advice based on the local waters to avoid eating PCB-containing fish.

Eat a variety of different types of fish to minimize the exposure to a particular toxin.

polychlorinated biphenyls (PCBs) Synthetic chemicals that have been shown to cause cancer and other adverse effects on the immune, reproductive, nervous, and endocrine systems in animals. PCBs may cause cancer in humans.

Potatoes that have been exposed to light and turned green, for example, contain increased amounts of solanine, a toxin that can cause fever, diarrhea, paralysis, and shock. (Luckily, peeling potatoes usually removes the green layer and the potato can be safely eaten. If it tastes bitter, however, throw it out.) Wild lima beans contain high amounts of cyanogenic glycosides, which can be converted to the poison cyanide. (The variety of lima beans sold commercially have minimal, nonthreatening amounts of this substance, so are safe to eat.) Cassava also contains cyanogenic glycosides and has been known to cause cyanide poisoning in people who eat large amounts of this root vegetable. Raw soybeans contain amylase inhibitors, which are inactivated when cooked or fermented.[84]

Other foods contain toxins that are harmful even in trace amounts, and so should be avoided altogether. Certain wild mushrooms, for example, are poisonous; they contain toxins that can cause nausea, vomiting, liver damage, and death.

Contamination Is Sometimes Due to Pollution

One person's trash can become another person's illness. Although industrial and household chemicals have useful purposes, if traces of these substances end up in the food supply, they can have negative health effects. Two pollutants of concern are PCBs and methylmercury.

Polychlorinated biphenyls (PCBs) are chemicals that occur in the food supply due to industrial pollution. A few decades ago, these chemicals were used as coolants and lubricants because they are good insulators and don't burn easily. They were banned in 1977 due to concerns about their toxicity.[85] For example, they may be responsible for promoting cancer in humans. Although PCBs are no longer manufactured in the United States, they can still make their way into the environment through hazardous waste sites, the burning of wastes, and the improper disposal of consumer products, such as old television sets and other electrical fixtures and devices.[86] PCBs have been shown to contaminate the sediments in rivers and lakes. Because PCBs don't break down over time, they bioaccumulate in small organisms and fish. In fact, PCBs are the major chemical risk associated with eating fish.[87]

Mercury occurs in nature, but it is also a by-product of industrial pollution. An airborne form of mercury can accumulate on the surface of streams and oceans and be transformed by the bacteria in the water into the toxic form of methylmercury. As fish either absorb the methylmercury from the water or eat smaller fish that contain methylmercury, they can bioaccumulate the substance to high levels.

LO 13.5 The Take-Home Message Toxins can occur naturally in foods and can cause harm to humans. Marine toxins can occur in certain varieties of spoiled fish and bioaccumulate in fish that feed on toxin-containing sea organisms. Chemicals can also get into the food supply as a result of environmental contamination. Polychlorinated biphenyls (PCBs) and methylmercury have been shown to bioaccumulate in fish.

What Is Bioterrorism and How Can You Protect Yourself?

LO 13.6 Explain how food can play a role in bioterrorism.

Food and water supplies are potential targets for **bioterrorism**. Agents such as the bacterium that causes anthrax and the virus that causes smallpox are examples of possible bioterrorist weapons. Until recently, scenarios of human-caused outbreaks of these diseases were thought to exist only in Hollywood movies. Today, Americans face the real threat of someone using plant or animal food supplies, or drinking water sources, to cause harm.[88]

Food can be the primary agent of bioterrorism by being contaminated with a biological or chemical toxin. In fact, the CDC lists several foodborne pathogens, such as botulism, *Salmonella, E. coli* O157: H7, and *Shigella* as potential bioterrorism agents.[89]

Food and water can also be used as secondary agents of bioterrorism by disrupting the availability of adequate safe amounts of these necessities and by limiting the fuel needed to safely cook and refrigerate perishable foods. Several years ago, London police arrested individuals involved in a plot to add poison to the food served at a British military base.[90] Tainted foods, or even the threat of such contamination, could cause a mandatory or self-imposed avoidance of a particular category of food and/or eating establishment and contribute to social disarray.[91]

To combat these threats, governmental agencies have made bioterrorism a national priority. Under the direction of the Department of Homeland Security, numerous local, state, and federal agencies, such as the Federal Emergency Management Agency (FEMA), FDA, and USDA, work together at each stage of the food continuum—from the farm to the table—to protect your foods.

As a consumer, you also play an important role in **food biosecurity**, and there are strategies you can employ if you should come into contact with suspicious-looking food items. Although food tampering is rare in the United States, a watchful consumer can spot it and avoid it. The Table Tips called "Avoid Foods that May Have Been Tampered With" lists ways you can identify such food items, and where to report suspicious items if you find them.

LO 13.6 The Take-Home Message Food and water can be primary agents of bioterrorism by being contaminated with a biological or chemical toxin. These necessities can also be used as secondary agents if a terrorist act disrupts their availability, or limits access to the fuel needed to safely cook and refrigerate perishable foods. If you come into contact with a tampered food, you should report the suspicious items to the appropriate authorities.

Clostridium botulinum, the bacterium that causes the deadly disease botulism, is classified by the CDC as a "Category A" biological agent posing the highest risk to national security.

Table TIPS

Avoid Foods that May Have Been Tampered With

Don't purchase a food product if the outer seal is broken, or the package is torn, dented, or otherwise damaged.

Purchase your foods by the "Sell By" date.

Don't buy canned items that are bulging or leaking.

Examine your food product packaging. Compare a suspect container with others on the shelf.

Report any suspicious store items to the store manager.

bioterrorism The use of a biological or chemical agent to frighten, threaten, coerce, injure, and/or kill individuals.

food biosecurity Protecting the food supply from bioterrorist attacks.

Is It Safe To Get Your Meals from a Food Truck?

Is It Safe To Get Your Meals from a Food Truck? Food trucks, food carts, mobile food—they all serve delicious, tempting food, ready-made, and, best of all, relatively cheap. They can be a great way to try new foods, and because they are right on the street, food trucks make getting a meal very convenient. As the trend has spread, the number of food trucks has grown accordingly.[1] However, some reports call into question the safety of food trucks, claiming that they are not always up to safe, public health standards.[2] Can food sold from a truck be safe? Take a close look at the arguments for both sides and see what you think.

yes

- In some states, every employee in a food truck is required to have a health department license, while in a restaurant only one person per shift is required to do so.[3]

- Food trucks must follow local rules for food safety.[4]

- Food trucks generally get good marks for cleanliness from health departments. In a survey of seven major U.S. cities, food trucks did as well as or better than restaurants in inspections.[5]

- Food truck owners must know their local health codes, and their staff must have current training on food safety practices, which includes how to handle and prepare food safely.[6]

no

- Even though there are regulations, and even though their record is better than restaurants', every year some food trucks still fail inspections.[7]

- It is difficult to inspect food trucks while they are in operation, so inspectors sometimes only look at them when they are not actually in use. This means inspectors cannot assess how food is handled and stored when serving the public. This makes it difficult to evaluate the safety of the food truck.[8]

- Food trucks are not covered under the FDA's menu labeling requirements so it's impossible to be sure of the nutrition content in your meal.[9]

- Keeping a small, mobile kitchen clean can be a major challenge, mainly because food trucks have to carry all their water.[10]

what do you think?

1. Do you buy food from food trucks, or do you know people who do? If so, what are some of the benefits and drawbacks of eating from a truck? **2.** If you have not eaten from a food truck, are you concerned about food safey, or are there other reasons? **3.** What are some ways you can tell whether the food truck you are eating at is following safe food-handling procedures?

VISUAL Chapter Summary

LO 13.1 Pathogens Are the Primary Cause of Foodborne Illness

Pathogens, which include viruses, bacteria, and parasites, as well as fungal agents and prions, all can cause foodborne illness. Noroviruses are the single largest cause of foodborne illness. The most common bacteria that cause foodborne illness are *Campylobacter*, *E. coli* O157: H7, and *Salmonella*.

LO 13.2 Practicing the Four Cs Can Prevent Foodborne Illness

Proper food-handling techniques during four critical steps—cleaning, combating cross-contamination, cooking, and chilling—can help reduce your risk of foodborne illness. Washing your hands and cleaning produce before eating it is important to prevent foodbornes illness. Separate cutting boards should be used for meat and nonmeat foods, and utensils and serving dishes that touch raw meat should not be used to handle cooked meat. The only way to tell if a meat product has been thoroughly cooked is to check its internal temperature with a meat thermometer. When serving foods, hot foods should be kept hot and cold foods should be kept cold. Leftovers should be divided and refrigerated quickly (within 1 to 2 hours), and frozen foods should never be thawed at room temperature. Refrigerators should always be set at 40°F or below and freezers should always be set at 0°F or below.

LO 13.3 Many Agencies Work Together to Keep Food Safe

Through the coordinated effort of the Food Safety Initiative, numerous United States government agencies work together to safeguard America's food supply against foodborne illness. Food manufacturers use preservation techniques such as pasteurization and irradiation to destroy contaminants. Food product dating can help you enjoy your foods at peak quality.

LO 13.4 Food Additives Can Help Keep Your Foods Safe and Healthy

Food additives are used as preservatives, antioxidants, flavoring, coloring, and leavening agents. They are also used to maintain a food's consistency and to add nutrients. The FDA must approve most additives before they can be used in foods, and all additives must be listed on the food label. Some additives are exempted from obtaining FDA approval by having attained GRAS or prior-sanctioned status based on their long history of safe consumption.

VISUAL Chapter Summary

LO 13.5 Toxins and Chemical Agents Can Contaminate Foods

In addition to pathogens, toxins and chemical agents can also cause foodborne illness. Naturally occurring toxins include marine toxins and toxins that can occur naturally in foods. Chemical agents such as polychlorinated biphenyls can occur as a by-product of industrial pollution.

Increasing accumulation of biotoxins

LO 13.6 Food and Water Supplies Are Potential Targets for Bioterrorism

The Department of Homeland Security coordinates the efforts of numerous local, state, and federal agencies to protect the United States, which includes safeguarding your food and water supply. Although food tampering is rare in the United States, a watchful consumer can play a role in spotting it and avoiding it.

Terms to Know

- foodborne illness
- food safety
- pathogens
- virus
- norovirus
- gastroenteritis
- bacteria
- parasites
- toxins
- cross-contaminate
- Food Safety Initiative (FSI)
- pasteurization
- irradiation
- closed or "coded" dating
- open dating
- food additives
- generally recognized as safe (GRAS)
- bioaccumulate
- polychlorinated biphenyls (PCBs)
- bioterrorism

MasteringNutrition™

Build your knowledge—and confidence—in the Study Area of MasteringNutrition with a variety of study tools.

MyDietAnalysis

Access MyDietAnalysis through MasteringNutrition™ and track your diet and daily activities. In addition, a dietary analysis activity is available for every chapter in your book.

Check Your Understanding

LO 13.1 1. Which of the following may cause a foodborne illness?
- a. MSG, sulfites, and nitrates
- b. parasites, viruses, bacteria, and naturally occurring chemicals and toxins
- c. ascorbic acid, carrageenan, annatto, and phosphoric acid
- d. none of the above

LO 13.2 2. The danger zone temperature range at which bacteria will multiply most rapidly is
- a. 40°F to 140°F.   b. 45°F to 140°F.
- c. 40°F to 145°F.   d. 50°F to 150°F.
- e. 50°F to 140°F.

LO 13.2 3. The four critical steps in the food-handling process that you need to take to help prevent foodborne illness are
- a. cutting, cleaning, chopping, and chilling.
- b. cleaning, combating cross-contamination, cutting, and chilling.
- c. clearing, combating cross-contamination, cutting, and chilling.
- d. cleaning, combating cross-contamination, cooking, and chilling.
- e. cooking, combating cross-contamination, cutting, and chilling.

LO 13.2 4. Though most bacteria will grow more slowly in a refrigerator set at 40°F and below, one of the following does not. Which one?
- a. *E. coli* O157: H7
- b. *Salmonella*
- c. Norwalk virus
- d. *Campylobacter*
- e. *Listeria*

LO 13.3 5. Which of the following U.S. government agencies is NOT involved in policing the food supply?
- a. the Internal Revenue Service (IRS)
- b. the Food and Drug Administration (FDA)
- c. the Centers for Disease Control and Prevention (CDC)
- d. the United States Department of Agriculture (USDA)

LO 13.3 6. The "Best if Used By" date on a food container refers to the date by which
- a. you should consume the product so that you don't get sick.
- b. you should consume the product to get your money's worth.
- c. you should purchase the product.
- d. to consume the product to enjoy it at its best quality.

LO 13.4 7. Two intentional food additives that some people are sensitive to are
- a. *Salmonella* and antioxidants.
- b. heat and lemon juice.
- c. sulfites and MSG.
- d. dioxins and MSG.

LO 13.4 8. Which of following is NOT a function of food additives?
- a. adding neurotoxins to foods
- b. preventing spoilage
- c. increasing the shelf life of a food
- d. enhancing the flavor of foods

LO 13.5 9. All of the following are examples of foodborne diseases caused by toxins that occur naturally in foods EXCEPT
- a. scombrotoxic poisoning.
- b. paralytic shellfish poisoning.
- c. sulfuric acid poisoning.
- d. ciguatera poisoning.

LO 13.6 10. Food can be the primary agent of bioterrorism by being contaminated with a biological or chemical toxin. Which of the following is NOT an example of bioterrorism?
- a. airborne mercury from a local factory accumulating in a body of water and being consumed by fish in the toxic form of methylmercury
- b. adding botulism to the food served at major national hospitals
- c. contamination of a nation's water supply with *Shigella*
- d. the spread of *E. coli* in the distribution of food via purposeful placement of a food item contaminated with *E. coli*

Answers

1. (b) Parasites, viruses, bacteria, and naturally occurring toxins and chemicals can cause foodborne illness. Food additives do not. In fact, they are either approved by the FDA prior to use or have GRAS or prior-sanctioned status based on a history of safe consumption.
2. (a) The danger zone is 40°F to 140°F.
3. (d) To prevent foodborne illness, it's important to employ proper food-handling strategies when cleaning, combating cross-contamination, cooking, and chilling the foods in your meal.
4. (e) *Listeria* can multiply at temperatures of 40°F or below.
5. (a) The IRS. The FDA, CDC, and USDA all play important roles in keeping the food supply safe.
6. (d) The "Best Used By" dated on the food container refers to the date by which to consume the product to enjoy it at its best quality.
7. (c) Sulfites and MSG are fine for most people but can cause unpleasant symptoms in people who are sensitive to them.
8. (a) Food additives help prevent spoilage, increase the shelf life of the product, and can enhance the flavor of foods.
9. (c) Sulfuric acid is not a naturally occurring toxin found in food products.
10. (a) Mercury occurs in nature, but is a by-product of industrial pollution. Mercury is transformed by bacteria in the water into the toxic form of methylmercury. Fish absorb methylmercury from the water or eat smaller fish that contain methylmercury and they bioaccumulate the substance to high levels.

Web Resources

- For food safety education for friends and family, visit www.fightbac.org
- For food safety tips for college students, visit www.fsis.usda.gov
- For foodborne illness fact sheets and food recalls, visit www.foodsafety.gov

Answers to True or False?

1. **False.** *Salmonella* is a bacterium, not a virus. To find out the most common virus that causes foodborne illness, turn to page 495.
2. **False.** An off smell in food is more likely a sign of food spoilage than that the food contains a pathogen that could cause foodborne illness. Unfortunately, a food that contains a disease-causing pathogen could smell perfectly fine. Turn to page 495 to find out more.
3. **False.** Running your hands under water for 10 seconds is not the correct way to wash your hands to reduce your risk of getting sick. To find out the correct method, turn to page 502.
4. **False.** It's not the color but rather the internal temperature of the chicken that will determine if it is safe to eat. Turn to page 505 to learn why color should not be used to determine if your food is safe to eat.
5. **True.** To be effective at keeping food safe, the temperature in your refrigerator should be 40°F or below. To find out why, turn to page 506.
6. **False.** Freezing doesn't kill bacteria, but only puts them in a dormant state. Find out what happens once the food is thawed on page 506.
7. **False.** Leftovers should be thrown out if they're not consumed within 3 to 5 days. To find out more about safe food storage, turn to page 507.
8. **False.** Irradiated food is treated with gamma rays that interrupt DNA and make cells unable to reproduce, thus killing harmful pathogens. It does not make foods radioactive. Learn more on page 513.
9. **False.** Package dates refer to food quality, not safety. To find out why consuming a food before the expiration date can't guarantee that the item is safe to eat, turn to page 514.
10. **True.** *E. coli* as well as other pathogens can be used in bioterrorism. To learn more, turn to page 521.

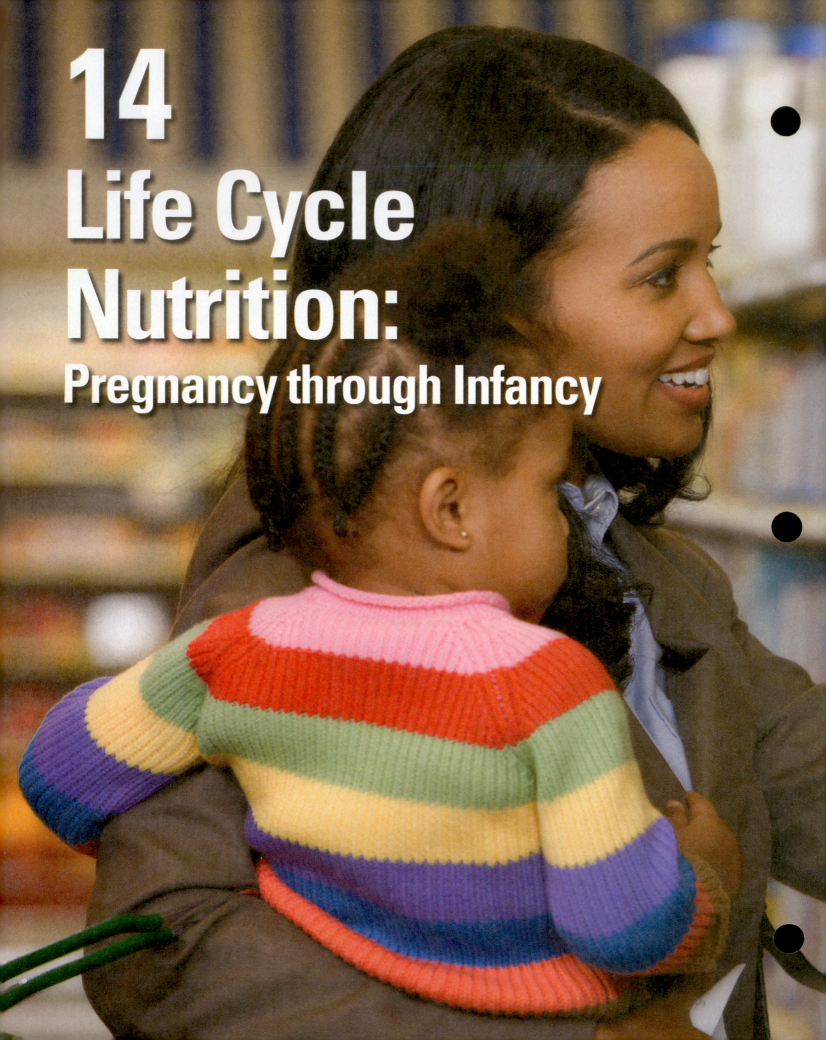

14
Life Cycle Nutrition:
Pregnancy through Infancy

True or False?

1. A father's health can impact the health of a developing fetus. T|F p. 528

2. Women who are obese may have more trouble becoming pregnant than women who are normal weight or only somewhat overweight. T|F p. 529

3. Morning sickness only happens before noon during the first trimester. T|F p. 533

4. Drinking red wine is healthy during pregnancy. T|F p. 537

5. Pregnant women should exercise through pregnancy. T|F p. 539

6. Infant formula is better for babies than breast milk. T|F p. 543

7. Chubby babies should be put on diets. T|F p. 552

8. Infants need dietary supplements. T|F p. 552

9. Commercial baby food is always less healthy than homemade. T|F p. 554

10. Raw carrots are a safe food for infants to help meet their need for vitamin A. T|F p. 555

See page 565 for the answers.

Learning Outcomes

After reading this chapter, you will be able to:

LO 14.1 Explain the importance of lifestyle factors, including diet, for both men and women and how they affect the likelihood of conception.

LO 14.2 Identify key nutrient needs for women and potential complications in the first trimester of pregnancy.

LO 14.3 Identify key nutrient needs for women and potential complications in the second trimester of pregnancy.

LO 14.4 Identify key nutrient needs for women and potential complications in the third trimester of pregnancy.

LO 14.5 List special concerns of younger and older mothers-to-be.

LO 14.6 Describe the benefits of breast-feeding.

LO 14.7 Identify key nutrient needs and lifestyle factors for breast-feeding women.

LO 14.8 Explain why formula can be a good alternative to breast milk.

LO 14.9 Discuss the nutritional needs of infants.

LO 14.10 Explain when and how solid foods may be introduced to infants.

When a woman is pregnant, her body facilitates the division, growth, and specialization of millions of new cells in her developing child. The raw materials for this rapid growth are provided by the nutrients she consumes in foods. Her diet, then, must not only maintain her own health, but also foster and maintain the health of her baby.

In this chapter, we will explore the specific nutrient requirements that a pregnant woman needs to ensure a healthy pregnancy. We'll also explore the diet and lifestyle factors in both the mother and father that can help ensure successful conception and healthy fetal development, as well as the nutritional needs and concerns of infants in their first year of life.

What Nutrients and Behaviors Are Important before Attempting a Healthy Pregnancy?

LO 14.1 Explain the importance of lifestyle factors, including diet, for both men and women and how they affect the likelihood of conception.

You're probably aware of at least a few things that women shouldn't do during pregnancy to support the baby's health. For instance, you probably know that pregnant women shouldn't smoke cigarettes or drink alcohol. But it might surprise you to learn that even before a couple attempt to get pregnant, they should both adopt some healthy behaviors, including several by the father-to-be. Let's review these now.

A Man's Diet and Lifestyle Affect the Health of His Sperm

The moment when a sperm fertilizes an egg is called **conception**. For conception to occur, the male's sperm has to be plentiful and motile—capable of "swimming" to the waiting egg. Thus, men who hope to father a child should take note: Their lifestyle and dietary habits may affect the number and motility of their sperm. Ⓣ Ⓕ Smoking cigarettes, abusing alcohol and drugs, and obesity have been associated with decreased production and function of sperm.[1] Stopping smoking, striving for a healthy body weight, drinking in moderation, and abstaining from drugs are all beneficial behaviors that promote conception.

As part of a healthy eating plan, an adequate intake of zinc and folate has been associated with the production of healthy sperm. In addition, antioxidants, such as vitamins E and C and carotenoids, may help protect sperm from damage by free radicals.[2] Men should make sure to eat a balanced diet that contains adequate amounts of fruits and vegetables (which provide antioxidants, vitamins, minerals, and folate), as well as whole grains and healthy protein foods, such as lean meats, fish, nuts, low-fat dairy foods, and legumes.[3] Men should avoid high intakes of saturated and *trans* fats as well as caffeine to promote sperm health.[4]

Women Need to Adopt a Healthy Lifestyle before Conception

If you have ever run a marathon or know someone who has, you know that a tremendous amount of effort and diligence goes into training for the event. Your commitment doesn't begin on the day of the race, but as far as a year in advance. In fact,

Are You Ready for a Healthy Pregnancy?

Both men and women should have healthy habits before becoming parents. Take the following self-assessment to see if you need some diet and lifestyle fine-tuning before trying to get pregnant.

For Both Men and Women

1. Are you overweight?

   Yes ☐ **No** ☐

2. Do you smoke cigarettes?

   Yes ☐ **No** ☐

3. Do you abuse alcohol?

   Yes ☐ **No** ☐

4. Do you consume less than 400 micrograms of folic acid daily?

   Yes ☐ **No** ☐

5. Do you use any illicit drugs such as marijuana, cocaine, or Ecstasy, or prescription painkillers?

   Yes ☐ **No** ☐

Additional Questions for Women Only

1. Do you drink alcohol?

   Yes ☐ **No** ☐

2. Do you take herb supplements or drink herbal teas?

   Yes ☐ **No** ☐

3. Do you drink more than 12 ounces of caffeinated coffee or energy drinks or four cans of caffeinated soft drinks daily?

   Yes ☐ **No** ☐

4. Do you eat albacore tuna, swordfish, mackerel, tilefish, and/or shark?

   Yes ☐ **No** ☐

Answers

If you answered yes to any of these questions, read on to find out how these diet and lifestyle habits can negatively affect a pregnancy.

---

the more time and effort the runner puts into preparing for the race, the better the results are likely to be.

Ask any woman who has had a baby, and she will tell you that planning, carrying, and delivering a healthy child was the marathon of her life. The commitment to change not-so-healthy behaviors is an extremely important part of prepregnancy preparation.

Let's look at the specific nutritional and lifestyle adjustments a woman needs to make to improve her chances of conceiving a healthy baby.

Attain a Healthy Weight

(T|F) Women who want to get pregnant should strive for the healthiest weight possible *before* conception. Women who begin pregnancy at a healthy weight are likely to conceive more easily, have an uncomplicated pregnancy,[5] and may have an easier time with breast-feeding.[6] Underweight women and overweight women may have a harder time getting pregnant, possibly because of irregular menstrual cycles. When they do become pregnant, they are at increased risk for fetal loss[7] and a variety of health problems, some of which can affect the baby.

Get Adequate Folic Acid

Folic acid is the synthetic form of the B vitamin, folate. Folate and folic acid are needed to create new cells and help the embryo grow and develop properly throughout pregnancy. During the first month after conception, consuming adequate folic acid plays a particularly important role in reducing the risk for neural tube defects (NTDs) in infants. NTDs, which include spina bifida, occur very early in pregnancy—when a woman may not know she is pregnant. For this reason, health experts recommend that all women who are capable of becoming pregnant should consume 400 micrograms of folic acid every day from dietary supplements, fortified foods, or both.[8]

conception The moment when a sperm fertilizes an egg.

Table 14.1

Fishing for a Healthy Baby

Pregnant and nursing women and women of childbearing age who may become pregnant should follow these guidelines for eating seafood:

Do Not Eat	Limit	Enjoy
• Shark • Swordfish • King mackerel • Tilefish (golden bass or golden snapper)	• Albacore (white) tuna to no more than 6 oz weekly • Locally caught fish from nearby lakes, rivers, and coastal areas. Check local advisories regarding its safety before consuming it. If no advice is available, eat up to 6 oz weekly. Don't consume any other fish during that week.	Up to 12 oz weekly of fish with low levels of methylmercury, such as: • Canned light tuna • Cod • Catfish • Crab • Pollock • Salmon • Scallops • Shrimp

Moderate Fish and Caffeine Consumption

The Food and Drug Administration (FDA) recommends that women of childbearing age who may become pregnant avoid certain fish that may contain high amounts of the toxin *methylmercury*. Methylmercury builds up in a woman's body and may be passed to an embryo during pregnancy. Methylmercury can harm the nervous system of a developing fetus, especially during the first trimester of pregnancy. Nearly all fish contain some methylmercury, but larger fish accumulate more of it in their bodies. **Table 14.1** summarizes the seafood consumption guidelines for women of childbearing age.

Caffeine consumption may affect a woman's fertility. Some research suggests that consuming 500 milligrams or more of caffeine daily may delay conception, but there is no definitive evidence that caffeine interferes with getting pregnant. Additionally, high daily caffeine intake may also contribute to miscarriage and growth restriction for the embryo.[9] Therefore, to be safe, women who are trying to conceive should consume fewer than 200 milligrams of caffeine per day.[10] This means limiting brewed coffee and energy drinks to no more than about 12 ounces a day—or better yet, switching to decaffeinated versions of these drinks. See **Table 14.2** for other common sources of caffeine in the diet.

Avoid Cigarettes and Other Toxic Substances

Cigarette smoking increases the risk of infertility, prolonging the time to conception.[11] If a female smoker is able to conceive, she'll face the difficulty of needing to quit smoking along with the many other challenges of pregnancy. The risks of maternal smoking are discussed later in this chapter.

Alcohol can affect an embryo within weeks of conception, before a woman is aware that she is pregnant. For this reason, the office of the Surgeon General has recommended that all women who may become pregnant abstain from alcohol.[12]

Smoking marijuana can reduce fertility in both men and women. Women who use marijuana should speak with their health care provider about how to stop. They can also access the National Drug and Alcohol Treatment Referral Routing Service through the National Institute on Alcohol Abuse and Alcoholism at www.niaaa.nih.gov.

Women should also avoid herbal supplements and teas, as no medicinal herbs have been established as safe in pregnancy, and even those that are generally safe in cooking can cause complications in highly concentrated supplements.[13] Some herbs are toxic in pregnancy, such as blue cohosh, so any women who routinely consumes herbs or herbal supplements should speak with their healthcare provider.

Now that you've learned which health habits are important to establish before trying to become parents, you and your partner might want to take the Self-Assessment to see if you're ready for a healthy pregnancy. Keep in mind that

Table 14.2

A Jolt of Caffeine

Beverage	Caffeine (mg)
Coffee, brewed, drip (8 oz)	85
"Energy" drinks (8 oz)	80
Espresso (1 oz)	40
Tea, brewed (8 oz)	40
Tea, iced (8 oz)	25
Soft drinks (8 oz)	24
Hot cocoa (8 oz)	6
Milk chocolate (1 oz)	6
Chocolate milk (8 oz)	5
Coffee, brewed, decaffeinated (8 oz)	3

The Stress of Infertility

Sofia and Matthew met in law school, and, because of their demanding careers, they put off having children. They are both 34 years old. After trying to get pregnant for a year, they scheduled an appointment with a fertility specialist. Before doing a physical exam with each of them, their fertility doctor, Dr. Baker, asks Sofia and Matthew to tell him a bit about their lifestyles. Sofia tells Dr. Baker that over the last year, she has been eating a healthy diet and has exercised at least four days per week. Sofia is taking a prenatal vitamin and has cut out alcohol, as they are eager to get pregnant. She does, however, continue to drink 4–5 cups of coffee each day, as she often works late into the night as a corporate lawyer. Matthew tells Dr. Baker that he has not really changed anything over the last year, as he has always thought that any issues getting pregnant would be due to Sofia and her reproductive health. Matthew also tells Dr. Baker that he has been really stressed at work recently, so he drinks 3–4 alcoholic beverages most nights of the week and does not eat a very healthy diet. During his exam, Dr. Baker remarks that Matthew's BMI is 31. Two weeks after their initial appointment, Dr. Baker calls Sofia and Matthew to discuss the results of their medical work-up. He reports that Matthew has a very low sperm count, which may be the reason why they have not been able to get pregnant. He explains that while all of Sofia's tests came back normal, she might benefit from some lifestyle changes.

Among American married women aged 35 to 39 years, who have never had a child before, as many as 39 percent have impaired fecundity (defined as physical difficulties getting pregnant or carrying a pregnancy to live birth). Among women aged 40 to 44, the prevalence of impaired fecundity increases to 47 percent. Among men age 25 to 44 years, 12 percent report struggling with fertility. Evidence supports that being overweight or obese, smoking cigarettes, and drug and alcohol use not only lower fertility in women, but also in men. Maintaining a healthy weight and following a healthy diet that is high in antioxidants found in fruits and vegetables can increase fertility for both men and women.

Think About It

In order to improve their chances of conceiving, Matthew and Sofia should make some lifestyle changes. If you were Dr. Baker, what would you recommend to each of them?

---

sometimes getting pregnant doesn't just happen; to read about one couple's struggles with conception, go to the Health Connection: A Case Study called "The Stress of Infertility." Then the next step is to learn about a woman's increased nutrition needs once she is pregnant.

LO 14.1 **The Take-Home Message** Good nutrition and healthy lifestyle habits are important for both men and women before conception. Smoking cigarettes, alcohol abuse, and obesity are associated with the decreased production and function of sperm. Conception is easier for women when they are at a healthy weight. Women should consume adequate amounts of folic acid prior to getting pregnant and throughout their pregnancy. Women should also avoid consuming fish that may contain high amounts of methylmercury and should consume caffeine only in moderation. They should not smoke cigarettes, drink alcohol, or use illicit drugs.

Virtual Stages of Pregnancy

For a summary of the developments during each stage of pregnancy, visit the pregnancy page at www.womenshealth.gov.

trimesters The three time periods of pregnancy.

embryo Term that refers to a fertilized egg during the third through the eighth week of pregnancy.

placenta The organ that allows nutrients, oxygen, and waste products to be exchanged between a mother and fetus.

umbilical cord Cord connecting the fetus to the placenta that allows the transfer of nutrients and waste products between the mother and the fetus.

fetus A developing embryo that is at least 8 weeks old.

What Nutrients and Behaviors Are Important in the First Trimester?

LO 14.2 Identify key nutrient needs for women and potential complications in the first trimester of pregnancy.

When a woman is pregnant, her diet must maintain her health and foster the health and growth of her baby. She is truly eating for two. To help you appreciate the increased nutrient needs during pregnancy, let's examine how a pregnancy begins and how the developing child obtains nutrients from the mother.

During the First Trimester, the Fertilized Egg Develops into a Fetus

A full-term pregnancy is approximately 40 weeks long and is divided into three **trimesters**. The moment of conception marks the beginning of the first trimester. During the first few days of this 13-week period, the fertilized egg travels down the fallopian tube to embed itself in the lining of the woman's uterus (**Figure 14.1**). This enables the developing **embryo** to obtain nutrients via the **placenta**, an organ of common tissue between the mother and the growing embryo that develops in the mother's uterus (**Figure 14.2**). The placenta is attached to the growing embryo via the **umbilical cord**. After the eighth week of pregnancy, the developing embryo is called a **fetus**. As the fetus develops, the mother's diet and lifestyle habits are critical in supporting and nurturing it.

By the end of the first trimester, the fetus's liver is already forming red blood cells, the heart is pumping blood, the limbs are taking shape, and the brain is

Conception	2 weeks	8 weeks	13 weeks
Zygote →	Preembryo →	Embryo →	Fetus

Figure 14.1 Fetal Development in the First Trimester
An embryo embeds itself into the uterine wall shortly after conception. After eight weeks, it is called a fetus.

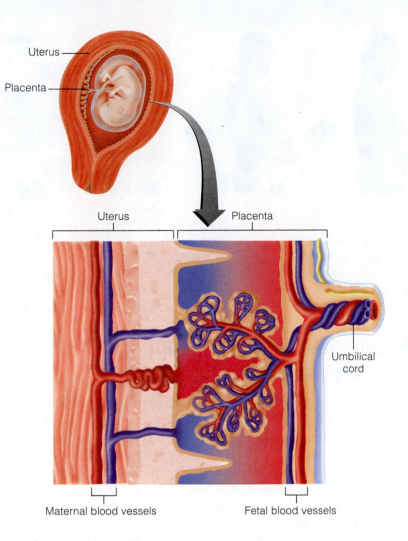

Figure 14.2 **The Placenta**
The placenta is the site of common tissue between the mother and the developing fetus where nutrients, oxygen, and waste products are exchanged.

Uterus

Placenta

Uterus

Placenta

Umbilical cord

Maternal blood vessels

Fetal blood vessels

growing rapidly. In spite of all the activity taking place, the fetus weighs just ½ ounce and measures about 3 inches long at this point. It has a lot more growing to do before being born.

"Morning Sickness" and Cravings Are Common

During the first trimester, the mother's body is also changing rapidly. She's beginning to notice some breast tenderness, a newly heightened sense of taste or smell, and perhaps some "morning sickness" or food cravings. One of the biggest myths of pregnancy is that morning sickness happens only in the morning. Ask any of the estimated 80 percent of women who experience nausea and vomiting during pregnancy and many will tell you that they wish their symptoms ended by noon. The cause of morning sickness is unknown, but fluctuating hormone levels may play a role.[14] There are no known dietary deficiencies that cause morning sickness, or diet changes that can prevent it. However, there are some behaviors that might help reduce it (see the Table Tips on "Alleviating Morning Sickness").

While some pregnant women develop an aversion to certain foods, such as coffee, tea, or fried or spicy foods, other women may have cravings for specific foods. Chocolate, citrus fruits, pickles, chips, and ice cream are foods that women commonly want when they are pregnant.[15] Sometimes women even crave and consume nonfood substances, such as cornstarch, clay, dirt, or baking soda, a condition called

Table TIPS

Alleviating Morning Sickness

Avoid fried and greasy foods.

Cook in areas with good ventilation to dissipate smells that can make you nauseated.

Try eating dry cereal or saltine crackers before getting out of bed in the morning.

Avoid large intakes of fluid in the morning.

Eat small, frequent meals that are high in carbohydrates, and avoid having an empty stomach.

Take prenatal vitamins with food. Cut pill in half; take half in morning and half before bed.

Figure 14.3 Components of Weight Gain during Pregnancy
Women who begin pregnancy at a healthy weight should gain between 25 and 35 pounds.

First trimester   Second trimester   Third trimester

Total weight gain 25–35 lbs
- Maternal fat stores (4–11 lbs)
- Uterus and breast (4 lbs)
- Blood (3–4 lbs)
- Fetus (7–8 lbs)
- Placenta, amniotic fluid, and other fluids (7–8 lbs)

pica. Experts are uncertain why pica occurs, but it may signal iron and zinc deficiencies in the diet. Women with the urge to eat nonfood items and large amounts of foods such as raw flour or cornstarch should tell their doctor immediately.[16]

Adequate Weight Gain Supports the Baby's Growth

Women who begin their pregnancies at a healthy weight are generally advised to gain 25 to 35 pounds (women having twins should gain between 37 and 54 pounds).[17] This is the approximate amount of weight needed to support the growth of the baby (**Figure 14.3**). The amount of weight an individual woman gains should be enough to ensure a healthy 6.5- to 8.5-pound baby, but not so much that she increases her risk for complications during delivery (see **Table 14.3**). Gaining excess weight will also make it more difficult to lose the weight once the baby is born, increases the likelihood of the mother's remaining overweight many years after childbirth, and also increases the risk that the baby will be obese later in life. While women may gain between 1 and 4.5 pounds during the first trimester, health experts do not suggest increasing calories during the first trimester.[18] However, pregnant women have an increased need for certain nutrients after conception.

The Need for Certain Nutrients Increases

From the moment of conception, a pregnant woman needs certain vitamins and minerals in higher quantities. Luckily, her body adjusts somewhat to help make this happen by increasing absorption of certain nutrients and slowing down digestion to allow for the increased absorption of others. Many of the increased nutrient requirements can be met easily through a healthy diet. However, the greater need for certain nutrients, including folate/folic acid, may not be achieved through food or increased absorption. Women who don't eat a balanced diet may also need additional iron, zinc, copper, calcium, and vitamin D.

Table 14.3

Recommended Weight Gain during Pregnancy

Body Mass Index (BMI) Prior to Conception	Recommended Weight Gain for a Single Baby* (in Pounds)	Recommended Rate of Weight Gain Weekly in the Second and Third Trimesters (Mean range in pounds)
< 18.5 kg/m² (Underweight)	28–40	1 (1.0–1.3)
18.5–24.9 kg/m² (Normal weight)	25–35	1 (0.8–1.0)
25.0–29.9 kg/m² (Overweight)	15–25	0.6 (0.5–0.7)
≥ 30.0 kg/m² (Obese)	11–20	0.5 (0.4–0.6)

Note: *Suggested weight gain is higher for multiple fetuses.

Let's examine these specific nutrients individually:

- *Folate/Folic acid.* If a woman is conscientious about consuming 400 micrograms of folic acid every day prior to conception and continues to take a dietary supplement and/or consume folic acid–fortified grains, in addition to eating foods rich in folate, she should be able to meet her increased needs for this vitamin. Foods high in folate include green leafy vegetables, legumes, and citrus fruits and juices.

- *Iron.* Pregnant women need extra iron to make additional red blood cells, prevent anemia, and provide for fetal growth and development. Although meat, fish, poultry, and enriched grains supply iron, the amount recommended during pregnancy is unlikely to be met from food alone, so an iron supplement is needed.[19] Many women take prescription and over-the-counter prenatal supplements with iron to help them satisfy their need for this mineral and other nutrients.

- *Zinc and copper.* Women who don't eat enough nutrient-rich foods may lack zinc and copper. Both of these minerals are key to a growing fetus's cell growth and development. An over the counter prenatal supplement can help fill in small dietary gaps in a mother's diet.

- *Calcium and vitamin D.* A pregnant woman absorbs more calcium from foods during pregnancy to offset the amount of calcium needed by the growing fetus, but she still needs to meet her own daily needs for calcium, as well as for vitamin D, to preserve bone mass and prevent osteoporosis later in life. One way to ensure adequate calcium and vitamin D intake is to drink milk or fortified orange juice, which are nutrient rich, rather than soda, juice beverages, and sports drinks, which are low in nutrients other than calories.

Prenatal supplements can help pregnant women meet their increased needs for iron, folic acid, and other essential nutrients.

Other nutrients, including omega-3 fatty acids, choline, and vitamin B_{12}, may be of concern during pregnancy, especially if the mother follows a vegetarian or vegan (a diet containing no animal products) diet.

Pregnant women who avoid seafood may not get enough of an omega-3 fat called docosahexaenoic acid (DHA). DHA is found in high concentrations in the brain and in the retina. The fetus accrues DHA rapidly during the second half of pregnancy and during the first two years of life.[20]

Choline, an essential nutrient, is important during pregnancy and breast-feeding. Choline is needed for healthy cells to divide and grow, especially in the brain.[21] Observational studies suggest choline may help to prevent neural tube defects, which occur in the first month of pregnancy.[22]

Vitamin B_{12} is necessary for healthy nerve and red blood cells and for the production of nucleic acids (DNA and RNA). Vitamin B_{12} is found naturally only in animal foods. Women who follow a vegan diet or who consume few or no animal foods may be at risk of vitamin B_{12} deficiency. They should make sure that to get adequate vitamin B_{12} from fortified foods, a dietary supplement, or both.

While it's important that pregnant women meet their nutrient needs, it is equally important that they not consume too much of some nutrients. Too much preformed vitamin A, found in dietary supplements and in certain foods, can be toxic and increase the risk for birth defects, especially when taken during the first trimester, a time when women may not realize they are pregnant. The Institute of Medicine recommends no more than 3,000 IU of vitamin A daily for pregnant women.[23]

Although vitamin and mineral supplements (multivitamins) are not suitable substitutes for a healthy diet at any time during the reproductive years, they are useful for filling nutrient gaps for nutrients that could affect pregnancy. Most prenatal supplements, including the over-the-counter variety that don't require a prescription, have higher levels of folic acid, iron, zinc, and calcium than regular supplements and may be a suitable choice for women who are at risk for not meeting their nutrient needs, including teens, women carrying multiple fetuses, older women, and women who did not eat an adequate diet before pregnancy or are not eating well during pregnancy.

To assist women in having healthy pregnancies, the USDA has created a program that personalizes dietary recommendations during pregnancy and lactation (available at www.choosemyplate.gov).[24] The site includes menu-planning tools that show how much and what women need to eat and provides links to additional topics and advice.

Figure 14.4 compares the nutrient needs of nonpregnant and pregnant women.

Figure 14.4 Nutrient Needs during Pregnancy
A balanced 2,000-calorie diet can meet most pregnant women's nutrient needs in the first trimester. They should add nutrient-rich foods to meet increased needs in their second and third trimesters.

Vegetables	Fruits	Grains	Protein	Dairy	Oils
2.5 cups	2 cups	6 oz eq	5.5 oz eq	3 cups	6 tsp

Nutrient	Recommended DRI for Nonpregnant Women Age 19–50 Years	Recommended Nutrient Intake during Pregnancy
Protein	46 g	71 g
Carbohydrates (minimum)	130 g	175 g
Dietary folate equivalents	400 µg	600 µg*
Thiamin	1.1 mg	1.4 mg
Riboflavin	1.3 mg	1.4 mg
Niacin equivalents	14 mg	18 mg
Vitamin B$_6$	1.3–1.5 mg	1.9 mg
Vitamin B$_{12}$	2.4 µg	2.6 µg
Vitamin C	75 mg	85 mg
Vitamin E	15 mg	19 mg
Vitamin A	700 µg	770 µg
Vitamin D	15 µg	15 µg
Calcium	1,000 mg	1,000 mg
Magnesium	310–320 mg	350–360 mg
Copper	900 µg	1,000 µg
Iron	18 mg	27 mg†
Phosphorus	700 mg	700 mg
Zinc	8 mg	11 mg
Calories	**2,000–2,200‡**	**§**

* Dietary supplements and/or fortified foods are recommended.
† Dietary supplements are usually needed to meet iron needs.
‡ Varies depending upon activity level and weight.
§ Add 340 calories/day in second trimester; 450 calories/day in third trimester.

Pregnancy Increases the Risk for Foodborne Illness

During pregnancy, a woman's immune system is weakened and the fetus's immune system is undeveloped, both of which set the stage for potential difficulties in fighting off pathogens that can cross the placenta. The bacterium *Listeria monocytogenes*, for example, may cause miscarriages, premature labor, low birth weight, developmental problems, and even infant death. Meat and dairy foods are most likely to be contaminated, but a variety of foods may contain *Listeria*. Pasteurization kills *Listeria*, which is why soft cheeses made from unpasteurized milk, such as Camembert, Brie, and blue cheeses, may be contaminated. Deli-style luncheon meats, salami, paté and other meat spreads, and smoked seafood may also harbor the bacteria. Pregnant women should avoid foods known to cause *Listeria* infection.

Raw meats and fish are more likely to carry pathogens and should be avoided during pregnancy. Sushi and sashimi, for example, contain raw fish, which are more likely to contain parasites or bacteria. Pregnant women should also avoid raw and undercooked meat, shellfish, and poultry; unpasteurized milk, cheeses, and juice; and raw sprouts, such as bean sprouts.

Food that may carry pathogens, such as sashimi and other undercooked animal foods, should be avoided by pregnant women for their own safety and the safety of the fetus.

Pregnant Women Should Avoid Many Other Substances

We noted earlier that smoking decreases the chance that a woman will conceive. When a woman continues smoking during pregnancy, her infant may weigh less than it should at delivery and has an increased risk of being born too soon or dying soon after birth. Prenatal exposure to cigarette smoke can also increase the risk for sudden infant death syndrome (SIDS)—the unexplained death of an infant less than one year of age—and may stunt the infant's growth. Even secondhand smoke can affect the health of a mom-to-be and her infant. Passive exposure to smoke can affect the infant's ability to grow properly.[25] Thus, pregnant women and new mothers should avoid secondhand smoke whenever possible.

The term fetal alcohol spectrum disorders (FASDs) describes a group of conditions that arise in infants whose mothers consume alcohol during pregnancy. The most severe effect of prenatal alcohol intake is fetal alcohol syndrome (FAS) in the baby, which you read about in Chapter 9. Children exposed to even low levels of alcohol during pregnancy can experience learning and behavioral disabilities later in life. Because there is no known safe level of alcohol consumption, pregnant women need to abstain completely to eliminate the chance of doing irreversible harm to their developing baby.

When used during pregnancy, illicit drugs, including marijuana, heroin, and prescription painkillers, can increase the risk for miscarriage, preterm labor, a **low birth weight baby**, and birth defects.[26] After birth, a baby exposed to illicit drugs in utero may experience drug withdrawal symptoms, such as excessive crying, trembling, and seizures, as well as long-term problems, including heart defects and behavioral and learning problems.

Pregnant women should restrict their intake of caffeine, which can be passed on to the fetus. Some research suggests that intakes greater than 200 milligrams (found in about 16 ounces of home-brewed coffee) daily may increase the risk for miscarriage. There is no conclusive evidence about how much caffeine during pregnancy is safe, but health experts advise pregnant women to limit their daily caffeine intake to 200 milligrams or less.[27]

As with smoking, drinking alcohol during pregnancy exposes the fetus to potentially toxic substances.

low birth weight baby A baby weighing less than 5½ pounds at birth.

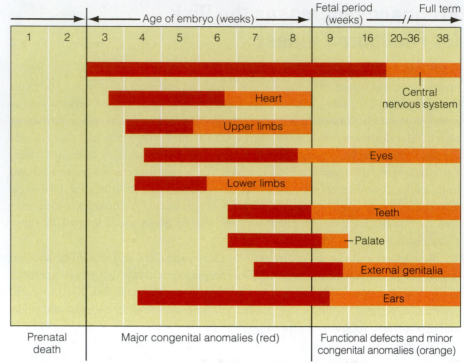

Figure 14.5 Critical Periods of Development
The damage caused by toxins or lack of nutrients during pregnancy can vary according to the stage of fetal development. Damage done during critical periods may be irreversible.

*Red indicates highly sensitive periods when teratogens may induce major anomalies.

The Importance of Critical Periods

The early part of pregnancy is when the main body systems and major organs are forming. Cells multiply, differentiate, and establish functional tissues and organs during various **critical periods** in the first trimester of pregnancy. During these times of rapid cellular activity, the embryo and the fetus are highly vulnerable to nutritional deficiencies, toxins, and other potentially harmful factors. It's also when the risk for spontaneous termination, also called miscarriage, is the greatest.

The harm that results from the influence of toxins, such as alcohol, or a nutrient deficiency, such as inadequate folic acid, during a critical developmental period is often irreversible and can affect health decades later (see **Figure 14.5**). For example, persons conceived during famines not only have a higher incidence of heart disease, but also an earlier onset of the condition. Inadequate fetal growth may have later, long-term effects on hypertension, glucose tolerance, and lipid metabolism. Further, inadequate maternal intake of calories, fat, protein, and a variety of vitamins and minerals may increase heart disease risk and time of onset in her child.[28] Poor iron intake in early pregnancy, when the central nervous system is starting to form, can also cause irreversible cognitive deficits.[29]

There is growing evidence that maternal nutrition can alter how genes are expressed during critical periods of gestation to permanently alter development.[30] This phenomenon is part of an emerging area of research about "fetal programming." The relationship between maternal nutrition and metabolic fetal programming is supported by studies showing that inadequate nutrient intakes during pregnancy may predispose the child to metabolic diseases in adulthood.[31] A mother's diet may even impact future generations.

LO 14.2 **The Take-Home Message** A pregnancy is divided into trimesters. During the first trimester, the fertilized egg develops into an embryo and eventually into a fetus. The placenta is the site of common tissue between the fetus and the mother, and is attached to the baby via the umbilical cord. Many women experience morning sickness,

critical periods Developmental stages during which cells and tissues rapidly grow and differentiate to form body structures.

food cravings, and food aversions during the first trimester. Women who begin pregnancy at a healthy weight should gain 25 to 35 pounds during pregnancy. Nutrient requirements, including folate, iron, and zinc, increase due to pregnancy. Pregnant women should avoid excess amounts of preformed vitamin A. They also need to avoid foods known to contain pathogens. Caffeine intake should be limited to no more than 200 milligrams daily. Tobacco, alcohol, and illicit drugs should be avoided throughout pregnancy but particularly in the first trimester. Potentially harmful toxins and other substances can cause irreversible damage to the fetus, especially during critical growth periods.

What Nutrients and Behaviors Are Important in the Second Trimester?

LO 14.3 Identify key nutrient needs for women and potential complications in the second trimester of pregnancy.

For many pregnant women, the nausea and fatigue of the first trimester subside during the second trimester, and appetite begins to improve. The baby is growing rapidly, and the mother's body is changing to accommodate this growth. The fetus is just under two pounds and measures about 13 inches long by the end of this trimester. During the second trimester, the mother should focus on consuming adequate calories and nutrients, participating in regular physical activity, and awareness of potential pregnancy complications.

Pregnant Women Need to Consume Adequate Calories, Carbohydrate, and Protein to Support Growth

Health experts advise pregnant women who begin their pregnancy at a healthy weight to consume 340 more calories per day during the second trimester than they did when not pregnant to support weight gain of about one pound per week. Pregnant women should choose nutrient-rich foods to get the additional calories they need. For example, a whole-wheat English muffin topped with peanut butter and paired with baby carrots supplies about 340 calories while providing complex carbohydrates, healthy fat, protein, fiber, iron, and zinc—nutrients that a woman needs more of during pregnancy (**Figure 14.6**).

Pregnant women require a minimum of 175 grams of carbohydrates per day (versus 130 grams for nonpregnant women) to provide the amount of glucose mom needs and to foster the growth and development of the embryo and fetus. Protein needs increase by about 35 percent, to about 71 grams daily, during the second and third trimesters, as you can see from Figure 14.4 on page 536. Women typically meet higher protein needs with a balanced diet.

Exercise Is Important for Pregnant Women

(T|F) Exercise during pregnancy is beneficial for improving the possibility of gaining weight within the targeted ranges.[32] It also helps to decrease minor aches and pains, lessen constipation, improve energy level, reduce stress, improve the quality of sleep, and reduce the risk for gestational diabetes.[33]

1 whole-wheat English muffin
2 tbs peanut butter
5 baby carrots

340 total calories

Figure 14.6 Adding Calories and Nutrients
The extra calorie needs and most increased nutrient needs of the second and third trimesters can be met with nutrient-rich foods.

Consult your health care provider before beginning an exercise program.

Begin slowly to avoid excessive fatigue and shortness of breath.

Exercise in the early morning or in the evening to avoid becoming overheated.

Drink plenty of fluids to stay hydrated.

Avoid any activity that involves lying on your back or puts you at risk for falling and other injuries to your abdomen.

Report any problems or unusual symptoms such as chest pains, contractions, dizziness, headaches, calf swelling, blurred vision, vaginal discharge or bleeding, and/or abdominal pain immediately to your health care provider.

Table 14.4

Safe and Unsafe Exercises during Pregnancy

Safe Activities	Unsafe Activities (Contact Sports and High-Impact Activities)
Walking	Hockey (field and ice)
Stationary cycling	Basketball
Low-impact aerobics	Football
Swimming	Soccer
Dancing	Gymnastics
	Horseback riding
	Skating
	Skiing (snow and water)
	Vigorous racquet sports
	Weight lifting

Healthy pregnant women should get at least 150 minutes (2 hours and 30 minutes) of moderate-intensity aerobic activity, such as brisk walking, each week. It's best to spread exercise over a 7-day period. Pregnant women who are healthy and already participate in vigorous-intensity aerobic activity, such as running, can continue provided they remain healthy and discuss adjustments in exercise with their health care provider as their pregnancy progresses.[34] Some forms of exercise are considered dangerous during pregnancy, however (**Table 14.4**). Pregnant women should check with their health care providers before exercising to see what type, and how much, is appropriate. See the Table Tips for more on exercising while pregnant.

Potential Complications: Gestational Diabetes and Hypertension

Sometimes a pregnant woman develops high blood glucose levels and is diagnosed with **gestational diabetes** (*gestation* = pregnancy-related). This type of diabetes occurs in an estimated 18 percent of pregnancies in the United States, typically toward the end of the second trimester or the early part of the third trimester.[35]

Though the cause of gestational diabetes is unknown, hormones from the placenta appear to lead to insulin resistance in the mother, which in turn causes hyperglycemia. Extra blood glucose crosses the placenta, stimulating the baby's pancreas to make more insulin, which leads to the storage of excess glucose as fat on the baby's body. Gestational diabetes can result in **macrosomia** (*macro* = large, *somia* = body), or a larger-than-normal baby. Large babies have an increased risk of shoulder injury during delivery and are more often born by Cesarean delivery. Gestational diabetes also increases the risk of the baby developing **jaundice**, breathing problems, and birth defects. Because the fetus produces extra insulin during pregnancy, this hormone is elevated after birth when the baby no longer has high levels of blood glucose, causing a rapid drop in blood glucose levels, which may lead to hypoglycemia.[36]

gestational diabetes Diabetes that occurs in women during pregnancy.

macrosomia A large baby, weighing more than 8 pounds, 13 oz.

jaundice A yellowish coloring of the skin due to the presence of bile pigments in the blood.

Certain factors can increase a woman's risk for gestational diabetes:

- Being overweight or obese
- Being over 25 years old
- Having a history of higher-than-normal blood glucose levels
- Having a family history of diabetes
- Being of Hispanic/Latina, African-American, American Indian, Alaska Native, Asian American, or Pacific Islander descent
- Having any of the following in a previous pregnancy: gestational diabetes, stillbirth, miscarriage, or large baby (weighing more than 9 pounds)
- Having polycystic ovary syndrome (PCOS) or another condition linked to problems with insulin
- Having ever had problems with insulin or blood glucose, such as insulin resistance, glucose intolerance, or prediabetes
- Having high blood pressure, high cholesterol, and/or heart disease

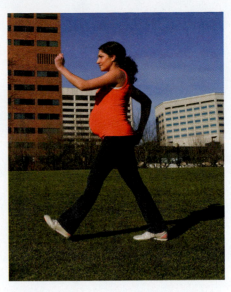

Walking is one form of exercise that is safe for most pregnant women. Regular exercise may help a pregnant woman maintain healthy blood glucose levels.

According to the National Institute of Child Health and Human Development, if a woman has two or more of these risk factors, she is at high risk for developing gestational diabetes and should contact her physician to be tested for the condition as soon as she knows she is pregnant. If she has one risk factor, she is at an average risk and should be tested for gestational diabetes between 24 and 28 weeks of her pregnancy. If she has no risk factors, she may not need testing for the condition.[37] Eating healthfully, gaining the appropriate pregnancy weight, and engaging in regular physical activity can help reduce the risk of developing diabetes during pregnancy.

Hypertension (high blood pressure) during pregnancy can damage the woman's kidneys and other organs and increase the risk for low birth weight and preterm delivery. **Pregnancy-induced hypertension** includes *gestational hypertension, preeclampsia,* and *eclampsia,* which vary in medical severity. Gestational hypertension is more likely to occur halfway through pregnancy and signal preeclampsia. Preeclampsia occurs when the pregnant woman has hypertension and her urine contains protein, which is a sign of damage to her kidneys. The cause of preeclampsia is not known. Preeclampsia is dangerous to the baby because it increases the risk of low birth weight babies, babies who are delivered early, and stillbirth. Women with hypertension prior to pregnancy or who developed it during a prior pregnancy, those who are obese, are under the age of 20 or over the age of 40, are carrying more than one baby, or have diabetes, kidney disease, rheumatoid arthritis, lupus, or scleroderma are at higher risk of developing preeclampsia. If left untreated, preeclampsia can lead to eclampsia, which can cause seizures in the mother and is a major cause of death of women during pregnancy.[38] The only cure for preeclampsia and eclampsia is to deliver the baby. However, delivery too early (before 32 weeks) is unsafe for the baby. Women are often confined to bed rest, managed with medications, and even hospitalized to treat preeclampsia until the baby can be safely born. Calcium supplements had been proposed to prevent preeclampsia, but research doesn't support that they reduce the risk, especially if the mother's diet is adequate in calcium. Some research suggests that antioxidants, specifically vitamins C and E, may reduce the risk, but more research is needed.[39]

LO 14.3 **The Take-Home Message** Pregnant women who begin pregnancy at a healthy weight need to consume about an additional 340 calories daily during the second trimester. A varied selection of nutrient-rich foods will help women meet most nutrient needs. Exercise can provide numerous benefits during pregnancy. Some women develop gestational diabetes and pregnancy-induced high blood pressure and need to be monitored closely by a health care professional to help manage these pregnancy complications.

pregnancy-induced hypertension A category of hypertension that includes *gestational hypertension* (occurs in pregnancy in a woman without a prior history of high blood pressure), *preeclampsia* (hypertension, severe edema, and protein loss occur), and *eclampsia* (can result in seizures; may be extremely dangerous for mother and baby).

What Nutrients and Behaviors Are Important in the Third Trimester?

LO 14.4 Identify key nutrient needs for women and potential complications in the third trimester of pregnancy.

At the end of the third trimester, the baby will weigh about 7 pounds, although healthy birth weights vary. Many pregnant women who conceived at a healthy weight should be eating 450 more calories each day than before pregnancy in order to gain about one pound per week.[40] A medium banana, whole-wheat English muffin with 2 tablespoons peanut butter, and a half cup of baby carrots supply about 450 calories.

As the growing baby exerts pressure on her intestines and stomach, and hormonal changes slow the movement of food through the gastrointestinal (GI) tract, pregnant women may experience heartburn and/or constipation. The large amount of iron in prenatal supplements and tendency toward less physical activity can also contribute to constipation. To minimize heartburn, pregnant women should eat frequent, small meals and avoid foods that may irritate the esophagus, such as spicy or highly seasoned foods. They should also avoid lying down after meals and elevate their heads during sleep. Eating more fiber-rich foods, along with drinking plenty of fluids, can help prevent and manage constipation.

Pregnancy also makes a woman more prone to hemorrhoids, in part because the growing uterus puts pressure on the pelvic veins and the large vein on the right side of the body that receives blood from the lower limbs. The increased pressure can slow the return of blood from the lower half of the body, which causes the veins below the uterus to become swollen. Straining to have a bowel movement because of constipation is also a cause of hemorrhoids.

LO 14.4 **The Take-Home Message** During the third trimester, women who begin pregnancy at a healthy weight need to eat 450 calories more per day than when not pregnant and should continue gaining about a pound per week. Heartburn and constipation commonly occur during the third trimester. Eating smaller meals and consuming more fiber can help.

What Special Concerns Might Younger or Older Mothers-to-Be Face?

LO 14.5 List special concerns of younger and older mothers-to-be.

Pregnancy and childbirth place demands on the body of a mother-to-be no matter what her age, but women who become pregnant during their teenage years face particular challenges. Women over the age of 35 also face some additional challenges.

A teenage girl's body is still growing, so she has higher nutrient needs than does an adult woman. In addition, teenage girls, like many adolescents, are more likely to eat on the run, skip meals, eat less-nutrient-dense snacks, and consume inadequate amounts of whole grains, fruits, vegetables, and lean dairy products. Pair this lower-nutrient diet to the increased needs of pregnancy, and these young girls are likely to fall short of many of their nutrient requirements, especially iron, folic acid, calcium, and potentially even calories. In some cases, a teenage girl may delay prenatal care because she is in denial of the pregnancy or fears telling others. She may also restrict her calorie intake to avoid weight gain as she attempts to hide her pregnancy.

Teenage mothers are also more likely to develop pregnancy-induced hypertension and deliver preterm and low birth weight babies, putting the baby at risk for health problems. They are more likely to engage in unhealthy lifestyle habits such as smoking, drinking alcohol, and taking illicit drugs, all of which can compromise the baby's health, as well as the mother's.[41]

Women who delay pregnancy until their 30s or beyond may also face additional challenges. Fertility typically begins to decline starting in a woman's early 30s, so conception may take longer. Women are not only at higher risk of having diabetes and high blood pressure after the age of 35, but also are at a greater risk of developing these conditions during pregnancy. Older mothers are also more likely to conceive multiples. Multiples are more likely to be born preterm, and, as a result, are at greater risk for low birth weight and medical complications.

Older mothers should try to achieve a healthy body weight prior to conception, avoid smoking, eat a balanced diet before and during pregnancy, and, like all potential mothers, consume adequate amounts of folic acid. Women over the age of 35 who may conceive should work closely with their doctors to manage health conditions, such as high blood pressure, to the best of their ability. As with all pregnant women, they should limit their caffeine intake and avoid alcohol and illicit drugs.

Regardless of age, as her due date draws near, an expectant mother needs to decide how to nourish her newborn after delivery: Should she breast-feed or use infant formula? Let's look at both of these options next.

Due to additional steps taken to ensure pregnancy, older mothers more often deliver multiples—twins, triplets, or quads—than do younger women.

LO 14.5 **The Take-Home Message** Teens who become pregnant are at higher risk of developing hypertension and delivering a premature and low birth weight baby. Because a teen is still growing, she may have a harder time satisfying her own nutrient needs and her baby's unless she is diligent about eating a well-balanced diet. Women over age 35 may have more difficulty conceiving and are at higher risk for high blood pressure and diabetes during pregnancy.

What Is Breast-Feeding and Why Is It Beneficial?

LO 14.6 Describe the benefits of breast-feeding.

A woman who has just given birth will begin a period of **lactation**; that is, her body will produce milk to nourish her new infant. Milk production is initially driven by hormonal changes following the delivery of the placenta and is subsequently stimulated by the infant's suckling at the mother's nipple. Signals sent from the nipple to the mother's brain prompt the release of two hormones: prolactin and oxytocin. Prolactin causes milk to be produced in the breast, while oxytocin causes the milk to be released in a **let-down response**, so the infant can receive it through the nipple (see **Figure 14.7**).[42]

The old adage "breast is best" when it comes to nourishing an infant is still true. The American Academy of Pediatrics recommends exclusive breast-feeding for the first six months of the baby's life for most women.[43] Through **breast-feeding**, or

Newborn babies may eat as often as 12 times a day!

lactation The production of milk in a woman's body after childbirth, and the period during which it occurs.

let-down response The release of milk from the mother's breast to feed the baby.

breast-feeding The act of feeding an infant milk from a woman's breast.

Figure 14.7 The Let-Down Response

Hypothalamus

2 Hypothalamus stimulates the release of prolactin and oxytocin

Pituitary

1 Sucking stimulates nerve that sends signal to mother's hypothalamus

3 Prolactin triggers milk production and oxytocin triggers the let-down response

nursing, mothers provide easily digestible food that is uniquely tailored to meet their infant's nutritional needs. Breast-feeding also provides many other advantages for both the mother and the baby.

Breast-Feeding Provides Physical, Emotional, and Financial Benefits for Mothers

Breast-feeding provides short- and long-term benefits for both mother and child. During infancy, breast-feeding can be cheaper, safer, and more convenient than infant formula. The long-term health and emotional benefits of breast-feeding can last for years after infancy.

Breast-Feeding Helps with Pregnancy Recovery and Reduces the Risk of Some Chronic Diseases

In addition to stimulating the release of breast milk, the hormone oxytocin stimulates contractions in the uterus, which helps the organ return to its pre-pregnancy size and shape. Breast-feeding also reduces blood loss in the mother after delivery, and may help some women return to their prepregnancy weight.[44] Observational studies suggest that the longer women breast-feed, the lower the risk for premenopausal breast cancer and ovarian cancer. Breast-feeding may also reduce a woman's risk of hip fractures later in life, as well as her risk of type 2 diabetes.[45]

Breast-feeding, especially if it is done exclusively (not in combination with formula-feeding), can also help delay the return of the menstrual cycle, which may decrease fertility. However, this does not mean that women who breast-feed their newborns should assume they won't get pregnant. They still need to take precautions if they wish to avoid pregnancy.

Breast Milk Is Less Expensive and More Convenient than Formula

Making breast milk costs significantly less than using infant formula to nourish a baby. Feeding a baby infant formula may cost $2,000 or more, depending on the formula, during the first year of life. The cost associated with the extra food required to promote breast-feeding, estimated at a minimum of $300 yearly, is significantly less than infant formula.[46]

There are other costs associated with formula-feeding beyond the price of the product. There are substantial environmental costs of dealing with the millions of formula containers and hundreds of thousands of pounds of paper packaging and waste that are disposed of in landfills each year. Health care costs are higher, too. One study concluded that if 90 percent of mothers breast-fed their children exclusively for the first six months of life, the United States would save $13 billion dollars a year, the majority of it in medical costs.[47] Finally, there are time costs associated with formula-feeding, whereas breast milk is always sterile and at the right temperature, and there isn't any need to prepare or clean bottles. Thus, for the family, environment, and society as a whole, breast-feeding is relatively less expensive all around than formula-feeding.

Breast-Feeding Promotes Bonding

The close interaction between mother and child during nursing promotes a unique bonding experience. The physical contact helps the baby feel safe, secure, and emotionally attached to the mother.

Breast-Feeding Provides Nutritional and Health Benefits for Infants

There are more than 200 compounds in breast milk that benefit infants. Numerous research studies have indicated that breast-feeding provides nutritional and health advantages that can last years beyond infancy.

Breast Milk Is Best for an Infant's Unique Nutritional Needs

The nutritional composition of breast milk changes as the infant grows. Right after birth, a new mother produces a carotenoid-rich, yellowish fluid called **colostrum** that has little fat but a lot of protein, vitamin A, and minerals. Colostrum also contains antibodies that help protect the infant from infections, particularly in the digestive tract.

Four to seven days after birth, breast milk production begins in earnest. Breast milk is high in lactose, fat, and B vitamins, and lower in fat-soluble vitamins, sodium, and other minerals. These nutrients are balanced to enhance their absorption. Breast milk is relatively low in protein so as not to stress the infant's immature kidneys with excessive amounts of nitrogenous waste products from protein digestion. The protein is also mostly in the form of alpha-lactalbumin, which is easier for the infant to digest. The nutrient composition of breast milk continues to change as the baby grows and his or her needs change.[48]

colostrum The fluid that is expressed from the mother's breast after birth and before the development of breast milk.

Breast-Feeding Protects Against Infections, Allergies, and Chronic Diseases and May Enhance Brain Development

Breast milk provides the infant with a disease-fighting boost as his or her immune system matures. Research supports that breast-feeding decreases the risk and severity of diarrhea and other intestinal disorders, respiratory infections, meningitis, ear infections, and urinary tract infections.[49] One protein in breast milk, lactoferrin, protects the infant against infection from a variety of bacteria, and viruses. Breast milk also contains the antioxidants, hormones, enzymes, and growth factors that help a child's immune system to grow and develop properly.[50]

Breast-feeding, especially if continued beyond six months, may help reduce the risk of childhood obesity. The reason for this isn't clear, but could be associated with the tendency of breast-fed infants to gain less weight during the first year of life than formula-fed infants. The lower weight gain may be due to breast-fed infants having more control over when they start and stop eating than their bottle-fed counterparts.[51] Babies at the breast may be allowed by their mothers to rely more on their internal cues to eat until they are full, and then stop eating, which may influence food intake later in life.

Lastly, breast milk may help infants with their intellectual development. The breast milk of mothers that consume an adequate diet provides two unsaturated fatty acids, docosahexaenoic acid (DHA) and arachidonic acid (AA), which are important for the development of the central nervous system, particularly the brain (see Chapter 5). The levels of these fatty acids vary in the mother's diet, and, therefore, in her breast milk. Research suggests that breast-fed infants may have greater cognitive function, measured by IQ and academic success in school through adolescence, than formula-fed babies, which may be due in part to DHA and AA.[52] DHA and AA are added in varying amounts to nearly all infant formula sold in the United States.

The breast-fed infant doesn't always need to consume breast milk directly from the breast. Milk can be pumped, or expressed, with a breast pump, refrigerated, and fed to the baby in a bottle by another caregiver at any time. This allows the mother to work outside the home or enjoy a few hours "off duty." The Nutrition in the Real World feature "Breast-Feeding at Work Can Work" addresses the challenges faced by nursing mothers who work outside the home. Fresh expressed breast milk should be refrigerated within 3 to 6 hours and used within three days, or stored in the freezer for up to six months. Breast milk should be stored in the back of the freezer, where there is less temperature fluctuation and it is less likely to defrost. Premature defrosting increases the risk of harmful bacteria multiplying.

LO 14.6 **The Take-Home Message** Breast-feeding provides numerous benefits for women and babies. It may help mothers return to their prepregnancy weight faster and reduce the risk of certain cancers, osteoporosis, and type 2 diabetes. Breast-feeding is the least expensive and most convenient way to nourish an infant, and helps the mother and baby to bond. Human milk is rich in nutrients, antibodies, and other compounds not available in formula that can protect the baby against infections, allergies, and chronic diseases, and may enhance the child's cognitive development. Women are advised to breast-feed exclusively for the first six months, and then breast-feed to supplement solid food through the rest of the first year.

Women can express breast milk using a breast pump and store the milk in the refrigerator or freezer for later use.

For many women, the decision to breast-feed their infants is an easy one. The bigger challenge is how to juggle breast-feeding with returning to work or school.

Women often feel uncomfortable about breast-feeding outside the home, especially in the workplace, and it's no wonder. Most companies don't offer support for working mothers, even though employer support for breast-feeding can extend the duration that a mother nurses her baby, which benefits both mother and child.[1] Sometimes, women have to choose between breast-feeding and a paycheck. But the attitude toward supporting breast-feeding mothers in the workplace is improving, albeit slowly. For example, in 1998, the state of Minnesota mandated that its companies aid and support breast-feeding moms. From 1998 to 2002, the percentage of women still breast-feeding at six months more than doubled within the state.[2] Forty-five

states, the District of Columbia, and the Virgin Islands have laws that specifically allow women to breast-feed in any public or private location, and 24 states, the District of Columbia, and Puerto Rico have laws related to breast-feeding in the workplace.[3]

Women who return to work while lactating require minimal worksite resources to accommodate their breast-feeding efforts. First, they need adequate break times and access to a private, comfortable room with an electrical outlet in order to pump their breast milk. They need a sink for cleaning their hands and the pumping equipment, and a refrigerator that runs at 40°F or below for storing expressed milk.

Worksite support of breast-feeding women is not only healthy for the infant but, in many ways, better for the corporate bottom line. Lactation support programs at work help to lower medical costs and health insurance costs for breast-feeding women and their infants,

and promote employee morale and loyalty to the company.[4] It is estimated that each $1 invested in a corporate breast-feeding program saves the company $2 to $3.[5]

What Are the Best Dietary and Lifestyle Habits for a Breast-Feeding Mother?

LO 14.7 Identify key nutrient needs and lifestyle factors for breast-feeding women.

During the first six months of breast-feeding, the mother produces about 24 ounces of breast milk daily and about 16 ounces a day during the second six months of breast-feeding. During this period, her body needs additional amounts of fluid and nutrients.

To meet her increased fluid needs, a breast-feeding woman should drink about 13 cups of water and beverages daily. It takes 500 calories a day to produce milk during the first six months of lactation. A combination of energy liberated from stored fat, and calories from food, provide the necessary fuel to make milk. Approximately 170 calories are mobilized daily from fat that was stored during pregnancy. A nursing woman who began her pregnancy at a healthy weight and gained a healthy amount of pregnancy weight needs just 330 more calories from food every day than when she was not pregnant.[53] Overweight and obese women and women who gained too much weight during pregnancy may not need to consume additional calories when breast-feeding, but need to eat a nutrient-rich diet.[54]

Practical Nutrition VIDEO

Take Care When Eating Fish

In many ways, nursing mothers are still "eating for two" so they need to be careful not to consume toxins. Joan spells out the guidelines for safe consumption of fish to avoid excess methylmercury. Scan this QR code with your mobile device to access the video. You can also access the video in MasteringNutrition™.

During the second six months of breast-feeding, fewer calories (theoretically) are available from stored body fat, so a lactating woman at a healthy weight prior to pregnancy needs to consume about 400 extra calories daily to meet her needs.[55] Although a breast-feeding woman's dietary carbohydrate, vitamin, and mineral requirements increase slightly, a well-balanced diet similar to the one she consumed during pregnancy will meet her needs. Lactating women who avoid or underconsume animal foods should make sure that they consume adequate amounts of vitamin B_{12}, iron, and zinc from dietary supplements, fortified foods, or a combination.

Anything that goes into a breast-feeding mother's body can potentially pass into her breast milk, and ultimately to her baby. Illicit drugs, such as cocaine, heroin, and marijuana, for example, can be transferred to a breast-fed infant and cause harm. Methylmercury, which a mother can overconsume if she doesn't avoid certain fish, can also be harmful. Nursing mothers should adhere to the FDA's guidelines about fish to minimize the infant's exposure, and her own, to methylmercury (see Table 14.1 on page 530).

A small amount of caffeine is transferred into breast milk, but caffeine consumption is generally considered safe for breast-feeding women. Coffee should be limited to no more than three cups daily, and possibly less, depending on how your child reacts, because caffeine can interfere with the baby's sleep and cause crankiness.[56]

Alcohol is transferred to breast milk and is capable of slowing infant growth. It also inhibits milk production and availability to the baby. An occasional drink when lactating probably presents little risk to a nursing child, but mothers should discuss alcohol consumption with their health care provider. The nicotine from cigarette smoking passes into breast milk and has been linked to decreased milk production and decreased weight gain in nursing infants.[57]

Breast milk can also reflect the foods a mother eats, and babies may become fussy if the mother has consumed certain spicy or gassy foods, such as garlic, beans, and broccoli. The mother can stop eating the food, wait a few days, and then try it again in her diet. If the infant reacts the same way, it's best to stop eating that food while nursing. If the mother's diet becomes too restrictive, she needs to consult with a registered dietitian nutritionist to tailor a diet that works to nourish her body and her baby's.

LO 14.7 **The Take-Home Message** A nursing mother who began her pregnancy at a healthy weight and gained the recommended pregnancy pounds needs to consume about 330 calories more daily during the first six months of lactation than she did when not pregnant and an extra 400 calories daily during the second six months. She needs to increase her fluid and nutrient intake to help her body produce breast milk. Anything a woman consumes can be passed on to her baby in breast milk, so nursing mothers should avoid all illicit drugs, caffeine, and smoking, and speak with their doctor about the use of alcohol.

When Is Infant Formula a Healthy Alternative to Breast Milk?

LO 14.8 Explain why formula can be a good alternative to breast milk.

If the infant isn't going to be breast-fed, the only other healthy option is infant formula. For some women, the choice is a personal preference. For others, breast-feeding may not be possible due to illness or other circumstances, and formula-feeding is necessary.

Some Women May Not Be Able to Breast-Feed

Women who are infected with HIV (human immunodeficiency virus), the virus that causes AIDS (acquired immune deficiency syndrome), should not breast-feed, as this virus can be transmitted to the child through breast milk. Women who have AIDS, human T-cell leukemia, active tuberculosis, are receiving chemotherapy and/or radiation, or use illicit drugs such as marijuana and cocaine should not breast-feed either. (Note: For HIV-infected women living in countries where there is inadequate food, an unsafe food supply, and/or frequent incidences of nutritional deficiencies and infectious diseases, the benefits of providing the infant with nutrient- and immune-rich breast milk may outweigh the risks of HIV infection for the baby.) An infant born with a genetic disorder called galactosemia can't metabolize lactose and shouldn't be breast-fed.[58] Lastly, any woman taking prescription or over-the-counter medications should check with her health care provider to ensure that they are safe to consume while breast-feeding.

Formula Can Be a Healthy Alternative to Breast-Feeding

The best alternative to breast-feeding is to feed an infant with a commercially made formula. Cow's milk should not be used to feed infants because it can't meet a baby's nutritional needs. Cow's milk is more difficult for the infant to digest, and even the full-fat variety is too low in total fat and the essential fatty acid linoleic acid, and too high in sodium and potassium. Also, the iron in cow's milk is poorly absorbed, and to make matters worse, cow's milk can cause intestinal blood loss in infants, which will cause iron loss and, possibly, anemia.[59]

Infant formula is developed to be as similar as possible to breast milk (see Table 14.5), and formula-fed infants grow and develop normally. The FDA regulates all infant formulas sold in the United States and has set specific requirements for the nutrients that the formula must contain.

Infant formula is available in several forms and varies in cost and ingredients. Infant formula is highly regulated by the FDA, so any formula on the market in the United States is considered safe.

Table 14.5

Nutritional Similarities between Infant Formula and Breast Milk

Nutrient	Amount in Breast Milk	Amount in Formula
Protein (g/100 ml)	1.1	1.8
Fat (g/100 ml)	4	4.8
Carbohydrate (g/100 ml)	7	7.3
Sodium (mg/100 ml)	1.3	0.7
Calcium (mg/100 ml)	22	53
Phosphorus (mg/100)	14	38
Iron (mg/100 ml)	0.03	0.1
Zinc (mg/100 ml)	3.2	5.1
Vitamin D (IU/100 ml)	4	41

Infant formula is typically made from cow's milk that has been altered to improve its nutrient content and digestibility. Soy protein–based formulas are free of cow's protein and lactose and can be used for infants who can't tolerate cow's milk protein–based formula or who are vegetarians. **Hypoallergenic infant formulas** are available for infants who can't consume cow's milk or soy formulas. The AAP and the American Academy of Family Physicians recommend that all formula-fed infants consume iron-fortified formulas to reduce the risk of iron deficiency.[60]

Formula can be purchased as powder, as a concentrated liquid, or as the ready-to-use variety. Powdered formula is the least expensive form and the ready-to-use form tends to be the most expensive. Care should be taken to mix the powdered or concentrated liquid with the correct amount of water so the formula will not be too diluted or too concentrated. (Water does not need to be treated by boiling first unless the infant's immune system is compromised.)

If the infant doesn't finish a formula bottle, it should be discarded rather than saved for another feeding. The bacteria in the infant's mouth can contaminate the formula and multiply to levels that could be harmful even if the formula is reheated. Reheating of infant formula can destroy some of the heat-sensitive nutrients. Also, formula should not be left out at room temperature for more than two hours, as any bacteria present can multiply to unhealthy levels.

Note that infants should not be allowed to sleep with a bottle containing milk, formula, or other sugary liquids (such as fruit juice, soda, or other sweetened drinks), as this practice can potentially lead to ear infections and to **early childhood caries** (see **Figure 14.8**). Liquids from bottles tend to pool in the mouth during sleep. The normal bacteria in the mouth change the sugar to an acid, which gradually dissolves the immature enamel and allows tooth decay to occur. The American Academy of Pediatric Dentistry recommends avoiding putting infants to sleep with bottles filled with sugar-containing beverages, among other strategies for reducing early childhood caries.[61]

LO 14.8 **The Take-Home Message** If a woman doesn't breast-feed, commercial iron-fortified infant formula is the only other healthy option. Cow's milk should not be offered before age one, as it is too high in protein and some minerals and too low in calories and fat. Powdered and concentrated infant formulas must be mixed carefully so they are not too diluted or concentrated for the baby's digestive system. Infants should never be given a bottle as they are put down to sleep, as this can lead to tooth decay and ear infections.

What Are the Nutrient Needs of an Infant and Why Are They So High?

LO 14.9 Discuss the nutritional needs of infants.

Whereas parents and caregivers can be confident that breast milk and commercial formulas are meeting their infants' unique nutritional needs, they would benefit from knowing exactly what those nutrient needs are, and what causes them to be so high. Let's explore these topics next.

Figure 14.8 Early Childhood Caries When infants are given a bottle shortly before sleep, the sugary beverage can pool in the mouth and dissolve developing tooth enamel, causing early childhood dental caries.

hypoallergenic infant formulas Specially developed formulas for infants who have food allergies and cannot tolerate regular formula.

early childhood caries Tooth decay from prolonged contact with formula, milk, fruit juice, or other carbohydrate-rich liquid offered to an infant in a bottle.

Infants Grow at an Accelerated Rate

During a child's **infancy**, or first year of life, he experiences a tremendous amount of growth. In fact, an infant doubles his birth weight by increase by 50 percent about 6 months of age, and triples it by the age of 12 months. Length will increase by 50 percent around the end of the first year as well. Let's try to imagine the physical growth of an infant in adult terms. On January first, you weigh 100 pounds. Around the month of June, you have grown to 200 pounds. By New Year's Eve, you would weigh 300 pounds! You would have to eat an enormous amount of food every day to actually make this happen. For an infant, though, this is a normal growth rate.

Infants are doing much more than just getting heavier and longer. Intellectual and social developments are also under way. As time goes by, infant communication skills go beyond crying, and at around three months of age a baby usually starts to smile. Preferences also become clearer: for particular people (such as the mom), for specific activities (getting kisses or being held), and for certain foods (such as mashed bananas).

An infant should reach certain stages of physical development within a distinct time frame. If an infant is not growing in the expected fashion, this may be a sign that something is wrong. Parents, caregivers, and health care providers need to be alert to infants who miss milestones and then look more deeply into the situation. The child may not be receiving sufficient nutrition. Perhaps an infant has a poor appetite, and the new mom has no idea that the child should be eating more frequently. Maybe an infant is having some digestive problems, and the new day care provider does not mention the frequency of dirty diapers.

Of course, optimal infant nutrition is sometimes hindered by circumstance. In less developed countries where poverty is the norm and food is scarce, problems such as protein-energy malnutrition (see Chapter 6) are common. Even in developed countries, such as the United States, there are problems with poor infant nutrition that may affect growth. For example, iron-deficiency anemia (see Chapter 8) sometimes occurs in infants when caregivers substitute juice or cow's milk for adequate amounts of breast milk or iron-fortified formula. Breast-fed infants who don't begin to consume iron-fortified foods, such as puréed meats and fortified cereals, at around 6 months may also have low iron levels in their blood, which may result in iron deficiency and iron-deficiency anemia.

Monitoring Infant Growth

An infant who does not receive adequate nutrition (whether in terms of quantity or quality) may have difficulty reaching developmental **milestones** (**Figure 14.9**). Think of developmental milestones as checkpoints, which can be physical, social, or intellectual. While most parents do not know the specific nutrient needs of their infant, it's important that the infant attain the specific milestones at the appropriate time. This assures parents that they are providing the right amount and type of nourishment.

If a child doesn't reach the appropriate milestones, he or she may eventually develop a condition called failure to thrive (FTT). A child with FTT is delayed in physical growth or size or does not gain enough weight. Poor appetite, an unbalanced diet, or a medical problem that has not yet been diagnosed can all be causes of FTT. Sometimes, FTT results from inappropriate care or neglect. Caregivers and health care providers need to be aware of the signs of this condition and watch for those signs in their children and patients.

infancy The age range from birth to 12 months.

milestones Objectives or significant events that occur during development.

Figure 14.9 Foods for Baby's First Year
During the first year after birth, as developmental milestones are being met, an infant's diet will progress from breast milk or infant formula to age-appropriate versions of family meals.

Foods	Breast milk or iron-fortified formula	Pureed or strained meat, vegetables, or fruit / Iron-fortified infant cereal	Pureed or strained vegetables, fruit, and meat or beans / Plain yogurt	Mashed or chopped food from family meal
Age (in months)	0–4	4–6	6–9	9–12
Infant milestones	Suckles	Controls head movements	Sits with support; sweeps food from spoon with upper lip	Chews and swallows lumpier foods	Feeds self; drinks from a cup

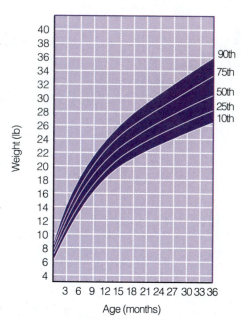

Figure 14.10 Growth Chart
Growth charts can help determine if a child is growing at a healthy rate for his or her age.

growth charts Series of percentile curves that illustrate the distribution of selected body measurements in U.S. children.

percentile The most commonly used clinical indicator to assess the size and growth patterns of children in the United States. An individual child is ranked according to the percentage of the reference population he equals or exceeds.

In addition to milestones, parents and health care providers use **growth charts** to track physical development. Typically, measures of head circumference, length, weight, and weight for length are used to assess growth. These measures are taken at each "well-check" visit to the health care provider, about once a month for the first year. The information obtained from the measurements is plotted on the growth chart, placing the child into a **percentile**. Percentiles rank the infant with regard to other infants of the same age in a reference group. For example, a four-month-old who is in the 25th percentile for weight for age weighs less than 75 percent of the four-month-olds and weighs the same as or more than 25 percent (see **Figure 14.10**).[62]

Infants Have Higher Nutrient Needs

Because they are growing rapidly, infants have a greater need for many nutrients, based on weight, including calories. For example, a 6-month-old boy requires about 82 calories for every kilogram (kg) of body weight.[63] A 35-year-old adult sedentary male who weighs 154 pounds needs about 34 calories per kilogram to maintain his weight.[64] As infants grow, their needs for carbohydrate and protein increase. Fat is a concentrated source of energy and should not be limited during infancy, and neither should overall calories. Doing so may restrict a child's physical and mental development.

Several nutrients in particular are important for an infant's health and well-being. As you recall from Chapter 7, all infants should receive an injection of vitamin K at birth to ensure that their blood clots properly. Vitamin K is produced by the bacteria in the gut. Infants are born with a sterile gut, so giving vitamin K at birth provides the infant with the vitamin K he needs until he is able to produce his own.[65]

The amount of vitamin D in breast milk is not enough to prevent rickets, so infants should receive 400 IU of vitamin D drops daily starting within the first few days of life. (Fortified infant formula contains adequate levels of vitamin D.) Once they reach age 1, children should drink vitamin D–fortified milk with meals and snacks. Even though vitamin D is produced in the body in response to strong ultraviolet rays from the sun, experts warn against exposing a child under the age of 6 months because of the risk for sunburn, which can lead to skin cancer in the future.[66]

Full-term infants are born with a six-month supply of iron. Iron-rich foods, such as fortified cereals and pureed meats, should be introduced to the infant's diet at about 6 months to provide adequate iron for growth and development.

Vitamin B$_{12}$ is found naturally only in animal foods. Breast-feeding women who avoid animal foods or eat insufficient amounts of animal foods rich in vitamin B$_{12}$ need to supplement their diets with vitamin B$_{12}$ supplements, fortified foods, or both to supply the infant with the vitamin B$_{12}$ she needs.

Infant formula is relatively low in fluoride. If the water used to make a child's infant formula is not fluoridated, she may need a fluoride supplement. However, before giving a child supplements, parents should check the fluoride levels in their water and speak with their pediatrician about the best course of action.[67]

Water (or, more correctly, fluid) needs generally are met with breast milk or formula. Extra fluid is only necessary to replenish stores following episodes of diarrhea, fever, or vomiting when the body loses fluid and electrolytes. Parents do not need to offer infants fluids other than breast milk or infant formula before the age of 6 months, as doing so may prevent the baby from being hungry for these nutrient-rich beverages.[68]

> "Colic" is characterized by an infant's chronic, inconsolable crying, often for long periods of time. Though the cause of colic is not known, some possible nutrition-related contributors include an immature digestive tract, cow's milk allergies or intolerance, food backup into the esophagus, increased intestinal gas, or the breast-feeding mother's diet.

LO 14.9 **The Take-Home Message** Infants grow at a dramatic rate during the first year of life. Caregivers and health care providers can monitor infant growth by making sure the child achieves appropriate developmental milestones and by using growth charts. Nutrient needs during the first year of life are substantial, and dietary supplements and fortified foods may be needed in some circumstances.

When Are Solid Foods Safe to Feed a Baby?

LO 14.10 Explain when and how solid foods may be introduced to infants.

Often, proud parents can hardly wait to show off how their baby is eating "real food." It is an exciting time, because eating **solid foods** represents maturing skills in the baby. Children typically start eating solid foods around 6 months of age.[69] However, parents should not suddenly decide to serve their baby steak or other foods that are difficult to chew and digest! The infant must be nutritionally, physiologically, and physically ready to eat solid foods. Let's take a look at what we mean by this.

Solid Foods May Be Introduced Once Certain Milestones Are Met

Infants must be developmentally ready for solid foods before parents introduce them into a child's diet. At about 6 months old, an infant has depleted his or her stored iron and will need to begin consuming iron from solid foods, such as pureed meats and fortified infant formula. Also, common sense tells us that as babies get bigger in size, they need more nutrients. Thus, an older, larger infant has higher nutrient needs than a younger, smaller one. Introducing solid foods will help to meet the infant's nutrient needs and help her develop feeding skills.

solid foods Foods other than breast milk or formula given to an infant, usually around 6 months of age.

The infant also needs to be physiologically ready; that is, his body systems must be able to process solid foods. At birth, and in early infancy, the GI tract and digestive organs cannot process solid foods.

These next questions are very specific to the individual child. Is the infant physically ready for solid foods? Has he or she met the necessary developmental milestones? To determine this, caretakers need to answer the following questions:

- Has the infant doubled his birth weight to at least 13 pounds?
- Has the infant's **tongue-thrust reflex** faded? This is a reflex infants have to protect against choking. The tongue automatically pushes outward when a substance is placed on it. The reflex fades at around 4 to 6 months of age.
- Does the infant have head and neck control? Without control, the infant is at greater risk for choking on solids.
- Have the infant's swallowing skills matured enough?
- Is the infant able to sit with support?
- Does the infant have the ability to turn his or her head to indicate "I'm full!"?

All of these questions should be answered with a "Yes" to know that it is safe and realistic to begin offering solid foods. If not, parents and caregivers would be wise to wait until the infant does develop these skills.[70] Still nervous about feeding an infant? See the Nutrition in the Real World feature "Feeding the Baby" for more information.

Solid Foods Should Be Introduced Gradually

Phasing in solid foods should take place over a period of several months. The food should initially be served pureed; eventually it can be served mashed so that the texture is soft, as the infant's chewing and swallowing skills are sharpened with practice and develop as she gets older. Pureed meat or fortified infant rice cereal are healthy first foods. Many parents choose infant cereal. Diluting infant cereal with breast milk or formula so there is a familiar taste along with the new taste helps to promote the infant's acceptance of the new food. Whole milk shouldn't be given to an infant until after 1 year of age.

Eating solid foods is new for infants, and they don't always accept certain foods on the first try. Rather than deciding that the infant does not like sweet potatoes because he spits it out upon the first taste, parents and caregivers should offer a given food more than once, over several days, to give the infant the opportunity to accept the food. After several days of feeding the infant a single food, proceed with other foods, such as pureed meats, fruits and vegetables, and barley or oat cereals. Parents and caregivers also need to consider the amount of salt, sugar, and butter in their infants' foods. Bland food is fine for infants. At this stage of the life cycle, infants can learn to find the natural flavors in whole foods satisfying, without added sugar or salt.

Many parents wonder if they should feed their child home-(T|F) made baby food for the sake of safety and better nutrition. It's good to know that commercially made baby foods are of high quality and often comparable to homemade. The choice is really up to the parent or caregiver. One benefit of homemade food that everyone might agree upon is the financial savings—there are no added costs for fancy packaging and labels. (See "Two Points of View" at the end of this chapter for more on this topic.)

Refer to Figure 14.9 on page 552 for suggested foods for a baby's first year of life.

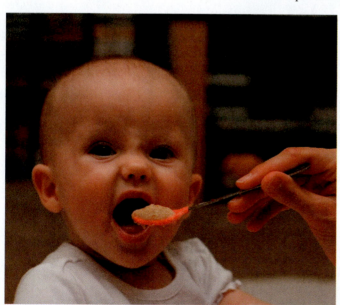
Solid foods like fortified infant rice cereal and oatmeal can be introduced between 4 and 6 months of age.

tongue-thrust reflex A forceful protrusion of the tongue in response to an oral stimulus, such as a spoon.

nutrition
IN THE
Real World   Feeding the Baby

New parents are often nervous when it comes to feeding their newborns. They may wonder if their baby is eating too much or too little, or swallowing too much air, and, if they are bottle-feeding, they may be worried about nipple confusion or other concerns they have heard about from well-meaning friends and relatives. The good news is that most parents can relax when it comes to feeding baby, as Mother Nature has built in numerous mechanisms to help babies healthfully consume the amount of food they need.

For example, infants are equipped with several reflexes that help them take in adequate amounts of breast milk (or infant formula) or solid foods and avoid choking. Among these reflexes are:

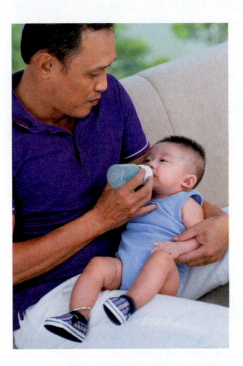

- Rooting reflex—When a baby's mouth, lips, cheek, or chin are touched by an object, such as a nipple, the head and mouth turn toward it.

- Suck/swallow reflex—After opening the mouth when a baby's lips and mouth area are touched, suckling movements begin and the tongue moves to the back of the mouth for swallowing.

- Tongue-thrust reflex—When the lips are touched, the baby's tongue moves forward in the mouth.

- Gag reflex—When an object such as a spoon or solid is placed in the mouth, it is pushed back out by the tongue.

Note that a baby should be fed when he indicates that he is hungry, rather than on a set schedule. Newborns may need to eat as often as every ½ hour to 2 hours, whereas older infants, who have larger stomachs, may taper off to 3 to 4 hours between feedings. Some cues that a baby is hungry include waking and tossing, sucking on a fist, crying or fussing, and looking like he is going to cry. Caregivers should respond early to the signs of hunger rather than waiting until the baby is crying. Infants are usually very clear about when they are ready to stop feeding, and use several techniques to communicate this to a caregiver. For example, they may spit out the nipple, close their lips, and decrease the rate of suckling.

When feeding an infant from a bottle, the baby should be gently and slowly positioned for feeding. The baby should be held upright in the cradle of the arm with the head higher than the rest of the body, to avoid choking. The bottle should be held and not propped during feeding because propping can cause choking or baby bottle tooth decay, and deprives the baby of human contact. To expel any excess swallowed air and alleviate potential gassiness, a baby needs to be burped after she eats. The best way to burp a baby is to gently pat or rub her back while she is resting on the caregiver's shoulder or sitting on the lap.

All babies develop at their own rate and each individual baby's developmental readiness should be used to determine which foods should be fed, what texture the foods should be, and what feeding styles should be used.

Some Foods Are Dangerous and Should Be Avoided

In spite of all the new skills an infant develops during the first year, becoming stronger, smarter, and more independent, parents and caregivers still need to "baby the baby" when it comes to eating. Many foods are just not appropriate for a baby. For example, some foods, like hot dog rounds or raw carrots, present a choking hazard for young infants and should be cut into very small pieces or avoided altogether. Because infants have few teeth, foods should be soft in texture so they do not require excessive chewing, and ideally should easily "melt" in the mouth, like a cracker. No matter what they are eating, infants should always be supervised.

Food Allergies

Once an infant is ready for solids, foods should be introduced gradually to make sure the child isn't allergic or intolerant. It's best to introduce one new single-ingredient food at a time, and wait for three to five days to see if the baby develops a food allergy.[71] If she develops hives or a rash, or starts sneezing or vomiting, food may be the culprit. Allergic reactions may also include a very mild tingling sensation in the mouth or swelling of the tongue and the throat, difficulty breathing, diarrhea, a drop in blood pressure, and loss of consciousness or death.

A **food allergy** is an abnormal physical reaction of the immune system in response to the consumption of a particular food allergen. **Food allergens** are proteins that are not broken down during cooking or by the gastric juices and enzymes in the body during digestion. Because they are not degraded, they enter the body intact, and can cause an adverse immune reaction if the allergen is perceived as a foreign invader.

A food allergy reaction occurs in two stages, the sensitization stage followed by the actual response or allergic reaction stage. In the first stage (see **Figure 14.11**), the food allergens don't provoke a reaction, but rather introduce themselves to the person's immune system. In response, the immune system creates an army of antibodies that enter the blood and stand ready for the next time the allergen appears. The antibodies attach to **mast cells**, setting the stage for a potential future allergic reaction. In the second stage, the allergic reaction stage, food allergens come into contact with mast cells, which release chemicals, including histamine, that trigger reactions in areas of the body where mast cells are most prevalent. This stage can only occur when a person is exposed to the food allergen for the second and subsequent times. In very sensitive individuals, a minute exposure of a food allergen—$^1/_{4,000}$ of a peanut, for example—can trigger an allergic reaction.

Reactions can appear as quickly as a few minutes after eating the food. In fact, itchiness in the mouth may occur as soon as the food touches the tongue. After the food reaches the stomach and begins to be digested, vomiting and/or diarrhea may result. When they enter the blood, the food allergens can cause a drop in blood pressure. When the allergens are near the skin, hives can develop, and as the allergens make their way to the lungs, asthma can ensue.

Individuals with allergies, or their caretakers, often carry a syringe injector of epinephrine (adrenaline) to be administered when severe reactions occur, to help treat these symptoms. Epinephrine constricts blood vessels, relaxes the muscles in the lungs to help with breathing, and decreases swelling and hives.

Eggs, milk, and peanuts are the most common sources of food allergens in children. In adults, shellfish, peanuts, tree nuts, fish, wheat, soy, and eggs are the most common sources of food allergens. These foods together cause 90 percent of all reactions to food allergens. Some children will outgrow their reaction to milk, eggs, or soy, but they generally do not outgrow a peanut allergy.[72] In the past, medical experts and organizations such as the AAP have advised against introducing so-called highly allergenic foods, such as eggs, peanuts, and peanut products, until after a child's first birthday. However, there is no convincing evidence for delaying the introduction of specific highly allergenic foods. In fact, there is evidence that delaying the introduction of solid foods may actually increase the risk of food allergy, not reduce it.[73]

Research suggests that the prevalence of food allergies among children in the United States has increased 18 percent over the last decade.[74] Estimates suggest that currently, 8 percent of American youth have at least one food allergy. The reason for the increase in food allergy prevalence is not well understood; however, it is

food allergy An abnormal reaction by the immune system to a particular food.

food allergens Proteins not broken down by cooking or digestion that enter the body intact, causing an adverse immune response.

mast cells Cells in connective tissue to which antibodies attach, setting the stage for potential future allergic reactions.

Stage 1: Sensitization

1 First allergen contact — Strawberry allergen

2 Immune system creates antibodies — Immune-system cell

Strawberry-specific antibodies

3 Antibodies attach to mast cells — Antibodies attached to mast cell — Mast cell

Stage 2: Allergic reaction

4 Subsequent allergen contact — Strawberry allergen

Strawberry allergen
Antibody

5 Strawberry allergens attach to antibody–mast cell complex — Mast cell

6 Histamine released from mast cells — Histamine

7 Allergic reaction triggered

- Itching
- Swelling
- Nausea
- Vomiting
- Cramps
- Diarrhea
- Blocked airways
- Hives
- Decreased blood pressure
- Irregular heart beat

Figure 14.11 Immune Response to a Food Allergen

hypothesized that the increase may be due, in part, to better diagnostic practices, environmental changes, and/or food manufacturing processes. Determining the cause of the rise in food allergies is an active area of research, as it will likely shed light on how to prevent them. In the United States, food allergies are the cause of 2,000 admittances to the hospital, approximately 30,000 **anaphylactic** (*ana* = without, no, *phylaxis* = protection) **reactions** (severe, life-threatening allergic reactions), and almost 200 deaths annually.[75] According to the Centers for Disease Control and Prevention, from 2004 to 2006, 9,500 hospital discharges a year carried a diagnosis related to food allergy.[76] Most of these visits to health care facilities were no doubt the result of an anaphylactic reaction. Anaphylactic reactions can cause vomiting and constriction or narrowing of the airways in the lungs, which inhibits breathing.

The symptoms of a **food intolerance** may mimic a food allergy, but they are different responses. A food intolerance does not involve the immune system. Recall from Chapter 4 that one common food intolerance, lactose intolerance, is caused by inadequate amounts of the enzyme lactase in the body.

anaphylactic reactions Severe, life-threatening reactions that cause constriction of the airways in the lungs, which inhibits the ability to breathe.

food intolerance Adverse reaction to a food that does not involve an immune response. Lactose intolerance is one example.

Proper food labeling can help reduce the risks associated with food allergy. The FDA requires that virtually all food ingredients be listed on the food label, and that the food label state whether the product contains protein from any of the major foods known to cause an allergic reaction: milk, egg, fish, shellfish, tree nuts, peanuts, soybeans, or wheat.[77]

Food Contamination

Some foods, including raw and undercooked meat, seafood, and eggs, are so dangerous as to be potentially fatal. Honey may contain the bacterium *Clostridium botulinum*, which can lead to a fatal disease called **botulism**. Though some cultures and families have used honey-dipped pacifiers to calm infants for generations, this is a dangerous practice. Infants with botulism become lethargic, feed poorly, and suffer from constipation. They will have a weak cry and poor muscle tone. Untreated symptoms may cause paralysis of the arms, legs, trunk, and respiratory muscles. The resulting respiratory failure is what makes this food potentially deadly. An infant's immune system is not developed enough to fight off botulism, but honey does not present problems for older children and adults, who have adequate amounts of intestinal microorganisms that compete with botulism and inhibit its growth in the intestines.[78]

LO 14.10 **The Take-Home Message** An infant must be physically, physiologically, and nutritionally ready before being introduced to solid foods. Solid foods should be introduced gradually and cautiously. Parents and caregivers must educate themselves about foods that are appropriate and those that are not to keep the infant safe and healthy.

Putting It All Together

Pregnancy, lactation, and infancy are periods of the life cycle during which women and babies have unique nutrient needs. Women need to refer to the DRIs for pregnancy and lactation (listed on the inside cover of this textbook) to make sure they consume adequate calories, protein, iron, and folate for both their own health and that of their developing baby. Babies have high nutrient and calorie needs during their first year to sustain their rapid growth and development. **Figure 14.12** summarizes the nutritional and lifestyle guidelines for babies and their parents. Both men and women should adopt healthier lifestyles before pregnancy in order to increase the likelihood of having a healthy baby.

botulism A rare but serious paralytic illness caused by the bacterium *Clostridium botulinum*. Infant botulism is caused by consuming the spores of the bacteria, which then grow in the intestines and release toxins. It can be fatal.

Prior to conception	First trimester	Second trimester	Third trimester	First year
Father • Stop smoking • Limit alcohol • Maintain a healthy weight • Consume a balanced diet				
Mother • Consume a balanced diet • Maintain a healthy weight • Add folic acid to diet • Limit caffeine • Avoid certain fish with high levels of methylmercury • Avoid alcohol, herbs, illicit drugs, and smoking • Exercise regularly	• Consume a balanced diet • Continue getting folic acid • Take an iron-rich supplement • Limit caffeine • Avoid too much vitamin A • Avoid foodborne illness • Continue exercising	• Consume a balanced diet with adequate calories for growth • Continue exercising	• Consume a balanced diet with adequate calories for growth • Eat frequent small meals if more comfortable • Choose high-fiber foods • Drink plenty of fluids • Continue nonimpact exercises	• Consume a balanced diet with adequate calories and fluids for breast-feeding • Nursing mothers should avoid illicit drugs, smoking, and alcohol • Limit caffeine • Avoid certain fish with high levels of methylmercury
Baby				• Supplement diet with vitamins K and D and sources of iron or iron-fortified foods • Avoid common food allergens, honey, and herbal tea • Consume breast milk or formula as primary source of calories • Do not start drinking cow's milk until after this year • Introduce solid foods gradually and one at a time • Avoid too much fiber and excessive amounts of juice

Figure 14.12 Summary of Nutritional Guidelines
Nutritional guidelines for both parents and infants are shown above.

Should Parents Make Their Own Baby Food? Many anxious parents worry about the foods they feed their babies, and when it comes to introducing solid foods, they often struggle with the question of whether to make their own baby food, buy organic versions of commercially produced products, or purchase regular, nonorganic (and usually less expensive) baby foods.

What concerns do parents have when it comes to commercially made baby food, and are those concerns valid? What other options are available? Are there advantages other than nutrition to making homemade baby food, or buying only organic products? Read through the arguments on both sides of the issue, and then consider the critical-thinking questions to decide for yourself!

yes

- Homemade baby foods may be more nutrient rich. Commercial baby foods often contain more water, starch, and sugar than homemade baby foods. The addition of these additives dilutes the nutrient content of commercial foods.[1]

- Commercially made baby foods are often processed with high heat during jarring, which can destroy some of the vitamins and other nutrients.[2]

- The average baby in the United States will consume 600 jars of baby food. Parents who use processed baby food spend an average of $300 during their infant's first year of life. On average, baby food prepared at home can cost as little as $55 in the first year.[3]

- Providing babies with homemade baby food made of fresh fruits and vegetables can help instill taste and preference for these healthy food choices. Babies will get used to the fresher tastes, and be less interested in the tastes of highly processed foods later on in life.[4]

no

- Pesticide levels in commercial baby foods are tightly regulated by U.S. law, which mandates a safety factor that is ten times the levels known to be safe.[5]

- Homemade baby foods may spoil more quickly and require refrigeration, which will take up room in the fridge or freezer if a lot of servings are made ahead of time. Prepackaged baby foods don't have to be refrigerated until they've been opened.[6]

- In preparing homemade food, adults may season it to their own tastes, adding enough salt or sugar to raise pediatric concerns.[7]

- Certain vegetables, particularly spinach, beets, and carrots, may contain high levels of nitrates, which can be harmful to young babies. There seems to be little or no risk of nitrate poisoning from commercially prepared infant foods in the United States. However, reports of nitrate poisoning from home-prepared vegetable foods for infants indicate that this does occur.[8]

what do you think?

1. Which side has the overall stronger argument? Why? **2.** Why might parents need to choose commercially prepared food over homemade food? **3.** Do you think making homemade baby food is worth the extra time and effort? Why or why not?

LO 14.1 Nutrient Intake and Healthy Behaviors Impact Fertility

Both the father and the mother should make healthy diet and lifestyle changes if needed prior to pregnancy. For healthy sperm, men should stop smoking, abstain from alcohol or drink only in moderation, strive for a healthy body weight, and consume a well-balanced diet with adequate amounts of fruits and vegetables, whole grains, lean meats, low-fat dairy foods, and legumes. Prior to pregnancy, women should also abstain from alcohol, smoking, and caffeine, and strive for a healthy weight. In addition, women should consume adequate amounts of folic acid prior to conception to reduce the risk of neural tube defects.

LO 14.2 Specific Nutrients and Behaviors Are Important during the First Trimester

Healthy women who begin pregnancy at a healthy weight should gain 25 to 35 pounds during pregnancy. A woman's needs for many nutrients including folate, iron, zinc, copper, and calcium increase up to 50 percent during pregnancy. Care should be taken to avoid consuming too much preformed vitamin A, which can cause birth defects.

Exercise during pregnancy can help improve sleep, lower the risk of hypertension and diabetes, prevent backaches, relieve constipation, shorten labor, reduce stress and depression, and possibly allow women to return more quickly to their prepregnancy weight after delivery.

Awareness of food safety is also important, as bacteria such as *Listeria monocytogenes* may cause miscarriages, premature labor, delivery of a low birth weight infant, developmental problems, or even infant death. Pregnant women should abstain from alcohol, herbal teas and herbal supplements, and illicit drugs, as these can all harm fetal growth and development. They should avoid fish that contain high amounts of methylmercury and consume caffeine only in moderation.

LO 14.3 Additional Carbohydrates and Protein Are Important during the Second Trimester

Many pregnant women find that the nausea and fatigue of the first trimester diminish during the second trimester, and appetite begins to increase. The mother's calorie needs also increase. A pregnant woman should consume an additional 340 calories daily during the second trimester and should gain around a pound per week. Pregnant women need about 175 grams of carbohydrate and 71 grams of protein. These needs can be met with a balanced diet. Sometimes a woman develops gestational diabetes and/or hypertension during pregnancy. Gestational diabetes increases the risk of delivering a larger-than-normal baby who may also be at risk for developing jaundice, breathing problems, and birth defects. Pregnancy-induced hypertension includes gestational hypertension, preeclampsia, and eclampsia, each progressively more medically serious. The risk of gestational diabetes and hypertension can be reduced during the second trimester with a healthy diet, daily exercise, and managing body weight.

1 whole-wheat English muffin
2 tbs peanut butter
5 baby carrots

340 total calories

LO 14.4 Healthy Eating Behaviors and Weight Gain Are Important Considerations during the Third Trimester

By the end of the last trimester, a pregnant woman should be taking in an extra 450 calories daily and continue to gain about 1 pound per week. The slower movement of food through the GI tract can contribute to heartburn and constipation. Reduced physical activity and iron supplementation can also contribute to constipation. To minimize heartburn, pregnant women should eat smaller but frequent meals, eliminate spicy foods that may irritate the esophagus, and avoid lying down immediately after meals. Exercise and consuming fiber-rich foods, along with plenty of fluids, can help prevent or alleviate constipation.

Total weight gain 25–35 lbs

- Maternal fat stores (4–11 lbs)
- Uterus and breast (4 lbs)
- Blood (3–4 lbs)
- Fetus (7–8 lbs)
- Placenta, amniotic fluid, and other fluids (7–8 lbs)

LO 14.5 Younger and Older Mothers-to-Be Face Special Challenges

Women younger or older than the physically optimal child-bearing age range of 20 to 35 may face additional challenges during pregnancy. Teenage mothers-to-be are at risk for pregnancy-induced hypertension, iron-deficiency anemia, and delivering premature and low birth weight babies. Older mothers-to-be are at risk of developing diabetes and high blood pressure. Their infants are more likely to have Down syndrome or other disabilities. Older women who use fertility-enhancing techniques are also more likely to give birth to multiples, which carries other increased risks, including premature birth, labor difficulties, and low birth weight.

LO 14.6 Breast-Feeding Benefits Both Mother and Child

Breast-feeding is the gold standard for feeding an infant. It provides physical, emotional, convenience, and financial benefits for the mother and nutritional and health benefits for the infant. Breast milk is rich in nutrients, antibodies, and other compounds that provide the infant with a disease-fighting boost until the baby's own immune system matures. Because of all the benefits, women are encouraged to exclusively breast-feed for the first six months. Breast-feeding women can also express their breast milk with a pump and store it for later use, allowing for more flexibility in their schedules.

LO 14.7 Breast-Feeding Mothers Have Increased Nutrient Needs

Breast-feeding mothers who began pregnancy at a healthy weight need to consume 330 to 400 extra calories daily to produce breast milk, and a breast-feeding woman should drink about 13 cups of water and beverages daily. Anything that goes into a breast-feeding mother's body can potentially pass into her breast milk, so she should limit caffeine consumption and discuss alcohol and medication intake with her health care provider. Breast-feeding mothers should also be careful to avoid over-consumption of fish that may contain methylmercury.

LO 14.8 Formula Can Be a Healthy Alternative to Breast Milk

If an infant isn't breast-fed, the only healthy alternative is commercially made formula. Commercially made formulas are modified from soy or cow's milk, and patterned after human breast milk. For some women, formula-feeding is a personal preference. For others it is necessary, as breast-feeding may not be possible due to illness or other circumstances. Tooth decay and ear infections can be prevented by avoiding bedtime bottle feedings when infants are placed in bed with a bottle.

LO 14.9 Infants Have Specific Nutrient Needs

An infant doubles his or her birth weight by around 6 months of age, and triples it by 12 months. With proper nutrition, an infant should reach certain stages of physical development within a distinct time frame. Poor infant nutrition (whether in quality or quantity) will likely prevent ideal growth and the ability of the child to reach milestones on time. All infants should receive a vitamin K injection at birth, and breast-fed infants need vitamin D supplements until 1 year of age. Infants older than 6 months need to begin taking in iron through food sources, as their stored iron supply is depleted around this time.

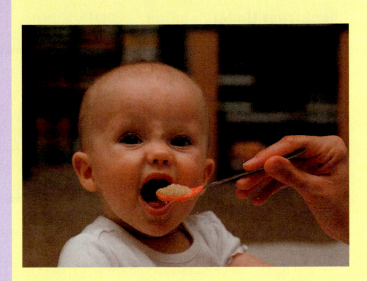

LO 14.10 Solid Foods Should Be Introduced Gradually after Certain Milestones Are Reached

Infants need to be nutritionally, physiologically, and physically ready before they begin eating solid foods. Foods should be introduced gradually and one at a time to monitor possible allergies or intolerances. Certain foods can be dangerous and should be avoided. Parents and caregivers should avoid adding heavy seasoning (such as sugar or salt) and offering excess amounts of fruit juice (which can lead to overconsumption of calories) to an infant's diet.

Age (in months)	0–4	4–6	6–9	9–12
Infant milestones	Suckles	Controls head movements	Sits with support; sweeps food from spoon with upper lip	Chews and swallows lumpier foods	Feeds self; drinks from a cup

Terms to Know

- trimesters
- embryo
- placenta
- fetus
- gestational diabetes
- pregnancy-induced hypertension
- lactation
- let-down response
- breast-feeding
- colostrum
- early childhood caries
- milestones
- food allergy

MasteringNutrition™ Build your knowledge—and confidence—in the Study Area of MasteringNutrition with a variety of study tools.

MyDietAnalysis Access MyDietAnalysis through MasteringNutrition™ and track your diet and daily activities. In addition, a dietary analysis activity is available for every chapter in your book.

Check Your Understanding

LO 14.1 **1.** To prevent neural tube birth defects, a woman should take 400 micrograms of folic acid daily
  a. during the first trimester.
  b. during the second trimester.
  c. throughout her childbearing years, if she's capable of conceiving.
  d. during the last trimester.

LO 14.2 **2.** To support the birth of a healthy 6.5- to 8.5-pound baby, how many pounds should a normal-weight woman gain during pregnancy?
  a. 10 to 15 pounds
  b. 25 to 35 pounds
  c. 15 to 25 pounds
  d. 37 to 54 pounds

LO 14.3 **3.** Two potential complications of pregnancy that must be closely monitored by a health care provider are
  a. cravings and morning sickness.
  b. gestational diabetes and preeclampsia.
  c. weight gain and exercise.
  d. constipation and heartburn.

LO 14.4 **4.** During the third trimester of pregnancy, a woman who begins pregnancy at a healthy weight should increase her daily calorie intake by
  a. 450 calories a day.
  b. 340 calories a day.
  c. 500 calories a day.
  d. No increase is needed.

LO 14.5 **5.** During pregnancy, a teenage mother's need for many nutrients increases. Which nutrient requirement is unlikely to be met through her diet alone?
  a. iron
  b. folic acid
  c. calcium
  d. all of the above

LO 14.6 **6.** Breast-feeding cannot
  a. help women reduce their risk of breast cancer.
  b. reduce women's risk of type 2 diabetes.
  c. prevent pregnancy.
  d. decrease the risk of the baby developing respiratory and ear infections.

LO 14.7 **7.** A breast-feeding mother should limit her intake of which of the following?
  a. fish, especially deep-sea fish high in mercury
  b. caffeine
  c. alcohol
  d. all of the above

LO 14.8 **8.** The best alternative to breast-feeding is to feed an infant with
  a. commercially made formula.
  b. cow's milk.
  c. soy or almond milk.
  d. pureed baby food.

LO 14.9 **9.** Andy is a healthy 3-month-old baby boy who is being breast-fed by his mother. Which of the following nutrients should be added to his diet in supplement form?
  a. vitamin D
  b. potassium
  c. vitamin C
  d. omega-3 fats

LO 14.10 **10.** Six-month-old Cathy is ready to take on solid foods. One healthy and safe first food that could be introduced in her diet is
  a. chopped meat.
  b. ready-to-eat crunchy cereal.
  c. iron-fortified rice cereal.
  d. scrambled eggs.

Answers

1. (c) To reduce the risk of these birth defects, folic acid should be consumed prior to conception and continue during the early weeks of pregnancy. Waiting until pregnancy occurs may be too late to help prevent birth defects during the first trimester. Because pregnancy increases the need for this vitamin, the mother should continue to make sure that folate intake is adequate throughout her pregnancy.

2. (b) Women who begin pregnancy at a healthy weight should gain from 25 to 35 pounds. This is the approximate amount of weight needed to ensure a healthy-weight baby while avoiding the risks of carrying excess weight.

3. (b) Gestational diabetes and pre-eclampsia are both potentially life-threatening complications that can be brought on by pregnancy and should be closely monitored by a physician. Cravings, morning sickness, constipation, and heartburn can all occur during pregnancy, but are not considered serious unless they are severe. Weight gain and exercise are not complications of pregnancy.

4. (a) A pregnant woman at a healthy weight before pregnancy needs 450 more calories than her pre-pregnancy energy needs every day during the third trimester. She doesn't require additional daily calories during the first trimester, but does have additional nutrient needs, so she should be sure to eat nutrient-rich foods. During the second trimester, she needs an extra 340 calories every day.

5. (d) A teenage girl's body is still growing, so she has higher nutrient needs than does an adult woman. Pair these higher needs with the increased needs of pregnancy, and these young mothers are likely to fall short of many of their nutrient requirements, especially iron, folic acid, calcium, and potentially even calories.

6. (c) Breast-feeding provides health advantages to both the mother and the baby. Breast-feeding reduces the risk of breast cancer and diabetes in the mother and the incidences of respiratory and ear infections in the baby. Breast-feeding cannot be relied upon to prevent pregnancy, however.

7. (d) Anything that goes into a breast-feeding mother's body can potentially pass into her breast milk. Mothers should avoid exposure to deep-sea fish, limit caffeine to no more than three cups per day, and limit alcohol intake to an occasional drink, if any at all.

8. (a) The best alternative to breast-feeding is commercially made formula. Cow's milk should not be used to feed infants because it is more difficult to digest than formula or breast milk.

9. (a) Although breast milk is an ideal food for baby Andy, it doesn't contain enough vitamin D, so Andy should receive daily drops in his diet. He doesn't need to be supplemented with vitamin C, potassium, or omega-3 fats.

10. (c) Iron-fortified rice cereal is a good choice and is unlikely to cause an allergic reaction. If Cathy tolerates the rice cereal well, oatmeal could be the next grain added to her diet, or she could try pureed meats, which are rich in iron.

Web Resources

- For more information on breast-feeding, visit the La Leche League International website at www.llli.org
- For more food safety guidance for during pregnancy and after the baby is born, visit the FDA's Center for Food Safety and Applied Nutrition website at www.fda.gov
- For more on infant nutrition, visit the USDA's Food and Nutrition Center website at www.nal.usda.gov
- For more information on children and their dietary needs, visit the American Academy of Pediatrics' consumer website at www.healthychildren.org
- For more information on food allergies, visit the Food Allergy and Anaphylaxis Network at www.foodallergy.org

Answers to True or False?

1. **True.** Fathers-to-be need to eat a healthy diet and avoid certain substances to help produce a healthy baby. Turn to page 528 to find out why this is the case.

2. **True.** Obese women may have more difficulty conceiving, possibly because of irregular menstrual cycles. Turn to page 529 to find out more.

3. **False.** Though it's called morning sickness, nausea can happen at any time of day, and sometimes occurs after the first trimester. To learn more about conditions during pregnancy, turn to page 533.

4. **False.** Any type of alcohol, including red wine, can harm a growing embryo and fetus. To find out what other substances can be harmful during pregnancy, turn to page 537.

5. **True.** Physical activity can be good for women expecting a baby, though some activities should be avoided. To find out which activities are safe, turn to page 539.

6. **False.** Infant formula is a healthy alternative, but breast milk is best for a baby. Turn to page 543 to find out why.

7. **False.** Infants should never be put on a weight-loss diet. Babies need calories and fat to support their rapid growth and development. To find out more about the demands of infant growth, turn to page 552.

8. **True.** Most infants receive an injection of vitamin K at birth, and there are other nutrients that infants may need to supplement their diet. Find out why this is the case on page 552.

9. **False.** Although there's probably nothing as delicious and fresh as homemade, most brands of jarred baby foods are just as healthy. Read more about commercially made versus homemade baby foods on page 554.

10. **False.** Although they're a good source of vitamin A and other nutrients, raw carrots are a potential choking hazard for an infant. For more on potentially dangerous foods, turn to page 555.

15
Life Cycle Nutrition: Toddlers through the Later Years

True or False?

1. Toddlers don't grow as quickly as infants do. **T/F** p. 568

2. Young children who fill up on low-iron foods, such as milk and juice, may have an iron deficiency. **T/F** p. 570

3. Once a child refuses a food, there is no point in offering it again. **T/F** p. 571

4. Young children often get "stuck" on particular foods. **T/F** p. 571

5. The increase in childhood obesity is due entirely to fast-food intake. **T/F** p. 574

6. Lunches served under the National School Lunch Program must meet certain nutritional standards. **T/F** p. 578

7. As long as teens drink diet soda, there's no need to be concerned about the negative health effects of carbonated soft drinks. **T/F** p. 580

8. Older adults don't need as many calories daily as they did when they were younger. **T/F** p. 582

9. Food insecurity among elders is not an issue in the United States. **T/F** p. 591

10. Alcohol abuse is extremely rare among older adults. **T/F** p. 594

See page 599 for the answers.

Learning Outcomes

After reading this chapter, you will be able to:

LO 15.1 Describe young children's nutrient needs, and discuss some of the nutrition-related issues they face.

LO 15.2 Describe school-aged children's nutrient needs, and discuss some of the nutrition-related issues they face, including childhood obesity.

LO 15.3 Describe adolescents' nutrient needs, and discuss some of the nutrition-related issues they face, including disordered eating.

LO 15.4 Summarize the nutrient needs of older adults, and discuss some of the nutrition-related health concerns common to old age.

LO 15.5 Describe the physical, economic, and psychological factors that can affect the health of older Americans.

Toddlers live busy lives. Their world is full of interesting things to explore and do, so sitting down at a table to eat isn't high on their list of priorities. In addition, their stomachs are still small, so a few bites of fruit, a handful of cereal, and a cup of milk may be enough to satisfy them before they are squirming in their seats, looking for the next adventure.

Just when parents think they've got a handle on good nutrition and eating habits for their toddlers, they find the toddler is no more and they have a young child heading off to kindergarten. During the elementary school years, providing healthy nutrition for a child begins to change dramatically and parents need to develop a whole new set of skills and knowledge. And so it goes through adolescence. As children grow, their nutritional needs change, sometimes because of physical changes and sometimes because of social and emotional changes. In the first part of this chapter, we'll explore the unique nutrition needs of toddlers, preschoolers, school-aged children, and adolescents as they grow and change.

The adult years, between the ages of 20 and 65, are a period of homeostasis and optimally functioning body systems for most people. After about age 65, body functions begin to slow and older adulthood begins. The experience of aging is unique for everyone, and changes in functions do not occur at the same rate or to the same degree in any two people. Although the risk of disease and disability increases with age, poor health is not inevitable. In the latter part of this chapter we'll discuss the physical, economic, and emotional aspects of aging, and the nutrient needs of older adults. We'll also examine the most common dietary challenges older adults face, and ways to minimize health risks and promote a healthier older age.

What Are the Issues Associated with Feeding Young Children?

LO 15.1 Describe young children's nutrient needs, and discuss some of the nutrition-related issues they face.

For the purposes of explaining growth, development, and nutritional needs, very young children may be categorized into two distinct groups: **toddlers** (1- to 3-year-olds) and **preschoolers** (aged 3 to 5 years). Toddlers and preschoolers develop relatively rapidly, but their growth rates have slowed significantly compared with infancy. For example, during the first year of life, a baby triples his/her birth weight and grows 5 to 8 inches, whereas[1] children ages 2 years and older gain between 4½ and 6½ pounds and grow 2½ to 3½ inches every year.[2] It's important to note that each child grows at her or his own pace, and that growth statistics serve as guidelines.

As a result of this slower growth, toddlers and preschoolers have smaller appetites and relatively lower calorie needs compared with those of infants. Parents and other caregivers may become concerned about this change, and think that their child is not eating enough to grow and develop properly. However, as long as parents and pediatricians monitor growth and stay alert for decreased energy levels, diarrhea, nausea, vomiting, changes in the quality of the child's hair, skin, or nails, or other changes in health, it is likely that the child's diet is sufficient.

Young Children Need to Eat Frequent, Small Meals with Nutrient-Rich Foods

Toddlers tend to be extremely active. They also have smaller stomachs than older children, and may eat less at mealtimes. The key to ensuring that a toddler consumes

Table 15.1

Calorie Needs for Children and Adolescents

| Age | Gender | Activity Level* | | |
		Sedentary	Moderately Active	Active
2–3 years	Male and Female	1,000–1,200	1,000–1,400	1,000–1,400
4–8 years	Female	1,200–1,400	1,400–1,600	1,400–1,800
4–8 years	Male	1,200–1,400	1,400–1,600	1,600–2,000
9–13 years	Female	1,400–1,600	1,600–2,000	1,800–2,200
9–13 years	Male	1,600–2,000	1,800–2,200	2,000–2,600
14–18 years	Female	1,800	2,000	2,400
14–18 years	Male	2,000–2,400	2,400–2,800	2,800–3,200

*Based on Estimated Energy Requirements (EER) equations, using reference heights (average) and reference weights (healthy) for each age/gender group. For children and adolescents, reference height and weight are based on median height and weight for ages up to 18 years. EER equations are from the Institute of Medicine. *Dietary Reference Intakes for Energy, Carbohydrate, Fiber, Fat, Fatty Acids, Cholesterol, Protein, and Amino Acids.* (Washington, D.C.: The National Academies Press, 2002).

adequate calories, protein, vitamins, minerals, and other nutrients is to offer him nutrient-rich foods at every meal and snack. Generally speaking, toddlers aged 2 to 3 require 1,000 to 1,400 calories per day (see **Table 15.1**). Meals and snacks should consist of small portions of protein-rich foods, such as lean meat, eggs, poultry, dairy products, and beans, as well as fruits, vegetables, and whole grains, rather than more processed, lower-nutrient foods such as chicken nuggets, prepared macaroni and cheese, french fries, sugary drinks, cookies, and crackers. (You can use MyPlate's Daily Food Plans for Preschoolers and Kids, discussed later in this chapter, for specific daily eating plans for young children. Also, check out the Table Tips "Tasty Treats for Toddlers" for some quick ideas.)

To establish a healthy relationship with food, parents and caregivers should avoid encouraging toddlers and preschoolers to eat more than they want at meals and snacks. Using child-sized plates and cups is one way to help ensure proper portion sizes. Caregivers should tailor portion sizes to each child's individual needs and pay attention to a child's cues about wanting less, or more, food.

By about 15 months, children are typically able to feed themselves and should be drinking from a cup. Between the first and second year, a child goes from holding a spoon to developing the fine motor skills needed to scoop the food and bring the spoon to her mouth. Younger children should always be offered a spoon at mealtimes to improve their feeding skills.

Allowing a child to self-feed is often messy and time-consuming, but it is important to his development and ability to regulate his own food intake. Choking and inhaling food is a top concern with toddlers and other young children, and close supervision is necessary. The American Academy of Pediatrics recommends that parents and other caregivers avoid offering to children under age 4 any foods that are easily lodged in the airway, including nuts, raw carrots, popcorn, peanuts and peanut butter, seeds, marshmallows, raisins and other dried fruit, chunks of meat or cheese, chewing gum, and round candy. Hot dogs are the leading cause of fatal food-related choking in children, but they, and other potentially problematic foods, such as whole grapes and string cheese, are less risky when cut into small pieces.[3] Children should always sit while eating to reduce the likelihood of food becoming lodged in the windpipe during a trip or fall. Children should not be allowed to eat while riding in the car because should the child begin choking, it may be difficult for the driver to pull over and assist the child.[4]

toddlers Children aged 1 to 3 years old.

preschoolers Children aged 3 to 5 years old.

Using child-sized dishes at mealtimes can help caregivers monitor portion sizes.

Children who attend day care may receive a substantial portion of their daily food in that setting. In some cases, day-care providers may offer menu items or snacks that are superior to what is given at home. Every state, with the exception of Idaho (which doesn't license child-care centers), requires that licensed child-care centers meet minimum standards for nutrition. The National Resource Center for Health and Safety in Child Care and Early Education website (http://nrckids.org) posts all child-care regulations for each state. Parents should know what is being offered at the day-care site and provide alternative foods for their child when necessary. This is particularly important for children with food allergies or food intolerances. Parents should ask day-care providers to alert them about special occasions, such as birthday parties, so they can bring in a treat for their own child if their child is allergic to certain foods. Even if children do not have special dietary concerns, parents have the right to be firm about what their child eats.

Young Children Have Special Nutrient Needs

The following nutrients are of special concern in the diets of young children:

- *Calcium*. Young children need calcium to develop healthy bones. Children between 1 and 3 years of age should consume 700 milligrams of calcium per day, and children aged 4 to 8 need 1,000 milligrams.[5] Milk and other dairy products, and calcium-added foods help children meet their calcium requirements. Eight ounces of milk, fortified soy beverage, or fortified orange juice each provide about 300 milligrams of calcium.[6]

- *Iron*. Children aged 1 to 3 need 7 milligrams of iron daily; those aged 4 to 8 require 10 milligrams.[7] Young children are prone to iron deficiency. Iron deficiency during infancy and early childhood can interfere with a child's cognition, behavior, and overall development, and have lasting effects.[8] In the United States, an estimated 14 percent of children aged 1 to 2 years old, and 4 percent of children aged 3 to 4 years old, experience iron deficiency.[9] Parents and caregivers should offer iron-rich foods including lean meats and poultry, and fortified grains such as breakfast cereal, to children on a daily basis and avoid allowing children to fill up on iron-poor foods, such as juice and milk. (See the Table Tips for more ideas for kid-friendly, iron-rich foods).

- *Vitamin D*. To build healthy bones, children over 1 year of age need 600 IU of vitamin D daily.[10] Very few foods are naturally high in vitamin D, so fortified foods, such as milk, provide most of the vitamin D in the American diet. One cup of fortified milk contains 100–125 IUs of vitamin D, so children often need a supplement to ensure adequate vitamin D intake.[11]

- *Fiber*. The recommended daily intake for fiber is 19 grams for children aged 1 to 3 years and 25 grams for 4- to 8-year-olds.[12] Like adults, toddlers and children need fiber to promote bowel regularity and prevent constipation. Fiber may also help with chronic disease prevention and weight control.[13] A balanced diet that contains whole fruits, vegetables, and whole grains helps a young child to meet his daily fiber needs.

- *Fluid*. Water, which makes up between 55 and 75 percent of body weight across the life span, is essential for life. Every day, children aged 1 to 3 years need about 4 cups of fluid including water, and those aged 3 to 5 years need about 5 cups of fluid. Milk and juice count toward daily fluid intake, and fruits and vegetables also supply fluid.[14] Caregivers need to monitor a child's beverage intake and provide water, milk, and no more than 4–6 ounces of 100% fruit juice daily, while avoiding soda and sugary drinks.[15]

picky eating Unwillingness to try unfamiliar foods.

food jags When a child will only eat the same food meal after meal.

Picky Eating and Food Jags Are Common in Small Children

Ellyn Satter is an expert on child feeding and nutrition. She has suggested an approach called Division of Responsibility, which proposes that parents and caregivers are responsible for what foods children are offered to eat, as well as when and where they eat, while children are responsible for how much they eat, if anything at all.[16] Food and power struggles can occur when parents and caregivers encourage a child to "clean their plate." Children are good self-regulators; they tend to listen to signals from their bodies, which tell them when to eat and when to stop. Encouraging a young child to overeat may inhibit the ability to self-regulate and result in the person becoming overweight later in life.

As young children grow and develop, they begin to feed themselves independently on a more regular basis. They also become more opinionated about their food preferences, especially when confronted with foods they have never tried before. For example, a child's first encounter with cooked mashed peas may result in the peas ending up on the floor. That doesn't mean that peas should be permanently off the menu, however. Health experts recommend a varied diet for people of all ages, and the toddler period is the ideal time to promote the acceptance of healthy foods, particularly fruits and vegetables. Therefore, though toddlers often demonstrate **picky eating**, parents should encourage them to try and accept new foods. To promote acceptance, parents and caregivers may need to repeatedly expose children to new foods (10 times or more).[17]

Parents and caregivers should also model healthy eating behaviors. Parents who eat a varied diet tend to have children who do the same, and eating meals together reinforces healthy eating habits.[18] Children often mimic adults' healthy—and unhealthy—eating behaviors. A mother who drinks diet soda for dinner instead of milk, or a father who insists that his 3-year-old eat asparagus but never puts it on his own plate, sends confusing messages about good nutrition. Involving children, even young ones, in food shopping, menu planning, and meal and snack preparation encourages them to enjoy a variety of foods.

While so-called "picky eating" is characterized by avoiding new foods, **food jags** are characterized by a child's tendency to favor certain foods to the exclusion of others. Did your parents ever mention that when you were small, all you wanted to eat was macaroni and cheese or peanut butter and jelly sandwiches on white bread? This behavior of getting "stuck" on a small selection of foods is quite common and normal in young children. It's important to note that food jags are usually temporary. A child who only wants to eat pretzels and oranges, or refuses to eat anything green, will likely emerge from the phase within a few days or weeks.

If a parent or other caregiver senses that the food jag is not going away in a reasonable amount of time, the child's eating pattern may pose a health threat. At that point, it is helpful to pay careful attention to what the child is eating as well as what he or she is avoiding. Is the child really "eating only crackers all day long," or is the parent forgetting that the child also drinks milk and eats chicken, green beans, and orange slices when they are offered? A parent or caregiver can keep a food diary of what the child eats and drinks for a few days to help identify any major problems. Sharing concerns (and the food diary) with the child's health care provider and asking for advice may prevent serious nutrient deficiencies in the long run.

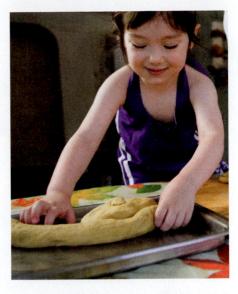

Having kids help in the kitchen is one way to get them excited about trying new foods and eating healthy meals.

When five-year-old girls (many of whom had dieting mothers) were asked, "What do people do when they are on a diet?" their responses included, "Eat more good things," "Can't eat any more snacks; smoke instead," and "Cook for the kids but don't eat the food they make." Caretakers should model healthy eating habits for all in view.[19]

Food jags, such as wanting to eat only one food (such as macaroni and cheese), or avoiding certain foods, are common among toddlers.

Practical Nutrition VIDEO

Marketing Foods to Preschoolers

Can marketers make healthy foods appeal more to preschoolers? At least one study suggests they may be able to do exactly that! Scan this QR code with your mobile device to access the video. You can also access the video in MasteringNutrition™.

Raising a Vegetarian Child

Young children can grow and develop normally on a vegetarian diet, as long as their eating pattern includes adequate vitamin D, calcium, iron, zinc, and other nutrients they may be missing by avoiding animal foods. Like any eating style, vegetarian diets should provide adequate servings of whole grains, vegetables, fruit, and lean protein sources, such as nuts and seeds, eggs, beans, and soy products. A vegetarian diet may be high in fiber, which can be so filling for children that they miss out on nutrients they need. Children who completely avoid animal foods or eat inadequate servings of animal foods require vitamin B_{12} from dietary supplements, fortified foods, or both, because vitamin B_{12} is found naturally only in animal foods.

LO 15.1 **The Take-Home Message** Toddlers grow at a slower rate than infants and have relatively reduced appetites. Parents and caregivers need to be sure that toddlers get adequate amounts of calcium, iron, vitamin D, and fiber. They also need to monitor a child's beverage intake and provide water and milk, limit 100% juice, and avoid soda and sugary drinks. Parents and caregivers should be sure to offer children appropriate portion sizes. Young children have the ability to stop eating when full and shouldn't be forced to clean their plates. Caregivers should be good role models when it comes to getting children to try new foods, which may need to be offered 10 times or more before they are accepted. Food jags are normal and usually temporary. Young children can grow and thrive on vegetarian diets as long as the diets are carefully planned.

What Are the Nutritional Needs and Issues of School-Aged Children?

LO 15.2 Describe school-aged children's nutrient needs, and discuss some of the nutrition-related issues they face, including childhood obesity.

School-aged children, those between the ages of 6 and 11, have plenty of growing to do and they, like their younger counterparts, require a high-quality diet to maximize growth and development. (See Table 15.1 on page 569 for the range of calorie needs for children in this age group.) School-aged children usually have a more rigid schedule than younger children and they may not eat as often throughout the day as toddlers and preschoolers.

At this point in the life cycle, children learn habits that often persist into adulthood, so encouraging a healthy lifestyle is essential. Parents and caregivers should capitalize on their role-model status, as children are heavily influenced by their parents and other adult caregivers. Although school-aged children have developed skills such as tying their own shoes or buckling their own seat belts, parents and caregivers are still responsible for providing a healthy diet.

While most children develop normally, some have developmental disabilities that may affect their eating patterns. The Examining the Evidence feature "Nutrition and Developmental Disabilities" on the next page explores the possible interconnections of nutrition and developmental disabilities. Children who have health issues may have special dietary concerns. For example, children with autism often become especially fixated on eating certain foods and may be reluctant to try new foods. Overcoming eating issues generally requires intervention and support from health professionals, such as registered dietitian nutritionists, who work with children with special needs.

school-aged children Children between the ages of 6 and 11.

Nutrition and Developmental Disabilities

An estimated 11 percent of children in the United States have **attention deficit/hyperactivity disorder (ADHD)**, also called attention deficit disorder, or ADD.[1] ADHD is a condition in which children have trouble paying attention, are impulsive, and are overly physically active. ADHD symptoms often appear in early childhood.[2] ADHD affects the child who has it, and, depending on its severity, ADHD may also cause difficulty for the entire family. ADHD is often treated with medication and behavioral therapy, and parents of children with the condition may wonder whether diet, particularly the amount of sugar and food additives a child consumes, also plays a role in managing ADHD.

Research suggests that the behavior of some children with ADHD improves with the avoidance of certain foods and food additives. In the early 1970s Dr. Benjamin Feingold, an allergist, promoted the idea that some foods triggered ADHD. Feingold's hypothesis generated interest among parents and controversy among health professionals. In 1982, the National Institutes of Health convened a panel to review the research on diet and hyperactivity, and concluded that food additives and some foods aggravated hyperactivity in some children.[3] The popularity of the so-called Feingold diet persists today, but it doesn't work for every child. See more about the Feingold diet at www.feingold.org.

Sugar has also been targeted for worsening behavioral problems. High-sugar foods elevate blood glucose levels, especially when eaten alone, and may cause temporary hyperactivity in children. However, there is little evidence that solidifies a direct relationship between sugar and ADHD.[4] According to the American Academy of Pediatrics, although one early study did reveal a link between high sugar consumption and hyperactive behavior, there was no evidence that one caused the other or that the behavior problems were not due to different parenting styles or other factors.[5] While sugar consumption has not been shown to cause or enhance ADHD-related behavior, it's a good idea for parents to limit added sugars and provide a balanced diet, which is a healthy strategy for all children.

Identifying and eliminating foods that may exacerbate ADHD can be challenging, especially because children don't eat the same foods every day, and limiting their diets to "special" foods draws attention to children. Parents of children with ADHD may want to consult with a registered dietitian nutritionist (RDN) to help their child with nutritional issues, such as underweight due to side effects of certain prescription medications used to treat ADHD that cause decreased appetite and lead to weight loss. Disruptive mealtimes may also be a concern from a nutritional standpoint because the child may not eat the amount of food he needs to grow and develop properly. Organizations such as the National Institute of Mental Health (www.nimh.nih.gov) and the American Academy of Child and Adolescent Psychiatry (www.aacap.org) provide information for families with children who have ADHD.

Autism is another developmental condition that is actually a group of developmental brain disorders, collectively called **autism spectrum disorder (ASD)**. "Spectrum" refers to the wide range of symptoms, skills, and levels of impairment, or disability, that children with ASD may exhibit. According to the Centers for Disease Control, 1 in 50 U.S. children aged 6 to 17 had diagnosed ASD per parental reports during the period of 2011 to 2012, up from 1 in 86 for the same age group in 2007.[6]

ASD symptoms often appear within the first three years of life, and ASD may result in impaired communication and social interaction, and repetitive behaviors. The symptoms and severity of autism vary greatly. There is no cure for ASD. Effective treatment includes intensive behavioral therapy during the toddler and preschool years to improve cognition and language skills.[7]

Parents of children with ASD may seek out alternative therapies, including specialized diets, to help their children. Several diet strategies have been suggested as possible treatments for reducing the behaviors associated with autism. Some researchers speculate that autism may also involve the gastrointestinal tract and the immune system, but the evidence is not conclusive. One of the most popular diets eliminates gluten (a protein found in most grains, including wheat) as well as casein (a milk protein). Other dietary interventions include restricting food allergens; including probiotics in the diet; following a yeast-free diet; and supplementing the diet with vitamin A, vitamin C, vitamin B_6, magnesium, folic acid, vitamin B_{12}, and omega-3 fatty acids.[8] More research is needed to determine the efficacy of dietary interventions, and parents of autistic children are encouraged to work with an RDN with expertise in this field.

WHAT DO YOU THINK?

1. How can developmental disorders affect the nutritional status of young children?
2. What are some possible explanations for the apparent increase in diagnoses of ADHD and ASD in recent years?
3. Why is it difficult for researchers to determine whether there is a relationship between nutrition and developmental disorders?

attention deficit/hyperactivity disorder (ADHD) Previously designated as attention deficit disorder (ADD). A condition in which an individual may be easily distracted, may have difficulty listening, following directions, and focusing and sustaining attention, and/or may have inconsistent performance in school.

autism spectrum disorder (ASD) Collective term for a group of brain disorders that make it difficult or impossible for a person to communicate and relate to others and may also be characterized by repetitive activities.

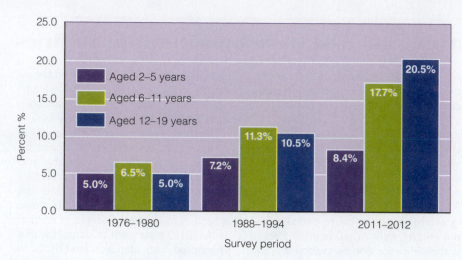

Figure 15.1 Increase in Obesity among U.S. Children and Adolescents

Note: Childhood obesity is defined as a BMI greater than or equal to the gender- and weight-specific 95th percentile from the CDC 2000 Growth Charts.

High Obesity Rates in School-Aged Children

Childhood obesity has more than doubled in children and tripled in adolescents in the past 30 years.[20] (See **Figure 15.1**.) Eighteen percent of children aged 6 to 11 were considered obese as of 2012.[21] Several factors contribute to the excess calories and inadequate activity that lead to **childhood overweight and obesity**.

Children Are Overeating

Children are taking in excess calories from several sources, including sugar-sweetened beverages such as soda and sports drinks, candy, chips, and baked goods such as cookies. Food seems to be everywhere, including in places where it was previously unavailable, making it easier to eat more often. As childhood obesity prevalence tripled from the 1970s to the present, eating frequency in children increased from three to five eating occasions per day.[22] Additionally, portion sizes, at home and in restaurants, are bigger than they were decades ago. For example, bagels were typically 3 inches in diameter and about 140 calories 20 years ago. Today, they measure about twice that and supply 350 calories.[23] On average, American children eat both more than the recommended amounts of solid fat, added sugar, and sodium, and fewer servings of whole grains, fruits, and vegetables than they should.[24] This not only contributes to excess weight gain, but also explains why many kids don't get enough calcium, vitamin D, potassium, and fiber.[25]

Children Are Not Getting Enough Physical Activity

In general, American children do not get the recommended amount of daily physical activity that is needed to support healthy growth and development and to balance calories consumed from foods and beverages. The following are two factors contributing to the decreased level of physical activity among children in America in recent years:

- *Increased screen time.* Research shows that 8- to 18-year-olds devote an average of 7½ hours daily to entertainment media, including television, computer time, video games, and movies.[26] The American Academy of Pediatrics recommends

childhood overweight and obesity
Excess body fat in children.

limiting combined screen time from television, computers, and video games to 1 to 2 hours per day and making sure that what is viewed is high-quality content.[27]

- *Fewer opportunities for activity.* Children and teens require at least 60 minutes of physical activity every day, but most are not reaching this suggested level of exercise. One recent study found that 42 percent of children and only 8 percent of adolescents engaged in moderate- to vigorous-intensity activity on 5 of the past 7 days for at least 60 minutes each day.[28] Schools are an ideal setting to provide physical activity, as a typical school day lasts about 7 hours for many kids. Yet academic achievement is often emphasized over exercise at school. For example, just six states (Illinois, Hawaii, Massachusetts, Mississippi, New York, and Vermont) require physical education in every grade, K–12.[29] Prioritizing physical activity as a family helps increase the likelihood that children are active and reduces the risk of children becoming overweight and obese. Parents and caregivers should encourage family activity, model healthy lifestyle habits that include regular exercise, and provide regular opportunities for children to be active.

Obesity Contributes to Type 2 Diabetes

Overweight and obesity in children is linked to several chronic conditions, including type 2 diabetes. Type 2 diabetes, historically seen in adulthood, is on the rise in U.S. children and teens, and obesity is often associated with a diagnosis of the condition.[30] Prediabetes, which is characterized as a fasting blood glucose level of $100 < 126$ mg/dL, is considered a marker for type 2 diabetes. From 2001 to 2009, the prevalence of type 2 diabetes in American youth increased by 30.5 percent.[31]

Early identification and adoption of a healthy lifestyle, including a balanced diet with adequate calories and regular physical activity, are necessary for children affected by prediabetes or type 2 diabetes. The sooner a family learns what the child should eat and how to manage the other aspects of the disease, the better off the child will be both immediately and in the long run. Managing type 2 diabetes involves dietary moderation, variety, and balance, as well as regular exercise, so that an entire family should consider eating in the same healthy fashion as the child. Taking a family walk or bike ride after dinner and enjoying weekend games of basketball or tennis instead of watching TV or playing sedentary video games are excellent ways to teach the importance of physical activity. Tackling any health issue as a family provides support for the child and increases the chance of controlling the effects of the condition. Children with type 2 diabetes, prediabetes, or weight-control issues should work with a registered dietitian nutritionist to determine the best eating plan for optimal growth and development.

Daily Food Plans for Kids Help Guide Food Choices

Most parents are not nutrition experts, and the idea of trying to meet a child's nutrient needs every day may be overwhelming and confusing. Consumer-friendly Daily Food Plans, available at ChooseMyPlate.gov, help parents and caregivers make good food choices for children. The 10 Tips Nutrition Education Series (see **Figure 15.2**), also available at ChooseMyPlate.gov in English and Spanish, provides useful tip sheets that address a number of important nutrition topics.

ChooseMyPlate.gov encourages children and adults to:

- *Eat foods from every food group every day.* Including an array of foods provides children and adults with the nutrients they need. See **Table 15.2** for ideas to help school-aged children get the fruits and vegetables they need every day.

We Can!

Want to learn more about programs that help families battle obesity? Visit the National Heart, Lung, and Blood Institute at www.nhlbi.nih.gov to learn about the We Can! program (Ways to Enhance Children's Activity & Nutrition) from the National Institutes of Health, which helps parents and caregivers prevent overweight and obesity in children.

Cut back on kid's sweet treats

1 Serve small portions
2 Offer healthy drinks
3 Use the check-out lane that does not display candy
4 Choose not to offer sweets as rewards
5 Make fruit the everyday dessert
6 Make food fun
7 Encourage kids to invent new snacks
8 Play detective in the cereal aisle
9 Make treats "treats," not everyday foods
10 If kids don't eat their meal, they don't need sweet "extras"

Be a healthy role model for children

1 Show by example
2 Go food shopping together
3 Get creative in the kitchen
4 Offer the same foods for everyone
5 Reward with attention, not food
6 Focus on each other at the table
7 Listen to your child
8 Limit screen time
9 Encourage physical activity
10 Be a good food role model

Figure 15.2 Tips for Helping Children Eat Healthfully from ChooseMyPlate.gov

- *Choose healthier foods from each group.* While all foods fit into a balanced diet, some foods are healthier than others, such as whole grains versus refined white grains, and low-fat dairy foods rather than higher-fat versions.
- *Make the right choices for you.* ChooseMyPlate.gov customizes eating advice for healthy people over the age of 2.
- *Take healthy eating one step at a time.* Start with one positive change that's easy to make, and wait until that new behavior becomes second nature. Add another change to your eating pattern when you're ready.
- *Use healthy fats.* Fats are not an official MyPlate food group, but they are part of a balanced diet for children and adults. Healthy fats, such as olive oil and canola oil, tub margarine, and the fat in avocados, nuts, and nut butters are encouraged.
- *Be physically active on a regular basis.* Physical activity balances calories consumed and helps to promote a healthy weight.

The Importance of Breakfast

It's difficult to overstate the importance of a nutritious morning meal for school-aged children, or for anyone, for that matter. Breakfast can positively benefit cognition (especially memory), academic performance, school attendance rates,

Table 15.2

TASTE: More Matters: Include Fruit and Vegetables in Meals and Snacks

T: Try something new	Add shredded carrots to casseroles, chili, meatloaf, soups, and stews. Purée beans and add to sauces, soups, and stews. Drop berries into cereal, yogurt, and pancake batter. Make fruit and vegetable smoothies. Enjoy bean and vegetable burritos. Use leftover veggies in salads, or add them to a can of soup. Keep grab-and-go snacks handy, such as snack-sized boxes of raisins, dried fruit, trail mix, and frozen 100% fruit juice bars. Cherry tomatoes and carrot sticks with hummus make a great pairing.
A: All forms of fruits and veggies count!	Consider fresh, frozen, 100% juice, canned, and dried. Cook fruits and veggies in different ways, including steamed, slow-cooked, sautéed, stir-fried, grilled, roasted, and microwaved.
S: Shop smart	Fresh produce in season is more affordable. Look for specials. Clean and cut up produce so it's ready to use. At a restaurant, substitute vegetables for rice or french fries.
T: Turn it into a family activity	Make fruit or vegetable kabobs with older kids. Add vegetables to homemade pizza. Take kids to farmers' markets.
E: Explore the bountiful variety	Use salad bars or buffets to try new flavors. When grocery shopping, encourage kids to choose a new produce item for meals and snacks.

psychosocial function, and mood. If a child is hungry during the midmorning hours, it may affect her ability to learn. Breakfast literally "breaks the fast" of going without eating for 10 to 12 hours overnight. That's why the morning meal improves blood glucose levels, which supports a child's energy levels and comprehension. Studies conducted by the USDA on the School Breakfast Program (SBP) have found that children who received a school breakfast performed better on standardized tests than children who did not eat breakfast.[32]

Research has also shown that eating breakfast may be associated with healthier body weight and a higher quality diet in children and adolescents. Nutrients missed at breakfast, including calcium, fiber, and certain vitamins and minerals, are rarely made up for during the rest of the day. The *Dietary Guidelines for Americans* (DGA) concluded that moderate evidence suggests that children who skip breakfast are at increased risk of overweight and obesity, and that the evidence is even stronger for adolescents. The DGA also concluded that moderate evidence supports a link between eating breakfast and the consumption of certain nutrients in children and teens.

Breakfast can be eaten at home before school or at school through the School Breakfast Program. Low-sugar, fortified cereal with low-fat milk and fruit is a quick and nutritious breakfast choice that provides several nutrients, including fiber. Fortified cereals are good or excellent sources of vitamins and minerals including iron, folic acid, zinc, and B vitamins. Many fortified cereals also contain added vitamin A, thiamin, niacin, calcium, phosphorus, and magnesium. If children don't have time to eat breakfast at home and don't receive breakfast at school, parents and other caregivers can also provide quick, nutritious morning meals that can be eaten on the way to school. See the Table Tips for some on-the-go breakfast ideas.

Table TIPS

Breakfast on the Go

Make a to-go yogurt parfait in a plastic cup with low-sugar ready-to-eat whole-grain cereal, a single-serving container of low-fat yogurt, and banana slices, berries, or dried fruit

Sprinkle reduced-fat cheese on a corn tortilla and melt it in the oven or microwave. Add some salsa and corn and roll it up into a portable tortilla tube.

Spread a thin layer of peanut butter or sunflower seed butter on a toasted whole-wheat waffle, and pair it with a travel cup of low-fat or fat-free milk.

The National School Lunch Program provides breakfast and noontime meals for millions of school-aged children.

School Meals Contribute to a Child's Nutritional Status

For some children, school meals are the healthiest—and perhaps the only significant—meals they eat all day. The SBP and the National School Lunch Program (NSLP) are federally assisted meal programs that provide nutritionally balanced, low-cost or free breakfast and lunch meals. In 2011, the SBP fed more than 12.1 million students breakfast, and the NSLP fed more than 31 million students lunch each school day. SBP and NSLP meals must meet nutrition standards based on the latest *Dietary Guidelines for Americans*. While school lunches must meet federal meal requirements, decisions about what foods to serve and how they are prepared are made by local school food authorities.[33] School gardens also positively contribute to a child's nutritional status. Research shows that they can increase consumption of and preferences for vegetables as well as willingness to try new fruits and vegetables.[34]

Imagine that you have the important job of being a school food-service director. On the one hand, you are running a business. You need to make enough money to pay your employees and meet your expenses. To help control the cost of school lunches, the USDA reimburses for breakfast and lunch meals if they meet published meal guidelines. That means the food-service director must adhere to the strict nutritional guidelines. On the other hand, you also need to satisfy your young customers, who have an array of food preferences. In addition, you may face competition from nearby fast-food restaurants, convenience stores, and vending machines vying for your customers' food dollars. School food-service directors must satisfy several different groups of people, so they have a lot to consider when deciding what to serve.

The job of school food-service directors got a bit easier in 2010 when the Healthy Hunger-Free Kids Act was passed, which limits competition coming from within their own cafeteria. Specifically, the *Smart Snacks in School* regulation of this act mandates that all foods sold at school during the school day (foods sold a la carte, in the school store, and from vending machines) meet certain nutrition standards based on calories and fat, as well as sodium and sugar content.[35] Foods such as candy, cookies, and soda are no longer allowed in school cafeterias or vending machines, and they have been replaced with a la carte snacks such as popcorn, fruit cups, and water.

When children do not choose a school lunch, it's up to the parents and other caregivers to provide lunch. Children who don't buy a school meal need a suitable substitute. Simply giving a child money may result in unhealthy food choices for lunch, which will shortchange him of about one-third of his nutrition for the day. It makes more sense for parents and kids to use the Daily Food Plans at ChooseMyPlate .gov as a guide for healthier brown-bag lunches. A lunch that the child has helped to plan has a better chance of being eaten. Without the child's input, the "healthy lunch" may end up being swapped for unhealthy foods, or worse, tossed in the trash. The Table Tips provide some useful ideas to improve the likelihood that a child will eat his or her packed lunch.

LO 15.2 **The Take-Home Message** Increasing obesity rates are contributing to rising rates of type 2 diabetes in children. Parents and caregivers need to be sure children limit their intake of low-nutrient foods and get enough physical activity. Daily Food Plans available at ChooseMyPlate.gov address the nutritional needs of preschool

TableTIPS

Tips for Packing School Lunches

Get children involved with their lunch by letting them pick out a fun lunch box or decorate a brown paper bag with stickers.

Involve the child in planning healthy lunches and then shop for the items together.

Make a lunch calendar and go over the specific days the child will eat a school-provided lunch and the days he or she will pack lunch.

Select healthy foods that the child likes and ask if there are new items he or she wants to try.

Be mindful of what the child is actually eating and what might be left behind or thrown away. If, for example, the apple keeps coming back day after day, it's time to try another type of fruit.

and school-aged children. Children who eat breakfast tend to have better concentration in class and better overall dietary habits, among other benefits, than those who do not eat breakfast. School meals provide nourishment for children. For children who don't eat school lunches, parents and caregivers need to provide a healthy alternative.

What Are the Nutritional Needs and Issues of Adolescents?

LO 15.3 Describe adolescents' nutrient needs, and discuss some of the nutrition-related issues they face, including disordered eating.

Adolescence is the stage of the life cycle between the start of puberty and adulthood. Adolescence is a time of transformation that includes the following physical and psychological changes:

- *Hormonal changes.* Hormones are responsible for the development of secondary sex characteristics, such as pubic hair, and a lower speaking voice in boys. Girls experience breast development and their first menstrual period (called *menarche*). Adolescents may also experience acne.
- *Physical changes.* During adolescence, children get taller and heavier. Lean muscle mass and body fat stores increase, and bones become longer and thicker. For example, by age 18, teens have accrued about 92 percent of their peak bone mass, which is important because peak bone mass is linked to risk of bone fracture later in life.[36] An adolescent's rapid rate of growth must be supported with a balanced eating plan that includes adequate amounts of protein, calcium, vitamin D, and iron. As with younger age groups, the rate of obesity is increasing among adolescents, and approximately 18 percent are now considered obese.[37]
- *Emotional changes.* Some nutrition-related issues that arise during adolescence may be related to a child's emotional growth. Adolescents experience a strong desire for independence and individuality, and they often want to make their own food choices, which may differ from what is typically served at home.

Peer Pressure and Other Factors Influence Teen Eating Behaviors

Parents and other caregivers have the most control over what children eat when they are young. As children get older, however, their peers become increasingly influential when it comes to food choices. Fitting in is very important to teens, including when eating with their friends; if a soft drink and a burger is what everyone else is eating, then a teen may be less likely to opt for a salad and a bottle of water. Young people may notice what, when, and how their peers eat and base their own eating decisions on how others in their group behave.

Some teens may defy authority or express their individuality by adopting different dietary eating choices than their parents, such as insisting on organically grown foods or adopting a vegan diet. They may also choose to smoke cigarettes, use illicit drugs, and drink alcohol as a result of influence from peers, the media, and adult role models. Teens who struggle with their body image may skip breakfast and other meals in an effort at weight control.

A teen's busy schedule may also influence his or her diet. Snacking—eating between meals—is typically part of an adolescent's eating style, and is useful when kids don't have the time for a full meal. However, snacks should be regarded as

Teen eating habits are often influenced by peers and social settings.

adolescence The developmental period between childhood and early adulthood.

Figure 15.3 Epiphyseal Plate in Long Bone
Adolescent bone growth takes place along the epiphyseal plate. Once the plates close, lengthening of the bone stops.

nutritious mini-meals, and not meal wreckers. For the most part, teens should avoid high-calorie foods that offer little in the way of nutrition, such as soda, sports drinks and energy drinks, cookies, chips, and candy, and reserve these foods for treats. Given that nearly 35 percent of adolescents are overweight or obese, excess calories from fast food or other lower-cost, nutrient-poor foods should be limited.

Adolescents Need Calcium and Vitamin D for Bone Growth

Adolescents experience rapid bone growth. Most of the growth occurs in the **epiphyseal plate** (**Figure 15.3**), the area of tissue near the end of the long bones in children and adolescents.[38] **Bone mineral density (BMD)** increases through early adulthood, and **peak bone mass** may not be reached until age 30.

More than 99 percent of total body calcium resides in the skeleton. Vitamin D promotes calcium absorption. During rapid periods of bone growth, such as adolescence, inadequate intakes of calcium and vitamin D can result in low peak bone mass and increase fracture risk both now and in later decades.

Adolescents require 600 IU of vitamin D daily from foods, dietary supplements, or a combination, and 1,300 milligrams of calcium daily.[39] Generally speaking, teenagers don't consume enough calcium and vitamin D. One reason for this trend is teens' increased preference for soft drinks, which are nearly devoid of calcium and vitamin D, over milk and other beverages, such as fortified soy beverages and fortified orange juice, that provide calcium and vitamin D. Consumption of sugar drinks is highest among people aged 12 to 19 (see **Figure 15.4**). Sodas and other sugar-sweetened beverages, such as energy drinks and sports drinks, may taste good and be popular with teens, but the beverages lack the nutrients that are crucial for bone health.

Teenage Girls Need More Iron

Compared with earlier in their childhood, adolescents need additional iron to support muscle growth and increased blood volume, and teen girls need more iron than boys to offset blood loss in menstruation. Many adolescent girls, especially those who restrict their calorie intake, have an inadequate iron intake. An estimated 9 percent of girls aged 12 to 19 have iron deficiency or iron-deficiency anemia.[40] Teens who limit

epiphyseal plate The growth plate of the bone. In puberty, growth in this area leads to increases in height.

bone mineral density (BMD) The amount of minerals, in particular calcium, per volume in an individual's bone.

peak bone mass The genetically determined maximum amount of bone mass an individual can build up.

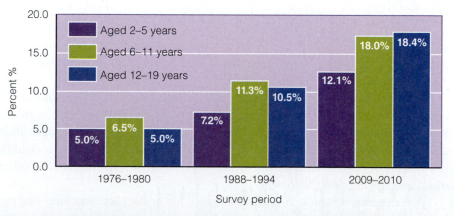

Figure 15.4 Daily Calorie Intake from Sugar Drinks, United States, 2005–2008
The rate of consumption of sugar drinks increases among both males and females until ages 12–19 years and then decreases with age.

their intake of fortified grains, such as breakfast cereal, and of lean meats, poultry, and seafood, may fail to meet iron needs unless they take a dietary supplement.

Adolescents: At Risk for Disordered Eating

Eating disorders such as anorexia nervosa, bulimia nervosa, and binge eating disorder, as well as disordered behaviors including restricting and purging (vomiting, laxative use, and excessive exercise), typically emerge during adolescence and have emotional as well as physical consequences. Teens who don't eat enough, eat and then purge, or just purge run the risk of severe nutrient deficiencies that affect their energy level and their health in the short term and the long run. Adolescents who are struggling with body image should seek help from a licensed mental health professional who specializes in disordered eating.

LO 15.3 **The Take-Home Message** Adolescents face hormonal, physical, and emotional changes. They typically want to have control over their food and lifestyle decisions, and peers and the media exert a tremendous amount of influence on eating habits. Calcium, vitamin D, and iron intakes are particularly important during adolescence to ensure adequate bone and muscle growth and to prevent deficiencies. Increased consumption of soft drinks and decreased milk consumption can compromise bone health. Adolescents are sometimes at risk of developing disordered eating patterns due to poor body image, emotional issues, and peer pressure. Because many adolescents live in the "here and now," they may not realize the long-term health consequences of poor diet and lifestyle habits they may adopt during their teenage years.

What Are the Nutritional Needs of Older Adults?

LO 15.4 Summarize the nutrient needs of older adults, and discuss some of the nutrition-related health concerns common to old age.

If you were born in the United States around 1900, you would have been lucky to see your fiftieth birthday, as the average **life expectancy** at the time was 47 years. When it comes to life expectancy, things have changed considerably since 1900.

Those born at the tail end of the so-called baby boom generation, between 1946 and 1964, are expected to be the fastest growing segment of the population in years to come (**Figure 15.5** on the next page). The number of people age 65 or older is expected to increase to an estimated 71 million in 2030, and the number of people over the age of 80 years is expected to increase to 19.5 million in 2030.[41]

Advances in medical research, health care, and public health policy are among the factors that have contributed to Americans' living longer. For example, the infectious and deadly diseases of the early twentieth century, such as tuberculosis, pneumonia, polio, mumps, and measles, have been dramatically reduced, thanks to widespread efforts to vaccinate children, as well as improved medical treatment for infectious diseases and other conditions, such as chronic illness. Public education campaigns that emphasize healthy lifestyle habits to prevent and manage conditions such as high blood pressure and elevated blood cholesterol levels to reduce the risk of heart disease, stroke, and certain cancers have also contributed to people living longer.

Good nutrition plays a key role in healthy aging. Seniors require a balanced eating plan with adequate amounts of protein, carbohydrate, and healthy fats. Calorie needs tend to decline with advancing age, but with the exception of a few vitamins

Table TIPS

Teen Table Tips

Encourage teens to read labels on sugar-sweetened drinks, such as soda, sports drinks, and energy drinks, to note the number of calories and the lack of other nutrients.

Talk to them about the short-lived effects of pills and other quick fixes to lose weight versus the long-term benefits of learning to eat healthfully.

Direct teens to credible websites for information, such as http://kidshealth.org or the *Take Charge of Your Health: A Guide for Teenagers* publication at www.win.niddk.nih.gov.

Be a role model! Eat well, get enough rest, exercise, be realistic about your body weight, and don't smoke.

Teach teens to look for healthy options, such as lower-fat sandwiches, salads, and low-sugar granola bars, at fast-food restaurants and in vending machines.

People are living longer today than in previous decades.

life expectancy The number of years that a person will live.

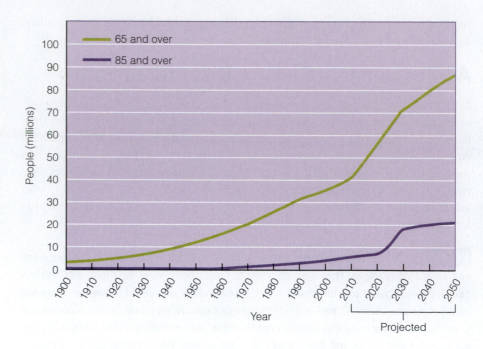

Figure 15.5 Aging of the Baby Boomers The number of older adults in the United States is expected to increase dramatically over the next several decades.

and minerals, other nutrient needs do not decrease, which makes it even more important for older adults to choose nutrient-rich foods every day.

Older Adults Need Fewer Calories, Not Less Nutrition

The body's metabolic rate declines with age, and generally speaking, older adults require fewer calories as time goes on. The decline in calorie needs is often a result of lean tissue loss, primarily muscle mass and less physical activity. For example, a 70-year-old moderately active man needs about 400 fewer calories—about the amount in a turkey sandwich—than his 40-year-old counterpart. By the age of 80, a sedentary female requires only about 1,600 calories a day, which is 600 fewer calories than she did when she was a moderately active 20-year-old.[42]

Protein intake tends to decline with age because people eat less food, and the oldest of the old have the lowest protein consumption. Adequate protein is necessary throughout the life cycle to support good health by providing amino acids to build cells and repair tissues, among other functions. As you get older, it's important to provide the body with the protein it needs to repair and produce lean tissue and to make bone tissue, too.

Though calorie needs may be reduced, the needs for vitamins, minerals, fiber, and other nutrients are not, and some nutrient requirements increase. **Figure 15.6** addresses the unique nutritional needs of older Americans. Foods rich in phytonutrients, such as fruits, vegetables, and whole grains, are as important as ever because phytonutrients play a role in reducing the risk of conditions that are more common in the aged, including certain cancers, heart disease, cataracts, and age-related macular degeneration.

Older Adults Need Adequate Fiber and Fluid

Adults of all ages need adequate fiber throughout the day. Fiber requirements are based on calorie needs, so adults may eat less fiber as they age. Recall from Chapter 4 that fiber may help reduce the risk of diverticulosis, heart disease, type 2 diabetes mellitus, obesity, and certain cancers, which are typically more common later in life.

MyPlate for Older Adults

Illustration by Betsy Hayes ©2011 Tufts University   http://now.tufts.edu/articles/eat-well-age-well

Figure 15.6 Older Adults Benefit from Good Nutrition and Physical Activity
Older adults need to focus on nutrient-dense foods that contain adequate fiber, calcium, vitamin B_{12}, and vitamin D. With a declining metabolic rate, they require fewer calories. Food choices should emphasize complex carbohydrates, lean protein foods, and healthy fats. They also need to ensure adequate fluid intake and regular participation in physical activity.

Fluid works with fiber to help prevent constipation. Consuming adequate fluid is important to prevent dehydration that may cause a lack of energy and may be confused with dementia. An older person's thirst mechanism also becomes blunted to the point where he doesn't detect that his body needs fluid, which can increase dehydration risk.

People in their 70s, 80s, and 90s may take diuretics, which prevent excess fluid buildup in the body. Diuretics may cause frequent urination and people who take them may drink less fluid to avoid frequent trips to the bathroom, which may contribute to inadequate hydration. Dehydration can also lead to constipation, another common condition in older adults, as the stool becomes hard and compacted in the colon.

As with most adults, there is little room for low-nutrient drinks, such as soda, and alcoholic beverages in an older adult's diet. Water and milk are the best beverages for meeting fluid needs and avoiding dehydration. **Table 15.3** summarizes some dietary needs of older adults.

Older Adults Should Monitor Their Micronutrients

Appropriate intakes of certain micronutrients become a concern as we age, including the following:[43]

- *Vitamin A.* Although the recommended daily amount of vitamin A doesn't change for people over the age of 50, too much preformed vitamin A (derived from animal sources), which is stored in the body, may increase the risk for osteoporosis and fractures. Older adults should be cautious when choosing supplements and fortified foods so as to prevent overconsuming this form of vitamin A. However, beta-carotene and other carotenoid precursors of vitamin A,

Table 15.3

Dietary Needs of Older Adults

What Older Adults Need	Why Older Adults Need It	How They Can Get It
Nutrient-rich food	Lower metabolic rate reduces daily calorie needs and makes higher quality food even more necessary to supply nutrients.	Choose foods in each food group that are low in added sugar, fat, and sodium.
Adequate protein	Provides the amino acids to preserve lean tissue and bones	Include protein-rich foods, such as dairy, eggs, seafood, and chicken, at every meal and snack.
Adequate fiber	Reduced calorie intake decreases fiber intake.	Choose whole-wheat bread, cereals, and grains such as brown rice, vegetables, and whole fruit.
Adequate fluid	Decreased ability of kidneys to concentrate urine and a blunted thirst mechanism, which can increase risk of dehydration	Drink milk or water with and between meals.
Vitamin D–rich foods	Decreased ability to make the active form of vitamin D, which decreases the absorption of calcium and phosphorus and increases the risk of osteoporosis	Choose vitamin D–fortified milk, yogurt, and cereals. Add a vitamin D supplement if needed.
Synthetic vitamin B_{12}	Reduced production of stomach acid that releases naturally occurring vitamin B_{12} from foods. Synthetic vitamin B_{12} does not require stomach acid.	Choose vitamin B_{12}–fortified cereals, breads, and soy milk. Add a dietary supplement if needed.
Adequate iron-rich foods	Necessary for strong immune system and transportation of oxygen to cells and tissues	Choose lean meat, fish, and poultry. Enjoy enriched grains and cereals along with vitamin C–rich foods (e.g., citrus fruits) to enhance iron absorption.
Adequate calcium	To help prevent the loss of bone mass with age	Consume 3 servings of dairy foods daily. Add a dietary supplement if necessary.

found in dietary supplements and in brightly colored fruits and vegetables, do not pose a threat to health and are considered beneficial.

- *Vitamin D.* The skin's ability to make vitamin D from sunlight declines with age. Further, the intestines and kidneys lose some ability to absorb and convert vitamin D into its active form. Vitamin D needs are age dependent. The suggested daily intake for vitamin D in the diet increases from 600 IU daily to 800 IU daily for those age 70 and older.[44]

- *Vitamin B_{12}.* Health experts estimate that a significant number of people over the age of 50 have trouble absorbing the naturally occurring form of vitamin B_{12}, which is found only in animal products. As you age, the stomach secretes less hydrochloric acid, which functions to separate vitamin B_{12} from the proteins in foods of animal origin, such as eggs, meat, and milk. To combat this change in body chemistry, people over age 50 should consume the majority of the daily recommended 2.4 micrograms of vitamin B_{12} in the synthetic form, found in fortified foods and dietary supplements. Synthetic vitamin B_{12} does not require hydrochloric acid to benefit the body.[45]

- *Iron.* Iron deficiency is uncommon among adult men and postmenopausal women who are not losing blood on a regular basis. However, iron deficiency can occur in older adults who do not consume adequate iron-rich foods, and those with chronic malabsorption, intestinal blood loss, or other ongoing conditions including kidney disease, cancer, and arthritis.[46]

- *Zinc.* Zinc is found in lean meat, poultry, fortified cereals, dairy foods, and legumes (dried beans and peas). A zinc deficiency may affect the immune system, as well as the sense of taste, which could reduce a person's intake of nutritious foods. Data from the National Health and Nutrition Examination Study (NHANES) III indicate that adults age 60 years or older from food-insufficient families had lower intakes of zinc and several other nutrients and were more likely to have zinc intakes below 50 percent of the RDA on a given day than those from food-sufficient families.[47]

- *Calcium.* Calcium absorption declines with age, and suggested intakes change with time. After age 50, experts suggest women consume 1,200 milligrams of calcium daily, up from the recommended 1,000 milligrams; men need 1,000 milligrams daily until age 70, and then should take in 1,200 milligrams of calcium daily after that.[48] Three daily servings of dairy, such as milk, yogurt, and cheese, or orange juice and soy beverages fortified with calcium as part of a balanced diet supplies nearly all the calcium older people require. However, many adults, especially older Americans, are calcium deficient, increasing their risk for bone disease. People who do not get the recommended daily calcium may need supplements to make up the difference between what they need and what they consume from foods.

- *Sodium.* The 2010 *Dietary Guidelines for Americans* recommends that everyone over the age of 50 reduce their daily sodium intake to 1,500 milligrams or less to help reduce the risk of high blood pressure, which is more common with advancing age. Keeping blood pressure in the normal range reduces an individual's risk of cardiovascular disease, congestive heart failure, and kidney disease. People who have high blood pressure, or who have diabetes or chronic kidney disease, may need to make further modifications in their sodium intake.[49]

LO 15.4 **The Take-Home Message** Life expectancy has increased in the last century due to improved research and health care, as well as dietary and lifestyle changes. Older adults need fewer calories but not less nutrition as they age. Nutrient-rich food selections are important to meet their fiber, fluid, vitamin, mineral, and phytonutrient needs.

What Additional Challenges Do Older Adults Face?

LO 15.5 Describe the physical, economic, and psychological factors that can affect the health of older Americans.

Many adults live productive, happy lives well into their eighties. But many seniors may not. Certain physical and emotional changes that accompany old age can make eating and exercise a challenge; such changes can include health conditions such as heart disease, cancer, and arthritis.

Eating Right for Health and to Prevent and Manage Chronic Disease

Eating right is important in every stage of the life cycle, especially in older adults. Nutrients such as fiber, vitamins, and minerals, in whole and lightly processed foods help to prevent chronic diseases, including certain cancers, heart disease, osteoporosis, cataracts, and age-related macular degeneration. The antioxidants found in plant products also help protect the body against free radicals, which damage cells, including those in the brain. Preliminary research suggests that, along with a healthy lifestyle, a varied, plant-based diet with plenty of phytonutrients, fiber, and essential nutrients is the best diet defense against the conditions and chronic diseases associated with aging.

The majority of older Americans are not eating the healthiest diet possible. When the diets of Americans 65 years of age and older were assessed to see if they adhered to recommendations, many fell short. On average, they consumed too much sodium, saturated fat, and calories from added sugars and alcohol. They also lacked adequate servings from several food groups including dairy, fruits, vegetables, and whole grains.[50]

Heart Disease and Stroke

Cardiovascular disease, which includes stroke, is more common with age. The most common cardiovascular disease is coronary heart disease, caused by a buildup of plaque that restricts the flow of blood to the heart; it is the number-one cause of death in the United States.[51] An ischemic stroke results from a clot, which may be the result of a piece of plaque that's been dislodged from a diseased blood vessel.

Millions of elderly people are living with coronary heart disease. They may also have diabetes and hypertension, adding to their risk for heart attack and stroke. Adults of any age who have coronary heart disease should be following a heart-healthy diet that limits saturated and *trans* fats, cholesterol, and sodium, and includes protein from plant sources, whole grains, lean meat, seafood, and low-fat dairy.

Type 2 Diabetes

The body's ability to maintain a normal blood level of glucose diminishes with age. The decline is typically gradual. If not corrected through lifestyle changes, medication, or both, prolonged elevated blood glucose concentrations can result in type 2 diabetes. Most people who have type 2 diabetes are overweight. Being overweight can trigger insulin resistance, which occurs when the body's cells are resistant to the effects of insulin, resulting in elevated blood glucose levels that can damage the eyes, kidneys, and heart, and the circulatory system.[52]

Hypertension

It's common for seniors to have hypertension, which is considered blood pressure above 120/80, and most are on medication to control it. The majority of high blood pressure is primary, or essential, hypertension, which probably cannot be cured but can be controlled. If left untreated or if poorly controlled, hypertension can result in heart attack, stroke, and kidney failure. Obesity, a high-sodium diet, and excessive alcohol use are among the major risk factors for hypertension. Some people can reduce their blood pressure by losing weight and being more active, and cutting down on alcohol and sodium.[53]

Arthritis

For people with **arthritis** (*arthr* = joint, *itis* = inflammation), simple activities, including getting out of bed, opening a jar, or climbing stairs, can be challenging. Arthritis causes painful and often debilitating swelling in the joints that restricts mobility.

Osteoarthritis is the most common form of the condition and often occurs in older people. As the population ages, the number of people with osteoarthritis will grow. By 2030, a projected 67 million people will have arthritis.[54] Osteoarthritis occurs when the cartilage, which covers the ends of the bones at the joints, wears down, causing bones to rub together. Friction between the bones causes swelling, loss of motion, and pain. Osteoarthritis commonly occurs in the fingers, neck, lower back, knees, and hips, which can interfere with the normal activities of daily living. Exercises that increase flexibility, keep joints limber, and improve the range of motion can help with osteoarthritis. Losing excess weight will also help relieve some of the stress at the hip and knee joints that bear most of the weight of the body.

Severe arthritis can make everyday activities, like writing, typing, and handling objects, a challenge.

arthritis Inflammation in the joints that can cause pain, stiffness, and swelling.

Dietary supplements, such as glucosamine sulfate, may help ease osteoarthritis. Glucosamine is present in tendons, ligaments, cartilage, and the fluid that surrounds and cushions joints. Taking glucosamine supplements, particularly glucosamine sulfate, may help to prevent the breakdown of cartilage and fluid, or may increase the body's production of both of these protective substances, although results vary. Several studies have suggested that chondroitin, especially when combined with glucosamine, may be effective for treating the pain, swelling, and stiffness of knee osteoarthritis in people who have mild pain. Chondroitin is a compound that the body produces naturally as a major component of cartilage, and is thought to help keep cartilage healthy and support joint health by allowing cartilage to absorb and retain water and by blocking enzymes that destroy cartilage, as well as providing the raw material for building new cartilage.[55]

People with osteoarthritis should speak with their health care provider to assess the benefits of taking either or both of these supplements. For safety's sake, they should also discuss their use of all dietary supplements, including herbs, with a health care provider prior to consuming them. The Nutrition in the Real World feature "Drug, Food, and Drug-Herb Interactions" on page 588–589 discusses the potentially harmful interactions between certain herbs, nutrients, and drugs.

Rheumatoid arthritis (RA), the second most common form of arthritis, affects an estimated 1.3 million U.S. adults. In rheumatoid arthritis the immune system attacks the tissues of the joints, leading to pain, inflammation, and joint damage and malformation. RA often begins in middle age and occurs with increased frequency in older people.[56]

With the exception of the omega-3 fatty acids in seafood and olive oil and other unsaturated fats, there is no scientific evidence that any specific food or nutrient helps or harms people with rheumatoid arthritis. A balanced diet with adequate calories, protein, and calcium is most beneficial. The omega-3 fatty acids in fish have anti-inflammatory effects and may help reduce the stiffness and joint tenderness characteristic of rheumatoid arthritis.[57] The current recommendation to eat at least two fish meals weekly to protect against heart disease may also be helpful to arthritis sufferers.

Alzheimer's Disease

Although it's normal for older adults to experience some cognitive changes, such as taking longer to learn new information, more drastic changes are cause for concern. Some adults forget where they live, become increasingly disoriented, have difficulty speaking, and may become emotionally unstable. These individuals may be experiencing **dementia**, which is the loss of cognitive functioning—thinking, remembering, and reasoning—and behavioral abilities, to such an extent that it interferes with a person's daily life and activities.

Alzheimer's disease (AD), an irreversible, progressive brain disease that slowly destroys memory and thinking skills, and eventually even the ability to carry out the simplest of daily tasks, is the most common form of dementia. Estimates vary, but experts suggest that as many as 5.1 million Americans may have Alzheimer's disease.[58]

Experts don't know how Alzheimer's disease begins, but it seems likely that damage to the brain starts a decade or more before problems become apparent in older adults. Some research suggests a connection between the risk for AD and heart disease, stroke, high blood pressure, diabetes, and obesity, but the evidence is preliminary. A nutritious diet, regular physical activity, social engagement, and mentally stimulating activities, such as reading and doing challenging puzzles, help people stay healthy as they age. New research suggests the possibility that these and other factors also might help to reduce the risk of Alzheimer's disease and other forms of cognitive decline.[59]

Exercise for Life!

Want to learn more about how to help an older relative or friend stay active and healthy? Visit www.asaging.org and search for "Physical Activity" to find information about how to increase physical activity in older people's lives.

dementia A disorder of the brain that interferes with a person's memory, learning, and mental stability.

Alzheimer's disease (AD) A type of dementia.

Drug, Food, and Drug-Herb Interactions

Seventy-nine-year-old Donald David uses a seven-day plastic pill box to remind him to take his four daily prescriptions. Because Donald takes pills for heart disease, high blood pressure, and diabetes, his local pharmacist works with him to make sure that the drugs do not interact with each other in a way that could harm his health. The pharmacist also reminds Donald that he needs to keep his dietary vitamin K intake at an even keel, as major fluctuations in blood levels of vitamin K affect his blood thinner medication, and he warns Donald about taking certain herbs that could also interfere with this, and other, drugs.

Donald is lucky to have a pharmacist to remind him how drugs, food, and herbs can interact and produce unhealthy effects. Some older adults aren't so lucky. Older adults who take prescription and nonprescription medications on a daily basis may use more than one pharmacy or order medications online or through the mail, and they may lack guidance about drugs and dietary supplements. In addition, there's

Daily pill containers like this one are often used by the elderly to remind them to take various medications.

Potential Interactions of Medications, Herbs, Nutrients, and Foods

Herb/ Nutrient/Food	Purported Use	Potential Side Effects	Drug Interactions
Astragalus	Enhance and support the immune system	Not well known	Medications that suppress immunity
Black cohosh	Reduce hot flashes and other menopausal symptoms	Possible headache, stomach discomfort, rash, possible liver dysfunction	Risk of interactions appears to be small
Calcium	Prevent osteoporosis	Constipation; calcium deposits in body	Decreases the absorption of antibiotics, bisphosphates, digoxin, high blood pressure medications, medications used to regulate heart beat, and more
Coenzyme Q10	Treatment of heart and blood vessel conditions	Mild stomach upset, decreased appetite, nausea, diarrhea, rash, low blood pressure	Decreased efficiency of some cancer medications; enhanced effect of drugs to lower blood pressure; decreases warfarin (anticoagulant) effectiveness
Dong quai root	Relieve menstrual and menopausal symptoms	Excessive bleeding. Skin sensitivity. May be carcinogenic with long-term use.	Enhances the blood-thinning effects of aspirin and anticoagulants as well as garlic and ginkgo biloba
Echinacea	Treat the common cold	Fever, nausea, vomiting, stomach pain. Allergic reaction if also allergic to ragweed and other plants.	Decreased effectiveness of immune-suppressing medications and drugs that are changed by the body
Fish oil	Reduce triglycerides and blood pressure; eye conditions; decrease inflammation	Excessive bleeding, fishy aftertaste in mouth, and allergic reaction in those with fish allergy	Enhances effectiveness of anticoagulant drugs such as warfarin and aspirin, and certain blood pressure drugs
Garlic, garlic supplements	Lower blood pressure and blood cholesterol levels	Possible stomach and intestinal discomfort	Do not take with drugs used to treat tuberculosis and certain HIV/AIDs drugs. Avoid with anticoagulant medication, such as warfarin.
Ginkgo biloba	Reduce memory loss, dementia	Possible stomach and intestinal discomfort	Blood-thinning drugs and aspirin. Enhances the blood-thinning actions of vitamin E and garlic.

little research assessing all the potential interactions between prescription drugs, food, and herbal remedies. When patients are not fully informed about the potential interactions between their diets and their medication or herbal supplements, the results may be dangerous.

Food can interact with medications in several ways. For example, it can delay or increase the absorption of a drug. Calcium, for instance, can bind with tetracycline (an antibiotic), decreasing its absorption. For this reason, this drug shouldn't be taken with milk or calcium-fortified foods.[9]

Drugs can also interfere with the metabolism of certain substances in foods. The compound tyramine, which is abundant in aged cheese, smoked fish, yogurt, and red wine, is metabolized by an enzyme called monoamine oxidase. Certain medications called monoamine oxidase inhibitors, sometimes prescribed to treat depression, prevent tyramine from being properly metabolized. High levels of tyramine in the blood can result in dangerously high blood pressure.

Herbs can also interact with medications. Herbs are regulated as food and not as drugs under the Dietary Supplement Health and Education Act of 1994. This act allowed manufacturers to be exempt from premarket safety and efficacy testing. Many people falsely assume that herbal remedies are safe because they are natural; however, dangerous interactions can occur when they are combined with prescription medications. For example, ginkgo biloba can interfere with blood clotting and shouldn't be consumed with the blood-thinning drug Coumadin (warfarin), or with aspirin, which also thins the blood. Consuming ginkgo with either or both of these medications can increase the risk of bleeding as well as hemorraghic stroke.[10]

The best way to avoid interactions is to make sure a health care provider and/or a pharmacist is aware of all the prescribed and over-the-counter medications, herbs, and dietary supplements that a person takes. See the accompanying table for a list of potential interactions.

Potential Interactions of Medications, Herbs, Nutrients, and Foods *continued*

Herb/ Nutrient/Food	Purported Use	Potential Side Effects	Drug Interactions
Ginseng	Stress reduction, enhance immunity, stimulant	Diarrhea, itchiness, insomnia, headache, nervousness, rapid heart rate	May enhance drugs used to reduce blood glucose levels in type 2 diabetes. Do not combine with the anticoagulant warfarin. Enhances the blood-thinning actions of vitamin E, garlic, and ginkgo biloba.
Grapefruit, grapefruit juice	Source of vitamin C and phytonutrients	None known	Enhances effect of certain heart medications (calcium channel blocking agents), corticosteroids, immunosuppressants
Hawthorn	Congestive heart failure	Rare, but may cause stomach upset, headache, dizziness	Not much evidence, but may interact with certain heart medications
Kava kava	Reduce anxiety, stress, insomnia	Liver damage; long-term use may result in scaly, yellowed skin; drowsiness.	Increases effectiveness of antianxiety drugs and sedatives
Licorice	Various disorders, including infections	Fatigue, headache, high blood pressure, weakness, among others	May reduce effectiveness of anticoagulant drugs such as warfarin
Milk thistle	Liver disorders	Allergic reactions in people who are allergic to ragweed and other plants; may lower blood glucose levels. Some gastrointestinal discomfort.	Medications that lower blood glucose levels
Saw palmetto	Treatment for benign prostatic hyperplasia	Stomach upset	Anticoagulants, birth control pills
St. John's wort	Reduce depression, anxiety, fatigue	Stomach upset, dry mouth, dizziness, headache, skin tingling	Must avoid with many medications. Alert pharmacist and doctor about St. John's wort use.
Vitamin E	Possibly preventing the risk of heart disease and Alzheimer's disease	Excessive amounts can interfere with blood clotting, causing bruising and bleeding. Also, nausea, diarrhea, stomach cramps, fatigue, rash.	Certain immunosuppressive drugs; anticoagulants, such as warfarin; statins used to lower cholesterol; and large amounts of niacin
Yohimbine	Erectile dysfunction and sexual dysfunction in women	Increases blood pressure, heart rate, headache, anxiety, stomach upset, sleeplessness	Do not combine with monoamine oxidase (MAO) inhibitors, as effect is additive. Interacts with high blood pressure medications, and certain drugs used to treat mental illness.

Depending on the stage of dementia, older adults may need part- or full-time supervision, and may not be allowed to take walks or to drive alone. However, accompanying an elder during any of these activities is a great way for both of you to get some exercise. While those with dementia experience mental deterioration, they should not be allowed to also experience physical deterioration.

Cancer

Cancer is the term used to identify a group of more than 100 diseases that are all characterized by the uncontrolled growth and spread of abnormal cells. Most of the time, the body quickly repairs or destroys a cell whose DNA has been altered or damaged, making it unable to reproduce and cause problems. However, cancer begins when the body cannot halt the growth of abnormal cells, which then multiply and form tumors, or, in the case of leukemia, a blood cancer, spur the growth of problematic cells in the bloodstream. Sometimes cells break off from the tumor and spread to other parts of the body.

Half of all men and one-third of all women in the United States will develop cancer during their lifetimes. Out of all cancer diagnoses, 78 percent are in people 55 years of age or older, as age increases cancer risk because it often takes many years for tumors to develop. The most common cancer among men is prostate cancer and, in women, breast cancer (men make up a small percentage of breast cancer cases). The second most common cancer in both men and women is lung cancer.[60]

Carcinogens Are Thought to Cause Most Cancers

All cancers involve the malfunction of genes that control cell growth and division, but only about 5 percent of cancers are strongly hereditary.[61] Most cases of cancer are not the result of inherited genes but of damage to DNA from carcinogens, a.k.a. cancer starters, that include the following:

- *Tobacco.* At least 69 chemicals in tobacco are known carcinogens, and cigarette smoking is the primary cause of lung cancer. Lung cancer also can occur in people who have never smoked, as about 3,000 lung cancer deaths occur each year among adult nonsmokers in the United States as a result of exposure to secondhand smoke.[62]
- *Alcohol.* Moderate to heavy alcohol consumption is associated with an increased risk for head and neck, breast, colorectal, esophageal, and liver cancers. The National Cancer Institute estimates that 3.5 percent of all cancers are caused by long-term heavy alcohol use.[63]
- *Radiation.* Excessive exposure to UV radiation, from sunlight and from tanning beds, is associated with an increased risk for skin cancer, and frequent exposure to other types of radiation—for instance, from X-rays—has long been associated with an increased risk for certain types of cancer.
- *Industrial chemicals.* Certain metals (such as nickel), some pesticides, and some chemical compounds (such as benzene) can act as carcinogens. People who are exposed to certain chemicals, including those who use them for work, are at the greatest risk.
- *Cancer-causing agents in foods and beverages.* Chemicals formed as a result of cooking meat, poultry, and fish at high temperatures, called heterocyclic amines (HCAs) and polycyclic aromatic hydrocarbons (PAHs), have caused cancer in animal studies, but their effects in humans are unclear.[64] Red and/or processed meats, nitrites, which are commonly used to preserve processed meats such as ham and bacon, and high salt intake are also associated with cancer risk.

cancer A group of diseases characterized by the uncontrolled growth and spread of abnormal cells.

Fighting Cancer with a Knife and Fork

An estimated one-third of cancer cases in the United States are related to being overweight or obese, physically inactive, and/or having a poor diet. Therefore, maintaining a healthy weight through regular physical activity and a healthy diet can help mitigate some of the increased cancer risk that comes with age. From a nutrition perspective, some compounds, found largely in fruits and vegetables, can help reduce your risk for numerous cancers:

- Certain *phytonutrients* can help reduce cancer risk. For example, the phytochemical lycopene, abundant in tomatoes and tomato products, is thought to help prevent certain cancers, including prostate cancer.
- *Antioxidants*, including carotenoids, the vitamins C and E, and the mineral selenium, neutralize free radicals, which can damage cellular DNA. They may also help prevent cancer from spreading to nearby tissues.
- *Retinoids* (vitamin A), *vitamin D*, and *folate* can stop the development of cancer by inhibiting the progression of damaged cells.
- *Omega-3 fatty acids*, found in fatty fish and some oils, may help reduce cancer cell growth.
- *Fiber* helps dilute waste products, which may contain cancer-promoting agents, in your intestinal tract and quickly move these out of your body. Also, the healthy bacteria that live in your colon feast on dietary fiber, creating a by-product that may also help in the fight against cancer, especially colorectal cancer.

The best strategy to reduce your risk for cancer is to follow the cancer-fighting recommendations listed in **Table 15.4**. Read about one woman's decision to change her lifestyle to reduce her risk of breast cancer in the Health Connection: A Case Study called "A Wake-Up Call."

Economic and Emotional Conditions Can Affect Nutritional Health

Staying active while managing chronic conditions is a common challenge for older adults, who may also be coping with food insecurity, depression, grief, or drug and alcohol abuse.

Food Insecurity

Between his medical and pharmaceutical costs and basic living expenses, Joe Powers exhausts his entire Social Security check by the twentieth day of each month. For the 10 days until he gets his next check, Joe is relegated to a stark menu of lower-cost foods such as oatmeal and eggs. His limited diet deprives him of the calories and other nutrients he needs until his next Social Security check arrives.

Joe is not alone. He is experiencing **food insecurity**, which means he does not have access at all times to enough food for an active, healthy life.[65] Research has shown that elders who consistently experience food insecurity not only have more than double the risk of not meeting their daily nutritional needs, but also tend to be in only fair to poor health.

Limited finances aren't always the cause of food insecurity. Some elders may be able to afford food but lack the physical means to obtain it, prepare it, or, because of health issues such as tooth loss, consume it. A quick and easy assessment of an older adult's diet can help determine whether he or she is at risk for food insecurity (see the Self-Assessment) on page 594.

food insecurity The chronic lack of sufficient resources to nutritiously feed oneself.

Table 15.4

Recommendations for Preventing Cancer

Recommendation	What to Do	How to Do It
1. Achieve and maintain a healthy weight, including during the teen years and young adulthood.	• Maintain a BMI between 21 and 23.* • Avoid weight gain, especially around your middle, as you age.	• Your pants are your best predictor of weight gain. If they begin to feel snug, assess your diet and your BMI. Is your diet heavy on the junk food? • See recommendation 3. • Review Chapters 10 and 11 for strategies to obtain and maintain a healthy BMI.
2. Be physically active as a part of everyday life.	• Incorporate at least 30 to 60 minutes of physical activity into your day. • Reduce the amount of screen time (TV, DVDs, computer, video games) spent daily.	• Set a timer at your computer and get up and move for at least 5 minutes every hour. • Watch one less TV show or play one less computer game daily. Spend that time cleaning, doing laundry, or running errands.
3. Limit consumption of energy-dense foods. Avoid sugary drinks.	• Cut back on sweets and treats that are energy (calorie) dense and serve up little nutrition besides calories. • Don't drink your calories by guzzling sodas, sports and energy drinks, fruit juices, or sweetened coffee beverages.	• If you want to snack on goodies, eat no more than about 100 calories of the item. That's typically one cookie or a small handful of chips or candy. • Drink one less sweetened beverage and one more glass of water daily.
4. Eat mostly foods of plant origin.	• Eat at least 5 cups of a variety of colorful fruits and veggies for phytochemicals, fiber, and nutrients. • At least half of your daily grain choices should be whole grains. • Eat dried peas and beans (legumes) as often as you can.	• Eat at least one salad with a minimum of three different colored veggies daily. • Choose only whole-grain cereals, such as raisin bran, oatmeal, and shredded wheat, in the morning. • Add beans to your daily salad.
5. Limit intake of red meat and avoid processed meat.	• Limit beef, lamb, and pork to no more than 18 ounces a week. • Avoid processed meats (bacon, salami, hot dogs, and sausages).	• Eat red meat only at lunch in a sandwich, as the portion size will be only about 3 ounces. • Try veggie or turkey sausages.
6. Limit alcoholic drinks.	If you choose to drink, • Women should consume no more than one alcoholic drink daily. • Men should consume no more than two alcoholic drinks daily.	• Make a glass of water the first drink, rather than alcohol, when you are socializing. • Alternate alcoholic beverages with nonalcoholic drinks to pace your evening. Make the nonalcoholic drink twice as big as the one containing the booze.
7. Limit salt consumption.	• Avoid salt and salt-preserved or salty foods. • Limit sodium to no more than 2,400 mg daily.	• Remove the salt from your salt shaker and fill it with a no-salt seasoning blend, such as Mrs. Dash.
8. Aim to meet nutritional needs through diet alone.	• Look to food, not supplements, to fight cancer. • Eat at least three meals a day to increase the variety and all the potential cancer-fighting compounds in food.	• Don't skip meals. • Eat at least three pieces of fruit daily. Challenge yourself to "eat the rainbow" by choosing fruits that are red, orange, yellow, green, blue, and purple.

Other Recommendations

• If you are pregnant, plan to breast-feed exclusively for up to six months and continue with complementary breast-feeding afterward to reduce your risk for breast cancer. Being breast-fed may also protect your child from becoming overweight.

• Cancer survivors should obtain nutritional recommendations from an appropriately trained professional, such as a registered dietitian nutritionist, and should eat a healthy diet, maintain a healthy weight, and be as physically active as they are able.

*See Chapter 10 to determine your BMI.

To help prevent food insecurity in seniors, Congress passed the Older Americans Act in 1965 to provide support and services, including nutritious meals and nutrition education, to those aged 60 years and older to help them maintain good health, an adequate quality of life, and an acceptable level of independence.[66] To see if you or someone you know is at risk of food insecurity, take the Self-Assessment titled "Are You at Nutritional Risk?"

Barbara is a 64-year-old African-American woman with a family history of cancer. Her mom passed away from breast cancer at 70 and her dad passed away from lung cancer at 63. Both of her parents were heavy smokers, but because Barbara doesn't smoke, she has never considered herself at high risk for cancer despite her family history. Barbara is a very busy woman. She works part-time as a nurse and helps care for her two small grandchildren two days a week. Because she is so busy, Barbara often eats out and she does not have time to regularly exercise.

At her annual physical, Barbara's doctor finds a lump in Barbara's breast and orders a mammogram. She also expresses concern over Barbara's diet and physical inactivity. While this lump turns out to be benign, Barbara decides to use this scare to motivate herself to make lifestyle changes that will hopefully reduce her risk of dying from breast cancer like her mom did.

In 2015, an estimated 232,000 cases of invasive breast cancer will be diagnosed among women in the United States.[11] Deaths from breast cancer are highest among African-American women and lowest among Asian/Pacific

Islander women. The American Cancer Society recommends that in order to prevent breast and other cancers, women and men should maintain a healthy weight throughout life, engage in regular physical activity, limit sedentary time, consume a healthy, plant-based diet, and limit alcohol consumption.[12]

Think About It
Barbara wants to reduce her cancer risk by making lifestyle changes. What changes relating to physical activity and diet do you think Barbara's doctor would recommend?

Congregate meals are one type of service available to elders as a result of the Older Americans Act. Nutritious hot meals are served at specified sites in the community, such as churches, synagogues, and senior centers, helping older adults meet their nutrient needs and offering opportunities for socializing. Often, transportation to these meals is available in the community.

Homebound elders can receive home meal delivery as part of the Meals on Wheels program. The Meals on Wheels Association of America is the largest organization in the United States providing meals to the homes of older adults who need them. Find out more about Meals on Wheels at www.mowaa.org.

Young people and others in the community can help make sure that older adults are aware of these meal programs and that they take advantage of the services available to them. Consider "adopting" an older adult in your neighborhood or a family member and, if need be, help him or her locate meal program services. Visit First .gov for Seniors at www.seniors.gov to locate these, and other, resources for seniors.

Programs such as Meals on Wheels provide hot meals to elderly adults who cannot leave their homes.

Depression and Grief
When Laura lost her husband at the age of 78, she stopped cooking dinner and took to opening a can of chicken soup for most of her evening meals. Her energy level dropped dramatically after his death, and on many days, she didn't even bother to get out of her pajamas. Like many elders who lose relatives and friends, Laura became depressed.

congregate meals Meals served at churches, synagogues, or other community sites where older adults can receive a nutritious meal and socialize.

Are You at Nutritional Risk?

Circle the number in the right column for the statements that apply to you (or someone you know if you are taking the assessment for a friend or relative). Add up the circled numbers to determine your score.

I have an illness or condition that has made me change the kind and/or amount of food I eat.	2
I eat fewer than two meals per day.	3
I eat few fruits or vegetables or milk products.	2
I have three or more drinks of beer, liquor, or wine almost every day.	2
I have tooth or mouth problems that make it hard for me to eat.	2
I don't always have enough money to buy food.	4
I eat alone most of the time.	1
I take three or more different prescribed or over-the-counter drugs a day.	1
Without wanting to, I have lost or gained 10 pounds in the last six months.	2
I am not always physically able to shop, cook, and/or feed myself.	2
Total =	____

Answers

If your score is

0–2: Good! Your diet and lifestyle don't appear to put you at risk of not meeting your nutritional needs.

3–5: You are at moderate nutritional risk. Your local office on aging, senior citizens' center, or health department can help you improve your nutritional health.

6 or over: You are at high nutritional risk. Bring this checklist the next time you see your doctor, dietitian, or other qualified health or social service professional. Ask for help to improve your nutritional health.

The loss of significant others and friends as well as chronic pain and concerns about their own health can add to feelings of sadness and isolation. Depression can interfere with an elder's motivation to eat, be physically active, and socialize—all of which can impact a person's mental and physical health. The risk of depression in older people increases with other illnesses and when their mobility and function is increasingly limited. Estimates of major depression in seniors range from less than 1 percent to about 5 percent, but rises to 13.5 percent in elderly people who require home health care and to 11.5 percent in elderly hospital patients.[67]

Alcohol Abuse

Increased alcohol consumption in an elderly person could be a sign of depression and grief. Chronic health problems, loss of friends and loved ones, and financial stress could make alcohol an appealing sedative to temporarily ease psychological pain. However, heavy drinking can worsen depression, which can lead to more drinking. Also, because alcohol impairs one's judgment and interferes with coordination and reaction time, elders who have been drinking are at a higher risk for stumbling, falling, and fracturing bones. Anyone of any age can abuse alcohol, and drinking too much is not uncommon in the elderly.

The National Institute on Alcohol Abuse and Alcoholism recommends that people over age 65 years limit their alcohol intake to seven drinks a week and no more than three drinks on any one day. People with certain health problems and those taking medications may need to drink less or avoid alcohol completely.[68]

Alcohol may interact with prescription or over-the-counter medications, intensifying or diminishing their effects. For example, alcohol increases the effectiveness of medication taken to prevent blood clots.

Alcohol abuse in elders may be mistaken as the forgetfulness and disorientation associated with normal aging. **Figure 15.7** lists the red flags from the National Institute of Aging that may signal alcohol abuse in an older adult.

Staying Physically Active

Joan loves to ski downhill and cross-country and has been attending exercise classes six days a week for the past decade—a rather active schedule for a 76-year-old. Robert, age 78, attends weekly fitness classes and plays tennis a few times a week.

Physical activity is not an option for older adults; it's a necessity. Regular physical activity can help lower the risk of heart disease, colon and breast cancer, diabetes, hypertension, osteoporosis, arthritis, and obesity. Exercise helps maintain healthy bones, muscles, and joints, and reduces anxiety, stress, and depression. It improves sleep, flexibility, and range of motion, and can help postpone the decline in cognitive ability that naturally occurs in aging. Elders in good physical shape are also able to live independently longer, reducing the need for assistance with everyday activities, such as food shopping and housework.

Despite the many health benefits of being physically active, older people don't always get the recommended amount of exercise they need. The 2008 *Physical Activity Guidelines for Americans* suggests that adults over the age of 65 years get at least 150 minutes (2 hours and 30 minutes) a week of moderate-intensity or 75 minutes (1 hour and 15 minutes) of vigorous-intensity aerobic physical activity, or the equivalent combination of moderate and vigorous activity. Older adults should also do muscle-strengthening activities on two or more days a week. When seniors are unable to get the suggested amount of exercise, they should be as physically active as their abilities and conditions allow.[69]

While regular physical activities that raise the heart rate and challenge the muscles are highly beneficial, it's important to be active all day long and to avoid sitting for long periods. Activities such as working in the garden, mowing the lawn, raking leaves, and dancing all provide health benefits.

LO 15.5 **The Take-Home Message** Older adults should consume a balanced diet to meet their nutrient needs and help prevent many of the chronic diseases associated with aging. Seniors also benefit from regular physical activity, and should do what they can to get exercise. Arthritis, Alzheimer's disease, food insecurity, depression, and alcohol abuse can challenge the abilities of older adults to maintain healthy diets and lifestyles.

Red Flags for Alcohol Abuse in Older Adults

- Drinks to calm nerves, reduce stress or depression, or forget his or her troubles.
- Gulps drinks.
- Frequently has more than one drink a day.
- Lies about or tries to hide his or her drinking habits.
- Hurts self or others when drinking.
- Needs increased amounts of alcohol to get high.
- Feels irritable, resentful, or unreasonable when not drinking.
- Has medical, social, or financial worries caused by drinking.

Figure 15.7 **Red Flags for Alcohol Abuse in Older Adults**

Although the cross sections of the thigh are similar in size, note the greatly reduced muscle area (in yellow) and increased fat area (in red) of the older, sedentary adult in the bottom image compared with that of a younger, more active adult. Most people lose a significant amount of muscle as they age, which could be prevented by engaging in regular physical activity.

Should School Meals Align with the *Dietary Guidelines for Americans?* Through the Healthy, Hunger-Free Kids Act of 2010, the USDA set new nutrition standards for school breakfast and lunch meals to align them with the *Dietary Guidelines for Americans.*[1] Specifically, the new standards increase servings of fruits, vegetables, whole grains, and fat-free or low-fat milk and reduce the levels of sodium, saturated fat, and *trans* fat in school meals. The new guidelines also limit the calories allowed in a lunch meal to 650 for children in kindergarten through fifth grade, 700 for sixth through eighth graders, and 850 for high school students. The new standards were developed in response to recommendations from the Institute of Medicine that school meals should improve the health and well-being of American school children.[2] While this seems straightforward, the new standards were somewhat controversial for many stakeholders, including students, school food service directors, and food purveyors. After you've read the arguments for and against these standards, answer the critical-thinking questions, and decide for yourself.

yes

- As many as 31 million American children eat school lunch each day. For some children, school lunch accounts for more than half of their daily calorie intake.

- The new guidelines increase the servings of fruits and vegetables that low-income students consume each day.[3]

- A recent study suggests that the new lunch standards have the potential to help in the fight against childhood obesity.[4]

no

- After the guidelines were adopted, high school students in states across the country protested that the new lunch standards left them hungry.[5]

- In a national survey, state authorities reported that the new meal standards resulted in higher food costs, challenges with menu planning, and difficulties in sourcing products that meet the federal portion and calorie requirements.[6]

- Participation in the National School Lunch Program declined by 1.2 million students from the 2010–2011 to 2012–2013 school years.

what do you think?

1. Which side do you think has the more compelling argument? Why? **2.** Do you think the benefits of the new meal standards outweigh the drawbacks? **3.** If you were a member of Congress, would you vote to amend the standards set forth in the Healthy, Hunger-Free Kids Act? If so, how?

LO 15.1 The Needs of Toddlers and Preschoolers Are Met with Small, Nutrient-Dense Meals

Toddlers and preschoolers grow and develop at a slower rate than infants. Children require small, frequent, nutrient-rich meals and snacks to fuel their busy lifestyles. Young children may be picky eaters and go on food jags, but these behaviors are normal and usually temporary. Caregivers may need to offer a new food up to 10 times before the child accepts it.

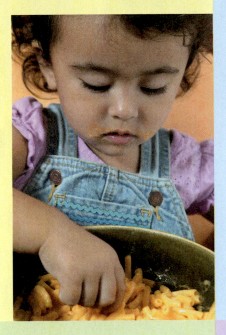

LO 15.2 The Nutritional Needs of School-Aged Children Can Be Guided by MyPlate

Young children and teens are prone to iron deficiency. Children of all ages need adequate calcium and vitamin D for bone growth, and fiber and fluid to prevent constipation. Milk, water, and diluted 100% fruit juices are better beverage choices than sweetened beverages. Obesity and type 2 diabetes are occurring more frequently in children and teens. Poor dietary choices and insufficient exercise are two of the key culprits of this problem. Parents and caregivers must provide healthy foods and encourage physical activity to reduce a child's risk for these conditions. The new standards for school meals support healthy meals in the context of age-specific calorie needs for American school children.

LO 15.3 Nutritional Needs of Adolescents Are Based on Hormonal and Physical Changes

Calcium, vitamin D, and iron intakes are particularly important during adolescence to ensure adequate bone and muscle growth and to prevent deficiencies. Adolescents are sometimes at risk of developing disordered eating patterns due to poor body image, emotional issues, and peer pressure. Because many adolescents live in the "here and now," they may not realize the long-term health consequences of the poor diet and lifestyle habits they adopt during their teenage years.

Epiphyseal plate (area of growth)

LO 15.4 Nutrient Needs Change along with the Physical and Cognitive Changes That Are Part of the Aging Process

Metabolism slows with age, so older adults need fewer calories than their younger counterparts. Staying physically active is important during a person's later years, though sometimes this is challenging due to the fact that many older people are managing at least one chronic condition, such as arthritis, dementia, or heart disease. Older adults need to be sure to consume adequate protein, fiber, fluid, vitamins D and B_{12}, and the minerals iron, calcium, and zinc. Prescription medications, over-the-counter medications, and herbal remedies can affect nutrient absorption, or otherwise interact with nutrients.

LO 15.5 Physical, Socioeconomic, and Psychological Issues Can Affect the Nutritional Health of Older Adults

Whereas a healthy diet is important across the entire life cycle, it is especially important for older adults, for whom chronic disease is most prevalent. Older adults sometimes suffer from food insecurity, due to decreased mobility, financial hardship, or health conditions such as tooth loss. Social programs can help ensure the proper nourishment of homebound adults by providing meals in the community. Alcohol abuse may be an issue with older adults and may affect how they manage daily life and chronic conditions.

Terms to Know
- toddlers
- preschoolers
- picky eating
- food jags
- school-aged children
- adolescence
- bone mineral density (BMD)
- peak bone mass
- life expectancy
- arthritis
- dementia
- food insecurity
- congregate meals

MasteringNutrition™

Build your knowledge—and confidence—in the Study Area of MasteringNutrition with a variety of study tools.

MyDietAnalysis

Access MyDietAnalysis through MasteringNutrition™ and track your diet and daily activities. In addition, a dietary analysis activity is available for every chapter in your book.

Check Your Understanding

LO 15.1 1. Because they are still growing but have diminished appetites (compared with infants), toddlers and preschoolers should
   a. consume large meals.
   b. consume nutrient-dense foods.
   c. consume foods high in fat.
   d. consume foods high in sugar.

LO 15.1 2. According to Ellyn Satter's Division of Responsibility, parents are responsible for
   a. what and how much a child eats.
   b. when and how much a child eats.
   c. when, where, and what a child is offered to eat.
   d. all aspects of feeding a child.

LO 15.2 3. Breakfast is important for school-aged children because
   a. it improves alertness and ability to concentrate throughout the day.
   b. it helps them slow down in the morning.
   c. it gives them energy for after-school activities.
   d. it prevents adult obesity.

LO 15.2 4. There appears to be a relationship between the rise in childhood obesity and the increase in
   a. childhood cancers.
   b. ADHD.
   c. type 2 diabetes in children.
   d. childhood cavities.

LO 15.3 5. Which mineral supports healthy bone development and is particularly important during adolescence?
   a. calcium
   b. iron
   c. vitamin D
   d. copper

LO 15.3 6. Teen boys and girls are at risk for a deficiency of which of the following?
   a. fat
   b. vitamin C
   c. iron
   d. vitamin A

LO 15.4 7. Which of the following two nutrient needs increase with age?
   a. water and lead
   b. calcium and vitamin D
   c. protein and lipids
   d. vitamin K and biotin

LO 15.4 8. Which of the following proba-bly has the most influence on older adults' ability to consume a nutritious diet?
  a. eating three meals a day
  b. working outside the home
  c. television-watching habits
  d. living on a fixed income

LO 15.5 9. Carcinogens, or cancer-causing agents, include which of the following?
  a. alcohol
  b. tobacco
  c. red and/or processed meats
  d. all of the above

LO 15.5 10. Congregate meals are
  a. meals delivered to the homes of older adults who are homebound.
  b. frozen meals that adults can pur-chase at the supermarket.
  c. hot meals that are served at a site in the community, such as at churches and synagogues.
  d. meals made at home and eaten with friends.

Answers

1. (b) Toddlers need to eat nutrient-dense foods in order to obtain all the nutrients they need. Their smaller appetites mean they aren't likely to eat large meals, and foods high in fat and sugar may add sig-nificant calories without contrib-uting many nutrients.
2. (c) The Division of Responsibil-ity suggests that it is a parent's responsibility to decide what foods children are offered to eat, as well as when and where they eat, while children are responsible for how much they eat, if anything at all.
3. (a) School-aged children who eat breakfast have been shown to per-form better in school and to have higher rates of physical activity and lower rates of obesity. Break-fast doesn't have to be eaten at the table, as caregivers can provide "to go" foods for children if they are in a hurry.
4. (c) Rates of type 2 diabetes among children have risen along with rates of overweight and obesity.
5. (a) Adolescents need adequate amounts of calcium to support their growing bones. Vitamin D is not a mineral, but is also very important for bone growth.

6. (c) Teenagers are growing at a rapid rate and they require adequate iron to make muscle mass. Teen girls need to replace monthly losses of iron caused by menstruation.
7. (b) The need for both vitamin D and calcium is increased in older adults. Lead is a toxin and should never be consumed. Vitamin K and biotin are necessary for health, but you don't need them in higher amounts as you age.
8. (d) Older adults who may have a limited income may not be able to purchase adequate amounts of healthy foods to meet their nutrient needs. Dental problems, including ill-fitting dentures and tooth loss, may limit their food choices based on their inability to chew certain nutritious foods such as meat. Excessive alcohol in the diet displaces nutritious foods, and alcohol use increases the risk of falls and injuries.
9. (d) Alcohol, tobacco, and red and/or processed meats are all associated with an increased risk for cancer.
10. (c) Congregate meals allow older adults in a community to meet and eat hot meals together. Older adults who are homebound can request that a healthy meal be delivered to their home. A variety of frozen meals can be purchased at the gro-cery store by adults of all ages.

Web Resources

- For more information on nutrition during the younger years, visit the Adolescent and School Health section at www.cdc.gov
- For more information on children's and teens' health, visit www.kidshealth.org
- For more about ADHD, search www.nimh.nih.gov
- For more about the USDA's National School Lunch Program, visit the Child Nutrition section at www.fns.usda.gov
- For more health information for older adults, visit the Aging section at www.cdc.gov
- For more information on herbs, visit the National Center for Complementary and Alternative Medicine, National Institutes of Health, at http://nccam.nih.gov

Answers to True or False?

1. **True.** Between the ages of 1 and 4, small children are extremely active and may not be interested in eating at meal-time. Turn to page 568 to find out how to make sure children get the nutrients they need.
2. **True.** In small children, iron deficiency is often caused by a limited diet that relies too heavily on milk or other iron-poor food sources. Read more about this condition on page 570.
3. **False.** Parents and caregivers may need to offer foods several times before a child accepts the food. This topic is covered in more detail on page 571.
4. **True.** Young children often go on food "jags" or may get hooked on particular foods and eat only those items. Learn more about these short-term habits and how to cope with them on page 571.
5. **False.** Fast food is only part of the problem. Too little exer-cise and too much screen time also contribute. Read more about the obesity epidemic among children on page 574.
6. **True.** Meals served as part of the National School Lunch Pro-gram must meet specific require-ments established by the USDA. Details are found on page 578.
7. **False.** Sugary sodas and diet soda are nutritionally empty beverages. Turn to page 580 to find which beverages will help adolescents achieve healthy adult bodies.
8. **True.** Because a person's metabolism slows naturally with age, older adults need fewer calories than their younger counterparts. Learn more about the altered energy and nutrient needs associated with aging on page 582.
9. **False.** Financial circum-stances or reduced mobility can cause older adults to experience food insecurity. Turn to page 591 to find out how this happens.
10. **False.** Older adults sometimes turn to alcohol to deal with dis-comfort, loneliness, or boredom. Find out more on page 594.

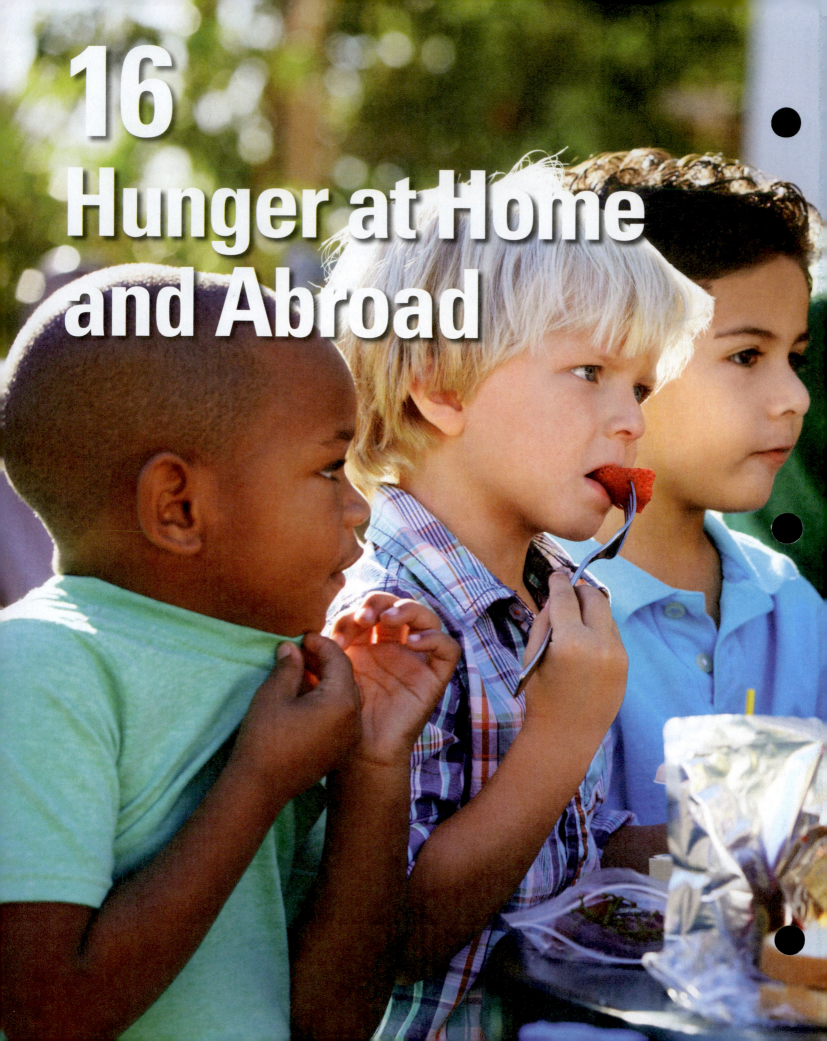

16
Hunger at Home and Abroad

True or False?

1. Food insecurity in the developing world is primarily due to poverty. T|F   p. 604

2. No hard-working American goes to bed hungry. T|F   p. 605

3. People who are obese don't experience food insecurity. T|F   p. 606

4. Not enough food is produced in the world to feed everyone. T|F   p. 607

5. Children are at a higher risk for food insecurity than are adults. T|F   p. 610

6. Older adults who are financially secure can still sometimes experience low food security and undernutrition. T|F   p. 611

7. Consuming inadequate nutrients won't affect mental development. T|F   p. 611

8. Agricultural advances can help increase food production. T|F   p. 614

9. Fortifying foods doesn't alter their nutritional content. T|F   p. 616

10. The only thing you can do to alleviate hunger is to give money to charities. T|F   p. 616

See page 621 for the answers.

After reading this chapter, you will be able to:

LO 16.1 Define food insecurity, food security, and hunger, and summarize the extent of food insecurity in the United States and worldwide.

LO 16.2 Explain some of the causes of food insecurity in the United States.

LO 16.3 Explain some of the causes of food insecurity worldwide.

LO 16.4 List populations at highest risk for experiencing undernutrition.

LO 16.5 Describe the effects of chronic malnutrition.

LO 16.6 Describe some of the strategies currently in use to reduce food insecurity.

We all know what "I'm hungry" feels like. After a long day, a grumbling or gnawing in the stomach, a feeling of fatigue, or maybe light-headedness are all signs that tell us we need to eat. How many of us, however, know what it is like to be hungry day in and day out, never to feel truly full, or to lose weight although we don't want to?

Who are the people in the United States and the rest of the world who are hungry? What are the effects of chronic hunger? And, once we understand the causes and scope of this problem, what can we do about it? Can one person's actions really help people who are hungry? In this chapter, we'll explore the conditions of hunger and malnutrition, their causes and effects, and potential solutions in the United States and around the world.

What Are Food Insecurity, Food Security, and Hunger?

LO 16.1 Define food insecurity, food security, and hunger, and summarize the extent of food insecurity in the United States and worldwide.

The U.S. Department of Agriculture (USDA) describes an American household as *food secure* if it has access at all times to enough food for an active, healthy life for all household members.[1] In contrast, a household is *food insecure* when any of its members do not have the resources they need to get adequate amounts of nutritious food. People who experience **food insecurity** may be at risk for undernutrition due to insufficient calories and nutrients in the diet. (You can see the range of definitions for high to very low food security in **Table 16.1**.)

Many People Experience Food Insecurity in the United States and Worldwide

Because the United States is one of the wealthiest countries in the world, it may not seem likely that some of its citizens would be unable to buy an adequate supply of healthy foods. However, food insecurity in the United States is a major problem: In 2013, 14.3 percent of American households—about 17.5 million households—were

Table 16.1

Ranges of Food Security

Level of Food Security	Description of Conditions in the Household
High food security	No reported indications of food access problems or limitations
Marginal food security	One or two reported indications—typically of anxiety over food sufficiency or shortage of food in the house. Little or no indication of changes in diets or food intake.
Low food security	Reports of reduced quality, variety, or desirability of diet. Little or no indication of reduced food intake.
Very low food security	Reports of multiple indications of disrupted eating patterns and reduced food intake.

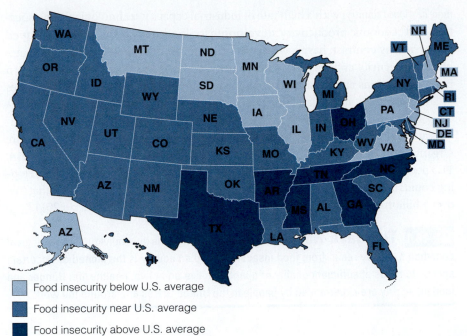

Food insecurity below U.S. average

Food insecurity near U.S. average

Food insecurity above U.S. average

food insecure at least some time during the year. Food-insecure households (those with low and very low food security) had difficulty at some time during the year providing enough food for all their members due to a lack of resources.[2] **Figure 16.1** illustrates the prevalence of food insecurity in the United States.

Also in 2013, 12.2 million adults lived in households with very low food security. In 2013 765,000 children lived in households with very low food security among children. However, according to the USDA, children are usually protected from substantial reductions in food intake even in households with very low food security.[3]

Food insecurity is a household-level economic and social condition of limited access to food, while **hunger** is an individual-level physiological condition that may result from food insecurity.[4] People who have very low food security are at significant risk for hunger. Prolonged hunger can lead to **starvation**, a state in which the body breaks down its own tissues for fuel. As shown in **Figure 16.2**, you can think of these states—from food security to starvation and death—as occurring along a continuum.

The number of Americans who experience food insecurity might surprise you, but it is much lower than the number of food insecure people in many other countries of the world. Whereas the United States is a **developed country** (also called a

> Enough food is available to provide at least 4.3 pounds of food per person per day worldwide.

Food | Food | Malnutrition | Hunger | Starvation | Death
security | insecurity

Figure 16.2 Spectrum of Food Security
Food insecurity and hunger are points along the continuum between being food secure and dying from starvation.

food insecurity The inability to satisfy basic food needs due to lack of financial resources or other problems. The USDA further defines food insecurity as falling into the categories of either *low food security* or *very low food security*.

hunger Physical discomfort that results from the lack of food associated with food insecurity.

starvation To suffer severely from lack of food; a state in which the body breaks down its own tissue for fuel.

developed country A nation advanced in industrial capability, technological sophistication, and economic productivity; also called *most developed country*.

What Are Food Insecurity, Food Security, and Hunger? **603** *more developed country*) with a high rate of industrial capacity, technological sophistication, and economic productivity, **developing** (or *less developed*) and **least developed countries**, by contrast, have lower levels of economic productivity, and higher rates of food insecurity and very low food security. Canada, Australia, and most western European nations are considered developed countries, while many of the countries in South America and Asia—for example, Brazil, China, India, and Saudi Arabia—are considered developing nations. The majority of the world's least developed countries are located in central and western Africa. Worldwide, the Food and Agriculture Organization of the United Nations (FAO) estimates that between 2012 and 2014, 11.3 percent of the world's population and 13.5 percent of the population of developing countries were undernourished.[5] As of 2014, the World Bank estimated that just over 1 billion people in developing countries lived on $1.25 a day or less in 2011.[6]

LO 16.1 The Take-Home Message Hunger is an individual physiological condition that may result from food insecurity. Food insecurity is the limited or uncertain access to foods of sufficient quality or quantity to live an active, healthy life. Hunger and food insecurity are experienced by people in the United States and around the world.

What Causes Food Insecurity in the United States?

LO 16.2 Explain some of the causes of food insecurity in the United States.

In developed countries, food insecurity typically results from factors affecting individuals, such as **poverty** or poor health. In developing and least developed countries, regional problems, such as discrimination, armed conflict, natural disasters, and population overgrowth, can be as significant as individual hardships. Let's take a closer look at these factors, beginning with those contributing to food insecurity in the United States.

In the United States, Food Insecurity Is Often Caused by Poverty

Poverty levels in the United States are defined according to strict guidelines. A family of four is considered impoverished if its annual income is at or below $24,008.[7] The U.S. Census Bureau reports that 45.3 million people (14.5 percent) lived in poverty in 2013, the first decrease in the poverty rate since 2006. In 2013, 19.9 percent of children under 18 lived in poverty.[8]

According to the U.S. Census Bureau, rates of food insecurity were greater for these groups:[9]

- Households with incomes below 185 percent of the poverty threshold (34.8 percent)
- Households with children headed by a single woman (34.4 percent)
- Black, non-Hispanic households (26.1 percent)
- Hispanic households (23.7 percent)

In addition, women and minorities may experience wage discrimination. Single mothers may feel "trapped," with very few options to explore different career paths, because of obligations to their children. Also, arranging for childcare can prompt additional stress and drain an already tight budget.

In the United States, poor single parents and their children can experience food insecurity due to unemployment, low wages, or other circumstances that lead to financial hardship.

developing country A nation having a relatively low level of industrial capability, technological sophistication, or economic productivity; also called *less developed country*.

least developed country A nation having a low level of economic productivity and technological sophistication within the contemporary range of possibility.

poverty Lacking the means to provide for material or comfort needs.

Which Is Cheaper: Fast Food or a Homemade Lunch?

Using the table below as an example, research the calories, fat, and cost of comparable items at your favorite fast-food restaurant and your local supermarket and total them up to find out for yourself what's cheaper.

Lunch Item	Total Calories	Total Fat (grams)	Cost
Fast-Food Burger Meal			
Fast-food burger: 2 beef patties on a sesame seed bun with lettuce, cheese, "special sauce," pickles, and onions	_____	_____	_____
Medium order of french fries	_____	_____	_____
Cost of a fast-food burger meal	_____	_____	_____
Homemade Packed Lunch			
Homemade turkey sandwich: 3 ounces oven-roasted turkey on 2 pieces of whole-wheat bread with 1 slice tomato, 1 leaf lettuce, and 1 tsp mustard	_____	_____	_____
Baby carrots, ½ cup	_____	_____	_____
Granola bar, 1, Oat & Honey	_____	_____	_____
Cost of a homemade packed lunch	_____	_____	_____

You may be surprised to learn that steady employment does not guarantee that an individual or a family won't experience food insecurity. In fact, in 2010 to 2011, almost 60 percent of households with food insecure children had one or more adults in the labor force.[10] In 2012, about 10.6 million Americans were classified among the **working poor**.[11] In these households, once the monthly expenses are paid, there is often too little money available to feed everyone adequately (see **Figure 16.3**). Additionally, even people with excellent jobs may experience food insecurity if they are laid off.

People on limited incomes may buy cheaper foods because they can buy more, or simply because that's what's available in their neighborhood. For those living on a limited budget, filling their cupboards with food, even if it is less nutrient-dense food, takes precedence over choosing foods with nutritional value. If they live in a *food desert*, they may not even have access to nutritious foods.

However, low-cost foods often lack nutrition. Fruit punch, for example, is about half the price of orange juice, and it is nutritionally inferior to orange juice. As you have learned from previous chapters, a diet high in empty calories and low in nutrient-dense foods can increase the risk of obesity and malnutrition. For an example showing the connection between food insecurity and obesity, see Health Connection: A Case Study on page 606. Also, buying nutritious food at a grocery store and using it to make healthy sandwiches, salads, and snacks can be cheaper than a daily trip through the drive-through (try the Self-Assessment to find out for yourself).

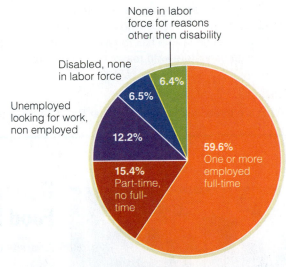

Figure 16.3 Employment Status of Food-Insecure Households
More than half of households with the greatest difficulty putting adequate food on the table include one or more employed adults.

working poor Individuals or families who are steadily employed but still experience poverty due to low wages or high dependent expenses.

Overweight and Undernourished

health CONNECTION

Tia, an African-American mother of two school-aged children, works full time for minimum wage at a fast-food restaurant, and is considered one of the working poor. She has difficulty making ends meet, especially during the winter months, when the cost of heating her one-bedroom apartment cuts into her monthly food budget. Tia eats breakfast and lunch at her job. She purposely fills up on french fries before she leaves work so that she can skip dinner without feeling hungry. With one less mouth to feed at supper, she can stretch her limited household food budget to feed her children and husband. Tia is obese.

According to the CDC, adults in situations similar to Tia's are at risk for being overweight. Non-Hispanic black women with low income have the greatest likelihood of being obese. The CDC also says that the less education women have, the more likely they are to be obese.[1] But they aren't alone. In 2011–2012, more than one-third of adults in the United States were obese. And obesity "now affects 17 percent of all children and adolescents in the United States."

The connection between food insecurity and obesity is thought to result from several contributing factors, a major one being lack of access to healthy food (living in a food desert). In the area where Tia lives, the nearest store with food is a convenience store where the fruits and vegetables are unappealing and expensive. The soda, chips, and prepackaged foods are more appealing and cheaper—and loaded with calories and fat. Tia has to take public transportation to reach a grocery store with reasonably priced fresh fruits and vegetables. At the end of a long workday with two tired children in tow, she often skips this more difficult option.

Lack of safe areas in which to exercise or for children to play is another factor contributing to obesity. Tia's kids are in the first and third grades. They have no safe outdoor place to play, so they tend to stay indoors watching TV. Because they are sedentary much of the time, they are gaining extra weight quickly.

Additional factors contributing to obesity include lack of access to basic health care, poor housing, low-wage work and long working hours, advertising of less-healthy foods, and increased stress that can lead to central adiposity and emotional eating. All of these stressors have impacted Tia as she tries to put healthy food on the table for her family.

Think About It

What are three lifestyle changes that Tia could make to give her kids a better chance of avoiding obesity?

People in poor, urban areas often find themselves in "food deserts," with little access to the fresh, healthy food found in supermarkets, and easy access to fast foods and snack foods like those found in drive-through restaurants and liquor or convenience stores.

Health Problems Contribute to Food Insecurity among Americans

A variety of health issues can also set the stage for food insecurity:

- *Chronic illness.* Adults who are chronically ill are less likely to earn a steady income and therefore are at risk of having a poor diet. Chronic illness in an elderly person can reduce mobility, making it difficult to get to a grocery store or to prepare nourishing meals.
- *Disability.* Many adults who are disabled lead highly productive lives, but others are limited to low-skilled, low-wage jobs. Some cannot work at all and must depend on disability income, which may not provide adequate money for nourishing food. Similar to chronic illness, disability can make it difficult for a person to shop for food and prepare meals.

Are You at Risk for Food Insecurity?

Take this quiz to find out if you are at risk for food insecurity and/or hunger.

In the past 12 months:

1. Have you ever run out of money to buy food?
   Yes ☐ **No** ☐
2. Have you ever eaten less than you felt you should because there was not enough money to buy food or enough food to eat?
   Yes ☐ **No** ☐
3. Have you ever completely depleted your food supply because there was not enough money to buy replacement groceries?
   Yes ☐ **No** ☐
4. Have you ever gone to bed hungry because there was not enough food to eat?
   Yes ☐ **No** ☐

5. Have you ever skipped meals because there was not enough money to buy food?
   Yes ☐ **No** ☐
6. Have you ever relied on a limited number of foods to feed yourself because you were running out of money to buy food?
   Yes ☐ **No** ☐

Answers

If there are zero "yes" replies, you are food secure. If there are one to three "yes" replies, you are at risk for food insecurity. If there are four or more "yes" replies, you are classified as "hungry."

- *Substance abuse.* Drug and alcohol abuse are common causes of food insecurity, in part because of the challenge these problems create in maintaining steady employment. Many people who abuse substances become unable to keep up their mortgage or rent, and they descend into homelessness. In fact, an estimated 85 percent of all homeless men and women in urban areas abuse substances and/or have a mental illness.
- *Mental illness.* Many mentally ill people, often including the **homeless**, are forced to rely on charity, church meals, or public assistance programs for most of their food. Even people with homes and jobs who suffer from mental illness can lose interest in eating or have decreased ability to prepare meals. For example, clinical depression among mothers, particularly those in low-income families, has been associated with food insecurity in households.[12]

Now that you've learned about the factors contributing to food insecurity in the United States, you may be wondering whether you're at risk. If so, take the Self-Assessment to find out.

Many hunger-relief programs work to provide food aid to needy nations. However, successfully delivering the food to those who need it is often challenging.

LO 16.2 **The Take-Home Message** The causes of food insecurity in the United States include individual hardships, such as poverty, unemployment, and health problems. Food insecurity and hunger are particularly prevalent in households headed by a single mother, minority households, households with children, those living in inner cities, and among those with unstable or seasonal professions.

What Causes Food Insecurity and Poverty around the Globe?

LO 16.3 Explain some of the causes of food insecurity worldwide.

(TF) Worldwide, food insecurity persists despite the fact that global food production exceeds the needs of the world's population. This sobering reality tells us that

homeless Individuals who are either "crashing" with friends or family members, or residing on the street or in their automobiles.

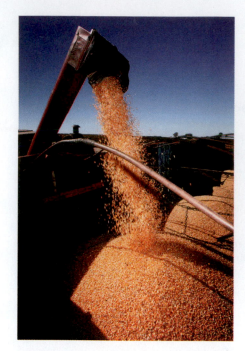

Thanks to agricultural advances, the world's farmers can grow plenty of food. However, distribution problems and other factors keep some people from getting enough to stave off hunger.

agricultural production is not the problem, and increasing it is not the sole solution. So, what causes global hunger?

Discrimination and Inequality Promote Poverty

Racial, gender, and ethnic discrimination can contribute to reduced employment, lower educational achievement, and fewer business opportunities. Vulnerable groups include women, the elderly, people with disabilities, refugees, orphans, migrant workers, and people who are illiterate. In many countries, such as Sudan, Afghanistan, Angola, and Ethiopia, discrimination exists at both the national and local levels.

At the national level, control over land and other assets is often unequal. At the local or household level, access to food is influenced by factors such as gender, control over income, education, birth order, and age.[13] Much of the inequity is due to educational disparities between boys and girls. Two-thirds of the almost 900 million illiterate adults in the world are women. Of the estimated 122 million illiterate youth, 60.7 percent are young women.[14]

Political Sanctions and Armed Conflicts

One government or country may try to force political change on another using **political sanctions**, such as boycotts and trade embargoes. Sanctions have various goals, including restoring democracy, condemning the abuse of human rights, and punishing groups that protect terrorists or international criminals. Although the goals of the sanctions may be noble, they can cause "indiscriminate economic impact and negative humanitarian consequences."[15] Agricultural embargoes, for example, can create food shortages by decreasing access to agricultural supplies, fuel, or crops. As with sanctions, embargoes more often hurt the average citizen than affect government authorities.

> Eighty percent of people who experience hunger around the world make their living from the land, and 50 percent are actually farmers.

War, armed conflict, and civil unrest may cause **famine** because of the disruption to agriculture, food distribution, and normal community activities. During wars and regional conflicts, governments often divert money from nutrition programs and food distribution efforts and redirect it toward weapons and military support. Conflicts cause increases in hunger and overwhelm the humanitarian safety network.[16]

Crop Failure, Natural Disasters, and Wasteful Agricultural Practices

Natural disasters, such as drought, floods, crop diseases, and insect infestations, can occur in any country, on any continent. However, the impact of natural disasters is much greater on least developed countries than on developed countries. There are several reasons for this, including the population's inability to relocate away from disaster-prone areas and people's inability to make their homes and farms less vulnerable to destructive natural forces. Additionally, the local economy and infrastructure tend to be less stable in least developed areas.[17] (See the Nutrition in the Real World feature "Natural Disasters and Food Insecurity: A Dire Combination" for a closer examination of efforts conducted to feed the hungry in the wake of severe natural disasters.)

Drought is one of the most common causes of severe food shortages in developing and least developed countries.[18] Lack of water can lead to famine and

political sanctions Boycotts or trade embargoes used by one country or international group to apply political pressure on another.

famine A severe shortage of food caused by crop destruction due to weather problems or poor agricultural practices so that the food supply is destroyed or severely diminished. Famine can also be caused by pestilence or war.

Natural Disasters and Food Insecurity: A Dire Combination

Natural disasters, including earthquakes, hurricanes, tsunamis, and floods, can be disastrous no matter where they occur, but when they strike a country or region that's particularly ill-prepared or impoverished, the impact can be devastating.

In 2008, 231 worldwide natural disasters, including one major (8.0) earthquake in the Sichuan province of China, killed almost 236,000 people and cost an estimated $181 billion.[2] In February 2010, a sizable (7.0) earthquake rocked the small, impoverished nation of Haiti, where more than 2 million people—over half the population—were already food insecure or undernourished. The earthquake resulted in more than 200,000 deaths, 300,000 injuries, and a million people being left homeless.[3] As people's homes and possessions were destroyed, they were often left wandering and destitute. They were afraid to reenter damaged housing for fear of aftershocks or further collapse. Those who sustained injuries were often untreated for days, without food and water, as relief workers struggled to find and rescue them.

Those lucky individuals who escaped the initial encounter were faced with a second crisis: shortages of food, clean water, and shelter. Aid workers rushed in with supplies, such as nutritious biscuits and bottled water, only to find that remote sites were largely inaccessible due to difficult terrain, extensive damage, or lack of infrastructure. Thus, widespread food insecurity developed. While some farmers were still producing food, damage to infrastructure such as roads and bridges prevented many of them from reaching markets with it. The food that did end up in the marketplace was often too expensive even for those who had a bit of money.[4]

The distribution of high-energy, nutritious biscuits was a lifeline in the first days after the 2010 disaster in Haiti.

As the situation stabilized and people returned home or left the cities to find shelter with families or friends in rural areas, the long-term consequences of the disaster began to be addressed. In the case of Haiti, 62 percent of the country's population lives in rural areas, and 80 percent relies on agriculture for its livelihood, including small-scale production in the form of backyard gardening and small animal rearing in urban areas.[5] International relief efforts therefore focused on:[6]

- Rapidly restoring food production through input distribution and technical support to small-scale urban and rural farmers in time for the planting season
- Reestablishing the livelihoods of about 1 million people living in urban and rural areas that were directly or indirectly hit by the earthquake, by supporting field-based and backyard food production, and providing assistance for small-scale agricultural and livestock production, including seeds, fertilizers, seedlings, and small animals
- Rehabilitating basic rural infrastructure in the affected areas, such as rural roads, irrigation facilities, food storage, and farm infrastructure, for about 1 million people

These efforts were not cheap, and the international relief community relied heavily on monetary and other assistance from nations, organizations, and charities to facilitate the repair and rebuilding necessary to restore a basic quality of life.

undernutrition. However, floods can also destroy food crops, and are major causes of food shortages.

Lack of irrigation also contributes to crop failures and low yields. The proper use of irrigation can increase crop yield by 100 to 400 percent. Only one fifth of the world's land used to grow crops is irrigated, and this land contributes nearly 50 percent of global crop production.[19]

Because of water's essential role in growing crops, water and food security are closely linked.

As the world's population continues to grow, demands on limited resources for food production will increase.

Wasteful agricultural practices also threaten limited resources. The depletion of natural resources through practices such as overcropping, overgrazing of livestock, aggressive timber harvesting, and the misuse of fertilizers, pesticides, and water may increase the yield of food in the short term at the cost of long-term sustainability.[20]

Population Overgrowth

The human population is growing by about 200,000 people a day, and the projected world population for 2025 is 8 billion people.[21] By 2050, the United Nations estimates, the world population will reach 8 to 12 billion people. Most of this growth is occurring in developing and least developed countries. Whenever rapid population growth occurs in areas that are strained for food production, the resulting **overpopulation** can take a toll on the local people's nutritional status.

LO 16.3 **The Take-Home Message** Factors that give rise to hunger and food insecurity around the world include poverty, discrimination, political sanctions, military conflicts, crop failures, natural disasters, wasteful agricultural practices, and overpopulation.

Who Is at Increased Risk for Undernutrition?

LO 16.4 List populations at highest risk for experiencing undernutrition.

Hunger and food insecurity usually result in **undernutrition**, in which a person's nutrient or energy needs are not being met by his or her diet. Some people are particularly susceptible to experiencing undernutrition because they have high nutrient needs or because they have a reduced ability to process nutrients. The following populations are at increased risk for undernutrition:

- *Pregnant and lactating women*. Pregnant women need extra calories and nutrients—in particular, protein, vitamins, and minerals—to support their own health and their growing baby. Many inadequately nourished pregnant women give birth to undernourished infants. Lactating women need even more calories than pregnant women if they are to maintain a healthy weight and produce adequate, nourishing breast milk. The global recommendation is for women to nurse their babies for the first six months and to continue nursing with supplemental foods into the second year of life or beyond.[22]

- *Infants and children*. Infants are vulnerable to undernutrition because they are growing rapidly, have high nutrient requirements (per unit of body weight), and may be breast-fed by mothers who are undernourished themselves. Because they are dependent on their caregivers to give them adequate breast milk, formula, or foods, they are particularly vulnerable to neglect. From 6 to 12 months of age, as an infant transitions from breast milk to a diet of breast milk plus solid foods, inadequate feeding can lead to diminished growth and the potential for severe undernutrition during the second year of life.[23] The risk for undernutrition continues into childhood if the family experiences food shortages or chronic disease. For example, AIDS can result in the death, and loss of income, of one or both parents. In 2009, the UN estimated that about 16.6 million children had lost one or both parents to AIDS.[24]

- *The critically ill*. Liver and kidney disease can impair the body's ability to process and use some nutrients. Loss of appetite, as seen in some cancer patients and most people with AIDS, can reduce patients' ability to eat, and complicate their treatment.

overpopulation When a region has more people than its natural resources can support.

undernutrition A state of inadequate nutrition whereby a person's nutrient and/or energy needs are not being met through the diet.

- *Older adults.* Older adults are at increased risk for undernutrition because of a decreased sense of taste and smell, dental problems, immobility, malabsorption, or chronic illnesses.[25] In addition, loneliness, isolation, confusion, or depression can diminish appetite or cause a person to lose interest in cooking and eating.

LO 16.4 **The Take-Home Message** Pregnant and lactating women, infants and children, and the ill and elderly are particularly vulnerable to the effects of undernutrition.

What Are the Effects of Chronic Malnutrition?

LO 16.5 Describe the effects of chronic malnutrition.

Once people move along the continuum from food insecurity and undernutrition to **malnutrition** and hunger, it can be extremely difficult to recover. That's because lack of food can lead to physical problems that interfere with a person's ability to earn an adequate income, a situation that leads to continued poverty and lack of adequate food (**Figure 16.4**).

In general, whenever the body experiences fasting, famine, serious disease, or severe malnutrition, it attempts to conserve energy and preserve body tissues. Over an extended period of fasting, however, the body breaks down stored fat, then muscle tissue and internal organs as sources of energy. In prolonged starvation, adults can lose up to 50 percent of their body weight. The greatest amount of organ deterioration occurs in the intestinal tract and the liver. The loss is moderate in the heart and kidneys, and the least damage occurs in the brain and nervous system.[26]

Let's look at some individual effects of chronic malnutrition.

Figure 16.4 **Downward Spiral of Poverty and Hunger**
Lack of food can lead to numerous other symptoms that compound the problem of hunger.

Children Suffer Impaired Growth and Development

When children do not receive the nutrients they need to grow and develop properly, they are likely to experience both physical and mental problems, including insufficient weight gain, improper muscle development, lowered resistance to infection, **growth stunting**, and impaired brain development (**Figure 16.5**).[27] Their bodies attempt to adapt to a lack of food by decreasing physical and intellectual growth. Children are more likely to show behavioral, emotional, and academic problems if they come from families that experience hunger and food insufficiency rather than families that do not report hunger experiences.[28] In particular, long-term undernutrition can slow behavioral and cognitive development, interfere with learning, impact reproductive health, and undermine future work productivity.[29]

If hunger persists or occurs at early, crucial times of brain development, cognitive development is impaired.[30] Research demonstrates that underweight and malnourished children perform poorly in school.[31] As a result, undernourished children may have a difficult time completing their basic elementary education. This is particularly unfortunate because school performance has a measurable impact on earning ability later in life.

Even if children are healthy enough to regularly attend school, hunger and malnutrition impair learning ability. For example, children who are deficient in iron suffer from reduced school performance.[32] Malnourished children also seem to be fatigued, inattentive, and unresponsive to their learning environment.

In 2012 an estimated 162 million children globally experienced stunted growth because of deficiencies in protein and other nutrients. Fifty-one million children

malnutrition The long-term outcome of consuming a diet that contains an imbalance of nutrients.

growth stunting Impaired growth and development primarily manifested in early childhood and including malnutrition during fetal development. Once growth stunting occurs, it is usually permanent.

Figure 16.5 Effects of Undernutrition
As hunger persists, physical symptoms set in and lead to further complications.

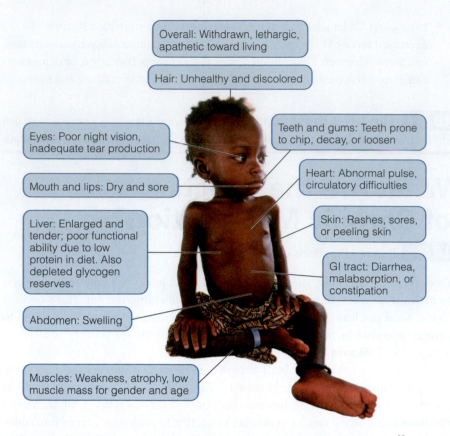

Overall: Withdrawn, lethargic, apathetic toward living

Hair: Unhealthy and discolored

Eyes: Poor night vision, inadequate tear production

Teeth and gums: Teeth prone to chip, decay, or loosen

Mouth and lips: Dry and sore

Heart: Abnormal pulse, circulatory difficulties

Liver: Enlarged and tender; poor functional ability due to low protein in diet. Also depleted glycogen reserves.

Skin: Rashes, sores, or peeling skin

GI tract: Diarrhea, malabsorption, or constipation

Abdomen: Swelling

Muscles: Weakness, atrophy, low muscle mass for gender and age

under age 5 had low weight for their height, a condition known as wasting.[33] Growth stunting may also have a negative impact on children over the long term, affecting cognitive development, school achievement, economic productivity, and maternal reproductive outcomes.[34]

Impaired Immunity Can Result in Disease

A malnourished individual has a weakened immune system, which increases his or her vulnerability to various infections. Fever, parasitic disease, pneumonia, measles, and malaria are examples of conditions that can occur because of weakened immune systems and chronic malnutrition (see **Table 16.2**).

In 2013, 6.3 million children under the age of 5 died.[35] The World Health Organization estimates that about 45 percent of all childhood deaths in developing countries are associated with malnutrition. The most common causes of death in postneonatal children (that is, those who survive birth and the first 28 days of life) are pneumonia, diarrhea, and malaria, all of which have malnutrition as an underlying contributing factor.[36]

Table 16.2

Common Illnesses in Malnourished Children

Disease/Condition	Cause	Effect
Diarrhea	Pathogenic infections	Severe dehydration
Acute respiratory infection	Virus or bacteria	Pneumonia, bronchitis, colds, fast breathing, coughing, and fever
Malaria	Parasite (transmitted by a mosquito)	Fever, weakness, sweating, shivering, shaking, nausea, liver failure, infected red blood cells, kidney failure or bleeding in the kidneys
Measles	Respiratory illness caused by a highly contagious virus, from airborne droplets (coughing/sneezing)	Pneumonia, brain inflammation, infection, diarrhea, and seizures

Table 16.3

Most Common Vitamin and Mineral Deficiencies among the Malnourished

Vitamin or Mineral	Effects	Incidence
Vitamin A	Eye disease; blindness	Vitamin A deficiency is the leading cause of preventable blindness in children in developing countries.
Iron	Iron-deficiency anemia	Most common nutritional disorder worldwide—affects over 30% of the world population. Half of pregnant women in developing countries are estimated to be anemic.
Iodine	Goiter, cretinism	Iodine-deficiency disorder is a serious public health threat. Households in 54 countries in the world are still iodine deficient.

Children experiencing malnutrition are especially vulnerable to respiratory problems.[37] Viruses or bacteria in the respiratory tract can cause acute respiratory infection. Pneumonia, the most serious respiratory infection, is the leading infectious killer of children worldwide,[38] and, when caused by bacteria, can be successfully treated with oral antibiotics.

Diarrhea—caused by viruses, parasites, and other harmful microorganisms— can result in severe dehydration (loss of fluids and electrolytes). The gastrointestinal infections that cause diarrhea kill around 2.2 million people globally each year, mostly children in developing countries. The use of contaminated water is a major cause of diarrhea.[39]

Malaria is carried by parasite-infected mosquitoes. Approximately 40 percent of the world's children under age 5 lack sufficient vitamin A, which makes them more susceptible to infection with malaria, as well as to diarrhea, impaired vision, and even blindness.[40] Vitamin and mineral deficiencies and their resulting diseases are serious concerns for people living in developing countries and in the United States. Iron and iodine deficiencies are also major world health issues that cause severe health problems. These micronutrient deficiencies are referred to as "hidden hunger." **Table 16.3** lists the most common vitamin and mineral deficiencies observed in those who are malnourished.

Infant and Child Mortality Rates Increase

As mentioned, malnutrition is part of a vicious cycle that passes hunger from one generation to the next. Unfortunately, many young women experience undernutrition during their own infancy and childhood. Girls who were low birth weight babies, premature, or were undernourished and ill during the first five years of life may be physically stunted and less able to support a healthy pregnancy when they become adults. The infants born to malnourished women are more likely to be malnourished, experience chronic illness, and have an increased risk of premature death.

LO 16.5 **The Take-Home Message** The effects of chronic malnutrition are devastating and can produce irreversible damage, depending on the stage of life. If malnutrition occurs during adulthood, the body tries to conserve nutrients and preserve its own organs, but eventually there could be irreversible organ damage. Physical effects of malnutrition among children include stunted growth, impaired mental development and immunity, and higher likelihood of disease. Mental effects include anxiety, irritability, and attention problems. Vitamin and mineral deficiency diseases can occur, and the impairment of the immune system increases vulnerability to infectious disease.

What Can Be Done to Reduce Food Insecurity?

LO 16.6 Describe some of the strategies currently in use to reduce food insecurity.

Everyone—from children to adults—can help eradicate hunger.

Global hunger harms all of us. When citizens of your community experience hunger, you are likely to see increased disease incidence, low ambition, poverty, and general apathy among the individuals affected. Additionally, from a humanitarian perspective, the painful physical symptoms of hunger are unacceptable when you consider that a surplus of food is grown each year.

At the local level, individuals, families, churches, and community relief agencies seek out and assist people who have insufficient resources. From providing free food and meals to education and job training, there are numerous ways such organizations can help alleviate hunger. Similarly, corporations and governments can help solve the hunger problem by providing food aid and creating economic opportunity to help people improve their lives. See **Table 16.4** for examples of programs that help combat hunger in the United States.

In addition to the human (person-to-person) help provided by people and organizations, technology also plays a role in alleviating malnutrition. As research and development provide new ways to pack more nutrition into food crops, hunger may be reduced. Enriched crops ultimately benefit hungry people by providing some of the common nutrients (iron, vitamin A, and iodine) that are in low supply in current crops.

Better Land Management and Proper Sanitation

Proper land management and appropriate crop selection can help increase agricultural production. For example, productive land is frequently used for nonconsumable crops, such as tobacco or flowers, for sale to industrialized nations. Raising edible, nutritious plants such as high-protein beans, vegetables, grains, seeds, nuts, or fruit instead of planting export crops like tea, coffee, and cocoa, or raising animal feed for livestock, would help reduce hunger.

Food security and land access are directly related, even if the land is not irrigated or of the highest quality. Farmers who own the land they farm may be more likely to make better farming decisions regarding irrigation, crop rotation, land fallowing (plowed, but unplanted, land), and appropriate soil management. Land ownership, and in particular female land ownership, is part of a long-term solution to a very complex problem. At this time, limited available data suggests that less than a quarter of land in developing countries is operated, let alone owned, by women.[41]

Most people think providing food is the primary means of reducing hunger, but safe water is equally important.

Better land and water management and appropriate crop selection can help eliminate hunger.

Table 16.4
Food Assistance Programs in the United States

Program	Eligibility	Description	Prevalence
Supplemental Nutrition Assistance Program (SNAP), (formerly the Food Stamp Program)	Low income (for a family of four, the net monthly income cannot exceed $1,988)	Individuals who are eligible for food stamps are issued a debit card to purchase specified foods, such as fruits, vegetables, cereals, meats, and dairy products, at their local authorized supermarket. (Items such as alcohol, tobacco, nonfood items, vitamins and medicines, and hot foods are not covered.)	In 2014, more than 46.5 million people per month in the United States
Special Supplemental Nutrition Program for Women, Infants and Children (WIC)	At-risk low-income pregnant and lactating women, infants, and children less than 5 years old	The program provides nutritious, culturally appropriate food, including tortillas, brown rice, soy-based beverages, and a wide choice of fruits and vegetables, to supplement the diet. There are even some organic forms of WIC-eligible foods. The program also emphasizes nutrition education and offers referrals to health care professionals.	8.6 million women, infants, and children per month in 2013
National School Lunch Program	Children with families with incomes at or below 130% of the poverty level are eligible for free meals and those with incomes between 130% and 185% of the poverty level are eligible for reduced-price meals.	Eligible children receive free or reduced-price lunches each year. A subsidized breakfast is sometimes also available at schools.	More than 31.6 million American children in 2012
Summer Food Service Program	Available to communities based on income data	Federal program that combines a meal or feeding program with a summer activity program for children	More than 2.28 million children at 39,000 sites in the summer of 2012
Child and Adult Care Food Program	Available to communities based on income data	Program provides nutritious meals to low-income children and senior adults who receive day care or adult care outside the home. There are income guidelines and specific menu requirements for program participation.	3.3 million children and 120,000 adults receive meals and snacks each day as part of this program.
Meals on Wheels America	Age 60 or over	The programs provide meals at a community site or delivered to the home.	Brings meals to nearly 2.5 million seniors across the country

According to the World Health Organization, "a significant proportion of diarrheal disease can be prevented through safe drinking water and adequate sanitation and hygiene."[42] More than 2.5 billion people lack basic sanitation facilities, and 780 million people lack access to safe water.[43] The consequences of unsanitary conditions are enormous. Each year, diarrhea kills about 760,000 children under 5,[44] and adult workers are less productive when they are ill themselves or caring for family members. Entire communities are often at risk for health problems from drinking contaminated water.

Various innovative solutions are being proposed to alleviate the world's water problems. For example, in Kenya, Latin America, and India, some villagers let the sun purify the water supply. They pour water into clear plastic bottles, then place the bottles in the sun for at least 6 hours. The combination of heat and UV radiation destroys common waterborne bacteria such as

Access to clean drinking water is just as important as adequate nutrition for human health.

Figure 16.6 Factors in Food Security

cholera, typhoid, and dysentery. This solution, called SODIS, for solar disinfection, is available, inexpensive, and accessible in countries with a warm climate.[45]

Other water sanitation solutions are more complex. They include chlorination of water, irrigation technology, river diversion projects, piped water systems, and community wells.

Fortification of Foods

Food fortification can help alleviate micronutrient deficiencies. Because they are the most commonly deficient (see Table 16.3), iodine, iron, and vitamin A are the three nutrients most often added to foods. For food fortification to work, the foods chosen to carry these extra nutrients must be a staple in the community's food supply (and therefore eaten often) and consistently available. The food should also be shelf stable and affordable. Rice, cereals, flours, salt, and even sugar are examples of foods that can be successfully fortified.

Food fortification is inexpensive, yet enormously beneficial. Countries across the globe, both developed and developing, have programs to fortify foods such as salt, flour, oil, sugar, and soy sauce with iron, iodine, and vitamin A.[46]

Education Is Key

Education plays an important role in ensuring food security (see **Figure 16.6**). Educated people are more likely to have increased economic and career opportunities, and less likely to fall into the trap of poverty. Literacy and education also build self-esteem and self-confidence, two qualities that help people overcome life's challenges.

Education also reduces poverty in other ways. For example, researchers found that societies with a more educated population enjoyed:[47]

- Better natural resource management
- More rapid technological adaptation and innovation
- greater diffusion of information leading to greater productivity
- better health and longer lives
- greater personal development and participation in civil society
- access to a wider range of opportunities

The curriculum and format for international education are somewhat different in the developing world than in the developed world. International education that aims to improve rates of food security ought to focus on literacy, technical knowledge, agricultural skills, horticulture, health education, and the development of natural resources. Agricultural education and increased agricultural production in developing countries help create jobs, which increases income, which then lifts people out of poverty.[48]

Meanwhile, education related to reducing food insecurity in the developed world should focus on land management, improved crop yields, boosting nutrient levels within crops, and continued development of drought-resistant and insect-repelling plants.

You Can Help Reduce Food Insecurity

Hunger can seem like an overwhelming problem, but there are specific things an individual person (you!) can do to help. If you have the funds, you can certainly give money or food to organizations that will distribute your offerings where they are needed. Just as important, and possibly more satisfying, is the idea of giving time.

Practical Nutrition VIDEO

Does It Cost More to Eat Healthy?

Having limited funds shouldn't have to mean poor nutrition. Sometimes the healthiest foods are among the least expensive. Let Joan show you how to stretch your food dollar for nutritional value. Scan this QR code with your mobile device to access the video. You can also access the video in MasteringNutrition™.

Food Insecurity among Us—and How You Can Help!

Food insecurity may be closer than you think. In fact, you may have friends, relatives, or neighbors who've experienced hunger sometime in their lives.

Feeding America, formerly called Second Harvest, is the nation's leading domestic hunger-relief charity. It is a national network of individuals, local food banks, and offices, as well as corporate and government partners, that helps distribute excess and donated food and grocery items annually to those who are hungry. Its mission is to feed America's hungry through a network of more than 200 member food banks and to continue the fight to end food insecurity in this country.

Feeding America collects surplus food from national food companies and other large donors and stores it in a centralized location. The food is then moved to local food pantries in order to reach those who need it.

When it comes to fighting hunger in America, everyone needs to pitch in. You can help your needy neighbors in three ways: give funds, give food, and/or give time. Funds can be donated online at www.feedingamerica.org. Every dollar donated helps provide 10 meals for those in need. You can also donate food by hosting a food drive. Finally, you can volunteer your time by helping out in your local community, perhaps tutoring children at a local afterschool feeding program, repackaging donated food, stocking shelves at a local food pantry, or transporting food to the hungry.

To find out where you can help, visit the Feeding America website and search for opportunities using the Volunteer Match service.

Contact a local food bank to ask how you can help with gathering and distributing food to those in need. For further tips on how you can contribute to reducing food insecurity, see the Nutrition in the Real World feature "Food Insecurity among Us—and How You Can Help!"

LO 16.6 **The Take-Home Message** Eradicating hunger benefits everyone, and local charities and community groups, including faith-based organizations, as well as corporations and governments, can provide aid and organize programs to alleviate hunger. Education of the world's population is also important, along with proper land management and proper crop selection.

Food vs Cash: Which Is More Effective for Alleviating Hunger?

As discussed in this chapter, food insecurity and hunger are major issues both in the United States and around the world. Numerous government agencies and nonprofit organizations attempt to remedy food insecurity with both food and monetary aid. However, experts differ as to which of these strategies is more effective.

Is the disbursement of food aid effective for alleviating hunger? Are cash payments more likely to be misused or abused? Read the two sets of arguments presented below, and then answer the questions to draw your own conclusions.

food aid

- Food aid has clearly had a significant role in reducing the loss of life during food emergencies in such countries as Ethiopia, Sudan, Somalia, Afghanistan, Rwanda, and Haiti.[1]

- Giving people money instead of food can upset local economies, fuel conflicts, and exclude the most needy.[2] For example, cash transfers can cause local food prices to rise, which may cause additional hardship for those who don't directly receive food aid.[3]

- Cash may be physically risky for those handling the money, and may disadvantage women who are less able to keep control of it.[4] In contrast, food aid that's given to women and children tends to be consumed by women and children.

- Food aid may be less vulnerable to corruption. Bags of maize cannot easily be swapped for cigarettes or beer, and stories of food being turned into fleets of Mercedes Benzes are few and far between.[5]

- Cash is not useful when there is no food to buy. Refugees fleeing war and living in camps or earthquake victims living amid rubble are better benefited by receiving food directly.[6]

monetary aid

- Cash aid has larger positive effects on household welfare, and benefits extended family members and not just the direct recipients of aid.[7]

- In cases where food is locally available, monetary donations are more cost effective than food donations, because the cost of shipping food internationally usually exceeds the cost of purchasing food locally.[8]

- Flooding a market with food aid can drive down the price for local farmers and therefore provide a disincentive to local food production.[9]

- Food often takes 4–6 months to arrive at its destination, far too late to save lives in an emergency situation.[10]

- U.S. law currently mandates that all food aid be grown by American farmers and shipped on American ships. Fifty-nine cents of every dollar we spend to send grain overseas gets spent dealing with red tape and regulations, rather than on food.[11]

what do you think?

1. What are the underlying causes of food insecurity in many countries around the world? **2.** Which approach do you think is likely to yield greater benefits—food aid or monetary aid? **3.** Why is food aid currently the preferred method of the U.S. government? Is this likely to change?

LO 16.1 Chronic Hunger Is Prevalent throughout the World

Food security is the access by all people at all times to enough food for an active, healthy life. Food insecurity is the inability to secure adequate amounts of nutritious foods to meet one's need due to lack of available resources. Hunger describes a feeling of discomfort or weakness caused by lack of food, coupled with the desire to eat. In the United States, about 14.9 percent of American households were food insecure at least some time in 2011. And the FAO estimates that between 2010 and 2012, 12 percent of the world's population was hungry.

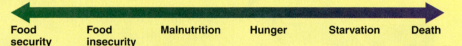

| Food security | Food insecurity | Malnutrition | Hunger | Starvation | Death |

LO 16.2 Food Insecurity in the United States Is Often Related to Poverty and Health Problems

In the United States, food insecurity often occurs among people in disadvantaged circumstances in rural areas, inner cities, and suburbs. Causes include poverty, disease or disability, lack of education, and inadequate wages. Mental illness and/or drug and alcohol abuse sometimes lead to homelessness, which in turn often results in hunger.

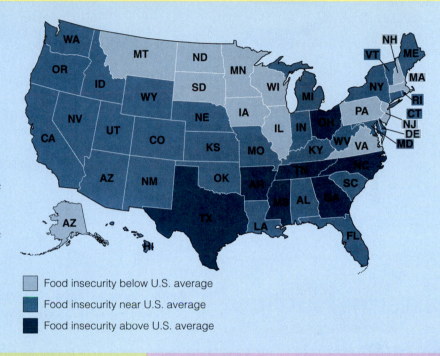

- Food insecurity below U.S. average
- Food insecurity near U.S. average
- Food insecurity above U.S. average

LO 16.3 Worldwide Food Insecurity Has Multiple Causes

Food insecurity and hunger are more prevalent in developing countries and least developed countries than in developed countries. In these nations, food insecurity may arise out of poverty or poor health, in addition to other risks, such as discrimination, armed conflict, natural disasters, poor agricultural practices, and population overgrowth.

LO 16.4 Pregnant and Lactating Women, Children, the Ill, and Older Adults Are at the Highest Risk for Undernutrition

Pregnant and lactating women have higher calorie and nutrient needs. If they are improperly nourished, their infants may be, too. Infants and children in general have high nutrient needs because they are growing rapidly. They are dependent on their caregivers for food, making them more susceptible to undernutrition. Chronically ill people may have malabsorption problems. Older adults may be at risk for undernutrition because of higher needs for several micronutrients, decreased senses of smell and taste, chronic illness, compromised immunity, and lack of mobility.

LO 16.5 Chronic Malnutrition Damages Your Health

Effects of chronic malnutrition include stunted growth, wasting, impaired immune function, infections, anemia, and nutrient deficiencies. A nutrient deficiency can lead to serious, permanent health damage, or even death, in both children and adults.

Lack of food → Fatigue, apathy, no ambition → Weight loss → Compromised health and disease → Anemia → Decreased growth → Malabsorption in GI tract → Loss of muscle mass

LO 16.6 Providing Greater Food Resources Can Reduce Hunger

Community and faith-based organizations can help ease hunger by providing free food and assistance programs to help people overcome poverty and food insecurity. Corporations and governments can invest in biotechnologies and education programs that provide more nutrient-dense foods and increase economic opportunity. Food assistance programs like the Supplemental Nutrition Assistance Program (SNAP), WIC, and the National School Lunch Program, among others, provide assistance to those who experience food insecurity in the United States.

Food security

Land management • Biotechnology • Fortification of foods • Water sanitation • Education

Terms to Know

- food insecurity
- hunger
- starvation
- developed country
- developing country
- least developed countries
- poverty
- working poor
- homeless
- political sanctions
- famine
- overpopulation
- undernutrition
- malnutrition
- growth stunting

MasteringNutrition™

Build your knowledge—and confidence—in the Study Area of MasteringNutrition with a variety of study tools.

MyDietAnalysis

Access MyDietAnalysis through MasteringNutrition™ and track your diet and daily activities. In addition, a dietary analysis activity is available for every chapter in your book.

Check Your Understanding

LO 16.1 1. What is food insecurity?
  a. Food insecurity happens only in developing countries, when they can't get enough food because of civil unrest.
  b. Food insecurity is the same thing as hunger.
  c. Food insecurity is a lack of adequate nutrition for an active, healthy life.
  d. Food insecurity describes a lack of sufficient calories in the diet for an active, healthy life.

LO 16.2 2. Food insecurity exists because
  a. not enough food is produced in the world to feed everyone adequately.
  b. food distribution is uneven, and some people do not have access to enough food.
  c. some people choose not to eat.
  d. people feel insecure about whether their food is safe.

LO 16.2 3. Who are the "working poor"?
  a. all individuals classified as low income by the United States Department of Labor
  b. all individuals who fall outside the middle-class range of income
  c. all individuals who are employed but have incomes that fall below the poverty line
  d. all minimum-wage workers

LO 16.3 4. What is one of the most common causes of food shortages?
  a. poverty
  b. lack of education and economic opportunity
  c. war, natural disaster, or civil unrest
  d. drought

LO 16.4 5. Which of the following groups is especially vulnerable to food insecurity–related illness?
  a. infants and young children
  b. adolescents
  c. adult men
  d. adult women

LO 16.4 6. Which of the following is a nutritional risk factor for older adults?
  a. increased metabolic rate
  b. rapid cell growth and turnover
  c. decreased sense of taste and smell
  d. increased energy needs

LO 16.5 7. What is the general term for the common condition in which micronutrients are consistently deficient in the diet?
  a. malaria
  b. hidden hunger

c. diarrhea

d. dehydration

LO 16.5 8. A lack of which micronutrient has been implicated in causing blindness in children?

 a. vitamin K

 b. vitamin A

 c. iodine

 d. iron

LO 16.6 9. Which nutrients are most likely to be used to fortify food?

 a. vitamins D, E, and K

 b. sodium, potassium, and chloride

 c. magnesium, phosphorus, and sulfur

 d. iron, iodine, and vitamin A

LO 16.6 10. Which of the following programs serves the greatest number of people in the United States?

 a. Meals on Wheels

 b. Supplemental Nutrition Assistance Program

 c. Feeding America

 d. the National School Lunch program

Answers

1. (c) Food insecurity is a lack of adequate nutrition for an active, healthy life. The USDA describes an American household as *food secure* if it has access at all times to enough food for an active, healthy life for all household members.

2. (b) Although enough food is produced to feed everyone in the world, the distribution of the world's food supply is uneven, and people in some parts of the world do not have access to, or cannot afford, adequate food. Everyone needs to eat to survive.

3. (c) The working poor includes individuals who are employed 27 or more weeks of each year, yet still have incomes below the official poverty line.

4. (d) Drought is one of the most common causes of food shortages. Poverty and lack of education are factors that can lead to individual hunger, but don't generally cause crop failure. While civil unrest may disturb food production, it may not have the widespread impact of a drought.

5. (a) Infants and young children have immature immune systems, making them more susceptible to illness related to undernutrition.

Adolescents and adults have mature immune systems that are stronger and better functioning.

6. (c) Older adults sometimes lose interest in food or have a diminished appetite because they cannot enjoy food's smells or tastes. Older people have a decreased basal metabolic rate and experience slower cell growth and decreased energy requirements.

7. (b) Hidden hunger refers to vitamin A, iron, or iodine deficiency. This condition affects more than 2 billion people in the world.

8. (b) Lack of vitamin A is implicated in preventable blindness. Deficiency in vitamin K can lead to excessive bleeding; deficiency in iodine can cause goiter and cretinism; and deficiency in iron can result in iron-deficiency anemia.

9. (d) Iron, iodine, and vitamin A are frequently used to fortify food because deficiencies of them are linked to many common and serious illnesses. The other nutrients listed are important, but are not generally incorporated into food fortification programs.

10. (b) All of these programs feed millions of people, but the program with the greatest number assisted is the Supplemental Nutrition Assistance Program (SNAP).

Web Resources

- For more on the state of food insecurity and hunger in the United States and around the world, visit the Bread for the World Institute at www.bread.org
- To learn more about one organization that is fighting global poverty, visit CARE at www.care.org
- To find out how the Food and Agriculture Organization of the United Nations leads international efforts to defeat hunger, visit www.fao.org
- To learn more about the efforts of the Global Health Council, visit the National Council for International Health website at www.globalhealth.org
- To learn more about an international children's group, visit the UNICEF website at www.unicef.org
- For more about the World Health Organization, visit www.who.int/en

Answers to True or False?

1. **True.** Poverty does play a significant role in food insecurity around the world. Additional factors like war, overpopulation, and disease can also affect people's access to sufficient food. Find out more on page 604.

2. **False.** Despite living in a wealthy nation, many people in the United States grapple with food insecurity. Turn to page 605 to find out why.

3. **False.** An overweight or obese individual can also experience a chronic shortage of food. To learn more, turn to page 606.

4. **False.** The world's farmers grow enough food to nourish every man, woman, and child on the planet. The challenge lies in distributing their products evenly. Learn more on page 607.

5. **True.** Children are dependent on the adults around them for adequate food, and therefore are susceptible to food insecurity. Children are also more prone to long-term consequences of nutrient deficiencies. Find out more on page 610.

6. **True.** Older adults may have sufficient funds for food, but may experience food insecurity due to mobility issues or emotional problems. Learn more on page 611.

7. **False.** Poor nutrition can negatively affect mental development, as well as physical development. Turn to page 611 to learn more.

8. **True.** Advances in agricultural processes do increase the amount of food grown per acre of farmland. Find out more on page 614.

9. **False.** Fortifying foods improves their nutritional value and can provide numerous nutrients that some populations wouldn't otherwise obtain. Learn which foods are being fortified on page 616.

10. **False.** You can also help the hungry by volunteering your time, hosting a food drive, or making a food donation to your local food bank. Learn more on page 616.

Appendices

Appendix A
Calculations and Conversions   A-2

Appendix B
Organizations and Resources   B-1

Calculation and Conversion Aids

Commonly Used Metric Units

millimeter (mm) : one-thousandth of a meter (0.001)
centimeter (cm) : one-hundredth of a meter (0.01)
kilometer (km) : one-thousand times a meter (1,000)
kilogram (kg) : one-thousand times a gram (1,000)
milligram (mg) : one-thousandth of a gram (0.001)
microgram (µg) : one-millionth of a gram (0.000001)
milliliter (ml) : one-thousandth of a liter (0.001)

Conversion Factors

Use the following table to convert U.S. measurements to metric equivalents:

Original Unit	Multiply By	To Get
ounces avdp	28.3495	grams
ounces	0.0625	pounds
pounds	0.4536	kilograms
pounds	16	ounces
grams	0.0353	ounces
grams	0.0022	pounds
kilograms	2.2046	pounds
liters	1.8162	pints (dry)
liters	2.1134	pints (liquid)
liters	0.9081	quarts (dry)
liters	1.0567	quarts (liquid)
liters	0.2642	gallons (U.S.)
pints (dry)	0.5506	liters
pints (liquid)	0.4732	liters
quarts (dry)	1.1012	liters
quarts (liquid)	0.9463	liters
gallons (U.S.)	3.7854	liters
millimeters	0.0394	inches
centimeters	0.3937	inches
centimeters	0.0328	feet
inches	25.4000	millimeters
inches	2.5400	centimeters
inches	0.0254	meters
feet	0.3048	meters
meters	3.2808	feet
meters	1.0936	yards
cubic feet	0.0283	cubic meters
cubic meters	35.3147	cubic feet
cubic meters	1.3079	cubic yards
cubic yards	0.7646	cubic meters

International Units

Some vitamin supplements may report vitamin content as International Units (IU).

To convert IU to:

➤ Micrograms of vitamin D (cholecalciferol), multiply the IU value by 0.025.
➤ Milligrams of vitamin E (alpha-tocopherol), multiply the IU value by 0.67 if vitamin E is from natural sources. Multiply the IU value by 0.45 if vitamin E is from synthetic sources.
➤ Vitamin A: 1 IU = 0.3 µg retinol or 0.3 µg RAE or 0.6 µg beta-carotene

Retinol Activity Equivalents

Retinol activity equivalents (RAE) are a standardized unit of measure for vitamin A. RAE account for the various differences in bioavailability from sources of vitamin A. Many supplements will report vitamin A content in IU, as shown above, or in retinol equivalents (RE).

1 µg RAE = 1 µg retinol
         12 µg beta-carotene

To calculate RAE from the RE value of vitamin carotenoids in foods, divide RE by 2. Divide the amount of beta-carotene by 12 to convert to RAE.

For vitamin A supplements and foods fortified with vitamin A, 1 RE = 1 RAE.

Folate

Folate is measured as dietary folate equivalents (DFE). DFE account for the different factors affecting bioavailability of folate sources.

1 µg DFE = 1 µg food folate
           0.6 µg folate from fortified foods
           0.5 µg folate supplement taken on an empty stomach
           0.6 µg folate as a supplement consumed with a meal

To convert micrograms of synthetic folate, such as that found in supplements or fortified foods, to DFE:

µg synthetic folate × 1.7 = µg DFE

For naturally occurring food folate, such as spinach, each microgram of folate equals 1 microgram DFE:

µg folate = µg DFE

Niacin

Niacin is measured as niacin equivalents (mg NE). NE reflects the amount of preformed niacin in foods or the amount that can be formed from a food's content of the amino acid niacin.

To calculate mg NE from a meal:

If you know the tryptophan and preformed niacin in a meal: (tryptophan × 1,000 ÷ 60) + preformed niacin = mg NE

If you know the total amount of protein in a meal but not the tryptophan content: (0.011 × g of protein) × 1,000 ÷ 60 + preformed niacin = mg NE

Length: U.S. and Metric Equivalents

¼ inch = 0.6 centimeters
1 inch = 2.5 centimeters
1 foot = 0.3048 meter
30.48 centimeters
1 yard = 0.9144 meter
1 millimeter = 0.03937 inch
1 centimeter = 0.3937 inch
1 decimeter = 3.937 inches
1 meter = 39.37 inches
1.094 yards
1 micrometer = 0.00003937 inch

Weights and Measures

Food Measurement Equivalencies from U.S. to Metric

Capacity

⅕ teaspoon = 1 milliliter
¼ teaspoon = 1.23 milliliters
½ teaspoon = 2.5 milliliters
1 teaspoon = 5 milliliters
1 tablespoon = 15 milliliters
1 fluid ounce = 30 milliliters
¼ cup = 59 milliliters
⅓ cup = 79 milliliters
½ cup = 118 milliliters
1 cup = 237 milliliters
1 pint (2 cups) = 473 milliliters
1 quart (4 cups) = 0.95 liter
1 liter (1.06 quarts) = 1,000 milliliters
1 gallon (4 quarts) = 3.79 liters

Weight

0.035 ounce = 1 gram
1 ounce = 28 grams
¼ pound (4 ounces) = 113 grams
1 pound (16 ounces) = 454 grams
2.2 pounds (35 ounces) = 1 kilogram

U.S. Food Measurement Equivalents

3 teaspoons = 1 tablespoon
½ tablespoon = 1½ teaspoons
2 tablespoons = ⅛ cup
4 tablespoons = ¼ cup
5 tablespoons + 1 teaspoon = ⅓ cup
8 tablespoons = ½ cup
10 tablespoons + 2 teaspoons = ⅔ cup
12 tablespoons = ¾ cup
16 tablespoons = 1 cup
2 cups = 1 pint
4 cups = 1 quart
2 pints = 1 quart
4 quarts = 1 gallon

Volumes and Capacities

1 cup = 8 fluid ounces
½ liquid pint
1 milliliter = 0.061 cubic inch
1 liter = 1.057 liquid quarts
0.908 dry quart
61.024 cubic inches
1 U.S. gallon = 231 cubic inches
3.785 liters
0.833 British gallon
128 U.S. fluid ounces
1 British Imperial gallon = 277.42 cubic inches
1.201 U.S. gallons
4.546 liters
160 British fluid ounces
1 U.S. ounce, liquid or fluid = 1.805 cubic inches
29.574 milliliters
1.041 British fluid ounces
1 pint, dry = 33.600 cubic inches
0.551 liter
1 pint, liquid = 28.875 cubic inches
0.473 liter
1 U.S. quart, dry = 67.201 cubic inches
1.101 liters
1 U.S. quart, liquid = 57.75 cubic inches
0.946 liter
1 British quart = 69.355 cubic inches
1.032 U.S. quarts, dry
1.201 U.S. quarts, liquid

Energy Units

1 kilocalorie (kcal) = 4.2 kilojoules
1 megajoule (MJ) = 239 kilocalories
1 kilojoule (kJ) = 0.24 kcal
1 gram carbohydrate = 4 kcals
1 gram fat = 9 kcals
1 gram protein = 4 kcals

Temperature Standards

	°Fahrenheit	°Celsius
Body temperature	98.6°	37°
Comfortable room temperature	65–75°	18–24°
Boiling point of water	212°	100°
Freezing point of water	32°	0°

Temperature Scales

To Convert Fahrenheit to Celsius

$[(°F - 32) \times 5]/9$

1. Subtract 32 from °F
2. Multiply (°F − 32) by 5, then divide by 9

To Convert Celsius to Fahrenheit

$[(°C \times 9)/5] + 32$

1. Multiply °C by 9, then divide by 5
2. Add 32 to (°C × 9/5)

Academic Journals

International Journal of Sport Nutrition and Exercise Metabolism
www.humankinetics.com/IJSNEM

Journal of Nutrition
http://jn.nutrition.org

Nutrition Research
www.journals.elsevierhealth.com/periodicals/NTR

Nutrition
www.journals.elsevierhealth.com/periodicals/NUT

Nutrition Reviews
http://onlinelibrary.wiley.com/journal/10.1111/(ISSN)1753-4887

Obesity
http://onlinelibrary.wiley.com/journal/10.1002/(ISSN)1930-739X

International Journal of Obesity
www.nature.com/ijo

Journal of the American Medical Association
http://jama.ama-assn.org

New England Journal of Medicine
http://content.nejm.org

American Journal of Clinical Nutrition
www.ajcn.org

Journal of the Academy of Nutrition and Dietetics
www.adajournal.org

Aging

Administration on Aging
www.aoa.gov

American Association of Retired Persons (AARP)
www.aarp.org

National Council on Aging
www.ncoa.org

International Osteoporosis Foundation
www.iofbonehealth.org

National Institute on Aging
www.nia.nih.gov

Osteoporosis and Related Bone Diseases National Resource Center
www.osteo.org

American Geriatrics Society
www.americangeriatrics.org

National Osteoporosis Foundation
www.nof.org

Alcohol and Drug Abuse

National Institute on Drug Abuse
www.nida.nih.gov

National Institute on Alcohol Abuse and Alcoholism
www.niaaa.nih.gov

Alcoholics Anonymous
www.alcoholics-anonymous.org

Narcotics Anonymous
www.na.org

National Council on Alcoholism and Drug Dependence
www.ncadd.org

Substance Abuse and Mental Health Services Administration
www.samhsa.gov

Canadian Government

Health Canada
www.hc-sc.gc.ca

Agricultural and Agri-Food Canada
www.agr.gc.ca

Canadian Food Inspection Agency
www.inspection.gc.ca/english/toce.shtml

Canadian Institute for Health Information
www.cihi.ca

Canadian Public Health Association
www.cpha.ca

Canadian Nutrition and Professional Organizations

Dietitians of Canada, Canadian Dietetic Association
www.dietitians.ca

Canadian Diabetes Association
www.diabetes.ca

National Eating Disorder Information Centre
www.nedic.ca

Canadian Paediatric Society
www.cps.ca

Disordered Eating/Eating Disorders

American Psychiatric Association
www.psych.org

Klarman Eating Disorders Center at McLean Hospital
www.mclean.harvard.edu/patient/child/edc.php

National Institute of Mental Health
www.nimh.nih.gov

National Association of Anorexia Nervosa and Associated Disorders (ANAD)
www.anad.org

National Eating Disorders Association
www.nationaleatingdisorders.org

Eating Disorder Referral and Information Center
www.edreferral.com

Overeaters Anonymous
www.oa.org

Exercise, Physical Activity, and Sports

American College of Sports Medicine (ACSM)
www.acsm.org

American Physical Therapy Association (APTA)
www.apta.org

Gatorade Sports Science Institute (GSSI)
www.gssiweb.com

National Coalition for Promoting Physical Activity (NCPPA)
www.ncppa.org

Sports, Cardiovascular, and Wellness Nutrition (SCAN)
www.scandpg.org

President's Council on Fitness, Sports & Nutrition
www.fitness.gov

American Council on Exercise
www.acefitness.org

IDEA Health & Fitness Association
www.ideafit.com

Food Safety

Food Marketing Institute
www.fmi.org

Agency for Toxic Substances and Disease Registry (ATSDR)
www.atsdr.cdc.gov

Food Allergy Research & Education
www.foodallergy.org

Foodsafety.gov
www.foodsafety.gov

The USDA Food Safety and Inspection Service
www.fsis.usda.gov

Consumer Reports
www.consumerreports.org

Center for Science in the Public Interest: Food Safety
www.cspinet.org/foodsafety/index.html

Center for Food Safety and Applied Nutrition
www.fda.gov/Food

Food Safety Project
www.extension.iastate.edu/foodsafety

Organic Consumers Association
www.organicconsumers.org

Infancy and Childhood

Administration for Children and Families
www.acf.hhs.gov

American Academy of Pediatrics
www.aap.org

Kidshealth: The Nemours Foundation
www.kidshealth.org

National Center for Education in Maternal and Child Health
www.ncemch.org

Birth Defects Research for Children, Inc.
www.birthdefects.org

USDA/ARS Children's Nutrition Research Center at Baylor College of Medicine
www.kidsnutrition.org

Centers for Disease Control—Healthy Youth
www.cdc.gov/healthyyouth

International Agencies

UNICEF
www.unicef.org

World Health Organization
www.who.int/en

The Stockholm Convention on Persistent Organic Pollutants
www.pops.int

Food and Agricultural Organization of the United Nations
www.fao.org

International Food Information Council Foundation
www.ific.org

Pregnancy and Lactation

San Diego County Breastfeeding Coalition
www.breastfeeding.org

National Alliance for Breastfeeding Advocacy
www.naba-breastfeeding.org

American Congress of Obstetricians and Gynecologists
www.acog.org

La Leche League
www.lalecheleague.org

National Organization on Fetal Alcohol Syndrome
www.nofas.org

March of Dimes Birth Defects Foundation
http://modimes.org

Professional Nutrition Organizations

Academy of Nutrition and Dietetics (AND)
www.eatright.org

American Dental Association
www.ada.org

American Heart Association
www.americanheart.org

The American Society for Nutrition (ASN)
www.nutrition.org

Dietitians in Integrative and Functional Medicine
www.complementarynutrition.org

The Institute for Functional Medicine
www.functionalmedicine.org

The Society for Nutrition Education and Behavior
www.sneb.org

American College of Nutrition
www.americancollegeofnutrition.org

The Obesity Society
www.obesity.org

American Council on Science and Health
www.acsh.org

American Diabetes Association
www.diabetes.org

Institute of Food Technologists
www.ift.org

ILSI Human Nutrition Institute
www.ilsi.org

Trade Organizations

American Meat Institute
www.meatami.com

National Dairy Council
www.nationaldairycouncil.org

United Fresh Produce Association
www.uffva.org

U.S.A. Rice Federation
www.usarice.com

U.S. Government

The USDA Agricultural Marketing Service
www.ams.usda.gov

U.S. Department of Health and Human Services
www.hhs.gov

Food and Drug Administration (FDA)
www.fda.gov

Environmental Protection Agency
www.epa.gov

Federal Trade Commission
www.ftc.gov

Office of Dietary Supplements
National Institutes of Health
http://dietary-supplements.info.nih.gov

Nutrient Data Laboratory
Beltsville Human Nutrition Research Center,
Agricultural Research Service
www.ars.usda.gov/nutrientdata

National Digestive Diseases Information Clearinghouse
http://digestive.niddk.nih.gov

National Cancer Institute
www.cancer.gov

National Eye Institute
www.nei.nih.gov

National Heart, Lung, and Blood Institute
www.nhlbi.nih.gov/index.htm

National Institute of Diabetes and Digestive and Kidney Diseases
www.niddk.nih.gov

National Center for Complementary and Alternative Medicine
http://nccam.nih.gov

U.S. Department of Agriculture (USDA)
www.usda.gov

Centers for Disease Control and Prevention (CDC)
www.cdc.gov

National Institutes of Health (NIH)
www.nih.gov

Food and Nutrition Information Center
Agricultural Research Service, USDA
www.nal.usda.gov/fnic

National Institute of Allergy and Infectious Diseases
www.niaid.nih.gov

Weight and Health Management

The Vegetarian Resource Group
www.vrg.org

The Obesity Society
www.obesity.org

Anemia Lifeline
www.ancmia.com

The Arc
www.thearc.org

Bottled Water Web
www.bottledwaterweb.com

Food and Nutrition
Institute of Medicine
www.iom.edu/Global/Topics/Food-Nutrition.aspx

The Calorie Control Council
www.caloriecontrol.org

TOPS (Take Off Pounds Sensibly)
www.tops.org

Shape Up America!
www.shapeup.org

World Hunger

Friedman School of Nutrition Science and Policy
http://nutrition.tufts.edu

Freedom from Hunger
www.freefromhunger.org

Oxfam International
www.oxfam.org

WorldWatch Institute
www.worldwatch.org

The Hunger Project
www.thp.org

U.S. Agency for International Development
www.usaid.gov

Feeding America
www.feedingamerica.org

Food First
www.foodfirst.org

Glossary

A

absorption The process by which digested nutrients move into the tissues where they can be transported and used by the body's cells.

Acceptable Macronutrient-Distribution Ranges (AMDR) A healthy range of intakes for the energy-containing nutrients—carbohydrates, proteins, and fats—in your diet, designed to meet your nutrient needs and help reduce the risk of chronic diseases.

acetaldehyde An intermediary by-product of the breakdown of ethanol in the liver.

acid group The COOH group that is part of every amino acid; also called the *carboxyl group.*

acromegaly A condition caused by excess growth hormone in which tissues, bones, and internal organs grow abnormally large.

active transport The process of absorbing nutrients across the intestinal cell membrane with the help of a carrier molecule and energy.

acute dehydration Dehydration starting after a short period of time.

added sugars Sugars that are added to processed foods and sweets.

adenosine triphosphate (ATP) A compound that is broken down to produce energy for working muscles and other tissues.

Adequate Intake (AI) The *approximate* amount of a nutrient that groups of similar individuals are consuming to maintain good health.

adolescence The developmental period between childhood and early adulthood.

aerobic With oxygen.

age-related macular degeneration (AMD) A disease that affects the macula of the retina, causing blurry vision.

agribusiness The businesses collectively associated with the production, processing, and distribution of agricultural products, including food.

alcohol A chemical class of substances that include ethanol, methanol, and isopropanol.

alcohol dehydrogenase One of the alcohol-metabolizing enzymes found in the stomach and the liver.

alcohol poisoning When the BAC rises to such an extreme level that a person's central nervous system is affected and his or her breathing and heart rate are interrupted.

alcohol tolerance When the body adjusts to long-term alcohol use by becoming less sensitive to the alcohol. You need to consume more alcohol in order to get the same effect.

alcohol use disorder (AUD) The continuation of alcohol consumption even though this behavior has created social, psychological, and/or physical health problems.

alcoholic hepatitis Stage 2 of alcoholic liver disease; due to chronic inflammation.

alcoholic liver disease A degenerative liver condition that occurs in three stages: (1) fatty liver, (2) alcoholic hepatitis, and (3) cirrhosis.

alpha-linolenic acid A polyunsaturated essential fatty acid; part of the omega-3 fatty acid family.

alpha-tocopherol (a-tocopherol) The most active form of vitamin E in the body.

Alzheimer's disease (AD) A type of dementia.

amine group The nitrogen-containing part (NH_2) of an amino acid.

amino acid pools A limited supply of amino acids stored in your blood and cells and used to build new proteins.

amino acid profile The types and amounts of amino acids in a protein.

amino acids The building blocks of protein. Amino acids contain carbon, hydrogen, oxygen, and nitrogen. All amino acids are composed of an acid group, an amine group, and a unique side chain.

anaerobic Without oxygen.

anaphylactic reactions Severe, life-threatening reactions that cause constriction of the airways in the lungs, which inhibits the ability to breathe.

anemia A condition in which your blood has a lower than normal number of red blood cells than it should to be healthy.

anencephaly A neural tube defect that results in the absence of major parts of the brain and spinal cord.

antibiotic-resistant bacteria Bacteria that have developed a resistance to an antibiotic such that they are no longer affected by antibiotic medication.

antibiotics Drugs that kill or slow the growth of bacteria.

antibodies Proteins made by your body to bind to and neutralize foreign invaders, such as harmful bacteria, fungi, and viruses, as part of the body's immune response.

anticoagulant A substance that interferes with blood coagulation.

antidiuretic hormone (ADH) A hormone that directs the kidneys to concentrate urine and reduce urine production in order to reduce water loss from the body.

antimicrobials Substances or a combination of substances, such as disinfectants and sanitizers, that control the spread of bacteria and viruses on nonliving surfaces or objects.

antioxidants Substances that neutralize free radicals. Vitamins A, C, and E and beta-carotene are antioxidants.

anus The opening at the end of the rectum where waste is eliminated from the body.

arthritis Inflammation in the joints that can cause pain, stiffness, and swelling.

ascorbic acid The active form of vitamin C.

atherosclerosis Narrowing of the coronary arteries due to buildup of debris along the artery walls.

attention deficit/hyperactivity disorder (ADHD) Previously designated as attention deficit disorder (ADD). A condition in which an individual may be easily distracted, may have difficulty listening, following directions, and focusing and sustaining attention, and/or may have inconsistent performance in school.

autism spectrum disorder (ASD) Collective term for a group of brain disorders that make it difficult or impossible for a person to communicate and relate to others and may also be characterized by repetitive activities.

B

bacteria Single-celled microorganisms without an organized nucleus. Some are benign or beneficial to humans, while others can cause disease.

bariatric surgery Surgical procedures that reduce the functional volume of the stomach so that less food is eaten. Such surgeries are sometimes used to treat extreme obesity.

basal metabolism The amount of energy the body expends to meet its basic physiological needs. Also referred to as *basal metabolic rate (BMR)*.

behavior modification Changing behaviors to improve health. Identifying and altering eating patterns that contribute to weight gain or impede weight loss is behavior modification.

beriberi A thiamin deficiency that can affect the cardiovascular and nervous systems and results in weakness in the body.

bile A yellowish-green fluid made in the liver and concentrated and stored in the gallbladder. It helps emulsify fat and prepare it for digestion.

bile A yellowish-green fluid made in the liver and concentrated and stored in the gallbladder. It helps emulsify fat and prepare it for digestion.

binge drinking The consumption of 5 or more alcoholic drinks by men, or 4 or more drinks by women, in a very short time.

bioaccumulate When a substance or chemical builds up in an organism over time, so that the concentration of the chemical is higher than would be found naturally in the environment.

bioavailability The degree to which a nutrient is absorbed from foods and used in the body.

biodiversity Having a wide variety of plant and animal species within an environment.

biopesticides Substances used to kill pests that are derived from natural materials such as animals, plants, bacteria, and certain minerals.

biotechnology The application of biological techniques to living cells, which alters their genetic makeup.

bioterrorism The use of a biological or chemical agent to frighten, threaten, coerce, injure, and/or kill individuals.

blackouts Periods of time when an intoxicated person cannot recall part or all of an event.

bleaching When light enters the eye and interacts with and changes rhodopsin.

blood alcohol concentration (BAC) The measurement of the amount of alcohol in your blood. BAC is measured in grams of alcohol per deciliter of blood, usually expressed as a percentage.

body composition The relative proportion of muscle, fat, water, and other tissues in the body.

body dysmorphic disorder A mental illness in which a person is excessively concerned about and preoccupied by a perceived defect in his or her body.

body mass index (BMI) A calculation of your weight in relationship to your height. A BMI between 18.5 and 24.9 is considered healthy.

bolus Chewed mass of food.

bone mineral density (BMD) The amount of minerals, in particular calcium, per volume in an individual's bone.

botulism A rare but serious paralytic illness caused by the bacterium *Clostridium botulinum*. Infant botulism is caused by consuming the spores of the bacteria, which then grow in the intestines and release toxins. It can be fatal.

bovine spongiform encephalopathy (BSE) A slow, degenerative, and deadly disease that attacks the central nervous system of cattle. Also known as *mad cow disease*.

bran The indigestible outer shell of the grain kernel.

breast-feeding The act of feeding an infant milk from a woman's breast.

buffers Substances that help maintain the proper pH in a solution by attracting or donating hydrogen ions.

C

cancer A group of diseases characterized by the uncontrolled growth and spread of abnormal cells.

canning The process of heating food to a temperature high enough to kill bacteria and then packing the food in airtight containers.

carbohydrate loading A diet and training strategy that maximizes glycogen stores in the body before an endurance event.

carcinogenic Cancer causing.

cardiorespiratory endurance The body's ability to sustain prolonged exercise.

carnitine A vitamin-like substance needed to properly utilize fat.

carotenodermia The presence of excess carotene in the blood resulting in an orange skin color, due to excessive intake of carotene-rich vegetables.

catalysts Substances that aid and speed up reactions without being changed, damaged, or used up in the process.

cataract A common eye disorder that occurs when the lens of the eye becomes cloudy.

celiac disease An autoimmune disease of the small intestine that involves the inability to digest the protein gluten.

cell differentiation The process that determines what a cell becomes in your body.

cellulite A nonmedical term that refers to fat cells under the skin that give it a ripplelike appearance. Contrary to popular belief, cellulite is no different from other fat in the body.

central obesity An excess storage of visceral fat in the abdominal area, which increases the risk of heart disease, diabetes, and hypertension.

chemical digestion Breaking down food with enzymes or digestive juices.

childhood overweight and obesity Excess body fat in children.

chlorophyll The green pigment in plants that absorbs energy from sunlight to begin the process of photosynthesis.

cholecystokinin A hormone released when the stomach is distended. It is associated with the feeling of satiation.

choline A vitamin-like substance needed for healthy cells and nerves.

chronic dehydration Dehydration over a long period of time.

chylomicron A type of lipoprotein that carries digested fat and other lipids through the lymph system into the blood.

chyme The semiliquid, partially digested food mass that leaves the stomach and enters the small intestine.

ciguatera poisoning A condition caused by marine toxins produced by *dinoflagellates* (microscopic sea organisms).

cirrhosis Stage 3 of alcoholic liver disease in which liver cells die, causing severe scarring.

closed or "coded" dating Refers to the packing numbers that are decodable only by manufacturers and are often found on nonperishable, shelf-stable foods.

clotting factors Substances involved in the process of blood clotting.

coagulation The process of blood clotting.

coenzyme Substances, often vitamins, that are needed by enzymes to perform many chemical reactions in your body.

coenzymes Substances needed by enzymes to perform many chemical reactions in your body. Many vitamins act as coenzymes.

collagen A ropelike, fibrous protein that is the most abundant protein in your body.

colostrum The fluid that is expressed from the mother's breast after birth and before the development of breast milk.

commodity crops Crop products such as corn and soybeans that can be used for commerce.

community-supported agriculture (CSA) An arrangement whereby individuals pay a fee to support a local farm, and in exchange receive a weekly or biweekly box of fresh produce from the farm.

complemented proteins Incomplete proteins that are combined with modest amounts of animal or soy proteins or with other plant proteins that are rich in the limiting amino acids to create a complete protein.

complete protein A protein that provides all the essential amino acids that your body needs, along with some nonessential amino acids. Soy protein and protein from animal sources, in general, are complete.

complex carbohydrates A category of carbohydrates that contain many sugar units combined. A polysaccharide is a complex carbohydrate.

conception The moment when a sperm fertilizes an egg.

conditionally essential amino acids Nonessential amino acids that become essential if the body cannot make them, such as during bouts of illness.

conditioning The process of improving physical fitness through repeated activity.

cones Light-absorbing cells responsible for color vision.

congeners Compounds in alcohol that enhance the taste but may contribute to hangover symptoms.

congregate meals Meals served at churches, synagogues, or other community sites where older adults can receive a nutritious meal and socialize.

connective tissue The most abundant tissue type in the body. Made up primarily of collagen, it supports and connects body parts as well as providing protection and insulation.

consensus The opinion of a group of experts based on a collection of information.

constipation Difficulty in passing stools.

control group The group given a placebo.

Corn Belt The parts of the United States where corn is grown in abundance. This includes Iowa, Indiana, most of Illinois, and parts of Kansas, Missouri, Nebraska, South Dakota, Minnesota, Ohio, and Wisconsin.

creatine phosphate A compound stored in the muscles that is broken down to replenish ATP stores.

cretinism A condition caused by a deficiency of thyroid hormone during prenatal development, resulting in abnormal mental and physical development in children. It is also known as *congenital hypothyroidism*.

critical periods Developmental stages during which cells and tissues rapidly grow and differentiate to form body structures.

Crohn's disease An inflammatory bowel disease involving inflammation and swelling of the intestines.

cross-contaminate Transfer pathogens from a food, utensil, cutting board, kitchen surface, and/or hands to another food.

D

Daily Values (DVs) Established reference levels of nutrients, based on a 2,000-calorie diet, that are used on food labels.

danger zone The range of temperatures (between 40°F and 140°F) at which foodborne bacteria multiply most rapidly. Room temperature falls within the danger zone.

dehydration The state whereby there is too little water in the body due to too much water being lost, too little being consumed, or a combination of both.

dementia Loss of memory along with confusion and disorientation.

denaturation The alteration of a protein's shape, which changes the structure and function of the protein.

dental caries The decay or erosion of teeth.

deoxyribonucleic acid (DNA) Genetic material within cells that directs the synthesis of proteins in the body.

dermatitis Inflammation or irritation of the skin.

developed country A nation advanced in industrial capability, technological sophistication, and economic productivity; also called *most developed country*.

developing country A nation having a relatively low level of industrial capability, technological sophistication, or economic productivity; also called *less developed country*.

diabetes mellitus A medical condition whereby an individual either doesn't have enough insulin or is resistant to the insulin available, causing the blood glucose level to rise.

diarrhea Frequent, loose, watery stools.

diastolic pressure The pressure of your blood against the artery walls when the heart is at rest between beats.

dietary fiber Nondigestible polysaccharides found naturally in foods.

dietary folate equivalents (DFE) A measurement used to express the amount of folate in a food or supplement.

Dietary Guidelines for Americans Guidelines published every five years that provide dietary and lifestyle advice to individuals aged 2 and older to maintain good health and prevent chronic diseases.

Dietary Reference Intakes (DRIs) Reference values for the essential nutrients needed to maintain good health, to prevent chronic diseases, and to avoid unhealthy excesses.

digestibility A food's capacity to be broken down so that it can be absorbed.

digestive process The breakdown of foods into absorbable components using mechanical and chemical means.

diglyceride A glycerol with only two attached fatty acids.

disaccharide Two sugar units combined. There are three disaccharides: sucrose, lactose, and maltose.

disordered eating Abnormal and potentially harmful eating behaviors that do not meet specific criteria for an eating disorder.

distillation The evaporation and then collection of a liquid by condensation.

diuretics Substances such as alcohol and some medications that cause the body to lose water.

diverticula Small bulges at weak spots in the colon wall.

diverticulitis Infection of the diverticula.

diverticulosis The existence of diverticula in the lining of the intestine.

DNA fingerprinting A technique in which DNA "gene patterns" (or "fingerprints") are detected and analyzed. Used in food safety to distinguish between different strains of a bacterium.

DNA The blueprint in cells that stores all genetic information. DNA remains in the nucleus of the cell and directs the synthesis of proteins.

double-blind, placebo-controlled study When the scientists and subjects in a research experiment can't distinguish between the treatments given to the subjects and don't know which group of subjects received which treatment.

duration The length of time of performing an activity.

dysphagia Difficult swallowing.

E

early childhood caries Tooth decay from prolonged contact with formula, milk, fruit juice, or other carbohydrate-rich liquid offered to an infant in a bottle.

early childhood tooth decay The decay of baby teeth in children due to continual exposure to fermentable sugary liquids.

eating disorders The term used to describe psychological illnesses that involve specific abnormal eating behaviors, such as anorexia nervosa (self-starvation), bulimia nervosa (bingeing and purging), and binge eating disorder.

edema The accumulation of excess fluid in the spaces surrounding your cells, which causes swelling of the body tissue.

eicosanoids Hormonelike substances in the body. Prostaglandins, thromboxanes, and leukotrienes are all eicosanoids.

eicosapentaenoic acid (EPA) and docosahexaenoic acid (DHA) Two omega-3 fatty acids that are heart healthy.

electrolytes Charged ions that conduct an electrical current in a solvent such as water. Sodium, potassium, and chloride are examples of electrolytes in the body.

embryo Term that refers to a fertilized egg during the third through the eighth week of pregnancy.

empty calories Calories that come with little nutrition. Jelly beans are an example of a food that provides lots of calories from sugar but few nutrients.

emulsifier A compound that keeps two incompatible substances, such as oil and water, mixed together.

endosperm The starchy part of the grain kernel.

endotoxin A damaging product produced by intestinal bacteria that travels in the blood to the liver and initiates the release of cytokines that damage liver cells, leading to scarring.

energy balance The state at which energy (calorie) intake and energy (calorie) output in the body are equal.

energy deficit Expending more energy than is consumed. Also called *negative energy balance*.

energy density A measurement of the calories in a food compared with the weight (grams) or volume of the food.

energy excess Consuming more energy than is expended. Also called *positive energy balance*.

energy gap The difference between the numbers of calories needed to maintain weight before and after weight loss.

enriched grains Refined grain foods that have folic acid, thiamin, niacin, riboflavin, and iron added.

enzymes Substances that speed up chemical reactions in your body.

epidemiological research Research that looks at populations of people; it is often observational.

epiglottis Flap of tissue that protects the trachea while swallowing.

epiphyseal plate The growth plate of the bone. In puberty, growth in this area leads to increases in height.

ergogenic aid A substance, such as a dietary supplement, used to enhance athletic performance.

esophagus Tube that extends from the throat to the stomach.

essential amino acids The nine amino acids that the body cannot synthesize; they must be obtained through dietary sources.

essential fatty acids The two polyunsaturated fatty acids that the body cannot make and therefore must be eaten in foods: linoleic acid and alpha-linolenic acid.

Estimated Average Requirement (EAR) The average amount of a nutrient that is known to meet the needs of 50 percent of the individuals in a similar age and gender group.

Estimated Energy Requirement (EER) The amount of daily energy needed to maintain a healthy body weight and meet energy (calorie) needs based on age, gender, height, weight, and activity level.

estrogen The hormone responsible for female sex characteristics.

ethanol The type of alcohol in alcoholic beverages such as wine, beer, and liquor.

exercise Any type of structured or planned physical activity.

experimental group The group given a specific treatment.

experimental research Research involving at least two groups of subjects.

extracellular fluid compartment The fluid located outside your cells. Interstitial fluids and fluids in the blood are extracellular fluids.

extreme obesity Having a BMI > 40.

F

facilitated diffusion The process of absorbing nutrients across the intestinal cell membrane with the help of a carrier molecule.

famine A severe shortage of food caused by crop destruction due to weather problems or poor agricultural practices so that the food supply is destroyed or severely diminished. Famine can also be caused by pestilence or war.

farm-to-table continuum Illustrates the roles that farmers, food manufacturers, food transporters, retailers, and consumers play in ensuring that the food supply, from the farm to the plate, remains safe.

farm An establishment that produces and sells at least $1,000 of agricultural products annually.

fat substitutes Substances that replace added fat in foods by providing the creamy properties of fat for fewer calories and fewer total fat grams.

fat The common name for triglycerides.

fatty acid The basic unit of triglycerides and phospholipids.

fatty liver Stage 1 of alcoholic liver disease.

fecal-to-oral transmission The spread of pathogens by putting something in the mouth that has been in contact with infected stool. Poor hygiene, such as not washing hands after using the bathroom, can lead to this type of contamination.

feedlot A facility where cattle are fed grain and other foods before being slaughtered.

female athlete triad A syndrome of the three interrelated conditions occurring in some physically active females: low energy availability, menstrual dysfunction, and low bone density.

fermentation The process by which yeast converts sugars in grains or fruits into ethanol and carbon dioxide.

fetal alcohol spectrum disorders (FASDs) A range of conditions that can occur in children who are exposed to alcohol in utero. Fetal alcohol

syndrome (FAS) is the most severe of the FASDs; children with FAS will display physical, mental, and behavioral abnormalities.

fetus A developing embryo that is at least 8 weeks old.

fiber The portion of plant foods that isn't digested in the small intestine.

flatulence Production of excessive gas in the stomach or the intestines.

flavonoids Phytochemicals found in fruits, vegetables, tea, nuts, and seeds.

flexibility A joint's ability to move freely through a full and normal range of motion.

fluid balance The equal distribution of water throughout your body and within and between cells.

fluorosis A condition caused by excess amounts of fluoride, resulting in mottling of the teeth.

flushing A reddish coloring of the face, arms, and chest.

folate The naturally occurring vitamin found in foods.

folic acid The form of folate used in vitamin supplements and fortification of foods.

food additives Substances added to food that affect its quality, flavor, freshness, and/or safety.

food allergens Proteins not broken down by cooking or digestion that enter the body intact, causing an adverse immune response.

food allergy An abnormal reaction by the immune system to a particular food.

food biosecurity Protecting the food supply from bioterrorist attacks.

food consumers Individuals who make decisions about which foods to buy.

food guidance systems Visual diagrams that provide a variety of food recommendations to help create a well-balanced diet.

food industry The collective efforts of various businesses that provide food to consumers.

food insecurity The chronic lack of sufficient resources to nutritiously feed oneself.

food intolerance Adverse reaction to a food that does not involve an immune response. Lactose intolerance is one example.

food jags When a child will only eat the same food meal after meal.

food preservation The treatment of foods to reduce deterioration and spoilage, and help prevent the multiplication of pathogens that can cause foodborne illness.

food safety Guidelines and procedures that help keep foods free from contaminants.

Food Safety Initiative (FSI) The program that coordinates the research, surveillance, inspection, outbreak response, and educational activities of the various government agencies that work together to safeguard food.

foodborne illness Sickness caused by consuming contaminated food or beverages. Also known as foodborne disease or food poisoning.

fortified foods Foods with added nutrients.

free radicals Unstable oxygen-containing molecules that can damage the cells of the body and possibly contribute to the increased risk of chronic diseases.

fructose The sweetest of the monosaccharides; also known as fruit sugar.

functional fiber The nondigestible polysaccharides that are added to foods because of a specific desired effect on health.

functional foods Foods that have a positive effect on health beyond providing basic nutrients.

fungicides Chemicals used to kill mold.

G

galactose A monosaccharide that links with glucose to create the sugar found in dairy foods.

gallbladder A pear-shaped organ located behind the liver. The gallbladder stores bile produced by the liver and secretes the bile through the bile duct into the small intestine.

gallstones Small, hard, crystalline structures formed in the gallbladder or bile duct due to abnormally thick bile.

gastric banding A type of bariatric surgery that uses a silicone band to reduce the size of the stomach so that less food is needed to feel full.

gastric bypass surgery A type of bariatric surgery that reduces the functional volume of the stomach to minimize the amount of food eaten.

gastrin A digestive hormone produced in the stomach that stimulates digestive activities and increases motility and emptying.

gastritis Inflammation of the stomach.

gastroenteritis Formal term for "stomach flu." Caused by a virus or bacteria and results in inflammation of the stomach and/or intestines.

gastroesophageal reflux disease (GERD) The backward flow of stomach contents past the lower esophageal sphincter into the esophagus.

gastroesophageal sphincter A circular band of muscle between the esophagus and the stomach that opens and closes to allow food to enter the stomach.

gastrointestinal (GI) tract Body area containing the organs of the digestive tract. It extends from the mouth to the anus.

gene–environment interaction The interaction of genetics and the environment that increases the risk of obesity in some people.

gene expression The processing of genetic information to create a specific protein.

gene A DNA segment that codes for a specific protein.

generally recognized as safe (GRAS) Describes a substance that is believed to be safe to consume based on a long history of use by humans or a substantial amount of research that documents its safety.

genetic engineering (GE) A biological technique that isolates and manipulates the genes of organisms to produce a targeted, modified product.

genetically modified organisms (GMOs) Organisms that have been genetically engineered to contain both original and foreign genes.

germ In grains, the seed of the grain kernel.

gestational diabetes Diabetes that occurs in women during pregnancy.

ghrelin A hormone produced mainly in the stomach that increases hunger.

globesity A blend of the words *global* and *obesity*, coined by the World Health Organization, which refers to the worldwide obesity epidemic.

glucagon The hormone that directs glycogenolysis and gluconeogenesis to increase glucose in the blood. Glucagon is produced in and released from the pancreas.

gluconeogenesis The creation of glucose from noncarbohydrate sources, predominantly protein.

glucose The most abundant sugar in foods and the primary energy source for your body.

glycerol The three-carbon backbone of a triglyceride.

glycogen The storage form of glucose in humans and animals.

glycogenesis The process of converting excess glucose into glycogen in your liver and muscle.

glycogenolysis The breakdown of glycogen to release glucose.

goiter Enlargement of the thyroid gland, mostly due to iodine deficiency.

growth charts Series of percentile curves that illustrate the distribution of selected body measurements in U.S. children.

growth hormone A protein-based hormone that stimulates cell growth and reproduction in humans and animals.

growth stunting Impaired growth and development primarily manifested in early childhood and including malnutrition during fetal development. Once growth stunting occurs, it is usually permanent.

Guillain-Barré syndrome A condition that can result from a *Campylobacter* infection. It causes the immune system to attack the body's own nerves and can lead to temporary paralysis.

H

hangover A collective term for the unpleasant symptoms, such as a headache and dizziness, that occur after drinking an excessive amount of alcohol.

health claim Claim on the label that describes a relationship between a food or dietary compound and a disease or health-related condition.

Healthy People 2020 A set of disease prevention and health promotion objectives for Americans to meet during the second decade of the new millennium.

healthy weight A body weight in relationship to your height that doesn't increase the risk of developing any weight-related health problems or diseases.

heart attack Permanent damage to the heart muscle that results from a sudden lack of oxygen-rich blood.

heartburn A burning sensation originating in the esophagus. Heartburn is usually caused by the reflux of gastric contents from the stomach into the esophagus. Chronic heartburn can lead to gastroesophageal reflux disease (GERD).

heavy drinking The consumption of 5 or more drinks on the same occasion in each of 5 or more days in the past month.

hemochromatosis A blood disorder characterized by the retention of an excessive amount of iron.

hemoglobin The oxygen-carrying, heme-containing protein found in red blood cells.

hemolytic uremic syndrome A rare condition caused by E. coli O157: H7 that results in the destruction of red blood cells and kidney failure.

hemorrhage Excessive loss of blood or bleeding.

hemorrhoids Swelling in the veins of the rectum and anus.

herbicides Substances that are used to kill and control weeds.

high-density lipoprotein (HDL) A lipoprotein that removes cholesterol from the tissues and delivers it to the liver to be used as part of bile and/or to be excreted from the body. Because of this, it is known as the *good* cholesterol carrier.

high-pressure processing (HPP) A method used to pasteurize foods by exposing the items to pulses of high pressure, which destroys the microorganisms that are present.

homeless Individuals who are either "crashing" with friends or family members, or residing on the street or in their automobiles.

hormones Chemical substances that regulate, initiate, or direct cellular activity.

host A living plant or animal (including a human) that a virus or parasite infects for the sake of reproducing.

Human Genome Project A project sponsored by the United States government to determine the complete set and sequencing of DNA in human cells and identify all human genes.

hunger Physical discomfort that results from the lack of food associated with food insecurity.

hydrochloric acid (HCl) A powerful acid made in the stomach that has digestive functions. It also helps to kill microorganisms and lowers the pH in the stomach.

hydrogenation Adding hydrogen to an unsaturated fatty acid to make it more saturated and solid at room temperature.

hydrophobic Having an aversion to water.

hypercalcemia A chronically high amount of calcium in the blood.

hyperkalemia Abnormally high levels of potassium in the blood.

hyperphosphatemia Abnormally high levels of phosphorus in the blood.

hypertension High blood pressure.

hypervitaminosis A The serious condition in which the liver accumulates toxic levels of vitamin A.

hypervitaminosis D A condition resulting from excessive amounts of vitamin D in the body.

hypoallergenic infant formulas Specially developed formulas for infants who have food allergies and cannot tolerate regular formula.

hypoglycemia A blood glucose level that drops to lower than 70 mg/dl. Hunger, shakiness, dizziness, perspiration, and light-headedness are some signs of hypoglycemia.

hypokalemia Abnormally low levels of potassium in the blood.

hyponatremia A condition of too little sodium in the blood.

hypotension Low blood pressure.

hypothesis An idea generated by scientists based on their observations.

I

ileocecal sphincter Gateway between the end of the small intestine and the beginning of the large intestine. The sphincter prevents backflow of fecal contents from the large intestine into the small intestine.

immunity The state of having built up antibodies to a particular foreign substance so that when particles of the substance enter the body, they are destroyed by the antibodies.

incomplete protein A protein that is low in one or more of the essential amino acids. Protein from plant sources tends to be incomplete.

infancy The age range from birth to 12 months.

inorganic Not containing carbon. Inorganic compounds include minerals, water, and salts.

inositol A vitamin-like substance synthesized in your body that helps to keep your cells and their membranes healthy.

insensible water loss The water that is lost from the body daily through exhalation from the lungs and evaporation off the skin.

insoluble fiber A type of fiber that doesn't dissolve in water and is not fermented by intestinal bacteria.

insulin resistance The inability of cells to respond to insulin.

insulin The hormone, produced in and released from the pancreas, that facilitates the movement of glucose from the blood into cells.

integrated pest management (IPM) Alternative to pesticides that uses the most economical and the least harmful methods of pest control to minimize risk to consumers, crops, and the environment.

intensity The level of difficulty of an activity.

international units (IU) A system of measurement of a biologically active ingredient such as a vitamin.

interstitial fluids Fluids located between cells.

intracellular fluid compartment The fluid located inside your cells.

intrinsic factor (IF) A protein secreted by the stomach that helps in the absorption of vitamin B_{12}.

iodopsin The compound found in the cones of the eye that is needed for color vision.

iron-deficiency anemia An anemia caused by low hemoglobin levels due to insufficient dietary intake and absorption of iron.

irradiation A process in which foods are placed in a shielded chamber, called an irradiator, and subjected to a radiant energy source. This kills specific pathogens in food by breaking up the cells' DNA.

irritable bowel syndrome (IBS) A functional disorder that involves changes in colon rhythm.

isoflavones Naturally occurring phyto-estrogens, or weak plant estrogens, that function in a fashion similar to the hormone estrogen in the human body.

J

jaundice A yellowish coloring of the skin due to the presence of bile pigments in the blood.

K

Keshan disease A disease related to a deficiency of selenium.

ketoacidosis The buildup of ketone bodies to dangerous levels, which can result in coma or death.

ketone bodies The by-products of the incomplete breakdown of fat.

ketosis The condition of increased ketone bodies in the blood.

kidney stone A solid mass formed in the kidneys from dietary minerals.

kilocalories The measurement of energy in foods. Commonly referred to as *calories*.

kwashiorkor A state of PEM where there is a severe deficiency of dietary protein.

L

laboratory experiment A scientific experiment conducted in a laboratory. Some laboratory experiments involve animals.

lactate A by-product of rapid glucose metabolism.

lactation The production of milk in a woman's body after childbirth, and the period during which it occurs.

lactose intolerant When maldigestion of lactose results in symptoms such as nausea, cramps, bloating, flatulence, and diarrhea.

lactose maldigestion The inability to digest lactose in foods due to low levels of the enzyme lactase.

lactose A disaccharide composed of glucose and galactose; also known as milk sugar.

lanugo Very fine, soft hair on the face and arms of people with anorexia nervosa.

large intestine Final organ of the GI tract. It consists of the cecum, appendix, colon, and rectum.

lean body mass The body mass once the fat mass has been subtracted. It contains mostly muscle but also organs and fluids.

least developed country A nation having a low level of economic productivity and technological sophistication within the contemporary range of possibility.

leptin A hormone produced in fat tissue that helps regulate body fat by signaling the reduction of food intake in the brain and interfering with the storage of fat in the cells.

let-down response The release of milk from the mother's breast to feed the baby.

licensed dietitian nutritionist (LDN) An individual who has met specified educational and experience criteria deemed necessary by a state licensing board to be considered an expert in the field of nutrition. An RDN would meet all the qualifications to be an LDN.

life expectancy The number of years that a person will live.

limiting amino acid The amino acid that is in the shortest supply in an incomplete protein.

linoleic acid A polyunsaturated essential fatty acid; part of the omega-6 fatty acid family.

lipids A category of carbon, hydrogen, and oxygen compounds that are insoluble in water.

lipoic acid A vitamin-like substance that your body needs for energy production; it may also act as an antioxidant.

lipoproteins Capsule-shaped carriers that enable fat and cholesterol to travel through the lymph and blood.

liposuction The surgical removal of subcutaneous fat with a penlike instrument. Usually performed on the abdomen, hips, and thighs, and/or other areas of the body.

listeriosis A disease caused by infection of the bacterium, *Listeria monocyotogenes*, typically caused by eating food contaminated with *Listeria*.

liver The largest gland of the body. It aids in digestive activity and is responsible for metabolism of nutrients, detoxification of alcohol, and some nutrient storage.

low birth weight baby A baby weighing less than 5½ pounds at birth.

low-density lipoprotein (LDL) A lipoprotein that deposits cholesterol in the walls of the arteries. Because this can lead to heart disease, LDL is referred to as the *bad* cholesterol carrier.

lumen The interior of the digestive tract, through which food passes.

lymph Watery fluid that circulates through the body in lymph vessels and eventually enters the blood.

M

macrocytes Abnormally large cells such as red blood cells.

macrocytic anemia A form of anemia characterized by large, immature red blood cells, due to a vitamin B_{12} deficiency.

macronutrients The energy-containing essential nutrients that you need in higher amounts: carbohydrates, lipids (fats), and proteins.

macrosomia A large baby, weighing more than 8 pounds, 13 oz.

major minerals Minerals needed from your diet and in your body in amounts greater than 100 milligrams per day. These include sodium, chloride, potassium, calcium, phosphorus, magnesium, and sulfur. Also called *macrominerals*.

malnourished The long-term outcome of consuming a diet that doesn't meet nutrient needs.

malnutrition The long-term outcome of consuming a diet that contains an imbalance of nutrients.

maltose A disaccharide composed of two glucose units joined together.

marasmus A state of PEM where there is a severe deficiency of calories that perpetuates wasting; also called starvation.

marine toxins Chemicals that occur naturally and contaminate some fish.

mast cells Cells in connective tissue to which antibodies attach, setting the stage for potential future allergic reactions.

mechanical digestion Breaking food down through chewing and grinding, or moving it through the GI tract with peristalsis.

medical nutrition therapy The integration of nutrition counseling and dietary changes based on an individual's medical and health needs to treat a patient's medical condition.

megadose A very large dose or amount.

megaloblasts Large, immature red blood cells.

menaquinone The form of vitamin K produced by bacteria in the colon.

messenger RNA (mRNA) A type of RNA that copies the genetic information encoded in DNA and carries it out of the nucleus of the cell to synthesize the protein.

metabolic syndrome Refers to a cluster of many factors such as abdominal obesity, insulin resistance, high blood pressure, elevated blood levels of triglycerides and slower clearance of this fat from the blood, a low HDL level, smaller and more dense LDL cholesterol particles, higher likelihood of blood clots, too much insulin, and, possibly, too much blood glucose.

metabolism The numerous reactions that occur within the cell. The calories in foods are converted to energy in the cells of the body.

micelles Small carriers in the intestine that enable fatty acids and other compounds to be absorbed.

micronutrients Essential nutrients that you need in smaller amounts: vitamins and minerals.

microsomal ethanol-oxidizing system (MEOS) The other major enzyme system in the liver that metabolizes alcohol.

microvilli Tiny projections on the villi in the small intestine that increase the surface area even more.

milestones Objectives or significant events that occur during development.

minerals Inorganic elements essential to the nutrition of humans.

moderate alcohol consumption An average consumption of up to one drink per day for women and up to two drinks per day for men, as well as no more than three drinks in any single day for women and no more than four drinks in a single day for men.

modified atmosphere packaging (MAP) A food preservation technique that changes the composition of the air surrounding the food in a package to extend the food's shelf life.

monoglyceride A glycerol with only one attached fatty acid.

monosaccharide One sugar unit. There are three monosaccharides: glucose, fructose, and galactose.

monosodium glutamate (MSG) A flavor enhancer.

monounsaturated fatty acid (MUFA) A fatty acid that has one double bond.

MSG symptom complex A series of reactions such as numbness, burning sensation, facial pressure or tightness, chest pain, rapid heart beat, and drowsiness that can occur in some individuals after they consume MSG.

mucus Viscous, slippery secretions found in saliva and other digestive juices.

muscle endurance The ability of a muscle to produce prolonged effort.

muscle strength The greatest amount of force exerted by a muscle at one time.

myoglobin The oxygen-carrying, heme-containing protein found in muscle cells.

MyPlate A tool that depicts five food groups using the familiar mealtime visual of a place setting. It is part of a USDA Web-based initiative to provide consumer information with a food guidance system to help you build a healthy diet based on the current *Dietary Guidelines for Americans.*

N

naturally occurring sugars Sugars such as fructose and lactose that are found naturally in fruit and dairy foods.

neural tube defects Any major birth defect of the central nervous system, including the brain, caused by failure of the neural tube to properly close during fetal development.

neurotoxins Toxins that affect the nerves and can cause symptoms including mild numbness or tingling in the face, arms, and legs, as well as headaches and dizziness. Severe cases could result in death.

niacin equivalents (NE) A measurement that reflects the amount of niacin and tryptophan in foods that can be used to synthesize niacin.

nicotinamide One of the two active forms of niacin that are derived from foods.

nicotinic acid One of the two active forms of niacin that are derived from foods.

night blindness The inability to see in dim light or at night due to a deficiency of vitamin A.

nitrates (nitrites) Substances that can be added to foods to function as a preservative and to give meats such as hot dogs and luncheon meats a pink color.

nitrogen balance The state in which an individual is consuming the same amount of nitrogen (from protein) in the diet as he or she is excreting in the urine.

nonessential amino acids The 11 amino acids that the body can synthesize.

nonexercise-associated thermogenesis (NEAT) The energy expenditure that occurs during nonexercise movements, such as fidgeting, standing, and chewing gum.

normal blood pressure Less than 120 mm Hg (systolic—the top number) and less than 80 mm Hg (diastolic—the bottom number). Referred to as 120/80.

norovirus The most common type of virus that causes foodborne illness. Noroviruses can cause gastroenteritis, or the "stomach flu." Also known as Norwalk-like viruses.

nutrient content claim Claim on the label that describes the level or amount of a nutrient in a food product.

nutrient density The amount of nutrients per calorie in a given food. Nutrient-dense foods provide more nutrients per calorie than do less-nutrient-dense foods.

nutrients Compounds in foods that sustain your body processes. There are six classes of nutrients: carbohydrates, fats (lipids), proteins, vitamins, minerals, and water.

nutrition The science that studies how the nutrients and compounds in foods that you eat nourish and affect your body functions and health.

Nutrition Facts panel The area on the food label that provides a uniform listing of specific nutrients obtained in one serving of the food.

nutritional genomics A field of study that researches the relationship between nutrition and genomics (the study of genes and gene expression).

nutritionist A generic term with no recognized legal or professional meaning. Some people may call themselves nutritionists without having any credible training in nutrition.

O

obesity Carrying an excessive amount of body fat above the level of being overweight. Clinically defined as having a body mass index (BMI) of 30 or higher.

observational research Research that involves looking at factors in two or more groups of subjects to see if there is a relationship to certain outcomes.

oils Fats that are liquid at room temperature.

open dating Typically found on perishable items such as meat, poultry, eggs, and dairy foods; must contain a calendar date.

organic Containing carbon.

organophosphates A group of synthetic pesticides that adversely affect the nervous systems of pests.

osmosis The movement of a solvent, such as water, from an area of lower concentration of solutes across a membrane to an area of higher concentration of solutes. It balances the concentration of solutes between the compartments.

osteocalcin The protein in bone that binds with bone-strengthening calcium.

osteomalacia The adult equivalent of rickets, causing muscle and bone weakness, and pain.

osteopenia A condition in which bone mineral density is lower than normal but not low enough to be classified as osteoporosis.

osteoporosis A condition in which bones become brittle and porous.

overnutrition A state of excess nutrients and calories in the diet.

overpopulation When a region has more people than its natural resources can support.

overweight Carrying extra weight on your body in relation to your height. Clinically defined as having a body mass index (BMI) of 25 to 29.9.

oxidation The process during which oxygen combines with other molecules.

P

pancreas Accessory organ of digestion that produces hormones and enzymes. It's connected to the duodenum via the bile duct.

paralytic shellfish poisoning A condition caused by consuming shellfish contaminated with neurotoxins.

parasites Organisms that live on or in another organism, obtaining nourishment from it.

parathyroid hormone (PTH) The hormone secreted from the parathyroid glands that activates vitamin D formation in the kidney.

passive diffusion The process of absorbing nutrients across the intestinal cell membrane from a high concentration to a low concentration.

pasteurization The process of heating liquids or food at high temperatures to destroy foodborne pathogens.

pathogens Collective term for disease--causing microorganisms (microbes). Includes viruses, bacteria, and parasites. The most common source of foodborne illness.

peak bone mass The genetically determined maximum amount of bone mass an individual can build up.

peer-reviewed journal A research journal in which fellow scientists (peers) review studies to assess if they are accurate and sound before they are published.

pellagra The disease caused by a deficiency of niacin in the body.

pendular movement A constrictive wave that involves both forward and reverse movements of chyme and enhances nutrient absorption.

pepsin A digestive enzyme produced in the stomach that breaks down protein.

peptic ulcers Sores, erosions, or breaks in the mucosal lining of the stomach.

peptide bonds The bonds that connect amino acids, created when the acid group of one amino acid is joined with the nitrogen-containing amine group of another amino acid.

percentile The most commonly used clinical indicator to assess the size and growth patterns of children in the United States. An individual child is ranked according to the percentage of the reference population he equals or exceeds.

peristalsis The forward, rhythmic motion that moves food through the digestive system. Peristalsis is a form of mechanical digestion because it influences motion, but it does not add chemical secretions.

pernicious anemia A form of anemia characterized by large, immature red blood cells, due to a lack of intrinsic factor.

pesticides Substances that kill or repel pests such as insects, weeds, microorganisms, rodents, or fungi.

pharynx The throat. Passageway for the respiratory (air) and digestive (food and beverages) tracts.

phospholipids Lipids made of two fatty acids and a phosphate group attached to a glycerol backbone.

photosynthesis A process by which green plants create carbohydrates using the energy from sunlight.

phylloquinone The form of vitamin K found in green plants.

physical activity Voluntary movement that results in energy expenditure (burning calories).

physical fitness The ability to perform physical activities requiring cardio-respiratory endurance, muscle endurance, and strength and/or flexibility; physical fitness is acquired through physical activity and adequate nutrition.

phytochemical Plant chemical that has been shown to reduce the risk of certain diseases such as cancer and heart disease. Beta-carotene is a phytochemical.

phytosterols Naturally occurring sterols found in plants. Phytosterols lower LDL cholesterol levels by competing with cholesterol for absorption in the intestinal tract.

picky eating Unwillingness to try unfamiliar foods.

placebo A sugar pill that has no impact on the individual's health when ingested.

placenta The organ that allows nutrients, oxygen, and waste products to be exchanged between a mother and fetus.

plant breeding A type of biotechnology in which two plants are crossbred to produce offspring with desired traits from both.

plaque The hardened buildup of cholesterol-laden foam cells, platelets, cellular waste products, and calcium in the arteries that results in atherosclerosis.

political sanctions Boycotts or trade embargoes used by one country or international group to apply political pressure on another.

polychlorinated biphenyls (PCBs) Synthetic chemicals that have been shown to cause cancer and other adverse effects on the immune, reproductive, nervous, and endocrine systems in animals. PCBs may cause cancer in humans.

polyneuritis Inflammation of the peripheral nerves.

polysaccharide Many sugar units combined. Starch, glycogen, and fiber are all polysaccharides.

polyunsaturated fatty acid (PUFA) A fatty acid with two or more double bonds.

poverty Lacking the means to provide for material or comfort needs.

precision agriculture A cost-efficient, precise farming method that uses new technologies to collect data about variations in field soil to better manage the use of appropriate seeds, fertilizer, water, and pesticides for the growing of crops with less waste. Also known as *satellite farming*.

precursor A substance that is converted into or leads to the formation of another substance.

preformed vitamin A The form of vitamin A that is readily used by the body.

preformed vitamins Vitamins that are found in active form in foods.

pregnancy-induced hypertension A category of hypertension that includes *gestational hypertension* (occurs in pregnancy in a woman without a prior history of high blood pressure), *preeclampsia* (hypertension, severe edema, and protein loss occur), and *eclampsia* (can result in seizures; may be extremely dangerous for mother and baby).

premenstrual syndrome (PMS) A variety of symptoms such as moodiness, irritability, bloating, and anxiety that some women may experience during the menstrual cycle.

preschoolers Children aged 3 to 5 years old.

prions Misfolded proteins that can act as disease agents. An abnormal prion protein is the cause of mad cow disease.

prior-sanctioned Having previous approval.

progressive overload principle A gradual increase in exercise demands resulting from modifications to the frequency, intensity, time, or type of activity.

proportionality The relationship of one entity to another. Vegetables and fruits should be consumed in a higher proportion than dairy and protein foods in the diet.

protein digestibility corrected amino acid score (PDCAAS) A score measured as a percentage that takes into account both digestibility and amino acid profile and gives a good indication of the quality of a protein.

protein quality The measure of a protein's digestibility and how its amino acid pattern compares with your body's needs. Proteins that are more easily digested and have a complete set of amino acids are of higher quality.

protein turnover The continual process of degrading and synthesizing protein. When the daily amount of degraded protein is equivalent to the amount that is synthesized, you are in protein balance.

protein-energy malnutrition (PEM) A lack of sufficient dietary protein and/or calories.

proteins Compounds in your body that consist of numerous amino acids and are found in all living cells.

provitamin A carotenoids The family of compounds that includes beta-carotene that can be used to make vitamin A in the body.

provitamins Substances found in foods that can be converted into an active vitamin form once they are absorbed.

public health nutritionist An individual who may have an undergraduate degree in nutrition but isn't an RDN.

purging Measures taken to prevent weight gain or to lose weight after consuming food; examples include self-induced vomiting, laxatives, diuretics (water pills), excessive exercise, and/or fasting.

pyloric sphincter Sphincter in the bottom of the stomach that separates the pylorus from the duodenum of the small intestine.

pyridoxine The major form of vitamin B_6 found in plants foods, supplements, and fortified foods.

R

rancidity The decomposition, or spoiling, of fats through oxidation.

rating of perceived exertion (RPE) A subjective measure of the intensity level of an activity using a numerical scale.

recombinant bovine somatotropin (rbST) A synthetically made hormone identical to a cow's natural growth hormone, somatotropin, that stimulates milk production. Also known as rbGH (recombinant bovine growth hormone).

Recommended Dietary Allowance (RDA) The average amount of a nutrient that meets the needs of 97 to 98 percent of individuals in a similar age and gender group. The RDA is higher than the EAR.

rectum The lowest part of the large intestine, continuous with the sigmoid colon and the anus.

refined grains Grain foods that are made with only the endosperm of the kernel. The bran and germ are not included.

registered dietitian nutritionist (RDN) A health professional who has completed at least a bachelor's degree in nutrition from an accredited university or college in the United States, completed a supervised practice, and passed an exam administered by the Commission on Dietetic Registration, the credentialing agency for the Academy of Nutrition and Dietetics (AND).

remineralization The repairing of teeth by adding back the minerals lost during tooth decay. Saliva can help remineralize teeth.

repetition maximum (RM) The maximum amount of weight that can be lifted for a specified number of repetitions.

retinoids The family or group of substances that include retinol, retinal, and retinoic acid.

retinol The most usable form of preformed vitamin A.

retinol activity equivalents (RAE) The unit of measure used to describe the total amount of all forms of preformed vitamin A and provitamin A carotenoids in food.

retort canning The process of subjecting already-canned foods to an additional high-temperature heat source to destroy potential pathogens.

rhodopsin A compound found in the rods of the eye that is needed for night vision.

rickets A vitamin D deficiency in children, resulting in soft bones.

risk assessment The process of determining the potential human health risks posed by exposure to substances such as pesticides.

RNA A molecule that carries out the orders of DNA.

rods Light-absorbing cells responsible for black-and-white vision and night vision.

S

saliva Watery fluid secreted by the salivary glands in the mouth. Saliva moistens food and makes it easier to swallow.

sashimi A type of sushi that primarily consists of raw seafood, sliced into thin pieces and served with a dipping sauce (soy sauce with wasabi paste) or other condiments (such as fresh ginger).

satiation The feeling during eating that determines how long and how much you eat.

satiety The sensation that you feel when you have had enough to eat. It determines how long you will go between meals and/or snacks.

saturated fats Fats that contain mostly saturated fatty acids.

saturated fatty acid A fatty acid that has all of its carbons bound with hydrogen.

school-aged children Children between the ages of 6 and 11.

scientific method A stepwise process used by scientists to generate sound research findings.

scombrotoxic fish poisoning A condition caused by consuming spoiled fish that contain large amounts of histamines.

scurvy A disease caused by a deficiency of vitamin C and characterized by bleeding gums and a skin rash.

segmentation A "sloshing" motion that thoroughly mixes chyme with the chemical secretions of the intestine.

selenosis The presence of toxic levels of selenium.

sex pheromones Naturally occurring chemicals secreted by one organism to attract another; used as a biopesticide to control pests by interfering with their mating.

sickle-cell anemia A blood disorder caused by a genetic defect in the development of hemoglobin. Sickle-cell anemia causes the red blood cells to distort into a sickle shape and can damage organs and tissues.

side chain The side group of an amino acid that provides it with its unique qualities; also referred to as the R group.

simple carbohydrates A category of carbohydrates that contain a single sugar unit or two sugar units combined. Monosaccharides and disaccharides are simple carbohydrates.

small intestine Comprised of the duodenum, jejunum, and ileum, the small intestine is the longest part of the GI tract. Most of the digestion and absorption of food occurs in the small intestine.

social drinking Drinking patterns that are considered acceptable by society.

solid foods Foods other than breast milk or formula given to an infant, usually around 6 months of age.

soluble fiber A type of fiber that dissolves in water and is fermented by intestinal bacteria. Many soluble fibers are viscous and have gummy or thickening properties.

solvent A liquid that acts as a medium in which substances dissolve. Water is considered the universal solvent.

spina bifida A serious birth defect in which the spinal cord is malformed and lacks the protective membrane coat.

spores Hardy reproductive structures that are produced by certain bacteria. Some bacterial spores can survive boiling temperature (212°F).

starch The storage form of glucose in plants.

starvation To suffer severely from lack of food; a state in which the body breaks down its own tissue for fuel.

sterol A lipid that contains four connecting rings of carbon and hydrogen.

stomach Digestive organ that holds food after it's moved down the esophagus and before it is propelled into the small intestine.

stool (feces) Waste products that are stored in the large intestine and then excreted from the body. Consists mostly of bacteria, sloughed-off gastrointestinal cells, inorganic matter, water, unabsorbed nutrients, food residue, undigested fibers, fatty acids, mucus, and remnants of digestive fluids.

strength training Exercising with weights or other resistance to build, strengthen, and tone muscle to improve or maintain overall fitness; also called *resistance training*.

stroke A condition caused by a lack of oxygen to the brain that could result in paralysis and possibly death.

stroke volume The amount of blood pumped by the heart with each heart beat.

structure/function claim Claim on the label that describes how a nutrient or dietary compound affects the structure or function of the human body.

subcutaneous fat The fat located under the skin.

sucrose A disaccharide composed of glucose and fructose; also known as table sugar.

sugar substitutes Alternatives to table sugar that sweeten foods for fewer calories.

sulfites Preservatives used to help prevent foods from turning brown and to inhibit the growth of microbes. Often used in wine and dried fruit products.

sushi A Japanese dish of cooked, vinegared rice served with fish or other seafood, vegetables, and/or seaweed.

sustainable Able to be maintained indefinitely.

sustainable food system A food-providing system that conserves natural resources and can be maintained indefinitely.

systolic pressure The force of your blood against the artery walls when your heart beats.

T

target heart rate A heart rate in beats per minute (expressed as a percentage of maximum heart rate) achieved during exercise that indicates the intensity of the exercise.

thermic effect of food (TEF) The amount of calories the body uses to digest, absorb, metabolize, and store food.

thermogenesis The production of heat in body cells.

thirst mechanism Various bodily reactions caused by dehydration that signal you to drink fluids.

toddlers Children aged 1 to 3 years old.

Tolerable Upper Intake Level (UL) The highest amount of a nutrient that can be consumed daily without harm in a similar age and gender group of individuals.

tongue-thrust reflex A forceful protrusion of the tongue in response to an oral stimulus, such as a spoon.

toxicity The level at which exposure to a substance becomes harmful.

toxins Poisons produced by living organisms.

trace minerals Minerals needed from your diet and in your body in small amounts, less than 20 milligrams daily. These include iron, zinc, selenium, fluoride, chromium, copper, manganese, and molybdenum. Also called *microminerals*.

trans fat Substance that contains mostly *trans* fatty acids.

trans fatty acids Substances that result from the hydrogenating of an unsaturated fatty acid, causing a reconfiguring of some of its double bonds. A small amount of *trans* fatty acids occur naturally in animal foods.

transfer RNA (tRNA) A type of RNA that collects the amino acids within the cell that are needed to make a specific protein.

transport proteins Proteins that carry lipids (fat and cholesterol), oxygen, waste products, and vitamins through the blood to various organs and tissues, or that serve as channels to allow substances to pass through cell membranes.

traveler's diarrhea A pathogen-induced intestinal disorder experienced by some travelers who visit areas with unsanitary conditions.

triglyceride Three fatty acids that are attached to a glycerol backbone.

trimesters The three time periods of pregnancy.

tryptophan An amino acid that can be converted to niacin in the body.

type 1 diabetes Autoimmune form of diabetes in which the pancreas does not produce insulin.

type 2 diabetes Form of diabetes characterized by insulin resistance.

U

U.S. Pharmacopeia (USP) A nonprofit organization that sets purity and reliability standards for dietary supplements.

ultraviolet (UV) rays The rays from sunlight that cause the production of vitamin D in the skin.

umbilical cord Cord connecting the fetus to the placenta that allows the transfer of nutrients and waste products between the mother and the fetus.

undernutrition A state of inadequate nutrition whereby a person's nutrient and/or calorie needs aren't met through the diet.

underweight Weighing less than is healthy for your height. Clinically defined as having a body mass index (BMI) below 18.5.

unsaturated fats Fats that contain mostly unsaturated fatty acids.

unsaturated fatty acid A fatty acid that has one or more double bonds between carbons.

urea A nitrogen-containing waste product that is excreted in urine.

V

vegetarian A person who doesn't eat meat, fish, or poultry or (sometimes) foods made from these animal sources.

very low-calorie diet A diet of fewer than 800 calories per day and high in protein.

very-low-density lipoprotein (VLDL) A lipoprotein that delivers fat made in the liver to the tissues. VLDL remnants are converted into LDLs.

villi Projections on the walls of the small intestine that increase the surface area over which nutrients can be absorbed.

virus A microscopic organism that carries genetic information for its own replication; can infect a host and cause illness.

visceral fat The fat stored in the abdominal area.

vitamins Non-energy-providing organic essential nutrients that your body needs in small amounts to grow, reproduce, and maintain good health.

VO₂ max The maximum amount of oxygen (ml) a person uses in one minute per kilogram of body weight.

W

warfarin An anticoagulant drug given to prevent blood from clotting.

water balance The state whereby an equal amount of water is lost and replenished daily in the body.

working poor Individuals or families who are steadily employed but still experience poverty due to low wages or high dependent expenses.

Wernicke-Korsakoff Syndrome A progressively damaging brain disorder due to chronic thiamin deficiency.

X

xerophthalmia Permanent damage to the cornea causing blindness, due to a prolonged vitamin A deficiency.

Z

zoochemical Compound in food products derived from animals that is beneficial to human health.

References

Chapter 1

1. Freeland-Graves, J., and S. Nitzke. 2013. Position Paper of the Academy of Nutrition and Dietetics: Total Diet Approach to Healthy Eating. *Journal of the Academy of Nutrition and Dietetics* 113: 307–317.
2. National Turkey Federation. 2012. Turkey Facts and Trivia. Available at www.eatturkey.com. Accessed April 2015.
3. Freeland-Graves. Position Paper of the Academy of Nutrition and Dietetics: Total Diet Approach to Healthy Eating.
4. National Restaurant Association. 2014. Restaurateurs View Super Bowl with Appetite for Sales. Available at www.restaurant.org. Accessed April 2015.
5. Smith, L., S. Ng, and B. Popkin. 2013. Trends in U.S. Home Food Preparation and Consumption: Analysis of National Nutrition Surveys and Time Use Studies from 1965–1966 to 2008–2009. *Nutrition Journal* 12: 45. doi:10.1186/1475-2891-12-45.
6. United States Department of Agriculture, Economic Research Service. 2013. Food Security in the U.S.: Key Statistics and Graphics. Available at www.ers.usda.gov. Accessed April 2015.
7. Freeland-Graves. Position Paper of the Academy of Nutrition and Dietetics: Total Diet Approach to Healthy Eating.; Carlson, A., and E. Frazao. 2012. Are Healthy Foods Really More Expensive? It Depends How You Measure the Price. Available at www.ers.usda.gov. Accessed April 2015.
8. Freeland-Graves. Position Paper of the Academy of Nutrition and Dietetics: Total Diet Approach to Healthy Eating.
9. The SBDC National Information Clearinghouse. 2012. Coffee Shop Business Overview and Trends, 2012. Available at www.sbdcnet.org/small-business-research-reports/coffee-shop-2012. Accessed April 2015.
10. Mintel International Group. 2012. Breakfast Foods-US; Mintel International Group. 2012. Fruit Juice and Juice Drinks-US. Available at www.reports.mintel.com. Accessed April 2015.
11. Centers for Disease Control and Prevention. 2015. Leading Causes of Death in the United States. Available at www.cdc.gov. Accessed April 2015.
12. U.S. Department of Health and Human Services. 2015. Scientific Report of the *Dietary Guidelines for Americans Advisory Committee*. Available at www.health.gov/dietaryguidelines/2015-scientific-report/. Accessed April 2015.
13. U.S. Department of Agriculture, Agricultural Research Service. 2015. Nutrient Intakes from Food: Mean Amounts Consumed per Individual, by Gender and Age, *What We Eat in America*, NHANES 2011–2012. Available at www.ars.usda.gov. Accessed April 2015.
14. U.S. Department of Health and Human Services. Scientific Report of the *Dietary Guidelines for Americans Advisory Committee*.
15. U.S. Department of Health and Human Services. Scientific Report of the *Dietary Guidelines for Americans Advisory Committee*; Marra, M., and A. Boyar. 2009. Position of the American Dietetic Association: Nutrient Supplement. *Journal of the American Dietetic Association* 109: 2073–2085.
16. U.S. Department of Agriculture, Economic Research Service. 2014. Foods Away from Home. www.ers.usda.gov/topics/food-choices-health/food-consumption-demand/food-away-from-home.aspx. Accessed April 2015.
17. U.S. Department of Health and Human Services. Scientific Report of the *Dietary Guidelines for Americans Advisory Committee*.
18. U.S. Department of Agriculture, Economic Research Service. Foods Away from Home.
19. U.S. Department of Health and Human Services. Scientific Report of the *Dietary Guidelines for Americans Advisory Committee*.
20. Ibid.
21. Centers for Disease Control and Prevention. 2015. Obesity and Overweight. Available at www.cdc.gov. Accessed April 2015.
22. Ibid.
23. U.S. Department of Health and Preventative Services. 2010. *Healthy People 2020*. Available at www.healthypeople.gov. Accessed April 2015.
24. Debusk, R. M., C.P. Fogarty, J.M. Ordovas, and K.S. Kornman. 2005. Nutritional Genomics in Practice: Where Do We Begin? *Journal of the American Dietetic Association* 105: 589–598.
25. Fox, S., and M. Duggan. 2013. Health Online 2013. Pew Research Center's Internet & American Life Project. Available at www.pewinternet.org. Accessed April 2015.
26. National Center for Complementary and Alternative Medicine. 2014. Finding and Evaluating Online Resources on Complementary Health Approaches. Available at www.nccam.nih.gov. Accessed April 2015.

Feature Box References

1. The Academy of Nutrition and Dietetics. 2012. Hungry and Overweight: How Is It Possible? Available at www.hendpg.org. Accessed February 2013.
2. Ibid.
3. Ibid.; USDA. April 2012. The Food Environment, Eating Out, and Body Weight: A Review of the Evidence. *Nutrition Insight 49*. Available at www.cnpp.usda.gov. Accessed February 2013.

Two Points of View References

1. Better Business Bureau. 2013. Children's Food and Beverage Advertising Initiative. Available at www.bbb.org. Accessed August 2013.
2. Veerman, J. L., et al. 2009. By How Much Would Limiting TV Food Advertising Reduce Childhood Obesity? *European Journal of Public Health* 19: 365–369; Children Now. 2009. The Impact of Industry Self-Regulation on the Nutritional Quality of Foods Advertised on Television to Children. Available at www.childrennow.org. Accessed August 2013; Harris, J. L., et al. 2013. Redefining "Child-Directed Advertising" to Reduce Unhealthy Television Food Advertising. *American Journal of Preventive Medicine* 44: 358–364.
3. Carter, O. B., et al. 2011. Children's Understanding of the Selling Versus Persuasive Intent of Junk Food Advertising: Implications for Regulation. *Social Science Medicine* 72: 962–968.
4. Graff, S., et al. 2012. Government Can Regulate Food Advertising to Children Because Cognitive Research Shows That It Is Inherently Misleading. *Health Affairs (Millwood)* 31: 392–398.
5. Committee on Food Marketing and the Diets of Children and Youth. Institute of Medicine of the National Academies. 2006. Food Marketing to Children and Youth: Threat or Opportunity? Available at www.nap.edu. Accessed August 2013.
6. Redish, M. H. 2011. Childhood Obesity, Advertising, and the First Amendment. Available at www.gmaonline.org. Accessed August 2013.
7. University of Michigan Health System. 2010. Your Child: Development and Behavior Resources: Television and Children. Available at www.med.umich.edu. Accessed August 2013.
8. Cheeseman, G. M. 2011. McDonald's Stands Its Ground: Advertising to Children Is OK. Available at www.triplepundit.com. Accessed August 2013.
9. Ashton, D. 2004. Food Advertising and Childhood Obesity. *Journal of the Royal Society of Medicine* 97: 51–52.

Chapter 2

1. Institute of Medicine. 2003. *Dietary Reference Intakes: Applications in Dietary Planning*. Washington, D.C.: The National Academies Press. Available at http://fnic.nal.usda.gov. Accessed April 2015.

2. Davis, C., and E. Saltos. Updated 2012. Chapter 2: Dietary Recommendations and How They Have Changed Over Time. In E. Frazo, ed., *America's Eating Habits: Changes and Consequences*. Agriculture Information Bulletin No. AIB750. Available at www.ers.usda.gov. Accessed April 2015.
3. Ibid.
4. U.S. Department of Agriculture. 2010. *2010 Report of the Dietary Guidelines Advisory Committee*. Available at www.cnpp.usda.gov. Accessed April 2015.
5. Ibid.
6. National Heart, Lung, and Blood Institute. 2014. What Is the DASH Eating Plan? Available at www.nhlbi.nih.gov/health/health-topics/topics/dash. Accessed April 2015.
7. Center for Food Safety and Applied Nutrition. 2013. A Food Labeling Guide. Available at www.fda.gov. Accessed April 2015.
8. Food and Drug Administration. 2013. Guidance for Industry: A Food Labeling Guide. Available at www.fda.gov. Accessed April 2015.
9. Ibid.
10. Food Safety and Inspection Service. 2013. A Guide to Federal Food Labeling Requirements: Guidance for Industry: A Food Labeling Guide (7. Nutrition Labeling; Questions G1 through P8). Available at www.fsis.usda.gov. Accessed April 2015.
11. United States Department of Agriculture. 2015. Labeling Policies. Available at www.fsis.usda.gov/wps/portal/fsis/topics/regulatory-compliance/labeling/Labeling-Policies. Accessed April 2015.
12. Food and Drug Administration. Guidance for Industry: A Food Labeling Guide.
13. Farley, D. 1993. Look for "Legit" Health Claims on Foods. *FDA Consumer Magazine; 27*: 21–28.
14. Center for Food Safety and Applied Nutrition. 2013. Claims That Can Be Made for Conventional Foods and Dietary Supplements. Available at www.fda.gov. Accessed May 2015.
15. Ibid.
16. Ibid.
17. International Food Information Council. 2014. Functional Foods. Available at www.foodinsight.org/Background_on_Functional_Foods. Accessed May 2015.
18. Riediger, N., R. Othman, M. Suh, and M. Moghadasian. 2009. A Systemic Review of the Roles of ω-3 Fatty Acids in Health and Disease. *Journal of the American Dietetic Association 109*: 668–679. http://www.sciencedirect.com/science/article/pii/S0002822308023353. Accessed November 2015.

Feature Box References

1. USDA Nutrition Insights. 2000. Servings Sizes in the Food Guide Pyramid and on the Nutrition Facts Label: What's Different and Why? Available at www.cnpp.usda.gov. Accessed May 2015.
2. USDA Nutrition Insights. 2012. The Food Environment, Eating Out, and Body Weight: A Review of the Evidence. Available at www.cnpp.usda.gov. Accessed May 2015.
3. Young, L. R., and M. Nestle. 2003. Expanding Portion Sizes in the U.S. Marketplace: Implications for Nutrition Counseling. *Journal of the American Dietetic Association 103*: 231–234.
4. Rolls, B. 2003. The Supersizing of America: Portion Size and the Obesity Epidemic. *Nutrition Today 38*: 42–53.
5. Rolls, B., L. S. Roe, and J. S. Meengs. 2006. Larger Portion Sizes Lead to a Sustained Increase in Energy Intake Over 2 Days. *Journal of the American Dietetic Association 106*: 543–549.
6. U.S. Department of Agriculture. 2015. 2015 Report of the Dietary Guidelines Advisory Committee. Available at www.cnpp.usda.gov. Accessed May 2015.
7. de Castro, J. M. 2003. The Time of Day of Food Intake Influences Overall Intake in Humans. *Journal of Nutrition 134*: 104–111.
8. Ibid.
9. Holt, S. H., J. C. Miller, P. Petocz, and E. Farmakalidis. 1995. A Satiety Index of Common Foods. *European Journal of Clinical Nutrition 49*: 675–690.
10. Kerver, J. M., E. Yang, S. Obayashi, L. Bianchi, and W. Song. 2006. Meal and Snack Patterns Are Associated with Dietary Intake of Energy and Nutrients in U.S. Adults. *Journal of the American Dietetic Association 106*: 46–54.
11. Boon, T. W., R. Zedek, and Z. M. Kais. 2012. Association between Snacking Patterns, Energy, and Nutrient Intakes, and Body Mass Index among School Adolescents in Kuala Lumpur. *American Journal of Food and Nutrition 2*: 69–70.
12. Center for Nutrition Policy and Promotion. 2011. Breakfast Consumption, Body Weight, and Nutrient Intake: A Review of the Evidence.

Available at www.cnpp.usda.gov/sites/default/files/nutrition_insights_uploads/Insight45.pdf. Accessed May 2015.
13. Wyatt, H. R., G. K. Grunwald, C. L. Mosca, M. L. Klem, R. R. Wing, and J. O. Hill. 2002. Long-Term Weight Loss and Breakfast in Subjects in the National Weight Control Registry. *Obesity Research 10*: 78–82.
14. Striegel-Moore, R. H., D. L. Franko, D. Thompson, S. Affenito, and H. C. Kraemer. 2006. Night Eating: Prevalence and Demographic Correlates. *Obesity 14*: 139–147.
15. Frank, A., J. L. Scheer, C. J. Morris, and S. A. Shea. 2013. The Internal Circadian Clock Increases Hunger and Appetite in the Evening Independent of Food Intakes and Other Behaviors. *Obesity 21*: 421–423.
16. Stockman, N. K. A., et al. 2005. Comparison of Energy and Nutrient Intakes Among Meals and Snacks of adolescent males. Preventive Medicine; 41:203–210.
17. Keim, N. L., M. D. Van Loan, W. F. Horn, T. F. Barbieri, and P. L. Mayclin. 1997. Weight Loss Is Greater with Consumption of Large Morning Meals and Fat-Free Mass Is Preserved with Large Evening Meals in Women on a Controlled Weight Reduction Program. *Journal of Nutrition 127*: 75–82.
18. Haines, P. S., M. Y. Hama, D. K. Guilkey, and B. M. Popkin. 2003. Weekend Eating in the United States Is Linked with Greater Energy, Fat, and Alcohol Intake. *Obesity Research 11*: 945–949.
19. International Food Information Council. 2013. 2013 Functional Foods Consumer Survey. Available at www.foodinsight.org. Accessed May 2015.
20. Crowe, C. 2013. Position of the Academy of Nutrition and Dietetics: Functional Foods. Journal of the Academy of Nutrition and Dietetics; 113:1096–1103.
21. Ibid.

Two Points of View References

1. Responsible Reform for the Middle Class. 2010. The Patient Protection and Affordable Care Act Detailed Summary. Available at www.dpc.senate.gov. Accessed August 2013.
2. Robert Wood Johnson Foundation. 2013. Impact of Menu Labeling on Consumer Behavior: A 2008–2012 Update. Available at www.rwjf.org. Accessed August 2013.
3. USDA Economic Research Service. 2011. Will Calorie Labeling in Restaurants Make a Difference? Available at www.ers.usda.gov. Accessed August 2013.
4. U.S. Food and Drug Administration. 2013. Questions and Answers on the New Menu and Vending Machines Nutrition Labeling Requirements. Available at www.fda.gov. Accessed August 2013.
5. Ibid.
6. Robert Wood Johnson Foundation. Impact of Menu Labeling on Consumer Behavior.
7. Stanford Graduate School of Business. 2011. New Stanford Study Shows Posting Calories on Restaurant Menu Boards Lowers Customers' Calorie Counts per Visit. Available at www.gsb.stanford.edu. Accessed August 2013.
8. Ibid.
9. Robert Wood Johnson Foundation. Impact of Menu Labeling on Consumer Behavior.
10. Sapatkin, D. 2013. Restaurants' Nutrition Labels: How Big an Impact? *The Philadelphia Inquirer*. Available at http://articles.philly.com. Accessed August 2013.

Chapter 3

1. Mahan, K., and S. Escott-Stump. 2012. *Krause's Food & The Nutrition Care Process*, 13th ed. St. Louis: Saunders Elsevier.
2. Marieb, E. N., and K. Hoehn. 2016. *Human Anatomy and Physiology*, 10th ed. San Francisco: Benjamin Cummings.
3. Tortora, G. J., and B. H. Derrickson. 2011. *Principles of Anatomy and Physiology*, 13th ed. New York: Harper & Row Publishers.
4. Marieb. *Human Anatomy and Physiology*, 10th ed.
5. Ibid.
6. Ibid.
7. Mahan. *Krause's Food & The Nutrition Care Process*, 13th ed.
8. Gropper, S. S., and J. L. Smith. 2012. *Advanced Nutrition and Human Metabolism*, 6th ed. Belmont, CA: Wadsworth Cengage Learning.
9. Marieb. *Human Anatomy and Physiology*, 10th ed.
10. Ibid.
11. Gropper. *Advanced Nutrition and Human Metabolism*, 6th ed.
12. Marieb. *Human Anatomy and Physiology*, 10th ed.
13. Ibid.
14. Mahan. *Food & The Nutrition Care Process*, 13th ed.
15. Gropper. *Advanced Nutrition and Human Metabolism*, 6th ed.

16. Ibid.
17. U.S. Department of Health and Human Services, 2010. Oral Health. Available at www.womenshealth.gov. Accessed August 2014.
18. National Digestive Diseases Information Clearinghouse (NDDIC). 2014. Gastroesophageal Reflux (GER) and Gastroesophageal Reflux Disease (GERD) in Adults. Available at http://digestive.niddk.nih.gov/ddiseases/pubs/gerd/index.aspx/. Accessed August 2014.
19. Ibid.
20. American Cancer Society. 2014. Esophagus Cancer Overview. Available at www.cancer.org. Accessed August 2014.
21. *Mosby's Medical Dictionary*, 8th ed. Elsevier. Available at http://medical-dictionary.thefreedictionary.com/borborygmi. Accessed August 2014.
22. National Institute of Diabetes and Digestive and Kidney Diseases (NIDDK). 2013. *H. pylori* and Peptic Ulcers. Available at http://digestive.niddk.nih.gov/ddiseases/pubs/hpylori/. Accessed August 2014.
23. Ford, A., et al. 2014. American College of Gastroenterology Monograph on the Management of Irritable Bowel Syndrome and Chronic Idiopathic Constipation. *American Journal of Gastroenterology* 109: S2–S26.
24. National Institute of Diabetes and Digestive and Kidney Diseases (NIDDK). 2013. Crohn's Disease. Available at http://digestive.niddk.nih.gov. Accessed August 2014.

Two Points of View References

1. Sanders, M. E., et al. 2013. An Update on the Use and Investigation of Probiotics in Health and Disease. *Gut*. Available at doi:10.1136/gutjnl-2012-302504. Accessed March 2013.
2. Chmielewska, A., and H. Szajewska. 2010. Systematic Review of Randomised Controlled Trials: Priiobiotics for Functional Constipation. *World Journal of Gastroenterology* 16: 69–75; Marteau, P., et al. 2002. Probiotics and Intestinal Health Effects: A Clinical Perspective. *British Journal of Nutrition* 88 Suppl 1: S51–S57.
3. Douglas, L. C., and M. E. Sanders. 2008. Probiotics and Probiotics in Dietetics Practice. *Journal of the American Dietetic Association* 108: 510–521.
4. American Gastroenterological Association, Patient Center. 2008. Probiotics: What They Are and What They Can Do For You. Available at www.gastro.org. Accessed May 2010.
5. McGee, E. 2009. Answers to Your Questions about Probiotics. Available at www.webmd.com. Accessed July 2010.
6. FDA. 2006. Guidance for Industry on Complementary and Alternative Medicine Products and Their Regulation by the Food and Drug Administration. Available at www.fda.gov. Accessed July 2010.
7. American Dietetic Association. 2009. Hot Topics Sheet on Probiotics and Digestion. Available at www.eatright.org. Accessed May 2010.
8. National Center for Complementary and Alternative Medicine. 2012. An Introduction to Probiotics. Available at http://nccam.nih.gov. Accessed May 2013.
9. Joint FAO/WHO Working Group Report on Drafting Guidelines for the Evaluation of Probiotics in Food, London, Ontario, Canada, April 30 and May 1, 2002. Available at www.who.int/foodsafety/fs_management/en/probiotic_guidelines.pdf. Accessed May 2014.

Chapter 4

1. Oldways. 2014. The Heritage Pyramids. Available at http://oldwayspt.org. Accessed September 2014.
2. Johnson, M. 2014. *Human Biology: Concepts and Current Issues.* 7th ed. San Francisco: Benjamin Cummings.
3. National Digestive Diseases Information Clearinghouse. 2014. Lactose Intolerance. Available at http://digestive.niddk.nih.gov/ddiseases/pubs/lactoseintolerance. Accessed June 2015; Joneja, J. 2013. *The Health Professional's Guide to Food Allergies and Intolerances.* Chicago: The Academy of Nutrition and Dietetics.
4. Ibid.
5. National Institutes of Health. 2010. NIH Consensus Development Conference: Lactose Intolerance and Health. Available at www.ncbi.nlm.nih.gov/pubmed/20186234. Accessed January 2015.
6. Institute of Medicine. 2002. *Dietary Reference Intakes for Energy, Carbohydrate, Fiber, Fat, Fatty Acids, Cholesterol, Protein, and Amino Acids.* Washington, D.C.: The National Academies Press; Agricultural Research Service. 2012. Nutrient Intakes from Food: Mean Amounts Consumed per Individual, by Gender and Age, *What We Eat in America,* NHANES 2009–2010. Available at www.ars.usda.gov. Accessed September 2014.
7. Ibid.
8. Centers for Disease Control and Prevention. 2012. How to Use Fruits and Vegetables to Manage Your Weight. Available at www.cdc.gov. Accessed September 2014.

9. Economic Research Service. 2014. Food Availability (Per Capita) Data System 2014. Available at www.ers.usda.gov. Accessed September 2014.
10. Fitch, C., and K. Keim. 2012. Position of the Academy of Nutrition and Dietetics: Use of Nutritive and Nonnutritive Sweeteners. *Journal of the Academy of Nutrition and Dietetics* 112: 739–758.
11. Horn, L., et al. 2010. Translation and Implementation of Added Sugars Consumption Recommendations. *Circulation* 122: 2470–2490.
12. Fitch. Position of the Academy of Nutrition and Dietetics: Use of Nutritive and Nonnutritive Sweeteners.
13. USDA. 2015. Scientific Report of the 2015 Dietary Guidelines Advisory Committee. Available at www.health.gov/dietaryguidelines/2015-scientific-report/.
14. Ibid.
15. American Heart Association. 2014. Added Sugars. Available at www.heart.org/HEARTORG/GettingHealthy/NutritionCenter/HealthyEating/Added-Sugars_UCM_305858_Article.jsp. Accessed September 2014; Horn. Translation and Implementation of Added Sugars; Johnson, R. K., et al. 2009. Dietary Sugars Intake and Cardiovascular Health. A Scientific Statement from the American Heart Association. *Circulation* 120: 1011–1020.
16. USDA. Scientific Report of the 2015 Dietary Guidelines Advisory Committee.
17. Centers for Disease Control and Prevention. 2014. National Diabetes Statistics Report, 2014. Available at www.cdc.gov. Accessed November 2015.
18. Ibid.
19. Ibid.
20. Ibid.
21. Centers for Disease Control and Prevention. 2014. Diabetes Report Card 2012: National and State Profile of Diabetes and its Complications. Available at http://www.cdc.gov/diabetes/pubs/pdf/DiabetesReport-Card.pdf Accessed June 2015.
22. National Diabetes Information Clearinghouse. 2012. Hypoglycemia. National Institutes of Health Publication. Available at http://diabetes.niddk.nih.gov. Accessed September 2014.
23. National Diabetes Information Clearinghouse (NDIC). 2013. DCCT and EDIC: The Diabetes Control and Complications Trial and Follow-Up. Available at http://diabetes.niddk.nih.gov/dm/pubs/control/. Accessed September 2014.
24. American Diabetes Association. 2014. Standards of Medical Care in Diabetes—2011. *Diabetes Care* 37: S14-S80.
25. Ibid.
26. Sheard, N., N. Clark, J. Brand-Miller, M. Franz, F. Pi-Sunyer, E. Mayer-Davis, et al. 2004. Dietary Carbohydrate (Amount and Type) in the Prevention and Management of Diabetes. *Diabetes Care* 27: 2266–2271.
27. Ludwig, D. 2002. The Glycemic Index: Physiological Mechanisms Relating to Obesity, Diabetes, and Cardiovascular Disease. *Journal of the American Medical Association* 287: 2414–2423.
28. Evert, A., J. Boucher, M. Cypress, S. Dunbar, M. Franz, E. Mayer-Davis, J. Neumiller, et al. 2014. Nutrition Therapy Recommendations for the Management of Adults with Diabetes. *Diabetes Care* 27: S120–to S143; Roberts, S. 2000. High-Glycemic-Index Foods, Hunger, and Obesity: Is There a Connection? *Nutrition Reviews* 58: 163–169; Foster-Powell, K., and J. Brand-Miller. 1995. International Tables of Glycemic Index. *American Journal of Clinical Nutrition* 62: 871S–893S.
29. Centers for Disease Control and Prevention. 2013. Diabetes Public Health Resources. Available at www.cdc.gov. Accessed September 2014.
30. Centers for Disease Control and Prevention. Diabetes Report Card 2012.
31. Centers for Disease Control and Prevention. National Diabetes Statistic Report.
32. Centers for Disease Control and Prevention. 2013. Diabetes Public Health Resources: Children and Diabetes—More Information. Available at www.cdc.gov. Accessed September 2014.
33. USDA. Scientific Report of the 2015 Dietary Guidelines Advisory Committee; Centers for Disease Control and Prevention. 2014. Children and Diabetes. Available at www.cdc.gov. Accessed September 2013.
34. Centers for Disease Control and Prevention. 2014. National Diabetes Program. Available at www.cdc.gov. Accessed September 2014; Diabetes Prevention Program Research Group. 2002. Reduction in the Incidence of Type 2 Diabetes with Lifestyle Intervention or Metformin. *New England Journal of Medicine* 346: 393–403.
35. Ibid.
36. Nabors, L., and T. Hedrick. 2012. Sugar Reduction with Polyols. *Food Technology Magazine* 66: 9; Calorie Control Council. Reduced-Calorie Sweeteners: Hydrogenated Starch Hydrolysates. Available at www.caloriecontrol.org. Accessed September 2014.

37. National Toxicology Program. 2000. Report on Carcinogens. 9th ed. Available at: http://www.nih.gov/news/pr/may2000/niehs-15.htm. Accessed June 2015.

38. Ajinomoto USA, Inc. The History of Aspartame. Available at www.aspartame.net. Accessed September 2014.

39. Fitch. Position of the Academy of Nutrition and Dietetics: Use of Nutritive and Nonnutritive Sweeteners.

40. Eunice Kennedy Shriver National Institute of Child Health and Development. 2013. Phenylketonuria (PKU): Condition Information. Available at www.nichd.nih.gov/Pages/index.aspx. Accessed September 2014.

41. March of Dimes. 2013. Birth Defects. Available at www.marchofdimes.com. Accessed September 2014.

42. Eunice Kennedy Shriver National Institute of Child Health and Development. Phenylketonuria.

43. Fitch. Position of the Academy of Nutrition and Dietetics: Use of Nutritive and Nonnutritive Sweeteners; The NutraSweet Company. 2008. Neotame: A Scientific Overview. Available at www.neotame.com. Accessed September 2014.

44. National Digestive Diseases Information Clearinghouse. 2014. Constipation. National Institutes of Health Publication No. 07-2754. Available at http://digestive.niddk.nih.gov. Accessed September 2014.

45. Ibid.

46. National Digestive Diseases Information Clearinghouse. 2013. Diverticulosis and Diverticulitis. National Institutes of Health Publication No. 08-1163. Available at http://digestive.niddk.nih.gov. Accessed September 2014.

47. U.S. Department of Agriculture and U.S. Department of Health and Human Services. 2010. Report of the Dietary Guidelines Advisory Committee on the *Dietary Guidelines for Americans, 2010*. Available at www.cnpp.usda.gov. Accessed September 2014.

48. Ibid.

49. Ibid.

50. Slavin, J. 2008. Position of the American Dietetic Association: Health Implications of Dietary Fiber. *Journal of the American Dietetic Association* 108: 1716–1731.

51. Ibid.

52. Ibid.

53. National Cancer Institute. 2014. Colorectal Cancer Prevention (PDQ®). Available at www.cancer.gov. Accessed September 2014.

54. National Cancer Institute. Colorectal Cancer Prevention (PDQ®); Ferguson, L., and P. Harris. 2003. The Dietary Fiber Debate: More Food for Thought. *The Lancet* 361: 1487–1488.

55. Bingham, S., et al. 2003. Dietary Fiber in Food and Protection Against Colorectal Cancer in the European Prospective Investigation into Cancer and Nutrition (EPIC): An Observation Study. *The Lancet* 361: 1496–1501.

56. Bingham. Dietary Fiber in Food and Protection Against Colorectal Cancer; Ferguson. The Dietary Fiber Debate.

57. Slavin. Position of the American Dietetic Association: Health Implications of Dietary Fiber.

Feature Box References

1. Economic Research Service. 2014. Food Availability (Per Capita) Data System. Available at www.ers.usda.gov. Accessed September 2014.

2. U.S. Department of Agriculture and U.S. Department of Health and Human Services. 2010. Report of the Dietary Guidelines Advisory Committee on the *Dietary Guidelines for Americans, 2010*. Available at www.cnpp.usda.gov. Accessed September 2014.

3. Ibid.

4. Ibid.

5. Slavin, J., D. Jacobs, L. Marquart, and K. Wiemer. 2001. The Role of Whole Grains in Disease Prevention. *Journal of the American Dietetic Association* 101: 780–785.

6. International Food Information Council Foundation. 2014. 2014 Food & Health Survey. Available at www.foodinsight.org/articles/2014-food-and-health-survey. Accessed September 2014.

7. Palmer, C., and J. Gilbert. 2012. Position of the Academy of Nutrition and Dietetics: The Impact of Fluoride on Health. *Journal of the Academy of Nutrition and Dietetics* 112: 1443–1453.

8. National Institute of Dental and Craniofacial Resarch. 2014. Dental Caries (Tooth Decay). Available at www.nidcr.nih.gov. Accessed September 2014.

9. Jain, P., P. Nihill, J. Sobkowski, and M. Z. Agustin. 2007. Commercial Soft Drinks: pH and in Vitro Dissolution of Enamel. *General Dentistry* 55: 150–154; Heller, K., B. Burt, and S. Ekund. 2001. Sugared Soda Consumption and Dental Caries in the United States. *Journal of Dental Research* 80: 1949–1953; American Dental Association. 2002. Diet and Tooth Decay. *Journal of the American Dental Association* 133: 527; Joint Report of the American Dental Association Council on Access, Prevention and Interprofessional Relations and the Council on Scientific Affairs to the House of Delegates. 2001. Response to Resolution 73H-200. Available at www.ada.org. Accessed September 2014.

10. Academy of General Dentistry. 2008. Popular Energy Drinks Cause Tooth Erosion, Study Shows. *Science Daily*. Available at www.sciencedaily.com. Accessed May 2010.

11. Duffy, R. 2012. *American Dietetic Association's Complete Food and Nutrition Guide*. 4th ed. Hoboken: John Wiley & Sons; American Dental Association. Early Childhood Tooth Decay (Baby Bottle Tooth Decay). Available at www.ada.org. Accessed June 2015.

12. Touger-Decker, R., and C. Mobley. 2013. Position of the Academy of Nutrition and Dietetics: Oral Health and Nutrition. *Journal of the Academy of Nutrition and Dietetics* 113: 693–701; Mallonee, L., L. Boyd, and C. Stegeman. 2014. Oral Health and Nutrition. Practice Paper of the Academy of Nutrition and Dietetics. Available at www.eatright.org; Kashket, S., and D. DePaola. 2002. Cheese Consumption and the Development and Progression of Dental Caries. *Nutrition Reviews* 60: 97–103.

13. Mallonee. Oral Health and Nutrition. Practice Paper of the Academy of Nutrition and Dietetics; Touger-Decker. Position of the Academy of Nutrition and Dietetics: Oral Health and Nutrition; Mandel, I. 1996. Caries Prevention: Current Strategies, New Directions. *Journal of the American Dental Association* 127: 1477–1488.

14. Centers for Disease Control and Prevention. 2014. *Adult Obesity Facts*. Available at www.cdc.gov.; Centers for Disease Control and Prevention. 2014. Childhood Obesity Facts. Available at www.cdc.gov. Accessed April 2015.

15. USDA. 2015. The Scientific Report of the 2015 *Dietary Guidelines for Americans* Advisory Committee. Available at www.health.gov/dietaryguidelines/2015-scientific-report/. Accessed April 2015.

16. Ogden, C. L., B. K. Kit, M. D. Carroll, and S. Park. 2011. "Consumption of Sugar Drinks in the United States, 2005–2008." *NCHS Data Brief* 2011: 1–8.

17. Han, E., and L. M. Powell. 2013. "Consumption Patterns of Sugar-Sweetened Beverages in the United States." *Journal of the Academy of Nutrition and Dietetics* 113: 43–53.

18. Miller, P. E., R. A. McKinnon, S. M. Krebs-Smith, et al. 2013. "Sugar-Sweetened Beverage Consumption in the U.S.: Novel Assessment Methodology." *American Journal of Preventive Medicine* 45: 416–421.

19. Ibid.

20. USDA. The Scientific Report of the 2015 *Dietary Guidelines for Americans* Advisory Committee.

21. Mozaffarian, D., T. Hao, E. B. Rimm, W. C. Willett, and F. B. Hu. 2011. "Changes in Diet and Lifestyle and Long-Term Weight Gain in Men and Women." *New England Journal of Medicine* 364: 2392–2404.

22. de Ruyter, J. C., M. R. Olthof, J. C. Seidell, and M. B. Katan. 2012. "A Trial of Sugar-Free or Sugar-Sweetened Beverages and Body Weight in Children." *New England Journal of Medicine* 367: 1397–1406.

23. Ibid.

24. Fowler, S. P., K. Williams, and H. P. Hazuda. 2011. "Diet Soft Drink Consumption Is Associated with Increased Waist Circumference in the San Antonio Longitudinal Study of Aging." *Diabetes Pro*. Available at http://professional.diabetes.org. Accessed February 2014; Njike, V. Y., Z. Faridi, K. Shuval, et al. 2011. "Effects of Sugar-Sweetened and Sugar-Free Cocoa on Endothelial Function in Overweight Adults." *International Journal of Cardiology* 149: 83–88.

25. Njike. "Effects of Sugar-Sweetened and Sugar-Free Cocoa.

26. Pan, A., V. S. Malik, T. Hao, W. C. Willett, D. Mozaffarian, and F. B. Hu. 2013. "Changes in Water and Beverage Intake and Long-Term Weight Changes: Results from Three Prospective Cohort Studies." *International Journal of Obesity* 37: 1378–1385.

27. Muckelbauer, R., G. Sarganas, A. Grüneis, and J. Müller-Nordhorn. 2013. "Association between Water Consumption and Body Weight Outcomes: A Systematic Review." *American Journal of Clinical Nutrition* 98: 282–299.

28. Page, K. A., O. Chan, J. Arora, R. Belfort-Deaguiar, J. Szuira, B. Roehmholdt, G. W. Cline, et al. 2013. "Effects of Fructose vs Glucose on Regional Cerebral Blood Flow in Brain Regions Involved with Appetite and Reward Pathways." *Journal of the American Medical Association* 309: 63–70.

29. Bray, G. A., S. J. Nielsen, and B. M. Popkin. 2004. "Consumption of High-Fructose Corn Syrup in Beverages May Play a Role in the Epidemic of Obesity." *American Journal of Clinical Nutrition* 79: 537–543.

30. Hu, B. 2013. "Resolved: There Is Sufficient Scientific Evidence that Decreasing Sugar-Sweetened Beverage Consumption Will Reduce the Prevalence of Obesity and Obesity-Related Diseases." *Obesity Review* 14: 606–619.

31. Ibid.

32. USDA. The Scientific Report of the 2015 *Dietary Guidelines for Americans* Advisory Committee.
33. Centers for Disease Control and Prevention. 2015. Prediabetes. Available at www.cdc.gov/diabetes/basics/prediabetes.html. Accessed January 2015.

Two Points of View References

1. U.S. Food and Drug Administration. 2014. Proposed Nutrition Facts Label Changes Are Based on Science and Research. Available at www.fda.gov/downloads/ForConsumers/ConsumerUpdates/UCM387438.pdf. Accessed July 2015.
2. U.S. Food and Drug Administration. 2014. Protecting and Promoting *Your* Health. Available at www.fda.gov/Food/GuidanceRegulation/GuidanceDocumentsRegulatoryInformation/LabelingNutrition/ucm385663.htm. Accessed July 2015.
3. World Health Organization. 2015. Healthy Diet. Available at www.who.int/mediacentre/factsheets/fs394/en. Accessed July 201510/27/15.
4. L.A. Times, Food Industry Waging a Bitter Battle over Proposal on Added-Sugar Labels. Available at www.latimes.com/nation/la-na-sugar-limits-20150317-story.html. Accessed July 2015.
5. World Health Organization. Healthy Diet.
6. Marketplace. 2014. 3 Ways the New Nutrition Label Will Change Food Marketing. Available at www.market-pl.com/nutrition-label. Accessed July 2015.
7. Canned Food Alliance. 2010. Sugar in Canned Fruit: Clearing Up Confusion. Available at www.mealtime.org/~/media/files/fact-sheets/23_sugar_facts_cfa.pdf?la=en. Accessed November 2015.
8. USDA Choose my plate.gov. 2015. Empty Calories. What are Added Sugars? Available at www.choosemyplate.gov/weight-management-calories/calories/added-sugars.html. Accessed July 2015.
9. Obesity Society. 2014. The Obesity Society (TOS) Supports All Proposed Changes to Food Nutrition Facts Labels and Commends the US Food & Drug Administration (FDA) for the Much-Needed Update. 2014. Available at www.obesity.org/news-center/us-adult-consumption-of-added-sugars-increased-by-more-than-30-over-three-decades.htm. Accessed November 2015.
10. Yang, Q., et al. 2014. Added Sugar Intake and Cardiovascular Diseases Mortality Among US Adults. *JAMA Internal Medicine*. Available at www.archinte.jamanetwork.com/article.aspx?articleid=1819573. Accessed July 2015.
11. The Huffington Post. 2014. Sorry, But There Is No Such Thing As a 'Healthy' Sugar. Available at www.huffingtonpost.com/2014/05/19/healthy-sugar-sugars_n_5315969.html. Accessed July 2015.
12. World Health Organization. Healthy Diet.
13. Sutherland, L., et al. 2010. Guiding Stars: The Effect of a Nutrition Navigation Program on Consumer Purchases at the Supermarket. *American Journal of Clinical Nutrition*. Available at www.ajcn.nutrition.org/content/91/4/1090S.full#ref-24. Accessed July 2015.
14. Hungry for Change. 2012. How to Spot Sugar on Food Labels. Available at www.hungryforchange.tv/article/how-to-spot-sugar-on-food-labels. November 2015.
15. L.A. Times. Food Industry Waging a Bitter Battle.

Chapter 5

1. Institute of Medicine. 2002. *Dietary Reference Intakes for Energy, Carbohydrate, Fiber, Fat, Fatty Acids, Cholesterol, Protein, and Amino Acids.* Washington, D.C.: The National Academies Press.
2. Gretchen, V., and H. Rasmussen. 2014. Position of the Academy of Nutrition and Dietetics: Dietary Fatty Acids for Healthy Adults. *Journal of the Academy of Nutrition and Dietetics* 114: 136–153.
3. Ibid.; Ramsden, C., D. Zamora, L. Boonseng, S. Majchrzak-Hong, K. Raurot, C. Sushindran, A. Ringel, et al. 2013. Use of dietary linoleic acid for secondary prevention of coronary heart disease and death: evaluation of recovered data from the Sydney Diet Heart Study and updated meta-analysis *British Medical Journal* 346: e8707
4. U.S. Department of Agriculture, Agricultural Research Service. 2012. Nutrient Intakes from Food: Mean Amounts Consumed per Individual, by Gender and Age. In *What We Eat in America*, NHANES 2009–2010. Available at www.ars.usda.gov. Accessed November 2014.
5. Institute of Medicine. *Dietary Reference Intakes for Energy.*
6. Ibid.
7. Ibid.
8. USDA. 2015. Scientific Report of the 2015 Dietary Guidelines Advisory Committee. Available at www.health.gov/dietaryguidelines/2015-scientific-report/. Accessed March 2015.
9. Gretchen. Dietary Fatty Acids for Healthy Adults; Food and Drug Administration. 2015. FDA Targets *Trans* Fat in Processed Foods. Available at www.fda.gov/ForConsumers/ConsumerUpdates/ucm372915.htm. Accessed March 2015.
10. Eckel, R., J. Jakicic, J. Ard, J. de Jesus, N. Miller, V. Hubbard, I. Lee, et al. 2014. 2013 AHA/ACC Guideline on Lifestyle Management to Reduce Cardiovascular Risk. *Circulation* 129: S76–S99; USDA. Scientific Report of the 2015 Dietary Guidelines Advisory Committee; Agricultural Research Service. Nutrient Intakes from Food.
11. Ibid.
12. International Food Information Council Foundation. 2014. 2014 Food & Health Survey. Available at www.foodinsight.org. Accessed November 2014.
13. Ibid.
14. American Heart Association. 2014. Fat Substitutes. Available at www.heart.org. Accessed November 2014; Mattes, R. D. 1998. Fat Replacers. *Journal of the American Dietetic Association* 98: 463–468.
15. Calorie Control Council. 2014. Fat Replacers. Available at www.caloriecontrol.org. Accessed November 2014; Mattes. Fat Replacers; Wylie-Rosett, J. 2002. Fat Substitutes and Health: An Advisory from the Nutrition Committee of the American Heart Association. *Circulation* 105: 2800–2804.
16. Calorie Control Council. Fat Replacers.
17. Ibid.
18. Mattes. Fat Replacers.
19. Ibid.
20. Food and Drug Administration. 2003. 21 CFR Part 172. Food Additives Permitted for Direct Addition to Food for Human Consumption; Olestra; Final Rules. *Federal Register.* Available at www.fda.gov. Accessed November 2014.
21. Calorie Control Council. 2015. Olestra. Available at www.caloriecontrol.org. Accessed November 2014; Sandler, R. S., N. L. Zorich, T. G. Filloon, H. B. Wisman, D. J. Leitz, M. H. Brock, et al. 1999. Gastrointestinal Symptoms in 3,181 Volunteers Ingesting Snack Foods Containing Olestra or Triglycerides: A 6-Week Randomized, Placebo-Controlled Trial. *Annals of International Medicine* 130: 253–261; Cheskin, L. J., R. Miday, N. Zorich, and T. Filloon. 1998. Gastrointestinal Symptoms Following Consumption of Olestra or Regular Triglyceride Potato Chips: A Controlled Comparison. *Journal of the American Medical Association* 279: 150–152.
22. Swithers, S., S. Ogden, Davidson, T., and L. Terry. 2011. Fat Substitutes Promote Weight Gain in Rats Consuming High-Fat Diets. *Behavioral Neuroscience* 125: 512–518; Patterson, R. E., A. R. Kristal, J. C. Peters, M. L. Neuhouser, C. L. Rock, L. J. Cheskin, D., et al. 2000. Changes in Diet, Weight, and Serum Lipid Levels Associated with Olestra Consumption. *Archives of Internal Medicine* 160: 2600–2604.
23. American Heart Association. 2014. Heart Disease and Stroke Statistics—2014 Update. Available at http://my.americanheart.org. Accessed November 2014.
24. Ibid.
25. U.S. Department of Health and Human Services. 2005. Your Guide to Lowering Your Cholesterol with TLC. NIH Publication No. 06-5235. Available at www.nhlbi.nih.gov. Accessed March 2015.
26. Sandmaier, M. Revised 2007. The Healthy Heart Handbook for Women. National Institutes of Health, National Heart, Lung, and Blood Institute. NIH Publication No. 07-2720. Available at: http://www.nhlbi.nih.gov/health/resources/heart/ht-women-healthy-heart.
27. Ibid.
28. U.S. Department of Health and Human Services. Your Guide to Lowering Your Cholesterol.
29. American Heart Association. Heart Disease and Stroke Statistics—2014 Update.
30. National Heart, Lung, and Blood Institute. 2011. How Does Smoking Affect Your Heart and Blood Vessels? Available at www.nhlbi.nih.gov. Accessed November 2014.
31. USDA. Scientific Report of the 2015 Dietary Guidelines Advisory Committee.
32. Sandmaier. The Healthy Heart Handbook for Women.
33. U.S. Department of Health and Human Services. Your Guide to Lowering Your Cholesterol.
34. Ibid.
35. Eckel, et al. 2013. AHA/ACC Guideline on Lifestyle Management to Reduce Cardiovascular Risk: A Report of the American College of Cardiology/American Heart Association Task Force on Practice Guidelines. *Circulation* 129: 576-599.

36. United States Department of Agriculture. 2015. Scientific Report of the 2015 Dietary Guidelines Advisory Committee. Available at: http://www.health.gov/dietaryguidelines/2015-scientific-report/. Accessed April 2015.

37. Shin, J., Y. Nakamura, and K. He. 2013. Egg Consumption in Relation to Risk of Cardiovascular Disease and Diabetes: A Systematic Review and Meta-Analysis. *American Journal of Clinical Nutrition* 98: 146–159; Eckel. 2013 AHA/ACC Guideline on Lifestyle Management to Reduce Cardiovascular Risk; USDA. Scientific Report of the 2015 Dietary Guidelines Advisory Committee.

38. Shin. Egg Consumption in Relation to Risk of Cardiovascular Disease and Diabetes.

39. Ibid.

40. Gretchen. Dietary Fatty Acids for Healthy Adults; Kramhout, D., E. B. Bosschieter, and C. Coulander. 1985. The Inverse Relation between Fish Consumption and 20-Year Mortality from Coronary Heart Disease. *New England Journal of Medicine* 312: 1205–1209.

41. Gretchen. Dietary Fatty Acids for Healthy Adults; American Heart Association. 2014. Fish and Omega-3 Fatty Acids. Available at www.heart.org. Accessed March 2015; Kris-Etherton, P., W. Harris, and L. Appel, 2002. Fish Consumption, Fish Oil, Omega-3 Fatty Acids, and Cardiovascular Disease. *Circulation* 106: 2747–2757.

42. Ibid.

43. Gretchen. Dietary Fatty Acids for Healthy Adults.

44. Kris-Etherton. Fish Consumption, Fish Oil, Omega-3 Fatty Acids, and Cardiovascular Disease.

45. Ibid.

46. Gretchen. Dietary Fatty Acids for Healthy Adults.

47. American Heart Association. 2014. Fish 101. Available at www.heart.org. Accessed November 2014.

48. Slavin, J. 2008. Position of the American Dietetic Association: Health Implications of Dietary Fiber. *Journal of the American Dietetic Association* 108: 1716–1731; Brown, L., B. Rosner, W. Willett, and F. Sacks. 1999. Cholesterol-Lowering Effects of Dietary Fiber: A Meta-Analysis. *American Journal of Clinical Nutrition* 69: 30–42.

49. U.S. Department of Health and Human Services. 2005. Your Guide to Lowering Your Cholesterol; National Cholesterol Education Program. 2001. Detection, Evaluation, and Treatment of High Blood Cholesterol in Adults (Adult Treatment Panel III). National Institutes of Health Publication No. 01-3290.

50. Eilat-Adar, S., T. Sinai, C. Yosefy, and Y. Henkin. 2013. Nutrition Recommendations for Cardiovascular Disease Prevention. *Nutrients* 5: 3646–3683; U.S. Department of Health and Human Services. Your Guide to Lowering Your Cholesterol.

51. Food and Drug Administration. 2000. FDA Authorizes New Coronary Heart Disease Health Claim for Plant Sterol and Plant Stanol Esters. FDA Talk Paper. Available at www3.scienceblog.com/community/older/archives/M/1/fda0642.htm. Accessed November 2014.

52. U.S. Department of Health and Human Services. Your Guide to Lowering Your Cholesterol.

53. Lichtenberg, D., and H. Pinchuk. 2013. Atherogenesis, the Oxidative LDL Modification. Hypothesis Revisited. *Advances in Bioscience and Biotechnology* 4: 48–61; Tribble, D. L. 1999. AHA Science Advisory. Antioxidant Consumption and Risk of Coronary Heart Disease: Emphasis on Vitamin C, Vitamin E, and β-Carotene. *Circulation* 99: 591–595.

54. Eilat-Adar. Nutrition recommendations for cardiovascular disease Prevention; Sabate, J., K. Oda, and E. Ros. 2013. *Archives of Internal Medicine* 170: 821–827.

55. Center for Food Safety and Applied Nutrition. 2003. Qualified Health Claims: Letter of Enforcement Discretion—Nuts and Coronary Heart Disease. Available at www.fda.gov. Accessed November 2013.

56. Eilat-Adar. Nutrition Recommendations for Cardiovascular Disease Prevention; Hollenberg, N., and N. Fisher. 2007. Is It the Dark in Dark Chocolate? *Circulation* 116: 2360–2362; Ariefdjohan, M., and D. Savaiano. 2005. Chocolate and Cardiovascular Health: Is It Too Good to Be True? *Nutrition Reviews* 63: 427–430.

57. Mostofsky, E., E. Levitan, A. Wolk, and M. Mittleman. 2010. Chocolate Intake and Incidence of Heart Failure: A Population-Based Prospective Study of Middle-Aged and Elderly Women. *Circulation: Heart Failure* 3: 612–616.

58. de Koning Gans, J., Y. Uiterwaal, J. van der Schouw, D. Boer, W. Verschuren, and J. Beulen. 2012. Tea and Coffee Consumption and Cardiovascular Morbidity and Mortality. *Arteriosclerosis, Thrombosis, and Vascular Biology* 30: 1665–1671.

59. Kim, A., A. Chiu, M. Barone, D. Avino, F. Wang, and C. Coleman. 2011. Green Tea Catechins Decrease Total and Low-Density Lipoprotein Cholesterol. A Systematic Review and Meta-Analysis. *Journal of the American Dietetic Association* 111: 1720–1729.

60. U.S. Department of Health and Human Services. 2008. 2008 Physical Activity Guidelines for Americans. Available at www.health.gov. Accessed November 2014.

61. Ibid.

62. Ibid.

63. Eilat-Adar. Nutrition Recommendations for Cardiovascular Disease Prevention; USDA. Scientific Report of the 2015 Dietary Guidelines Advisory Committee; Rimm, E., A. Klatsky, D. Grobbee, and M. J. Stampfer. 1996. Review of Moderate Alcohol Consumption and Reduced Risk of Coronary Heart Disease: Is the Effect Due to Beer, Wine or Spirits? *British Medical Journal* 312: 731–736.

64. Ibid.; Costano, S., A. Di Castelnuovo, M. Donati, L. Iacovielle, and G. de Gaetano. 2010. Cardiovascular and Overall Mortality Risk in Relation to Alcohol Consumption in Patients with Cardiovascular Disease. *Circulation* 121: 1951–1959; American Heart Association. 2011. Alcoholic Beverages and Cardiovascular Disease. Available at www.heart.org. Accessed March 2013; Goldberg, I. J., L. Mosca, M. R. Piano, and E. A. Fisher. 2001. Wine and Your Heart: A Science Advisory for Healthcare Professionals from the Nutrition Committee, Council on Epidemiology and Prevention, and Council on Cardiovascular Nursing of the American Heart Association. *Circulation* 103: 472–475.

65. Karatzi, K., V. Rontoyanni, A. Protogerou, A. Georgoulia, K. Xenos, J. Chrysou, P. Sfikakis, and L. Sidossis. 2013. Acute Effects of Beer on Endothelial Function and Hemodynamics: A Single-Blind, Crossover Study in Healthy Volunteers. *Nutrition* 29: 1122–1126; Rimm, E., and R. C. Ellison. 1995. Alcohol in the Mediterranean Diet. *American Journal of Clinical Nutrition* 61: 1378S–1382S.

66. USDA. Scientific Report of the 2015 Dietary Guidelines Advisory Committee; American Heart Association. Alcoholic Beverages and Cardiovascular Disease; Mukamal, K. J., K. M. Conigrave, M. A. Mittleman, C. A. Camaro, M. J. Stampfer, W. C. Willett, and E. B. Rimm. 2003. Roles of Drinking Pattern and Type of Alcohol Consumed in Coronary Heart Disease in Men. *New England Journal of Medicine* 348: 109–118.

67. U.S. Department of Health and Human Services. Your Guide to Lowering Your Cholesterol; Jenkins, D. J., C. W. Kendal, A. Marchie, D. A. Faulkner, J. M. Wong, R. de Souza, et al. 2003. Effects of a Dietary Portfolio of Cholesterol-Lowering Foods vs. Lovastatin on Serum Lipids and C-Reactive Protein. *Journal of the American Medical Association* 290: 502–510.

68. U.S. Department of Health and Human Services. Your Guide to Lowering Your Cholesterol; Anderson, J. W. 2003. Diet First, Then Medication of Hypercholesterolemia. *Journal of the American Medical Association* 290: 531–533.

Feature Box References

1. USDA. Scientific Report of the 2015 Dietary Guidelines Advisory Committee; Sofi, F., R. Abbate, G. Gensini, and A Casini. 2010. Accessing Evidence on Benefits of Adherence to the Mediterranean Diet on Health: An Updated Systematic Review and Meta-Analysis. *Journal of Clinical Nutrition* 92: 1189–1196.

2. Trichopoulou, A. N., T. Costacou, C. Bamia, and D. Trichopoulos. 2003. Mediterranean Diet, Traditional Risk Factors, and the Rate of Cardiovascular Complications after Myocardial Infarction: Final Report of the Lyon Diet Heart Study. *Circulation* 99: 779–785; Kris-Etherton, P., R. H. Eckel, B. V. Howard, S. St. Jeor, and T. L. Bazzarre. 2001. Lyon Diet Heart Study. Benefits of a Mediterranean-Style, National Cholesterol Education Program/American Heart Association Step I Dietary Pattern on Cardiovascular Disease. *Circulation* 103: 1823–1825.

3. Willett, W. C., F. Sacks, A. N. Trichopoulou, G. Drescher, A. Ferro-Luzzi, E. Helsing, and D. Trichopoulos. 1995. Mediterranean Diet Pyramid: A Cultural Model for Healthy Eating. *American Journal of Clinical Nutrition* 61: 1402S–1406S.

4. Ibid.

5. Nestle, M. 1995. Mediterranean Diets: Historical and Research Overview. American Journal of Clinical Nutrition; 61: 1313S–1320S

6. Willett. Mediterranean Diet Pyramid; Nestle. Mediterranean Diets.

7. Ibid.; Gretchen. Dietary Fatty Acids for Healthy Adults.

8. Food and Drug Administration. 2014. Fish: What Pregnant Women and Parents Should Know. Available at www.fda.gov. Accessed November 2014.

9. Ibid.

10. Ibid.

11. Ibid.

12. Ibid.

13. Environmental Protection Agency. 2014. Fish Consumption Advisories. Available at http://water.epa.gov. Accessed November 2014.

Two Points of View References

1. Indiana University. 2004. Farmed Salmon More Toxic Than Wild Salmon, Study Finds. *Science Daily*. Available at www.sciencedaily.com. Accessed May 2013.
2. Crinnion, W. J. 2011. The Role of Persistent Organic Pollutants in the Worldwide Epidemic of Type 2 Diabetes Mellitus and the Possible Connection to Farmed Atlantic Salmon (*Salmo salar*). *Alternative Medicine Review* 16: 301–313.
3. Monterey Bay Aquarium. 2010. Seafood Watch: Salmon Fact Sheet. Available at www.montereybayaquarium.org. Accessed May 2013.
4. The Cornucopia Institute. 2009. How Farm-Raised Salmon Are Turning Our Oceans into Dangerous and Polluted Feedlots. Available at www.cornucopia.org. Accessed May 2013.
5. Pew Environment Group. 2009. Pew Environment Group Calls for a Crackdown on Unapproved Drug Use by Salmon Farms. Available at www.pewtrusts.org. Accessed May 2013.
6. Monterey Bay Aquarium Seafood Watch. 2013. Seafood Watch: Atlantic Salmon: Farmed Atlantic Salmon. www.montereybayaquarium.org. Accessed May 2013.
7. Ziccarelli, V. 2009. Nutritional Health Benefits of Salmon. Available at www.salmonfarmers.org. Accessed May 2013.
8. Hites, R., and B. Hamilton. 2004. Global Assessment of Organic Contaminants in Farmed Salmon. *Science* 303: 226–229.
9. Ziccarelli. Nutritional Health Benefits of Salmon.
10. Harvard School of Public Health. 2006. Benefits of Eating Fish Greatly Outweigh the Risks, New Study Says. *Science Daily*. Available at www.sciencedaily.com. Accessed May 2013.
11. University of California Cooperative Extension. 2010. Commercially Farmed and Wild-Caught Salmon—Bon Appetit! Available at http://seafood.ucdavis.edu. Accessed May 2013.
12. Ibid.

Chapter 6

1. Johnson, M. D. 2014. *Human Biology: Concepts and Current Issues*. 7th ed. San Francisco: Benjamin Cummings.
2. Institute of Medicine. 2002. *Dietary Reference Intakes for Energy, Carbohydrate, Fiber, Fat, Fatty Acids, Cholesterol, Protein, and Amino Acids*. Washington, D.C.: The National Academies Press.
3. Bennion, M. 1980. *The Science of Food*. New York: Harper & Row.
4. Food Safety and Inspection Service. 2013. Poultry: Basting, Brining, and Marinating. Available at www.fsis.usda.gov. Accessed February 2015.
5. Institute of Medicine. *Dietary Reference Intakes for Energy*.
6. National Human Genome Research Institute. 2014. Learning about Sickle-Cell Disease. Available at www.genome.gov.
7. Koster, M. 2009. Managing an Epidermis. *Annals of the New York Academy of Sciences* 1107: 7–10.
8. Murray, R. K., D. Bender, P. J. Kennelly, and V. Rodwell. 2012. *Harper's Illustrated Biochemistry*. 29th ed. New York: Lange Medical Books/McGraw-Hill.
9. Joneja, J. 2013. *The Health Professional's Guide to Food Allergies and Intolerances*. Chicago: Academy of Nutrition and Dietetics.
10. Paddon-Jones, D., E. Westman, R. Mattes, R. Wolfe, A. Astrup, and M. Westerterp-Plantenga. 2008. Protein, Weight Management and Satiety. *American Journal of Clinical Nutrition* 87: 1558S–1561S; Astrup, A. 2006. Carbohydrates as Macronutrients in Relation to Protein and Fat for Body Weight Control. *International Journal of Obesity* 30: S4–S9.
11. Vedlhorst, M., A. Smeets, S. Soenen, A. Hochstenback-Waelen, R. Hursel, K. Diepvens, et al. 2008. Protein-Induced Satiety: Effects and Mechanisms of Different Proteins. *Physiology & Behavior* 94: 300–307.
12. Stipanuk, M., and M. Caudill. 2013. *Biochemical, Physiological, and Molecular Aspects of Human Nutrition*. 3rd ed. Philadelphia: Saunders Elsevier.
13. U.S. Department of Agriculture, Agricultural Research Service. 2014. Nutrient Intakes from Food: Mean Amounts Consumed per Individual, by Gender and Age. In *What We Eat in America, NHANES 2011–2012*. Available at www.ars.usda.gov. Accessed February 2015.
14. Ibid.
15. American Dietetic Association, Dietitians of Canada, and the American College of Sports Medicine. 2009. Nutrition and Athletic Performance. *Journal of the American Dietetic Association* 109: 509–527.
16. Economic Research Service (ERS). 2014. Food Availability per Capita Data System. Available at www.ers.usda.gov. Accessed February 2015.
17. Ibid.
18. U.S. Department of Health and Human Services, National Kidney and Urologic Diseases Information Clearing House. 2013. Kidney Stones in Adults. Available at http://kidney.niddk.nih.gov. Accessed February 2015.
19. Heaney, R., and D. Layman. 2008. Amount and Type of Protein Influences Bone Health. *American Journal of Clinical Nutrition* 87: 156S–170S; Institute of Medicine. *Dietary Reference Intakes for Energy*.
20. Heaney. Amount and Type of Protein; Heaney, R. P. 1998. Excess Dietary Protein May Not Adversely Affect Bone. *Journal of Nutrition* 128: 1054–1057.
21. Kushi, L., C. Doyle, M. McCullough, C. Rock, W. Denmark-Wahnefried, E. Bandera, S. Gapstu, et al. 2012. American Cancer Society Guidelines on Nutrition and Physical Activity for Cancer Prevention: Reducing the Risk of Cancer with Healthy Food Choices and Physical Activity. *CA: A Cancer Journal for Clinicians* 62: 30–67; World Cancer Research Fund/American Institute for Cancer Research. 2007. Food, Nutrition, Physical Activity, and the Prevention of Cancer: A Global Prospective. Available at www.dietandcancerreport.org. Accessed May 2015.
22. Bertstein, M., and N. Munoz. 2012. Food and Nutrition for Older Adults: Promoting Health and Wellness. *Journal of the Academy of Nutrition and Dietetics* 112: 1255–1277.
23. Food and Agriculture Organization of the United Nations. 2013. The State of Food Insecurity in the World 2013. Available at www.fao.org. Accessed February 2015.
24. Nordin, S., M. Boyle, and T. Kemmer. 2013. Position of the Academy of Nutrition and Dietetics: Nutrition Security in Developing Nations: Sustainable Food, Water, and Health. *Journal of the Academy of Nutrition and Dietetics* 113: 581–595.
25. Ibid.
26. Scheinfeld, N. 2014. Protein-Energy Malnutrition Treatment and Management. *Medscape*. Available at http://emedicine.medscape.com/article/1104623-overview. Accessed February 2015; Grover, A., and L. C. Ee. 2009. Protein-Energy Malnutrition. *Pediatric Clinics of North America* 56: 1055–1068; Shils, M., J. Olson, M. Shike, and A. Ross. 1999. *Modern Nutrition in Health and Disease*. 9th ed. Baltimore: Williams & Wilkins.
27. Rabinowitz, S. 2014. Marasmus. *Medscape*. Available at http://emedicine.medscape.com/article/984496-overview. Accessed February 2015; Grover. Protein-Energy Malnutrition; Shils. *Modern Nutrition*.
28. Grover. Protein-Energy Malnutrition.
29. Food and Agriculture Organization of the United Nations. The State of Food Insecurity.
30. American Dietetic Association and Dietitians of Canada. 2009. Position of the American Dietetic Association and Dietitians of Canada: Vegetarian Diets. *Journal of the American Dietetic Association* 109: 1266–1282.
31. Gallup Wellbeing. 2012. Gallup's July 9–12 Consumption Habits Survey. Available at www.gallup.com. Accessed February 2015.
32. Ginsberg, C. 2011. The Market for Vegetarian Foods. Available at www.vrg.org. Accessed April 2013.
33. American Dietetic Association and Dietitians of Canada. Position of the American Dietetic Association and Dietitians of Canada: Vegetarian Diets.
34. Ibid.
35. Ibid.
36. Kushi. American Cancer Society Guidelines on Nutrition and Physical Activity for Cancer Prevention.

Feature Box References

1. 2012. Moo-ve Over Milk: Plant Alternatives Primed to Benefit from Protein Supplement Demand. *Euromonitor International*. Available at www.blog.euromonitor.com. Accessed February 2015.
2. ConsumerLab.com. 2015. 31% of Protein Powders and Drinks Flunk Test of Quality. Available at www.consumerlab.com/reviews/Protein_Powders_Shakes_Drinks_Sports_%20Meal_Diet/NutritionDrinks/. Accessed February 2015.
3. 2010. Alert! You Don't Need the Extra Protein or the Heavy Metals Our Tests Found. *Consumer Reports* 75: 24. Accessed February 2015.
4. Maughan, R. J., and S. M. Shirreffs. 2012. Nutrition for Sports Performance: Issues and Opportunities. *Proceedings of the Nutrition Society* 71: 112–119.
5. Graf, S., S. Egert, and M. Heer. 2011. Effects of Whey Protein Supplements on Metabolism: Evidence from Human Intervention Studies. *Current Opinion in Clinical Nutrition and Metabolic Care* 14: 569–580.
6. Spillane, M., N. Schwarz, S. Leddy, T. Correa, M. Minter, V. Longoria, and D. S. Willoughby. 2011. Effects of 28 Days of Resistance Exercise while Consuming Commercially Available Pre- and Post-Workout

Supplements, NO-Shotgun® and NO-Synthesize®, on Body Composition, Muscle Strength and Mass, Markers of Protein Synthesis, and Clinical Safety Markers in Males. *Nutrition & Metabolism* 8: 78.

7. Mintel Oxygen. 2014. Snack and Nutrition Bars – US – March 2014. Available at http://store.mintel.com/snack-and-nutrition-bars-us-march-2014. Accessed February 2015.

8. United Soybean Board. 2014. Bite. The Data is Delicious. Available at www.soyconnection.com/sites/default/files/Consumer%20Attitudes_Med_062714.pdf. Accessed February 2015.

9. Ibid.

10. Ibid.

11. McCullough, M. 2012. The Bottom Line on Soy and Breast Cancer Risk. American Cancer Society. Available at www.cancer.org/cancer/news/expertvoices/post/2012/08/02/the-bottom-line-on-soy-and-breast-cancer-risk.aspx. Accessed February 2015; Munro, I. C., M. Harwood, J. J. Hlywka, A. M. Stephen, J. Doull, W. G. Flammn, and H. Adlercrutz. 2003. Soy Isoflavones: A Safety Review. *Nutrition Reviews* 61: 1–33.

12. Sacks, F., A. Lichtenstein, L. Van Horn, W. Harris, P. Kris-Etherton, M. Winston, and the American Heart Association Nutrition Committee. 2006. Soy Protein, Isoflavones, and Cardiovascular Health: An American Heart Association Science Advisory for Professions from the Nutrition Committee. *Circulation* 113: 1034–1044.

13. He, J., M. Wofford, K. Reynolds, J. Chen, C. Chen, L. Myers, et al. 2011. Effect of Dietary Protein Supplementation on Blood Pressure: A Random Controlled Trail. *Circulation* 124: 589–595.

14. McCullough. The Bottom Line on Soy; American Institute of Cancer Research. 2014. Foods that Fight Cancer. Available at www.aicr.org. Accessed February 2015; Messina, M. J., V. Persky, K. D. R. Setchell, and S. Barnes. 1994. Soy Intake and Cancer Risk: A Review of the In Vitro and In Vivo Data. *Nutrition and Cancer* 21: 113–131; Messina, M. J., and C. L. Loprinzi. 2001. Soy for Breast Cancer Survivors: A Critical Review of the Literature. *Journal of Nutrition* 131: 3095S–3108S.

15. McCullough. The Bottom Line on Soy; Kushi. American Cancer Society Guidelines on Nutrition and Physical Activity for Cancer Prevention.

16. American Cancer Society. 2013. Soybean. Available at www.cancer.org. Accessed February 2015; McCullough. The Bottom Line on Soy; Shu, X. O., F. Jin, Q. Dai, W. Wen, J. D. Potter, L. H. Kushi, et al. 2001. Soy-food Intake during Adolescence and Subsequent Risk of Breast Cancer among Chinese Women. *Cancer Epidemiology, Biomarkers & Prevention* 10: 483–488; Maskarinec, G. 2005. Soy Foods for Breast Cancer Survivors. *Journal of the American Dietetic Association* 105: 1524–1528.

17. American Institute of Cancer Research. Foods that Fight Cancer; Maskarinec. Soy Foods for Breast Cancer Survivors; McMichael-Phillips, D. F., C. Harding, M. Morton, S. A. Roberts, A. Howell, C. S. Potten, and N. J. Bundred. 1998. Effects of Soy-Protein Supplementation on Epithelial Proliferation in the Histologically Normal Human Breast. *American Journal of Clinical Nutrition* 68: 1431S–1436S.

18. American Cancer Society. Soybean; American Institute of Cancer Research. Foods that Fight Cancer.

19. American Cancer Society. Soybean.

20. American Institute of Cancer Research. Foods that Fight Cancer.

Two Points of View References

1. The Paleo Diet. 2012. What to Eat on the Paleo Diet. Available at http://thepaleodiet.com. Accessed June 2013.

2. The Vegetarian Resource Group. 2000. Vegetarianism in a Nutshell: Humans Are Omnivores. Available at www.vrg.org. Accessed June 2013.

3. The Paleo Diet. What to Eat on the Paleo Diet; Liu, S., et al. 2000. A Prospective Study of Whole-Grain Intake and Risk of Type 2 Diabetes Mellitus in U.S. Women. *American Journal of Public Health* 90: 1409–1415; Jenkins, D. J., H. Ghafari, and T. M. Wolever, et al. 1982. Relationship between Rate of Digestion of Foods and Post-Prandial Glycaemia. *Diabetologia* 22: 450–455.

4. The Paleo Diet. What to Eat on the Paleo Diet.

5. Ibid.; Centers for Disease Control and Prevention. 2011. Americans Consume Too Much Sodium (Salt). Available at www.cdc.gov. Accessed June 2013; Activist Post. 2012. What Is the Average American Diet? Infographic. Available at www.activistpost.com. Accessed June 2013.

6. U.S. News and World Report. 2013. Health. Health and Wellness. Paleo Diet. Available at http://health.usnews.com. Accessed June 2013.

7. U.S. News and World Report. 2013. Health. Health and Wellness. Paleo Diet. Expert Reviews. Available at http://health.usnews.com. Accessed June 2013; Baik, I., et al. 2013. A Healthy Dietary Pattern Consisting of a Variety of Food Choices Is Inversely Associated with the Development of Metabolic Syndrome. *Nutrition Research and Practice* 7: 233–241.

8. Cunningham, E. 2012. Are Diets from Paleolithic Times Relevant Today? *Journal of the Academy of Nutrition and Dietetics* 112: 8.

9. GoodReads. 2013. Interview with Michael Pollan. Available at www.goodreads.com. Accessed June 2013; Perry, G. H., et al. 2007. Diet and the Evolution of Human Amylase Gene Copy Number Variation. *Nature Genetics* 39: 1256–1260.

Chapter 7

1. Rosenfeld, L. 1997. Vitamine-Vitamin. The Early Years of Discovery. *Clinical Chemistry* 43: 680–685.

2. Lobo, V., A. Patil, A. Phatak, and N. Chandra. Jul–Dec, 2010. Free Radicals, Antioxidants and Functional Foods: Impact on Human Health. *Pharmacognosy Review* 4: 118–126.

3. Ibid.

4. National Eye Institute, National Institutes of Health. 2013. Facts About Age-Related Macular Degeneration. Available at www.nei.nih.gov. Accessed May 2015.

5. Ibid.

6. National Institutes of Health, Senior Health. 2013. Cataract. Available at http://nihseniorhealth.gov. Accessed May 2015.

7. Ibid.

8. Kuski, L., C. Doyle, M. McCullough, C. Rock, W. Demark-Wahnefried, E. Bandera, S. Gapstur, S., A. Patel, K. Andrews., T. Gansler et al., and The American Cancer Society. 2012. American Cancer Society Guidelines on Nutrition and Physical Activity for Cancer Prevention. *CA: A Cancer Journal for Clinicians* 62: 30–67.

9. Freeland-Graves, J., and S. Nitzke. 2013. Position of the Academy of Nutrition and Dietetics: Total Diet Approach to Healthy Eating. *Journal of the Academy of Nutrition and Dietetics* 113: 307–317.

10. Prodanow, M., I. Sierra, and C. Vidal-Valverde. 2004. Influence of Soaking and Cooking on the Thiamin, Riboflavin, and Niacin Contents of Legumes. *Food Chemistry* 84: 271–277.

11. Lee, S. K., and A. A. Kader. 2000. Preharvest and Postharvest Factors Influencing Vitamin C Content of Horticultural Crops. *Postharvest Biology and Technology* 20: 207–220.

12. Pandrangi, S., and L. E. LaBorde. 2004. Retention of Folate, Carotenoid, and Other Quality Characteristics in Commercially Packaged Fresh Spinach. *Journal of Food Science* 69: C702–C707.

13. National Institutes of Health. 2013. Vitamin A. Available at http://ods.od.nih.gov. Accessed May 2015; Institute of Medicine, Food and Nutrition Board. 2001. *Dietary Reference Intakes: Vitamin A, Vitamin K, Arsenic, Boron, Chromium, Copper, Iodine, Iron, Manganese, Molybdenum, Nickel, Silicon, Vanadium, and Zinc.* Washington, D.C.: The National Academies Press.

14. Institute of Medicine. *Dietary Reference Intakes: Vitamin A.*

15. National Institutes of Health. Vitamin A; Ross, A. C. 1993. Vitamin A as Hormone: Recent Advances in Understanding the Actions of Retinol, Retinoic Acid, and Beta-Carotene. *Journal of the American Dietetic Association* 93: 1285–1290.

16. Layton, A. 2009. The Use of Isotretinoin in Acne. *Dermato-Endocrinology* 1: 162–169.

17. National Institutes of Health. Vitamin A; Institute of Medicine. *Dietary Reference Intakes: Vitamin A.*

18. Institute of Medicine. *Dietary Reference Intakes: Vitamin A.*

19. Institute of Medicine, Food and Nutrition Board. 2000. *Dietary Reference Intakes: Vitamin C, Vitamin E, Selenium, and Carotenoids.* Washington, D.C.: The National Academies Press.

20. Brown, M., M. Ferruzzi, M. Nguyen, D. Cooper, A. Eldridge, S. Schwartz, and W. White. 2004. Carotenoid Bioavailability Is Higher from Salads Ingested with Full-Fat Than with Fat-Reduced Salad Dressings as Measured with Electrochemical Detection. *American Journal of Clinical Nutrition* 80: 396–403.

21. Institute of Medicine. *Dietary Reference Intakes: Vitamin A.*

22. Ibid.; National Institutes of Health. Vitamin A.

23. Ibid.

24. National Institutes of Health. Vitamin A; Brinkley, N., and D. Krueger. 2000. Hypervitaminosis A and Bone. *Nutrition Reviews* 58: 138–144; Genaro, P., and L. A. Martini. 2004. Vitamin A Supplementation and Risk of Skeletal Fracture. *Nutrition Reviews* 62: 65–67; Melhus, H., K. Michaelsson, K. Mark, A. Kindmark, R. Berstrom, L. Holmber, H. Mallmin, et al. 1998. Excessive Dietary Intake of Vitamin A Is Associated with Reduced Bone Mineral Density and Increased Risk for Hip Fractures. *Annals of Internal Medicine* 129: 770–778.

25. Joo N. S., S. W. Yang, B. C. Song, and K. J. Yeum. 2015. Vitamin A Intake, Serum Vitamin D and Bone Mineral Density: Analysis of the Korea National Health and Nutrition Examination Survey (KNHANES,

2008–2011). *Nutrients* 10: 1716–1727; National Institutes of Health. Vitamin A; Feskanich, D., V. Singh, W. Willett, and G. Colditz. 2002. Vitamin A Intake and Hip Fractures among Postmenopausal Women. *Journal of the American Medical Association* 287: 47–54; Lips, P. 2003. Hypervitaminosis A and Fractures. *New England Journal of Medicine* 348: 347–349; Michaelsson, K., H. Lithell, B. Bvessby, and H. Melhus. 2003. Serum Retinol Levels and the Risk of Fractures. *New England Journal of Medicine* 348: 287–294.

26. National Institutes of Health. Vitamin A; Institute of Medicine. *Dietary Reference Intakes: Vitamin C.*

27. National Institutes of Health. Vitamin A; The Alpha-Tocopherol, Beta-Carotene Cancer Prevention Study Group. 1994. The Effects of Vitamin E and Beta-Carotene on the Incidence of Lung Cancer and Other Cancers in Male Smokers. *New England Journal of Medicine* 330: 1029–1035.

28. National Institutes of Health. Vitamin A; World Health Organization. 2009. Global Prevalence of Vitamin A Deficiency in Populations at Risk 1995–2005. WHO Global Database on Vitamin A Deficiency, Geneva. Available at www.who.int. Accessed May 2015.

29. National Institutes of Health. 2013. Vitamin E. Available at http://ods .od.nih.gov. Accessed May 2015.

30. Ibid.

31. Ibid.

32. Ibid.

33. U.S. Department of Agriculture. 2014. Nutrient Intakes from Food: Mean Amounts Consumed per Individual, by Gender and Age, What We Eat in America, NHANES 2011–2012. Available at www.ars.usda .gov. Accessed May 2015.

34. National Institutes of Health. Vitamin E.; Miller, E. R., R. Pastor-Barriso, D. Dalal, R. A. Riemersma, L. J. Appel, and E. Guallar. 2005. Meta-Analysis: High-Dosage Vitamin E Supplementation May Increase All-Cause Mortality. *Annals of Internal Medicine* 142: 37–46.

35. National Institutes of Health. 2013. Vitamin K. Available at: http://ods .od.nih.gov/factsheets/VitaminK-HealthProfessional/#en34. Accessed May 2015; Shea, M., and S. Booth. 2008. Update on the Role of Vitamin K in Skeletal Health. *Nutrition Reviews* 66: 549–557; Feskanich, D., P. Weber, W. C. Willet, H. Rockett, S. L. Booth, and G. A. Colditz. 1999. Vitamin K Intake and Hip Fractures in Women: A Prospective Study. *American Journal of Clinical Nutrition* 69: 74–79.

36. Institute of Medicine. *Dietary Reference Intakes: Vitamin A.*

37. National Institutes of Health. 2012. Important Information to Know When You Are Taking Warfarin (Coumadin) and Vitamin K. Available at www.cc.nih.gov. Accessed May 2015.

38. National Institutes of Health. Vitamin K; Institute of Medicine. *Dietary Reference Intakes: Vitamin A.*

39. Institute of Medicine. 2011. *Dietary Reference Intakes for Calcium and Vitamin D.* Washington, D.C.: The National Academies Press.

40. National Institutes of Health. 2014. Vitamin D. Available at http://ods .od.nih.gov. Accessed May 2015; Toner, C., C. Davis, and J. Milner. 2010. The Vitamin D and Cancer Conundrum: Aiming at a Moving Target. *Journal of the American Dietetic Association* 110: 1492–1500.

41. National Institutes of Health. Vitamin D.

42. Ibid.

43. Manson, J., and S. Bassuk. 2015. Vitamin D Research and Clinical Practice. *Journal of the American Medical Association* 313: 1311–1312; Ross, A., C. Taylor, A. Yaktine, and H. Del Valle. 2010. *Dietary Reference Intakes for Calcium and Vitamin D.* Committee to Review Dietary Reference Intakes for Vitamin D and Calcium. Available at www.ncbi.nlm.nih.gov. Accessed May 2015.

44. National Institutes of Health. Vitamin D; Institute of Medicine. *Dietary Reference Intakes for Calcium and Vitamin D.*

45. Ibid.

46. U.S. Department of Agriculture, Agricultural Research Service. Nutrient Intakes from Food: Mean Amounts Consumed per Individual, by Gender and Age.

47. National Institutes of Health. Vitamin D; Institute of Medicine. *Dietary Reference Intakes for Calcium and Vitamin D.*

48. Ibid.

49. Wagner, C., and F. Greer. 2008. Prevention of Rickets and Vitamin D Deficiency in Infants, Children, and Adolescents. *Pediatrics* 122: 11421152.

50. Voorman, T., E. van den Hooven, A. Heijboer, A. Hofman, V. Jaddoe, and O. Franco. 2015. Vitamin D Deficiency in School-Age Children Is Associated with Sociodemographic and Lifestyle Factors. *Journal of Nutrition* 145: 791–798.

51. Centers for Disease Control and Prevention. 2015. How Can I Protect my Children from the Sun? Available at www.cdc.gov. Accessed May 2015.

52. American Cancer Society. 2015. How Do I Protect Myself from UV Rays? Available at www.cancer.org. Accessed May 2015.

53. American Academy of Pediatrics. 2011. Policy Statement—Ultraviolet Radiation: A Hazard to Children and Adolescents. DOI:10.1542/peds .2010-3501.

54. Institute of Medicine. *Dietary Reference Intakes for Calcium and Vitamin D.*

55. Rosenfeld, L. 1997. Vitamine-Vitamin. The Early Years of Discovery. *Clinical Chemistry* 43: 680–685.

56. U.S. Department of Agriculture, Agricultural Research Service. Nutrient Intakes from Food: Mean Amounts Consumed per Individual, by Gender and Age.

57. U.S. National Library of Medicine, National Institutes of Health. 2014. Beriberi. Medline Plus. Available at www.nlm.nih.gov. Accessed May 2015.

58. U.S. National Library of Medicine, National National Institutes of Health. 2014. Wernicke-Korsakoff Syndrome. Available at www.nlm .nih.gov. Accessed May 2015.

59. Herreid, E. O., B. Ruskin, G. L. Clark, and T. B. Parks. 1952. Ascorbic Acid and Riboflavin Destruction and Flavor Development in Milk Exposed to the Sun in Amber, Clear, Paper, and Ruby Bottles. *Journal of Dairy Science* 35: 772–778.

60. U.S. Department of Agriculture, Agricultural Research Service. Nutrient Intakes from Food: Mean Amounts Consumed per Individual, by Gender and Age.

61. Ibid.

62. Cervantes-Laurean, D., G. McElvaney, and J. Moss. 1999. Niacin. In M. E. Shils, J. Olson, M. Shike, and A. C. Ross, eds., *Modern Nutrition in Health and Disease.* 9th ed. Baltimore: Williams and Wilkins.

63. Institute of Medicine, Food and Nutrition Board. 1998. *Dietary Reference Intakes: Thiamin, Riboflavin, Niacin, Vitamin B_6, Folate, Vitamin B_{12} Pantothenic Acid, Biotin, and Choline.* Washington, D.C.: The National Academies Press.

64. Ibid.

65. Ibid.

66. National Institutes of Health. 2011. Vitamin B_6. Available at http://ods .od.nih.gov. Accessed May 2015.

67. Ibid.

68. National Institutes of Health. 2012. Folate. Available at http://ods. od.nih.gov. Accessed May 2015; Institute of Medicine. *Dietary Reference Intakes: Thiamin.*

69. Centers for Disease Control and Prevention. 2015. Folic Acid. Available at www.cdc.gov. Accessed May 2015.

70. National Institutes of Health. Folate.

71. Ibid.

72. Institute of Medicine. *Dietary Reference Intakes: Thiamin.*

73. National Institutes of Health. Folate.

74. Ibid.

75. National Institutes of Health. Folate; Ebbing, M., K. Bonaa, O. Nygard, E. Arnesen, P. Ueland, J. Nordrehaug, et al. 2009. Cancer Incidence and Mortality After Treatment with Folic Acid and Vitamin B_{12}. *Journal of the American Medical Association* 302: 2119–2126; Cole, B., et al. 2007. Folic Acid for the Prevention of Colorectal Adenomas. A Randomized Clinical Trial. *Journal of the American Medical Association* 297: 2351–2359.

76. Institute of Medicine. *Dietary Reference Intakes: Thiamin.*

77. Ibid.; National Institutes of Health. 2011. Vitamin B_{12}. Available at http://ods.od.nih.gov. Accessed May 2015.

78. National Institutes of Health. Vitamin B_{12}.

79. Institute of Medicine. *Dietary Reference Intakes: Thiamin;* National Institutes of Health. Vitamin B_{12}.

80. Institute of Medicine. *Dietary Reference Intakes: Vitamin C.*

81. National Institutes of Health. 2013. Vitamin C. Available at http://ods .od.nih.gov. Accessed May 2015; Iqbal, K., A. Khan, and M. Khattak. 2004. Biological Significance of Ascorbic Acid (Vitamin C) in Human Health. *Pakistan Journal of Nutrition* 3: 5–13.

82. Ibid.

83. National Institutes of Health. Vitamin C; Institute of Medicine. *Dietary Reference Intakes: Vitamin C.*

84. National Institutes of Health. Vitamin C; Rosenfeld. Vitamine-Vitamin.

85. Zempleni, J., S. Wijeratne, and Y. Hassan. 2009. Biotin. *Biofactors* 35: 36–46; Institute of Medicine. *Dietary Reference Intakes: Thiamin.*

86. Glusman, M. 1947. The Syndrome of "Burning Feet" (Nutritional Melagia) as a Manifestation of Nutritional Deficiency. *American Journal of Medicine* 3: 211–223.

87. Sweetmna, L. 2000. Pantothenic Acid and Biotin. In M. H. Stipanuk, ed., *Biochemical and Physiological Aspects of Human Nutrition.* Philadelphia: Saunders.

88. Mock, D. M. 1999. Biotin. In M. E. Shils, J. Olson, M. Shike, and A. C. Ross, eds., *Modern Nutrition in Health and Disease.* 9th ed. Baltimore: Williams and Wilkins.

89. Zeisel, S., and K. da Costa. 2009. Choline: An Essential Nutrient for Public Health. *Nutrition Reviews* 67: 615–623; Institute of Medicine. 1998. *Dietary Reference Intakes for Thiamin, Riboflavin, Niacin, Vitamin B₆, Folate, Vitamin B₁₂, Pantothenic Acid, Biotin, and Choline.* Washington, D.C.: The National Academies Press.

90. National Institutes of Health. 2013. Carnitine. Available at http://ods .od.nih.gov. Accessed May 2015.

91. Koh, E., W. Lee, S. Lee, E. Kim, E. Cho, E. Jeong, D. Kim, et al. 2011. Effects of Alpha-Lipoic Acid on Body Weight in Obese Subjects. *American Journal of Medicine* 124: 85.e1–85.e8.

92. U.S. Department of Agriculture. 2015. 2015 Scientific Report of the Dietary Guidelines Advisory Committee. Available at www.health.gov/ dietaryguidelines/2015-scientific-report. Accessed May 2015.

93. Office of Dietary Supplements. National Institutes of Health. 2013. Dietary Supplement Fact Sheet: Multivitamin/Mineral Supplements. Available at http://ods.od.nih.gov. Accessed May 2015.

94. Mintel International Group Limited. 2014. Vitamin and Supplement US–December 2014. Available at http://store.mintel.com. Accessed May 2015.

95. Marra, M., and A. Boyar. 2009. Position of the American Dietetic Association: Nutrient Supplementation. *Journal of the American Dietetic Association* 109: 2073–2085.

96. National Institutes of Health. 2011. Dietary Supplements. Available at http://ods.od.nih.gov. Accessed May 2015.

97. United States Pharmacopoeia. USP's Dietary Supplement Verification Program. Available at: http://www.usp.org/usp-verification-services/ usp-verified-dietary-supplements Accessed May 2015.

Feature Box References

1. U.S. National Library of Medicine, National Institutes of Health. 2013. Common Cold. Available at www.nlm.nih.gov. Accessed May 2015.

2. National Institute of Allergy and Infectious Diseases. 2011. Common Cold. Available at www.niaid.nih.gov. Accessed May 2015.

3. Hemila, H., and E. Chalker. 2013. Vitamin C for Preventing and Treating the Common Cold. The Cochrane Library. Available at www .thecochranelibrary.com. Accessed May 2015.

4. Ibid.

5. Karsch-Völk M, B. Barrett, D. Kiefer, R, Bauer, K. Ardjomand-Woelkart, and K. Linde. 2014. *Echinacea* for Preventing and Treating the Common Cold. Available at www.cochrane.org. Accessed May 2015.

6. Ranjan, R., and M. Singh. 2014. Oral Zinc for the Common Cold. *Journal of the American Medical Association* 311: 1440–1441.

Two Points of View References

1. Langan, R. C., and K. Zawistoski. 2011. Update on Vitamin B₁₂ Deficiency. *American Family Physician.* Available at www.aafp.org/ afp/2011/0615/p1425.html. Accessed July 2015.

2. Ibid.

3. National Institutes of Health, U.S. National Library of Medicine. 2013. Medline Plus. Vitamin B₁₂. Available at www.nlm.nih.gov/medlineplus/ ency/article/002403.htm. Accessed July 2015.

4. Centers for Disease Control and Prevention. 2009. Vitamin B₁₂ Deficiency. Screening Patients. Available at www.cdc.gov/ncbddd/b12/ screening.html. Accessed July 2015.

5. WebMD. 2005–2015. Vitamin B₁₂ Deficiency Anemia. Available at www.webmd.com/a-to-z-guides/vitamin-b12-deficiency-anemia-topic- overview. Accessed June 2015.

6. WebMD. Ask the Nutritionist. 2005–2015. Available at www.webmd .com/vitamins-and-supplements/nutrition-vitamins-11/help-vitamin- supplement. Accessed July 2015.

7. Mayo Clinic. 1998–2015. Nutrition and Healthy Eating. Available at www.mayoclinic.org/healthy-lifestyle/nutrition-and-healthy-eating/ in-depth/supplements/art-20044894. Accessed July 2015.

8. Mayo Clinic. 2013. Drugs and Supplements. Vitamin B₁₂. Available at www.mayoclinic.org/drugs-supplements/vitamin-b12/safety/ hrb-20060243. Accessed July 2015.

9. Centers for Disease Control and Prevention. 2009. Vitamin B₁₂ Deficiency. Risk Factors for Vitamin B₁₂ Deficiency. Available at www.cdc .gov/ncbddd/b12/risks.html. Accessed July 2015.

10. National Institutes of Health. 2011. Office of Dietary Supplements. Vitamin B₁₂ Fact Sheet for Consumers. Available at www.ods.od.nih.gov/ factsheets/VitaminB12-Consumer/#h8. Accessed June 2015.

Chapter 8

1. Marieb, E., and K. Hoehn. 2013. *Human Anatomy and Physiology.* 9th ed. San Francisco: Pearson Education, Inc.

2. Ibid.

3. Institute of Medicine. 2004. *Dietary Reference Intakes: Water, Potassium, Sodium, Chloride, and Sulfate.* Washington, D.C.: The National Academies Press. Available at www.nap.edu. July 2015.

4. Ibid.; Marieb. *Human Anatomy and Physiology.*

5. Marieb. *Human Anatomy and Physiology.*

6. Ibid.

7. Institute of Medicine. *Dietary Reference Intakes: Water, Potassium, Sodium, Chloride, and Sulfate.*

8. Ibid.

9. Casa, D. J., L. E. Armstrong, S. K. Hillman, S. J. Montain, R. C. Reiff, B. S. E. Rich, W. O. Roberts, and J. A. Stone. 2000. National Athletic Trainers Association Position Statement: Fluid Replacement for Athletes. *Journal of Athletic Training* 35: 212–224. Accessed May 2015.

10. Institute of Medicine. *Dietary Reference Intakes: Water, Potassium, Sodium, Chloride, and Sulfate.*

11. Arnold, D. 2002. To the End, Marathon Was at Center of Student's Life. *The Boston Globe.* April 18, 2002; Aucoin, D. 2002. Tribute to a Fallen Champion of the Needs of the Afflicted. *The Boston Globe.* October 26, 2002; Noakes, T. D. 2003. Overconsumption of Fluids by Athletes. *British Medical Journal* 327: 113–114; Zeller, T. 2007. Too High a Price for a Wii. *The New York Times.* Available at www.nytimes.com. Accessed May 2015; Smith, S. 2002. Marathon Runner's Death Linked to Excessive Fluid Intake. *The Boston Globe.* August 13, 2002.

12. Marieb. *Human Anatomy and Physiology.*

13. Institute of Medicine. *Dietary Reference Intakes: Water, Potassium, Sodium, Chloride, and Sulfate.*

14. Ibid.

15. Ibid.

16. Ibid.

17. Gallagher, M. 2012. The Nutrients and Their Metabolism. In *Krause's Food, Nutrition and Diet Therapy.* 13th ed. St. Louis: Saunders Elsevier.

18. Ibid.; Institute of Medicine. 2001*Dietary Reference Intakes: Vitamin A, Molybdenum, Nickel, Silicon, Vanadium, and Zinc.* Washington, D.C.: The National Academies Press. Available at www.nap.edu. Accessed August 2015.

19. Institute of Medicine. *Dietary Reference Intakes: Vitamin A, Molybdenum, Nickel, Silicon, Vanadium, and Zinc.*

20. Institute of Medicine. *Dietary Reference Intakes: Water, Potassium, Sodium, Chloride, and Sulfate.*

21. Ibid.

22. Dietary Guidelines Advisory Committee. 2010. Report of the Dietary Guidelines Advisory Committee on the *Dietary Guidelines for Americans, 2010.* Available at www.cnpp.usda.gov. Accessed May 2015.

23. Ibid.

24. Coxson, P., N. Cook, M. Joffres, Y. Hong, D. Orenstein, S. Schmidt, and K. Bibbins-Domingo. 2013. Mortality Benefits from U.S. Population-Wide Reduction in Sodium Consumption. *Hypertension* 61: 564–570.

25. National Heart, Lung, and Blood Institute. 2012. What Is High Blood Pressure? Available at www.nhlbi.nih.gov. Accessed May 2015.

26. U.S. Department of Health and Human Services. 2015. Physical Activity Guidelines. Available at www.health.gov/paguidelines. Accessed May 2015; Wharton, S. P., A. Chin, X. Xin, and J. He. 2002. Effect of Aerobic Exercise on Blood Pressure: A Meta-Analysis of Randomized Controlled Trials. *Annals of Internal Medicine* 136: 493–503.

27. Xin, X., J. He, M. G. Frontini, L. G. Ogden, O. I. Motsamai, and P. K. Whelton. 2001. Effects of Alcohol Reduction on Blood Pressure: A Meta-Analysis of Randomized Controlled Trials. *Hypertension* 38: 1112–1117.

28. National Heart, Lung, and Blood Institute. 2014. What Is the DASH Eating Plan? Available at www.nhlbi.nih.gov. Accessed May 2015; Harsha, D. W., P. Lin, E. Obarzanek, N. M. Karanja, T. J. Moore, and B. Caballero. 1999. Dietary Approaches to Stop Hypertension: A Summary of Study Results. *Journal of the American Dietetics Association* 99: S35–S39.

29. National Heart, Lung, and Blood Institute. What Is the DASH Eating Plan?

30. U.S. Department of Agriculture, U.S. Department of Health and Human Services. 2015. Scientific report of the 2015 Dietary Guidelines for Americans Advisory Committee. Available at www.health.gov/ dietaryguidelines/2015-scientific-report. Accessed May 2015.

31. Mitchell, A., J. Cole, P. McArdle, Y. Cheng, K. Ryan, M. Sparks, B. Mitchell, and S. Kittner. 2015. Obesity Increases Risk of Ischemic Stroke in Young Adults. *Stroke* DOI:10.1161/StrokeAHA.115.008940.

32. American Heart Association. 2011. ACCF/AHA 2011 Expert Consensus Document on Hypertension in the Elderly. *Circulation* 123: 2434–2506; Franklin, S. S., et al. 1997. Hemodynamic Patterns of Age-Related Changes in Blood Pressure. *Circulation* 96: 308–315.

33. National Heart, Lung, and Blood Institute. What Is High Blood Pressure?; National Heart, Lung, and Blood Institute. National High Blood Pressure Education Program Coordinating Committee. 2004. The Seventh Report of the Joint National Committee on Prevention, Detection, Evaluation, and Treatment of High Blood Pressure. Available at www.nhlbi.nih.gov. Accessed May 2015.

34. Tucker, K. 2014. Vegetarian Diets and Bone Status. *American Journal of Clinical Nutrition* 100: 329S–335S.

35. Institute of Medicine. *Dietary Reference Intakes: Water, Potassium, Sodium, Chloride, and Sulfate.*

36. U.S. Department of Agriculture. Agricultural Research Service. 2014. Nutrient Intakes from Food: Mean Amounts Consumed per Individual, by Gender and Age, What We Eat in America, NHANES 2011–2012. Available at www.ars.usda.gov. Accessed May 2015.

37. Lehnhardt, A., and M. Kemper. 2011. Pathogenesis, Diagnosis and Management of Hyperkalemia. *Pediatric Nephrology* 26: 377–384.

38. U.S. National Library of Medicine and National Institutes of Health. 2013. Low Potassium Levels. Available at www.nlm.nih.gov. Accessed May 2015.

39. Zhu, K., and R. Prince. 2014. Lifestyle and Osteoporosis. *Current Osteoporosis Reports* 13: 52–59; Dietary Guidelines Advisory Committee. Report of the Dietary Guidelines Advisory Committee on the *Dietary Guidelines for Americans, 2010.*

40. Institute of Medicine. 2011. *Dietary Reference Intakes for Calcium and Vitamin D.* Washington, D.C.: The National Academies Press. Available at www.nap.edu. Accessed July 2015

41. Institute of Medicine. *Dietary Reference Intakes for Calcium and Vitamin D*; Office of Dietary Supplements. 2013. Dietary Supplement Fact Sheet: Calcium. Available at http://ods.od.nih.gov. Accessed May 2015; Institute of Medicine. 1997. *Dietary Reference Intakes for Calcium, Phosphorus, Magnesium, Vitamin D, and Fluoride.* Washington, D.C.: The National Academies Press. Available at www.nap.edu. Accessed July 2015.

42. Office of Dietary Supplements. Dietary Supplement Fact Sheet: Calcium.

43. Ibid.; Institute of Medicine. *Dietary Reference Intakes for Calcium and Vitamin D*; Miller, G. D., G. D. DiRienzo, M. E. Reusser, and D. A. McCarron. 2000. Benefits of Dairy Product Consumption on Blood Pressure in Humans: A Summary of the Biomedical Literature. *Journal of the American College of Nutrition* 19: 147S–164S.

44. Office of Dietary Supplements. Dietary Supplement Fact Sheet: Calcium; Baron, J. A., M. Beach, J. S. Mandel, R. U. van Stolk, R. W. Haile, R. S. Sandler, et al. 1999. Calcium Supplements for the Prevention of Colorectal Adenomas. *New England Journal of Medicine* 340: 101–107; Wu, K., W. C. Willet, C. S. Fuchs, G. A. Colditz, and E. L. Giovannucci. 2002. Calcium Intake and Risk of Colon Cancer in Women and Men. *Journal of the National Cancer Institute* 94: 437–446.

45. National Kidney and Urologic Diseases Information Clearinghouse. 2013. Kidney Stones in Adults. Available at http://kidney.niddk.nih.gov. Accessed May 2015.

46. Office of Dietary Supplements. Dietary Supplement Fact Sheet: Calcium; Borghi, L., R. Schianchi, T. Meschi, A. Guerra, U. Maggiore, and A. Novarini. 2002. Comparison of Two Diets for the Prevention of Recurrent Stones in Idiopathic Hypercalciuria. *New England Journal of Medicine* 346: 77–84; Bushinsky, D. A. 2002. Recurrent Hypercalciuric Nephrolithiasis: Does Diet Help? *New England Journal of Medicine* 346: 124–125; Curhan, G. C., W. C. Willett, E. B. Rimm, and M. J. Stampfer. 1993. A Prospective Study of Dietary Calcium and Other Nutrients and the Risk of Symptomatic Kidney Stones. *New England Journal of Medicine* 328: 833–838.

47. Office of Dietary Supplements. Dietary Supplement Fact Sheet: Calcium.

48. Institute of Medicine. *Dietary Reference Intakes for Calcium and Vitamin D*; Office of Dietary Supplements. Dietary Supplement Fact Sheet: Calcium.

49. Ibid.

50. Ibid.

51. USDA. Agricultural Research Service. Nutrient Intakes from Food.

52. USDA. Economic Research Service. 2014. Trends in U.S. per Capita Consumption of Dairy Products, 1970–2012. Available at www.ers.usda.gov/amber-waves/2014-june/trends-in-us-per-capita-consumption-of-dairy-products,-1970-2012.aspx#. Accessed June 2015.

53. National Osteoporosis Foundation. Osteoporosis and Your Spine. Available at http://nof.org/articles/18. Accessed May 2015; Patlak, M. 2001. Bone Builders: The Discoveries behind Preventing and Treating Osteoporosis. *The FASEB Journal* 15: 1677.

54. U.S. Department of Health and Human Services. Office of the Surgeon General. 2012. The Surgeon General's Report on Bone Health and Osteoporosis. Available at www.niams.nih.gov. Accessed May 2015; National Institutes of Health. 2012. Osteoporosis Overview. Available at www.niams.nih.gov/Health_Info/Bone/Osteoporosis/overview.pdf. Accessed June 2015; U.S. Department of Health and Human Services. 2004. *Bone Health and Osteoporosis: A Report of the Surgeon General.* Washington, D.C.: U.S. Department of Health and Human Services, Office of the Surgeon General.

55. Office of the Surgeon General. The Surgeon General's Report on Bone Health and Osteoporosis; U.S. Department of Health and Human Services. *Bone Health and Osteoporosis: A Report of the Surgeon General.*

56. Office of Dietary Supplements. Dietary Supplement Fact Sheet: Calcium.

57. Institute of Medicine. *Dietary Reference Intakes for Calcium and Vitamin D*; Office of Dietary Supplements. Dietary Supplement Fact Sheet: Calcium.

58. Ibid.

59. Office of Dietary Supplements. Dietary Supplement Fact Sheet: Calcium. National Institutes of Health. 2012. Osteoporosis Overview; U.S. Department of Health and Human Services. 2004. *Bone Health and Osteoporosis: Osteoporosis in Postmenopausal Women: Diagnosis and Monitoring Evidence.* Report/Technology Assessment No. 28. Agency for Healthcare Research and Quality, 2001. Publication No. 01-E032.

60. Lewiecki, E. 2011. In the Clinic. Osteoporosis. *Annals of Internal Medicine* 155: ITC1–ITC16; U.S. Department of Health and Human Services. *Bone Health and Osteoporosis: Osteoporosis in Postmenopausal Women*; U.S. Department of Health and Human Services. *Bone Health and Osteoporosis: A Report of the Surgeon General.*

61. Miller, K. K. 2003. Mechanisms by Which Nutritional Disorders Cause Reduced Bone Mass in Adults. *Journal of Women's Health* 12: 145–150; U.S. Department of Health and Human Services. *Bone Health and Osteoporosis: Osteoporosis in Postmenopausal Women*; U.S. Department of Health and Human Services. *Bone Health and Osteoporosis: A Report of the Surgeon General.*

62. U.S. Department of Health and Human Services. 2012. The Surgeon General's Report on Bone Health and Osteoporosis:.; U.S. Department of Health and Human Services. *Bone Health and Osteoporosis: A Report of the Surgeon General.*

63. Ibid.

64. Ibid.

65. USDA. Agricultural Research Service. Nutrient Intakes from Food.

66. Institute of Medicine. *Dietary Reference Intakes for Calcium, Phosphorus, Magnesium, Vitamin D, and Fluoride.*

67. Office of Dietary Supplements. 2013. Magnesium. Available at http://ods.od.nih.gov. Accessed June 2015.

68. Ibid.; Appel, L. J., T. J. Moore, E. Obarzanek, W. M. Vollmer, L. P. Svetkey, F. M. Sacks, et al. 1997. A Clinical Trial of the Effects of Dietary Patterns on Blood Pressure. *New England Journal of Medicine* 336: 1117–1124.

69. Office of Dietary Supplements. Magnesium; Harsha. Dietary Approaches to Stop Hypertension: A Summary of Study Results.

70. Office of Dietary Supplements. Magnesium.

71. USDA. Agricultural Research Service. Nutrient Intakes from Food.

72. Institute of Medicine. *Dietary Reference Intakes for Calcium, Phosphorus, Magnesium, Vitamin D, and Fluoride.*

73. Institute of Medicine. *Dietary Reference Intakes: Water.*

74. Mahan, L., S. Escott-Stump, and J. Raymond. 2012. *Krause's Food and the Nutrition Care Process.* 13th ed. St. Louis: Saunders Elsevier.

75. Institute of Medicine. 2001. *Dietary Reference Intakes for Vitamin A, Vitamin K, Arsenic, Boron, Chromium, Copper, Iodine, Iron, Manganese, Molybdenum, Nickel, Silicon, Vanadium, and Zinc.* Washington, D.C.: The National Academies Press. Available at www.nap.edu. Accessed July 2015.

76. Ibid.

77. Office of Dietary Supplements. 2015. Iron. Available at http://ods.od.nih.gov. Accessed June 2015; Beard, J. 2003. Iron Deficiency Alters Brain Development and Functioning. *Journal of Nutrition* 133: 1468S–1472S; Black, M. M. 2003. Micronutrient Deficiencies and Cognitive Function. *Journal of Nutrition* 133: 3972S–3931S.

78. USDA. Agricultural Research Service. Nutrient Intakes from Food.

79. Ibid.

80. Institute of Medicine. *Dietary Reference Intakes for Calcium, Phosphorus, Magnesium, Vitamin D, and Fluoride.*

81. USDA. Agricultural Research Service. Nutrient Intakes from Food.
82. Office of Dietary Supplements. Iron.
83. Institute of Medicine. 2001. *Dietary Reference Intakes for Vitamin A, Vitamin K, Arsenic, Boron, Chromium, Copper, Iodine, Iron, Manganese, Molybdenum, Nickel, Silicon, Vanadium, and Zinc.*
84. Office of Dietary Supplements. Iron.
85. Institute of Medicine. *Dietary Reference Intakes for Vitamin A, Vitamin K, Arsenic, Boron, Chromium, Copper, Iodine, Iron, Manganese, Molybdenum, Nickel, Silicon, Vanadium, and Zinc;* Turnlund, J. R. 2006. Copper. In Shils, M. E., M. Shike, A. C. Ross, B. Caballero, and R. J. Cousins, eds. *Modern Nutrition in Health and Disease.* 10th ed. Philadelphia: Lippincott Williams & Wilkins; Uaruy, R., M. Olivares, and M. Gonzalez. 1998. Essentiality of Copper in Humans. *American Journal of Clinical Nutrition* 67: 952S–959S.
86. Office of Dietary Supplements. 2013. Zinc. Available at http://ods.od.nih.gov. Accessed June 2015; Institute of Medicine. *Dietary Reference Intakes for Vitamin A, Vitamin K, Arsenic, Boron, Chromium, Copper, Iodine, Iron, Manganese, Molybdenum, Nickel, Silicon, Vanadium, and Zinc;* Ranjan, R., and M. Singh. 2014. Oral Zinc for the Common Cold. *Journal of the American Medical Association* 311:1440–1441.
87. Office of Dietary Supplements. Zinc; Ibs, K., and L. Rink. 2003. Zinc-Altered Immune Function. *Journal of Nutrition* 133: 1452S–1456S; Schwartz, J. R., R. G. Marsh, and Z. D. Draelos. 2005. Zinc and Skin Health: Overview of Physiology and Pharmacology. *Dermatological Surgery* 31: 837–847; Walravens, P. A. 1979. Zinc Metabolism and Its Implications in Clinical Medicine. *Western Journal of Medicine* 130: 133–142.
88. Russell, R. M., M. E. Cox, and N. Solomons. 1983. Zinc and the Special Senses. *Annals of Internal Medicine* 99: 227–239.
89. Ranjan R. Oral Zinc for the Common Cold; Office of Dietary Supplements. Zinc.
90. Ibid.
91. Office of Dietary Supplements. Zinc.
92. Ibid.
93. Prasad, A. 2003. Zinc Deficiency. *British Medical Journal* 326: 409–410.
94. Office of Dietary Supplements. 2013. Selenium. Available at http://ods.od.nih.gov. Accessed June 2015; Institute of Medicine. 2000. *Dietary Reference Intakes for Vitamin C, Vitamin E, Selenium, and Carotenoids.* Washington, D.C.: The National Academies Press. Available at www.nap.edu. Accessed July 2015
95. Office of Dietary Supplements. Selenium; Beck, M. A., O. A. Levander, and O. Handy. 2003. Selenium Deficiency and Viral Infection. *Journal of Nutrition* 133: 1463S–1467S; Li, H., M. J. Stampfer, E. L. Giovannucci, J. S. Morris, W. C. Willett, M. Gaziano, and J. Ma. 2004. A Prospective Study of Plasma Selenium Levels and Prostate Cancer Risk. *Journal of the National Cancer Institute* 96: 696–703; Center for Food Safety and Applied Nutrition. 2013. Qualified Health Claims Subject to Enforcement Discretion. Available at www.fda.gov. Accessed June 2015; Wei, W., C. C. Abnet, Y. Qiao, S. M. Dawsey, Z. Dong, X. Sun, et al. 2004. Prospective Study of Serum Selenium Concentrations and Esophageal and Gastric Cardia Cancer, Heart Disease, Stroke, and Total Death. *American Journal of Nutrition* 79: 80–85.
96. Office of Dietary Supplements. Selenium.
97. Palmer, C., and J. Gilbert. 2012. Position of the Academy of Nutrition and Dietetics: The Impact of Fluoride on Health. *Journal of the Academy of Nutrition and Dietetics* 112:1443–1453.
98. Centers for Disease Control and Prevention. 1999. Achievements in Public Health, 1900–1999: Fluoridation of Drinking Water to Prevent Dental Caries. *Morbidity and Mortality Weekly Report* 48: 933–940. Available at www.cdc.gov. Accessed June 2015.
99. Palmer. Position of the Academy of Nutrition and Dietetics: The Impact of Fluoride on Health.
100. Institute of Medicine. *Dietary Reference Intakes for Calcium, Phosphorus, Magnesium, Vitamin D, and Fluoride.*
101. Office of Dietary Supplements. 2013. Chromium. Available at http://ods.od.nih.gov. Accessed June 2015; Hopkins, L. L., O. Ransome-Kuti, and A. S. Majaj. 1968. Improvement of Impaired Carbohydrate Metabolism by Chromium (III) in Malnourished Infants. *American Journal of Clinical Nutrition* 21: 203–211; Jeejeebhoy, K. N., R. C. Clu, E. B. Marliss, G. R. Greenberg, and A. Bruce-Robertson. 1977. Chromium Deficiency, Glucose Intolerance, and Neuropathy Reversed by Chromium Supplementation in a Patient Receiving Long-Term Total Parenteral Nutrition. *American Journal of Clinical Nutrition* 30: 531–538; Mertz, W. 1998. Interaction of Chromium with Insulin: A Progress Report. *Nutrition Reviews* 56: 174–177.
102. Office of Dietary Supplements. Chromium; Cefalu, W. T., and F. B. Hu. 2004. Role of Chromium in Human Health and in Diabetes. *Diabetes Care* 27: 2741–2751.
103. Food and Drug Administration. 2014. Summary of Qualified Health Claims Subject to the Enforcement Discretion. Available at www.fda.gov. Accessed June 2015.
104. Office of Dietary Supplements. Chromium.
105. Ibid.
106. Ibid.
107. Office of Dietary Supplements. 2011. Iodine. Available at https://ods.od.nih.gov/factsheets/Iodine-HealthProfessional/. Accessed June 2015; Institute of Medicine. *Dietary Reference Intakes for Vitamin A, Vitamin K, Arsenic, Boron, Chromium, Copper, Iodine, Iron, Manganese, Molybdenum, Nickel, Silicon, Vanadium, and Zinc.*
108. Ibid.
109. Institute of Medicine. *Dietary Reference Intakes for Vitamin A, Vitamin K, Arsenic, Boron, Chromium, Copper, Iodine, Iron, Manganese, Molybdenum, Nickel, Silicon, Vanadium, and Zinc.*
110. Ibid.; Barceloux, D. G. 1999. Manganese. *Clinical Toxicology* 37: 293–307.
111. Institute of Medicine. *Dietary Reference Intakes for Vitamin A, Vitamin K, Arsenic, Boron, Chromium, Copper, Iodine, Iron, Manganese, Molybdenum, Nickel, Silicon, Vanadium, and Zinc.*

Feature Box References

1. U.S. Environmental Protection Agency. 2009. Water on Tap. Available at http://water.epa.gov. Accessed May 2015.
2. Ibid.; U.S. Environmental Protection Agency. 2012. Current Drinking Water Regulations. Available at http://water.epa.gov/lawsregs/rulesregs/sdwa/currentregulations.cfm. Accessed May 2015.
3. Centers for Disease Control and Prevention. 2013. Community Water Fluoridation: Statistics 2012. Available at www.cdc.gov. Accessed May 2015.
4. Food and Drug Administration. 2009. Regulation of Bottled Water. Available at www.fda.gov/NewsEvents/Testimony/ucm170932.htm. Accessed May 2015.
5. Saylor, A., L. Prokopy, and S. Amberg. 2011. What's Wrong with the Tap? Examining Perceptions of Tap Water and Bottled Water at Purdue University. *Environmental Management* 48: 588–601.

Two Points of View References

1. Fitbie. 2015. 10 Fancy Waters You Shouldn't Drink. Available at www.fitbie.com/slideshow/10-fancy-waters-you-shouldnt-drink. Accessed July 2015.
2. Statista. 2015. Sales of the Leading 10 Bottled Still Water Brands of the United States in 2015 (in billion U.S. dollars). Available at www.statista.com/statistics/188312/top-bottled-still-water-brands-in-the-united-states. Accessed June 2015.
3. How Stuff Works. 2015. How Vitamin Water Works. Available at www.science.howstuffworks.com/innovation/edible-innovations/vitaminwater2.htm. Accessed July 2015.
4. WebMD. 2014. Heat Exhaustion. Available at www.webmd.com/fitness-exercise/heat-exhaustion?page=3. Accessed July 2015.
5. Wanjek, C. 2007. The Truth about 'Healthy' Bottled Water. Available at www.livescience.com/4470-truth-healthy-bottled-water.html. Accessed June 2015.
6. Mayo Clinic. 2015. Dehydration. Available at www.mayoclinic.org/diseases-conditions/dehydration/basics/definition/con-20030056. Accessed July 2015.
7. Dachner, N., et al. 2015. An Examination of the Nutrient Content and On-Package Marketing of Novel Beverages. *Applied Physiology, Nutrition, and Metabolism.* Available at www.nrcresearchpress.com/doi/abs/10.1139/apnm-2014-0252#.VW2hbGAmfQc. Accessed July 2015.
8. Nestle, M. 2014. Food Politics. Available at www.foodpolitics.com/2014/07/coconut-water. Accessed July 2015.
9. U.S. Department of Health and Human Services.2010. Dietary Guidelines for Americans. Available at www.cnpp.usda.gov/sites/default/files/dietary_guidelines_for_americans/PolicyDoc.pdf. Accessed July 2015.
10. Zelman, K. 2015. What Vitamin and Mineral Supplements Can and Can't Do. Available at www.webmd.com/vitamins-and-supplements/nutrition-vitamins-11/help-vitamin-supplement. Accessed July 2015.
11. CDC. 2012. Nutrition for Everyone. Available at www.cdc.gov/nutrition/everyone/basics/water.html. Accessed July 2015.

Chapter 9

1. Distilled Spirits Councils in the United States. 2007. Distilled Spirits Industry Primer. Available at www.discus.org. Accessed June 2015.
2. Centers for Disease Control and Prevention. 2012. Alcohol and Public Health: Data, Trends and Map. Available at www.cdc.gov. Accessed June 2015.
3. National Institute on Alcohol Abuse and Alcoholism. Alcohol and Your Health. Available at www.niaaa.nih.gov/alcohol-health. Accessed June 2015.
4. Mandelbaum, D. G. 1965. Alcohol and Culture. *Current Anthropology* 6: 281–288; National Institute on Alcohol Abuse and Alcoholism. 1992. Moderate Drinking. Available at http://pubs.niaaa.nih.gov. Accessed June 2015.
5. Arranzm, S., G. Chiva-Blanch, P. Valderas-Martinez, A. Medina-Remon, R. Lamuela-Raventos, and R. Estruch. 2012. Wine, Beer, Alcohol and Polyphenols on Cardiovascular Disease and Cancer. *Nutrients* 4: 759–81. U.S. Department of Agriculture. 2010. Report of the Dietary Guidelines Advisory Committee, 2010. Available at www.cnpp.usda.gov. Accessed June 2015; Goldberg, I. J., L. Mosca, M. R. Piano, and E. A. Fisher. 2001. Wine and Your Heart. A Science Advisory for Healthcare Professionals from the Nutrition Committee, Council on Epidemiology and Prevention, and Council on Cardiovascular Nursing of the American Heart Association. *Circulation* 103: 472–475.
6. Dodd, T. H., and S. Morse. 1994. The Impact of Media Stories Concerning Health Issues on Food Product Sales. *Journal of Consumer Marketing* 11: 17–24.
7. U.S. Department of Agriculture. Report of the Dietary Guidelines Advisory Committee; Goldberg. Wine and Your Heart.
8. U.S. Department of Agriculture. Report of the Dietary Guidelines Advisory Committee.
9. National Institute on Alcohol Abuse and Alcoholism. 2000. Alcohol Alert: Alcohol Metabolism. Available at http://pubs.niaaa.nih.gov. Accessed June 2015.
10. Jones, A. W., and K. A. Jonsson. 1994. Food-Induced Lowering of Blood-Ethanol Profiles and Increased Rate of Elimination Immediately After a Meal. *Journal of Forensic Sciences* 39: 1084–1093.
11. National Institute on Alcohol Abuse and Alcoholism. Alcohol Alert: Alcohol Metabolism.
12. Ibid.
13. National Institute on Alcohol Abuse and Alcoholism. 2010. Beyond Hangovers. Available at http://pubs.niaaa.nih.gov/publications/Hangovers/beyondHangovers.htm. Accessed June 2015; National Institute on Alcohol Abuse and Alcoholism. 2004. Alcohol Alert: Alcohol and the Brain. Available at www.pubs.niaaa.nih.gov. Accessed June 2015; National Institute on Alcohol Abuse and Alcoholism. 2000. Alcohol Alert: Imaging and Alcoholism: A Window on the Brain. Available at http://pubs.niaaa.nih.gov. Accessed June 2015.
14. O'Brien, M., T. McCoy, S. Rhodes, A. Wagoner, and M. Wolfson. 2008. Caffeinated Cocktails: Energy Drink Consumption, High-Risk Drinking, and Alcohol-Related Consequences Among College Students. *Academy of Emergency Medicine* 15: 453–460.
15. Ferreira, S., T. deMello, S. Pompeia, and M. deSouza-Formigoni. 2006. Effects of Energy Drink Ingestion on Alcohol Intoxication. *Alcoholism: Clinical and Experimental Research* 30: 598–605.
16. Frezza, M., C. diPadova, G. Pozzato, M. Terpin, E. Baraona, and C. S. Lieber. 1990. High Blood Alcohol Levels in Women: The Role of Decreased Gastric Alcohol Dehydrogenase Activity and First-Pass Metabolism. *New England Journal of Medicine* 332: 95–99.
17. Brooks, P. J., M. A. Enoch, D. Goldman, T. K. Li, and A. Yokoyama. 2009. The Alcohol Flushing Response: An Unrecognized Risk Factor for Esophageal Cancer from Alcohol Consumption. *PLoS Medicine* 6: e1000050. doi:10.1371/journal.pmed.1000050; Makimoto, K. 1998. Drinking Patterns and Drinking Problems Among Asian-Americans and Pacific Islanders. *Alcohol Health & Research World* 22: 270–275.
18. Subgketibm, R., and A. Wolfson. 2009. Alcohol Consumption, Sleep, and Academic Performance Among College Students. *Journal of Studies on Alcohol and Drugs* 70: 355–363; National Institute on Alcohol Abuse and Alcoholism. 2000. Alcohol Alert: Alcohol and Sleep. Available at www.niaaa.nih.gov. Accessed June 2015.
19. National Institute on Alcohol Abuse and Alcoholism. Alcohol Alert: Alcohol and Sleep; Roehrs, T., D. Beare, F. Zorick, and T. Roth. 1994. Sleepiness and Ethanol Effects on Simulated Driving. *Alcoholism: Clinical and Experimental Research* 18: 154–158.
20. Verster, J., D. van Duin, E. Volkerts, A. Schreuder, and M. Verbaten. 2003. Alcohol Hangover Effects on Memory Functioning and Vigilance Performance after an Evening of Binge Drinking. *Neuropsychopharmacology* 28: 740–746; Swift, R. S., and D. Davidson. 1998. Alcohol Hangover, Mechanisms and Mediators. *Alcohol Health & Research World* 22: 54–60. Available at http://pubs.niaaa.nih.gov. Accessed June 2015.
21. Swift. Alcohol Hangover.
22. Food and Drug Administration. 2015. Acetaminophen and Liver Injury: Q & A for Consumers. Available at www.fda.gov. Accessed June 2015; Food and Drug Administration. 2013. Careful: Acetaminophen in Pain Relief Medicines Can Cause Liver Damage. Available at www.fda.gov. Accessed June 2015; National Institute on Alcohol Abuse and Alcoholism. Alcohol Alert: Alcohol Metabolism; Swift. Alcohol Hangover.
23. Chen, W., B. Rosner, S. Hankinson, G. Colditz, and W. Willet. 2011. Moderate Alcohol Consumption during Adult Life, Drinking Patterns, and Breast Cancer Risk. *Journal of the American Medical Association* 306: 1884–1890.
24. Muthusami, K., and P. Chinnaswamy. 2005. Effect of Chronic Alcoholism on Male Fertility Hormones and Semen Quality. *Fertility and Sterility* 84: 919–924; USDA. Report of the Dietary Guidelines Advisory Committee; National Institute on Alcohol Abuse and Alcoholism. 2004. Alcohol Alert: Alcohol—An Important Women's Health Issue. Available at http://pubs.niaaa.nih.gov. Accessed June 2015.
25. Lieber, C. S. 2000. Alcohol: Its Metabolism and Interaction with Nutrients. *Annual Review of Nutrition* 20: 394–430.
26. National Institute on Alcohol Abuse and Alcoholism. 2010. Beyond Hangovers; Jarl, J., and U. Gerdtham. 2011. Time Pattern of Reduction in Risk of Oesophageal Cancer Following Alcohol Cessation—A Meta Analysis. *Addiction* 107: 1234–1243; Pelucchi, C., S. Gallus, W. Garavello, C. Bosetti, and C. LaVecchia. 2006. Cancer Risk Associated with Alcohol and Tobacco Use: Focus on Upper Aero-Digestive Tract and Liver. *Alcohol Research & Health* 29: 193–198.
27. Bagnardi, V., M. Blangiardo, C. LaVecchia, and G. Corrao. 2001. Alcohol Consumption and the Risk of Cancer. *Alcohol Research and Health* 25: 263–270.
28. National Institute on Alcohol Abuse and Alcoholism. 2010. Beyond Hangovers; Templeton, A., K. Carter, N. Sheron, P. Gallagher, and C. Verrill. 2009. Sudden Unexpected Death in Alcohol Misuse—An Unrecognized Public Health Issue? *International Journal of Environmental Research and Public Health* 6: 3070–3081.
29. National Institute on Alcohol Abuse and Alcoholism. 2010. Beyond Hangovers; Zakhari, S. 2006. Overview: How Is Alcohol Metabolized by the Body? *Alcohol Research & Health* 29: 245–255; Lieber. Alcohol: Its Metabolism and Interaction with Nutrients.
30. Nolan, J. 2010. The Role of Intestinal Endotoxin in Liver Injury: A Long and Evolving History. *Hepatology* 52: 1829–1835; National Institute on Alcohol Abuse and Alcoholism. 2000. Alcohol and the Liver: Research Update. Available at http://pubs.niaaa.nih.gov. Accessed June 2015.
31. National Institute on Alcohol Abuse and Alcoholism. 2005. Alcohol Alert: Alcohol and the Liver. Available at http://pubs.niaaa.nih.gov. Accessed June 2015.
32. National Vital Statistics Systems. 2014. Deaths, Percent of Total Deaths and Death Rates for the 15 Leading Causes of Death: United States and Each State, 1999–2013. Available at www.cdc.gov/nchs/data/dvs/LCWK9_2013.pdf. Accessed June 2015.
33. Jones, K., and D. Smith. 1973. Recognition of the Fetal Alcohol Syndrome in Early Infancy. *The Lancet* 2: 999–1001; Bertrand, J., R. L. Floyd, and M. K. Weber. 2005. Guidelines for Identifying and Referring Persons with Fetal Alcohol Syndrome. *Morbidity and Mortality Weekly Report* 54 (RR11): 1–10. Available at www.cdc.gov. Accessed June 2015.
34. Centers for Disease Control and Prevention. 2014. Fetal Alcohol Spectrum Disorders. Available at www.cdc.gov. Accessed June 2015; Bertrand. Guidelines for Identifying and Referring Persons.
35. National Institute on Alcohol Abuse and Alcoholism. 2012. Alcohol Use Disorder. Available at www.niaaa.nih.gov/alcohol-health/overview-alcohol-consumption/alcohol-use-disorders. Accessed June 2015.
36. Centers for Disease Control and Prevention. 2014. Vital Signs. Binge Drinking. Available at www.cdc.gov. Accessed June 2015.
37. National Institute on Alcohol Abuse and Alcoholism. 2015. College Drinking. Available at http://pubs.niaaa.nih.gov. Accessed June 2015.
38. Ibid.
39. Centers for Disease Control and Prevention. Vital Signs. Binge Drinking.
40. White, A. M., D. W. Jamieson-Drake, and H. S. Swartzwelder. 2002. Prevalence and Correlates of Alcohol-Induced Blackouts Among College Students: Results of an E-Mail Survey. *Journal of American College Health* 51: 117–131.
41. National Institute on Alcohol Abuse and Alcoholism. 2015. College Drinking

42. B.R.A.D. 21 website. 2013. Available at www.brad21.org. Accessed June 2015.
43. National Institute on Alcohol Abuse and Alcoholism. 2000. Alcohol Tolerance. Available at http://pubs.niaaa.nih.gov. Accessed June 2015.
44. National Highway Traffic Safety Administration. 2013. Traffic Safety Facts 2014: Alcohol-Impaired Driving. Available at www-nrd.nhtsa.dot .gov. Accessed June 2015.
45. Centers for Disease Control and Prevention. 2011. Drinking and Driving. Available at www.cdc.gov. Accessed June 2014; Centers for Disease Control and Prevention. 2015. Impaired Driving: Get the Facts. Available at www.cdc.gov. Accessed June 2015.
46. National Institute on Alcohol Abuse and Alcoholism. 2013. Underage Drinking. Available at http://pubs.niaaa.nih.gov. Accessed June 2015.
47. Ibid.
48. Ibid.
49. National Highway Traffic Safety Administration. 2014. Traffic Safety Facts 2012: Young Drivers. Available at www-nrd.nhtsa.dot.gov. Accessed June 2015.
50. Ibid.
51. American Medical Association. 2003. The Minimum Legal Drinking Age: Facts and Fallacies. Available at www.alcoholpolicymd.com. Accessed June 2015.
52. Wagenaar, A. C., A. L. Tobler, and K. A. Komro. 2010. Effects of Alcohol Tax and Price Policies on Morbidity and Mortality: A Systematic Review. *American Journal of Public Health* 100: 2270–2278.
53. Centers for Disease Control and Prevention. 2014. Underage Drinking. Available at www.cdc.gov. Accessed June 2015.
54. Spithoff, S. 2015. Primary Care Management of Alcohol Use Disorder and At-Risk Drinking. *Canadian Family Physician* 61: 515–521.
55. Ibid.
56. Alcoholics Anonymous. 2013. Membership Survey. Available at www .aa.org. Accessed June 2015.
57. U.S. Department of Agriculture. Report of the Dietary Guidelines Advisory Committee.

Feature Box References

1. Austin, E., and S. Hust. 2005. The Content and Frequency of Alcoholic and Nonalcoholic Beverage Ads in Magazine and Video Formats November 1999–April 2000. *Journal of Health Communications* 10: 769–785.
2. Johns Hopkins Bloomberg School of Public Health, Center on Alcohol Marketing and Youth. 2012. Youth Exposure to Alcohol Advertising on Television, 2001–2009. Available at www.camy.org. Accessed June 2015.
3. Austin, E., M. Chen, and J. Grube. 2006. How Does Alcohol Advertising Influence Underage Drinking? The Role of Desirability, Identification, and Skepticism. *Journal of Adolescent Health* 38: 376–384.

Two Points of View References

1. Elkind, M. S., R. Sciacca, et al. 2006. Moderate Alcohol Consumption Reduces Risk of Ischemic Stroke. *Stroke* 37: 13; Goldberg, I. J., et al. 2001. AHA Science Advisory: Wine and Your Heart: A Science Advisory for Healthcare Professionals from the Nutrition Committee, Council on Epidemiology and Prevention, and Council on Cardiovascular Nursing of the American Heart Association. *Circulation* 103: 472–475.
2. Hanson, D. J. 2013. Alcohol: Problems and Solutions. Available at www2.potsdam.edu. Accessed July 2013.
3. Ibid.
4. Koppes, L. L., et al. 2005. Moderate Alcohol Consumption Lowers the Risk of Type 2 Diabetes: A Meta-analysis of Prospective Observational Studies. *Diabetes Care* 28: 719–725.
5. Goldberg. AHA Science Advisory: Wine and Your Heart; Academy of Nutrition and Dietetics. 2011. The Buzz on Beer. American Dietetic Association Offers a Toast to Good Health during American Heart Month. Available at www.eatrightpro.org/resource/media/press-releases/new-in-food-nutrition-and-health/ada-times-beer-article-release. Accessed July 2015.
6. National Institute on Alcohol Abuse and Alcoholism. 2015. College Drinking. Available at http://niaaa.nih.gov/alcohol-health/special-populations-co-occurring-disorders/college-drinking. Accessed July 2015.
7. Ibid.
8. Masten, A., V. Faden, and R. Zucker. 2009. *A Developmental Perspective on Underage Alcohol Use*. Available at http://pubs.niaaa.nih.gov. Accessed July 2013.
9. Centers for Disease Control and Prevention. 2014. Alcohol and Public Health: Frequently Asked Questions. Available at www.cdc.gov. Accessed July 2015.

Chapter 10

1. Yang, L., and G. Colditz. 2015. Prevalence of Overweight and Obesity in the United States, 2007–2012. *JAMA Internal Medicine*. 2015. Aug; 175(8):1412–1413. doi:10.1001/jamainternmed. 2015. 2405. Centers for Disease Control and Prevention. Obesity and Overweight. Available at www.cdc.gov. Accessed June 2015.
2. IFIC Foundation. Updated 2014. Food for Thought VI: Reporting of Diet, Nutrition, and Food Safety News. Available at www.foodinsight .org. Accessed June 2015.
3. Mintel Oxygen. 2012. Diet Trends—US—November 2012. Available at http://oxygen.mintel.com. Accessed June 2015.
4. Centers for Disease Control and Prevention. 2012. Economic Consequences of Overweight and Obesity. Available at www.cdc.gov. Accessed June 2015.
5. Centers for Disease Control and Prevention. 2014. Healthy Weight. Available at www.cdc.gov. Accessed June 2015.
6. Centers for Disease Control and Prevention. Overweight and Obesity; American Medical Association. 2013. AMA Adopts New Policies on Second Day of Voting at Annual Meeting. Available at www.ama-assn .org. Accessed June 2015.
7. National Heart, Lung, and Blood Institute. 1998. Clinical Guidelines on the Identification, Evaluation, and Treatment of Overweight and Obesity in Adults. Available at www.nhlbi.nih.gov. Accessed June 2015.
8. Ibid.
9. Centers for Disease Control and Prevention. Healthy Weight.
10. Gee, M., L. Mahan, and S. Escott-Stump. 2008. Weight management. In L. Mahan and S. Escott-Stump, eds., *Krause's Food, Nutrition, and Diet Therapy*. 12th ed. Philadelphia: Saunders.
11. Hammond, K. 2008. Assessment: Dietary and clinical data. In L. Mahan and S. Escott-Stump, eds., *Krause's Food, Nutrition, and Diet Therapy*. 12th ed. Philadelphia: Saunders.
12. U.S. Department of Health and Human Services. 2002. A Century of Women's Health, 1900–2000. Available at www.womenshealth.gov. Accessed June 2015.
13. National Heart, Lung, and Blood Institute. Clinical Guidelines on the Identification, Evaluation, and Treatment of Overweight and Obesity in Adults.
14. Ibid.
15. Ibid.
16. McFarlane, S. I., M. Banerji, and J. R. Sowers. 2001. Insulin Resistance and Cardiovascular Disease. *Journal of Clinical Endocrinology & Metabolism* 86: 713–718.
17. Institute of Medicine. 2002. *Dietary Reference Intakes for Energy, Carbohydrate, Fiber, Fat, Fatty Acids, Cholesterol, Protein, and Amino Acids*. Available at www.iom.edu. Accessed March 2010.
18. Hoffer, L. J. 2006. Metabolic consequences of starvation. In M. Shils, et al., eds., *Modern Nutrition in Health and Disease*. 10th ed. Philadelphia: Lippincott Williams & Wilkins.
19. Mattes, R., J. Hollis, D. Hayes, and A. Stunkard. 2005. Appetite: Measurement and Manipulations Misgivings. *Journal of the American Dietetic Association* 105 (supplement): S87–S97.
20. Smith, G. 2006. Controls of food intake. In M. Shils, et al., eds., *Modern Nutrition*.
21. Mattes. Appetite: Measurement and Manipulations Misgivings.
22. Smith. Controls of food intake.
23. Geliebter, A., S. Schachter, C. Lohmann-Walter, et al. 1996. Reduced Stomach Capacity in Obese Subjects After Dieting. *American Journal of Clinical Nutrition* 63: 170–173.
24. Centers for Disease Control and Prevention. 2013. Genomics and Health. Available at www.cdc.gov. Accessed June 2015.
25. Ibid.; Hill, J., V. Catenacci, and H. Wyatt. 2006. Obesity: Etiology. In M. Shils, et al., eds., *Modern Nutrition*.
26. Hill. Obesity: Etiology.
27. Bray, G., and C. Champagne. 2005. Beyond Energy Balance: There Is More to Obesity than Kilocalories. *Journal of the American Dietetic Association* 105 (supplement): S17–S23.
28. Brodsky, I. 2006. Hormones and growth factors. In M. Shils et al., eds., *Modern Nutrition*.
29. Hill. Obesity: Etiology.
30. Ibid.
31. Bray. Beyond Energy Balance; Loos, R., and T. Rankinen. 2005. Gene-Diet Interactions on Body Weight Changes. *Journal of the American Dietetic Association* 105 (supplement): S29–S34.
32. Gale, S., T. Van Itallie, and I. Faust. 1981. Effects of Palatable Diets on Body Weight and Adipose Tissue Cellularity in the Adult Obese Female Zucker Rat (fa/fa). *Metabolism* 30: 105–110.

33. Ravussin, E., M. Valencia, J. Esparza, P. Bennett, and L. Schulz. 1994. Effects of a Traditional Lifestyle on Obesity in Pima Indians. *Diabetes Care* 17: 1067–1074; Wang, S., and K. Brownell. 2005. Public Policy and Obesity: The Need to Marry Science with Advocacy. *Psychiatric Clinics of North America* 28: 235–252.

34. The Keystone Group. 2006. The Keystone Forums on Away-From-Home Food, Opportunities for Preventing Weight Gain and Obesity. Available at www.fda.gov. Accessed June 2015.

35. Smith, L., S. Ng, and B. Popkin. 2013. Trends in U.S. Home Food Preparation and Consumption: Analysis of National Nutrition Surveys and Time Use Studies from 1965–1966 to 2007–2008. *Nutrition Journal* 12: 45.

36. U.S. Department of Agriculture and U.S. Department of Health and Human Services. 2015. Scientific Report of the Dietary Guidelines for Americans Advisory Committee. Available at http://health.gov/dietaryguidelines/2015-scientific-report. Accessed June 2015; U.S. Department of Agriculture, Economic Research Service. 2012. Food and Nutrient Intake Data. Taking a Look at the Nutritional Quality of Foods Eaten at Home and Away from Home. Available at www.fda.gov. Accessed June 2015.

37. Ibid.

38. U.S. Department of Agriculture and U.S. Department of Health and Human Services. Scientific Report of the Dietary Guidelines for Americans Advisory Committee.

39. The Keystone Group. The Keystone Forums on Away-From-Home Food.

40. The Keystone Group. The Keystone Forums on Away-From-Home Food; Rolls, B. 1986. Sensory-Specific Satiety. *Nutrition Reviews* 44: 93–101.

41. U.S. Department of Agriculture and U.S. Department of Health and Human Services. 2010. *Dietary Guidelines for Americans, 2010.* 7th ed. Washington, DC: U.S. Government Printing Office; Rolls, B. 2003. The Supersizing of America. *Nutrition Today* 38: 42–53.

42. Wansink, B. 2006. Ice Cream Illusions: Bowls, Spoons, and Self-Served Portion Sizes. *American Journal of Preventative Medicine* 31: 240–243; Wansink, B. 1996. Can Package Size Accelerate Usage Volume? *Journal of Marketing* 60: 1–14.

43. Rolls, B., L. Roe, and J. Meengs. 2006. Larger Portion Sizes Lead to a Sustained Increase in Energy Intake over 2 Days. *Journal of the American Dietetic Association* 106: 543–549.

44. U.S. Department of Agriculture and U.S. Department of Health and Human Services. *Dietary Guidelines for Americans, 2010*; French, S., M. Story, and R. Jeffery. 2001. Environmental Influences on Eating and Physical Activity. *Annual Reviews of Public Health* 22: 309–335.

45. French. Environmental Influences on Eating.

46. Mummery, W., G. Schofield, R. Steele, E. Eakin, and W. Brown. 2005. Occupational Sitting Time and Overweight and Obesity in Australian Workers. *American Journal of Preventive Medicine* 29: 91–97.

47. French. Environmental Influences on Eating.

48. Wang. Public Policy and Obesity.

49. Lanningham-Foster, L., L. Nysse, and J. Levine. 2003. Labor Saved, Calories Lost: The Energetic Impact of Domestic Labor-Saving Devices. *Obesity Research* 11: 1178–1181.

50. Ibid.

51. Centers for Disease Control and Prevention. 2012. Facts About Physical Activity. Available at www.cdc.gov. Accessed June 2014.

52. Centers for Disease Control and Prevention. 2012. Prevalence and Trends Data. Exercise 2012. Available at www.cdc.gov. Accessed June 2015.

53. Nielsen Media Research. 2013. Free to Move Between Screens. Available at www.nielsen.com. Accessed June 2015.

54. The Kaiser Family Foundation. 2010. Daily Media Use Among Children and Teens Up Dramatically from Five Years Ago. Available at www.kff.org. Accessed June 2015.

55. National Heart, Lung, and Blood Institute. Clinical Guidelines on the Identification, Evaluation, and Treatment of Overweight and Obesity in Adults.

56. Centers for Disease Control and Prevention. 2015. Eat More, Weigh Less? Available at www.cdc.gov. Accessed June 2015; Mattes. Appetite: Measurement and Manipulations Misgivings; Lissner, L., D. Levitsky, B. Strupp, H. Kalkwarf, and D. Roe. 1987. Dietary Fat and the Regulation of Energy Intake in Human Subjects. *American Journal of Clinical Nutrition* 46: 886–892.

57. Centers for Disease Control and Prevention. Eat More, Weigh Less?; Tohill, B., J. Seymour, M. Serdula, L. Kettel-Khan, and B. Rolls. 2004. What Epidemiologic Studies Tell Us about the Relationship between Fruit and Vegetable Consumption and Body Weight. *Nutrition Reviews* 62: 365–374.

58. Centers for Disease Control and Prevention. Eat More, Weigh Less?; Rolls, B., E. Bell, and E. Thorwart. 1999. Water Incorporated into a Food but Not Served with a Food Decreases Energy Intake in Lean Women. *American Journal of Clinical Nutrition* 70: 448–455.

59. Slavin, J. 2008. Position of the American Dietetic Association: Health Implications of Dietary Fiber. *Journal of the American Dietetic Association* 108: 1716–1731; Burton-Freeman, B. 2000. Dietary Fiber and Energy Regulation. *Journal of Nutrition* 130: 272S–275S.

60. Davis, J., V. Hodges, and B. Gillham. 2006. Normal-Weight Adults Consume More Fiber and Fruit than Their Age- and Height-Matched Overweight/Obese Counterparts. *Journal of the American Dietetic Association* 106: 833–840.

61. Paddon-Jones, D., E. Westman, R. Mattes, R. Wolfe, A. Astrup, and M. Westerterp-Plantenga. 2008. Protein, Weight Management, and Satiety. *American Journal of Clinical Nutrition* 87: 1558S–1561S; Snoek, H., L. Huntjens, L. van Gemert, C. Graaf, and H. Weenen. 2004. Sensory-Specific Satiety in Obese and Normal-Weight Women. *American Journal of Clinical Nutrition* 80: 823–831; Mattes. Appetite: Measurement and Manipulations Misgivings.

62. U.S. Department of Agriculture, U.S. Department of Health and Human Services. *Dietary Guidelines for Americans, 2010*; Saries, W., S. Blair, M. van Baak, et al. 2003. How Much Physical Activity Is Enough to Prevent Unhealthy Weight Gain? Outcome of the IASO Stock Conference and Consensus Statement. *Obesity Reviews* 4: 101–114.

63. Keim, N., C. Blanton, and M. Kretsch. 2004. America's Obesity Epidemic: Measuring Physical Activity to Promote an Active Lifestyle. *Journal of the American Dietetic Association* 104: 1398–1409.

64. Jakicic, J., and A. Otto. 2005. Physical Activity Consideration for the Treatment and Prevention of Obesity. *American Journal of Clinical Nutrition* 82: 226S–229S.

65. Shape Up America! 2006. 10,000 Steps. Available at www.shapeup.org. Accessed June 2015.

66. Vella-Zarb, R., and F. Elgar. 2009. The "Freshman 15": A Meta-Analysis of Weight Gain in the Freshman Year of College. *Journal of American College Health* 58: 61–66; Edwards, J., and H. Meiselman. 2003. Changes in Dietary Habits during the First Year at University. *British Nutrition Foundation Nutrition Bulletin* 28: 21–34.

67. Zagorsky, J., and P. Smith. 2011. The Freshman 15: A Critical Time for Obesity Intervention or Media Myth? *Social Science Quarterly* 92: 1389–1407; Graham, M., and A. Jones. 2002. Freshman 15: Valid Theory or Harmful Myth? *Journal of American College Health* 50: 171–173.

68. Kong, A., S. Beresford, C. Alfano, K. Foster-Schubert, M. Neuhouser, D. Johnson, et al. 2012. Self-Monitoring and Eating-Related Behaviors Are Associated with 12-Month Weight Loss in Postmenopausal Overweight-to-Obese Women. *Journal of the Academy of Nutrition and Dietetics* 112: 1428–1435.

69. Schlundt, D., J. Hill, T. Sbrocco, J. Pope-Cordle, and T. Sharp. 1992. The Role of Breakfast in the Treatment of Obesity: A Randomized Clinical Trial. *American Journal of Clinical Nutrition* 55: 645–651.

70. Seagle. Position of the American Dietetic Association: Weight Management; National Heart, Lung, and Blood Institute. Clinical Guidelines on the Identification, Evaluation, and Treatment of Overweight and Obesity in Adults.

71. DeWald, T., L. Khaodhiar, M. Donahue, and G. Blackburn. 2006. Pharmacological and Surgical Treatments for Obesity. *American Heart Journal* 151: 604–624.

72. U.S. Food and Drug Administration. 2015. Medications Target Long-Term Weight Control. Available at www.fda.gov. Accessed July 2015.

73. National Center for Complementary and Integrative Medicine. 2015. Edpedra. Available at: https://nccih.nih.gov/health/ephedra. Accessed September 2015.; FDA. 2004. FDA Issues Regulation Prohibiting Sale of Dietary Supplements Containing Ephedrine Alkaloids and Reiterates Its Advice That Consumers Stop Using these Products. Available at www.cfsan.fda.gov. Accessed July 2015.

74. American Society for Metabolic and Bariatric Surgery. 2015. Estimate of Bariatric Surgery Numbers, 2011–2014. Available at http://asmbs.org. Accessed July 2015.

75. Pournaras, D., and C. le Roux. 2010. Ghrelin and Metabolic Surgery. *International Journal of Peptides*. Available at www.hindawi.com. Accessed July 2015.

76. American Society for Metabolic and Bariatric Surgery. 2013. Metabolic and Bariatric Surgery. Available at http://asmbs.org. Accessed July 2015.

77. National Institute of Diabetes and Digestive and Kidney Diseases. 2013. Dieting and Gallstones. Available at http://niddk.nih.gov. Accessed June 2015; Delahanty, L., Q. Pan, K. Jablonski, V. Aroda, K. Watson, G. Bray, S. Kahn, et al. 2014. Effects of Weight Loss, Cycling and Weight Loss

Maintenance on Diabetes Incidence and Change in Cardiometabolic Traits in the Diabetes Prevention Program. *Diabetes Care* 37: 2738–2745; Rosenbaum, M., R. Leibel, and J. Hirsch. 1997. Obesity. *New England Journal of Medicine* 337: 396–407.

78. Mehta, T., D. Smith, J. Muhammad, and K. Casazza. 2014. Impact of Weight Cycling on Risk of Morbidity and Mortality. *Obesity Reviews* 15: 870–881.

79. Wing, R., and S. Phelan. 2005. Long-Term Weight Loss Maintenance. *American Journal of Clinical Nutrition* 82: 222S–225S; Rosenbaum. Obesity; Klem, M. L., R. R. Wing, M. T. McGuire, H. M. Seagle, and J. O. Hill. 1997. A Descriptive Study of Individuals Successful at Long-Term Maintenance of Substantial Weight Loss. *American Journal of Clinical Nutrition* 66: 239–246.

80. Ibid.

81. Hill, J., J. Peters, and H. Wyatt. 2009 Using the Energy Gap to Address Obesity: A commentary. *Journal of the American Dietetic Association* 109: 1848–1853; Hill, J., H. Wyatt, G. Reed, and J. Peters. 2003. Obesity and the Environment: Where Do We Go from Here? *Science* 299: 853–897.

82. Hill, J., H. Thompson, and H. Wyatt. 2005. Weight Maintenance: What's Missing? *Journal of the American Dietetic Association* 105: S63–S66.

83. U.S. Department of Health and Human Services. 2008. Physical Activity Guidelines for Americans. Available at www.health.gov. Accessed June 2015.

84. Ibid.

85. Wade, T. D., A. Keski-Rahkonen, and J. Hudson. 2011. Epidemiology of eating disorders. In M. Tsuang and M. Tohen, eds. *Textbook in Psychiatric Epidemiology*. 3rd ed. New York: Wiley, 343–360.

86. Chamorro, R., and Y. Flores-Ortiz. 2000. Acculturation and Disordered Eating Patterns among Mexican American Women. *International Journal of Eating Disorders* 28: 125–129; Crago, M., C. M. Shisslak, and L. S. Estes. 1996. Eating Disturbances among American Minority Groups: A Review. *International Journal of Eating Disorders* 19: 239–248; Kjelsås, E., C. Bjornstrom, and K. G. Gotestam. 2004. Prevalence of Eating Disorders in Female and Male Adolescents (14–15 Years). *Eating Behaviors* 5: 13–25; O'Dea, J., and S. Abraham. 2002. Eating and Exercise Disorders in Young College Men. *Journal of American College Health* 50: 273–278.

87. Spettigue, W., and K. A. Henderson. 2004. Eating Disorders and the Role of Media. *Canadian Child and Adolescent Psychiatry Review* 13: 16–19.

88. Rubenstein, S., and B. Cabellero. 2000. Is Miss America an Undernourished Role Model? *Journal of the American Medical Association* 382: 1569.

89. Strober, M., and C. M. Bulik. 2002. Genetic epidemiology of eating disorders. In D. G. Fairburn and K. D. Brownell, eds. *Eating Disorders and Obesity: A Comprehensive Handbook*. 2nd ed. New York: Guilford Press, 238–242.

90. Mangweth, B., J. I. Hudson, H. G. Pope, Jr., A. Hausmagn, C. DeCol, N. M. Laird, and M. T. Tsuang. 2003. Family Study of the Aggregation of Eating Disorders and Mood Disorders. *Psychological Medicine* 33: 1319–1323; McElroy, S. L. O., R. Kotwal, and P. E. Keck, Jr. 2006. Comorbidity of Eating Disorders with Bipolar Disorder and Treatment Implications. *Bipolar Disorders* 8: 686–695.

91. Altman, S. E., and S. A. Shankman. 2009. What Is the Association between Obsessive-Compulsive Disorder and Eating Disorders? *Clinical Psychology Review* 29: 638–646.

92. Woodside, D. B., P. E. Garfinkel, E. Lin, P. Goering, A. S. Kaplan, D. S. Goldbloom, and S. H. Kennedy. 2001. Comparisons of Men with Full or Partial Eating Disorders, Men without Eating Disorders, and Women with Eating Disorders in the Community. *American Journal of Psychiatry* 158: 570–574.

93. Harrop, E. N., and G. A. Marlatt. 2010. The Comorbidity of Substance Use Disorders and Eating Disorders in Women: Prevalence, Etiology, and Treatment. *Addictive Behaviors* 35: 392–398.

94. Reiff, D., and K. Reiff. 1997. *Eating Disorders: Nutrition Therapy in the Recovery Process*. Aspen, CO: Aspen Publishers.

95. Arcelus, J., A. J. Mitchell, J. Wales, and S. Nielsen. 2011. Mortality Rates in Patients with Anorexia Nervosa and Other Eating Disorders. *Archives of General Psychiatry* 68: 724–731.

96. Reiff. *Eating Disorders.*

97. Ibid.

98. Birketvedt, G. S., J. Florholmen, J. Sundsfjord, B. Osterud, D. Dinges, W. Bilker, and A. Stunkard. 1999. Behavioral and Neuroendocrine Characteristics of the Night Eating Syndrome. *Journal of the American Medical Association* 282: 657–663.

99. Birketvedt. Behavioral and Neuroendocrine Characteristics of the Night Eating Syndrome.

100. National Eating Disorders Association. 2013. Treatment. Available at www.nationaleatingdisorders.org. Accessed July 2013.

Feature Box References

1. Marketdata Enterprises, Inc. 2014. The U.E. Weight Loss Market: 2014 Status Report and Forecast. Available at www.marketresearch.com/Marketdata-Enterprises-Inc-v416/Weight-Loss-Status-Forecast-8016030. Accessed July 2015.

2. Johnston, B., S. Kanters, K. Bandayrel, P. Wu, F. Naji, R. Siemieniuk, G. Ball, et al. 2014. Comparison of Weight Loss Among Named Diet Programs in Overweight and Obese Adults: A Meta-Analysis. *Journal of the American Medical Association* 312: 923–933; Sacks, F., G. Bray, V. Carey, S. Smith, D. Ryan, S. Anton, K. McManus, et al. 2009. Comparison of Weight-Loss Diets with Different Compositions of Fat, Protein, and Carbohydrates. *New England Journal of Medicine* 360: 859–873; Freedman, M., J. King, and E. Kennedy. 2001. Popular Diets: A Scientific Review. *Obesity Research* 9: 1S–40S.

3. Dansinger, M., J. Gleason, J. Griffith, H. Selker, and E. Schaefer. 2005. Comparison of the Atkins, Ornish, Weight Watchers, and Zone Diets for Weight Loss and Heart Disease Risk Reduction. *Journal of the American Medical Association* 293: 43–53.

4. Ibid.

5. Seagle, H., G. Strain, A. Makris, and R. Reeves. 2009. Position of the American Dietetic Association: Weight Management. *Journal of the American Dietetic Association* 109: 330–346.

6. Ornish, D. 2004. Was Dr. Atkins Right? *Journal of the American Dietetic Association* 104: 537–542.

7. Denke, M. 2001. Metabolic Effects of High-Protein, Low-Carbohydrate Diets. *The American Journal of Cardiology* 88: 59–61.

8. Ibid.

9. Federal Trade Commission. 2015. Federal Court Rules Affiliate Marketing Network and Its Parent Company Must Turn over $11.9 Million They Received from Deceptive Marketing Scheme. Available at www.ftc.gov. Accessed July 2015; Federal Trade Commission. 2010. Marketers of Unproven Weight Loss Products Ordered to Pay Nearly $2 Million. Available at www.ftc.gov. Accessed July 2015.

10. National Center for Complementary and Alternative Medicine. 2012. Green Tea. Available at http://nccam.nih.gov. Accessed July 2015.

11. National Center for Complementary and Integrative Medicine. 2015. Weight Control and Complementary and Integrative Approaches. Available at http://nccam.nih.gov. Accessed July 2015; Pittler, M., and E. Ernst. 2004. Dietary Supplements for Body-Weight Reduction: A Systematic Review. *American Journal of Clinical Nutrition* 79: 529–536.

12. National Center for Complementary and Integrative Medicine. Weight Control and Complementary and Integrative Approaches.

13. National Eating Disorders Association. 2012. What Is Body Image? Available at www.nationaleatingdisorders.org. Accessed July 2013.

14. Ibid.

15. Ibid.

16. Koran, L. M., E. Abujaoude, M. D. Large, and R. T. Serpe. 2008. The Prevalence of Body Dysmorphic Disorder in the United States Adult Population. *CNS Spectrums* 13: 316–322.

17. Cafri, G., R. Olivardia, and J. K. Thompson. 2008. Symptom Characteristics and Psychiatric Comorbidity among Males with Muscle Dysmorphia. *Comprehensive Psychiatry* 48: 374–379.

18. National Eating Disorders Association. 2012. Enhancing Male Body Image. Available at www.nationaleatingdisorders.org. Accessed July 2013; National Eating Disorders Association. 2012. Every Body Is Different. Available at www.nationaleatingdisorders.org. Accessed July 2013.

Two Points of View References

1. WebMD. Weight-Loss Surgery Health Center. 2012. Facts about Weight-Loss Surgery. Available at www.webmd.com. Accessed June 2013.

2. Mayo Clinic Staff. 2011. Definition of Gastric Bypass Surgery. Available at www.mayoclinic.com. Accessed June 2013.

3. Wolters Kluwer Health, Lippincott Williams & Wilkins. 2012. Obesity Epidemic Means Bariatric Surgery Rates Continue to Rise, Reports *Plastic and Reconstructive Surgery*. Available at www.sciencedaily.com. Accessed June 2013.

4. Centers for Disease Control and Prevention. 2013. Adolescent and School Health: Childhood Obesity Facts. Available at www.cdc.gov. Accessed October 2013.

5. Reeves, G. M., et al. 2008. Childhood Obesity and Depression: Connection between These Growing Problems in Growing Children. *International Journal of Child Health and Human Development* 1: 103–114.

6. Han, J., D. Lawlor, and S. Kimm. 2010. Childhood Obesity. *The Lancet* 375: 1737–1748.

7. Inge, T., J. Bean, et al. 2009. Reversal of Type 2 Diabetes Mellitus and Improvements in Cardiovascular Risk Factors After Surgical Weight Loss in Adolescents. *Pediatrics* 123: 214–222.

8. O'Brien, P., S. Sawyer, et al. 2010. Laparoscopic Adjustable Gastric Banding in Severely Obese Adolescents. *Journal of the American Medical Association* 303: 519–526.

9. Cleveland Clinic. 2013. Adolescent Bariatric Surgery. Available at http://weightloss.clevelandclinic.org. Accessed July 2013.

10. Beil, L. 2010. Surgery for Obese Children? *The New York Times*. Available at www.nytimes.com. Accessed July 2013; Ippisch, H., T. Jenkins, T. Inge, and T. Kimball. 2009. Do Acute Improvements in LV Mass and Diastolic Function Following Adolescent Bariatric Surgery Persist at Two Years Post-Op? *Circulation* 120: S474.

11. Beil. Surgery for Obese Children?

12. Ibid.

13. Kaulfers, A. M., et al. 2011. Bone Loss in Adolescents after Bariatric Surgery. *Pediatrics* 127: e956–e961.

Chapter 11

1. U.S. Department of Health and Human Services. 2011. Healthy People 2020. Available at www.healthypeople.gov. Accessed April 2013.

2. U.S. Department of Health and Human Services. 2008. Physical Activity Guidelines for Americans. Available at www.Health.gov/paguidelines. Accessed March 2015.

3. Bushman, B. 2014. Promoting Exercise as Medicine for Prediabetes and Prehypertension. *Current Sports Medicine Report* 13: 233–239.

4. Sousa, N., R. Mendes, C. Abrantes, J. Sampaio, and J. Oliveira. 2014. A Randomized Study on Lipids Response to Different Exercise Programs in Overweight Older Men. *International Journal of Sports Medicine* DOI: 10.1055/s-0034-1374639.

5. Janssen, I., P. T. Katzmarzyk, R. Ross, A. S. Leon, J. S. Skinner, D. C. Rao, et al. 2004. Fitness Alters the Associations of BMI and Waist Circumference with Total and Abdominal Fat. *Obesity* 12: 525–537.

6. Van Dijk, J. W., M. Venema, W. van Mechelen, C. D. Stehouwer, F. Hartgens, and L. L. van Loon. 2013. Effect of Moderate-Intensity Exercise versus Activities of Daily Living on 24-Hour Blood Glucose Homeostasis in Male Patients with Type 2 Diabetes. *Diabetes Care* 36: 3448–3453.

7. U.S. Department of Health and Human Services. 2008. *Physical Activity Guidelines Advisory Committee Report*. Washington, DC: ODPHP Publication No. U0049. Available from www.health.gov/paguidelines/Report/pdf/CommitteeReport.pdf. Accessed March 2015.

8. Tucker, L. A., J. E. Strong, J. D. Lecheminant, and B. W. Bailey. 2014. Effect of Two Jumping Programs on Hip Bone Mineral Density in Premenopausal Women: A Randomized Controlled Trial. *American Journal of Health Promotion* DOI: 10.4278/ajhp; Saravi, F. D., and F. Sayegh. 2013. Bone Mineral Density and Body Composition of Adult Premenopausal Women with Three Levels of Physical Activity. *Journal of Osteoporosis* DOI: 10.1155/2013/953271.

9. Menicucci, D., A. Piarulli, F. Mastorci, L. Sebastiani, et al. 2013. Interactions between Immune, Stress-Related Hormonal and Cardiovascular Systems Following Strenuous Physical Exercise. *Archives Italiennes de Biologie* 151930: 126–136.

10. U.S. Department of Health and Human Services. *Physical Activity Guidelines Advisory Committee Report*.

11. Akbari Kamrani, A. A., D. Shamsipour Dehkordi, and R. Mohajeri. 2014. The Effect of Low and Moderate Intensity Aerobic Exercises on Sleep Quality in Male Older Adults. *Pakistan Journal of Medical Sciences* 30: 417–421.

12. Herbert, R. D., and M. de Noronha. 2007. Stretching to Prevent or Reduce Muscle Soreness after Exercise. *Cochrane Database of Systematic Reviews* 4.

13. Thacker, Stephen B., et al. 2004. The Impact of Stretching on Sports Injury Risk: A Systematic Review of the Literature. *Medicine & Science in Sports & Exercise* 3: 371–378.

14. American College of Sports Medicine. 2011. Quantity and Quality of Exercise for Developing and Maintaining Cardiorespiratory, Musculoskeletal, and Neuromotor Fitness in Apparently Healthy Adults: Guidance for Prescribing Exercise. Position Stand. *Medicine & Science in Sports & Exercise* 43: 1334–1359.

15. Jensen, T. E., and E. A. Ritcher. 2012. Regulation of Glucose and Glycogen Metabolism During and After Exercise. *Journal of Physiology* 590:1069–1076.

16. Costill, D., R. Thomas, R. Roergs, D. Pascoe, C. Lambert, S. Barr, and W. Fink. 1991. Adaptations to Swimming Training: Influence of Training Volume. *Medicine & Science in Sports & Exercise* 23: 371–377; Sherman,

W., M. Peden, and D. Wright. 1991. Carbohydrate Feedings 1 Hour Before Exercise Improves Cycling Performance. *American Journal of Clinical Nutrition* 54: 866–870.

17. Coyle, E. F., A. R. Coggan, M. K. Hemmert, and J. L. Ivy. 1986. Muscle Glycogen Utilization during Prolonged Strenuous Exercise When Fed Carbohydrate. *Journal of Applied Physiology* 61: 165–172; Jensen. Regulation of Glucose and Glycogen Metabolism.

18. Burke, L., B. Kiens, and J. Ivy. 2004. Carbohydrate and Fat for Training and Recovery. *Journal of Sports Science* 22: 15–30.

19. American College of Sports Medicine, American Dietetic Association, and Dietitians of Canada. 2009. Nutrition and Athletic Performance Joint Position Statement. *Medicine & Science in Sports & Exercise* 41: 709–731.

20. Ibid.

21. Brownell, K. D., S. N. Steen, and J. H. Wilmore. 1987. Weight Regulation Practices in Athletes: Analysis of Metabolic and Health Effects. *Medicine & Science in Sports & Exercise* 19: 546–556; Horvath, P. J., C. K. Eagen, S. D. Ryer-Calvin, and D. R. Pendergast. 2000. The Effects of Varying Dietary Fat on the Nutrient Intake in Male and Female Runners. *Journal of the American College of Nutrition* 19: 42–51.

22. American College of Sports Medicine, American Dietetic Association, and Dietitians of Canada. Nutrition and Athletic Performance Joint Position Statement.

23. Yaspelkis, B. B., J. G. Patterson, P. A. Anderla, Z. Ding, and J. L. Ivy. 1993. Carbohydrate Supplementation Spares Muscle Glycogen During Variable-Intensity Exercise. *Journal of Applied Physiology* 75: 1477–1485; Coyle, E. F., J. M. Hagberg, B. F. Hurley, W. H. Martin, A. A. Ehsani, and J. O. Holloszy. 1983. Carbohydrate Feeding During Prolonged Strenuous Exercise Can Delay Fatigue. *Journal of Applied Physiology* 55: 230–235.

24. Miller, S. L., K. D. Tipton, D. L. Chinkes, S. E. Wolf, and R. R. Wolfe. 2003. Independent and Combined Effects of Amino Acids and Glucose After Resistance Exercise. *Medicine & Science in Sports & Exercise* 35: 449–455.

25. Temesi, J., N. A. Johnson, J. Raymond, C. A. Burdon, and H. T. O'Connor. 2011. Carbohydrate Ingestion during Endurance Exercise Improves Performance in Adults. *Journal of Nutrition* 141: 890–897.

26. Koopman, R., D. L. Pannemans, A. E. Jeukendrup, A. P. Gijsen, J. M. Senden, D. Halliday, et al. 2004. Combined Ingestion of Protein and Carbohydrate Improves Protein Balance During Ultra-Endurance Exercise. *American Journal of Physiology - Endocrinology and Metabolism* 287: E712–E720.

27. Ivy, J. L., A. L. Katz, C. L. Cutler, W. M. Sherman, and E. F. Coyle. 1988. Muscle Glycogen Synthesis After Exercise: Effect of Time of Carbohydrate Ingestion. *Journal of Applied Physiology* 64: 1480–1485.

28. Roy, B. D., M. A. Tarnopolsky, J. D. MacDougall, J. Fowles, and K. E. Yarasheski. 1997. Effect of Glucose Supplement Timing on Protein Metabolism After Resistance Training. *Journal of Applied Physiology* 82: 1882–1888.

29. Rasmussen, B. B., K. D. Tipton, S. L. Miller, S. E. Wolf, and R. R. Wolfe. 2000. An Oral Essential Amino Acid-Carbohydrate Supplement Enhances Muscle Protein Anabolism after Resistance Exercise. *Journal of Applied Physiology* 88: 386–392; Zawadzki, K. M., B. B. Yaspelkis, and J. L. Ivy. 1992. Carbohydrate-Protein Complex Increases the Rate of Muscle Glycogen Storage after Exercise. *Journal of Applied Physiology* 72: 1854–1859.

30. Zawadzki. Carbohydrate-Protein Complex; Ivy, J. L., H. W. Goforth, B. M. Damon, T. R. McCauley, E. C. Parsons, and T. B. Price. 2002. Early Postexercise Muscle Glycogen Recovery Is Enhanced with a Carbohydrate-Protein Supplement. *Journal of Applied Physiology* 93: 1337–1344.

31. Pritchett, K., and R. Pritchett. 2012. Chocolate Milk: A Post-Exercise Recovery Beverage for Endurance Sports. *Medicine and Sport Science* 59: 127–134.

32. McAnulty, S. R., L. S. McAnulty, D. C. Nieman, J. D. Morrow, L. A. Shooter, S. Holmes, et al. 2005. Effect of Alpha-Tocopherol Supplementation on Plasma Homocysteine and Oxidative Stress in Highly Trained Athletes Before and After Exhaustive Exercise. *Journal of Nutritional Biochemistry* 16: 530–537; Mariacher C., H. Gatterer, J. Greilberger, R. Djukic, M. Greilberger, M. Philippe, and M. Burtscher. 2014. Effects of Antioxidant Supplementation on Exercise Performance in Acute Normobaric Hypoxia. *International Journal of Sport Nutrition and Exercise Metabolism* 24: 227–235.

33. DellaValle, D. M., and J. D. Haas. 2011. Impact of Iron Depletion without Anemia on Performance in Trained Endurance Athletes at the Beginning of a Training Season: A Study of Female Collegiate Rowers. *International Journal of Sport Nutrition and Exercise Metabolism* 21: 501–506.

34. Gropper, S. S., D. Blessing, K. Dunham, and J. M. Barksdale. 2006. Iron Status of Female Collegiate Athletes Involved in Different Sports. *Biological Trace Element Research* 109: 1–14; Dubnov, G., Constanini, N.W. 2004. Prevalence of iron depletion and anemia in top-level basketball players. *International Journal of Sport Nutrition and Exercise Metabolism* 14.1 2004: 30–37. DellaValle, D.M., Haas, J.D., 2011. Impact of Iron Depletion Without Anemia on Performance in Trained Endurance Athletes at the Beginning of a Training Season: A Study of Female Collegiate Rowers. *International Journal of Sport Nutrition and Exercise Metabolism*, 2011, 21, 501–506.

35. Nasri, R., S. Hassen Zrour, H. Rebai, F. Neffeti, M. F. Najjar, N. Bergaoui, H. Mejdoub, and Z. Tabka. 2013. Combat Sports Practice Favors Bone Mineral Density among Male Athletes. *Journal of Clinical Densitometry* doi: 10.1016/j.jocd.2013.09.012.

36. Herbold, N. H., B. K. Visconti, S. Frates, and L. Bandini. 2004. Traditional and Nontraditional Supplement Use by Collegiate Female Varsity Athletes. *International Journal of Sport Nutrition and Exercise Metabolism* 14: 586–593; Darvishi, L., G. Askari, M. Hariri, M. Bahreynian, R. Ghiasvand, S. Ehsani, N. S. Mashhadi, et al. 2013. The Use of Nutritional Supplements among Male Collegiate Athletes. *International Journal of Preventive Medicine* 4 (Supplement 1): S68–S72.

37. Fry, A. C., R. J. Bloomer, M. J. Falvo, C. A. Moore, B. K. Schilling, and L. W. Weiss. 2006. Effect of a Liquid Multivitamin/Mineral Supplement on Anaerobic Exercise Performance. *Research in Sports Medicine* 14: 53–64.

38. Gatorade.com. 2015. Gatorade History. Available at www.gatorade .com/company/heritage. Accessed March 2015.

39. C. Rosenbloom, and E. J. Coleman. 2012. *Sports Nutrition: A Practice Manual for Professionals.* Chicago, IL: Academy of Nutrition and Dietetics.

40. Wilk, B., and O. Bar-Or. 1996. Effect of Drink Flavor and NaCl on Voluntary Drinking and Hydration in Boys Exercising in the Heat. *Journal of Applied Physiology* 80: 1112–1117.

41. American College of Sports Medicine. 2007. Position Stand on Exercise and Fluid Replacement. *Medicine & Science in Sports & Exercise* 39: 377–390.

42. National Institutes of Health. 2013. *Caffeine in the Diet.* National Institutes of Health Medline Plus Medical Encyclopedia. Available at www.nlm .nih.gov/medlineplus/ency/article/002445.htm. Accessed March 2015.

43. USA Track & Field. Press Release April 19, 2003. USATF Announces Major Change in Hydration Guidelines. Available at www.usatf.org. November 2015.

44. Casa, Douglas J. 2003. Proper Hydration for Distance Running— Identifying Individual Fluid Needs, A USA Track and Field Advisory. Available at www.usatf.org.

45. Greenhaff, P. L., A. Casey, A. H. Short, R. Harris, K. Söderlund, and E. Hultman. 1993. Influence of Oral Creatine Supplementation on Muscle Torque During Repeated Bouts of Maximal Voluntary Exercise in Man. *Clinical Science* 84: 565–571.

46. Antonio, J., and V. Ciccone. 2013. The Effects of Pre Versus Post Workout Supplementation of Creatine Monohydrate on Body Composition and Strength. *Journal of the International Society of Sports Nutrition.* doi:10.1186/1550-2783-10-36.

47. Williams, J., G. Abt, and A. E. Kilding. 2014. Effects of Creatine Monohydrate Supplementation on Simulated Soccer Performance. *International Journal of Sports Physiology and Performance* 9: 503–510; Kreider, R. B., M. Ferreira, M. Wilson, P. Grindstaff, S. Plisk, J. Reinardy, et al. 1998. Effects of Creatine Supplementation on Body Composition, Strength, and Sprint Performance. *Medicine & Science in Sports & Exercise* 30: 73–82.

48. Buford, T. W., R. B. Kreider, J. R. Stout, M. Greenwood, B. Campbell, M. Spano, et al. 2007. International Society of Sports Nutrition Position Stand: Creatine Supplementation and Exercise. *Journal of the International Society of Sports Nutrition* doi: 10.1186/1550-2783-4-6; Kreider, R. B., C. Melton, C. J. Rasmussen, M. Greenwood, S. Lancaster, E. C. Cantler, et al. 2003. Long-Term Creatine Supplementation Does Not Significantly Affect Clinical Markers of Health in Athletes. *Molecular and Cellular Biochemistry* 244: 95–104.

49. Hogervorst, E., S. Bandelow, J. Schmitt, et al. 2008. Caffeine Improves Physical and Cognitive Performance during Exhaustive Exercise. *Medicine & Science in Sports & Exercise* 49: 1841–1851.

50. Brown, S. J., J. Brown, and A. Foskett. 2013. The Effects of Caffeine on Repeated Sprint Performance in Team Sport Athletes—A Meta-Analysis. *Sport Science Review* 22: 25–32.

51. Crist, D. M., G. T. Peake, P. A. Egan, and D. L. Waters. 1988. Body Composition Responses to Exogenous GH During Training in Highly Conditioned Adults. *Journal of Applied Physiology* 65: 579–584; Foss, M., and S. Keteyian. 1998. *Physiological Basis for Exercise and Sport.* 6th ed. McGraw-Hill: 498.

52. Deyssig, R., H. Frisch, W. Blum, and T. Waldorf. 1993. Effect of Growth Hormone Treatment on Hormonal Parameters, Body Composition, and Strength in Athletes. *Acta Endocrinologica* 128: 313–318; Lange, K., J. Andersen, N. Beyer, F. Isaksson, B. Larsson, M. Rasmussen, et al. 2002. GH Administration Changes Myosin Heavy Chain Isoforms in Skeletal Muscle but Does Not Augment Muscle Strength or Hypertrophy, Either Alone or Combined with Resistance Exercise Training in Healthy Elderly Men. *Journal of Clinical Endocrinology & Metabolism* 87: 513–523.

53. Woodhouse, L. J., S. L. Asa, S. G. Thomas, and S. Ezzat. 1999. Measures of Submaximal Aerobic Performance Evaluate and Predict Functional Response to Growth Hormone (GH) Treatment in GH-Deficient Adults. *Journal of Clinical Endocrinology & Metabolism* 84: 4570–4577.

54. Thomsen, J. J., R. L. Rentsch, P. Robach, J. A. Calbert, R. Boushel, P. Rasmussen, C. Juel, and C. Lundy. 2007. Prolonged Administration of Recombinant Human Erythropoietin Increases Submaximal Performance More than Maximal Aerobic Capacity. *European Journal of Applied Physiology* 101: 481–486.

Feature Box References

1. Wisemann, J., and D. Willoughby. 2006. Gender Differences in Carbohydrate Metabolism and Carbohydrate Loading. *Journal of the International Society of Sports Nutrition* 3: 28–34.

2. Goforth, W. H., D. Laurent, W. K. Prusaczyk, K. E. Schneider, K. F. Peterson, and G. I. Shulman. 2003. Effects of Depletion Exercise and Light Training on Muscle Glycogen Supercompensation in Men. *American Journal of Physiology - Endocrinology and Metabolism* 285: E1304–1311.

3. Houmard, J. A., D. L. Costill, J. B. Mitchell, S. H. Park, R. C. Hickner, and J. N. Roemmich. 1990. Reduced Training Maintains Performance in Distance Runners. *International Journal of Sports Medicine* 11: 46–52.

4. K. N. Brown, H. J. Wengreen, and K. A. Beals. 2014. "Knowledge of the Female Athlete Triad and Prevalence of Triad Risk Factors." *Journal of Pediatric and Adolescent Gynecology.* doi: 10.1016/j.jpag.2013.11.014.

5. E. M. Lanser, K. N. Zach, and A. Z. Hoch. 2011. "The Female Athlete Triad and Endothelial Dysfunction." *Physical Medicine and Rehabilitation* 3(5): 458-465.

6. M. T. Barracj, J. C. Gibbs, M. J. De Souza, N. I. Williams, J. F. Nichols, M. J. Rauh, and A. Nattive, 2014. Higher Incidence of Bone Stress Injuries with Increasing Female Athlete Triad-Related Risk Factors: A Prospective Multisite Study of Exercising Girls and Women." *American Journal of Sports Medicine* 42(4): 949–958.

Two Points of View References

1. Bloomberg. 2013. Top Doctors Tell FDA to Limit Caffeine in Energy Drinks. Available at www.bloomberg.com/news/articles/2013-03-19/ top-doctors-tell-fda-to-limit-caffeine-in-energy-drinks. Accessed June 2015.

2. Banerjee, P., et al. 2014. Fatal Caffeine Intoxication: A series of Eight Cases from 1999 to 2009. *Journal of Forensic Science.* Available at www .ncbi.nlm.nih.gov/pubmed/24502704. Accessed June 2015.

3. Seifert, S. M., et al. 2011. Health Effects of Energy Drinks on Children, Adolescents, and Young Adults. *Pediatrics.* Available at www.pediatrics .aappublications.org/content/127/3/511.full. Accessed July 2015.

4. Reissig, C. J., et al. 2009. Caffeinated Energy Drinks—A Growing Problem. *Drug and Alcohol Dependence.* Available at www.ncbi.nlm.nih.gov/ pmc/articles/PMC2735818. Accessed July 2015.

5. Consumer Reports. 2012. The Buzz on Energy-Drink Caffeine. www .consumerreports.org/cro/magazine/2012/12/the-buzz-on-energy-drink-caffeine/index.htm. Accessed June 2015.

6. Consumer Reports. The Buzz on Energy-Drink Caffeine.

7. Martz, M., et al. 2015. Alcohol Mixed with Energy Drink Use among U.S. 12th-Grade Students: Prevalence, Correlates, and Associations with Unsafe Driving. Available at www.jahonline.org/article/S1054-139X(15)00059-2/abstract. Accessed June 2015.

8. Velazquez, C.E., et al. 2012. Associations between Energy Drink Consumption and Alcohol Use Behaviors among College Students. *Drug and Alcohol Dependence.* Available at www.ncbi.nlm.nih.gov/ pubmed/22138539. Accessed July 2015.

9. Pomeranz, J. L., et al. 2013. Energy Drinks: An Emerging Public Health Hazard for Youth. *Journal of Public Health Policy.* Available at www .palgrave-journals.com/jphp/journal/v34/n2/abs/jphp20136a.html. Accessed June 2015.

10. Mayo Clinic. 2015. Nutrition and Healthy Eating. Can Energy Drinks Really Boost a Person's Energy? Available at www.mayoclinic.org/ healthy-lifestyle/nutrition-and-healthy-eating/expert-answers/ energy-drinks/faq-20058349. Accessed June 2015.

11. FDA. 2013. FDA to Investigate Added Caffeine. Available at www.fda.gov/ForConsumers/ConsumerUpdates/ucm350570.htm. Accessed July 2015.
12. Caffeine Informer. 2015. Caffeine Content of Drinks. Available at www.caffeineinformer.com/the-caffeine-database. Accessed July 2015.
13. Mayo Clinic. Nutrition and Healthy Eating. 2014. Available at www.mayoclinic.org/healthy-lifestyle/nutrition-and-healthy-eating/in-depth/caffeine/art-20049372. Accessed July 2015.

Chapter 12

1. USDA. 2012. Global Food Markets, Global Food Industry. Available at www.ers.usda.gov. Accessed May 2013.
2. Gallo, A. 1999. Food advertising in the United States. In Franzao, E., ed., *America's Eating Habits: Changes and Consequences.* Washington, D.C.: United States Department of Agriculture. Available at www.ers.usda.gov. Accessed May 2013.
3. SOS eMarketing. 2009. Red Bull: The Stuff of Beverage Marketing Legends. Available at www.sosemarketing.com. Accessed March 2010.
4. Garner, J. 2009. Using Social Media to Market Your Products: The Case of Red Bull. ComputerWeekly.com. Available at www.computerweekly.com. Accessed March 2010.
5. USDA. 1999. Blisard, N. Advertising and What We Eat, The Case of Dairy Products. *America's Eating Habits: Changes and Consequences.* Agriculture Information Bulletin No. (AIB-750), May 1999. www.ers.usda.gov/publications/aib-agricultural-information-bulletin/aib750.aspx.
6. Harmon, A. H., and B. L. Gerald. 2007. Position of the American Dietetic Association: Food and Nutrition Professionals Can Implement Practices to Conserve Natural Resources and Support Ecological Sustainability. *Journal of the American Dietetic Association* 107: 1033–1043; Sobal, J., L. Kahn, and C. Bisogni. 1998. A Conceptual Model of the Food and Nutrition System. *Social Science & Medicine* 47: 853–863.
7. U.S. Environmental Protection Agency. Updated April 2013. Ag 101: Demographics. Available at www.epa.gov. Accessed June 2013.
8. USDA Census of Agriculture. 2012. 2012 Census Highlights. Available at www.agcensus.usda.gov/Publications/2012/Online_Resources/Highlights. Accessed May 2015.
9. U.S. Environmental Protection Agency. Updated April 2013. Ag 101: Economic Overview. Available at www.epa.gov. Accessed May 2015.
10. U.S. Environmental Protection Agency. Ag 101: Demographics.
11. International Food Information Council. 2009. Food Insight. Background on Agricultural Practices and Food Technologies. Available at www.foodinsight.org. Accessed January 2010.
12. Rickman, D., J. Luvall, J. Shaw, P. Mask, D. Kissel, and D. Sullivan. 2003. Precision Agriculture: Changing the Face of Farming. *GeoTimes.* Available at www.geotimes.org. Accessed January 2010.
13. USDA. 2015. Food Expenditure. Available at www.ers.usda.gov/data-products/food-expenditures.aspx#.UuE9EHn0Ay5. Accessed May 2015.
14. U.S. Environmental Protection Agency. Ag 101: Economic Overview.
15. Ibid.
16. Ibid.
17. U.S. Environmental Protection Agency. 2009. Agribusiness: Sectors Strategies Program, June 29, 2009. Available at www.epa.gov. Accessed January 2010.
18. U.S. Department of Agriculture, Economic Research Service. 2013. FAQs. Available at www.ers.usda.gov. Accessed November 2013.
19. U.S. Environmental Protection Agency. Agribusiness.
20. U.S. Environmental Protection Agency. 2009. Ag 101: Crop Production. Available at www.epa.gov. Accessed May 2015.
21. Ibid.
22. U.S. Environmental Protection Agency. 2009. Ag 101: Beef Production. Available at www.epa.gov. Accessed May 2015.
23. U.S. Environmental Protection Agency. 2009. Ag 101: Pork Production. Available at www.epa.gov. Accessed May 2015.
24. U.S. Environmental Protection Agency. 2009. Ag 101: Poultry Production. Available at www.epa.gov. Accessed May 2015.
25. Ibid.
26. International Food Information Council. Food Insight. Background on Agricultural Practices and Food Technologies.
27. Hendrickson, M., and H. James. 2008. Does the World Need U.S. Farmers Even If Americans Don't? *Journal of Agricultural and Environmental Ethics* 21: 311–328.
28. United States Department of Agriculture, Economic Research Service. 2013. Outlook for U.S. Agricultural Trade. Available at www.ers.usda.gov. Accessed August 2013.
29. United States Department of Agriculture, Economic Research Service. 2009. Global Food Markets: International Consumer and Retail Trends.
Available at www.ers.usda.gov. Accessed January 2010; Regmi, A., H. Takeshima, and L. Unnevehr. 2008. Convergence in Global Food Demand and Delivery. *Economic Research Report No. ERR-56.* Available at www.ers.usda.gov. Accessed January 2010.
30. Popkin, B. 2007. The World Is Fat. *Scientific American.* Available at www.sciam.com. Accessed February 2010; Centers for Disease Control and Prevention. 2013. FastStats: Obesity and Overweight. Available at www.cdc.gov. Accessed August 2013.
31. World Health Organization. 2010. Controlling the Global Obesity Epidemic. Available at www.who.int. Accessed January 2010.
32. United States Department of Agriculture, Economic Research Service. 2013. Value of U.S. Food Imports: Fruits and Fruit Preparations. Available at www.ers.usda.gov. Accessed August 2013.
33. Hendrickson. Does the World Need U.S. Farmers?
34. USDA. 2013. Report on U.S. Agricultural Trade Import Share of Consumption. Available at www.ers.usda.gov. Accessed June 2013.
35. Hendrickson. Does the World Need U.S. Farmers?; Blank, S. 1998. *The End of Agriculture in the American Portfolio.* Westport, CT: Quorum Books.
36. Mundell, E. 2008. U.S. Food Safety: The Import Alarm Keeps Sounding. *U.S. News & World Report.* Available at http://health.usnews.com. Accessed January 2010.
37. U.S. FDA. 2013. 2013 Annual Report on Food Facilities, Food Imports, and FDA Foreign Offices. Available at www.fda.gov/Food/GuidanceRegulation/FSMA/ucm376478.htm?source=govdelivery&utm_medium=email&utm_source=govdelivery. Accessed May 2015.
38. Martin, A. 2007. FDA Curbs Sale of 5 Seafoods Farmed in China. *The New York Times.* Available at www.nytimes.com. Accessed January 2010.
39. Regmi. Convergence in Global Food Demand and Delivery.
40. IFIC. 2014. Consumer Perceptions of Food Technology Survey. Available at www.foodinsight.org/2014ConsumerPerceptionsofTechnologySurvey. Accessed May 2015.
41. Tagtow, et al. 2014. Academy of Nutrition and Dietetics: Standards of Professional Performance for RDNs in Sustainable, Resilient, and Healthy Food and Water Systems. *Journal of the Academy of Nutrition and Dietetics* 114: 475–488.
42. Horrigan, L., R. Lawrence, and P. Walker. 2002. How Sustainable Agriculture Can Address the Environmental and Human Health Harms of Industrial Agriculture. *Environmental Health Perspectives* 110: 445–456.
43. Hendrickson. Does the World Need U.S. Farmers?
44. Pirog, R., T. Van Pelt, K. Enshayan, and E. Cook. 2001 Food, Fuel, and Freeways: an Iowa perspective on how far food travels, fuel usage, and greenhouse gas emissions. Available at http://www.leopold.iastate.edu/pubs-and-papers/2001-06-food-fuel-freeways. Accessed July 2015.
45. Ibid.
46. An Introduction to Climate Change. National Resources Defense Council. 2011. Available at www.nrdc.org/globalwarming/climatebasics.asp. Accessed May 2015.
47. Heller, Martin C., and Gregory A. Keoleian. 2000. *Life Cycle-Based Sustainability Indicators for Assessment of the U.S. Food System.* Ann Arbor, MI: Center for Sustainable Systems, University of Michigan; The Sustainable Table, GRACE Communications Foundation. 2009. Local and Regional Food Systems. Available at www.sustainabletable.org. Accessed August 2013.
48. Harmon. Position of the American Dietetic Association: Food and Nutrition Professionals Can Implement Practices.
49. Pimentel, D., P. Hepperly, J. Hanson, D. Douds, and R. Seidel. 2005. Environmental, Energetic, and Economic Comparisons of Organic and Conventional Farming Systems. *BioScience* 55: 573–582.
50. Brown, L. 2008. *Plan B 3.0. Mobilizing to Save Civilization.* New York: WW Norton & Company.
51. Howard, A. 1940. *The Agricultural Testament.* London: Oxford University Press.
52. Environmental Protection Agency. 2009. What on Earth Is Soil? Available at www.epa.gov. Accessed August 2013.
53. Tagtow, A., and A. Harmon. 2009. *Healthy Land, Healthy Food and Healthy Eaters.* Available at www.uwyo.edu. Accessed February 2010.
54. Nemecek, T., F. Hayer, E. Bonnin, B. Carrouee, and C. V. Schneider. 2015. Designing Eco-Efficient Crop Rotations Using Life Cycle Assessment of Crop Combinations. *European Journal of Agronomy* 65: 40–51.
55. EPA. 2010. Watersense. Available at www.epa.gov. Accessed February 2010.
56. Ibid.
57. Ibid.
58. Eshel, G., A. Shepon, T. Makoz, and R. Milo. 2014. Land, Irrigation, Water, Greenhouse Gas, and Reactive Nitrogen Burdens of Meat, Eggs, and Dairy Production in the U.S. *Proceedings of the National Academy of Sciences* 111: 1196–2001.

59. Scientific Report of the 2015 Dietary Guidelines for Americans. 2015. Available at www.health.gov/dietaryguidelines/2015-scientific-report/PDFs/Scientific-Report-of-the-2015-Dietary-Guidelines-Advisory-Committee.pdf. Accessed May 2015.

60. Harmon. Position of the American Dietetic Association: Food and Nutrition Professionals Can Implement Practices.

61. Know Your Farmer Know Your Food. www.usda.gov/wps/portal/usda/knowyourfarmer?navid=KNOWYOURFARMER. Accessed October 2015.

62. United Nations. 2012. World Population Prospects, the 2012 Revision. Available at http://esa.un.org/wpp. Accessed May 2015.

63. Collier, R. J., and D. E. Bauman. 2014. Update on Human Health Concerns of Recombinant Bovine Somatotropin Use in Dairy Cows. *Journal of Animal Science* 92: 1800–1807.

64. FDA, Center for Veterinary Medicine. 2009. Report on the Food and Drug Administration's Review of the Safety of Recombinant Bovine Somatotropin. Available at www.fda.gov. Accessed February 2010; Collier. Update on Human Health Concerns.

65. American Cancer Society. 2011. Recombinant Bovine Growth Hormone. Available at www.cancer.org. Accessed October 2013.

66. FDA, Center for Veterinary Medicine. Updated 2009. Steroid Hormones. Available at www.fda.gov. Accessed October 2010.

67. U.S. Environmental Protection Agency. Ag 101: Beef Production.

68. Ibid.

69. Centers for Disease Control, National Antimicrobial Resistance Monitoring System. 2015. Antibiotic Resistance Threats Report and Foodborne Germs. Available at www.cdc.gov/narms/resources/threats.html. Accessed May 2015.

70. FDA, Center for Veterinary Medicine. 2013. National Antimicrobial Resistance Monitoring System. Available at www.fda.gov. Accessed August 2013.

71. FDA, Center for Veterinary Medicine. 2012. Judicious Use of Antimicrobials. Available at www.fda.gov. Accessed August 2013.

72. USDA, Agricultural Marketing Service. 2013. National Organic Program. Available at www.ams.usda.gov. Accessed June 2013.

73. Smith-Spangler, C., et al. 2012. Are Organic Foods Safer or Healthier than Conventional Alternatives? *Annals of Internal Medicine* 157: 348–366.

74. EPA. 2013. What Are Biopesticides? Available at www.epa.gov. Accessed August 2013.

75. Ibid.

76. Beseler, C., L. Stallones, J. Hoppin, M. Alavanja, A. Blair, T. Keefe, and F. Kamel. 2008. Depression and Pesticide Exposures among Private Pesticide Applicators Enrolled in the Agricultural Health Study. *Environmental Health Perspectives* 116: 1713–1719.

77. U.S. Fish and Wildlife Service. 2013. Bald Eagle Fact Sheet. Available at www.doi.gov. Accessed October 2013.

78. U.S. Environmental Protection Agency. 2012. Pesticides and Food: Health Problems Pesticides May Pose. Available at www.epa.gov. Accessed August 2013.

79. U.S. Environmental Protection Agency. 2012. Pesticides and Food: Why Children May Be Especially Sensitive to Pesticides. Available at www.epa.gov. Accessed October 2013.

80. Smith-Spangler. Are Organic Foods Safer or Healthier than Conventional Alternatives?

81. U.S. Environmental Protection Agency. Updated 2012. Pesticides: Environmental Effects. Available at www.epa.gov. Accessed May 2015.

82. International Food Information Council. Food Insight. Background on Agricultural Practices and Food Technologies.

83. U.S. Environmental Protection Agency. 2012. Pesticides: Topical and Chemical Fact Sheets. Integrated Pest Management (IPM) Principles. Available at www.epa.gov. Accessed August 2013.

84. Pew Initiative on Food and Biotechnology. 2004. Genetically Modified Crops in the United States. Available at www.pewtrusts.org. Accessed August 2013.

85. International Food Information Council. 2013. Food Insight. Questions and Answers about Food Biotechnology. Available at www.foodinsight.org. Accessed August 2013.

86. International Food Information Council. 2009. Food and Agricultural Biotechnology. Health Impacts in Developing Nations CPE Program. Available at www.foodinsight.org. Accessed January 2010.

87. Fernandez-Cornejo, J., and W. McBride. 2002. Adoption of Bioengineered Crops. *Agricultural Economic Report No. AER-810*. Available at www.ers.usda.gov. Accessed January 2010.

88. USDA, Economic Research Service. 2013. Adoption of Genetically Engineered Crops in the U.S. Available at www.ers.usda.gov. Accessed August 2013.

89. Bruh, C. 2006. Position of the American Dietetic Association: Agricultural and Food Biotechnology. *Journal of the American Dietetic Association* 106: 285–293.

90. The American Oil Chemists' Society. 2012. High-Oleic Canola Oils and Their Food Applications. Available at www.aocs.org. Accessed October 2013.

91. Phillips, T. 2008. Genetically Modified Organisms (GMOs): Transgenic Crops and Recombinant DNA Technology. *Nature Education* 1. Available at www.nature.com. Accessed August 2013.

92. Ibid.

93. Ibid.

94. International Food Information Council. 2014. Food Biotechnology: A Study of U.S. Consumer Trends. Available at www.foodinsight.org. Accessed May 2015.

95. Golan, E., L. Mancino, and L. Unnevehr. 2009. Food Policy: Check the List of Ingredients. *Amber Waves*. Available at www.ers.usda.gov. Accessed March 2010.

96. Ibid.

97. O'Neil, C. E., et al. 2010. Whole-Grain Consumption Is Associated with Diet Quality and Nutrient Intake in Adults: The National Health and Nutrition Examination Survey, 1999–2004. *Journal of the American Dietetic Association* 110: 1461–1468.

98. Whole Grains Council. 2009. Report from the Make Half Your Grains Whole Conference, April 2009. Available at http://wholegrainscouncil.org. Accessed June 2013.

99. Golan. Food Policy: Check the List of Ingredients.

100. Ibid.

101. Ibid.

102. National School Lunch Program. National School Lunch Program Fact Sheet. 2013. Available at www.fns.usda.gov/sites/default/files/NSLP-FactSheet.pdf. Accessed May 2015.

103. Ibid.

104. Nestle, M. 2002. *Food Policy*. Berkeley: University of California Press.

105. Brownell, K., T. Farley, W. Willett, B. Popkin, F. Chaloupka, J. Thompson, and D. Ludwig. 2009. The Public Health and Economic Benefits to Taxing Sugar-Sweetened Beverages. *New England Journal of Medicine* 361: 1599–1605.

106. Eaton, J. 2009. The Food Lobby's War on a Soda Tax. The Center for Public Integrity. Available at www.publicintegrity.org. Accessed March 2010.

107. USDA. 2013. Meat and Poultry Labeling Terms. Available at www.fsis.usda.gov. Accessed August 2013.

108. USDA, Economic Research Service. 2014. Organic Market Overview. Available at www.ers.usda.gov/topics/natural-resources-environment/organic-agriculture/organic-market-overview.aspx. Accessed May 2015.

109. Hartman Group. 2012. Organic and Natural Report. Available at www.hartman-group.com. Accessed June 2013.

110. USDA, Agricultural Marketing Service, National Organic Program. 2012. USDA Oversight of Organic Products. Available at www.ams.usda.gov. Accessed August 2013.

111. USDA, Agricultural Marketing Service, National Organic Program. 2013. National List of Allowed and Prohibited Substances. Available at www.ams.usda.gov. Accessed August 2013.

112. USDA, Agricultural Marketing Service, National Organic Program. USDA Oversight of Organic Products.

113. Smith-Spangler. Are Organic Foods Safer or Healthier than Conventional Alternatives?

114. Ibid.

115. Greene, C., C. Dimitri, B. Lin, W. McBride, L. Oberholtzer, and T. Smith. 2009. Emerging Issues in the U.S. Organic Industry. United States Department of Agriculture, Economic Research Service, Bulletin No. 55. Available at www.ers.usda.gov. Accessed February 2010.

116. USDA, Agricultural Marketing Service, National Organic Program. 2013. International Agreements. Available at www.ams.usda.gov. Accessed June 2013.

117. Greene. Emerging Issues in the U.S. Organic Industry.

Feature Box References

1. Cotner, S., and J. Masabni. 2009. Vegetable Gardening in Containers. AgriLife Extension, Texas A&M System. Available at http://repository.tamu.edu. Accessed August 2013; Iowa State University Extension. 2005. Container Vegetable Gardening. Available at www.extension.iastate.edu. Accessed August 2013.

Two Points of View References

1. USDA. 2014. Economic Research Services. Title 1 - Crop Commodity Programs. Available at HYPERLINK "http://www.ers.usda.gov/topics/crops/wheat/policy.aspx" \t "_blank" www.ers.usda.gov/topics/crops/wheat/policy.aspx. Accessed October 2015.

Chapter 13

1. U.S. Department of Agriculture, U.S. Department of Health and Human Services. 2010. *Dietary Guidelines for Americans, 2010.* 7th ed. Washington, D.C.: U.S. Government Printing Office.
2. Centers for Disease Control and Prevention. 1999. Safer and Healthier Foods: 1900–1999. *Journal of the American Medical Association* 48: 905–913; Food and Drug Administration. 2009. About the FDA: The Long Struggle for the Law. Available at www.fda.gov. Accessed May 2015.
3. Ibid.
4. Johnson, R. 2012. The Federal Food Safety System: A Primer. Available at www.fas.org. Accessed May 2015.
5. Centers for Disease Control and Prevention. Safer and Healthier Foods.
6. Food and Drug Administration. 2013. Food Protection Plan of 2007. Available at www.fda.gov. Accessed May 2015.
7. Johnson, M. 2014. *Human Biology: Concepts and Current Issues.* Boston: Pearson Education, Inc.
8. Ibid.
9. Centers for Disease Control and Prevention. 2013. Norovirus. Available at www.cdc.gov. Accessed May 2015.
10. Centers for Disease Control and Prevention. 2003. Public Health Dispatch: Multistate Outbreak of Hepatitis A among Young Adult Concert Attendees, United States, 2003. *Morbidity and Mortality Weekly Report* 52: 844–845.
11. Grice, E. A., H. H. Kong, G. Renaud, et al. 2008. A Diversity Profile of the Human Skin Microbiota. *Genome Research* 18: 1043–1050. Available at http://genome.cshlp.org. Accessed May 2015.
12. Centers for Disease Control and Prevention. 2012. Food Safety. Available at www.cdc.gov. Accessed May 2015.
13. National Center for Zoonotic, Vector-Borne, and Enteric Diseases. 2013. General Information: *Campylobacter.* Available at www.cdc.gov. Accessed July 2013.
14. Ibid.
15. Ibid.
16. National Center for Zoonotic, Vector-Borne, and Enteric Diseases. Updated July 2012. *E. coli.* Available at www.cdc.gov. Accessed July 2013.
17. Ibid.
18. Centers for Disease Control and Prevention. 2006. Traveler's Diarrhea. Available at www.cdc.gov. Accessed June 2015.
19. National Center for Zoonotic, Vector-Borne, and Enteric Diseases. 2009. Salmonellosis. Available at www.cdc.gov. Accessed July 2013.
20. Food Safety and Inspection Service. 2013. Parasites and Foodborne Illness. Available at www.fsis.usda.gov. Accessed July 2013; Food and Drug Administration. 2012. Bad Bug Book. Available at www.fda.gov. Accessed 2013.
21. Ibid.
22. U.S. Department of Agriculture, Animal and Plant Health Inspection Service. 2012. Bovine Spongiform Encephalopathy (BSE). Available at www.aphis.usda.gov. Accessed May 2015.
23. Ibid.
24. Ibid.
25. Food and Drug Administration. 2013. Bovine Spongiform Encephalopathy. Available at www.fda.gov. Accessed June 2015.
26. USDA, Animal and Plant Health Inspection Service. 2006. Bovine Spongiform Encephalopathy Ongoing Surveillance Plan. Available at www.aphis.usda.gov. Accessed June 2015.
27. Ibid.
28. Food and Drug Administration. Bovine Spongiform Encephalopathy.
29. Centers for Disease Control and Prevention. 2013. vCJD. Available at www.cdc.gov. Accessed June 2015.
30. Food and Drug Administration. 2013. Food Safety for Older Adults. Available at www.fda.gov. Accessed July 2013; Buzby, J. C. 2003. Older Adults at Risk of Complications from Microbial Foodborne Illness. *Food Review* 25: 30–35.
31. The Pew Health Group and the American Academy of Pediatrics. 2009. Children and Foodborne Illness. Available at www.pewtrusts.org. Accessed July 2013; Buzby, J. C. 2002. Children and Microbial Foodborne Illness. *Food Review* 24: 32–37.
32. Food and Drug Administration. 2013. Food Safety: It's Especially Important for At-Risk Groups. Available at www.fda.gov. Accessed June 2015.
33. Food and Drug Administration. Bad Bug Book.
34. Ibid.
35. Curtis, V., and S. Cairncross. 2003. Effect of Washing Hands with Soap on Diarrhoea Risk in the Community: A Systematic Review. *The Lancet Infectious Diseases* 3: 275–281.
36. Borchgrevink, C., J. Cha, and S. Kim. 2013. Hand Washing Practices in a College Town. *Environment* 5: 18–24.
37. U.S. Department of Agriculture. 2010. Report of the Dietary Guidelines Advisory Committee on the *Dietary Guidelines for Americans, 2010.* Available at www.cnpp.usda.gov. Accessed July 2013.
38. Godwin, S., F. Chen, and R. Coppings. 2006. Correlation of Visual Perceptions of Cleanliness and Reported Cleaning Practices with Measures of Microbial Contamination in Home Refrigerators. *Food Protection Trends* 26: 474–480.
39. Food Safety and Inspection Service. 2010. Refrigeration and Food Safety. Available at www.fsis.usda.gov. Accessed June 2015.
40. Food Safety and Inspection Service. 1998. Premature Browning of Cooked Ground Beef. Available at www.fsis.usda.gov. Accessed June 2015.
41. Food Safety and Inspection Service. 2011. The Color of Meat and Poultry. Available at www.fsis.usda.gov. Accessed June 2015.
42. Centers for Disease Control and Prevention. 2013. Vital Signs: *Listeria* Illnesses, Death, and Outbreaks—United States, 2009–2011. *Morbidity and Mortality Weekly Report (MMWR)* 62: 448–452.
43. Centers for Disease Control and Prevention. 2013. Vital Signs: Recipe for Food Safety. Available at www.cdc.gov. Accessed August 2013.
44. Ibid.
45. The Partnership for Food Safety Education. 2010. Chill: Refrigerate Promptly! Available at www.fightbac.org. Accessed June 2015.
46. Food and Drug Administration. Bad Bug Book.
47. Food and Drug Administration and U.S. Department of Agriculture. 2000. A Description of the U.S. Food Safety System. Available at www.fsis.usda.gov. Accessed June 2015.
48. Centers for Disease Control and Prevention. Foodborne Disease Active Surveillance Network (FoodNet): FoodNet Surveillance. 2012. Report for 2011. Atlanta, Georgia: U.S. Department of Health and Human Services, CDC.
49. Food and Drug Administration and U.S. Department of Agriculture. A Description of the U.S. Food Safety System.
50. Centers for Disease Control and Prevention. 2013. PulseNet & Foodborne Diseases Outbreak Detection. Available at www.cdc.gov. Accessed June 2015.
51. Bracket, R. 2006. Statement before the Committee on Health, Education, Labor and Pensions, United States Senate. Ensuring Food Safety: FDA's Role in Tracking and Resolving the Recent *E. coli* Spinach Outbreak. Available at www.hhs.gov. Accessed June 2015; Food and Drug Administration. 2006. FDA Statement on Foodborne *E. coli* O157:H7 Outbreak in Spinach. Available at www.fda.gov. Accessed June 2015.
52. Food and Drug Administration. 2013. Hazard Analysis and Critical Control Points (HACCP). Available at www.fda.gov. June 2015.
53. Food and Drug Administration. 2013. FDA Food Code. Available at www.fda.gov. Accessed June 2015.
54. Food and Drug Administration. 2013. Talking about Juice Safety: What You Need to Know. Available at www.fda.gov. Accessed June 2015.
55. Centers for Disease Control and Prevention. 2006. Botulism: Control Measures Overview for Clinicians. Available at www.bt.cdc.gov. Accessed July 2015.
56. Food and Drug Administration. 2013. Analysis and Evaluation of Preventive Control Measures for the Control and Reduction/Elimination of Microbial Hazards on Fresh and Fresh-Cut Produce. Available at www.fda.gov. Accessed July 2015.
57. Food and Drug Administration. 2011. Kinetics of Microbial Inactivation for Alternative Food Processing Technologies. High-Pressure Processing. Available at www.fda.gov. Accessed July 2015.
58. U.S. Environmental Protection Agency. 2012. Food Irradiation. Available at www.epa.gov. Accessed July 2015.
59. Ibid.
60. Food and Drug Administration. 2013. Irradiated Food and Packaging: Consumer Information. Available at www.fda.gov. Accessed July 2015.
61. Centers for Disease Control and Prevention. 2009. Food Irradiation. Available at www.cdc.gov. Accessed July 2015; Tauxe, R. 2001. Food Safety and Irradiation: Protecting the Public from Foodborne Infections. *Infectious Diseases* 7: 516–521.
62. Tauxe. Food Safety and Irradiation; Centers for Disease Control and Prevention. Food Irradiation.

63. Food and Drug Administration. Irradiated Food and Packaging. Available at www.fda.gov. Accessed July 2015.
64. Tauxe. Food Safety and Irradiation.
65. Food and Drug Administration. Irradiated Food and Packaging. Available at www.fda.gov. Accessed July 2015.
66. Ibid.
67. Olson, D. G. 1998. Irradiation of Food Scientific Status Summary. *Food Technology* 52: 56-62.
68. Food Safety and Inspection Service. 2013. Food Product Dating. Available at www.fsis.usda.gov. Accessed July 2015.
69. Ibid.
70. Grotheer, P., M. Marshall, and A. Simonne. 2005. Sulfites: Separating Fact from Fiction. Institute of Food and Agricultural Sciences, University of Florida. Available at http://edis.ifas.ufl.edu. Accessed July 2015.
71. Ibid.
72. Ibid.
73. Meadows, M. 2003. MSG: A Common Flavor Enhancer. *FDA Consumer* 37: 35.
74. Ibid.
75. Rados, C. 2004. GRAS: Time Tested and Trusted Food Ingredients. *FDA Consumer* 38: 20.
76. FDA. Updated 2010. Food Additives. Available at www.fda.gov. Accessed July 2015.
77. Ibid.
78. Rados. GRAS.
79. Centers for Disease Control and Prevention. 2012. Dioxins, Durans and Dioxin-Like Polychlorinate Biphenyls. Available at www.cdc.gov. Accessed July 2013; Food and Drug Administration. 2013. Questions and Answers about Dioxins and Food Safety. Available at www.fda.gov. Accessed July 2015.
80. Centers for Disease Control and Prevention. 2005. Marine Toxins. Available at www.cdc.gov. Accessed July 2015.
81. Ibid.
82. Ibid.
83. Ibid.
84. Taylor, S. 2006. Food additives, contaminants, and natural toxicants and their risk assessment. In Shils, M., M. Shike, A. Ross, B. Caballero, and R. Cousins. *Modern Nutrition in Health and Disease.* 10th ed. Philadelphia: Lippincott Williams & Wilkins.
85. U.S. Environmental Protection Agency. Updated 2013. Polychlorinated Biphenyls (PCBs). Available at www.epa.gov. Accessed July 2015.
86. Ibid.
87. Ibid.
88. Food and Drug Administration. 2013. Food Defense. What's Your Plan? Available at http://blogs.fda.gov. Accessed July 2015.
89. Centers for Disease Control and Prevention. 2007. Bioterrorism Overview. Available at http://emergency.cdc.gov. Accessed July 2015.
90. Risen, J. 2003. Threats and Responses: Terror Network Plot to Poison Food of British Troops Is Suspected. *New York Times.* Available at www.nytimes.com. Accessed July 2013.
91. Bruemmer, B. 2003. Food Biosecurity. *Journal of the American Dietetics Association* 103: 687–691.

Feature Box References

1. FDA. 2011. *Fish and Fisheries Products Hazards and Controls Guidance.* 4th ed. Available at www.fda.gov. Accessed June 2015.
2. FDA. 2013. Fresh and Frozen Seafood: Selecting and Serving It Safely. Available at www.fda.gov. Accessed June 2015.
3. Ibid.
4. Centers for Disease Control and Prevention. 2013. *Listeria* (Listeriosis): Prevention. Available at www.cdc.gov. Accessed August 2013.

Two Points of View References

1. Direct from CDC Environmental Health Services Branch. 2014. Available at www.cdc.gov/nceh/ehs/docs/jeh/2014/april-food-trucks.pdf. Accessed July 201510/27/15.
2. CNN. 2013. Are Food Trucks Safe? Available at www.edition.cnn.com/2013/04/08/health/food-trucks-safety. Accessed July 2015.
3. NY Times. 2013. The Food Truck Business Stinks. Available at www.nytimes.com/2013/05/12/magazine/the-food-truck-business-stinks.html?pagewanted=all&_r=0. Accessed July 2015.
4. CDC. 2013. Your Health – Your Environment. Find Out about Food Trucks in Your Area. Available at www.blogs.cdc.gov/yourhealthyourenvironment/2013/08/14/find-out-about-food-trucks-in-your-area. Accessed July 2015.
5. Institute for Justice. 2012. Seven Myths and Realities about Food Trucks. http://ij.org/report/seven-myths-and-realities-about-food-trucks/#1. Accessed November 2015.
6. Myrick, R. 2015. Running a Food Truck for Dummies. Prepare Your Food Truck for Health Inspections. Available at www.dummies.com/how-to/content/prepare-your-food-truck-for-health-inspections.html. Accessed July 2015.
7. Institute for Justice. Erickson, A. C. 2014. Street Eats, Safe Eats. Available at www.ij.org/street-eats-safe-eats-results. Accessed July 2015.
8. Faw, B. V., and J. L. Tuttle, Direct From CDC Environmental Health Services Branch. 2014. Mobile Food Trucks: California EHS-Net Study on Risk Factors and Inspection Challenges. Available at www.cdc.gov/nceh/ehs/docs/jeh/2014/april-food-trucks.pdf. Accessed July 2015.
9. FDA. 2014. Questions and Answers on the Menu and Vending Machines Nutrition Labeling Requirements. Available at www.fda.gov/Food/IngredientsPackagingLabeling/LabelingNutrition/ucm248731.htm. Accessed July 2015.
10. Food Safety News. 2015. Food Safety on Food Trucks Called 'A Little More of a Challenge.' Available at www.foodsafetynews.com/2015/05/food-safety-on-food-trucks-a-little-more-of-a-challenge/#.VXV1Y-WAmfQc. Accessed July 2015.

Chapter 14

1. Hammoud, A., N. Wilde, M. Gibson, D. T. Carrell, and A. W. Meikle. 2008. Male Obesity and Alteration in Sperm Parameters. *Fertility and Sterility* 90: 2222–2225.
2. Eskenazi, B., S. Kidd, A. Marks, E. Sloter, G. Block, and A. Wyrobek. 2005. Antioxidant Intake Is Associated with Semen Quality in Healthy Men. *Human Reproduction* 20: 1006–1012.
3. Centers for Disease Control and Prevention. 2012. Preconception Care and Health Care, Information for Men. Available at www.cdc.gov. Accessed March 2013.
4. Barazani, Y., B. F. Katz, H. M. Nagler, and D. S. Stember. 2014. Lifestyle, Environment, and Male Reproductive Health. *Urologic Clinics of North America* 41: 55–66.
5. Kaiser, L., and L. Allen. 2008. Position of the American Dietetic Association: Nutrition and Lifestyle for a Healthy Pregnancy Outcome. *Journal of the American Dietetic Association* 108: 553–561.
6. Kitsantas, P., and L. R. Pawloski. 2010. Maternal Obesity, Health Status during Pregnancy, and Breast-Feeding Initiation and Duration. *Journal of Maternal and Fetal Neonatal Medicine* 23: 135–141.
7. Gaskins, A. J., J. W. Rich-Edwards, D. S. Colaci, M. C. Afeiche, T. L. Toth, M. W. Gillman, et al. 2014. Prepregnancy and Early Adulthood Body Mass Index and Adult Weight Change in Relation to Fetal Loss. *Obstetrics & Gynecology* 124: 662–669.
8. Centers for Disease Control and Prevention. 2014. Folic Acid. Available at www.cdc.gov/ncbddd/folicacid/recommendations.html. Accessed March 2015.
9. American College of Obstetricians and Gynecologists. 2010. Moderate Caffeine Consumption during Pregnancy. Committee Opinion No. 462. *Obstetrics & Gynecology* 116: 467–468.
10. March of Dimes Foundation. 2015. Caffeine in pregnancy. Available at www.marchofdimes.com. Accessed November 2015.
11. U.S. Department of Health and Human Services. 2004. *The Health Consequences of Smoking: A Report of the Surgeon General.* Atlanta: National Center for Chronic Disease Prevention and Health Promotion, Office on Smoking and Health.
12. U.S. Department of Health and Human Services. 2005. U.S. Surgeon General Advisory on Alcohol Use in Pregnancy. Available at www.cdc.gov. Accessed July 2010.
13. Beth Israel Deaconess Medical Center. 2015. Herbs and Supplements to Avoid During Pregnancy and Breast Feeding. Available from http://www.bidmc.org/YourHealth/Therapeutic-Centers/Pregnancy.aspx?ChunkID=35536. Accessed June 2015.
14. National Library of Medicine. National Institutes of Health. 2012. Morning Sickness. Available at www.nlm.nih.gov. Accessed March 2013.
15. Kaiser. Position of the American Dietetic Association: Nutrition and Lifestyle for a Healthy Pregnancy Outcome.
16. National Center for Biotechnology Information, U.S. National Library of Medicine. 2012. Pica. Available at www.ncbi.nlm.nih.gov. Accessed March 2013.
17. American College of Obstetricians and Gynecologists. 2013. Weight Gain during Pregnancy. Committee Opinion No. 548. *Obstetrics & Gynecology* 121: 210–212.
18. Institute of Medicine. 2009. Weight Gain during Pregnancy: Reexamining the Guidelines. Available at www.iom.edu. Accessed March 2013.

19. U.S. Department of Agriculture, U.S. Department of Health and Human Services. 2010. *Dietary Guidelines for Americans, 2010*. 7th ed. Washington, D.C.: U.S. Government Printing Office.

20. Koletzko B., E. Lien, C. Agosoni, et al. 2008. The Roles of Long-Chain Polyunsaturated Fatty Acids in Pregnancy, Lactation, and Infancy: Review of Current Knowledge and Consensus Recommendations. *Journal of Perinatal Medicine* 36: 5–14.

21. Zeisel, S. H., and M. D. Niculescu. 2006. Perinatal Choline Influences Brain Structure and Function. *Nutrition Reviews* 64: 197–203.

22. Shaw, G. M., S. L. Carmichael, W. Yang, S. Selvin, and D. M. Schaffer. 2004. Periconceptional Dietary Intake of Choline and Betaine and Neural Tube Defects in Offspring. *American Journal of Epidemiology* 160: 102–109.

23. Institute of Medicine. 2001. *Dietary Reference Intakes for Vitamin A, Vitamin K, Arsenic, Boron, Chromium, Copper, Iodine, Iron, Manganese, Nickel, Silicon, Vanadium, and Zinc*. Washington, D.C.: National Academies Press.

24. USDA. 2013. Health and Nutrition Information for Pregnant and Breast-Feeding Women. Available at www.choosemyplate.gov. Accessed March 2013.

25. Kaiser. Position of the American Dietetic Association: Nutrition and Lifestyle for a Healthy Pregnancy Outcome.

26. March of Dimes Foundation. 2008. Alcohol and Drugs. Available at www.marchofdimes.com. Accessed March 2013.

27. Weng, X., R. Odouli, and D. K. Li. 2008. Maternal Caffeine Consumption during Pregnancy and the Risk of Miscarriage: A Prospective Cohort Study. *American Journal of Obstetrics and Gynecology* 198: 279. e1–e8.

28. Painter, R. C., S. R. de Rooij, P. M. Bossuyt, T. A. Simmers, C. Osmond, D. J. Barker, et al. 2006. Early Onset of Coronary Artery Disease after Prenatal Exposure to the Dutch Famine. *American Journal of Clinical Nutrition* 84: 322–327.

29. Ames, B. N. 2006. Low Micronutrient Intake May Accelerate the Degenerative Diseases of Aging through Allocation of Scarce Micronutrients by Triage. *Proceedings of the National Academy of Sciences* 103: 17589–17594.

30. Wu, G., F. W. Bazer, T. A. Cudd, C. J. Meininger, and T. E. Spencer. 2004. Recent Advances in Nutritional Sciences: Maternal Nutrition and Fetal Development. *Journal of Nutrition* 134: 2169–2172.

31. Stover, P. J., and M. A. Caudill. 2008. Genetic and Epigenetic Contributions to Human Nutrition and Health: Managing Genome-Diet Interactions. *Journal of the American Dietetic Association* 108: 1480–1487.

32. Institute of Medicine. Weight Gain during Pregnancy: Reexamining the Guidelines.

33. March of Dimes Foundation. 2012. Physical Activity. Available at www.marchofdimes.com. Accessed March 2013.

34. Centers for Disease Control and Prevention. 2011. Physical Activity, Healthy Pregnant or Postpartum Women. Available at www.cdc.gov. Accessed March 2013.

35. American Diabetes Association. 2013. What Is Gestational Diabetes? Available at www.diabetes.org. Accessed March 2013.

36. Ibid.

37. American College of Obstetricians and Gynecologists. 2013. Gestational Diabetes Mellitus. Practice Bulletin No. 137. *Obstetrics & Gynecology* 122: 406–416.

38. National Heart, Lung, and Blood Institute. 2000. High Blood Pressure in Pregnancy. Available at www.nhlbi.nih.gov. Accessed November 2015.

39. Kaiser. Position of the American Dietetic Association: Nutrition and Lifestyle for a Healthy Pregnancy Outcome.

40. Institute of Medicine. 2002. *Dietary Reference Intakes for Energy, Carbohydrate, Fiber, Fat, Fatty Acids, Cholesterol, Protein, and Amino Acids*. Washington, D.C.: National Academies Press.

41. Story, M., and J. Stang, eds. *Nutrition and the Pregnant Adolescent: A Practical Reference Guide*. 2000. Minneapolis, MN: HRSA.

42. Shabert, J. 2000. Nutrition during pregnancy and lactation. In Krause, *Food, Nutrition, & Diet Therapy*. 11th ed. Philadelphia: Saunders.

43. American Academy of Pediatrics. Section on Breast-Feeding. 2012. Breast-Feeding and the Use of Human Milk. *PEDIATRICS* 115: 496–506. doi: 10.1542/peds.2004-2491. Available at http://pediatrics.aappublications.org. Accessed March 2013.

44. Ibid.

45. U.S. Breast-Feeding Committee. 2002. Benefits of Breast-Feeding. Available at www.ehd.org. Accessed March 2013.

46. Economic Research Service. 2001. Economic Benefits of Breast-Feeding: A Review and Analysis. Available at www.ers.usda.gov. Accessed March 2013.

47. Bartick, M., and A. Reinhold. 2010. The Burden of Suboptimal Breast-Feeding in the United States. *PEDIATRICS* 125: e1048–e1056.

48. James, D. C. S., and R. Lessen. 2009. Position of the American Dietetic Association: Promoting and Supporting Breast-Feeding. *Journal of the American Dietetic Association* 109: 1926–1942.

49. American Academy of Pediatrics. Section on Breast-Feeding. Breast-Feeding and the Use of Human Milk.

50. Picciano, M., and S. S. McDonald. 2006. Lactation. In Shils, M. *Modern Nutrition in Health and Disease*. 10th ed. Philadelphia: Lippincott Williams & Wilkins.

51. James. Position of the American Dietetic Association: Promoting and Supporting Breast-Feeding.

52. Ibid.

53. Institute of Medicine. *Dietary Reference Intakes for Energy, Carbohydrate, Fiber, Fat, Fatty Acids, Cholesterol, Protein, and Amino Acids*.

54. Institute of Medicine. Weight Gain during Pregnancy: Reexamining the Guidelines.

55. Institute of Medicine. *Dietary Reference Intakes for Energy, Carbohydrate, Fiber, Fat, Fatty Acids, Cholesterol, Protein, and Amino Acids*.

56. American Academy of Pediatrics. 2012. Things to Avoid When Breast-Feeding. Available at www.healthychildren.org. Accessed March 2013.

57. American Academy of Pediatrics. Section on Breast-Feeding. Breast-Feeding and the Use of Human Milk.

58. Ibid.

59. Heird, W. C., and A. Cooper. 2006. Infancy and Childhood. In Shils, M. *Modern Nutrition in Health and Disease*. 10th ed. Philadelphia: Lippincott Williams & Wilkins.

60. O'Connor, N. R. 2009. Infant Formula. *American Family Physician* 79: 565–570.

61. American Academy of Pediatric Dentistry. 2011. Policy on Early Childhood Caries (ECC): Classification, Consequences and Preventive Strategies. Available at www.aapd.org. Accessed March 2013.

62. Centers for Disease Control and Prevention. 2010. Growth Charts. Available at www.cdc.gov. Accessed March 2013.

63. Institute of Medicine. *Dietary Reference Intakes for Energy, Carbohydrate, Fiber, Fat, Fatty Acids, Cholesterol, Protein, and Amino Acids*.

64. U.S. Department of Agriculture, Department of Health and Human Services. 2010. *Dietary Guidelines for Americans, 2010*. Available at www .health.gov. Accessed March 2013.

65. Institute of Medicine. *Dietary Reference Intakes for Vitamin A, Vitamin K, Arsenic, Boron, Chromium, Copper, Iodine, Iron, Manganese, Nickel, Silicon, Vanadium, and Zinc*.

66. American Academy of Pediatrics. 2008. Prevention of Rickets and Vitamin D Deficiency in Infants, Children, and Adolescents. Available at http://pediatrics.aappublications.org. Accessed March 2010.

67. Centers for Disease Control and Prevention. 2012. Overview: Infant Formula and Fluorosis. Available at www.cdc.gov. Accessed March 2013.

68. American Academy of Pediatrics. Section on Breast-Feeding. Breast-Feeding and the Use of Human Milk.

69. Ibid.

70. American Academy of Pediatrics. 2012. Switching to Solid Foods. Available at www.healthychildren.org. Accessed March 2013.

71. Fleischer, D. M., J. M. Spergel, A. H. Assa'ad, and J. A. Pongracic. 2013. Primary Prevention of Allergic Disease through Nutritional Interventions. *Journal of Allergy and Clinical Immunology: In Practice* 1: 29–36.

72. National Institute of Allergy and Infectious Diseases. Updated 2012. Food Allergy: Common Food Allergens in Infants, Children, and Adults. Available at www.niaid.nih.gov. Accessed June 2013.

73. Ibid.

74. Branum, A., and S. Lukacs. 2008. Food Allergy among U.S. Children: Trends in Prevalence and Hospitalizations. National Center for Health Statistics Data Brief. Available at www.cdc.gov/nchs/data/databriefs/db10.htm. Accessed April 2015.

75. Long, A. 2002. The Nuts and Bolts of Peanut Allergy. *New England Journal of Medicine* 346: 1320–1322.

76. Branum. Food Allergy among U.S. Children: Trends in Prevalence and Hospitalizations.

77. Food and Drug Administration. 2006. Food Allergen Labeling and Consumer Protection Act of 2004 (Title II of Public Law 108–282). Report to the Committee on Health, Education, Labor, and Pensions, United States Senate, and the Committee on Energy and Commerce, United States House of Representatives. Available at www.cfsan.fda.gov. Accessed June 2013.

78. Centers for Disease Control and Prevention. 2010. Botulism. Available at www.cdc.gov. Accessed March 2013.

Feature Box References

1. Slusser, W., L. Lange, V. Dickson, C. Hawkes, and R. Cohen. 2004. Breast Milk Expression in the Workplace: A Look at Frequency and Time. *Journal of Human Lactation* 20: 164–169.
2. Johnson, M. 2006. Letter to the Editor: Twentieth Anniversary Issue. *Journal of Human Lactation* 22: 14.
3. National Council of State Legislatures. 2011. Breast-Feeding Laws. Available at www.ncsl.org. Accessed June 2013.
4. U.S. Department of Health and Human Services, Maternal and Child Health Bureau. 2008. Easy Steps to Supporting Breast-Feeding Employees. Available at www.womenshealth.gov. Accessed June 2013.
5. American Academy of Pediatrics. 2012. Policy Statement: Breast-Feeding and the Use of Human Milk. *PEDIATRICS* 129: e827–e841.

Two Points of View References

1. Health and Human Services Division, Municipality of Anchorage, Alaska. 2008. Why Homemade? Available at www.hhs.muni.org. Accessed June 2013; Stallone, D., and M. Jacobson. 1995. Cheating Babies: Nutritional Quality and Cost of Baby Food. *CSPI Reports*. Available at www.cspinet.org. Accessed June 2013.
2. Freshbaby.com. 2002. Benefits of Homemade Baby Food. Available at http://freshbaby.com. Accessed November 2015.
3. Municipality of Anchorage. Why Homemade?; Stallone. Cheating Babies.
4. Fountain, B., University of Mississippi Extension Service. 2010. Homemade Baby Food Benefits Entire Family. Available at http://msucares.com. Accessed June 2013.
5. USDA, Agricultural Research Service. 2006. The New Food Quality Protection Act, 2006. Available at www.ars.usda.gov. Accessed August 2010.
6. Shaw, G. 2010. Homemade Baby Food: Is it Right for You? *WebMD*. Available at www.webmd.com. Accessed June 2013.
7. Schaefer, E., and N. Fradgley, National Network for Child Care. 1995. Feeding Your Baby. Available at www.nncc.org. Accessed June 2013.
8. Greer, F., and M. Shannon. 2005. Infant Methemoglobinemia: The Role of Dietary Nitrate in Food and Water. *PEDIATRICS* 116: 784–786.

Chapter 15

1. MedlinePlus. 2015. Normal Growth and Development. Available at www.nlm.nih.gov. Accessed April 2015.
2. American Academy of Pediatrics. 2004. *Pediatric Nutrition Handbook*. 5th ed. American Academy of Pediatrics.
3. Baker, R. D., F. R. Greer, and the Committee on Nutrition. 2010. Clinical Report—Diagnosis and Prevention of Iron Deficiency and Iron-Deficiency Anemia in Infants and Young Children (0–3 Years of Age). Available at http://pediatrics.aappublications.org. Accessed May 2013.
4. Ibid.
5. Institute of Medicine. 2011. *Dietary Reference Intakes for Calcium and Vitamin D*. Washington, D.C.: The National Academies Press.
6. Ibid.
7. Institute of Medicine. 2001. *Dietary Reference Intakes for Vitamin A, Vitamin K, Arsenic, Boron, Chromium, Copper, Iodine, Iron, Manganese, Nickel, Silicon, Vanadium, and Zinc*. Washington, D.C.: The National Academies Press.
8. Ibid.
9. Centers for Disease Control and Prevention. 2013. FastStats. Available at www.cdc.gov. Accessed May 2013.
10. Institute of Medicine. *Dietary Reference Intakes for Calcium and Vitamin D*.
11. Office of Dietary Supplements. 2015. Dietary Supplement Fact Sheet: Vitamin D. Available at http://ods.od.nih.gov/factsheets/VitaminD-HealthProfessional. Accessed April 2015.
12. Institute of Medicine, Food and Nutrition Board. 2002. *Dietary Reference Intakes for Energy, Carbohydrate, Fiber, Fat, Fatty Acids, Cholesterol, Protein, and Amino Acids*. Washington, D.C.: The National Academies Press.
13. Kranz, S., M. Brauchla, J. L. Slavin, and K. B. Miller. 2012. What Do We Know about Dietary Fiber Intake in Children and Health? The Effects of Fiber Intake on Constipation, Obesity, and Diabetes in Children. *Advances in Nutrition* 3: 47–53.
14. Institute of Medicine, Food and Nutrition Board. *Dietary Reference Intakes for Water, Potassium, Sodium, Chloride, and Sulfate*.
15. American Academy of Pediatrics. 2012. Fruit Juice and Your Child's Diet. Available at www.healthychildren.org. Accessed May 2013.
16. Satter, E. 2003. *Child of Mine: Feeding with Love and Good Sense*. Boulder, CO: Bull Publishing.
17. Birch, L. L., and A. E. Doub. 2014. Learning to Eat: Birth to Age 2 y. *American Journal of Clinical Nutrition* 99: 723S–728S.
18. Larson, N., J. Fulkerson, M. Story, and D. Neumark-Sztainer. 2012. Shared Meals among Young Adults Are Associated with Better Diet Quality and Predicted by Family Meal Patterns during Adolescence. *Public Health Nutrition* 3: 1–11.
19. Abramovitz, B., and L. Birch. 2000. Five-Year-Old Girls' Ideas about Dieting Are Predicted by Their Mothers' Dieting. *Journal of the American Dietetic Association* 100: 1157–1163.
20. Ogden, C. L., M. D. Carroll, B. K. Kit, and K. M. Flegal. 2014. Prevalence of Childhood and Adult Obesity in the United States, 2011–2012. *Journal of the American Medical Association* 311: 806–814.
21. Ibid.
22. Popkin, B. M., and K. J. Duffy. 2010. Does Hunger and Satiety Drive Eating Anymore? Increasing Eating Occasions and Decreasing Time between Eating Occasions in the United States. *American Journal of Clinical Nutrition* 91: 1342–1347.
23. Ibid.
24. Reedy, J., and S. M. Krebs-Smith. 2010. Dietary Sources of Energy, Solid Fats, and Added Sugars among Children and Adolescents in the United States. *Journal of the American Dietetic Association* 110: 1477–1484.
25. U.S. Department of Health and Human Services. 2010. *Dietary Guidelines for Americans, 2010*. 7th ed. Washington, D.C.: U.S. Government Printing Office.
26. Henry J. Kaiser Family Foundation. 2010. Generation M2: Media in the Lives of 8- to 18-Year-Olds: Report. Available at www.kff.org. Accessed May 2013.
27. American Academy of Pediatrics. 2013. Media and Children. Available at www.aap.org. Accessed May 2013.
28. U.S. Department of Health and Human Services. 2010. *Physical Activity Guidelines for Americans* Midcourse Report. Strategies to Increase Physical Activity among Youth. Available at www.health.gov. Accessed May 2013.
29. National Association for Sport and Physical Education and the American Heart Association. 2012. 2012 Shape of the Nation Report: Status of Physical Education in the USA. Available at www.aahperd.org. Accessed May 2013.
30. Centers for Disease Control and Prevention. 2012. Diabetes Public Health Resource. Available at www.cdc.gov. Accessed May 2013.
31. Dabelea, D., E. J. Mayer-Davis, S. Saydah, et al. 2014. Prevalence of Type 1 and Type 2 Diabetes among Children and Adolescents from 2001 to 2009. *Journal of the American Medical Association* 311: 1778–1786.
32. Rampersaud, G. C., M. A. Pereira, B. L. Girard, J. Adams, and J. D. Metzl. 2005. Breakfast Habits, Nutritional Status, Body Weight, and Academic Performance in Children and Adolescents. *Journal of the American Dietetic Association* 105: 743–760.
33. U.S. Department of Agriculture, Food and Nutrition Service. 2012. National School Lunch Program. Available at www.fns.usda.gov. Accessed April 2015.
34. Davis, J. N., et al. 2015. Sustenance and Sustainability: Maximizing the Impact of School Gardens on Health Outcomes. *Public Health Nutrition* (Epub ahead of print).
35. U.S. Department of Agriculture, Food and Nutrition Service. 2015. Smart Snacks in School. Available at www.fns.usda.gov. Accessed April 2015.
36. Treuth, M. S., and I. J. Griffin. 2006. Adolescence. In M. Shils, ed., *Modern Nutrition in Health and Disease*. 10th ed. Philadelphia: Lippincott Williams & Wilkins.
37. Centers for Disease Control and Prevention. 2015. Childhood Obesity Facts. http://www.cdc.gov/healthyschools/obesity/facts.htm.
38. Treuth. Adolescence.
39. Office of Dietary Supplements. Dietary Supplement Fact Sheet: Vitamin D.
40. Centers for Disease Control and Prevention. FastStats.
41. U.S. Census Bureau. 2012. International Database. Table 094. Midyear Population, by Age and Sex. Available at www.census.gov. Accessed May 2013.
42. U.S. Department of Health and Human Services. *Dietary Guidelines for Americans, 2010*.
43. National Institute on Aging. 2010. Vitamins and Minerals. Available at www.nia.nih.gov. Accessed April 2015.
44. Office of Dietary Supplements. Dietary Supplement Fact Sheet: Vitamin D.
45. Institute of Medicine. 1998. Vitamin B₁₂. In *Dietary Reference Intakes: Thiamin, Riboflavin, Niacin, Vitamin B₆, Vitamin B₁₂, Pantothenic Acid, Biotin, and Choline*. Washington, D.C.: The National Academies Press.
46. Office of Dietary Supplements. 2007. Dietary Supplement Fact Sheet: Iron. Available at http://ods.od.nih.gov. Accessed May 2013.

47. Office of Dietary Supplements. 2011. Dietary Supplement Fact Sheet: Zinc. Available at http://ods.od.nih.gov. Accessed May 2013.
48. Institute of Medicine. *Dietary Reference Intakes for Calcium and Vitamin D*.
49. U.S. Department of Health and Human Services. *Dietary Guidelines for Americans, 2010*.
50. Hiza, H. A. B., P. M. Guenther, K. Connell, and C. A. Davis. 2010. Diet Quality of Americans 65 Years and Older. Available at www.fasebj.org. Accessed May 2013.
51. American Heart Association. 2013. Heart Attack and Stroke Statistics. Available at www.heart.org. Accessed May 2013.
52. American Diabetes Association. 2013. Facts about Type 2. Available at www.diabetes.org. Accessed May 2013.
53. National Heart, Lung, and Blood Institute. 2012. What Is High Blood Pressure? Available at www.nhlbi.nih.gov. Accessed May 2013.
54. National Institute of Arthritis and Musculoskeletal and Skin Diseases (NIAMS). 2010. Handout on Health: Osteoarthritis. Available at www.niams.nih.gov. Accessed May 2013.
55. National Center for Complementary and Alternative Medicine. 2008. Questions and Answers: NIH Glucosamine/Chondroitin Arthritis Intervention Trial Primary Study. Available at http://nccam.nih.gov. Accessed October 2013.
56. National Institute of Arthritis and Musculoskeletal and Skin Diseases. 2009. Rheumatoid Arthritis. Available at www.niams.nih.gov. Accessed July 2010.
57. Choi, H. 2005. Dietary Risk Factors for Rheumatic Diseases. *Current Opinion in Rheumatology* 17: 141–146.
58. National Institute on Aging. 2013. Alzheimer's Disease Fact Sheet. Available at www.nia.nih.gov. Accessed May 2013.
59. Ibid.
60. American Cancer Society. 2015. Cancer Facts & Figures 2015. Available at www.cancer.org. Accessed April 2015.
61. Ibid.
62. National Cancer Institute. 2011. Secondhand Smoke and Cancer. Available at www.cancer.gov. Accessed May 2013.
63. National Cancer Institute. 2015. Alcohol and Cancer Risk. Available at www.cancer.gov. Accessed April 2015.
64. National Institutes of Health. National Cancer Society. 2010. Chemicals in Meat Cooked at High Temperatures and Cancer Risk. Available at www.cancer.gov. Accessed May 2013.
65. U.S. Department of Agriculture, Economic Research Center. 2012. Food Security in the U.S. Available at www.ers.usda.gov. Accessed May 2013.
66. Administration on Aging. 2009. Older Americans Act. Available at www.aoa.gov. Accessed July 2010.
67. National Institute of Mental Health. 2007. Older Adults: Depression and Suicide Facts (Fact Sheet). Available at www.nimh.nih.gov. Accessed May 2013.
68. National Institute on Aging. 2012. Alcohol Use in Older People. Available at www.nia.nih.gov. Accessed May 2013.
69. U.S. Department of Health and Human Services. 2008. *Physical Activity Guidelines for Americans*. Available at www.health.gov. Accessed May 2013.

Feature Box References

1. Centers for Disease Control and Prevention. 2015. Attention-Deficit/Hyperactivity Disorder (ADHD). Available at www.cdc.gov. Accessed April 2015.
2. Ibid.
3. U.S. Department of Health & Human Services. National Institutes of Health. 1982. Defined Diets and Childhood Hyperactivity. Available at http://consensus.nih.gov. Accessed May 2013.
4. Kim, Y., and H. Chang. 2011. Correlation between Attention Deficit Hyperactivity Disorder and Sugar Consumption, Quality of Diet, and Dietary Behavior in School Children. *Nutrition Research and Practice* 5: 236–245.
5. American Academy of Pediatrics. 2011. Your Child's Diet: A Cause and a Cure of ADHD? Available at www.healthychildren.org. Accessed May 2013.
6. Centers for Disease Control and Prevention. National Health Statistics Reports. 2013. Changes in Prevalence of Parent-Reported Autism Spectrum Disorder in School-Aged U.S. Children: 2007 to 2011–2012. No. 65. Available at www.cdc.gov. Accessed May 2013.
7. National Institute of Mental Health. 2011. A Parent's Guide to Autism Spectrum Disorder. Available at www.nimh.nih.gov. Accessed May 2013.
8. Mayo Clinic. 2010. Autism. Available at www.mayoclinic.com. Accessed May 2013.

9. U.S. Department of Health & Human Services. U.S. Food and Drug Administration. 2012. Drug Interactions: What You Should Know. Available at www.fda.gov. Accessed May 2013.
10. U.S. Food and Drug Administration. 2009. Dietary Supplements: Tips for Older Dietary Supplement Users. Available at www.fda.gov. Accessed July 2010.
11. American Cancer Society. Cancer Facts & Figures 2015.
12. American Cancer Society. 2015. Breast Cancer Facts & Figures 2015–2016. Available at www.cancer.org. Accessed April 2015.

Two Points of View References

1. Department of Agriculture. 2012. Nutrition Standards in the National School Lunch and School Breakfast Programs; Final Rule In: Federal Register. Available at www.gpo.gov/fdsys/pkg/FR-2012-01-26/pdf/2012-1010.pdf. Accessed May 2015.
2. Institute of Medicine. 2009. *School Meals: Building Blocks for Healthy Children*. Washington, D.C.: National Academies Press.
3. Cohen, J. F. W., et al. 2014. Impact of the New U.S. Department of Agriculture School Meal Standards on Food Selection, Consumption, and Waste. *American Journal of Preventive Medicine* 46: 388–394.
4. Taber, D. R., et al. 2013. Association between State Laws Governing School Meal Nutrition Content and Student Weight Status: Implications for New USDA School Meal Standards. *Journal of the American Medical Association Pediatrics* 167: 513–519.
5. Yee, V. 2012. No Appetite for Good-for-You School Lunches. *The New York Times*.
6. U.S. Government Accountability Office. 2014. Implementing Nutrition Changes Was Challenging and Clarification of Oversight Requirements Is Needed. Available at www.gao.gov/assets/670/660427.pdf. Accessed May 2015.

Chapter 16

1. Nord, M., M. Andrews, and S. Carlson. 2008. Household Food Security in the United States, 2007. United States Department of Agriculture (USDA), Economic Research Report No. (ERR-66), November 2008. Available at www.ers.usda.gov. Accessed January 2009.
2. USDA, Economic Research Service. 2014. Household Food Security in the United States in 2013. Available at www.ers.usda.gov/media/1565410/err173_summary.pdf. Accessed January 2015.
3. USDA, Economic Research Service. 2015. Food Security in the United States: Key Statistics and Graphics. Available at www.ers.usda.gov/topics/food-nutrition-assistance/food-security-in-the-us/key-statistics-graphics.aspx. Accessed January 2015.
4. USDA, Economic Research Service. 2014. Food Security in the U.S.: Measurement. Available at www.ers.usda.gov/topics/food-nutrition-assistance/food-security-in-the-us/definitions-of-food-security.aspx. Accessed January 2015.
5. Food and Agriculture Organization of the United Nations. 2014. The State of Food Insecurity in the World. Available at www.fao.org/3/a-i4030e.pdf. Accessed January 2015.
6. World Bank. 2014. Poverty. Poverty Overview. Available at www.worldbank.org/en/topic/poverty/overview. Accessed January 2015.
7. United States Census Bureau. 2015. Poverty Data: Poverty Thresholds. Available at www.census.gov/hhes/www/poverty/data/threshld/. Accessed January 2015.
8. United States Census Bureau. 2014. Income and Poverty in the United States: 2013. Data and Publications. Hunger and Poverty. Available at www.census.gov/content/dam/Census/library/publications/2014/demo/p60-249.pdf. Accessed January 2015.
9. USDA, Economic Research Service. Food Security in the United States: Key Statistics and Graphics.
10. USDA, Economic Research Service. 2013. Food Insecurity in Households with Children, EIB-113. Available at www.ers.usda.gov/media/1120651/eib-113.pdf. Accessed May 2015.
11. U.S. Bureau of Labor Statistics. 2014. A Profile of the Working Poor, 2012. Available at www.bls.gov/cps/cpswp2012.pdf. Accessed May 2015.
12. Whitaker, R. C., S. M. Phillips, and S. M. Orzol. 2006. Food Insecurity and the Risks of Depression and Anxiety in Mothers and Behavior Problems in their Preschool-Aged Children. *PEDIATRICS* 118: e859–e868.
13. Smith, L. C., and L. Haddad. 2000. *Explaining Child Malnutrition in Developing Countries: A Cross-Country Analysis of International Food Policy*. Washington, D.C.: International Food Policy Research Institute.
14. UNESCO. 2014. Education. Statistics on Literacy. Available at www.unesco.org/new/en/education/themes/education-building-blocks/literacy/resources/statistics. Accessed May, 2015.

15. Biersteker, Thomas, et al. 2013. The Effectiveness of UN Targeted Sanctions. Available at http://graduateinstitute.ch/files/live/sites/iheid/files/sites/internationalgovernance/shared/Effectiveness%20of%20UN%20Targeted%20Sanctions%20-%206.Nov.2013%20.pdf. Accessed January 2015.
16. World Food Programme. 2015. What Causes Hunger? Available at www.wfp.org/hunger/causes. Accessed January 2015.
17. Food and Agriculture Organization of the United Nations. 2014. The State of Food Insecurity in the World, 2014. Available at www.fao.org/publications/sofi/2014/en/. Accessed January 2015.
18. World Food Programme. What Causes Hunger?
19. Food and Agriculture Organization of the United Nations. *How to Feed the World in 2050.* http://www.fao.org/fileadmin/templates/wsfs/docs/expert_paper/How_to_Feed_the_World_in_2050.pdf. Available at fao.org. Accessed May 2015.
20. World Food Programme. What Causes Hunger?
21. U.S. Department of Commerce. 2013. U.S. Census Bureau. World POPClock Projection. Notes on the World POPClock and World Vital Events. Available at www.census.gov/population/popwnotes.html. Accessed January 2015.
22. Kramer, M. S., and R. Kakuma. 2012. The Optimal Duration of Exclusive Breast-Feeding. *Cochrane Database of Systematic Reviews.* Available at www.ncbi.nlm.nih.gov/pubmed/22895934. Accessed May 2015.
23. Caulfield, L., et al. 2006. Stunting, Wasting, and Micronutrient Deficiency Disorders. In *Disease Control Priorities in Developing Countries,* 2nd ed. Washington, D.C.: World Bank.
24. United Nations, Economic and Social Council. 2015. Combat HIV/AIDS, Malaria and Other Diseases: MDG 6. Available at www.un.org/en/ecosoc/about/mdg6.shtml. Accessed January 2015.
25. Merck Manual Professional Edition. 2015. Overview of Undernutrition. Available at www.merckmanuals.com/professional/nutritional_disorders/undernutrition/overview_of_undernutrition.html. Accessed January 2015.
26. *The Merck Manual.* 2014. *Protein-Energy Undernutrition: Pathophysiology.* Available at www.merckmanuals.com/professional/nutritional_disorders/undernutrition/protein-energy_undernutrition.html. Accessed January 2015.
27. Doctors without Borders. 2013. Malnutrition. Available at www.doctorswithoutborders.org. Accessed January 2015.
28. Kleinman, R. E., et al. 1998. Hunger in Children in the United States: Potential Behavioral and Emotional Correlates. *PEDIATRICS* 101: 3–10.
29. The World Bank. 2014. Early Childhood Development Overview. Available at www.web.worldbank.org. Accessed January 2015.
30. Bhoomika, R., L. Kar, R. Shobini, and B. A. Chandramouli. 2008. Cognitive Development in Children with Chronic Protein-Energy Malnutrition. *Behavioral and Brain Functions* 4: 31. Available at www.ncbi.nlm.nih.gov/pmc/articles/PMC2519065. Accessed May 2015.
31. UNICEF. 2009. Tracking Progress on Child and Maternal Nutrition. Available at www.unicef.org. Accessed April 2013.
32. World Health Organization. 2015. Nutrition. Micronutrient Deficiencies. Available at www.who.int/nutrition/topics/ida/en/. Accessed May 2015.
33. WHO. 2015. Infant and Young Child Feeding. Available at www.who.int/mediacentre/factsheets/fs342/en/. Accessed January 2015.
34. Dewey, K. G., and K. Begum. 2011. Long-Term Consequences of Stunting in Early Life. *Maternal & Child Nutrition.* Available at www.ncbi.nlm.nih.gov/pubmed/21929633. Accessed May 2015.
35. World Health Organization, Media Centre. 2014. Children: Reducing Mortality. Available at www.who.int/mediacentre/factsheets/fs178/en/. Accessed January 2015.
36. Ibid.
37. World Health Organization, Media Centre. 2014. Pneumonia. Available at www.who.int/mediacentre/factsheets/fs331/en/. Accessed January 2015.
38. World Health Organization. Pneumonia.
39. World Health Organization. 2015. Water Sanitation Health. Water-Related Diseases. Diarrhoea. Available at www.who.int/water_sanitation_health/diseases/diarrhoea/en/. Accessed January 2015.
40. Micronutrient Initiative. 2015. Vitamin A. Available at www.micronutrient.org/English/View.asp?x=577&id=440. Accessed January 2015.
41. Food and Agriculture Organization of the United Nations. 2010. Policy Briefs. Female Land Ownership. Available at www.fao.org. Accessed January 2015.
42. World Health Organization, Media Centre. 2013. Diarrhoeal Disease. Available at www.who.int. Accessed January 2015.
43. Ibid.
44. Ibid.
45. CDC. 2008. Household Water Treatment Options in Developing Countries: Solar Disinfection (SODIS). Available at www.cdc.gov.
46. Flour Fortification Initiative. 2014. Global Progress. Available at www.ffinetwork.org/global_progress/. Accessed May 2015.
47. United Nations. 2003. Department of Economic and Social Affairs. Population Division. Population, Education and Development: A concise report. Available at http://www.un.org/esa/population/publications/concise2003/Concisereport2003.pdf Accessed May 2015.
48. Struble, et al. Addressing World Hunger.

Feature Box References

1. Centers for Disease Control and Prevention. 2010. Obesity and Socioeconomic Status in Adults: United States, 2005–2008. NCHS Data Brief, Number 50, December 2010. Available at www.CDC.gov.
2. World Health Organization. 2009. World Health Day 2009. Available at www.who.int. Accessed January 2015.
3. BBC News. 2010. Haiti Will Not Die, President Rene Preval Insists. Available at news.bbc.co.uk. Accessed February 2015.
4. Friends of the World Food Program. 2010. Latest Assessment Reveals Widespread Food Insecurity in Haiti. Available at http://friendsofwfp.typepad.com. Accessed February 2015.
5. Food and Agriculture Organization of the United Nations (FAO). 2010. Haiti: Earthquake Flash Appeal, 2010. Available at www.fao.org. Accessed January 2015.
6. Ibid.

Two Points of View References

1. United States Department of Agriculture, Economic Research Service. 2004. Amber Waves: 50 Years of U.S. Food Aid and Its Role in Reducing World Hunger. Available at http://ageconsearch.umn.edu. Accessed January 2015.
2. Center for Global Development. 2009. Cash (or Food?) for Thought: The Debate on Cash versus Food Isn't Over (Yet). Available at www.cgdev.org. Accessed January 2015.
3. Bretton Woods Project. 2010. Farming Furor: World Bank Launches New Agriculture Fund. Available at www.brettonwoodsproject.org. Accessed April 2013.
4. Ibid.
5. Center for Global Development. Cash (or Food?) for Thought.
6. Ibid.
7. A. Gelan. 2006. Cash or Food Aid? A General Equilibrium Analysis for Ethiopia. *Development Policy Review* 24: 601–624.
8. Oxfam America, Inc. 2015. Food Aid: A Critical Program, Ripe for Reform. Available at www.oxfamamerica.org/take-action/campaign/food-farming-and-hunger/food-aid/. Accessed February 2015.
9. Gelan. Cash or Food Aid?; International Policy Network. 2013. New IPN Study Shows Foreign Aid Does More Harm than Good. Available at www.policynetwork.net. Accessed April 2013.
10. Oxfam America, Inc. Food Aid: A Critical Program, Ripe for Reform.
11. Ibid.

Index

Page references followed by *fig* indicate illustrated figures or photographs; followed by *t* indicates a table.

A

absorption
    alcohol, absorption of, 345*fig*–346
    fatty acids, 152*fig*
    iron and, 316
    in large intestine, 78*fig*
    minerals, bioavailability of, 296
    overview of digestive process, 74*fig*, 81–82*fig*
    proteins, 192–194*fig*, 193*fig*
    in small intestine, 76–77*fig*
    vitamins, 229*fig*, 230*t*, 246, 247
Academy of Nutrition and Dietetics (AND), 21
acai berries, 390
Acceptable Macronutrient Distribution Range (AMDR). *See also* Dietary Reference Intakes (DRIs)
    carbohydrates, 110
    fat intake, 157–158
    overview of, 34–36, 37*t*
accessory organs, digestion, 70, 79*fig*
access to food. *See* food insecurity
Accutane, 235, 237
acesulfame-K, 131*t*, 133
acetaldehyde, 346
acetaminophen, 351
acid-base balance, 198
acid group, amino acids, 188–189*fig*
acid reflux, 86
acne, vitamin A and, 235, 237
acromegaly, 447
active transport, 82*fig*
activity, physical. *See* physical activity
acute dehydration, defined, 442–444, 443*fig*. *See also* fluid balance
added, food label terminology, 56*t*
added sugars
    diabetes and, 129
    food labels and, 119*fig*–120, 139
    overview, 115–121, 116*fig*, 119*fig*, 120*fig*
    protein and energy bars, 207*t*
    sugar-sweetened beverages, 122–123
adenosine diphosphate (ADP), 426*fig*
adenosine triphosphate (ATP), 426*fig*, 427*fig*, 445
Adequate Intake (AI), 34–36. *See also* Dietary Reference Intakes (DRIs)
adipose tissue, 430–432
adolescents
    calorie needs, 569*t*
    disordered eating, 581
    eating behavior, influences on, 579–580
    gastric bypass, debate about, 410
    nutritional needs, overview, 579, 580–581
    obesity and overweight, 13, 574*fig*–575
    pregnancy and, 542–543
ADP (adenosine diphosphate), 426*fig*
adrenaline, 109
advantame, 131*t*, 134
advertising
    alcohol use and, 349, 350

body image and, 372, 402, 404
    food choices and, 5, 458–459
    regulation of, 25
aerobic energy, 426*fig*, 427*fig*
aerobic exercise, 420, 430. *See also* physical activity
age-related macular degeneration (AMD), 231*fig*, 320
aging. *See* older adults
agribusiness, 462
agriculture
    antibiotics in food supply, 474
    biotechnology, use of, 477–481, 478*fig*, 480*t*
    energy use, 468*fig*
    exports, 464–465
    farm subsidies, 487
    farm-to-table continuum, 512*fig*
    food policy, effects of, 481–484, 482*t*
    global practices and problems, 608–610
    hormones in food supply, 473
    imports, 465*fig*–466
    land management, 614–616
    organic, food labels and, 485*fig*–486*t*
    pesticides, use of, 474–477, 476*fig*
    sustainable food system, 466–471*t*, 467*fig*, 468*fig*, 470*t*
    in United States, overview of, 459*fig*–465, 460*fig*, 461*t*, 462*fig*, 463*fig*, 463*t*
AIDS/HIV, 549
air, vitamin exposure to, 232
alanine (Ala), 190*t*
alcohol
    alcohol poisoning, 359
    alcohol tolerance, 359
    alcohol use disorder (AUD), 356–357*t*
    Asian ethnicity and, 348
    benefits vs. risks, debate about, 363
    binge drinking, 356, 357*fig*–359
    blood alcohol concentration (BAC), 346, 347*t*, 348*t*
    blood pressure and, 303–304*t*
    bone health and, 310
    brain, effect on, 346–348*fig*, 348*t*
    breast-feeding mothers, 548
    cancer risk and, 590
    drinking and driving, 359–360
    exercise and, 442
    food insecurity and, 607
    heart disease and, 169, 178
    heavy drinking, 360
    hormones, effect on, 351
    Made Over Made Better, 362
    magnesium loss and, 314
    Mediterranean diet, 173
    metabolism of, 344–346, 345*fig*
    older adults, alcohol abuse in, 594–595*fig*
    overnutrition and malnutrition, 351–353*fig*, 352*t*
    pregnancy and, 355–356*fig*, 530–531, 537
    problem drinking, counseling for, 361
    production process, 342
    reasons for use, 342–344
    sleep disturbances and hangovers, 349, 351
    standard drink measures, 343*fig*, 344*fig*
    underage drinking, 360
    vitamin deficiencies and, 249, 254
alcohol dehydrogenase (ADH), 345*fig*–346, 348

alcohol flush, defined, 348
alcoholic hepatitis, 354*fig*
alcoholic liver disease, 354*fig*
Alcoholics Anonymous (AA), 361
alginates, 517*t*
allergies
    breast-feeding, benefits of, 546
    hypoallergenic infant formulas, 550
    infant food allergies, 556–558, 557*fig*
    sulfites, 515–516
Alli (orlistat), 71, 72, 396
allicin, 232*t*
allium, 232*t*
almonds, 161*fig*
alpha-carotene, 235
alpha-linolenic acid, 147*fig*, 148, 156*fig*, 161*fig*, 175
alpha-tocopherol, 240*fig*–241*fig*. *See also* vitamin E
Alzheimer's disease, 231, 587, 590
AMD (age-related macular degeneration), 231*fig*, 320
American Academy of Child and Adolescent Psychiatry, 573
American Academy of Pediatric Dentistry, 550
American Academy of Pediatrics, 543, 569
American diet, overview of, 12–15*t*, 13*fig*
amine group, amino acids, 188–189*fig*
amino acid pools, 192–196, 193*fig*, 194*fig*, 195*fig*
amino acid profile, proteins, 202–203
amino acids
    essential, nonessential, and conditional, 190*t*
    exercise, energy for, 427*fig*, 433
    protein degradation and synthesis, 192–196, 193*fig*, 194*fig*, 195*fig*
    proteins, structure of, 188–190, 189*fig*
    sulfur intake and, 315
    supplements, 206–207
    sweeteners from, 132–133
    vitamin C and, 260
amylase, 73–75*fig*, 74*fig*, 80*t*, 104–105*fig*
amylase inhibitors, 520
amylopectin, 102*fig*
amylose, 102*fig*
anabolic steroids, 446, 448*t*
anaerobic energy, 426*fig*, 427*fig*
anaphylactic reactions, 557*fig*
androgenic effects, steroids, 446
anemia
    defined, 254
    folate deficiencies, 256–257
    iron-deficiency, 318*fig*, 438
    macrocytic anemia, 257*fig*, 259
    pernicious anemia, 258–259
    sickle-cell anemia, 195–196
    sports anemia (pseudoanemia), 438
anencephaly, 256
Animal and Plant Health Inspection Service (APHIS), 482*t*
animal feed, 463*fig*–464
animals raised for food, 463*fig*–464
animal studies, 16
annatto, 517*t*
anorexia nervosa, 306, 401–408, 402*t*, 403*fig*, 407*t*
anthocyanin, 61*t*, 232*t*
antibiotic-resistant bacteria, 474

antibiotics, food safety and, 474, 485
antibodies, 199
anticoagulants, 240–241, 243, 589
antidiuretic hormone (ADH), 288, 349, 350
antimicrobials, food production and, 475–477, 476fig
antioxidants
  benefits of, 591
  breast milk and, 546
  as food preservatives, 515
  functions and sources, 177fig, 231, 232t
  overview of, 229–231fig, 230fig
  pregnancy, intake needs, 541
  in red wine, 344
  selenium, 322
  sperm production and, 528
  vitamin C, 260
  vitamin E, 240fig–241fig
anus, 78fig, 88
anxiety, eating disorders and, 403fig
apolipoprotein B (ApoB), 170
appendix, 78fig
appetite
  environment and, 384–386
  medications for weight loss, 396
  protein and, 199–200t
  regulation of, 85, 381–382fig
  sugar-sweetened beverage consumption, 122–123
apple body shape, 374fig
arachidonic acid, 156fig, 546
arginine (Arg), 190t
Armstrong, Lance, 447
arsenic, 298, 300t
arteries, atherosclerosis and, 167. See also cardiovascular disease
arthritis, 231, 371, 586–587
ascending colon, 78fig
ascorbic acid. See vitamin C
asparagine (Asn), 190t
aspartame, 131t, 132–133, 134, 517t
aspartic acid (Asp), 132, 133, 189fig, 190t
assault, alcohol use and, 357fig
astragalus, 588
atherosclerosis. See also cardiovascular disease
  red wine consumption and, 344
  risk factors, 167
  vitamin E and, 240fig
athletes. See also physical activity; physical fitness
  body mass index and, 373–374
  calorie intake needs, 433–435
  carbohydrate loading, 429, 430–431
  female athlete triad, 434–435
  protein, energy from, 433
  timing of meals, 435–437
  vegetarian diet and, 219
  vitamin and mineral needs, 437–439
Atkins diet, 388–389
ATP (adenosine triphosphate), 426fig, 427fig, 445
attention deficit hyperactivity disorder (ADHD), 573
authoritative statements, food label claims, 57t
authorized health claims, food labels, 57t, 58
autism spectrum disorder (ASD), 572, 573
autoimmune diseases
  celiac disease, 90–91
  rheumatoid arthritis, 541, 587
  type 1 diabetes, 124fig–125
avidin, 262

B

Bacillus thuringiensis, 479
bacteria. See also food safety; specific bacteria names
  cooking temperature, 504–505fig, 505t, 506fig
  cross-contamination, 503–504fig
  foodborne illness and, 494–499, 496t, 497t, 498t
  food preservation techniques, 512–514
  food safety practices, 501–509t, 502fig, 504fig, 505fig, 505t, 506fig, 508t
  food storage, 505–509t, 506fig, 508t
  intestinal microflora, 78, 88, 106
  probiotics, 93
baking soda, 301
balanced diet, defined, 32

ballistic stretching, 422
bariatric surgery, 396–397fig, 410
basal metabolic rate (BMR), 378t
basal metabolism, defined, 378
Bechler, Steve, 396
beef, cooking of, 504–505t, 505fig
beef tallow (fat), 163fig
beer, 342, 344. See also alcohol
behavior modification, 394–395fig
Belviq, 396
benzoate, 517t
beriberi, 248–249, 264
beta-carotene
  as antioxidant, 229–231fig, 230fig
  functions and sources, 60, 61t, 232t, 235–238, 236fig, 237fig
  orlistat, effects of, 72
  as provitamin, 233
  recommended intake, 237
  summary chart, 264t
beta-cryptoxanthin, 235
beta-glucan, 60, 61t, 103, 232t
Better Business Bureau, 25
beverages. See also milk
  aspartame in, 132–133
  caffeine content in, 451, 530t
  energy drinks, 347, 451
  exercise, fluid needs, 441–442
  sports drinks, 436–437, 440, 441–442
  sugar content, 122–123, 129
  tap water vs. bottled water, 292–293
bicarbonate ions, 80t
bile
  cholesterol in, 157
  defined, 151
  digestive system, overview, 74fig, 79
  fat digestion, 80t–81t, 151–152fig
  fiber and, 136
  gallbladder disease, 87
binge drinking, 343, 356, 357fig–359, 360
binge eating, 401–408, 402t, 403fig, 407t
bioaccumulation, toxins, 519fig
bioavailability, minerals, 296
bioavailability, vitamins, 231
biodiversity, 467
bioelectrical impedance, 375t
biopesticides, 475–477, 476fig, 477
biosecurity, food, 521
biotechnology, food production, 477–481, 478fig, 480t
bioterrorism, 521
biotin
  absorption and transport of, 229fig, 230t
  functions and sources, 247fig, 262
  summary chart, 265t
birth defects, 256, 535, 537
bitter orange, 390
black cohosh, 588
blackouts, alcohol and, 356
bladder, excretory system, 84fig
blood. See also anemia
  anticoagulant, 240–241
  calcium, role of, 307
  cholesterol levels in, 160, 167t–169, 168fig
  clotting of, 242–243fig
  folate intake, 255, 257fig
  iron, functions of, 316, 318fig
  ketosis, 109
  life span of red blood cells, 197
  lipoprotein transport, 153–155fig
  nutrient transport, 83fig–84
  phosphorus and, 311
  sickle-cell anemia, 195–196
  vitamin B$_{12}$ and, 258–259
blood alcohol concentration (BAC), 346, 347t, 348t, 359–360
blood doping, 447
blood glucose. See also diabetes mellitus
  alcohol and, 351
  gestational diabetes, 540–541
  glycemic index and load, 128–129fig
  regulation of, 85, 106–109, 107fig, 108fig, 197

blood pressure
  alcohol, effects of, 354
  calcium intake, 307
  choline and, 263
  DASH diet, 40
  exercise, benefits of, 421
  heart disease and, 169
  magnesium, role of, 313
  normal level, 303
  obesity and overweight, 370–371, 375
  older adults, dietary needs and, 586
  potassium intake, 305
  pregnancy and, 541, 543
  sodium intake, 302–304fig, 304t
  vegetarian diets, 216
blue cohosh, 530
BMR (basal metabolic rate), 378t
BodPod, 375t
body composition
  body fat measurements, 374fig–376fig, 375t
  defined, 419
  minerals, 297fig
  physical fitness and, 419, 420t
  strength training and, 421–422
  water, nutrients, protein, and fat, 284fig
body dysmorphic disorder (BDD), 404
body fat. See also eating disorders; obesity; weight management
  body composition, 284fig
  body storage of, 84
  chemical composition, 146–151fig, 147fig, 148fig, 149fig, 150fig
  exercise, energy for, 427fig, 429–432
  female athlete triad, 434–435
  functions of, 146, 154, 156–157
  heart disease, risk factors, 166–170, 167t, 168fig
  measurement and location of, 374fig–376fig, 375t
  percent body composition, 9fig
  sugar intake and, 117
body image, 402, 403–404. See also disordered eating
body mass index (BMI), 372–374, 373t
body temperature
  heat exhaustion and heat stroke, 440t
  regulation of, 285fig–286
body water. See fluid balance
body weight. See also obesity and overweight; weight management
  blood pressure and, 303, 303–304t
  body mass index (BMI) and, 372–374, 373t
  factors affecting, 380–386fig, 382fig
  genetics and, 383–384
  preconception health, 529
  pregnancy weight gain, 533fig, 533t
  water loss and, 289
bolus, 73–75fig, 74fig
bonding, 545
bone health
  adolescents, 580fig
  calcium and, 307–310, 308fig, 309fig, 438–439
  female athlete triad, 434–435
  mineral storage in bone, 84
  osteoporosis, 308fig–310, 309fig
  phosphorus and, 311
  physical fitness, benefits of, 421t
  potassium and, 305
  protein intake and, 210
  vitamin A and, 235, 237
  vitamin D and, 244, 246
  vitamin K and, 242–243fig
bone mineral density (BMD), 309, 580fig
boron (B), 298, 300t
bottled water, 292–293
botulism, 521, 558
bovine spongiform encephalopathy (BSE), 499–500
bowels. See large intestine
brain
  alcohol, effects of, 346–348fig, 348t
  Alzheimer's disease and dementia, 587, 590
  breast-feeding and, 546
  iron, role of, 316
brain stem, 346–348fig, 348t

bran, 112–113
breakfast, 13, 48–49, 576–577
breast cancer. *See also* cancer
  alcohol use and, 351
  breast-feeding benefits, 544
  fiber, benefits of, 136–137
  obesity and overweight, 371
  physical fitness, benefits of, 420t
  vitamin D and, 244
breast-feeding
  benefits of, 543–546
  mother's diet needs, 547–548
breast milk, 545–546
broccoli, nutrients in, 9fig, 60
brown rice, 7
brush border enzymes, 104–105fig
brussels sprouts, 60
bulimia nervosa, 306, 401–408, 402t, 403fig, 407t
butter, 163fig, 174fig
butylated hydroxyanisole (BHA), 515, 517t
butylated hydroxytoluene (BHT), 515, 517t

C

caffeine
  breast-feeding women, 548
  content by beverage, 530t
  energy drinks, 347, 451
  fluid balance and, 294, 442
  physical activity and, 445–446, 448t
  pregnancy consumption, 530t, 537
  sperm production and, 528
calcium
  adolescents, intake of, 580fig
  alcohol, effects of, 353
  American diet, 13
  bioavailability of, 308
  body content, 297fig
  bone health, 310
  drug interactions, 588
  exercise and, 438–439
  food labels, 51–54, 52fig
  functions and sources, 297t, 307–310, 308fig, 309fig
  gastric bypass surgery and, 397
  hypercalcemia, 246
  infant formula, 549t
  older adults, intake, 584t, 585
  osteoporosis and, 210
  pregnancy, intake, 533–535, 536fig, 541
  recommended intake, 307, 308fig
  remineralization, teeth, 118
  in spinach, 296
  supplements, 309, 439
  toddlers and preschoolers, intake, 570
  vegetarian diets, 218t
  vitamin D and, 244, 296
calcium carbonate, 517t
calories. *See also* kilocalories (kcal)
  breast-feeding mothers, 547–548
  childhood overweight and obesity, 574fig–575
  daily need by weight and lifestyle, 36
  energy balance, overview of, 376–380, 378fig, 378t
  energy from, 9–10
  energy used by activity, 393t
  estimated energy requirement (EER), 379
  exercise and intake needs, 433–435
  female athlete triad and, 434–435
  food labels in restaurants, 63
  infant needs, 552
  Nutrition Facts Panel, 51–54, 52fig
  older adults, intake needs, 582
  pregnancy, intake needs, 536fig, 539fig, 542
  reduced-fat products and, 165–166t
  serving size estimates by food group, 47t
  time of day for eating, impact of, 48–49
  for weight loss, 387–393, 391fig, 391t, 392fig
Campylobacter, 474, 498, 513
Campylobacter jejuni, 496t
cancer
  alcohol and, 351
  antioxidants and, 231

breast cancer, 351, 544
  calcium intake and, 307
  colon, 91, 92t, 307
  esophagus, 86, 353
  fiber, benefits of, 136–137
  folate intake and, 256, 257
  obesity and overweight, 371
  ovarian cancer, 544
  physical fitness, benefits of, 420t
  protein consumption and, 210
  risk factors and reduction, 590–591, 592t
  saccharin and, 132
  selenium intake and, 322
  skin cancer, 246
  soy and, 214
  vegetarian diets, 216
  vitamin D and, 244
canning, 512–513
canola oil, 161fig, 163fig, 175
capillaries, skin, 285fig–286
capillaries, small intestine, 77fig
caramel, 517t
carbohydrate loading, 429, 430–431
carbohydrates. *See also* fiber
  Acceptable Macronutrient Distribution Range (AMDR), 36
  breast-feeding mother, needs of, 548
  chemical composition, 9fig–10
  digestion and absorption, 76, 78, 80t, 88, 104–106, 105fig
  energy from, 426–429, 427fig
  as fat substitutes, 164–165t
  food labels, 51–54, 52fig, 139
  functions of, 9fig–10, 100
  glycemic index, 128–129fig
  glycogen, 103
  infant formula, 549t
  infant needs, 552
  lactose intolerance, 104, 106
  natural and added sugars, 115–121, 116fig, 119fig, 120fig, 139
  percent body composition, 9fig
  polysaccharides, 101, 102fig
  popular weight loss diets, 388–389
  pregnancy, intake needs, 536fig, 539fig
  recommended intake, 36, 110–111fig, 111t
  simple carbohydrates, 100–102fig
  sources of, 100, 111fig–115, 114fig
  sports drinks, 442
  storage in body, 84
  timing of meals, exercise and, 435–437
carboxypeptidase, 80t
carcinogenic, defined, 515
cardiorespiratory conditioning, 420–421, 423t
cardiorespiratory endurance, 418, 419
cardiovascular disease
  alcohol use and, 178, 344, 354
  antioxidants and phytochemicals, benefits of, 177, 231
  DASH diet, 40
  diabetes, effects of, 125, 127–128
  exercise, benefits of, 421, 432
  fat intake and, 158
  fiber, benefits of, 136
  obesity and overweight, 370–371, 375
  older adults, dietary needs and, 586
  omega-3 fatty acids, 156fig
  physical fitness, benefits of, 420t
  protein intake and, 209–210
  risk factors, 166–170, 167t, 168fig
  risk reduction strategies, 170–179, 171fig, 174fig, 177fig, 178t
  sodium intake and blood pressure, 302–304fig, 304t
  Table Tips, 179
  trans fats and, 158
  vegetarian diet and, 216
  vitamin E and, 240fig
carnitine, 263
carotenodermia, 239

carotenoids, 12, 235, 238–239, 528, 591. *See also* vitamin A
carrageenan, 517t
Case Study
  alcohol abuse, 358
  cancer risks, 593
  diabetes, risk for, 127
  dietary fat, types of, 175
  extreme obesity, management of, 398
  fast-food city, 21
  functional foods and cholesterol, 62
  gluten, 89
  hypertension, 303
  infertility, stress of, 531
  overweight and undernourished, 607
  vegetarian diets, 213
cassava, 520
catalysts, 197fig
cataracts, 231fig
catechins, 177
cecum, 78fig
celiac disease, 89–91, 92t
cell membranes
  phospholipid bilayer, 149–150fig
  transport proteins, 198fig–199
cells
  cell differentiation, 235
  cell growth, vitamin A and, 235, 237
  tissues and, 71
cellulite, 397
cellulose, 103fig, 114, 164–165t
Center for Veterinary Medicine (CVM), 474
Centers for Disease Control and Prevention (CDC), 474, 482t, 510–512fig, 511t
central obesity, 374fig
cerebellum, alcohol and, 348fig, 348t
cerebral cortex, alcohol and, 348fig, 348t
certified, food label terminology, 484
cheese, 118, 537. *See also* dairy products
chemical agents, cancer and, 590
chemical digestion, 70–71fig, 73–75fig, 74fig
chicken. *See* poultry
chickpeas, 114
Child and Adult Care Food Program, 615t
child-care centers, food offered at, 570
children. *See also* adolescents; infants; preschoolers; toddlers
  advertising regulations, 25
  childhood overweight and obesity, 574fig–575
  child mortality, 613
  fish consumption, 176
  foodborne illness and, 500–501
  malnutrition, effects of, 611–613t, 612fig, 612t
  obesity and overweight, 13
Children's Food and Beverage Advertising Initiative, 25
chitosan, 390
chloride, 297fig, 297t, 315, 440t
chlorophyll, 100–101fig
chocolate, 148, 177
choking hazards, 569
cholecystokinin (CCK), 80t, 381–382fig
cholesterol
  antioxidants and phytochemicals, benefits of, 177fig
  bile and, 80–81
  dietary *vs.* blood levels, 160
  exercise, benefits of, 421, 432
  fat storage in body, 375
  fiber intake and, 136
  food labels, 51–54, 52fig
  functional foods and, 62
  functions of, 154, 157
  Mediterranean diet and, 172–173
  niacin and, 252–253fig
  oats and, 60
  obesity and overweight, 371
  recommended intake, 171–173
  sugar intake and, 117
  trans fats and, 158
  transport of, 152fig–155fig
  vitamin E and, 240

Index   **I-3**

choline, 263, 535
chondroitin, 587
ChooseMyPlate.gov, 39–47
chromium, functions and sources, 299t, 326–327
chronic dehydration, defined, 442–444, 443fig. See also fluid balance
chronic illness. See also cancer; cardiovascular disease; diabetes mellitus; hypertension
  food insecurity and, 606
  undernutrition and, 610–611
chylomicrons, 153–155fig, 229fig
chyme, 71, 74fig, 75–76
chymotrypsin, 80
cigar/cigarette smoking
  bone health and, 310
  cancer and, 590
  heart disease and, 169
  pregnancy and, 530–531, 537
ciguatera poisoning, 518–519fig
circular folds, small intestine, 77fig
circulatory system
  diabetes, effects of, 125, 127–128
  digestion and, 81–84, 82fig, 83fig
cirrhosis, 354fig–355
citric acid, as food additive, 517t
claims, health, 51, 54–58fig, 55fig, 56t, 57t
closed dating, food safety, 514fig–515
Clostridium botulinum, 119, 496t, 512, 515, 558
Clostridium perfringens, 496t
clotting factors, blood, 242–243fig
cloves, 517t
coagulation, blood, 242–243fig
cobalamin. See vitamin B₁₂ (cobalamin)
cocoa butter, 148
coconut oil, 163fig
cod-liver oil, 17fig–18
coenzyme Q10, 588
coenzymes
  B vitamins as, 247fig
  protein, functions of, 197fig
  vitamin B₆ as, 254
  vitamin C as, 260
collagen, 196–197, 260, 437
colon, 78fig
  disorders of, 89–92t
  fiber, benefits of, 134–137, 135t, 136fig
  lactose intolerance and, 106
colon cancer
  calcium intake, 307
  fiber and, 136–137
  folate intake, 256
  obesity and overweight, 371
  overview of, 91, 92t
  physical fitness, benefits of, 420t
  vitamin D and, 244
color, food additives, 516, 517t
colostrum, 545
commodity crops, 462
common cold, 266–267, 320
community-supported agriculture (CSA), 470
complemented proteins, 202–203
complete proteins, 202–203
complex carbohydrates, overview, 101. See also carbohydrates
conception, defined, 528, 529
conditionally essential amino acids, 190t. See also amino acids
conditioning, physical fitness, 422
cones, eye, 235, 236fig
congeners, 351
congenital hypothyroidism, 328
congregate meals, 593
connective tissue, 196–197
consensus, defined, 15
constipation, 88, 92t, 134–137, 135t, 136fig
control group, 18–20
convenience, food choice and, 6–7
cooking temperature, 231–233, 501, 504–505fig, 505t, 506fig
copper (Cu)
  body content, 297fig

functions and sources, 299t, 319fig
  pregnancy, intake needs, 533–535, 536fig
  vision and, 231fig
  zinc intake and, 296
corn, growing of, 463fig–464, 487
Corn Belt, 462, 463fig–464
cornea, 236fig, 239
corn oil, 163fig
coronary heart disease, 166–170, 167t, 168fig, 586
cost, food choices and, 6–7
cottonseed oil, 163fig
Coumadin, 243, 589
cravings, pregnancy and, 533–534
C-reactive protein (CRP), 170
creatine, supplements, 445, 448t
creatine phosphate (CP), 426fig, 427fig
cretinism, 328, 613t
critical periods, fetal development, 538fig
Crohn's disease, 91, 92t
crop failures, 608–610
cross-contamination, food handling, 503–504fig
Cryptosporidium parvum, 498t, 499
culture
  alcohol consumption and, 342–343
  disordered eating and, 402
  food choices and, 5–6
cyanide, 520
cyanogenic glycosides, 520
Cyclospora cayatenensis, 498t, 499
cysteine (Cys), 190t
cytokines, 354

D

Daily Values (DVs), overview, 52fig, 53–54
dairy products
  calcium and, 307, 308fig
  carbohydrates in, 115
  daily intake guidelines, 44t
  exercise and, 437
  milk allergies, 556, 557fig
  minerals in, 298
  riboflavin (vitamin B₂), 250–251fig
  serving size estimates, 47t
  vitamins in, 228fig
danger zone, food storage temperature, 505–509t, 506fig, 508t
DASH (Dietary Approaches to Stop Hypertension) diet, 40, 304fig, 307, 313
DASH-Sodium study, 304
day-care providers, 570
death, leading causes of, 8t
de Castro, John, 48
defecation, 78
dehydration
  alcohol and, 349, 350
  exercise, fluid needs for, 441t, 442–444, 443fig
  overview, 287–289fig, 440
Delaney Clause, 518
dementia, 253, 587, 590
denaturation, proteins, 191fig
dental caries, 117, 118, 550
dental health. See teeth
deoxyribonucleic acid. See DNA (deoxyribonucleic acid)
Department of Health and Human Services (DHHS), 38, 482t
depression, 350, 403fig, 593–594
dermatitis, 253
descending colon, 78fig
developed country, 603
developing country, 604. See also food insecurity
developmental disabilities, 572–573
diabetes, gestational, 540–541
Diabetes Control and Complications Trial (DCCT), 128
diabetes mellitus
  childhood obesity and, 575
  chromium, role of, 326
  effects on body, 125, 127–128
  fiber, benefits of, 136
  forms of, 123–125, 124fig

heart disease and, 169
  magnesium, role of, 313
  obesity and overweight, 370–371
  older adults, dietary needs and, 586
  overview of, 121–122
  physical fitness, benefits of, 420t
  prevention, 129
  rates of, 13, 129
  sugar intake and, 117
  treatment and control of, 128–129fig
  vegetarian diets, 216
diabetic ketoacidosis, 122
diarrhea, 88, 92t, 253, 496t, 497t, 498t
diastolic pressure, 303
diet. See also vegetarian and vegan diet; weight management; individual nutrient names
  American diet, 12–15t, 13fig
  attention-deficit and hyperactivity disorder (ADHD), 573
  autism spectrum disorder and, 572, 573
  breast-feeding mother, needs of, 547–548
  disordered eating, 401–408, 402t, 403fig, 407t
  female athlete triad, 434–435
  global obesity rates, 464–465
  Paleo Diet, 221
  popular weight loss diets, 388–390
  sample daily food plan, 45fig
  time of day for eating, impact of, 48–49
  tools for healthy eating, overview, 32–33, 59t
  using MyPlate, 42–47t, 44fig, 44t, 45fig
  very low-calorie diet, 395
  weight gain, strategies for, 399–401, 400fig
  weight loss and, 387–393, 391fig, 391t, 392fig, 399
  well-balanced diet, defined, 11–12
dietary folate equivalent (DFE), 256
Dietary Guidelines for Americans. See also MyPlate
  breakfast, importance of, 577
  nutrient intake recommendations, summary, 267, 268fig
  overview, 33, 37–39, 59t, 64
  school lunches and, 596
  sugar intake, 121–123
Dietary Reference Intakes (DRIs). See also individual nutrient names
  Daily Values and, 52fig, 53–54
  overview, 33, 34–37, 59t
Dietary Supplement Health and Education Act (1994), 589
digestibility, proteins, 202–203
digestion. See also foodborne illness
  carbohydrates, 104–106, 105fig
  digestive disorders, overview, 85–92t
  excretory system, 84fig
  fiber and, 103
  hormone regulation of, 79–80
  large intestine, 78fig
  liver, gallbladder, and pancreas, 79fig
  in mouth, 73–75fig, 74fig
  nutrient absorption, 81–82fig
  nutrient transport, 83fig–84
  orlistat, effects of, 71, 72, 396
  overview of, 70–71fig, 80t, 81t
  proteins, 191, 192–194fig, 193fig
  small intestine and, 76–77fig
  stomach and, 75fig–76
digestive process, defined, 70, 71
diglyceride, 151–152fig, 517t
dining out, 6, 13, 46–47, 63, 384–385
dinoflagellates, 519fig
dioxins, 518
dipeptides, 188
disability, food insecurity and, 606
disaccharides, 101, 102fig
disordered eating, 401–408, 402t, 403fig, 407t, 434–435, 581
distillation, alcohol, 342, 343
distilled water, 292–293
distributors, food industry, 459fig
diuretics, 287, 314, 349, 350
diverticula, 135, 136fig
diverticulitis, 135, 136fig

diverticulosis, 135, 136*fig*
DNA (deoxyribonucleic acid). *See also* genes/genetics
  defined, 20
  folate and, 255
  genetically modified organisms (GMOs), 478*fig*–481, 480*t*
  phosphorus, 311
  protein synthesis, 194–196, 195*fig*
  zinc and, 320
DNA fingerprinting, food safety, 511
docosahexaenoic acid (DHA), 156*fig*, 174–175, 535, 546
dong quai root, 588
Double-blind, Randomized Intervention Study in Kids (DRINK), 123
double-blind placebo-controlled study, defined, 19
drinking and driving, 359–360
driving under the influence (DUI), 359–360
drought, food insecurity and, 608–610
drug interactions, 588–589
drug use and abuse
  food insecurity and, 607
  pregnancy and, 537
  withdrawal symptoms, 537
dual-energy X-ray absorptiometry (DXA), 375*t*
duodenal ulcers, 87, 92*t*
duodenum, 76–77*fig*, 80
duration, FITT principle, 422–425*t*, 423*t*, 424*fig*
DXA (dual-energy X-ray absorptiometry), 375*t*
dynamic stretching, 422
dysphagia, 86

E

early childhood caries, 550
early childhood tooth decay, 118
earthquakes, food insecurity and, 609
eating disorders, 401–408, 402*t*, 403*fig*, 407*t*, 434–435, 581
Echinacea, 267, 588
eclampsia, 541
edamame, 214–215
edema, 198*fig*, 211*fig*
education, food security and, 616
eggs
  allergies to, 556, 557*fig*
  avidin and biotin, 262
  cholesterol in, 171
  cooking temperature, 505*t*
  farming and, 464
  food safety, 508
  proteins in, 191*fig*, 205
eggs, human pregnancy, 532*fig*
eicosanoids, 156*fig*
eicosapentaenoic acid (EPA), 156*fig*, 174–175
Eijkman, Christiaan, 248
electrolytes
  absorption in large intestine, 78*fig*
  alcohol and, 349, 350
  anorexia nervosa and, 405
  bulimia nervosa and, 405
  defined, 284, 285
  diarrhea and, 88
  exercise, fluid needs for, 439–444, 440*t*, 441*t*, 443*fig*
  hyponatremia, 443
  sports drinks, 436–437
elimination, digestive system, 74*fig*
embryo, 532*fig*
emotion, food choices and, 7
empty calories, 115, 117
emulsifiers, 150*fig*, 164–165*t*
endocrine system, 85
endocytosis, 82*fig*
endometrial cancer, 420*t*
endosperm, grains, 112–113
endotoxins, 354
energy
  basal metabolic rate (BMR), 378*t*
  B-complex vitamins and, 247*fig*
  carbohydrate loading, 430–431
  from carbohydrates, 426–429*t*, 427*fig*

copper, role of, 319*fig*
energy-yielding nutrients, 9*fig*–10
estimated energy requirement (EER), 36, 379, 385–386
  for exercise, 425–427*fig*, 426*fig*
  from fat, 154, 429–432
  glycogen, 107–109, 108*fig*
  ketosis and, 109
  natural and added sugars, 115–117, 116*fig*
  niacin and, 252–253*fig*
  from nutrients, 9*fig*–10
  phosphorus and, 311
  photosynthesis and, 100–101*fig*
  from protein, 194*fig*, 199
  protein-energy malnutrition, 210–212, 211*fig*
  thermogenesis, 383
  timing of meals, exercise and, 435–437
  weight loss and, 387
energy, food industry use of, 468*fig*
energy balance, overview of, 376–380, 378*fig*, 378*t*
energy bars, 206–207
energy deficit, 376, 377*fig*
energy density, 40–41, 390–391*t*
energy drinks, 347, 451
energy excess, 376, 377*fig*
energy gap, 399
enhanced water, 292–293
enriched grains, 112–113
enterohepatic circulation, 81
enterotoxigenic *E. coli*, 497*t*, 499
environment, body weight and, 383–384
environment, food choices and, 5
Environmental Protection Agency (EPA), 176, 292, 475–477, 476*fig*, 482*t*, 510–512*fig*, 511*t*
enzymes
  alcohol dehydrogenase (ADH), 345*fig*–346, 348
  amylase, 73–75*fig*, 74*fig*, 80*t*, 104–105*fig*, 520
  B vitamins as coenzymes, 247*fig*
  copper, role of, 319*fig*
  defined, 10
  digestion and, 80*t*
  gastric lipase, 80*t*, 152*fig*
  lactase, 104–105*fig*, 106
  lipase, 72, 80*t*, 152*fig*
  maltase, 104–105*fig*
  pancreatic enzymes, 104–105*fig*, 152*fig*
  protein, functions of, 197*fig*
  sucrase, 104–105*fig*
ephedra, 390, 396
ephedrine, 396
epidemiological research, 18–20
epiglottis, 75*fig*
epinephrine, 109
epiphysial plate, 580*fig*
Equal, 131*t*, 132–133
ergogenic aids, 444–447, 448*t*
erythropoietin, 447, 448*t*
Escherichia coli, 497*t*, 498, 499, 511, 513
esophageal cancer, 86, 353
esophagus, 75*fig*, 86, 353
essential amino acids, 190*t*. *See also* amino acids
essential fatty acids, 148, 156*fig*, 158, 161*fig*
essential nutrients, 9
Estimated Average Requirement (EAR), 34–35. *See also* Dietary Reference Intakes (DRIs)
estimated energy requirement (EER), 36, 379, 385–386
estrogen
  alcohol use and, 351
  body fat storage and, 374*fig*–375
  bone health and, 310
  heart health and, 169
  from soy, 214–215
ethanol, defined, 342, 343. *See also* alcohol
Examining the Evidence
  alcohol and advertising, 350
  common cold, myths about, 266–267
  evaluating nutrition news, 16
  fat-burning zone, 432
  Mediterranean diet, 172–173

nutrition and developmental disorders, 573
  popular weight loss diets, 388–390
  protein supplements, 206–207
  sugar-sweetened beverages, 122–123
  time of day for eating, impact of, 48–49
excellent source of, food label terminology, 56*t*
excretory system, 84*fig*
exercise, defined, 418, 419. *See also* physical activity
experimental group, 18–20
experimental research, 18–20
exports of food, 464, 465
extra, food label terminology, 56*t*
extracellular fluid (ECF), 284, 285*fig*
extra lean, food label terminology, 56*t*
extreme obesity, 398
eyes
  age-related macular degeneration (AMD), 231*fig*, 320
  cataracts, 231*fig*
  diabetes, effects of, 125, 127–128
  fetal development, 538*fig*
  night blindness, 239
  vitamin A and, 235, 236*fig*
  xerophthalmia, 239

F

facilitated diffusion, 82*fig*
fad diets, 388–389
failure to thrive (FTT), 551–552*fig*
fallopian tube, 532*fig*
family health history, 8
famine, 608
farm, defined, 459–460
farmers' markets, 470
farming. *See* agriculture
farm-to-table continuum, 512*fig*
fasting, ketosis and, 109
fat, body. *See also* eating disorders; obesity; weight management
  body composition, 284*fig*
  body storage of, 84
  chemical composition, 146–151*fig*, 147*fig*, 148*fig*, 149*fig*, 150*fig*
  exercise, energy for, 427*fig*, 429–432
  female athlete triad, 434–435
  functions of, 146, 154, 156–157
  heart disease, risk factors, 166–170, 167*t*, 168*fig*
  measurement and location of, 374*fig*–376*fig*, 375*t*
  percent body composition, 9*fig*
  sugar intake and, 117
fat, defined, 149
fat, dietary
  Acceptable Macronutrient Distribution Range (AMDR), 36
  American diet, 13
  carbohydrate loading and, 431
  chemical composition, 10, 146–151*fig*, 147*fig*, 148*fig*, 149*fig*, 150*fig*
  digestion of, 76, 80*t*–81, 151–153, 152*fig*
  fat substitutes, 164–166*t*, 165*t*
  food labels, 174*fig*
  functions of, 9*fig*–10, 146, 154, 156*fig*–157
  heart disease, risk reduction strategies, 170–179, 171*fig*, 174*fig*, 177*fig*, 178*t*
  heart disease and, 166–170, 167*t*, 168*fig*
  infant formula, 549*t*
  Made Over Made Better, 180
  Mediterranean diet and, 172–173
  Nutrition Facts Panel, 51–54, 52*fig*
  orlistat and, 72, 396
  protein and energy bars, 207*t*
  recommended intake, 36, 44*t*, 157–161, 158*fig*, 159*t*, 160*fig*
  sources of, 161*fig*–163*fig*, 162*fig*
  timing of meals, exercise and, 435–437
  trans fatty acids, 158*fig*–160*fig*
  transport in lymph and blood, 153–155*fig*
  types of, 41
  vitamin absorption and, 238
fat-burning zone, 432

fat-soluble vitamins, 229fig, 230t, 234. *See also*
	vitamin A; vitamin D; vitamin E; vitamin K
fatty acids
	in breast milk, 546
	chemical structure, 146–151fig, 147fig, 148fig,
		149fig, 150fig
	defined, 146, 147
	energy for exercise, 429–432
fatty liver, 354fig
fecal-to-oral transmission, 494–500, 496t, 497t, 498t
feces, 78fig
Federal Food, Drug and Cosmetic Act (1938),
	517–518
Federal Trade Commission (FTC), 23, 482t
Feeding America, 617
feedlot, 464
female athlete triad, 434–435
females. *See* women
fermentation, 342, 343
fertility, 530–531, 543
fertilization, human pregnancy, 532fig
fertilizers, food production and, 468
fetal alcohol spectrum disorders (FASDs), 356fig, 537
fetal alcohol syndrome (FAS), 355–356fig, 537
fetal development. *See also* pregnancy
	alcohol, effects of, 355–356fig, 530–531
	critical periods in, 538fig
	first trimester, 532fig–539, 533fig, 534fig, 534t,
		536fig, 538fig
	fish consumption and, 176, 530t
	folate deficiency and, 256
	foodborne illness and, 506, 507
	gestational diabetes, effects of, 540
	gestational hypertension, effects of, 541
	preconception choices and, 528–531, 530t
	second trimester, 539fig–541, 540t
	summary of nutrition guidelines, 559fig
	third trimester, 542
fetus, defined, 532fig
fiber
	American diet, 13
	cancer risk reduction, 591
	carbohydrate digestion, 104–105fig
	cholesterol levels and, 176
	constipation and, 88
	defined, 12, 102–103
	diet for weight loss, 390
	digestion of, 76, 78
	as fat substitute, 164–165t
	flatulence and, 88
	food labels, 51–54, 52fig
	function of, 12, 60, 102–103, 134–137, 135t, 136fig
	glycemic index and, 128–129fig
	older adults, intake, 582–583
	polysaccharides, overview, 101, 102fig–103
	protein and energy bars, 207t
	recommended intake, 110–111t
	satiety and, 116
	sources of, 12, 102–103, 113–114fig, 138
	toddlers and preschoolers, needs of, 570
	types of, 102–103
	whole grains, 112–113
Fight Bac!, 502fig
fight-or-flight hormones, 109
fish
	adding to diet, 176
	antioxidants in, 231
	breast milk, toxins in, 548
	essential fatty acid intake, 156fig
	health benefits of, 173–175
	imports of, 465fig–466
	Mediterranean diet, 173
	mercury and, 176, 520
	omega-3 fatty acids and, 60
	pregnancy, consumption of, 530t, 537
	sushi and sashimi, 501
	toxins and chemical agents, food safety, 518–520,
		519fig
	wild *vs.* farmed salmon, 181
fish oil supplements, 588

fitness. *See* physical fitness
FITT principle, 422–425t, 423t, 424fig
flatulence, 88
flavanols, 61t
flavonoids, 177, 232t, 344
flavored water, 292–293
flavor enhancers, 516, 517t
flaxseed, 161fig, 175, 177fig
flexibility, 419, 422
flood, food insecurity and, 608–610
fluid balance. *See also* water
	breast-feeding mothers, 547–548
	exercise and, 439–444, 440t, 441t, 443fig
	infant needs, 553
	maintaining, 286–291, 287fig, 288fig, 289fig, 290fig
	older adults, 582–583
	potassium and, 305
	protein and, 197–198fig
	Self-Assessment, 291
	toddlers and preschoolers, 570
flukes, 501
fluoride, 299t, 324fig–325, 553
fluorosis, 325
flushing, 252
foam cells, 167, 168fig
Focus Figure
	blood glucose regulation, 108fig
	diabetes, 124fig
	dietary reference intakes (DRIs), 35
	energy balance, 377fig
	energy for exercise, 427fig
	fat digestion and absorption, 152fig
	fluid balance and exercise, 290fig
	lipoprotein transport and distribution, 155fig
	Nutrition Facts panel, 52fig
	protein digestion and absorption, 193fig
	protein synthesis, 195fig
	retinal and vision, 236fig
	small intestinal wall, 77fig
folate and folic acid
	absorption and transport of, 229fig, 230t
	alcohol, effects of, 353
	celiac disease and, 90
	enriched grains, 112–113
	functions and sources, 228fig, 247fig, 255–257fig,
		517t
	preconception intake of, 529
	pregnancy intake, 533–535
	recommended intake, 256–257fig
	sources of, 228fig
	sperm production and, 528
	storage concerns, 233
	summary chart, 265t
Food Additive Amendment (1958), 518
food additives, 301
	color and flavor enhancers, 516, 517t
	nitrates and nitrites, 505
	nutrient additives, 516, 517t
	preservatives, 515–516
	for texture, 516, 517t
food allergies
	breast-feeding, benefits of, 546
	hypoallergenic infant formulas, 550
	infants and, 556–558, 557fig
	sulfites, 515–516
Food and Agriculture Organization, United Nations,
	604
Food and Drug Administration (FDA)
	aspartame research, 132–133
	bottled water regulation, 292–293
	Center for Veterinary Medicine, 474
	food additive regulation, 517–518
	food labels, 49–51, 50fig
	Food Quality Protection Act (1996), 475
	food safety and, 510–512fig, 511t
	fraud detection, 22, 23
	genetically engineered food and, 480t
	role of, 482t
	saccharin regulation, 132
	vitamin safety and regulation, 270–272fig

food assistance programs, 614, 615t
food biosecurity, 521
foodborne illness. *See also* food safety
	DNA fingerprinting, 511
	handwashing and, 502–503
	overview of, 494, 495
	pathogens, overview of, 494–500, 496t, 497t, 498t
	pregnancy and, 501, 537
	risk factors, 500–501
	risk reduction tips, 501–509t, 502fig, 504fig, 505fig,
		505t, 506fig, 508t
	toxins and chemical agents, 500, 518–520, 519fig
food choices, drivers of, 4–7, 5fig
Food Code, 511
food consumers, defined, 458, 459fig
food deserts, 606
food diary, 571
food guidance systems, MyPlate, 40–47
food industry
	antibiotics in food supply, 474
	biotechnology, use of, 477–481, 478fig, 480t
	defined, 458, 459fig
	energy use, 468fig
	exports, 464–465
	farming, United States, 459fig–465, 460fig, 461t,
		462fig, 463fig, 463t
	farm subsidies, 487
	food policy, effects of, 481–484, 482t
	hormones, in food supply, 473fig
	imports, 465fig–466
	organic, food labels and, 485fig–486t
	pesticides, use of, 474–477, 476fig
	sustainable food system, 466–471t, 467fig, 468fig,
		470t
food insecurity
	actions for reducing, 614–617, 615t, 616fig
	defined, 602t, 603
	food *vs.* cash assistance, 618
	global rates and causes, 607–610
	health problems from, 606–607
	older adults, 591–593
	undernutrition and, 610–611
	in the United States, 602t–607, 603fig, 605fig
food intolerance, 557
food jags, 571
food labels
	added sugars, 119fig–120, 139
	Daily Values (DVs), 52fig, 53–54
	fat content, 174fig
	food policy and, 482t–483
	food production information, 484
	genetically engineered food, 480
	health claims, 177
	nutrient content claims, 54–55fig
	Nutrition Facts Panel, overview, 33, 51–54, 52fig, 59t
	organic, terms and standards, 485fig–486t
	overview of, 48–51, 50fig, 59t
	product dating, 514fig–515
	in restaurants, 63
	serving sizes, 46–47
	supplement labels, 270–272fig
	trans fats, 159
food log, 394–395fig
FoodNet, 510–512fig, 511t
food preservation, 315, 512–514
food processors, 459fig, 462fig, 512fig
	food preservation techniques, 512–514
	food production, labels and, 484
Food Quality Protection Act (1996), 475
food safety
	biotechnology in agriculture, 477–481, 478fig, 480t
	bioterrorism and, 521
	botulism, 558
	breast milk storage, 546, 547
	cooking temperature, 504–505fig, 505t, 506fig
	cross-contamination, 503–504fig
	foodborne illness, overview, 494, 495, 500–501
	food policy, effects of, 481–484, 482t
	food storage, 505–509t, 506fig, 508t
	food truck meals, 522

government regulations, 510–512*fig*, 511*t*
handwashing, 502–503
hormones and antibiotics, 473–474
imported foods, 466
pathogens, overview of, 494–500, 496*t*, 497*t*, 498*t*
pesticides, 476*fig*
pollution and, 520
pregnancy and, 537
preservation techniques, 512–514, 515–516
product dating, 514*fig*–515
Self-Assessment, 510
toxins and chemical agents, 500, 518–520, 519*fig*
Food Safety Initiative (FSI), 510–512*fig*, 511*t*
Food Stamp Program, 615*t*
food storage, 501
food tampering, 521
food thermometers, 505*fig*
food trucks, 522
forebrain, alcohol and, 348*fig*, 348*t*
fortified foods, 267–269*fig*, 616
fractures, bone, 309, 310, 434, 438–439
fraud, food claims, 22, 23
free, food label terminology, 56*t*
free radicals, 230*fig*–231, 240*fig*
free range, food label terminology, 484
freezing, food storage, 505–509*t*, 506*fig*, 508*t*
French Paradox, 343–344
frequency, FITT principle, 422–425*t*, 423*t*, 424*fig*
fresh poultry, food label terminology, 484
fructose, 100–102*fig*, 104–105*fig*, 123, 342
fruits. *See also* carbohydrates
    American diet, 13
    antioxidants and, 231, 232*t*
    carbohydrates from, 113–114
    daily intake guidelines, 44*t*
    diet for weight loss, 390
    imports of, 465*fig*–466
    minerals in, 298
    potassium source, 306
    preservatives, 515
    serving size estimates, 47*t*
    TASTE, meal and snack mnemonic, 577*t*
    vitamins in, 228*fig*
    washing, food safety, 503
fruit sugar, 101–102*fig*
fumaric acid, 517*t*
functional fiber, types of, 102–103
functional foods
    cholesterol and, 62
    defined, 58, 60
    role in diet, 60–61*t*
function claims, food labels, 58*fig*
fungicides, food production and, 475–477, 476*fig*
Funk, Casimir, 232

G
gag reflex, 555
galactose, 100–102*fig*, 104–105*fig*
galactosemia, 549
gallbladder, 74*fig*, 79*fig*, 80*t*, 81*t*, 151–153, 152*fig*
gallbladder disease, 370–371
gallstones, 87, 92*t*
garlic, 588
gastric banding, 397*fig*, 410
gastric bypass surgery, 396–397*fig*, 410
gastric lipase, 80*t*, 152*fig*
gastrin, 75, 79–80*t*
gastritis, 353
gastroenteritis, 87, 88, 494, 496*t*
gastroesophageal reflux (GERD), 75*fig*, 86, 92*t*
gastroesophageal sphincter, 75*fig*
gastrointestinal (GI) tract. *See also* foodborne illness
    digestive disorders, overview, 85–92*t*
    digestive process, overview, 70–71*fig*, 80*t*, 81*t*
    fiber and, 103
    liver, gallbladder, and pancreas, 79*fig*
    mouth, 73–75*fig*, 74*fig*
    nutrient absorption, 81–82*fig*
    small intestine, digestion and, 76–77*fig*
    stomach, 75*fig*–76

gelatin, 202
gender differences. *See* men
gene-environment interaction, body weight and, 383–384
generally recognized as safe (GRAS), 516, 517–518
genes/genetics
    biotechnology in food production, 477–481, 478*fig*, 480*t*
    body weight and, 383–384
    eating disorders and, 402–403*fig*
    fetal development, critical periods, 538*fig*
    gene expression, 20
    nutritional genomics, 20*fig*
    phenylketonuria (PKU), 196
    protein synthesis, 194–196, 195*fig*
genetically modified organisms (GMOs), 478*fig*–481, 480*t*
genetic engineering, 478*fig*–481, 480*t*
germ, grains, 112–113
gestational diabetes, 540–541
gestational hypertension, 541
ghrelin, 80*t*, 85, 381–382*fig*
Giardia duodenalis, 498*t*, 499
ginger, 517*t*
gingivitis, 86
ginkgo biloba, 588
ginseng, 589
global nutrition, food insecurity, 607–610
Global Positioning System (GPS), 461
globesity, 465
glossitis, 251
glucagon
    alcohol use and, 351
    blood glucose regulation, 197
    fat metabolism, 154
    pancreas production of, 79
    roles of, 85
glucomannan, 390
gluconeogenesis, 108*fig*–109
glucosamine sulfate, 587
glucose. *See also* diabetes mellitus
    alcohol production and, 342
    energy from, 100
    exercise, energy for, 426–429*t*, 427*fig*
    gestational diabetes, 540–541
    from photosynthesis, 100–101*fig*
glucose load, 128–129*fig*
glutamic acid (Glu), 190*t*
glutamine (Gln), 190*t*
gluten, 89–91, 573
glycemic index (GI), 128–129*fig*
glyceride, 517*t*
glycerol, 149*fig*
glycine (Gly), 189*fig*, 190*t*
glycogen
    blood glucose regulation, 106–109, 107*fig*, 108*fig*
    carbohydrate loading and, 430–431
    exercise, energy for, 426–429*t*, 427*fig*
    polysaccharides, overview, 101, 102*fig*–103
    storage of, 84, 103
glycogenesis, 107–109, 108*fig*
glycogenolysis, 108*fig*–109
GMOs (genetically modified organisms), 478*fig*–481, 480*t*
goiter, 328*fig*, 613*t*
golden rice, 479
good source, food label terminology, 56*t*
government role, food safety, 510–512*fig*, 511*t*, 517–518. *See also* specific agency names
grains. *See also* carbohydrates
    American diet, 13
    daily intake guidelines, 44*t*
    diet for weight loss, 390
    export of, 464–465
    as functional foods, 61*t*
    minerals in, 298
    serving size estimates, 47*t*
    vitamins in, 228*fig*
    whole grains, 7, 112–113
grapefruit, medication interactions, 589

green tea, 177
grief, 593–594
growth charts, 551–552*fig*
growth hormone, human, 446–447, 448*t*
growth hormone, in food supply, 473*fig*
growth stunting, 611–612*fig*
guar gum, 390, 517*t*
Guillain-Barré syndrome, 498

H
habits, food choices and, 7
Haiti, food insecurity, 609
handwashing, 502–503
hangovers, alcohol use, 349, 351
hard water, 292–293
hawthorn, 589
Hazard Analysis and Critical Control Points (HACCP), 511
HDL. *See* high-density lipoproteins (HDL)
health claims
    defined, 56
    food labels, 51, 54–58*fig*, 55*fig*, 56*t*, 57*t*, 177
Healthy Hunger-Free Kids Act (2010), 578
Healthy People 2020, 14–15*t*
healthy weight, defined, 370, 371
heart. *See also* heart disease
    alcohol, effects of, 354
    cardiorespiratory exercise, 420–421, 423*t*
    fetal development, 538*fig*
    Keshan disease, 323
heart attack, 167
heartburn, 75*fig*, 86
heart disease
    alcohol, effects of, 178, 344, 354
    antioxidants and phytochemicals, benefits of, 177, 231
    DASH diet, 40
    diabetes, effects of, 125, 127–128
    exercise, benefits of, 421, 432
    fat intake and, 158
    fiber, benefits of, 136
    obesity and overweight, 370–371, 375
    older adults, dietary needs and, 586
    omega-3 fatty acids, 156*fig*
    physical fitness, benefits of, 420*t*
    protein intake and, 209–210
    risk factors, 166–170, 167*t*, 168*fig*
    risk reduction strategies, 170–179, 171*fig*, 174*fig*, 177*fig*, 178*t*
    sodium intake and blood pressure, 302–304*fig*, 304*t*
    Table Tips, 179
    trans fats and, 158
    vegetarian diet and, 216
    vitamin E and, 240*fig*
heat exhaustion, 440*t*
heat stroke, 440*t*
heavy drinking, 360
Helicobacter pylori, 87
heme group, 316, 318*fig*
hemochromatosis, 261, 318
hemoglobin, 189*fig*, 195–196, 316, 318*fig*, 319*fig*, 438
hemolytic uremic syndrome (HUS), 499
hemorrhage, vitamin E and, 240–241. *See also* blood, clotting of
hemorrhoids, 88, 542
hepatic portal vein, 83*fig*
hepatitis, foodborne illness, 494, 496*t*
herbal remedies
    drug and food interactions, 588–589
    pregnancy and, 530
herbicides, 475–477, 476*fig*
heroin, 537
heterocyclic amines (HCAs), 590
high, food label terminology, 56*t*
high-density lipoproteins (HDL)
    alcohol use and, 344
    fat storage in body, 375
    obesity and overweight, 371
    overview of, 153–155*fig*
high-fructose corn syrup, 119*fig*, 123

high-pressure processing (HPP), 513
histidine (His), 190t
HIV/AIDS, 549
homeless, 607
homocysteine, 170
honey, 119, 558
hoodia, 390
hormones
    alcohol and, 351
    anabolic steroids, 446
    blood glucose regulation, 106–109, 107fig, 108fig
    breast-feeding and, 544fig, 546
    defined, 106
    digestion and, 79–80t
    endocrine system, overview, 85
    erythropoietin, 447
    fight-or-flight hormones, 109
    in food supply, 473fig
    gastrin, 75
    growth hormone, 446–447
    hunger and satiety, regulation of, 381–382fig
    organic food labels and, 485
    protein, functions of, 197
Human Genome Project, 20
human studies, 16
hunger. See also food insecurity
    ghrelin and, 80t
    malnutrition, effects of, 611–613t, 612fig, 612t
    medications for weight loss, 396
    regulation of, 85, 381–382fig
    undernutrition, 610–611
hydrochloric acid (HCl), digestion, 75fig–76, 80t, 86
hydrogenated starch hydrolysates (HSH), 131t, 132
hydrogenation, 158fig–160fig
hydrophilic compounds, 149fig, 190
hydrophobic compounds, 146, 147
hyperactivity, sugar and, 117, 573
hypercalcemia, 246, 307
hyperkalemia, 305–306
hyperphosphatemia, 311–312
hypertension
    alcohol, effects of, 354
    calcium intake, 307
    choline and, 263
    DASH diet, 40
    defined, 169, 303
    exercise, benefits of, 421
    heart disease and, 169
    magnesium, role of, 313
    obesity and overweight, 370–371, 375
    older adults, dietary needs and, 586
    potassium intake, 305
    pregnancy and, 541, 543
    sodium intake, 302–304fig, 304t
    vegetarian diets, 216
hypervitaminosis, 238–239
hypervitaminosis D, 246
hypoallergenic infant formulas, 550
hypoglycemia, 127
hypokalemia, 306
hyponatremia, 289, 443
hypotension, 263
hypothesis, defined, 17fig–18

I
ibuprofen, 351
ileocecal sphincter, 78fig
ileum, 76–77fig, 91
immune system
    alcohol, effects of, 354
    breast milk and, 546
    copper, role of, 319fig
    food allergies, causes of, 556–558, 557fig
    malnutrition and, 612t–613
    physical fitness, benefits of, 421t
    proteins and, 199
    rheumatoid arthritis, 587
    vitamin A and, 235
    vitamin C and, 260
    zinc and, 320

immunity, 199
implantation, embryo, 532fig
imports, food, 465fig–466
incomplete proteins, 202–203
indoles, 232t
industrial chemical exposure, 590
infancy, defined, 551
infant formula, 548–550, 549t, 553
infant mortality, 613
infants
    breast-feeding, benefits of, 543–546
    food allergies, 556–558, 557fig
    growth rate, 551–552fig
    honey consumption, 119, 558
    malnutrition, effects of, 611–613t, 612fig, 612t
    nutrient needs, 550–553, 552fig
    solid foods, 553–558, 560
    tongue-thrust reflex, 554
    undernutrition, 610
infertility, 530–531, 543
inflammation, heart disease and, 170
ingredients, food labels, 50fig, 119fig–120
injury, alcohol and, 357fig
inorganic substances, defined, 10, 295. See also
            minerals
inositol, 263
insensible water loss, 287fig
insoluble fiber, 103, 114
intrinsic factor, 75
insulin. See also diabetes mellitus
    alcohol use and, 351
    blood glucose regulation, 106–109, 107fig, 108fig,
            197
    chromium, role of, 326
    diabetes, overview, 121–122
    diabetes, types of, 124fig–125
    genetic engineering and, 479
    gestational diabetes, 540–541
    hunger and satiety regulation, 381–382fig
    pancreas production of, 79
    roles of, 85
insulin-like growth factor, 473
insulin resistance, 121–122, 124fig–125, 371, 375
integrated pest management (IPM), 476–477
intensity, FITT principle, 422–425t, 423t, 424fig
intentional food additives, 518
international units (IU), vitamin A intake, 237
Internet, information on, 22–24
interstitial fluid, 284, 285fig
intestines. See large intestine
intracellular fluid (ICF), 284, 285fig
intravascular hemolysis, 438
intrinsic factor (IF), 258–259
iodine and iodide
    body content, 297fig
    fortified foods, 616
    functions and sources, 299t, 327–328fig
    malnutrition and, 613t
iodopsin, 235, 236fig
iron (Fe)
    adolescents, intake, 580–581
    alcohol, effects of, 353
    body content, 297fig
    enriched grains, 112–113
    food labels, 51–54, 52fig
    fortified foods, 616
    functions and sources, 299t, 316–318fig, 317fig, 438
    gastric bypass surgery and, 397
    golden rice, 479
    infant formula, 549t
    infant needs, 553
    malnutrition and, 613t
    older adults, intake, 584t
    phytates and, 296
    pica and, 533
    pregnancy, intake, 533–535, 536fig
    toddlers and preschoolers, intake, 570
    vegetarian diets, 217t
    vitamin C and, 261, 296, 316
iron-deficiency anemia, 318fig, 438

irradiation, food safety, 513fig–514
irritable bowel syndrome (IBS), 89–90, 92t
isoflavones, 214
isoleucine (Ile), 190t
isopropyl alcohol, 342
isothiocyanates, 60

J
jaundice, 540
jejunum, 76–77fig
joints
    obesity and overweight, 371
    osteoarthritis and, 231, 586–587
Jones, Kenneth, 355

K
kava kava, 589
kernel, 112–113
Keshan disease, 323
ketoacidosis, 122
ketone bodies, 109
ketosis, 109
kidney disease, 541
kidneys
    diabetes, effects of, 125, 127–128
    excretory system, overview, 84fig
    gluconeogenesis, 108fig–109
    magnesium regulation, 314
    potassium balance, 305
    sodium regulation, 301
    vitamin D metabolism, 244
    water balance, 287fig
kidney stones, 210, 305fig, 307
kilocalories (kcal). See also calories
    defined, 5
    energy needs and sources, 9fig–10
konjac plant, 390
Kosher, food labels, 484
kwashiorkor, 211fig

L
labels, food
    added sugars, 119fig–120, 139
    Daily Values (DVs), 52fig, 53–54
    fat content, 174fig
    food policy and, 482t–483
    food production information, 484
    genetically engineered food, 480
    health claims, 177
    nutrient content claims, 54–55fig
    Nutrition Facts Panel, overview, 33, 51–54,
            52fig, 59t
    organic, terms and standards, 485fig–486t
    overview of, 48–51, 50fig, 59t
    product dating, 514fig–515
    in restaurants, 63
    serving sizes, 46–47
    supplement labels, 270–272fig
    trans fats, 159
laboratory experiment, 18–20
lactase, 104, 104–105fig, 106
lactate, exercise and, 428
lactation, 543–546
lactic acid, 517t
lacto-ovo vegetarian diet, 212t–219t, 217fig,
            217t, 218t
lactose, 101–102fig, 104–105fig
lactose intolerance, 104, 106
lactose maldigestion, 104, 106
lacto-vegetarian diet, 212t–219t, 217fig, 217t, 218t
land management, 614–616
lanugo, 405
lard, 163fig
large intestine
    carbohydrate digestion, 104–106, 105fig
    constipation, 88
    diarrhea, 88
    digestive process, 78fig, 80t, 81t
    digestive system, overview, 74fig
    disorders of, 89–92t

fiber, benefits of, 103, 134–137, 135t, 136fig
  flatulence, 88
  lactose intolerance and, 106
  water balance, 287fig
laxatives, 405
LDL. See low-density lipoproteins (LDL)
LDN (licensed dietitian nutritionist), 22
lean, food label terminology, 56t
lean body mass, 378t
least developed country, 604
lecithin, 150, 517t
legumes, 114, 176. See also carbohydrates
leptin, 123, 381–382fig
less, food label terminology, 56t
let-down response, 543
letdown response, 544fig
leucine (Leu), 189fig, 190t
licensed dietitian nutritionist (LDN), 22
licorice, 589
life expectancy, 581
lifestyle. See also physical activity
  behavior modification, 394–395fig
  body weight and, 383–384
  childhood obesity and, 574–575
  infertility and, 531
  Mediterranean diet, 172–173
  obesity and overweight, 13
  preconception choices, 528–531, 530t
light, food label terminology, 56t
lignans, 232t
lima beans, 520
limiting amino acids, 202–203
limonene, 517t
lingual lipase, 152fig
linoleic acid, 147fig, 148, 156fig, 161fig
lipase, 72, 80t, 152fig
lipids
  chemical composition, 146–151fig, 147fig, 148fig, 149fig, 150fig
  defined, 146, 147
  functions of, 9fig–10, 146
lipoic acid, 263
lipoprotein lipase, 153–155fig
lipoproteins, 153–155fig. See also high-density lipoproteins (HDL); low-density lipoproteins (LDL); very low-density lipoproteins (VLDL)
liposuction, 397
liquor. See alcohol
Listeria monocytogenes, 497t, 498, 506, 507, 537
listeriosis, 506, 507
liver
  acetaminophen use and, 351
  alcohol, effects of, 354fig–355
  alcohol metabolism, 345fig–346
  anatomy, 374fig
  bile, recycling of, 81
  carbohydrate digestion, 104–106, 105fig
  digestion and, 74fig, 79fig, 80t, 81t
  fat digestion, 151–153, 152fig
  glycogenesis, 107–109, 108fig
  glycogen storage, 84, 428–429
  lipid digestion, 153–155fig
  nutrient transport, 83fig–84
  protein digestion, 192, 193fig
  vitamin A toxicity, 238
  vitamin storage, 234
  weight loss medications, risks of, 396
lobbyists, food industry, 483–484
local food movement, 469–471, 470t
locavore, 469
low, food label terminology, 56t
low birth weight baby, 537
low-density lipoproteins (LDL)
  alcohol use and, 344
  antioxidants and phytochemicals, benefits of, 177fig
  diet and, 171–173
  fat storage in body, 375
  heart disease, risk factors, 167, 168fig
  heart-healthy diet, 176
  niacin and, 252–253fig

obesity and overweight, 371
  overview of, 153–155fig
  trans fats and, 158
  vitamin E and, 240fig
lubrication, water and, 286
lumen, intestines, 70
lung cancer, 420t
lungs, water balance, 287fig
lupus erythematosus, 541
lutein, 231fig, 232t, 235
lycopene, 61t, 232t, 235, 591
lymph, 153, 153–155fig
lymphatic system, 77fig, 81–84, 82fig, 83fig
lysine (Lys), 190t, 206

M

macrocytes, 257fig
macrocytic anemia, 257fig, 259
macronutrients, defined, 9
macrosomia, 540
macula, 236fig
Made Over Made Better
  fat intake, 180
  fiber intake, 138
  food for exercise, 450
  mineral intake, increasing, 331
  nonalcoholic beverages, 362
  protein intake, 220
  vitamin intake, 273
  for weight loss, 409
magnesium
  alcohol, effects of, 353
  body content, 297fig
  functions and sources, 297t, 313–314fig
  pregnancy, intake needs, 536fig
ma huang, 396
major minerals, 296, 297t
malabsorption, celiac disease, 90–91
malaria, 612t–613
males. See men
malnourished, defined, 32, 33
malnutrition. See also food insecurity
  alcohol, long-term effects of, 351–353fig, 352t
  effects of, 611–613t, 612fig, 612t
  protein-energy malnutrition (PEM), 210–212, 211fig
  underweight and, 371
maltase, 104–105fig
maltose, 101–102fig, 104–105fig, 342
manganese, 299t, 329fig
mannitol, 130–132, 131t
marasmic kwashiorkor, 211fig
marasmus, 211fig
margarine, 163fig
marijuana, 530–531, 537
marinades, 191
marine toxins, 518–519fig
mast cells, 556, 557fig
meal replacers, 447–449fig
Meals on Wheels, 593, 615t
measles, 612t–613
meat, food labels, 51. See also food safety; protein
Meat Inspection Act, 494
meat substitutes, 214–215
mechanical agitation, 191
mechanical digestion, 70–71fig, 73–75fig, 74fig
media information
  advertising, regulation of, 25
  alcohol advertising, 349, 350
  body image and, 372, 402, 404
  evaluating, 15–24
  food choices and, 5fig, 458–459
medical nutrition therapy, defined, 21
medications
  drug-food interactions, 588–589
  for weight loss, 71, 72, 396
Mediterranean diet, 40, 172–173
megadose, vitamins, 233
megaloblasts, 257fig
melanin, 192, 244
memory, alcohol and, 353

men
  added sugar intake, 121
  alcohol, intake recommendations, 347t, 348fig
  anabolic steroid use, 446
  body composition, 284fig, 374fig
  body image, media and, 372
  calorie needs, children and adolescents, 569t
  carbohydrate intake, 110–111fig, 111t
  carbohydrate loading, 430–431
  daily calorie requirements, 36
  eating disorders, 401–408, 402t, 403fig, 407t
  fiber intake, 111t
  folate intake, 256–257fig
  heart disease, risk for, 167t–169, 168fig
  hypertension, risk of, 303
  iodine intake, 327–328fig
  iron intake, 316–317fig
  magnesium intake, 313, 314fig, 329fig
  molybdenum intake, 330
  niacin intake, 252–253fig
  potassium intake, 305, 306fig
  preconception diet and lifestyle, 528
  riboflavin (vitamin B_2) intake, 250–251fig
  selenium intake, 322–323fig
  sugar-sweetened beverage consumption, 122t
  thiamin intake, 248–249fig
  vitamin A intake, 237fig
  vitamin B_6 intake, 254
  vitamin B_{12} intake, 258–259fig
  vitamin C intake, 260–261fig
  vitamin D intake, 244–245fig
  vitamin E intake, 240, 241fig
  vitamin K intake, 242–243fig
  water intake, 291, 294fig–295fig
  zinc intake, 320–321fig
menaquinone, 242–243fig
menarche, 579
menopause, 167, 310, 317fig
menstrual cycle
  body fat storage and, 374fig–375
  breast-feeding and, 545
  female athlete triad, 434–435
  iron intake, 316–317fig
  menarche, 579
  vitamin B_6 intake, 254
mental health
  eating disorders and, 401–408, 402t, 403fig, 407t
  food insecurity and, 607
  physical fitness, benefits of, 421t
mercury, 176, 181, 520, 530t, 548
Meridia, 396
messenger RNA (mRNA), 194–196, 195fig
metabolic syndrome, 170
metabolism
  of alcohol, 344–346, 345fig
  defined, 5
  energy for exercise, 425–427fig, 426fig
  magnesium, role of, 313
  phosphorus, role of, 311
methanol, 342
methionine (Met), 190t
methyl cellulose, 517t
methylmercury, 176, 181, 520, 530t, 548
micelles, 152fig–153fig
micronutrients. See also minerals; vitamins
  American diet, 13
  defined, 9
microsomal ethanol-oxidizing system (MEOS), 346
microvilli, intestines, 76–77fig
milestones, infant growth, 551–552fig
milk and dairy products
  allergies to, 556, 557fig
  calcium and, 307, 308fig
  carbohydrates in, 115
  daily intake guidelines, 44t
  exercise and, 437
  minerals in, 298
  riboflavin (vitamin B_2), 250–251fig
  serving size estimates, 47t
  vitamins in, 228fig

milk thistle, 589
minerals. *See also* specific mineral names
  bioavailability, 296
  body composition, 297*fig*
  chemical composition, 11
  food labels and, 52*fig*
  functions of, 10–11, 295–300*t*, 297*fig*, 297*t*, 299*t*
  liver storage of, 79
  Made Over Made Better, 331
  major and trace, 296, 297*t*, 299*t*
  percent body composition, 9*fig*
  vision and, 231*fig*
mineral water, 292–293
miso, 214–215
moderate alcohol consumption, 343*fig*–344
moderate diet, defined, 32
modified atmosphere packaging (MAP), 513
molybdenum, 299*t*, 330
monk fruit, 131*t*, 134
monoglycerides, 151, 151–152*fig*, 517*t*
monosaccharides, 100–102*fig*
monosodium glutamate (MSG), 301, 516–517*t*
monounsaturated fatty acids (MUFA), 146–148*fig*,
      147*fig*, 148
more, food label terminology, 56*t*
morning sickness, 533–534
mortality rates, 613
motor vehicles, alcohol use and, 359–360
mouth
  carbohydrate digestion, 104–106, 105*fig*
  digestive process, 80*t*, 81*t*
  disorders of, 85–86
  fat digestion, 151–153, 152*fig*
  protein digestion, 192, 193*fig*
MSG complex syndrome, 517
mucus, digestive process, 75–76, 80*t*
  in mouth, 73–75*fig*, 74*fig*
muscle dysmorphia, 404
muscle endurance, 305, 418, 419, 421–422
muscles
  calcium, role of, 307
  carbohydrate loading, 430–431
  chromium and, 326
  exercise, energy for, 427*fig*, 428–429, 433
  fats, energy from, 429–432
  glycogenesis, 107–109, 108*fig*
  older adults, physical activity and, 595
muscle strength, 418, 419, 421–422, 433
mushrooms, toxins from, 520
My Family Health Portrait, 8
myoglobin, 316, 318*fig*, 504–505*fig*
MyPlate. *See also* individual nutrient intake
      recommendations
  for children, 575–576*fig*, 577*t*
  diet for weight loss, 392–393
  fat sources, 161*fig*
  nutrient intake recommendations, 267, 268*fig*
  for older adults, 583*fig*
  overview of, 33, 39–47*t*, 40*fig*, 41*fig*, 42*fig*, 43*fig*,
      44*fig*, 44*t*, 45*fig*, 59*t*
  vs. Mediterranean diet, 173
MyVeganPlate, 217

N

National Antimicrobial Resistance Monitoring
      System-Enteric Bacteria (NARMS), 474
National Cancer Institute, 232*t*
National Drug and Alcohol Treatment Referral
      Routing Service, 530
National Institute of Child Health and Human
      Development, 541
National Institute of Mental Health, 573
National Institute on Alcohol Abuse and Alcoholism,
      530, 594–595
National List of Allowed and Prohibited Substances, 485
National Marine Fisheries Service (NMFS), 482*t*
National Organic Standards (NOS), 485
National Resource Center for Health and Safety in
      Child Care and Early Education, 570
National School Lunch Program (NSLP), 483, 578, 615*t*

National Toxicology Program (NTP), 132
natural, food label terminology, 484
natural disasters, food insecurity and, 608–610
natural sugars, 115–121, 116*fig*, 119*fig*, 120*fig*
Naturlose, 131*t*
NEAT (nonexercise-associated thermogenesis), 383
Nectresse, 131*t*
nematodes, 501
Neotame, 131*t*, 133
nervous system
  alcohol, effects of, 346–348*fig*, 348*t*
  appetite and, 85
  calcium, role of, 307
  diabetes, effects of, 125, 127–128
  essential fatty acids, 156*fig*
  fetal development of, 535, 538*fig*
  folate intake, 256–257
  manganese toxicity, 329
  potassium, role of, 305
  thiamin (vitamin B$_1$) and, 248
  vitamin B$_{12}$ and, 258–259
net weight, food labels, 50*fig*
neural tube defects, 256, 529, 535
neurotoxins, 519*fig*
New Atkins for a New You diet, 388–389
niacin
  absorption and transport of, 229*fig*, 230*t*
  enriched grains, 112–113
  functions and sources, 228*t*, 247*fig*, 252–253*fig*
  pregnancy, intake needs, 536*fig*
  recommended intake, 252–253*fig*
  sources, 228*fig*
  summary chart, 264*t*
  vitamin B$_6$ and, 254
niacin equivalents (NE), 252
nickel, 298, 300*t*
nicotine, 548
night blindness, 239
night eating syndrome, 406
nitrates, 505, 515–516, 517*t*
nitrites, 505, 515–516, 517*t*, 590
nitrogen balance, 200–201*fig*
no hormones, food label terminology, 484–485
nonessential amino acids, 190*t*. *See also* amino acids
nonexercise-associated thermogenesis (NEAT), 383
No Oven Needed Energy Bars, 449*fig*
norepinephrine, 109
normal blood pressure, defined, 169
norovirus, 494, 496*t*
Norwalk virus, 494, 496*t*
Nutrasweet, 131*t*, 132–133
nutrient content claims, food labels, 54–55*fig*
nutrient density, 40–41, 42*t*
nutrients. *See also* digestion; individual nutrient names
  defined, 4, 5
  dietary sources, 11–12
  energy from, 9*fig*–10
  supplements and, 12
nutrition. *See also* individual nutrient names
  defined, 8
  information sources, 15–24
nutritional genomics, 20*fig*
nutrition experts, 20–22
Nutrition Facts Panel, 50*fig*
  added sugars, 119*fig*–120, 139
  fat content, 174*fig*
  food policy and, 482*t*–483
  overview of, 33, 51–54, 52*fig*, 59*t*
  serving sizes, 46–47
  trans fats, 159
Nutrition in the Real World
  babies, feeding of, 555
  body image, 404
  breast-feeding at work, 547
  carbohydrate loading, 430–431
  consumer scams, 23
  dental caries, 118
  Dietary Guidelines for Americans, overview, 38–39
  digestive process, tinkering with, 72
  drug, food, and herb interactions, 588–589

fish and mercury, 176
food insecurity, 617
natural disasters and food insecurity, 609
obesity and poverty, 14
portion sizes, 46–47
soy foods, 214–215
sushi, food safety and, 501
tap *vs.* bottled water, 292–293
vegetable container gardening, 472
whole grains, 112–113
nutritionist, defined, 22
nuts
  allergies to, 556, 557*fig*
  antioxidants in, 177*fig*
  carbohydrate source, 114
  fats from, 161*fig*
  Table Tips, 178

O

oats, 60, 176
obesity and overweight
  alcohol use and, 351–353*fig*, 352*t*
  arthritis and, 586–587
  body mass index (BMI), 372–374, 373*t*
  breast-feeding and, 546
  in childhood, 574*fig*–575
  defined, 13, 370, 371
  economic costs of, 370
  environmental factors, 386
  extreme obesity, 398
  fiber, benefits of, 135–137
  food labels in restaurants, 63
  global rates of, 464–465
  health risks of, 370–371
  high-fructose corn syrup and, 119
  medications for weight loss, 396
  metabolic syndrome, 170
  2 Points of View, gastric bypass, 410
  poverty and, 14
  pregnancy and, 529
  rates of, 13*fig*–15, 607
  sugar-sweetened beverages and, 122–123
  surgical interventions, 396–397*fig*
  undernourishment and, 607
  vegetarian diet and, 216
  very low-calorie diet, 395
observational research, 18–20
obsessive-compulsive disorder (OCD), 403*fig*
oils, 163*fig*. *See also* fat, dietary
  defined, 149
  fats, sources of, 174*fig*
  fatty acid chemistry, 146–151*fig*, 147*fig*, 148*fig*,
      149*fig*, 150*fig*
  functions of, 146
older adults
  alcohol abuse, 594–595*fig*
  chronic disease and, 585–587, 590–591
  depression and grief, 593–594
  drug, food, and herb interactions, 588–589
  foodborne illness and, 500–501
  food insecurity, 591–593
  micronutrient needs, 583–585, 584*t*
  nutritional needs, 581–585, 582*fig*, 583*fig*, 584*t*
  physical activity, 595
  undernutrition, 611
Older Americans Act (1965), 592–593
Olean, 164–165*t*
oleic acid, 147*fig*, 148, 149*fig*
olestra, 164–165*t*
olive oil, 148, 163*fig*, 173
omega-3 fatty acids
  cancer risk reduction, 591
  chemical structure of, 147*fig*
  functional foods, 60
  functions and sources, 61*t*, 156*fig*
  pregnancy, intake needs, 535
  sources, 173–175, 177*fig*
  vegetarian diets, 218*t*
  wild *vs.* farmed salmon, 181
omega-6 fatty acids, 147*fig*, 156*fig*

open dating, food safety, 514fig–515
optic nerve, 236fig
organic compounds, 10
organic food labeling, 473, 474, 476, 485fig–486t
organophosphates, 475–477, 476fig
organs, 71
organ systems, 71
orlistat, 71, 72, 396
Ornish diet, 388–389
orthorexia, 406
osmosis, 288fig
osteoarthritis, 370–371, 586–587
osteocalcin, 242
osteomalacia, 246
osteopenia, 309
osteoporosis
   celiac disease and, 90
   female athlete triad, 434
   overview of, 308fig–310, 309fig
   protein intake and, 210
   vitamin A and, 238
   vitamin K and, 242
Osymia, 396
ovarian cancer, 544
ovaries, 532fig, 541
overhydration, 444
overnutrition, 32, 33, 351–353fig, 352t
overpopulation, 610
overweight, defined, 370, 371. See also obesity and
      overweight
ovo-vegetarian diet, 212t–219t, 217fig, 217t, 218t
oxalates, 296, 307, 308
oxidation, antioxidants and, 230fig–231
oxidative stress, 231
oxygen, cardiorespiratory exercise, 421
oxytocin, 544, 544fig

P

packaged foods
   added sugars, 117, 119fig–121, 120fig, 120t
   carbohydrates in, 115
PAHs (polycyclic aromatic hydrocarbons), 590
Paleo Diet, 221, 388–389
palmitic acid, 149fig
palm kernel oil, 163fig
palm oils, 163fig
pancreas
   blood glucose regulation and, 85
   carbohydrate digestion, 104–106, 105fig
   diabetes, types of, 124fig–125
   digestion, overview, 74fig, 79fig, 80t, 81t
   fat digestion, 151–153, 152fig
   hunger and satiety, regulation of, 382fig
   obesity and overweight, 371
   protein digestion, 192, 193fig
pancreatic amylase, 104–105fig
pancreatic cancer, 244
pancreatic lipase, 152fig
pantothenic acid, 229fig, 230t, 247fig, 262, 265t
paralytic shellfish poisoning, 519fig
parasites, 498t, 499, 501
parathyroid hormone (PTH), 244
Partnership for Food Safety Education (PFSE), 511
passive diffusion, 82fig
pasteurization, 512, 537
pathogens, foodborne illness
   cooking temperature, 505fig, 505t
   overview of, 494–500, 496t, 497t, 498t
   pregnancy and, 537
   toxins from, 518–519fig
Patient Protection and Affordable Care Act (2010), 63
PCBs (polychlorinated biphenyls), 181, 520
peak bone mass, 309, 580fig
peanut butter, 159
peanut oil, 163fig
peanuts, allergies to, 556, 557fig
pear body shape, 374fig
pectin, 103, 176, 517t
peer-reviewed journals, 16, 18
pellagra, 253

PEM (protein-energy malnutrition), 210–212, 211fig
pendular movement, 71
pepsin, 76, 192, 193fig
pepsinogen, 192, 193fig
peptic ulcers, 87, 92t
peptide bonds, 189fig–190
peptides, protein structure, 188–190, 189fig
percentile rank, growth charts, 552fig
perfectionism, 403
periodontal disease, 86
peristalsis, 70–71fig, 74fig, 78
pernicious anemia, 258–259
pesco-vegetarian diet, 212t–219t, 217fig, 217t, 218t
pesticides, food production and, 468, 474–477,
      476fig, 485fig–486t
pharynx, 73–75fig, 74fig
Phelps, Michael, 433
phenolics, 232t
phenols, 232t
phentermine, 396
phenylalanine (Phe), 132–133, 134, 189fig, 190t
phenylketonuria (PKU), 133, 196
phospholipids
   chemical structure, 146–151fig, 147fig, 148fig,
      149fig, 150fig
   defined, 149fig
   phosphorus intake and, 311fig
   transport of, 152fig–155fig
phosphoric acid, 517t
phosphorus
   body content, 297fig
   functions and sources, 297t, 311fig–321fig
   infant formula, 549t
   intake recommendations, 311–312fig
   pregnancy, intake needs, 536fig
   vitamin D and, 244
photosynthesis, 100–101fig
phylloquinone, 242–243fig
physical activity. See also physical fitness
   benefits of, 418–419, 420t, 421t
   blood pressure and, 303–304t
   calorie intake needs, 433–435
   calorie needs, children and adolescents, 569t
   calories used by activity, 393t
   carbohydrate loading, 429, 430–431
   carbohydrates, energy from, 426–429t, 427fig
   childhood obesity and, 574fig–575
   Dietary Guidelines for Americans and, 38, 42
   energy for, 379, 425–427fig, 426fig
   environmental factors, 386
   ergogenic aids, 444–447, 448t
   fat, energy from, 429–432
   fat-burning zone, 432
   fluid intake and, 439–444, 440t, 441t, 443fig
   heart disease and, 169, 178
   older adults, 595
   pregnancy and, 539–540t
   protein, energy from, 433
   protein supplements, 449t
   recommended levels of, 178
   sports bars, shakes, and meal replacers, 447–449fig
   timing of meals, 435–437
   water balance, maintaining, 289–290fig
   weight loss and, 393t–394
Physical Activity Guidelines for Americans, 178, 419,
      423–424fig, 595
physical fitness
   components of, 418–419
   ergogenic aids, 444–447
   fitness program, elements of, 420–425t, 423t, 424fig
   FITT principle, 422–425t, 423t, 424fig
   terminology, 418–419
   vitamins and minerals, benefits of, 437–439
phytates, 296, 321
phytochemicals
   antioxidant properties of, 229–231fig, 230fig, 232t
   defined, 12, 60, 231
   functions and sources, 177fig, 231, 232t
   in red wine, 344
   whole grains, 112–113

phytoestrogens, sources of, 232t
phytonutrients, 582, 591
phytosterols, 176, 177
pica, 406, 533
picky eating, 571
Pima Indians, 383–384
pituitary gland, 349, 446–447
placebo, defined, 19
placenta, 532fig–533fig
plant breeding, 477–481, 478fig, 480t
plants
   antioxidants and phytochemicals, 177fig, 231, 232t
   carbohydrates from, 100
   estrogens from, 214–215
   heart healthy diet and, 175–177
   Paleo Diet, 221
   photosynthesis, 100–101fig
   protein, amino acid profile of, 202–203
   protein, digestibility of, 202
   protein, soy products, 214
   starch, 102fig
   vitamin K, 242–243fig
plant sterols and stanols, 61t, 176, 232t
plaque, arteries, 167, 168fig
plus, food label terminology, 56t
political sanctions, food insecurity and, 608
politics, food industry and, 483–484
pollution, 520
polychlorinated biphenyls (PCBs), 181, 520
polycyclic aromatic hydrocarbons (PAHs), 590
polycystic ovary disease, 541
polyneuritis, 248
polyols, 130–132, 131t
polypeptides, defined, 188
polyphenols, 296
polysaccharides, defined, 101, 102fig
polyunsaturated fatty acids (PUFA), 146–148fig, 147fig
population, food insecurity and, 610
pork, 464, 484, 505t, 508t, 509t
pork fat (lard), 163fig
portion size, 42, 43, 44fig, 46–47, 385
   standard alcohol drink, 343fig, 344fig
potassium (K)
   acesulfame-K, 133
   American diet, 13
   body content, 297fig
   cell membrane transport, 198fig–199
   exercise, fluid needs for, 440t
   functions and sources, 297t, 305–306fig
   recommended intake, 305, 306fig
potatoes, 520
poultry
   antibiotics in food supply, 474
   chicken, fat in, 163fig
   chicken, nutrients in, 9fig
   cooking of, 505, 505t
   farming of, 464
   food labels, 51, 484
   food storage, 508t
poverty
   defined, 604
   food insecurity and, 602t–607, 603fig, 605fig
   global data on, 607–610
   malnutrition and, 611–613t, 612fig, 612t
   obesity and overweight, 14
   undernutrition, 610–611
precision agriculture, 461
precursor, defined, 150–151, 190
preeclampsia, 541
preformed vitamins, 233, 235
pregnancy
   alcohol, effects of, 355–356fig
   first trimester, 532fig–539, 533fig, 534fig, 534t,
      536fig, 538fig
   fish consumption, 176, 530t
   folate intake, 256
   foodborne illness and, 501, 506, 507
   gestational diabetes, 540–541
   iron intake, 316–317fig
   morning sickness and cravings, 533–534

pregnancy (*continued*)
    nutrient needs, 534–536*fig*
    older mothers, 542–543
    preconception diet and lifestyle, 528–531, 530*t*
    second trimester, 539*fig*–541, 540*t*
    summary of guidelines, 559*fig*
    teenage mothers, 542–543
    third trimester, 542
    undernutrition and, 610
    vitamin A intake, 238
    vitamin supplements, 270
    weight gain recommendations, 533*fig*, 533*t*
pregnancy-induced hypertension, 541, 543
premenstrual syndrome (PMS), 254
preschoolers
    food jags, 571
    nutrient needs, overview, 568–570, 569*t*
preservation, food, 301, 315, 515–516
prions, 499–500
prior-sanctioned status, food additives, 517–518
Pritikin diet, 388–389
probiotics, 61*t*, 91, 93
processed foods
    added sugars, 117, 119*fig*–121, 120*fig*, 120*t*
    carbohydrates in, 115
    sodium content, 301, 302*fig*
product dating, 514*fig*–515
progressive overload principle, 424–425
prolactin, 544*fig*
proline (Pro), 190*t*
propionic acid, 517*t*
proportionality, defined, 40
propulsion, digestive system, 74*fig*
prostate cancer, 244, 256, 591
proteases, 80*t*
protein
    Acceptable Macronutrient Distribution Range (AMDR), 36
    alcohol, effects of, 353
    body composition, 284*fig*
    carbohydrate loading and, 431
    chemical composition, 10, 188–190, 189*fig*
    copper, role of, 319*fig*
    daily intake guidelines, 44*t*
    defined, 188, 189
    denatured proteins, 191*fig*
    diet for weight loss, 392
    digestion and absorption, 76, 80, 80*t*, 192–194*fig*, 193*fig*
    exercise, energy for, 427*fig*, 433
    as fat substitutes, 164–165*t*
    food labels, 51–54, 52*fig*
    functions of, 9*fig*–10, 188, 196–200*t*, 197*fig*, 198*fig*
    gluconeogenesis, 108*fig*–109
    growth hormone and, 446–447
    infant formula, 549*t*
    infant needs, 552
    ketosis and, 109
    Made Over Made Better, 220
    minerals in, 298
    older adults, recommended intake, 582
    over consumption, 209–210
    Paleo Diet, 221
    percent body composition, 9*fig*
    pregnancy, intake needs, 536*fig*, 539*fig*
    recommended intake, 200–204, 201*fig*, 203*t*
    Self-Assessment, 208
    serving size estimates, 47*t*
    sources of, 199, 204*fig*–205*fig*
    supplements, 206–207, 449*t*
    timing of meals, exercise and, 435–437
    transport proteins, 198*fig*–199
    turnover in body, 192–196, 193*fig*, 194*fig*, 195*fig*
    vegetarian diet, 212*t*–219*t*, 217*fig*, 217*t*, 218*t*
    vitamin C and collagen, 260
    vitamins in, 228*fig*
    in whole grains, 112–113
protein digestibility corrected amino acid score (PDCAAS), 203
protein-energy malnutrition (PEM), 210–212, 211*fig*

protein quality, defined, 202–203
protein-sparing modified fast, 395
provitamin A carotenoids, 235
provitamins, 233
pseudoanemia, 438
psyllium, 103, 176
puberty, 579
public health nutritionists, 22
PUFA (polyunsaturated fatty acids), 146–148*fig*, 147*fig*
PulseNet, 511
PureVia, 131*t*
purging, 405
pyloric sphincter, 76
pyridoxal. *See* vitamin B$_6$
pyridoxal phosphate. *See* vitamin B$_6$
pyridoxamine. *See* vitamin B$_6$
pyridoxine. *See* vitamin B$_6$

Q

quackery, 22, 23
qualified health claims, food labels, 57*t*, 58

R

radiation, cancer risk, 590
rancidity, 158
rating of perceived exertion (RPE), 423
RDN (registered dietitian nutritionist), 21
rebaudioside A, 131*t*, 133
recombinant bovine somatotropin (rbST), 473*fig*
Recommended Dietary Allowance (RDAs). *See also* Dietary Reference Intakes (DRIs)
    overview of, 34–35*fig*, 37*t*
    protein, 204, 206
    vitamin A, 239
    vitamin B$_1$ (thiamin), 248
rectum, 74*fig*, 78*fig*, 88
red blood cells (RBCs). *See also* blood; iron-deficiency anemia
    life span of, 197
    sickle-cell anemia, 195–196
Red Bull, 458–459
red tide, 519*fig*
reduced, food label terminology, 56*t*
red wine, benefits of, 178, 343–344
refined grains, 112
reflexes, 555
refrigeration, food safety, 505–509*t*, 506*fig*, 508*t*
registered dietitian nutritionist (RDN), 21
remineralization, teeth, 118
repetition maximum (RM), 423*t*
research, nutrition, 15–24, 17*fig*, 18*fig*, 19*fig*, 20*fig*
resistance training, 421–422, 433
respiratory infection, malnutrition and, 612*t*–613
restaurants, 13, 46–47, 63, 384–385
resveratrol, 344
retailers, food safety, 512*fig*
retina, 235, 236*fig*
Retin-A, 235
retinal, 236*fig*. *See also* vitamin A
retinoic acid, 235. *See also* vitamin A
retinoids, 235, 591. *See also* vitamin A
retinol, 235. *See also* vitamin A
retinol activity units (RAE), 237
retort canning, 513
rheumatoid arthritis, 541, 587
rhodopsin, 235, 236*fig*
riboflavin (vitamin B$_2$)
    absorption and transport of, 229*fig*, 230*t*
    alcohol, effects of, 353
    enriched grains, 112–113
    functions and sources, 228*fig*, 247*fig*, 250–251*fig*
    pregnancy, intake needs, 536*fig*
    recommended intake, 250–251*fig*
    summary chart, 264*t*
ribonucleic acid (RNA), 194–196, 195*fig*, 311
rice, golden, 479
rich in, food label terminology, 56*t*
rickets, 17*fig*–18, 246, 552
risk assessment, pesticides, 475–477, 476*fig*
RNA (ribonucleic acid), 194–196, 195*fig*, 311

rods, eye, 235, 236*fig*
rooting reflex, 555
roundworms, 501
Russell's sign, 406

S

saccharin, 131*t*, 132, 517*t*
Safety, food. *See* Food safety
safflower oil, 163*fig*
saliva, 73–75*fig*, 74*fig*, 80*t*, 104–105*fig*
salivary glands, 73, 74*fig*
salmon, 181
Salmonella, 474, 494, 497*t*, 498, 499, 513
salt, 301*fig*–302*fig*, 328
sanitation, food security and, 614–616
saponins, 232*t*
sashimi, 501, 537
satellite farming, 461
satiety
    diet for weight loss, 390, 392
    eating and time of day, 48–49
    fiber content of food and, 116
    hunger, regulation of, 381–382*fig*
    protein and, 199–200*t*
    sugar-sweetened beverage consumption, 122–123
saturated fats. *See also* fat, dietary
    American diet, 13
    defined, 148
    energy density and, 41
    food labels, 51–54, 52*fig*
    recommended intake, 171
saturated fatty acids, chemical structure, 146–148*fig*, 147*fig*
saw palmetto, 589
Schlatter, James, 132
school-aged children
    breakfast, 576–577
    developmental disabilities, 572–573
    food choices, 575–576*fig*, 577*t*
    nutritional needs, overview, 572
    obesity and overweight, 574*fig*–575
school meals, 577, 578, 596
scientific method, defined, 17*fig*–18
scleroderma, 541
scombrotoxic fish poisoning, 518–519*fig*
screen time, 574–575
scurvy, 261
Second Harvest, 617
secretin, 80*t*
segmentation, 70–71*fig*
selenium (Se)
    as antioxidant, 229–231*fig*, 230*fig*
    functions and sources, 299*t*, 322–323*fig*
    intake recommendations, 322–323*fig*
selenosis, 323
Self-Assessment
    diet proportionality, 41
    eating disorders, risk of, 408
    environment and energy balance, 384
    estimated energy requirement (EER), 379
    exercise, fluid needs for, 443
    family medical history, 8
    fat intake, 161
    fitness and diet needs for exercise, 445
    food choices, 7
    food cost, fast food *vs.* homemade lunch, 605
    food insecurity, risk for, 607
    food safety habits, 510
    nutritional risk, 594
    osteoporosis, risk for, 310
    pregnancy, readiness for, 529
    protein-friendly diet, 208
    sustainable food shopping, 471
    type 2 diabetes, risk of, 126
    vitamin intake, fat-soluble, 234
    vitamin intake, water-soluble, 247
    water intake, 291
sellers, food industry, 459*fig*
semivegetarian diet, 212*t*–219*t*, 217*fig*, 217*t*, 218*t*
serine (Ser), 189*fig*, 190*t*

serving size, 42, 43, 44fig, 46–47, 385
   food labels, 51–52fig
set-point theory, weight, 383
sex pheromones, 475
sexual assault, binge drinking and, 357fig
sexually transmitted infections, 357fig
shellfish, 171–172, 519fig, 556, 557fig
Shigella, 497t
short bowel syndrome, 93
shortening, 163fig
sickle-cell anemia, 195–196
side chain, amino acids, 188–189fig
sigmoid colon, 78fig
silbutramine, 396
silicon, 298, 300t
simple carbohydrates, 100–102fig
Sinclair, Upton, 494
skin
   body temperature regulation, 285fig–286
   carotenodermia, 239
   skin cell life cycle, 196–197
   vitamin A and, 235, 237
   water balance, 287fig
skin cancer, 246
skinfold measurement, 375t
sleep
   alcohol use and, 349, 351
   physical fitness, benefits of, 421t
sleep apnea, 370–371
small intestine
   alcohol metabolism, 345fig–346
   carbohydrate digestion, 104–106, 105fig
   digestive process, 74fig, 76–77fig, 80t, 81t
   disorders of, 89–92t
   fat digestion, 151–153, 152fig
   fiber and, 103, 134–137, 135t, 136fig
   hunger and satiety, regulation of, 382fig
   nutrient absorption and transport, 83fig
   orlistat, effects of, 72
   protein digestion, 192, 193fig
   vitamin absorption, 229fig
   weight loss surgeries, 396–397fig
Smith, David, 355
Smith, Robert, 361
smoking, tobacco
   bone health and, 310
   cancer and, 590
   heart disease and, 169
   pregnancy and, 530–531, 537
social drinking, 343
social life, food choices and, 6
socioeconomic status
   food insecurity, United States, 602t–607, 603fig, 605fig
   malnutrition and, 611–613t, 612fig, 612t
   obesity and overweight, 14
   undernutrition, 610–611
soda, sugar in, 121
sodium (Na)
   American diet, 13
   body content, 297fig
   cell membrane transport, 198fig–199
   exercise, fluid needs for, 440t
   food labels, 51–54, 52fig, 55fig
   function and sources, 297t, 301fig–302fig
   hyponatremia, 289, 443
   infant formula, 549t
   older adults, recommended intake, 585
   recommended intake, 301fig, 302fig
sodium aluminosilicate, 517t
sodium bicarbonate, 301, 517t
sodium carbonate, 301
sodium nitrite, 517t
sodium phosphate, 301
soft drinks, 122–123, 294, 530t. See also beverages
soft water, 292–293
soil, sustainable food system, 468–469
solanine, 520
solid fats, defined, 41
solid foods, infants, 553–558, 560

soluble fiber, 103, 114
solvent, water as, 284–285
sorbitol, 130–132, 131t
South Beach diet, 388–389
soybean oil, 148, 161fig, 175
soybeans
   growing of, 463fig–464
   toxins, 520
soy products, types and uses, 214–215
soy protein, 61t, 161t, 202
soy protein-based formula, 550
sparkling water, 292–293
Special Supplemental Nutrition Program for Women, Infants, and Children (WIC), 615t
sperm, 528
spina bifida, 256, 529
spinach, 296, 308
Splenda, 131t, 133
sponges, 503
spores, 513
sports anemia, 438
sports bars, shakes, and meal replacers, 447–449fig
sports drinks, 436–437, 440, 441–442
spring water, 292–293
St. John's wort, 589
standard drink, 343fig, 344fig
Staphylococcus aureus, 498t
starch, 101, 102fig, 104–105fig, 113–114, 164–165t
starvation, 603fig
static stretching, 422
stearic acid, 147fig, 148, 149fig
steroid hormones, 446
sterols, 150–151fig
stevia, 133
stomach
   alcohol, effects of, 353–354
   alcohol metabolism, 345fig–346
   anatomy, 374fig
   carbohydrate digestion, 104–106, 105fig
   digestive process, 80t, 81t
   digestive system, overview, 74fig, 75fig–76
   disorders of, 87
   fat digestion, 151–153, 152fig
   heartburn, 86
   hunger and satiety, regulation of, 381–382fig
   protein digestion, 192, 193fig
   ulcers of, 92t, 353
   weight loss surgeries, 396–397fig
stool, 78fig
strength training, 418–419, 421–422, 433
stress fractures, 434
stretching, 422
stroke
   alcohol, effects of, 354
   DASH diet, 40
   exercise and, 432
   obesity and overweight, 371
   older adults, dietary needs and, 586
   overview of, 167
stroke volume, 421
structure claims, food labels, 58fig
subcutaneous fat, 374fig
subsidies, agriculture, 462, 487
suck/swallow reflex, 555
sucralose, 131t, 133
sucrase, 104–105fig
sucrose, 101–102fig, 123, 131t
sudden infant death syndrome (SIDS), 537
sugar
   alcohol production and, 342
   American diet, 13
   behavior and, 573
   dental caries and, 117, 118
   diabetes and, 129
   food labels, 51–54, 52fig, 139
   fruit and vegetable sources of, 113–114
   functions of, 117
   natural and added sugars, 41, 115–121, 116fig, 119fig, 120fig
   protein and energy bars, 207t

sugar-sweetened beverages, 122–123
   tips for lower consumption of, 117
sugar alcohols, 130–132, 131t
sugarless gum, 118
sugar substitutes, 130fig–134, 131t
sulfites, 515–516
sulfur, 297fig, 297t, 315
Summer Food Service Program, 615t
Sunette, 131t, 133
sunflower oil, 163fig
sunlight, vitamin D and, 244–245
Supplemental Nutrition Assistance Program (SNAP), 615t
supplements
   American diet and, 13
   antioxidants, 231
   athlete's need for, 439
   calcium, 309, 439
   chromium, 326
   creatine, 445
   drug, food, and herb interactions, 588–589
   ergogenic aids, 444–447, 448t
   fish oil, 174–175
   folate, 256
   gastric bypass surgery and, 397
   iron, 318
   for joint health, 587
   minerals, 298
   niacin, 252–253
   pregnancy and, 530, 535–536fig
   protein, 206–207, 449t
   role of, 12
   vitamin A (beta-carotene), 237
   vitamin E, 240, 241
   vitamins, benefits and risks, 269–272fig, 271t
sushi, 501, 537
sustainable food system, 466–471t, 467fig, 468fig, 470fig, 472
swallowing, 73–75fig, 74fig, 86
sweat, 285fig–286, 287fig, 439, 440
sweat glands, 285fig–286
sweeteners
   food labels and, 119fig–120
   sugar substitutes, overview, 130fig–134, 131t
   sugar-sweetened beverage consumption, 122–123
Sweet'N Low, 131t
syndrome X, 170
systolic pressure, 169, 303

T

Table Tips
   breakfast on the go, 577
   chromium intake, 327
   copper intake, 319
   digestion, improving, 85
   eat more to weigh less, 393
   fiber, increasing intake, 115
   fish, adding to diet, 176
   fluid intake, 295
   fluoride intake, 325
   folate intake, 257
   foodborne illness, avoiding, 500
   food tampering, signs of, 521
   get up and move, 394
   gluten free eating, 90
   healthy habits, weight management and, 395
   heart-healthy eating, 179
   iodine intake, 328
   iron intake, 318
   iron-rich foods for children, 570
   magnesium intake, 314
   manganese intake, 329
   moderate alcohol intake, 361
   morning sickness, alleviating, 533
   niacin intake, 253
   nut consumption, 178
   nutrition tips, 37
   phosphorus intake, 312
   physical activity, 425

Table Tips (continued)
potassium intake, 306
pregnancy, exercise and, 540
protein sources, 199
riboflavin intake, 251
school lunches, 578
scrub away pathogens, 503
seafood toxins, avoiding, 520
selenium intake, 323
snacks for health weight gain, 400
sodium intake, 303
sugar consumption, lowering, 117
teen table tips, 581
thiamin intake, 249
toddlers, treats for, 569
vegetarian diet, 217t–218t
vitamin A intake, 239
vitamin B_6 intake, 255
vitamin B_{12} intake, 259
vitamin C intake, 261
vitamin D intake, 245
vitamin E intake, 241
vitamin K intake, 243
vitamins, cooking tips, 233
whole grains, 113
zinc intake, 321
tagalose, 131t, 132
tapeworms, 501
tap water, 292–293
target heart rate, 423t
tartrate, 517t
taste, food choices and, 5fig
TASTE, fruit and vegetable mnemonic, 577t
taste, sense of, 320
tea, 177
teeth
calcium intake, 307
dental caries, 117, 118
early childhood caries, 550
fetal development, 538fig
fluoride intake, 324fig–325
phosphorus intake, 311
teff, 90
tempeh, 214–215
temperature, body, 285fig–286, 440t
temperature, cooking, 231–233, 501, 504–505fig, 505t, 506fig
testosterone, 446
texture, food, 164–165t, 516, 517t
textured soy protein, 214–215
thermic effect of food (TEF), 379
thermogenesis, 383
thermometers, food, 505fig
thiamin (vitamin B_1)
alcohol, effects of, 353
enriched grains, 112–113
functions and sources, 228fig, 247fig, 248–249fig, 517fig
pregnancy, intake needs, 536fig
recommended intake, 248–249fig
summary chart, 264t
thirst mechanism, 288
threonine (Thr), 190t
throat, disorders of, 85–86
thyroid, 322, 327–328fig
time, FITT principle, 422–425t, 423t, 424fig
time, food choice and, 6–7
time of day for eating, impact of, 48–49
tissues, 71
tobacco use
bone health and, 310
cancer and, 590
heart disease and, 169
pregnancy and, 530–531, 537
tocotrienols, 232t
toddlers
foodborne illness and, 500–501
food jags, 571
nutrient needs, overview, 568–570, 569t
tofu, 214–215

Tolerable Upper Intake Level (UL), 233
iron, 299t, 318
minerals, summary table, 297t, 299t
overview of, 34–36, 37t, 233
vitamin C, 260–261, 265t
vitamin D, 246, 264t
vitamins, summary table, 264t–265t
tongue, 251
tongue-thrust reflex, 554, 555
topiramate, 396
topsoil, 468–469
total fat, food labels, 51–54, 52fig
toxicity, minerals, 298, 318, 323, 329
summary table, 297t, 299t
toxicity, vitamins, 233, 264t–265t
toxins, food safety, 500, 518–520, 519fig, 548
Toxoplasma gondii, 498t, 499
trace minerals, 296, 298, 299t
trans fats, 41, 51–54, 52fig, 158fig–160fig, 171. See also fat, dietary
trans fatty acids, 158fig–160fig
transfer RNA (tRNA), 194–196, 195fig
transport, of nutrients, 285fig
transportation of food, 468fig, 470t, 512fig
transport proteins, 198fig–199
transverse colon, 78fig
traveler's diarrhea, 497t, 499
trends, food choices, 6
Trichinella spiralis, 498t, 499
triglycerides
chemical structure, 146–151fig, 147fig, 148fig, 149fig, 150fig
defined, 149fig
energy from, 429–432
lipoprotein transport and distribution, 153–155fig
sugar intake and, 117
trimesters, prenatal development
defined, 532fig
first trimester, 532fig–539, 533fig, 534fig, 534t, 536fig, 538fig
second trimester, 539fig–541, 540t
third trimester, 542
tripeptides, 188
Truvia, 131t, 133
trypsin, 80
tryptophan (Trp), 190t, 206, 252
tumeric, 517t
turkey. See poultry
2 Points of View
alcohol risks and benefits, 363
baby food, making your own, 560
designer water, 332
energy drinks and caffeine, 451
farm subsidies, 487
food advertising, regulation of, 25
food labels and added sugars, 139
food trucks, food safety and, 522
food vs. cash for hunger, 618
gastric bypass for adolescents, 410
Paleo Diet, 221
probiotics, 93
restaurants and food labels, 63
school meals, 596
vitamin B_{12} supplements and vegetarian diets, 274
wild vs. farmed salmon, 181
type 1 diabetes. See also diabetes mellitus
effects on body, 125, 127–128
overview, 124fig–125
rates of, 129
treatment and control of, 128–129fig
type 2 diabetes. See also diabetes mellitus
childhood obesity and, 575
effects on body, 125, 127–128
heart disease and, 169
magnesium and, 313
obesity and overweight, 370–371
older adults, dietary needs and, 586
overview, 124fig–125
physical fitness, benefits of, 420t
prevention of, 129

rates of, 129
sugar intake and, 117
treatment and control of, 128–129fig
vegetarian diet and, 216
typhoid fever, 494
tyrosine (Tyr), 190t

U

ulcers, stomach, 87, 92t
ultraviolet (UV) light
free radicals and, 230fig–231
vitamin D synthesis, 244
umbilical cord, 532fig–533fig
underage drinking, 360
undernutrition, 32, 33, 211fig, 610–611. See also food insecurity
underwater weighing, 375t
underweight
body mass index (BMI) and, 372–374, 373t
defined, 371
pregnancy and, 529
weight gain strategies, 399–401, 400fig
unintentional food additives, 518
United Nations Food and Agriculture Organization, 604
United States
American diet, 13
food insecurity, 602t–607, 603fig, 605fig
unsaturated fatty acids, 146–148fig, 147fig. See also fat, dietary
urea, 194fig
ureter, 84fig
urethra, 84fig
urine, dehydration and, 289fig
U.S. Department of Agriculture (USDA)
antibiotics in the food supply, 474
Dietary Guidelines for Americans, 38
food safety, 510–512fig, 511t
MyPlate, 50fig–55, 51fig, 52fig, 52t, 53fig, 53t, 54fig, 54t
role of, 482t
school lunches, 578
USDA Organic Seal, 485fig
U.S. Department of Health and Human Services (DHHS), 38, 482t
U.S. Pharmacopoeia (USP), 270–272fig
uterus, 371, 532fig, 544

V

valine (Val), 189fig, 190t
vanadium, 298, 300t
vanillin, 134
variant Creutzfeldt-Jakob Disease (vCJD), 500
varied diet, defined, 32
vegetables
American diet, 13
antioxidants and, 231, 232t
carbohydrates from, 113–114
container gardening of, 472
daily intake guidelines, 44t
diet for weight loss, 390
imports of, 465fig–466
minerals in, 298
potassium source, 306
preservatives, 515
serving size estimates, 47t
TASTE, meal and snack mnemonic, 577t
vitamins in, 228fig
washing, food safety, 503
vegetarian and vegan diet
athletes, iron intake and, 438
children and, 572
overview of, 212t–219t, 217fig, 217t, 218t
pregnancy and, 535
vitamin A intake, 237
vitamin B_{12} supplements and, 274
vitamin supplements, 270
very low-calorie diet, 395
very low-density lipoproteins (VLDL), 153–155fig
villi, intestines, 76–77fig, 83fig

viruses
   common cold, myths about, 266–267
   foodborne illness, 494, 496t
   food safety practices, 501–509t, 502fig, 504fig, 505fig, 505t, 506fig, 508t
visceral fat, 374fig
vision
   age-related macular degeneration (AMD), 231fig, 320
   cataracts, 231fig
   diabetes, effects of, 125, 127–128
   night blindness, 239
   vitamin A and, 235, 236fig
   xerophthalmia, 239
vitamin A. See also vitamins
   absorption and transport of, 229fig, 230t
   alcohol, effects of, 353
   as antioxidant, 229–231fig, 230fig
   cancer risk reduction, 591
   cooking and storage concerns, 232–233
   fats and, 154, 156
   food labels, 51–54, 52fig
   fortified foods, 616
   functions and sources, 60, 228fig, 235–238, 236fig, 237fig
   golden rice, 479
   malnutrition and, 613t
   older adults, intake, 583–584
   orlistat, effects of, 72
   over- and underconsumption of, 238–239
   pregnancy, intake needs, 535, 536fig
   as provitamin, 233
   recommended intake, 237fig
   storage in body, 234
   summary chart, 264t
   vegetarian diets, 218t
vitamin B1 (thiamin). See also vitamins
   absorption and transport of, 229fig, 230t
   alcohol, effects of, 353
   enriched grains, 112–113
   functions and sources, 247fig, 248–249fig
   pregnancy, intake needs, 536fig
   recommended intake, 248–249fig
   summary chart, 264t
vitamin B2 (riboflavin). See also vitamins
   absorption and transport of, 229fig, 230t
   alcohol, effects of, 353
   enriched grains, 112–113
   functions and sources, 228fig, 247fig, 250–251fig
   recommended intake, 250–251fig
   summary chart, 264t
vitamin B3 (niacin). See also vitamins
   absorption and transport of, 229fig, 230t
   enriched grains, 112–113
   functions and sources, 228fig, 247fig, 252–253fig
   pregnancy, intake needs, 536fig
   recommended intake, 252–253fig
   summary chart, 264t
   vitamin B6 and, 254
vitamin B6 (pyridoxine). See also vitamins
   absorption and transport of, 229fig, 230t
   functions and sources, 228fig, 247fig, 254–255fig
   pregnancy, intake needs, 536fig
   summary chart, 265t
vitamin B7 (biotin). See also vitamins
   absorption and transport of, 229fig, 230t
   functions and sources, 247fig, 262
   summary chart, 265t
vitamin B9 (folate/folic acid)
   absorption and transport of, 229fig, 230t
   alcohol, effects of, 353
   celiac disease and, 90
   enriched grains, 112–113
   functions and sources, 228fig, 247fig, 255–257fig, 517t
   preconception intake of, 529
   pregnancy intake, 533–535
   recommended intake, 256–257fig
   sources of, 228fig
   sperm production and, 528

storage concerns, 233
   summary chart, 265t
vitamin B12 (cobalamin). See also vitamins
   functions and sources, 228fig, 247fig
   gastric bypass surgery and, 397
   infant needs, 553
   older adults, intake, 584t
   pregnancy, intake, 535, 536fig
   recommended intake, 258–259fig
   summary chart, 265t
   supplements, 270, 274
   vegetarian diet, 218t
   vitamin B6 and, 258–259fig
vitamin C. See also vitamins
   absorption and transport of, 229fig, 230t
   alcohol, effects of, 353
   as antioxidant, 229–231fig, 230fig
   cancer risk reduction, 591
   common cold and, 266–267
   cooking and storage concerns, 233
   as food additive, 515, 517t
   food labels, 51–54, 52fig
   functions and sources, 228fig, 247fig, 260–261fig, 437
   iron and, 296, 316
   megadoses of, 233
   pregnancy, intake needs, 536fig, 541
   recommended intake, 260–261fig
   sperm production, 528
   summary chart, 265t
vitamin D. See also vitamins
   absorption and transport of, 229fig, 230t
   adolescents, intake of, 580fig
   alcohol, effects of, 353
   American diet, 13
   bone health and, 310
   calcium absorption and, 296
   cancer risk reduction, 591
   cholesterol and, 157
   fats and, 154, 156
   functions and sources, 9, 244–246, 245fig
   infant formula, 549t
   infant needs, 552
   older adults, intake, 584t
   orlistat, effects of, 72
   pregnancy, intake, 533–535, 536fig
   recommended intake, 244–245fig
   rickets, 17fig–18
   storage in body, 234
   summary chart, 264t
   supplements, 270
   toddlers and preschoolers, needs of, 570
   vegetarian diets, 218t
vitamin E. See also vitamins
   absorption and transport of, 229fig, 230t
   as antioxidant, 229–231fig, 230fig
   cancer risk reduction, 591
   cooking and storage concerns, 232–233
   drug interactions, 589
   fats and, 154, 156
   as food preservative, 515
   functions and sources, 228fig, 240fig–241fig, 437
   orlistat, effects of, 72
   pregnancy, intake, 536fig, 541
   recommended intake, 240, 241fig
   sperm production, 528
   storage in body, 234
   summary chart, 264t
vitamin K. See also vitamins
   absorption and transport of, 229fig, 230t
   alcohol, effects of, 353
   blood clotting, 241
   cooking and storage concerns, 232–233
   fats and, 154, 156
   functions and sources, 228fig, 242–243fig
   infant needs, 552
   orlistat, effects of, 72
   recommended intake, 242–243fig
   storage in body, 234
   summary chart, 264t

vitamins. See also specific vitamin name
   antioxidant function, 229–231fig, 230fig
   bioavailability, 231
   body storage of, 84
   chemical composition, 11
   common cold and, 266–267
   cooking and storage concerns, 231–233
   developmental disorders and, 573
   fat-soluble, 154, 156, 229fig, 230t, 234
   food and supplement sources of, 266–272, 271t
   food labels and, 52fig
   fortified foods, 267–269fig, 616
   functions of, 10–11
   large intestine, production in, 78
   liver storage of, 79
   Made Over Made Better, 273
   overview of, 228fig
   percent body composition, 9fig
   provitamins and preformed vitamins, 233
   Self-Assessment, fat-soluble vitamins, 234
   summary chart, 264t–265t
   supplements, overview of, 269–272fig, 271t
   toxicity and megadosing, 233
   vegetarian diet and, 216–219t, 217t, 218t
   water-soluble, 229fig, 230t, 247
   in whole grains, 112–113
vitamin water, 292–293
VLDL (very low-density lipoproteins), 153–155fig
VO2 max, 421
vomiting, 349, 351, 405. See also dehydration

W

waist circumference, body fat and, 375–376fig
walnuts, 161fig, 175
war, food insecurity and, 608
warfarin, 243, 589
water. See also fluid balance
   absorption in large intestine, 78fig
   conservation and quality of, 469
   excretory system, 84fig
   exercise, fluid needs for, 439–444, 440t, 441t, 443fig
   fluoride in, 324fig–325
   functions of, 284–286, 285fig
   intake recommendations, 291, 294fig–295fig
   as nutrient, 11
   pathogens in, 499
   percent body composition, 9fig
   2 Points of View, designer water, 332
   Self-Assessment, water intake, 291
   tap water vs. bottled water, 292–293
   water balance, maintaining, 286–291, 287fig, 288fig, 289fig, 290fig
water-soluble vitamins, 229fig, 230t, 247. See also B vitamin names; vitamin C
websites, evaluating information on, 22–24
weight, body. See also obesity and overweight
   blood pressure and, 303, 303–304t
   body mass index (BMI) and, 372–374, 373t
   factors affecting, 380–386fig, 382fig
   genetics and, 383–384
   preconception health, 529
   pregnancy weight gain, 533fig, 533t
   water loss and, 289
weight cycling, 399
weight management. See also Made Over Made Better
   alcohol use and, 351–353fig, 352t
   basal metabolic rate (BMR), 378t
   behavior modification, 394–395fig
   body fat measurement and location, 374fig–376fig, 375t
   body mass index (BMI), 372–374, 373t
   defined, 370, 371
   diet and weight loss, 387–393, 391fig, 391t, 392fig
   Dietary Guidelines for Americans, recommendations of, 38–39
   disordered eating, 401–408, 402t, 403fig, 407t
   economic data on, 370
   energy balance, overview of, 376–380, 378fig, 378t
   environmental factors, 386
   estimated energy requirement (EER), 379

weight management (*continued*)
  exercise, benefits of, 421
  heart health and, 178
  medication for weight loss, 396
  orlistat, 71, 72
  physical fitness, benefits of, 420t
  2 Points of View, gastric bypass, 410
  pregnancy and, 533fig, 533t
  reduced-fat products and, 165–166t
  sugar intake and, 117
  surgery for, 396–397fig
  time of day for eating, impact of, 48–49
  very low-calorie diet, 395
  weight gain strategies, 399–401, 400fig
  weight loss, maintaining, 399
Weight Watchers, 388–389
well-balanced diet, defined, 11–12
well-established health claims, food labels, 57t
Wernicke-Korsakoff syndrome, 249, 353
wheat, 463fig–464, 487
white blood cells (WBCs), 260
whole grains, 13, 61t, 112–113, 390
Wilson, Bill, 361
wine, 173, 178, 342, 343–344. *See also* alcohol
Winfrey, Oprah, 395
women
  added sugars, intake of, 121
  alcohol, intake recommendations, 347t, 348fig
  anabolic steroid use, 446
  body composition, 284fig, 374fig
  body image, media and, 372
  calorie needs, children and adolescents, 569t
  carbohydrate intake, 110–111fig, 111t

carbohydrate loading, 430–431
daily calorie requirements, 36
eating disorders, 401–408, 402t, 403fig, 407t
female athlete triad, 434–435
fiber intake, 111t
fish consumption, 176
folate intake, 256–257fig
heart disease, risk for, 167t–169, 168fig
hypertension, risk of, 303
iodine intake, 327–328fig
iron-deficiency anemia, 438
iron intake, 316–317fig, 580–581
magnesium intake, 313, 314fig, 329fig
molybdenum intake, 330
niacin intake, 252–253fig
potassium intake, 305, 306fig
preconception diet and lifestyle, 528–531, 530t
riboflavin intake, 250–251fig
selenium intake, 322–323fig
sugar-sweetened beverage consumption, 122t
thiamin intake, 248–249fig
vitamin A intake, 237fig
vitamin B_6 intake, 254
vitamin B_{12} intake, 258–259fig
vitamin C intake, 260–261fig
vitamin D intake, 244–245fig
vitamin E intake, 240, 241fig
vitamin K intake, 242–243fig
water intake, 291, 294fig–295fig
zinc intake, 320–321fig
Women, Infants, and Children (WIC), 615t
working poor, food insecurity and, 606fig, 607
wound healing, 320

X
Xenical, 72, 396
xerophthalmia, 239
xylitol, 118, 130–132, 131t

Y
yeast, alcohol production and, 342
yoga, 422
yohimbine, 589

Z
Zailckas, Koren, 358
zeaxanthin, 231fig, 232t, 235
zinc
  alcohol, effects of, 353
  body content, 297fig
  common cold and, 266–267
  copper absorption and, 296
  functions and sources, 299t, 320–321fig
  infant formula, 549t
  older adults, recommended intake, 584
  phytates and, 296
  pica and, 533
  pregnancy, intake needs, 533–535, 536fig
  sperm production and, 528
  vegetarian diets, 218t
  vision and, 231fig
Zone diet, 388–389
zoochemicals, 60

Credits

Photo Credits

Source; **p. 201:** Dorling Kindersley, Ltd.; **p. 201:** Monkey Business Images/Shutterstock; **p. 201:** Science Source; **p. 201:** Dorling Kindersley, Ltd.; **p. 206:** Pearson Education, Inc.; **p. 206:** Pearson Education, Inc.; **p. 206:** Mike Flippo/Shutterstock; **p. 210:** Mbongo/Fotolia; **p. 211:** Dai Kurokawa/Newscom; **p. 212:** Elenathewise/Fotolia; **p. 213:** Elenathewise/Fotolia; **p. 214:** Lilyana Vynogradova/Fotolia; **p. 214:** Dorling Kindersley, Ltd.; **p. 214:** Uckyo/Fotolia; **p. 214:** Pearson Education, Inc.; **p. 215:** Akalong Suitsuit/Fotolia; **p. 215:** Stockstudios/Shutterstock; **p. 215:** Dorling Kindersley, Ltd.; **p. 215:** Pearson Education, Inc.; **p. 216:** AGE Fotostock America Inc.; **p. 217:** Reed Mangels PhD, RD; Lindsey Siferd; **p. 217:** Pearson Education, Inc.; **p. 217:** Fotohunter/Shutterstock; **p. 217:** Valentyn Volkov/Shutterstock; **p. 220:** MSPhotographic/Fotolia; **p. 220:** ElliotKo/Shutterstock; **p. 220:** Christopher Elwell/Shutterstock; **p. 220:** Janet Faye Hastings/Shutterstock; **p. 220:** A9photo/Shutterstock; **p. 220:** Erickson/Getty Images; **p. 220:** RoJo Images/Fotolia; **p. 220:** Serghei Starus/Getty Images; **p. 220:** Fotolia; **p. 221:** Subbotina Anna/Shutterstock; **p. 222:** Frederic Cirou/PhotoAlto/Alamy; **p. 222:** Monkey Business Images/Shutterstock; **p. 223:** Dorling Kindersley, Ltd.; **p. 223:** Dai Kurokawa/Newscom; **p. 223:** Vegetarian Resource Group, Reed Mangels PhD, RD; Lindsey Seiferd

Chapter 7

p. 226: OlegDoroshin/Shutterstock; **p. 227:** OlegDoroshin/Shutterstock; **p. 229:** Mtsyri/Shutterstock; **p. 229:** Stockbyte/Getty Images; **p. 229:** Best view Stock/Alamy; **p. 231:** National Eye Institute; **p. 231:** National Eye Institute; **p. 231:** National Eye Institute; **p. 233:** Manceau/StockFood GmbH/Alamy; **p. 234:** Timolina/Shutterstock; **p. 235:** Timmary/Shutterstock; **p. 236:** Siri Stafford/Digital Vision/Getty Images; **p. 237:** hriana/Fotolia; **p. 238:** Sarsmis/Shutterstock; **p. 238:** Envision/Corbis; **p. 239:** James Stevenson/ Science Source; **p. 240:** Ian O'Leary/Dorling Kindersley, Ltd.; **p. 240:** VIPDesign/Fotolia; **p. 241:** Rachel Epstein/PhotoEdit, Inc.; **p. 241:** Brian Hagiwara/Photolibrary/Getty Images; **p. 242:** Eye of Science/Science Source; **p. 242:** Cristina Pedrazzini/Science Source; **p. 242:** Ted Kinsman/Science Source; **p. 242:** Barry Gregg/keepsake/Corbis; **p. 243:** Joerg Beuge/Fotolia; **p. 244:** Farah Abdi Warsameh/AP Images; **p. 244:** Science Source; **p. 244:** Alamy; **p. 245:** Jacek Chabraszewski/Shutterstock; **p. 246:** Science Source; **p. 246:** Pearson Education, Inc.; **p. 248:** AGE Fotostock; **p. 248:** Fotolia; **p. 248:** Viktor/Fotolia; **p. 249:** Dr. P. Marazzi/Science Source; **p. 250:** Ralph Morse/Getty Images; **p. 250:** Sea Wave/Fotolia; **p. 250:** Johner/Getty Images; **p. 251:** SPL/Science Source; **p. 251:** JJAVA/Fotolia; **p. 252:** Elena Elisseeva/Shutterstock; **p. 253:** M.A. Ansary/Science Source; **p. 253:** D. Hurst/Alamy; **p. 254:** Jules Frazier/Stockbyte/Getty Images; **p. 255:** Barry Gregg/ Spirit/Corbis; **p. 256:** Tim Ridley/Dorling Kindersley, Ltd.; **p. 256:** Biophoto Associates/Science Source; **p. 258:** Lew Robertson/Photolibrary/Getty Images; **p. 258:** Souders Studios/Photolibrary/Getty Images; **p. 258:** Pearson Education, Inc.; **p. 259:** Corbis; **p. 259:** Martin Jacobs/Getty Images; **p. 260:** Dimitri Otis/Getty Images; **p. 260:** Corbis; **p. 260:** SPL/Science Source; **p. 260:** Barry Gregg/Keepsake/Corbis; **p. 261:** Edyta Pawlowska/Shutterstock; **p. 261:** Biophoto Associates/Science Source; **p. 262:** AGE Fotostock; **p. 262:** Justin Lightley/Getty Images; **p. 262:** C Squared Studios/Getty Images; **p. 262:** Smileus/Shutterstock; **p. 264:** AGE Fotostock; **p. 264:** Anitasstudio/Fotolia; **p. 264:** AGE Fotostock; **p. 266:** Jason Stitt/Shutterstock; **p. 266:** Pearson Education, Inc.; **p. 267:** Antagain/E+/Getty Images; **p. 268:** Pearson Education, Inc.; **p. 269:** Pearson Education, Inc.; **p. 269:** Gvictoria/Shutterstock; **p. 269:** Mtsyri/Shutterstock; **p. 270:** United States Pharmacopeial Convention; **p. 271:** Julian Rovagnati/Shutterstock; **p. 271:** Pearson Education, Inc.; **p. 271:** Smal Marina/Shutterstock; **p. 272:** Pearson Education, Inc.; **p. 273:** Foodfolio/Alamy; **p. 273:** Mariontxa/Fotolia; **p. 273:** Ciaran Griffin/Stockbyte/Getty Images; **p. 273:** Olga Popova/Shutterstock; **p. 273:** Smneedham/Photolibrary/Getty Images; **p. 273:** James Nesterwitz/Alamy; **p. 273:** fkruger/Fotolia; **p. 273:** Mbongo/Fotolia; **p. 274:** Nenad.C/Shutterstock; **p. 275:** Stockbyte/Getty Images; **p. 275:** Timolina/Fotolia; **p. 275:** Sarsmis/Shutterstock; **p. 276:** Cristina Pedrazzini/Science Source; **p. 276:** Science Scource; **p. 277:** AGE Fotostock; **p. 277:** Sea Wave/Fotolia; **p. 277:** Dr. M.A. Ansary/Science Source; **p. 278:** Lew Robertson/Photolibrary/Getty Images; **p. 278:** Jules Frazier/Getty Images; **p. 278:** Edyta Pawlowska/Shutterstock; **p. 278:** Biophoto Associates/Science Source; **p. 279:** Smileus/Shutterstock; **p. 279:** Gvictoria/Shutterstock; **p. 279:** Martin Jacobs/Stockbyte/Getty Images; **p. 281:** OlegDoroshin/Shutterstock

Chapter 8

p. 282: Africa Studio/Shutterstock; **p. 282:** Africa Studio/Shutterstock; **p. 285:** Radius Images/Alamy; **p. 286:** Claude Edelmann/Science Source; **p. 288:** Getty Images; **p. 290:** Sergey Peterman/Shutterstock; **p. 290:** George Dolgikh/Shutterstock; **p. 290:** Peter Bernik/Shutterstock; **p. 290:** Jeremy Pembrey/Alamy; **p. 292:** finallast/Fotolia; **p. 293:** Fotosearch/Getty Images; **p. 301:** Pearson Education,Inc.; **p. 301:** Richard Megna/Fundamental Photographs; **p. 301:** Pearson Education,Inc.; **p. 303:** Ken Weingart/Alamy; **p. 305:** Steve Sant/Alamy; **p. 305:** John Lund/Tiffany Schoepp/Getty Images; **p. 305:** keko64/Shutterstock; **p. 306:** Joe Gough/Shutterstock; **p. 307:** M.studio/Fotolia; **p. 307:** D. Hurst/Alamy; **p. 308:** Michael Klein/Getty Images; **p. 308:** Surgeon General; **p. 309:** Surgeon General; **p. 311:** Vaivirga/Fotolia; **p. 311:** Nitr/Shutterstock; **p. 312:** Brent Hofacker/Shutterstock; **p. 313:** Getty Images; **p. 313:** Nick Emm/Alamy; **p. 313:** Ingram Publishing/Alamy; **p. 314:** Stockbyte/Getty Images; **p. 314:** Image Werks/Corbis; **p. 315:** Brand X Pictures/Getty Images; **p. 315:** Photogal/Shutterstock; **p. 316:** Comstock/Getty Images; **p. 316:** Grafnata/Shutterstock; **p. 317:** Phoebe_Lapine/Getty Images; **p. 318:** Eric Grave/Science Source; **p. 318:** Joaquin Carrillo Farga/Science Source; **p. 319:** Smileus/Shutterstock; **p. 320:** bajita111122/Fotolia; **p. 320:** lidante/Fotolia; **p. 320:** Pearson Education, Inc.; **p. 321:** Alamy; **p. 322:** Foodcollection/Getty Images; **p. 322:** Getty Images; **p. 322:** Papkin/Shutterstock; **p. 323:** Motorlka/Fotolia; **p. 325:** Don Farrall/Getty Images; **p. 325:** AGE Fotostock America Inc.; **p. 325:** Dr. P. Marazzi/Science Source; **p. 326:** AGE Fotostock America Inc.; **p. 327:** Stockbyte/Getty Images; **p. 327:** AGE Fotostock America Inc.; **p. 327:** Richard Megna/Fundamental Photographs; **p. 328:** Mike Goldwater/Alamy; **p. 328:** Centers for Disease Control and Prevention (CDC); **p. 329:** Foodcollection/Getty Images; **p. 329:** Viktor/Fotolia; **p. 330:** Anna Hoychuk/Shutterstock; **p. 330:** Marco Mayer/Shutterstock; **p. 331:** Imageman/Shutterstock; **p. 331:** marekuliasz/Shutterstock; **p. 331:** Melinda Fawver/Shutterstock; **p. 331:** D. Hurst/Alamy; **p. 331:** Nick Emm/Alamy; **p. 331:** Valentyn Volkov/Shutterstock; **p. 331:** Shutterstock; **p. 331:** Blue Lemon/Shutterstock; **p. 332:** Mark Lennihan/AP Images; **p. 333:** Fuse/Getty Images; **p. 334:** John Lund/Tiffany Schoepp/Getty Images; **p. 334:** D. Hurst/ALamy; **p. 335:** Stockbyte/Getty Images; **p. 335:** Brand X Pictures/Getty Images; **p. 336:** Bajita111122/Fotolia; **p. 336:** Comstock/Getty Images; **p. 336:** Foodcollection/Getty Images; **p. 337:** Foodcollection/Alamy; **p. 337:** Mike Goldwater/Alamy; **p. 337:** Foodcollection/Getty Images; **p. 337:** Dr. P. Marazzi/Science Source; **p. 338:** Anna Hoychuk/Shutterstock; **p. 339:** Africa Studio/Shutterstock

Chapter 9

p. 340: Jack Andersen/Digital Vision/Getty Images; **p. 342:** Jack Andersen/Digital Vision/Getty Images; **p. 343:** Steve Gorton/Dorling Kindersley, Ltd.; **p. 343:** Adam Woolfitt/Corbis; **p. 344:** Johnfoto18/Shutterstock; **p. 344:** Getty Images; **p. 344:** Pearson Education, Inc.; **p. 344:** Pearson Education, Inc.; **p. 345:** Digital Vision/Getty; **p. 345:** Alamy; **p. 346:** Jim Varney/Science Source; **p. 347:** Joe Raedle/Getty Images; **p. 348:** Corbis; **p. 350:** Pearson Education, Inc.; **p. 351:** 68/Bluemoon Stock/Ocean/Corbis; **p. 352:** Joy Brown/Shutterstock; **p. 352:** Valentyn Volkov/Shutterstock; **p. 352:** Viktorija/Fotolia; **p. 352:** JJAVA/Fotolia; **p. 352:** Ron Chapple Stock/Alamy; **p. 352:** Unpict/Fotolia; **p. 352:** Danny Hooks/Fotolia; **p. 352:** AmpFotoStudio/Fotolia; **p. 353:** Richard Megna/Fundamental Photographs; **p. 353:** Richard Megna/Fundamental Photographs; **p. 354:** Arthur Glauberman/Science Source; **p. 355:** Image Source/Corbis; **p. 356:** University of Washington, Fetal Alcohol and Drug Unit; **p. 358:** Pearson Education, Inc.; **p. 360:** USDA Center for Nutrition Policy and Promotion; **p. 360:** Dmitry Kalinovsky/Shutterstock; **p. 361:** Les/Shutterstock; **p. 362:** vsl/Shutterstock; **p. 362:** Dibrova/Shutterstock; **p. 362:** BeautyStockPhoto/Shutterstock; **p. 362:** Clive Streeter/Dorling Kindersley, Ltd.; **p. 362:** Vsl/Shutterstock; **p. 362:** BeautyStockPhoto/Shutterstock; **p. 362:** I food and drink/Alamy; **p. 362:** vsl/Shutterstock; **p. 363:** Ol vic/Shutterstock; **p. 364:** Adam Woolfitt/Corbis; **p. 364:** Steve Gorton/Dorling Kindersley, Ltd.; **p. 364:** Digital Vision/GettyGetty Images ; **p. 365:** Image Source/Corbis; **p. 365:** Dmitry Kalinovsky/Shutterstock; **p. 367:** Jack Andersen/Digital Vision/Getty Images

Chapter 10

p. 369: Robert Llewellyn/Getty Images; **p. 370:** Robert Llewellyn; **p. 371:** Dan Kosmayer/Fotolia; **p. 371:** Bill Aron; **p. 372:** Remy de la Mauviniere/AP Images; **p. 372:** Fairchild Photo Service/Condé Nast/Corbis; **p. 372:** Biological Psychiatry Research Laboratory; **p. 372:** Bettmann/

Text Credits

Chapter 1   **p. 8**: Based on "Leading Causes of Death," Centers for Disease Control and Prevention web-site, 2015.; **p. 13**: Source: Centers for Disease Control and Prevention. 2014. Obesity Prevalence Maps. Available at: http://www.cdc.gov/obesity/data/prevalence-maps.html.; **p. 15**: Healthy People 2020, U.S. Department of Health and Human Services, 2015.; **p. 23**: U.S. Department of Health and Human Services, U.S. Food and Drug Administration. 2015. Health Fraud Scams. Available at www.fda.gov. Accessed April 2015.; **p. 25**: Better Business Bureau. 2013. Children's Food and Beverage Advertising Initiative. Available at www.bbb.org. Accessed August 2013.; IF-**p. 1**: Reprinted with permission from Dietary Reference Intakes for Energy, Carbohydrate, Fiber, Fat, Fatty Acids, Cholesterol, Protein, and Amino Acids (2002/2005) and Dietary Reference Intakes for Water, Potassium, Sodium, Chloride, and Sulfate (2005). Copyright © 2005 by the National Academy of Sciences, Courtesy of the National Academies Press, Washington, D.C.; IF-**p. 1**: U.S. Food and Drug Administration.; IFC-**p. 1**: Reprinted with permission from DIETARY REFERENCE INTAKES SERIES. Copyright © (year) by the National Academy of Sciences, Courtesy of the National Academies Press, Washington, D.C.

Chapter 2   **p. 36**: U.S. Department of Agriculture, 2015 Dietary Guidelines for Americans, advisory committee. Note: These calorie levels are based on the Institute of Medicine's Estimated Energy Requirements from the Dietary Reference Intakes: Macronutrients Report, 2002.; **p. 37**: "The Do's and Don'ts of the DRIs" from Dietary Reference Intakes: Applications in Dietary Planning by Institute of Medicine of the National Academies. Reprinted with permission from the National Academies Press. Copyright © 2003, National Academy of Sciences.; **p. 43**: U.S. Department of Agriculture, "Finding Your Way to a Healthier You." Based on the Dietary Guidelines for Americans and MyPlate.gov.; **p. 44**: Adapted from "Empty Calories: How Do I Count the Empty Calories I Eat?" from U.S. Department of Agriculture, MyPlate. Available at www.ChooseMyPlate.gov.; **p. 44**: U.S. Department of Agriculture, 2015 Dietary Guidelines for Americans advisory committee.; **p. 46**: Data from L. R. Young and M. Nestle, "Expanding Portion Sizes in the U.S. Marketplace: Implications for Nutrition Counseling," *Journal of the American Dietetic Association* 103 (2003): 231–234; 47.: U.S. Department of Agriculture, Mixed Dishes in MyPyramid. Available at www.ChooseMyPlate.gov.; **p. 49**: Data from S. H. Holt, J. C. Miller, P. Petocz, and E. Farmakalidis, "A Satiety Index of Common Foods," *European Journal of Clinical Nutrition* 49 (1995): 675–690.; **p. 50**: U.S. Food and Drug Administration.; **p. 52**: U.S. Food and Drug Administration. 2012. Understanding and Using the Nutrition Facts Label. Available at www.fda.gov. Accessed January 2014.; **p. 52**: U.S. Food and Drug Administration. 2012. Understanding and Using the Nutrition Facts Label. Available at www.fda.gov. Accessed Jaunary 2014.; **p. 55**: U.S. Food and Drug Administration.; **p. 56**: Data from "Guidance for Industry: A Food Labeling Guide" by U.S. Food and Drug Administration, from the FDA website. Revised January 2013. Accessed April 2015.; **p. 57**: FDA, 2014. Available at: www.fda.gov. Accessed May 2015.; **p. 61**: Based on "International Food Information Council (IFIC) Foundation Functional Foods Component Chart" from the IFIC website, accessed May 2015.; **p. 64**: U.S. Department of Agriculture.; **p. 65**: U.S. Department of Agriculture.; IFC- **p. 2**: Reprinted with permission from DIETARY REFERENCE INTAKES SERIES. Copyright © 1997, 1998, 2000, 2001, 2005, 2011 by the National Academy of Sciences, Courtesy of the National Academies Press, Washington, D.C.

Chapter 3   **p. 593**: Based on A. Rubio-Tapia, et al., "The Prevalence of Celiac Disease in the United States," *American Journal of Gastroenterology* 107, no. 10 (2012): 1538–1544.

Chapter 4   **p. 111**: Based on data from Institute of Medicine, Dietary Reference Intakes for Energy, Carbohydrate, Fiber, Fat, Fatty Acids, Cholesterol, Protein, and Amino Acids (Washington, D.C.: The National Academies Press, 2005).; **p. 114**: Harvard University Health Services. "Fiber Content of Foods in Common Portions." 2004. Available at www.huh.harvard.edu; Tufts University School of Medicine. HIV Resources: Fiber. www.tufts.edu.; **p. 120**: U.S. Department of Health and Human Services.; **p. 120**: USDA, Dietary Guidelines for Americans, 5th ed. (Home and Garden Bulletin No. 232, 2000); Manufacturers' labels.; **p. 126**: Based on American Diabetes Association,

"Type 2 Diabetes Risk Test." 2014. Available at www.diabetes.org/are-you-at-risk/diabetes-risk-test/. Accessed September 2013.; **p. 130**: Calorie Control Council, "Trends and Statistics," 2012. www.caloriecontrol.org.

Chapter 5   **p. 160**: USDA and HHS. Dietary Guidelines for Americans, 2010. Available at www.health.gov/dietaryguidelines.; **p. 163**: USDA and HHS. Dietary Guidelines for Americans, 2010. Available at www.health.gov/dietaryguidelines.; **p. 165**: Data from Calorie Control Council. 2013. Glossary of Fat Replacers. Available at www.caloriecontrol.org. Accessed March 2013.; R. D. Mattes, "Fat Replacers," *Journal of the American Dietetic Association* 98 (1998): 463–468; J. Wylie-Rosett, "Fat Substitutes and Health: An Advisory from the Nutrition Committee of the American Heart Association," Circulation 105 (2002): 2800–2804.; **p. 171**: National Cholesterol Education Program. Detection, Evaluation, and Treatment of High Blood Cholesterol in Adults (Adult Treatment Panel III). May 2001. National Institutes of Health Publication No. 01-3290.; **p. 172**: MEDITERRANEAN DIET PYRAMID ©2009 Oldways Preservation and Exchange Trust. Reprinted with permission.

Chapter 6   **p. 203**: Based on data from Institute of Medicine, Dietary Reference Intakes for Energy, Carbohydrate, Fiber, Fat, Fatty Acids, Cholesterol, Protein, and Amino Acids (Washington, D.C.: The National Academies Press, 2002).; **p. 204**: Based on data from Committee to Ensure Safe Food from Production to Consumption, Institute of Medicine, and National Research Council, "Ensuring Safe Food: From Production to Consumption." Washington, D.C., The National Academies Press (1998).; **p. 208**: Dietary Guidelines for Americans, 2010, by the US Department of Agriculture and the Department of Health and Human Services, 2010.; Pearson Education, Inc.

Chapter 7   **p. 228**: U.S. Department of Agriculture.; **p. 237**: U.S. Department of Agriculture.; **p. 241**: U.S. Department of Agriculture.; **p. 243**: U.S. Department of Agriculture.; **p. 245**: U.S. Department of Agriculture.; **p. 249**: U.S. Department of Agriculture.; **p. 251**: U.S. Department of Agriculture.; **p. 253**: U.S. Department of Agriculture.; **p. 255**: U.S. Department of Agriculture.; **p. 257**: U.S. Department of Agriculture.; **p. 259**: U.S. Department of Agriculture.; **p. 261**: U.S. Department of Agriculture.; **p. 268**: Source: Scientific Report of the 2015 Dietary Guidelines advisory committee; What We Eat in America, NHANES 2007–2010.

Chapter 8   **p. 288**: Janice J. Thompson et. al., *The Science of Nutrition*, 3rd Edition, Pearson Education, Inc.; **p. 292**: Environmental Protection Agency. 2005. Water Health Series: Bottled Water. Available at www.epa.gov. Accessed May 2015; Food and Drug Administration. 2010. Bottled Water Everywhere: Keeping it Safe. Available at www.fda.gov/ForConsumers/ConsumerUpdates/ucm203620.htm. Accessed May 2015.; **p. 294**: Pearson Education, Inc.; **p. 300**: based on data from Institute of Medicine. Dietary Reference Intakes: Vitamin A, Vitamin K, Arsenic, Boron, Chromium, Copper, Iodine, Iron, Manganese, Molybdenum, Nickel, Silicon, Vanadium, and Zinc. (Washington, D.C.: The National Academies Press, 2001). Available at www.nap.edu.; **p. 304**: Based on A. V. Chobanian, et al., The Seventh Report of the Joint National Committee on Prevention, Detection, Evaluation, and Treatment of High Blood Pressure, *Journal of the American Medical Association* 289 (2003): 2560–2572.; **p. 324**: Figure 8.33 Percentage of Americans Living in Communities with a Fluoridated Water Supply, by State. 2012.; **p. 331**: Source: USDA National Nutrient Database for Standard Reference. U.S. Department of Agriculture

Chapter 9   **p. 347**: Adapted from "Blood Alcohol Concentration (BAC) Tables" from Pennsylvania Liquor Control Board's Bureau of Alcohol Education, published by the Pennsylvania Liquor Control Board, with data gathered from The National Clearinghouse for Alcohol and Drug Information, Substance Abuse, and Mental Health Services Administration. Adapted with permission.; **p. 348**: National Institute on Alcohol Abuse and Alcoholism. 2003. Understanding Alcohol: Investigations into Biology and Behavior. Available at http://science.education.nih.gov. Accessed June 2015.; **p. 352**: Pearson Education, Inc.; **p. 357**: Based on data from National Institute on Alcohol Abuse and Alcoholism. 2015. College Drinking. Available at http://pubs.niaaa.nih.gov. Accessed June 2015.; **p. 357**: National Institute on Alcohol Abuse and Alcoholism. 2013. Alcohol Use Disorder: A comparison between DSM-IV and DSM-5. Available at: National Institute on Alcohol Abuse and

Alcoholism. 2013. Alcohol Use Disorder: A comparison between DSM-IV and DSM-5. Accessed July 2015.; **p. 359:** based on data from National Institute on Alcohol Abuse and Alcoholism. 2003. Understanding Alcohol: Investigations into Biology and Behavior. Available at http://www.ncbi.nlm.nih.gov/books/NBK20360/. Accessed June 2015; U.S. Department of Health and Human Services. 1997. Ninth Special Report of the U.S. Congress on Alcohol and Health. Bethesda, MD: National Institute on Alcohol Abuse and Alcoholism.

Chapter 10 **p. 378:** Based on data from Committee to Ensure Safe Food from Production to Consumption, Institute of Medicine, and National Research Council, "Ensuring Safe Food: From Production to Consumption." Washington, D.C., The National Academies Press (1998).; **p. 391:** Based on data from the Centers for Disease Control and Prevention, "Can Eating Fruits and Vegetables Help People to Manage Their Weight?" 2012. Available at www.cdc.gov. Accessed July 2015.; **p. 393:** Based on data from Centers for Disease Control and Prevention, "Physical Activity for a Healthy Weight" 2015. Available at www.cdc.gov. Accessed July 2015.; **p. 402:** The Alliance for Eating Disorders Awareness. 2013. Available at www.allianceforeatingdisorders.com. Accessed July 2013.; **p. 409:** Based on data from USDA National Nutrient Database for Standard Reference.

Chapter 11 **p. 425:** Data from American College of Sports Medicine, "Position Stand: Quantity and Quality of Exercise for Developing and Maintaining Cardiorespiratory, Musculoskeletal, and Neuromotor Fitness in Apparently Healthy Adults: Guidance for Prescribing Exercise," *Medicine & Science in Sports & Exercise* 43 no. 7 (2011).; **p. 429:** Data from L. Burke, B. Kiens, and J. Ivy. "Carbohydrate and Fat for Training and Recovery," *Journal of Sports Science* 22 (2004): 15–30.; **p. 431:** Data from N. Clark, *Nancy Clark's Sports Nutrition Guidebook*, 3rd ed. (Champaign, IL: Human Kinetics, 2003).; **p. 441:** Copyright © 2011 American College of Sports Medicine. This brochure is a product of ACSM's Consumer Information Committee.; **p. 443:** Adapted from "USA Track & Field Self-Testing Program for Optimal Hydration for Distance Running" by Douglas Casa, from USA Track and Field website. Copyright © 2003 by Douglas Casa. Reprinted with permission.; **p. 443:** data based on L. Burke. 2007. Practical Sports Nutrition. Champaign, IL: Human Kinetics.; **p. 449:** Based on "Eating for Recovery" by Sports, Cardiovascular, and Wellness Nutrition (SCAN) – a dietetic practice group of the Academy of Nutrition and Dietetics, from NUTRITION FACT SHEET, Issue 1, April 2009; "Gaining Weight and Building Muscle" by SCAN, from NUTRITION FACT SHEET, Issue 8, January 2010; and "Nutrition for Muscle Mass" by R. Skinner, from Gatorade Sports Science Institute website, 2008.

Chapter 12 **p. 431:** Data from N. Clark, *Nancy Clark's Sports Nutrition Guidebook*, 3rd ed. (Champaign, IL: Human Kinetics, 2003).; **p. 460:** United States Department of Agriculture, "2012 Census of Agriculture." 2012. Available at www.agcensus.usda.gov.; **p. 461:** United States Environmental Protection Agency, "Ag 101: Demographics." Updated April 2013. Available at www.epa.gov. Accessed June 2015.; **p. 462:** United States Environmental Protection Agency, "Location of U.S. Facilities." Available at http://www.epa.gov/sectors/sectorinfo/sectorprofiles/agribusiness/map.html Accessed May 2015.; **p. 463:** Data from United States Department of Agriculture, "2007 Census of Agriculture." 2009. Available at www.agcensus.usda.gov.; **p. 463:** 2012 Census of Agriculture Highlights. Farms and Farmland. Numbers, Acreage, Ownership, and Use. September 2014. Available at http://www.agcensus.usda.gov/Publications/2012/Online_Resources/Highlights/Farms_and_Farmland/Highlights_Farms_and_Farmland.pdf. Accessed May 2015.; **p. 465:** Data from USDA, Economic Research Service, "Import Share of Consumption." 2009. Available at http://ers.usda.gov. Accessed August 2013.; **p. 467:** Tagtow et al. Standards of professional performance for RDNs In sustainable, resilient, and healthy food and water systems. *Journal of the Academy of Nutrition and Dietetics.* 2014;114:475–488.; **p. 468:** Based on data from "Food, Fuel, and Freeways: An Iowa Perspective on How Far Food Travels, Fuel Usage, and Greenhouse Gas Emissions" from Iowa State University Leopold Center for Sustainable Agriculture website, 2002.; **p. 471:** Source: Adapted from Angie Tagtow, MS, RD, LD, "Shades of Green: Looking at the Food System with a Critical Eye" in "Healthy Land, Healthy Food & Healthy Eaters" by A. Tagtow and A. Harmon. Available at University of Wyoming website, 2009. Copyright © 2009 Angie Tagtow and Alison Harmon. Adapted with permission from

the author.; **p. 472:** Based on data from S. Cotner and J. Masabni, "Vegetable Gardening in Containers," AgriLife Extension, Texas A&M System (March 2009). Available at http://repository.tamu.edu. Accessed June 2013; Iowa State University Extension, "Container Vegetable Gardening." (2005). Available at www.extension.iastate.edu. Accessed June 2013.; **p. 480:** Based on FDA, "Policy for Food Developed by Biotechnology," 1995. Available at http://vm.cfsan.fda.gov; J. H. Maryanski, "Bioengineered Foods: Will They Cause Allergic Reactions?" 1997. Center for Food Safety and Applied Nutrition. Available at www.cfsan.fda.gov; FDA, "Plant Biotechnology for Food and Feed. FDA's Biotechnology Policy." 2009. Available at www.fda.gov. Accessed January 2010; C. Bruh, "Position of the American Dietetic Association: Agricultural and Food Biotechnology." *Journal of the American Dietetic Association* 106 (2006): 285–293.; **p. 482:** Based on data from Committee to Ensure Safe Food from Production to Consumption, Institute of Medicine, and National Research Council, "Ensuring Safe Food: From Production to Consumption." Washington, D.C., The National Academies Press (1998).; **p. 487:** USDA, The Farm Bill http://www.usda.gov/wps/portal/usda/usdahome?navid=farmbill. Accessed June 2015.

Chapter 13 **p. 498:** Data from the Food and Drug Administration, "Bad Bug Book," 2nd ed. 2012. Available at www.fda.gov. Accessed June 2015; Centers for Disease Control and Prevention (CDC), "Diagnosis and Management of Foodborne Illness: A Primer for Physicians," 2004. Available at www.cdc.gov. Accessed June 2015.; **p. 500:** Data from Centers for Disease Control, "Travelers' Diarrhea." Available at www.cdc.gov. Accessed June 2015.; **p. 523:** Partnership for Food Safety Education. Reprinted with Permission.; **p. 506:** Food Safety Information: Kitchen Thermometers"" from USDA's Food Safety and Inspection Service website, 2013. Accessed June 2015.; **p. 509:** USDA Food Safety and Inspection Service, "Cold Storage Chart" from "Keep Food Safe! Food Safety Basics," 2013. Available at www.fsis.usda.gov. Accessed June 2015.; **p. 511:** Data from Food and Drug Administration and the U.S. Department of Agriculture, "A Description of the U.S. Food Safety System," 2000. Available at www.fsis.usda.gov. Accessed July 2013.; **p. 513:** U.S. Food and Drug Administration.; **p. 517:** FDA, "Food Additives and Ingredients," 2010. Available at www.fda.gov. Accessed June 2015.; **p. 521:** FDA, "Food Tampering, an Extra Ounce of Caution," 2013. Available at www.fda.gov. Accessed July 2013.

Chapter 14 **p. 530:** Data from Food and Drug Administration. 2004. What You Need to Know About Mercury in Fish and Shellfish: EPA and FDA Advice for Women Who Might Become Pregnant, Women Who Are Pregnant, and Nursing Mothers. Available at www.fda.gov. Accessed March 2013.; **p. 530:** Data from National Toxicology Program, Department of Health and Human Services, http://ntp-server.niehs.nih.gov; the International Food Information Council (IFIC), www.ific.org.; **p. 531:** Chandra A, Copen CE, Stephen EH. Infertility and impaired fecundity in the United States, 1982–2010: Data from the National Survey of Family Growth. National Health Statistics Reports; no 67. Hyattsville, MD: National Center for Health Statistics. 2013.; **p. 534:** based on data from: Weight gain during pregnancy. Committee Opinion No. 548. American College of Obstetricians and Gynecologists. *Obstet Gynecol* 2013;121:210–2.; **p. 536:** U.S. Department of Agriculture.; **p. 540:** Adapted from "Exercise During Pregnancy" by T. Wang and B. Apgar, from AMERICAN FAMILY PHYSICIAN, 1998, Volume 57. Copyright © 1998 by American Academy of Family Physicians. Adapted with permission.; **p. 555:** USDA. 2002. Feeding Infants: A Guide for Use in Child Nutrition Programs. Available at www.fns.usda.gov.

Chapter 15 **p. 569:** based on Dietary Guidelines for Americans, 2010. www.cnpp.usda.gov. Accessed May 2013.; **p. 571:** Abramovitz, B., and L. Birch. 2000. Five-Year-Old Girls' Ideas about Dieting Are Predicted by Their Mothers' Dieting. *Journal of the American Dietetic Association* 100: 1157–1163.; **p. 574:** Data from Ogden CL, Carroll MD, Kit BK, Flegal KM. Prevalence of childhood and adult obesity in the united states, 2011–2012. JAMA. 2014; 311(8):806–14.; 576: Adapted from USDA, 10 Tips Nutrition Education Series. 2011. Available at www.choosemyplate.gov.; **p. 580:** C. L. Ogden, B. K. Kit, M. D. Carroll, and S. Park, "Consumption of Sugar Drinks in the United States, 2005–2008." NCHS Data Brief no. 71 (Hyattsville, MD: National Center for Health Statistics, 2011).; **p. 582:** Federal Interagency Forum on Aging-Related

Statistics, www.agingstats.gov.; **p. 583:** My Plate for Older Adults, © 2011 Tufts University; **p. 592:** based on data from the World Cancer Research Fund/American Institute for Cancer Research (AICR), Food, Nutrition, Physical Activity, and the Prevention of Cancer: A Global Perspective (Washington, D.C.: AICR, 2007).; **p. 594:** American Academy of Family Physicians, Academy of Nutrition and Dietetics, and National Council on Aging, Inc. 2002. The Nutrition Screening Initiative is available at www.aafp.org. Accessed July 2010.; **p. 595:** National Institute on Aging, "Alcohol Use and Abuse." Available at www.niaPublications.org. Accessed July 2010.

Chapter 16

p. 602: Adapted from USDA Economic Research Service. 2014. Food Security in the U.S. Available at www.ers.usda.gov. Accessed February 2015.; **p. 603:** United States Department of Agriculture Economic Research Service. Prepared by ERS using data from the December 2011, December 2012, and December 2013 Current Population Survey Food Security Supplements.; **p. 605:** USDA Economic Research Service, "Food Insecurity in Households with Children," 2010–11. www.ers.usda.gov. Accessed January 2015.; **p. 606:** Publications and Information Products; NCHS Data Brief, Number 50, December 2010, Obesity and Socioeconomic Status in Adults: United States, 2005–2008) available at CDC.gov.; **p. 607:** Source: Adapted from USDA. 2014. Food Security in the U.S., U.S. HOUSEHOLD FOOD SECURITY SURVEY MODULE. Available at http://www.ers.usda .gov/datafiles/Food_Security_in_the_United_States/Food_Security_Survey_ Modules/hh2012.pdf.; **p. 613:** Data from World Health Organization. 2015. Nutrition. Micronutrient Deficiencies. Available at www.who.int.; **p. 615:** Data from USDA, Food and Nutrition Service. 2014. Snap to Health FAQ. http://www.snaptohealth.org. www.fns.usda.gov; Meals on Wheels America. 2015. http://www.mealsonwheelsamerica.org.